Celebrity Obituaries, 2023

Celebrity Obituaries, 2023
Film, Television, Radio, Theatre, Dance, Music, Cartoons and Pop Culture

****

Harris M. Lentz, III

DANCING GRIFFIN

PRESS
Horseshoe Lake, Arkansas

This book is dedicated to the memory of those friends and family lost during 2023 -

Pam Zanone, John Ernest, Vincent Astor, Mickey Keep, Ben Newell, Gene Branham, Mitch Foust, Nan Lambert, Marie Lovelace, Emma Shackelford, Ann Kyle Wade, Arun Gahdhi, Gerry Fleming, Marsha Jane Siders, Bill Harlow, Betty Jack, Eric Setbacken, Tip Senhausen

and Margia Dean, Lisa Montell, Sara Lane, Dean Smith, Michael Bishop

Front cover: **Top Row: Matthew Perry, Harry Belafonte, Sinead O'Connor, Tony Bennett**
Bottom Row: Raquel Welch, Pee-wee Herman, Suzanne Somers, Tina Turner

ISBN: 9798326774163

Dancing Griffin Press, Publishers
119 Horseshoe Point
Horseshoe Lake, Arkansas 72348

hml111@aol.com

ACKNOWLEDGMENTS

I greatly appreciate the invaluable assistance of my friend and co-conspirator Carla Clark. Special thanks also go to my sister, Nikki Walker. Also, thanks to Kayla Hugel, Bob King, Tom Weaver, John Beifuss, Ray Neilson, Jimmie Covington, John Whyborn, Boyd Magers at Western Clippings, Andrew 'Captain Comics' Smith, Hobo Timmy, Tony & Lynn Pruitt, Carol Baird, Jason 'the Doctor' Heath, Greg & Dana Bridges, Kent Nelson, George & Leona Alsup, Betty Alsup, Toni Cerrito, Vicki & Ed Bennett, Darla & Randy Sellars, Dink Walker, Jay & Shirley Vincent, Abbey Vincent, Vickie Edwards, Mike & Cindy Callan, Beth Latham, Kelsey Latham, Dale Warren, Andrew Clark, Aarin Prichard, Dr. Mark Heffington, Anne Taylor, Pat Branham, Joy Martin, Denise Tansil, Jennifer Brewer, Lance Oliver, Mike McCarthy, Dale Morton, Paul & Sam Geary, Ian, Shannon & Dacey Geary, Mr. Robert Walker, Carlin and Renee Stuart, Maggie Hernandez, Scott & Dawn Graves, Wade & Allison Pace DeHart, Bill Dabbs, Chuck & Michelle Kist, Dia Barbee, Ray and Judy Herring, Grace Garcia Adams, Brett Fleming, John Beck, Polly Sharp, Tammy Lambdin, Verlinda Hennings, Ed Witherspoon, Josh Cleary, Sean & Amber Hart, Kira Christensen, Heather Rich, Pat Cohen, Ali Meyer, Kristen Williams, Stephanie Godman, Jamie Bromley, Katelyn Pearce, Ashley Essary, Dave & Lisa Hansen, the Memphis Film Festival, Bryan Burgess, Keith Hurd, the gang at Classic Horror Film Board, Tommy & Julie Gattas, James & Linda Gattas, Emma Brown, Horseshoe Lake Public Libraries, Debbe Davenport, Cathy Forester, Cassey Clayman, Mackenzie Chrestman, and the Crittenden County Library, the folks at Bond's Store and Kamp Karefree, and all my friends at Horseshoe Lake, Garry & Gayle Hahne, Bill & Barbara McKee, Suzanne & Pete Seal, Jim & Gina Good, Jerry & Melinda Akins, Paul Pipkin, Molly Coffee, Annie Edwards, Betty Duncan, Trina Scarborough, Fred 'Truckerfred' Plaisted, Scott Plaisted, Pat & Nancy Bond, Dennis & Pam Ellis, Nina Mack, Shawn & Marsha Siders, Woodis Dunn, Milton Hardy, Bill & Katherine Clarke, Herb & Mika Hyman, Skip & Billie Gaia, Stacy Grubbs, Donna Hooker, Charmain Murphy, Ronnie & Gail Faulkner, Greg & Kathy Davenport, Terry Tarr, Billy Raines, Billy & Cheri Thomen, Kathy Baker, Kenneth & Stacy McDermott, Terry & Natalie Taylor, Whitney Taylor, Sherry May, Tim & Belynda Dwyer, Sherry Dodd, Brian Bracken, Betsy Bracken, Larry & Holly Spiotta, Mary Ann Pittman, Chuck Smith, Chris Beleu, Lavelle Frost, Bobbie Jean Coleman, Walter Pipkin, Leila Dodge, Lee Askey, Kay Rhodes, Eddie Smith, Jennifer Smith Burns, Billy & Jeannie Shull, Nick Cross & Joanie McCaleb, Carol Adams, Cana Able, Natalie King & Whit Hyman, David & Glenda Harlow, Jason Harlow, Greg and Rachel Hill, Lisa Fox, Shawn Fox, Christian James & Kate Cook, Silvia Romo and Jorge Ornelas, Jorge Jr., Genesis & Sebastian Ornelas, Mariana Romo and Raul Diaz, Jeremy Hitchcock, Charles Daugherty, Kaylie Malone, Taylor Webb, Tim Edwards, Kristen Sparrow, Courtney May, Allie Hartness, Shelli Conlee, Kaytlin Thorpe, Hailey Williams, Bubba & Kindale Briggs, DK & Blade Briggs, Reagan Walls, Milly Harden, Camryn Hart, Marcella Garza, Kaitlyn Bain, Carlee Moore, Brittany Rios, Christina Frazier, Abygail Williams, Emily Blankenship, Danielle Blakely Strange, Robyn Hood, Briana Lopez, Jose Rubio, Maddie Herrington, and Chase Herrington.

INTRODUCTION

This book provides a single source that notes the deaths of all major, and many minor, figures in the fields of film, television, cartoons, theatre, music, and popular literature throughout the world. The obituaries within this volume contain pertinent details of deaths including date, place and cause, of over 1370 celebrities who died in 2023. Biographical information and career highlights and achievements are also provided. I have also included a complete-as-possible filmography for film and television performers. Both print and on-line resources used are listed below and in the bibliography. A photograph has been included for the vast majority of the individuals within. A handful of individuals whose deaths in previous years that had not been recorded are found in the addendum.

The year 2023 saw the passing of numerous luminaries in the fields of films, television, music, literature, and the arts. The past years losses include singer, actor, and political activist Harry Belafonte, who popularized Calypso in the United States, and starred in the films "Carmen Jones" and "The World, the Flesh and the Devil"; actor Matthew Perry, who starred as Chandler Bing in the hit comedy series "Friends"; television writer and producer Norman Lear, who was noted for such hit series as "All in the Family" and Sanford and Son"; legendary singer and actress Tina Turner, who was noted for such hits as "Proud Mary" and "What's Love Got to Do with It"; Scottish actor David McCallum, who was noted for his roles as secret agent Illya Kuryakin in the 1960s television series "The Man from U.N.C.L.E." and as medical examiner Dr. Donald 'Ducky' Mallard in "NCIS"; television personality Bob Barker, who was host of the game shows "The Price is Right" and "Truth or Consequences"; legendary singer Tony Bennett, who recorded the hit song "I Left My Heart in San Francisco"; actress Cindy Williams, who starred as Shirley Feeney on the television comedy series "Laverne & Shirley"; Irish singer and political activist Sinead O'Connor, who had a hit song with "Nothing Compares to You"; comedian and actor Paul Reubens, who portrayed Pee-wee Herman, the child-like host of the children's television series "Pee-wee's Playhouse"; British actress Glenda Jackson, who received Academy Awards for her roles in the films "Women in Love" and "A Touch of Class"; Oscar-winning songwriter and composer Burt Bacharach, who wrote such songs as "What's New Pussycat?", "The Look of Love", and "Raindrops Keep Fallin' On My Head"; actress and sex symbol Raquel Welch, who starred in such films as "Fantastic Voyage" and "One Million Years B.C."; actress Piper Laurie, who received Academy Award nominations for her roles in films "Hustler", "Carrie", and "Children of a Lesser God"; actress Stella Stevens, who starred with Jerry Lewis in "The Nutty Professor" and Elvis Presley in "Girls! Girls! Girls!"; singer and songwriter David Crosby, who was a member of the groups the Byrds and Crosby, Stills & Nash; Israeli actor Chaim Topol, who received an Oscar nomination for his role as Tevye in the film production of the musical "Fiddler on the Roof"; actress Suzanne Somers, who starred as Chrissy Snow on the popular television comedy series "Three's Company"; actress Phyllis Coates, who starred as Lois Lane on the television series "Adventures of Superman" during its first season in 1952; singer and songwriter Jimmy Buffett, who was noted for the hits "Margaritaville" and "Cheeseburger in Paradise"; actor Lance Reddick, who starred as Cedric Daniels in "The Wire" television series and was Charon, concierge at the Continental hotel, in the "John Wick" film franchise; actress Lara Parker, who starred as Angelique in the gothic soap opera "Dark Shadows"; comedian and musician Tom Smothers, who formed the popular musical comedy duo The Smothers Brothers with his brother, Dick, and starred in the ground-breaking variety series "The Smothers Brothers Comedy Hour"; child actress Lisa Loring, who starred as Wednesday Addams in the television series "The Addams Family" in the mid-1960s; film director William Friedkin, who was noted for the films "The French Connection" and "The Exorcist"; Irish-English actor Michael Gambon, who was noted for is role as Albus Dumbledore in the "Harry Potter" film series; television producer Marty Krofft, who teamed with his brother Sid to create such children's series as "H.R. Pufnstuf" and "Land of the Lost"; Italian actress Gina Lollobrigida, who was an international sex symbol in the 1950s and starred as Esmeralda in the 1956 version of "The Hunchback of Notre Dame"; actor Richard Roundtree, who starred as detective John Shaft in the 1971 action film "Shaft"; actor Alan Arkin, who received a Tony Award for the 1963 play "Enter Laughing" and an Oscar for 2006's "Little Miss Sunshine"; actor Ryan O'Neal, who was a leading star in the 1970s with such films as "Love Story", "Paper Moon", and "Barry Lyndon"; television host and former Cincinnati mayor Jerry Springer, who oversaw a controversial tabloid talk show for three decades; actor Andre Braugher, who starred as Detective Frank Pembleton in the television series "Homicide: Life on the Street" and was Captain Raymond Holt on the comedy police series "Brooklyn Nine-Nine"; actor Robert Blake, who began his career as a child actor in the "Our Gang" comedy shorts and starred as police detective Tony Baretta in the television series "Baretta"; singer Lisa Marie Presley, who was the daughter of Elvis and Priscilla Presley; football player turned actor Jim Brown, who starred as one of "The Dirty Dozen" in the 1967 World War II film; actor Charles Kimbrough, who starred as anchorman Jim Dial on the "Murphy Brown" sitcom; Northern Irish actor Ray Stevenson, who starred as Titus Pullo in the television series "Rome" and was Volstagg in Marvel's "Thor" films; actor Mark Goddard, who starred as Major Don West in the science fiction series "Lost in Space" in the 1960s; actor Frederic Forrest, who received an Academy Award nomination for his role in the 1979 film "The Rose", and appeared in "Apocalypse Now" and "It Lives Again"; actor Barry Newman, who starred in the 1971 cult film "Vanishing Point" and the television legal drama "Petrocelli"; South Korean actor Lee Sun-Kyun, who starred in Bong Joon-ho's Oscar-winning 2019 film "Parasite"; concert pianist and conductor Peter Nero; British film director Hugh Hudson, who helmed such features as "Chariots of Fire" and "Greystoke: Legend of Tarzan, Lord of the Apes"; British guitarist Jeff Beck, who was a member of the rock bands the Yardbirds and the Jeff Beck Group; actress Melinda Dillon, who earned Oscar nominations for her roles in "Close Encounters of the Third Kind" and "Absence of Malice"; Irish singer Shane MacGowan, who was lead singer for the band the Pogues; actor Burt Young, who was featured as Paulie, the brother-in-law of Sylvester Stallone's Rocky Balboa, in the "Rocky" film franchise; Australian comedian and actor Barry Humphries, who was noted for such satirical alter egos as Dame Edna Everage and Sir Les Patterson; actor Richard Moll, who was featured as Bailiff Bull Shannon on the television comedy series "Night Court"; comic book artist John Romita, Sr., who co-created such Marvel Comic characters as Wolverine, the Punisher, and Luke Cage; experimental filmmaker Kenneth Anger, who was noted for such works as "Invocation of My Demon Brother" and "Lucifer Rising" and wrote the gossip book "Hollywood Babylon"; Canadian singer and songwriter Gordon Lightfoot, who was best known for the songs "The Wreck of the Edmund Fitzgerald" and "If You Could Read My Mind"; British fashion designer Mary Quant, who was credited with designing the miniskirt; political satirist and comedian Mark Russell; songwriter Sheldon Harnick, who worked with Jerry Bock on such hit Broadway musicals as "Fiorello!" and "Fiddler on the Roof"; and actor and singer Ed Ames, who performed with the musical quartet the Ames Brothers and starred as the half-Cherokee Mingo in the 1960's television series "Daniel Boone".

Many other stars of stage and screen are found within including actor Michael Lerner, who received an Academy Award nomination for Best Supporting Actor for his role in the 1991 film "Barton Fink"; British actor Tom Wilkinson, who was noted for his roles in the films "The Full Monty" and "In the Bedroom"; actor Tom Sizemore, who appeared in such films as "Saving Private Ryan" and "Black Hawk Down"; actress Cindy Morgan, who starred in such films as "Tron" and "Caddyshack" in the early 1980s; actor Treat Williams who starred in such films as "Hair", "Dead Heat", and "The Phantom"; British-Pakistani actor Zia Mohyeddin who was featured in the films "Lawrence of Arabia", "Khartoum", and "They Came from Beyond Space"; British actress Anne Heywood, who starred in the 1967 film "The Fox"; actress Janet Landgard, who starred with Burt Lancaster in the 1968 film "The Swimmer"; actress Carole Cook, who starred as the wife of Don Knott's "The Incredible Mr. Limpet" in 1964; singer and songwriter Sandy Farina, who was featured as Strawberry Fields in the 1978 musical film "Sergeant Pepper's Lonely Hearts Club Band"; actor Lew Palter, who was featured as Isidor Straus in the 1997 film "Titanic"; actress Miiko Taka, who was noted for her role opposite Marlon Brando in the 1957 Korean War drama "Sayonara"; British actor Murray Melvin, who was featured in Ken Russell's "The Devils" and Stanley Kubrick's "Barry Lyndon"; Italian actress Marisa Pavan, who received an Academy Award nomination for her role in the 1955 film "The Rose Tattoo"; British-French actress and singer Jane Birkin, who was noted for her personal and professional relationship with singer Serge Gainsbourg and appeared in the films "Seven Deaths in the Cat's Eye" and "Death on the Nile"; Puerto Rican actor Eugene Iglesias, who

appeared in such films as "Taza, Son of Cochise" and "Rio Bravo"; actress Dodie Heath, who was noted for her roles on the Broadway stage; actress Carlin Glynn, who earned a Tony Award for her role as Madam Mona Stangley in the 1978 Broadway production of "The Best Little Whorehouse in Texas"; British actress Hildegarde Neil, who was Cleopatra to Charlton Heston's Mark Antony in 1972's "Antony and Cleopatra"; child actor Marc Gilpin, who was featured as young Sean Brody in the 1978 sequel "Jaws 2"; Brazilian actress Lea Garcia de Aguiar, who was noted for her role as Serafina in the 1959 film "Black Orpheus"; South African political leader and Zulu Prince Mangosuthu Gatsha Buthelezi who was featured as Zulu King Cetshwayo, his great-grandfather, in the 1964 film "Zulu"; actor Michael McGrath, who earned a Tony Award for his performance in the Broadway musical "Nice Work If You Can Get It" in 2012; Austrian actress Nadja Tiller, who starred in the films "The Burning Court" and "Lulu"; comedian and actor Shecky Greene; British stuntman and actor Dinny Powell, who worked on numerous films for the James Bond franchise; Pamela Blair, who starred as Val in the original Broadway musical "A Chorus Line"; French actor Henri Serre, who starred as Jim in Francois Truffaut's classic film "Jules and Jim"; dancer and actor Maurice Hines, who appeared with brother Gregory Hines in the 1984 film "The Cotton Club"; actress Sheila Smith, who was noted for her roles in such Broadway productions as "Mame" and "Follies"; British actor Paxton Whitehead, who received a Tony Award nomination for his role as King Pelinore in the Broadway play "Camelot" in 1980; British actress Sylvia Syms, who appeared in the film "Expresso Bongo" and the Amicus horror anthology "Asylum"; Canadian actor George R. Robertson, who starred as Commissioner Henry Hurst in the "Police Academy" film series; actress Dorothy Tristan, who was featured as prostitute Arlyn Page in the 1971 film "Klute"; rapper Nashawn Breedlove, who was featured as Lotto in the 2002 film "8 Mile" starring Eminem; child actor Ted Donaldson, who starred in the "Rusty" film series in the 1940s; juvenile actor Lanny Rees, who starred as Junior Riley in the "Life of Riley" film and television series; Betty Ann Bruno, who appeared as a child Munchkin in the 1939 film "The Wizard of Oz"; child actor Tad Devine, who appeared with his father Andy Devine in the 1946 western film "Canyon Passage"; Mexican actress Ana Ofelia Murguia, who was the voice of Mama Coco in the 2017 animated film "Coco"; actor Richard Romanus, who was the voice of Weehawk in Ralph Bakshi's 1977 animated fantasy classic "Wizards"; Spanish actress and singer Carmen Sevilla, who was featured as Mary Magdalene in the 1961 film "King of Kings"; actor J. Patrick McNamara, who was featured as Mr. Preston in the film "Bill & Ted's Excellent Adventure"; Filipino actor John Regala, who was noted for his roles as villains in action and crime films; actress Betty Sturm, who was featured in Timothy Carey's off-beat 1962 film "The World's Greatest Sinner"; South Korean actress Yoon Jeong-hee, who appeared in over 200 films during her career; adult actor Herschel Savage, who starred in the 1978 porn classic "Debbie Does Dallas"; and Japanese martial artist and actor Fumio Demura, who was stunt double for Pat Morita's Mr. Miyagi in several of "The Karate Kid" films.

Numerous individuals who worked behind the camera also passed in 2023 including screenwriter Bo Goldman, who received Academy Awards for scripting "One Flew Over the Cuckoo's Nest" and "Melvin and Howard"; screenwriter Julian Barry, who was nominated for an Academy Award for the 1974 film "Lenny"; Scottish-Australian film director George T. Miller, who helmed the 1982 film "The Man from Snowy River", and the 1990 fantasy classic "The NeverEnding Story II: The Next Chapter"; film editor Mike Hill, who shared an Academy Award for his work on the 1995 film "Apollo 13"; cinematographer Bill Butler, who received an Oscar nomination for his work on "One Flew Over the Cuckoo's Nest"; television writer Peter S. Fischer, who was co-creator of the series "Murder, She Wrote"; television producer and writer David Jacobs, who was a creator of the prime-time soap operas "Dallas" and Knots Landing; film producer Walter Mirisch, who won the Academy Award for the 1967 film "In the Heat of the Night"; television producer Stan Rogow, who was noted for the Disney series "Lizzie McGuire"; cinematographer Victor J. Kemper who worked on the films "The Candidate" and "Dog Day Afternoon"; Herman Raucher, who wrote the novel and screenplay for the 1971 film "Summer of '42"; Italian art director Osvaldo Desideri, who received an Academy Award for the 1984 film "The Last Emperor"; British costume designer Charles Knode, who received an Academy Award nomination for his work on "Braveheart"; cinematographer Owen Roizman, who received Oscar nominations for the films "The French Connection" and "The Exorcist"; film editor David Finfer, who received an Oscar nomination for his work on the 1993 film "The Fugitive"; British production designer Norman Reynolds, who shared Academy Awards for his work on "Star Wars" and "Raiders of the Lost Ark"; Spanish film director Carlos Saura Atares, who was nominated for three Academy Awards for Best Foreign Language Film; screenwriter Edward Hume, who scripted the 1983 tele-film "The Day After"; film editor Donn Cambern, who earned an Academy Award nomination for his work on the 1984 film "Romancing the Stone"; film editor Robert Dalva, who won an Oscar for his work on the 1979 film "The Black Stallion"; screenwriter Arnold Schulman, who earned Oscar nominations for his scripts for "Love with a Proper Stranger" and "Goodbye, Columbus"; Japanese composer and pianist Ryuichi Sakamoto, who earned an Academy Award for his score to the 1987 film "The Last Emperor"; television producer Bill Geddie, who was co-creator of television's "The View" with Barbara Walters; screenwriter and producer Norman Steinberg, who co-wrote Mel Brooks' 1974 comedy classic "Blazing Saddles"; businessman Alexander W. Dreyfoos, Jr., who received an Academy Award for co-creating the Video Color Negative Analyzer; film and television producer Kevin Turen who produced the "Euphoria" television series and Ti West's "X" horror film trilogy; film editor John Refoua, who received an Oscar nomination for his work on the 2009 film "Avatar"; Japanese film director Sadao Nakajima, who was noted for his numerous yakuza crime films; television director Robert Butler, who helmed the pilot episodes of such series as "Star Trek", "Batman", and "Remington Steele"; television writer Nathan Louis Jackson, who wrote and produced Netflix's "Luke Cage" series; film producer Mort Engelberg, who was noted for the 1977 film "Smokey and the Bandit"; film editor Arthur Schmidt, who received Academy Awards for his work on the films "Who Framed Roger Rabbit" and "Forrest Gump"; British television and music video director Bruce Gowers, who helmed the live episodes of "American Idol" for its first decade; animator Burny Mattinson, who worked at Walt Disney Studios for seven decades; producer Edward R. Pressman, who produced such films as "The Crow" and "American Psycho"; film producer Lawrence Turman, who received an Academy Award nomination for the 1967 film "The Graduate"; Austrian director Wolfgang Gluck, who earned an Academy Award nomination for Best Foreign Language Film for 1987's "'38 - Vienna Before the Fall"; film and television director Elliot Silverstein, who was noted for the films "Cat Ballou" and "A Man Called Horse"; television writer and producer Manny Coto, who worked on the series "Star Trek: Enterprise" and "Dexter"; British cinematographer Brian Tufano, who was noted for his work with director Danny Boyle; British composer Christopher Gunning, who scored numerous film and television productions; screenwriter Stu Silver, who was noted for the 1987 film "Throw Momma from the Train"; animator and designer Rolly Crump, who was known for his work with Walt Disney Studios; conductor and composer Carl Davis, who worked on numerous film and television productions; screenwriter Gregory Allen Howard, who was noted for the 2000 film "Remember the Titans"; British special effects artist Ian Wingrove, who received an Academy Award nomination for his work on the film "Return to Oz"; scenic designer Robin Wagner, who was recipient of three Tony Award for his works on Broadway; experimental psychologist Lloyd Morrisett, who helped create the children's television show "Sesame Street"; television producer Robert Precht, who produced the popular variety series "The Ed Sullivan Show" for over twenty years; Japanese art director Nizo Yamamoto, who worked on numerous animated films with Hayao Miyazaki; film costumer Eddie Marks, who was president of Western Costume Company; film producer Tom Luddy, who was co-founder of the Telluride Film Festival; Canadian sound engineer Rob Young, who received an Academy Award nomination for his work on the 1992 film "Unforgiven"; set designer Eugene Lee, who was production designer for "Saturday Night Live" for over four decades, and his former wife, Franne Lee, who frequently worked with him on the show; Austrian film director Rudolf Zehetgruber, who was noted for directing and writing the "Superbug" fantasy comedy film series; adult film producer and home video pioneer Arthur Morowitz; and Canadian songwriter and composer Philip Balsam, who was noted for his work on the "Fraggle Rock" television series.

Many familiar names and faces from the television screen also passed in 2023 including actor and comedian Richard Belzer, who starred as Detective John Munch on the television series "Homicide: Life on the Street" and "Law & Order: Special Victims Unit" for over twenty years; actor George Maharis, who starred as Buz Murdock in the television series "Route 66" in the early 1960s; child actor Adam Rich, who starred as Nicholas Bradford on the television series "Eight Is Enough"; juvenile actor Lance Kerwin, who starred in the 1977 television series "James at 15"; actor Angus Cloud, who was featured as drug dealer Fezco in the HBO series

"Euphoria"; actress Inga Swenson, who was featured as Gretchen Kraus in the television comedy series "Benson"; actress Sara Lane, who starred as Elizabeth Grainger on the television western series "The Virginian"; actor Ron Cephus Jones, who received two Emmy Awards for his role as William Hill in the drama series "This Is Us", and was chess-playing Bobby Fish in the Netflix Marvel superhero series "Luke Cage"; British actor John Nettleton, who was noted for his role as Sir Arnold Robinson in the British television comedy series "Yes Minister" and "Yes, Prime Minister" in the 1980s; comedian Kelly Monteith, who was star of several British comedy series in the 1980s; actor and comedian Johnny Hardwick, who was the voice of Dale Dribble on the animated television series "King of the Hill"; actress Annette McCarthy, who starred as Evelyn Marsh in the second season of television's "Twin Peaks" in 1990; dancer and television personality Len Goodman, who was a judge on the reality television series "Strictly Come Dancing" and "Dancing with the Stars"; child actor Austin Majors who was featured as Theo Sipowicz on the television police series "NYPD Blue"; Indian actor Sajid Khan, who co-starred with Jay North in the 1966 film "Maya" and the subsequently television series; actor Jack Hogan, who starred the World War II series "Combat!" as Private William G. Kirby from 1962 to 1967; actress Jacky O, who was a regular performer on Nick Cannon's improvisational comedy series "Wild 'n Out"; football player and actor Dick Butkus who starred as Richard 'Ski' Butowski in the "Blue Thunder" action series and Coach Mike Katowinski in the comedy "Hang Time; actor John Mengatti, who was featured as Nick Vitaglia on the television series "The White Shadow"; actor Kevin O'Neal, who starred as Private Ben Whitledge in the 1964 comedy series "No Time for Sergeants"; Barbara Bosson, who was noted for her role as Fay Furillo in the series "Hill Street Blues" in the early-1980s; Scottish actress Brigit Forsyth, who was noted for her role as Thelma Ferris in the BBC comedy series "Whatever Happened to the Likely Lads?"; actor James McCaffrey, who was featured as deceased firefighter Jimmy Keefe on the television series "Rescue Me"; actress Frances Sternhagen, who was featured in the recurring role of Cliff Claven's mother, Esther, on the television comedy series "Cheers"; British actress Barbara Young, who was noted for her role as Agrippina, the mother of Nero, in the 1976 "I, Claudius" television mini-series; actor Michael Norell, who starred as Captain Hank Stanley on the television series "Emergency!"; British actress Haydn Gwynne, who starred as Camilla in the comedy series "The Windsors"; Japanese-American actress Eileen Saki, who portrayed the proprietor of Rosie's Bar in the television series "M*A*S*H"; actress Judy Farrell, who appeared in the recurring role of Nurse Able on the television series "M*A*S*H"; British actor Geoffrey Davies, who starred as Dr. Dick Stuart-Clark in the television series "Doctor in the House" and its sequels; Japanese-American actor Yoshio Yoda, who was featured as Fuji in the television series "McHale's Navy"; British actor Benjamin Zephaniah, who was featured as Jeremiah Jesus in the BBC crime drama "Peaky Blinders"; tap dancer Arthur Duncan, who performed on "The Lawrence Welk Show" for two decades; actress and fashion model Shelley Smith, who starred as Sara James in the short-lived television comedy series "The Associates" in 1979; child actress Judy Nugent, was featured as Ann Carson,

the little blind girl who flies around the world with Superman in a 1954 episode of "Adventures of Superman"; actress Hersha Parady, who was featured as Alice Garvey in the television series "Little House on the Prairie"; New Zealand actor Jason 'Levi' Holley, who was featured as Lock in the television series "Shortland Street"; broadcast journalist and reporter Bernard Kalb; bodybuilder Tonya Knight, who was featured as Gold on "American Gladiators" from 1989 to 1992; Bernadette Hunt, who was featured as Falcon on the British version of "Gladiators" in the 1990s; comedian Bill Saluga, who was noted for his comic persona Raymond J. Johnson, Jr., known for the catchphrase "You Can Call Me Ray, or You Can Call Me Jay, or You Can Call Me..."; French actor Guy Marchand, who starred in the "Nestor Burma" detective television series in the 1990s; ventriloquist and voice actor Jimmy Weldon, who created the character of Webster Webfoot the duck; Mike Batayeh, who was featured as Dennis Markowski, the manager of Gus Frings' laundromat, in the "Breaking Bad" television series; actor and comedian Pat Cooper; and radio and television personality Don Kennedy, who hosted the children's series "The Popeye Club" in Atlanta under the name Officer Don.

Soap opera passings include Nicholas Coster, who was noted for his role as Eduardo Grimaldi on "As the World Turns"; Elizabeth Hubbard, who starred as Lucinda Walsh on "As the World Turns"; Jacklyn Zeman, who starred as nurse Bobbie Spencer on "General Hospital"; Brett Hadley, who starred as Detective Carl Williams on "The Young and the Restless"; Jeffrey Carlson, who starred as Zoe Luper, the first transgendered character on a soap opera, in "All My Children" in 2006; Nick Benedict, who starred as Curtis Reed in "Days of Our Lives" in the 1990s; Tyler Christopher, who was best known for his role as Nikolas Cassadine on "General Hospital" for nearly 20 years; Nancy Frangione, who was featured as Cecile de Poulignac on "Another World"; Ellen Holly, who was featured as Carla Gray-Hall on "One Life to Live"; Michael Levin, who starred as Jack Fenelli in "Ryan's Hope"; Ben Masters, who starred as wealthy womanizer Julian Crane on "Passions"; Billy Miller, who was featured as Billy Abbott on "The Young and the Restless"; Kamar de los Reyes, who was featured as Antonio Vega in "One Life to Live"; Peter White, who starred as Linc Tyler on "All My Children"; Andrea Evans, who starred as Tina Lord in "One Life to Live"; Dean Sullivan, who starred as Jimmy Corkhill on the British soap opera "Brookside"; and stars of the ITV soap opera "Emmerdale" including Steve Halliwell (Zak Dingle), Meg Johnson (Pearl Ladderbanks), Peter Martin (Len Reynolds), and Dale Meeks (Simon Meredith).

Many singers, songwriters, musicians, and other notables of the music world are included in this year's compilation including musician and singer Randy Meisner, who was a founding member of the Eagles; Canadian musician Robbie Robertson, who was lead guitarist and songwriter with the rock group the Band; guitarist Gary Rossington, who was co-founder of the southern rock band Lynyrd Skynyrd; Brazilian singer Astrud Gilberto, who was noted for her rendition of the bossa nova song "The Girl from Ipanema"; British musician Les Maguire, who played piano for the band Gerry and the Pacemakers; rapper Lola Chantrelle Mitchell, who performed under the name Gangsta Boo with the group Three 6 Mafia; British singer and musician Denny Laine, who was a founding member of the rock bands the Moody Blues and Wings, Canadian rock drummer Robbie Bachman and rock guitarist Tim Bachman, who performed with the band Bachman-Turner Overdrive; singer Rudolph Isley, who was a founding member of the musical group the Isley Brothers; pianist Huey 'Piano' Smith, who was noted for the classic song "Rockin' Pneumonia and the Boogie Woogie Flu"; singer and musician Laura Lynch, who was a founding member of the country music group the Dixie Chicks; Australian musician and actor Rolf Harris, who recorded the hit song "Tie Me Kangaroo Down, Sport"; British musician Top Topham, who was lead guitarist for the Yardbirds; musician and songwriter Gary Wright, who was the keyboardist and singer for the band Spooky Tooth and wrote the hit song "Dream Weaver"; singer Jerrold Samuels, who performed the hit novelty song "They're Coming to Take me Away, Ha-Haaa!" under the name Napoleon XIV; singer and songwriter Terry Kirkman, who performed with the band The Association; Iranian classical guitarist Lily Afshar; Canadian musician and singer Chad Allan, who was a founding member of the band the Guess Who; songwriter Tom Whitlock, who received an Academy Award for the song "Take My Breath Away" from the film "Top Gun"; Jamaican musician Lester Sterling, who was a founding member of the band the Skatalites; rapper Melvin Barcliff, who was half of the duo Timbaland and Magoo; musician Sixto Rodriguez, who was the subject of the 2012 Oscar-winning documentary "Searching for Sugar Man"; singer Katherine Anderson, who was co-founder of the Motown singing group the Marvelettes; musician Bruce Barthol, who was the original bass player for the rock band Country Joe and the Fish; disc jockey DJ Casper, who created the hit song "Cha Cha Slide"; guitarist Wayne Swinny, who was co-founder of the band Saliva; rock musician Steve Harwell, who was lead singer for the band Smash Mouth; British lyricist Pete Brown, who co-wrote the Cream songs "Sunshine of Your Love" and "White Room"; rapper Jaime Brugada Valdez, who performed under the name MoneySign Suede; country musician Buck Trent, who appeared regularly on the "Hee Haw" television series; British guitarist Bernie Marsden, who was noted for his work with the band Whitesnake; singer Jean Knight, who was noted for the 1971 hit "Mr. Big Stuff"; Australian rock drummer Colin Burgess, who was a founding member of the band AC/DC; drummer George 'Funky' Brown, who was a founding member of the band Kool & the Gang; keyboardist and singer Joseph 'Amp' Fiddler, who performed with George Clinton's Parliament and Funkadelic groups; singer Clarence 'Fuzzy' Haskins, who performed with Parliament-Funkadelic; guitarist and singer Sheldon Reynolds and drummer Fred White, who performed with the band Earth, Wind & Fire; musician Jack Sonni, who played the guitar with the band Dire Straits; British songwriter Richard Kerr, who co-wrote Barry Manilow's hit songs "Mandy" and "Looks Like We Made It"; singer Howie Kane, who performed with the band Jay and the Americans; British songwriter Keith Reid, who co-wrote the lyrics for most of Procol Harum's albums; South Korean singer and actor Moonbin; singer and songwriter Essra Mohawk, who wrote several tunes for the "Schoolhouse Rock" television series, including "Mother Necessity" and "Sufferin' Till Suffrage"; guitarist George Tickner, who was a founding member of the band Journey; British guitarist Ronnie Caryl, who performed with Phil Collins and in the band Flaming Youth; British singer and musician Roger Whittaker; guitarist Dennis Budimir, who performed with the session group the Wrecking Crew; jazz saxophonist and composer Wayne Shorter; British drummer and keyboardist Jon Povey, who played with the rock band Pretty Things; keyboardist Dean Daughtry, who performed with the bands the Classics IV and the Atlanta Rhythm Section; drummer Lee Rauch, who performed with the thrash metal band Megadeath; singer and songwriter Billy 'The Kid' Emerson, who was noted for the hit song "Red Hot"; Canadian drummer Floyd Sneed, who was a member of the band Three Dog Night; Canadian singer and musician Care Failure, who was founder of the alternative rock band Die Mannequin; British musician and songwriter Ray Shulman, who was co-founder of the band Gentle Giant; singer Charlie Thomas, who performed with the vocal group the Drifters from the late-1950s; Scottish musician Alan Rankine, who was keyboardist for the rock band the Associates; classical pianist Andre Watts; rapper and MC C-Knight, who was a founding member of the hip hop ensemble Dove Shack; guitarist and music producer Jeffrey Foskett, who worked frequently with the Beach Boys; Irish musician Sean Keane, who performed with the Irish folk band the Chieftains; British singer and musician Pete Lucas, who performed with the bands Dave Dee, Dozy, Beaky, Mick & Tich and the Troggs; lyricist Tom Jones, who was noted for the hit Off-Broadway musical "The Fantasticks"; British musician Andy Rourke, who was bassist for the indie rock band the Smiths; jazz pianist and composer Ahmad Jamal; guitarist and singer Tom Verlaine, who led the rock band Television in the 1970s; musician and songwriter Jim Gordon, who was drummer for the group Derek and the Dominos; singer Ray Hildebrand, who was half of the duet Paul and Paula; drummer Kirk Arrington, who performed with the heavy metal band Metal Church; jazz drummer Isaac 'Redd' Holt, who played with the Ramsey Lewis Trio; Scottish musician Ian Bairnson, who performed with the Alan Parsons Project; Christian musician and radio personality Ron Hamilton, who was known as Patch the Pirate; opera singer Grace Bumbry; soul singer Spencer Wiggins; bluegrass musician Bobby Osborne, who was half of the duo the Osborne Brothers who were noted for their recording of the hit song "Rocky Top"; drummer Dickie Harrell, who played with Gene Vincent's band the Blue Caps; rapper David 'Trugoy the Dove' Jolicoeur, who performed with the hip hop trio De La Soul; Canadian musician Myles Goodwyn, who was lead singer and guitarist for the band April Wine; music executive Jerry Bradley, who was head of RCA Records in Nashville from 1973 to 1982; musician Gary Young, who was the original drummer for the indie rock band Pavement; recording executive Jerry Moss, who was co-founder of A&M Records; Japanese drummer and singer Yukihiro Takahshi, who was a pioneer of electronic pop music; singer Leon Hughes, who was a founding member of the vocal group the Coasters; rapper Milton Powell, who performed under the name Big Pokey; jazz composer and pianist Carla Bley; British rock musician Geordie Walker, who was the guitarist for the post-punk group Killing Joke; guitarist Tom Leadon, who was a founding member of Tom Petty's first band, Mudcrutch; rock drummer and actress Teresa Taylor, who performed with the experimental band Butthole Surfers; bluegrass musician Jesse McReynolds; British guitarist and singer Tony McPhce, who was founder of the band the Groundhogs; musician James Harvey, who was bassist for the band Goatwhore; singer James Lewis, who performed with the Trans-Siberian Orchestra; South African rapper and dancer Costa Titch; and composer David Del Tredici, who received the 1980 Pulitzer Prize for Music.

Cult horror and science fiction films and television lost such leading figures as actor and stuntman Ricou Browning, who starred in the title role of the Gill-man in underwater scenes in the 1954 Universal horror film classic "Creature from the Black Lagoon" and actress and model Ginger Stanley, who was the underwater stunt double for leading lady Julie Adams in the film; film producer and director Bert I. Gordon, who was known for such cult science fiction films as "The Amazing Colossal Man" and "Attack of the Puppet People"; British actor Julian Sands, who starred in such horror films as "Warlock", "Arachnophobia", and 1998's "The Phantom of the Opera"; actress Gayle Hunnicutt, who starred in the horror films "Eye of the Cat" and "The Legend of Hell House"; actress Margia Dean who starred in the Hammer science fiction film "The Creeping Unknown"; Japanese actor and stuntman Kenpachiro Satsuma, who portrayed Godzilla in films from 1984 to 1995; actor Wally Campo, who starred in Roger Corman's cult-classics "The Little Shop of Horrors" and "Beast from Haunted Cave"; actress Linda Haynes who was noted for her role in the 1970s films "Rolling Thunder" and "Human Experiments"; actress Marlene Clark, who starred in the horror films "Ganja & Hess" and "Night of the Cobra Woman"; British actress Shirley Anne Field, who starred in the horror films "Horrors from the Black Museum", "Peeping Tom", and "These Are the Damned"; British actor Oscar Quitak, who starred as the crippled hunchback Karl in the Hammer horror film "The Revenge of Frankenstein"; actress Annie Wersching, who starred as Leslie Dean in the series "Runaways" and was the Borg Queen in "Star Trek: Picard"; actress Arleen Sorkin, who provided the inspiration and the voice for the Batman cartoon character Harley Quinn; actress Noreen Nash, who starred in the 1953 science fiction film "Phantom from Space"; actress Nan Peterson, who was featured in Robert Clarke's 1958 science fiction film "The Hideous Sun Demon"; actor and stuntman George P. Wilbur, who was featured as masked killer Michael Myers in "Halloween 4: The Return of Michael Myers"; British film director Anthony Hickox, who helmed such horror films as "Waxwork", "Sundown: The Vampire in Retreat", and "Hellraiser III: Hell on Earth"; author and screenwriter Laird Koenig, who wrote the 1974 novel "The Little Girl Who Lives Down the Lane", and Nicolas Gessner, who helmed the 1976 film version; British actress Margaret Whiting, who was the evil Zenobia in 1977's "Sinbad and the Eye of the Tiger"; actor Joe Patridge, who starred as Detective Sgt. Dave Kennedy in 1960 horror film "The Hypnotic Eye"; British actor Robert Crewdson, who starred in the horror films "Blood Beast from Outer Space" and "The Psychopath"; actress Sharon Farrell, who starred in the cult horror films "It's Alive" and "The Premonition"; actor Brandon Smith, who was featured as police officer Davis Tubbs in the 2001 horror film

"Jeepers Creepers"; Canadian actor Gordon Pinsent, who was featured in the films "Colossus: The Forbin Project" and "Blacula'" British actor Darren Kent, who starred as the Scholar in the cult horror series "Blood Drive"; Canadian actress Patricia Hamilton, who was featured as the ill-fated Mabel Osbourne in the 1981 horror film "My Bloody Valentine"; British director Piers Haggard, who directed the horror films "Blood on Satan's Claw" and "Venom"; actress Lelia Goldoni who appeared in the Hammer thriller "Hysteria" and the horror film "Theatre of Death"; actor Baird Stafford, who starred in the extreme 1981 slasher film "Nightmare"; British actor Richard Franklin, who was featured as Captain Mike Yates in the "Doctor Who" series from 1971 to 1974; Austrian actor Helmut Berger, who starred in the 1970 film adaptation of "Dorian Gray"; actress Deborah Reed, who starred as the Goblin Queen in the 1990 cult classic "Troll 2"; Scottish actor Ewan Hopper, who was noted for his role in the 1968 Hammer horror film "Dracula Has Risen from the Grave"; British actress Sarah Lawson, who was featured in the Hammer horror film "The Devil Rides Out"; actress Pamela Curran who starred in the 1965 science fiction film "Mutiny in Outer Space"; cinematographer Jacques Haitkin, who was noted for his work on Wes Craven's horror film classic "A Nightmare on Elm Street"; actress Elaine Devry who appeared in the films "The Atomic Kid" and "Diary of a Madman"; actor and bodybuilder Ed Fury, who starred in the sword and sandal films "Colossus and the Amazon Queen" and "Ursus in the Land of Fire"; British singer and actor Dennis Lotis, who starred in the 1960 horror film "Horror Hotel"; actress Lynn Loring who starred in the horror tele-films "Black Noon" and "The Horror at 37,000 Feet"; Japanese film producer Shuji Abe, who produced the 2023 hit film "Godzilla Minus One"; actress Lisa Montell, who starred in the science fiction film "World Without End"; actor Peter Spellos, who was the unkillable Orville Ketchum in the 1990 slasher film "Sorority House Massacre II"; Jamaican-British screenwriter Evan Jones who scripted the films "These Are the Damned" and "Modesty Blaise"; actress Elizabeth Hoffman, who was Margaret Buchanan in the 1981 horror film "Fear No Evil"; Italian film director and writer Aldo Lado who helmed the science fiction film "The Humanoid"; costume designer Shawna Trpcic, who was noted for her work on the television series "Firefly" and "The Mandalorian"; actress Sandra Dorsey, who was featured as decapitated camp counselor Lily Miranda in the 1989 horror film "Sleepaway Camp III: Teenage Wasteland"; film director and writer Avery Crounse, who was noted for the 1983 western horror film "Eyes of Fire"; actor Earl Boen, who was featured as psychologist Dr. Peter Silberman in "The Terminator" film franchise and was the alien Nestor in "Battle Beyond the Stars"; Spanish film director Eugenio Martin Marquez, who was noted for the 1972 horror film "Horror Express"; British actor Joss Ackland who was featured in the horror films "Rasputin, the Mad Monk", "Crescendo", and "The House That Dripped Blood"; Irish-Canadian actress Nuala Fitzgerald, who was featured in David Cronenberg's 1979 horror film "The Brood"; Italian actor Giovanni Lombardo Radice, who was sometimes billed as John Morghen and starred in such horror films as "Cannibal Apocalypse" and "The House on the Edge of the Park"; Italian screenwriter Giorgio Mariuzzo, who worked with director Lucio Fulci on the horror films "The Beyond" and "The House by the Cemetery"; special effects artist Marc Thorpe, who worked in the "Star Wars" and "Indiana Jones" franchises; actor David McKnight, who was featured as resurrected gangster J.D. Walker in the 1976 blaxploitation horror film "J.D.'s Revenge"; actress Betta St. John, who was featured in the horror films "Corridors of Blood" and "Horror Hotel"; actress Zoe Trilling, who starred as Shirley Finnerty in the 1994 horror film "Night of the Demons 2"; poet R.H.W. Dillard, who co-wrote the 1965 cult-classic film "Frankenstein Meets the Space Monster"; actor Steve Barkett, who was noted for his role in the science fiction films "The Aftermath", "Wizards of the Demon Sword", and "Dinosaur Island"; actor and makeup artist Byrd Holland, who was featured as the Sheriff in the notorious 1964 horror classic "The Creeping Terror"; actress Joan McCall who appeared in the horror films "Devil Times Five" and "Grizzly"; French actress Juliette Mayniel who was featured as Edna Gruber, the ill-fated donor of a face transplant in Georges Franju's horror classic "Eyes Without a Face"; actor Camden Toy, who was noted for horror roles under special effects makeup in such series as "Buffy the Vampire Killer" and "Angel"; Japanese actor Jiro Dan, who starred as Hideki Go and Ultraman Jack in the television series "The Return of Ultraman" in the early 1970s; film director Jeff Burr, who helmed such horror films as "Leatherface: The Texas Chainsaw Massacre III" and "Pumpkinhead II"; Egyptian-American film director and producer Frank Agrama, who was noted for the low-budget horror films "Queen Kong" and "Dawn of the Mummy"; British television director and stuntman Ray Austin, who was stunt coordinator for the television series "The Avengers" in the 1960s; actor Cody Longo, who was featured in the 2010 cult film "Piranha 3D"; special effects artist Bill Basso, who was noted for his work on such films as "Jurassic Park" and "Tremors"; actress Sharon Acker, who starred as Odona in the 1969 "Star Trek" episode "The Mark of Gideon"; film and television writer Stephen Kandel who wrote the "Star Trek" episodes "Mudd's Women" and "I, Mudd"; actor John Copage who appeared in "Star Trek" as Elliott in the 1967 episode "The Doomsday Machine"; South Korean actress Jung Chae-yul, who starred in the television series "Zombie Detective"; British actor Terrence Hardiman, who starred in the title role in the children's horror series "Demon Headmaster"; Filipino actor Ronaldo Valdez, who was featured in the 1969 horror film "The Mad Doctor of Blood Island"; Welsh filmmaker Andrew Jones, whose low-budget horror films include "Werewolves of the Third Reich" and the "Robert the Doll" series; actress Josephine Chaplin, who starred in the films "Shadowman" and 1976's "Jack the Ripper"; director and screenwriter Michael De Gaetano, whose films include the cult classics "UFO: Target Earth" and "Haunted"; television writer and producer Jeff Vlaming, who was noted for his work on the series "The X-Files" and "Hannibal"; South Korean actor Byun Hee-Bong, who was featured as the grandfather in the 2006 monster movie "The Host"; Rev. William O'Malley, who was a technical advisor and actor for the 1973 film "The Exorcist"; Canadian actor Len Birman, who was Dr. Simon Mills in the "Captain America" tele-films in 1979; British actor Peter Vaughan-Clarke, who starred as Stephen Jameson in the juvenile science fiction series "The Tomorrow People" in the 1970s; British stuntman and actor Chris Webb, who worked on over a dozen James Bond films; Japanese actress Miyuki

Ichijo, who was noted for her voice role as Jodie Starling in the "Detective Conan" anime franchise; Japanese actor Hiroshi Inuzuka, who starred in the 1972 kaiju fantasy film "Daigoro vs. Goliath"; artist Roger Kastel, who was noted for designing posters for such films as "Jaws", and "The Empire Strikes Back"; and Terry Byrd, who was noted as the internet horror host Riggor Mortiss.

Literary figures who died in 2023 include author Cormac McCarthy, who wrote the novel "No Country for Old Men" and received a Pulitzer Prize in 2007 for "The Road"; Japanese writer Kenzaburo Oe, who received the Nobel Prize in Literature in 1994; John Jakes, who was noted for the civil war trilogy "North and South"; Greek author Vassilis Vassilikos, who wrote the 1967 political novel "Z"; British author Fay Weldon, who was noted for her 1983 novel "The Life and Loves of a She-Devil"; Czech-French novelist Milan Kundera, who was noted for his 1984 book "The Unbearable Lightness of Being"; author and screenwriter Vincent Patrick, who was noted for the crime novel "The Pope of Greenwich Village"; Paul Brodeur, whose novel was adapted for the 1980 film "The Stunt Man"; Russell Banks, who was noted for the novels "Continental Drift" and "The Sweet Hereafter"; oboist and author Blair Tindall, who wrote the 2005 memoir "Mozart in the Jungle"; novelist John Nichols, who was best known for his books "The Milagro Beanfield War" and "The Sterile Cuckoo"; mystery writer Carol Higgins Clark; poet Louise Gluck, who received the Nobel Prize in Literature in 2020; Serbian-American poet Charles Simic, who received the Pulitzer Prize for Poetry in 1990; South African playwright Mbongeni Ngema, who was noted for the musical "Sarafina!"; David Drake, who was noted for the military science fiction series "Hammer's Slammers"; and the science fiction writers D.G. Compton, Michael Bishop, Richard Bowes, Suzy McKee Charnas, Michael Flynn, and Eric Brown.

Comic book and cartoon passings include comic book artist and writer Keith Giffen, who was co-creator of the comic characters Rocket Raccoon, Lobo, and the Jaime Reyes version of the Blue Beetle; comic book artist Lee Moder, who was co-creator of the DC superhero Courtney 'Stargirl' Whitmore; cartoonist Al Jaffee, who contributed to "Mad" magazine for over 60 years and created the magazine's parody back cover Fold-In feature; comic book artist Joe Giella, who was noted for inking tales featuring Batman, the Flash, and Green Lantern; science fiction and comic book writer Rachel Pollack who was noted for her work on the "Doom Patrol" comic; comic book artist Gerry Shamray, who worked with Harvey Pekar on the series "American Splendor"; comic book artist Steve Erwin, who was co-creator of the DC comics "Checkmate" and "Gunfire"; cartoonist Joe Matt, who was noted for the autobiographical comic "Peepshow"; comic book writer Steve Skeates who co-created DC's Hawk and Dove; British comic artist John M. Burns, who was noted for his work on the "Judge Dredd" series; Italian comic book artist Giuseppe Montanari, who was noted for his work on the "Dylan Dog" comic series; Japanese manga artist Leiji Matsumoto, who created "Space Pirate Captain Harlock" and "Galaxy Express 999"; fantasy artist Mitch Foust; comic book artist Dan Green; comic book writer and artist Ian McGinty; British comic artist Ian Gibson, who was noted for his work on the series "Judge Dredd" and "The Ballad of Halo Jones"; cartoonist Chris Browne, who took over the comic strip "Hagar the Horrible" from his father Dik Browne in 1989; and cartoonist Sam Gross.

Reality television losses include singer C.J. Harris, who was a contestant on the 13th season of the television talent competition "American Idol" in 2014; Jody Kelly, who was a contestant on the television reality competition show "The Amazing Race"; Bobbie Jean 'B.J.' Carter, the sister of singers Nick and Aaron Carter and star of the reality series "House of Carters"; Anna 'Chickadee' Cardwell, who was the eldest sister of reality television star Honey Boo Boo; Alaska bush pilot Jim Tweto, who starred in the Discovery Channel television reality series "Flying Wild Alaska"; Japanese chef Chen Kenichi, who starred on the "Iron Chef" reality series; British antiques experts Henry Sandon and Judith Miller, who were featured frequently on the BBC's "Antiques Roadshow"; socialite and television personality Anna Shay, who starred on the television reality series "Bling Empire"; Scottish chef Barry 'Jock' Zonfrillo who hosted the television series "Nomad Chef" and "Restaurant Revolution"; Larry Myers, Jr., who was featured on the television series "My 600-lb. Life"; Stan Ellsworth, who was host of the history series "American Ride"; country music singer and songwriter Kyle Jacobs, who starred with his wife on the reality series "I Love Kellie Pickler"; Dakota Fred Hurt, who starred in the reality television franchise "Gold Rush"; and Marvin 'Jim Tim' Hedrick, who starred in the Discovery Channel series "Moonshiners".

Sports stars found within include baseball player and sports commentator Tim McCarver; college basketball coach Bobby Knight, who was head coach for the Indiana Hoosiers from 1971 to 2000; and basketball player Larry 'Gator' Rivers, who performed with the Harlem Globetrotters. The world of sports entertainment lost the wrestling champions Terry Funk and Superstar Billy Graham; Windham Rotunda, who was best known for his work with WWE under the names Bray Wyatt and the Fiend; Iranian professional wrestler Hossein Khosrow Ali Vaziri, who competed under the name the Iron Sheik; Welsh professional wrestler Exotic Adrian Street; Lanny Poffo, who was known in the ring as Leaping Lanny and the Genius; Jamin Dale Pugh, who teamed with his brother Mark as the Briscoe Brothers; wrestler and promoter Jerry Jarrett; leading female wrestlers Joyce Grable, Peggy Lee Leather, and Beverly Shade; Darren Drozdov, who competed in the ring under the name Droz and became a quadriplegic from a neck injury received during a wrestling match; New Zealand wrestler Robert 'Butch' Miller, who competed as Bushwhacker Butch in a tag team with Bushwhacker Luke; Japanese professional wrestler Masashi Ozawa, who was known in the ring as the Mongolian giant Killer Khan; Canadian Mohawk wrestler Billy Two Rivers; Mike Halac, who competed in the WWE under the name Mantaur; wrestler and manager Adnan Al-Kaissie; New Zealand professional wrestler Abe Jacobs; Mexican wrestler Black Warrior; Canadian wrestler Emile Dupree; and wrestlers Brett Sawyer, Jeff Gaylord, and Charlie Norris.

Other passings of note include attorney Newton N. Minow, who declared that television was a "vast wasteland" in a speech while chairman of the Federal Communications Commission in the early 1960s; military analyst and political activist Daniel Ellsberg, who was noted for leaking the Pentagon Papers to the press in 1971; Italian media mogul Silvio Berlusconi, who was three-time Prime Minister of Italy; astronauts Frank Borman, who was commander of the Apollo 8 mission that became the first to fly around the Moon in 1968, Walter Cunningham, who was pilot of the lunar module for the Apollo 7 mission in 1968, and Ken Mattingly, who was Command Module Pilot for the Apollo 16 lunar mission in 1972; Sal Piro, the founder and president of "The Rocky Horror Picture Show" Fan Club who helped turn the film into an interactive cult phenomenon; Spanish fashion designer Paco Rabanne; actor Brendan O'Brien, who was noted as the original voice of Crash Bandicoot in video games; German supermodel Tatjana Patitz; female bodybuilding pioneer and model Lisa Lyon; Canadian model Pamela Anne Gordon, who was Playboy Playmate of the Month in March of 1962; actress and model Teri Hope, who was Playboy Playmate of the Month in September of 1958; model Karen Velez, who was Playboy's Playmate of the Year in 1985; Uruguayan model Sherika de Armas, who represented Uruguay in the 2015 Miss World pageant; model Leina'ala Drummond, who was Miss Hawaii in 1964; Puerto Rican television personality Marisol Malaret, who was crowned Miss Universe in 1970; Linda Kasabian, a former Manson Family member who was a key witness for the prosecution in the trial of Charles Manson and the Manson Family for a series of brutal murders in 1969; British writer Anne Perry, who helped murder her best friend's mother as a teenager in a crime that was depicted in the 1994 film "Heavenly Creatures"; diplomat and Nobel Prize winner Henry Kissinger, who served as U.S. Secretary of State from 1973 to 1977; religious broadcaster and political commentator Pat Robertson; Methodist clergyman Donald Wildmon, who was an outspoken critic of immorality in media and the founder of the American Family Association; motorcycle stunt performer Robbie Knievel, who was the son of daredevil Evel Knievel; rodeo cowboy and actor Larry Mahan; attorney Frank W. 'Sonny' Seiler, who was the owner of the University of Georgia Bulldog's Uga bulldog mascots; British astrologer Margaret Anne Lake, who was known by the name Mystic Meg; British circus owner John Hayes Mabley, who was known as Doktor Haze and was ringmaster of the Circus of Horrors; magicians Milt Larsen, who was co-creator of the Magic Castle, a clubhouse for magicians, Harry Lorayne, who was noted for his mastery of memory recall, Gloria Dea, and mentalist David Berglas; political commentator Lynnette Hardaway, who was half of the black conservative duo Diamond and Silk; British role-playing game designer Bryan Ansell, who was co-creator of "Warhammer" and role-playing game designer Teeuwynn Woodruff; British scientist Nick Hitchon, who was featured in the long-running documentary film series "Seven Up!"; professional poker player Doyle Brunson; Japanese social medial personality, singer, and LGBTQ advocate ryuchell; British comedian and television personality Paul O'Grady, who was noted for his drag persona Lily Savage; British comedian George Logan, who was best known as half of the drag duo Hinge and Bracket; drag queen and actor Stefan Grygelko, who performed under the name

Heklina; mixed-martial artist Aaron Brink, who also performed in adult films under the name Dick Delaware; adult actor Paul F. Little, who was known by the stage name Max Hardcore; adult film actress Anna Ventura; and Spanish dancer and vaginal magician Sticky Vicky.

Celebrities of the animal world who passed in 2023 are also found within including Balltze, a Shiba Inu dog from Hong Kong who was the subject of the Cheems internet memes; Tater Tot, an orange tabby kitten whose physical deformities made him an internet sensation; Ricochet, the surfing Golden Retriever; Lolita the orca, a popular attraction at the Miami Seaquarium; French bulldog and internet celebrity Manny the Frenchie; Zeus, a Great Dane who was recognized as the tallest dog in the world; and groundhog Fred la Marmotte, who predicted the coming of spring,

I have been writing obituaries of film personalities for over forty years, beginning with a column in Forry Ackerman's Famous Monsters of Filmland in the late 1970s.

Many of the film obituaries in this work are taken from my monthly column in Classic Images (P.O. Box 809, Muscatine, IA 52761), a newspaper devoted to classic films and their performers. Information on the passing of the individuals found in this volume has been gathered from a myriad of sources. Primary sources include The New York Times, The Los Angeles Times, Times (of London), The Washington Post, Variety, Time, People, and TV Guide. Other sources include Boyd Mager's Western Clippings, The Memphis Commercial Appeal, The Hollywood Reporter, The (Manchester) Guardian, Locus, Pro Wrestling Torch, and Facts on File. Several sources on the internet have also been helpful, including Obits - Celebs & Otherwise (hosted by Teller) (http://www.voy.com/220428/), Life in Legacy (http://www.lifeinlegacy.com/), and the Internet Movie Database, Ltd. (http://us.imdb.com/).

REFERENCES

Internet References

Newspapers and Periodicals:
BBC News: http://news.bbc.co.uk/
Chicago Tribune: http://www.chicagotribune.com/
Commercial Appeal (Memphis, TN):
www.commercialappeal.com/
Der Standard: http://derstandard.at/
Guardian Unlimited: www.guardian.co.uk/
Hollywood Reporter:
www.hollywoodreporter.com/hr/index.jsp
Independent, The: http://independent.co.uk/
International New York Times:
http://international.nytimes.com/
La Repubblica: http://www.repubblica.it/
Los Angeles Times: www.latimes.com/
Nation, The: www.nationmultimedia.com/
New York Times: www.nytimes.com/
Online Newspapers: www.onlinenewspapers.com/
Playbill: www.playbill.com/news/
RTE Entertainment: www.rte.ie/
Scotsman: http://www.scotsman.com/
Seattle Post-Intelligencer: http://seattlepi.nwsource.com/
Stage, The: www.thestage.co.uk/
Star Tribune (Minneapolis-St. Paul, MN):
www.startribune.com/
Telegraph: www.telegraph.co.uk/
Time: www.time.com/
Times of India: http://timesofindia.indiatimes.com/
TimesOnline: www.timesonline.co.uk/tol/news/
TMZ: http://www.tmz.com/
Variety: www.variety.com/
Xinhua News: http://news.xinhuanet.com/english/
Yonhap News: http://english.yonhapnews.co.kr/

Other Sites:
1WrestlingLegends: www.1wrestlinglegends.com/
alt.obituaries:
http://groups.google.com/group/alt.obituaries/
Aveleyman: http://www.aveleyman.com/Default.aspx
Barbara's Obits & Memorials (Chronicler):
www.voy.com/221392/
Boot Hill: http://westernboothill.blogspot.com/
Bruisermania: http://bruisermania.com/
Caskets on Parade: http://daggy.name/cop/index.htm
Cauliflower Alley Club: www.caulifloweralleyclub.org/
Classic Horror Film Board:
http://monsterkidclassichorrorforum.yuku.com/
Dead Famous: https://deadfamous.info/

Dead People Server: http://dpsinfo.com/dps/
Dead Porn Stars: www.rame.net/faq/deadporn/
Dead Rock Stars Club: http://thedeadrockstarsclub.com/
Famous Monsters: www.famousmonstersoffilmland.com/
Find a Grave: www.findagrave.com/
Gary Will: Deceased Pro Wrestlers:
www.garywill.com/wrestling/decwres.htm
Internet Broadway Database: http://www.ibdb.com/
Internet Movie Database: www.imdb.com/
Jersey Girls Sing:
http://www.jerseygirlssing.com/GoneButNotForgotten.html
Legacy.com: http://legacy.com/NS/
Life in Legacy: www.lifeinlegacy.com/
Memphis Film Festival: www.memphisfilmfestival.com/
Obits - Celebs & Otherwise (Teller): www.voy.com/220428/
Outpost Gallifrey: http://gallifreyone.com/
Ranker: http://www.ranker.com/list/dead-actors-2015-list-
of-actor-deaths/ranker-death-lists
Satellite News: http://www.mst3kinfo.com/
Screen Actors Guild: http://www.sagaftra.org/
Seeing Stars in Hollywood: http://www.seeing-stars.com/
Social Security Death Index:
http://search.ancestry.com/search/db.aspx?dbid=3693
Toonopedia: www.toonopedia.com/index.htm
Westerns... all'Italiana!:
http://westernsallitaliana.blogspot.com/
Wikipedia: http://en.wikipedia.org/
Young Hollywood Hall of Fame:
www.younghollywoodhof.com

Abe, Shuji

Japanese film producer Shuji Abe, who was founder of the Robot Communications production company and produced the 2023 hit film "Godzilla Minus One", died in Japan on December 11, 2023. He was 74. Abe was born in Chiba, Japan, on August 7, 1949. He was founder of Robot

Communications in 1986, initially working on graphics design and television commercials. Robot became involved in film production the following decade and Abe served as executive producer of such features as "Love Letter" (1995), "Juvenile" (2000), "Laundry" (2002), "Bayside Shakedown 2" (2003), "Gyakkyo Nine" (2005), "Always: Sunset on Third Street" (2005), "Always: Sunset on Third Street 2" (2007), "Gin Iro No Shizun" (2008), the action film "K-20: The Fiend with Twenty Faces" (2008), "Honokaa Boi" (2009), "Oppai Bare" (2009), the animated mystery "Professor Layton and the Eternal Diva" (2009), "Space Battleship Yamato" (2010), "Flowers" (2010), "Crossroads" (2011), "Wild 7" (2011), "Always: Sunset on Third Street '64" (2012), the war drama "The Eternal Zero" (2013), the animated "Stand by Me Doraemon" (2014) based on the popular manga, the science fiction films "Parasyte: Part 1" (2014) and "Parasyte: Part 2" (2015), "The Lies She Loved" (2017), "Our Departures" (2018), "Lupin III: The First" (2019), "Stand by Me Doraemon 2" (2020), "Ghost Book" (2022), and the kaiju epic "Godzilla Minus One" (2023).

Abraham, Jake

British actor Jake Abraham died of prostate cancer in England on October 1, 2023. He was 56. He was born in

Toxteth, Liverpool, England, on July 12, 1967, and was raised in Kensington. He began his career at the Everyman Youth Theatre in the 1980s. He was seen often on television with roles in episodes of "Help!" as Davva from 1986 to 1988, "Making Out", "Screenplay", "The Brittas Empire", "Red Dwarf", "Sharpe", "Backup", "The Governor" as Brian Samora from 1995 to 1996, "Trial & Retribution", "Liverpool 1", "The Bill", "Merseybeat", "Holby City", "Prisoners Wives", "Moving On", and "The Responder". His other television credits include productions of "G.B.H." (1991), "Blood on the Dole" (1994), "Sardines" (1995), "The Commander" (2003), and "Justice" (2011). Abraham was featured in such films as "Blonde Fist" (1991), Guy Ritchie's directing debut "Lock, Stock and Two Smoking Barrels" (1998) as Dean, "The Parole Officer" (2001), "Formula

51" (2001), "Mean Machine" (2001), "Revengers Tragedy" (2002), "Oh Marabella!" (2003), "American Cousins" (2003), "The Virgin of Liverpool" (2003), "London Boulevard" (2010), "Spike Island" (2012), "Tamla Rose" (2013), "Ghetto Heaven" (2017), and "Fighter from the Docks" (2018). He married Joanna Taylor in 2002 and is survived by her and two children.

Abrams, Patsy Grady

Actress Patsy Grady Abrams died of a heart attack in Rockville, Maryland, on January 3, 2023. She was 89. She was

born Patsy Grady in Philadelphia, Pennsylvania, on October 25, 1933. She appeared on the local Philadelphia television program "Paul Whiteman's TV Teen Club" as a teenager. She also performed at Grossinger's Catskill Resort before serving in the U.S. Navy. She moved to Washington, D.C., after her discharge where she sang at nightclubs. She married Earle Abrams, who played piano in her band, in 1957, and they continued to perform together throughout her life. She began appearing in films in the early 1990s including several with director John Waters. Her films include "Serial Mom" (1994), "First Kid" (1996), "Pecker" (1998), "Enemy of the State" (1998), "Liberty Heights" (1999), "Cecil B. Demented" (2000), "Head of State" (2003), and "A Dirty Shame" (2004). Abrams was also seen in episodes of "America's Most Wanted: America Fights Back", "Homicide: Life on the Street", and "Veep". She is survived by her husband and two sons, Mike and Jeff, who often performed with the family band.

Absolute Andy

German professional wrestler Andreas Ullman, who competed under the name Absolute Andy with the Westside Xtreme Wrestling (wXw), died in Germany on November 23,

2023. He was 40. Ullman was born in Nuremberg, West Germany, on September 22, 1983. He began his wrestling career in 2003 and competed as Absolute Andy for wXw from 2006. He defeated Bryan Danielson for the promotion's World Heavyweight Championship in 2009 and held it for seven months before losing to Steve Douglas. He teamed with Marius Al-Ani as A4 to win the tag team titles in 2017. He later feuded with Al-Ani, Matt Riddle, and Ilja Dragunov. He won the Unified World Wrestling Championship from Dragunov and later lost the belt to Bobby Gunns in 2019. He and Jay FK formed the tag team Jay-AA to win the tag title. Andy defeated Norman Harras for the promotion's Shotgun Championship in 2021.

Acker, Sharon

Canadian actress Sharon Acker died at a residential home in Toronto, Ontario, Canada, on March 16, 2023. She was 87. Acker was born in Toronto on April 2, 1935. She began appearing on Canadian television in the mid-1950s with roles in episodes of "On Camera" and "Folio". She was featured in productions of "Ruth" (1955) and "Anne of Green Gables" (1956) as Mrs. Stacey. She joined the Stratford Theatre and accompanied the troupe to England. She made her film debut in the 1957 comedy "Lucky Jim". Acker returned to Canada to continue her career on television as Lady MacDuff in a 1961 production of "Macbeth". Her other television credits include episodes of "The Unforeseen", "Encounter", "Heritage",  "Playdate", "Shoestring Theatre", "Quest", "The Serial" as Helen Whitley in 1964, "Time of Your Life" (1964), "Wojeck" (1966), "The Wild Wild West", "Festival", "Star Trek" as Odona in the 1969 episode "The Mark of Gideon", "Get Smart", "It Takes a Thief", "Lancer", "The Bold Ones: The Senator" as Ellen Stowe, the wife of Hal Holbrook's Senator Hays Stowe, from 1970 to 1971, "Alias Smith and Jones", "Gunsmoke", "Cade's County", "The F.B.I.", "Love, American Style", "Mission: Impossible", "Mod Squad", "McMillan & Wife", "Hec Ramsey", "Marcus Welby, M.D.", "The Delphi Bureau", "The New Perry Mason" as Della Street, secretary for Monte Markham's Perry Mason, from 1973 to 1974, "Harry O", "Cannon", "Barnaby Jones", the short-lived prime-time soap opera "Executive Suite" as Helen Walling from 1976 to 1977, "The Streets of San Francisco", "The Love Boat", "The Rockford Files", "Police Story", "Stone", "Galactica 1980", "The Great Detective", "Matt and Jenny", "The Incredible Hulk", "Quincy", "Flamingo Road", "Shannon", the soap opera "Texas" as Judith Wheeler in 1982, "The Powers of Matthew Star", "Matt Houston", "Trapper John, M.D.", "Whiz Kids", "Simon & Simon", "Crazy Like a Fox", "Knight Rider", "Murder, She Wrote", "You Again!", "Adderly", "Days of Our Lives" as Pamela Fouchier from 1987 to 1988, "Street Legal", "Rin Tin Tin: K-9 Cop", and "The Young and the Restless" as Dr. Grace Sundell in 1992. She also appeared in the tele-films "Power Trip" (1969), "A Clear and Present Danger" (1970), "The Stranger" (1973), "The Hanged Man" (1974), "Our Man Flint: Dead on Target" (1976), "The Hostage Heart" (1977), "Battles: The Murder That Wouldn't Die" (1980), and "Off Your Rocker" (1982). Acker was also seen in the films "One Plus One" (1961), John Boorman's "Point Blank" (1967) as the unfaithful wife of Lee Marvin's character, "Don't Let the Angels Fall" (1969), "The First Time" (1969), "Waiting for Caroline" (1969), "Ace of Heart" (1970), the science fiction film "Threshold" (1981), and the horror film "Happy Birthday to Me" (1981) with Glenn Ford and Melissa Sue Anderson. She largely retired from acting by the early 1990s. Acker was married to Austin R. Macdonald from 1956 until their divorce in 1973 and is survived by their two daughters. She was married to Peter J. Elkington from 1973 until his death in 2001 and is also survived by two stepdaughters.

Ackland, Joss

British actor Joss Ackland died in Clovelly, Devon, England, on November 19, 2023. He was 95. Ackland was born in North Kensington, London, England, on February 29, 1928. He trained as an actor at the Central School of Speech and Drama and began his career on stage in regional theatrical companies. He worked in Africa from 1954 until 1957, where  he continued his stage career. He appeared in numerous productions with the Old Vic after returning to England. He was seen on Broadway in "Twelfth Night" (1958), "Hamlet" (1958), and "King Henry V" (1958). Ackland made his film debut in the late 1940s and appeared in "Landfall" (1949), "Seven Days to Noon" (1950), "Ghost Ship" (1952), "Next to No Time!" (1958), "In Search of the Castaways" (1962), Hammer's "Rasputin, the Mad Monk" (1966) starring Christopher Lee, "Crescendo" (1970), the horror anthology "The House That Dripped Blood" (1971) as Rogers in the "Waxworks" segment, "Villain" (1971), "Mr. Forbush and the Penguins" (aka "Cry of the Penguins") (1971), the science fiction film "The Mind Snatchers" (aka "The Happiness Cage") (1972), "Hitler: The Last Ten Days" (1973) as General Burgdorf, "Penny Gold" (1973), "England Made Me" (1973), "The Three Musketeers" (1973) as the father of Michael York's D'Artagnan, the spy thriller "The Black Windmill" (1974), "S*P*Y*S" (1974), the musical fantasy "The Little Prince" (1974) as the King, the Disney comedy "One of Our Dinosaurs Is Missing" (1975), "Royal Flash" (1975), "Operation Daybreak" (1975), "Silver Bears" (1977), "The Strange Case of the End of Civilization as We Know It" (1977), "The Greek Tycoon" (1978), "Who Is Killing the Great Chefs of Europe?" (1978), the animated fantasy "Watership Down" (1978) as the voice of Black Rabbit, "Saint Jack" (1979), "Caligula" (1979) as a voice in the English language version, "A Nightingale Sang in Berkeley Square" (1980), "Rough Cut" (1980), the science fiction musical "The Apple" (1980) as Mr. Topps, Peter Greenaway's "A Zed & Two Noughts" (1985), "Lady Jane" (1986), the historical crime drama "The Sicilian" (1987), "White Mischief" (1987) earning a BAFTA Award nomination for his supporting role as Jock Delves Broughton, the Pet Shop Boys' musical "It Couldn't Happen Here" (1987), "To Kill a Priest" (1988), "Olympus Force: The Key" (1988), the buddy cop action film "Lethal Weapon 2" (1989) as ill-fated South African villain Arjen Ruud, "The Palermo Connection" (1990), the submarine thriller "The Hunt for Red October" (1990) as Russian Ambassador Andrei Lysenko, "Tre Colonne in Cronaca" (1990), "The Sheltering Desert" (1991), "The Object of Beauty" (1991), the comic fantasy "Bill & Ted's Bogus Journey" (1991) as terrorist Chuck De Nomolos, "The Bridge" (1991), the animated "The Princess and the Goblin" (1991) as the voice of King Papa, "Once Upon a Crime..." (1992), "Shadowchaser" (1992), the Disney sports comedy "The Mighty Ducks" (1992) as Hans, the old mentor of Emilio Estevez's Gorgon Bombay, "Nowhere to Run" (1993), the animated "The Thief and the Cobbler" (1993), "Mother's Boys" (1993), "Giorgino" (1994), "Miracle on 34th Street" (1994), "OcchioPinocchio" (1994), "Mad Dogs and Englishmen" (1995), "A Kid in King Arthur's Court" (1995) as King Arthur, "Surviving Picasso" (1996) as Henri Matisse, "D3: The Mighty Ducks" (1996) reprising his role as Hans, "Swept from the Sea" (1997), "Fireflight" (1997), "My Giant" (1998), "Milk" (1999),

"Passion of Mind" (2000), "The Mumbo Jumbo" (2000), "No Good Deed" (2002), "K-19: The Widowmaker" (2002), "I'll Be There" (2003), "A Different Loyalty" (2004), "Asylum" (2005), "The Christmas Eve Snowfall" (2005), "These Foolish Things" (2006), "Moscow Zero" (2006), "Flawless" (2007), "How About You" (2007), "In Search of the Great Beast 666" (2007) as the Narrator, "Prisoners of the Sun" (2013), and "Decline of an Empire" (2014). Ackland was frequently soon on television with roles in episodes of "Destination Downing Street", "On Trial", "About Religion", "First Night", "Detective", "The Indian Tales of Rudyard Kipling" as William Stevens in 1964, "Sherlock Holmes", "Londoners", "Gaslight Theatre", "Blackmail", "No Hiding Place", "Dr. Finlay's Casebook", "Lord Raingo", "Thirteen Against Fate", "Theatre 625", "Armchair Theatre", "The Further Adventures of the Musketeers" as d'Artagnan in 1967, "Trapped", "The Wednesday Play", "The Troubleshooters" (aka "Mogul"), "Mystery and Imagination", "Z Cars" as Detective Inspector Todd from 1967 to 1968, "The Avengers", "W. Somerset Maugham", "Canterbury Tales" as the host in 1969, "One Pair of Eyes", "Shirley's World", "Justice", "The Persuaders!", "Thirty-Minute Theatre", "Country Matters", "Six Faces", "Late Night Theatre", "Play for Today", "The Rivals of Sherlock Holmes", "Orson Welles' Great Mysteries "The Protectors", "Centre Play", "Aquarius", "This Is Your Life", "The Crezz" as Charles Bronte in 1976, "Maggie and Her", "Enemy at the Door", "Return of the Saint", "The Sweeney", "Turtle's Progress", "A Question of Guilt" as Samuel Kent in 1980, "The Gentle Touch", "Thicker Than Water", "BBC2 Playhouse", "The Adventures of Sherlock Holmes", "Omnibus", "Tales of the Unexpected", "The Justice Game", "Jackanory", "The Young Indiana Jones Chronicles", "Shakespeare: The Animated Tales" as the voice of Julius Caesar in 1994, "Screen Two", "Testament: The Bible in Animation", "Blue Peter", "Midsomer Murders", "Ghostly Tales of the Unexpected" as host in 2004, "Kingdom", and "Crusoe" in the recurring role of Judge Jefferies from 2008 to 2001. His other television credits include productions of "Hamlet" (1959), "The Violent Years" (1959), "All My Own Work" (1961), "Death of a Salesman" (1966), "The Gold Robbers" (1969), "The Three Sisters" (1970), "Consequences" (1972), "Miss Nightingale" (1974), "Great Expectations" (1974), John LeCarre's "Tinker Tailor Soldier Spy" (1979) as Jerry Westerby, "Closing Ranks" (1980), "Dangerous Davies: The Last Detective" (1981), "Thicker Than Water" (1981), "The Confessions of Felix Krull" (1982), "Escape to the West" (1982), "The Barretts of Wimpole Street" (1982) as Edward Moulton-Barrett, "Shroud for a Nightingale" (1984), "The Tragedy of Coriolanus" (1984), "The Great White Mountain" (1986), "Shadowlands" (1986) as C.S. Lewis, "A Killing on the Exchange" (1987), "Queenie" (1987), "When We Are Married" (1987), "Codename: Kyril" (1988), "A Quiet Conspiracy" (1989), "The Man Who Lived at the Ritz" (1989) as Hermann Goering, "First and Last" (1989) receiving a BAFTA nomination for best actor, "Jekyll and Hyde" (1990) as Dr. Charles Lanyon, "Spymaker: The Secret Life of Ian Fleming" (1990), "Never the Sinner" (1990) as Clarence Darrow, "A Murder of Quality" (1991), "A Woman Named Jackie" (1991) as Aristotle Onassis, "Miss Marple: They Do It with Mirrors" (1991), "Ashenden" (1991), the animated "Brown Bear's Wedding" (1991) and "White Bear's Secret" (1992) as the voice of Brown Bear, "Sherlock Holmes: Incident at Victoria Falls" (1992), "Citizen Locke" (1994), "Jacob" (1994), "Citizen X" (1995), "Daisies in December" (1995), "Hidden in Silence" (1996), "To the End of Times" (1996), "Heat of the Sun" (1998), "Il Figlio di Sandokan" (1998), "Tales from the Madhouse" (2000), "Gioco di Spechi" (2000), "Othello" (2001), "A World in Arms" (2002), "Lionheart: The Crusade" (2003), "Henry VIII" (2003) as Henry VII, "Icon" (2005), Terry Pratchett's "Hogfather" (2006), "Above and Beyond" (2006) as Winston Churchill, and "Pinocchio" (2009). He provided the voice of Pieter Van Eckhardt for the video game "Tomb Raider: The Angel of Darkness" in 2003. Ackland continued his career on stage throughout his career. He created the role of Juan Peron in the Andrew Lloyd Webber musical "Evita". He also appeared in the London productions of Stephen Sondheim's "A Little Night Music". Ackland was married to Rosemary Kirkcaldy from 1951 until her death in 2002. They had seven children together. Their eldest son, Paul Ackland, died of a heroin overdose in 1982. He is survived by daughters, Melanie, Antonia, Penelope, Samantha, and Kirsty, and son Toby.

Adam, Peter R.

German film editor Peter R. Adam, whose work includes "An American Werewolf in Paris" and "Good Bye, Lenin!", died in Berlin, Germany, on December 4, 2023. He was 56.

Adam was born in Pirmasens, West Germany, on May 29, 1957. He worked in films as a sound editor for such features as "The Noah's Ark Principle" (1984), "Last Exit to Brooklyn" (1989), "The Handmaid's Tale" (1990), "The NeverEnding Story II: The Next Chapter" (1990), "Werner - Beinhart!" (1990), "Nordkurve" (1992), and "Felidae" (1994). Adam edited the films "Yol" (1982), "The Record" (1984), "Versteckte Liebe" (1986), "Kinder aus Stein" (1987), "Rotlicht!" (1987), "Taxi Nach Kairo" (1987), "Superstau" (1991), "Alles Luge" (1992), "No More Mr. Nice Guy" (1993), "Mute Witness" (1995), "Gimlet" (1995), "Ludwig & Richard" (1995), "Jailbirds" (1996), "14 Days to Life" (1997), the horror film "An American Werewolf in Paris" (1997), "The Harmonists" (1997), "Love Your Neighbour!" (1998), "Nichts als die Wahrheit" (1999), "The Little Vampire" (2000), "Der Tunnel" (2001), "Angel of Death" (2001), "Good Bye, Lenin!" (2003), "Berlin Blues" (2003), "Erbsen Auf Halb 6" (2004), "The Ninth Day" (2004), "The Thief Lord" (2006), "Elementarteilchen" (2006), "My Fuhrer" (2007), "Ulzhan" (2007), "Warum Manner Nicht Zuhoren und Frauen Schlecht Einparken" (2007), "The Silent Army" (2008), "Germany 09: 13 Short Films About the State of the Nation" (2009) for the "Krankes Haus" segment, "Dinosaurier" (2009), "Anonymous" (2011), "Russendisko" (2012), "Sources of Life" (2013), "Four Senses" (2013), "Punk berlin 1982" (2015), "Me and Kaminski" (2015), "The White King" (2016), "Vier Gegen die Bank" (2016), "Bye Bye Germany" (2017), "Hansel & Gretel: Don't Let Fear Eat You" (2017), "Herrliche Zeiten" (2018), "Die Schneekonigin - Zusammen Erreichen Wir Alles!" (2018), "Berlin, I Love You" (2019), "Bekenntnisse des Hochstaplers Felix Krull" (2021), "A Stasi Comedy" (2022),

"Measure of Men" (2023), "Die Unscharferelation der Liebe" (2023), and "The Piper" (2023). Adam was a founding member of the Deutsche Filmakademie in 2003.

Adnan Al-Kaissie

Iraqi-American professional wrestler and manager Adan Al-Kaissie died in Minnesota on September 8, 2023. He was 84. He was born Adnan bin Abdul Kareem Ahmed Alkaissy El Farthie in Baghdad, Iraqi, on March 1, 1939. He played football and wrestled while in high school. He came to

the United States to play football with the University of Houston in Texas. He later transferred to Oklahoma State University where he wrestled. He began wrestling professionally under the name Billy White Wolf in the Oklahoma territory in 1959. He competed with Pacific Northwest Wrestling in the 1960s. He frequently brought wrestling events to Iraq in the early 1970s under Saddam Hussein, who was his high school classmate. He competed in Japan as the Sheik of Sheiks of Baghdad, frequently teaming with Nikolai Volkoff from 1974 to 1975. He wrestled as Billy White Wolf in the World Wide Wrestling Federation (now WWE) and teamed with Chief Jay Strongbow to capture the tag team titles in 1976. He appeared Hawaii and England later in the decade and made his final tour of Iraq. He debuted with the American Wrestling Federation (AWA) under as Sheik Adnan Al-Kaissey in 1981. He failed to capture the AWA championship from Nick Bockwinkel and his tag team with Crusher Jerry Blackwell also were unsuccessful in championship bouts. Adnan became manager of the tag team of Blackwell and Ken Patera and led them to victory over Greg Gagne and Jim Brunzell for the AWA Tag Team Championship in June of 1983. He continued to work in the AWA, battling Verne Gagne and teaming with Boris Zhukov against the Midnight Rockers. He joined the WWE in 1990 as General Adnan, managing Sgt. Slaughter during his pro-Iraqi gimmick. Slaughter won the WWF title from the Ultimate Warrior in January of 1991 but dropped the belt to Hulk Hogan two months later. Adnan and Slaughter were joined by the Iron Sheik, now known as Colonel Mustafa, to form the anti-American Triangle of Terror. He left the WWE in 1992. He wrestled with the American Wrestling Federation (AWF) in the 1990s until his retirement in 1998. His memoirs, "The Sheik of Baghdad: Tales of Celebrity and Terror from Pro Wrestling's General Adnan", were published in 2005. Adnan married Kathy Davis in 1964 and they had four children.

Afshar, Lily

Iranian classical guitarist Lily Afshar died of cancer in Iran on October 24, 2023. She was 63. She was born Lily Afshar Azardad in Tehran, Iran, on March 9, 1960. She became interested in classical guitar as a child. She came to the United States to study guitar at Boston University in 1977. She remained in the United States following the ouster of the Shah

of Iran in 1979 and the establishment for a Islamic theocracy. She received a master's degree in music from the New England Conservatory. She continued her studies at Florida State University where she earned a Doctor of Music degree for her

guitar performance. She also studied under classic guitar virtuoso Andres Segovia at the University of Southern California in 1986. Afshar joined the faculty as director of the guitar program for the University of Memphis in 1989. She continued to perform and teach around the world. She was noted for performing music ranging from Persian and Azerbaijani folk music to collaborations with such contemporary artists as Carlo Domeniconi, Gerard Drozd, Marilyn Siffrin, and Salvador Brotons. She recorded several albums from Memphis' Archer Records label including "A Jug of Wine and Thou" (1999), "Possession" (2002), "Hemispheres" (2006), "One Thousand and One Nights" (2012), "Musica da Camera" (2013), and "Bach on Fire" (2019). Afsar retired from teaching at the University of Memphis after 34 years due to a long struggle with cancer earlier in 2023 and returned to Iran.

Agrama, Frank

Egyptian-American film director and producer Frank Agrama, who was noted for the low-budget horror films

"Queen Kong" and "Dawn of Mummy", died in Los Angeles, California, on April 25, 2023. He was 93. He was born Farouk Agrama in Arish, Egypt, on January 1, 1930. He began his career as an actor in Egyptian cinema with roles in the films "Saut Min el Madi" (1956), "Ayyami el Saida" (1958), "Malish Gherak" (1958), "Mugarem Fi Ijaza" (1958),
"Gharam Fil cirque" (1960), and "Hub Fi Hub" (1960) which he also produced. He studied medicine at the University of Cairo and became a doctor in the 1950s. He left medicine to concentrate on a career in films and received a degree in theater arts from the University of California at Los Angeles. He returned to the Middle East in 1964. He directed the films "El Ainab el Murr" (1965), "Al Kahirun" (1966), "Love Game" (1966), "The Adventures of Filfila" (1966), "Wadi al Mot" (1967), "Storm Over Petra" (1968), "Gang of Women" (1968), "Game of Chance" (1968), "Fire of Love" (1968), and "Khata-Karan" (1968). He produced, directed, and scripted the films "The Godfather's Friend" (1972) and the horror film "Dawn of the Mummy" (1981). He also directed and wrote the 1976 comedy spoof "Queen Kong". Agrama distributed the 1983 television mini-series "Shaka Zulu", which was produced by the South African Broadcasting Corporation. He founded the film and television production company Harmony Gold USA. He was executive producer for such productions as "Time Patrol"

(1985), "Captain Harlock and the Queen of a Thousand Years" (1985-1986), "Robotech: The Movie" (1986), "Robotech II: The Sentinels" (1988), "Around the World in 80 Days" (1989), "The Man Who Lived at the Ritz" (1989), "Dragon Ball" (1989), "Sherlock Holmes and the Leading Lady" (1991), "Sherlock Holmes: Incident at Victoria Falls" (1992), "The Lost World" (1992), "Return to the Lost World" (1992), "Heidi" (1993), "American Strays" (1996), "Road Ends" (1997), "Heart of Fear" (2006), "Robotech: The Shadow Chronicles" (2006), and "Stepping High" (2013). Agrama supplied the broadcasting rights for films from Paramount Pictures to Silvio Berlusconi's Mediaset broadcasting company in Italy from the 1980s. He and Berlusconi, a former Prime Minister of Italy, were among a group of people involved with Mediaset that were indicted by a court in Milan for tax fraud, embezzlement, and false accounting in 2005. He was convicted and sentenced to three years but was never imprisoned due to an amnesty due to his age. He and several others, including Berlusconi's son, Pier Silvio, were tried for tax evasion and embezzlement in 2013 but were acquitted due to the statute of limitations. Subsequent charges against Agrama were dropped in 2016. He is survived by his wife, Olfat El Sergany, and two children.

Ah Kin, Camilla

Australian actress Camilla Ah Kin died in Sydney, Australia, on June 9, 2023. Ah Kin was born in Australia in 1964. She was 58. She graduated from the Western Australian Academy of Performing Arts. She also studied at the L'Ecole Internationale du Theatre Jacdques Lecoq in Paris, France, in the early 1990s and earned a Master of Arts degree from the University of Sydney's Department of Performance Studies.

She performed frequently on stage in productions with the Sydney Theatre Company, Melbourne Theatre Company, Bell Shakespeare, and the Belvoir St. Theatre. Ah Kin appeared on television in episodes of "Halifax f.p.", "Blue Heelers", "Murder Call", "Going Home" as Najette Malek in 2001, "Stories from the Golf", "All Saints", "Stupid Stupid Man", "Tough Nuts: Australia's Hardest Criminals", "Rake", "Here Come the Habibs!" as Mariam Habib from 2016 to 2017, and "Doctor Doctor". She was also seen in the mini-series "Fighting Season" (2018) and "Wakefield" (2021). Ah Kin was featured in the films "Holding the Man" (2015), "The Greenhouse" (2021), and "What About Sal" (2023).

Ahlin, Per

Swedish animation director Per Ahlin died in Malmo, Sweden, on May 1, 2023. He was 91. Ahlin was born in Hofors, Sweden, on August 7, 1931. He left school to work as a draftsman before moving to Malmo in 1952. He became an illustrator of stories for the Swedish newspaper "Sydsvenskan". He was a self-taught animator and began working in films for Hasse & Tage's animated production "Senska Bilder"

("Swedish Portraits") in 1964. He also worked on the Hasse & Tage animated films "Out of an Old Man's Head" (1968), which was Sweden's first animated, feature, and "The Adventures of Picasso" (1978), where he animated various Picasso paintings. Ahlin began his own animation studio, PennFilm Studio AB, in 1970, where he directed the films and shorts "Dunderklumpen!" (1974), "Christopher's Christmas Mission" (1975), "Voyage to Melonia" (1989), "The Dog Hotel" (2000), and "That Boy Emil" (2013). He was co-creator of the animated series "Alfons Aberg", based on the children's books by Gunilla Bergstrom", in 1981. He illustrated the book covers for numerous Agatha Christie novels published in Sweden. He also directed numerous "Lilla Spoket Laban" shorts in the 2000s. Ahlin worked on the film "Hoffmann's Eyes", based on Jacques Offenbach's opera, "The Tales of Hoffmann", but the film was never completed.

Aidoo, Ama Ata

Ghanaian playwright and author Ama Ata Aidoo died in Accra, Ghana, on May 31, 2023. She was 81. Aidoo was born in Abeadzi Kyiakor, Ghana, on March 23, 1942. She graduated from the University of Ghana in Leon and wrote her

first play, "The Dilemma of a Ghost", in 1965. She attended Stanford University in California on a fellowship in creative writing before returning to Ghana to teach at the University of Ghana in 1969. She also taught at the University of Cape Coast. She wrote the 1970 play "Anowa" and the 1977 novel "Our Sister Killjoy: or Reflections from a Black-Eyed Squint" (1977). Aidoo served as Secretary of Education of Ghana under Jerry Rawlings' government from 1982 to 1983. She lived in Harare, Zimbabwe, for several years from 1983, where she published the poetry collection "Someone Talking to Sometime" in 1985 and the children's book "The Eagle and the Chickens and Other Stories" in 1986. She went to London, England, in 1986, and was writer in residence at the University of Richmond, Virginia, in 1989. She also taught at Hamilton College in Clinton, New York, in the mid-1990s. She was a visiting professor at Brown University from 2004 to 2011. Aidoo was author of the 1991 novel "Changes: A Love Story", the poetry collections "Birds and Other Poems" (9187) and "An Angry Letter in January" (1992), and the short story collections "The Girl Who Can and Other Stories" (1997) and "Diplomatic Pounds & Other Stories" (2012).

AKA

South African rapper Kiernan Jarryd Forbes, who performed under the name AKA, was shot to death outside of a restaurant in Durban, South Africa, on February 10, 2023. He  and his friend, Tebello Motsoane, were standing outside a restaurant when two gunmen shot and killed both. He was 35. Forbes was born in Cape Town, South Africa, on January 28, 1988. He moved to Johannesburg in his youth and was educated at St. John's College. He began performing with Vice Versa and Greyhound Sizwe Mpofu-Walsh as the hip hop group Entity in 2002. They disbanded in 2006 and he was co-founder of the production collective The I.V. League. Forbes released several singles in 2009 including "In My Walk", "I Do", and "My Mistakes Killed Me". He recorded his debut album, "Altar Ego", in 2010 which included the singles "I Want It All", "All I Know", and "Victory Lap". His other albums include "Levels" (2014), "Be Careful What You Wish For" (2017), "Touch My Blood" (2017), and "Mass Country" (2022). He appeared at a live event for World Wrestling Entertainment (WWE) in South Africa in April of 2018. AKA had a daughter from a relationship with producer DJ Zinhle that lasted from 2014 to 2015. They briefly reunited from 2018 to 2019. He was engaged to Nelli Tembe before her death from a fall at a Cape Town hotel in April of 2012.

Alexander, James

South African actor James Alexander, who was frequently billed under the name James Gracie later in his  career, died of cancer in South Africa on April 28, 2023. He was 45. Alexander was born in Boksburg, South Africa, on January 8, 1978. He appeared in films and television from the late 1990s. He was featured as Christopher Hawkins in the series "Isidingo" from 1998 and was Dr. Rico Maartens in "Binnelanders" in 2005. He was featured in television productions of "To the Ends of the Earth" (2005), "The Sinking of the Laconia" (2011), "Women in Love" (2011), "The Runaway" (2011), "Donkerland" (2013), "The Book of Negroes"(2015), "The Gamechangers" (2015), "Roots" (2016), "Madiba" (2017), and "Rita" (2020). His other television credits include episodes of "Home Affairs", "Scandal!" as Graham Wilson in 2008, "Strike Back", "Wild at Heart", "The Wild", "Leonardo", "Geraamtes in die Kas", "Homeland", "The Wrong Mans", "Black Sails" in the recurring role of Juan Antonio Grandal in 2016, "Trackers" as Lemmer in 2019, and "Alex Rider" as Langham in 2020. He was the voice of Jesus in several "Adventures of Toby" animated shorts from 2005 to 2009. He also appeared in the films "Discreet" (2008),

"Leading Lady" (2014), "Eye in the Sky" (2015), "Sy Klink Soos Lente" (2016), "The Journey Is the Destination" (2016), and "Siberia" (2018). He married actress Anel Alexander in 2003 and she survives him.

Allan, Chad

Canadian musician and singer Chad Allan, who was a founding member of the Guess Who, died in Canada on November 21, 2023. He was 80. He was born Allan Kowbel  in Winnipeg, Manitoba, Canada, on March 29, 1943. He attended Miles MacDonnell Collegiate in Winnipeg in the late 1950s and formed his first band, Allan and the Silvertones, in 1958. He soon formed a new band and changed his stage name with Chad Allan and the Reflections. They became Chad Allan and the Expressions in 1963. A promotion for the band's 1965 release "Shakin' All Over" with the artist identified as Guess Who?. The band was soon being billed as the Guess Who. They recorded the albums "Hey Ho (What You Do to Me!)" in 1965 and "It's Time" in 1966 before Allan left the band. He briefly returned to college before becoming host of the CBC-TV weekly music program "Let's Go" in 1967. He continued to perform and record and teamed with Karen Marklinger and Corrine Cyca as the Metro-Gnomes in 1968. Allan reunited with former Guess Who bandmate Randy Bachman to form Brave Belt in 1971 and they recorded "Brave Belt" (1961) and "Brave Belt II" (1972). He recorded the solo album "Sequel" in 1973 and performed the lead character in the musical adaptation of "Beowulf" in 1974. He remained involved in the music industry and hosted a local children's program in Winnipeg. He released an album and several singles on his own label, Seabreeze Records. He also began teaching songwriting at Kwantien University College in Surrey, British Columbia, in 1982. Allan released the 1992 Christian rock album "Zoot Suit Monologue" and much of his earlier work was reissued by Regenerator Records in 2007. He continued to perform until suffering a stroke in 2017. Allan is survived by his wife, Christine.

Allen, Tony

British comedian Tony Allen died in England on December 1, 2023. He was 78. Allen was born in Hayes,  Middlesex, England, on March 4, 1945. He began acting with the West London Theatre Workshop in the early 1970s and formed the Rough Theatre in 1973. He co-wrote their plays and scripted several BBC radio plays including 1975's "Two Fingers Finnegan Comes Again". He became a popular stand-up comic later in the decade and worked with Alexei Sayle to promote the Comedy Store in Soho. Allen also formed the Alternative Cabaret, helping establish England's live comedy circuit. He appeared on television in episodes of "The Comic Strip" and "The Young Ones". His comedy routines highlighted his radical anarchist approach. He and writing partner Max Handley wrote scripts for the television and radio shows "Spitting Image", "Naked Video", "Week Ending", and "Alas Smith and Jones". He wrote several comic strips for the science fiction comic magazines "Crisis" and "Judge Dredd Megazine". He also performed as a street clown under the name Tofu the Zany and helped Banksy create the parody them park Dismaland in 2015. Allen was author of the books "Attitude! Wanna Make Something of it? The Secret of Stand-up Comedy" (2002) and "A Summer in the Park. A Journal of Speakers' Corner" (2004).

Almada, Fernando

Mexican actor Fernando Almada Otero died in Mexico City, Mexico, on October 30, 2023. He was 94. Almada was born in Mexico on February 26, 1929. He was the younger brother of actor and producer Mario Almada. Fernando appeared in nearly 200 productions from the late 1950s through

the early 2000s. His films, which were frequently westerns or action thrillers, include "Milagros de San Martin de Porres" (1959), "El Correo del Norte" (1960), "Il Terror de la Frontera" (1963), "Los Hijos del Condenado" (1964), "Nido de Aguilas" (1965), "Los dos Cuatreros" (1965), "Los Jinetes de la Bruja (En el Viego Guanajuato)" (1966) the first of many films he made with his brother Mario, "Crisol" (1967), "El Tesoro de Atahualpa" (1968), "Todo por Nada" (1969), "Nido de Fieras" (1971), "Los Desalmados" (1972), "Todo el Horizonte Para Morir" (1971), "Por Eso" (1972) which he also produced, "Pistoleros Bajo el Sol" (1974), "Debieron Ahorcarlos Antes" (1974), "El Pistolero del Diablo" (1974), "El Valle de los Miserables" (1975), "Dinastia de la Muerte" (1977), "Mariachi - Fiesta de Sangre" (1977), "El Hechizo del Pantano" (1978) which he also directed and wrote, "La Banda del Carro Rojo" (1978), "El Arracadas" (1978), "Puerto Maldito" (1979), "Perros Callejeros II" (1979), "Under Siege" (1980), "La Venganza de un Maton" (1980), "Treinta Segundos Para Morir" (1981), "357 Magnum" (1981), "Pistoleros Famosos" (1981), "Herencia de Muerte" (1981), "Una Leyenda de Amor" (1982), "Contrabando Humano" (1982), "El Canto de los Humildes" (1982), "El Traficante" (1983), "Todos Eran Valientes" (1983), "El Vengador del 30-06" (1983), "La Muerte del Chacal" (1984), "Hombres de Accion" (1984), "Encuentro Con la Muerte" (1984), "Siete en la Mira" (1984), "Gatilleros del Rio Bravo" (1985), "El Gatillo de la Muerte" (1985), "Que Me Maten de Una Vez" (1985), "Rafaga de Plomo" (1985), "La Venganza del Rojo" (1986), "El Trailer Asesino" (1986), "Cartucho Cortado" (1986), "Los Dos Frailes" (1986), "Perseguido Por la Ley" (1986), "Y... Se Hizo Justicia" (1986), "Camino al infierno" (1987), "Pasaporte a la Muerte" (1988), "La Jaula de Oro" (1988), "Masacre en Rio Grande" (1988), "Cargamento Mortal" (1989), "Los Hijos del Criminal" (1980), "Grave Robbers" (1989), "La Diosa del Puerto" (1989), "Al Margen de la Ley" (1989), "Pistolero a Sueldo" (1989), "Al Filo del Terror" (1990), "La Camioneta Gris" (1990), "Milagro en el Barrio" (1990), "El Fugitivo de Sonora" (1990), "Calles Sangrientas" (1990), "Emboscada" (1990), "Mision Sangrienta" (1990), "Exterminador Implacable" (1990), "Los Demonios del Desierto" (1990), "Comando de Federales" (1990), "Tengo Que Matarlos" (1991), "Three Roosters" (1991), "Muerte en Tijuana" (1991), "Martir de Mexicali" (1991), "El Amarrador" (1991), "Encuentro de Valientes" (1991), "Tierra Sin Ley" (1991), "Asalto Mortal" (1991), "Estrella Negra" (1992), "Testigo Silencioso" (1992), "Ansiedad Asesina" (1992), "La Furia de un Gallero" (1992), "Comando de Federales II" (1992), "Alla en el Rancho Chico" (1992), "Destino Homicida" (1992), "El Corrido de los Perez" (1992), "Halcones de la Frontera II" (1992), "Mi Destino es la Violencia" (1992), "Muerte en los Canaverales" (1992), "En la Mira del Odio" (1992), "38 Special" (1992), "El Guardian de la Ley" (1992), "Con la Muerte en los Ojos" (1992), "Ajuste de Cuentas" (1992), "Mariachi" (1993), "El Ultimo Gatillero" (1993), "Misa de Cuerpo Presente" (1993), "Ranger II: El Narcotunel" (1993), "A las Puertas del Infierno" (1993), "Y... Donde Esta la Comadre?" (1993), "La Venganza del Silla de Ruedas" (1993), "Bajado del Cerro a Tamborazos" (1993), "Waco Texas: Apocalipsis" (1993), "Angustia Fatal" (1993), "Por la Gloria o la Muerte" (1994), "La Dinastia de Los Perez" (1994), "Que Me Entierren Con la Banda" (1994), "Estuches de Madera" (1994), "Rencilla Mortal" (1994) which he also wrote, "Mestizo" (1995), "Demoledor" (1995), "Fotografiando a la Muerte" (1995), "Velocidad Mortal" (1995), "Traficantes de Michoacan" (1995), "Muerte en el Tovara" (1995), "Justicia Violenta" (1995), "Sin Retorno" (1995), "El Amarrador 3" (1995), "Venganza Mortal" (1995), "Crimen en Chihuahua" (1995), "Amigos Hasta la Muerte" (1995), "El Emperador de la Muerte" (1995), "Fugitivo Sin Salida" (1995), "Duelo de Serpientes" (1995), "El Cartel de Michoacan" (1996), "Un Indio Quiere Llorar 2" (1996), "Cruz de Madera" (1996), "Fatal Lottery" (1997), "El Corrido de Silviano Bernal" (1997), "El Bufalo de Jalisco" (1997), "La Camioneta Azul de la Mafia" (1997), "Regalo Caro" (1998), "La Leyenda del Pistolero" (1998), "El Gatillero" (1998), "Juego Con la Muerte" (1998), "La Pantera de Michoacan" (1998), "Unidos Por el Destino" (1998), "Regreso Sangriento" (1998), "Persecucion" (1998), "El Ultimo Cartucho" (1999), "El Extermindaor de la Mafia" (1999), "Cien Kilos de Oro Verde" (1999), "El Ultimo Secuestro" (1999), "Dos Cruces" (1999), "Ambicion y Exterminio" (1999), "La Camioneta Gris 2" (2000), "De Mi Rancho a Zurrancho" (2000), "Era Cabron el Viejo" (2000), "Tierra de Escorpiones" (2000), "El Rey de la Mota" (2001), "Perro No Come Perro" (2001), and "La Viuda de Chihuahua" (2003).

Ambrosini, Carlo

Italian comic book artist Carlo Ambrosini died in Brescia, Italy, on November 1, 2023. He was 69. Ambrosini was born in Azzano Mella, Italy, on April 15, 1954. He graduated from the Academy of Fine Arts in Brera in 1975. He soon began working in comics drawing war stories for Dardo

publishers. He also worked on comics for Ediperiodici and Editoriale Corno. He began working for Sergio Bonelli Editore in 1980, illustrating "Ken Parker" comics. He created the medieval series "Nico Macchia" for the "Orient Express" magazine in 1984. He also wrote western comics for Paolo Eleuteri-Sepeirri. Ambrosini teamed with writer Franco Mescola on the "Il Tesoro Degli Imbala" comic for "Corto Maltese" in 1986. He created the character "Barokko" for the French publisher Casterman in 1988. He was an artist for the "Dylan Dog" series at Bonelli in 1987. He and Graziano Origa created "Videomax" for Fumetti d'Italia in 1992. He returned to Bonelli to create "Napoleone", which ran from 1997 through 2006.

Amelina, Victoria

Ukrainian novelist Victoria Amelina was seriously injured in a Russian missile attack on Kramatorsk, Ukraine,

while dining at a pizza restaurant on June 27, 2023. She was 37. She died of her injuries several days later at a hospital in Dnipro, Ukraine. Amelina was in Lviv, Ukraine (then part of the Soviet Union), on January 1, 1986. She briefly emigrated to Canada with her family in her early teens before returning to earn a degree in computer science in Lviv. She worked in the international technology industry for over a decade. Amelina wrote her first book, "The Fall Syndrome: About Homo Compatients", in 2015. Her children's book "Someone, or Water Heart" was published in 2016. She also wrote the 2017 novel "Dom's Dream Kingdom". She began writing poetry in 2022 and was also a war crimes researcher after the Russian invasion of Ukraine.

Ames, Ed

Actor and singer Ed Ames, who starred as the half-Cherokee Mingo in the 1960's television series "Daniel

Boone", died of complications from Alzheimer's disease at his home in Los Angeles, California, on May 21, 2023. He was 95. He was born Edmund Dantes Urick in Malden, Massachusetts, on July 8, 1927. He and three of his older brothers, Joe, Gene, and Vic, formed a singing quartet while in high school. They were originally known as the Amory Brothers in

the late 1940s and performed at local clubs in Boston. They relocated to New York City and began performing with Art Mooney's band. They became known as the Ames Brothers when they began recording with Coral Records. They also performed on Robert Q. Lewis' radio program and the CBS musical quiz program "Sing It Again". The quartet scored a hit with their 1950 record "Rag Mop" and soon became regulars on radio's "Arthur Godfrey and His Friends". They were featured on such television variety shows as "The Ed Sullivan Show", "Perry Como's Kraft Music Hall", "Cavalcade of Stars", "The Arthur Murray Party", "The Dave Garroway Show", "The Steve Allen Plymouth Show", and "The Eddie Fisher Show". They were stars of their own syndicated television series, "The Ames Brothers Show", in 1956. They continued to record such hit songs as "Sentimental Me", "(Put Another Nickel In) Music! Music! Music!", "Can Anyone Explain? (No, No, No)", "The Thing", "Hawaiian War Chant", "Undecided", "You, You, You", "The Man with the Banjo", "The Naughty Lady of Shady Lane", "My Bonnie Lassie", "It Only Hurts for a Little While", "Tammy", "A Very Precious Love", and "China Doll" during the 1950s. They were also featured in episodes of the series "State Trooper" and "Mike Hammer". The Ames Brothers disbanded in 1963 and Ed continued a solo career as a singer and actor. He trained as an actor at the Herbert Berghoff School and appeared in off-Broadway productions of "The Crucible" and "The Fantastics". He appeared on Broadway in the musical "Carnival!" and the play "One Flew Over the Cuckoo's Nest" as Chief Bromden in the early 1960s. He recorded several hit songs as a solo artist including "Try to Remember", "My Cup Runneth Over", "Time, Time", "When the Snow Is on the Roses", and "Who Will Answer?". He sang the theme song, "Ballad of the War Wagon", for the 1967 film "The War Wagon" starring John Wayne. He was featured in episodes of such television series as "The Rifleman", "Redigo", and "The Travels of Jaimie McPheeters". He was also seen in the 1967 television production of "Androcles and the Lion" and the animated "Cricket on the Hearth" (1967) in a voice role. Ames

was best known for his role as Mingo, the half-Cherokee friend of Fess Parker's Daniel Boone on the series of the same name from 1964 to 1968. Ames also continued to appear in various television variety series and game shows including "That Regis Philbin Show", "What's This Song?", "I'll Bet", "The Pat Boone Show", "Personality", "The Jonathan Winters Show", "Gypsy", "The Kraft Music Show", 'What's My Line?, "You Don't Say", "The Johnny Cash Show", "Della", "The Joey Bishop Show", "The Hollywood Squares", "Jimmy Durante Presents the Lennon Sisters", "Jerry Lewis MDA Labor Day Telethon",. "Stand Up and Cheer", "Dinah's Place", "The David Frost Show", "Celebrity Tennis", "The Merv Griffin Show", "Dinah!", "The Mike Douglas Show", "Celebrity Bowling", and "The Bob Braun Show". He made multiple appearances on "The Tonight Show Starring Johnny

Carson" including a memorable moment in 1965 when demonstrating his tomahawk throwing skills he landed the weapon in the crotch of outline of a cowboy on a wooden plank. The segment was frequently repeated during highlight showings over the decades. He was a guest actor in episodes of "The Starlost", "McCloud", "Kodiak", "Greatest Heroes of the Bible", "Murder, She Wrote", "It's Garry Shandling's Show.", "In the Heat of the Night", "Jake and the Fatman", and "The Marshal". he was also seen in the 1975 tele-film "The Impersonation Murder Case" ion "The Wide World of Mystery". Ames continued to perform on stage with the Kenley Players summer stock circuit in productions of "Shenandoah", "Fiddler on the roof", "Camelot", "South Pacific", and "Man of La Mancha" in the 1970s and 1980s. Ed and his brothers were inducted into the Vocal Group Hall of Fame in 1998. Brother Vic died in an automobile accident in 1978, Gene died of cancer in 1997, and Joe died of a heart attack in 2007. Ames was married to Sara Cacheiro from 1947 until their divorce in 1973. He is survived by their children, Sonya and Ronald. Another daughter, Marcila, died in 2007. He married Jeanne Arnold Saviano in 1998 and she also survives him.

Amis, Martin

British novelist and screenwriter Martin Amis died of esophageal cancer at his home in Lake Worth Beach, Florida, on May 19, 2023. He was 73. Amis was born in Oxford,

England, on August 25, 1949. He was the son of novelist Kingsley Amis. He attended school in Spain and Great Britain and divorce of his parents in the early 1960s. He made his film debut as an actor in his early teens as John Thornton in the 1965 film adaptation of Richard Hughes' "A High Wind in Jamaica". Amis attended Exeter College, Oxford, graduating in 1971. He began reviewing science fiction novels under the name Henry Tilney for "The Observer". He joined the staff of "The Times Literary Supplement" in 1972 and became literary editor of "New Statesman" in 1976. His first novel, "The Rachel Papers", was published in 1973. It was adapted for a 1989 film of the same name. His 1975 novel "Dead Babies" was the basis of a 2000 film of the same name starring Paul Bettany. The film was also known as "Mood Swingers". Amis wrote the novels "Success" (1977) and "Other People" (1981) and scripted the 1980 science fiction film "Saturn 3". His novels "Money" (1984) a comic satire about consumerism that was adapted for a television mini-series in 2010, "London Fields" (1989), and "The Information" (1995) became known as the London Trilogy. "London Fields" was adapted for a 2018 film co-scripted by Amis and starring Amber Heard and Jason Isaacs. His other novels include "Time's Arrow: Or the Nature of the Offence" (1991), "Night Train" (1997) which was adapted for the 2017 film "Out of Blue", "Yellow Dog" (2003), "House of Meetings" (2006), "The Pregnant Widow" (2010), "Lionel Asbo: State of England"

(2012), "The Zone of Interest" (2014) which was adapted by Jonathan Glazer as a 2023 film and received five Academy Award nominations including Best Picture, and the novelized autobiography "Inside Story" (2020). Much of his short fiction with featured in the collections "Einstein's Monsters" (1987), "God's Dice" (1995), and "Heavy Water and Other Stories" (1998). Amis wrote the non-fiction books "Invasion of the Space Invaders" (1982) about video games", "The Moronic Inferno: And Other Visits to America" (1986), "Visiting Mrs. Nabokov: And Other Excursions" (1993), "Experience" (2000), "The War Against Cliche: Essays and Reviews 1971-2000" (2001), "Koba the Dread: Laughter and the Twenty Million" (2002), "The Second Plane" (2008), and "The Rub of Time: Bellow, Nabokov, Hitchens, Travolta, Trump. Essays and Reportage, 1986–2016" (2017). He starred in the 2014 television documentary "Martin Amis's England". He was also seen on television in episodes of "The South Bank Show", "The Last Resort with Jonathan Ross", "Late Night with David Letterman", "Late Night with Conan O'Brien", "Celebrity Poker Club", "Bill Moyer on Faith & Reason", and "Mark Lawson Talks To...", "Charlie Rose". Amis was married to author and scholar Antonia Phillips from 1984 until their divorce in 1993 and is survived by their two sons. He married writer Isabel Fonseca in 1996 and is also survived by her and their two daughters.

Anderson, Katherine

Singer Katherine Anderson, who was co-founder of the Motown singing group the Marvelettes, died in Dearborn, Michigan, on September 20, 2023. She was 79. Anderson was

born in Inkster, Michigan, on January 16, 1944. She sang in gospel and glee club groups in her youth. She attended Inkster High School and formed the Casinyets singing groups in 1960 with several of her classmates, including Gladys Horton, Georgeanna Tillman, Juanita Cowart, and Georgia Dobbins, who was soon replaced by Wanda Young. They signed with Motown the following year and recorded the hit song "Please Mr. Postman" as the Marvelettes. Anderson and the Marvelettes recorded several hit songs in the early 1960s including "Playboy", "Beachwood 45789", "Don't Mess with Bill", and "The Hunter Gets Captured by the Game". She left the group later in the decade and moved to Las Vegas with her husband, Joe Schaffner. She later returned to Detroit, where she worked with troubled youth. She and Schaffner remained married until his death in 2021, and she is survived by her daughters, Keisha and Kalaine.

Anderson, Sophie

British adult actress and internet personality Sophie Anderson died in England on December 4, 2023. She was 36. Anderson was born in Bristol, England, on November 23, 1987. She was abandoned by her mother from an early age and said she was sexually abused at the age of ten. She began working in adult films in 2017 with several lesbian scenes for "Fake Taxi".

She and fellow adult performer Rebecca More were noted by a viral video in October of 2013 calling themselves the Cock Destroyers and promoting a gangbang. The two also hosted the British reality series "Slag Wars: The Next Destroyer" in 2020. Anderson was also seen in television productions of "Pure CFNM", "Public Agent", "House of Taboo", "Fakehub Originals", "Hands on Hardcore", "The Men", and "Brazzers Extras". She was noted for her extreme body modification including increasing her bust size to 32J. She was involved in a relationship with soccer player turned adult actor Oliver Spedding until his death in November of 2023.

Anger, Kenneth

Experimental filmmaker Kenneth Anger, who was noted for such works as "Invocation of My Demon Brother" and "Lucifer Rising" and wrote the gossip book "Hollywood Babylon", died at a care facility in Yucca Valley, California, on May 11, 2023. He was 96. He was born Kenneth Anglemyer in Santa Monica, California, on February 3, 1927. He developed a fascination with films at an early age. He was ten

years old when he used scraps of 16 mm film to make the short "Ferdinand the Bull". He made the film "Who Has Been Rocking My Dreamboat" several years later in 1941 and directed and starred in the short science fiction "Prisoner of Mars" in 1942. Many of his earlier films as presumed lost as he burned much of his earlier work in 1967. He moved to Hollywood with his family in 1944 where he continued to make films including the occult-based "Escape Episode". He soon met fellow director Curtis Harrington and they formed Creative Film Associates (CFA) to promote underground and experimental films. Anger also became interested in the occult writing of Aleister Crowley, which inspired many of his later films. He became aware of his homosexuality in the mid-1940s which influenced his 1947 homoerotic experimental short "Fireworks". He was arrested on obscenity charges when the film was exhibited the following year but was eventually acquitted when the Supreme Court of California ruled the film was art and not pornography. His subsequent film, "Puce Women", resulted in only one scene being produced due to lack of funding and "The Love That Whirls" was destroyed at an Eastman-Kodak film lab developing it when technicians decided that it was obscene. He moved to France in 1950 where he worked with Henri Langlois at the Cinematheque Francaise and became friends with Jean Cocteau. He began filming

"Rabbit's Moon", which remained unfinished until he retrieved the earlier footage in 1970. He went to Rome, Italy, in 1953 where he completed a single scene for a proposed film about occultist Cardinal d'Este which was exhibited as "Eaux d'Artifice". He returned to the United States later in 1953 after the death of his mother. He created one of his best-known films, 1954's "Inauguration of the Pleasure Dome", with a cast that included occultists Samson De Brier and Marjorie Cameron playing various pagan gods. Anger appeared as the Greek goddess Hekate in the film, which was exhibited at film festivals in Europe. He made a short documentary about Aleister Crowley, "Thelema Abbey", in Sicily in 1955, but it was later lost. He and ghostwriter Elliot Stein wrote the book "Hollywood Babylon" later in the 1950s which recounted often unlikely tales of alleged Hollywood scandals. It was initially published in France in 1959 and a pirated version arrived in the United States in 1965. An official U.S. version was printed in 1974. He again returned to the United States in the early 1960s and his 1963 film, "Scorpio Rising", which featured a biker gang preparing for an evening out to the accompaniment of a soundtrack of popular 1960s songs. Anger was again charged with obscenity, but a ban was eventually overturned by the California Supreme Court. His 1965 film "Kustom Kar Kommandos" was funded by a Ford Foundation grant. He had long been involved in the use of mind-altering drugs and became a popular figure in the underground art and film community. He began work on the film "Lucifer Rising" in 1966 and cast Bobby Beausoleil as the lead. He claimed that much of the footage he shot for the film had been stolen and accused Beausoleil of the theft. Beausoleil denied complicity, claiming Anger had failed to shoot the film and was trying to evade creditors. Beausoleil later became involved with the Charles Manson Family and was convicted of murder in 1969. Anger claimed to have burned all of his previous films in 1967 and attempted to reinvent himself as a filmmaker. He went to London where he utilized remaining footage for "Lucifer Rising" for a new film, "Invocation of My Demon Brother" (1969), which starred Anger, Mick Jagger, Keith Richards, and Church of Satan leader Anton Sandor LaVey. He filmed another version of "Lucifer Rising" in 1972 starring Marianne Faithfull as Lilith, Donald Cammell as Osiris, and Anger as the Magus. It was eventually released in 1981. He was the subject of the PBS documentary "Kenneth Anger's Magick" in 1982. He released a sequel for his earlier book, "Hollywood Babylon II", in 1984. He sold the video rights to his existing films in 1986, making many of them available to the general public for the first time. He was featured in the BBC documentary film "Kenneth Anger's Hollywood Boulevard" later in the year. He began making new short films following a two-decade hiatus in the late 1990s with "Don't Smoke That Cigarette" (1999) and "The Man We Want to Hang" (2002). Other works soon followed including "Anger Sees Red" (2004), "Mouse Heaven" (2004) a montage of Mickey Mouse memorabilia, "Elliot's Suicide" (2007), "Foreplay" (2008), "My Surfing Lucifer" (2009), "Brush of Baphomet" (2009), "Magic Lantern Cycle" (2009), "Missioni" (2010), "42 One Dream Rush" (2010), and "Airships" (2013). He appeared in Nik Sheehan's 2008 documentary feature "FLicKeR" and Brian Butler's 2009 short "Night of Pan".

Anobile, Richard J.

Television producer and writer Richard J. Anobile died of idiopathic pulmonary fibrosis in Toronto, Ontario, Canada, on February 10, 2023. He was 76. Anobile was born in the Bronx, New York, on February 6, 1947. He studied film at City College of New York and worked on retrospectives of the Marx Brothers and Laurel and Hardy at the Gallery of Modern Art in Manhattan. His first book, "Drat: Being the Encapsulated View of Life by W.C. Fields in His Own Words", was published in 1969. He wrote the book "Why a Duck? Visual and Verbal Gems from the Marx Brothers Movies", combining frame blowups and dialogue from eight of the Marx Brothers' comedy films, in 1971. Groucho Marx wrote the introduction and the two began working together on 1973's "The Marx Bros. Scrapbook". Groucho later sued to try and stop the distribution of the book that featured his unedited caustic remarks about people he worked with. Anobile provided the court with tapes of his interviews with the comedian and an injunction was never issued. He continued to utilize the technique of combining dialogue with pictures from a film for various books from "The Film Classics Library". His books include "A Flask Of Fields - Verbal And Visual Gems From The Films Of W. C. Fields" (1972), Who's on First?: Verbal and Visual Gems from the Films of Abbott & Costello" (1972), "Hooray for Captain Spaulding! Verbal & Visual Gems from 'Animal Crackers" (1974), "Alfred Hitchcock's Psycho" (1974), "James Whale's Frankenstein" (1974), "John Houston's The Maltese Falcon" (1974), "Michael Curtiz's Casablanca" (1974), "Rouben Mamoulian's Dr. Jekyll & Mr. Hyde, Starring Fredric March" (1975), "Ernst Lubitsch's Ninotchka, starring Greta Garbo" (1975), "John Fords Stagecoach: Starring John Wayne" (1975), "Godfrey Daniels: W.C. Fields" (1975), "Buster Keaton's The General" (1976), "The Best of Buster: The Classic Comedy Scenes Direct from the Films of Buster Keaton" (1976), "Woody Allen's Play It Again, Sam" (1977), "The Wiz Scrapbook" (1978), "Alien" (1979), "Mork & Mindy: A Video Novel" (1979), "Popeye, the Movie Novel" (1980), "Outland: The Movie Novel" (1981), and "Star Trek II: The Wrath of Khan - Photostory" (1982). Anobile moved into television production in the 1980s. He served as a production supervisor or executive on the tele-films "Liberace: Behind the Music" (1988), "Sweet Bird of Youth" (1989), "A Husband, a Wife and a Lover" (1996), "Aladdin" (1999), "Captive Heart: The James Mink Story" (1996), "Blackout" (2001), "Going for Broke" (2003), "On Thin Ice" (2003), "Brave New Girl" (2004), "Man in the Mirror: The Michael Jackson Story" (2004), "A Friend of the Family" (2005), "Confessions of a Sociopathic Social Climber" (2005), "Cool Money" (2005), "Murder at the Presidio" (2005), "Plague City: SARS in Toronto" (2005),

"Fighting the Odds: The Marilyn Gambrell Story" (2005), "The House Next Door" (2006), "A Family Lost" (2007), "Matters of Live & Dating" (2007), "Holiday Switch" (2007), "Never Cry Werewolf" (2008), "Smoke Screen" (2010), "On Strike for Christmas" (2010), and "Lucky Christmas" (2011). He also worked on the series "1st & Ten", "Catwalk", "Stunt Dawgs", "High Tide", "Adventure Inc.", "1-800-Missing", "Aaron Stone", "The Bridge", "Murdoch Mysteries", "The Listener", "My Babysitter's a Vampire", and "X Company". Anobile served as post-production supervisor for the films "Pound Puppies and the Legend of Big Paw" (1988), "Picture Claire" (2001), and "My Babysitter's a Vampire" (2010). He was associate producer for the television series "Acapulco H.E.A.T.", "The Hoop Life", "1-800-Missing", "Aaron Stone", "Unnatural History", "Flashpoint", "The Strain", "Sex/Life", "The Kings of Napa", "The Big Door Prize", and "Fellow Travelers". He was also associate producer for the tele-films and mini-series "Submerged" (2001), "Atomic Twister" (2002), "The Gathering" (2007), and "Before You Say 'I Do'" (2009), and the features "Living with the Dead" (2002) and "Cypher" (2002). Anobile is survived by his wife, Elizabeth Golfman, and a stepdaughter.

Ansell, Bryan

British role-playing game designer Bryan Ansell, who was co-creator of "Warhammer", died in England on December 30, 2023. He was 68. Ansell was born in Nottingham, England, on October 11, 1955. He began his career as a sculptor of miniatures at Conquest Miniatures and was co-founder of Asgard Miniatures in 1976. He left Asgard in 1978 to team with Games Workshop to form Citadel Miniatures. He designed "Warhammer Fantasy Battle" with Rick Priestley and Richard Halliwell in 1983. Ansell became managing director of Games Workshop in 1985. The company was concentrating on "Warhammer" games by the early 1990s and he sold his shares to Tom Kirby in 1991. He subsequently founded Guernsey Foundry to produce figures from the Old West, the Seven Years' War, and Darkest Africa. He continued to work in historical and fantasy miniatures until his retirement in 2005.

Anthony, Jackson

Sri Lankan actor Jackson Anthony died at a hospital in Colombo, Sri Lanka, of injuries he had received in an accident the previous year in Colombo, on October 9, 2023. He was 65. He had been severely injured when the vehicle he was traveling in collided with a wild elephant while shooting the film "Singhabahu" in Thalawa, Sri Lanka, on July 2, 2022. Anthony was born in Podiwee Kumbura, Sri Lanka, on July 8, 1958. he graduated from the University of Colombo and earned a master's degree from the University of Sri Jayewardenepura. He began performing on stage while attending university. He remained a popular stage performer throughout his career.

Anthony began appearing in films in the early 1990s with such credits as "Guru Gedara" (1993), "Loku Duwa" (1994), "Bawa Duka" (1997), "The Fishing Net" (1997), "Gini Avi Saha Gini Keli" (1998), "Bawa Karma" (1998), "Aswesuma" (2001), "Fire & Water" (2002), "Mille Soya" (2004), "Randiya Dahara" (2004), "Guerilla Marketing" (2005), "Dheevari: Fisherman's Daughter" (2006), "Kurulu Phihatu" (2006), "Kreshma Bhumi" (2010), "Kusa-Paba" (2012), "Ahelepola Kumarihami" (2014), "Maharaja Bemunu" (2015), "Pravegaya" (2015), "No Address" (2015), "Dharmayuddhaya" (2017), "Gharasarpa" (2018), "Udumbara" (2018), "The Other Half" (2019), "Dada Ima - End of the Hunt" (2019), "Little Miss Puppet" (2020), and "Ksheera Sagaraya Kalabina" (2023). He wrote and directed several films including "Jullietge Bhoomikawa" (1998), "Aba" (2008), and "No Address" (2015). Anthony was a judge for the television talent series "Sri Lank's Got Talent" in 2018. He was producer and star of several travel documentaries including "Roma Puranaya" and "Kalu Ganga Dige". He was seen on television in productions of "Akalasandya" (1995) and "Bandara Deyyo" (2013). Anthony is survived by his wife, actress and singer Kumari Sandalatha Munasinghe, and three children, all of whom are in the entertainment industry.

Antoniou, Peter

Actor Peter Antoniou died in Tampa, Florida, on October 29, 2023. He was 53. Antoniou was born in Titusville, Florida, on December 4, 1969. He was a graduate of the University of Southern Mississippi, where he played football.

He played professional football with the Arena League North Carolina Charlote Rage. He subsequently earned a master's degree in fine arts at Louisiana State University and began a career in acting in the mid-1990s. Antoniou appeared on television in episodes of "The Big Easy", "The Bold and the Beautiful", "Orleans", "Beverly Hills, 90210", "Saved by the Bell: The New Class", "Star Trek: Deep Space Nine", "Air America", "JAG", "Providence", and "Strong Medicine". He was also seen in the television productions "Things That Go Bump" (1997) and "Thunderdome" (2003). He was divorced from Stephanie Swiniarski and is survived by two sons and a daughter.

Applegate, Phyllis

Actress Phyllis Applegate died in Los Angeles, California, on January 13, 2023. She was 92. Applegate was born in Providence, Rhode Island, on May 8, 1930. She

appeared frequently on television from the late 1970s with roles in productions of "Love Is Not Enough" (1978), "Centennial" (1979), "Robert Kennedy and His Times" (1985), "Kate's Secret" (1986), "Revenge of the Nerds III: The Next Generation" (1992), and "ATF" (1999). Applegate was also seen in episodes of such series as "What's Happening!!", "Mrs. Columbo", "Lou Grant", "Quincy", "Whiz Kids", "ABC Weekend Specials", "Hill Street Blues", "Highway to Heaven", "Cagney & Lacey", "Knight Rider", "Valerie", "Life with Lucy", "Karen's Song", "L.A. Law", "thirtysomething", "Snoops", "China Beach", "In Living Color", "Wings", "Dream On", "Sister, Sister", "Murder One", "The Pretender", "Felicity", "City of Angels", "Any Day Now", "Scrubs", "Cedric the Entertainer Presents", "All About the Andersons", "That's So Raven", "Medical Investigation", "South of Nowhere", "ER", "Just Jordan", "My Name Is Earl" in the recurring role of Darnell's Grandmother in 2007, "The Sarah Silverman Program", "Southland", "Conan", "Awake", "Glee", "Mike & Molly", "See Dad Run", "Hollywood Square", and "Better Call Saul". She was featured in the films "Jagged Edge" (1985), "Ruthless People" (1986), "The Five Heartbeats" (1991), "Hitz" (1992), "Mother" (1995), "The Arrival" (1996), "Big Momma's House" (2000), "Black Dynamite" (2009), "The Undershepherd" (2012), the horror film "Insidious: Chapter 3" (2015) as Grace, "The Mortuary Collection" (2019), and "DOMINO: Battle of the Bones" (2021).

Arabov, Yuri

Russian screenwriter Yuri Arabov died in Russia after a long illness on December 27, 2023. He was 69. Arabov was born in Moscow, Russia, on October 25, 1954. He studied

screenwriting at the Gerasimov Institute of Cinematography (VGIK) and graduated in 1980. He became friends with filmmaker Alexander Sokurov while attending school. They worked together on their first feature, "The Lonely Voice of Man", which was completed in 1978 but remained unreleased until 1987. Their 1983 film "Mournful Unconcern" was also not released until 1987. The two continued to work frequently together throughout their careers. They were noted for a quartet of films they made together that includes "Moloch" (1999) about Adolf Hitler, "Taurus" (2001) about Vladimir Lenin, "The Sun" (2005) about Emperor Hirohito, and a 2011 retelling of "Faust". Arabov also wrote such films as "Gospodin Oformitel" (1987), "Days of Eclipse" (1988), "Save and Protect" (1989), "The Initiated" (1989), "The Second Circle" (1990), "The Sphinx" (1990), "The Stone" (1992), "Prisutstvie" (1993), "Whispering Pages"

(1994), "Mother and Son" (1997), "Apokrif: Muzyka Dlya Petra i Pavla" (2005), "Uzhas, Kotoryy Vsegda s Toboy" (2007), "Yurev Den" (2008), "Poltory Komnaty ili Sentimentalnoe Puteshestvie na Rodinu" (2009), "Chudo" (2009), "The Horde" (2012), "Zerkala" (2013), "Orlean" (2015), "Kletka" (2015), "Okhrana" (2016), "The Monk and the Demon" (2016), "The Imagined Wolf" (2019), "The Nose or Conspiracy of Mavericks" (2020), and "Gjiroskastra" (2022) which he also directed. He wrote the television productions "Delo o Myortvykh Dushakh" (2005), "Doktor Zhivago" (2006), and "Zeveshchanie Lenina" (2007). Arabov also wrote several novels including "Big-Beat" (2003), "Wonder" (2009), "Orlean" (2011), and "A Butterfly Encounter" (2014). He was on the faculty of VGIK from 1992 and headed the screenwriting department until his death.

Archerd, Selma

Actress Selma Archerd died in Los Angeles, California, on December 14, 2023. She was 98. She was born Selma Fenning in Newark, New Jersey, on February 26, 1925.

She moved to Los Angeles with her family in the mid-1930s. She was educated at the University of California at Los Angeles. She married Howard M. Rosenblum in 1943 and they had two sons before their divorce in 1968. She married "Variety" columnist Army Archerd the following year. She made her film debut in an uncredited role in 1974's "Airport 1975". She continued to appear in small roles in such films as "W.C. Fields and Me" (1976), "Harry and Walter Go to New York" (1976), "The Big Bus" (1976), "Fun with Dick and Jane" (1977), "Fire Sale" (1977), "New York, New York" (1977), "The Concorde... Airport '79" (1979), "Americathon" (1979), "Meteor" (1979), "Can't Stop the Music" (1980), "Underground Aces" (1981), "Mommie Dearest" (1981), "Hard to Hold" (1984), "The Ladies Club" (1985), "Lethal Weapon" (1987), "Die Hard" (1988), "Scrooged" (1988), "Side Out" (1990), "Taking Care of Business" (1990), "Live Wire" (1992), "Lethal Weapon 3" (1992), "Born Yesterday" (1993), "Indecent Proposal" (1993), and "The Brady Bunch Movie". Archerd was seen on television in episodes of "It's Your Bet", the game show "Tattletales" frequently teaming with her husband Army Archerd, "The Brady Bunch", "Kolchak: The Night Stalker", "Marcus Welby, M.D.", "Serpico", "Westside Medical", "The Amazing Spider-Man", "Hotel", "Knots Landing", "E/R", "Cagney & Lacey", "The Love Boat", "The Trials of Rosie O'Neill", "Roseanne", "Melrose Place", and "Charmed". Her other television credits include the tele-films "Perfect Gentlemen" (1978), "Rainbow" (1978), "Crisis in Mid-Air" (1979), "The Kid from Nowhere" (1982), "Fantasies" (1982), "Malibu" (1983), the mini-series "Alice in Wonderland" (1985) as the Queen of Diamonds, "Outrage!" (1986), "The Children of Times Square" (1986), "A Very Brady Christmas" (1988), and "Cagney & Lacey: The Return" (1994). She was married

to Army Archerd from 1969 until his death in 2009. She is survived by her two sons from her first marriage.

Arkin, Alan

Actor Alan Arkin, who received a Tony Award for the 1963 play "Enter Laughing" and an Oscar for 2006's "Little Miss Sunshine", died of heart problems at his home in San Marcos, California, on June 29, 2023. He was 89. Arkin was born in Brooklyn, New York, on March 26, 1934. He moved

to Los Angeles with his family in 1945 where his father briefly worked as a set designer. His father was accused of being a Communist in the 1950s and his refusal to submit to questioning about his politics led to his being fired as a teacher. Alan began studying acting in his youth and later attended Los Angeles State College and Bennington College. He teamed with Erik Darling and Bob Carey to form the folk band the Tarriers and they scored a hit with the 1956 recording of "The Banana Boat Song". He appeared with the Tarriers in a small role in the 1957 film "Calypso Heat Wave". He joined the comedy improv troupe Second City in the early 1960s and appeared with them in the 1961 Broadway production of "From the Second City". Arkin also appeared on Broadway in Carl Reiner's semi-autobiographical "Enter Laughing" (1963) receiving a Tony Award for his role as David Kolowitz, and Mike Nichols "Luv" (1964) with Eli Wallach and Anne Jackson. He directed the Broadway plays "Hail Scrawdyke!" (1966), "The Sunshine Boys" (1972) earning a Tony Award nomination, "Molly" (1973), and "Taller Than a Dwarf" (2000). Arkin proved adept in both comedy and drama in the films "The Russians Are Coming the Russians Are Coming" (1966) earning an Oscar nomination as stranded Russian submarine officer Lt. Yuri Rozanov, and the psychological thriller "Wait Until Dark" (1967) as the murderous Roat threatening a blind Audrey Hepburn. His other films include "Woman Times Seven" (1967), "Inspector Clouseau" (1968) briefly replacing Peter Sellars in the title role of the third "Pink Panther" film, "The Heart Is a Lonely Hunter" (1968) earning another Oscar nomination for his tragic role as John Singer, a deaf mute in a small southern town, "Popi" (1969), the science fiction satire "The Monitors" (1969), and Mike Nichols' adaptation of Joseph Heller's anti-war satire "Catch-22" (1970) as Captain John Yossarian. Arkin also began directing in the late 1960s with the shorts "T.G.I.F." (1967) and "People Soup" (1969) which earned an Academy Award nomination and featured his sons, Adam and Matthew Arkin. He directed Jules Feiffer's satire "Little Murders" in 1971 and appeared in the role of Lieutenant Practice, having previously received an Obie Award for helming an off-Broadway production in 1969. Arkin continued his film career in "Deadhead Miles" (1972), Neil Simon's comedy "Last of the Red Hot Lovers" (1972), "Freebie and the Bean" (1974) as Detective Dan 'Bean' Delgado, "Rafferty and the Gold Dust Twins" (1975), the western comedy "Hearts of the West" (1975), "The Seven-Per-Cent Solution" (1976) as Dr. Sigmund Freud with Nicol Williamson as Sherlock Holmes and Robert Duvall as Dr. Watson, "Fire Sale" (1977) which he also directed, the comedy "The In-Laws" (1979) with Peter Falk, the drama "The Magician of Lublin" (1979) as Jewish stage magician and con man Yasha Mazur, the science fiction comedy "Simon" (1980) in the title role, "Improper Channels" (1981), "Chu Chu and the Philly Flash" (1981) opposite Carol Burnett, the comedy horror "Full Moon High" (1981), the animated fantasy "The Last Unicorn" (1982) as the voice of Schmendrick, "The Return of Captain Invincible" (1983) in the title role, "Joshua Then and How" (1985), "Bad Medicine" (1985), "Big Trouble" (1986), "Coupe de Ville" (1990), Tim Burton's "Edward Scissorhands" (1990), "Havana" (1990), "The Rocketeer" (1991), "Glengarry Glen Ross" (1992), "Indian Summer" (1993), "So I Married an Axe Murderer" (1993), the short "Samuel Beckett Is Coming Soon" (1993) which he also directed, "North" (1994), "The Jerky Boys" (1995), "Steal Big Steal Little" (1995) "Mother Night" (1996), "Grosse Pointe Blank" (1997), "Four Days in September" (1997), the science fiction film "Gattaca" (1997) as Detective Hugo, "Slums of Beverly Hills" (1998), "Jakob the Liar" (1999), "Magicians" (2000), "American Sweethearts" (2001), "Thirteen Conversations About One Thing" (2001), "Eros" (2004), "Noel" (2004), "Little Miss Sunshine" (2006) receiving the Academy Award for Best Supporting Actor for his role as inappropriate grandfather Edwin Hoover, "Firewall" (2006), "The Novice" (2006), "The Santa Clause 4: The Escape Clause" (2006), "Raising Flagg" (2006), "Rendition" (2007), "Sunshine Cleaning" (2008), the film version of "Get Smart" (2008) as the Chief, "Marley & Me" (2008), "The Private Lives of Pippa Lee" (2009), "City Island" (2009), "Thin Ice" (2011), "The Change-Up" (2011), "The Muppets" (2011), Ben Affleck's "Argo" (2012) receiving another Oscar nomination for his supporting role as movie producer Lester Siegel, "Stand Up Guys" (2012), "The Incredible Burt Wonderstone (2013), "Armed Response (2013), "Grudge Match" (2013), "Million Dollar Arm" (2014), "Love the Coopers" (2015), the remake "Going in Style" (2017) with Morgan Freeman and Michael Caine, "Dumbo" (2019) as J. Griffin Remington, "Spenser Confidential" (2020), and the animated "Minions: The Rise of Gru" (2022) as the voice of Wild Knuckles. Arkin appeared on television in episodes of "East Side/West Side", "What's My Line?", "The Les Crane Show", "ABC Stage 67" earning an Emmy Award nomination for his starring role in the 1967 episode "The Love Song of Barney Kempinski", "Sesame Street" as Larry from 1970 to 1971, "The David Frost Show", "Donahue", "The Merv Griffin Show", "The Great American Dream Machine", "Captain Kangaroo", "Busting Loose", "Dinah!", "The Mike Douglas Show", "The Dick Cavett Show, "The Muppet Show", "Carol

Burnett & Company", "St. Elsewhere" in the recurring role of Jerry Singleton in 1983, "American Playhouse" as Flagg Purdy in a 1984 production of "A Matter of Principle, "Faerie Tale Theatre", "A Year in the Life", the short-lived comedy series "Harry" as Harry Porschak in 1987, "Picture Windows", "The Charles Grodin Show", "The Rosie O'Donnell Show", "Chicago Hope" receiving an Emmy nomination for his role as Zoltan Karpathein in the 1997 episode "The Son Also Rises", the legal drama "100 Centre Street" as Joe Rifkind from 2001 to 2002, "Will & Grace", "The Late Late Show with Craig Ferguson", "Tavis Smiley", "Jimmy Kimmel Live!", "Up Close with Carrie Keagan", "Kevin Pollak's Chat Show", "The View", the animated "BoJack Horseman" in the recurring voice role of J.D. Salinger from 2015 to 2016, and "Get Short". He starred as Norman Newlander, the agent of Michael Douglas' Sandy Kominsky, in the show business comedy series "The Kominsky Method" from 2018 to 2019 and received two Emmy nominations for his supporting role. Arkin's other television credits include productions of "It Couldn't Happen to a Nicer Guy" (1974), "The Other Side of Hell" (1978), "The Defection of Simas Kudirka" (1978) in the title role, "The Fourth Wise Man" (1984), "A Deadly Business" (1986), "Escape from Sobidor" (1987) earning an Emmy Award nomination for his role as Leon Feldhendler, "Necessary Parties" (1988) which he also scripted, "Cooperstown" (1993), "Taking the Heat" (1993), "The Doomsday Gun" (1994), "Heck's Way Home" (1996), "Blood Money" (2000), "Varian's War: The Forgotten Hero" (2001), "The Pentagon Papers" (2003) earning another Emmy nomination for his role as Harry Rowen, and "And Starring Pancho Villa as Himself" (2003). Arkin also directed the 1975 tele-film "Twigs" and episodes of "Fay" and "Trying Times". He helmed the 2004 comedy short film "Blood (Thinner Than Water)". Arkin was author of several books including "Tony's Hard Work Day" (1972), "The Lemming Condition" (1976), "Halfway Through the Door: An Actors Journey Toward Self" (1979), "The Clearing" (1986), and the memoirs "An Improvised Life" (2011) and "Out of My Mind" (2018). He was married to Jeremy Yaffe from 1955 until their divorce in 1961 and is survived by their two sons, actors Adam Arkin and Matthew Arkin. He was married to actress and screenwriter Barbara Dana from 1964 until their divorce in 1994 and is survived by their son Tony Arkin. Arkin married psychotherapist Suzanne Newlander in 1996 and she also survives him.

Arleen, Joyce

Child actress Joyce Arleen, who was also credited under the names Mary Thomas and Arleen Joyce, died in Bakersfield, California, on February 17, 2023. She was 91. She was born Joyce Arleen Novotny in Hackensack, New Jersey, on May 20, 1931. She signed with Paramount in the late 1930s and made her film debut as a child in 1939's "The Star Maker". She continued to appear in films over the next several years, frequently billed as Mary Thomas. Her films include "Our Neighbors - The Carters" (1940), "The Great McGinty" (1940), "Birth of the Blues" (1941), "Wild Bill Hickok Rides" (1942), "Kings Row" (1942) as Betty Field's Cassandra Tower as a

child, "Reap the Wild Wind" (1942), "The Gay Sisters" (1942) as Barbara Stanwyck's character as a child, "Wake Island" (1942), "Mrs. Wiggs of the Cabbage Patch" (1942), "This Is the Life" (1944), and "Till We Meet Again" (1944). She briefly returned to the screen in the early 1950s and was seen in small roles in "Take Care of My Little Girl" (1951), "The Proud Ones" (1956), and "The Best Things in Life Are Free" (1956). She was married to Al Baldock from 1953 until his death in 2009 and is survived by their daughter.

Armour, Norman

Canadian actor Norman Armour died of lung cancer in Vancouver, British Columbia, Canada, on November 19, 2023.

He was 63. Armour was born in Canada on February 19, 1959. He performed frequently on stage from the 1980s and was co-founder of the small local venue Rumble Theatre in 1990. Armour was co-founder of the PuSh International Performing Arts Festival in Vancouver in 2003. He retired from PuSh in 2019 but remained involved with the local theater. Armour was featured in the films "Bliss" (1997), "Beautiful Joe" (2000), "Trixie" (2000), "Suspicious River" (2000), "Saving Silverman" (2001), "Say It Isn't So" (2001), "Living with the Dead" (20020, and "Capote" (2005). He appeared on television in productions of "Omen IV: The Awakening" (1991), "Broken Badges" (1991), "Sherlock Holmes Returns" (1993), "Final Appeal" (1993), "Voices from Within" (1994), "The Surrogate" (1995), "Atomic Train" (1999), "The Linda McCartney Story" (2000), "Damaged Care" (2002), "A Wrinkle in Time" (2003), and "The Book of Ruth" (2004). His other television credits include episodes of "Heritage Minutes", "The Commish", "M.A.N.T.I.S.", "Strange Luck", "The X-Files", "Viper", "Millennium", "Strange World", "First Wave", "Cold Squad", "Stargate SG-1", "Dark Angel", "Breaking News", "Kingdom Hospital" as Myron Overdick in 2004, and "Supernatural". His survivors include his partner, artist Lorna Brown.

Armstrong, George

British actor George Armstrong died of leukemia in London, England, on July 11, 2023. He was 60. Armstrong was born in England on September 7, 1962. He made his television debut as Hubert Lane in a 1977 production of "Just William". He was featured as Alan Humphries in

the BBC series "Grange Hill" from 1978 to 1982 and reprised the role in the spin-off series "Tucker's Luck" from 1983 to 1985. Armstrong appeared as a thief in the 1984 television production of "Aladdin and the Forty Thieves" and was seen in episodes of "Honky Tonk Heroes" and "The Bill". He largely abandoned acting in the early 1990s and worked at a public school as a technical theater manager.

Aronberg, Charles

Actor and physician Charles Aronberg died in Beverly Hills, California, on November 9, 2023. He was 93. Aronberg

was born in Neptune, New Jersey, on August 30, 1930, and moved to Los Angeles in 1940. He graduated from the University of California at Los Angeles and completed medical school at the University of California at San Francisco. He became an ophthalmology specialist with a practice in Beverly Hills. He was also involved in sports medicine as team doctor for the Los Angeles sports teams the Lakers, Kings, and Raiders. Aronberg was active in civic affairs and served twelve years on the Beverly Hills City Council. He served as two terms as mayor from 1974 to 1975 and from 1979 to 1980. Aronberg was also an actor in films and television during the 1990s. He was seen in the films "Double Trouble" (1992), "Miracle Beach" (1992), "Grey Knight" (1993), the horror film "Pumpkinhead II: Blood Wings" (1993) as the ill-fated Fred Knox, "Till the End of the Night" (1995), "Cover Me" (1995), and "Soldier Boyz" (1995). He appeared in the tele-films "Ring of the Musketeers" (1992), "Love, Cheat & Steal" (1993), and "Sketch Artist II: Hands That See" (1995). He is survived by his wife, Dr. Sandra Aronberg, and daughter Cindy.

Arrington, Kirk

Drummer Kirk Arrington, who performed with the heavy metal band Metal Church, died on May 22, 2023. He

was 61. Arrington was born on January 23, 1962. Rhythm guitarist and keyboardist Kurdt Vanderhoof formed the first incarnation of Metal Church in 1980. He was joined by lead guitarist Craig Wells and bassist Duke Erickson in 1981. Arrington joined the band as drummer in 1982 and David Wayne became lead singer the following year.

Metal Church released their self-titled debut album in 1985. Arrington remained with the band until they broke up in 1996. He rejoined Metal Church when they regrouped in 1998. He was drummer for many of the group's albums including "The Dark" (1986), "Blessing in Disguise" (1989), "The Human Factor" (1991), "Hanging in the Balance" (1993), "Live"

(1998), "Masterpeace" (1999), and "The Weight of the World" (2004). Arrington also played drums on Vanderhoof's solo albums "Vanderhoof" (1997) and "A Blue in Time" (2002). He left Metal Church in 2006 due to health complications from diabetes.

Astor, Vincent

Author, actor, historian, and flamboyant gay activist Vincent Astor was found dead at his apartment in Memphis, Tennessee, on January 16, 2023. He was 69. Astor was born in Memphis on December 6, 1953. He graduated from

Southwestern University (now Rhodes College) in 1975. He was involved in restoring the Malco Theater in downtown Memphis to its former identity as the Orpheum theatrical venue. Astor was an accomplished organist and played the Wurlitzer organ at the Orpheum from the 1970s. He was seen frequently on the local stage, working with Circuit Playhouse and Playhouse on the Square during the 1970s and 1980s. He was a pioneer in gay activities including participating the Miss Gay Memphis Pageant. He often appeared in his drag persona, known as Lady A. He was a founding member of OUTMemphis: The LGBTQ+ Community Center of the Mid-South in 1989. He was a vast resource of knowledge about local history, appearing frequently at history and heritage lectures. Astor appeared frequently on the local PBS network, WKNO, for documentary programs about the city's heritage. He was also a recurring guest as Chancellor Grimm in the station's horror film showcase series "Professor Ghoul's Horror School". He was author of the 2013 book "Images of America: Memphis Movie Theatres". He was featured in the 2019 short film "How I Came Out". He was involved with Elmwood Cemetery, often giving tours and performing as deceased residents during Elmwood's "Soul of the City" events. Astor was buried at Elmwood with a gray granite obelisk monument he designed at his gravesite with the epitaph "sacred to the memory of a proud gay man".

Atadeniz, Yilmaz

Turkish film director and writer Yilmaz Atadeniz died of complications from COVID-19 in Sanyer, Turkey, on December 13, 2023. He was 91. Atadeniz was born in Istanbul, Turkey, on February 1, 1932. He studied engineering at Robert College before leaving school to work in the film industry. He worked with his brother, director Orhan Atadeniz, serving as a writer and editor for the 1952 film "Tarzan in Istanbul". Atadeniz continued to work in films as an assistant director or editor for "Hickirik" (1953), "Ahretten Gelen Adam" (1954), "Findikci Gelin" (1954), "Simal Yildizi" (1954), "Funda" (1958), "Cumbadan Rumbaya" (1960), "Hazreti Omer'in Adaleti" (1961), "Kucuk Hanimefendi" (1961), "Hayat Bazen Tatlidir" (1962), "Kucuk Hanimin Soforu" (1962), "Leyla ile Mecnun Gibi" (1963), "Canakkale Arslanlari" (1964), "Ask ve

Kin" (1964), "Erkekler Aglamaz" (1964), "Kasimpasali Recep" (1965), "Gonul Kusu" (1965), and "Dokunma Bozulurum" (1965). He made his directorial debut with the 1963 film "Yedi Kocali Hurmuz". Atadeniz helmed over 100 films during the next sixty years. His films include "Ike Sene Mektep Tatili" (1964), "Yuz Karasi" (1964), "Son of the Mountains" (1965), "Kan Govdeyi Goturdu" (1965), "Kahreden Kursun" (1965), "Kibar Haydut" (1966), "Kovboy Ali" (1966), "Silaharin Kanunu" (1966), "Yedi Dagin Aslani" (1966), "The Ugly King" (1966), "Arslanlarin Donusu" (1966), the fantasy adventure "Killing in Istanbul" (1967), "Oyna Bebegim Oyna" (1967), "The Ugly King Doesn't Forgive" (1967), "Kilink Ucan Adama Karsi" (1967), "Kilink: Strip and Kill" (1967), "Killing Caniler Krali" (1967), "Olumsuz Adamlar" (1968), "Casus Kiran" (1968), "Aci Intikam" (1968), "Kafkas Kartali" (1968), "Maskeli Besler" (1968), "Maskeli Beslerin Donusu" (1968), "Guney Olum Saciyor" (1969), "Zoro Kamcili Suvari" (1969), "Ringo Vadiler Aslani" (1969), "Zorro'nun Intikami" (1969), "Ebu Muslim Horasani" (1969), "Cakircali Mehmet Efe" (1969), "Sampiyon" (1970), "Kan Yagmuru" (1970), "Belanin Krali" (1971), "Kara Cellat" (1971), "Jilet Kazim" (1971), "Bes Hergele" (1971), "Bicirik Is Basinda" (1971), "Cehenneme Dolmus Var" (1971), "Tuzsuz Deli Bekir" (1972), the action film "Yilmayan Seytan" (aka "The Deathless Devil") (1972), "Baskin" (1972), "Zalim" (1973), "Dag Kanunu" (1973), "Komando Behcet" (1974), "Dort Hergele" (1974), "Sev Beni Behcet" (1974), "Opme Sev" (1974), "Kadi Han" (1976), "Tatli Melek" (1977), "Olum Cemberi" (1978), "Bionik Ali Futbolcu" (1978), "Super Selami" (1979), "Karpuzcu" (1979), "Tatli ve Guzel: Istanbul Geceleri" (1979), "Akrep" (1980), "Kader Arkadasi" (1981), "Kader Arkadasi" (1981), "Kanije Kalesi" (1982), "Son Akin" (1982), "Kobra" (1983), "Care Sende Allahim" (1984), "Ikizler" (1985), "Guldur Yuzumu" (1985), "Kuskunum" (1986), "Sevmek Neye Yarar" (1986), "Hayat Merdiveni" (1986), "Hapishane Gulu" (1986), "Kader Ruzghari" (1986), "Cilali Ibo Maceralar Pesinde" (1986), "Muallim" (1986), "Talihsizler" (1987), "Hasret" (1987), "Yalvaris" (1987), "Meaner" (1988), "Acilar" (1988), "Afacan" (1989), "Kinali Hanzo" (1989), "Sah Mat" (1990), "Afacan Ates Parcasi" (1990), "Afacan Tatli Bela" (1994), "Babami Ariyorum" (1997), "Acilar" (2000), "Tokat Ballica Magarasi" (2005), "Istanbul Arkeoloji Muzeleri" (2009), and "Ikimize Bir Dunya" (2016).

Auer, Hannelore

Austrian actress and singer Hannelore Auer died of cardiac arrest in Kitzbuhel, Austria, on November 8, 2023. She was 81. Auer was born in Linz, Austria, on May 30, 1942. She became a popular singer in Austria from the late 1950s. She also appeared frequently in films in the 1960s including "I'm Marrying the Director" (1960), "Willy, der Privatetektiv" (1960), "Das ist die Liebe der Matrosen" (1962), "Ohne Krimi

Geht die Mimi Nie ins Bett" (1962), "Only a Woman" (1962), "Sing, Aber Spiel Nicht Mit Mir" (1963), "Our Crazy Nieces" (1963), "Don't Fool with Me" (1963), "...Denn die Musik und

die Liebe in Tirol" (1963), "The Merry Wives of Tyrol" (1964), "Schweik's Awkward Years" (1964), "Holiday in St. Tropez" (1964), "Die Lustigen Weiber von Triol" (1964), "Hotel der Toten Gaste" (1965), "Tausend Takte Ubermut" (1965), "Ich Kauf Mir Lieber Einen Tirolerhut" (1965), "Come to the Blue Adriatic" (1966), "The Sinful Village" (1966), "Spukschloss im Salzkammergut" (1966), "Susanne, die Wirtin von der Lahn" (1967), "Kommissar X - Drei Blaue Panther" (1968), "Otto ist auf Frauen Scharf" (1968), "Sexy Susan Sins Again" (1968), "Three Golden Serpents" (1969), Franz Antel's "Sexy Susan Sins Again" (1970), and "Ausser Rand und Band am Wolfgangsee" (1972). Auer performed on television in productions of "Eheinstitut Harmonie" (1963), "Der Ton(film) Macht die Musik" (1963), "Komm Mit Auf den Rummelplatz" (1963), "Der Arme Prinz" (1965), "Vom Ersten das Beste" (1965), "Der Nachste Urlaub Kommt Bestimmt" (1966), "Saison in Salzburg" (1966), and "Die Eitagsfliege" (1969). She was also seen on television in episodes of "Omkring et Flygel", "Nachmittsgsparty", "Treffpunkt Telebar, "Musik Erklingt...", "Musik aus Studio B", "Die Braute Meiner Sohne", Luftsprunge", and "Diamantendektiv Dick Donald". Auer was married to Austrian Prince Alfred von Auersperg from 1968 until their divorce in 1979. She married German singer Heinz 'Heino' Kramm in 1979 and served as his manager until her death.

Augsberger, Thomas

German-born film producer Thomas Augsberger died suddenly at his home in Hollywood Hills, California, on November 28, 2023. He was 60. Augsberger was born in

Munich, Germany, in 1963. He was an attorney who served as consultant and North American representative for Herbert Kloiber's German Tele Muenchen Group (TMG). He helped acquire numerous film and television projects for the German Market including "Iron Man", "The Hunger Games", "Twilight", and "John Wick". He was also involved in TMG's investments in the United States including Lionsgate Entertainment, serving on the board from 2002 to 2004, and the acquisition of Mutual Film Library in 2006. Augsberger founded the media consulting film Eden Rock Media in 2002. He served as an executive producer or producer for such films as "The Alarmist" (1997), "Judas Kiss" (1998), "Operation Splitsville" (1998), "Coming Soon" (1999), "Girls on Top" (2001), "She

Gets What She Wants" (2002), "Love and a Bullet" (2002) also appearing on screen in a small role, "Till Human Voices Wake Us" (2002), "Strange Bedfellows" (2004), "Incident at Loch Ness" (2004), "Waiting..." (2005), "Mr. Brooks" (2007), "Salute" (2008), "Still Waiting..." (2009), "Humans" (2009), "Charlie & Boots" (2009), "Tucker and Dale vs. Evil" (2010), "Swinging with the Finkel's" (2011), "Solace" (2015), "Reinventing Mirazur" (2021), and "Bonnie" (2022). Augsberger produced television productions of "USA's Cannonball Run 2001" (2001), "Have No Fear: The Life of Pope John Paul II" (2005), "To Appomattox" (2015), and "The Crime of the Century" (2021). He was also executive producer of the series "Spy City" and "Professionals". He was a founding partner of Filmaka, BestEverChannels, and Liquid Light. Augsberger is survived by his wife, Jana, two daughters, and a son.

August 08

Singer and songwriter Ray Davon Jacobs, who performed under the name August 08, died in Los Angeles on

August 28, 2023. He was 31. Jacobs was born in Los Angeles on January 2, 1992. He achieved success as a member of the 88 Rising artists collective and appeared on tracks with musicians Higher Brothers, Joji, and Rich Brian. He released his debut solo album "Father" in 2018. He co-wrote the songs "Sorry" for Justin Bieber and "I'm the One" by DJ Khaled. His songs were also recorded by Quavo and Chance the Rapper. He recorded the album "Emotional CUH" in 2020. August 08 released the 2002 album "Seasick" on the Def Jam label and featured collaborations with Aiko, Schoolboy Q, and Joji.

Augusta, Dan

Canadian actor Dan Augusta died after a long illness at his home in Winnipeg, Manitoba, Canada, on May 26, 2023.

He was 34. Augusta was born in Winnipeg on May 8, 1989. He suffered from various physical conditions including non-Hodgkin Lymphoma that compromised his immune system and affected his growth. He performed on stage with the Shakespeare Company of the Manitoba Theatre for Young People from an early age. He was co-founder of the Struts and Frets Players and stage shows for the Winnipeg Fringe Theatre. He graduated from the University of Winnipeg with a degree in theatre and film. He was a member of the Sick & Twisted theatre company from 2017. He often used his disabilities while playing characters ranging from an underworld demon named Doug to a brick wall of a sentient house. Augusta was featured in the 2008 television mini-series "The Capture of the Green River Killer" and the 2009 film "New in Town". He also appeared in several episodes of the television series "Tayo, the Little Bus" in 2010.

Austin, Ray

British television director and stuntman Ray Austin, who was stunt coordinator for the television series "The Avengers" in the 1960s, died at his home in Virginia on May 17, 2023. He was 90. Austin was born in London, England, on  December 5, 1932. He began his career working in films in the late 1950s as a stunt double for Alfred Hitchcock's "North by Northwest". He performed stunts and appeared in small roles in the films "Operation Petticoat" (1969), "Tunes of Glory (1960), Stanley Kubrick's "Spartacus" (1960), "Saturday Night and Sunday Morning" (1960), "The Sundowners" (1960), "Never Take Candy from a Stranger" (1960), "Return of a Stranger" (1961), "The Loneliness of the Long Distance Runner" (1962), "Cleopatra" (1963), "Tom Jones" (1963), "The V.I.P.s" (1963), "Escape by Night" (1963), and "The Curse of the Mummy's Tomb" (1964). Austin was a stuntman and actor for the television series "The Cheaters", "24-Hour Call", "Sergeant Cork", "Ghost Squad", "Drama '64", "The Wednesday Play", "The Avengers", "Love Story", "Blackmail", "Cooperama", and "The Saint". He also began working as a second unit director for episodes of "The Avengers" and "The Champions" and became a director for both series. He became a prolific director for series in England and the United States including "The Saint", "The Ugliest Girl in Town", "Department S", "My Partner the Ghost", "Shirley's World", "The Adventures of Black Beauty", "Space: 1999", "The New Avengers" also serving as a coordinating producer, "W.E.B.", "Sword of Justice", "The Professionals", "The Hardy Boys/Nancy Drew Mysteries", "Return of the Saint", "Barnaby Jones", "Wonder Woman", "Hawaii Five-O", "B.J. and the Bear", "A Man Call Sloane", "Salvage 1", "The Yeagers", "From Here to Eternity", "B.A.D. Cats", "House Calls", "Vega$", "The Love Boat", "Simon & Simon", "Tales of the Gold Monkey", "King's Crossing", "Quincy", "The Master", "Hart to Hart", "Jessie", "The Fall Guy", "Airwolf", "V", "Spenser: For Hire", "Lime Street", "Magnum, P.I.", "Our House", "The Dirty Dozen", "Alfred Hitchcock Presents", "A Fine Romance", "Snoops", "The Boys of Twilight", "Zorro" also serving as producer, "Highlander", "Heaven Help Us", "JAG", "Silk Stalkings", "Pensacola: Wings of Gold", "Police Academy: The Series", and "CI5: The New Professionals". He appeared in episodes of several series including "Magnum, P.I.", "Snoops", "Prison Break", and "Crisis". His other television credits as director include the tele-films "The Return of the Man from U.N.C.L.E.: The Fifteen Years Later Affair" (1983), "The Zany Adventures of Robin Hood" (1984), and "The Return of the Six Million Dollar Man and the Bionic Woman" (1987). Austin directed several films including "1,000 Convicts and a Woman" (1971), "Virgin Witch" (1972), and "House of the Living Dead" (1974). He largely retired from directing by the early 2000s. He was married to actress Alison Seebohm from 1966 until their divorce in 1970 and they had two children. He was married to actress Yasuko Nagazumi from 1976 until their divorce in the early 1980s. He married novelist Wendy DeVere Knight-Wilton in 1984 and she survives him.

Avant, Clarence

Music executive Clarence Avant died at his home in Los Angeles, California, on August 13, 2023. He was 92. Avant was born in Climax, North Carolina, on February 25, 1931. He moved to New Jersey in his teens in 1947 and worked as a clerk at Macy's and as a clerk for a law directory publisher.  He became manager of Teddy P's Lounge in Newark in the early 1950s. He was trained by Joe Glaser, Louis Armstrong's music manager. Avant began managing such artists as Little Willie John and jazz organist Jimmy Smith. He assisted pianist Lalo Schifrin's career in Hollywood in 1964. He was founder of Sussex Records in 1969 which released early records from Bill Withers. Avant became active in civil rights and politics. He was instrumental in assisting Andrew Young's race of U.S. Congress in Georgia in the early 1970s. His Avant Garde Broadcasting bought the first black owned FM radio station in Los Angeles, KTYM-FM, in 1973. He helped guide the careers of such music stars as Quincy Jones, Janet Jackson, and Whitney Houston. He assisted baseball player Hank Aaron in getting endorsement deals and aided Jim Brown transition from football to films. Avant was executive producer of the films "Save the Children" (1973), "Deliver Us from Evil" (1975), "Stalingrad" (1990), and "Jason's Lyric" (1994). He was also a producer for the tele-films "Heart and Soul" (1988) and "Livin' Large" (1989), and the television series "New Attitude" in 1990. He appeared as an African musician in the 1985 film "The Color Purple". He was the subject of the 2019 Netflix documentary "The Black Godfather", which was produced by his daughter, Nicole. Avant was given a star on the Hollywood Walk of Fame in 2016 and was inducted into the Rock and Roll Hall of Fame in 2021. He was married to model Jacqueline 'Jackie' Gray from 1967 until she was shot and killed during a home invasion in December of 2021. He is survived by their daughter, Nicole, a former U.S. Ambassador to the Bahamas, and son, Alexander.

Axelrod, Jack

Character actor Jack Axelrod, who was featured as crime boss Victor Jerome on the soap opera "General Hospital" in the late 1980s, died in Los Angeles, California, on November 28, 2023. He was 93. Axelrod was born in Los Angeles on January 25, 1930. He attended the University of California at

Berkley where he studied architecture. He served in the U.S. Army from 1953 to 1955 and was stationed in Germany. Axelrod worked as an architect in Washington state before moving to New York City to pursue an acting career. He

studied under Uta Hagen at HB Studios for six years. He performed frequently on stage and appeared on Broadway in productions of "Gandhi" (1970) and "Herzl" (1976). He became a popular character performer in films and television in the 1970s. Axelrod was seen on television in episodes of "Kojak", "Hill Street Blues", "Dallas", "The Judge", "Dynasty", "Outlaws", "Night Court", the daytime soap opera "General Hospital" as Victor Jerome from 1987 to 1989, "Knots Landing" in the recurring role of Arnie Zimmer from 1989 to 1990, "Murphy Brown", "Everybody Loves Raymond", "Boy Meets World", "Good vs Evil", "Jack & Jill", "Dharma & Greg", "Star Trek: Voyager", "Gideon's Crossing", "The Division", "Philly", "Alias", "In-Laws, "Frasier" as an elderly Fraser Crane in a 2003 episode, "It's All Relative", "The Help" as Grandpa Eddie in 2004, "Malcolm in the Middle", "Scrubs", "It's Always Sunny in Philadelphia", "Grey's Anatomy", "My Name Is Earl" in the recurring role of the Electrolarynx Guy from 2005 to 2008, "Eli Stone", "Star-ving" as Ira Silver in 2009, "Secret Girlfriend", "Private Practice", "Hawthorne", "Criminal Minds: Suspect Behavior", "Franklin & Bash", "Love Bites", "Hot in Cleveland", "Dexter", "Shameless", "The Office", "The Beauty Inside", "Raising Hope", "Animal Practice", "NCIS", "Family Tools", "Hawaii Five-O", "Kirstie", "Legit", "Mystery Girls", "Mulaney", "Playing House", "Brooklyn Nine-Nine", "Animals.", "Ray Donovan", "Gilmore Girls: A Year in the Life", "Baskets", "Dice", "Speechless", "Station 19", "No Activity" in the recurring role of Steve in 2018, and "Modern Family". His other television credits include the tele-films "Not My Kid" (1985), "Hammer, Slammer & Slade" (1990), "Love, Cheat & Steal" (1993), "Something to Sing About" (2000), "Blowing Smoke" (2004), and "Christmas Do-Over" (2006). Axelrod was seen in such films as Woody Allen's "Bananas" (1971), "Faith" (1990), "Vice" (2000), "Road to Redemption" (2001), "Hancock" (2008), "Winged Creatures" (2008), "Labor Pains" (2009), "Table for Three" (2009), "Little Fockers" (2010), "Fred & Vinnie" (2011), "Super 8" (2011), "Transformers: Dark of the Moon" (2011), "J. Edgar" (2011), "The Lone Ranger" (2013), "Coffee Town" (2013), "Adulthood" (2015), and "Bad Therapy" (2020). Axelrod taught acting at the University of Wisconsin, Boston University, Penn State, Temple State, Brandeis University, CalState, and the Aaron Speiser Acting Studio in Los Angeles.

Azagaia

Mozambican rapper Edson Amandio Maria Lopes da Luz, who performed under the name Azagaia, died of complications from epilepsy at his home in Matola,

Mozambique, on March 9, 2023. He was 38. He was born in Namaacha, Mozambique, on May 6, 1984. He moved to

Maputo in 1994, where he attended high school. He also studied at Eduardo Mondlane University. He started performing in his early teens with the group Dinastia Bantu, and they recorded the 2005 album "Siavuma". Azagaia released the 2007 solo album "Babalaze" which contained several successful songs. He released the controversial political song "Combatentes de Fortuna" in 2009. His other songs include "Arriiii" (2010) and "Emboscada" (2012). He released his second album, "Cubaliwa", in 2013. Azagaia suffered from epilepsy and was diagnosed with a brain tumor on 2014, which was successfully removed in India.

Bacharach, Burt

Oscar-winning songwriter and composer Burt Bacharach, who wrote such songs as "What's New Pussycat?", "The Look of Love", and "Raindrops Keep Fallin' On My Head", died at his home in Los Angeles, California, on February 8, 2023. He was 94. Bacharach was born in Kansas City, Missouri, on May 12, 1928, and was raised in Forest Hills,

Queens, New York. He learned to play piano and other musical instruments as a child and became interested in jazz during his teens. He graduated from McGill University in Montreal, Canada, with a degree in music in 1948. He also studied at the Mannes School of Music in New York City under Helmut Blume and the Music Academy of the West in Montecito, California. Bacharach served two years in the U.S. Army in the late 1940s and was stationed in Germany. He began playing the piano at clubs there and arranged music for dance bands. He began working with singer Vic Damone, who he met during his time in the service, and was his pianist and conductor for three years after their discharge. He also accompanied such performers as Polly Bergen, Steve Lawrence, the Ames Brothers, and Joel Grey. He became music director for Marlene Dietrich in 1956 and toured with her nightclub shows around the world through the early 1960s. He also began a twenty-year songwriting collaboration with lyricist Hal David in 1956 with the songs "I Cry More", "The Morning Mail", and "Peggy's in the Pantry". Marty Robbin's rendition of their song "The Story of My Life" and Perry Como's recording of "Magic Moments" were major hits in 1957. Bacharach and Mack David, Hal's brother, wrote the title song for the 1958 horror film "The Blob". He and lyricist Bob Hilliard wrote several hits in the early 1960s including the Drifters "Please Stay" and "Mexican Divorce", Gene McDaniels' "Tower of Strength", Chuck Jackson's "Andy Day

Now (My Wild Beautiful Bird)", and Dick Van Dyke's "Three Wheels on My Wagon". He began a long association with Dionne Warwick in 1961 after discovering her working as a backup session singer. They and sister Dee Dee Warwick released the single "Move It on the Backbeat" under the name Burt and the Backbeats. Bacharach and David wrote Warwick's debut solo recording "Don't Make Me Over" in 1962. The songwriting duo and the singer scored numerous hits over the next two decades with such songs as "Walk On By", "Anyone Who Had a Heart", "I Say a Little Prayer", "I'll Never Fall in Love Again", and "Do You Know the Way to San Jose". He and David shared Oscar nominations for Best Original Song for the themes for "What's New Pussycat" (1965) and "Alfie" (1966) and for "The Look of Love" from the 1967 James Bond spoof "Casino Royale". Bacharach won the Oscar for Best original Score for "Butch Cassidy and the Sundance Kid" (1969) and shared another with David for the film's song "Raindrops Keep Fallin' on My Head". He shared another Academy Award for Best Original Song for "Arthur's Theme (Best That You Can Do)" from "Arthur" (1981). He released the 1965 solo album "Hit Maker!: Burt Bacharach Plays the Burt Bacharach Hits" and scored the 1966 film "After the Fox". He and David wrote the 1966 television musical "On the Flip Side" for "ABC Stage 67". They earned a Tony Award nomination for the 1968 Broadway musical "Promises, Promises" which included the hit song "I'll Never Fall in Love Again". Herb Alpert scored a hit with their song "This Guy's in Love with You" in 1968. He earned Emmy nominations for the variety shows "The Sound of Burt Bacharach" (1969) and "Another Evening with Burt Bacharach" (1970). He won the Emmy for 1971's "Singer Presents Burt Bacharach" and starred in the 1972 television special "Burt Bacharach: Close to You". He and David ended their long collaboration in the mid-1970s after work on the unsuccessful 1973 film musical remake of "Lost Horizon" and on Stephanie Mills' album "For the First Time" in 1975. He worked with such lyricists as James J. Kavanaugh, Libby Titus, Anthony Newley, and Paul Anka later in the decade. He began working with lyricist Carol Bayer Sager in the early 1980s and the two soon married. They collaborated on the hit songs as "Where Did the Time Go" by the Pointer Sisters, "Heartlight" by Neil Diamond, "Making Love" by Roberta Flack, "On My Own" by Patti LaBelle and Michael McDonald, and "That's What Friends Are For" reuniting Bacharach with Warwick in 1985. Other hits include "A House Is Not a Home", "(There's) Always Something There to Remind Me", and "Any Day Now". He was composer for the films "Night Shift" (1982), "Arthur 2: On the Rocks" (1988), and "Love Hurts" (1990). He worked with singer and musician Elvis Costello on the 1998 album "Painted from Memory", and the album's song "I Still Have that Other Girl" earned the duo a Grammy Award for Best Pop Collaboration. Bacharach appeared in a cameo role in an episode of the television series "The Nanny" in 1996 and appeared in cameos in the films "Austin Powers: International Man of Mystery" (1997), "Austin Powers: The Spy Who Shagged Me" (1999), and "Austin Powers in Goldmember" (2002). He was featured in an episode of the television series "Nip/Tuck" in 2006. He

was a guest on numerous variety and talk shows during his career including "Ready, Steady, Go!", "Top of the Pops", "The Joey Bishop Show", "The David Frost Show", "Della", "The Hollywood Palace", "Dinah's Place", "This Is Tom Jones", "This Is Your Life", "The Tonight Show Starring Johnny Carson", "The Vin Scully Show", "The Mike Douglas Show", "The Muppets Go Hollywood", "American Bandstand", "The John Davidson Show", "The Merv Griffin Show", "Saturday Night Live", "Solid Gold", "Late Show with David Letterman", "60 Minutes", "The Tonight Show with Jay Leno", "Biography", "Late Night with Conan O'Brien", "The Ellen DeGeneres Show", "Later... with Jools Holland", "Tavis Smiley", "The South Bank Show", and "American Idol". He wrote the music and lyrics for his 2005 solo album "At This Time" and was subject of the 2015 special "Burt Bacharach: A Life in Song". His autobiography, "Anyone Who Had a Heart", was published in 2013. He worked with Joseph Bauer to score the 2016 film "A Boy Called Po". He and musician Daniel Tashian received a Grammy nomination for Best Traditional Pop Vocal Album for 2020's "Blue Umbrella". Bacharach was recipient of six Grammy Awards and an additional sixteen nominations during his career. He was given the Grammy Lifetime Achievement Award in 2008 and shared the Library of Congress' Gershwin Prize for Popular Song with Hal David in 2012. Bacharach was married to actress Paula Stewart from 1953 until their divorce in 1958. He was married to actress Angie Dickinson from 1965 until their divorce in 1981. Their daughter, Lea Nikki Bacharach, suffered from depression and committed suicide in 2007. He was married to lyricist Carol Bayer Sager from 1982 until their divorce in 1991 and is survived by their adopted son Cristopher Elton Bacharach. He married Jane Hansen in 1993 and is survived by her and their son and daughter.

Bachman, Robbie

Canadian rock drummer Robbie Bachman, who performed with the band Bachman-Turner Overdrive, died in Vancouver, British Columbia, Canada, on January 12, 2023. He was 69. Bachman was born in Winnipeg, Manitoba, Canada, on February 18, 1953. He was the younger brother of

singer and guitarist Randy Bachman who performed with the Guess Who in the 1960s. He joined Randy in the Winnipeg band Brave Belt in 1971 along with accompanied by former Guess Who singer Chad Allan and bassist Fred Turner. They were joined by brother Tim Bachman on second guitar in 1972 after Allan's departure. The band was renamed Bachman-Turner Overdrive (BTO) in 1973. They recorded numerous hit songs in the next several years including "Roll on Down the Highway" which Robbie co-wrote, "Take It Like a Man", and "Takin' Care of Business". Randy left BTO in 1977 and the group disbanded after touring for their 1979 album "Rock n' Roll Nights". He declined to rejoin his brothers in the reformed BTO in 1984. He did rejoin the group for reunion tours from 1988 to 1991 when Randy left the band. Robbie continued to tour with the new lineup through 2004. He teamed with Fred Turner to tour and record as Bachman & Turner in 2009. Robbie is survived by his wife, Chrissy.

Bachman, Tim

Canadian rock guitarist Tim Bachman, who performed with the band Bachman-Tuner Overdrive, died of cancer in Canada on April 28, 2023. He was 71. Bachman was born in Winnipeg, Manitoba, Canada, on August 1, 1951. He played with several bands in the Winnipeg area in the late 1960s. He joined his brothers, guitarist and singer Randy and drummer Robbie Bachman, with bassist Fred Turner in the band Brave Belt in 1972. The band was renamed Bachman-Turner Overdrive (BTO) the following year. Tim recorded the group's first two self-named albums before leaving in 1974. He rejoined with Randy Bachman and Fred Turner for a BTO reunion album and tour and they were accompanied by Garry Peterson on drums when brother Robbie declined. Tim briefly led the band from 1987 to 1988 after Randy again departed.

Baer, Donald A.

Television producer and assistant director Donald A. Baer died in Denver, Colorado, on October 25, 2023. He was 91. Baer was born in Chicago, Illinois, on September 26, 1932. He graduated from the University of California at Los Angeles before pursuing a career in television. He worked as an assistant director from the late 1950s on such series as "M Squad", "Markham", "Johnny Midnight", "Bachelor Father", "General Electric Theater", "The Deputy", "The Tall Man", "Alfred Hitchcock Presents", "Tales of Wells Fargo", "Checkmate", "Thriller", "Alcoa Premiere", "Wide Country", "Laramie", "The Virginian", "Wagon Train", "Bob Hope Presents the Chrysler Theatre", "The Alfred Hitchcock Hour", "Kraft Suspense Theatre", "Laredo", "Run for Your Life", and "The Tony Randall Show". He was also assistant director for the 1966 Alfred Hitchcock film "Torn Curtain" and the 1968 tele-film "Shadow Over Elveron". Baer was a unit production manager for the 1968 film "Jigsaw" and the tele-films "Stranger on the Run" (1967), "I Love a Mystery" (1973), Panache" (1976), and "The Critical List" (1978). He was also production manager for such television series as "Run for Your Life", "My World and Welcome To It", "That Girl", "Mayberry R.F.D.", "Sanford and Son", "The Manhunter", and Lou Grant". Baer was producer

for the tele-films "The Boy Who Drank Too Much" (1980), "Fighting Back: The Story of Rocky Bleier" (1980), and "Tomorrow's Child" (1982), and the series "Tales of the Gold Monkey" (1982-1983) and "Blue Thunder" (1984). He taught at Denver University and the Osher Lifelong Learning Institute after retiring from the film industry. Baer's survivors include his life partner Diana Arendrup and three children.

Bailey, John

Cinematographer John Bailey, who served as president of the Academy of Motion Picture Arts and Sciences from 2017 to 2019, died at his home in Los Angeles, California, on November 10, 2023. He was 81. Bailey was born in Moberly, Missouri, on August 10, 1942, and was raised in Norwalk, California. He briefly attended Santa Clara University before going to Loyola University in Los Angeles, where he graduated in 1964. He continued his education at the University of Southern California School of Cinematic Artist and received a graduate degree in 1968. He worked for such cinematographers as Vilmos Zsigmond and Nester Almendros in the 1960s and served as a camera operator for television productions of "The New Cinema" (1968), "The Night They Took Miss Beautiful" (1977), "Forever" (1978), "The Initiation of Sarah" (1978), and "A Question of Guilt" (1978). He was also camera operator for the films "Two-Lane Blacktop" (1971), "Posse" (1975), "Hollywood Boulevard" (1976), "Welcome to L.A." (1976), "The Late Show" (1977), "3 Women" (1978), and "Winter Kills" (1979). Bailey was a cinematographer and director of photography by the early 1970s on such films as "Premonition" (1972), "End of August" (1974), "Legacy" (1975), "The Mafu Cage" (1978), "Boulevard Nights" (1979), "American Gigolo" (1980), "Ordinary People" (1980), "Honky Tonk Freeway" (1981), "Continental Divide" (1981), "Cat People" (1982), "That Championship Season" (1982), "Without a Trace" (1983), "The Big Chill" (1983), "Racing with the Moon" (1984), "The Pope of Greenwich Village" (1984), "Mishima: A Life in Four Chapters" (1985), "Silverado" (1985), "Crossroads" (1986), "Brighton Beach Memoirs" (1986), "Light of Day" (1987), "Swimming to Cambodia" (1987), "Tough Guys Don't Dance" (1987), "Vibes" (1987), "The Accidental Tourist" (1988), "Hollywood Mavericks" (1990), "My Blue Heaven" (1990), "A Brief History of Time" (1991), "Groundhog Day" (1993), "In the Line of Fire" (1993), "Nobody's Fool" (1994), "Extreme Measures" (1996), "As Good As It Gets" (1997), "Living Out Loud" (1998), "The Out-of-Towners" (1999), "Forever Mine" (1999), "For Love of the Game" (1999), "Michael Jordan to the Max" (2000), "Antitrust" (2001), "The Anniversary Party" (2001), "The Kid Stays in the Picture" (2002), "Divine Secrets of the Ya-Ya Sisterhood" (2002), "How to Lose a Guy in 10 Days" (2003), "Digital Babylon" (2003), "Incident at Loch Ness" (2004), "The Cutting Edge: The Magic of Music Editing" (2004), "The Sisterhood of the Traveling Pants" (2005), "Must Love Dogs" (2005), "The

Producers" (2005), "The Architect" (2006), "Bobby Z" (2007), "License to Wed" (2007), "Mad Money" (2008), "Over Her Dead Body" (2008), "The Greatest" (2009), "Brief Interviews with Hideous Men" (2009), "He's Just Not That Into You" (2009), "When in Rome" (2010), "Ramona and Beezus" (2010), "Country Strong" (2010), "Big Miracle" (2012), "The Way Way Back" (2012), "A.C.O.D." (2013), "Snake & Mongoose" (2013), "The Angriest Man in Brooklyn" (2014), "The Forger" (2014), "A Walk in the Woods" (2015), "Burn Your Maps" (2016), "How to Be a Latin Lover" (2017), "An Actor Prepares" (2018), "Phil" (2019), and "Ten Tricks" (2022). He was cinematographer for the tele-films "Battered" (1978), "City in Fear" (1980), "Time Flies When You're Alive" (1989), "Passion" (1996), "Always Outnumbered" (1998), and "Searching for Michael Cimino" (2003). Bailey also directed several films including "The Search for Signs of Intelligent Life in the Universe" (1991), "China Moon" (1994), "Via Dolorosa" (2000), the music documentary "NSync: Bigger Than Life" (2001), and "Mariette in Ecstasy" (2019). He received a lifetime achievement award from the American Society of Cinematographers in 2015. He became the first cinematographer to serve as president of the Academy of Motion Picture Arts and Sciences from 2017 to 2019. Bailey married film editor Carol Littleton in 1972 and she survives him.

Bairnson, Ian

Scottish musician Ian Bairnson, who performed with the Alan Parsons Project, died of complications from dementia in Surrey, England, on April 7, 2023. He was 69. Bairnson was  born in Lerwick, Scotland, on August 3, 1953. He learned to play the guitar at an early age and worked as a session guitarist in the early 1970s. He and musicians David Paton and Billy Lyall of the Bay City Rollers formed the band Pilot in 1973. They recorded a self-named album and had a hit with the song "Magic". He began working with Alan Parsons and Eric Woolfson in the Alan Parsons Project in 1975. Bairnson was featured on all of the band's albums including "Tales of Mystery and Imagination" (1976), "I Robot" (1977), "Pyramid" (1978), "Eve" (1979), "The Turn of a Friendly Card" (1980), "Eye in the Sky" (1982), "Ammonia Avenue" (1984), "Vulture Culture" (1985), "Stereotomy" (1985), "Gaudi" (1987), and "Freudiana" (1990). He played on Kate Bush's early albums including "The Kick Inside" (1978), "Lionheart" (1978), "Never for Ever" (1980), and "The Dreaming" (1982). He played with the pop band Bucks Fizz in the early 1980s and co-wrote their hits "If You Can't Stand the Heat" and "Run for Your Life". He toured and recorded with various bands and had a recording studio while living in Spain from 2003 to 2013. He returned to England in 2013 and recorded the album "A Pilot Project" with David Paton. He retired in 2018 after being diagnosed with a neurological condition. His survivors include his wife, Leila.

Bakewell, Michael

British radio and television producer Michael Bakewell died of complications from Alzheimer's disease in East Sussex, England, on July 11, 2023. He was 92. Bakewell was born in Birmingham, Warwickshire, England, on June 7,  1931. He served in the Royal Air Force during National Service and attended King's College, Cambridge, where he graduated in 1954. He soon began working with the BBC Third Programme (now BBC Radio 3). He served as Head of Plays for the BBC in the 1960s. He was a producer and director for such television productions as "The Men from Room 13" (1961), "Hedgehog" (1962), "Where I Live" (1965), "Hold My Hand, Soldier" (1965), "Eh, Joe?" (1966), "Troilus and Cressida" (1966), "Zigger Zagger" (1967), and "Pitchi Poi" (1967). Bakewell was producer of the series "Theatre 625" from 1965 to 1968 and directed episodes of "Canterbury Tales" in 1969. He also worked in radio drama, adapting "The Lord of the Rings" for a radio series in 1981. He adapted many of Agatha Christie's Poirot and Miss Marple novels for radio plays from the 1980s through 2000s. Bakewell served as dubbing director for the English language version of numerous Japanese productions including "Devilman" (1987), "Dominion Tank Police" (1988), "Crying Freeman" (1988), "Goku Midnight Eye" (1989), "Megazone 23 III" (1989), "Patlabor" (1989), "Venus Wars"(1989), "Angel Cop" (1989), "The Dark Myth" (1990), "AD Police Files" (1990), "RG Veda" (1991), "Cyber City Oedo 808" (1991), "Sohryuden: Legend of the Dragon Kings" (1991), "Mad Bull 34" (1992), "Battle Angel" (1993), "New Dominion Tank Police" (1993), "Tokyo Babylon" (1994), "Genocyber" (1994), and "X" (1996). He was married to television host Joan Bakewell from 1955 until their divorce in 1972 and is survived by their children, Matthew and Harriet. He married Melissa Dundas in 1975 and she also survives him.

Bakos, John

Actor John Bakos died of complications from pneumonia in Tacoma, Washington, on April 25, 2023. He was  85. Bakos was born in Chicago, Illinois, on August 1, 1937. He trained as an actor at the Art Institute of Chicago's Goodman School of Drama, graduating in 1963. He joined Ellen Stewart's La Mama theatrical troupe in New York City and toured in various plays throughout Great Britain. He starred as the title character in La Mama's Off-Off Broadway production of "Futz" in the late 1960s and starred in the film version in 1969. He also appeared in the 1971 film "Josie's Castle". Bakos appeared on television in episodes of "The Young Rebels", "The Most Deadly Game", "Ryan's Hope", "Missing Persons", and "ER". He was also seen in the 1971 tele-film "The Impatient Heart". He continued to perform on stage throughout his career, appearing in Shakespeare in the Park, numerous Off-Off Broadway productions, and regional and summer stock. Bakos is survived by his wife, Jude Kelley, and daughter, Daisy.

Balaban, Judy

Actress Judy Balaban died in Los Angeles, California, on October 19, 2023. She was 91. Balaban was born in Chicago, Illinois, on October 13, 1932. He father was Barney

Balaban, a film executive who served as president of Paramount Pictures. Her brothers were jazz musician Leonard 'Red' Balaban and film producer and director Burt Balaban. She moved to New York City with her family in her youth and later worked there in the fashion industry. She dated actor Montgomery Clift and singer

Merv Griffin in the early 1950s. She married Jay Kanter, Grace Kelly's talent agent, in 1953. She became close friends with Kelly and was one of her bridesmaids when she married Prince Rainier of Monaco in April of 1956. She later wrote about her experience in the 1989 books "The Bridesmaids: Grace Kelly, Princess of Monaco, and Six Intimate Friends". She was featured in several documentaries including "Montgomery Clift" (1983), "Grace Kelly: The American Princess" (1987), "Hollywoodism: Jews, Movies and the American Dream" (1998), "The Story of Film: An Odyssey" (2011), "Becoming Cary Grant" (2017), and "Making Montgomery Clift" (2018). Balaban was married to Kanter from 1953 until their divorce in 1961 and is survived by their daughter Amy Kanter. Another daughter, Victoria Kanter, died in June of 2020. She was married to actor Tony Franciosa from 1961 until their divorce in 1967, and is survived by their daughter, Nina Franciosa. She was married to actor Don Quine from 1971 until their divorce in 1996.

Balabanian, Aracy

Brazilian actress Aracy Balabanian died of lung cancer in Rio de Janeiro, Brazil, on August 7, 2023. She was 87. Balabanian was born in Campo Grande, Brazil, on February 22, 1940. She moved to Sao Paoulo with her family in her early teens. She studied acting at the Escola de Arte Dramatica and began her career on stage in the early 1960s. She appeared frequently on television with roles in series and telenovelas. Her credits include "Mercados Pelo Amor" (1964), "Um Rosto Perdido" as Alba from 1965 to 1966, "O Amor Tem Cara de Mulher" as Matilde in 1966, "Sublime Amor" (1967), "Angustia de Amar" as Jane in 1967, "Meu Filho, Minha Vida" as Nellie in 1967, "O Coacao Nao Envelhece" (1968), "Antonio Maria" as Heloisa from 1968 to 1969, "Nino, o Italianinho" as Branca from 1969 to 1970, "A Fabrica" as Isabel from 1971 to

1972, "Vila Sesamo" (1972), "O Primeiro Amor" as Giovana in 1972, "Corrida do Ouro" as Teresa from 1974 to 1975, "Bravo!" as Cristina Lemos from 1975 to 1976, "O Casarao" (1976),

"Locomotivas" as Milena in 1977, "Pecado Rasgado" as Teca from 1978 to 1979, "Coracao Alado" as Maria Faz-Favor from 1980 to 1981, "Brilhante" (1981), "Elas Por Elas" as Helena in 1982, "Guerra dos Sexos" as Greta from 1983 to 1984, "Transas e Caretas" (1984), "The Buzz" as Marta from 1985 to 1986, "Mania de Querer" as Lucia from 1986 to 1987, "Helena" as Ursula in 1987, "Que Rei Sou Eu?" as Lenoe Gaillard

and Maria Fromet in 1989, "Rainha da Sucata" as Dona Armenia in 1990, "Felicidade" as Paquita from 1991 to 1992, "Deus Nos Acuda" (1992), "Caso Especial" (1993), "Patria Minha" (1994), "Cutie Pie... Her Loves and Sins" as Dona Geninha in 1995, "The Next Victim" as Filomena Ferreto in 1995, "Uma Professora Muito Maluquinha" as Mosqueteira in 1996, "Sai de Baixo" as Cassandra Mathias Sayao from 1996 to 2002 and again in 2013, "Brava Gente" (2001), "The Taste of Passion" as Herminia Lemos from 2002 to 2003, "Hot Line" (2003), "Shades of Sin" as Germana in 2004, "Once in a Blue Moon" as Leontina in 2005, "Eterna Magia" as Inacia in 2007, "Dear Friends" as Teresa in 2008, "Casos e Acasos" (2008), "Take It, Give It" (2008), "O Natal do Menino Imperador" (2008), "Passione" as Gema Mattoli from 2010 to 2011, "Sparkling Girls" as Maslova Tilman in 2012, "Crazy About Them" (2013), "Saramandaia" as Dona Pupu in 2013, "Now Generation" (2014), "Dangerous Liaisons" as Consuelo in 2016, "Rising Sun" as Geppina from 2016 to 2017, "The Big Catch" as Mariazinha Pires de Saboia in 2017, "Marhalcao" (2018), and "Juntos a Magic Acontece: Especial de Natal" (2019). Balbanian was seen in several films during her career including "A Primeira Viagem" (1972), the short "Caramujo-Flor" (1988), "Policarpo Quaresma, Heroi do Brasil" (1997), "De Corpo Inteiro Enteristas (2010), and "Sai de Baixo: O Filme" (2019).

Balltze

Balltze, a Shiba Inu dog from Hong Kong who was the subject of the Cheems internet memes, died during surgery for

respiratory problems on August 18, 2023. He was 12. Balltze was born on January 9, 2011, and was adopted at the age of one. He became an internet sensation in 2019 when he was featured in the Cheems "cheemsburgers" memes. Balltze was seen in numerous other memes, including "Swole Doge vs Cheems". His owners signed deals with two companies

to create Balltze toys, tee shirts, and other merchandise. In May of 2022, Balltze was diagnosed with pancreatitis but recovered soon after. He had cancer and was undergoing treatments at the time of his death.

Balsam, Philip

Canadian songwriter and composer Philip Balsam, who was noted for his work on the "Fraggle Rock" television series, died of complications of giant cell arteritis in Toronto, Canada on March 31, 2023. He was 79. Balsam was born in Siberia on December 23, 1943. He came to Toronto, Canada, as a child after escaping Europe at the end of World War II. He attended the Ontario College of Art and pursued a career as a musician and composer. He and poet Dennis Lee wrote nearly 200 songs for Jim Henson's "Fraggle Rock". The songs were sung by a variety of puppet characters from 1983 to 1987. A collection of songs from the show, "Jim Henson's Muppets Present Fraggle Rock", was released in 1984 and he received a Grammy Award. An extended version of the series' theme was released as a hit single in 1984. Balsam provided the voice of Phil Fraggle on the series. He and Lee wrote the songs for the stage production of Mordecai Richler's "Jacob Two Two Meets the Hooded Fang" in 1984. They also wrote the songs for Henson's 1986 television production "The Tale of the Bunny Picnic" and for the series "Dog City" in 1994. They provided songs for the Canadian puppet series "Groundling Marsh" from 1994 to 1997. Balsam married Carol Hall in 1980 and she survives him.

Bandit

Thai drag performer and costume designer Bandit Janthawan died in Thailand on December 26, 2023. She was 38. Bandit was born in Phrae, Thailand, on July 10, 1985. She was a fashion designer who released the 2011 collection the Men from the Venus. She also designed costumes for stage performances and was a fashion lecturer at several universities. Bandit was a contestant on the second season of "Drag Race Thailand" in 2019 and tied for fourth place in the competition.

Banks, Russell

Author Russell Banks, who was noted for the novels "Continental Drift" and "The Sweet Hereafter", died of cancer at his home in Saratoga Springs, New York, on January 7, 2023. He was 82. Banks was born in Newton, Massachusetts, on March 28, 1940, and was raised in Barnstead, New Hampshire. He attended Colgate University in Hamilton, New York, on scholarship but dropped out after six weeks. He moved to Lakeland, Florida, where he worked in a department store. He returned to New England in 1964 before settling in North Carolina. He attended the University of North Carolina at

Chapel Hill. Banks was co-founder of the small literary label Lillabulero Press in 1966 and his poetry collection, "Waiting to Freeze", was published there in 1969. He also wrote the poetry collection "Snow: Meditations of a Cautious Man in Winter" in 1974. He penned his first novel, "Family Life", in 1975, and a collection of short stories, "The New World", was published in 1978. He wrote the novel "Hamilton Stark" in 1978. His 1981

story collection, "Trailerpark", was adapted for a film in 2010. Banks' other novels include "The Book of Jamaica" (1980), "The Relation of My Imprisonment" (1984), "Continental Drift" (1985) which earned a Pulitzer Prize nomination, "Affliction" (1989) which was adapted for a short film in 1997, "The Sweet Hereafter" (1991) which was adapted for a film in 1997 by director Atom Egoyan and featured Banks in a small role as a doctor, "Rule of the Bone" (1995), and "Cloudsplitter" (1998) again earning a Pulitzer nomination. His later works include "The Darling" (2005), "The Reserve" (2008), "Lost Memory of Skin" (2011), and "Foregone" (2021). His short fiction appeared in the collections "The Angel on the Roof" (2000) and "A Permanent Member of the Family" (2013). He wrote the nonfiction "Dreaming of America" in 2008 and a collection of his travel writings, "Voyager", was published in 2016. He taught at Princeton University and was artist-in-residence at the University of Maryland. He was named New York State Author from 2004 to 2006. Banks was married to Darlene Bennett from the 1950s until their divorce in 1963 and is survived by their daughter, Lea. He was married to poet Mary Gunsts from 1963 until their divorce in 1977, and is also survived by their three daughters, Caerthan, Maia, and Danis. He was married to book editor Kathy Walton from 1982 until their divorce in 1988. He married poet Chase Twitchell in 1989 and she also survives him.

Barker, Bob

Television personality Bob Barker, who was host of the game shows "The Price is Right" and "Truth or

Consequences", died complications from Alzheimer's disease and other health issues at his home Los Angeles, California, on August 26, 2023. He was 99. Barker was born in Darrington, Washington, on December 12, 1923. His father was one-quarter Rosebud Sioux and Bob spent much of his youth on the Rosebud Indian Reservation in Mission, South Dakota. He attended high school in Missouri and Drury College in Springfield, Missouri. He joined the U.S. Navy Reserve in 1943 to train as a fighter pilot during World War II but did not see combat. He returned to Drury to complete his education after the war. He worked at KTTS-FM Radio in Springfield while attending college. He moved to Lake Worth Beach, Florida, in the late 1940s and was an announcer and news editor at WWPG-AM in Palm Beach. He went to California in 1950 where he hosted "The Bob Barker Show" on radio in Burbank for six years. He made his debut as a game show host in 1956, when he was hired by producer Ralph Edwards to replace Jack Bailey on "Truth or Consequences". Barker remained with the show through 1975. He was featured in the role of Mort in the "Bonanza" episode "Denver McKee" in 1960. He joined the revival of Mark Goodson and Bill Todman's gameshow "The Price Is Right" on CBS in 1972. He remained host of the long-running series for 35 years until retiring in 2007. He was succeeded by Drew Carey and made occasional return appearances including briefly taking over for Carey for April Fools' Day in 2015. Barker was author of the 2009 autobiography "Priceless Memories". He was an active animal rights proponent and encouraged viewers of "The Price Is Right" to spay or neuter their pets from the early 1980s. He created the DJ&T Foundation to help fund such programs in 1994. He gave millions of dollars to animal rescue and animal rights organizations including PETA. His funding for the Sea Shepherd Conservation Society in 2010 in its efforts to halt Japanese whaling operations resulted in a ship to be used for that purpose that was christened MY Bob Barker. He served as host of the Miss Universe Pageant from 1967 and the Miss USA Pageant from 1979. He severed ties with both events over the contestant's use of furs. He served as host of the Pillsbury Bake-Off and CBS coverage of the Tournament of Roses Parade in the 1970s and 1980s. Barker had cameo roles in such television series as "The Nanny", "Bailey Kipper's P.O.V.", "Something So Right", "Martial Law", "Futurama", "Yes, Dear", "How I Met Your Mother", "Family Guy", "The Bold and the Beautiful", and "SpongeBob SquarePants" as the voice of Bob Barnacle. He was a frequent panelist on the gameshows "Tattletales" and "Match Game" in the 1970s. Barker was a guest on various talk and game shows including "This Is Your Lie", "I'll Bet", "Today", "Dream Girl of '67", "You Don't Say", "The Ed Nelson Show", "The Mike Douglas Show", "The Woody Woodbury Show", "Betty Hughes and Friends", "Philbin's People", "Jerry Lewis MDA Labor Day Telethon", "The Pet Set", "It's Your Bet", "I've Got a Secret", "The Cross-Wits", "The Jim Nabors Show", "Dinah!", "That's My Line", "Tomorrow Coast to Coast", "The John Davidson Show", "The Tonight Show Starring Johnny Carson", "The Hollywood Squares", "The Arsenio Hall Show", "One on One with John Tesh", "The Chuck Woolery Show", "Family Feud", "Vicki!", "The Suzanne Somers Show", "Late Night with Conan O'Brien", "Maury", "Biography", "The Rosie O'Donnell Show", "The Wayne Brady Show", "The Reichen Show", "The Tyra Banks Show", "The Early Show", "Square Off", "The Ellen DeGeneres Show", "Late Show with David Letterman", "Larry King Live", "WWE Raw" as guest host in 2009, "The Bonnie Hunt Show", "Rachael Ray", "The Morning Show with Mike & Juliet", "The Late Late Show with Craig Ferguson", and "Lorena". He had a memorable cameo role in the 1996 comedy film "Happy Gilmore" when he engaged in a fistfight

with star Adam Sandler on the golf course. He received fourteen Daytime Emmy Awards for Outstanding Game Show Host for his work on "The Price Is Right" and an additional four awards as executive producer of the show. He was given a Daytime Emmy Lifetime Achievement Award in 1999. He was inducted into the Academy of Television Arts & Sciences Hall of Fame in 2004. He was the subject of a several lawsuits brought by former model Dian Parkinson from "The Price Is Right" who accused Barker of sexual harassment. The 1994 lawsuit was later dropped by Parkinson. Model Holly Hallstrom sued Barker in 1995 claiming that she had been fired from the show when she refused to give false testimony in the Parkinson lawsuit. He suffered from bouts of poor health in later years including a stroke, prostate surgery, and injuries from several falls. Barker was married to Dorothy Jo Gideon from 1945 until her death from lung cancer in 1981. He began an long relationship with animal rights activist Nancy Burnet in 1983 which lasted until his death.

Barkett, Steve

Actor Steve Barkett, who was noted for his role in science fiction films in the 1990s, died of pneumonia in Reno, Nevada, on March 3, 2023. He was 73. Barkett was born in

Oklahoma City, Oklahoma, on January 1, 1950. He produced, directed, wrote, and starred as Newman in the 1982 apocalyptical zombie film "The Aftermath", also featuring Sid Haig and Forrest J Ackerman. Barkett appeared in the low-budget films "Beverly Hills Vamp" (1989), "Empire of the Dark" (1990) which he also produced, directed, and wrote, "Wizards of the Demon Sword" (1991), "Dark Universe" (1993), Fred Olen Ray's "Dinosaur Island" (1994) also serving as miniature supervisor, "Bikini Drive-In" (1995), "Hard Bounty" (1995), "Attack of the 60 Foot Centerfolds" (1995) also serving as special effects supervisor, "Droid Gunner" (1995), "Masseuse" (1996), "Star Hunter" (1996), "Invisible Mom" (1996), and "Rapid Assault" (1997). Barkett married Denise Gibson in 2008 and she survives him. He is also survived by his children, production designer Christopher Barkett and director Laura McQuay.

Barlow, Tim

British actor Tim Barlow died in England on January 20, 2023. He was 87. Barlow was born in Blackpool, Lancashire, England, on January 18, 1936. He joined the British army after graduating high school and served for fifteen years. He lost his hearing while testing a high velocity rifle for the army in the 1950s. He regained some of his hearing with a cochlear implant in 2008 and his experiences were recounted on the BBC Radio 4 series "It's My Story" episode "Earfull - From Silence into Sound". He left the army in 1969 and pursued an acting career. He wrote and performed in a one-man show entitled "My Army".

Barlow appeared frequently on television with roles in episodes of "Emmerdale Farm", "The Nearly Man", "Dixon of Dock Green", "Victorian Scandals", "The Experts", "Secret Army", "Poldark", "The Prime of Miss Jean Brodie", "Wings", "Within These Walls", "A Horseman Riding By", "Grange Hill", "The Omega Factor", "Doctor Who" as Tyssan in the 1979 serial "Destiny of the Daleks", "Buccaneer", "Escape", "Crown Court", "In Loving Memory", "The Adventures of Sherlock Holmes", "Hannay", "Screenplay", "Screen Two", "Moon and Son", "Screen One", "Frank Stubbs promotes", "Cracker", "Health and Efficiency", "Inside Victor Lewis-Smith" as Mr. Lobley from 1993 to 1995, "North Square", "My Uncle Silas", "The Bill", "Mile High", "Blue Murder", "My Life in Film", "Mike Bassett: Manager" as Sir Denzil Quartermaine in 2005, "Rome", "Wire in the Blood", "Waterloo Road", "Holby City", "Derek" as Jack from 2012 to 2014, "Sherlock", and "The Alienist". He was also seen in television productions of "Meriel, the Ghost Girl" (1976), "Return Fare" (1978), "Fanny by Gaslight" (1981), "Swallows and Amazons Forever!: The Big Six" (1984), "Eight Hours from Paris" (1997), "The History of Tom Jones, a Foundling" (1997), "Cleopatra" (1999), "Gormenghast" (2000), "The Life and Adventures of Nicholas Nickleby" (2001), "The Gentleman Thief" (2001), "White Heat" (2012), and "The New Pope" (2019). Barlow appeared in such films as "Brannigan" (1975), "The Eagle Has Landed" (1976), "Who Is Killing the Great Chefs of Europe?" (1978), "Privates on Parade" (1983), "The Tall Guy" (1989), "Anchoress" (1993), "Mary Reilly" (1996), "The Ugly" (1997), "Les Miserables" (1998), "Cousin Bette" (1998), "A Kind of Hush" (1999), "Tube Tales" (199), "The Nine Lives of Tomas Katz" (2000), "Kiss Kiss Bang Bang" (2001), "The Emperor's New Clothes" (2001), "The Rocket Post" (2004), "Kingdom of Heaven" (2005), "Lie Still" (2005), "Hot Fuzz" (2007), "10,000 BC" (2008), "Lezione 21" (2008), "Cockneys vs Zombies" (2012), "The Christmas Candle" (2013), "Automata" (2014), and "My Cousin Rachel" (2017). He was featured in the autobiographical stage production "Him" in 2016.

Barrett, Katherine

Actress Katherine Barrett died of cancer in Shingletown, California, on October 22, 2023. She was 91. Barrett was born in Hibbing, Minnesota, on January 21, 1932. She moved to California after college in the 1950s to pursue an acting career. She was featured in several films including "Bundle of Joy" (1956), "The Wayward Girl" (1957), "Eighteen and Anxious" (1957), and "The Shakiest Gun in the West" (1968). Barrett appeared on television in episodes of

"Dragnet", "The Millionaire", "Maverick", "Man with a Camera", "Frontier Doctor", "Bonanza", "My Three Sons", and "Family Affair". She largely abandoned acting in the late 1960s and served as a production assistant on the series "Mission Impossible". She developed an interest in photography and became noted for her pictures of horses. Barrett was photographer of racetrack at Santa Anita Park for over forty years.

Barry, Julian

Screenwriter Julian Barry, who was nominated for an Academy Award for the 1974 film "Lenny", died of complications from congestive heart failure and kidney disease at his home in Beverly Hills, California, on July 25, 2023. He was 92. He was born Julian Barry Mendelsohn, Jr. in New York City on December 24, 1930. He briefly attended Syracuse

University and Emerson College in Massachusetts, where he performed on stage in college productions. He was drafted into the U.S. Army during the Korean War and was discharged in 1953. Barry pursued an acting career and appeared in Orson Welles' production of "King Lear" on Broadway in 1955. He was a performer and stage manager for the Broadway productions of "Shinbone Alley" (1957) and "Compulsion" (1957). He continued to work on Broadway as a stage manager for "The Disenchanted" (1958), "The Andersonville Trial" (1959), "A Cook for Mr. General" (1961), "Write Me a Murder" (1961), "Sophie" (1963), and "The Chinese Prime Minister" (1964). Barry appeared on television in episodes of "Suspense" and "Goodyear Playhouse" in the 1950s. He began writing for television in the mid-1960s, penning episodes of "The Wackiest Ship in the Army" and "Mission: Impossible". He wrote the screenplay adaptation for Eugene Ionesco's play "Rhinoceros" in 1974. He wrote the play "Lenny", about controversial comedian Lenny Bruce, which was staged on Broadway in 1971. He wrote the screenplay for the 1974 film version starring Dustin Hoffman and earned one of the films six Academy Award nominations. Barry also wrote the 1978 slasher film "Eyes of Laura Mars", "The River" (1984), the tele-film "A Marriage: Georgia O'Keeffe and Alfred Stieglitz" (1991), and "Me Myself and I" (1992) which he also directed. He wrote the book for the short-lived musical biography "Jean Seberg" in 1983 and co-authored the opera "Born Again" with Peter Hall in 1990. He wrote the libretto and Peter King composed the music for the 2005 opera "Zyklon". His autobiography, "My Night with Orson", was published in 2011. Barry was married and divorced four times. He is survived by a son, Michael, and daughters, Sally and Jennifer, from his marriage to actress Patricia Foley. He is survived by his daughter, Julia, from his marriage to film producer Laura Ziskin. He is also survived by his longtime partner, Samantha Harper Macy.

Barthol, Bruce

Musician Bruce Barthol, who was the original bass player for the rock band Country Joe and the Fish, died in

hospice care in Sebastopol, California, on February 20, 2023. He was 75. Barthol was born in Berkeley, California, on November 11, 1947. He attended the University of California at Berkeley in 1964 where he was an active member of the Free Speech Movement and other radical causes. He left school to join Country Joe McDonald and Barry 'The Fish' Melton in the psychedelic rock band Country Joe and the Fish. He played the bass for the band through November of 1968. He remained in England following a European tour and joined Gary Peterson and Phil Greenberg in the band Formerly Fat Harry. He returned to California in 1972, where he formed the Energy Crisis Band. He became musical director for the San Francisco Mime Troupe in 1976. He worked on over three dozen shows with the mime troupe until his retirement in 2009. Barthol reunited with some members of Country Joe and the Fish for occasional tours from 2004 to 2006.

Barzman, Norma

Screenwriter and author Norma Barzman died at her home in Beverly Hills, California, on December 17, 2023. She was 103. She was born Norma Levor in New York City on September 15, 1920. She attended Radcliffe College in

Cambridge, Massachusetts. She married acclaimed mathematician Claude Shannon in 1940 and resided with him in Princeton, New Jersey, until their divorce the following year. She then moved to Los Angeles where she studied at the School for Writers. She soon married fellow writer Ben Barzman. Norma wrote the original story for the films "Never Say Goodbye" (1946) and "The Locket" (1946), which was based on her story "What Nancy Wanted". She and her husband had ties to leftist organizations and came under the scrutiny of Senator Joe McCarthy's blacklist. The couple moved to Europe in 1949, living in London and Paris. Norma wrote the 1953 French-Italian comedy film "Luxury Girl" (aka "Fanciulle di Lusso"), which was originally credited to the front name of Ennio Flaiano. She also wrote for the Italian television series "Il Triangolio Rosso" in the late 1960s. She and her family returned to the United States in 1976. She was active in having credits restored to writers who had films released under front names, including her own "Luxury Girls", in 1999. She was an

outspoken critic of the honorary Academy Award presented to Elia Kazan in 1998, who had testified before the House Committee of Un-American Activities in the 1950s. Barzman helped organized the Hollywood Blacklist exhibit for the Academy in 2001 and authored the 2003 book "The Red and the Blacklist: The Intimate Memoir of a Hollywood Expatriate". She also wrote the 2006 book "The End of Romance: A Memoir of Love, Sex, and the Mystery of the Violin". She was married to screenwriter Ben Barzman from 1942 until his death in 1989, and is survived by their seven children, including director and writer Paolo Barzman.

Basso, Bill

Special effects artist Bill Basso, who was noted for his work on such films as "Jurassic Park" and "Tremors", died at a hospital in Freehold, New Jersey, on May 4, 2023. He was 60.

Basso was born in Manalapan, New Jersey, on December 8, 1962. He attended college at the Parsons School of Design. He moved to Glendale, California, in the late 1980s to pursue a career in the film industry. He began working at Stan Winston Studio and was an effects artist, sculptor, and puppeteer on numerous films. Basso's film credits include "Tremors" (1990), "Bride of the Re-Animator" (1990), "Edward Scissorhands" (1990), "Predator 2" (1990), "Tales from the Darkside: The Movie" (1990), "Terminator 2: Judgment Day" (1991), "Batman Returns" (1992), "Jurassic Park" (1993), "Interview with the Vampire" (1994), "Congo" (1995), "The Island of Dr. Moreau" (1996), "The Relic" (1997), "The Lost World: Jurassic Park" (1997), "Small Soldiers" (1998), "Lake Placid" (1999), "Inspector Gadget" (1999), "Lost Souls" (2000), and "Reign of Fire" (2002). He also worked on the "Monsters" television series and the 1998 mini-series "Creature". Basso left films in the early 2000s and worked as a mixed media artist, utilizing drawing, sculpture, photography, collage, and painting.

Bastien, Charles E.

Canadian animation director Charles E. Bastien died of cancer in Toronto, Ontario, Canada, on March 21, 2023. He

was 60. Bastien was born in Sarnia, Ontario, Canada, on October 14, 1962. He studied animation at Sheridan College in Toronto and began working at the animation studio Nelvana in the mid-1980s. He worked as a storyboard artist, art director, designer, and animation director for numerous cartoon series and animated videos. His numerous television credits include "Star Wars: Droids", "Star Wars: Ewoks", "My Pet Monster", "Babar", "Beetlejuice", "Rupert",

"Little Rosey", "The Rosey & Buddy Show", "Fievel's Adventures in the West", "Cadillacs and Dinosaurs", "Tales from the Cryptkeeper", "Gargoyles", "Journey to the Center of the Earth", "Extreme Ghostbusters", "The Magic School Bus" sharing a Daytime Emmy Award nomination in 1997, "Anatole", "Freaky Stories", "Little Bear", "Pelswick", "Cyberchase", "Roswell Conspiracies: Aliens, Myths & Legends", "Elliot Moose", "Quads!", "Seven Little Monsters", "Clone High", "Larry Boy: The Cartoon Adventures", "Jacob Two-Two", "6Teen", "Braceface", "Bigfoot Presents: Meteor and the Mighty Monster Trucks", "My Gym Partner's a Monkey", "Johnny Test", "The Replacements", "Handy Manny", "Rescue Heroes", "Mike the Knight", "Wayside", "Magic Adventures of Mumfie", "Miraculous: Tales of Ladybug & Cat Noir", "True and the Rainbow Kingdom", "Brain Dump", "Abby Hatcher, Fuzzly Catcher", and "PAW Patrol". Bastien also worked on the animated films and videos "Clifford's Fun with Letters" (1988), "Babar: The Movie" (1989), "Call of the Wild" (1996), "An Angel for Christmas" (1996), "The Adventures of Moby Dick" (1996), "The Pirates and the Prince" (1997), "The Suite Life of Hudson & James: Taking Over the Lipton" (2004), "Treasure of the Hidden Planet" (2004), and "Mike the Knight: Journey to Dragon Mountain" (2014), and features in the "Little Bear", "Care Bears" and "PAW Patrol" series. He was also artist for the online comic strip "Bugsport".

Batayeh, Mike

Actor Mike Batayeh, who was featured as Dennis Markowski, the manager of Gus Frings' laundromat in the "Breaking Bad" television series, died of a heart attack at his

home in Ypsilanti, Michigan, on June 1, 2023. He was 52. Batayeh was born in Detroit, Michigan, on December 27, 1970. He began performing as a comedian and an actor in the 1990s. He appeared at comedy clubs around the country including Los Angeles' Laugh Factory, Comedy Story, and the Improv. Batayeh was seen on television in episodes of "Everybody Loves Raymond", "Boy Meets World", "Something So Right", "Two Guys, a Girl and a Pizza Place", "Power Rangers Lost Galaxy", "JAG, "The Pitts", "Baby Bob", "The Shield", "The Bernie Mac Show", "Night Stalker", "Pepper Dennis", "CSI: Miami", "Sleeper Cell" in the recurring role of Ziad from 2005 to 2006, "Life", "Touch", "Breaking Bad" as the manager of Gus' laundromat that served as a cover for Walter White's meth lab in several episodes from 2011 to 2012, "It's Always Sunny in Philadelphia", "Real Husbands of Hollywood", "Jessie", "Marco Polo", and "Battle Creek". He was also seen in the tele-films "The Apostles" (2008) and "Prank of America" (2018). Batayeh was featured in such films as "Gas" (2004), "American Dreamz" (2006), "You Don't Mess with the Zohan" (2008), "AmericanEast" (2008), "This Narrow Place" (2011), "Detroit

Unleaded" (2012), "Misled" (2015), "Sharia" (2016), "Namour" (2016), and "Dirty" (2016). he was one of the first American comics to perform in the Middle East, with shows in Egypt, Lebanon, and Jordan. He was also featured in a Showtime Arabia special filmed in Dubai.

Baumann, Heinz

German actor Heinz Baumann, who was noted for his work in crime television series, died in Munich, Germany, on March 4, 2023. He was 95. Baumann was born in Oldenburg,

Germany, on February 12, 1928. He performed frequently on stage and screen from the 1950s. He was featured in the films "Schloss Hubertus" (1954), "The Haunted Castle" (1960), "I'm an Elephant, Madame" (1969), "Und Jimmy Ging Zum Regenbogen" (1971), "Alle Menschen Werden Bruder" (1973), "Die Antwort Kennt Nur der Wind" (1974), "Der Gartner von Toulouse" (1982), "Diebinnen" (1996), and "Doppelspiel" (2006). Baumann was seen often on television with roles in productions of "Becket oder Die Ehre Gottes" (1962) as Thomas Becket, "Penthesilea" (1963), "Der Arme Mann Luther" (1965), "Die Karussell" (1965), "Der Schwarze Schwan" (1965), "Die Chinesische Mauer" (1965), "Irrungen - Wirrungen" (1966), "Drei Schwestern" (1966), "Stella" (1966), "Jeanne Oder Die Lerche" (1966), "Moral" (1967), "Im Lemgo 89" (1967), "Bahnwarter Thiel" (1968), "Mordergesellschaft" (1968), "Fragestunde" (1969), "Langeweile" (1969), "Fememord" (1969), "Der Ruckfall" (1969), "Lauf Doch Nicht Splitternackt Herum" (1969), "Die Verschworung" (1969), "Floup Oder Der Hang Zur Redlichkeit" (1970), "Der Selbstmorder" (1971), "Willy und Lilly" (1971), "Letzte Mahnung" (1971), "Die Messe der Erfullten Wunsche" (1971), "Bluten der Gesellschaft" (1972), "Eine Egoistische Liebe" (1973), "Macbett" (1973), "Nie Wieder Mary" (1974), "Polly Oder Die Bataille am Bluewater Creek" (1975), "Der Biberpelz" (1975), "Eine Frau Zieht Ein" (1975), "Lobster" (1976), "Der Winter, der Ein Sommer War" (1976), "Nicht von Gestern" (1977), "Kleine Geschichten Mit Grossen Tieren" (1978), "Der Geist der Mirabelle. Geschichten von Bollerup" (1978), "Tochter des Schweigens" (1978), "Im Schlaraffenland. Ein Roman Unter Feinen Leuten" (1981), "Ich Bin Wie Othello - Mein Tagewerk Ist Vorbei" (1983), "Die Funfte Jahreszeit" (1983), "Zeig' Was du Kannst - Eine Komodie Aus den 50er Jahren" (1983), "In der Sackgasse" (1983), "Der Snob" (1984), "Treffpunkt im Unendlichen" (1984), "250.000 Mucken im Pappkarton" (1985), "Reichshauptstadt Privat" (1987), "Dem Tod auf der Spur" (1988), "Der Spatzenmorder" (1989), "Ich Will Lebcn" (1990), "Der Unschuldesengel" (1992), "Wehner - Die Unerzahlte Geschichte" (1993), "Die Elefantebraut" (1993), "Vater Werden Ist Nicht Schwer" (2004), "Bettis Bescherung" (2006), "Spate Aussicht" (2007), "Die Letzte Fahrt" (2013), and "Just Married - Hochzeiten Zwei" (2013). His other television credits include episodes of "Die Perle - Aus dem Tagebuch Einer Hausgehilfin", "Der Kommissar", "Stadt Ohne Sheriff" as Antonio Colani in 1972, "Sonderdezernat K1", "Hoftheater", "Kara Ben Nemsi Effendi" as Bybar Aladschi in 1975, "Eine Ganz Gewohnliche Geschichte", "Partner Gesucht", "Die Falle des Herrn Konstantin", "Jorg Preda Berichtet" as James Reuther in 1977, "Tochter des Schweigens", "Achtung Kunstdiebe" as Gerd Wieland in 1979, "Buddenbrooks", "Felix und Oskar" as Oskar Martens in 1980, "St. Pauli-Landungsbrucken", "The Old Fox", "Die Krimistunde", "Georg Thomallas Geschichten", "Ich, Christian Hahn", "Ich Heirate Eine Familie..." as Bernie Graf from 1983 to 1986, "Derrick", "Der Fahnder", "Tatort", "Wolffs Revier", "Florida Lady", "Blankenese", "Schlosshotel Orth", "Das Traumschiff", "Heimatgeschichten", and "Pfarrer Braun". Bauman played detective Jurgen Sudmann in the police series "SOKO Munchen" from 1984 to 2008 and in the short-lived 1997 series "Solo fur Sudmann". He was featured as Chief Inspector Ewald Strobel in the series "Adelheid und Ihre Morder" from 1993 to 2007. Baumann was married to actress Gardy Brombacher from 1963 until her death in 2003. His survivors include his daughter with comedian Beatrice Richter, actress Judith Richter.

Baxter, Keith

British actor Keith Baxter died of a heart attack while swimming on vacation in Corsica, France, on September 24, 2023. He was 90. He was born Keith Baxter-Wright in Newport, Wales, on April 29, 1933. He trained in London at

the Royal Academy of Dramatic Art in the mid-1950s. He appeared on television in a 1956 production of "She Stoops to Conquer" and was featured in the 1957 version of "The Barretts of Wimpole Street" starring John Gielgud. He was soon appearing on stage in repertory in Oxford and Worthing and toured in a 1957 production of Noel Coward's "South Sea Bubble". He had a small role in the 1960 psychological horror film "Peeping Tom". Baxter was featured as Prince Hal opposite Orson Welles' Falstaff in a stage production of "Chimes at Midnight" in 1960. He reprised the roles with Welles in the 1965 film version. He was also cast as Doctor Livesey in Welles' unfinished version of Robert Louis Stevenson's "Treasure Island" in 1965. He performed frequently on stage throughout his career and was seen in Broadway productions of "A Man for All Seasons" (1961) as King Henry VIII, "The Affair" (1962), "Avanti!" (1968), "Sleuth" (1970) earning a Drama Desk Award for his role as Milo Tindle, "A Meeting by the River" (1979), "Romantic Comedy" (1980), and "Corpse!" (1986). Baxter continued to appear in such films as "With Love in Mind" (1970), "Ash Wednesday" (1973) starring Elizabeth Taylor, "La Regenta" (1974), "Golden Rendezvous" (1988), "Berlin Blues" (1988), and "Killing Time" (1999). His other television credits include productions of "Six Stayed the Night"

(1957), "Incident at Echo Six" (1958), "The Troublemakers" (1958), "The Young May Moon" (1958), "Man and Superman" (1958), "A Dead Secret" (1959), "The Extra Grave" (1959), "Sweet Poison" (1959), "Square Dance" (1960), "After the Party" (1960), "The Reward of Silence" (1963), "For Tea on Sunday" (1963), "Where Angels Fear to Tread" (1963), "Curtains for Sheila" (1965), "Hold My Hand, Soldier" (1965), "Saint Joan" (1968), "Nightmare for a Nightingale" (1975), "Will Shakespeare" (1978) as the Earl of Essex, "Six Characters in Search of an Author" (1992), and "Merlin" (1998) as Sir Hector. Baxter also appeared in episodes of "The Sentimental Agent", "The Hidden Truth", "Gideon C.I.D.", "Armchair Theatre", "Public Eye", "Love Story", "Thirty-Minute Theatre", "The Avengers", "Orson Welles' Great Mysteries", "Dial M for Murder", "Do You Remember?", and "Hawaii Five-O". He wrote the 1987 play "Barnaby and the Old Boys" and the memoir "My Sentiments Exactly" in 1999. Baxter served frequently as a director for stage productions and worked with the Shakespeare Theatre Company in Washington, D.C., in the early 2000s. He began a long relationship with restaurateur Brian Holden while visiting Florida in 1979. The two married in 2016 and Holden survives him.

Bean, Reathel

Actor Reathel Bean died of cancer in Chicago, Illinois, on October 4, 2023. He was 81. Bean was born in West Plains, Missouri, on August 24, 1942. He began performing on stage in high school and graduated from Drake University in 1964. He was active in the civil rights movement in the 1960s and was a conscientious objector during the Vietnam War. He performed on stage from the late 1960s and appeared in Broadway productions of "Doonesbury" (1983), "Big River"

(1985), "Inherit the Wind" (1996), "Our Town" (2002), and "Caroline, or Change" (2004). He was featured in such films as Adolfas Mekas' "Windflowers" (1968), "Going in Style" (1979), "Alamo Bay" (1985), "Static" (1985), "Cocktail" (1988), "Brenda Starr" (1989), "The Boy Who Cried Bitch" (1991), "Flodder in Amerika!" (1992), "The Gun in Betty Lou's Handbag" (1992), "Killer: A Journal of Murder" (1995), "Box of Moonlight" (1996), "Just One Time" (1998), "Company Man" (2000), "Dancer in the Dark" (2000), "Almost Famous" (2000), "Revolution #9" (2001), "Dead Dog" (2001), "Knots" (2004), "The Good Shepherd" (2006), "The Nanny Diaries" (2007), "The Life Before Her Eyes" (2007), "Home" (2008), "Das Vaterspiel" (2009), and "Handsome Harry" (2009). He was seen on television in the tele-films "Apology" (1986) and "Our Town" (2003), and episodes of "The Wright Verdicts", "Remember WENN", "Spin City", "Third Watch", "Ed", "Law & Order", "Guiding Light", "30 Rock", "As the World Turns", "Rescue Me", "Nurse Jackie", "White Collar", "Law & Order: Criminal Intent", "One Life to Live", "Law & Order: Special

Victims Unit", "The Blacklist", and "Madam Secretary". Bean is survived by his wife of over sixty years, Holly Vincent, and their two children.

Beasley, John

Actor John Beasley died at a hospital in Omaha, Nebraska, on May 30, 2023. He was 79. Beasley was born in Omaha on June 26, 1943. He worked with the Union Pacific Railroad until pursuing an acting career in the mid-1980s. He was founder of the John Beasley Theater and Workshop in South Omaha where he worked for over a decade. He was seen in numerous films including "Rapid Fire" (1989), "V.I. Warshawski" (1991), "The Mighty Ducks" (1992), "Untamed Heart" (1993), "Rudy" (1993), "Little Big League" (1994), "Losing Isaiah" (1995), "The Cure" (1995), "The Apostle" (1997), "Overnight Delivery" (1998), "The General's Daughter" (1999), "The Living Witness" (1999), "Crazy in Alabama" (1999), "The Operator" (2000), "Lost Souls" (2000), "The Gift" (2000), "The Journeyman" (2001), "The Sum of All Fears" (2002), "Walking Tall" (2004), "Daddy's Little Girls" (2007), "For Love of Amy" (2009), "Haunted Maze" (2013), "The Purge: Anarchy" (2014), "I'll See You in My Dreams" (2015), "Sinister 2" (2015), "The Turkey Bowl" (2019), "Cowboys" (2020), "Spell" (2020), "Stoker Hills" (2020), "Firestarter" (2022), an "It Snows All the Time" (2022). Beasley was seen on television in episodes of "Brewster Place" as Mr. Willie in 1990, "Angel Street", "The Untouchables", "Missing Persons", "EZ Streets", "Early Edition", "The Pretender", "Millennium" in the recurring role of James Edward Hollis in 1999, "CSI: Crime Scene Investigation", "Judging Amy" in the recurring role of Judge Henry Bromell in the early 2000s, "Everwood" as Irv Harper from 2002 to 2006, "NCIS", "Boston Legal", "CSI Miami", "Harry's Law", "Detroit 1-8-7", "House of Payne", "Treme" as Don Encalade in 2011, "The Soul Man" as Barton Ballentine from 2012 to 2016, "Shorts Fired" as Mr. Dabney in 2017, "The Resident", "Limetown", "The Mandalorian", and "Your Honor". His other television credits include productions of "Lucky Day" (1991), "Laurel Avenue" (1993), "To Sir, with Love II" (1996), "Traces of Insanity" (1998), "ATF" (1999), "Freedom Song" (2000), "The Moving of Sophia Myles" (2000), "Disappearing Acts" (2000), "The Lost Room" (2006), "Chasing a Dream" (2009), and "The Immortal Life of Henrietta Lacks" (2017). Beasley is survived by his wife, Judy, of nearly sixty years and their two sons.

Becerril, Fernando

Mexican actor Fernando Becerril, who was featured in the films "Ravenous" and "The Legend of Zorro", died in Mexico on February 7, 2023. He was 78. Becerril was born in San Luis Potosi, Mexico, on May 30, 1945. He began performing in a choir during his youth. He studied at the School of Fine Arts Theatre in Mexico City before traveling to France. He continued his studies in Paris, where he remained for two decades. Becerril returned to Mexico in the mid-1990s and was featured in the films "The Mask of Zorro" (1998) and "Ravenous" (1999). He continued his film career with such

credits as "Rito Terminal" (2000), "Los Maravillosos Olores de la Vida" (2000), "The Crime of Padre Amaro" (2002), "Zapata - El Sueno del Heroe" (2004) as Presidente Francisco Madero, "Cero y Van 4" (2004), "La Ultima Noche" (2005), "The Legend of Zorro" (2005), "Don de Dios" (2005), "Drama/Mex" (2006), "Morirse en Domingo" (2006), "KM 31: Kilometro 31" (2006), "The Night Buffalo" (2007), "Corazon Marchito" (2007), "Ano Una" (2007), "Esperame en Otro Mundo" (2007), "The Zone" (2007), "Todos los Dias Son Tuyos" (2007), "Amor Letra por Letra" (2008), "Arrancame la Vida" (2008), "Caja Negra" (2009), "La Mitad del Mundo" (2009), "Depositarios" (2010), "180o" (2010), "The Attempt Dossier" (2010), "By Day and by Night" (2010), "To Presento a Laura" (2010), "Fragmentos Sobre El Vertigo" (2010), "Against the Wind" (2011), "Mariachi Gringo" (2012), "Tooth for a Tooth" (2012), "Get the Gringo" (2012) starring Mel Gibson, "Portion" (2012), "Tlatelolco, Verano de 68" (2013), "Potosi" (2013), "Pulling Strings" (2013), "Actores S.A." (2013), "Los Fabulosos 7" (2013), "Huerfanos" (2014), "Tiempos Felices" (2014), "Hilda" (2014), "The Obscure Spring" (2014), "Hyena's Blood" (2014), "The Thin Yellow Line" (2015), "Por Mis Bigotes" (2015), the supernatural thriller "The Similars" (2015), "Purasangre" (2016), "Hysteria" (2016), "Vive Por Mi" (2016), "Casi Una Gran Estafa" (2017), "The Inhabitant" (2017), "Champs" (2018), "El Club de los Insomnes" (2018), "Ni Tu Ni Yo" (2018), "Sonora, the Devil's Highway" (2018), "Souvenir" (2019), "The Gasoline Thieves" (2019), "Close Quarters" (2020), "Mutiny of the Worker Bees" (2020), "You've Got This" (2020), "Dance of the 41" (2020) as Porfirio Diaz, "Aztech" (2020), "Los Dias Que No Estuve" (2021), "Book of Love" (2022), "Courage" (2022), "El Sueno de Ayer" (2022), "Donde los Pajaros Van a Morir" (2022), "La Vida en el Silencio" (2022), and "Death's Roulette" (2023). Becerril was seen on television in productions of "La Duchesse de Langeais" (1995), "Les Brumes de Manchester" (1998), "Tres Veces Sofia" (1998), "Hablame de Amor" as Alonso in 1999, "Amores Querer con Alevosia" as Guillermo Herreros in 2001, "In the Time of the Butterflies" (2001), "Fidel", "Por Ti" (2002) as Arturo Montalban, "And Starring Pancho Villa as Himself" (2003), "Zapata: Amor en Rebeldia" (2004), "Linea Nocturna" (2006), "Capadocia" (2008) as Juez Diego Cedeno, "Nochc Eterna" (2008), "Eternamente Tuya" (2009), "Fierce Angel" (2010), "Drenaje Profundo" as Roman Milosz from 2010 to 2011, "Querete Asi" (2012), "Los Rey" (2012), "XY. La Revista" as Artemio Miranda, Sr. from 2009 to 2012, "Secretos de Familia" (2013), "Sr. Avila" in the recurring role of Sr. Moreira from 2013 to 2018, "Meister des Todes" (2015),

"Hasta Que Te Conoci" (2016), "Un Dia Cualquiera" (2016), "Su Nombre era Dolores, la Jenn que yo Conoci" (2017), "Run Coyote Run" (2017), "Dos Lagos" (2017), "An Unknown Enemy" (2018) as Alfonso Corna del Rosal, "Casino Mex" (2018), "El Candidato" (2020), "The Five Juanas" as Rogelio Marroquin in 2021, "The Envoys" as Monsenor Benavent from 2021 to 2022, and "El Rey, Vicente Fernandez" (2022) as Honorio Dalton.

Beck, Jeff

British guitarist Jeff Beck, who was a member of the rock bands the Yardbirds and the Jeff Beck Group, died from a bacterial meningitis infection at a hospital in East Sussex, England, on January 10, 2023. He was 78. Beck was born in Wallington, Surrey, England, on June 24, 1944. He learned to play the guitar in his youth. He studied at the Wimbledon School of Art and worked at odd jobs while pursuing a music career. He played with the bands the Nightshift, the Rumbles, the Tridents, and Screaming Lord Sutch and the Savages in the early 1960s. He joined the Yardbirds in 1965, replacing Eric Clapton as lead guitarist. He performed on the band's hit singles "Heart Full of Soul", "Evil Hearted You"/"Still I'm Sad", a cover of Bo Diddley's "I'm a Man", "Shapes of Things", and "Over Under Sideways Down", and the band's 1966 album "Roger the Engineer" (aka Over Under Sideways Down"). He appeared while performing with the Yardbirds in Michelangelo Antonioni's 1966 film "Blow Up". The Yardbirds soon had dual lead guitarists when Jimmy Page joined the group. Beck left the band in November of 1966 while on a tour in the United States. He recorded several solo singles in 1967 before forming the Jeff Beck Group. The new band included Rod Stewart on vocals, Ronnie Wood on bass, Nicky Hopkins on piano, and Aynsley Dunbar on drums. They recorded the albums "Truth" (1968) and "Beck-Ola" (1969) from Columbia Records. Micky Waller replaced Dunbar on Drums before the group disbanded in July of 1969. His career was interrupted when he suffered a fractured skull in an automobile accident later in the year. He recovered to form a new Jeff Beck Group in 1971 with Bobby Tench on lead vocals and Cozy Powell on drums. They recorded the albums "Rough and Ready" (1971) and "Jeff Beck Group" (1972). He teamed with Vanilla Fudge members Carmine Appice and Tim Bogert for the 1973 album "Beck, Bogert & Appice". He recorded the solo album "Blow by Blow" in 1975 and performed with the band Upp's self-named debut album. Beck recorded the 1976 album "Wired" with Mahavishnu Orchestra drummer and composer Narada Michael Walden and keyboardist Jan Hammer. He later toured with the Jan Hammer Group that resulted in a live album in 1977. He continued to perform and record and his album "There & Back" was released in 1980. He performed with Eric Clapton in the early 1980s at the benefit concert "The Secret Policeman's Other Ball", and appeared on

the subsequent album and film in 1982. He had a hit with his 1985 album "Flash" which included the Grammy Award-winning song "Escape" and a cover of "People Get Ready" with Rod Stewart on vocals. Beck returned to the studio for the 1989 instrumental music album "Jeff Beck's Guitar Shop". He played the guitar solo for Jon Bon Jovi's solo debut album "Blaze of Glory" in 1990 and was a featured performer for the score for the 1990 film "Days of Thunder". He played lead guitar on Roger Waters' album "Amused to Death" (1992), Kate Bush's "The Red Shoes" (1993), and Beverley Craven's "Love Scenes" (1993). He was inducted with the Yardbirds into the Rock and Roll Hall of Fame in 1992. He toured and recorded with Jennifer Batten for the 1999 album "Who Else!" and "You Had It Coming" (2001). He won Grammy Awards for his work on the songs "Dirty Mind" (2001), "Plan B" (2003), "A Day in the Life" (2009), "Imagine" (2010), "Nessun Dorma" (2010), and "Hammerhead" (2010). Beck was inducted into the Rock and Roll Hall of Fame as a solo artist in 2009. He toured and recorded with Beach Boys founder Brian Wilson in 2013. His final solo album, "Loud Hailer", was released in 2016. He began collaborating with actor Johnny Depp in 2020 and they released the 2022 album "18". Beck was seen on numerous television variety series including "Ready, Steady, Go!", "Top of the Pops", "Beat-Club", "In Concert", "The Arsenio Hall Show", "The Comic Strip Presents", "Late Show with David Letterman", "Late Night with Conan O'Brien", "Later... With Jools Holland", "American Idol" where he accompanied Kelly Clarkson for her rendition of "Up to the Mountain" in 2007, "Breakfast", "The Tonight Show with Jay Leno", "Arena", "Great Performances", "Late Night with Jimmy Fallon", and "Celebrity Page". He starred in the television specials "Jeff Beck at Ronnie Scott's" (2008), "Jeff Beck: Live in Tokyo" (2014), "Jeff Beck: Live at the Hollywood Bowl" (2017), and "Jeff Beck: Still on the Run" (2018). He was featured as a guitarist in the 1988 film "Twins". He composed music for the 1991 film "The Pope Must Diet" and appeared in a small role. He scored the 1994 film "Blue Chips" and the television mini-series "Frankie's House" (1992) and "Catterick" (2004). Beck was married to Patricia Brown from 1963 until their divorce in 1967. He was involved with model Celia Hammond from 1968 through the mid-1980s. He married Sandra Cush in 2005 and she survives him.

Belafonte, Harry

Singer, actor, and political activist Harry Belafonte, who popularized Calypso in the United States, died of congestive heart failure at his home in the Upper West Side of Manhattan, New York, on April 25, 2023. He was 96. He was born Harold George Bellanfanti, Jr., in Harlem, New Yok, on March 1, 1927. He was raised by a grandmother in Jamaica for nearly a decade in his youth. He attended high school after returning to New York City but dropped out to serve in the U.S. Navy during World War II. He became interested in acting after attending a performance of the American Negro Theater later in the 1940s. He also became friends with fellow aspiring actor Sidney Poitier. He took acting classes at the Dramatic Workshop of the New School in New York City, studying under

Erwin Piscator. He performed with the American Negro Theater, playing the lead in a production of "Juno and the Paycock". He earned a Tony Award for Best Featured Actor in

a Musical for his role in the musical revue "John Murray Anderson's Almanac" in 1954. Belafonte also starred in the 1955 musical "3 for Tonight". He was a singer in New York night clubs and made his recording debut on the Roost label in 1949. He signed with RCA Victor in 1953 and recorded the hit single "Matilda" later in the year. His 1956 album "Calypso" was a major hit becoming the first to sell over a million copies in a year. The album contained the hit songs "Day-O" (aka "Banana Boat Song") and "Jamaica Farewell". He starred in the 1959 television special "Revlon Revue: Tonight with Belafonte" and performed a duet of "There's a Hole in My Bucket" with Odetta. He became the first Jamaican to earn an Emmy Award for the production. He recorded songs from various genres including blues, folk, gospel, and American standards. Belafonte made his film debut in 1953's "Bright Road" opposite Dorothy Dandridge. The duo also starred together in Otto Preminger's production of the hit musical "Carmen Jones" (1954). He starred with Joan Crawford and James Mason in the 1957 film "Island in the Sun" and starred in and produced, through his HarBel Productions company, the 1959 film "Odds Against Tomorrow". He starred opposite Inger Stevens in the end of the world classic "The World, the Flesh and the Devil" in 1959. He left acting for nearly a decade in the 1960s to concentrate on his music. He released the popular albums "Swing Dat Hammer" (1960) earning a Grammy Award, "Jump Up Calypso" (1961), "Midnight Special" (1962), "Belafonte at The Greek Theatre" (1964), "An Evening with Belafonte/Makeba" (1965) receiving another Grammy Award, and "Calypso Carnival" (1971). He performed on television in such variety series and specials as "Cavalcade of Stars", "The Colgate Comedy Hour", "America After Dark", "The Nat King Cole Show", "The Steve Allen Plymouth Show", "Perry Como's Kraft Music Hall", "The Ed Sullivan Show", "The New Les Crane Show", "The Bell Telephone Hour", "The Danny Kaye Show", "What's My Line?", "ABC Stage 67", "Petula" igniting a controversy when the white Clark touched the black Belafonte while singing a song, "Rowan & Martin's Laugh-In", "The Smothers Brothers Comedy Hour", "An Evening with Julie Andrews and Harry Belafonte" in 1969, "Harry and Lena" in 1970, "The David Frost Show", "The Real Tom Kennedy Show", "The Diahann Carroll Special", "Jerry Lewis MDA Labor Day Telethon", "The Lee Phillip Show", "Soul!", "The Dick Cavett Show", "The Merv Griffin Show", "The New Bill Cosby Show", "The Julie Andrews Hour", "The Rowan and Martin Special", "RCA's Opening Night", "Flip", "Free to Be... You & Me", "The Mike Douglas Show", "The Muppet Show", "Night of 100 Stars", "Ebony/Jet Showcase", 1985's "Harry Belafonte in Concert", "Live! Dick Clark Presents", "Lou Rawls Parade of Stars", "The Arsenio Hall Show", "Live with Regis and Kathie Lee", "The Rosie O'Donnel Show", "Sesame Street", "Biography", "60 Minutes", 1997's "An Evening with Harry Belafonte & Friends", "The Marion Anderson Award Honoring Harry Belafonte" in 1998, 2000's "An Evening with Harry Belafonte", "Petula Clark: This Is My Song", "Live from Lincoln Center", "Real Time with Bill Maher", "Larry King Live", "The Colbert Report", "Charlie Rose", "Tavis Smiley", and "Today". He was a frequent guest on "The Tonight Show Starring Johnny Carson", including a stint as guest host in February of 1968 when he had Martin Luther King, Jr., and Sen. Robert F. Kennedy as guests. He returned to the big screen in the 1970s, starring in 1970's "The Angel Levine". He starred with Sidney Poitier in the films "Buck and the Preacher" (1972) which he also produced and "Uptown Saturday Night" (1974). He starred as Coach Eddie Robinson in the 1981 tele-film "Grambling's White Tiger". He produced and scored the 1984 musical film "Beat Street". His later films include "The Player" (1992), "Ready to Wear" (1994), "White Man's Burden" (1995), Robert Altman's "Kansas City" (1996), the tele-film "Swing Vote" (1999), "Bobby" (2006), and Spike Lee's "BlacKkKlansman" (2018) as Jerome Turner. Belafonte was an outspoken advocate for civil rights and opposed the South

African apartheid system and western colonialism in Africa. He was a confidant of Martin Luther King, Jr., bailing him out of a jail in Birmingham, Alabama, in 1963. He supported John F. Kennedy for U.S. President in 1960 and was named cultural advisor to the Peace Corps. He was one of the organizers of the Grammy Award-winning song "We Are the World" to raise money for Africa in 1985 and participated in the Live Aid concert later in the year. He was also involved with the Hands Across America human-chain campaign in 1986. He served as a UNICEF Goodwill Ambassador from 1987 until his death. He was the subject of the 2011 documentary film "Sing Your Song". His memoir, "My Song", was published in 2011. Belafonte received the Kennedy Center Honors in 1989 and was awarded the National Medal of Arts in 1994. He was given a Grammy Lifetime Achievement Award in 2000 and received the BET Humanitarian Award in 2006. He was given the Jean Hersholt Humanitarian Award at the Academy of Motion Picture Arts and Sciences in 2014 and was inducted into the Rock and Roll Hall of fame in the early influences category in 2022. Belafonte is a rare EGOT honoree, having earned Emmy, Grammy, Oscar, and Tony Awards during his career, though his Oscar, the Jean Hersholt Humanitarian Award, was a non-competitive honor. He was married to Marguerite Byrd from 1948 until their divorce in 1957 and is survived by their two daughters, Adrienne Belafonte and actress Shari Belafonte. He was married to dancer Julie Robinson from 1957 until their divorce in 2005 and is survived by their daughter Gina and son David. He married photographer Pamela Frank in 2008 and she also survives him.

Bell, Alan J.W.

British television producer and director Alan J.W. Bell, who worked on the comedy series "Last of the Summer Wine" for nearly thirty years, died in England on October 19, 2023. He was 85. Bell was born in Battersea, London, England, on November 14, 1937. He began working in films at BBC as an editor at Ealing Studios in 1958 and soon moved to Television Centre. He was producing and directing television productions by the end of the 1960s. His credits include "Mirror for Our Dreams" (1968), "Scene" (1969), "The Curious Character of Britain" (1970), "Trials of Life" (1971), "One Pair of Eyes" (1971), "All in a Day" (1971-1974), "The Chinese Puzzle" (1974), "Couples" (1975-1976), "The Yugoslav Way" (1976), "The World About Us" (1977), "Call My Bluff" (1977-1982), "Fallen Hero" (1978), "Crackerjack!" (1978), "Crown Court" (1979), "Ripping Yarns" (1979), "Parkinson" (1980), the 1981 adaptation of Douglas Adams' "The Hitchhiker's Guide to the Galaxy", "Rule Britannia" (1981), "There's a Lot of It About" (1982), "There's a Lot of It About" (1982), "Gaskin" (1983), "The Climber" (1983), "Getting Sam Home" (1983), "The Hello Goodbye Man" (1984), "The Fainthearted Feminist" (1984), "Murder Not Proven?" (1984), "The Clairvoyant" (1984-1986), "King & Castle" (1986), "Gems" (1986-1988), "C.A.T.S. Eyes" (1987), "Dogfood Dan and the Carmarthen Cowboy" (1988), "Wyatt's Watchdogs" (1988), "The Customer Connection: Who Cares Wins" (1988), "The Beiderbecke Connection" (1988), the documentary "Peter Cushing: A One-Way Ticket to Hollywood" (1989), "Split Ends" (1989), "Children's Ward" (1990-1991), "The Bill" (1991-1995), "Taggart" (1993), "Crime Story" (1995), "Casualty" (1996), and "Emmerdale" (1997). He took over directing and producing the BBC sitcom "Last of the Summer Wine" in 1983 and remained with the series until it ended in 2010. Bell directed Deric Longden's autobiographical drama "Lost for Words" for ITV in 1999 and produced and directed episodes of the 2014 series "Cooper and Walsh". He wrote the books "Last of the Summer Wine: From the Director's Chair" (2012) and "A Hitch in the Galaxy" (2016). Bell married actress Constance (Bell) Carling in 1970 and is survived by her and their daughter, Cheraine.

Bell, Ted

Author Ted Bell, who was noted for the Lord Alexander Hawke espionage thrillers, died of an intercerebral hemorrhage in Hartford, Connecticut, on January 20, 2023. He was 76. Bell was born in Tampa, Florida, on July 3, 1946. He graduated from Randolph-Macon College in Ashland, Virginia. He began his career in advertising at the Doyle Dane Bernbach Agency in 1972. He joined the Leo Burnett Company in 1982 as a creative director and became president and chief creative

officer in 1986. He was also vice-chairman of the board and creative director of Yung & Rubicam from 1993 until his retirement in 2000. Bell began a series of spy novels featuring the character of Lord Alexander Hawke with 2003's "Hawke". The series continued with the novels "Assassin" (2004), "Pirate" (2005), "Spy" (2006), "Tsar" (2008), "Warlord" (2010), "Phantom" (2012), "Warriors" (2014), "Patriot" (2015), "Overkill" (2018), "Dragonfire" (2020), and "Sea Hawke" (2021). He wrote a pair of juvenile novels featuring time traveling adventurer Nick McIver which included "Nick of Time" (2008) and "The Time Pirate" (2010). Bell married photographer Evelyn Byrd Lorentzen in 1978 and they had a daughter, actress and model Byrdie Bell before their divorce. He was also married and divorced from artist Page Lee Hufty and author Lucinda Watson.

Belzer, Richard

Actor and comedian Richard Belzer, who starred as Detective John Much on the television series "Homicide: Life on the Street" and "Law & Order: Special Victims Unit" for over twenty years, died at his home in Bozouls, France, on February 19, 2023. He was 78. Belzer was born in Bridgeport, Connecticut, on August 4, 1944. He worked as a reporter for the "Bridgeport Post" after graduating high school. He attended Dean College in Franklin, Massachusetts, until he was expelled. He moved to New York City to work as a stand-up comic at such comedy clubs as the Improv and Catch a Rising Star. He also worked with the Channel One comedy group and was featured in the 1974 cult film "The Groove Tube". He performed comedy sketches on the "National Lampoon Radio Hour" from 1973 to 1975. Belzer served as an audience warm-up comedian for "Saturday Night Live" and was a guest on three episodes between 1975 to 1980. He also opened for musician Warren Zevon's tour promoting his "Excitable Boy" album in 1978. He co-hosted the "Brink & Belzer" program on WNBC-AM radio in New York City in the late 1970s and was a frequent guest on "The Howard Stern Show". He was seen on television in episodes of "Sesame Street", "Not Necessarily the News", "The Mike Douglas Show", "Make Me Laugh", "The Midnight Special", "The Alan Thicke Show", "Everything Goes", "The Tonight Show with Johnny Carson", "Friday Night", "Moonlighting", "Miami Vice", "D.C. Follies", "Tattinger's", "What a Dummy", "Comic Relief", "The Late Show", "Showtime at the Apollo", "Camp Midnight", "The Dick Cavett Show", "Monsters", "The Flash" as television reporter Joe

Kline from 1990 to 1991, "Good Sports", "Night After Night", "The A-List", "An Evening at the Improv", "Later with Bob Costas", "The Arsenio Hall Show", "Late Night with David Letterman", "Human Target", "Nurses", "Lois & Clark: The New Adventures of Superman" in the recurring role of Inspector Henderson in 1994, "The Larry Sanders Show", "Jerry Lewis MDA Labor Day Telethon", "Crook & Chase", "Politically Incorrect", "Mad About You", "Today", "The Rosie O'Donnell Show", "Howard Stern", "Hollywood Squares", "Late Night with Conan O'Brien", ""The Caroline Rhea Show", "The Tonight Show with Jay Leno", "Tough Crowd with Colin Quinn", "Celebrity Blackjack", "Celebrity Poker Showdown", the animated "South Park" as the voice of Loogie, "Minding the Store", "Late Show with David Letterman", "Last Comic Standing", "The Daily Show", The View", "The Real Housewives of New York City", "Tavis Smiley", "Jimmy Kimmel Live!", "Late Night with Jimmy Fallon", "Real Time with Bill Maher", "The Green Room with Paul Provenza", "Iron Chef America", "Piers Morgan Live", "Celebrity Wife Swap", "Tom Green Live", "PoliticKING with Larry King", and the animated "American Dad!". Belzer was best known for his role as Police Detective John Munch on the Baltimore-based police series "Homicide: Life on the Street" from 1993 to 1999 and the New York-based "Law & Order: Special Victims Unit" from 1999 to 2013. He also played the role of Munch in guest appearances on such series as "Law & Order", "The X-Files", "The Beat", "Law & Order: Trial by Jury", "Arrested Development", "The Wire", "30 Rock", "Jimmy Kimmel Live!", and "Unbreakable Kimmy Schmidt". He was a frequent participant in television broadcasts of Friars Club roasts on Comedy Central and was himself roasted in 2001. He hosted the short-lived series "The Richard Belzer Show" in 1984 and "Hot Properties" in 1985. He had wrestler Hulk Hogan on an episode of the latter series and badgered him into showing him a wrestling move. Hogan put him in a front face lock and the comedian passed out, hitting the back of his head when released. Belzer sued for $5 million but eventually settled from $400,000 in 1990. He also starred in the television specials "Belzer Behind Bars" (1983), "Richard Belzer in Concert" (1986), "Richard Belzer: Another Lone Nut" (1997), "Richard Belzer's Town Hall" (1997), and "The Belzer Connection" (2003). Belzer also appeared in the tele-films "Bandit: Bandit Bandit" (1994), "Hart to Hart: Crimes of the Hart" (1994), "Not of This Earth" (1995), "Prince for a Day" (1995), "The Invaders" (1995), and "Deadly Pursuits" (1996). He was featured in small and cameo roles in the films "Fame" (1980), "Author! Author!" (1982), "Night Shift" (1982), "Cafe Flesh" (1982), "Likely Stories, Vol. 3" (1983), "Flicks" (1983), "Scarface" (1983), "America" (1986), "The Wrong Guys" (1988), "Freeway" (1988), "The Big Picture" (1989), "Fletch Lives" (1989), "The Bonfire of the Vanities" (1990), "Off and Running" (1991), "Missing Pieces" (1991), "Mad Dog and Glory" (1993), "Dangerous Game" (1993), "North" (1994), "The Puppet Masters" (1994), "Girl 6" (1996), "A Very Brady Sequel" (1996), "Get on the Bus" (1996), "Species II" (1998) as the U.S. President, "Jump" (1999), "Man on the Moon" (1999), "Bitter Jester" (2003), "My Dog: An Unconditional Love Story"

(2009), "Polish Bar" (2010), "Santorini Blue" (2013), "Drunk Stoned Brilliant Dead" (2014), "Eccentric Eclectic" (2015), "King Kill 63" (2015), and "The Comedian" (2016). Belzer held controversial opinions about conspiracy series and was a frequent guest on Alex Jones' right-wing radio program. He was co-author of the books "UFOs, JFK, and Elvis: Conspiracies You Don't Have to Be Crazy to Believe" (1999), "Dead Wrong: Straight Facts on the Country's Most Controversial Cover-Ups" (2012), "Hit List: An In-Depth Investigation into the Mysterious Deaths of Witnesses to the JFK Assassination" (2013), "Someone Is Hiding Something: What Happened to Malaysia Airlines Flight 370?" (2015), and "Corporate Conspiracies: How Wall Street Took Over Washington" (2017). Belzer was married to Gail Susan Ross from 1966 until their divorce in 1972 and to Dalia Danoch from 1976 until their divorce in 1978. He married actress Harlee McBride in 1985 and she survives him.

Benedict, Nick

Actor Nick Benedict, who starred as Curtis Reed in the soap opera "Days of Our Lives" in the 1990s, died of complications from emergency spinal cord surgery in Arizona  on July 14, 2023. He was 77. He was born Nicholas Sciurba in Los Angeles, California, on July 14, 1946, the son of actor Richard Benedict. He appeared with his father as a child in the 1955 film "Wiretapper". He was also featured in the 1964 fantasy film "Mike and the Mermaid" which was written and directed by his father. Benedict served in the U.S. Navy before resuming his acting career on television with roles in episodes of "Iron Horse", "Mission: Impossible", "Hawaii Five-O", "Ironside", "The Bold Ones: The Lawyers", "Dan August", "Alias Smith and Jones", "Adam-12", "Medical Center", "Ozzie's Girls", "The Carol Burnett Show", "Dinah", "The Mike Douglas Show", "The Fall Guy", "The Dukes of Hazzard", "The Toni Tennille Show", "Tales from the Darkside", "Knots Landing", and "Tribes". He was best known for his work in soap operas. He starred as Philip Brent, a husband of Susan Lucci's Erica Kane, on "All My Children" from 1973 to 1978 and earned a Daytime Emmy Award nomination for the role in 1979. He was Michael Scott on "The Young and the Restless" from 1981 to 1982, Ron Washington on "Another Life" from 1982 to 1983, and Boots on "Santa Barbara" in 1990. Benedict starred as Curtis Reed on "Days of Our Lives" from 1993 to 2001. He also appeared in the tele-films "Frankie & Annette: The Second Time Around" (1978), "Memories of Murder" (1990), and "Devil's Food" (1996). Benedict appeared frequently in films throughout his career with roles in "Little Cigars" (1973), "Slaughter's Big Rip-Off" (1973), "Disconnected" (1984), "The Naked Cage" (1986), "Rachel River" (1987), "An American Summer" (1990), "The Pistol: The Birth of a Legend" (1991) as Pistol Pete's father Press Maravich, "East Meets West" (1995), "Beach House"

(1996), "Angela Mooney Dies Again" (1996), "Obsession" (1997), "Courting Courtney" (1997), "Get a Job" (1998), "Route 66" (1998), "Perfect Fit" (2000), "Mars and Beyond" (2000), "Entourage" (2000), and "Kept" (2001). Benedict was briefly married to Michelle Dow in 1976 until their marriage was annulled. He married Ginger Loli in 2001 and she survives him.

Benedictus, David

British author David Benedictus, who wrote the Winnie-the-Pooh novel "Return to the Hundred Acre Wood" in 1989, died in England on October 4, 2023. He was 85. Benedictus was born in London, England, on September 16,  1938. He attended Eton College, Balliol College, Oxford, and the University of Iowa. He became a trainee at the BBC in 1962 and worked in radio news. His first novel, "The Fourth of June", inspired by his days attending Eton, was published in 1962. It was adapted as a play for the London stage in 1964. His next novel, "You're a Big Boy Now", was published in 1963 and was adapted for film by director Francis Ford Coppola in 1966. He remained at the BBC, directing episodes of "Moonstrike" and "The Wednesday Play". He wrote the tele-play adaptation of "Gordon of Khartoum" for "BBC Play of the Month" in 1966. Benedictus directed for the stage later in the 1960s including a season with the Royal Shakespeare Company. He was writer-in-residence at the Sutton Library from 1976. He became commissioning editor for drama at Channel 4 in 1984, where he promoted the adaptation of Tom Sharpe's "Porterhouse Blue". He returned to BBC Radio as readings editor in 1989 and directed several radio plays. He also oversaw the "Book at Bedtime" series for BBC Radio 4 before leaving the company in 1995. He taught drama at Putney High School in the 1990s. His other books include "The Guru and the Golf Club" (1969), "The Rabbi's Wife" (1977), "Lloyd George: A Novel" (1981), the 1983 novelization of the film "Local Hero", "Floating Down to Camelot" (1985), "Little Sir Nicholas" (1990) with C.A. Jones, "Odyssey of a Scientist" (1991) with Hans Kalmus, and "The Stamp Collector" (1994). He was granted permission by the A.A. Milne estate to create the first new Winnie-the-Pooh volume in eighty years, "Return to the Hundred Acre Wood", in 2009. His autobiography, "Dropping Names", was published in 2005. Benedictus was married to actress Yvonne Antorbus from 1971 until their divorce in 2002 and is survived by their son and daughter. He is survived by another son and daughter from other relationships.

Bennett, Tony

Legendary singer Tony Bennett, who recorded the hit song "I Left My Heart in San Francisco", died from complications of Alzheimer's disease at his home in New York City on July 21, 2023. He was 96. He was born Anthony Benedetto in New York City on August 3, 1926. He began

singing in his youth and worked as a singing waiter at Italian restaurants in the Queens area in his early teens. He studied painting and music at New York's School of Industrial Art but  dropped out in the early 1940s to help support his family. He worked at various jobs while aspiring to be a singer and won amateur contests around New York. He was drafted into the U.S. Army in November of 1944 and saw active duty in France and Germany during World War II. He remained in Germany with the occupying forces after the war and entertained the troops with the Army Special Services Band under the name Joe Bari. He returned to the United States after the war in 1946 and studied at the American Theatre Wing. He got his break when he opened for Pearl Bailey in Greenwich Village in 1949. Bob Hope saw the show and took him on the road with him, changing his name to Tony Bennett. He was signed by Mitch Miller to a recording contract at Columbia Records in 1950 and had a hit with his rendition of "Because of You" the following year. He continued to be accompanied by Percy Faith's orchestra on subsequent hits including "Cold, Cold Heart", "Blue Velvet", "Rags to Riches", and "Stranger in Paradise". His first album, "Cloud 7", was released in 1955 with guitarist Chuck Wayne as his musical director. Ralph Sharon became Bennett's pianist and arranger in 1957 and his music featured more jazz elements. He recorded the 1957 album "The Beat of My Heart" and worked with the Count Basie Orchestra on "Basie Swings, Bennett Sings" (1958) and "In Person!" (1959). He became a popular nightclub performer and sang in concert in Carnegie Hall in June of 1962. He released his signature song, "I Left My Heart in San Francisco", in 1962, earning a Grammy Award for the song and his vocal performance. His 1963 album "I Wanna Be Around..." contained hits including the title song and "The Good Life". He recorded several albums of show tunes over the next few years. Bennett was active in the civil rights movement and participated in the Selma to Montgomery marches in 1965. His musical success waned as the Beatles and other rock groups took over the charts. He tried an album covering contemporary songs in 1970 with little success. He left Columbia and moved to the Verve label at MGM Records in 1972. He formed his own record label, Improv, soon after and recorded the albums "The Tony Bennett/Bill Evans Album" (1975) and "Together Again" (1976) with jazz pianist Bill Evans. His record label folded by 1977 and Bennett suffered a near-fatal cocaine overdose in 1979. His son, Danny, took over as his business manager and helped him battle his drug addiction and settle his outstanding debt with the Internal Revenue Service. He reunited with Ralph Sharon as pianist and music director and re-signed with Columbia Records to release the popular 1986 album "The Art of Excellence". Bennett maintained his singing style and choice of songs, frequently performing material from the Great American Songbook. He appeared on television shows and at concerts around the country. He released the 1990 album "Astoria: Portrait of the Artist" and earned Grammy Awards for the albums "Perfectly Frank" (1992) and "Steppin' Out" (1993). His music video of "Steppin' Out with My Baby" was featured on MTV and helped establish his popularity with a younger generation. He was featured on "MTV Unplugged" in 1994 and the subsequent album, "MTV Unplugged: Tony Bennett" earned him another Grammy Award and received the Grammy for Album of the Year. His popularity increased as he continued to record and perform and received another Grammy Award for his 2006 album "Duets: An American Classic". "Duets II" followed in 2011 and he sang with such artists as Willie Nelson, Aretha Franklin, Queen Latifah, Lady Gaga, Carrie Underwood, and Amy Winehouse. His "Viva Duets" album in 2012 included such Latin stars as Vicente Fernandez and Juan Luis Guerra. The 88-year-old Bennett received a Grammy Award for his collaborative album with Lady Gaga, "Cheek to Cheek" in 2014. They performed together in concert and released the concert special album "Tony Bennett and Lady Gaga: Cheek to Cheek Live". NBC televised a special concert, "Tony Bennett Celebrates 90: The Best Is Yet to Come", in 2016, and teamed with Diana Krall for the collaborative album "Love Is Here to Stay" in 2018. He reunited with Lady Gaga for his final album, "Love for Sale", in 2021. He made his final concerts in August of 2021 and failing health and a battle with Alzheimer's disease took its toll. A television special featuring excerpts from the concerts, "One Last Time: An Evening with Tony Bennett and Lady Gaga", aired later in the year. Bennett made his acting debut at Hymie Kelly in the 1966 film "The Oscar". He also appeared in episodes of "The Danny Thomas Show" and "77 Sunset Strip". He was seen in cameo roles in

the films "The Scout" (1994), "Analyze This" (1999), "Bruce Almighty" (2003), and "Muppets Most Wanted" (2014). He appeared as himself in the 1978 television mini-series "King" and had cameo roles in episodes of "The Doris Day Show", "Evening Shade", "Cybill", "Suddenly Susan", "Cosby", "Entourage", "Blue Bloods", and "30 Rock". He was a voice performer in episodes of "The Simpsons" and "Wallykazam!". Bennett performed on numerous variety and talk shows including "Star of the Family", "The Milton Berle Show", "Cavalcade of Stars", "Songs for Sale", "TV Teen Club", "The Dave Garroway Show", "The Name's the Same", "The Colgate Comedy Hour", "Max Liebman Spectaculars", "Stage Show", "The Julius LaRosa Show", "The Jackie Gleason Show", "The Nat King Cole Show", "Val Parnell's Sunday Night at the London Palladium", "The Patrice Munsel Show", "The Big Record", "The Ed Sullivan Show", "Make Me Laugh", "The Pat Boone-Chevy Showroom", "The Dick Clark Show", "The Steve Lawrence-Eydie Gorme Show", "The Garry Moore Show", "The Jimmie Rodgers Show", "Perry Presents", "The Arthur Murray Party", "The Steve Allen Plymouth Show", "Celebrity Talent Scout", "The Tennessee Ernie Ford Show", "The Tonight Show Starring Jack Paar", "The Dinah Shore Chevy Show", "The Adam Faith Show" 'Perry Como's Kraft Music Hall", "Play Your Hunch", "Jackie Gleason: American Scene Magazine", "American Bandstand", "The Judy Garland Show", "The Hollywood Palace", "The Red Skelton Hour", "What's My Line?", "The Danny Kaye Show", "Shindig!", "Juke Box Jury", "The Eamonn Andrews Show", "The Andy Williams Show", "The Bob Hope Show", "The Clay Cole Show", "The Jonathan Winters Show", "The Dick Cavett Show", "The London Palladium Show", "George Jessel's Here Come the Stars", "The Jackie Gleason Show", "The Barbara McNair Show", "The Tommy Leonetti Show", "This Is Tom Jones", "The Kraft Music Hall", "The Joey Bishop Show", "The Glen Campbell Goodtime Hour", "Della", "The Engelbert Humperdinck Show", "Playboy After Dark", "The Mike Walsh Show", "The Dean Martin Show", "The Pearl Bailey Show", "The David Frost Show", "The Lee Phillip Show", "Mister Rogers' Neighborhood", "Dinah!", "The Val Doonican Music Show", "The Mike Douglas Show", "The Merv Griffin Show", "Jerry Lewis MDA Labor Day Telethon", "Lou Rawls Parade of Stars", 'Night of 100 Stars", "SCTV Network", "Harty", "Lifestyles of the Rich and Famous", "Des O'Connor Tonight", "Doris Day's Best Friends", "Wogan", "The Howard Stern Show", "The Tonight Show Starring Johnny Carson", "The Whoopi Goldberg Show", "Late Night with David Letterman", "The Arsenio Hall Show", "The Danny Baker Show", "Muppets Tonight", "The Gaby Roslin Show", "Mundo VIP", "The Big Breakfast", "TFI Friday", "Space Ghost Coast to Coast", "Arena", "Intimate Portrait", "Sesame Street", "The Rosie O'Donnell Show", "The Lesley Garrett Show", "A Night at the Apollo", "V Graham Norton", "Good Morning Australia", "Live from Lincoln Center", "The Apprentice", "The Tony Danza Show", "Richard & Judy", "Canadian Idol", "The X Factor UK", "Saturday Night Live" as the musical guest in 2006, "Charlie Rose", "Later... With Jools Holland", "The Oprah Winfrey Show", "Late Night with Conan O'Brien", "The Tonight Show with Conan O'Brien", "American Idol", "The One Show", "America's Got Talent", "The Daily Show", "The Alan Titchmarsh Show", "The Tonight Show with Jay Leno", "Late Show with David Letterman", "Late Night with Jimmy Fallon", "Piers Morgan Live", "Katie", "Strictly Come Dancing", "American Masters", "The Colbert Report", "The View", "Today", "Tavis Smiley", "Jimmy Kimmel Live!", "Live with Kelly and Mark", "The Tonight Show with Jimmy Fallon", "Rachael Ray", "Great Performances", "The Late Show with Stephen Colbert", "Unplugged", and "60 Minutes". He was host of "The Tony Bennett Show" in 1956 and the mini-series "Tony Bennett at the Talk of the Town" in 1972. He appeared in numerous television specials including "Tony & Lena" (1973), "Sinatra and Friends" (1977), "Tony Bennett with Love: At the Sahara Lake Tahoe" (1985), "Mancini and Friends" (1987), "Irving Berlin's 100th Birthday Celebration" (1988), "Sinatra 75: The Best Is Yet to Come" (1990), "Sinatra Duets" (1994), "Tony Bennett: Here's to the Ladies, a Concert of Hope" (1995), "Tony Bennett Live by Request: A Valentine's Special" (1996), "Tony Bennett Live by Request: An All-Star

Tribute" (1998), "Garth Brooks & the Magic of Christmas" (1999), "Elizabeth Taylor: A Musical Celebration" (2000), "Christmas in Vienna" (2000), "Tony Bennett: An American Classic" (2006), "A Very Gaga Thanksgiving" (2011), "Tony Bennett: Duets II" (2012), "Merry Christmas with Our People... Tony Bennett and Friends" (2012), "Tony Bennett Celebrates 90: The Best Is Yet to Come" (2016), and "Tony Bennett & Diana Krall: Love Is Here to Stay" (2018). His autobiography, "The Good Life: The Autobiography of Tony Bennett", was published in 1998. He also wrote the books "Tony Bennett in the Studio: A Life of Art & Music" (2007), "Life Is a Gift: The Zen of Bennett" (2012), and "Just Getting Started" (2016). He was awarded the Grammy Lifetime Achievement Award in 2001 and was a Kennedy Center Honoree in 2005. Bennett married Patrica Beech in 1952 and they divorced in 1971 after being separated for several years. He is survived by their two sons, Danny and Dae. He was married to actress Sandra Grant from 1971 until their divorce in 1983 and is survived by their daughters, Joanna and Antonia. He became involved with Susan Crow in the late 1980s and they co-founded the charitable organization Exploring the Arts and the Frank Sinatra School of the Arts in Queens. He and Crow married in 2007 and she also survives him.

Berezin, Tanya

Actress Tanay Berezin died of lung cancer in San Francisco, California, on November 29, 2023. She was 82.

Berezin was born in Philadelphia, Pennsylvania, on March 25, 1941. She attended Boston University College of Fine Arts. She moved to New York City in the early 1960s where she began her career on stage. She performed in summer stock and at La MaMa Experimental Theatre Club. She appeared in productions of Lanford Wilson's "Rimers of Eldrige", "Spring Play", and Wilson's "The Sand Castle, or There Is a Tavern in the Town, or Harry Can Dance". She was a co-founder of the Circle Repertory Company with her husband, Rob Thirkield, Wilson, and Marshall Mason. Many of the Circle's productions ended up on Broadway and Berezin appeared in "Fifth of July" (1980) and "Angels Fall" (1983). She served as artistic director of the Circle Repertory Company from 1987 to 1994. He numerous off-Broadway performances include "Sympathetic Magic", "The Mound Builders" earning an Obie Awar in 1975, "Balm in Gilead", "Battle of Angels", "Serenading Louie", "Caligua", and "The Beaver Coat". She was seen in several films including "Girlfriends" (1978), "A Little Sex" (1982), "Compromising Positions" (1985), "Longtime Companion" (1989), "Awakenings" (1990), "He Said, She Said" (1991), and "Dead Funny" (1994). Berezin appeared in a 1976 television production of "The Mound Builders" and episodes of "NBC Special Treat", "Search for Tomorrow", "The Equalizer", "Spenser: For Hire", "St. Elsewhere", "Law & Order: Special Victims Unit", "Law &

Order: Criminal Intent", "Crossing Jordan", and "Law & Order" in the recurring roles of both Trial Judge Rosalyn Lenz and Trial Judge Janine Pate from 1991 through the early 2000s. She worked as an acting teacher and coach for over two decades. Berezin was married to producer Rob Thirkield from 1969 until their divorce in 1977. Thirkield died in 1986 and she is survived by their son and daughter.

Berger, Helmut

Austrian actor Helmut Berger, who starred in the 1970 film adaptation of "Dorian Gray", died in Salzburg, Austria, on May 18, 2023. He was 78. He was born Helmut Steinberger in Bad Ischi, Austria, on May 29, 1944. He worked with his

family in the hotel industry before leaving for London in his late teens. He began taking acting classic and moved to Italy to study language at the Universita der Stranieri di Perugia. He met director Luchino Visconti in 1964, who became his mentor and cast him in the 1967 anthology film "Le Streghe" (aka "The Witches"). He was also seen in the films "I Giovani Tigri" (1968), "Love Circle" (1969), and "Sai Cosa Faceva Stalin Alle Donne?" (1969). Berger starred as Martin Von Essenbeck in Visconti's 1969 production of "The Damned", giving a notable impersonation of Marlene Dietrich. He starred in the title role in the 1970 film adaptation of Oscar Wilde's "Dorian Gray" and starred in Vittorio De Sica's "The Garden of the Finzi-Continis" (1970). He continued to appear in such films as "Love Me Strangely" (1971), Duccio Tessari's giallo film "The Bloodstained Butterfly" (1971), "Les Voraces" (1973), Visconti's "Ludwig" (1973) earning a David di Donatello award for his role as King Ludwig II of Bavaria, "La Colonna Infame" (1973), "Merry-Go-Round" (1973), "Ash Wednesday" (1973) with Elizabeth Taylor and Henry Fonda, "Conversation Piece" (1974) with Burt Lancaster, "Order to Assassinate" (1975), "The Romantic Englishwoman" (1975) with Michael Caine and Glenda Jackson, Tinto Brass' controversial war drama "Madam Kitty" (1976) with Ingrid Thulin, "Beast with a Gun" (1977), "Paperback" (1977), "The Biggest Battle" (1978), "Das Funfte Gebot" (1978), "Eroina" (1980), "Mia Moglie e Una Strega" (1980), "Die Jager" (1982), "Femmes" (1983), "Veliki Transport" (1983), "Victoria! La Gran Aventura d'Un Poble" (1983) as Tinent Rodriguez Haro, "Victoria! 2: La Disbauxa del 17" (1983), "Victoria! 3: El Seny i la Rauxa" (1984), the World War II spy drama "Code Name: Emerald" (1984), Jess Franco's horror film "Faceless" (1988), "La Puritana" (1989), Francis Ford Coppola's "The Godfather Part III" (1990) as Frederick Keinszig, "Adelaide" (1992), "Ludwig 1881" (1993) reprising his role as King Ludwig II, "L'Ombre du Pharaon" (1996), "Ultimo Taglio" (1997), "Die 120 Tage von Bottrop" (1997), "Unter den Palmen" (1999), "Honey Baby" (2004), "Initiation" (2009), "Zapping-Alien@Mozart-Balls" (2009), "Beautiful Blue Eyes" (aka "Iron Cross") (2009), "Murder Sisters" (2011), "The Devil's

Violinist" (2013), "Saint Laurent" (2014) as Yves Saint Laurent", the science fiction film "Timeless" (2016), "Libere" (2019), and "Portae Infernales" (2019). Berger appeared on television in productions of "Victory at Entebbe" (1976), "La Rose di Danzica" (1979), "Fantomas" (1980) in the title role, "Fluchtige Bekanntschaften" (1982), "Skipper" (1987), "The Betrothed" (1989), "Boomtown" (1993), "L'Affaire Dreyfus" (1995), "Abgrunde" (1995), "Teo" (1997), and "Damals Warst Du Still" (2005). His other television credits include episodes of "Return of the Saint", "Dynasty" as Peter De Vilbis from 1983 to 1984, "Veliki Transport", "Helena", and "Van Loc: Un Grand Flic de Marseille". Berger suffered from depression following the death of Visconti in 1976 and tried to commit suicide exactly one year later. He survived the attempt but continued to suffer from drug and alcohol abuse. He was the subject of the 2008 television production of "Helmut Berger - A Life in Pictures". He was briefly a contestant on the reality series "Ich bin Ein Star - Holt Mich Hier Raus!", the German version of "I'm a Celebrity - Get Me Out of Here", in 2013 until a health issue forced him to withdraw. He was the subject of the documentary films "Helmut Berger, Actor" (2015) and "Helmut Berger, Meine Mutter und Ich" (2019). He made his theatrical debut in a production of the play "Liberte" in 2018. He retired from acting the following year. Berger was a bisexual who had long relationships with director Luchino Visconti and actress Marisa Berenson. His autobiography, "Ich. Die Autobiographie", was published in 1998 and recounted affairs with Ursula Andress, Rudolf Nureyev, Tab Hunter, Linda Blair, Anita Pallenberg, Jerry Hall, and Bianca and Mick Jagger. He was married to Italian writer and model Francesca Guidato from 1994 until their separation in 2020.

Bergjagen, Lasse

Swedish singer and songwriter Lars 'Lasse' Berghagen, who represented Sweden in the 1975 EuroVision Song Contest, died of complications from heart surgery in Stockholm, Sweden, on October 19, 2023. He was 78. Berghagen was born in Stockholm on May 13, 1945. He began performing at local venues in his teens and was signed by the Karusell record label in 1964. He released his first record the following year and scored hits with the 1969 songs "Teddbjornen Fredriksson" and "Gunga Gunga". His other songs include "En Enkel Sang Om Frihet", "Halligang i Skogen", and "Du Som Vandrar Genom Livet". Berghagen represented Sweden in the 1975 Eurovision Song Contest where he placed eighth with the song "Jennie, Jennie". He was host of the Sveriges Television variety shows "Strapetz" (1971), "Positiva Klubben" (1984), and "Tjocka Slakten" (1991). He hosted "Allsang pa Skansen" from 1994 to 2003. He appeared on stage in various musical revues and was seen in the films "Company Party" (1972), "Dante - Akta're for Hajen!" (1978), "Spanska Flugan" (1983), "Bert: The Last Virgin" (1995), and "O Som i

Markoolio" (1999). He was married to singer Barbro Svensson, who performed under the name Lill-Babs, from 1965 until their divorce in 1968 and is survived by their daughter, actress Malin Berghagen-Nilsson. He married Eva Strand in 1976 and is also survived by her and their daughter, Maria Berghagen Enander.

Berglas, David

German-British magician and mentalist David Berglas died in London, England, on November 3, 2023. He was 97. Berglas was born in Berlin, Germany, on July 30, 1926. He was Jewish and escaped from Nazi Germany to England in 1937.

He joined the U.S. Army Intelligence Service at the end of World War II and spent 18 months working with them in the denazification of Germany. He studied textiles at Bradford Technical College after returning to England. He became interested in magic in the late 1940s. He trained as a psychotherapist at Tavistock Clinic, London, and gave demonstrations in clinical hypnosis. He became a professional magician in 1952, performing at the Windmill Theatre in London. He was noted for creating the card magic trick of allowing someone to name a playing card and a position in the deck and the magician finds the specified card in the specified position. The magic trick was later named the Berglas Effect in his honor. He became one of the first magicians to appear on British television and starred in the series "Meet David Berglas" in 1954. He was also seen in such series as "Men of Mystery", "Garrison Theatre", "The Centre Show', "Variety Parade", "Call Boy", "Crackerjack!", "Sandler and Young's Kraft Music Hall", "The David Nixon Show", "Starburst", "Look Who's Talking", "After Dark", "The Best of Magic", "The Secret Cabaret", "This Is Your Life", "Magic", and "Brain Hacker". Berglas was a technical adviser and magic consultant for the 1964 television production of "The Rise and Fall of Nellie Brown" for "ITV Play of the Week" and for the films "Casino Royale" (1967), "Barry Lyndon" (1975), "Octopussy" (1981), "Willow" (1988), and Tim Burton's "Batman" (1989). He hosted the series "The Mind of David Berglas" in 1986 and appeared in the television specials "50 Greatest Magic Tricks" (2002), "The Magic Show Story" (2015), and "How Magic Changed TV" (2017). He was the subject of Martin T. Hart's documentary videos "The David Berglas Scrapbooks" from 2018. Berglas was president of the Magic Circle from 1989 to 1998. He married actress Ruth Shiell in 1956, and she survives him. He is also survived by their son, magician Marvin Berglas, who is current president of the Magic Circle, and daughter, Irena. His son, Peter, predeceased him in 2013.

Bergstrom, Sheldon

Canadian actor Sheldon Bergstrom died in Canada on June 18, 2023. He was 51. Bergstrom was born in Prince Albert, Saskatchewan, Canada, in 1971. He performed frequently on stage and was a member of the Souris Valley Theatre in Saskatchewan. He appeared in productions of "Rob Ford: The Musical", "Hairspray",

"The Producers", and "Seussical". Bergstrom was also a frequent host of the Telemiracle telethons in Saskatchewan. He was featured in such films as "Held Up" (1999), "The Impossible Elephant" (2001), "Shot in the Face" (2001), "A.R.C.H.I.E." (2016), "The Humanity Bureau" (2017), "Welcome to Nowhere" (2018), "A.R.C.H.I.E. 2" (2018), and "SueprGrid" (2018). Bergstrom appeared on television in episodes of "Body & Soul", "Corner Gas", and "InSecurity", and the tele-films "I Downloaded a Ghost" (2002), "Without Malice" (2003), and "Touch the Top of the World" (2006).

Berlusconi, Silvio

Italian media mogul Silvio Berlusconi, who was three-time Prime Minister of Italy, died of complications from leukemia in Milan, Italy, on June 12, 2023. He was 86.

Berlusconi was born in Milan on September 29, 1939. He studied law at the University of Milan and graduated in 1961. He became wealthy in the 1960s in real estate and construction and built a huge residential apartment complex near Milan in the 1970s. He also began a small cable television company in the 1970s which evolved into the first private Italian system Canale 5. He formed the media group Finnivest and continued to expand his media empire. He entered politics in the early 1990s and formed a conservative new party, Forza Italia. He was elected to the Chamber of Deputies in 1994 and soon became Italy's prime minister. His government collapsed the following year, and he left office in January of 2005. He returned as prime minister in 2001, serving until 2006. Berlusconi again became prime minister in May of 2008, and remained head of the government until November of 2011. He was a controversial figure in Italy and his governments were often turbulent. He was involved in various sex scandals including a criminal charge for involvement with a teenage prostitute. He was charged with various other crimes including tax evasion, bribery, corruption, and abuse of office during his political career. Berlusconi was elected to the European Parliament in 2019, serving until 2022. He was producer of several films including "Preferisco Vivere" (1989), "Mediterraneo" (1991), "Folks!" (1992), and "Man Trouble" (1992). He also produced the 1992 television series "Micaela". The controversial media tycoon and politician was played by Elio De Capitani in the 2006 comedy film "The Caiman" and was portrayed by Toni Servillo in the 2018 film "Loro". Berlusconi was married to Carla Elvira Lucia Dall'Oglio from 1965 until their divorce in 1985 and is survived by their two children. Marina and Pier Silvio. He was married to actress Veronica Larrio from 1990 until their divorce in 2014 and is also survived by their three children, Barbara, Eleonora, and Luigi.

Berlyn, Michael

Video game designer Michael Berlyn, who was noted for designing the "Bubsy the Bobcat" video games, died of cancer died on March 30, 2023. He was 73. Berlyn was born

in Brookline, Massachusetts, on October 21, 1949. He was author of the science fiction novels "The Integrated Man" (1980), "Crystal Phoenix" (1980), "Blight" (1981) under the name Mark Sonders, and "The Eternal Enemy" (1990). He began working in the game industry with "Oo-Topos" for Sentient Software in 1981. Berlyn was co-founder of Brainwave Creations studios in the mid-1980s and created "Tass Times in Tone Town" with Interplay's Rebecca Heineman and his wife, Muffy McClung. He teamed with Marc Blank to form Blank, Berlyn & Co. in 1992, which later became known as Eidetic and Bend Studio. They developed Playstation's "Syphon Filter" series". He created the "Bubsy" platformer series and was designer of the games "Bubsy in Claws Encounters of the Furred Kind" in 1993 and "Bubsy 3D" in 1996. He also worked on such games as "Zork" and "Altered Destiny". He headed Cascade Mountain Publishing from 1998 to 2000, publishing e-books and interactive fiction. He later returned to game developing, concentrating on interactive games for Windows and mobile devices. He is survived by his wife, fellow game designer Muffy McClung.

Bertel, Dick

Radio and television personality Dick Bertel died at a hospital in Rockville, Maryland, on September 11, 2023. He was 92. He was born Richard Bertelmann in the Bronx, New

York, on January 6, 1931. He moved with his family to Darien, Connecticut, in the early 1940s. He graduated from high school in 1948 and was soon working at the new Norwalk, Connecticut, radio station, WNLK. He was host of the Saturday morning program "The Hi Teen Show". He worked with the Community Radio Workshop to produce the series "The Mystery Theater of the Air" on WNLK and wrote their 1950 series "The House of Retribution". Bertel left for WNAB in Bridgeport in 1951 and graduated from New York University with a degree in broadcasting in 1952. He continued to work at WNAB as an announcer and continuity director until joining WSTC in Stamford in 1954. He began using the name Dick Richards at WSTC, where he hosted his own show. He moved to Hartford in 1955 where he joined WGTH. He became a senior announcer and was host of the programs "The Uprising" and "Luncheon with Dottie and Dick". He began working at WTIC in 1956 where he became known on air as Dick Bertel. He hosted the station's program "Conversation Piece" from 1956 to 1969. He was host of the "Americana" interview program in 1962 and was host of the annual Christmas Eve Shows from 1962 to 1976. Bertel was also host of the series "Saturday Showcase", "'TIC Afternoon Edition", and "The Golden Age of Radio". He served as news anchor and public affairs host at WTIC-TV from 1957 until 1974. He served as manager of the WKKS Radio station and hosted "Good Morning, New England," from 1978 to 1984. Bertel moved to Washington, D.C., in 1984 where he served as executive producer for the Voice of America (VOA). He continued to work with VOA in Munich, Germany, from 1991 to 1993 and created the international call-in show, "Talk to America", after his return to Washington. He retired from VOA in 2006. He is survived by his wife of 67 years, Jean Bertelmann, two sons, and two daughters.

Bertho, Jean

French actor and director Jean Bertho died in France on January 4, 2023. He was 94. Bertho was born in Pont-a-Mousson, France, on January 23, 1928. He trained at the

Conservatoire d'Art Dramatique in Nancy and began his acting career on stage in screen in the late 1940s. He appeared in the 1950 film "La Marie du Port" and the 1959 horror production "The Doctor's Horrible Experiment" (aka "The Testament of Dr. Cordelier"). Bertho was also seen in television episodes of "La Camera Explore le Temps", "Si c'Etait Vous?", "Meurtre au Ralenti", and "L'Inspecteur Leclerc Enquete". He served as assistant director for the television series "Airs de France" in 1959 and for the 1962 film "Nous Irons a Deauville". He began producing reports for the television news program "Cinq Colonnes a la Une" in 1961 and was soon hosting such shows as "Lectures Pour Tous" and "En Votre Ame et Conscience". He was host of "C'est pas Serieux" from 1974 to 1982 and produced and hosted "Tele a la Une" and "Des Choses du Lundi" from 1984 to 1985. Bertho also directed episodes of "Pour le Plaisir", "Dim Dam Dom", "En Direct de,,,", "La Nuit Ecoute", and "Serleux s'Abstenir". He helmed the tele-films "Le Miroir a Trois Faces: Louise" (1967), "Les Balances" (1974), "Le Commissaire est Bon Enfant" (1974), "Le Droit Aux Etrennes" (1974), and "Monsieur Badin" (1974). He became more involved with writing in the early 1990s and penned a biography of the poet Yvan Goll.

Big Pokey

Rapper Milton Powell, who performed under the name Big Pokey, collapsed and died on June 18, 2023, while

performing at a bar in Beaumont, Texas. He was 48. Powell was born in Houston, Texas, on November 29, 1974. He became involved with rap in the early 1990s as part of DJ Screw's rap collective Screwed Up Click. He was featured on DJ Screw's mixtape "June 27th Freestyle". Pokey make his solo debut with the 1999 album "Hardest Pit in the Litter". He recorded the album "D-Game 2000" in 2000 and collaborated with the Wreckshop Wolfpack for "The Collabo" in 2002. He recorded the solo album "Da Sky's Da Limit" in 2002. His later albums include "Evacuation Notice" (2008) and "Sensei" (2021). He collaborated with Megan Thee Stallion on the 2022 song "Southside Royalty Freestyle". Pokey is survived by his wife and three children.

Biondi, Dick

Radio disc jockey Dick Biondi died in Chicago, Illinois, on June 26, 2023. He was 90. Biondi was born in Endicott, New York, on September 13, 1932. He aspired to be a sportscaster from an early age and began working behind the

scenes at Binghampton, New York, station WINR in his youth. He began his on-air career at WCBA in Corning, New York. He spent the next several years working at stations in Alexandria, Louisiana; York, Pennsylvania; Youngstown, Ohio; and Buffalo, New York. He joined WLS in Chicago in 1960 as a disc jockey as they changed their format to rock 'n' roll. He soon became a popular personality in the Chicago area where he was noted for his screaming delivery and wild antics. He called himself the Wild-Itralian, and hosted area dances and charity events. He recorded the 1961 novelty song "On Top of a Pizza". His penchant for argument led to his firing, despite his popularity, in 1963. He subsequently moved to Los Angeles where he had two stints at KRLA. He returned to Chicago to work at WCFL in 1967. He moved to Cincinnati in 1972 and spent time at stations in Boston and North Myrtle Beach, South Carolina, before returning to Chicago. He hosted a show on WJMK-FM, a new oldies station, from 1983 until 2004. He returned to WLS, where he broadcast until 2018. Biondi was inducted into the Chicago Radio Hall of Fame in 1998. He was the subject of a forthcoming documentary film, "The Voice That Rocked America: The Dick Biondi Story". He is survived by his wife, Maribeth Biondi.

Birkin, Jane

British-French actress and singer Jane Birkin was found dead at her home in Paris, France, on July 16, 2023. She was 76. Birkin was born in Marylebone, London, England, on

December 14, 1946. She was the daughter of Royal Navy officer David Birkin and actress Judy Campbell. Her older brother, Andrew Birkin, became a screenwriter and director.

She attended boarding school on the Isle of Wight. She met composer John Barry in her late teens, and they married in 1965. They had a daughter in 1967 and divorced the following year. Birkin pursued an acting career and appeared in small roles in the films "The Knack... and How to Get It" (1965), "The Idol" (1966), "Kaleidoscope" (1966), and Michelangelo Antonioni's "Blow-Up" (1966) as a blonde model. She was seen on television in episodes of "Armchair Mystery Theatre" and "Armchair Theatre". She starred as Penny Lane in the 1968 psychedelic film "Wonderwall". Birkin starred with Serge Gainsbourg in the 1969 French film "Slogan" and they performed the film's theme song, "La Chanson de Slogan". She moved to France permanently and began a personal and professional partnership with Gainsbourg. The couple had a major hit with their duet "Je t'Aime... Moi Non Plus" in 1969. She was featured on Gainsbourg's 1971 album "Histoire de Melody Nelson". Birkin released three solo albums, "Di Doo Dah" (1973), "Lolita Go Home" (1975), and "Ex Fan des Sixties" (1978), all of which were written by Gainsbourg. She became a popular actress in French films with roles in Jacques Deray's "La Piscine" (1969) opposite Alain Delon, "The Pleasure Pit" (aka "Les Chemins de Katmandou") (1969), "Sex-Power" (1970), "May Morning" (1970), the crime film "French Intrigue" (aka "Cannabis") (1970), "Trop Petit Mon Ami" (1970), "Devetnaest Djevojaka i Jedan Mornar" (1971), "Romance of a Horserthief" (1971), "Trop Jolies Pour Etre Honnets" (1972), Roger Vadim's "Don Juan, or If Don Juan Were a Woman" (1973) as Brigitte Bardot's lover, Antonio Margheriti's horror film "Seven Deaths in the Cat's Eyes" (1973), "Private Screening" (1973), "Love at the Top" (1974), the psychological horror film "Dark Places" (1974) with Christopher Lee and Joan Collins, "Comment Reussir... Quand on Est Con et Pleurnichard" (aka "How to Do Well When You Are a Jerk and a Crybaby") (1974), "I'm Losing My Temper" (aka "Lucky Pierre") (1974), "Serieux Comme le Plaisir" (1975), "La Course a l'Echalote" (1975), the sex comedy "Catherine & Co." (1975), "7 Morts Sur Ordonnance" (1975), "Je t'Aime Moi Non Plus" (1976) directed by Gainsbourg, "The Devil in the Heart" (1976), "Burnt by a Scalding Passion" (1976), "Animal" (1977), the Agatha Christie adaptation as "Death on the Nile" (1978) starring Peter Ustinov as detective Hercule Poirot, "Au Bout du Bout di Banc" (1979), "Melancoly Baby" (1979), "La Miel" (1979), "Egon Schiele: Excess and Punishment" (1980), Jacques Doillon's "The Prodigal Daughter" (1981), "Rends-Moi la Cle!" (1981), the Christie adaptation "Evil Under the Sun" (1982) again with Ustinov as Poirot, "Nestor Burma, Detective de Choc" (1982), "Move Along, There Is Nothing to See" (1983), "A Friend of Vincent" (1983), "The Bodyguard" (1984), Doillon's "The

Pirate" (1984), "Love on the Ground" (1984), "Dust" (1985), "Beethoven's Nephew" (1985), "Leave All Fair" (1985), "La Femme de Ma Vie" (1986), "Soigne ta Droite" (1987), "Comedie!" (1987), "Kung-Fu Master!" (1988), Agnes Varda's docudrama "Jane B. for Agnes V." (1988), "Daddy Nostalgia" (1990), "The Beautiful Troublemaker" (1991), "Divertimento" (1992), Varda's comedy "One Hundred and One Nights" (1995), "Between the Devil and the Deep Blue Sea" (1995), "Noir Comme le Souvenir" (1995), "Same Old Song" (1997), "A Soldier's Daughter Never Cries" (1998), "The Last September" (1999), "This Is My Body" (2001), "A Hell of a Day" (2001), "Merci Docteur Rey" (2002), "Marlees Mais pas Trop" (aka "The Very Merry Widows") (2003), "La Tete de Maman" (2007), "Boxes" (2007) which she also directed and wrote, "Around a Small Mountain" (2009), "Thelma, Louise et Chantal" (2010), "Si tu Meurs, Je Te Tue" (2011), "Twice Born" (2012), "The French Minister" (2013), and the Oscar-nominated short film "La Femme et le TGV". Birkin was seen on television in productions of "Melody" (1971), "Les Maudits Rois Faineants" (1973), "Bons Baisers de Tarzan" (1974), "Scarface" (1982), "Dorothee - Le Show" (1983), "La Fausse Suivante" (1985), "L'ex-Femme de Ma Vie" (1990), "Red Fox" (1991), "Quand le Chat Sourit" (1997), "Cinderella" (2000), "The Stevensons" (2006), and "Les Saisons Meurtrieres" (2011). She was a frequent guest on European variety and talk shows. Birkin separated from Gainsbourg after a dozen years in 1980. He continued writing music for her including the albums "Baby Alone in Babylone" (1983) and "Amours des Feintes" (1990) until his death in 1991. She later released the 2006 album "Fictions" and recorded "Birkin/Gainsbourg: Le Symphonique" in 2017. She was the star of the 2021 docudrama "Jane by Charlotte" directed by her daughter, Charlotte Gainsbourg. She had suffered from health issues in recent years, having been diagnosed with leukemia in 2002 and suffering a stroke in 2021. Birkin was married to composer John Barry from 1965 until their divorce in 1968. Their daughter, photographer Kate Barry, died from a fall from her fourth floor Paris apartment in 2013. Her relationship with Serge Gainsbourg lasted from 1968 until 1980 and she is survived by their daughter, actress and singer Charlotte Gainsbourg. She was subsequently involved with director Jacques Doillon until separating in 1993, and is survived by their daughter, actress and singer Lou Doillon.

Birman, Len

Canadian actor Len Birman died at a hospital in Los Angeles, California, on February 10, 2023. He was 90. Birman was born in Montreal, Quebec, Canada, on September 28, 1932. He graduated from high school in 1949 and decided on a career as an actor. He performed on the local stage from the early 1950s and was soon appearing on television for the Canadian Broadcasting Corporation. Birman was seen in episodes of "Encounter", "On Camera", "Tomahawk", "A Midsummer Theatre", "Folio", "R.C.M.P.", "Naked City", "Shoestring Theatre", "Playdate", "Quest", "Seaway", "The Forest Rangers", "Festival", "Judd for the Defense", "It Takes a Thief", "Cowboy in Africa", "Adventures in Rainbow County",

"Festival of Family Classics", "Police Surgeon" as Lt. Dan Palmer from 1971 to 1973, "Mannix", "The Collaborators", "Most Wanted", "Serpico", "The Streets of San Francisco",  "Young Dan'l Boone", "Logan's Run", "The Six Million Dollar Man", "The Paper Chase", "Sword of Justice", "A Man Called Sloane", "Buck Rogers in the 25th Century", "B.J. and the Bear", "Knots Landing", "Nero Wolfe", "Dallas", "Titans", "Airwolf", "Generations" as Eddie in 1990, "Tropical Heat", "Days of Our Lives" as Judge Milton Bartlett in 1992, and "E.N.G.". His other television credits include productions of "Twelfth Night" (1964), "Julius Caesar" (1966), "She Cried Murder" (1973), "The Rhinemann Exchange" (1977), "The Man Inside" (1977), "Killer on Board" (1977), "Escapade" (1978), "Evening in Byzantium" (1978), "Captain America" (1979) and "Captain American II: Death Too Soon" (1979) as Dr. Simon Mills, "Draw!" (1984), "Passions" (1984), "The Undergrads" (1985), "Picking Up the Pieces" (1985), "Assassin" (1986), "Without Her Consent" (1990), and "Web of Deceit" (1990). He was a voice performer for the animated series "The Marvel Super Heroes", "Mighty Thor", and "Rocket Robin Hood". He starred in numerous radio dramas on Mutual Radio Theatre and Sears Radio Theatre. Birman appeared in several films during his career including "Lies My Father Told Me" (1975), "Silver Streak" (1976) and "The Great Brain" (1978). He was married to Harriet Jane Takefman from 1956 until their divorce in 1963 and is survived by their son, actor Matt Birman. He was married to actress Ruby Renaut from 1977 until her death in 2020.

Bishop, Michael

Science fiction writer Michael Bishop died of cancer in LaGrange, Georgia, on November 13, 2023. He was 78.  Bishop was born in Lincoln, Nebraska, on November 12, 1945, where his father was stationed with the Army Air Corps. He spent his childhood in bases around the world. Bishop graduated from the University of Georgia in 1967 and earned a master's degree the following year. He taught English at a the United States Air Force Academy Preparatory School in Colorado Springs, Colorado from 1968 to 1972. He then joined the faculty at the University of Georgia at Athens until becoming a full-time writer in 1974. He began writing short stories in the late 1960s and his first published story, "Pinon Fall", was published in "Galaxy Science Fiction" magazine in 1970. His first novel, "A Funeral for the Eyes of Fire", was published in 1975, and revised as "Eyes of Fire" in 1980. He received a Nebula Award for his 1981 novelette in 1981. His other novels include "And Strange at Ecbatan the Trees" (1976), "Under Heaven's Bridge" (1981), "No Enemy But Time" (1982) earning a Nebula Award for best novel, "Who Make Stevie Crye" (1984), "Ancient of Days" (1985), "Philip K. Dick Is Dead, Alas" (1987), "Unicorn Mountain" (1988), "Count Geiger's Blues" (1992), "Brittle Innings" (1994), and "Joel-Brock the Brave and the Valorous Smalls" (2016). Some of his short fiction appeared in the collections "Windows & Mirrors" (1977), "Blooded on Arachne" (1982), "One Winter in Eden" (1984), "Close Encounters with the Deity" (1986), "Emphatically Not SF. Almost" (1990), "At the City Limits of Fate" (1996), "Time Pieces" (1998), "Blue Kansas Spy" (2000), "Brighten to Incandescence: 17 Stories" (2003), "The Door Gunner and Other Perilous Flights of Fancy: A Michael Bishop Retrospective" (2012), "The Sacerdotal Owl and Three Other Long Tales of Calamity, Pilgrimage, and Atonement" (2018), and "A Few Last Words for the Late Immortals: 50 Short Stories & Poems" (2021). His short story, "Seasons of Belief", was adapted for a 1986 episode of the television anthology series "Tales from the Darkside", and he wrote the "Their Divided Self" episode of "Monsters" in 1989. Bishop and Paul Di Filippo wrote a pair of noir mystery novels under the pseudonym Philip Lawson, "Would It Kill You to Smile?" (1998) and "Muskrat Courage" (2000). He published a collection of stories, "Other Arms Reach Out to Me: Georgia Stories", in 2019. He also edited seven anthologies and two volumes of poetry. His collection of nonfiction, "A Reverie for Mister Ray", was published in 2005. Bishop married Jeri Ellis Whitaker in 1969 and is survived by her and daughter Stephanie. Their son, Jamie Bishop, was a graphic artist who illustrated the cover of several of his books. He was a teacher at Virginia Tech when he was killed by a gunman on campus during a spree shooting in April of 2007.

Black Warrior

Mexican professional wrestler Jesus Toral Lopez, who competed under the name Black Warrior, died in Mexico on January 10, 2023. He was 54. Lopez was born in Torreon,  Mexico, on January 7, 1969. He began his wrestling career in 1984 as the masked wrestler Destroyer. He worked for Empresa Mexicana de la Lucha Libre (EMLL) under a mask as Camorra from 1985 to 1988 and became La Mascara when he joined the Universal Wrestling Association (UWA). He returned to EMLL, now known as Consejo Mundial de Lucha Libre (CMLL), in 1991 where he used the name Bronce (Bronze). He teamed with wrestlers Oro and Plata as the trio "Los Metalicos". They captured in Trios Championship in early 1992 and held the belts for nearly a year. He joined Antonio Pena's new promotion Asistencia Asesoria y Administracion (AAA) later in the year where had a variety of aliases including Super Star, Dragon de Oro, Bali, and Vegas. He returned to

CMLL in 1995 as the Black Panther, and teamed with his uncle, who was known as the Blue Panther. He again changed his alias to the Black Warrior the following year and competed as a villain. He captured the NWA World Light Heavyweight Championship from El Dandy later in the year. He lost the title to Shocker in May of 1997 but regained the belt in March of 1998. He teamed with Blue Panther and Wagner, Jr. to capture the CMLL World Trios Championship in December of 1998. They were known collectively as Ola Laguenero and held the trios title for over three years. Black Warrior lost the light heavyweight title to Tarzan Boy in March of 2000. He became a fan favorite soon after and was ejected for Ola Laguenero. Warrior teamed with Mr. Niebla and Atlantis to capture the trios belt from his old team in June of 2002. They lost the belts in March of 2003, but Warrior joined with El Canek and Rayo de Jalisco, Jr. to regain the belts in July of 2004. His new team lost the titles the following November. He soon began teaming with Mistico until a feud developed between the two. He captured the NWA World Middleweight Championship from Mistico in May of 2006 but lost a mask versus mask match with him the following September. Mistico recaptured the title in April of 2007. He teamed with Bucanero to lose a hair hatch against Shocker and Lizmark Jr. later in the year. Black Warrior joined with Sangre Azteca and Dragon Rojo Jr. to form the trio Poder Mexica. They won the Mexican National Trios Championship in February. He teamed with Naito and Yujiro of No Limit in July of 2009 but became feuding with them a few months later. He had his hair shaved in October of 2009 after losing a hair match with Yujiro. He again held the trios title from June to October of 2012 while teaming with Mr. Aguila and Volador Jr. as Los Depredadores del Aire. He returned to AAA in February of 2014 and joined Lucha Libre Elite in November of 2015. He continued to make occasional ring appearances in his later years. Black Warrior was married to the daughter of wrestler Mano Negra. Their son, Ramces de Jesus Toral, wrestled as Warrior Jr. until his death in 2022.

Blackman, Lonie

Actress Lonie Blackman died in Concord, California, on November 5, 2023. She was 91. Blackman was born in San

Francisco, California, on February 25, 1932. She trained to be an actor at the Pasadena Playhouse and appeared frequently on the local stage. She was seen in episode of numerous television series including "Science Fiction Theatre", "Highway Patrol", "The Adventures of Ozzie and Harriet", "Sugarfoot", "Lawman", "Tales of Wells Fargo", "The Man from Blackhawk", "Hennesey", "Bat Masterson", "Johnny Midnight", "Miami Undercover" in the recurring role of Dusty in 1961, "Ripcord", "Dr. Kildare", and "Perry Mason". Blackman was featured in the 1961 film "The Sergeant Was a Lady". She largely retired from the screen in the early 1960s. She and her

husband, E. Douglas Ward, wrote the 2007 science fiction novel "Lightspeed: The Quest". Blackman was married to H. William Hunt from 1953 until their divorce in 1958 and to Robert Lee Johnston from 1959 until their divorce in 1976. She was married to Edward Douglas Ward from 1979 until his death in 2015.

Blair, Pamela

Actress Pamela Blair, who starred as Val in the original Broadway musical "A Chorus Line", died of complications from colon surgery in Phoenix, Arizona, on July

23, 2023. She was 73. Blair was born in Bennington, Vermont, on December 5, 1949. She moved to New York City in the mid-1960s to attend the National Academy of Ballet. She made her Broadway debut as a dancer in Michael Bennett's musical "Promises, Promises" in 1968. She continued to appear in Broadway productions of "Wild and Wonderful" (1971), "Sugar" (1972), "Seesaw" (1973), and "Of Mice and Men" (1974) as Curly's Wife. She starred as Valerie Clark in Bennett's hit musical "A Chorus Line" in 1974, in a role that was partially based on her own life. Blair also appeared in "The Best Little Whorehouse in Texas" (1978) as Amber, "King of Hearts" (1978), "The Nerd" (1987), and "A Few Good Men" (1989). Blair was seen in the films "Annie" (1982) as Annette, "Me and Veronica" (1992), Woody Allen's "Mighty Aphrodite" (1995), "Before and After" (1996), the animated "Beavis and Butt-Head Do America" (1996) in a voice role, "Angelo" (1999), "21 Grams" (2003), "42nd Street The Musical" (2019), and "Tomorrow Morning" (2022). She was seen in several television soap operas including "Ryan's Hope" as Elizabeth Shrank Ryan in 1980, "Loving" as Rita Mae Bristow from 1983 to 1985, "All My Children" earning a Daytime Emmy Award nomination for her role as Maida Andrews in 1987, and "Another World" as Bonnie Broderick in 1994. She also appeared in the tele-films "Svengali" (1983), "The Last Dance" (2000), and "Maneater" (2002), and episodes of "Family Feud", "The Days and Nights of Molly Dodd", "The Cosby Show", "Law & Order", "The Cosby Mysteries", and "Sabrina the Teenage Witch". She continued to perform on stage in musicals in regional theaters. Blair married Alfred Anthony Feola in 1977 and they later divorced. She was married to actor Don Scardino from 1984 until their divorce in 1991.

Blake, Robert

Actor Robert Blake, who began his career as a child actor in the "Our Gang" comedy shorts and starred as police detective Tony Baretta in the television series "Baretta" in the 1970s, and saw his career overshadowed when he was tried and acquitted of the murder of his wife in 2001, died of heart disease in Los Angeles, California, on March 9, 2023. He was 89. He was born Michael Gubitosi in Nutley, New Jersey, on

September 18, 1933. He claimed to have been abused by his parents as a child. He and his older brother and sister danced for money in parks while their father played guitar as a young child. The family moved to Hollywood in 1938 and he began his acting career at the age of five in the 1939 film "Bridal Suite". He was billed as Mickey Gubitosi when he began  appearing in Hal Roach's "Our Gang" (aka "The Little Rascals") comedy shorts. He played Mickey in "Joy Scouts" (1939), "Auto Antics" (1939), "Captain Spanky's Show Boat" (1939), "Dad for a Day" (1939), "Time Out for Lessons" (1939), "Alfalfa's Double" (1940) "The Big Premiere" (1940), "All About Hash" (1940), "The New Pupil" (1940), "Bubbling Troubles" (1940), "Good Bad Boys" (1940), "Waldo's Last Stand" (1940), "Goin' Fishin'" (1940), "Baby Blues" (1941), "Ye Olde Minstrels" (1941), "1-2-3-Go!" (1941), "Robot Wrecks" (1941), "Helping Hands" (1941), "Come Back, Miss Phipps" (1941), "Wedding Worries" (1941), "Melodies Old and New" (1942), "Going to Press" (1942), "Don't Lie" (1942), "Surprised Parties" (1942), "Doin' Their Bit" (1942), "Rover's Big Chance" (1942), "Mighty Lak a Goat" (1942), "Unexpected Riches" (1942), "Benjamin Franklin, Jr." (1943), "Family Troubles" (1943), "Calling All Kids" (1943), "Farm Hands" (1943), "Election Daze" (1943), "Little Miss Pinkerton" (1943), "Three Smart Guys" (1943), "Radio Bugs" (1944), "Tale of a Dog" (1944), and "Dancing Romeo" (1944). He was also a child actor in the films and shorts "Spots Before Your Eyes" (1940), "I Love You Again" (1940), "Main Street on the March!" (1941), "Kid Glove Killer" (1942), "Mokey" (1942) in the title role, "China Girl" (1942), "Andy Hardy's Double Life" (1942) as Tooky Stedman, "Slightly Dangerous" (1943), "Salute to the Marines" (1943), "Lost Angel" (1943), "Meet the People" (1944), "The Seventh Cross" (1944), "The Big Noise" (1944) with Laurel and Hardy, and "The Woman in the Window" (1944). He took the stage name Bobby Blake in 1942 and starred as Little Beaver, the Native American boy sidekick to western comic strip hero Red Ryder, played by Wild Bill Elliott and Allan 'Rocky' Lane during the course of the film series. Blake was featured as Little Beaver in "Tucson Raiders" (1944), "Marshal of Reno" (1944), "The San Antonio Kid" (1944), "Cheyenne Wildcat" (1944), "Vigilantes of Dodge City" (1944), "Sheriff of Las Vegas" (1944), "Great Stagecoach Robbery" (1945), "Lone Texas Ranger" (1945), "Phantom of the Plains" (1945), "Marshal of Laredo" (1945), "Colorado Pioneers" (1945), "Wagon Wheels Westward" (1945), "California Gold Rush" (1946), "Sheriff of Redwood Valley" (1946) "Sun Valley Cyclone" (1946), "Conquest of Cheyenne" (1946), "Santa Fe Uprising" (1946), "Stagecoach to Denver" (1946), "Vigilantes of Boomtown" (1947), "Homesteaders of Paradise Valley" (1947), "Oregon Trail Scouts" (1947), "Rustlers of Devil's Canyon" (1947), and "Marshal of Cripple Creek" (1947). His other film credits include "The Horn Blows

at Midnight" (1945), "Pillow to Post" (1945), "Dakota" (1945), "A Guy Could Change" (1946), "Home on the Range" (1946), "In Old Sacramento" (1946), "Out California Way" (1946), "Humoresque" (1946) as John Garfield's character as a child, "The Return of Rin Tin Tin" (1947), "The Last Round-Up" (1947), the classic "The Treasure of the Sierra Madre" (1948) as a Mexican boy selling lottery tickets to Humphrey Bogart, "The Black Rose" (1950), and "Black Hand" (1950). Blake was drafted into the U.S. Army in 1950. He tried to resume his acting career after his discharge and studied acting under Jeff Corey after battling drug addiction. He continued to appear in such films as "Apache War Smoke" (1952), "Treasure of the Golden Condor" (1953), "The Veils of Bagdad" (1953), "Screaming Eagles" (1956), "The Rack" (1956), "Three Violent People" (1956), "Rumble on the Docks" (1956), "The Tijuana Story" (1957), "The Beast of Budapest" (1958), "Revolt in the Big House" (1958), "Pork Chop Hill" (1959), "Battle Flame" (1959), the crime thriller "The Purple Gang" (1959) as William 'Honeyboy' Willard "Town Without Pity" (1961), "PT 109" (1963), "The Greatest Story Ever Told" (1965) as Simon the Zealot, and "This Property Is Condemned" (1966). He was seen on television in episodes of "Adventures of Wild Bill Hickok", "Your Favorite Story", "Fireside Theatre", "The Cisco Kid", "The Roy Rogers Show", "Whirlybirds", "The Court of Last Resort", "26 Men", "Men of Annapolis", "Official Detective", "The Millionaire", "Broken Arrow", "The Restless Gun", "The Californians", "Black Saddle", "Playhouse 90", "Zane Grey Theatre", "The Rebel", "One Step Beyond", "Bat Masterson", "Naked City", "Wagon Train", "Laramie", "Ben Casey", "Straightaway", "Cain's Hundred", "The New Breed", "Have Gun - Will Travel", "The Richard Boone Show", "Slattery's People", "The Trials of O'Brien", "Rawhide", "The F.B.I.", "12 O'Clock High", and "Death Valley Days". Blake earned acclaim for his role as murderer Perry Smith in the 1967 adaptation of Truman Capote's true-crime book "In Cold Blood". His other films include "Tell Them Willie Boy Is Here" (1969), "The Boxer" (1972), "Corky" (1972), "Electra Glide in Blue" (1973), "Busting" (1974), "Second-Hand Hearts" (1980), "Coast to Coast" (1980), "Money Train" (1995), and David  Lynch's "Lost Highway" (1997). He starred as plain clothes police detective Tony Baretta, accompanied by a pet cockatoo named Fred, in the television series "Baretta" from 1975 to 1978. He received an Emmy Award for his performance in 1975 and another nomination in 1978. He starred as private detective Joe Dancer and served as executive producer for a trio of tele-films, "The Big Black Pill" (1981), "The Monkey Mission" (1981), and "Murder 1, Dancer 0" (1983). He starred as George opposite Randy Quaid's Lenny in the 1981 television adaptation of John Steinbeck's "Of Mice and Men" and earned another Emmy nomination for his role as Jimmy Hoffa in the 1983 tele-film "Blood Feud". Blake starred as Father Noah 'Hardstep' Rivers in the 1985 tele-film and the subsequent short-lived television series of the same name that he also created under the name Lyman P. Docker. He also appeared in the tele-films "Heart of a Champion: The Ray Mancini Story" (1985) and "Judgment Day: The John List Story" (1993) earning another Emmy nomination for starring in the title role. He was a guest on such television series as "The Hollywood Squares", "Tattletales", "Sammy and Company", "Dinah!", "Jerry Lewis MDA Labor Day Telethon", "The Mike Douglas Show", "The Merv Griffin Show", "The John Davidson Show", "The Toni Tennille Show", "Saturday Night Live" hosting a show in 1982, and "The Tonight Show Starring Johnny Carson". Blake earned a reputation as a troublesome presence on film and television sets, threatening producers and fighting with directors and fellow actors. He would frequently mock his own career and demean other actors as a guest on television talk shows. He met Bonnie Lee Bakley in 1999 at a Los Angeles nightclub. She later had a daughter which was initially thought to be by Christian Brando, but DNA tests later indicated it was Blake. They married in 2000 and Bakely was found shot to death in her husband's vehicle outside an Italian restaurant in Los Angeles on May 4, 2001. Blake said he was not present at the time of the shooting as he had returned to the restaurant where they had dined to retrieve a gun he had left in their booth. He was charged with murder in April of 2002 and held without bail for 11 months until it was granted in March of 2003. The trial resulted in his acquittal in March of 2005. Bakley's family later won a civil court judgment for wrongful death against Blake, who filed for bankruptcy in 2006. Blake resurfaced with an autobiography, "Tales of a Rascal: What I Did for Love", in 2012. He was interviewed on "Piers Morgan Tonight" in 2012 and on "20/20" in 2019. He discussed his life and career on a YouTube channel called "Robert Blake: I ain't dead yet, so stay tuned" in 2019. Blake was married to Sondra Kerr from 1961 until their divorce in 1983 and is survived by their son, actor Noah Blake, and daughter, Delinah Blake. He married Bonnie Lee Bakley in 2000 and they remained together until her murder in 2001. He is survived by their daughter, Rose Blake. He reportedly married Pamela Hudak in 2017 and they divorced in 2019.

Bleier, Edward

Television executive Edward Bleier died at his home in East Hampton, New York, on October 17, 2023. He was 94.

Bleier was born in New York City on October 16, 1929. He began working in radio in while in high school and was an ABC News copy boy while attending Syracuse University. He wrote for several local radio stations and for the "Syracuse Herald Journal". He dropped out of college in 1949 and began working in television at the DuMont Television Network. He worked with ABC's New York Channel 7 in advertising in the early 1950s and soon moved to the ABC television network. He became a senior executive with the network in daytime and children's programming, general sales management and marketing, and public relations in the 1960s. He left ABC in 1968 to join Warner Bros. Television. He became President of Domestic Pay TV, Cable & Network Features and headed network programming and sales in 1969. He spent over three decades with the network and was instrumental in developing basic and pay television networks including MTV, Nickelodeon, and the Movie Channel. He repackaged numerous versions of the Looney Tunes cartoons library while president of Warner Bros. Animation. He collaborated with Steven Spielberg to produce several new cartoons featuring the characters including "Tiny Toon Adventures". He was co-creator of the plans for Warner Home Video and pioneered new digital media markets. He was also involved in Warner's merger with Time Inc. in 1990. Bleier served as senior advisor at Warner from 2002 until retiring in 2005. He was author of the 2003 book "The Thanksgiving Ceremony". Bleier married French-language journalist Magda Palacci in 1973 and she survives him.

Bley, Carla

Jazz composer and pianist Carla Bley died of brain cancer at her home in Willow, New York, on October 17, 2023. She was 67. She was born Lovella May Borg to Swedish

parents in Oakland, California, on May 11, 1936. She sang from an early age and moved to New York City in the early 1950s. She became a cigarette girl at the jazz club Birdland. She began touring with jazz pianist Paul Bley, who encouraged her to compose music. She married Bley in 1957 and became known as Carla Bley. Her compositions include "Bent Eagle", recorded by George Russell in 1960, and "Ictus", recorded by Jimmy Giuffre in 1961. She helped form the Jazz Composers Guild in 1964 and was co-leader of the Jazz Composers' Orchestra with Michael Mantler. They recorded her jazz opera "Escalator Over the Hill" in 1971. She and Mantler formed several independent record labels including WATT Records and New Music Distribution Service. She wrote the 1967 composition "A Genuine Tong Funeral" and played with vibraphonist Gary Burton on the recording. Bley wrote Nick Mason's solo debut album "Nick Mason's Fictitious Sports" in 1981. She continued to record with her own big band and several smaller ensembles including the Lost Cords. Bley received the National Endowment for the Arts Jazz Masters Award in 2015. Her last album, "Life Goes On", was released in 2020. She was the subject of Amy C. Beal's 2011 biography "Carla Bley". She was married to Paul Bley from 1957 until their divorce in 1967. She was married to Austrian trumpeter Michael Mantler from 1967 until their divorce in 1991 and is survived by their daughter, singer and pianist Karen Mantler. She is also survived by bassist Steve Swallow, her partner for thirty years.

Blumhagen, Lothar

German actor Lothar Blumhagen, who was noted as a dubbing performer for such stars as Roger Moore and Christopher Plummer, died at a hospital in Berlin, Germany, on January 10, 2023. He was 95. Blumhagen was born in Leipzig, Germany, on July 16, 1927. He began his career on stage in 1947, performing in Leipzig, Halle, and Berlin. He was part of the Deutsches Theater Berlin from 1954 to 1956. He appeared in the films "Hexen" (1954) and "Sommerliebe" (1955). Blumhagen moved to West Berlin in 1956 and performed at the Schillertheater and the Schlossparktheater. He became best known as a dubbing actor for over 600 films and television productions. He provided the German voice for such stars as Christopher Plummer, Roger Moore, Alan Rickman, John Hillerman on the "Magnum, P.I." television series, Christopher Lee, and Andreas Katsulas as G'Kar in "Babylon 5". Blumhagen appeared on television in productions of "Die Erbin" (1958), "1913" (1961), "Das Vergnugen, Anstandig Zu Sein" (1962), "Zweierlei Mass" (1964), "The Garden Party" (1966), "Die Schwarze Hand" (1966), "Bericht Uber Zyskar" (1966), "Nathan der Weise" (1967), "Unwiederbringlich" (1968), "Waterloo" (1969), "Bischof Ketteler" (1969), "Ein Sonntag am See" (1971), "Auf den Spuren der Anarchisten" (1972), "Die Geschichte Einer Dicken Frau" (1973), "Unter Ausschluss der Offentlichkeit" (1974), "Frau von Bebenburg" (1975), "Vor den Sturm" (1984), and "Die Schwarmer" (1985). He was featured in the 1986 documentary film "Boundaries of Time: Caspar David Friedrich".

Boen, Earl

Actor Earl Boen, who was featured as psychologist Dr. Peter Silberman in "The Terminator" film franchise, died of lung cancer in Hawaii on January 5, 2023. He was 81. Boen was born in New York City on August 8, 1941. He performed frequently on television from the early 1970s with roles in episodes of "The Streets of San Francisco", "What's Happening!!", "Kojak", "Rafferty", "Hawaii Five-O", "Wonder Woman", "Police Woman", "Richie Brockelman, Private Eye", "Eight Is Enough", "Lou Grant", "The Paper Chase", "Barnaby Jones", "The Jeffersons", "Buck Rogers in the 25th Century", "A Man Called Sloane", "Angie", "I'm a Big Girl Now", "The Dukes of Hazzard", "Soap", "Code Red", "King's Crossing", "M*A*S*H", "Barney Miller", "It's a Living", "The Powers of Matthew Star", "Gavilan", "Too Close for Comfort", "Voyagers!", "Madame's Place", "Three's Company", "Fantasy Island", "It Takes Two", "Just Our Luck", "Benson", "Amanda's", "St. Elsewhere", "Night Court", "Family Ties", "Street Hawk", "Otherworld", "Me and Mom", "Newhart", "Remington Steele", "Growing Pains", "Silver Spoons", "1st & Ten", "Punky Brewster", "What's Happening Now!", "Hill Street Blues", "Who's the Boss?" in the recurring role of Jim Peterson from 1984 to 1986, "Knots Landing", "Dynasty", "Gung Ho", "Isabel's Honeymoon Hotel", "ALF", "Scarecrow and Mrs. King", "thirtysomething", "Mr. President", "Mama's Family" in the recurring role of Reverend Lloyd Meechum from 1983 to 1987, "Crime Story", "The Oldest Rookie", "The New Gidget", "The Law and Harry McGraw" as Howard Sternhagen from 1987 to 1988, "Boys Will Be Boys", "Hotel", "Dallas", "The Bold and the Beautiful", "Webster", "Star Trek: The Next Generation", "Murder, She Wrote", "Baywatch", "Life Goes On", "227", "Tales from the Crypt", "Sydney", "Matlock", "WIOU", "Seinfeld", "The Wonder Years", "Amen", "The New WKRP in Cincinnati", "Family Matters", "Herman's Head", "Get a Life", "Santa Barbara", "The Golden Girls", "Rhythm & Blues", "The Fresh Prince of Bel-Air", "The Golden Palace", "L.A. Law", "Hangin' with Mr. Cooper", "ABC Weekend Specials", "Lois & Clark: The New Adventures of Superman", "On Our Own", "Blue Skies", "Empty Nest", "The 5 Mrs. Buchanans", "Living Single", "Deadly Games", "Ellen", "Silk Stalkings", "California Dreams", "Sparks", "Working", "The Good News", "Boy Meets World", "The West Wing", "Family Law", "State of Grace", and "The Practice". Boen was also seen in television productions of "Cyrano de Bergerac" (1974), "The Taming of the Shrew" (1976), "Last of the Good Guys" (1978), Disney's "Donovan's Kid" (1979), "The Children Nobody Wanted" (1981), "Adams House" (1982), "I Take These Men" (1983), "For Members Only" (1983), "Getting Physical" (1984), "Antony and Cleopatra" (1984), "Royal Match" (1985), "Annihilator" (1986), "She's with Me" (1986), "Tales from the Hollywood Hills: A Table at Ciro's" (1987), "Going to the Chapel" (1988), "Double Your Pleasure" (1989), "Perry Mason: The Case of the Poisoned Pen" (1990), "Opposites Attract" (1990), "Menu for Murder" (1990), "Darkness Before the Dawn" (1993), "The Companion" (1994), "Norma Jean & Marilyn" (1996), "Within the Rock" (1996), "Ali: An American Hero" (2000) as Howard Cosell, and "The Jennie Project" (2001). Boen appeared in the films "Mr. Billion" (1977), "The Fifth Floor" (1978), "The Main Event" (1979), the science fiction classic "Battle Beyond the Stars" (1980) as Nestor 1, "9 to 5" (1980), "Soggy Bottom, U.S.A." (1981), "Airplane II: The Sequel" (1982), "The Man with Two Brains" (1983) with Steve Martin, "To Be or Not to Be" (1983), "The Terminator" (1984) as Dr. Peter Silberman, "Movers & Shakers" (1985), "Touch and Go" (1986), "Stewardess School" (1986), "Walk Like a Man" (1987), "18 Again!" (1988), "Miracle Mile" (1988), "Alien Nation" (1988), "My Stepmother Is an Alien" (1988), "Chopper Chicks in Zombietown" (1989), "Marked for Death" (1990), "Guilty as Charged" (1991), "Terminator 2: Judgment Day" (1991) reprising his role as Dr. Silberman, "Samantha" (1991), "Naked Gun 33 1/3: The Final Insult" (1994), "Sioux City" (1994), "Gordy" (1994) as the voice of Minnesota Red, "The Dentist" (1996), "The Prince" (1996), "Living in Peril"

(1997), "The Odd Couple II" (1998), "Nutty Professor II: The Klumps" (2000), "The Majestic" (2002), "Now You Know" (2002), and "Terminator 3: Rise of the Machines" (2003) again as Dr Silberman. He was a prolific voice actor for films, television, and video games. He voiced roles for the animated films "Porco Rosso" (1992), "Dot & Spot's Magical Christmas Adventure" (1996) as Santa, "Poseidon's Fury: Escape from the Lost City" (1999), "Little Shepherd" (2002), "The Wild Thornberrys" (2002), and "Clifford's Really Big Movie" (2004) as Mr. Bleakman. He was also a voice performer on television for the animated series "G.I. Joe", "A Pup Named Scooby-Doo", "The Further Adventures of SuperTed", "Pryde of the X-Men" as Magneto in 1989, "Fantastic Max", "Paddington Bear", "The Pirates of Dark Water", "3x3 Eyes", "Capitol Critters", "Swat Kats: The Radical Squadron", "The Addams Family", "Bonkers" as Police Chief Leonard Kanifky from 1993 to 1994, "Problem Child", "Skeleton Warriors", "Batman: The Animated Series", "Animaniaccs", "What-a-Mess", "Wing Commander Academy", "The Mask", "The Real Adventures of Jonny Quest", "Bruno the Kid", "Extreme Ghostbusters", "Pinky and the Brain", "The New Batman Adventures", "Spider-Man: The Animated Series" as the Beyonder and the Red Skull, "The Sylvester & Tweety Mysteries", "Oh Yeah! Cartoons", "Zorro", "I Am Weasel", "The Fantastic Voyages of Sinbad the Sailor", "Cow and Chicken", "The Adventures of Jesus and His Brother", "Buzz Lightyear of Star Command", "The Zeta Project", "Captain Sturdy: Back in Action", "The Wild Thornberrys", "Dexter's Laboratory", "Johnny Bravo", "Time Squad", "Justice League" as Simon Stagg, "Clifford the Big Red Dog" as Horace Bleakman from 2000 to 2003, "Evil Con Carne", "Citizen Tony", "The Grim Adventures of Billy & Mandy", "Kim Possible", and "Megas XLR". He was also a voice actor for numerous video games including "The Secret of Monkey Island" as Captain LeChuck, "Zork: Grand Inquisitor", "Return to Krondor", "Baldur's Gate", "Revenant", "Alundra 2: A New Legend Begins", "Toy Story 2", "Sword of the Berserk: Guts' Rage", "Soldier of Fortune", "Orphen: Scion of Sorcery", "Tenchu 2: Birth of the Stealth Assassins", "Star Trek Voyager: Elite Force", "Escape from Monkey Island", "Invictus: In the Shadow of Olympus", "Clifford the Big Red Dog: Thinking Adventures", "Kingdom Under Fire: A War of Heroes", "Fallout Tactics: Brotherhood of Steel", "Black & White", "Atlantis: The Lost Empire", "Metal Gear Solid 2: Sons of Liberty", "Baldur's Gate: Dark Alliance", "Star Trek: Armada II", "Blood Omen 2", "New Legends", "Star Trek: Bridge Commander", "Bloody Roar: Primal Fury", "Soldier of Fortune II: Double Helix", "Eternal Darkness: Sanity's Requiem", "Icewind Dale II", "The Scorpion King: Rise of the Akkadian", "Metal Gear Solid 2: Substance", "Kim Possible: Revenge of Monkey Fist", "Tenchu: Wrath of Heaven", "RTX Red Rock", "Lionheart", "Extreme Skate Adventure", "Call of Duty", "Fallout: Brotherhood of Steel", "Daredevil: The Man Without Fear", "Tenchu: Return from Darkness", "XX-Men Legends", "EverQuest II", "World of Warcraft: Mists of Pandaria", "Psychonauts", "Hearthstone: Heroes of Warcrafrt", and "Girls Mode 4: Star Stylist". His voice was heard on the Disneyland Railroad from 2002 to 2016 and on the Walt Disney World Railroad from 2002 to 2010. He was the voice of Edwin and Regis Blackgaard on the Focus on the Family's "Adventures in Odyssey" radio serial for many years. Boen was married to actress Carole Keane from 1970 until her death in 2001 and is survived by their daughter Ruby. He married Cathy Boen in 2008 and she also survives him.

Bogachyov, Gennadi

Russian actor Gennadi Bogachyov died in Saint Petersburg, Russia, on April 25, 2023. He was 78. Bogachyov was born in Shatsk, Russia (then part of the Soviet Union), on

March 6, 1945. He studied at the Leningrad State Institute of Theatre, Music, and Cinema and began his career on stage with the Leningrad Drama Theater. He was seen on television in productions of "Provody Belykh Nochey" (1969), "Khanuma" (1978), "Tri Nenastnykh Dnya" (1978), "Otpusk v Sentyabre" (1979), "Bal" (1979), "Karl Marks. Molodye Gody" (1980), "Pikvikskiy Klub" (1986), "Isklyuchenie Bez Pravil" (1986), "To Muzhchina, to Zhenshchina" (1989), "Vospominanie o Sherloke Kholmse" (2000), "Nero Wolfe i Archie Goodwin" (2002), "Brezhnev" (2005), and "Master i Margarita" (2005). Bogachyov appeared in the films "Sergey Ivanovich Ukhodit Na Pensiyu" (1980), "Olenya Okhotta" (1982), "Skorost" (1983), "Mera Presecheniya" (1983), "Moonzund" (1988), "Khmel - Film Vtoroy: Ishkod" (1991), "Ispoved Neznakomtsu" (1995), and "Prostye Veshchi" (2007). Bogachyov also provided the Russian dubbing voice for such actors as Robin Williams, Tommy Lee Jones, Cliff Robertson, Mel Gibson, and Richard Gere. He continued to perform on Stage with the Bolshoi Drama Theatre throughout his career.

Boht, Jean

British actress Jean Boht, who starred in the television comedy series "Bread" as Nellie Boswell, died of complications from Alzheimer's disease at Denville Hall in Northwood,

London, England, on September 12, 2023. She was 91. She was born Jean Dance in Bebington, Cheshire, England, on March 6, 1932. She trained as an actress at the Liverpool Playhouse and began her career on stage. She performed in repertory and in productions on the West End from the early 1960s. Boht was seen frequently on television in episodes of "Mr. Rose", "Scene", "Softly Softly: Task Force", "Six Days of Justice", "Z Cars", "Couples", "Esther Waters", "Last of the Summer Wine", "Grange Hill" (1978), "The Sweeney", "Some Mothers Do 'Ave 'Em", "Mother Nature's Bloomers", "Funny Man" as Elsie in 1981, "Triangle" as Mrs.

Carter in 1982, "Goodnight and God Bless", "Maybury", "Juliet Bravo", "Bergerac", "Blankety Blank", "I Woke Up One Morning" as Mrs. Hamilton from 1985 to 1986, "Screenplay", "Bread" as matriarch Nellie Boswell from 1986 to 1991, "This Is Your Life", "Jackanory", "Cluedo", "Comedy Playhouse", "Brighton Belles" as Josephine from 1993 to 1994, "Celebrity Squares", "Trial & Retribution", "Holby City", "The Bill", "Missing", "Skins", "Casualty", and "Doctors". Her other television credits include productions of "Ego Hugo" (1973), "Where Adam Stood" (1976), "Bill Brand" (1976), "Sons and Lovers" (1981), "Boys from the Blackstuff" (1982), "Spyship" (1983), "Scully" (1984), "Arthur's Hallowed Ground" (1984), "Agatha Christie's Miss Marple: 4:50 from Paddington" (1987), "The Cloning of Joanna May" (1992), "The Big Game" (1995), "Jim's Gift" (1996), "Celebrate 'Oliver!'" (2005), and "Justice" (2011). Boht was seen in a handful of films including "Rapunzel Let Down Your Hair" (1978), "Distant Voices, Still Lives" (1988), "The Girl in a Swing" (1988), "Heaven's a Drag" (1994), "The Asylum" (2000), "Mothers and Daughters" (2004), "The Understudy" (2008), "Kin" (2009), and the short "Bad Night for the Blues" (2010). She was married to William Boht from 1954 until their divorce in 1970. She married conductor and composer Carl Davis in 1970 and they had two daughters, Hannah and Jessie. She and Davis served as executive producers for their daughter Hanah's 2008 black comedy film "The Understudy" and appeared as a married couple.

Boigelot, Jacques

Belgian film director Jacques Boigelot died in Belgium on March 4, 2023. He was 93. Boigelot was born in Uccle, Belgium, on August 23, 1929. He began his film career

in the late 1940s as an assistant director and writer for advertising films. He served in the Belgian military for several years, where he worked with the film services in the early 1950s. Boigelot was co-director of the short films "The Surprise Box" (1951) and "A Black Country" (1953) with Jean Delire. He also directed the shorts "Francoise and the City" (1956) and "Wellington, Here I Am" (1956). He joined the Belgian film and television service RTB in 1958 as a programmer. He directed the short "On These Paths' in 1961. His 1970 feature film "Paix sur les Champs" ("Peace on the Fields") (1970) was nominated for the Academy Award for Best Foreign Language Film. He also directed the 1975 television series "The Fox and the Golden Ring". Boigelot was married to Simone Allebosch until her death in 19897 and they had three children together.

Bollmann, Hannelore

German actress Hannelore Bollmann died in Santa Barbara, California, on April 7, 2023. She was 97. Bollmann was born in Hamburg, Germany, on May 10, 1925. She was

the daughter of opera singer Hans-Heinz Bollmann. She began her film debut in the 1947 comedy "King of Hearts". She was seen in numerous romantic comedies and musicals over the next two decades. Bollmann's films include "Hello, Fraulein!" (1949), "Love on Ice" (1950), "Czardas of Hearts" (1951), "Holiday from Myself" (1952), "Carnival in White" (1952), "On the Green Meadow" (1953), "Marriage for One Night" (1953), "The Sweetest Fruits" (1954) the first of several directed by her then-husband Franz Antel, "The Big Star Parade" (1954), "Roses from the South" (1954), "The Congress Danes" (11955), "Espionage" (1955), "The Happy Village" (1955), "Emperor's Ball" (1956), "All the Sins of the Earth" (1958), "Our Crazy Aunts" (1961), and "Two Bavarians in Bonn" (1962). She retired from the screen in the early 1960s. Bollmann was married to director Franz Antel from 1953 until their divorce in 1958. She subsequently married producer Rudolf Travnicek. They had a son together, Alexander Sasha, who died in 2021. Her third marriage was to director Francis Cantor in the early 1970s.

Booth, Bronwen

British actress Bronwen Booth died of ampullary cancer on April 4, 2023. She was 59. Booth was born in Marylebone, London, England, on February 21, 1964, the

daughter of actor Anthony Booth and producer Julie Allan. Booth appeared in a handful of films including "Eternal Evil" (1985), "Kayla" (1997), "Snowboard Academy" (1997), "For Hire" (1998), "Airspeed" (1999), "Babel" (1999), "Pact with the Devil" (2003), and "What's Your Number?" (2011). She was featured as Andy Harrison in the daytime soap opera "One Life to Live" from 1989 to 1991. Booth appeared in the tele-films "The Call of the Wild" (1997), "Glory & Honor" (1998), "Jackie Bouvier Kennedy Onassis" (2000) as Jackie's sister Lee Bouvier, "Voices" (2008), and "The Healing Project" (2008). Her other television credits include episodes of "Ask Harriet", "Law & Order: Criminal Intent", "Scrubs", "Naked Josh", and "Nurse Jackie". She was featured as Jacqueline Kennedy in the Los Angeles production of the musical "First Lady Suite" in 2002. Booth is survived by her husband, producer and actor Nick Miscusi.

Borman, Frank

Astronaut Frank Borman, who was commander of the Apollo 8 mission that became the first to fly around the Moon in 1968, died of complications from a stroke at a clinic in

Billings, Montana, on November 7, 2023. He was 95. Borman was born in Gary, Indiana, on March 14, 1928. He moved to Tucson, Arizona, with his family as a child and attended elementary and high school there. He entered West Point

Military Academy in July of 1946 and was commissioned as a second lieutenant in the U.S. Air Force after graduating in 1950. He qualified as fighter pilot and served in the Philippines. He earned a master's degree in science at the California Institute of Technology in 1957 and became an assistant professor of thermodynamics and fluid mechanics at West Point. Borman qualified as a test pilot at the USAF Experimental Flight Test Pilot School at Edwards Air Force Base in California in 1960. He was part of the second group of astronauts selected by NASA in 1962. He was command pilot of the 1965 Gemini 7 mission and spent nearly 14 days in space with James Lovell. He was selected to crew a lunar mission for Project Apollo, but a cabin fire during a launch rehearsal test killed the crew of the first planned Apollo mission in January of 1967. Borman was the only astronaut to serve on the review board investigating the accident. The fire delayed successive Apollo lunar missions for over a year. Borman served as commander of the second manned Apollo mission, Apollo 8, which launched on December 21, 1968, along with crewmates James Lovell and William Anders. The spacecraft was the first manned mission to leave low Earth orbit and the first to reach the Moon. He and his crew were the first humans to observe and photograph the far side of the Moon during their six-day mission. The mission was also noted for the crew reading the first ten verses from the Bible's Book of Genesis on a Christmas Eve television broadcast. Borman served as NASA liaison to President Richard Nixon during the Apollo 11 lunar landing mission in July of 1969. He retired from NASA and the U.S. Air Force as a colonel in June of 1970. He subsequently joined Eastern Air Lines and became senior vice president for operations. He was named chief executive officer of Eastern in 1975 and chairman of the board the following year. He resigned from Eastern in 1986 and later operated a Ford dealership in Las Cruces, New Mexico, and a cattle ranch in Bighorn, Montana. Borman was recipient of numerous awards and medals for his role as an astronaut including the Congressional Space Medal of Honor and induction into the National Aviation Hall of Fame and the U.S. Astronaut Hall of Fame. He appeared as himself in numerous film and television documentaries including "Spaceflight" (1985), "Moon Shot" (1994), "The Century" (1999), "Apollo 8: Christmas at the Moon" (2003), "Race to the Moon" (2005), "Project Gemini: Bridge to the Moon" (2008), "NASA: Triumph and Tragedy" (2009), "When We Left Earth: The NASA Missions" (2009), "The Apollo Years" (2009), "The Apollo Chronicles" (2019), "Chasing the Moon" (2019), and "Armstrong" (2019). He was a guest on the television talk shows "The Dick Cavett Show", "The Mike Douglas Show",

"V.I.P.-Schaukel", and "Today". Borman was portrayed by actor David Andrews in the 1989 HBO mini-series "From the Earth to the Moon". He was married to Susan Bugbee from 1950 until her death in 2021 and is survived by their sons, Frederick and Edwin.

Borre, Odd

Norwegian pop singer Odd Borre died in Norway on January 28, 2023. He was 83. Borre was born in Harstad, Norway, on August 9, 1939. He began his career singing with the Kjell Karlsen Orchestra from 1962 to 1970. He was best known for the song "Stress" which he performed at the Eurovision Song Contest in 1968, placing 16th. He largely left professional singing in 1970 to work as an insurance agent.

Bos, Burny

Danish film and television producer Burny Bos, who was best known for his works geared for younger audiences, died of mesothelioma in Amsterdam, Netherlands, on

December 1, 2023. He was 79. Lar Korean novels. Bos was born in Haarlem, Netherlands, on April 8, 1944. He began his career with AVRO public radio with the series "Ko de Boswachtershow" from 1974 to 1984 and "Radio Lawaaipapegaai" from 1976 to 1978. He became head of juvenile television programming for VPRO, developing such series as "Theo en Thea", "Mevrouw Ten Kate", "Max Laadevermogen", "Rembo en Rembo", "Achterwerk in de Kast", and "Buurmand Bolle". He founded the Ben Bros production company in 1989. He produced such series as "Kinderen van Waterland" (1990), "Mus" (1993), "Dag Juf, Tot Morgen" (1995), "Mijn Franse Tante Gazeuse" (1996), "Groot Licht" (1998), "Otje" (1998-1999), "The Flying Liftboy" (2000), "Knofje" (2002-2003), "Ibbeltje" (2004), "Waltz" (2006), "Annie MG" (2010), "Zusjes" (2013), "Vrolijke Kerst" (2016), "Voetbalmeisjes" (2016), and "Papadag" (2017-2018). Bos also produced numerous films including "The Penknife" (1991), "Vinayaz" (1992), "The Boy Who Stopped Talking" (1996), "Always Yours, for Never" (1996), "The Flying Liftboy" (1998) which he also wrote, "Miss Minoes" (2001), "Yes Nurse! No Nurse!" (2002), "Mein bruder Ist ein Hund" (2004), "Pluk van de Petteflet" (2004), "Gruesome School Trip" (2005) which he also wrote, "Het Paard van Sinterklaas" (2005), "Ben X" (2007), "Breath" (2007), "Waar is Het Paard van Sinterklaas?" (2007), "Morrison Krijgt Een Zusje" (2008), "Hoe Overleef Ik...?" (2008), "Los" (2008), "Zwemparadijs" (2009), "Dolfje Weerwolfje" (2011), "Allez, Eddy!" (2012), "Fidgety Bram" (2012), "The Zigzag

Kid" (2012), "Chez Nous" (2013), "Sickos" (2014), "Zwemmen of Verzulpen" (2014), "The Amazing Wiplala" (2014), "Mr. Frog" (2016), "Adios Amigos" (2016), "Romy's Salon" (2019), "Marionette" (2020), "Lucy Ist Jetzt Gangster" (2022), and "Rocco y Sjuul" (2023). Bos was also the author of over forty childrens books. His survivors include his daughter, screenwriter Tamara Bos.

Bosley, Randall

Actor Randall Bosley died on May 10, 2023. He was 75. Bosley was born in Van Nuys, California, on August 1, 1947. He appeared frequently in films and television from the early 1990s. His films include "Illegal Entry: Formula for Fear" (1994), "Kazaam" (1996), "Legally Exposed" (1997), "MP Da Last Don" (1998), "Monkeybone" (2001), "The United States of Leland" (2003), Envy" (2004), "Neighborhood Watch" (2005), "Veritas, Prince of Truth" (2006), "An American Carol" (2008), and the horror film "Death Factory" (2014). Bosley appeared on television in episodes of "Homefront", "Star Trek: Voyager", "Mad TV", "Click", "The X-Files", "Jack & Jill", "Malcolm in the Middle", and "Mind of Mencia".

Bosson, Barbara

Actress Barbara Bosson, who was noted for her role as Fay Furillo in the series "Hill Street Blues" in the early-1980s, died in Los Angeles, California, on February 18, 2023. She was 83. Bosson was born in Charleroi, Pennsylvania, on November 1, 1939. She moved to Florida with her family in her teens and graduated from high school in Gulfport. She went to New York and took various jobs while pursuing an acting career. She worked as a secretary and Playboy Bunny and studied acting with Milton Katselas and Herbert Berghof. She attended Carnegie Tech on scholarship in 1965. She began working with the Committee, and improvisational group in San Francisco. She appeared in small roles in the films "Bullitt" (1968), "Where It's At" (1969), and "The Love God?" (1969). She was also seen on television in episodes of "The Smothers Brothers Comedy Hour" and "Mannix", and the tele-film "The Impatient Heart" (1971). Bosson married television writer and producer Steven Bochco in 1970 and appeared frequently in series he was involved with. She was seen in episodes of "Longstreet", "Emergency!", "Alias Smith and Jones", "Ironside", "Griff", "Sunshine", "McMillan & Wife", and "Delvecchio". She was featured as Sharon in the 1976 tele-film "Richie Brockelman: The Missing 24 Hours" and the subsequent series "Richie

Brockelman, Private Eye" in 1978. Bosson appeared in the tele-films "Operating Room" (1978), "Calendar Girl Murders" (1984), "Hostage Flight" (1985), and "Jury Duty: The Comedy" (1990). She was best known for her role as Fay Furillo, wife of Daniel J. Travanti's Captain Frank Furillo, on her husband's police series "Hill Street Blues" from 1981 to 1986. She earned five successive Emmy Award nominations for Outstanding Supporting Actress in a Drama Series for her role. She continued her career in episodes of such series as "Crazy Like a Fox", "L.A. Law", "The New Mike Hammer", "ABC Afterschool Specials", "The New Hollywood Squares", "Hotel", "Murder, She Wrote", "CBS Schoolbreak Special", Bochco's "Hooperman" as Captain C.Z. Stern from 1987 to 1989, the short-lived police musical series "Cop Rock" as Mayor Louise Plank in 1990, "Civil Wars" in the recurring role of Judge Babyak from 1992 to 1993, "Star Trek: Deep Space Nine" as Roana in the 1994 "Rivals" episode, "NYPD Blue", "Lois & Clark: The New Adventures of Superman", and "Total Security". Bosson starred as Miriam Grasso on the series "Murder One" from 1995 until 1997 and received another Emmy Award nomination. She reprised the role in the 1997 mini-series "Murder One: Diary of a Serial Killer". She was seen in several more films during her career including "Mame" (1974), "Capricorn One" (1977), "Imps*" (1983), "The Last Starfighter" (1984) as Jane Rogan, "The Education of Allison Tate" (1986), and "Little Sweetheart" (1988). She wrote and produced the 1998 tele-film "Scattering Dad". Bosson was married to Steven Bochco from 1970 until their divorce in 1998 and is survived by their two children, producer Jesse Bochco and Melissa Bochco.

Bostick, Cynthia

Actress Cynthia Bostick died in Marshfield, Wisconsin, on January 24, 2023. She was 70. Bostick was born in Owensboro, Kentucky, on June 3, 1952. She began performing on stage while in her teens. She competed in beauty pageants and was crowned Miss Owensboro and became Miss Kentucky in 1970. She moved to New York City where she trained at the American Academy of Dramatic Arts. Bostick was featured in the 1975 film "That's the Way of the World". She was also seen in the television soap operas "For Richer, for Poorer" as Connie Ferguson from 1977 to 1978, "As the World Turns" as Marcia Campbell in 1979, and "Texas" as Margaret Hansen in 1981. She left acting to work in public relations in the early 1980s. She worked at Proctor and Gamble in Cincinnati and the S.C. Johnson company in Racine. Bostick married John Georgeson in 1988 and is survived by him and their daughter. She is also survived by a son from a previous relationship and a stepson.

Bould, Bruce

British actor Bruce Bould, who starred as David Harris-Jones in the British television comedy series "The Rise and Rise of Reginald Perrin" in the late 1970s, died in England on May 15, 2023. He was 73. Bould was born in Bradford, West Yorkshire, England, on May 19, 1949. He began

performing on stage with the Birmingham Repertory in 1966. He trained at the Royal Academy of Dramatic Art and graduated in 1969. He was featured in a small role in a 1969 television production of "Julius Caesar". Bould was also seen in episodes of "Z Cars", "Thirty-Minute Theatre", "Six Days of Justice", "Play for Today", "Van der Valk", "Special Branch", "New Scotland Yard", "Village Hall", "Churchill's People", "The Good Life", "Hadleigh", "The New Avengers", "Coronation Street", "Rings on Their Fingers", "The Fall and Rise of Reginald Perrin" as David Harris-Jones from 1976 to 1979, "The Dick Emery Show", "Strangers" as Det. Insp. Tom Casey in 1980, "Prisoners of Conscience", "To the Manor Born", "The Consultant", "Now and Then", "Shelley", "The Hello Goodbye Man", "Shine on Harvey Moon" in the recurring role of Tom Chavan in 1984, "Me and My Girl", "Howards' Way" as David Lloyd from 1985 to 1987, "Close to Home", "Harry Endfield's Television Programme", "The Upper Hand", "Drop the Dead Donkey", "As Time Goes By", and "The Legacy of Reginald Perrin" reprising his role as David Harris Jones in 1996. His other television credits include the 1974 mini-series "QB VII" and the tele-film "The Alchemists" (1999). Bould married Theresa Watson, who was featured as his character's wife in "The Fall and Rise of Reginald Perrin", in 1972. He is survived by her and their two children,

Boulogne, Christian Aaron

French actor Christian Aaron 'Ari' Boulogne was found dead of a heroin overdose at his apartment in Paris, France, on May 20, 2023. He

reportedly has been dead for over a month before his discovery. He was 60. He was born Christian Aaron Passgen in Neuilly-sur-Seine, France, on August 11, 1962. His mother was German singer Nico and his father was French actor Alain Delon, but he denied paternity. He was raised by his mother until he was adopted by Delon's mother and second husband, Edith and Paul Boulogne. He appeared with his mother in Philippe Garrel's 1972 surrealist film "The Inner Scar". He also worked as a model and was featured in the films "L'Enfant Secret" (1979), "Mixed Blood" (1984), "Nico Icon" (1995), "La Repentie" (2002), "Nathalie..." (2003), and "Pas Sages" (2004). He was frequently billed under the name Ari Paffgen. He worked as a photographer after he quit acting. Boulogne's memoir, "Love

Never Forgets", was published in 2001. He is survived by two children, Charles and Blanche.

Bowes, Richard

Science fiction writer Richard Bowes died in Massachusetts on December 24, 2023. He was 79. Bowes was born in Boston, Massachusetts, on January 8, 1944. He graduated from Hofstra University in Hempstead, New York,

in 1965 and moved to New York City. He worked at various jobs including writing fashion copy, designing board games, and serving as a librarian at New York University. His debut novel, "Warchild", was published in 1986 and was followed by the sequel, "Goblin Market", in 1988. Bowes wrote the 1987 fantasy novel "Feral Cell". His other works include "Minions of the Moon" (1999), "From the Files of the Time Rangers" (2005), and "Dusty Devil on a Quiet Street" (2013). He penned numerous works of short fiction with many appearing in the pages of "The Magazine of Fantasy & Science Fiction". He received the World Fantasy Award for his novellas "If Angels Fight" (2008) and "Streetcar Dreams" (1997). Many of his stories appeared in the collections "Transfigured Night and Other Stories" (2001), "Streetcar Dreams and Other Midnight Fancies" (2006), "The Queen, the Cambion, and Seven Others" (2013), and "If Angels Fight: Stories" (2013).

Bradley, Brian

Actor and comedian Brian Bradley died in Orlando, Florida, on March 31, 2023. He was 68. Bradley was born near Philadelphia, Pennsylvania, on October 19, 1954, and moved to

Florida with his family as a child. He graduated from the University of Florida before moving to Los Angeles in the 1970s. He began his career as a comic performing with the Comedy Store Players and appeared on television in A&E's "Comedy on the Road" and Showtime's "Comedy Club Network". Bradley was also seen on television in episodes of "We Got It Made", "That Was the Week That Was", "The Twilight Zone", "Amazing Stories", "Nine to Five", "It's a Living", "Parker Lewis Can't Lose", "Seinfeld" as Jerry's butler, and "Angel". He appeared in the 1987 television special "Jonathan Winters: On the Ledge" and the 1991 unsold pilot "Lookwell" starring Adam West. He performed on Broadway as Vince Fontaine in the 1994 revival of "Grease". Bradley subsequently performed with an improv troupe at Disney World's Comedy Warehouse for nearly a decade. He also spent several years performing aboard cruise ships with Holland America.

Bradley, Jerry

Music executive Jerry Bradley, who was head of RCA Records in Nashville from 1973 to 1982, died in Mount Juliet, Tennessee, on July 17, 2023. He  was 83. Bradley was born in Nashville, Tennessee, on January 30, 1940. He was the son of musician and record producer Owen Bradley. He served for two years in the U.S. Army after graduating high school. He began working for his father's recording studio, known as the Bradley Barn, after his discharge. He became a staff assistant to Chet Atkins at RCA Nashville in 1970. He succeeded Atkins as head of RCA Nashville when he stepped down for health reasons in 1973. Bradley was instrumental in furthering the careers of such country artists as Ronnie Milsap, Dolly Parton, Charley Pride, and Alabama. His 1976 album, "Wanted! The Outlaws", featured previously recorded songs of Willie Nelson, Waylon Jennings, Jessie Colter, and Tompall Glaser. It became the first certified platinum country music album. RCA Nashville also released such later Elvis Presley songs as "Moody Blue", "Way Down", and "Guitar Man". Bradley left RCA Records in 1982 and became head of Opryland Music Group in 1985. He retired in 2004 when Sony Music Group purchased the label. He was inducted into the Country Music Hall of Fame in 2019. Bradley married Gwynn Hastings in 1963 and they later divorced. He is survived by their son Clay and daughter Leigh. He was married to Connie Bradley from 1979 until her death in 2021.

Braugher, Andre

Actor Andre Braugher, who starred as Detective Frank Pembleton in the television series "Homicide: Life on the Street" from 1993 to 1998 and was Captain Raymond Holt on the comedy police series  "Brooklyn Nine-Nine" from 1993 to 2022, died after a brief illness on December 11, 2023. He was 61. Braugher was born in Chicago, Illinois, on July 1, 1962. He began acting while attending Stanford University and graduated with a degree in theater in 1984. He subsequently attended Juilliard School's Drama Division, where he graduated in 1988. Braugher appeared frequently on stage with roles in Shakespeare in the Park productions of "Much Ado About Nothing" (1988), "King John" (1988), "Twelfth Night" (1989), and "Measure for Measure" (1993). His other off-Broadway credits include the plays "Coriolanus" (1989), "The Tragedy of Richard II" (1994), "Henry V" (1996) earning an Obie Award for his role as King Henry V, "Hamlet" (2008) as Claudius, "The Whipping Man" (2011), and "As You Like It" (2012). He made his film debut in the 1989 Civil War drama "Glory" as Cpl. Thomas Searles. Braugher was featured as Detective Winston Blake with Telly Savalas' Theo Kojak in the tele-films "Kojak: Ariana" (1989), "Kojak: Fatal Flaw" (1989), "Kojak: Flowers for Matty" (1990), "Kojak: It's Always Something" (1990), and "Kojak: None Are So Blind" (1990). He was also seen in the tele-films and mini-series "Murder in Mississippi" (1990), "Somebody Has to Shoot the Picture" (1990), "The Court-Martial of Jackie Robinson" (1990), "Class of '61" (1993), "Without Warning: Terror in the Towers" (1998), "The Tuskegee Airmen" (1995) receiving an Emmy Award nomination for his role as Benjamin O. Davis, "Passing Glory" (1999), "Love Song" (1999) also directing a segment, "10,000 Black Men Named George" (2002) as A. Philip Randolph, "Soldier's Girl" (2003), Stephen King's "Salem's Lot" (2004) as Matt Burke, "Thief" (2006) winning an Emmy Award for his role as Nick Atwater, and "The Andromeda Strain" (2008) as General George W. Mancheck. Braugher starred as Detective Frank Pembleton in the crime series "Homicide: Life on the Street" from 1993 to 1998, earning an Emmy nomination in 1996 and winning the Emmy in 1998. He reprised the role in an episode of "Law & Order" and the 2000 tele-film "Homicide: The Movie". He starred as Dr. Ben Gideon in the medical series "Gideon's Crossing" from 2000 to 2001, receiving another Emmy nomination. He also appeared in the role in a crossover episode of "The Practice". He was Detective Marcellus Washington in the series "Hack" from 2002 to 2004 and appeared in episodes of "The Jury", "Miami Medical", "Men of a Certain Age" from 2009 to 2011 receiving two more Emmy nominations for his role as Owen Thoreau Jr., "House" in the recurring role of psychiatrist Dr. Darryl Nolan from 2009 to 2012, "Law & Order: Special Victims Unit" in the recurring role of Defense Attorney Bayard Ellis from 2011 to 2015, the military drama "Last Resort" as Captain Marcus Chaplin from 2012 to 2013, "American Experience", and "The Good Fight" as Ri'Chard Lane in 2022. Braugher starred as Captain Raymond Holt in the comedy cop series "Brooklyn Nine-Nine" from 2013 to 2021. He earned four additional Emmy nominations for his work in the series and appeared in a cameo as Holt in an episode of "New Girl". He was a voice actor in the animated series "Happily Ever After: Fairy Tales for Every Child", "Jackie Chan Adventures" as Derge from 2000 to 2001, "Axe Cop", and "BoJack Horseman" in the recurring voice role of Woodchuck Coodchuck-Berkowitz in 2017. He was seen in numerous films including "Striking Distance" (1993), "Primal Fear" (1996), Spike Lee's "Get on the Bus" (1996), "City of Angels" (1998) as the angel Cassiel, "Thick as Thieves" (1999), "All the Rage" (1999), the science fiction thriller "Frequency" (2000) as Satch DeLeon, "Duets" (2000), "A Better Way to Die" (2000), "Poseidon" (2006) as Captain Bradford, "Live!" (2007), the horror film "The Mist" (2007) as Brent Norton, "Fantastic Four: Rise of the Silver Surfer" (2007) as General Hager, "Passengers" (2008), the animated "Superman/Batman: Apocalypse" (2010) as the voice of Darkseid, "Salt" (2010), "The Baytown Outlaws" (2012), "The Gambler" (2014), "Emily & Tim" (2015), the animated "Spirit Untamed" (2021) as the voice of Al Granger, and "She Said" (2022). Braugher married actress Ami Brabson in 1991 and she was featured as his character's wife, Mary Whelan

Pembleton, on the series "Homicide: Life on the Street". He is survived by his wife and three sons, Michael, Isaiah, and John Wesley.

Bredin, Patricia

British actress and singer Patricia Bredin died in Nova Scotia, Canada, on August 13, 2023. She was 88. Bredin was born in Hull, East Riding of Yorkshire, England, on February  14, 1935. She began her career as a singer and was the United Kingdom's first representative to the Eurovision Song Contest in 1957. She placed seventh in the competition with her rendition of the song "All". Bredin appeared on stage in the 1957 musical "Free as Air". She appeared in a handful of films including "Left Right and Centre" (1959), "The Bridal Path" (1959), "Make Mine a Million" (1959), "Desert Mice" (1959), "The Secret of Monte Cristo" (1961), and "To Have and to Hold" (1963). Bredin was seen on television in productions of "Samson by Moonshine" (1964), "Ninety Years On" (1964), and "Titi-Pu" (1967). Her other television credits include episodes of "Ivanhoe", "Charlie Drake", "Juke Box Jury", and "The Edgar Wallace Mystery Theatre". Her memoirs about her life as a cattle breeder after her second marriage, "My Fling on the Farm", was published in 1989. Bredin was married to Welsh singer Ivor Emmanuel from 1964 until their divorce in 1966. She married Canadian businessman Charles MacCulloch in 1979 and he died on their honeymoon.

Breedlove, Nashawn

Rapper Nashawn Breedlove, who was featured as Lotto in the 2002 film "8 Mile" starring Eminem, died in his  sleep of an overdose of alcohol and drugs at his home in Newark, New Jersey, on September 24, 2023. He was 46. Breedlove was born in Newark on February 17, 1977. He was a rapper who was known by the name Ox. He contributed to the soundtrack for the 2001 comedy film "The Wash". Breedlove was featured as rapper Lotto, a member of The Free World rap group and rival to Eminem's character in the 2002 film "8 Mile". He and Eminem face down in a battle rap near the films end.

Bridger, Grant

New Zealand actor Grant Bridger died in Devonport, New Zealand, on March 7, 2023. He was 75. Bridger was born in Wellington, New Zealand, in 1947. He began his career as a radio disc jockey. he later performed as a singer and released several singles. He appeared on television from the mid-1970s with roles in episodes of "A Going Concern", "Fuller's Earth", "Radio Waves" as Win Savage in 1978, "Gather Your Dreams"

as Lester Lovegrove in 1978, "Heroes", "The Ray Bradbury Theater", "High Tide", "Hercules: The Legendary Journeys", "Xena: Warrior Princess", "Cleopatra 2525", "Revelations: The  Initial Journey", and "Shortland Street". His other television credits include productions of "Which Way Home" (1991), "The Rainbow Warrior" (1993), "Hercules in the Underworld" (1994), and "Atomic Twister" (2002). Bridger was featured in several films including "Merry Christmas Mr. Lawrence" (1983), "Second Time Lucky" (1984), "Jubilee" (2000), "Treasure Island Kids: The Monster of Treasure Island" (2006), and "We're Here to Help" (2007). Bridger performed frequently on stage during his career in stage musicals and wrote 2019's "Petty Crime".

Bridges, Rand

Actor Rand Bridges died of complications from Parkinson's disease in Cookeville, Tennessee, on March 24,  2023. He was 81. Bridges was born in Clarendon Hills, Illinois, on January 19, 1942. He began his career on stage and appeared frequently in regional theater. He appeared on Broadway in productions of "Major Barbara" (1980) and "Macbeth" (1982). Bridges appeared in several films including "Phantom of the Paradise" (1974) and "Doc Savage: The Man of Bronze" (1975). He was featured in the tele-films "Black Bart" (1975) and "Young Pioneers' Christmas" (1976), and episodes of "Gunsmoke", "Karen", "Harry O", and "Greatest Heroes of the Bible". Bridges' survivors include his wife of 36 years, Giulia Pagano.

Brink, Aaron

Mixed-martial artist Aaron Brink, who also performed in adult films under the name Dick Delaware, died of pancreatic cancer in El Cajon, California, on May 26, 2023. He was 48.  Brink was born in Newport Beach, California, on November 12, 1974. He was expelled from high school and had numerous arrests as a juvenile. He was incarcerated for smuggling marijuana from Mexico in the late 1990s where he began training on a heavy bag. He entered mixed martial arts after his release from prison. He fought in 58 matches during his career with 29 wins, 27 losses, and 2 no contests. He competed in the promotions King of the Cage, RINGS, World Extreme Cagefighting, and Gladiator Challenge. He lost a bout with

Andrei Arlovski in the UFC in 2000. His last match was in June of 2019 with a win over Cody Sons at the California Cage Wars. Brink entered the adult film business in the early 2000s under the name Dick Delaware. He appeared in hundreds of adult films and videos over the next decade including "Not Just Another 8 Teen Movie" (2003), "Erotique" (2003), "Hellcats" (2003), "Oops... You Took My Innocence" (2003), "Mystified" (2003), "Sleeping with Sin" (2003), "Grand Theft Anal" (2003), "18 and Lost in Detroit" (2004), "Twisted Cheerleader Tryouts" (2003), "Candy Store Coeds" (2003), "Dominating Baby Dolls" (2003), "The Masseuse" (2003), "Reality Teens Gone Crazy" (2003), "Beverly Hills Dolls" (2004), "The Sex Therapist" (2004), "Blonde Ambition" (2004), "The Evil Vault" (2004), "Sex in the Sun" (2004), "Wife Swappers" (2004), "The Maintenance Girls" (2004), "As Nasty As It Gets" (2005), "Sweet Lolita" (2005), "Gigi" (2005), "Women's Pen" (2005), "Valley Vixens" (2005), "How the West Was Hung" (2006), "My Happy Ending" (2006), "Frosty Finish" (2006), "Double Bubble" (2006), "Nurse Nasty" (2007), "Cheating Housewives" (2007), "Boobzilla" (2007), "Paris Behind Bars" (2007), "Don't 'Cha Wish Your Girlfriend Was Hot Like Her?" (2007), "Cougar Hunt" (2007), "Nurse Devon" (2007), "A Thorn in My Ass" (2007), "Porn Valley P.T.A." (2007), "Farmer's Daughter" (2007), "Chubby Chasers" (2007), "Boobzilla 3" (2008), "Stimulus Package" (2008), "In the Army Now" (2009), "Spider-Man XXX: A Porn Parody" (2011) as Electro, "Family Guy: The XXX Parody" (2012), "This Ain't Terminator XXX" (2013), and "Thor XXX: A Axel Braun Parody (2013). His problems with drug addiction led to an appearance on the television series "Intervention". Brink was married to Laura Voepel from 1999 until their divorce in 2001. He married fellow adult performer Cassandra Cruz in 2007. They later divorced after appearing in an episode of the television series "Divorce Court" in 2011. His son by his first marriage, Anderson Lee Aldrich, who was originally named Nicholas Franklin Brink, entered Club Q, an LGBTQ bar in Colorado Springs, in November of 2022 and opened fire with a semi-automatic rifle. Five people were killed and 17 were wounded before he was subdued by patrons. He was tried and convicted of the shootings and sentenced to life in prison.

Briscoe, Jay

Professional wrestler Jamin Dale Pugh, who teamed with his brother Mark as the Briscoe Brothers, died in an

automobile accident in Laurel, Delaware, on January 17, 2023. He was 38. Another car driving in the opposite lane crossed the center line and struck Pugh's vehicle head on. The driver of the other vehicle was also killed, and Pugh's two young daughters were severely injured. They were released from the hospital after a month. Pugh was born in Salisbury, Maryland, on January 25, 1984. He began his career in his teens wrestling with younger brother Mark in the East

Coast Wrestling Association in Delaware in 2000. They debuted as the Briscoe Brothers with Combat Zone Wrestling (CZW) in 2001. They briefly captured the CZW tag championship in 2001 and worked as the Midnight Outlaws in the promotion over the next year. The brothers wrestled frequently with Jersey All Pro Wrestling in the 2000s. Jay wrestled in singles and tag matches with the promotion and teamed with Insane Dragon to capture the JAPW tag championship in 2002. The Briscoe Brothers were best known for their time with Ring of Honor (ROH), losing title matches to AJ Styles and Amazing Red in 2003. They held the tag team title there during the year, feuding with Samoa Joe, Bryan Danielson, and Jerry Lynn before losing the belts to CM Punk and Colt Cabana. They returned to ROH in 2006 where they battled Austin Aries and Roderick Strong for the tag belts. They also became enforcers for Jim Cornette's role as ROH Commissioner. They were again ROH tag champions, beating Christopher Daniels and Matt Sydal in February of 2007. They lost the belts in their first title defense soon after to Naruki Doi and Shingo Takagi. They soon recaptured the belts in a rematch and Jay teamed with Erick Stevens when Mark was injured. They reunited to lose the titles to Jimmy Jacobs and Tyler Black in December of 2007, but recaptured the belts the following April, beating Davey Richards and Rocky Romero. Another injury kept Mark out of action for a while and Jay teamed with Austin Aires. The tag championship was declared vacant in May of 2008. The Briscoes regained the titles in December of 2009 after Mark resumed wrestling. They defeated Davey Richards and Eddie Edwards but again lost the belts in April of 2010 to Claudio Castagnoli and Chris Hero. They earned their seventh victory for the ROH tag championship, defeating Charlie Haas and Shelton Benjamin in December of 2011. They lost a rematch in May of 2012 but regained the belts in a three-way match the following December. They were defeated for the titles by Bobby Fish and Kyle O'Reilly in March of 2013. Jay Brisco became the ROH World Champion in a battle against Kevin Steen in April of 2013. He defeated Adam Cole, Matt Hardy, and brother Mark for the title before being stripped of the championship in July of 2013. Jay defeated Michael Elgin to again become ROH champion in September of 2014. He was defeated by Jay Lethal for the belt in June of 2015. Jay and Mark were again crowned tag champions after defeating Alex Shelley and Chris Sabin, the Motor City Machine Guns, in March of 2018. The Briscoes also competed with New Japan Pro-Wrestling from 2016 to 2019 and Impact Wrestling in 2022. The brothers were inducted into the ROH Hall of Fame in March of 2022. They defeated Cash Wheeler and Dax Harwood (FTR) to claim their final ROH World Tag Team Championship in December of 2022. Pugh married Ashley Crothers in 2008 and is survived by her and their three children.

Brodeur, Paul

Author Paul Brodeur, whose novel was adapted for the 1980 film "The Stunt Man", died of complications from pneumonia and hip replacement surgery at a hospital in Hyannis, Massachusetts, on August 2, 2023. He was 92. Brodeur was born in Boston, Massachusetts, on May 16, 1931.

He graduated from Harvard College in 1953. He served in the U.S. Army as part of the Counterintelligence Corps in West Germany after college. He spent a year in Paris after his discharge where he wrote the short story "The Sick Fox", which was published in "The New Yorker" in 1957. He joined the magazine's staff the following year and was a reporter for the Talk of the Town segment. Brodeur's novel "The Stunt Man" was published in 1970 and was adapted for a film starring Peter O'Toole and Steve Railsback in 1980. His 1968 article "The Magic Mineral" brought national attention to the health problems caused by asbestos. He continued to research and write about the hazards of asbestos over the next two decades. He also wrote cautionary articles about the depletion of the ozone layer, the hazards of microwave radiation, and the electromagnetic fields generated from power lines. Brodeur retired from "The New Yorker" in the mid-1990s. His memoirs, "Secrets: A Writer in the Cold War", was published in 1997. He married Malabar Schleiter in 1960 and they later divorced. He is survived by their son, Stephen Brodeur, and daughter, author Adrienne Brodeur. He was also married and divorced from Margaret Staats. His third wife, Milane Christiansen, died in 2013.

Brook, Apple

British actress Apple Brook died in England on January 6, 2023. She was 91. She was born Anita Burman in Leeds, England, on January 20, 1931. She moved to London in the late 1940s and studied acting at the Joan Collins Drama Academy. She began performing on stage in repertory and appeared frequently with the Unity Theatre. She was featured as Charlotte in the premiere of Lionel Bart's "Oliver!" in the West End in 1960. She also performed as a comedian on the cabaret stage. Brook appeared frequently on television from the late 1950s with roles in episodes of "Charlesworth", "Winning Widows", "The Wednesday Play", "The Further Adventures of the Musketeers", "Life with Cooper", "Z Cars", "Cranford", "Within These Walls", "Midnight Is a Place", "London's Burning", "The Robinsons", "Blessed", "No Signal", "Life of Riley", "Dani's Castle", "Benidorm", "Patrick Melrose", "Doctors", "Cuckoo", and "Andor" (2022). Her other television credits include productions of "North and South" (1966), "Wives and Daughters" (1971), and "The Miser" (1988). Brook appeared in several films during her career including "Half a Sixpence" (1967), "The Colour of Funny" (1999), and "Harry Potter and the Order of the Phoenix" (2007) as Professor Wilhelmina Grubly-Plank. She also appeared in the shorts "Little Red and the Wolfe" (2014) as Grandma Hood and "A Sea of Change" (2015). She is survived by a daughter, Melanie.

Brown, Al

Actor Al Brown died of complications from Alzheimer's disease at his home in Las Vegas, Nevada, on January 13, 2023. He was 83. Brown was born in Reading, Pennsylvania, in 1939. He studied English and theater at Dennison University in Ohio. He began working in construction after his marriage in 1961 and later earned a college degree from La Salle University in Philadelphia in 1964. He subsequently served six years of active duty with the U.S. Air Force, including two tours in Vietnam. He retired from the U.S. Air Force Reserves in 1992. He and his family moved to Doylestown, Pennsylvania, in 1972 where he worked for pharmaceutical companies. He began performing on stage with the local State Street Players in 1978. He moved to the Washington, D.C., area in the 1990s where he worked with the Environmental Protection Agency until his retirement in 2003. Brown also began pursuing an acting career with roles in the films "12 Monkeys" (1995), "Liberty Heights" (1999), "The Replacements" (2000), "Red Dragon" (2002), and "Play the Favorite" (2012). He appeared on television in episodes of "Homicide: Life on the Street", "The F.B.I. Files", "Forensic Files", "Rescue Me", "Commander in Chief", "Law & Order: Special Victims Unit", "The Hustler", and "Maron". He was best known for his role as Baltimore City Police Major Stan Valchek in the series "The Wire" from 2002 to 2008. He was seen in the tele-films "The Adversaries" (1998), "Shot in the Heart" (2001), "Something the Lord Made" (2004), and "Sunset Bar" (2012). Brown was married to Barbara Eberz from 1961 until their divorce in 1990 and is survived by their two sons and daughter. He subsequently married Janet Newhart who also survives him.

Brown, Eric

British science fiction writer Eric Brown died of sepsis and complications from non-Hodgkin lymphoma in England on March 21, 2023. He was 62. Brown was born in Haworth, Yorkshire, England, on May 24, 1960. His first publication, the children's play "Noel's Ark", was published in 1982. He wrote numerous short stories for "Interzone" magazine later in the decade. His first novel, "Meridian Days of Pan", was published in 1992. His other novels include "Engineman" (1994), "Penumbra" (1999), "Helix" (2007), "Kethani" (2008), "Guardians of the Phoenix" (2010), "The Kings of Eternity" (2011), "Helix Wars" (2012), and "Serene

Invasion" (2013). His "Virex" trilogy included "New York Nights" (2000), "New York Blues" (2001), and "New York Dreams" (2004). His 2004 novel "Bengal Station" was followed by the trilogy that included "Necropath" (2009), "Xenopath" (2010), and "Cosmopath" (2010). Brown also wrote the "Weird Space" trilogy including "The Devil's Nebula" (2012), "Satan's Reach" (2013), and "The Baba Yaga" (2015). He wrote the "Langham and Dupre" mystery series that included "Murder by the Book" (2013), "Murder at the Chase" (2014), "Murder at the Loch" (2016), "Murder Take Three" (2017), "Murder Takes a Turn" (2018), "Murder Served Cold" (2018), "Murder by Numbers" (2020), "Murder at Standing Stone Manor" (2021), and "Murder Most Vile" (2022). He was the author of numerous children's books and short-story collections. Brown was the science fiction reviewer for the "Guardian" newspaper for many years. He is survived by his wife, Finn, and daughter Freya.

Brown, George 'Funky'

Drummer George 'Funky' Brown, who was a founding member of the band Kool & The Gang, died of lung cancer in Los Angeles, California, on November 16, 2023. He

was 74. Brown was born in Jersey City, New Jersey, on January 15, 1949. He began performing in a jazz band with future Kool bandmates keyboardist Ricky West, saxophonist Robert 'Kool' Bell, and trumpeter Robert Mickens while in high school. They were joined by Bell's brother, Ronald, on keyboards, Dennis 'D.T.' Thomas on saxophone, and Charles Smith on guitar for the music group the Jazziacs in the early 1960s. They performed in New York City under various names before becoming Kool & the Gang in 1968. They released their self-named debut album in 1970. They scored major hits with the songs "Jungle Boogie" and "Hollywood Swinging" from their fourth album, "Wild and Peaceful" in 1973. Brown wrote many of the band's hits including "Celebration", "Ladies Night", "Jungle Boogie", "Get Down on It", and "Too Hot". Kool & the Gang were given a star on the Hollywood Walk of Fame in 2015. He continued to perform and record with the band throughout his life and produced their 2023 album "People Just Wanna Have Fun". Brown was inducted into the Songwriters Hall of Fame in 2018. His memoir, "Too Hot: Kool & the Gang & Me", was released earlier in 2023. He is survived by his wife, Hanh Brown, and five children.

Brown, Jim

Football player turned actor Jim Brown, who starred as one of "The Dirty Dozen" in the 1967 World War II film, died at his home in Los Angeles, California, on May 18, 2023. He was 87. He was born on St. Simons Island, Georgia, on February 17, 1936. He was initially raised by his grandmother and moved to Manhasset, New York, to live with his mother at age eight. He played football, lacrosse, baseball, basketball, and ran track while attending high school. He continued to excel in sports when he entered Syracuse University in 1953, where he became a leading football star. He was drafted by the Cleveland Browns in the 1957 NFL draft. He was considered to be one of the greatest football running backs of all time while playing with the Browns through 1965. He led the league in rushing yards for eight of his nine seasons and won an NFL championship with the team in 1964. He made his film debut in the 1964 western film "Rio Conchos". He left football to concentrate on his acting career and starred as convict Robert

T. Jefferson who is sent on a suicide mission behind enemy lines in the World War II drama "The Dirty Dozen" in 1967. He continued to appear in such films as "Dark of the Sun" (1968), "Kenner" (1968), the espionage film "Ice Station Zebra" (1968) starring Rock Hudson, "The Split" (1968), "Riot" (1969), the western "100 Rifles" (1969) in an early interracial film romance with Raquel Welch, "...tick...tick...tick..." (1970), "The Grasshopper" (1970), "El Condor" (1970), the blaxploitation classic "Slaughter" (1972) in the title role, "The Slams" (1973), "I Escaped from Devil's Island" (1973), "Three the Hard Way" (1974), "Take a Hard Ride" (1975), "Vengeance" (1976), "Fingers" (1978), "Pacific Inferno" (1979) also serving as executive producer , "One Down, Two to Go" (1982), "The Running Man" (1987) as Fireball opposite Arnold Schwarzenegger, "I'm Gonna Git You Sucka" (1988), "Killing American Style" (1988), "L.A. Heat" (1989), "Crack House" (1989), "Twisted Justice" (1990), "Original Gangstas" (1996), Tim Burton's science fiction film "Mars Attacks!" (1996) as Byron Williams, "He Got Game" (1998), "Small Soldiers" (1998) as the voice of Butch Meathook, "Any Given Sunday" (1999), "New Jersey Turnpikes" (1999), "On the Edge" (2002), "She Hate Me" (2004), "Dream Street" (2010), and "Draft Day" (2014). Brown appeared on television in episodes of "Valentine's Day", "I Spy", "Police Story", "CHiPs", "Knight Rider", "T.J. Hooker", "Cover Up", "Lady Blue", "The A-Team", "Good Sports", "Living Single", "Between Brothers", "Arli$$", and "Soul Food" as Willie White in 2004. He was also seen in the tele-films "Hammer, Slammer & Slade" (1990), "Sucker Free City" (2004), and "Sideliners" (2006). Brown appeared on television in the talk and variety shows "The Ed Sullivan Show", "The Milton Berle Show", "The Woody Woodbury Show", "Pat Boone in Hollywood", "The Beautiful Phyllis Diller Show", "Playboy After Dark", "The Joey Bishop Show", "Philbin's People", "The David Frost Show", "The Merv Griffin Shoe", "The Dean Martin Show", "The Dick Cavett Show", "The Mike Douglas Show", "The Sonny and Cher Comedy Hour", "Flip", "The Tonight Show Starring Johnny Carson", "Soul Train", "The Bob Braun Show", "Jerry Lewis MDA Labor Day Telethon", "The Hollywood Squares", "Later with Bob Costas", "The Arsenio Hall Show", "Charlie

Rose", "The Tonight Show with Jay Leno", "Larry King Live", "The Late Show with Stephen Colbert", "The James Brown Show", "Fox and Friends", and "PoliticsNation with Al Sharpton". He was active in the civil rights movement from the 1950s. He was founder of the Black Economic Union in 1966. Brown's activism earned him and the organizations he supported investigation by the Federal Bureau of Investigation in an attempt to damage his reputation. He was a nude centerfold for "Playgirl" magazine in September of 1974. He became a color analyst for NFL telecasts on CBS in 1978. He served as a color commentator for six fights for the Ultimate Fighting Championship in 1993. Brown was arrested several times for assaults against women from the 1960s. He was charged with making terroristic threats against his wife Monique in 1999 and was sentenced to three years' probation, counseling, and community service. He served three months in jail in 2002 after failing to follow the terms of his probation. Brown was inducted into the Pro Football Hall of Fame in 1971 and the College Football Hall of Fame in 1995. He was also inducted into the National Lacrosse Hall of Fame in 1983. He co-authored his autobiographies "Off My Chest" (1964) and "Out of Bounds" (1989) and was the subject of the books "Jim Brown: The Fierce Life of an American Hero" (2006) by Mike Freeman and "Jim: The Author's Self-Centered Memoir on the Great Jim Brown" (2009) by James Toback. Brown was portrayed by Aldis Hodge in the 2020 film "One Night in Miami...". He married Sue Jones in 1959 and they had three children. They separated in 1968 and divorced in 1972. He married Monique Brown in 1997 and they had two children together. He is survived by his wife and five children.

Brown, Les, Jr.

Actor and musician Les Brown, Jr., died of cancer at his home in Branson, Missouri, on January 9, 2023. He was 82.

Brown was born in New York City on February 15, 1940. He was the son of band leader Les Brown who was leader of Les Brown and His Band of Renown. Les Jr. worked as an actor in the 1960s, appearing on television in episodes of "The Many Loves of Dobie Gillis", "Death Valley Days", "The Gertrude Berg Show", "Fair Exchange", "Ensign O'Toole", "My Three Sons", "The Lieutenant", "My Great Adventure", "Profiles in Courage", the comedy series "The Baileys of Balboa" as Jim Bailey from 1964 to 1965, the soap opera "The Young Marrieds" as Buzz Coleman in 1965, "Gilligan's Island", "Gunsmoke", "The Patty Duke Show", "F Troop", "12 O'Clock High", "The Lucy Show", "Green Acres", "Police Story", and "Lassie". He was also seen in the films "The Nutty Professor" (1963) and "Wild Wild Winter" (1966). He was also a rock musician with the Rockin' Foo band from 1969 to 1970 and was a producer and promoter for numerous music artists including Merle Haggard, Shirley Jones, Loretta Lynn, and the Lettermen. Les Jr. took over as

leader of Les Brown and His Band of Renown following his father's death in 2001. He continued to perform around the world and led a regular big band show in Branson, Missouri. He was host of a national radio show on the Music of Your Life network. Brown is survived by his wife of 21 years, Alexa Brown, and two children.

Brown, Pete

British lyricist Pete Brown, who co-wrote the Cream songs "Sunshine of Your Love" and "White Room", died of cancer in Hastings, Sussex, England, on May 19, 2023. He was 82. Brown was born in Ashtead, Surrey, England, on December

25, 1940. He began writing poetry in his teens and became a part of the beat poetry scene in Liverpool in the 1960s. He frequently teamed with Michael Horovitz writing poetry and reciting together. He and Horovitz performed with the musical group the New Departures. Brown later formed the First Real Poetry Band and was soon writing for the band Cream. He initially wrote with the band's drummer, Ginger Baker, before joining with bassist Jack Bruce. The duo penned many of Cream's best-known hits including "I Feel Free", "White Room", and "SWLABR". They joined with Eric Clapton to write the 1967 song "Sunshine of Your Love". Brown wrote the lyrics for most of Bruce's solo albums after Cream disbanded. He recorded the albums "A Mean You Can Shake Hands with in the Dark" and "Mantlepiece" with the band Pete Brown and His Battered Ornaments in 1969. He formed the band Piblokto!, the Inuit word for arctic hysteria, after being dismissed from the Battered Ornaments. They performed and recorded with various line-ups from 1969 to 1971. They recorded the albums "Things May Come and Things May Go but the Art School Dance Goes on Forever" and "Thousands on a Raft" in 1970. He recorded the album "Two Heads Are Better Than One" with Graham Bond in 1972. He worked with the bands Brown and Friends, Flying Tigers, and Back to the Front before leaving music in 1977. He wrote the script for the 1989 animated film "Felix the Cat: The Movie". Brown collaborated with Phil Ryan for over a decade. They formed the Interoceter label and released the 2003 albums "Ardours of the Lost Rake" and "Coals to Jerusalem". Brown and Ryan released the album "Road to Cobras" in 2010. His autobiography, "White Rooms & Imaginary Westerns: On the Road with Ginsberg, Writing for Clapton and Cream — An Anarchic Odyssey", was published in 2010. He released a new volume of poetry, "Mundane Tuesday and Freudian Saturday", in 2016. He teamed with Gary Brooker to write lyrics for Procol Harum's final album, "Novum", in 2017. Brown is survived by his wife, actress Sheridan MacDonald, and his daughter, Jessica, from a previous relationship.

Browne, Chris

Cartoonist Chris Browne, who took over the comic strip "Hagar the Horrible" from his father Dik Browne in 1989, died in Sioux Falls, South Dakota, on February 5, 2023. He was 70. Browne was born in South Orange, New Jersey, on May

16, 1952. He assisted his father on the "Hagar the Horrible" and "Hi and Lois" comic strips in his youth. He as co-author of the 1985 publication "Hagar the Horrible's Very Nearly Complete Viking Handbook". He took over the Hagar strip after his father's death in 1989. His brother, Chance Browne, took over the "Hi and Lois" strip. Browne also created the short-lived autobiographical strips "Chris Browne's Comic Strip" from 1993 to 1994 and "Raising Duncan" from 2000 to 2004. He worked with artist Garry Hallgren on "Hagar" from 2005 until his death. He was author of the illustrated children's book "The Monster Who Ate the State" in 2015. He was predeceased by his wife, Carroll Browne.

Browning, Ricou

Actor, stuntman, and underwater cinematographer Ricou Browning, who starred as the title Gill-man in underwater scenes in the 1954 Universal horror film classic "Creature from the Black Lagoon", died at his home in

Southwest Ranches, Florida, on February 27, 2023. He was 93. Browning was born in Fort Pierce, Florida, on February 16, 1930. He attended Florida State University before taking a job at Wakulla Springs as an underwater performer in the late 1940s. He also appeared in underwater newsreels filmed by Newt Perry. Browning was tasked with assisting a Hollywood film scouting crew looking for locations in 1953. He was soon asked to don the costume of the Gill-man in 1954's "Creature from the Black Lagoon". He portrayed the Creature in underwater sequences while Ben Chapman played him on land. Julie Adams starred as the love interest for both the monster and human leading men and Ginger Stanley was frequently Adams' stunt double for underwater sequences with Browning. He returned as the Creature for the sequel films "Revenge of the Creature" (1955) and "The Creature Walks Among Us" (1956). Browning was also a stunt diver for the 1954 Disney film "20,000 Leagues Under the Sea" and was Jerry Lewis' swimming double for "Don't Give Up the Ship" in 1959. He served as an underwater photography supervisor for the television series "Sea Hunt" starring Lloyd Bridges and was featured onscreen in an episode in 1958. He also supervised underwater sequences for "The Aquanauts" from 1960 to 1961. He worked with Ivan Tors' studio in Florida in the early 1960s and co-wrote and co-produced the 1963 film "Flipper" about an intelligent bottlenose dolphin. He was associate producer for the 1964 sequel "Flipper's New Adventure" and appeared onscreen as Dr. Burton. Browning also wrote and directed for the subsequent "Flipper" television series from 1964 to 1967. He was second unit director for underwater sequences for the 1965 James Bond film "Thunderball" and the films "Around the World Under the Sea" (1966), "Island of the Lost" (1967), "Daring Game" (1968), "Lady in Cement" (1968), and "Hello Down There" (1969). He directed episodes of the series "Gentle Ben" from 1967 to 1967 and "Primus" in 1971. Browning directed and co-wrote the 1973 film "Salty" with a friendly sea lion as the title character and directed episodes of the subsequent series from 1974 to 1975. He helmed the off-beat crime drama "Mr. No Legs" in 1978 and co-wrote the 1980 giant crab horror film "Island Claws". He directed underwater sequences for the 1970 tele-film "The Aquarians" and worked on the films "Lucky Lady" (1975), "Joe Panther" (1976), "Hot Stuff" (1979), "Raise the Titanic" (1980), "Caddyshack" (1980), "Nobody's Perfekt" (1981), "Never Say Never Again" (1983), "The Heavenly Kid" (1985), "Opposing Force" (1986), and "Police Academy 5: Assignment: Miami Beach" (1988). He was credited with the story for the 1996 "Flipper" remake. His wife of over forty years, Fran Browning, died in March of 2020. He is survived by two sons, Ricou Browning, Jr., who also works as an underwater actor and stuntman, and Kelly Browning, and two daughters, Renee and Kim.

Brubaker, James D.

Film producer James D. Brubaker died of

complications from several strokes at his home in Beverly Hills, California, on January 3, 2023. He was 85. Brubaker was born in Los Angeles, California, on March 30, 1937. He attended California State University in Los Angeles before serving in the U.S. Army. He began working in films with the Teamsters delivering horses to John Wayne's 1971 film "Big Jake". He was a driver and transportation coordinator throughout the 1970s on such films as "Diamonds Are Forever" (1971), "Harold and Maude" (1971), "Lady Sings the Blues" (1972), "Thumb Tripping" (1972), "Up the Sandbox" (1972), "Walking Tall" (1973), "Cahill U.S. Marshal" (1973), "McQ" (1974), "The Godfather Part II" (1974), "Against a Crooked Sky" (1975), "Embryo" (1976), "Won Ton Ton, the Dog Who Saved Hollywood" (1976), "Nickelodeon" (1976), and "Capricorn One" (1977). Brubaker moved into production by the end of the decade, working on such films as "Comes a Horseman" (1978), "Uncle Joe Shannon" (1978), "Raging Bull" (1980), "True Confessions" (1981), "Rocky III" (1982), "Staying Alive" (1983), "The Right Stuff" (1983), "The Right Stuff" (1983), "Rhinestone" (1984), "Beer" (1985), "Rocky IV" (1985), "Cobra" (1986), "Over the Top" (1987), "Patty Hearst" (1988), "K-9" (1989), "Problem Child" (1990), "Brain Donors" (1992), "Mr. Baseball" (1992), "Above the Rim" (1994), "D2: The Mighty Ducks" (1994), "A Walk in the Clouds" (1995), "Liar

Liar" (1997), "Life" (1997) also appearing on screen as a judge, "Nutty Professor II: The Klumps" (2000) appearing on screen as a reporter, "F-Stops" (2001), "Her Majesty" (2001), "Dragonfly" (2002), "Bruce Almighty" (2003), "Turn Me on, Dead Man" (2009), "Jayne Mansfield's Car" (2012), "Standing Up" (2013), and "Chef" (2014). Brubaker was also producer for the tele-films "Running Mates" (1992) and "Gia" (1998) earning an Emmy Award nomination. Brubaker married Marcy Kelly in 1992 and is survived by her and their three children.

Brummel, David

Actor David Brummel died in Flagler Beach, Florida, on October 5, 2023. He was 80. Brummel was born in Brooklyn, New York, on November 1, 1942. He served in the U.S. Navy and ran a furniture business before pursuing a career on stage. He was an actor and singer in such Broadway musicals as "The Pajama Game" (1973), "Music Is" (1976), "Annie" (1977), "Oklahoma!" (1979), "Nine" (1982), "Bells Are Ringing" (2001), and "Sweet Smell of Success" (2002). Brummel was seen in the films "A Stranger Is Watching" (1982) and "Everyday People" (2004), and television episodes of "Third Watch" and "Law & Order".

Bruno, Betty Ann

Journalist Betty Ann Bruno, who appeared as a child Munchkin in the 1939 film "The Wizard of Oz", died of a heart attack in Sonoma, California, on July 30, 2023. She was 91. She was born Betty Ann Cain (Ka'ihilani) in Wahiawa, Hawaii, on October 1, 1931, and was raised in Hollywood. She appeared as a child in John Ford's 1937 film "The Hurricane". She and a handful of children joined over 100 little people as Munchkins in the 1939 film classic "The Wizard of Oz" starring Judy Garland. She later graduated from Stanford University and had a long career in local television. She worked with KTVU in the Bay Area from 1971 and reportedly earned three local new Emmy Awards. She began teaching hula after her retirement and founded the Hula Mai dance troupe. Bruno published the 2020 book "The Munchkin Diary: My Personal Yellow Brick Road". She appeared in an episode of "To Tell the Truth" in 2022 relating to her experiences as a Munchkin. She is survived by her husband craig Scheiner and their three children.

Brunson, Doyle

Professional poker player Doyle Brunson died in Las Vegas, Nevada, on May 14, 2023. He was 89. Brunson was born in Longworth, Texas, on August 10, 1933. He attended

Hardin-Simmons University in Abilene, Texas, graduating in 1954. He aspired to be a professional basketball player until a knee injury sidelined him. He began working in sales but was soon making more money playing poker. He left the company to become a professional card player. He played primarily in illegal games in Texas, Oklahoma, and Louisiana. Brunson moved to Las Vegas in the 1960s and was a regular player at the World Series of Poker since its start in 1970. He won the tournament in 1976 and 1977. He was author of the 1979 book on poker, "Super/System". A revised edition, "Super/System 2", was released in 2004. He also wrote the 1984 book "Poker Wisdom of a Champion". He was featured in cameo roles in the films "Lucky You" (2007) and "The Grand" (2007). He remained a leading competitor in poker, appearing in numerous televised events, until his retirement from tournament events in 2018. His winnings reportedly exceeded $6,000,000 during his career. Brunson married Louise Carter in 1962 and is survived by her and their son, Todd, who also plays poker professionally. Their daughter, Doyla, died in 1982.

Brustein, Robert

Theatrical critic and playwright Robert Brustein died at his home in Cambridge, Massachusetts, on October 29, 2023. He was 96. Brustein was born in New York City on April 21, 1927. He graduated from the High School of Music & Art and Amherst College, earning a degree in medieval history in 1948. He spent time in the Merchant Marine before continuing his education at the Yale School of Drama for a year. He earned a master's degree in dramatic literature from Columbia in 1950. He attended the University of Nottingham in England on a Fulbright fellowship before returning to Columbia to earn a Ph.D. in 1957. He taught at Cornell University, Vassar College, and Columbia in the 1950s and early 1960s. He became dean of the Yale School of Drama in 1966 and was founder of the Yale Repertory Theatre. He also served as artist director of the Yale Repertory during his tenure. He remained at Yale until 1979 when he became a professor at Harvard University. He was founder of the American Repertory Theater (ART) and the Institute for Advanced Theater Training. He was artistic director of ART from 1980 to 2002 and supervised over 200 productions during his career. He adapted productions of the Henrik Ibsen plays "The Wild Duck", "The Master Builder", and "When We Dead Awaken". He directed Luigi Pirandello's trilogy, "Six Characters in Search of an Author", Right You Are (If You Think You Are)", and "Tonight We Improvise". His original plays include "Demons", "Shlemiel the First", "Nobody Dies on

Friday", "The Face Lift", "Spring Forward, Fall Back", "The English Channel", "Mortal Terror", and "The Last Will". Brustein served as theater critic for "The New Republic" from 1959 to the late 1990s. He was writer and narrator for the WNET television series "The Opposition Theatre" in 1966. He was author of various books and collections of essays on theater including "The Theatre of Revolt: An Approach to Modern Drama" (1964), "The Third Theatre" (1969), "Revolution as Theatre: Notes on the New Radical Style" (1971), "Making Scenes: A Personal History of the Turbulent Years at Yale, 1966–1979" (1981), "Reimagining American Theatre" (1991), "Dumbocracy in America: Studies in the Theatre of Guilt, 1987–1994" (1994), "The Siege of the Arts: Collected Writings, 1994–2001" (2001), "Letters to a Young Actor: A Universal Guide to Performance" (2005), and "The Tainted Muse: Prejudices and Preconceptions in Shakespeare's Work and Times" (2009). He was a recipient of the National Medal of Arts in 2010. He was married to actress Norma Ofstrock until her death in 1979 and is survived by their son, Daniel Brustein. Brustein married South African human rights activist and documentary film professor Doreen Beinart in 1996 and is also survived by her and two stepchildren.

Bryne, Barbara

British-American actress Barbara Bryne died in Minneapolis, Minnesota, on May 2, 2023. She was 94. She was born Barbara Birkinshaw in London, England, on April 1, 1929. She trained at the Royal Academy of Dramatic Arts

before relocating to Canada in the early 1960s. She performed frequently with the Stratford Shakespeare Festival in Ontario and joined the Guthrie Theater in Minneapolis, Minnesota, in 1966. She was nominated for a Drama Desk Award for the first U.S. production of Joe Orton's "Entertaining Mr. Sloane" in 1982. Byrne starred on Broadway in Stephen Sondheim's musical "Sunday in the Park with George" in 1984. She also appeared in the Broadway productions "Hay Fever" (1985) and "Into the Woods" (1987) as Jack's Mother. She continued to perform with the Guthrie Theater for fifty years and appeared in such productions as "Arsenic and Old Lace", "Mother Courage", "The Glass Menagerie", "She Stoops to Conquer", "Design for Living", and "Pygmalion". Byrne was featured in the films "The Bostonians" (1984), "Amadeus" (1984), and "Two Evil Eyes" (1990) as Martha in Dario Argento's "The Black Cat" segment. She appeared on television in episodes of "Mister Rogers", "CBS Children's "Mystery Theatre", "Best of the West", the short-lived comedy "Love, Sidney" as Mrs. Gaffney from 1982 to 1983, and the 1995 animated series "The Neverending Story" as the voice of Urgl the gnome. Her other television credits include the tele-films "Back to Beulah" (1974), "The School for Scandal" (1975), "Maid in America" (1982), "Svengali" (1983), "Sunday in the Park with George" (1986), "Into the Woods"

(1991), and "Romeo & Juliet" (1993). Byrne was married to producer Denny Spence from 1953 until his death in 2018 and is survived by her daughter, Susan.

Budimir, Dennis

Guitarist Dennis Budimir, who performed with the session group the Wrecking Crew, died on January 10, 2023. He was 84. Budimir was born in Los Angeles, California, on June 20, 1938. He played guitar and piano in his youth and was

performing professionally in his early teens. He performed with La Monte Young, Billy Higgins, and Don Cherry in a quartet in the mid-1950s and played in bands led by Harry James, Ken Hanna, and Chico Hamilton later in the decade. He was accompanist for singer Peggy Lee from 1960 to 1961. Budimir served in the military from 1961 to 1963. He later toured Japan with Bobby Troup. He began working as a studio musician after returning to Los Angeles. He was considered part of the collective of studio musicians who became known as the Wrecking Crew. He was a sideman for the 5th Dimension for most of their albums from 1967 to 1975 and played for the Partridge Family in the early 1970s. He recorded with such artists as Barbra Streisand, Frank Zappa, Jonny Mathis, Ella Fitzgerald, Brian Wilson, Joni Mitchell, Julie London, Quincy Jones, George Harrison, Cher, and Dusty Springfield. Budimir played guitar on numerous television soundtracks including "The Shoes of the Fisherman" (1968), "Kelly's Heroes" (1970), "Klute" (1971), "Duel" (1971), "The Poseidon Adventure" (1972), "The Getaway" (1972), "Enter the Dragon" (1973), "The Paper Chase" (1973), "Magnum Force" (1973), "Earthquake" (1974), "The Towering Inferno" (1974), "The Eiger Sanction" (1975), "Rooster Cogburn" (1975), "All the President's Men" (1976), "The Big Bus" (1976), "Murder by Death" (1976), "Swashbuckler" (1976), "King Kong" (1976), "Airport '77" (1977), "The Deep" (1977), "Damnation Alley" (1977), "Telefon" (1977), "The Driver" (1978), "Jaws 2" (1978), "Rocky II" (1979), "Breaking Away" (1979), "North Dallas Forty" (1979), "One from the Heart" (1981), "Raggedy Man" (1981), "Twilight Zone: The Movie" (1983), "Strange Invaders" (1983), "The Right Stuff" (1983), "Sudden Impact" (1983), "Ghostbusters" (1984), "The Karate Kid" (1985), "Harry and the Hendersons" (1987), "Jaws: The Revenge" (1987), "Last Rites" (1988), the television mini-series "Lonesome Dove" (1989), "The 'Burbs" (1989), "Young Guns II" (1990), "The Addams Family" (1991), "Indecent Proposal" (1993), "Jurassic Park" (1993), "The Shadow" (1994), "Toy Story" (1995), "Sabrina" (1995), "The Truth About Cats & Dogs" (1996), "Chain Reaction" (1996), "Mars Attacks!" (1996), "The Lost World: Jurassic Park" (1997), "Mousehunt" (1997), "Small Soldiers" (1998), "A Bug's Life" (1998), and "Pearl Harbor" (2001).

Buffett, Jimmy

Singer and songwriter Jimmy Buffett, who was noted for the hits "Margaritaville" and "Cheeseburger in Paradise", died of complications from a rare form of skin cancer at his  home in Sag Harbor, New York, on September 1, 2023. He was 76. Buffett was born in Pascagoula, Mississippi, on December 25, 1946. He decided he wanted to be a musician in the early 1960s and was soon playing guitar at a hootenanny. He graduated from high school in 1964 and attended Auburn University for a year before dropping out. He learned to play the guitar and performed with the rock band Upstairs Alliance. He later attended Pearl River Community College and graduated from the University of Southern Mississippi in Hattiesburg, Mississippi, in 1969. He moved to New Orleans where he was a street performer and settled in Nashville, Tennessee. He signed with Barnaby Records and recorded the album "Down to Earth" in 1970. His second album from Barnaby, "High Cumberland Jubilee", was recorded the following year. He spent some time performing at a Nashville night club before moving to Key West, Florida. He worked as first mate on a private yacht during the ay and performed at bars in the evening. He began recording with ABC/Dunhill Records in 1973 and released the album "A White Sport Coat and a Pink Crustacean". The album featured the hit singles "Why Don't We Get Drunk", "Grapefruit - Juicy Fruit", and "I Have Found Me a Home". Buffett's album "Lying & Dying in 3/4 Time" was released in 1974 and included the singles "A Pirate Looks at Forty" and "Come Monday". He formed the Coral Reefer Band in 1975 and recorded the 1976 album "Havana Daydreamin'". He had a hit with the title track of his 1977 album "Changes in Latitudes, Changes in Attitudes", which also included the signature song "Margaritaville". He moved to Saint Barts Island in the Caribbean in 1978. The popular tune "Cheeseburger in Paradise" was included on his 1978 album "Son of a Son of a Sailor", and the 1979 release "Volcano" had the song "Fins". He released the compilation album "Songs You Know by Heart" in 1985. Buffett sang a duet with Frank Sinatra on the song "Mack the Knife" for Sinatra's "Duets II" album in 1984. He co-created a musical theater production of Herman Wouk's novel, "Don't Stop the Carnival", and the 1998 album was a hit. His duet with Alan Jackson, "It's Five O'Clock Somewhere", was a major success in 2003 as was his 2004 album "License to Chill". He was founder of the online station Radio Margaritaville in 1998 which joined Sirius Satellite Radio in 2005. His song honoring the survivors of Hurricane Katrina, "Breath In, Breath Out", was featured on his 2006 album "Take the Weather with You". He teamed with Alan Jackson and George Strait for the song "Hey Good Lookin'" in 2007. He recorded the song "Knee Deep" with the Zac Brown Band for his 2010 album "You Get What You Give". He was the voice of Mark Twain on the 2011 album "Mark Twain: Words & Music" and released "Songs from St. Somewhere" in 2013. He rerecorded some of his lesser-known songs for the 2020 album "Songs You Don't Know by Heart". Buffett remained a popular concert performer and his legion of fans became known as Parrot Heads as they followed him from venue to venue. He retired from the road in spring of 2023 and his final album, "Equal Strain on All Parts", was released posthumously in November of 2023. Buffett was the musical guest for "Saturday Night Live" in 1978. He also performed on such television series as "Your Hit Parade", "Austin City Limits", "Fridays", "SCTV Network", "Late Night with David Letterman", "Cinemax Sessions", "The Tonight Show Starring Johnny Carson", "The Whoopi Goldberg Show", "The Tonight Show with Jay Leno", "60 Minutes", "Late Night with Conan O'Brien", "Life with Kelly and Mark", "Late Show with David Letterman", "Late Night with Jimmy Fallon", "CMT Crossroads", "The Ellen DeGeneres Show", "The View", "Megyn Kelly Today", "Watch What Happens Live with Andy Cohen", "The Late Late Show with James Corden", and "The Tonight Show Starring Jimmy Fallon". He starred in the television specials Sesame Street's "Elmopalooza" (1998) singing "Caribbean Amphibian" with Kermit the Frog, "Jimmy Buffett & Friends: Live from the Gulf Coast" (2010) and "Sharking Around with Jimmy Buffett" (2018). He was featured in several films including "Rancho Deluxe" (1975), "FM" (1978), "Repo Man" (1984), "Hook" (1991), "Cobb" (1994), "Congo" (1995), "Hoot" (2006) which he also co-produced and wrote the soundtrack for, "Jurassic World" (2015), the documentary "Parrot Heads" (2017), "Billionaire Boys Club" (2018), and "The Beach Bum" (2019). Buffett appeared in a small role in the 1998 television mini-series "From the Earth to the Moon". He was seen in cameo roles in episodes of "NCIS: New Orleans", "Hawaii Five-O" in the recurring role of helicopter pilot Frank Bama from 2011 to 2020, "Blue Bloods", and "Life & Beth". He penned the songs "Hello, Texas" for the 1980 film "Urban Cowboy", "I Don't Know (Spicoli's Theme)" for "Fast Times at Ridgemont High" (1982), "Turning Around" for "Summer Rental" (1985), and "If I'm Gonna Eat Somebody (It Might As Well Be You)" for the 1992 animated film "FernGully: The Last Rainforest". He wrote the theme song for the 1993 television series "Johnny Bago". He was author of the books "Tales from Margaritaville" (1989), "Where Is Joe Merchant?" (1992), the memoir "A Pirate Looks at Fifty" (1998), the novel "A Salty Piece of Land" (2004), and "Swine Not?" (2008). He penned the children's books "The Jolly Mon" (1988) and "Trouble Dolls" (1991) with his young daughter, Samantha Buffett. He opened several restaurant chains including Jimmy Buffett's Margaritaville, LandShark Bar & Grill, and Cheeseburger in Paradise Restaurant. He had his own beer brand, Land Shark Lager, from Anheuser-Busch from 2006. He was co-creator of the Coral Reefer marijuana brand in 2019. He was diagnosed with Merkel-cell carcinoma, an aggressive skin cancer, in 2019, but had kept his illness private and continued to tour while receiving treatment. Buffett was married to Margie Washichek from 1969 until their divorce in 1972. He married Jane Slagsvol in 1977 and is survived by her, their two daughters, Savannah

Buffett and Sarah Delaney, and an adopted son, Cameron Marley.

Buirski, Nancy

Documentary filmmaker Nancy Buirski died in New York City on August 29, 2023. She was 78. She was born Nancy Cohen in New York City on June 23, 1945. She graduated from Adelphi University in Garden City, New York, in 1967. She began her career as an editor at the Magnum photo agency. She soon began working as picture editor at the international desk of the "New York Times". She was founder of the Full Frame Documentary Film Festival at Duke University in Durham, North Carolina, in 1998. She made the 2011 documentary feature, "The Loving Story", about an interracial couple who face prison in Virginia in the late 1950s due to their relationship being illegal. Their plight resulted in the Supreme Court voiding state anti-miscegenation laws in a landmark ruling in 1967. The film was aired on HBO in 2012 and earned an Emmy Award and a Peabody Award for outstanding historical programming. The documentary served as inspiration for Jeff Nichols 2016 film "Loving", and Buirski was a producer. She co-produced, directed, and wrote the 2013 documentary "Afternoon of a Faun" about polio-stricken ballerina Tanaquil Le Clerq, and "By Sidney Lumet", about the filmmaker, in 2015. They were both aired on the PBS series "American Masters". Her other documentaries include "The Rape of Recy Taylor" (2017), "A Crime on the Bayou" (2021), and "Desperate Souls, Dark City and the Legend of Midnight Cowboy" (2023). Buirski served as an adviser for Questlove's 2021 Oscar-winning concert documentary film "Summer of Soul". Buirski was also a photographer who produced the 1994 book "Earth Angels: Migrant Children in America". She was married and divorced from Peter Buirski and Kenneth Friedlein.

Bumbry, Grace

Opera singer Grace Bumbry died of complications from a stroke at a hospital in Vienna, Austria, on May 7, 2023. She was 86. Bumbry was born in St. Louis, Missouri, on January 4, 1937. She was inspired by singer Marian Anderson and began singing with a local church choir as a child. She was a soloist in her grade school production of Handel's "Messiah". The won a teen talent contest from a St. Louis radio station at age 17, which included a scholarship to the St. Louis Institute of Music. The institute did not accept African American students at the time and the embarrassed promoters arranged an appearance on Arthur Godfrey's "Talent Scouts" radio program instead. Her performance of Verdi's "O Don Fatale" gained her entrance into the Boston University College of Fine Arts in 1954. She subsequently studied under Lotte Lehmann at Northwestern University and continued to study under her at the Music Academy of the West in Santa Barbara, California, for over three years. She made her operatic debut with the Paris Opera in 1960, performing Amneris in Verdi's "Aida". She soon joined the Basel Opera in Switzerland where she performed Dalili in Saint-Saens' "Samson et Dalila", Orfeo in Christoph Gluck's "Orfeo ed Euridice", Lady Macbeth in Verdi's "Macbeth", and the title role in Bizet's "Carmen". She became the first black singer to perform with the Bayreuth Festival in Germany, performing Venus in Richard Wagner's "Tannhauser" in 1961. The casting was initially met with controversy, but her powerful performance earned her 42 curtain calls. Bumbry performed the title role in a London studio cast album of the musical "Carmen Jones" in 1962. She made her debut with the London Royal Opera House the following year as Eboli in Verdi's "Don Carlo". She was Santuzza in Mascagni's "Cavalleria Rusticana" with the Vienna State Opera and Lady Macbeth at the Salzburg Festival in 1964. She debuted with the Metropolitan Opera as Eboli in 1965. She was a leading mezzo soprano at such venues as the San Francisco Opera, the Opera Bastille in Paris, and La Scala in Milan. Her major roles also include Laura Adorno in Ponchielli's "La Gioconda", Ulrica in Verdi's "Un Ballo in Maschera", Cassandre and Didon in Berlioz's "Les Troyens", and the title role in Massenet's "Herodiade". She transitioned to soprano roles in the 1970s, starring in Richard Strauss' "Salome" at the Royal Opera House in 1970. She starred in Puccini's "Tosca" at the Metropolitan Opera the following year. Her other roles with the Met include Leonora in Verdi's "Il Trovatore" and "La Forza del Destino" and Bess in George Gershwin's "Porgy and Bess". She was noted for her many performances in the title role of Vincenzo Bellini's "Norma". Bumbry's other roles as a soprano include Ariane in Paul Dukas' "Ariane et Barbe-Bleue", Selika in Giacomo Meyerbeer's "L'Africaine", Abigaille in Verdi's "Nabucco", and Chimene in Jules Massenet's "Le Cid". She appeared in film and television productions of "Don Carlo" (1965), "Carmen" (1969), "Aida" (1977), "Nabucco" (1979), "Don Carlo" (1984), and "La Gioconda" (1988). She also appeared on television in the series "The Merv Griffin Show", "The Tonight Show Starring Johnny Carson", "The David Frost Show", "The Mike Douglas Show", and "Great Performances". She was founder of the Grace Bumbry Black Musical Heritage Ensemble in the 1990s and frequently toured with the group. She was also a teacher and served as a judge at various international competitions. She returned to the opera stage in 2010 in a production of Scott Joplin's "Treemonisha" at the Theatre du Chatelet in Paris. She retired from the operatic stage following her role as the Countess in Tchaikovsky's "Pique Dame" at the Vienna State Opera in 2013. Bumbry received a Grammy Award for Best Opera Recording in 1972. She was a recipient of the Kennedy Center Honors in 2009. She was married to tenor Erwin Jaeckel from 1963 until their divorce in 1972.

Bunch, Pat

Country music songwriter Pat Bunch died at her home in Cross Plains, Tennessee, on January 30, 2023. She was 83. Bunch was born on June 22, 1939. She began er songwriting

career in Nashville in the 1970s. She became noted as a lyricist and frequently collaborated with such fellow songwriters as Mary Ann Kennedy, Pam Rose, and Doug Johnson. She co-wrote such songs as "Ten Thousand and One" (1979) for Connie Smith, "Me Against the Night"(1984) for Crystal Gayle, Jane Fricke's "The First Word in Memory Is Me" (1985) and "Somebody Else's Fire" (1985), Restless Heart's "I'll Still Be Loving You" (1987) which earned a Grammy Award nomination, "Wild One" (1993) for Faith Hill, "You Wouldn't Say That to a Stranger" (1994) for Suzy Bogguss, "Safe in the Arms of Love" (1995) for Martina McBride, "Slow Dance More" (1999) for Kenny Rogers, "She Didn't Have Time" (2005) for Terri Clark, and "Better I Don't" (2013) for Chris Janson. Bunch co-wrote Ty Herndon's hit songs "I Want My Goodbye Back" (1995), "Living in a Moment" (1996), and "I Have to Surrender" (1997). She is survived by her husband of 45 years, James Price, and three sons.

Bunting, Eve

Irish-American writer Eve Bunting, who was noted for her books for children and young adults, died of pneumonia in Santa Cruz, California, on October 1, 2023. She was 94. She was born Anne Evelyn Bolton in Maghera, Northern Ireland, on

December 19, 1928. She graduated from Methodist College in Belfast in 1945. She subsequently attended Queen's University. She married business executive Edward Bunting in 1950 and moved with him to Scotland to begin a family. She and her family moved to the United States in 1958. She continued her studies as Pasadena City College and began taking a writing course. Her first book, "The Two Giants", was published in 1971. She wrote over 250 books for children and young adults during her career. Her fiction includes "One More Flight" (1976), "Terrible Things: An Allegory of the Holocaust" (1980), "Someone Is Hiding on Alcatraz Island" (1984), "Face at the Edge of the World" (1985) which was adapted for the "ABC Afterschool Special" episode "A Desperate Exit" in 1986, "Sixth-Grade Sleepover" (1986), "Is Anybody There?" (1988), "A Sudden Silence" (1988), "The Ghost Children" (1989), "How Many Days to America" (1989), "Fly Away Home" (1991), "Night Tree" (1991), "Gleam and Glow" (1991), "Coffin on the Case!" (1992) which earned the Edgar Award for Best Juvenile Mystery, "Nasty, Stinky Sneakers" (1994),

"Smoky Night" (1994), "Spying on Miss Muller" (1995), "S.O.S. Titanic" (1996), "The Blue and the Gray" (1996), "Twinnies" (1997), "Moonstick: The Seasons of the Sioux" (1997), "So Far from the Sea" (1998), "A Picnic in October" (1999), "The Memory String" (2000), "The Summer of Riley" (2001), "The Presence: A Ghost Story" (2003), "The Lambkins" (2005), "That's What Leprechauns Do" (2006), "One Green Apple" (2006), "The Man with the Red Bag" (2007), and "The Cart That Carried Martin" (2013). Her non-fiction includes" The Great White Shark" (1982), "The Sea World Book of Sharks" (1984), and "The Sea World Book of Whales" (1987). She and Bunting were married from 1951 until his death in 2014. She is survived by their two sons and a daughter.

Burgess, Colin

Australian rock drummer Colin Burgess, who was a founding member of the band AC/DC, died on December 16,

2023. He was 77. Burgess was born in Sydney, Australia, on November 16, 1946. He and his brother, guitarist Denny Burgess, teamed with guitarist Joe Travers and bass guitarist Bill Verbaan to form the psychedelic band Honeybunch in 1967. They became known as the Haze the following year. Colin became

drummer of the Masters Apprentices in 1968. He was joined by his brother for the band's year in 1982. He teamed with Malcolm Young, Angus Young, Dave Evans, and Larry Van Kriedt to form the hard rock band AC/DC in November of 1973. He was released from the band the following year but briefly filled in on drums for an injured Phil Rudd in September of 1975. He and brother Denny teamed with Japanese singer Yukiko Davis and guitarist Spike Williams for the hard rock band His Majesty from 1983 to 1988. He joined a new lineup of the band in 1992 and the backing group of Tiny Tim's album. The band changed its name to Good Time Charlie in 1998 and recorded the album "Adults Only". He and his brother survived a major vehicle collision in 1998 but largely recovered. They were the subject of the 2005 documentary "The Comeback Kings" and continued to perform and record as the Burgess Brothers Band. Burgess was part of the Dead Singer Band, a tribute band dedicated to deceased Australian singers, in recent years.

Burns, John M.

British comic artist John M. Burns, who was noted for his work on the "Judge Dredd" series, died in England on December 29, 2023. He was 85. Burns was born in Essex, England, in 1938. He began his career working at Link Studios as an apprentice to Doris White in 1954. He contributed to such titles as "Girls' Crystal" and "School Friend" for Amalgamated Press before serving in the Royal Air Force in Singapore. He returned to England in 1960 and illustrated the novels "Wuthering Heights" and "Great Expectations" for the comic magazine "Diana" for D.C. Thomson. He worked on such newspaper comic strips as "The Seekers" for "The Daily Sketch" from 1966 to 1971, "Danielle" for "Evening News"

from 197 to 1974, "George and Lynne" from 1977 to 1984, and "Jane" for "The Daily Mirror" from 1985 to 1989. He also was artist for the "Modesty Blaise" strip from 1978 to 1979. He illustrated the German newspaper strip "Julia" (later titled "Lilli") in 1987. He also drew various television strips for "T 21", "Look-In", and "TV Action", including "The Tomorrow People", "Space: 1999", "The Bionic Woman", "Buck Rogers", and "The Tripods". He worked for Eagle on such titles as "Wrath of God", "The Fists of Danny Pike", "Dolebusters", and "Roving Reporter". He teamed with Dutch writer Martin Lodewijk for the fantasy series "Zetari". Burns worked with Fleetway from the 1980s on the series "Dan Dare", "Judge Dredd", and "Trueno". He teamed with Robbie Morrison to co-create the "Bendatti Vendetta" series for "Judge Dredd Megazine" in 2002. He worked for Marvel on the titles "Doctor Who - Age of Chaos" and "Sable and Fortune".

Burr, Jeff

Film director Jeff Burr, who helmed such horror films as "Leatherface: The Texas Chainsaw Massacre III" and "Pumpkinhead II", died of stroke at his home in Dalton, Georgia, on October 10, 2023. He was 60. Burr was born in

Aurora, Ohio, on July 18, 1963, and was raised in Dalton. He was a fan of horror films and magazines in his youth and began making his own amateur films on Super-8. He attended the University of Southern California for several years before dropping out to make the Civil War film "Divided We Fall" with Kevin Meyer in 1982. Burr directed and wrote the 1987" horror anthology "From a Whisper to a Scream" (aka "The Offspring"), starring Vincent Price as the storyteller Julian White. He helmed the 1989 horror sequel "Stepfather II: Make Room for Daddy" and 1990's "Leatherface: The Texas Chainsaw Massacre III" starring R.A. Mihailoff in the title role. Burr directed the off-beat comedy "Eddie Presley" starring Duane Whitaker in 1992. He continued to direct such horror and action films as "Pumpkinhead II: Blood Wings" (1993), "Puppet Master 4" (1993), "Puppet Master 5" (1995), "Night of the Scarecrow" (1995), "American Hero" (1997), "Johnny Mysto: Boy Wizard" (1987), "Spoiler" (1998), "The Werewolf Reborn!" (1998), "The Boy with the X-Ray Eyes" (1999) which he also wrote and appeared in as science teacher Mr. Wright, "Phantom Town" (1999), the World War II drama "Straight into Darkness" (2004) which he also co-wrote, "Frankenstein & the

Werewolf Reborn!" (2005), "Devil's Den" (2006), "Mil Mascaras vs. the Aztec Mummy" (2007), "Resurrection" (2010), "Gun of the Quiet Sun" (2011), "Puppet Master: Blitzkrieg Massacre" (2018), "American Resurrection" (2022), and "Tales of the Fantastic" (2023). He directed television episodes of "Land of the Lost" and "BeetleBorgs", and the 2012 tele-film "Tornado Warning". Burr appeared in cameo roles in several of the films he directed as well as "The Lost Empire" (1984), "The Summoned" (1992), "Fear of the Black Hat" (1993), "Things" (1993), "Saturday Night Special" (1994), "High Tomb" (1995), "With Criminal Intent" (1995), "Witchouse II: Blood Coven" (2000), "Dark Asylum" (2001), "Zombiegeddon" (2003), "The Mangler Reborn" (2005), "Creepies 2" (2005), "Have Love, Will Travel" (2007), "The Curse of Lizzie Borden 2: Prom Night" (2008), "Sutures" (2009), "The Dry Spell" (2015), "Paranormal Chasers Legend of the Black Cross" (2015), "Making Out" (2016), "The Litch" (2018) as Uncle Jeff, "Cool as Hell 2" (2020), and "Edge of Town" (2021).

Burrows, Vinnie

Actress Vinie Burrows, who was noted for her performances on the Broadway stage, died on December 25,

2023. She was 99. She was born Vinie Harrison in New York City on November 15, 1928. She began performing on stage and radio as a child. She graduated from Harlem High School in the late 1930s. She continued to perform on stage and made her Broadway debut in the 1950 drama "The Wisteria Trees". Her other Broadway credits include "The Green Pastures" (1951), "Mrs. Patterson" (1954), "The Skin of Our Teeth" (1955), "The Ponder Heart" (1956), and "Mandingo" (1961). Burrows starred in off-Broadway productions of Jean Genet's "The Blacks" and "The Words of Shakespeare". She was dissatisfied with roles for black actresses and began writing her own one-woman plays and monologues. Her solo work "Walk Together Children" appeared off-Broadway in 1968, and her other shows include "Dark Fire" and "Sister Sister". She was also seen in such stage productions as "A Midsummer Night's Dream", "Good Person of Szechwan", "Light Shining in Buckinghamshire", "The Homecoming Queen", and her final appearance, "Chekhov/Tolstoy: Love Stories", in 2020. Burrows received a Lifetime Achievement Obie Award in 2020.

Bushwhacker Butch

New Zealand professional wrestler Robert 'Butch' Miller, who competed as Bushwhacker Butch in a tag team with Bushwhacker Luke, died at a hospital while visiting in Los Angeles, California, on April 2, 2023. He was 78. Miller was born in Auckland, New Zealand, on October 21, 1944. He began wrestling in 1964 with NWA New Zealand. He and his partner, Luke Williams (aka Brian Wickens) soon began wrestling in the United States and Canada. Butch became known as Nick Carter and Luke was Sweet William in the  Kiwis tag team for Stu Hart's Stampede Wrestling in Canada. They held the Stampede International Tag Team Championship several times in 1974. The Kiwis began competing with International Wrestling Enterprise in Japan and returned to New Zealand in 1975, where they appeared on television's "On the Mat" wrestling program. The returned to the United States in 1979 and were known as the Kiwi Sheepherders with NWA Pacific Northwest. They won the tag titles three times before leaving the area in 1980. They moved to Mid Atlantic Championship Wrestling where they captured the tag team championship from Matt Borne and Buzz Sawyer. They held the belts for three months until December of 1980. They also held the tag team belts with the World Wrestling Council in Puerto Rico, where they were known as Los Pastores. Butch left for Australia and Luke continued to wrestle as the Sheepherders with Lord Jonathan Boyd. Boyd was injured in 1983 and Butch and Luke reunited in Southwest Championship Wrestling. They defeated the Fabulous Ones (Stan Lane & Steve Keirn) for the promotion's World Tag Team Championship, which they held from March to September of 1984. They again held the tag belts in a return visit to Puerto Rico and signed with Bill Watt's Universal Wrestling Federation (UWF) in early 1986. They captured the tag titles from Ted DiBiase and Steve Williams and feuded with the Fantastics. They had stints with Championship Wrestling of Florida and the Continental Wrestling Association (CWA), where the briefly captured the titles from Badd Company (Paul Diamond and Pat Tanaka) in Memphis in 1987. They left the promotion after another feud with the Fabulous Ones. A return to Puerto Rico saw a feud with Chris and Mark Youngblood resulting in another tag title reign from April to May of 1987. They captured the NWA Florida Tag Team Championship from Mike Graham and Steve Keirn later in the summer. They had another title run with the UWF, defeating Brad Armstrong and Tim Horner in October of 1987. The promotion merged into Jim Crockett Promotions, and they competed against the Midnight Express and the Fantastics. Luke and Butch entered the World Wrestling Federation (WWF/now WWE) in December of 1988 where they were known as the Bushwhackers. Their previously violent screen personas were replaced by a family friendly comedic style that often included them licking the faces of their opponents. They battled such teams as the Headshrinkers, the Beverly Brothers, Rhythm and Blues (Honky Tonk Man and Greg Valentine), the Fabulous Rougeau Brothers, Well Done, and the Bodydonnas. They left the WWF in 1996 and continued to appear on the independent circuit until Butch retired from the ring in 2001. He soon returned to New Zealand where he served as a commissioner for Kiwi Pro Wrestling. He and Luke were inducted into the WWE Hall of Fame in 2015. The Bushwhackers were featured as themselves in an episode of the comedy television series "Family Matters" in 1994. They released their autobiography, "The Bushwhackers: Blood, Sweat & Cheers", in 2022. Butch is survived by his wife of 18 years, Butch Miller, and two daughters from a previous marriage.

Buthelezi, Prince Mangosuthu

South African political leader and Zulu Prince Mangosuthu Gatsha Buthelezi died at his home in Ulundi, South Africa, on September 9, 2023. He was 95. Buthelezi was born Mahlabathini in southeastern Natal, South Africa, on August 27, 1928. He was educated in Nongoma and at the  mission school Adams College in Amanzimtoti from 1944 to 1946. He continued his education at the University of Fort Hare in the eastern Cape Province from 1948 to 1950. He was an opponent of the apartheid system in South Africa when it was implemented in the late 1940s. His political activities led to his expulsion from Fort Hare in 1950. He later graduated from the University of Natal. He returned to Mahlabathini in 1953 and became hereditary chief of the Buthelezi clan. He served as traditional prime minister of the Zulu royal family from 1954 until his death. He was also chief minister of the semi-independent KwaZulu (formerly Zululand until 1970) during South Africa's apartheid system until it was abolished in 1994. He was founder of the Inkatha Freedom Party in 1975 and remained as president until stepping down in 2019. He joined Nelson Mandela's government as Minister of Home Affairs from 1994 to 2004. Buthelezi was featured as Zulu King Cetshwayo, his great-grandfather, in the 1964 film "Zulu". He was also featured as a Zulu chief in the 1965 film "Tokoloshe". He was author of the 1990 book "South Africa: My Vision of the Future". Buthelezi was married to Irene Audrey Thandekile Mzila from 1952 until her death in 2019. He is survived by three of their children, Princess Phumzile Nokuphiwa, Prince Ntuthukoyezwe Zuzifa, and Princess Sibuyiselwe Angela. He was predeceased by five other children, Mabhuku Sinikwakonke in 1966, Mandisi Sibukakonke in 2004, Lethuxolo Bengitheni in 2008, Nelisuzulu Benedict in 2004, and Phumaphesheya Gregory in 2012.

Butkus, Dick

Professional football player and actor Dick Butkus died at his home in Malibu, California, on October 5, 2023. He was 80. Butkus was born in Chicago, Illinois, on December 9, 1942. He was a star football player in high school and attended the University of Illinois. He played center and linebacker for the Illinois Fighting Illini football team from 1962 through 1964. He was chosen as the Illini's most valuable player two years in a row. He signed with the Chicago Bears after the NFL draft in 1965. He was a highly regarded lineman and was considered one of the meanest and most feared players in football. He released a memoir of the final week of the 1971

season, "Stop-Action", that proved controversial with his criticisms of the rival Detroit Lions. He suffered from a knee injury later in his career which forced his retirement in 1974. Butkus was inducted into the Pro Football Hall of Fame in 1979, and his No. 51 jersey was retired by the Bears. He embarked on a successful acting career, appearing in the films "Cry, Onion" (1975), "Mother, Jugs & Speed" (1975), "Gus" (1976), "Deadly Games" (1982), "Cracking Up" (1983), "Johnny Dangerously" (1984), "Hamburger: The Motion Picture" (1986), "Spontaneous Combustion" (1989), "Gremlins 2: The New Batch" (1990), "Necessary Roughness" (1991), "The Last Boy Scout" (1991), "Let's Kill All the Lawyers" (1992), "Any Given Sunday" (1999), and "Teddy Bears' Picnic" (2001). Butkus appeared on television in episodes of "The Dean Martin Show", "The Mike Douglas Show", "The Hollywood Squares", "Emergency!", "McMillan & Wife", "Police Story", "Bronk", "The Six Million Dollar Man", "Joe Forrester", "Petrocelli", "The Rockford Files", "Wonder Woman", "Taxi", "Fantasy Island", "Vega$", "Magnum, P.I.", "Matt Houston", "The Greatest American Hero", "Simon & Simon", the action series "Blue Thunder" as Richard 'Ski' Butowski in 1984, "The Love Boat", "Murder, She Wrote", "Half Nelson" as Beau in 1985, "Night Court", "Matlock", "Growing Pains", "D.C. Follies", "Kate & Allie", the comedy series "My Two Dads" as Ed Klawicki from 1987 to 1989, "MacGyver" in the recurring role of Earl Dent from 1990 to 1991, "Burke's Law", "Charlie Grace", "Chicago Sons", "Coach", "Early Edition", "Malibu, CA", "Hang Time" as Coach Mike Katowinski from 1998 to 2000, "Inside Schwartz", "The Bernie Mac Show", and "I Didn't Do It". He was also seen in the tele-films and mini-series "A Matter of Wife... and Death" (1975), "Rich Man, Poor Man" (1976), "Superdome" (1978), "The Legend of Sleepy Hollow" (1980) as Brom Bones, "Cass Malloy" (1982), "The Stepford Children" (1987), and "Time Out for Dad" (1987). He was noted for a series of ads for Miller Lite with Bubba Smith in the late 1970s and early 1980s. He also promoted Prestone antifreeze, Echo Tools, and the Quick-Cook Grill. He became color analyst for the Bears on radio in 1985 and replaced Jimmy 'the Greek' Snyder of the CBS pregame Show "The NFL Today" from 1988 to 1989. He was briefly named head coach of the XLF's Chicago Enforcers in 2001. He was head coach for a Pennsylvania high school team in the ESPN reality series "Bound for Glory" in 2005. Butkus married Helen Essenhart in 1963 and is survived by her and their three children.

Butler, Bill

Cinematographer Wilmer Cable 'Bill' Butler, who received an Oscar nomination for his work on "One Flew Over the Cuckoo's Nest", died in Los Angeles, California, on April 5, 2023. He was 101. Butler was born in Cripple Creek, Colorado, on April 7, 1921. He was raised in Mount Pleasant, Iowa, and graduated high school there in 1940. He served in the U.S. Army Signal Corps during World War II. He received a medical discharge and graduated from the University of Iowa was a degree in engineering. Butler worked as an engineer at a radio station in Gary, Indiana. He went to Chicago, where he was instrumental in designing the ABC affiliate television station. He also worked at WGN-TV, where he was live video camera operator for local programming and commercials. He began working with director William Friedkin and was cinematographer for his television documentaries "The People vs. Pau Crump" (1962) and "The Bold Men" (1965). He made his feature debut as cinematographer for 1967's "Fearless

Frank". Butler worked with director Francis Ford Coppola on the 1969 film "The Rain People". He moved to California in 1970 where he was cinematographer for the tele-film "A Clear and Present Danger" (1970) and episodes of the supernatural anthology series "Circle of Fear" in 1972. He worked on two of Steven Spielberg's earliest works, the tele-films "Something Evil" (1972) and "Savage" (1973). He was cinematographer or director of photography for numerous films including "Adam's Woman" (1970), "Drive, He Said" (1971), "The Return of Count Yorga" (1971), "Deathmaster" (1972), "Melinda" (1972), "The Godfather" (1972) as an uncredited second unit photographer, "Hickey & Boggs" (1972), "Deliverance" (1972) working second unit, "Running Wild" (1973), Coppola's "The Conversation" (1974), "The Manchu Eagle Murder Caper Mystery" (1975), Spielberg's summer blockbuster "Jaws" (1975), "One Flew Over the Cuckoo's Nest" (1975) replacing Haskell Wexler and earning an Academy Award nomination, "Lipstick" (1976), "The Bingo Long Traveling All-Stars & Motor Kings" (1976), "Alex & the Gypsy" (1976), "Demon Seed" (1977), "Capricorn One" (1977), "Damien: Omen II" (1978), "Grease" (1978), "Uncle Joe Shannon" (1978), "Ice Castles" (1978), "Rocky II" (1979), "Can't Stop the Music" (1980), "It's My Turn" (1980), "The Night the Lights Went Out in Georgia" (1981), "Stripes" (1981), "Rocky III" (1982), "The Sting II" (1983), "Beer" (1985), "Rocky IV" (1985), "Big Trouble" (1986), "Legal Eagles" (1986) providing additional photography, "Biloxi Blues" (1988), "Wildfire" (1988), "Child's Play" (1988), "Graffiti Bridge" (1990), "Hot Shots!" (1991), "Sniper" (1993), "Cop & 1/2" (1993), "Beethoven's 2nd" (1993), "Flipper" (1996), "Mother" (1996), "Anaconda" (1997), "Deceiver" (1997), "Ropewalk" (2000), "Frailty" (2001), "Berserker" (2005), the short "Zombie Prom" (2006), "The Plague" (2006), "Funny Money" (2006), "Redline" (2007), "Limousine" (2008), "Evil Angel" (2009), and "The Boys at the Bar" (2016). Butler continued to work in television as cinematographer for the tele-films and mini-series "Sunshine" (1973), "Deliver Us from Evil" (1973), "I Heard the Owl Call My Name" (1973), "Indict and Convict" (1974), "The Execution of Private Slovik" (1974), "Target Risk" (1975), "Hustling" (1975), "Fear on Trial"

(1975), "Raid on Entebbe" (1976) earning an Emmy Award, "Mary White" (1977), "Death Ray 2000" (1980), "Killing at Hell's Gate" (1981), "The Thorn Birds" (1983) receiving an Emmy nomination, "A Streetcar Named Desire" (1984) earning another Emmy Award, "Bates Motel" (1987), "When We Were Young" (1989), "A Walton Wedding" (1995), "Don King: Only in America" (1997), "Passing Glory" (1999), "Hendrix" (2000), and "Joe and Max" (2002). His other television credits include episodes of "McCoy", "Brooklyn Bridge", "Dark Skies", and "Good v Evil". He received the Lifetime Achievement Award from the American Society of Cinematographers in 2003. He was married to Alma Smith from 1943 until their divorce in 1984 and is survived by their two daughters, Judy and Pam. Another daughter, Patricia Pekau, died in 2021. He married Iris Schwimmer Butler in 1984 and is also survived by her and their two daughters, Genevieve and Chelsea.

Butler, Robert

Television director Robert Butler, who helmed the pilot episodes of such series as "Star Trek", "Batman", and "Remington Steele", died in Los Angeles, California, on

November 3, 2023. He was 95. Butler was born in Los Angeles on November 16, 1927. He began playing the trombone in his teens and was part of the band on Hoagy Carmichael's variety show on NBC Radio. He graduated from the University of California at Los Angeles and began working at CBS as an usher. He had several

jobs at the network before serving as an assistant director for the anthology series "Climax!" and "Playhouse 90" in the late 1950s. He made his directorial debut with an episode of Jackie Cooper's comedy series "Hennesey" in 1959. He continued to helm episodes of such series including "The Many Loves of Dobie Gillis", "Happy", "The DuPont Show with June Allyson", "Peter Loves Mary", "Have Gun - Will Travel", "Michael Shayne", "Bonanza", "The Dick Van Dyke Show", "The Dick Powell Theatre", "The Gertrude Berg Show", "The Rifleman", "Follow the Sun", "The Detectives", "Stoney Burke", "The Untouchables", "Dr. Kildare", "The Richard Boone Show", "The Greatest Show on Earth", "Ben Casey", "Espionage", "The Lieutenant", "Arrest and Trial", the 1964 episodes of "The Twilight Zone" entitled "Caesar and Me" and "The Encounter", "The Defenders", "Run for Your Life", "The Virginian", "Mister Roberts", "Hogan's Heroes" including the 1965 pilot episode, "The Fugitive", "Blue Light", "Shane", and "I Spy". Butler directed the original pilot, "The Cage", for "Star Trek" in 1964, which starred Jeffrey Hunter as Captain Christopher Pike. The series was recast, starring William Shatner as Captain James T. Kirk and only retaining Leonard Nimoy's Mr. Spock from the original pilot. "The Cage" was re-edited for the two-part episode "The Menagerie" during "Star Trek"'s first season in 1966. He directed the premiere episodes of "Batman", "Hi Diddle Riddle" and "Smack in the Middle", featuring Frank Gorshin as the Bat-villain the Riddler, in 1966.

He also helmed episodes featuring the villains Mr. Freeze and the Penguin. He continued to direct episodes of "Bob Hope Presents the Chrysler Theatre", "The Invaders", "N.Y.P.D.", "Judd for the Defense", "Ironside", "Cimarron Strip", "The Felony Squad", "Mission: Impossible", "CBS Playhouse", "The Outcasts", Disney's "Kilroy", "Then Came Bronson", "Lancer", "Nichols", "Gunsmoke", "Hawaii Five-O", "Doc Elliot", "Kung Fu", "Roll Out", "The Blue Knight" winning two Emmy Awards for directing the pilot episode in 1974, "The Waltons", "Columbo", "Insight", "Hill Street Blues" receiving another Emmy Award for directing the premiere episode in 1981 and earning an Emmy nomination in 1982, "Remington Steele" which he also co-created in 1982, "Moonlighting" earning another Emmy nomination for the pilot episode in 1985, "Our Family Honor", "Midnight Caller" also serving as executive consultant from 1989 to 1991, "Sisters" also serving as executive consultant from 1991 to 1996, "Sirens" receiving an Emmy nomination in 1993, "Lois & Clark: The New Adventures of Superman" earning an Emmy nomination in 1994 for directing the pilot episode, and "The Division". Butler also directed the tele-films "Death Takes a Holiday" (1971), "McMasters of Sweetwater" (1974), "Black Bart" (1975), Gene Roddenberry's "Strange New World" (1975), "Dark Victory" (1976), "James Dean" (1976), "Mayday at 49,000 Feet!" (1976), "In the Glitter Palace" (1977), "A Question of Guilt" (1978), "Lacy and the Mississippi Queen" (1978), "Concrete Beat" (1984), "Long Time Gone" (1986), the mini-series "Out on a Limb" (1987), (On the Edge" (1987), "Out of Time" (1988), "The Brotherhood" (1991), "White Mile" (1994), "Glory, Glory" (1998), and "St. Michael's Crossing" (1999). Butler directed a handful of films for Walt Disney Productions, most starring Kurt Russell, including "Guns in the Heather" (aka "The Secret of Boyne Castle") (1969), "The Computer Wore Tennis Shoes" (1969), "The Barefoot Executive" (1971), the western comedy "Scandalous John" (1971), and "Now You See Him, Now You Don't (1972). His other films include "The Ultimate Thrill" (1974), "Hot Lead and Cold Feet" (1978), "Night of the Juggler" (1980), "Underground Aces" (1981), "Up the Creek" (1984), and the thriller "Turbulence" (1997). He received a Lifetime Achievement Award for Distinguished Achievement in Television Direction from the Directors Guild of America in 2015. Butler married Adrienne Hepburn in 1957 and is survived by her and their two children. Robert Jr. and Cornelia.

Byatt, A.S.

British author Dame Antonia Susan Duffy, who was known for her works as A.S. Byatt, died at her home in London, England, on November 16, 2023. She was 87. She was born Antonia Susan Drabble in Sheffield, West Riding of Yorkshire, England, on August 24, 1936. She was educated in boarding schools and later attended Newnham College, Cambridge, Bryn Mawr College in Pennsylvania, and Somerville College, Oxford. She married Ian Byatt in 1959 and moved to Durham, England. She began writing while attending college and her first published books were "Shadow of a Sun" (1964) and "The Game" (1967). Byatt was lecturer for the Department of Extra-

Mural Studies of the University of London from 1962 to 1971) the Central School of Art and Design, and University College London from 1972 to 1983. She began her series of novels known as "The Quartet" with "The Virgin in the Garden" in 1978. The series continued with "Still Life" (1985), "Babel

Tower" (1996), and "A Whistling Woman" (2002). Her 1990 novel "Possession: A Romance" received the Booker Prize for Fiction. It was adapted for a 2002 film starring Gwyneth Paltrow and Aaron Eckhart and for a radio play for BBC Radio 4 in 2011. Her 1992 novella "Morpho Eugenia" was adapted for the 1995 "Angels & Insects" starring

Mark Rylance and Kristin Scott Thomas. Her short story, "The Djinn in the Nightingale's Eye", was included in a collection of the same name in 1994. It was adapted for the 2022 film "Three Thousand Years of Longing", directed by George Miller and starring Tilda Swinton and Idris Elba as a Djinn. The 2018 short film "Medusas Ankles" was also based on one of her short stories. Her other novels include "The Biographer's Tale" (2000), "The Children's Book" (2009), and "Ragnarok: The End of the Gods" (2011). Byatt wrote several works of non-fiction including "Degrees of Freedom: The Early Novels of Iris Murdoch" (1965), "Wordsworth and Coleridge in Their Time" (1970), "Iris Murdoch: A Critical Study" (1976), "Passions of the Mind: Selected Writings" (1991), "Portraits in Fiction" (2001), and "Peacock & Vine: On William Morris and Mariano Fortuny" (2016). She was recipient of numerous literary awards including the Aga Khan Prize for Fiction in 1995, Germany's Shakespeare Prize in 2002, Netherland's Erasmus Prize in 2016, and Denmark's Hans Christian Andersen Literature Award in 2018. Byatt was appointed Commander of the Order of the British Empire (CBE) in 1990 and Dame Commander of the Order of the British Empire (DBE) in 1999. She was married to Ian Byatt from 1959 until their divorce in 1969. They had two children, a daughter who survives her, and a son, Charles, who was killed by a drunk driver at age 11. She married Peter Duffy in 1969 and is survived by him and their two daughters.

Byrd, Terry

Actor Terry Byrd, who was noted as the internet horror host Riggor Mortiss, died at his home in Seymour, Indiana, on

July 5, 2023. He was 58. Byrd was born in Indianapolis, Indiana, on August 13, 1964. He began hosting horror films with "Riggor Mortiss Presents" on the internet with Vimeo in 2010. He was accompanied by his wife, Waylaree, who appeared in the guise of Nyte Angel. Riggor

Mortis and Nyte Angel were inducted into the Horror Host Hall of Fame in 2022. He also worked in heating and air conditioning and was with the Columbus Regional Hospital in environmental services. Byrd is survived by his wife and nine children.

Byrne, Terry

Irish actor Terry Byrne died at a hospital in Dublin, Ireland, on November 16, 2023. He was noted for his work on the Irish stage as an actor and director from the 1980s. He was

featured in a handful of films including "Agnes Browne" (1999), "Mad About Mambo" (2000), "When Brendan Met Trudy" (2000), "The Abduction Club" (2002), "Veronica Guerin" (2003), "Penance" (2018), and "Kindred" (2020). Byrne was seen on television in episodes of the series "Ros na Run" as Freddie Victor from 1996 to 1997, "The

Ambassador", "Ballykissangel", "Bachelors Walk", "The Tudors", and "Game of Thrones". He appeared in the mini-series "Relative Strangers" (1999) and "Titanic: Blood and Steel" (2012) and the tele-films "The Man Who Crossed Hitler" (2011) and "Chasing Leprechauns" (2012). He is survived by his wife, Eileen, and six children.

Byun Hee-Bong

South Korean actor Byun Hee-Bong, who was featured in the grandfather in the 2006 monster movie "The Host", died of pancreatic cancer in Seoul, South Korea, on

September 18, 2023. He was 81. He was born Byun In-chul in Sinchang Village, South Korea, on June 8, 1942. He studied law at Chosun University before dropping out to become an actor. He began his career as a voice actor in the early 1960s. He was featured in the television police series "Chief Inspector" in 1971. He

appeared in numerous television productions including "113 Investigation Division" (1973), "Wealthy Merchant Im Sang-Ok" (1976), "Season of Love" (1979), "Last Witness" (1979), "The End of the Line" (1980), "Power Diary" (1980), "New Madam" (1981), "1st Republic" (1981), "Market People" (1982), "Trade King Choi Bong-joon" (1983), "Sunflower in Winter" (1983), "Five Hundred Years of the Joseon Dynasty" (1984), "Governor-General of Korea" (1984), "Chusa Kim Jung-hee" (1984), "Wild Orchid" (1985), "White-Haired Youth" (1985), "The Season of Men" (1985), "Beautiful Secret Love Affair" (1987), "Three Women" (1988), "Our Town" (1988), "The 2nd Republic" (1989), "The Fifth Row" (1989), "Legacy" (1989), "Anti-People Special Committee" (1990), "The Handmaid and the Gainae" (1990), "Eyes of Dawn" (1991), "Three Day Promise" (1991), "We're Middle Class" (1991), "For the Poet" (1993), "The 3rd Republic" (1993), "Moonlight Hometown" (1993), "Close One Eye" (1994),

"Relationship Is" (1995), "Seoul Nightsangok" (1995), "Asphalt Man" (1995), "Glorious Dawn" (1995), "Halt" (1996), "Tears of the Dragon" (1996), "Desire" (1997), "Scamper" (1997), "Love and Success" (1998), "The King's Path" (1998), "Legend of Ambition" (1998), "Hur Jun" (1999), "Secret" (2000), "Foolish Princes" (2000), "The Dawn of the Empire" (2002), "Lovers" (2002), "Something About 1%" (2003), "Good Morning Confucius" (2004), "New Human Market" (2004), "Choice" (2004), "A Second Proposal" (2004), "Green Rose" (2005), "My Girl" (2005), "Wolf" (2006), "Great Inheritance" (2006), "Behind the White Tower" (2007), "Witch You Hee" (2007), "My Too Perfect Sons" (2009), "Master of Study" (2010), "My Girlfriend Is a Gumiho" (2010), "The President" (2010), "Glory Jane" (2011), "Ohlala Couple" (2012), "Princess Aurora" (2013), "Goddess of Fire" (2013), "Flower Grandpa Investigation Unit" (2014), "Pinocchio" (2014), "Save the Family" (2015), "Madame Antoine: The Love Therapist" (2016), "Blow Breeze" (2016), and "Mr. Lawyer, Mr. Jo 2: Crime and Punishment" (2019). Byun was seen frequently in films, often portraying eccentric characters, with roles in "Dull Servant Pal Bul-chul" (1980), "Hotel at 00:00" (1983), "A Man with Color" (1985), "Eunuch" (1986), "No Woman Is Afraid of the Night" (1986), "We Are Going to Geneva Now" (1988), "Karma" (1988), "The World of Women" (1988), "A Surrogate Father" (1993), Bong Joon-ho's directorial debut "Barking Dogs Never Bite" (2000), "Volcano High" (2001), "Scent of Love" (2003), "My Teacher, Mr. Kim" (2003), "Memories of Murder" (2003), "Spring Breeze" (2003), "Au Revoir, UFO" (2004), "To Catch a Virgin Ghost" (2004), "Lovely Rivals" (2004), "Another Public Enemy" (2005), "Crying Fist" (2005), "Detective Mr. Gong" (2005), Bong's hit monster film "The Host" (2006) as Park Hee-bong, "Mission Sex Control" (2006), "Small Town Rivals" (2007), "The Devil's Game" (2009), "Lifting King Kong" (2009), "Searching for the Elephant" (2009), "Haunters" (2010), "In Love and War" (2011), "I Am the King" (2012), "The Spies" (2012), "Mr. Go" (2013), "Okja" (2017), and "By Quantum Physics: A Nightlife Venture" (2019).

Caillaud, Gerard

French actor Gerard Caillaud died in Montrouge, France, on January 27, 2023. He was 76. Caillaud was born in Poitiers, France, on April 10, 1946. He trained at the

Conservatoire National Superieur d'Art Dramatique. He performed with the Comedie-Francaise from 1971 until 1978 and was a director at the Theatre des Mathurins from 1984 to 1986. He appeared frequently in films with roles in "On s'est Trompe d'Histoire d'Amour" (1974), "L'Imprecateur" (1977), "Black Journal" (1977), "L'Argent des Autres" (1978), "Un Si Joli Village..." (1979), "The Dogs" (1979), "Us Two" (1979), "Bete, Mais Discipline" (1979), "La Femme Flic" (1980), "T'inquiete Pas, Ce Se Soigne" (1980), "Prends Ton Passe-Montagne, On Va a la

Plague" (1983), "Y a-t-il un Pirate sur l'Antenne?" (1983), "L'Addition" (1984), "Until September" (1984), "La Galette du Roi" (1986), "Paulette, la Pauvre Petite Milliardaire" (1986), "La Maison Assassinee" (1988), "Fanfan" (1993), "Les Palmes de M. Schutz" (1997), "My Wife Maurice" (2002), "Le Grand Role" (2004), and "Madame Irma" (2006). Caillaud was seen in such television productions as "Les Femmes Savantes" (1972), "Les Precieuses Ridicules" (1972), "La Station Champbaudet" (1972), 'Le Medecin Volant" (1973), "Les Fourberies de Scapin" (1973), "Paul Gauguin" (1975), "Monsieur Teste" (1975), "Marie-Antoinette" (1975), "Destinee de Monsieur de Rochambeau" (1976) as King Louis XVI, "Diner de Familie" (1976), "Histoire de la Grandeur et de la Decadence de Cesar Birotteau" (1977), "Le Misanthrope" (1977), "Lorenzaccio" (1977), "Ce Diable d'Homme" (1978), "Histoire du Chevalier Des Grieux et de Manon Lescaut" (1978), "Dickie-Roi" (1981), "Malesherbes, Avocat du Roi" (1982), "Marcheloup" (1982), "Histoire de Therese" (1983), "Dernier Banco" (1984), "La Methode Rose" (1986), "Pognon Sur Rue" (1992), "Balle Perdue" (1994), "Accuse Mendes France" (2011), and "A Child's Battle" (2011). His other television credits include episodes of "Les Grands Detectives", "L'Inspecteur Mene l'Enquete", "Commissaire Moulin", "Les Grandes Conjurations", "Les Enquetes du Commissaire Maigret", "Les Heritiers", "Julien Fontanes, Magistrat", "Messieurs les Jures", "Les Dossiers de l'Ecran", "Au Theatre ce Soir", "L'Affaire Marie Besnard", "Le Petit Docteur", "La Belle Anglaise", "Coplan", "Cinema 16", "Nouvelles de Marcel Ayme", "Les Mercredis de la Vie" (1993), "Louis Page" (2006), "Au Siecle de Maupassant: Contes et Nouvelles du XIXeme Siecle", "SoeurTherese.com" as Commandant Mazaud from 2003 to 2011, and "Chez Maupassant".

Cairney, John

Scottish actor John Cairney died in Scotland on September 7, 2023. He was 93. Cairney was born in Glasgow, Scotland, on February 16, 1930. He trained at the Royal

Scottish Academy of Music and Drama in Glasgow. He began his career on the stage in Scotland in the 1950s, appearing in roles in "Hamlet" and "Macbeth". Cairney was seen television in productions of "Knock" (1954), "Au Clair de la Lune" (1954), "Wild Decembers" (1956), "The Fisherman King" (1956), "MacAdam and Eve" (1956), "Home Is the Hero" (1958), "Mr. Gillie" (1960), "The Nightwalkers" (1960), "Drop Dead" (1961), "Design for a Headstone" (1962), "My Bonnie Jean" (1969) as poet Robert Burns, "Elizabeth R" (1971), "Henry IV Part I" (1979), "Silent Mouse" (1988), "The Torch" (1992), "The Chosen" (1998), and "Nightmare" (1999). His other television credits include episodes of "Stage by Stage", "Nom-de-Plume", "General Electric Theatre", "Boyd Q.C.", "Armchair Theatre", "Redgauntlet" as Alan Fairford in 1959, "Interpol Calling", "Target Luna" as Ian Murray in 1960, "Here

Lies Miss Sabry", "The Edgar Wallace Mystery Theatre", "Ghost Squad", "The Pursuers", "Barbara in Black" as Dr. Dave Sharland in 1962, "The Master of Ballantrae" as James Dune in 1962, "Dr. Finlay's Casebook", "Secret Agent", "Gideon C.I.D.", "Emergency-Ward 10", "Glaister", "Court Martial", the drama series "This Man Craig" as schoolteacher Ian Craig from 1966 to 1967, "Man in a Suitcase", "The Avengers", "ITV Playhouse", "Jamie", "The Persuaders!", "Late Night Theatre", "Scotch on the Rocks" as John Mackie in 1973, "Special Branch", "Churchill's People", "Jackanory", "Taggart", "Brond", "Shark in the Park", "White Fang", "High Tide", "Mysterious Island" as Captain Nemo in 1995, "Riding High", and "Plainclothes". Cairney appeared frequently in films from the late 1950s through the 1960s with roles in "Night Ambush" (1957), "Miracle in Soho" (1957), "Lucky Jim" (1957), "Windom's Way" (1957), "A Night to Remember" (1958) based on the sinking of the Titanic, "Shake Hands with the Devil" (1959) with James Cagney, "Operation Bullshine" (1959), the horror film "The Flesh and the Fiends" (aka "Mania") (1960) as Chris Jackson, a victim of the murderous grave-robbing duo Burke (George Rose) and Hare (Donald Pleasence), "Marriage of Convenience" (1960), "Victim" (1961), "Cleopatra" (1963) starring Elizabeth Taylor and Richard Burton, "Jason and the Argonauts" (1963) as Hylas, the ill-fated friend of Nigel Green's Hercules, the Hammer adventure film "The Devil-Ship Pirates" (1964) with Christopher Lee, the science fiction films "Spaceflight IC-1" (1965), and "A Study in Scarlet" (1965) starring John Neville as Sherlock Holmes. He performed on stage frequently throughout his career and wrote and starred in one-man shows as Robert Burns, Robert Louis Stevenson, Robert Service, and William McGonagall. He portrayed Burns in the 1965 play "There Was a Man" at the Traverse Theatre in Edinburgh in 1965. The play was later televised and Cairney recorded an album of his performance. He also wrote the books "Worlds Apart", "A Scottish Football Hall of Fame", "Heroes Are Forever", "A Year Out in New Zealand", "Glasgow by the Way, But", and "Flashback Forward". His autobiography, "The Man Who Played Burns", was published in 1987. Cairney earned a Master of Letters degree from Glasgow University for a "History of Solo Theatre" in 1988. He received a PhD from Victoria University in Wellington, New Zealand, in 1994. Cairney married Susan Cowan in the 1950s and they had five children before their divorce. He married New Zealand writer and actress Alannah O'Sullivan in 1980 and they spent 17 years together inn New Zealand before returning to Glasgow in 2008. He is survived by Alannah and his five children from his previous marriage.

Calderon, Sergio

Mexican-American actor Sergio Calderon died of pneumonia in Los Angeles, California, on May 31, 2023. He was 77. Calderon was born in Coatlan del Rio, Mexico, on July 21, 1945. He trained as an actor at the Instituto Andrés Soler of the Asociación Nacional de Actores. He made his film debut in 1970's "The Bridge in the Jungle". He was seen in numerous films including Sergio Leone's "Duck, You Sucker!" (1971), "The Revengers" (1972), "Mecanica Nacional" (1972), "Los Caciques" (1975), "Las Vuerzas Vivas" (1975), "Canoa: A Shameful Memory" (1976), "El Apando" (1978), "La India" (1976), "Las Poquianchis (De los Pormenores y Otros Sucedidos del Dominio Publico que Acontecieron a las Hermanas de Triste Memoria a Quienes la Maledicencia asi las Bautizo)" (1976), "La Casta Divinaa" (1977), "The Children of Sanchez" (1978), "El Complot Mongol" (1978), "Anacrusa" (1979), "Players" (1979), "The In-Laws" (1979) with Peter Falk and Alan Arkin, "Para Usted Jefa" (1980), "High Risk" (1981), "Las Siete Cucas" (1981), "La Chevre" (1981), "Valentin Lazana" (1982), "Erendira" (1983), John Huston's "Under the Volcano" (1984), "Buster" (1988), "Blood Red" (1989), "Old Gringo" (1989) with Gregory Peck and Jane Fonda, "Border Shootout" (1990), "The Man in the Golden Mask" (1991), "Pure Luck" (1991), "Highway Patrolman" (1991), the science fiction

comedy "Men in Black" (1997) starring Tommy Lee Jones and Will Smith, "El Aroma del Copal" (1997), "The Missing" (2003), "Pirates of the Caribbean: At World's End" (2007) as Captain Eduardo Villanueva, Pirate Lord of the Adriatic Sea, "The Ruins" (2008), "Little Fockers" (2010), and "The Seven Faces of Jane" (2022). Calderon appeared on television in episodes of "The A-Team", "Land's End", "Funny or Die Presents...", "Better Things", and "The Resort", He was also seen in the tele-films "A Home of Our Own" (1975), "Oceans of Fire" (1986), "Nurses on the Line: The Crash of Flight 7" (1993), "Have You Seen My Son" (1996), "Warden of Red Rock (2001), and "Hard Ground" (2003).

Caldwell, Bobby

Singer and songwriter Bobby Caldwell, who was noted for the hit single "What You Won't Do for Love", died at his home in Great Meadows, New Jersey, on March 14, 2023. He was 71. Caldwell was born in Manhattan, New York, on

August 15, 1951, and was raised in Miami, Florida. He began playing the piano and guitar from an early age and was rhythm guitarist for Little Richard in the early 1970s. He soon moved to Los Angeles where he played with various bands in local bars. He signed with TK Records in Miami in 1978 and recorded his first album. He scored a hit with his song "What You Won't Do for Love". He also recorded the albums "Cat in the Hat" (1980) and "Carry On" (1982). He became concentrating on writing songs for other artists including "The Next Time I Fall", which was a hit for Amy Grant and Peter Cetera. His songs were recorded by Boz Scaggs, Chicago, Natalie Cole, Neil Diamond, Roberta Flack, and many others. Caldwell appeared on television in episodes of "American Bandstand", "The Toni Tenille Show", and "Sara". He was featured as himself in the 1988 film "Salsa" and performed the song "Every Teardrop". He also provided songs for various film soundtracks including "Never Give Up" for "Night of the Comet" (1984), "Educated Girl" for "Back to School" (1986), "Bad Girl" for "The Hidden" (1987), "Take Me, I'll Follow You" for "Mac and Me" (1988), "One Love" for "The Raffle" (1994), "The Girl I Dream About" for "My First Mister" (2001) and "S1m0ne" (2002). He married Mary Beth Caldwell in 2004 and is survived by her and their two children.

Calvert, Rosalee

Actress Rosalee Calvert died in Oceanside, California, on April 25, 2023. She was 96. She was born Rosalee Coughenour in Dearborn, Michigan, on December 13, 1926. She moved to California with her family in the mid-1930s. She soon began modeling, working with such designers as Jean Louis, Irene, Galanos, Travilla, and Edith Head. She appeared in small roles in a handful of films from the 1950s including "Little Women" (1949), "East Side, West Side" (1949), "The Lemon Drop Kid" (1951), "Here Comes the Groom" (1951), "Two Tickets to Broadway" (1951), "Lovely to Look At" (1952), "Sound Off" (1952), "The Louisiana Hussy" (1959) opposite then husband Peter Coe, "If a Man Answers" (1962), "Made in Paris" (1966), "The Oscar" (1966), and "Save the Tiger" (1973). She also continued to work as a model through the 1970s. Calvert was married to actor Peter Coe from 1951 until their divorce in 1965 and is survived by their three sons.

Cambern, Donn

Film editor Donn Cambern, who earned an Academy Award nomination for his work on the 1984 film "Romancing the Stone", died of complications from a fall at a hospital in Burbank, California, on January 18, 2023. He was 93. Cambern was born in Los Angeles, California, on October 9, 1929. He earned a degree in music from the University of California at Los Angeles. He began his career working as a messenger at Disney in the 1950s. He moved to the music department at 20th Century Fox in 1959 and joined United Productions of America in the early 1960s. He worked on the animated film "Mr. Magoo's Christmas Carol" in 1962 and the Desilu television series "The Untouchables". He worked in television as a music editor, often with composer Dearle Hagan, for such series as "Margie", "The Andy Griffith Show", "Gomer Pyle, USMC", "I Spy", "That Girl", and "The Ghost and Mrs. Muir". He served as an editor for the television specials "The Bob Hope Christmas Special" (1968) sharing an Emmy Award nomination and "Debbie Reynolds and the Sound of Children"

(1969). Cambern made his debut as a film editor on the comedy feature "2000 Years Later" in 1969 and was editor for Dennis Hopper's 1969 counterculture classic "Easy Rider". He also edited the films "Follow Me" (1969), "A Session with the Committee" (1969), Jack Nicholson's directorial debut "Drive, He Said" (1971), "The Last Picture Show" (1971), "Blume in Love" (1973), "Steelyard Blues" (1973), "Cinderella Liberty" (1973), "The Hindenburg" (1975), "Alex & the Gypsy" (1976), "The Other Side of Midnight" (1977) also serving as second unit director, Burt Reynolds' directorial debut "The End" (1978), "Hooper" (1978), "Time After Time" (1979), "Smokey and the Bandit II" (1980), "Willie & Phil" (1980), "Excalibur" (1981), "Cannonball Run" (1981), "Paternity" (1981), "Tempest" (1982) also serving as second unit director, "Going Berserk" (1983), "Romancing the Stone" (1984) sharing an Oscar nomination, Richard Pryor's "Jo Jo Dancer, Your Life Is Calling" (1986), "Big Trouble" (1986), "Harry and the Hendersons" (1987), "Casual Sex?" (1988), "Feds" (1988), "Twins" (1988), "Ghostbusters II" (1989), "Eyes of an Angel" (1991) also serving as co-producer, "The Butcher's Wife" (1991), "The Bodyguard" (1992), "Rookie of the Year" (1993), "Bound by Honor" (1993), "Major League II" (1994), "Little Giants" (1994), "The Glimmer Man" (1996), and "A Thousand Acres" (1997). He also taught editing at the American Film Institute and was president of the Motion Picture Editors Guild from 1991 to 2002. Cambern received a Career Achievement Award from the American Cinema Editors in 2004. He was married to Patricia Lee Cambern from 1950 until her death in 2018, and is survived by their two children, Sharon and Wade. Another son, editor Clay Cambern, died in 2011.

Campeotto, Dario

Danish singer Dario Campeotto, who was a contestant in the 1961 Eurovision song contest, died in Denmark on April 1, 2023. He was 84. Campeotto was born in Frederiksberg, Copenhagen, Denmark, to Italian parents on February 1, 1939. He began singing as a child in the late 1940s. He represented Denmark in the Eurovision Song Contest in 1961 performing the song "Angelique". He placed fifth in the competition. Campeotto was featured in such films as "Eventyrrejsen" (1960), "Peter's Baby" (1961), "Han, Hun, Dirch og Dario" (1962), "Flagermusen" (1966), "Min Kones Ferie" (1967), "Onkel Joakims Hemmelighed" (1967), "Hopla Pa Sengekanten" (1976), "Kaerlighed Ved Forste Desperate Blik" (1994), "Flyvende Farmor" (2001), and "Gooseboy" (2019). He appeared on television in productions of "Et Moderne Maskespil" (1962) and "Musikken er af Noel Coward" (1968), and episodes of "Omkring et Flygel", "Bla Time", "Kik Ind!", and "Station 13". Campeotto was married to actress Ghita Norby from 1963 until their divorce in 1969, and is survived by their son, director

Giacomo Campeotto. He married Gertrude in 1977 and is also survived by her and their two children.

Campo, Wally

Actor Wally Campo, who starred in Roger Corman's cult-classics "The Little Shop of Horrors" and "Beast from Haunted Cave", died in Los Angeles, California, on January 14, 2023. He was 99. He was born Wallace Campodonico in Stockton, California, on April 23, 1923. He performed on stage while attending high school. He served in the U.S. Army during World War II. He embarked on a career on stage after his discharge and performed with the Stockton Community Players in a production of "Ah, Wilderness!" in 1948. He moved to Los Angeles in the early 1950s where he worked with the Orchard Gables Repertory Theatre Company and Showplace Theater. He made his film debut in the mid-1950s and appeared in the features "Inside Detroit" (1956), Roger Corman's crime drama "Machine-Gun Kelly" (1958), "Hell Squad" (1958), "Tank Commandos" (1959), and "Warlock" (1959). He was best known for his roles in a pair of Roger Corman horror films, "Beast from Haunted Cave" (1959) as gangster henchman Byron Smith, and the man-eating plant comedy "The Little Shop of Horrors" (1960) as Sgt. Joe Fink, the Narrator. His other films include Corman's "Ski Troop Attack" (1960), "Master of the World" (1961) adapted from a science fiction adventure by Jules Verne, "War Is Hell" (1961), Corman's horror anthology "Tales of Terror" (1962) in a segment based on Edgar Allan Poe's "The Black Cat", Sam Fuller's "Shock Corridor" (1963), the psychological horror "The Strangler" (1964) starring Victor Buono, the outlaw biker thriller "Devil's Angels" (1967), and the long-lost western "Mark of the Gun" (1969) which he also directed. Campo appeared on television in episodes of "The Lawless Years" and "Bat Masterson". He largely retired in the late 1960s but returned in television in episodes of "Berrenger's" and "The Fall Guy" in the 1980s, and "First Monday" and "Bram and Alice" in the early 2000s. He also appeared as himself in the 2011 comedy short "Actors Anonymous". He married actress Geraldine Matthews, his occasional stage co-star, in the 1950s and she predeceased him. He is survived by his son, musician Tony Campodonico.

Cantieni, Ursula

Swiss-German actress Ursula Cantieni died in Baden-Baden, Germany, on August 15, 2023. She was 75. Cantieni was born in Zurich, Switzerland, on December 5, 1947. She trained as an actor with the University of Music and Performing Arts in Stuttgart. She began her career on stage, working as an assistant director. She appeared frequently on television from the 1980s with roles in episodes of "Fest im Sattel", "Utta Danella", "High Society Murder", and "Tatort". She was also

featured in the tele-films "Der Letzte Gast" (1989), "Der Fischerkrieg" (1997), "Ein Mann Zum Bernaschen" (2004), and "Mama und der Millionar" (2005). Cantieni was seen in the 1986 film "Der Polenweiher. She was best known for her role as Black Forest farmer Johanna Faller on the television series "Die Fallers – Eine Schwarzwaldfamilie" from 1994 through 2022. She was also a member of the quiz show team for the television series "Sag die Wahrheit" from 2003 to 2022.

Capece Minutolo, Irma

Italian opera singer Irma Capece Minutolo died in Rome, Italy, on June 7, 2023. She was 87. Capece Minutolo was born in Naples, Italy, on August 6, 1935. She appeared in several films in the early 1950s including "Napoletani a Milano" (1953) and "Siamo Ricchi e Poveri" (1953). She was crowned Miss Naples in 1953. She was the long-time companion of deposed King Farouk of Egypt from the mid-1950s. She claimed that the two had been married after his death in 1965, though it was never substantiated. She began giving singing recitals in the early 1960s and was soon performing in such operas as "Il Trovatore" and "Gianni Schicchi". She returned to the screen as Signora Mantelli in Franco Zeferilli's 1988 film "Young Toscanini" starring Elizabeth Taylor. Her other films include "Crystal or Ash, Fir or Wind, as Long as It's Love" (1989), "Mutande Pazze" (1992), "Boom" (1999), and "Fantozzi 2000 - La Clonazione" (1999).

Capps, Mark

Music producer and sound engineer Mark Capps was shot to death in the doorway of his home in Hermitage, Tennessee, by a SWAT team member responding to reports that he was holding his wife and stepdaughter hostage, on January 5, 2023. He was 54. Capps was born in Nashville, Tennessee, on December 14, 1968. His father was Jimmy Capps, the house band guitarist for the Grand Ole Opry. Mark worked frequently as an engineer for country and gospel artists from the late 1980s. He worked on recordings by Amy Grant, Alabama, Neil Diamond, the Dixie Chicks, Barry Manilow, Conway Twitty, the Oak Ridge Boys, Kenny Rogers, Donna Summer, Olivia Newton-John, and many others. He shared four Grammy Awards for Best Polka Album for his work with Jimmy Sturr & His

Orchestra from 2005 to 2008. Capps had reportedly been suffering from depression prior to the shooting partially due to the death of his brother, Jeffrey Capps, two days earlier. He had been drinking beer while taking medication when he engaged in an altercation with his wife, Tara Capps, and stepdaughter, McKenzie Acuff. Despite some tense moments and threats with a gun during the morning the situation had deescalated and the two were allowed to leave the house in the morning. The police SWAT team were then sent to the location and reportedly did little to persuade Capps to surrender peacefully before shooting him. A controversy on whether the police shooting was justified remained a point of controversy and his wife filed a lawsuit against the city of Nashville later in the year.

Carcano, Alvaro

Mexican actor Alvaro Carcano died in Meridan, Mexico, on October 5, 2023. He was 85. He was born Alvaro de Jesus Carcano Ricalde in Mexico City, Mexico, on March 29, 1938. He was noted for his various roles in the children's television program "Odyssey Bubbles" in the 19870s and early 1980s. He was featured as such characters as Professor Memelovsky, Mafafa Musquito, and Mimoso Raton. He provided the Spanish dubbing voice for numerous animated series including "The Pink Panther Show" as the Ant, "Looney Tunes", and "Archie and Friends". Carcano appeared in numerous films including "El Aguila Descalza" (1971), "San Simon de los Magueyes" (1973), "Fe, Esperanza y Caridad" (1974), "Canoa: A Shameful Memory" (1976), "El Apando" (1976), "Meridiano 100" (1976), "Las Poquianchis (De los Pormenores y Otros Sucedidos del Dominio Publico que Acontecieron a las Hermanas de Triste Memoria a Quienes la Maledicencia Asi las Bautizo)" (1976), "La Palomilla al Rescate" (1976), "Vacaciones Misteriosas" (1977), "The In-Laws" (1979) with Peter Falk and Alan Arkin, "High Risk" (1981), "Yellowbeard" (1984), "Frankenstein's Great Aunt Tillie" (1984), "Mission Kill" (1985), "Firewalker" (1986) with Chuck Norris, "Manana de Cobre" (1986), "Verdugo de Traidores" (1986), "Ni de Aqi, Ni de Alla" (1988), "Buster" (1988), "La Furia de un Dios" (1988), "El Jinete de la Dinina Providencia" (1989), "Romero" (1989), "Solo Para Adulteros" (1989), "Como Fui a Enamorarme de Ti" (1990), "Ni Parientes Somos - Contagio de Amor" (1990), "Viernes Tragico" (1990), "The Man in the Golden Mask" (1991), "Kino" (1993), "The Wrong Man" (1993), "The Queen of the Night" (1994), "Midaq Alley" (1995), "Sin Remitente" (1995), "Los Talacheros" (1995), "Solo" (1996), "Deep Crimson" (1996), "Luces de la Noche" (1998), "A Sweet Scent of Death" (1999), "Pilgrim" (2000), 'Inspiracion' (2001), and "La Boda de Valentina" (2018). He was seen on television in episodes of "Sabado Loco, Loco", "Un Original y Veinte Copias", "No Empujen", "El Rincon de los Prodigios", "Trying Times",

"Hora Marcada", "Palace Guard", "Cuentos de Borges", "Tenias Que Ser Tu", "Papa Soltero", "Prisionera de Amor", "Retrato de Familia", "Conan the Adventurer", "Serafin", "Ramona", "Agua y Aceite", "Amy, la Nina de la Mochila Azul", "Gritos de Muerte y Libertad", "El Encanto del Aguila", and "Un dia Cualquiera". He also appeared in the tele-films "A Home of Our Own" (1975) and "One Man's War" (1991).

Cardwell, Anna 'Chickadee'

Anna 'Chickadee' Cardwell, who was the eldest sister of reality television star Honey Boo Boo, died of cancer in Georgia on December 9, 2023. She was 29. She was born Anna Shannon in Georgia on August 29, 1994. She appeared with her sister on the reality series "Toddlers & Tiaras" from 2012 to 2014 and was seen regularly with her family on the TLC series "Here Comes Honey Boo Boo" from 2012 to 2014. Her younger sister, Alana 'Honey Boo Boo' Thompson, and mother, Mama June Shannon, were the stars of the show along with sister Lauryn 'Pumpkin' Shannon and Jessica 'Chubbs' Shannon, and stepfather Mike 'Sugar Bear' Thompson. Anna was also seen in the We TV reality series "Mama June: From Not to Hot" in 2017. She was a guest on the series "Steve Harvey", "Family Feud", and "Dr. Phil". Anna was married to Michael Cardwell from 2014 until their divorce in 2017. She is survived by her daughters, Kaitlyn Elizabeth and Kylee Madison.

Carey, Anita

British actress Anita Carey died of breast cancer in New York on July 19, 2023. She was 75. Carey was born in Halifax, England, on April 16, 1948. She worked as a typist after attending secondary school and began performing on stage with the Bradford Civic Playhouse. She trained at the Central School of Speech and Drama in London from 1967 to 1970. She continued to perform on stage and became a familiar face on television from the early 1970s. She was seen in episodes of "Kate", "Please Sir!", "Z Cars", "Queenie's Castle", "The Flaxton Boys", "Whatever Happened to the Likely Lads?" as Susan Chambers from 1973 to 1974, "Billy Liar", "Marked Personal", "Dixon of Dock Green", "Centre Play", "Horizon", "Loner", "One-Upmanship", "I Didn't Know You Cared" as Pat from 1975 to 1976, "Beryl's Lot" as Babs Humphries from 1975 to 1977, "Coronation Street" as Brenda Summers in 1978, "Ripping Yards", "Premiere", "Strangers", "Play for Today", "Juliet Bravo", "The Spoils of War" as Martha Blaze from 1980 to 1981, "Roger Doesn't Live Here Anymore", "Andy Robson", "Miracles Take Longer", "Screen Two", "A Kind of Living" as Linda in 1990, "Poirot", "The Good Guys", "Virtual Murder",

"The Bill", "Band of Gold" as Glennis Minkin in 1996, "Rescue Me", "Where the Heart Is", "Heartbeat", "Last of the Summer Wine", "Midsomer Murders", "Casualty", and "Talk to Me". She returned to "Coronation Street" as Joyce Smedley from 1996 to 1997 and starred as receptionist Vivien March in the medical soap opera "Doctors" from 2007 to 2009. Carey also appeared in television productions of "But Fred, Freud Is Dead" (1973), "Napoleon and Love" (1974), "Mr. & Ms. Bureaucrat" (1978), "Some Enchanted Evening" (1978), "The History of Mr. Polly" (1980), "First Among Equals" (1986), "The Wyvern Mystery" (2000), "Perfect Strangers" (2001), "The Murder Room" (2005), and "The State Within" (2006). She was featured in several films during her career including "Ordeal by Innocence" (1984), "Still Crazy" (1998), "Crust" (2003), the short "Candlesticks" (2011), and "The Last Witness" (2018). Carey began living with actor Mark Wing-Davey in 1974 and the two married in 2002. She moved with him to the United States several years later. She is survived by her husband and their two children.

Carey, Gabrielle

Australian writer Gabrielle Carey, who co-wrote the 1979 novel "Puberty Blues", died in Sydney, Australia, on May 2, 2023. She was 64. Carey was born in Sydney on January 10, 1959. She and childhood friend Kathy Lette left school in their teens and shared an apartment together. They wrote the 1979 novel "Puberty Blues" about the lives of young surfers in Sydney. The book was adapted for a film by Bruce Beresford in 1981. She wrote the autobiographical book "Just Us" in 1984 which was adapted for a tele-film in 1986. She also wrote the memoirs "In My Father's House" (1992), "Moving Among Strangers" (2013), and "Falling Out of Love with Ivan Southall" (2018). Carey penned the 1994 novel "The Borrowed Girl". The wrote occasional articles for newspapers in Australia and lectured at the University of Sydney and the University of Canberra. Her survivors include her son Jimmy and daughter Bridgette.

Carlson, Jeffrey

Actor Jeffrey Carlson, who starred as Zoe Luper, the first transgendered character on a soap opera, in "All My Children" in 2006, died of complications from an enlarged heart in Chicago, Illinois, on July 8, 2023. He was 48. Carlson was born in Long Beach, California, on June 23, 1975. He graduated from the University of California at Davis in 1997, where he studied acting. He continued his training at the Juilliard School in New York City from 1997 to 2001. He performed on stage at the Guthrie Theatre in Minneapolis, Minnesota. He made his Broadway debut in the 2002 play "The Goat, or Who Is Sylvia?". He also appeared in Broadway productions of "Tartuffe" (2003) and "Taboo" (2003). Carlson was featured in several films including "Happy End" (2003), "Hitch" (2005), "Backseat" (2005), and "The Killing Floor" (2007). He was seen on television in the 2004 tele-film "Plainsong" and an episode of "Law & Order: Special Victims Unit". He was best known for his work on the soap opera "All My Children" from 2006 to 2007. He originally arrived on the series as Zarf, a British rock star. It was later revealed that Zarf was actually a transgender woman named Zoe Luper. Carlson continued to perform on stage, starring in the title role of the play "Lorenzaccio" at the Shakespeare Theatre Company in Washington, D.C. in 2005. He also appeared in productions with the Shakespeare Theatre Company of "Hamlet" (2008) and "Romeo and Juliet" (2016) as Mercutio. He performed frequently with regional theaters including Yale Repertory Theatre, the Charlotte Repertory Theatre, the Paper Mill Playhouse in Milburn, New Jersey, Chicago's Goodman Theater, and the Philadelphia Theatre Company. He appeared Off-Broadway in productions of "Antony and Cleopatra", "Bach at Leipzig", "Manuscript", "Last Easter", and "Thief River".

Carlyle, Simon

Scottish television writer Simon Carlyle, who created the series "Two Doors Down", died in Scotland on August 8, 2023. He was 48. Carlyle was born in Irvine, Scotland, on May 6, 1975. He was an ice skater in his youth and later attended Strathclyde University. He began working as a model and was an extra on the television police series "Taggart". He began working for BBC Scotland as a researcher for the program "Fully Booked" in 1997. He began working in television on the series "Terri McIntyre" which he wrote and starred in the title role from 2001 to 2003. He also began a long collaboration with writer Gregor Sharp, who produced the series. Carlyle was also a writer and performer in the series "Fran's People" in 2002. He and Sharp created the short-lived series "Thin Ice" in 2006 and "Happy Holidays" in 2009. He wrote the tele-films "No Holds Bard" (2009) and the mini-series "Psychobitches" (2013). He and Sharp created "Two Doors Down", starring Arabella Weir and Alex Norton, as a special for the BBC in 2013. It became a series in 2016 with its seventh season airing in late 2023. Carlyle was script editor for the comedy series "Benidorm" from 2010 to 2012, "Bad Education" from 2012 to 2013, and "Walking and Talking" in 2012. He was co-writer for episodes of "Boy Meets Girl" from 2015 to 2016. He was co-creator of the comedy series "Changing Ends" with Alan Carr in 2023.

Carraway, Bob

Actor Bob Carraway died in Woodland Hills, California, on March 26, 2023. He was 92. Carraway was born on December 7, 1930. He

appeared frequently on television in episodes of such series as "Decoy", "The Investigator", "Men of Annapolis", "Pistols 'n' Petticoats", and "Nero Wolfe". Carraway starred as Scott Banning in the daytime soap p[era "Days of Our Lives" in 1968. He was featured as Lt. Simpson in U.S. footage added to the Japanese kaiju film "Gammera the Invincible" in 1966. His other films include "The Reluctant Astronaut" (1967) starring Don Knotts and the western film "Soldier Blue" (1970). Carraway also performed on stage and appeared in the 1962 Broadway production of "Never Too Late".

Carter, Bobbie Jean

Bobbie Jean 'B.J.' Carter, the sister of singers Nick and

Aaron Carter, was found dead at her home in Florida on December 23, 2023. She was 41. Carter was born in Jamestown, New York, on January 12, 1982. She appeared with her four siblings in the E! reality series "House of Carters" in 2006. Older brother Nick was a member of the popular singing group the Backstreet Boys. Younger brother Aaron was a leading singer from an early age. The series also featured sisters Leslie and Angel. Bobbie Jean served as makeup artist and wardrobe stylist for Aaron Carter's concert tours in the early 2000s. She Jean reportedly suffered from addiction and substance abuse and had several legal difficulties relating to her problems. Sister Leslie Carter died of a drug overdose in 2012 and Aaron Carter drowned in his bathtub due to drugs in 2022. Her survivors include her 8-year-old daughter, Bella. She is also survived by brother Nick Carter and sister Angel.

Carvey, Dex

Comedian Dex Carvey, who was the son of comic

Dana Carvey, died of an accidental drug overdose in Los Angeles, California, on November 15, 2023. He was 32. He was born in 1991, the son of "Saturday Night Live" star Dana Carvey and his wife, Paula Zwagerman. Dex aspired to be a comedian like his father. He was the opening comic for his father's 2016 special "Dana Carvey: Straight White Male, 60" on Netflix. He was also seen in the television mini-series "The Funster" (2013) and "Beyond the Comics" (2014), and the 2015 film "Joe Dirt 2: Beautiful Loser".

Caryl, Ronnie

British guitarist Ronnie Caryl, who performed with Phil Collins and in the band Flaming Youth, died on December 18, 2023. He was 70. Caryl was born in Liverpool, England, on February 10, 1953. He was friends with drummer Phil Collins, and they accompanied singer John Walker on a tour of

Great Britain in the early 1970s. He and Collins joined with fellow musicians on the tour, bassist Gordon 'Flash' Smith and organist Brian Chatton, to form the band Hickory. They recorded the single "Green Light/The Key" in 1969. They changed their name to Flaming Youth and released the 1969 album "Ark 2". They disbanded in early 1970. Caryl subsequently auditioned with Collins for the band Genesis to make the group. They performed with several other bands including Sanctuary and Zox & the Radar Boys. He moved to France in 1995. He rejoined Collins in 1996, becoming a backing vocalist and rhythm guitarist for his group. He also worked with such artists as David Hentschel, Michel Polnareff, Lulu, Eric Clapton, Gary Brooker, Maggie Bell, and John Otway. Caryl released the solo albums "Leave a Light On" (1994) and "One Step at a Time" (2003). He is survived by his wife, Melanie.

Casper, DJ

Disc jockey William Perry, Jr., who was known by the name DJ Casper and created the hit song "Cha Cha Slide", died

of kidney and liver cancer in Hazel Crest, Illinois, on August 7, 2023. He was 58. Perry was born in Chicago, Illinois, on May 31, 1965. He was a DJ who became known as Casper due to appearing dressed in all white while on stage. He created the song "Casper Slide Pt. 1" in 1998 as a workout track for his nephew, who was a personal trainer. The song, which became known as "Cha Cha Slide" was soon being played on Chicago radio and became a hit. He released a sequel, "Casper Slide Pt. 2", in 2000. He had a minor hit with the 2004 single "Oops Up Side Your Head". Casper appeared in a cameo role in a 2018 episode of television's "Orange Is the New Black". He is survived by his wife, Kim Bradshaw.

Castillo, Gerald

Actor Gerald Castillo died at his home in Houston, Texas, on May 4, 2023. He was 90. Castillo was born in Chicago, Illinois, on December 23, 1932. He studied acting at the Goodman Theater in Chicago in the 1960s and performed frequently on the local stage. He moved to Los Angeles in the late 1970s and made his television debut in a small role in an episode of "The Jeffersons". He was seen frequently on

television with roles in episodes of "What Really Happened to the Class of '65?", "All in the Family", "Barnaby Jones", "Trapper John, M.D.", "Vega$", "Sanford", "The White Shadow", "M*A*S*H", "Chicago Story", "Dynasty", "Our Family Honor", "Scarecrow and Mrs. King", "The Paper Chase", "Night Court", "Hill Street Blues" in the recurring role of Detective Michael Benedict in 1987, "Our House", "Simon & Simon", "Houston Knights", "Beauty and the Beast", "Something Is Out There", "Hunter", "Perfect Strangers", "Dallas", "Dragnet", "Knots Landing" in the recurring role of Dr. Herrara in 1990, "The New Adam-12", "2000 Malibu Road", "Saved by the Bell" in the recurring role of Major Slater, the father of Mario Lopez's character from 1989 to 1992, "FBI: The Untold Stories", "General Hospital" as Judge Davis Wagner from 1992 to 1994, "Profiler", and "CSI: Crime Scene Investigation". His other television credits include productions of "Jacqueline Susann's Valley of the Dolls" (1981), "The Renegades" (1982), "Through Naked Eyes" (1983), "Right to Die" (1987), and "State of Emergency" (1994). Castillo appeared in a handful of films including "Hero at Large" (1980), "Death Wish 4: The Crackdown" (1987), "Kinjite: Forbidden Subjects" (1989), "Delta Force 2: The Colombian Connection" (1990), "Above Suspicion" (1995), "2084" (2009), and "Troubled Child" (2012). He retired from the screen and moved to Houston in 2013. Castillo is survived by his wife of 36 years, Dayna Quinn-Castillo. He was predeceased by a daughter from his first marriage, Lisa, in 2022.

Castro, Benito

Mexican comedian and musician Benito Castro died of complications from a fall in Mexico City, Mexico, on September 11, 2023. He was 77. He was born Arturo Castro

Hernandez in Mexico City on June 5, 1946. His father was comedian Arturo 'El Bigoton' Castro. His cousins Arturo, Javiere, Jorge, and Gualberto Castro formed the musical group Los Hermanos Castro in the late 1950s. Benito joined his cousins in the group while they were performing in Las Vegas, singing and playing the guitar. He continued to performer with Los Hermanos Castro after they returned to Mexico and also formed the duo Benito and Kiko with Kiko Campos. He appeared on the television series "La Carabina de Ambrosio" as the comic character Kin Kin from Acapulco in the late 1970s and early 1980s. He was also seen frequently on the series "La Ensalada de Locos". He played El Papirigo in several series including "Andale" (1992), "La Guereja y Algo Mas" (1998), and "Guereja de Mi Vida" (2001-2002). He also appeared in such television productions as "Siempre Te Amare" (2000), "Asi Son Ellas" as Roque Delfino in 2002, "Chiquiti Bum" (2006), "Mujer, Casos de la Vida Real" (2006), "Adictos" (2009), "Como Dice el Dicho" (2014), and "Nosotros los Guapos" (2016). Castro appeared in several films during his career including "El Zangano" (1968), "El Misterio de los Hongos Alucinantes" (1968), "La Criada Maravilla" (1979), "La Sangre de los Inocentes" (1995), and "El Nacotraficante" (2023). He was married to Karen Kaczmarczyk from 1974 until their divorce in 2008 and is survived by their son. He later married Deborah Ochoa and is survived by her and their daughter. He is also survived by a daughter from another relationship.

Castro, Itziar

Spanish actress Itziar Castro i Rivadulla died of a heart attack in a swimming pool in Lloret de Mar, Spain, while

rehearsing for a synchronized swimming performance on December 8, 2023. Castro was born in Barcelona, Spain, on February 14, 1977. She was 46. She began her acting career in the early 2000s with a role in the 2002 film "Noche de Fiesta". Her numerous film credits include "Inconscientes" (2004), "The Tulse Luper Suitcases, Part 3: From Sark to Finish" (2004), "Pretextos" (2008), "Sing for Darfur" (2008), "The Vazquez" (2010), "Red Eagle" (2011), the horror comedy "[REC] 3: Genesis" (2012), "Blancanieves" (2012), "Witching and Bitching" (2013), "Transeuntes" (2015), "La Sexta Alumna" (2016), "Pieles" (aka "Skins") (2017), "Killing God" (2017), "Champions" (2018), "Escape from Marwin" (2018), "Get Her... If You Can" (2019), "El Cerro de los Dioses" (2019), "Asylum: Twisted Horror and Fantasy Tales" (2020) in the "RIP" segment, Woody Allen's "Rifkin's Festival" (2020) in a cameo role, "The Barcelona Vampiress" (2020), "Historias Lamentables" (2020), "A Todo Tren! Destino Asturias" (2021), "La Mesita del Comedor" (2022), and "Campeonex" (2023). Castro produced, directed, and starred in the short films "La Soledad" (2022) and "L@ Cita" (2023). She appeared on television in episodes of "Hospital Central", "El Cor de la Ciutat", "Algo Que Celebrar", "El Crac", "Paquita Salas", "Vis a Vis" as Goya Fernandez from 2018 to 2019, "Terror y Feria", "Vida Perfecta", "Validas", "Vis a Vis: El Oasis" reprising her role as Goya in 2020, "Benidorm", "True Story Espana", "La Que se Avecina", and "One Way or Another" as Choni from 2020 to 2023. Her other television credits include productions of "Rumors" (2007), "Otra Ciudad" (2009), "Laia" (2016), and the Netflix musical mini-series "Once Upon a Time... Happily Never After" (2022).

Catt, Michael

Film producer and pastor Michael Catt died of prostate cancer in Albany, Georgia, on June 12, 2023. He was 70. Catt  was born in Pascagoula, Mississippi, on December 25, 1952. He graduated from Mississippi College and earned a Master of Divinity degree from Luther Rice Bible Seminary. He received a Doctor of Ministry degree from Trinity Theological Seminary of South Florida. Catt became senior pastor of Sherwood Baptist Church in Albany, Georgia, in 1989. He formed Sherwood Pictures to make faith-based films in 2003. He served as executive producer of the films "Flywheel" (2003) also appearing onscreen as a pastor, "Facing the Giants" (2006), "Fireproof" (2008), "Courageous" (2011), and "Woodlawn" (2015). Catt was also noted as a writer and orator. He remained pastor at Sherwood Baptist until his retirement in 2021. He married Terri Catt in 1974 and is survived by her and their two daughters, Erin and Hayley.

Cavezzali, Massimo

Italian comic book artist Massimo Cavezzali died in  Florence, Italy, on May 10, 2023. He was 73. Cavezzali was born in Ravenna, Italy, on February 11, 1950. He began his career in comics with the magazine "Il Mago" in 1976. He also illustrated comics for the magazines "Il Monello", "Lupo Alberto", "Orient Express", "Tango", and "Comix". He was noted for his comic strips "Ivan Timbrovic", "Ava", about an anthropomorphic duck, and "DIO S.p.a.", about a fictional God. His comics were seen in various newspapers including "La Stampa", "L'Unita", and "La Repubblica". He illustrated a comic biography of singer Vasco Rossi, "Ogni Volta Che Sono Vasco", in 2004.

Chambers, Joy

Australian actress Joy Chambers died in Queensland, Australia, on September 17, 2023. She was 76. Chambers was born in Ipswich, Australia, on November 18, 1947. She was a model and became the first Miss Surf Girl of the Queensland Surf Life Saving Club in 1965. She became a regular panelist on the Australian version of "I've Got a Secret" in 1967. She married television tycoon Reg Grundy in 1971 and worked as his production assistant. She also appeared in several of his game shows including "Everybody's Talking", "The Celebrity Game", and "Graham Kennedy's Blankety Blanks". Chambers was featured in the 1977 tele-film "All at Sea". She starred as Rita Merrick in the television soap opera "The Restless Years" from 1977 to 1979. She was also seen in the soaps "The Young

Doctors" as Robyn Porter from 1981 to 1982, and "Neighbours" in the recurring role of Rosemary Daniels from 1986 to 2010.  Chambers began writing historical novels in the 1990s including "Mayfield" (1993), "My Zulu, Myself" (1995), "Vale Valhalla" (2000), "None But the Brave" (2003), "For Freedom" (2007), and "The Great Deception" (2012). She served on the board of her husband's media company Grundys Worldwide until it was sold in 1995. The couple subsequently formed the media investment company RG Capital Holdings. Chambers and Grundy were married until his death in 2016.

Chance, Larry

Singer Larry Chance, who performed with the doo-wop group the Earls, died of lung cancer in Orlando, Florida,  on September 4, 2023. He was 82. He was born Lawrence Figueiredo in the Bronx, New York, on October 19, 1940. He was raised in Philadelphia, Pennsylvania, but returned to New York to form the doo-wop group the High Hatters in the 1957. The group evolved into the Earls and Figueiredo changed his last name to Chance. They had a major hit with their 1962 single "Remember Then". The Earls also recorded the songs "Never", "Life Is But a Dream", "I Believe", "Looking for My Baby", and "Kissing". Chance continued to perform with the frequently changing roster of the group. They played on the revival circuit by the 1990s and Chance remained with them until his death.

Chaplin, Josephine

Actress Josephine Chaplin, who was the daughter of legendary comedian Charlie Chaplin, died in Paris, France, on  July 13, 2023. She was 74. Chaplin was born in Santa Monica, California, on March 28, 1949. She was the third of eight children of Charlie Chaplin and his fourth wife, Oona O'Neill. Her grandfather was famed playwright Eugene O'Neill. She appeared as a child in a small role in her father's 1952 film "Limelight". She was later seen in her father's 1967 film "A Countess from Hong Kong". She was featured as May in Pier Paolo Pasolini's 1972 film "The Canterbury Tales" and co-starred with Laurence Harvey in the drama "Escape to the Sun" (1972). Her other films include "L'Odeur des Fauves"

(1972), "Les Quatre Charlots Mousquetaires" (1974) as Charlotte, "Les Charlots en Folie: A Nous Quatre Cardinal!" (1974), Georges Franju's science fiction thriller "Shadowman" (1974), "Docteur Francoise Gailland" (1976), "The Peaks of Zelengore" (1976), the German horror film "Jack the Ripper" (1976) with Klaus Kinski in the title role, "A l'Ombre d'un Ete" (1976), "La Guerillera" (1982), "The Bay Boy" (1984), "Cop Au Vin" (1985), "Coincidences" (1986), and "Ciudad Baja (Downtown Heat)" (1994). Chaplin appeared on television in productions of "The Man Without a Face" (1975) as Martine Leduc, "Les Annees d'Illusion" (1977), "Donatien-Francois, Marquis de Sade" (1985), and "Hemingway" (1988) as Hadley Richardson, the first wife of Stacy Keach's Ernest Hemingway. Her other television credits include episodes of "Histoires Insolites", "Histoires Extraordinaires", "Les Enquetes du Commissaire Maigret", "Symphonie", and "Le Masque". She was married to Greek furrier Nicholas Sistovaris from 1969 until their divorce in 1977 and is survived by their son, Charly. She lived with French actor Maurice Ronet from 1977 until his death in 1983 and is survived by their son, Julien. She was married to French archaeologist Jean-Claude Gardin from 1989 until his death in 2013 and is survived by their son Arthur. She is also survived by her seven siblings including actress Geraldine Chaplin. Half-brother Charles Chaplin III died in 1968 and Sydney Chaplin died in 2009.

Chapman, Kurtis

British professional wrestler Kurtis Chapman, who competed in the ring as Mad Kurt, died in Portsmouth, England, on December 29, 2023. He was 26. Chapman was born in Portsmouth on December 19, 1997. He began his career with Revolution Pro Wrestling in 2014. He frequently teamed with his brother, Harry, as the Chapman Brothers. He held the RevPro Wrestling British Cruiserweight Championship from 2017 until May of 2018. Chapman also held the promotions Arthouse Championship and made his most recent appearance in the ring defending the title in June of 2023.

Charles, Maria

British actress Maria Charles died in England on April 21, 2023. She was 93. She was born Maria Zena Schneider in London, England, on September 22, 1929. She graduated from the Royal Academy of Dramatic Art in 1946. She began her career on stage the previous year as the Dormouse in a production of "Alice in Wonderland". She made her West End debut in 1946's "Pick Up Girl". She appeared frequently on the West End, starring as Dulcie in the original London production of "The Boy Friend" in 1954. Charles appeared frequently on television with roles in productions of "The Likes of 'Er" (1947), "The Moon in the Yellow River" (1947), "Down Our Street" (1949), "A Man's House" (1949), "The Timorous Rake"

(1969), "Anne of Green Gables" (1972), "Pollyanna" (1973), "Great Expectations" (1974), "Anne of Avonlea" (1975), "Bar

Mitzvah Boy" (1976), "Disraeli: Portrait of a Romantic" (1978), "Sheppey" (1980), "Brideshead Revisited" (1981), "La Ronde" (1982), "Elphida" (1987), "A Perfect Spy" (1987), ""Great Expectations" (1989), "Anna" (1990), "Oliver Twist" (1997), "Crime and Punishment" (1998), "The 10th Kingdom" (2000), and "Cor, Blimey!" (2000). Her other television credits include episodes of "Nicholas Nickleby", "ITV Television Playhouse", "Saturday Playhouse", "Crossroads", "Angel Pavement", "ITV Playhouse", "Rogues' Gallery", "Kate", "Country Matters", "The Song of Songs", "Z Cars", "Within These Walls", "Six Days of Justice", "Doctor on the Go", "Ten from the Twenties", "Crown Court" as Joyce Farrington in 1975, "The Prince and the Pauper" as Grandma Canty in 1976, "Plays for Britain", "Play for Today", "Angels", "The Galton & Simpson Playhouse", "Jubilee", "Seven Faces of Woman", "Yanks go Home", "Secret Army", "Parables", "A Soft Touch", "Thomas and Sarah" as Madge in 1979, the ITV comedy series "Agony" as Bea Fisher from 1979 to 1981, "Whoops Apocalypse", "Shine on Harvey Moon", "Dream Stuffing" as May in 1984, "Weekend Playhouse", "The Two Ronnies", "Never the Twain" as Mrs. Sadler from 1982 to 1988, "Boon", "Casualty", "Alas Smith & Jones", "Woof!", "Screenplay", "The Young Indiana Jones Chronicles", "Lovejoy", "Agony Again" reprising her role as Bea Fisher in 1995, "London's Burning", "Shades", "Down to Earth", "Doctors", "Bad Girls" as Noreen Biggs from 2002 to 2003, "The Basil Brush Show", "Coronation Street" as Lena Thistlewood in 2005, "Holby City", "Ruddy Hell! It's Harry and Paul", and "Skins". Charles appeared in occasional films during her career including "A Gunman Has Escaped" (1948), "Folly to Be Wise" (1952), "The Deadly Affair" (1967), "The Strange Case of the End of Civilization as We Know It" (1977), "Revenge of the Pink Panther" (1978), "Cuba" (1979), "Victor/Victoria" (1982), "Under the Bed" (1988), "The Fool" (1990), "Savage Hearts" (1995), "Ten Minutes Older: The Cello" (2002), "Sixty Six" (2006), the short "Little Claus and Big Claus" (2006) as Granny Claus, "Hot Fuzz" (2007) as Mrs. Reaper, "In Your Dreams" (2008), and "Sisterhood" (2008). Charles was married to actor Robin Hunter from 1952 until their divorce in 1966 and is survived by two daughters, actress Kelly Hunter, and stage manager Samantha Hunter.

Charles, Walter

Actor Walter Charles died of complications from frontotemporal dementia at a hospital in Cleveland, Ohio, on August 3, 2023. He was 78. Charles was born in East Strousberg, Pennsylvania, on April 4, 1945. He studied piano at Bucknell University before transferring to Boston College. He graduated in 1966 and worked at performed at dinner theaters and touring companies for several years. He made his

Broadway debut as a replacement for the role of Vince Fontaine in the first road company production of "Grease" in 1972. He

was featured in numerous Broadway musicals including "1600 Pennsylvania Avenue" (1976), "Sweeney Todd" (1979), "Cats" (1982), "La Cage aux Folles" (1983), "Me and My Girl" (1986), "Aspects of Love" (1990), "Kiss Me, Kate" (1999), "The Boys from Syracuse" (2002), "Big River" (2003), "The Woman in White" (2005), "The Apple Tree" (2006), and "Anything Goes" (2011). Charles was featured in the 1982 television production of "Sweeney Todd: The Demon Barber of Fleet Street". He was also seen in episodes of "Cagney & Lacey", "Kate & Allie", "Law & Order", "The $treet", and "Law & Order: Criminal Intent". He appeared in several films including "A Fine Mess" (1986), "Weeds" (1987), "Fletch Lives" (1989), and "Prancer" (1989). Charles married his longtime companion, Leslie Thompson, in 2019 and she survives him.

Charnas, Suzy McKee

Science fiction and fantasy writer Suzy McKee Charnas died of a heart attack in New Mexico on January 2,

2023. She was 83. She was born Suzy McKee in New York City on October 22, 1939. She graduated from Barnard College om 1961. She subsequently joined the Peace Corps and taught in Nigeria for two years. She then earned a master's degree in education from New York University in 1965. She wrote the first book of what would be "The Holdfast Chronicles", a feminist post-apocalyptic epic, with "Walk to the End of the World" in 1974. Later volumes include "Motherlines" (1978), "The Furies" (1994), and "The Conqueror's Child" (1999). Charnas received a Nebula Award for her 1980 novella "Unicorn Tapestry" and a Hugo Award for the 1989 werewolf short story "Boobs". Her other novels include "The Vampire Tapestry" (1980), "Dorothea Dreams" (1986), "The Kingdom of Kevin Malone" (1993), and "The Ruby Tear" (1997). She wrote the young adult "Sorcery Hall" fantasy trilogy consisting of "The Bronze King" (1985), "The Silver Glove" (1988), and "The Golden Thread" (1989). Much of her short fiction appeared in the collections "Moonstone and Tiger-Eye" (1992), "Music of the Night" (2001), and "Stagestruck Vampires and Other Phantasms" (2004). She penned the 2002 memoir "My Father's Ghost: The Return of My Old Man and Other Second Chances". She was married to lawyer Stephen Charnas from 1968 until his death in 2018.

Chen Kenichi

Japanese chef Chen Kenichi, who starred on the "Iron Chef" reality series, died of interstitial pneumonia at a hospital

in Tokyo, Japan, on March 11, 2023. He was 67. He was born Ken'ichi Azuma in Tokyo on January 5, 1956. His father was Chen Kenmin, a chef from China, who introduced Sichuan cuisine to Japan. He followed in his father's footsteps and became chairman of the Szechwan Restaurant group with locations around Japan. He was one of three chefs to star in the cooking competition show "Iron Chef" from 1993. He wore a yellow outfit and was known as Iron Chef Chinese. He was the only chef to remain with the series until its completion in 1999. His survivors include his son, Chen Kentaro, who operated a Szechwan Restaurant branch in Singapore.

Chen Wei-ling

Taiwanese film director Chen Wei-ling died of cervical cancer at a hospital in Taipei, Taiwan, on November 1,

2023. She was 48. Chen was born in Taipei on March 4, 1975. She was best known for her work on television, directing productions of "Autumn's Concerto" (2009), "Year of the Rain" (2010), "Your Eyes, My Hands" (2011), "Material Queen" (2011), "Fiancee" (2013), "You Light Up My Star" (2014), "Rock Records in Love" (2016), "On Children" (2018), and "Mom, Don't Do That!" (2022). Chen also directed several films including "The Moonlight of Jilin" (2012) and "One Minute More" (2014).

Chesser, Chris

Film producer Chris Chesser died in Los Angeles, California, on February 2, 2023. He was 74. Chesser was born

on September 16, 1948. He graduated from Dartmouth College and earned a master's degree from the American Graduate School of International Management. He began working in films at Columbia in New York in 1974 as an executive in international sales. He became general manager of the American Film Institute in Los Angeles in 1976 and soon became an executive at Orion Pictures. He served as a production executive for such features as "The Great Santini" (1979), "Caddyshack" (1980), "On Golden Pond" (1981), "Wolfen" (1981), "Arthur" (1981), "Sharky's Machine" (1981),

"Excalibur" (1981), "Absence of Malice" (1981), "Yellowbeard" (1983), and "Spinal Tap" (1984). He was producer for the films "Kansas" (1988), "War Party" (1988), "Major League" (1989) also appearing onscreen in the small role of a Yankees baseball player, "Eyes of an Angel" (1991), "The Wrong Man" (1993), "The Surgeon" (1995), "Bad Day on the Block" (1997), "The Rundown" (2003), "Safari Tracks" (2005), "Bloodwork" (2012), and "Absolutely Anything" (2015). Chesser was producer of the tele-films "Silhouette" (1990), "Under Pressure" (1997), and "The Face of Evil: Reinhard Heydrich" (2002), and the documentary series "The Color of War", "Celebrity Wings", and "Secrets of War".

Chiarello, Michael

Celebrity chef Michael Chiarello died of anaphylaxis at a hospital in Napa, California, on October 6, 2023. He was 61. Chiarello was born in Red Bluff, California, on January 16,  1962. He graduated from the Culinary Institute of America in 1982 and earned a degree in hospitality management from Florida International University in 1984. He soon opened several restaurants in Florida including the Grand Bay and Toby's Bar and Grill. He settled in Napa Valley, California, in the mid-1980s and opened the Tra Vigne restaurant in 1987. He also served as executive chef at such restaurants as Ajax Tavern and Bump's in Aspen, Colorado, Bistecca Italian Steakhouse in Scottsdale, Arizona, and Caffe Museo in San Francisco, California. Chiarello hosted the PBS cooking show "Season by Season" in 2001. He also hosted "Napa Style" in 2004 and "Easy Entertaining with Michael Chiarello" from 2006 to 2008. He was a contestant on "Top Chef Masters" in 2009. Chiarello was also seen in episodes of "The Early Show", "The Best Thing I Ever Ate", "The Next Iron Chef", "The Perfect 3", "Unique Eats", "The Best Thing I Ever Made", "Restaurant: Impossible", "Barefoot Contessa", "Bringing It Home with Laura McIntosh", "Steve Harvey", "Late Night with Jimmy Fallon", and "Chopped". He was married and divorced from Ines Bartel and is survived by their three daughters. He married Eileen Gordon in 2004 and is also survived by her and their son.

Choi, Abby

Hong Kong model and internet influencer Abby Choi  was found murdered in the village of Tai Po, a suburb of Hong Kong, on February 24, 2023. She was 28. Some of her body parts were found in a refrigerator near where her headless corpse was located. The head and several of her ribs were found inside a pot of cooked soup. She had been reported missing on February 21. Her former husband, Alex Kwong, his brother, their parents, and other family members were charged in the killing. Choi was born in Hong Kong on July 15, 1994. She was a socialite and model and appeared in several magazines including "Elle", "Harper's Bazaar", and "Vogue". She was described as a fashion icon and influencer in a featured article in the magazine "L'Officiel Monaco" published shortly before her death. She was married to Alex Kwong from 2012 until their divorce in 2015 and they had two children together. She was later involved with Chris Tam Fong-Chun and they also had two children.

Chow, Kathy

Hong Kong actress Kathy Chow Hoi Mei died of complications from lupus in Beijing, China, on December 11, 2023. She was 57. Chow was born in Hong Kong on December  6, 1966. She was a contestant in the Miss Hong Kong pageant in the mid-1980s. She soon became a leading actress in films and television. Her film credits include "Zhu Zai Chu Geng" (1986), "The Truth" (1988), "How to Pick Girls Up" (1988), "My Dear Son" (1989), "Qing Yi Wo Xin Zhi" (1989), "Do Wong" (1990), "B u Wen Xiao Zhang Fu" (1990), the horror film "Holy Virgin vs. the Evil Dead" (1991), "Fight Back to School III" (1993), "Insanity" (1993), "The Private Eye Blues" (1994), "Ai Qing Se Xiang Wei" (1994), "Don't Give a Damn" (1995), "First Option" (1996), "The Legend of the Dragonslayer Sword 3" (1996), "Kau Luen Kei" (1997), "Beast Cops" (1998), "Nude Fear" (1998), "Oi Joi Yue Lok Guen Dik Yat Ji" (1998), "Sleepless Town" (1998), "Cheap Killers" (1998), "Wu Fa Wu Tian" (2000), "Sound from the Dark" (2000), "Vampire Controller" (2001), and "Memento" (2002). She was seen on television in productions of "The Yangs' Saga" (1985), "Lau Man Dai Hung" (1986), "Sung Meng Chi Loi" (1987), "The Saga of the Lost Kingdom" (1988), "Yee But Yung Ching" (1989), "Siu Giu Zoi Ming Tin" (1990), "Nagarete Yamazu" (1992), "Heaven Sword and Dragon Sabre" (1994) as Zhou Zhi-ruo, "Love Is Blind" (1994) as Leung Kwai, "Plain Love" (1995), "Time Before Time" (1997), "Secret of the Heart" (1998) as Ching Ka Wa, and "Chung Wan Sei Hoi" (1999). Chow moved to Beijing in the early 2000s where she continued her acting career in the films "Yi Ye Wei Liao Qing" (2011), "Legendary Amazons" (2011), "Hot Blood Band" (2015), "Mr. Pride vs. Miss Prejudice" (2017), "The Magic School" (2019), "The Rookies" (2019), "Gu Ci" (2019), "Asura Bride" (2020), and the action comedy "Heroes Return" (2021). Her later television credits include "Asian Heroes" (2003), "Legend of the Condor Heroes" (2008), "Hok King Shiu Kik" (2009), "Wang Yang Ming" (2012), "The Empress of China" (2014-2015) as Consort Yang Shu Fei, "72 Floors of Mystery" (2017), "Ashes of Love" (2018), "Heavenly Sword and Dragon Slaying Sabre" (2019) as Abbess Mie Jue, and "Count Your Lucky Stars" (2020). Chow was married to actor Ray Lui from 1988 until their divorce in 1989.

Christopher, Jamie

British assistant director Jamie Christopher died of heart complications in Los Angeles, California, on August 29, 2023. He was 52. Christopher was born in London, England,

on July 1, 1971. His parents, Malcolm J. Christopher and Penny Christopher, both worked in film production. Jamie began working in television as a production runner for the tele-films "Just Another Secret" (1989) and "Pride and Extreme Prejudice" (1989). He made his film debut as third assistant director for "Alien 3". He continued to work as an assistant director on such films as "Black Beauty" (1994), "First Knight" (1995), "GoldenEye" (1995), "The Ghost and the Darkness" (1996), "The Fifth Element" (1997), "Mortal Kombat: Annihilation" (1997), "Legionnaire" (1998), "The Mummy" (1999), "Woman Wanted" (1999), "Shadow of the Vampire" (2000), "102 Dalmatians" (2000), "Just Visiting" (2001), "The Mummy Returns" (2001), "Harry Potter and the Sorcerer's Stone" (2001), "Killing Me Softly" (2002), "Harry Potter and the Chamber of Secrets" (2002), "Hidalgo" (2004), "Harry Potter and the Prisoner of Azkaban" (2004), "Harry Potter and the Goblet of Fire" (2005), "The Da Vince Code" (2006), "Fantastic Four: Rise of the Silver Surfer" (2007), "Harry Potter and the Order of the Phoenix" (2007), "The Bourne Ultimatum" (2007), "Harry Potter and the Half-Blood Prince" (2009), "Ondine" (2009), "Harry Potter and the Deathly Hallows: Part 1" (2010), "Harry Potter and the Deathly Hallows: Part 2" (2011), "The Three Musketeers" (2011), "Resident Evil: Retribution" (2012), "Jack the Giant Slayer" (2013), "Justice League" (2017), "Star Wars: Episode VIII - The Last Jedi" (2017) also appearing onscreen as X-Wing Pilot Tubbs, "Holmes & Watson" (2018), "Murder Mystery" (2019), and "Knives Out" (2019). Christopher began working with the Marvel Cinematic Universe as first assistant director and associate producer for 2013's "Thor: The Dark World". He also worked on the Marvel films "Guardians of the Galaxy" (2014), "Avengers: Age of Ultron" (2015), "Black Widow" (2021), "Doctor Strange in the Multiverse of Madness" (2022), "Ant-Man and the Wasp: Quantumania" (2023), and "The Marvels" (2023). Christopher is survived by his wife, Carly, and their son and daughter. He is also survived by three children from a previous marriage.

Christopher, Julian

Actor Julian Christopher died on February 26, 2023. He was 78. Christopher was born in Philadelphia, Pennsylvania, on November 7, 1944. He appeared frequently in films and television from the early 1970s. He was originally billed under the name James Louis 'Jim' Watkins through the 1980s. He was featured in the films "Cool Breeze" (1972), "Black Gunn" (1972), "McQ" (1974), "Caged Heat" (1974), "J.D.'s Revenge" (1976), "The Night Stalker" (1986),

"Spellbinder" (1988), "Timebomb" (1991), "Sexual Predator" (2001), "The Lazarus Child" (2004), "The Exorcism of Emily Rose" (2005), "Severed" (2005), "The Hard Corps" (2006), "-Men: The Last Stand" (2006), "88 Minutes" (2007), "Whisper" (2007), "Beneath" (2007), "Lullaby for Pi" (2010), "Elysium" (2013), and "Crash Pad" (2017). He appeared on television in episodes of "Cannon", "The Bob Newhart Show", "The Magician" as Jerry Anderson from 1973 to 1974, "Get Christie Love!", "Baretta", "Joe Forrester", "Police Story", "1st & Ten", "Three's a Crowd", "Who's the Boss?", "Dynasty", "Webster", "Tall Tales & Legends", "Stingray", "Hill Street Blues", "Our House", "Star Trek: The Next Generation", "Jake and the Fatman", "Supercarrier", "A Man Called Hawk", "227", "Doogie Howser, M.D.", "Amen", "Dream On", "Dangerous Women" as Ron Webb in 1991, "Street Justice", "The Commish", "Murder, She Wrote", "Star Trek: Deep Space Nine", "Robin's Hoods", "The Outer Limits", "The Marshal", "Saved by the Bell: The New Class", "The Associates", "Touching Evil", "The Dead Zone", "Masters of Horror", "The 4400", "Three Moons Over Milford", "Smallville" in the recurring role of Dr. MacIntyre from 2002 to 2006, "Masters of Science Fiction", "Bionic Woman", "Fear Itself", "Knights of Bloodsteel", "Human Target", "Fringe", "Endgame", "Flashpoint", "Supernatural", "Emily Owens M.D.", "Cult" as Ben Quinn in 2013, "Rogue", "Continuum", "Once Upon a Time", "Gracepoint", "Motives & Murders: Cracking the Case", "Lost Girl", "American Lawmen", "The X-Files", "Aurora Teagarden Mysteries" as Lemaster Cane from 2015 to 2016, "When We Rise", "When Calls the Heart" in the recurring role of George Edwards from 2016 to 2017, "A Million Little Things", and "Upload" as Ernie in 2020. His other television credits include the tele-films "The Keegans" (1976), "Killer in the Mirror" (1986), "Who Is Julia?" (1986), "Working Tra$h" (1990), "Majority Rule" (1992), "Sherlock Holmes Returns" (1993), "Serving in Silence: The Margarethe Cammermeyer Story" (1995), "Broken Trust" (1995), "Meltdown" (2004), "Our Fathers" (2005), "The Engagement Ring" (2005), "Passion's Web" (2007), "Crossroads: A Story of Forgiveness" (2007), "Fireball" (2009), "Christmas in Canaan" (2009), "Freshman Father" (2010), "One Angry Juror" (2010), "Christmas Comes Home to Canaan" (2011), "The Mystery Cruise" (2013), "Wedding Planner Mystery" (2014), "Autumn in the Vineyard" (2016), "Undercover Angel" (2017), and "A Gingerbread Romance" (2018).

Christopher, Tyler

Actor Tyler Christopher, who was best known for his role as Nikolas Cassadine on the soap opera "General Hospital" for nearly 20 years, died of cardiac arrest in San Diego, California, on October 31, 2023. He was 50. He was born Tyler

Baker in Joliet, Illinois, on November 11, 1972. He attended college for two years at Ohio Wesleyan University before moving to Los Angeles in the early 1990s to pursue an acting

career. He was cast in the role of Nikolas Cassadine in "General Hospital" in 1996 and remained with their series through 1999. He returned to "General Hospital" from 2003 to 2011 and again from 2013 to 2016. He starred as Stefan DiMera on the soap opera "Days of Our Lives" from 2017 to 2019. Christopher was a five-time Daytime Emmy Award nominee and received the Emmy for his role as Nikolas Cassadine in 2016. He was also seen in episodes of such series as "Family Law", "Charmed", "Angel", "The Pretender", "Felicity", "Special Unit 2", "The Division", "The Twilight Zone", "JAG", "Boomtown", "CSI: Crime Scene Investigation", "One for the Money", "Crossing Jordan", "Secrets of a Small Town", and the teen mystery drama "The Lying Game" as Dan Whitehorse from 2011 to 2013. His other television credits include the tele-films "Sam's Circus" (2001), "One for the Money" (2002), the mini-series "Into the West" (2005), "The Other Mother" (2017), "Super Volcano" (2022), "20.0 Megaquake" (2022), and "Ice Storm" (2023). Christopher was featured in the films "Common Bonds" (1997), "Catfish in Black Bean Sauce" (1999), "Face the Music" (2011), "Out of the Black" (2011), "Frogmen Operation Stormbringer" (2002), "Raven" (2010), "Stage 4" (2010), "Shouting Secrets" (2011), "Beyond the Lights" (2014), "Pretty Broken" (2018), "F.R.E.D.I." (2018), "Max Winslow and the House of Secrets" (2019), the science fiction adventure "Moon Crash" (2022), "Thor: God of Thunder" (2022) (not to be confused with the Marvel Comics franchise), and "Murder, Anyone?" (2022). Christopher was married to actress Eva Longoria from 2002 until their divorce in 2004. He was married to auto racing reporter Brienne Pedigo from 2008 until their divorce in 2021 and is survived by their son and daughter.

Chronopoulou, Mary

Greek actress Mary Chronopoulou died of complications from a fall at a hospital in Athens, Greece, on

October 6, 2023. She was 90. Chronopoulou was born in Athens on July 16, 1933. She graduated from the National Theatre Drama School and began her career on stage. She was a popular performer on stage and screen throughout her career. She made her film debut in a small role in Michael Cacoyannis' "A Matter of Dignity" in 1958 for Finos Films. Chronopoulou continued to appear in such films as "Stournara 288" (1959), "Horis Taftotita" (1963), "The Red Lanterns" (1963), "Anishya Neiata" (1963), "To Tempeloskylo" (1963),

"Ta Paliopaida" (1963), "Kravgi..." (1964), "I Kypros Stis Floges" (1964), "To Koritsi Tis Kyriakis" (1964), "The Naked Brigade" (1965), "Adistaktoi" (1966), "Blood on the Land" (1965), "The Fear" (1966), "Tears for Electra" (1966), "Society Hour Zero" (1966), "The Blue Beads from Greece" (1967), "Psomi Gia Ena Drapeti" (1967), "A Lady in Sirtaki Dance" (1968), "A Woman's Past" (1968), "Too Late for Tears" (1968), "The Avenue of Hatred" (1968), "Gorgones Kai Mages" (1968), "When the City Dies" (1969), "Oratotis Miden" (1970), "In the Name of the Law" (1970), "The City Jungle" (1970), "Ippokratis Kai Dimokratia" (1972), "I Gynaikokratia" (1973), "Oi Kynigoi" (1977), "Porsklitirio tis Manas" (1979), "The Hemline" (1980), "Savage Hunt" (1980), "Kathenas Me Tin Trella Tou..." (1980), "Panikos Sta Sholeia" (1981), "O Zigolo Tis Athinas" (1982), "The Children of the Swallow" (1987), "Ehete Gia Vrisoules" (1990), and "Pros Tin Elefteria" (1996). She was seen on television in productions of "Vradya Epitheorisis" (1984), "Oi Palioi Mas Filoi" (1985), "Mora Mou Kalispera, Voggame Oli Mera" (1993), "Mana Einai Mono Mia" as Mairi Moisiadou from 1993 to 1994, "Emeis Ki Emeis" (1994), "Simiste Mas... Kai Afiste Mas" (1997), "Skaei Nyfi... SKAI Gabros" (1998), and "The Other Me" as Matron from 2022 to 2023.

Churikova, Inna

Russian actress Inna Churikova died in Moscow, Russia, on January 14, 2023. She was 79. Churikova was born in Belebey, Bashkortostan, Russia, on October 5, 1943. She

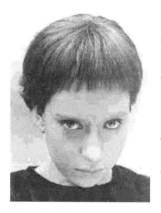

moved to Moscow with her mother in the early 1950s. She studied drama and attended the Shchepkin Drama School, graduating in 1965. She appeared frequently in films and television from the early 1960s. Her credits include "Clouds Over Borsk" (1963), "Walking the Streets of Moscow" (1963), "Jack Frost" (1964), "Where Are You Now, Maxim?" (1964), "Cook" (1965), "Thirty Three" (1965), "Head Nurse" (1966), "The Elusive Avengers" (1966), "No Path Through Fire" (1967), "The Beginning" (1970), "Request to Speak" (1967), "The Very Same Munchhausen" (1979), "The Theme" (1979), "Valentina" (1981), "Wartime Romance" (1983), "Vassa" (1983), "Dead Souls" (1984), "Courier" (1987), "Mother" (1990), "Adam's Rib" (1990), "Casanova's Raincoat" (1993), "The Year of the Dog" (1994), "Assia and the Hen with the Golden Eggs" (1994), "Shirli-Myrli" (1995), "Bless the Woman" (2003), "The Idiot" (2003), "Casus Belli" (2003), "Narrow Bridge" (2004), "Moscow Saga" (2004), "The First Circle" (2005), "Spiral Staircase" (2005), "Carnival Night-2, or 50 Years Later" (2006), "Guilty Without Fault" (2008), "Secrets of Palace Overturns. Part 7. 'Vivat, Anna!'" (2008), and "Burnt by the Sun 2: Citadel" (2011), "The Land of Oz" (2015), "Bez Granits" (2015), "Samyy Luchshiy Den!" (2015), "Pamyat Oseni" (2016), "100 Minutes" (2021), and "Myatnyy Pryanik"

(2022). Churikova performed frequently on stage throughout her career and was a member of the Lenkom Theatre troupe in Moscow from 1974. She was named a People's Artist of the USSR in 1991. Churikova married director Gleb Panfilov in the 1960s and he survives her.

Cicogna, Marina

Italian film producer Marina Cicogna died in Rome, Italy, on November 4, 2023. She was 89. Cicogna was born in Rome on May 29, 1934. Marina attended Sarah Lawrence College in Yonkers, New York. She left school to work as a photographer in Hollywood. She became involved in films in the mid-1960s when her mother, Countess Annamaria Volpi di Misurata, purchased Euro International Films. Cicogna was involved with the distribution of the 1967 West German film "Helga". She was involved in the production and distribution of such films as Luis Bunuel's "Belle de Jour" (1967), "I Giovani Tigri" (1968), Sergio Leone's "Once Upon a Time in the West" (1968), Pier Paolo Pasolini's "Teorema" (1968) and "Medea" (1969), "My Uncle Benjamin" (1969), Elio Petri's Academy Award winning Best Foreign Language Film "Investigation of a Citizen Above Suspicion" (1970), "Incontro" (1971), Franco Zeffirelli's "Brother Sun, Sister Moon" (1972), "We'll Call Him Andrea" (1972), "The Master Touch" (1972), and "A Brief Vacation" (1973). She stopped producing films in the early 1970s. She was the subject of the 2021 documentary film "Marina Cicogna: La Vita e Tut il Resto" and her autobiography, "I Still Hope: A Story of Life and Cinema" was published in 2023. Cicogna was involved with Brazilian actress Florinda Bolkan for over two decades. She was subsequently involved with Benedetta Gardona who she later legally adopted for inheritance purposes as same-sex unions were not allowed in Italy.

Cirella, Ralph

Stylist and radio personality Ralph Cirella, who was Howard Stern's personal stylist who made frequent appearances on his radio program, died of cancer on December 5, 2023. He was 58. Cirella was born on April 20, 1965. He first became associated with Howard Stern by calling into his WNBC radio show in 1985. He worked with Stern to create a penis puppet for the 1986 New Year's Eve event at the New York City Felt Forum. He continued to work with Stern creating special effects for his television series "The Channel 9 Show". Cirella also became personal stylist, wardrobe consultant, and set designer for Stern's shows. He was frequently heard on "The Howard Stern Show". He worked as a makeup artist for the films "She's Back" (1989) and "Alien Space Avenger" (1989) and was a production consultant for Stern's 1997 film "Private Parts". Cirella briefly hosted "The Friday Show" on Howard 101 radio in 2006 and was host of the network's "Geek Time". He remained a close friend of Sterns' for over thirty years.

C-Knight

Rapper and MC Arnez Blount, who was a founding member of the hip hop ensemble Dove Shack under the name C-Knight, died of complications from diabetes and a stroke in Las Vegas, Nevada, on November 7, 2023. He was 52. Blount was born in Long Beach, California, on June 15, 1971. He formed the Dove Shack with Bo-Roc and 2Scoops in the early 1990s and they performed their debut song "This Is the Shack" on Warren G's 1995 album "Regulate... G Funk Era". They released their own album soon after which included the hits "Summertime in the LBC", "We Funk (The G Funk)", and "Bomb Drop". C-Knight recorded the solo album "Knight Time" in 2001. The Dove Shack later released the 2006 album "Reality Has Got Me Tied Up". Blount had been hospitalized in October for problems with diabetes. He subsequently suffered a stroke and was put on life support from which he never recovered.

Clark, Carol Higgins

Mystery writer Carol Higgins Clark, who frequently worked with her mother, acclaimed author Mary Higgins Clark, died of appendix cancer at a hospital in Los Angeles, California, on June 12, 2023. She was 66. Clark was born in New York City on July 28, 1956, and was raised in Washington Township, New Jersey. She graduated from Mount Holyoke College in South Hadley, Massachusetts. She began assisting her mother with typing her book manuscripts while in college. She studied acting at the Beverly Hills Playhouse. She also began performing on stage and appeared in a small role in the 1986 film version of her mother's book "Where Are the Children?". She was featured in a handful of tele-films, many based on her mother's novels. She was seen in "Stillwatch" (1987), "Night of the Fox" (1990), "A Cry in the Night" (1992), "While My Pretty One Sleeps" (1997), "The Cradle Will Fall" (2004), "Deck the Halls" (2011), "The Mystery Cruise" (2013), and "My Gal Sunday" (2014). Clark also appeared in the 1990 film "Fatal Charm" and an episode of "Secret Service" in 1993. She was a contestant on the game show "To Tell the Truth" in 2001. She made her writing debut with "Decked" in 1992 which introduced her recurring protagonist private investigator Regan Reilly. Other novels in her Regan Reilly series include

"Snagged" (1993), "Iced" (1997), "Twanged" (1998), "Fleeced" (2001), "Jinxed" (2002), "Popped" (2003), "Burned" (2005), "Hitched" (2006), "Laced" (2008), "Zapped" (2009), "Cursed" (2009), "Wrecked" (2010), "Mobbed" (2012), "Gypped" (2012), and "Knocked" (2015). She and her mother co-wrote the novels "Deck the Halls" (2000), "The Christmas Thief" (2006), "Santa Cruise: A Holiday Mystery at Sea" (2006), and "Dashing Through the Snow" (2008) which featured Carol's Regan Reilly and Mary's Willy & Alvirah characters. The two also wrote the 2001 novel "He Sees You When You're Sleeping" and the story collections "The Christmas Collection" (2010) and "A Holiday Collection" (2010). Mary Higgins Clark died in January of 2020.

Clark, Erin K.

Actress Erin K. Clark died after a brief illness at her home in Long Beach, California, on September 13, 2023. She  was 34. Clark was born in Moline, Illinois, on November 2, 1988, and was raised in Port Byron, Illinois. She graduated from Western Illinois University in 2011. She performed in plays while in high school and college. She moved to Los Angeles in 2016 to pursue an acting career. She was featured in various films and shorts including "Birthday Girl" (2017), "UniversitE" (2017), "Ouija House" (2018) as Evelyn the Evil Witch, "Outside Park" (2018), "A Beauty & the Beast Christmas" (2019), "Cigarette Daydreams" (2020), "The Rockside Files" (2020), "The Ushers" (2021), and "Forest Giants" (2022). Clark was seen on television in the tele-films "Mommy, I Didn't Do It" (2017) and "Dying to Be a Cheerleader" (2020), and episodes of "Most Likely" and "What Brings You In?".

Clark, Marlene

Actress Marlene Clark, who starred in the horror films "Ganja & Hess" and "Night of the Cobra Woman", died in Los Angeles, California, on May 18, 2023. She was 85. Clark was  born in New York City on December 19, 1937. She attended Morristown Jr. College in Tennessee and City College in New York City. She worked as a fashion model before pursuing an acting career in the 1960s. She made her film debut in a small role in the 1968 film "For Love of Ivy" starring Sidney Poitier. Clark also appeared in the films "Midnight Cowboy" (1969), "Putney Swope" (1969), "Stop!" (1970), "The Landlord" (1970), "Clay Pigeon" (1971), the horror film "Night of the Cobra Woman" (1972) as Lena Aruza, the horror-comedy "Beware! The Blob" (aka "Son of the Blob") (1972), the blaxploitation film "Slaughter" (1972) starring Jim Brown, the vampire film

"Ganja & Hess" (1973) as Ganja Meda, "Enter the Dragon" (1973) starring Bruce Lee, the British werewolf film "The Beast Must Die" (1974), "Newman's Law" (1974), "Black Mamba" (1974), "Lord Shango" (1975), "Switchblade Sisters" (aka "The Jezebels") (1975), and "The Baron" (1977). Clark was featured in the tele-films "Lost Flight" (1970), "Parachute to Paradise" (1972), "Incident on a Dark Street" (1973), and "Bunco" (1977). Her other television credits include episodes of "The Bill Cosby Show", "The Governor & J.J.", "Marcus Welby, M.D.", "The Immortal", "Bonanza", "Mod Squad", "McCloud", "The Rookies", "Sanford and Son" in the recurring role of Lamont's girlfriend, Janet Lawson, from 1976 to 1977, "The Richard Pryor Show", "What's Happening!!", "Barnaby Jones", "Flamingo Road", "Highway to Heaven", and "Head of the Class". She owned a clothing store in Los Angeles in the 1980s and later worked as a manager at Hal's Bar and Grill in Venice Beach for over a decade. Clark was married to actor Billy Dee Williams from 1968 until their divorce in 1971.

Cleve, Jenny

French actress Jenny Cleve died in Tourcoing, France, on February 17, 2023. She was 92. Cleve was born in Roubaix, France, on April 3, 1930. She studied at the Conservatoire de  Roubaix and trained as an actress. She performed on stage from the 1950s and was seen on television in productions of "Adrian et Jusemina" (1958), "En Famille" (1966), "Deslouettes Pere et Fils" (1967), "Le Renard et les Grenouilles" (1973), "Ma Femme et l'Enfant" (1973), "L'Enfant de l'Automne" (1973), "Chronique Villageoise" (1973), "La Colonie" (1974), "La Nuit de Winterspelt" (1974), "Le Silence des Armes" (1976), "Le Coeur au Ventre" (1976), "Inutile d'Envoyer Photo" (1977), "Le Loup-Cervier" (1979), "Le Dernier Train" (1979), "Les Yeux Bleus" (1979), "Les Petits Soirs" (1979), "Les Aventures d'Yvon Dikkebusch" (1980), "Vincendon" (1980), "Histoires Etranges" (1980), "L'Epreuve" (1980), "Le Carton Rouge" (1980), "Quatre Femmes, Quatre Vies" (1981), "Un Temps Ailleurs" (1981), "L'Ennemi de la Mort" (1981), "Rioda" (1981), "Ursule Mirouet" (1981), "Paris Saint-Lazare" (1982), "L'Adelaide" (1982), "Bonbons en Gros" (1982), "La Steppe" (1982), "Toile de Fond" (1983), "Le Dancing" (1983), "Lace" (1984), "La Gourmande" (1984), "Mort Carnaval" (1985), "Une Vie Comme Je Veux" (1986) "Felicien Greveche" (1986), "Des Toques et des Etoiles" (1986), "Le Clan" (1988), "Liberte, Libertes" (1989), "B Comme Bolo" (1994), "Un Crime de Guerre" (1994), "Un Ange Passe" (1995), "Des Gens Si Bien Eleves" (1997), "Le Mystere Parasuram" (2000), "Les Rencontres de Joelle" (2001), "Retour a Locmaria" (2003), "Zodiaque" (2004), and "Les Pieds Dans le Plat" (2012). Her other television credits include episodes of "Rue Barree", "Adieu, Mes Quinze Ans...", "La Malle de Hambourg", "Dossiers: Danger Immediat", "L'Inspecteur Mene l'Enquete", "Les Heritiers", "Messieurs les Jure", "Les Dossiers Eclates",

"Les Amours des Annees Folles", "Les Cinq Dernieres Minutes", "Camera Une Premiere", "Les Enquetes du Commissaire Maigret", "Les Amours desAnnees 50", "Neo Polar", "Cinema 16", "Mysteress et Bulles de Gomme" as Nounou Rose in 1988, "Commissaire Moulon", "Beaumanoir", "Puissance 4", "V Comme Vengeance", "C'est Mon Histoire", "Les Mercredis de la Vie", "L'Histoire du Samedi", "Melissol", "Dossier: Disparus", "The School Teacher", "Sur le Fil", and "Baron Noir". Cleve was also seen in numerous films including the obscure horror film "Love Bride of the Blood Mummy" (1973), "The Flesh of the Orchid" (1975), "Docteur Francoise Gailland" (1976), "Femmes Fatales" (1976), "F... Comme Fairbanks" (1976), "Mr. Klein" (1976), "The Ambassadors" (1976), "L'Ombre des Chateaux" (1976), "La Communion Solennelle" (1977), "La Nuit de Saint-Germain-des-Pres" (1977), "Dossier 51" (1978), "Like a Turtle on Its Back" (1978), "Mais ou et Donc Ornicar" (1979), "Plurielles" (1979), "Temporale Rosy" (1980), "Cocktail Molotov" (1980), "Anthracite" (1980), "One Deadly Summer" (1983), "La Derelitta" (1983), "Hiver 60" (1983), "La Garce" (1984), "Partenaires" (1984), "Le Meilleur de la Vie" (1985), "Code Name: Emerald" (1985), "La Maison Assassinee" (1988), "Dark Woods" (1989), "Un Ascenseur Pour l'an Neuf" (1990), "Les Enfants du Naufrageur" (1992), "IP5: The Island of Pachyderms" (1992), "Far from Brazil" (1992), "La Cavale des Fous" (1993), "Faut-il Aimer Mathilde?" (1993), "Germinal" (1993), "Elisa" (1995), "XY, Drole de Conception" (1996), "Lucie Aubrac" (1997), "XXL" (1997), "The Children of the Marshland" (1999), "Un rime au Paradis" (2001), "Itineraires" (2005), "Welcome to the Sticks" (2008), "Arretez-Moi" (2013), "Baby Balloon" (2013), "Breves de Comptoir" (2014), and "A Mother" (2015). Cleve was married to actor Claude Talpaert from 1951 until his death in 2016 and is survived by their four children.

Cloud, Angus

Actor Angus Cloud, who was featured drug dealer Fezco in the HBO series "Euphoria" was found dead of a drug overdose at his family's home in Oakland, California, on July 31, 2023. He was 25. He was born Conor Angus Cloud Hickey in Oakland on July 10, 1998. He attended the School of Production Design at Oakland School of Arts. He moved to New York City in the late 2010s where he worked at a restaurant in Brooklyn. A casting director for "Euphoria" approached him for the role of the kind-hearted drug dealer Fezco. Cloud initially thought it was some kind of scam before accepting the role. He appeared in "Euphoria" with Zendaya during its first two seasons from 2019 to 2022. He was seen in an episode of the television series "The Perfect Soman" and the independent films "North Hollywood" (2021) and "The Line" (2023). Cloud also appeared in music videos for Noah Cyrus' "All Three", Juice Wrid's "Cigarettes", and Becky G and Karol G's "Miamiii". He had been cast in several upcoming films including an untitled Universal Monsters film, "Freaky Tales", and "Your Lucky Day" which are in various stages of post-production. He had been in mourning because of the death of his father in Ireland a few weeks prior to his own death.

Coates, Phyllis

Actress Phyllis Coates, who starred as Lois Lane on the television series "Adventures of Superman" during its first season in 1952, died at the Motion Picture & Television Country House and Hospital in Woodland Hills, California, on October 11, 2023. She was 96. She was born Gypsie Ann Stell in Wichita Falls, Texas, on January 15, 1927. She moved to California with her mother after high school and attended Los Angeles City College. She was working in a restaurant when she was discovered by comedian Ken Murray in the mid-1940s. She worked with him as a dancer and comedienne in skits for his variety shoe "Blackouts" for nearly a year. She also performed in a revue by Earl Carroll and the USO touring production of "Anything Goes" in 1946. She was featured as Alice McDoakes, the wife of George O'Hanlon's Joe McDoakes, in a series of comedy shorts including "So You Want to Be in Politics" (1948), "So You Want to Be on the Radio" (1948), "So You Want to Be a Baby Sitter" (1949), "So You Want to Be Popular" (1949), "So You Want to Be a Muscle Man" (1949), "So You're Having in-Law Trouble" (1949), "So You Want to Get Rich Quick" (1949), "So You Want to Throw a Party" (1950), "So You Think You're Not Guilty" (1950), "So You Want to Hold Your Husband" (1950), "So You Want to Move" (1950), "So You Want a Raise" (1950), "So You want to Be a Cowboy" (1951), "So You Want to Be a Paper Hanger" (1951), "So You Want to Buy a Used Car" (1951), "So You Want to Be a Bachelor" (1951), "So You Want to Be a Plumber" (1951), "So You Want to Get It Wholesale" (1952), "So You Want to Go to a Convention" (1952), "So You Never Tell a Lie" (1952), "So You Want to Wear the Pants" (1952), "So You Want a Television Set" (1953), "So You Love Your Dog" (1953), "So You Think You Can't Sleep" (1953), "So You Want to Be a Heir" (1953), "So You're Having Neighbor Trouble" (1954), "So You Want to Be Pretty" (1956), "So You Want to Play the Piano" (1956), and "So Your Wife Wants to Work" (1956). Coates was also seen in the films "Smart Girls Don't Talk" (1948), "A Kiss in the Dark" (1949), "Look for the Silver Lining" (1949), "The House Across the Street" (1949), "My Foolish Heart" (1949), "My Blue Heaven" (1950), "Blues Busters" (1950) with the Bowery Boys, "Outlaws of Texas" (1950), "Valentino" (1951), "Man from Sonora" (1951), "Canyon Raiders" (1951), "Nevada Badmen" (1951), "Oklahoma Justice" (1951), "The Longhorn" (1951), and "Stage to Blue River" (1951). She starred as Daily Planet reporter Lois Lane opposite George Reeves' Man of Steel in the 1951 film "Superman and the Mole-Men". It served as a pilot for the subsequent "Adventures of Superman" television series and Coates continued her role as Lois Lane for the first season from 1952 to 1953. She left the series for the remainder of its run and was replaced by Noel Neill, who had previously portrayed Lois Lane in a pair of Columbia serials in the late 1940s. Coates continued to appear in such films as "The Gunman" (1952), "Fargo" (1952), "Canyon Ambush" (1952), "Flat Top" (1952), "Wyoming Roundup" (1952), the Cold War science fiction "Invasion, U.S.A." (1952), "The Maverick" (1952), "Scorching Fury" (1952), the Republic serial "Jungle Drums of Africa" (1953), "Marshal of Cedar Rock" (1953), "She's Back on Broadway" (1953), "Perils of the Jungle" (1953) opposite Clyde Beatty, "Topeka" (1953), "Here Come the Girls" (1953), "El Paso Stampede" (1953), the western serial "Gunfighters of the Northwest" (1954), the Republic adventure serial "Panther Girl of the Kongo" (1955) in the title role of Jean Evans, "Girls in Prison" (1956), the religious short "God Is in the Streets" (1956), "Chicago Confidential" (1957), Herman Cohen's cult horror film "I Was a Teenage Frankenstein" (1957) as the ill-fated secretary to Michael Gough's Professor Frankenstein, "Blood Arrow" (1958), "Cattle Empire" (1958) starring Joel McCrea, and Jerry Warren's science fiction film "The Incredible Petrified World" (1959). Her later films include "The Baby Maker" (1970) and "Goodnight, Sweet Marilyn" (1989) as Gladys Pearl Baker, the mother of Misty Rowe's Marilyn Monroe. Coates was a familiar face on television from the late 1940s. She starred as Louise Willow in the early television soap opera "Faraway Hill", which briefly aired on the DuMont Television Network in late 1946. Her other television credits include episodes of "Your Show Time", "The Cisco Kid", "Stars Over Hollywood", "Hollywood Opening Night", "Racket Squad", "Schlitz Playhouse", "Craig Kennedy, Criminologist", "The Range Rider", "The Files of Jeffrey Jones", "Ramar of the Jungle", "I'm the Law", "The Red Skelton Hour", "Your Jeweler's Showcase", "The Abbott and Costello Show", "Summer Theatre", "Terry and the Pirates", "Crown Theatre with Gloria Swanson", "The Adventures of Kit Carson", "The Duke" as Gloria opposite Paul Gilbert's boxer-turned-nightclub owner in 1954, "Public Defender", "Professional Father", "Topper", "Cavalcade of America", "The Millionaire", "The Lone Ranger", "Willy", "Stage 7", "Science Fiction Theatre", "Lassie", "The Great Gildersleeve", "Frontier", "Western Union", "This Is the Life", "TV Reader's Digest", "Navy Log", "Four Star Playhouse", "It's a Great Life", "Crossroads", "Chevron Hall of Stars", "Leave It to Beaver", "The Sheriff of Cochise", "General Electric Theater", "Richard Diamond, Private Detective", the comedy series "This Is Alice" as Clarissa Mae Holliday, mother of Patty Ann Gerrity's Alice Holliday, from 1958 to 1959, "Westinghouse Desilu Playhouse", "Black Saddle", "Lux Playhouse", "Hennesey", "The DuPont Show with June Allyson", "Hawaiian Eye", "The Best of the Post", "Gunslinger", "Tales of Wells Fargo", "Rawhide", "The Untouchables", "Perry Mason", "The Virginian", "The Patty Duke Show", "Gunsmoke", "Death Valley Days", "Slattery's People", and the unsold pilot "Thompson's Ghost" on "Summer Fun" in 1966. She was also seen in the tele-films "Whisper Kill" (1988), "Kiss Shot"

(1989), "Mrs. Lambert Remembers Love" (1991). Coates was featured as Mrs. Howard in a two-part episode of "Dr. Quinn, Medicine Woman" in 1994 and was Ellen Lane, mother of Teri Hatcher's Lois, in an episode of "Lois & Clark: The New Adventures of Superman". She was married to director Richard L. Bare from 1948 until their divorce in 1949. Coates was married to jazz pianist Robert Nelms from 1950 until their divorce in 1953 and is survived by their daughter Zoe. She was married to producer and director Norman Tokar from 1955 until their divorce in 1960 and was predeceased by their son, David, in 2011. She was married to Dr. Howard Press from 1962 until their divorce in 1986 and is also survived by their daughter, Laura.

CoConis, Ted

Illustrator Ted CoConis, who was noted for his work with children's books and movie posters, died in Cedar Key, Florida, on March 28, 2023. He was 95. CoConis was born in Chicago, Illinois, on August 31, 1927. He attended the Art  Institute of Chicago while in grade school. He joined the U.S. Air Force in his early teens. He attended the American Academy of Arts after his discharge, then joined the U.S. Merchant Marine. He began working as an illustrator for the publicity department of the Fifth Army in Chicago. He created magazine covers, posters, and brochures. He transferred to the Sixth Army in San Francisco in the early 1950s and continued to work as an illustrator. He joined a commercial art studio in New York City later in the decade. He was cover artist for such books as Nelson Algren's "A Walk on the Wild Side" (1960), Vladimir Nabokov's "Ada, or Ardor" (1969), William Goldman's "The Princess Bride" (1973), and A.C.H. Smith's "Labyrinth" (1986). He illustrated Betsy Cromer Byars' 1971 Newberry Award-winning children's book "The Summer of the Swans" and Doris Gates' "The Golden God, Apollo" (1973). He was poster artist for numerous films including "Petulia" (1968), "Finian's Rainbow" (1968), "The Prime of Miss Jean Brodie" (1969), "The Picture of Dorian Gray" (1970), "Fiddler on the Roof" (1971), "Man of La Mancha" (1972), "Lady Caroline Lamb" (1972), "Breezy" (1973), "A Matter of Time" (1976), "Joseph Andrews" (1977), "The Other Side of Midnight" (1977), "Cuba" (1979), and "Labyrinth" (1986). CoConis also worked as a fine artist from the early 1980s, creating the series "Women in Paris" and "Exotic Ladies of Rue St. Denis".

Coggins, Howard

British actor Howard Coggins died of cancer in England on November 1, 2023. He was 52. Coggins was born in Backwell, Somerset, England, on August 2, 1971. He graduated from the Royal Welsh College of Music and Drama and performed frequently on stage with the Bristol Old Vic from the late 1990s. He and Stu Mcloughlin co-founded the Bristol theatrical company Living Spit in 2012 and created numerous comic characters together. Coggins was featured in an advertising campaign for the National Lottery. He appeared

on television in episodes of "The Bill", "Dalziel and Pascoe", "Mr. Charity", "Black Books", "Teachers", "Casualty", "The Worst Week of My Life", "Clatterford", "Gina's Laughing Gear", "Doc Martin", "Doctors", "Beautiful People", "Being Human", "Sherlock", "Waking the Dead", "Law & Order: UK", and "The Coroner". His other television credits include productions of "Othello" (2001), "Doc Martin" (2001), "Every Time You Look at Me" (2004), "Bleak House" (2005), "Beau Brummell: This Charming Man" (2006), "Moses Jones" (2009), "Runaway" (2009), and "The Lost Honour of Christopher Jefferies" (2014). He was seen in several films including "The Ghost of Greville Lodge" (2000), "Acres and Acres" (2016), and the short "Choose Your Weapon" (2021). Coggins is survived by his wife, Kirstyn, and daughter, Betty.

Coler, Douglas

Actor Douglas Coler died of pancreatic cancer in Mathews, North Carolina, on August 19, 2023. He was 63.

Coler was born in Cincinnati, Ohio, on February 3, 1960. He began his career on stage and performed with regional theater. He was also a radio voice actor. Coler was a founding member of the Actors' Art Theatre in Los Angeles and directed the touring company Chamber Theatre Productions. He was Manager of Shows and Floor Programming at Discovery Place Science in Charlotte, North Carolina, from 2008 to 2020. Coler was featured as Dr. Piccard on the daytime soap opera "Days of Our Lives" in the late 1990s. He was also seen in the films "Coldfire" (1990), "The Perfect Shadow" (1998), and "Foreign Correspondents" (1999), and the 2000 short "Mars and Beyond". He was a voice actor in the video games "Star Trek: Judgment Rites" and "M.U.G.E.N" in the 1990s. Coler married Jo St. James in 2009 and they had two daughters before their subsequent divorce.

Collin, Pierre

Canadian actor Pierre Collin died in Canada on July 27, 2023. He was 85. Collin was born in Montreal, Quebec, Canada, on July 18, 1938. He began his career on stage in the 1960s with the avant garde theatrical troupe Les Apprentis-Sorciers. He continued to appear in stage productions throughout his career. Collin was seen on television in productions of "Onzieme Speciale" (1988), "Si Belles" (1994), "Omerta, la Loi du Silence" (1996), "L'Enfant des Appalaches"

(1997), and "Rene Levesque" (2006). His other television credits include episodes of "Archibald", "Scoop", "Les Grands Proces", "Le Sorcier", "Virginie", "Radio Enfer", "Reseaux", "Fred-dy", "La Vie, la Vie", "Les Bougon: C'est Aussi Ca la Vie", "Rumeurs", "Le Negociateur", "Francois en Serie", "Vice

Cache", "Camera Cafe", "La Brigadiere", "Unite 9" as Yvon Lamontagne from 2012 to 2013, "Toute la Verite", "Au Secours de Beatrice", "Les Beaux Malaises", "Victor Lessard", and "Madame Lebrun" as Adelard Lebrun from 2015 to 2019. Collin appeared in such films as "Post Mortem" (1999), "Maelstrom" (2000), "Karmina 2" (2001), "How My Mother Gave Birth to Me During Menopause" (2003), "Seducing Doctor Lewis" (2003), "Dans Une Galaxie Pres de Chez Vous - Le Film" (2004), "L'Esperance" (2004), "Ma Vie en Cinemascope" (2004), "Le Survenant" (2005), "Niagara Motel" (2005), "Aurore" (2005), "The Novena" (2005), "Saint Martyrs of the Damned" (2005), "Histoire de Famille" (2006), "Delivrez-Moi" (2006), "Dans les Villes" (2006), "La Lachete" (2007), "La Lili a Gilles" (2007), "Father and Guns" (2009), "Le Technicien" (2009), "Route 132" (2010), "Le Sens de l'Humour" (2011), "Columbarium" (2012), "Esimesac" (2012), "Henri Henri" (2014), "Ego Trip" (2015), and "And the Birds Rained Down" (2019). He married Sylvie Houle in 2001 and is survived by her and three sons.

Compton, D.G.

British science fiction writer David Guy Compton, whose 1974 novel "The Continuous Katherine Mortenhoe" was adapted for Bertrand Tavernier's 1979 film "Death Watch", died in Maine on November 10, 2023. He was 93. Compton was

born in London, England, on August 19, 1930. He began writing crime novels in the early 1960s under the name Guy Compton including "Too Many Murderers" (1962), "Medium for Murder" (1963), "Dead on Cue" (1964), "High Tide for Hanging" (1965), "Disguise for a Dead Gentleman" (1966), and "And Murder Came Too" (1967). He was best known for his science fiction novels, using the name D.G. Compton. They include "The Quality of Mercy" (1965), "Farewell, Earth's Bliss" (1966), "The Silent Multitude" (1966), "Synthajoy" (1968), "The Palace" (1969), "The Steel Crocodile" (1970), and "Chronocules" (1971). His 1974 novel "The Continuous Katherine Mortenhoe" was published by DAW books in the United States under the title "The Unsleeping Eye". It was adapted for Bertrand Tavernier's 1980 film "Death Watch" starring Romy Schneider, Harvey Keitel, and Max von Sydow. Compton also wrote the books "The Missionaires" (1975), "A Usual Lunacy" (1978), "Windows" (1979), "Ascendancies"

(1980), "Scudder's Game" (1988), "Ragnarok" (1991) with John Gribbin, "Nomansland" (1993), the non-fiction "Stammering: It's Nature, History, Causes and Cures" (1993), "Justice City" (1994), "Back of Town Blues" (1996), and "The Masters of Talojz" (1997). He also penned several Gothic romance novels under the pseudonym Frances Lynch including "Twice Ten Thousand Miles" (1984), "The Fine and Handsome Captain" (1975), "Stranger at the Wedding" (1976), "A Dangerous Magic" (1978), and "In the House of Dark Music" (1979).

Constant, Yvonne

French actress and singer Yvonne Constant died in Larmor-Plage, France, on February 28, 2023. She was 92. Constant was born in Paris, France, on June 15, 1930. She trained in ballet before transitioning to musical comedy. She

performed in cabaret productions in Europe and New York. She made her film debut in a small role in 1953's "Their Last Night". She was also seen in "Father, Mother, the Maid and I" (1954), "Nana" (1955), "Ce Soir les Jupons Volent..." (1956), "The Hunchback of Notre Dame" (1956) starring Anthony Quinn, and "Maxime" (1958). Constant appeared on Broadway in productions of "La Plume de Ma Tante" (1958) and received a special award in 1959, "The Gay Life" (1961), "No Strings" (1962), and "Come Live with Me" (1967). She was a frequent guest on "The Tonight Show Starring Johnny Carson", appearing in 45 episodes. She was also seen in episodes of "The Mike Douglas Show" and "The Merv Griffin Show". Constant appeared with Jackie Gleason in the 1962 film "Gigot" and co-starred with Maurice Chevalier and Dean Jones in the 1967 Disney comedy "Monkeys, Go Home!". She was featured as Annette in the television mini-series "Sins" (1986) and was a prostitute in the 1991 film "The Favour, the Watch and the Very Big Fish". She toured with the one-woman show "Yvonne Constant Sings Yves Montand" and continue to perform in cabarets in New York in her later years. She was married and divorced from Yannick Pinguet and composer Gershon Kingsley, and is survived by a son, Gerard Pinguet. Her husband of 45 years, producer Mike Lanin, died in 2014.

Cook, Carole

Actress Carole Cook, who starred as the wife of Don Knott's "The Incredible Mr. Limpet" in 1964, died of heart failure in Beverly Hills, California, on January 11, 2023. She was 98. She was born Mildred Frances Cook in Abilene, Texas, on January 14, 1924. She graduated from Baylor University in 1945 and began her career on stage in regional theater. She moved to New York City in 1954 where she appeared off-Broadway in a 1954 revival production of "Threepenny Opera" as Mrs. Peachum. Lucille Ball saw Cook in a production of "Annie Get Your Gun" and she soon began working for Desilu

Productions. She was seen in episodes of "Westinghouse Desilu Playhouse", "U.S. Marshal", "The Many Loves of Dobie Gillis", "The New Phil Silvers Show", "The Hollywood Palace", "Password" teaming with Lucille Ball, "Kentucky Jones", the "Vacation Playhouse" unsold pilot of "The Hoofer"

in 1966, "Daniel Boone", "The Joey Bishop Show", "Dean Martin Presents the Golddiggers", "The Merv Griffin Show", "Rhyme and Reason", and "The Paul Ryan Show". Cook was featured as Thelma Green in a handful of episodes of "The Lucy Show" from 1963 to 1964 and appeared in various roles in subsequent episodes through 1968. She was also seen in episodes of "My World and Welcome to It", "That Girl", "Here's Lucy" in various roles from 1969 to 1974, "Sarge", "Griff", "McMillan & Wife" in the recurring role of Carole Crenshaw in 1974, "Maude", "Baretta", "Ellery Queen", "Chico and the Man" in the recurring role of Flora from 1975 to 1976, "Bronk", "This Is the Life", "Starsky and Hutch", "Charlie's Angels", "Kojak" in the recurring role of bar owner Marie Stella in 1977, "Darkroom", "Laverne & Shirley", "Strike Force", "The Zertigo Diamond Caper" on "CBS Children's Mystery Theatre" in 1982, the soap opera "Capitol" as Sugar Lane from 1983 to 1984, "Trapper John, M.D.", "Knight Rider", "Hart to Hart", "The Love Boat", "Quincy", "The A-Team", "Magnum, P.I.", "Dynasty" in the recurring role of Cora Van Heusen from 1986 to 1987, "Cagney & Lacey", "Murder, She Wrote", "A Family for Joe", "Strip Mall", "Grey's Anatomy", "Major Crimes", and "Break a Hip". Her other television credits include the tele-films "Lady Luck" (1973), "In the Glitter Palace" (1977), "Rendezvous Hotel" (1979), "Make Me an Offer" (1980), "Something So Right" (1982), and "Gloria Vane" (1993). Cook appeared in such films as "Palm Springs Weekend" (1963), "The Incredible Mr. Limpet" (1964) as Bessie Limpet, "The Gauntlet" (1977) starring Cling Eastwood, "American Gigolo" (1980) starring Richard Gere, "Summer Lovers" (1982), "Sixteen Candles" (1984) as Molly Ringwald's Grandma Helen, "Grandview, U.S.A." (1984), "42nd Street" (1986), "Fast Money" (1996), "Lost & Found" (1999), the animated "Home on the Range" (2004) as the voice of Pearl Gesner, "A Very Sordid Wedding" (2017), and "Still Waiting in the Wings" (2018). Cook continued to appear on stage throughout her career and starred as Dolly Levi in a touring production of "Hello, Dolly!" in Australia in 1965. She also appeared in Broadway productions of "Romantic Comedy" (1979), and "42nd Street" (1980). Cook married actor Tom Troupe in 1964 and they performed on stage together in productions of "The Lion in Winter" and "Father's Day". She is survived by her husband.

Cooper, Pat

Actor and comedian Pat Cooper died at his home in Las Vegas, Nevada, on June 6, 2023. He was 93. He was born

Pasquale Vito Caputo in New York City on July 31, 1929. He was drafted into the U.S. Army in 1952 and was stationed at Fort Jackson, South Carolina, but was soon discharged. He returned to New York, where he worked as a cab driver while

developing a stand-up comedy routine. He performed at the Catskills from the 1950s and took the name Pat Carroll. He had a poor relationship with his parents and siblings which was acerbated by the name change. He had two children from his first marriage that ended in divorce in 1961, and he continued his history of family difficulties with his own son and daughter. He often utilized his estranged family as part of his comedy routines. He recorded several comedy albums including "Our Hero" (1965) and 1966's "Spaghetti Sauce and Other Delights". He was a regular opening act for numerous entertainers including Frank Sinatra, Bobby Darin, Jerry Lewis, Tony Bennett, Paul Anka, and Sammy Davis, Jr. Cooper made his television debut as a guest of "Jackie Gleason: American Scene Magazine" in 1963. He also performed in episodes of "Today", "The Dean Martin Show", "The Dom DeLuise Show", "The Joan Rivers Show", "The Kraft Music Hall", "The Dennis Wholey Show", "This Is Tom Jones", "The Hollywood Palace", "The David Frost Show", "The Ed Sullivan Show", "The Virginia Graham Show", "The Tonight Show Starring Johnny Carson", "Jack Paar Tonite", "The Merv Griffin Show", "Dinah!", "Vaudeville", "Rhyme and Reason", "Celebrity Sweepstakes", "The Bobby Vinton Show", "The Mike Douglas Show", "Late Night with David Letterman", "Late Night with Conan O'Brien", "Howard Stern", "The Rat Pack", "Jerry Lewis MDA Labor Day Telethon", "Tough Crowd with Colin Quinn", "All Night with Joey Reynolds", and "Hey Moe, Hey Dad!". Cooper was an actor in episodes of "Vega$", "Charlie's Angels", "It's a Living", "ABC Afterschool Specials", "Throb", and "L.A. Law". He also appeared in the tele-films "Charlie and the Great Balloon Chase" (1981) and "Recipe for Disaster" (2002). He was featured in a handful of films including "Uncle Scam" (1981), "Fighting Back" (1982), "Silent Predator" (1997), "Code of Ethics" (1998), "Analyze This" (1999) as Salvatore Masiello, "The Boys Behind the Desk" (2000), "Ankle Bracelet" (2001), "This Thing of Ours" (2002), "Analyze That" (2002), and "The Aristocrats" (2005). He began criticizing stars that he had worked with later in his career, claiming Dionne Warwick, Tony Bennett, Paul Anka, Lola Falana, and others had disrespected him when he opened for them. He became a frequent guest on Howard Stern's radio show from the mid-1980s, and he argued with his estranged mother and two children when they called in to the show. He continued to perform at casinos and clubs until his retirement in 2012. His memoirs, "How Dare You Say How Dare Me!" was published in 2011. Cooper was married to Dolores Nola from 1952 until their divorce in 1961 and is survived by their two children, Michael and Louise Caputo. He was married to singer Patti

Prince from 1964 until their divorce in 2005 and is survived by his adopted daughter. He married Emily Connor i 2018 and she also survives him.

Coopersmith, Jerome

Television writer and playwright Jerome Coopersmith died in Rochester, New York, on July 21, 2023. He was 97. Coopersmith was born in New York City on August 11, 1925.

He began working as an office boy at the Schubert Theatrical Company in the early 1940s. He served with distinction in the U.S. Army for two years during World War II. He earned a Purple Heart after being shot in the chest in January of 1945. He returned to college after his discharge later in the year and graduated from New York University. He began working with television producer Martin Stone in 1947 on the quiz show "Americana". He worked with Horton Foote as co-writer for the NBC series "The Gabby Hayes Show" in 1951. He scripted the 1952 production of "The Story of Roger Williams" for "Hallmark Hall of Fame". He was script editor and occasional voice actor and producer for the science fiction children's series "Johnny Jupiter" from 1953. Coopersmith also wrote for the series "Justice", "Appointment with Adventure", "Goodyear Playhouse", "Encounter", "The Alcoa Hour", "The Big Story", "Harbourmaster", "Lamp Unto My Feet", "Decoy", "Kraft Theatre", "Brenner", "Deadline", "The United States Steel Hour", "Combat!", "The Doctors and the Nurses", and David Susskind's "The Armstrong Circle Theatre" serving as principal writer from 1955 to 1963. He continued to write for television during the 1970s and 1980s, penning episodes of "Medical Center", "The Streets of San Francisco", "Hawaii Five-O" writing over thirty episodes from 1968 to 1976, "The Andros Target" which he created in 1977, "Nurse", "Spenser: For Hire", and "A Man Called Hawk". Coopersmith also wrote the tele-films "Mr. Inside/Mr. Outside", the animated "'Twas the Night Before Christmas" (1974), "The Impostor" (1975), "Have I Got a Christmas for You" (1977), "An American Christmas Carol" (1979), "The Cradle Will Fall" (1983), "The Sins of Dorian Gray" (1983), "Islands" (1984), and "Betrayed by Innocence" (1986), sometimes using the pseudonym Ken August. He wrote book material for several Broadway musicals including "Baker Street" (1965) earning a Tony Award nomination, and "The Apple Tree" (1966). He was author of the 1969 children's book "A Chanukah Fable for Christmas", with illustrations by Syd Hoff. Coopersmith married Judy Loehnberg in 1956 and is survived by their two daughters.

Copage, John

Actor John Copage died in Arcadia, California, on June 26, 2023. He was 98. Copage was born in Chicago, Illinois, on March 25, 1925. He was seen frequently on television from the early 1960s with roles in episodes of such series as "The Many Loves of Dobie Gillis" in various roles from 1962 to 1963, "Bewitched" (1964), "The Man from U.N.C.L.E.", "Star Trek" as Elliott in the 1967 episode "The Doomsday Machine", "Mission: Impossible", "Judd for the

Defense", "The Ghost & Mrs. Muir", "Julia", "Night Court", "Cheers", "Mr. Belvedere", "The Colbys", and "Falcon Crest". He also appeared in various roles in multiple episodes of "Star Trek: The Next Generation" from 1991 to 1994 and "Star Trek: Voyager" as a science division officer from 1995 to 1997. He appeared in small roles in a handful of films during his career including "PT 109" (1963), "The Killers" (1964), "With Six You Get Eggroll" (1968), "Simon, King of Witches" (1971), "City Heat" (1984), "The Naked Gun: from the Files of Police Squad!" (1988), "Repossessed" (1990), and "The Distinguished Gentleman" (1992). Copage also worked in real estate while continuing to pursue an acting career. He was married to Alise J. Peak from 1954 until their divorce in 1964 and is survived by their two sons, reporter Eric Copage and child actor Marc Copage, who starred with Diahann Carroll in the television series "Julia" from 1968 to 1971. Copage married Elaine Gonzales McDoanld in 1970.

Cordes, Michel

French actor Michel Cordes died of a suicide by gunshot at his home in Grabels, France, on May 5, 2023. He was 77. Cordes was born in Siran, France, on October 20, 1945.

He studied at the Montpellier Theatre Conservatory. He appeared in films and television from the late 1980s. His film credits include "Sunfish" (1993), "The Horseman on the Roof" (1995), "Didier" (1997), "A Matter of Taste" (2000), "Under the Sand" (2000), "Mon Pere, il M'a Sauve la Vie" (2001), "L'Illa de l'Holandes" (2001), "Carnages" (2002), "Strange Gardens" (2003), and "La Fin du Regne Animal" (2003). Cordes was seen in television productions of "Le Roi Mysere" (1991), "La Cavaliere" (1993), "Les Louves" (1995), "Mauvaises Affaires" (1997), "La Femme de l'Italien" (1998), "Tramontane" (1999), "Permission Moisson" (2001), "The Costly Truth" (2001), "Fragile" (2003), "La Parenthese Interdite" (2005), "Les Filles du Desert" (2009), "Petits Arrangements Avec l'Amour" (2013), "Une Vie en Nord" (2014), "Infiltration" (2016), and "Troubled Waters" (2019). His other television credits include episodes of "V Comme Vengeance", "Police Secrets", "The School Teacher", "Sara", "L'Avocate", "Le Selec", "L'Histoirie du Samedi", "Cuentame Como Paso", "La Camarguais", "Une Femme d'Honneur", "Nos Chers Voisins", "Burning Crimes", and "La Seria". Cordes was best known for his role as Roland Marci in the soap opera "Plus Belle la Vie" from 2004 to 2022.

Costa Titch

South African rapper and dancer Costantinos Tsobanoglou, who performed under the name Costa Titch,

collapsed and died on stage at a music festival in Johannesburg, South Africa, on March 11, 2023. He was 27. Tsobanoglou was born in Nelspruit, South Africa, on September 10, 1995. He began performing as a dancer in his youth. He moved to Johannesburg in 2014 where he became a rapper. He recorded his popular debut album, "Made in Africa", in 2020. He collaborated with other South African rappers including AKA, Riky Rick, and Boity. He and Nigerian afrobeats singer O.L.A. recorded the 2022 single "Data" and he teamed with Senegalese-American singer Akon for a remix of the song "Big Flexa" in 2023. Costa Titch was performing at the Ultra South Africa music festival in Johannesburg in March of 2023 when he collapsed on stage and died.

Costanzo, Maurizio

Italian television host and screenwriter Maurizio Costanzo died of complications from surgery at a clinic in Rome, Italy, on February 24, 2023. He was 84. Costanzo was born in Rome on August 28, 1938. He began his career as a

journalist for the newspaper Paese Sera and became managing editor of the weekly women's magazine "Grazia". He became founding editor of "L'Occhio" newspaper in the late 1980s. Costanzo worked in films from the late 1960s, writing "The Vatican Affair" (1968), "I Quattro del Pater Noster" (1969), "Cerca di Capirmi" (1970), "La Madama" (1976), "Bordella" (1976), "Lunatics and Lovers" (1976), "The House with Laughing Windows" (1976), "Al Piacere di Riverderla" (1976), "L'Altra Meta del Cielo" (1977), "Tutti Defunti... Tranne i Morti" (1977), "Stato Interessante" (1977), "A Special Day" (1977), "Kolossal - I Magnifici Macisti" (1977), "Melodrammore" (1978) which he also directed, "Le Strelle Nel Fosso" (1979), Pupi Avanti's horror film "Zeder" (aka "Revenge of the Dead") (1983), "Per Sempre" (2003), "Passo a Due" (2005), "Too Beautiful" (2005), "Voce dek Verbo Amore" (2007), and "Parlami di Me" (2008). He wrote television productions of "Riuscira il Cav. Papa Ubu?" (1971), "Jazz Band" (1978), "Cinema!!!" (1979), "Preferisco Vivere" (1989), "Ovidio" (1989), and "Madame" (2004). He was host of the series "Bonta Loro" from 1976 to 1978. He joined Silvio Berlusconi's television station Canale 5 as host of the talk show "The Maurizio Costanzo Show" from 1982 to 2021. He was host of

105

"Buona Domenica" from 1996 to 2005 and "Domenica In" from 2009 to 2021. Costanzo married journalist and photographer Lori Sammartino in 1963 and they later divorced. He was married to journalist Flaminia Morando from 1973 until their divorce in 1984. He married television host Marta Flavi in 1989. They separated the following year and divorced in 1995. He married television host and producer Maria De Filippi in 1995 and is survived by her and their adopted son.

Coster, Nicholas

British-American actor Nicholas Coster, who was noted for his roles in the soap operas as Paul Britton on "The Secret Storm" and Eduardo Grimaldi on "As the World Turns", died in Florida on June 26, 2023. He was 89. Coster was born in London, England, on December 3, 1933. He was largely raised in the United States in California. He returned to England to study at the Royal Academy of Dramatic Art. He also trained with Lee Strasberg in New York City. Coster appeared on the Broadway stage in productions of "Becket" (1961), "Ross" (1961), "The Ninety Day Mistress" (1967), "But, Seriously..." (1969), "Happy Birthday, Wanda June" (1970), "Twigs" (1971), "Seesaw" (1973), "Otherwise Engaged" (1977), "The Little Foxes" (1981), and "Getting Married" (1991). He was seen in numerous films including "Titanic" (1953), "The Desert Rats" (1953), "Sea of Lost Ships" (1953), "The Black Shield of Falworth" (1954), "The Outcast" (1954), "The Eternal Sea" (1955), "City of Shadows" (1955), "Light Fantastic" (1964), the psychological thriller "My Blood Runs Cold" (1965), "the Sporting Club" (1971), "1776" (1972), "All the President's Men" (1976) as Markham, "MacArthur" (1977), "The Big Fix" (1978), "Slow Dancing in the Big City" (1978), "Goldengirl" (1979), "Just You and Me, Kid" (1979), "The Concorde... Airport '79" (1979), "The Electric Horseman" (1979), "Little Darlings" (1980), "The Hunter" (1980), "Why Would I Lie?" (1980), "Stir Crazy" (1980), "The Pursuit of D.B. Cooper" (1981), "Reds" (1981), "Big Business" (1988), "How I Got Into College" (1989), "Betsy's Wedding" (1990), "Freedom Strike" (1998), "Love Happens" (1999), "Plot 7" (2007), "Race" (2008), "Dancing on a Dry Salt Lake" (2010), "Cold Turkey" (2013), "A Winter Rose" (2014), "The Southside" (2015), "Chemical Cut" (2016), "Con Man" (2018), "Blood Type" (2018), the H.P. Lovecraft-based horror film "The Deep Ones" (2020) also serving as co-producer, and "The Last Exorcist" (2020). Coster starred in numerous daytime soap operas including "The Secret Storm" as Prof. Paul Britton in 1954 and from 1967 to 1969, "Our Private World" as John Eldridge in 1965, "Somerset" as Robert Delaney from 1970 to 1972, "Another World" reprising his role as Robert Delaney from 1980 to 1980, "One Life to Live" as Anthony Makana from 1983 to 1984, "All My Children" as Steve Andrews from 1988 to 1989, "Santa

Barbara" as Lionel Lockridge from 1984 to 1993, and "As the World Turns" as Eduardo Grimaldi from 1993 to 1995. His other television credits include episodes of "Your Favorite Story", "Naked City", "The United States Steel Hour", "The Defenders", "Young Dr. Malone", "Directions", "Brenner", "No Time for Sergeants", "Wendy and Me", the 1966 unsold pilot "Where's Everett", "The Felony Squad", "Occasional Wife", "The Green Hornet", "N.Y.P.D.", "The Blue Knight", "Charlie's Angels", "Little House on the Prairie:, "On Our Own", "Baretta", "Husbands, Wives & Lovers", "Grandpa Goes to Washington", "The Amazing Spider-Man", "Family", "The Rockford Files", "One Day at a Time", "Wonder Woman", "The Runaways", "The Incredible Hulk", "Mrs. Columbo", "Paris", "Buck Rogers in the 25th Century", "Dallas", "Tenspeed and Brown Shoe", "When the Whistle Blows", "The Misadventures of Sheriff Lobo" as Chief of Detectives J.E. Carson from 1980 to 1981, "Today's F.B.I.", "Hart to Hart", "Police Squad!", "Shannon", "Quincy", "Simon & Simon", "Magnum, P.I.", "The Mississippi", "Teachers Only", "Ryan's Four" as Dr. Morris Whitford in 1983, "Nine to Five" in the recurring role of Bill Spangler from 1982 to 1983, "Hardcastle and McCormick", "T.J. Hooker", "Knight Rider", "Alfred Hitchcock Presents", "You Are the Jury", "L.A. Law", "The Facts of Life" in the recurring role of the father of Lisa Whelchel's Blair Warner from 1982 to 1988, "Smart Guys", "Hooperman", "thirtysomething", "Murder, She Wrote", "Who's the Boss?", "Hunter", "War of the Worlds", "Life Goes On", "Star Trek: The Next Generation" as Admiral Anthony Haftel in the 1990 episode "The Offspring", "Midnight Caller", "MacGyver", "Matlock", "Jake and the Fatman", "Beverly Hills, 90210", "Reasonable Doubts", "Dark Justice", "Law & Order", "Nurses", "South of Sunset", "Coach", "Mr. & Mrs. Smith", "Silk Stalkings", "Tracey Takes On...", "Gun", "Pensacola: Wings of Gold", "Dr. Quinn, Medicine Woman", "Michael Hayes", "Timecop", "3rd Rock from the Sun" in the recurring role of Chancellor Stevens from 1998 to 1999, "Women: Stories of Passion", "L.A. Heat", "Gideon's Crossing", "Judging Amy" (2001), "The Lyon's Den", "Crumbs", "The Bay" as Mayor Jack Madison from 2010 to 2019, "Cold Case", "Trust Me", "My Synthesized Life", "Better Things", "American Crime Story", "Dead to Me", and "The Rookie: Feds". Coster also appeared in the tele-films and mini-series "The Court-Martial of George Armstrong Custer" (1977) as General Philip Sheridan, "The Word" (1978), "A Fire in the Sky" (1978), "Long Journey Back" (1978), "Friendly Fire" (1979), "Ebony, Ivory and Jade" (1979), "Bender" (1979), "The Solitary Man" (1979), "The Women's Room" (1980), "The Day the Bubble Burst" (1982), "M.A.D.D.: Mothers Against Drunk Drivers" (1983), "Princess Daisy" (1983), "Beverly Hills Madam" (1986), "Incident at Dark River" (1989), "By Dawn's Early Light" (1990), "Natural Selection" (1994), "Hearts Adrift" (1996), "Full Circle" (1996), "The Dukes of Hazzard: Hazzard in Hollywood" (2000), and "Flower Girl" (2009). Coser was married to actress Candace Hilligoss from 1960 until their divorce in 1981 and is survived by their two children. He married Beth Pantel in 1982 and is also survived by her and their child.

Cote, Michel

Canadian actor Michel Cote died of complications from a bone marrow disease in Montreal, Quebec, Canada, on May 29, 2023. He was 72. Cote was born in Alma, Quebec, on June 25, 1950. He began performing on stage in amateur productions while in college. He later trained at the National Theater School of Canada. He continued to perform on stage and appeared in numerous productions of the comic play "Broue" from 1979 through 2017. Cote was seen in numerous films including "Au Clai de la Lune" (1983) which he also wrote, "Exit" (1986), "La Fuite" (1986), "Dans le Ventre du Dragon" (1989), "Cruising Bar" (1989), "The Scorpio Factor" (1989), "Moody Beach" (1990), "You're Beautiful, Jeanne" (1990), "A Wind from Wyoming" (1994), "Liste Noire" (1995), "Erreur Sur la Personne" (1996), "La Vie Apres l'Amour" (2000), "Evil Words" (2003), "Le Dernier Tunnel" (2004), "C.R.A.Z.Y." (2005), "My Daughter, My Angel" (2007), "Cruising Bar 2" (2008) which he directed and wrote, "Father and Guns" (2009), "Piche: Entre Ciel et Terre" (2010), "Le Sens de l'Humour" (2011), "Omerta" (2012), "Les Maitres du Suspense" (2014), "Mon Ami Dino" (206), and "De Pere en Flic 2" (2017). He appeared on television in episodes of "La Petite Patrie", "The Newcomers", "Le Pont", "Du Tac au Tac", "Les Brillant", "Les Girouettes", "Vaut Mieux en Rire", "Omerta, la Loi du Silence" as Pierre Guathier from 1996 to 1999, "Si la Tendance se Maintient" as Alain Gagnon in 2001, "Et Dieu Crea Laflaque", "La Petite Vie" as Jean-Lou Pichette from 1994 to 2009, "En Audition Avec Simon", "Les Pecheur", "La Theorie du K.O." as Carol Hebert from 2014 to 2015, and "Bye-Bye". He was also featured in television productions of "La Fille du Maquignon" (1991), "Miss Moscou" (1992), and "Montreal Ville Ouverte" as Pax Plante in 1992. Cote married French actress Veronique Le Flaguais in 1972 and is survived by her and their two sons, Charles and actor Maxime Le Flaguais.

Coto, Manny

Cuban-American television writer and producer Manny Coto, who worked on the series "Star Trek: Enterprise" and "Dexter", died of pancreatic cancer in Pasadena, California, on July 9, 2023. He was 62. Coto was born in Havana, Cuba, on June 10, 1961. He and his family fled the Castro regime and settled in Orlando, Florida, when he was an infant. He became interested in making films in his teens and moved to Los Angeles to pursue a career. He was a graduate of the American Film Institute in 1990. He worked in television from the late 1980s directing episodes of "Monsters" and "Tales from the Crypt" and the tele-films "The Other Me" (2000) and "Zenon: The Zequel" (2001). He also scripted episodes of "Alfred Hitchcock Presents", "Tales from the Crypt", "Tales from the Cryptkeeper", and "Dead at 21". Coto was a producer and writer for the series "The Outer Limits", "Strange World", and "Odyssey 5". He wrote and directed the 1992 horror film "Dr. Giggles" and the 1997 juvenile science fiction "Star Kid". He also directed the films "Playroom" (1990) and "Cover-Up" (1991) and scripted 1997's "Hostile Intent". He was producer and writer for the "Star Trek: Enterprise" series from 2003 to 2005 and appeared onscreen in a cameo role as an admiral in an episode. He was executive producer and occasional writer for the final five seasons of the series "24" and shared an Emmy Award for his work on the series in 2006. He returned to the franchise to produce and write the mini-series "24: Live Another Day" (2014) and "24: Legacy" (2016). He was co-creator of the short-lived Fox series "The 1/2 Hour New Hour" in 2007. Coto was executive producer and writer for "Dexter" on Showtime from 2010 to 2013 and shared an Emmy nomination in 2011. He scripted an episode of the horror series "The Exorcist" and wrote and produced the science fiction crime series neXt in 2020. He was producer and writer for the "American Horror Story" serials "Apocalypse" (2018), "1984" (2019), "Double Feature" (2021), and "NYC" (2022). He also wrote and produced for "American Horror Stories" from 2021 to 2022. Coto married Robin Trickett in 2004 and she survives him.

Cotterill, Ralph

British-Australian actor Ralph Cotterill died in Cairns, Queensland, Australia, on May 7, 2023. He was 91. Cotterill was born in Yorkshire, England, on March 26, 1932. He worked in amateur dramatics in his youth and trained at the Bristol Old Vic and the Drama Centre London. He served in the Royal Air Force and joined the Royal Shakespeare Company after his discharge. He settled in Australia after the company staged a production of "A Midsummer Night's Dream" there in 1973. Cotterill continued to perform on stage throughout his career. He also appeared frequently in films with roles in "Deathcheaters" (1976), "Journey Among Women" (1977), "Blue Fin" (1978), "The Chain Reaction" (1980), "Alison's Birthday" (1981), "The Survivor" (1981), "Hoodwink" (1981), "Going Down" (1982), "The City's Edge" (1983), "Prisoners" (1983), "Where the Green Ants Dream" (1984), the science fiction "Lorca and the Outlaws"(1984), "Burke & Wills" (1985), "Comrades" (1986), "The Right Hand Man" (1987), "The Lighthorsemen" (1987), the horror film "Howling III: The Marsupials" (1987) as Professor Sharp, "Nice Coloured Girls" (1987), "Rikky and Pete" (1988), "Sons of Steel" (1988), "Vicious!" (1988), "Resistance" (1992), "Bad Boy Bubby" (1993), "This Won't Hurt a Bit" (1993), "The Proposition" (2005), and "December

Boys" (2007). He was seen frequently on television with roles in episodes of "Homicide", "Behind the Legend", "Shannon's Mob", "King's Men", "Chopper Squad", "Cop Shop", "Punishment", "Patrol Boat", "Five Mile Creek", "Carson's Law", "Special Squad", "The Fast Lane", "The Flying Doctors", "Mission: Impossible", "Rafferty's Rules", the science fiction series "Ultraman: Towards the Future" as Arthur Grant in 1990, "A Country Practice", "E Street", "Halifax f.p.", and "Murder Call". His other television credits include productions of "Essington" (1974), "Shannon's Mob" (1976), "Luke's Kingdom" (1976), "Beyond a Reasonable Doubt" (1977), "The Timeless Land" (1980), "Water Under the Bridge" (1980), "The Boy in the Bush" (1984), "Waterfront" (1984), "The Last Bastion" (1984), "The Blue Lightning" (1986), "My Brother Tom" (1986), "Shark's Paradise" (1986), "I've Come About the Suicide" (1987), "All the Way" (1988), "The Four Minute Mile" (1988), "Trouble in Paradise" (1989), "CrimeBroker" (1993), "Whipping Boy" (1996), and "The Broken Shore" (2013). He was cast as the long-lost father of Leonardo DiCaprio's Jay Gatsby in Baz Luhrmann's 2013 film version of "The Great Gatsby" but his scenes were not included in the final cut. Cotterill's interest in Buddhist philosophy led him to spend much time in Thailand and Myanmar, where he mentored acting students with the New Yangon Theatre. He settled in Cairns in his later years and continued to perform in local community theaters.

Country Boy Eddie

Singer and television personality Gordon Edward Burns, who performed under the name Country Boy Eddie, died

at his home in Warrior, Alabama, on January 13, 2023. He was 92. Burns was born in Warrior on December 13, 1930. He served in the U.S. Army during the Korean War. He performed as a musician and entertainer from his teens and worked in radio. He was noted in the Birmingham, Alabama, area for hosting the long-running local variety series "The Country Boy Eddie Show" on WBRC from 1957 to 1993. Burns hosted numerous country musicians including such big names as Dolly Parton and Tammy Wynette. He usually opened his show by braying like a mule and jingling cow bells. WBRC released a television special, "Absolutely Alabama: Country Boy Eddie's 90th Birthday Celebration", in 2020. He was preceded in death by his wife of 61 years, Edwina Acton Burns, and is survived by their son, Doyle.

Courtney, Dave

British gangster Dave Courtney, who later became an author and actor, died of a self-inflicted gunshot wound at his home in Plumstead, London, England, on October 22, 2023. He was 64. Courtney was born in Bermondsey, London, England, on February 17, 1959. He made numerous claims about his links with criminals and gangsters, though few of them could

be substantiated. He claimed to have worked in such criminal enterprises as debt collection, assault, smuggling, and murder. He was charged with possession of live ammunition and a prohibited weapon in 2009 and filed for bankruptcy in 2009. He was author of the books "Stop the Ride I Want to Get Off:

An Autobiography" (1999), "Raving Lunacy: Clubbed to Death - Adventures on the Rave Scene" (2000), "The Ride's Back On" (2002), "Dave Courtney's Little Black Book" (2005), "Dave Courtney's Heroes and Villains" (2005), and "F**k the Ride" (2006). Courtney had a small role in the 1990 film "The Krays". He was also seen in the films "Triads, Yardies & Onion Bhajees!" (2003), "Cathula II: Vampires of Sex" (2004) as the Devil, "The Baby Juice Express" (2004), "Hell to Pay" (2005) which he also wrote and produced, "Six Bend Trap" (2007), "The Dead Sleep Easy" (2007), "Clubbing to Death" (2008), "Killer Bitch" (2010), "The Estate" (2011), "Sacrifice" (2013), "Full English Breakfast" (2014) also serving as producer, "Looters, Tooters and Sawn-Off Shooters" (2014), "Mob Handed" (2016), "Gangsters Gamblers Geezers" (2016), "Gatwick Gangsters" (2017), "Roofied" (2017), "Bangers and Cash" (2017), "Cream" (2018), "198 Grand" (2019), "The Seven" (2019), "Mother's Child" (2020), "Social Media" (2021), and "Legacy" (2022). He was seen on television in episodes of "The Paradise Club", "Minder", "The Bill", and "Wrongfully Convicted". Courtney appeared in numerous documentaries about the British criminal scene. He reportedly was in severe pain from rheumatoid arthritis and other health issues and had been filming farewell videos for friends and family in the weeks before his suicide. He is survived by his wife, Jennifer Pinto, though they had long been separated. He is also survived by his most recent girlfriend, Angela Hoy.

Cray, Patricia

Actress Patricia Cray died of complications from Parkinson's disease and a fall at her home in Allentown, Pennsylvania, on October 7, 2023. She was 82. She was born

Patricia Cratty in Pittsburgh, Pennsylvania, on August 13, 1941. She performed on stage from an early age and appeared in national productions of "Take Her, She's Mine" and "A Streetcar Named Desire". She graduated from college at Quinnipiac University in Connecticut in 1971. She also worked as a field manager for Reader's Digest. She returned to the stage and was featured in the 1980 Broadway production of "John Gabriel Borkman". She earned a law degree from the University of Pittsburgh School of Law in 1981 and served as a law clerk at the Allegheny County Court of Common Pleas for over two decades. Cray was featured in small roles in several films including "Houseguest" (1995), "Wonder Boys" (2000), "Love & Other Drugs" (2010), and "Won't Back Down" (2012). She also appeared on television in episodes of "The Doctors", "The Kill Point", and "One Dollar". Cray's survivors include her son, John Gabriel Lloyd.

Crayton, Robert

Actor Robert Crayton killed himself after shooting his wife and three children to death at their home in High Point, North Carolina, on January 7, 2023. He was 45. Crayton was born in Brooklyn, New York, in 1978. He began performing

for family and friends from an early age. He began appearing in films with roles in the 2008 short "Chains" and the 2009 feature "Paranormal" as a demon. His other films include "The 5th Quarter" (2010), "Consumption" (2010), "Inara, the Jungle Girl" (2012), "Life of a Struggling Actor" (2013), "We're the Millers" (2013), "10 Rules for Sleeping Around" (2013), "Are You Here" (2013), "Operation Z: Volume 1" (2013), "My Name Is Paul" (2013), "Spirit in the Woods" (2014), "A Long Way Off" (2014), "Dark Awakening" (2014), "Crazed" (2014), "The Sin Seer" (2015), "Koch Daddy" (2015), "Paper Towns" (2015), "Ant-Man" (2015) as Peachy, "Athena" (2015), "Barbershop: The Next Cut" (2016), "Survival T.V. The Movie!" (2016), "Obamaland Part 1: Rise of the Trumpublikans" (2017), "Hit a Lick" (2017), "Empire of the Heart" (2017), "Shifting Gears" (2018), "Edge of Fear" (2018), "Safety" (2020), "Murdersville, USA" (2021), "Motorvation" (2022), "Airborn" (2022), and "I Got Problemz" (2023). Crayton appeared on television in productions of "Trinity Goodheart" (2011), "Let the Church Say Amen" (2013), "When Love Kills: The Falicia Blakely Story" (2017), and "The Chronicles of Jesus" (2021). He was also seen in episodes of "Sid Roth's It's Supernatural", "Teen Wolf", "History Detectives", "Homeland", "The Haves and the Have Nots", "Royal Pains", "Under the Dome", "Constantine", "Banshee", "Amnesia", "Born Again Virgin", "Here We Go Again", "Saints & Sinners", "Star", "Six", "Underground", "Being Mary Jane", "The Inspectors", "The Quad", "Love Is_", "Ballers", "Wu-Tang: An American Saga" as Attila in 2019, "La Guerra Silenciosa", "The I Ching Lawyer", "Fostering Dad", "Young Rock" as football player Warren Sapp in 2021, "Swagger", and "The Staircase" as Ron Guerette in 2022. Crayton had a long battle with mental illness and had been visited by authorities five times over the last decade. He shot his wife, Athalia Crayton, and their three children at their home before shooting himself.

Crewdson, Robert

British actor Robert Crewdson, who starred in the horror films "Blood Beast from Outer Space" and "The

Psychopath", died of complications from Alzheimer's disease at a care facility in Galloway, Scotland, on February 7, 2023. He was 96. Crewdson was born in Lambeth, London, England, on January 20, 1927. He appeared frequently in films from the mid-1950s with such credits as "Oh... Rosalinda!!" (1955), "Escape from the Iron Curtain" (1956), "Pursuit of the Graf Spee" (1956), "Million Dollar Manhunt" (1956), "The Beasts of Marseilles" (1957), "The One That Got Away" (1957), "The Two-Headed Spy" (1958), "Room 43" (1958), "Chance Meeting" (1959), "Devil's Bait" (1959), "The Battle of the Sexes" (1960), "Peeping Tom" (1960), "Strip Tease Murder" (1961), "Highway to Battle" (1961), "The Pursuers" (1961), the science fiction film "Blood Beast from Outer Space" (aka "The Night Caller") (1965) as the alien Medra, the Amicus psycho-thriller "The Psychopath" (1966) as ill-fated artist Victor Ledoux, "Here Private Hell" (1968), and "Trog" (1970). Crewdson appeared on television in productions of "Bless the Bride" (1956), "The Power and the Glory" (1957), "Million Dollar Smile" (1957), and "The Gentle Shade" (1961). His other television credits include episodes of "The Adventures of Sir Lancelot", "The Errol Flynn Theatre", "Overseas Press Club - Exclusive!", "Escape", "Pride and Prejudice", "Hotel Imperial", "Mary Britten, M.D.", "The Edgar Wallace Mystery Theatre", "Probation Officer", "One Step Beyond", "Top Secret", "The Cheaters", "The Plane Makers", "Tales of Mystery", "Epitaph for a Spy" as Koche in 1963, "No Hiding Place", "Crane", "The Third Man", "The Baron", "The Man Who Never Was", "The Saint", "Crossroads" as Rupert Bonnamy in 1967, "Armchair Theatre", "Virgin of the Secret Service", "Man in a Suitcase", "The Champions", and "The Flaxton Boys". He largely retired from the screen in the early 1970s and worked as a fine art dealer. Crewdson is survived by his wife, Lucy, and three sons.

Crosby, David

Singer and songwriter David Crosby, who was a member of the groups the Byrds and Crosby, Stills & Nash, died of complications from COVID-19 in Santa Ynev, California, on

January 18, 2023. He was 81. Crosby was born in Los Angeles, California, on August 14, 1941. His father was Oscar-winning cinematographer Floyd Crosby. He performed in high school dramatics before flunking out and graduated through a correspondence course. He briefly attended Santa Barbara City College before dropping out to pursue a career in music. He formed a folk duo with singer Terry Callier and they performed in Chicago and Greenwich Village. Crosby was part of Les Baxter's Balladeers from 1964 to 1965 and recorded several singles with the group. He was a founding member of the folk-rock band the Byrds in 1964, joining Roger McGuinn on lead guitar, Gene Clark on tambourine, Chris Hillman on bass guitar, and Michael Clarke on drums. Crosby played rhythm guitar and provided vocals. The Byrds had a major hit with their rendition of "Mr. Tambourine Man" in 1965. He soon became a songwriter for the group, co-writing "I See You", "What's Happening", and "Why". The Byrds continued to score hits with "Turn! Turn! Turn!" and "Eight Miles High". Crosby's conflicts with other members of the band led to him leaving the group in mid-1967 after recording several songs on "The Notorious Byrd Brothers" album. He soon began performing with Stephen Stills and they were joined by Graham Nash. They became known as the trio Crosby, Stills & Nash and recorded their first self-named album in 1969 which contained the major hits "Suite: Judy Blue Eyes" and "Marrakesh Express". The trio performed at the Woodstock Music Festival in August of 1969 and were seen in the "Woodstock" film the following year. Crosby wrote several songs for the band including "Guinnevere", "Almost Cut My Hair", "Long Time Gone", and "Delta", and co-wrote "Wooden Ships". Neil Young joined the band in 1969 and performed at the ill-fated Altamont Free Concert in September of 1969. The quartet recorded the 1970 hit album "Deja Vu". The album featured the hits "Woodstock", "Teach Your Children", and "Our House". They disbanded after the 1971 double album "4 Way Street". Crosby released the 1971 solo album "If I Could Only Remember My Name". He and Nash continued to perform together as a duo and released the 1972 album "Graham Nash David Crosby". He produced a reunion album with the Byrds in March of 1973. The quartet reunited later in 1973 and embarked on a reunion tour. The compilation album, "So Far", featuring the hit song "Ohio", was released in 1974. They again disbanded but soon reunited as the original trio without Young. They released the albums "CSN" (1977) and "Daylight Again" (1982). There later albums include "American Dream" (1988) which also included Young, "Live It Up" (1990), "After the Storm" (1994), and "Looking Forward" (1999) again with Young. The "Crosby & Nash" album was released in 2004. Crosby was also a session musician in the 1970s, working with such artists as Jackson Browne, James Taylor, Art Garfunkel, Dave Mason, Elton John, and Carole King. He also sang backup on various projects with Phil Collins in the late 1980s and with the Indigo Girls on the 1992 "Rites of Passage" album. He teamed with guitarist Jeff Pevar and his son, pianist James Raymond, in the band CPR from 1996 to 2004, recording several albums together. He and Nash were backing vocalists on David Gilmour's 2006 album "On an Island". Crosby released the solo album "Croz" in 2014 and "Lighthouse" in 2016. His later solo albums include "Sky Trails" (2017), "Here If You Listen" (2018), and "For Free" (2021). He appeared and performed on television in such series as "Shindig!", "The Ed Sullivan Show", "Ready, Steady, Go!", "The Dick Cavett Show", "This Is Tom Jones", "Tomorrow Coast to Coast", "The Mike Douglas Show", "One on One with John Tesh", "The Whoopi Goldberg Show", "The Arsenio Hall Show", "Hollywood Squares", "Larry King Live", "Live with Kelly and Mark", "The Tonight Show with Jay Leno", "Later... With Jools Holland", "The Colbert Report", "Late Show with David Letterman", "Late Night with Jimmy Fallon", "The Big Interview with Dan Rather", "Tavis Smiley", and "The Tonight Show Starring Jimmy Fallon". Crosby was an actor in the films "Backdraft" (1991), "Hook" (1991), "To Cross the Rubicon" (1991), and "Thunderheart" (1992). He also appeared in television episodes of "Shannon's Deal", "Roseanne", "Flying Blind", the animated "The Simpsons", "The John Larroquette Show" in the recurring role of Alcoholic Anonymous sponsor Chester from 1993 to 1994, "Ellen", and "Chicago Hope". He was featured in the 1996 tele-film "Suddenly". He was the subject of the 2019 documentary film "David Crosby: Remember My Name". He co-wrote the memoirs "Long Time Gone: The Autobiography of David Crosby" (2005) and "Since Then: How I Survived Everything and Lived to Tell About It" (2007). He was active in political affairs, condemning the war in Vietnam and promoted conspiracy theories regarding the assassination of President John F. Kennedy. He was later an opponent of Donald Trump's presidency. He was frequently involved with drug and alcohol abuse and spent nine months in prison in Texas in 1985 for possession of cocaine and heroin. He was also arrested on such charges as drunken driving, hit-and-run, weapons offenses, and drug possession. He suffered a long battle with hepatitis C that resulted in a liver transplant in 1994. He also suffered from type 2 diabetes and heart disease. He was inducted into the Rock and Roll Hall of Fame as a member of the Byrds in 1991 and with Crosby, Stills and Nash in 1997. Crosby is survived by his son, James Raymond, who was adopted shortly after his birth in 1962. He later reunited with his father as an adult. He also had a daughter, Erika, with Jackie Guthrie, and daughter Donovan Crosby, with Debbie Donovan. He married Jan Dance in 1987, and they had a son, Django Crosby.

Cross, Perry

Television producer Perry Cross, who was the first producer of "The Tonight Show Starring Johnny Carson" in the early 1960s, died of kidney cancer in Los Angeles, California, on March 9, 2023. He was 95. Cross was born in Brooklyn, New York, on February 26, 1928. He was the son of vaudeville

comic Alan Cross. He attended the University of Rhode Island and began working in television as a NBC page at Rockefeller enter in 1949. He worked at NBC as a production coordinator and produced Ernie Kovacs' weekday morning program on CBS in 1956. He briefly hosted "The Tonight Show Starring Jack Paar" in 1957 but left due to friction with the host. He returned to "The Tonight Show" after Paar quit in 1962 and oversaw a line-up of guest hosts until a replacement could be found. The guest hosts included Jerry Lewis, Groucho Marx, Mort Sahl, Art Linkletter, Merv Griffin, and Robert Cummings. He remained producer when Carson took the helm in 1962. Cross left "The Tonight Show" the following year to produce the short-lived variety series "The Jerry Lewis Show". He also served as producer of the series "Producers' Showcase", "County Fair", "Be Our Guest", "The Spike Jones Show", "The Chevy Show", "The Dinah Show Chevy Show", "The Jonathan Winters Specials", "Hollywood Talent Scouts", "The Garry Moore Show", "Rowan & Martin's Laugh-In", "Life with Linkletter", "The Soupy Sales Show", "The Red Skelton Hour", "Can You Top This", and "The Ice Palace". He was producer of "The 26th Annual Primetime Emmy Awards" in 1974 and the "NBC 50th Anniversary Special" in 1976. Cross left television in the mid-1970s and became successful in real estate. His survivors include his son, Larry Cross.

Crounse, Avery

Film director and writer Avery Crounse, who was noted for the 1983 western horror film "Eyes of Fire", died in

Charleston, South Carolina, on March 20, 2023. He was 71. Crounse was born in Paducah, Kentucky, on April 15, 1951. He began working in films in the early 1980s and formed his own production company, Elysian Pictures. He produced, directed, and wrote the 1983 horror film "Eyes of Fire". He also helmed the 1988 science fiction comedy film "The Invisible Kid" and the 1996 drama "Sister Island" (aka "Cries of Silence"). He was also noted as photographer whose works appeared in the pages of "American Photographer" magazine. Crounse is survived by his partner, Jessica Sater, and two daughters.

Crowley, Ann

Singer and actress Ann Crowley died on April 24, 2023. She was 93. Crowley was born in Olyphant, Pennsylvania, on April 24, 1929. She went to New York City

on a singing scholarship and graduated from Julia Richman High School in 1947. She began performing in nightclubs in the mid-1940s and made her Broadway debut in a production of "Oklahoma!" in 1946, filling in for Betty Jane Watson in the role of Laurey. Crowley was also seen in such Broadway musicals as "Carousel" (1947), "Seventeen" (1951), "Paint Your Wagon" (1951), and "Music Is" (1976). She starred in numerous regional and touring productions. She performed on television in episodes of "Musical Comedy Time", "Studio One" in a production of "Cinderella '53", "Your Chevrolet Showroom", and "Footlights and Kleiglights". She was featured in "The Marriage of Figaro" on "NBC Television Opera Theatre" in 1954. Crowley largely retired from performing following her marriage to Dr. Stephen N. Jones. They had five children together before his death in 2003. Their

son Christopher died as an infante in 1960 and son Stephen died in 2018. She is survived by daughter Elisa and sons Thomas and Blaise. She was married to Jim Simpson from 2006 until his death in 2016. She is also survived by her younger sister, actress Patricia Crowley.

Crump, Rolly

Animator and designer Rolly Crump, who was known for his work with Walt Disney Studios, died at his home in Carlsbad, California, on March 12, 2023. He was 93. Crump was born in Alhambra, California, on February 27, 1930. He began working at Walt Disney Studios in 1952 and served as an

inbetweener on the film "Peter Pan" (1953) and the animated short "Ben and Me" (1953). He moved up to assistant animator and worked on such films as "Lady and the Tramp" (1955), "Sleeping Beauty" (1959), and "101 Dalmatians" (1961). He became a designer for WED Enterprises, which later became Walt Disney Imagineering, in 1959. He designed the architectural piece called the Tower of the Four Winds for the "It's a Small World" attraction at the New York World's Fair in 1964. The attraction moved to Disneyland in 1966 and Crump added a large, animated clock at the entrance featuring puppet children on parade. He also worked on the Disneyland attractions "The Enchanted Tiki Room", the "Adventureland Bazaar", and "The Haunted Mansion". He was involved with the early designs for the Magic Kingdom at Walt Disney World in Florida. He left Disney in the early 1970s to work on other projects including Busch Gardens, The ABC Wildlife Preserve in Maryland, the Ringling Brothers & Barnum and Bailey Circus World in Florida, and Knott's Berry Farm's "Knott's Bear-y Tales". Crump returned to Disney in 1976 and designed the Land and Wonders of Life pavilions at Epcot Center. He again left Disney in 1981 and was involved in the design for the proposed Cousteau Ocean Center in Norfolk, Virginia. He formed the Mariposa Design Group, which developed projects in Las Vegas, Denver, and Oman. He again returned to Disney in 1992 to work on the Epcot Center as executive designer at Imagineering. He retired from Disney in 1996 and was named a Disney Legend in 2004. His autobiography, "It's Kind of a Cute Story", was published in 2012. Crump is survived by his second wife, Marie, and three children. Crump appeared as himself in several episodes of "The Magical World of Disney" in the 1960s and was featured in various film and television documentaries about Disneyland.

Cunningham, Bill

Singer Bill Cunningham, who was the original voice of Mattel's Ken doll in the 1960s, died at his home in West Hollywood, California, on July 15, 2023. He was 96. Cunningham was born in San Francisco, California, on January 2, 1927. He served in the U.S. Navy during World War II. He performed as a singer and entertained troops in the Pacific theater. He later performed with NBC's "Voices of Walter

Schumann" and "The Tennessee Ernie Ford Show". He was best known for supplying the voice of Ken, Barbie's doll boyfriend, in Mattel Toys commercials in the early 1960s. He released his debut album, "I'm Always Chasing Rainbows", in 1962, and toured with Judy Garland. He began the voice-over talent agency Pacific Artists Agency in Los Angeles in 1963. It became Cunningham & Associates in 1967, and later was known as CESD. Cunningham retired in 1989. His autobiography, "I Wonder What Became of Me", was published in 2014.

Cunningham, Walter

Astronaut Walter Cunningham, who was pilot of the lunar module for the Apollo 7 mission in 1968, died of complications from a fall in Houston, Texas, on January 3,

2023. He was 90. Cunningham was born in Creston, Iowa, on March 16, 1932. He graduated from high school in Los Angeles in 1950 and attended Santa Monica College. He joined the U.S. Navy in 1951 and began flight training the following year. He was a fighter pilot with the U.S. Marine Corps in Korea from 1953 to 1954. He served with the U.S. Marine Corps Reserve from 1956 until retiring with the rank of colonel in 1975. He resumed his education at Santa Monica College and transferred to the University of California at Los Angeles in 1960. He graduated in 1960 and earned a master's degree in physics in 1961. He worked with the Rand Corporation before being chosen in the third group of astronauts by NASA in October of 1963. He was part of the first manned Apollo mission, Apollo 7, with Donn Eisele and Wally Schirra, from October 11-22, 1968. He later served as head of the Flight Crew Directorate for the Skylab branch before leaving NASA in 1971. Cunningham later worked in business and investments, becoming a senior executive at financial and real estate companies. His memoirs, "The All-American Boys", was published in 1977. He was also a contributor and wrote the forward for the 2007 book "In the Shadow of the Moon". He was portrayed by Fredric Lehne in the HBO mini-series "From the Earth to the Moon" in 1998. Cunningham married LoElla Irby in 1956, and they later divorced. He is survived by their two children, Brian and Kimberley. He is also survived by his second wife, Dorothy 'Dot' Cunningham.

Curran, Pamela

Actress Pamela Curran died in West Hollywood, California, on September 3, 2023. She was 93. Curran was born in New York city on February 6, 1930. She was a socialite

and was named debutante of the year in 1948. She began working in films and television in the late 1950s with small roles in the films "Desk Set" (1957) and "The Blob" (1958).

She continued to appear in such films as "Who Was That Lady?" (1960), "The Thrill of It All" (1963), "Under the Yum Yum Tree" (1963), the science fiction film "Mutiny in Outer Space" (1965), "Girl Happy" (1965), "The Loved One" (1965), and "The Chase" (1966). Curran was seen on television in episodes of "Kraft Theatre", "Michael Shayne", "Checkmate", "Tallahassee 7000", "Surfside 6", "87th Precinct", "The Detectives", "Target: The Corruptors!", "Bachelor Father", "Perry Mason", "Thriller", "Alfred Hitchcock Presents", "Laramie", "The Dick Powell Theatre", "My Favorite Martian", "The Alfred Hitchcock Hour", "Kraft Suspense Theatre", "The Bing Crosby Show", "I Dream of Jeannie", "Branded", "Run for Your Life", "The Green Hornet", "The Man from U.N.C.L.E.", "The Felony Squad", "The Invaders", "The F.B.I.", "Hogan's Heroes", "Adam-12", "The Merv Griffin Show", and "Love, American Style". She largely retired from the screen in the early 1970s. Curran was married to Joseph Wade, Jr., from 1951 until their divorce in 1955 and they had two children. She was married to Bob Sweeney from 1957 until their divorce in 1961.

Curtis, Dick

Actor and comedian Dick Curtis died of congestive heart failure in Los Angeles, California, on September 16, 2023.

He was 95. He was born Richard Byrd Laub in Detroit, Michigan, on May 24, 1928. He served as a U.S. Marine during World War II. He began performing as a comic in nightclubs after leaving the military. He appeared frequently on television from the 1950s with roles in episodes of "The Jack Benny Program", "Waterfront", "Network", "Revue '61", "The Dick Van Dyke Show", "Batman", "Vacation Playhouse", "The Andy Griffith Show", "Captain Nice", and "He & She". Curtis was a regular performer on the comedy variety series "The Jonathan Winters Show" from 1967 to 1969, often serving as Winters straight man. He was also seen in episodes of "That Girl", "The Ray Stevens Show", "The New Andy Griffith Show", "The Partners", "Love, American Style", "The New Dick Van Dyke Show", and "The Odd Couple". He was featured in the 1971 tele-film "Confessions of a Top Crime Buster" and was a voice actor in such animated series as "Skyhawks", "Cattanooga Cats", and "Motormouse and Autocat". Curtis was seen in several films including "Support Your Local Gunfighter" (1971), "The Day It Came to Earth" (1977), the cult horror film "Motel Hell" (1980), and "What Waits Below" (1984). He was married to Barbara Ruth Hislop from 1950 until their divorce in 1973 and is survived by three daughters.

Curval, Philippe

French science fiction writer Philippe Tronche, who wrote under the pseudonym Philippe Curval, died in Paris, France, on August 5, 2023. He was 93. Tronche was born in Paris on December 27, 1929. He was a journalist and writer from the mid-1950s. His first science fiction story, "Elduo's Egg", was published in 1955 and his debut novel, "Les Fleurs de Venus", appeared in 1960. His other novels include "Le Ressac de l'Espace" (1962), "La Forteresse de Colon" (1967), "Les Sables de Falun" (1970), "L'Homme a Rebours" (1974), "Cette Chere Humanite?" (aka "Brave Old World") (1976), "Un Soupcon de Neanf" (1977), "Rut Aux Etoiles" (1979), "Le Dormeur s'Eveillera-t-il?" (aka "Will the Sleeper Awake?") (1979), "La Face Cachee du Desir" (1980), "Tous Vers l'Extase" (1981), "L'Odeur de la Bete" (1981), "En Souvenir du Futur" (aka "Remembrance of Time to Come") (1982), "Akiloe" (1988), "Les Evades du Mirage" (1995), "Voyance Aveugle" (1998), "MACNO Emmerede la Mort" (1998), "Voyage a l'Envers" (2000), and "Lothar Blues" (2008). He wrote numerous works of short fiction which appeared in such collections as "Take a Lood, Boy, If There's an Alien Behind the Wine Bottle" (1980), "The Golden Book of Science Fiction: Philippe Curval" (1980), "On Your Feed, Dead Men, the Phantom Train Is Pulling In" (1984), and "Do We Really Live Somewhere?" (1990).

Cutogno, Toto

Italian singer and songwriter Salvatore 'Toto' Cutugno died of prostate cancer at a hospital in Milan, Italy, on August 22, 2023. He was 80. Cutugno was born in Fosdinovo, Italy, on July 7, 1943. He began performing in bands as a drummer in his teens and formed the band Toto e i Tati in the early 1960s. He became co-writer of numerous popular songs by the 1970s that became hits for such artists as Joe Dassin, Johnny Halliday, Michel Sardou, and Claude Francois. He formed the band Albatross to record his own material in 1976 and they released a self-named album. He performed frequently as a solo artist at the San Remo Music Festival with such songs as "Solo Noi" ("Only Us"), "Serenata", "Figli" ("Sons"), "Emozioni", and "Le Mamme" ("The Mothers"). His song "Insieme 1992" ("Together 1992") won the Eurovison Song Contest. His numerous albums include "Innamorata, Innamorato, Innamorati" (1980), "L'Italiano" (1983), "Azzura Malinconia"

(1986), "Toto Cutugno" (1990), "Voglio Andarea Vivere in Campagna" (1995), "Il Treno Va" (2002), "Cantando" (2004), "Come Noi Nessuno al Mondo" (2005), and "Un Falco Chiuso in Gabbia" (2009). He married Carla Cutugno in 1971 and she survives him. He is also survived by a son for another relationship.

Dainton, Patricia

British actress Patricia Dainton died in England on May 31, 2023. She was 93. She was born Margaret Bryden Pate in Hamilton, Lanarkshire, Scotland, on April 12, 1930. She moved to London in 1940 where she studied at the Italia Conti Academy of Theatre Arts and the Cone School of Dance. She soon began her career on stage, appearing in productions at Stratford-Upon-Avon and at the Theatre Royal in London. Dainton appeared frequently in films from the late 1940s through the early 1960s. Her films include "Dancing with Crime" (1947), "The Inheritance" (1947), "Love in Waiting" (1948), "A Piece of Cake" (1948), "The Dancing Years" (1950), "Hammer the Toff" (1952), "Castle in the Air" (1952), "Bombay Waterfront" (1952), "Tread Softly" (1952), "Operation Diplomat" (1953), "No Road Back" (1957), "A Novel Affair" (1957), "At the Stroke of Nine" (1957), "Witness in the Dark" (1959), "The House in March Road" (1960), "Ticket to Paradise" (1961), and "The Third Alibi" (1961). She was featured as Sally Norton in the ITV television soap opera "Sixpenny Corner" from 1955 to 1956. She was also seen in a 1950 television production of "The Song in the Forest" and episodes of "The Inch Man" and "White Hunter". Dainton largely retired from acting in the early 1960s and worked as a bookseller for two decades. She was married to producer Norman Williams from 1952 until his death in 2010 and is survived by their four children.

D'Alatri, Alessandro

Italian film director Alessandro D'Alatri died in Rome, Italy, on May 3, 2023. He was 68. D'Arlatri was born in Rome on February 24, 1955. He began his career in his teens as an actor on stage and screen. He was seen in television productions of "I Fratelli Karamazov" (1969), "Viaggio di Ritorno" (1970), and "Una Mattina Come le Altre" (1981). He also appeared in the films "Il Ragazzo Dagli Occhi Chiari" (1970) and "The Garden of the Finzi-Continis" (1970). D'Alatri began training as a director in the 1970s and helmed various commercials. He directed his first feature film, "Red American", in 1991. He continued to direct, and frequently write, such films include "Senza Pelle" (1994),

"I Giardini dell'Eden" (1998), "Casomai" (2002), "La Febbre" (2005), "Commediasexi" (2006), "Sul Mare" (2010), and "The Startup: Accendi il Tuo Futuro" (2017). D'Alatro worked in television, directing episodes of "Ritratti d'Autore", "Alfabeto Italiano", "I Bastardi di Pizzofalcone", "Inspector Ricciardi", and "A Professor". He also helmed television productions of "La Scuola Della Notte" (2017), "La Legge del Numero Uno" (2017), and "On Your Tiptoes" (2018).

Dalva, Robert

Film editor Robert Dalva, who won an Oscar for his work on the 1979 film "The Black Stallion", died of lymphoma in Larkspur, California, on January 27, 2023. He was 80. Dalva was born in New York City on April 14, 1942. He graduated from Colgate University in Hamilton, New York, in 1964 and

studied film at the University of Southern California for three years. Dalva served as a key grip on the low-budget horror film "The Undertaker and His Pals" in 1966. He began working with editor Verna Fields at the U.S. Information Agency after school. He made his feature debut editing Agnes Varda's "Lions Love (... and Lies)" in 1969. He handled second-unit photography for George Lucas' "Star Wars" in 1977, filming a land speeder crossing the desert. He received an Academy Award for editing Francis Ford Coppola's "The Black Stallion" in 1979 and provided additional photography for the film. He directed the 1983 sequel "The Black Stallion Returns" and television episodes of "Crime Story", "Nova", and "Star Wars: The Clone Wars". Dalva also served as second-unit photographer for the films "Heat and Sunlight" (1987), "True Believer" (1989), and "The War of the Roses" (1989). He was editor of the films "Latino" (1985), "Raising Cain" (1992), "The Joy Luck Club" (1993), Joe Johnston's "Jumanji" (1995), "Conceiving Ada" (1998), "October Sky" (1999), "Jurassic Park III" (2001), "Hidalgo" (2004), "The Prize Winner of Defiance, Ohio" (2005), "Touching Home" (2008), "Captain America: The First Avenger" (2011), "Immortals" (20), "Knife Fight" (2012), "Lovelace" (2013), "Sweetwater" (2013), "Heist" (2015), "Precious Cargo" (2016), "Evolution of Organic" (2017), and "San Francisco Stories" (2021). Dalva was cinematography for the "Nash Bridges" television series from 1999 to 2000. He married Marcia Smith in 1964 and is survived by her and their four children.

Damroth, John

Actor John Damroth died in Maywood, New Jersey, on August 21, 2023. He was 59. Damroth was born in the Bronx, New York, on April 2, 1964. He began performing on stage in school plays and community theater in his teens. He served in the U.S. Marine Corps and was later the embarked on a career in films. He appeared in the films "Blood Ties" (2013), "Vengeance" (2013), "Once Upon a Time in Queens" (2013),

"Monica Z" (2013), "Revenge of the Green Dragons" (2014), "Love Like This" (2014), "Flowers in the Snow" (2015), and "Courier X" (2015). Damroth was seen on television in episodes of such series as "Deadly Sins", "True Crimes with Aphrodite Jones", "Alien Dawn", "Fatal Encounters", "Changelings", "Blindspot", and "The Blacklist". Damroth is survived by his wife, Linda Powell, their son.

Dan, Jiro

Japanese actor Jiro Dan, who starred as Hideki Go and Ultraman Jack in the television series "The Return of Ultraman" in the early 1970s, died of lung cancer in Japan on March 22, 2023. He was 74. He was born Hideo Murata in Kyoto, Japan, on January 30, 1949. He began his career as an actor on

television in the early 1970s. He was featured as Hideki Go, the human host of Ultraman Jack, in the television series "Return of Ultraman" from 1971 to 1972. He reprised the role in episodes of many of the subsequent series including "Ultraman Ace" (1972), "Ultraman Taro" (1973-1974), "Ultraman Leo" (1974), and "Ultraman Mebius" (2007). Dan was featured in numerous other television series including "Edogawa Rampo Shirizu: Akechi Kogoro" as Golden Mask in 1970, "Super Robert Mach Baron" as Dr. Murano from 1974 to 1975, Sejun Kamen Mashinman" (1984), "Godzilla Island" (1997), "Teppen" (1999), "Tengoku No Kiss" as Koichi Okazaki in 1999, "Hanamura Daisuke", "The Files of the Young Kindaichi 3", "Shomuni", "Ninpuu Sentai Hurricaneger" as Ikki Kasumi in 2002, "The Aaah Detective Agency", "Pazuru", "Shitsuji Kissa ni Okaerinasaimase" as Kuromisaki in 2009, "Homicide Team 9", "The Tax G-Men" 19", "Wasted Land", "Ryomaden", "Lieutenant Kenzo Yabe", "Atami No Sosakan", "Dr. Irabu Ichiro", "Carnation", "Madame Butterfly", "Monsters", "Perfect Blue", "Doubles: Futari No Keiji", "Gunshi Kanbee", "Ginnikan", "TEAM - Keishicho Tokubetsu Sosa Honbu", "Anonymous Detective", "Nobunaga Concerto", "Doctors: Saikyo No Meii", "Hamon" as Tokuhisa kanda in 2015, "Liquid: Oni No Sake, Miseki No Kura", "Otosan to Yobasete", "Keishicho 0 Gakari: Seikatsu Anzen Ka Nandemo Sodanshitsu", "Gu.Ra.Me! - Sori No Ryoriban", "Doctor X", "Honjitsu Wa, Ohigara Mo Yoku", "Beppin San" as Nemoto from 2016 to 2017, "Bushi No Tamashii", "CSI: Crime Scene Talk", "Aishitetatte, Himitsu Wa Aru", "Red Beard", "Special Investigation Nine", "Konya, Latteni Dakisimetemo Iidesuka?", "Mampuka", "Inosenusu Enzai Bengoshi", "AIBOU: Tokyo Detective Duo", "Kishiryu Sentai Ryusoulger", "Byoshitsu de Nembutsu o Tonaenaide Kudasai", as Enmei in 2020, "Tokkai - Furyo Saiken Tokubetsu

Kaishu Bu -", and "Tada Rikon-Shitenai Dake" as Toshimichi Kakino in 2021.

Danneberg, Thomas

German actor Thomas Danneberg, who was noted as the German dubbing voice for such stars as Arnold Schwarzenegger, Sylvester Stallone, John Travolta, and Nick Nolte, died of complications from a stroke in Berlin, Germany, on September 30, 2023. He was 81. Danneberg was born in Berlin on June 2, 1942. He appeared in films and television from the early 1960s. His film credits include "Ferien Wie Noch Nie" (18963), "Verdammt Zur Sunde" (1964), Edgar Wallace's horror mystery "Creature with the Blue Hand" (1967) as Charles Emerson, Wallace's "Im Banne des Umheimlichen" (aka "The Hand of Power", "The Zombie Walks") (1968), "Heimlichkeiten" (1968), "Dr. Med. Fabian - Lachen Ist die Beste Medizin" (1969), "Die Liebestollen Baronessen" (1970), "Praise, What Makes You Hard" (1972), "Code Name: Wild Geese" (1984), "Kommando Leopard" (1985), and "The Commander" (1988). Danneberg was seen on television in productions of "Aktion Brieftaube - Schicksale im Geteilten Berlin" (1964), "Das Blaue vom Himmel" (1964), "Der Fall Michael Reiber" (1965), "Die Geschichte dses Rittmeisgters Schach von Wuthenow" (1966), and "Marco W. - 247 Tage im Turkischen Gefangnis" (2011). His other television credits include episodes of "Paul Klinger Erzahlt Abenteuerliche Geschichten", "Unser Pauker" as Dietrich Hellmann in 1965, "Den Lieben Langen Tag", "Geisterjager John Sinclair: Edition 2000", and "Heff der Chef - Horspielserie". He provided the German voices for numerous characters in animated film television, and video game productions. Danneberg was also the dubbing voice for such actors as Arnold Schwarzenegger, Sylvester Stallone, Dennis Quaid, Terence Hill, John Cleese, Dan Aykroyd, Nick Nolte, and Bruce Willis.

Danon, Ambra

Italian costume designer Ambra Danon died of cancer in Rome, Italy, on April 12, 2023. She was 75. Danon was born in Rome in 1947. She was the daughter of film producer Marcello Danon. She worked in costume design for stage productions and operas. She was costume designer for the 1975 film "Il Caso Raoul". Danon shared an Academy Award nomination for her work on the 1978 French comedy film "La Cage aux Folles", which was produced by her father. She was also costume designer for the sequels "La Cage aux Folles II" (1980) and "La Cage aux Folles

3: The Wedding" (1985), and the 1992 film "Quando Eravamo Repressi".

Daughtry, Dean

Keyboardist Dean Daughtry, who performed with the bands the Classics IV and the Atlanta Rhythm Section, died in Huntsville, Alabama, on January 26, 2023. He was 76. Daughtry was born in Kinston, Alabama, on September 8, 1946. He began performing with the band the Candymen in the mid-1960s. They recorded several minor hits including "Georgia Pines" and "Ways" later in the decade. They often served as Roy Orbison's backing band. Daughtry joined the Classics IV under Dennis Yost in 1968 and was heard on the hits "Stormy" and "Traces". He and his bandmates from the Candymen, singer Rodney Justo and drummer Robert Nix, and guitarist James B. Cobb, Jr., from Classics IV, joined to become the session band for the new Studio One recording label in Georgia. The band became known as the Atlanta Rhythm Section in 1970, with guitarist Barry Bailey and bassist Paul Goddard. The band released their first self-named album in 1972 with little success. They scored a success with their 1978 album "Champagne Jam", which featured the hits "Imaginary Lover" and "I'm Not Gonna Let It Bother Me Tonight". He continued to perform and record with the Atlanta Rhythm Section, becoming the only consistent member of the band until his retirement in 2020.

Davies, Dickie

British television personality Dickie Davies, who was host of ITV's "World of Sport", died in England on February 19, 2023. He was 94. Davies was born in Wallasey, Cheshire, England, on April 30, 1928. He served in the Royal Air Force for National Service and was a purser for ocean liners after his discharge. He began his career working as an announcer for Southern Television. He joined ITV Sport in 1965 and worked with Eamonn Andrews, the host of the network's "World of Sport". Davies took over as host from Andrews in 1968 and remained with the series through 1985. He continued to work with the network covering various sporting events, including the 1988 Seoul Olympics, until leaving ITV in 1989. He subsequently joined the original version of Eurosport and provided snooker coverage. Davies presented sports bulletins for Classics FM from 1992 until suffering a stroke in 1995. He also appeared on television in cameo roles in episodes of "Pardon My Genie", "Budgie", and "The New Statesman". He married Elisabeth Mann in 1962 and is survived by her and their twin sons.

Davies, Geoffrey

British actor Geoffrey Davies, who starred as Dr. Dick Stuart-Clark in the television series "Doctor in the House" and its sequels, died in England on July 13, 2023. He was 84. Davies was born in Leeds, Yorkshire, England, on December 15, 1934. He trained to be a commercial artist before embarking on an acting career. He began performing in repertory and attended the Royal Academy of Dramatic Art for two years. He appeared frequently on television from the late 1960s. He starred as Dr. Dick Stuart-Clark in the comedy series "Doctor in the House" from 1969 to 1970, "Doctor at Large" in 1971, "Doctor in Charge" from 1972 to 1973, "Doctor at Sea" in 1974, "Doctor on the Go" from 1975 to 1977, "Doctor Down Under" in 1979, and "Doctor at the Top" in 1991. His other television credits include episodes of "The Other 'Arf", "Bergerac", "The Bretts", "Woof!", "The Labours of Erica" as Dexter Rook from 1989 to 1990, "Law and Disorder", "Paul Merton's Life of Comedy", "EastEnders" as Judge Phelps-Gordon in 2002, "Casualty", "Doctors", and "Not Going Out". Davies appeared in a handful of films including "Oh! What a Lovely War" (1969), "1917" (1970), "Doctor in Trouble" (1970), the horror anthology "The Vault of Horror" (1973), and "Run for Your Wife" (2012). He married Ann Wheeler in 1962 and is survived by her and their daughter, actress Emma Davies.

Davies, Terence

British screenwriter and director Terence Davies died of cancer at his home in Mistley, England, on October 7, 2023. He was 77. Davies was born in Liverpool, England, on

November 11, 1945. He left school in his teens and worked as a shipping office clerk for a decade. He moved to Liverpool in 1971 and attended Coventry Drama School. He wrote and directed his first autobiographical short film, "Children", in 1976. He continued his training at the National Film School and continued his autobiographical trilogy with "Madonna and Child" (1980) and "Death and Transfiguration" (1983). He wrote and directed the features "Distant Voices, Still Lives" (1988) and "The Long Day Closes" (1992). He adapted the 1995 film "The Neon Bible" from a novel by John Kennedy Toole and 2000's "The House of Mirth" from a book by Edith Wharton. Davies wrote the radio plays "A Walk to the Paradise Garden" (2001) and a two-part adaptation of Virginia Woolf's "The Waves" in 2007. He directed and wrote the documentary film "Of Time and the City" in 2008. His later films include "The Deep Blue Sea" (2011) based on a play by Terence Rattigan, "Sunset Song" (2015), "A Quiet Passion" (2016) based on the life of poet Emily Dickinson, and "Benediction" (2021) a biographical drama of poet Siegfried Sassoon. He made the short films "But Why?" (2021) and "Passing Time" (2023), also serving as narrator.

Davis, Carl

American-British conductor and composer Carl Davis, who worked on numerous film and television productions, died from a brain hemorrhage in Oxford, England, on August 3,

2023. He was 86. Davis was born in Brooklyn, New York, on October 28, 1936. He attended Bard College in New York and studied musical composition with Paul Hordoff, Hugo Kauder, and Per Norgard. He worked with the New York City Opera and the Robert Shaw Chorale in the 1950s. He co-wrote the revue "Diversions" which was performed off-Broadway in 1959. He worked as a composer for the British television satire series "That Was the Week That Was" in the early 1960s. He continued to work frequently for British television throughout his career. He composed the title music for the BBC anthology series "The Wednesday Play" and "Play for Today". Davis also composed and sometimes conducted for such series as "Armchair Theatre", "Theatre 625", "Five More", "Omnibus", "Report", "Away from It All", "ITV Saturday Night Theatre", "The World at War", "Shades of Greene", "Out of Bounds", "The Lively Arts", "In the Looking Glass", "BBC2 Play of the Week", "Horse in the House", "The Commanding Sea", "Private Schulz", "BBC2 Playhouse", "All for Love", "Arena", "All Our Working Lives", "The Pickwick Papers", "Oscar", "Late Starter", "Horizon", "Screenplay", "The Play on One", "Screen One", "The Royal Collection", "Covington Cross" earning an Emmy Award nomination in 1993, "American Masters", "The English Programme", "Performance", "Real Women", "Comedy Lab", "Cranford", "Upstairs Downstairs", and "The Queen's Nose". His other television credits include compositions for productions of "The Other World of Winston Churchill" (1964), "Edward II" (1970), "The Snow Goose" (1971) receiving an Emmy Award nomination, "The Grievance" (1972), "War & Peace" (1972), "The Gangster Show: The Resistible Rise of Arturo Ui" (1972), "The Merchant of Venice" (1973), "The Cay" (1974), "The Canterville Ghost" (1974), "The Naked Civil Servant" (1975), "Our Mutual Friend" (1976), "Where Adam Stood" (1976), "Lorna Doone" (1976), "The Lady of the Camellias" (1976), "The Snow Queen" (1976), "Marie Curie" (1977), "The Eagle of the Ninth" (1977), "Tresure Island" (1977), "The Mayor of Casterbridge" (1978), "Wuthering Heights" (1978), "Thank You, Comrades" (1978), "The Light Princess" (1978), "Brecht and Co." (1979), "Marya" (1979), "Prince Regent" (1979), "The Old Curiosity Shop" (1979), "The Misanthrope" (1980), "Hollywood" (1980), "Moving Pictures" (1980), "Fair Stood the Wind for France"

(1980), "Staying On" (1980), "Oppenheimer" (1980), "The Merchant of Venice" (1980), "The Mystery of the Disappearing Schoolgirls" (1980), "Winston Churchill: The Wilderness Years" (1981), "La Ronde" (1982), "The Hound of the Baskervilles" (1982), "Praying Mantis" (1982), "Schoolgirl Chums" (1982), "Arms and the Man" (1983), "Unknown Chaplin" (1983), "Landscape" (1983), "Macbeth" (1983), "The Aerodrome" (1983), "The Weather in the Streets" (1983), "St. Ursula's in Danger" (1983), "The Tales of Beatrix Potter" (1983), "The Far Pavilions" (1984), "Sakharov" (1984), "A Kind of Alaska" (1984), "Vicious Circle" (1985), "The Day the Universe Changed" (1985), "A Song for Europe" (1985), "Silas Marner" (1985), "Murrow" (1986), "Fire & Ice" (1986), "The First Eden" (1987), "Buster Keaton: A Hard Act to Follow" (1987), "Once in a Life Time" (1988), "Journey's End" (1988), "Somewhere to Run" (1989), "Skullduggery" (1989), "The Yellow Wallpaper" (1989), "Crossing to Freedom" (1989), "Spymaker: The Secret Life of Ian Fleming" (1990), "Separate But Equal" (1991), "The Black Velvet Gown" (1991), "Ghosts of the Past" (1991), "The Crucifer of Blood" (1991), "Ashenden" (1991), "A Sense of History" (1992), "A Year in Provence" (1993), "Voyage" (1993), "Thatcher: The Downing Street Years" (1993), "Red Eagle" (1994), "George Stevens: D-Day to Berlin" (1994), "The Return of the Native" (1994), "The Buried Mirror" (1994), "Oliver's Travels" (1995), "Cinema Europe: The Other Hollywood" (1995), "Pride and Prejudice" (1995), "An Audience with Charles Dickens" (1996), "A Dance to the Music of Time" (1997), "Seesaw" (1988), "Coming Home" (1998), "The Face of Russia" (1998), "Goodnight Mr. Tom" (1998), "Cold War" (1998), "The Greatest Store in the World" (1999), "The Great Gatsby" (2000), "Back Home" (2001), "An Angel for May" (2002), and "Promoted to Glory" (2003). He was composer and often conductor for the films "The Bofors Gun" (1968), "Praise Marx and Pass the Ammunition" (1970), "The Only Way" (1970), "Up Pompeii" (1971), "I, Monster" (1971), "The Chastity Belt" (1972), "What Became of Jack and Jill?" (1972), "Rentadick" (1972), "The National Health" (1973), "The Lovers!" (1973), "What Next?" (1974), "Man Friday" (1975), "The Sailor's Return" (1978), "Birth of the Beatles" (1979), "The French Lieutenant's Woman" (1981), "Champions" (1984), "King David" (1985), "The Girl in a Swing" (1988), "Scandal" (1989), "The Rainbow" (1989), "Fragments of Isabella" (1989), "Frankenstein Unbound" (1990), "Le Radeau de la Meduse" (1990), "Diary of a Madman" (1990), "Echoes That Remain" (1991), "The Trial" (1993), "Genghis Cohn" (1993), "Widows' Peak" (1994), "Liberation" (1994), "Anne Frank Remembered" (1995), "Satan at His Best" (1995), "The Book of Eve" (2002), "Mothers and Daughters" (2004), "Garbo" (2005), "I'm King Kong!: The Exploits of Merian C. Cooper" (2005), "The Understudy" (2008), "Three Hours That Shook the World: Observations on Intolerance" (2013), and "Ethel & Ernest" (2016). Davis provided new scores for numerous silent films including "Intolerance", "The Four Horsemen of the Apocalypse", "Safety Last!", "Our Hospitality", "Greed", 1925's "The Phantom of the Opera", "The Big Parade", "The Eagle", "Ben-Hur: A Tale of Christ", "The Strong Man", "Flesh

and the Devil", "The General", "The Kid Brother", "It", "Napoleon", "The Student Prince of Old Heidelberg", "The Crowd", "Speedy", "The Godless Girl", "The Wind", "Show People", "A Woman of Affairs", "The Iron Mask", and Charles Chaplin's "City Lights". Davis appeared onscreen in small roles in several films including "Praise Marx and Pass the Ammunition" (1970), "The Understudy" (2008), and "Florence Foster Jenkins" (2016). He composed the 1997 symphonic "A Circle of Stones" and the dance works "Nijinsky" (2016), "Chaplin, the Tramp" (2019), "The Great Gatsby" (2019), and "Le Fantome et Chritine" (2023). His other stage works include the ballet "Lipizzaner" (1989), "The Liverpool Oratorio" (1991) with Paul McCartney, "Aladdin" (2000), the musicals "The Mermaid" (2003) and "Alice in Wonderland" (2005), the ballet "Cyrano" (2006), and "The Last Train to Tomorrow" for children's choir and orchestra in 2012. Davis married actress Jan Boht in 1970 and is survived by her and their two daughters, filmmaker Hannah Davis and Jessie Jo Davis.

Davis, Jennifer

Actress and makeup artist Jennifer Davis died on April 4, 2023. She was 85. Davis was born in December of 1938. She began working as an actress in the 1970s and appeared in a

small role in the 1974 film "Foxy Brown". She was featured as a nurse in numerous episodes of the Korean War comedy series "M*A*S*H*" from 1975 to 1983. She was also seen in an episode of "Trapper John, M.D.". Davis married Marvin Westmore of the famed Hollywood makeup Westmore family. She worked as a makeup artist from the early 1990s on such series as "Space Rangers", "Lois & Clark: The New Adventures of Superman", "Sweet Justice", "Childhood", "Sweetheart", "The Jessie Lansky Story", "St. Michael's Crossing", "Off Today", "13 Days", "The Practice", and "Ally McBeal". She retired in 2005. She and Marvin Westmore were married until his death in 2020.

Day, Peter

British television visual effects designer Peter Day died in England on March 13, 2023. He was 95. Day was born

in Richmond, Surrey, England, on July 9, 1927. He served with the Royal Army Service Corps as a driver after high school. He was discharged in 1948 and attended art schools in Kingston and Wimbledon. He worked at various jobs over the next decade including scenic design for theatrical productions. He joined the BBC in 1958 in the newly formed visual effects department. Hall worked as a special effects assistant in the 1958 science fiction mini-series

"Quatermass and the Pit" and appeared onscreen in a small role. He worked on numerous television series through the early 1980s including "Thursday Theatre", "Adam Adamant Lives!", "Doomwatch", "Out of the Unknown", "Some Mothers Do 'Ave 'Em", "Dad's Army", "Survivors", "The Goodies", "Doctor Who" also appeared in small roles in several episodes between 1967 to 1977, "Wings", and "The Little and Large Show". He also worked on television productions of "The Stone Tape" (1972), "Great Big Groovy Horse" (1975), "Running Blind" (1979), "The Twenty-First Century Show" (1979), and "Icebound in the Antarctic" (1983). Day married Elizabeth Wallis in 1954 and is survived by her and their two sons.

Dayman, Leslie

Australian actor Leslie Dayman died in Australia on October 20, 2023. He was 85. Dayman was born in Footscray, Victoria, Australia, on January 19, 1938. He began his career working on stage in the mid-1950s. He appeared on television in productions of "Weather at Pinetop" (1964) and "Dark Corridor" (1965). He was featured as Detective Bill Hudson on the detective series "Homicide" from 1966 to 1968. He was also seen in episodes of "Division 4", "Cop Shop", "Holiday Island", "Possession", "Special Squad", "Prisoner: Cell Block H" as Geoff Macrae from 1984 to 1985, "Son and Daughters" as Roger Carlyle from 1984 to 1985, "Rafferty's Rules", "William and Abel", "A Country Practice", "E Street" as Sergeant George Sullivan from 1989 to 1993, "Big Sky", "Water Rats", "Stingers", "Blue Heelers", and "All Saints". His other television credits include productions of "The Last Outlaw" (1980), "I Can Jump Puddles" (1981), "Bellamy" (1981), "Sara Dane" (1982), "Bodyline" (1984), "The Last Frontier" (1986), "Witch Hunt" (1987), "Blue Murder" (1995), "The Silence" (2006), and "Stepfather of the Bride" (2006). Dayman was seen in the films "Weekend of Shadows" (1978), "Gallipoli" (1981), "Molly" (1983), "With Prejudice" (1983), "Stanley: Every Home Should Have One" (1984), "I Can't Get Started" (1985), "Oscar and Lucinda" (1997), "In the Winter Dark" (1998), "Holy Smoke" (1999), and "Footy Legends" (2006). He was married and divorced from actress Diane Chamberlain and is survived by their two sons. He married Rosie Dayman in 1989 and she also survives him.

Dea, Gloria

Actress and magician Gloria Dea died at her home in Las Vegas, Nevada, of heart disease on March 18, 2023. She was 100. She was born Gloria Metzner in Alameda, California, on August 25, 1922. Her father was a magician who performed at local venues under the name The Great Leo. Gloria began performing magic tricks from an early age. She was noted for her hat trick that included the cooperation of two guinea pigs and a pigeon. She was billed as "the youngest working

magician in the world" by the age of seven. She became the first magician to perform on the Las Vegas Strip in May of 1941 with an appearance at El Rancho Vegas. She soon began her career in films, appearing in small roles and as a dancer in "The Story of Dr. Wassell" (1944), "I'll Remember April" (1945), "Mexicana" (1945), "An American in Paris" (1951), "Something to Live For" (1952), "Singin' in the Rain" (1952), the Columbia serial "King of the Congo" (1952) as Princess Pha opposite Buster Crabbe, "Down Among the Sheltering Palms" (1952), "The Prodigal" (1955), "The Sea Chase", "Around the World in 80 Days" (1956), Ed Wood's "Plan 9 from Outer Space" (1957), and "The Girl Most Likely" (1957). Dea later worked in sales with an insurance agency and at used car dealerships. She returned to Las Vegas in the early 1980s with her husband, fellow car dealer Sam Anzalone. She continued to perform occasionally in Las Vegas and celebrated her 100th birthday with other magicians at Westgate Las Vegas in August of 2022. Her husband, Sam Anzalone, died in 2022.

Dean, Margia

Actress Margia Dean died in Rancho Cucamonga, California, on June 23, 2023. She was 101. She was born Marguerite Louise Skliris in Chicago, Illinois, on April 7, 1922, and was raised in San Francisco. She began performing on stage from an early age and her role as Juliet in a production of

"Romeo and Juliet" won her the Women's National Shakespeare Contest. She was a contestant in beauty pageants, earning the titles of Miss San Francisco and Miss California and finishing first runner-up in 1939's Miss America competition. She performed on stage in Los Angeles in the early 1940s and made her film debut in the 1944 Republic Picture "Casanova in Burlesque". She took the screen name Margia Dean and appeared in small roles in the films "Call of the South Seas" (1944), "Taking It Big" (1944), "The Desert Hawk" (1944), "Delinquent Daughters" (1944), "Minstrel Man" (1944), "Earl Carroll Vanities" (1945), "The Power of the Whistler" (1945), "The Crime Doctor's Warning" (1945), "Who's Guilty?" (1945), and "Living in a Big Way" (1947). She became involved personally and professionally with producer Robert L. Lippert in the late 1940s and starred as Martha Langley in 1948's Shep Comes Home". She appeared frequently in films for Lippert over the next several years. Dean's other films include Sam Fuller's directorial debut "I Shot Jesse James" (1949), "Rimfire" (1949), "Grand Canyon" (1949), "Ringside" (1949), "Treasure of Monte Cristo" (1949), "Tough Assignment" (1949), "Red Desert" (1949), "The Baron of Arizona" (1950) with Vincent Price, "Western Pacific Agent" (1950), "Motor Patrol" (1950), "Hi-Jacked" (1950), "The Return of Jesse James" (1950), "Bandit Queen" (1950), "Fingerprints Don't Lie" (1951), "Mask of the Dragon" (1951), "Tales of Robin Hood" (1951), "Pier 23" (1951), "Inside the Walls of Folsom Prison" (1951), "Kentucky Jubilee" (1951), "Savage Drums" (1951), "Take Care of My Little Girl" (1951), "Leave It to the Marines" (1951), "Sky High" (1951), "F.B.I. Girl" (1951), "Superman and the Mole Men" (1951) starring George Reeves, "Loan Shark" (1952), "Mr. Walkie Talkie" (1952), the short "Love's A-Poppin'" (1953), "Mesa of the Lost Women" (1953), "Sins of Jezebel" (1953), "Fangs of the Wild" (1954), "The Lonesome Trail" (1955), and "Last of the Desperados" (1955). She starred as Judith Carroon, the wife of an ill-fated astronaut in the early Hammer horror science fiction film "The Quatermass Experiment" (aka "The Creeping Unknown") (1955). She also appeared in the films "The Revolt of Mamie Stover" (1956), "Frontier Gambler" (1956), "Stagecoach to Fury" (1956), "Badlands of Montana" (1957), "Ambush at Cimarron Pass" (1958), "Villa!!" (1958), "The Secret of the Purple Reef" (1960), "The Big Show" (1961), "7 Women from Hell" (1961), and "Moro Witch Doctor" (1964) with Jock Mahoney. Dean was seen on television in episodes of "Dick Tracy" as Police Officer Mary Faelb from 1950 to 1951, "Racket Squad", "Adventures of Superman", "The Revlon Mirror Theater", "The Pepsi-Cola Playhouse", "The Joe Palooka Story", and "I Spy". She served as a producer for several films including "The Long Rope" (1961) and the horror comedy "The Horror of It All" (1964) starring Pat Boone. She retired from acting in the mid-1960s after her second marriage. She later worked in a real estate agency and as an interior decorator. She also owned a dress shop and a coffee shop in Beverly Hills. Dean was married to baseball player Hal Fischer from 1939 until their divorce in 1945. She later married Spanish architect Felipe Alvarez in 1965 and he survives her.

de Armas, Sherika

Uruguayan model Sherika de Armas, who represented Uruguay in the 2015 Miss World pageant, died after a two-year battle with uterine cancer in Uruguay on October 16, 2023. She was 26. De Armas was born Montevideo, Uruguay, on March 29, 1997. She was crowned Miss Mundo Uruguay in a 2015 competition at the age of 18. She was unsuccessful in the subsequent Miss World contest, held in Sanya, China, in 2015, and failed to make the top 30. De Armas subsequently operated the Shey De Armas Beauty Studio, selling cosmetics and hair items. She also pursued a modeling career.

Dearborn, Philip

Film producer Philip Dearborn died in Chicago, Illinois, on March 14, 2023. He was 78. Dearborn was born in

New York City on March 15, 1944. He attended Harvard University and served in the U.S. Army during the Vietnam War after his graduation. He worked with Time Life's book department following his discharge. He moved to Los Angeles where he became involved in the film industry with partner Anthony Fingleton. Dearborn served as executive producer of the films "Blood Bath" (1975), "Young Lust" (1984), and "Drop Dead Fred" (1991). He also worked in sports marketing and helped form the U.S. bobsled team for the 1982 Olympics. Dearborn was married to Angelica Gerry until their divorce in 1995 and is survived by their two daughters. He married Mark Bereyso in 2014 and he also survives him.

Debever, Emmanuelle

French actress Emmanuelle Debever died of a suicide by drowning in the Seine River in Paris, France, on November 29, 2023. She was 60. Debever was born in Marseille, France,

on August 8, 1963. She began her acting career in the early 1980s, appearing in the film "Sweet Inquest on Violence" (1982) and the 1982 television mini-series "Joelle Mazart". She was featured as Louison Danton, the wife of Gerard Depardieu's Georges Jacques Danton, in Andrzej Wajda's historical epic "Danton". Her other films include "My Other Husband" (1983), "A Brutal Game" (1983), "Vive la Sociale!" (1983), "Grain of Sand" (1983), and "Paris Seen By... 20 Years After" (1984). Debever appeared on television in productions of "Quidam" (1984) and "La Barbe-bleue" (1986), and episodes of "Medecins de Nuit", "Marc et Sophie", and "Les Enquetes du Commissaire Maigret". She largely retired from the screen by the late 1980s. She accused French actor and co-star Gerard Depardieu of sexual assault during the filming of "Danton". Other actresses followed suit and Debever was featured in a France 2 television documentary, "Gerard Depardieu, la Chute d'un Ogre", which aired the day her death was announced. Debever was reported missing on November 29, 2023, after leaving a note at her home. The police were later alerted about a woman jumping from a bridge into the Seina. She was revived by paramedics and taken to a hospital, where she later died. Her death was confirmed by authorities on December 7, 2023.

De Gaetano, Michael

Director and screenwriter Alessandro 'Michael' De Gaetano, whose films include the cult classics "UFO: Target Earth" and "Haunted", died of complications from a fall at his

home in Arizona on June 11, 2023. He was 85. De Gaetano began working in films in the early 1970s and was producer, director, and writer of the science fiction feature "UFO: Target Earth" in 1974. He also produced, directed, and wrote the horror film "Haunted" (1977) and the comedy "Scoring" (1979). He later directed and scripted the films "Bloodbath in Psycho Town" (1989), "Project: Metalbeast" (1995), and "Butch Camp" (1996).

de Groot, Bob

Belgian comic book artist Bob de Groot died in Ottignies, Belgium, on November 17, 2023. He was 82. De Groot was born in Brussels, Belgium, on October 26, 1941. He

began working in comics as an assistant to cartoonist Maurice Tillieux at the publisher Dupuis in the early 1960s. He helped Tillieux redesign earlier "Felix" comics under the new title "Ange Signe". De Groot also began writing and illustrating his own comics for "Spirou".
He created a trilogy of serials featuring the character Jonas in the mid-1960s. He and writer Fred created the espionage feature "4x4= 31. L'Agent Cameleon" which ran from 1968 to 1969. He began a collaboration with cartoonist Turk in the late 1960s creating the comic "Robin Dubois", a parody of Robin Hood, for "Tintin" magazine. The comic ran from 1969 to 1989 and again from 2007 to 2008. Their comics series about Leonardo Da Vinci, "Leonard", ran from 1974 to 2015. The duo collaborated on the secret agent series "Clifton" from 1970 to 1984. De Groot continued to work on "Clifton" with artist Bedu after Turk left the series. He and Walli worked on the series "Chlorophylle" for "Tintin" and wrote several "Lucky Luke" stories. His later comics include "Doggyguard" with Michel Rodrigue from 1999 to 2000, "Pere Noel & Fils" with Philippe Bercovici from 2006 to 2008, and "Le Bar de Acariens" with Godi from 2008 to 2009.

Delaney, Leon

Actor and stuntman Leon Delaney died in Orem, Utah, on July 14, 2023. He was 76. Delaney was born in Houston, Texas, on February 18, 1947. He worked as a roadie for the band KISS and began his career in films and television with a small role in the 1978 tele-film "KISS Meets the Phantom of the Park". Delaney continued to perform stunts and appear in small roles in such films as "The Warriors" (1979), "Commando" (1985), "Predator" (1987), "Action Jackson" (1988), "Road House" (1989), "Ghostbusters II" (1989), "Far Out Man" (1990), "Dark Angel" (1990), "Total Recall" (1990), "Die Hard 2" (1990), "Home Alone" (1990) as stunt double for Daniel Stern, "Stone Cold" (1991), "Highway to Hell" (1991),

"Cape Fear" (1991), "Home Alone 2: Lost in New York" (1992), "Hoffa" (1992), "Universal Soldier" (1992), "Excessive Force" (1993), "Joshua Tree" (1993), "Mrs. Doubtfire" (1993), "Baby's Day Out" (1994), "Stargate" (1994), "Radioland Murders" (1994), "Rumpelstiltskin" (1995), "Cutthroat Island" (1995), "Sometimes They Come Back... Again" (1996), "Celtic

Pride" (1996), "Shadow Conspiracy" (1997), "The Maker" (1997), "Titanic" (1997), "Starship Troopers" (1997), "Black Dog" (1998), "The Thin Red Line" (1998), "Galaxy Quest" (1999), "Charlie's Angels" (2000), "Osmosis Jones" (2001), "Terminator 3: Rise of the Machines" (2003). Delaney also worked on the tele-films "Dangerous Passion" (1990), "The Adventures of Young Indiana Jones: Hollywood Follies" (1994), and "Under Wraps" (1997), and episodes of such series as "The Dukes of Hazard" and "The A-Team". He was predeceased by his wife, Melanie, and is survived by a son and two daughters.

de los Reyes, Kamar

Puerto Rican actor Kamar de los Reyes, who was featured as Antonio Vega in the soap opera "One Life to Live" from 1995 to 2009, died of cancer in Los Angeles, California, on December 24, 2023. He was 56. De los Reyes was born in

San Juan, Puerto Rico, on November 8, 1967. His father was Cuban percussionist Walfredo de los Reyes. Kamar was raised in Las Vegas, Nevada. He began his acting career in the late 1980s and was a featured dancer in the 1988 film "Salsa". His other films include "Ghetto Blaster" (1989), "East L.A. Warriors" (1989), "Coldfire" (1990), "Lethal Ninja" (1991), "The Silencer" (1992), "Street Knight" (1993), "Da Vinci's War" (1993), "Father Hood" (1993), "Nixon" (1995), the short "Daedalus Is Dead" (1996), "In Search of a Dream" (1997), "Mambo Cafe" (2000), "The Cell" (2000), "Love & Suicide" (2005), "Cayo" (2005), "Salt" (2010), "Hot Guys with Guns" (2013), "LA Apocalypse" (2015), and "Amelia 2.0" (2017). De los Reyes was featured as Ray Ariaz in the short-lived syndicated soap opera "Valley of the Dolls" in 1994. He was also seen in episodes of "ER" in the recurring role of Hernandez in 1995, "New York Undercover", "Swift Justice", "Four Corners" as Tomas Alvarez in 1998, "Promised Land" in the recurring role of Leon Flores from 1998 to 1999, "Total Recall 2070", "Touched by an Angel", "Early Edition", "Law & Order", the soap opera "One Life to Live" as Antonio Vega from 1995 to 2009, "CSI: Miami", "Law & Order: Criminal Intent", "The Mentalist", "Reed Between the Lines" as Anthony Guillory in 2011, "Blue Bloods", "Pretty Little Liars", "Major

Crimes", "Castle", "Kingdom", "Shooter", "Sleepy Hollow" as the demon Jobe in 2017, "MacGyver", "The Gifted", "SEAL Team", "The Passage" as Julio Martinez in 2019, "The Rookie" as Ryan Caradinc in 2021, and "All American" as Coach Montes from 2022 to 2023. He appeared in the tele-films "The Corpse Had a Familiar Face" (1994), "Blood on Her Hands" (1998), "The Way She Moves" (2001), "Undefeated" (2003), and "Abducted" (2015). De los Reyes was the voice of Raul Menendez in several video games in the "Call of Duty" franchise since 2012. He and his wife, Sherri Saum, formed MaPa Productions and starred in an produced the 2017 short film "First Strike Butcher Knife". De los Reyes married actress Sherri Saum in 2007 and is survived by her and their twin sons. He is also survived by another son from a previous relationship.

Delson, Sarah

Actress and artist Sarah Delson died of ovarian cancer in Stanford, California, on May 4, 2023. She was 61. Delson

was born in Manhattan, New York, on July 5, 1961. She graduated from Sarah Lawrence College with a degree in drama. She began performing on stage and television. Delson was frequently seen on the USA Network's movie series "Commander USA's Groovie Movies" from 1987 to 1989. She appeared with Jim Hendricks' Commander USA in various roles including a Beach Bunny, Dr. Moist Brothers, a Fiesta Dancer, Nurse Nancy, Moth Woman, Pearl Necklace, and a Beatnik. She also began working in graphic arts, creating greeting cards and book covers. She became art director at St. Martin's Press. She left New York for Stanford, California, in 2004, where she became noted as a painter and sculptor. Delson is survived by her husband, Larry Kramer, and their daughter, Kiki.

Del Tredici, David

Composer David Del Tredici, who received the 1980 Pulitzer Prize for Music, died of complications from Parkinson's disease at his home in Manhattan, New York, on

November 18, 2023. He was 86. Del Tredici was born in Cloverdale, California, on March 16, 1937. He was trained by German pianist Bernhard Abramovitch from an early age. He performed with the San Francisco Symphony at age 16. He continued studying piano at the University of California at Berkeley. He also attended the Aspen Music Festival and School where he began composing. Del Tredici graduated from Berkeley in 1959 and studied composition with Earl Kim and Roger Sessions for a year at

Princeton University. He earned a master's degree from Princeton in 1963. He soon began teaching at Harvard University from 1966 to 1972. He used the literary works of James Joyce as the setting of his experimental compositions "Night-Conjure Verse" (1965) and "Syzygy" (1966). He was inspired by the works of Lewis Carroll resulting in his compositions "Pop-Pourri" (1968), "An Alice Symphony" (1969), "Adventures Underground" (1971), and "Vintage Alice" (1972). His "Alice" series culminated with the composition "Final Alice" for soprano and orchestra in 1975. His composition "In Memory of a Summer Day" earned him the Pulitzer Prize for Music in 1980. Del Tredici's compositions also include the "Tattoo" (1986), "Steps" (1990), opera "Dum Dee Tweedle" (1990), "Cabbage and Kings" (1996), "The Spider and the Fly" (1998), "Dracula" (1999), "Gay Life" (2001), and "Paul Revere's Ride" (2005). He taught at Boston University from 1973 to 1984 and City College of New York from 1984 to 2015. He was composer in residence at the New York Philharmonic from 1988 to 1990.

Delville, Michel

French film director Michel Delville died in Boulogne-Billancourt, France, on February 16, 2023. He was 91. Delville was born in Boulogne-Billancourt on April 13, 1931. He began working in films as an assistant director in the

early 1950s, frequently working with Henri Decoin. His films include "The Lovers of Toledo" (1953), "Girls' Dormitory" (1953), "The Scheming Women" (1954), "The Bed" (1954), "One Step to Eternity" (1954), "Razzia" (1955), "The Case of Poisons" (1955), "Le Feu Aux Poudres" (1957), "Everybody Wants to Kill Me" (1957), "Charmants Garcons" (1957), "La Chatte" (1958), and "Would-Be Gentleman" (1958). Delville directed and wrote the 1958 film "A Bullet in the Gun Barrel". He directed and frequently scripted numerous films including "Ce Soir ou Jamais" (1961) the first of a series of light comedies co-written with Nina Companeez, "Adorable Liar" (1962), "Because, Because of a Woman" (1963), "Girl's Apartment" (1963), "Lucky Jo" (1964), "Il Ldro della Gioconda" (1966), "Martin Soldat" (1966), "Zartliche Haie" (1967), "The Diary of an Innocent Boy" (1968), "Bye Bye, Barbara" (1969), "The Bear and the Doll" (1970), "Raphael ou le Debauche" (1971), "La Femme en Bleu" (1973), "Love at the Top" (1974), "L'Apprenti Salaud" (1977), "Dossier 51" (1978), "A Sweet Journey" (1980), "Deep Water" (1981), "The Little Bunch" (1983), "Death in a French Garden" (1985), "Le Paltoquet" (1986), "The Reader" (1988), "Nuit d'Ete en Ville" (1990), "Lest We Forget" (1991), "Sweetheart" (1992), "Aux Petits Bonheurs" (1994), "The Gods Must Be Daring" (1997), "La Maladie de Sachs" (1999), "Un Monde Presque Paisible" (2002), and "The Art of Breaking Up" (2005). He retired from filmmaking in 2005. He was married to Rosalinde Deville from

1976 until his death, and she frequently worked with him as a screenwriter and producer.

Demura, Fumio

Japanese martial artist and actor Fumio Demura, who was stunt double for Pat Morita's Mr. Miyagi in several of "The Karate Kid" films, died in Santa Ana, California, on April 24, 2023. He was 84. Demura was born in Yokohama, Japan, on

September 15, 1938. He began training in karate and kendo at an early age and won the East Japan Championships in 1957. He later trained in kobudo, a style of Okinawan weapons fighting. Demura came to the United States in 1965 where he taught and competed. He was author of several books on martial arts including "Shito-Ryu Karate" (1971), "Advanced Nunchaku" (1976), "Tonfa: Karate Weapon of Self-Defense" (1982), "Bo: Karate Weapon of Self-Defense" (1987), and "Sai: Karate Weapon of Self-Defense" (1987). He was featured as the Hyena Man in the 1977 film "The Island of Dr. Moreau" and performed stunts in the films "The Bad News Bears Go to Japan" (1978) and "The Nude Bomb" (1980). He performed the martial arts stunts for Pat Morita's Mr. Miyagi in "The Karate Kid" (1984), "The Karate Kid Part III" (1989), and "The Next Karate kid" (1994). Demura performed stunts and appeared in small parts in the films "Shootfighter: Fight to the Death" (1993), "Rising Sun" (1993), "Mortal Kombat" (1995), "Ninja" (2009), and "Blood and Bone" (2009). He worked on the television series "Walker, Texas Ranger" in 2000. He was the subject of the 2015 documentary "The Real Miyagi".

De Niro Rodriguez, Leandro

Actor Leandro De Niro Rodriguez was found dead of a drug overdose in Manhattan, New York, apartment on July 2, 2023. He was 19. De Niro was born in New York City on June 25, 2004. He was the son of actress Drena De Niro, the adopted daughter of acclaimed actor Robert De Niro, and artist Carlos (Mare) Rodriguez. Leandro also appeared with his mother in several films as a child including "The Collection" (2005), "Cabaret Maxime" (2018), and Bradley Cooper's 2018 remake of "A Star Is Born".

de Rousse, Marcia

Diminutive actress Marcia de Rousse died of complications from a hiatal hernia in Altadena, California, on September 2, 2023. She was 70. De Rousse was born in Donithan, Missouri, in July of 1953. She graduated from the University of Missouri and moved to Los Angeles with her

mother in 1980. The 4'4" actress made her film debut in the 1981 comedy "Under the Rainbow". She was also seen in the films "Tiptoes" (2002) and "The Disappointments Room". De Rousse was featured in episodes of "The Fall Guy", "St. Elsewhere", and "Schooled". She appeared in the recurring role of Dr. Ludwig in the HBO series "True Blood" from 2009 to 2014

Desideri, Osvaldo

Italian art director Osvaldo Desideri, who received an Academy Award for the 1984 film "The Last Emperor", died in Italy on October 18, 2023. He was 84. Desideri was born in Rome, Italy, on February 16, 1939. He studied to be an industrial technician in college. He began working in films as

a set decorator and assistant production designer in the late 1960s and worked frequently with Ferdinando Scarfiotti. His films include "Bandits in Rome" (1968), "Carnal Circuit" (1969), "The Conformist" (1970), "Death in Venice" (1971), "1870" (1972), the prehistoric sex comedy "When Women Played Ding Dong" (1971), Billy Wilder's "Avanti!" (1972), "The Night Porter" (1974), "Till Marriage Do Us Part" (1974), "The Passenger" (1975), "Fantozzi" (1975), Roberto Rossellini's "The Messiah" (1975), Pier Paolo Pasolini's "Salo, or the 120 Days of Sodom" (1975), "Todo Modo" (1976), "Beyond Good and Evil" (1977), "Viva Italia!" (1977), the action comedy "They Call Him Bulldozer" (1978), "Flatfoot in Egypt" (1980), Federico Fellini's "City of Women" (1980), "Io e Caterina" (1980), "Buddy Goes West" (1981), "Fuga Dall'Arcipelago Maledetto" (1982), "Bomber" (1982), Sergio Leone's "Once Upon a Time in America" (1984), "Nothing Left to Do But Cry" (1984), "Segreti Segreti" (1985), "Il Camorrista" (1986), Bernardo Bertolucci's "The Last Emperor" (1987) sharing an Academy Award with Scarfiotti and Bruno Cesari, "Young Toscanini" (1988), "Fair Game" (1988), "Night Sun" (1990), "Sognando la California" (1992), "Comincio Tutto per Caso" (1993), and "L'Educazione di Giulio" (2000). Desideri was production designer for the films "Hot Stuff" (1976), "Strange Occasion" (1976), "Towards Evening" (1990), "Vacanze di Natale '90" (1990), "Vacanze di Natale '91" (1991), "Fantozzi 2000 - La Clonazione" (1999), "The Piano Player" (2002), "The Good War" (2002), "The Undesirables" (2003), "Per Sempre" (2003), "La Passione di Giosue l'Ebreo" (2005), and "I Bambini Della Sua Vita" (2010). He served as a set decorator or production designer on television productions of "Tre Donne - La Sciantosa" (1971), "Tre Donne - 1943: Un Incontro" (1971), "The Automobile" (1971), "Patto Con la Morte" (1982), "Ci Vediamo in Tribunale" (1996), "We Are Angels" (1997),

"Thinking About Africa" (1999), "Shaka Zulu: The Citadel" (2001), "L'Uomo Della Carita" (2007), "Senza Via d'Uscita - Un Amore Spezzato" (2007), "Il Maresciallo Rocca e l'Amico d'Infanzia" (2008), "Artemisia Sanchez" (2008), and "Al di la del Lago" (2009).

Destouches, Bernard

French actor Bernard Destouches died in France on December 14, 2023. He was 63. Destouches was born in  France on December 1, 1960. He appeared frequently in films and television from the 1990s. He was featured in the films "Taxi" (1998), "Taxi 3" (2003), "Nos Amis les Flics" (2014), "Taxi 4" (2007), "Gomez vs. Tavares" (2007), "Je Deteste les Enfants des Autres" (2007), "Visions Interdites" (2013), "Fanny" (2013), "Promise at Dawn" (2017), "To Each, Her Own" (2018), "Le Temps des Secrets" (2022), and "Sexygenaires" (2023). He was seen in television productions of "Association de Bienfaiteurs" (1994), "Les p'Tits Gars Ladouceur" (2001), "Une Ferrari Pour Deux" (2002), "The Psychic" (2014), "La Tueuse Cameleon" (2015), and "Collection Mary Higgins Clark, la Reine du Suspense" (2018). Destouches also appeared in episodes of "L'Avocate", "Le Juste", "Mafiosa" as Pascal Santini from 2008 to 2010, "No Limit" as Bago from 2012 to 2015, and "Plus Belle la Vie" as Janou in 2020.

de Valk, Reiky

Dutch actor Reiky de Valk died of a suicide in the Netherlands on September 24, 2023. He was 23. De Valk was born in Amsterdam, Netherlands, on March 5, 2000. He studied at the Amsterdamse Jeugdtheaterschool and made his television  debut in the teen drama series "Skam NL" as Kes de Beus from 2018 to 2019. He also starred in the series "Hunter Street" as Josh in 2021, "Fellow de SOA" as Jacob in 2021, "Hockeyvaders" as Yannick El Ghazi in 2023, and "Dertigers" as Thomas in 2023. His other television credits include episodes of "Onze Straat", "Nerds with Attitude", "Oogappels", "Modern Love Amsterdam", and "Panduloria". De Valk was featured in the short films "Voltooid Verleden Tijd" (2021), "De Overkammer" (2021), and "Jerry" (2021), and the 2022 horror film "#No_Filter".

Devine, Tad

Child actor Tad Devine, who appeared with his father Andy Devine in the 1946 western film "Canyon Passage", died in Newport Beach, California, on March 22, 2023. He was 88. Devine was born in Los Angeles, California, on November 26, 1934. He was the son of Andy and Dorothy Devine. He and his younger brother Denny joined his gravelly-voiced character  actor father in the 1946 film "Canyon Passage". They played his onscreen sons in the film that starred Dana Andrews and Susan Hayward. Tad later graduated from Stanford University where he competed in the swimming trials for the 1956 U.S. Olympics. He served in the U.S. Navy as part of the underwater demolition team. He later owned a property management company. His father died in 1977. Devine married Donna Allis Starling in 1963 and is survived by her and their son and daughter.

Devlin, David

Cinematographer David Devlin died following a lengthy illness in Bozeman, Montana, on August 14, 2023. He was 56. Devlin was born in Rome, New York, on March 27,  1967. He graduated from New York University's Tisch School of the Arts in 1990. He interned with Jim Henson and served as his assistant on the productions "Labyrinth" (1986), "The Storyteller" (1988), and "Sesame Street: Monster Hits!" (1990). He began working in films as an electrician and gaffer on the films "Diplomatic Immunity" (1991), "Weird Nightmare" (1993), "The Stoned Age" (1994), "Grace of My Heart" (1996), "Psycho" (1998), "Minority Report" (2002), "Funny People" (2009), and "How Do You Know" (2010). He was a lighting director or assistant cameraman on "Jerry Maguire" (1996), "The Lost World: Jurassic Park" (1997), "Amistad" (1997), "Saving Private Ryan" (1998), "The Hunted" (1998), "Lost Souls" (2000), "A.I. Artificial Intelligence" (2001), "Catch Me If You Can" (2002), "The Terminal" (2004), "War of the Worlds" (2005), "Shine a Light" (2008), "Indiana Jones and the Kingdom of the Crystal Skull" (2008), "War Horse" (2011), and "Lincoln" (2012). Devlin served as cinematographer on numerous music videos including Madonna's "Get Stupid" (2008), Justin Bieber's "As Long as You Love Me" (2012), Taylor Swift's "I Knew You Were Trouble" (2012), Lady Gaga's "Applause" (2013), Jay-Z and Justin Timberlake's "Holy Grail", Lenny Kravitz's "The Chamber" (2014), Bruno Mars' "Versace on the Floor" (2017), and the Jonas brothers' "Only Human" (2019). He was cinematographer for the 2016 music documentary "Madonna: Rebel Heart Tour" and the films "Monster" (2018), "Semper Fi" (2019), "Happiness Continues" (2020), and "Survive" (2022). Devlin is survived by his wife, Aimee, and daughter, Wilhelmina.

Devry, Elaine

Actress Elaine Devry, who was the fourth wife of actor Mickey Rooney, died in Grants Pass, Oregon, on September 20,

2023. She was 93. She was born Thelma Elaine Mahnken in Compton, California, on January 10, 1930. She worked as a model while attending high school and Compton Community College. She married Dan Ducich in 1948 and they moved to

Butte, Montana. Ducich was soon arrested and convicted of armed robbery. He was sentenced to probation and the couple divorced in 1952. Ducich died of a self-inflicted gunshot wound two years later. She met actor Mickey Rooney in 1952 and became his fourth wife the following September. She soon began appearing in films under the name Elaine Davis with a small part in 1953's "A Slight Case of Larceny". She co-starred with Rooney in the 1954 science fiction comedy "The Atomic Kid". They divorced by the end of the decade. She continued to appear in such films as "China Doll" (1958) and "The Last Time I Saw Archie" (1961), and was seen on television in episodes of "General Electric Theater", "The People's Choice", "The Great Gildersleeve", "Bourbon Street Beat", "Bachelor Father", "Death Valley Days", "Laramie", "Tales of Wells Fargo", "Lock Up", and "Dante". She took the name Elaine Devry in the early 1960s and was seen in the films "Man-Trap" (1961), the horror film "Diary of a Madman" (1963) with Vincent Price, the comedy "A Guide for the Married Man" (1967) with Walter Matthau, "With Six You Get Eggroll" (1968), "Once You Kiss a Stranger..." (1969), "The Cheyenne Social Club" (1970), "Bless the Beasts & Children" (1971), the horror film "The Boy Who Cried Werewolf" (1973), and "Herbie Rides Again" (1974). She was also seen in television episodes of "The Dick Powell Theatre", "Target: The Corruptors!", "77 Sunset Strip", "Surfside 6", "I'm Dickens, He's Fenster", "Hawaiian Eye", "Ripcord", "Arrest and Trial", "Burke's Law", "Perry Mason", "Bonanza", "I Dream of Jeannie", "Lassie", "This Is the Life", "Dragnet", "Family Affair", "My Three Sons", "To Rome with Love", "Cannon", "Marcus Welby, M.D.", and "Project U.F.O." She largely retired from the screen in the late 1970s. Devry was married to actor Will J. White from 1975 until his death in 1992.

de Ycaza, Michael

Actor Michael de Ycaza died in Honolulu, Hawaii, on July 24, 2023. He was 72. De

Ycaza graduated from high school in Barrington, Illinois, in 1969. He moved to Hawaii in 1973 where he worked various jobs. He began performing on stage several years later and appeared in productions with the Diamond Head Theatre. De Ycaza appeared on television in episodes of "Lost", "Hawaii Five-O", "Magnum, P.I.", and Disney's "Doogie Kamealoha, M.D."

Deyle, John

Actor John Deyle died of esophageal cancer in Mount Kisco, New York, on June 22, 2023. He was 68. Deyle was born in Rochester, New York, on July 6, 1954. He graduated

from the University of North Carolina School of Art in 1976 and moved to New York City to pursue a career on stage. He made his Broadway debut in the musical "Annie" in 1979. He was also seen in Broadway productions of "Camelot" (1980), "Footloose" (1998), and "Urinetown" (2001) as Senator Fipp. He toured in the play "How to Succeed in Business Without Really Trying" in 1996 and performed Off-Broadway in the 2006 revival of "The Fantasticks". Deyle was featured in several films including "Wall Street" (1987), "Before and After" (1996), "One True Thing" (1998), "Wirey Spindell" (1999), "Tio Papi" (2013), and "The Rewrite" (2014). He was seen on television in episodes of "Late Night with Conan O'Brien" as a bumbling Mr. Science in 1993, "Law & Order", "The Good Wife", "All My Children", and "Law & Order: Special Victims Unit". He appeared in numerous television commercials including Skippy Peanut Butter, Kraft Macaroni & Cheese, Just for Men Hair Color, and Hoover Vacuum Cleaners. Deyle married Rebecca Paller in 1991 and is survived by her and their son, Oleg.

DiBenedetto, Tony

Actor Tony DiBenedetto died at his home in Pooler, Georgia, on April 3, 2023. He was 78. DiBenedetto was born in Manhattan, New York, on July 1, 1944. He began his acting career in the late 1970s and was seen in the films "Short Eyes"

(1977), "Nunzio" (1978), "Going in Style" (1979), "Defiance" (1980), "Windows" (1980), "The Exterminator" (1980), "Fort Apache the Bronx" (1981), "Prince of the City" (1981), "Paternity" (1981), "Deathtrap" (1982), "My Favorite Year" (1982), "Splash" (1983), "The Pope of Greenwich Village" (1984), "Garbo Talks" (1984), "Raw Deal" (1986), "Someone to Watch Over Me" (1987), "Hero and the Terror" (1988), "Last Rites" (1988), "Family Business" (1989), "My Blue Heaven" (1990), "Maked for Death" (1990), "Bloodfist III: Forced to Fight" (1991), "The Hidden II" (1993), "In the Kingdom of the Blind, the Man with One Eye Is King" (1995), "Gloria" (1999), and "Analyze This" (1999). DiBenedetto was seen on television in episodes of "The Equalizer", "L.A. Law", "Fame", "The Famous Teddy Z" in the recurring role of Uncle Nikos from 1989 to 1990, "Mancuso, FBI", "Murphy Brown", "Hardball", "Cheers", "Jack's Place", "Walker, Texas Ranger", "Lois & Clark: The New Adventures of Superman", "Hot Line",

"New York Undercover", and "Law & Order". His other television credits include the tele-films "Just Me and You" (1978), "...and Your Name Is Jonah" (1979), "Johnny Garage" (1983), "Kojak: The Price of Justice" (1987), "Dangerous Passion" (1998), and the mini-series "Lucky Chances" (1990). He is survived by his wife, Bonnie, and six children.

Dillard, R.H.W.

Poet R.H.W. Dillard, who co-wrote the 1965 cult-classic film "Frankenstein Meets the Space Monster", died in Roanoke, Virginia, on April 4, 2023. He was 85. Dillard was born in Roanoke on October 11, 1937. He graduated from Roanoke College and earned a master's degree and a Ph.D. from the University of Virginia. He began teaching creative writing and literature at Hollins University in Virginia in 1964 and was editor of the Hollins Critic from 1996. Dillard was noted for his poetry which was featured in such collections as "The Day I Stopped Dreaming About Barbara Steele and Other Poems" (1966), "News of the Nile" (1971), "After Borges" (1972), "The Greeting: New and Selected Poems" (1981), "Just Here, Just Now" (1994), "A New Pleiade: Selected Poems" (1998), "Sallies" (2001), "What Is Owed the Dead" (2011), and "Not Ideas" (2014). He wrote the novels "The Book of Changes" (1974) and "The First Man on the Sun" (1983), and the short story collection "Omniphobia" (1995). He was also author of the non-fiction works "Horror Films" (1976) and "Understanding George Garrett" (1988). Dillard was also co-writer of the 1965 cult science fiction film "Frankenstein Meets the Space Monster".

Dillon, Melinda

Actress Melinda Dillon, who earned Oscar nominations for her roles in "Close Encounters of the Third Kind" and "Absence of Malice", died in Los Angeles, California, on January 9, 2023. She was 83. She was born Melinda Clardy in Hope, Arkansas, on October 13, 1939, and was raised in Cullman, Alabama. Her stepfather served in the U.S. Army, and she lived on several military basis, including in Nuremberg, Germany, for four years. She graduated high school in Chicago, Illinois, and attended the Goodman School of Drama at the Art Institute of Chicago. She began performing as an improvisational comedy with the Second City. She studied acting at DePaul University and moved to New York City. She was featured in the 1959 short film "The Cry of Jazz". Dillon appeared on Broadway in productions of "Who's Afraid of Virginia Woolf?" (1962) earning a Tony Award nomination for her role as Honey, "You Know I Can't Hear You When the Water's Running" (1967), "A Way of Life" (1969) which never opened officially, "Paul Sills' Story Theatre" (1970), and "Ovid's Metamorphoses" (1971). She made her feature film debut in the 1969 romantic comedy "The April Fools". She was also seen in the films "Bound for Glory" (1976) as Woody Guthrie's wife Mary, and "Slap Shot" (1977). She starred as Jillian Guiller, whose son is abducted by aliens, in Steven Spielberg's 1977 science fiction classic "Close Encounters of the Third Kind" and earned an Academy Award nomination for Best Supporting Actress. She appeared in the films "F.I.S.T." (1978) and "The Muppet Movie" (1979) and earned another Oscar nomination for her supporting role as suicidal Teresa Perrone in 1981's legal drama "Absence of Malice". She starred as Mother Parker, the mother of Ralphie Parker, in the 1983 Christmas classic "A Christmas Story". Her other films include "Songwriter" (1984), "Harry and the Hendersons" (1987) as Nancy Henderson, "Spontaneous Combustion" (1989), "Staying Together" (1989), "Captain America" (1990) as Steve Rogers' mother, "The Prince of Tides" (1991) as Savannah Wingo, the suicidal sister of Nick Nolte's character, "Sioux City" (1994), "To Wong Foo, Thanks for Everything! Julie Newmar" (1995), "How to Make an American Quilt" (1995), "Entertaining Angels: The Dorothy Day Story" (1996), "The Effects of Magic" (1998), "The Adventures of Elmo in Grouchland" (1999), "Magnolia" (1999), "Cowboy Up" (2001), "Debating Robert Lee" (2004), "Adam & Steve" (2005), and "Reign Over Me" (2007). Dillon appeared frequently on television from the early 1960s with roles in episodes of "The Defenders", "East Side/West Side", "Bonanza", "Men at Law", "Story Theatre", "The Jeffersons", "Sara", "The Mississippi", "Insight", "The Twilight Zone", "The Client", "Picket Fences", "Tracey Takes On...", "Judging Amy", "The Lyon's Dean", "Law & Order: Special Victims Unit", and "Heartland" in the recurring role of Janet Jacobs in 2007. Her other television credits include the tele-films "Enigma" (1977), "The Critical List" (1978), "Transplant" (1979), "Marriage Is Alive and Well" (1980), "The Shadow Box" (1980), "Fallen Angel" (1981), "Hellinger's Law" (1981), "The Juggler of Notre Dame" (1982), "Right of Way" (1983), "Space" (1985), "Shattered Spirits" (1986), "Shattered Innocence" (1988), "Nightbreaker" (1989), "Judgment Day: The John List Story" (1993) as Eleanor List opposite Robert Blake, "Confessions: Two Faces of Evil" (1994), "State of Emergency" (1994), "Naomi & Wynonna: Love Can Build a Bridge" (1995) as Polly Judd, and "A Painted House" (2003). Dillon largely retired from acting in the late 2010s. She was married to actor Richard Libertini from 1963 until their divorce in 1978 and is survived by their son.

Donaldson, Ted

Child actor Ted Donaldson, who starred in the "Rusty" film series in the 1940s, died of complications from a fall at his apartment in Los Angeles, California, on March 1, 2023. He was 89. Donaldson was born in New York City on August 20, 1933. He was the son of singer and composer Will Donaldson.

His mother died when he was a child, and his stepmother was radio musician and composer Muriel Pollock. Donaldson attended the Professional Children's School in New York City.

He began his career in radio at NBC in December of 1937. He starred as Tiny Tim in a radio presentation of "A Christmas Carol" on "Wheatena Playhouse" in 1941. He appeared on Broadway in the original Broadway production of "Life with Father" in 1941. He returned to Broadway in the 1943 play "Sons and Soldiers". He made his film debut opposite Cary Grant in the 1944 film "Once Upon a Time" as youngster Pinky Thompson, whose pet caterpillar Curly stands on his tail and dances when he plays on the harmonica. Donaldson was best known for his role as Danny Mitchell in the "Rusty" film series about a German Shepherd Dog. He starred in the "Rusty" films "Adventures of Rusty" (1945), "The Return of Rusty" (1946), "For the Love of Rusty" (1947), "The Son of Rusty" (1947), "My Dog Rusty" (1948), "Rusty Leads the Way" (1948), "Rusty Saves a Life" (1959), and "Rusty's Birthday" (1949). His other films include "Mr. Winkle Goes to War" (1944), "A Tree Grows in Brooklyn" (1945) as Neeley Nolan, the son of Dorothy McGuire and James Dunn's characters, "A Guy, a Gal and a Pal" (1945), "Personality Kid" (1946), "The Red Stallion" (1947), "Pal's Adventure" (1948), "The Decision of Christopher Blake" (1948) in the title role, "The Green Promise" (1949), "Phone Call from a Stranger" (1952), and "Flight Nurse" (1953). Donaldson appeared on television in television productions of "Ah, Wilderness!" (1955) on "Front Row Center" and "Midsummer" (1955) and "The Bright Boy" (1956) and "Matinee Theatre". He also appeared in a 1958 episode of "The Silent Service". He starred as Bud Anderson in the radio version of "Father Knows Best" starring Robert Young from 1949 to 1954 but declined an offer to continue the role in the subsequent television series. Donaldson later worked as an acting teacher and at a bookstore on Hollywood Boulevard. He was featured as a guest at Several TCM Classic Film Festivals in recent years.

Dorsey, Sandra

Actress Sandra Dorsey, who was featured as decapitated camp counselor Lily Miranda in the 1989 horror

film "Sleepaway Camp III: Teenage Wasteland", died of pancreatic cancer on September 26, 2023. She was 83. She was born Sandra Ellenburg in Atlanta, Georgia, on September 28, 1939. She moved to New York City to pursue a career in show business. She was an actress and singer in the Broadway musicals "Drat! The Cat!" (1965), "Illya Darling"

(1967), "Gantry" (1970), and "On the Town" (1971). She also taught acting and singing in New York. Dorsey made her film debut in the 1976 horror film "Grizzly". Her other film credits include "They Went That-A-Way & That-A-Way" (1978), "Norma Rae" (1979), "Impure Thoughts" (1986), the slasher film "Sleepaway Camp III: Teenage Wasteland" (1989), "Gordy" (1994), "The Three Stooges" (2012), and "Dumb and Dumber To" (2014). She was seen on television in a 1979 episode of "The Dukes of Hazard" and in the tele-films "The Georgia Peaches" (1980), "Angel City" (1980), "Maid in America" (1982), "Passing Glory" (1999), and "Frankenstein" (2004). She also appeared on stage in regional theater and in national television commercials. She was founder of Dorsey Studios in Atlanta in 1977 where she was an acting and voice instructor. She also taught at the Alliance Theatre in Atlanta and Emory University. She is survived by her husband, actor Joe Dorsey.

Douglas, Ross

Canadian actor Ross Douglas died in Canada on March 20, 2023. He was 72. Douglas was born in Vancouver,

British Columbia, Canada, on February 22, 1951. He was best known as a voice actor in such animated productions as "Mobile Suit Gundam" as the Narrator, "Master Keaton" as Daniel O'Connell, "Project ARMS" as Keith Blue, "Hikaru no Go", "MegaMan: NT Warrior" as TorchMan, "Inuyasha", "Elemental Gelade", "Black Lagoon" as Kageyama, "The Story of Saiunkoku", "InuYasha: The Final Act", "The Little Prince", and "Tara Duncan". Douglas appeared in the tele-films "Higher Ground" (1988), "The Angel of Pennsylvania Avenue" (1996), and "In the Doghouse" (1998). He was also featured in episodes of "The Commish", "The X-Files", "Police Academy: The Series", "The New Addams Family", "The Outer Limits", "Beggars and Choosers", "Seven Days", "Just Cause", "The 4400", "Psych", "Smallville" as the voice of Booster Gold's robotic sidekick Skeets, and "Supernatural". He also supplied voices for various video games including "Pajama Sam", "Spy Fox", "Mobile Suit Gundam", "The Suffering", "Sly 2: Band of Thieves" as Jean Bisson, and "Nancy Drew: The Creature of Kapu Cave". Douglas appeared in the films "Beat Angel" (2004) and "A Christmas Story 2" (2012), and the 2014 short film "The Devil Walks in Salem". He married actress Robin Douglass in 1990 and she survives him.

Dox, Chip

Television production designer Chip Dox, who was noted for his work in soap operas, died in Burbank, California, on August 15, 2023. He was 89. Dox was born on March 14, 1943. He graduated from Carnegie Institute of Technology and served in the U.S. Army for two years. He taught at the Carnegie Institute before moving to Hollywood. He began

working in television as art director for "Days of Our Lives" from 1989 to 1989. He was production designer for "Days of Our Lives" from 1990 and shared a Daytime Emmy Award for his work in 1997. He received another Daytime Emmy for his work on "General Hospital" in 2011 and received six additional Emmy nominations for "General Hospital between 2008 and 2016. He earned an Emmy Award nomination for the comedy series "Tracey Takes On..." in 1998. Dox was also production designer for the soaps "Nightshift" and "Port Charles", the comedy series "Oh Baby", and the Telemundo sitcoms "Los Beltran" and "Viva Vegas!". He retired in 2015. Dox is survived by his wife of 29 years, Jeanne Haney, and two daughters.

Doyle, Wally

Actor Wally Doyle died in Chesapeake, Virginia, on June 13, 2023. He was 89. Doyle was born on September 4, 1933. He worked in construction and later became a teacher. He was also an actor who appeared frequently on the local stage in the Virginia area. He was featured in the television mini-series "George Washington" (1984) and the tele-film "My Name Is Bill W." (1989). Doyle appeared in the films "Metamorphosis" (1990) and "Invader" (1991) and was seen in a 1999 episode of the television series "The F.B.I. Files".

Drake, David

Writer David Drake, who was noted for the military science fiction series "Hammer's Slammers", died in Silk Hope, North Carolina, on December 10, 2023. He was 78. Drake was born in Dubuque, Iowa, on September 23, 1945. He graduated from the University of Iowa and studied at the Duke University School of Law. His studies were interrupted when he was drafted into the U.S. Army. He served in Vietnam and Cambodia as an interrogator with the 11th Armored Cavalry. Drake completed his law degree after his discharge. He worked as the assistant town attorney in Chapel Hill, North Carolina, from 1972 to 1980. He was best known for the 1979 military science fiction "Hammer's Slammers". He continued the series with the novels "At Any Price" (1985), "Counting the Cost" (1987), "Rolling Hot" (1989), "The Warrior" (1999), "The Sharp End"

(1993), "Cross the Stars" (1984), "The Voyage" (1994), and "Paying the Piper" (2002). He wrote a pair of novels featuring Tom Kelly, "Skyripper" (1983) and "Fortress" (1987), and the trilogy that included "Northworld" (1990), "Vengeance" (1991), and "Justice" (1992). His novels "Surface Action" (1990) and "The Jungle" (1991) were part of his "Seas of Venus" series. The "Crisis of Empire" series consisted of four novels, each with a different co-author. They included "An Honorable Defense" (1988) with Thomas T. Thomas, "Cluster Command" (1989) with William C. Dietz, "The War Machine" (1989) with Roger MacBride Allen, and "Crown of Empire" (1994) with Chelsea Quinn Yarbro. The military science fiction series "The General" starred Raj Whitehall as the main character. The first seven books were co-written with S.M. Stirling and included "The Forge" (1991), "The Hammer" (1992), "The Anvil" (1993), "The Steel" (1993), "The Sword" (1995), "The Chosen" (1996), and "The Reformer" (1999). Subsequent works in the series include "The Tyrant" (2002) with Eric Flint, "The Heretic" (2013) and "The Savior" (2014) with Tony Daniels. His "Reaches" trilogy includes "Igniting the Reaches" (1994), "Through the Breach" (1995), and "Fireships" (1996). Drake teamed with Janet Morris to co-write "Arc Riders" (1995) and the sequel "The Fourth Rome" (1996). He wrote the fantasy novel "Lord of the Isles" in 1987 and the series continued with "Queen of Demons" (1998), "Servant of the Dragon" (1999), "Mistress of the Catacombs" (2001), "Goddess of the Ice Realm" (2003), and "Master of the Cauldron" (2004). The "Crown of the Isles" series followed including "The Fortress of Glass" (2006), "The Mirror of Worlds" (2007), and "The Gods Return" (2008). He and Eric Flint co-wrote the "Belisarius" series including "An Oblique Approach" (1998), "In the Heart of Darkness" (1998), "destiny's Shield" (1999), "Fortune's Stroke" (2000), "The Tide of Victory" (2001), and "The Dance of Time" (2006). Drake's series, "Republic of Cinnabar Navy (RCN)" included the novels "With the Lightnings" (1998), "Lt. Leary, Commanding" (2000), "The Far Side of the Stars" (2003), "The Way to Glory" (2005), "Some Golden Harbor" (2006), "When the Tide Rises" (2008), "In the Stormy Red Sky" (2009), "What Distant Deeps" (2010), "The Road of Danger" (2012), "The Sea Without a Shore" (2014), "Death's Bright Day" (2016), "Though Hell Should Bar the Way" (2018), and "To Clear Away the Shadows" (2019). His novels "The Legions of Fire" (2010), "Out of the Waters" (2011), "Monsters of the Earth" (2013), and "Air and Darkness" (2015) were part of "The Books of Elements" series. He co-wrote the "Citizen" series with John Lambshead that included "Into the Hinterlands" (2011) and "Into the Maelstrom" (2015). Drake's other novels include "The Dragon Lord" (1979), "Birds of Prey" (1984), "The Forlorn Hope" (1984), "Active Measures" (1985) with Janet Morris, "Strangers and Lovers" (1985), "Killer" (1985) with Karl Edward Wagner, "Bridgehead" (1986), "Lacey and His Friends" (1986), "Kill Ratio" (1987) with Janet Morris, "The Sea Hag" (1988), "Vettius and His Friends" (1989), "Target" (1989) with Janet Morris, "The Undesired Princess and the Enchanted Bunny" (1990) with L Sprague de Camp, "The Hunter Returns" (1991) with Jim Kjelgaard, "Old Nathan"

(1991), "Starliner" (1992), "Tyrannosaur" (1994), "Enemy of My Enemy" (1995) with Ben Ohlander, "Redliners" (1996), "All the Way to the Gallows" (1996), "Patriots" (1996), "Other Times Than Peace" (2006), and "Dinosaurs & a Dirigible" (2014). He stopped writing in November of 2021 due to reasons of health. Drake is survived by his wife, Joanne Kammiller, and son, Jonathan Drake.

Draper, Eamonn

Irish actor Eamonn Draper died in Cork, Ireland, on December 27, 2023. He was 83. Draper was born in Dublin, Ireland, in 1940, and was raised in Cork. He attended the

University College at Cork and served in the Irish Army in the early 1960s. He continued his interest in acting and performed on stage with the Daimler Theatre and the Abbey Theatre later in the decade. Draper appeared on television in episodes of such series as "The Riordans", "The Burke Enigma", "Ros Na Run" as Muiris O Baoill from 1999 to 2000, "Foreign Exchange", "Teenage Cics", "The Clinic", "Uncle Max", "Mobs Mheiricea", "An Crisis", "1916 Seachtar na Casca", "Bothar go dti an White House", "Jack Taylor", "Scup", "Sceal", "Game of Thrones" as a sick maester in a 2017 episode, and "Vikings". His other television credits include productions of "Teangabhail" (1975), "Eagla" (1977), "Teresa's Wedding" (1980), "House of the Damned" (1996), "Showbands II" (2006), "The Running Mate" (2007), and "The Irish Mob" (2008). Draper was also featured in several films including "The Sleep of Death" (1980), "Anne Devlin" (1984), "Warlock III: The End of Innocence" (1999), "Moving Target" (2000), "The Game of Death" (2000), and "Dangerous Curves" (2000).

Dresner, Hal

Screenwriter Hal Dresner died of cancer in Ashland, Oregon, on March 17, 2023. He was 85. Dresner was born in New York City on June 4, 1937. He graduated from the

University of Florida and moved to Los Angeles to work as a screenwriter. He began his career as an uncredited writer for Paul Newman's 1967 classic "Cool Hand Luke". Dresner also scripted the films "The Extraordinary Seaman" (1969), "The April Fools" (1969), "Sssssss" (1973), "The Eiger Sanction" (1975), and "Zorro: The Gay Blade" (1981) starring George Hamilton. He wrote several episodes of Rod Serling's anthology series "Night Gallery" in the early 1970s. He also wrote episodes of "M*A*S*H" and was a writer and producer for the tele-films "Husbands and Wives" (1977), "Husbands, Wives & Lovers" (1978), and "Poor Richard" (1984), and

episodes of "The Harvey Korman Show", "Joe & Valerie", and "CBS Summer Playhouse". Dresner's survivors include his daughter, Amy.

Dreyfoos, Alexander W., Jr.

Businessman Alexander W. Dreyfoos, Jr., who received an Academy Award for co-creating the Video Color Negative Analyzer, died in West Palm Beach, Florida, on May 28, 2023. He was 91. Dreyfoos was born in New York City on March 22, 1932. His father was photographer and inventor

Alexander W. Dreyfoos, Sr., who died in 1951. The younger Dreyfoos graduated from the Massachusetts Institute of Technology (MIT) in 1954. He served in the U.S. Air Force in Sembach, Germany, from 1954 to 1956. He attended Harvard Business School after his discharge, earning a master's degree in 1958. He was co-founder with George W. Mergens of Photo Electronics Corporation in 1963. They developed the Video Color Negative Analyzer (VCNA) for color print reproduction. VCNA was marketed by Eastman Kodak and earned Dreyfoos an Academy Award for the film version in 1970. He and his son, Robert Dreyfoos, later developed a digital version of the VCNA. He also invented the LaserColor Printer. Dreyfoos owned the West Palm Beach, Florida, CBS television affiliate, WPEC TV-12, from 1973 to 1996. He also developed the Sailfish Marina Resort in Palm Beach in 1977. He was instrumental in funding the Raymond F. Kravis Center for the Performing Arts in 1992 as head of the Cultural Council of Palm Beach County from 1978 to 2007. He founded the philanthropic organization, the Dreyfoos Group, in 1996. Dreyfoos was also a photographer noted for his works while traveling and underwater. Many of his photos were published in the 2015 book "A Photographic Odyssey: Around the World with Alexander W. Dreyfoos". His biography, "Alexander W. Dreyfoos: Passion & Purpose" by Lise M. Steinhauer and David Randal Allen, was published in 2016. Dreyfoos was divorced his first wife, Joan, in 1975 and is survived by their two children, Catherine and Robert. He was married to Barbara Lee Murphy from 1981 until their divorce in 1986. He was married to Carolyn Buckley from 1986 until their divorce their divorce in 1999. He married Renate Destler Hanson Jaspert in 1999 and she also survives him.

Drozdov, Darren

Professional wrestler Darren Drozdov, who competed in the ring under the name Droz and became a quadriplegic from a neck injury received during a wrestling match, died at a medical center in Pomona, New Jersey, on June 30, 2023. He was 54. Drozdov was born in Mays Landing, New Jersey, on April 7, 1969. He was a leading football player in high school and was a defensive tackle for the Terrapins football team at the University of Maryland. He played briefly in the National

Football League after graduating in 1992. He had short stints with the Denver Broncos, New York Jets, and Philadelphia Eagles. He was noted for an incident when he vomited on the  football during a televised game in 1993. Drozdov briefly played in the Canadian Football League with the Montreal Alouettes in 1996. He began a career as a professional wrestler with Extreme Championship Wrestling (ECW) in 1997. He was signed by the World Wrestling Federation (WWF/now WWE) the following year. His penchant for regurgitating on the football field earned him the ring name Puke. He was originally an ally of Animal and Hawk of the Legion of Doom. His ring name soon became Droz and he began wrestling as a villain. His ring career came to an end in October of 1999 when he broke his neck during a match with D'Lo Brown. The injury left him a quadriplegic though he later gained some movement in his upper body and arms. He had a specially designed wheelchair, described as "tank-like", and was still able to go into the woods and hunt. He continued to work for the WWE as a writer and penned columns for the promotion's website and magazine. He also appeared on the "WWE Byte This!" internet show. Drozdov was married to WWE seamstress Julie Youngberg from 1999 until their divorce in 2005. His survivors include his sister, Rommi Drozdov, who cared for him after his accident, and her four children.

Drummond, Leina'ala

Model Leina'ala Drummond, who was Miss Hawaii in 1964, died of cancer at a hospital in Hilo, Hawaii, on September  18, 2023. She was 77. She was born Leina'ala Teruya in Puunene, Hawaii, on May 28, 1946. She graduated from Cannon's Business College and became a flight attendant for Hawaiian Airlines in 1964. She soon was crowned Miss Hawaii and represented her state in the Miss American competition in 1965. Drummond became the face of Hawaiian Airlines when they adopted the Pualani logo in 1973. She was married to John Robert 'Ian' Drummond from 1976 until his death in 2000, and is survived by their children, Kawika and Christina.

Duncan, Arthur

Tap dancer Arthur Duncan, who performed on "The Lawrence Welk Show" for two decades, died of complications from pneumonia and a stroke in Moreno Valley, California, on January 4, 2023. He was 97. Duncan was born in Pasadena, California, on September 25, 1925. He became part of a dance quartet while attending high school. He later studied pharmacy at Pasadena City College for leaving to pursue a career in show business. He performed in Europe for several years and toured with the Jimmie Rodgers Show. He appeared on Betty White's daily television series "Hollywood on Television" in Los Angeles. It became "The Betty White Show" when it gained a national audience from NBC in 1954 and he soon became a  regular performer. White was pressured to fire Duncan when the show was threatened by a boycott in the South due to Duncan's race. She refused the request and instead featured him more often. He toured military bases with Bob Hope's troupe later in the decade. He began appearing on "The Lawrence Welk Show" in 1964 and was a featured dancer on the series through 1984. Duncan was also seen on television in episodes of "The Bob Hope Show", "The Red Skelton Hour", "The General Motors Hour", "The Good Old Days", "The Folk World of Jimmie Rodgers", "Dream Girl of '67", "The Joey Bishop Show", "The Rosey Grier Show", and "Jerry Lewis MDA Labor Day Telethon". He was featured in the 1989 film "Tap" and the 2004 short film "Tap Heat". He was an actor in the 1992 tele-film "Diagnosis Murder: Diagnosis of Murder" and an episode of "Columbo" in 1998. He remained a frequent performer at stage events around the country and was featured in several regional musical productions. He continued to dance for audiences until shortly before his death. Duncan married Carole Carbone in 2019 and she survives him. A previous marriage to Donna Pena ended in divorce.

Dupree, Emile

Canadian professional wrestler Emile Dupree died in Canada on September 17, 2023. He was 86. He was born Emile  Goguen in Shediac, New Brunswick, Canada, on October 20, 1936. He began training as a wrestler with Vic Butler and Reggie Richard in 1955. He made his wrestling debut in the Boston, Massachusetts, area. He also competed with Stampede Wrestling in Calgary. He started the Grand Prix Wrestling promotion in the Maritimes in 1977. Many stars were featured at Grand Prix events including Killer Kowalski, Andre the Giant, Randy Savage, Lanny Poffo, and Ric Flair. He eventually sold the promotion to World Wrestling Entertainment (WWE). Dupree was selected for the Canadian Pro-Wrestling Hall of Fame in 2023. His survivors include his son, wrestler Rene Dupree.

DuPree, Lynette

Actress Lynette DuPree died in Los Angeles, California, on February 6, 2023. She was 58. DuPree was born in Rochester, New York, on February 15, 1964. She performed in a church choir in her youth. She attended SUNY Brockport for two years after graduating high school. She began her career on stage as an actress and singer in musicals. She appeared on Broadway in productions of "Truly Blessed" (1990) and "Bring in 'Da Noise, Bring in 'Da Funk" (1996). She also performed in national tours of "Dreamgirls", "The Color Purple", "Josephine", and "Broadway's Best". She was seen often on television from the late 1990s with roles in episodes of "Law & Order" in the recurring role of Judge Joyce Randall from 1998 to 1999, "Bette", "NYPD Blue", "The Division", "Philly" as Nancy from 2001 to 2002, "State of Grace", "The Brotherhood of Poland, New Hampshire", "ER", "Karen Sisco", "Medium", "Everybody Hates Chris", "Desperate Housewives", "Southland", "The Middle", "See Dad Run", "Scandal", "Legit", "Anger Management", "Maron", "Extant", "The Mindy Project", "Faking It", "The Haunted Hathaways", "One Big Happy", "Idiotsitter", "Mike & Molly", "It's Always Sunny in Philadelphia", "Shameless", "Heartbeat", "Angie Tribeca", "How to Get Away with Murder",. "Workaholics", "Fresh Off the Boat", "Grace and Frankie", "Man with a Plan", "Doubt", "The Good Place", "Abby's", the animated "The Lion Guard" as the voice of the elephant Ma Tembo from 2016 to 2019, "Single Parents", "Light as a Feather", "The Goldbergs", "S.W.A.T.", "Snowfall", and "Family Reunion". Her other television credits include the tele-films "Back When We Were Grownups" (2004), "Their Eyes Were Watching God" (2005), "Petty Offense" (2012), and "Carole's Christmas" (2019). DuPree was featured in several films including "Random Hearts" (1999), "Zig Zag" (2002), "Sugar" (2013), "American Idiots" (2013), "Best Night Ever" (2013), "About Scout" (2015), and "Beckman" (2020). She was also seen in the shorts "Last Time We Met" (2005), "Lyla Wolf: Infractus" (20111), "To Beauty" (2011), "Petals in the Wind" (2011), and "Fall from LA" (2018). DuPree married Charles Richardson in 2006 and he survives her.

Dussault, Louisette

Canadian actress and writer Louisette Dussault died in Montreal, Quebec, Canada, on March 14, 2023. She was 82. Dussault was born in Thetford Mines, Quebec, on June 11, 1940. She trained with the National Theatre School of Canada. She was co-founder of Les Enfants de Chenier in 1969 and performed in their stage production of "Grand Spectacle d'Adieu". She appeared in numerous stage productions including her own monologue "Moman" (1979). Dussault appeared frequently in films from the late 1960s with roles in "Poussiere sur la Ville" (1968), "IXE-13" (1972), "Francoise Durocher, Waitress" (1972), "Bingo" (1974), "L'Absence" (1976), "Le Soleil Se Leve en Retard" (1977), "Bonheur d'Occasion" (1983), "Rencontre Avec Une Femme

Remarquable" (1983), the short "L'Etau-Bus" (1985) which she also wrote, "Le Dernier Havre" (1986), "Simon les Nuages" (1990), "Le Silence des Fusils" (1996), "L'Homme Ideal" (1996), "Nuit de Noces" (2001), "Secret de Banlieue" (2002), "Dans l'Oeil du Chat" (2004), "La Brunante" (2007), and "Une Constitution" (2013). She was seen on television in such series as "L'Heure du Concert", the children's series "La Souris Verte", "Picotine", "Le Gutenberg", "Chez Denise" as Therese Tremblay from 1979 to 1980, "Avec un Grand A", "Chop Suey", "Le Parc des Braves" as Mado Coulombe from 1984 to 1988, "Marilyn", "Bouledogue Bazar", "Les Heritiers Duval" as Reine Lorange from 1995 to 1996, "Y'a Plein d'Soleil", "Les Super Mamies", "Rumeurs", "Les Etoiles Filantes", and "Trauma" as Cecile Meilleur from 2013 to 2014. Her other television credits include productions of "Un Simple Soldat" (1972), "Le Grand Jour" (1988), "L'Incompris" (1997), and "Mon Meilleur Ami" (2013).

Duvall, Carol

Television host Carol Duvall, who was noted for her arts and crafts programs, died in Traverse City, Michigan, on July 31, 2023. She was 97. She was born Carol-Jean Reihmer in Milwaukee, Wisconsin, on January 10, 1926, and was raised in Grand Rapids, Michigan. She graduated from Michigan State University. She began working in television in the early 1950s on a children's show in Grand Rapids. She worked on numerous live local shows during the decade. She moved to WWJ-TV in Detroit in 1962 and remained there for 18 years. She was a news anchor and producer and hosted the craft show "Here's Carol Duvall". She became the crafts expert on the "Home Show" on ABC from 1988 to 1994. She subsequently hosted "The Carol Duvall Show" on HGTV from 1994 to 2005 and on the DIY Network from 2005 to 2009. She married Carl Duvall in 1945 and they had two sons before their divorce. She was predeceased by her son, Michael, in 2011, and is survived by son Jack.

Dynevor, Shirley

British actress Shirley Dynevor died of complications from dementia in England on January 10, 2023. She was 89. She was born Shirley Teague in Cardiff, Wales, on May 15, 1933. She aspired to be an actress from an early age and performed in repertory at Pontypridd after leaving school. She later moved to London and worked with Joan Littlewood's Theatre Workshop company from 1953. She married fellow actor Gerard Dynevor in 1954. She performed on television in

130

episodes of "Charlesworth", "Scotland Yard", "Armchair Theatre", "Family Solicitor" as Helen in 1961, "The Liars", "The Wednesday Play", and "Crown Court" as the jury foreman in 1972. She also appeared in the 1976 tele-film "Rogue Male". Dynevor also worked at Granada Television where she served as stage manager for the soap opera "Coronation Street". She was married to Gerard Dynevor from 1954 until his death in 1966 and is survived by their two children. She married guitarist Simon White in 1989 and he also survives her.

Eckstein, Paul

Television writer and producer Paul Eckstein, who was co-creator of the series "Godfather of Harlem", died in Kingston, Jamaica, on June 6, 2023. He was 59. Eckstein was born in Brooklyn, New York, on September 11, 1963. He

graduated from Brown University and began his career on stage. He was a founding member of the Naked Angels Theater Company. He appeared on Broadway in the 1991 play "Mule Bone". Eckstein was seen in the films "The Cabinet of Dr. Ramirez" (1991), "The Refrigerator" (1991), "Se7en" (1995), "Black Rose of Harlem" (1996), and "Hoodlum" (1997) which he co-produced. He appeared on television in episodes of "Law & Order", "The Steve Harvey Show", "413 Hope St.", "Star Trek: Deep Space Nine", "First Wave", and "Star Trek: Voyager", and the tele-films "Suspect Device" (1995) and "Bella Mafia" (1997). Eckstein began writing for television in the late 1990s, penning episodes of "First Wave", "The Dead Zone", "Street Time", and "Law & Order: Criminal Intent". He wrote and produced the series "Narcos" and "Godfather of Harlem". He produced and directed the 2012 documentary "Obama: What He's Done". He also served as a producer for the series "Of Kings and Prophets" and the 2020 mini-series "By Whatever Means Necessary: The Times of Godfather of Harlem". He was producer of the forthcoming detective series "August Snow" starring Keegan-Michael Key. He was in Jamaica leading a screenwriting workshop at the time of his death. Eckstein is survived by his wife, Hala, and two sons.

Edgeworth, Patrick

British-Australian screenwriter Patrick Edgeworth died in Australia on May 22, 2023. He was 80. Edgeworth was born in London, England, on December 25, 1942. He moved to Australia in 1969 and soon began working as an actor on television. He was seen in episodes of "The Long Arm",

"Homicide", "Matlock Police", "Division 4", "Cash and Company", "Cop Shop" as David Lambert in 1979, and

"Lawson's Mates". He also appeared in the 1978 mini-series "Against the Wind". Edgeworth was also writing for television by the early 1970s, scripting episodes of "Homicide", "Matlock Police", "Cash and Company" and "Tandarra" which he also produced, "Taxi", "Cop Shop", "Special Squad", "Chances", "Ship to Shore", "Newlyweds", "Blue Heelers", "Snowy River: The McGregor Saga", "State Coroner", and "Neighbours". He produced, wrote, and appeared in the 1977 film "Raw Deal" and wrote the films "BMX Bandits" (1983), "Cool Change" (1986), "Driving Force" (1989), and "A Sting in the Tale" (1989). The 2017 film "Bad Blood" was based on his screenplay. Edgeworth wrote several plays including "Boswell for the Defence" (1989), "Girl Talk" (2000), and "Georgy Girl - The Seekers Musical" (2015).

Edmunds, John

British television host and announcer John Edmunds died in Brighton, England, on May 3, 2023. He was 94. Edmunds was born in London, England, on April 3, 1929. He

graduated from the University College of Wales in Aberystwyth in the early 1950s. He worked as a grammar schoolteacher and performed on the local stage. He worked for ABC Weekend TV in the 1960s and was host of the BBC Children's series "Television Top of the Form" from 1966 to 1967. Edmunds was a newscaster for the BBC from 1968 to 1973 and again from 1974 to 1979. He was host of the BBC London television magazine "Town and Around" from 1968 to 1969 and BBC Radio 4's "You and Yours" in 1972. He was featured in cameo roles in the films "Lifeforce" (1985), "Love in Limbo" (1993), "Rendezvous with Zack" (2000), and "The Faces of the Moon" (2002). Edmunds served as head of the drama department at the University College of Wales in Aberystwyth from 1973 to 1985 and was professor of drama at the University of the Americas and the University of California at Santa Cruz from 1985 to 1997.

Eggert, Almut

German actress Almut Eggert died in Berlin, Germany, on February 7, 2023. She was 85. Eggert was born in Rostock, Germany, on June 7, 1937. She was the daughter of stage director Walter Eggert and actress Agnes-Marie Grisebach. She moved to Heidelberg with her family in 1951 where she trained to be a beautician. She later embarked on an acting career and trained at the Olly Rummel-Pickschneider drama school in Berlin from 1956 to 1959. She began

performing on stage in the late 1950s with the Vaganten Buhne Berlin and the Kleinen Theater im Zoo in Frankfurt. She performed with the Tribune Berlin from 1961 to 1966, the Theater Baden-Baden from 1966 to 1968, and the Schillertheater in Berlin from 1968 to 1975. She continued to perform on stage throughout her career. Eggert was also noted as a radio and dubbing actress. Eggert was seen frequently on television from the late 1950s with roles in productions of "Wie es Eucxh Gefallt" (1958), "Die Geburtstagsfeier" (1961), "Wiedersehen auf Raten" (1963), "Lebenskunstler" (1964), "Bezaubernde Mama" (1964), "Spatsommer" (1964), "Ich Fahre Patschold" (1964), "Auf Einem Bahnhof Bei Dijon" (1965), "Mrs. Cheney's Ende" (1965), "Der Mann, der Sich Abel Nannte" (1966), "Die Liebenden von Flrenz" (1966), "Der Tod Eines Mitburgers" (1967), "Ein Mann, der Nichts Gewinnt" (1967), "Crumbles Letzte Chance" (1967), "Die Reisegesellschaft" (1968), "Ostern" (1968), "Die Ruckkehr" (1969), "Startsprunge - Die Geschichte Einer Meisterschwimmerin" (1970), "Knast" (1972), "Berlin Alexanderplatz" (1980), "Der Urlaub" (1980), "Drei Schlafzimmer" (1980), "250.000 Mucken im Pappkarton" (1985), "Was Zu Beweisen War" (1986), "Der Knick - Die Geschichte Einer Wunderheilung" (1988), and "Ich Melde Einen Selbstmord" (1989). Her other television credits include episodes of "Unser Vater, der Tierarzt", "1... 2... 3... Rideau!", "Von Null Uhr Eins Bis Mitternacht - Der Abenteuerliche Urlaub des Mark Lissen", "Die Funfte Kolonne", "Alle Hunde Lieben Theobold", "Die Ivan-Rebroff-Show", "Ein Verrucktes Paar", "Kommissariat IX", "Locker vom Hocker", "Cafe Wernicke" as Marie Lampe from 1980 to 1981, "Diese Drombuschs", "Leute Wie du und Ich", "Turf", "Ich Heirate Eine Familie...", "Liebling Kreuzberg", "The Country Doctor", "Jakob und Adele", "The Adventures of Dr. Bayer" as Edith Sommer from 1987 to 1989, "Hals Uber Kopf", "Tucken des Alltags", "Auto Fritze", "Immer Wieder Sonntag", "SK Babies", "Praxis Bulowbogen" as Dr. Birgit Solms from 1995 to 1996, and "Alarm fur Cobra 11 - Die Autobahnpolizei" as Highway Police Chief Inspector Katharina Lamprecht from 1996 to 1997. She provided the German dubbing for such actresses as Sally Field, Ursula Andress, Lee Remick, Madeline Kahn, Raquel Welch, Stella Stevens, Candice Bergen, Farrah Fawcett, Samantha Eggar, Patty Shepard, and Stephanie Beacham. Eggert was married to actor and director Wolfgang Spier from 1959 until 1965. She had two daughters, actress Miriam Bettina Spier, who died in 2008, and Nana Spier.

Elliard, Leslie

Actor Leslie Elliard died of heart disease at his home in Los Angeles, California, on July 15, 2023. He was 46. Elliard was born in Indianapolis, Indiana, on June 20, 1977. He

was raised in Detroit, Michigan, where he graduated from high school in 1995. He attended Dillard University in New Orleans and earned a master's degree from the Yale School of Drama in 2002. He moved to New York City to pursue an acting career. He was featured in the off-Broadway musical "Crowns" and the Broadway musical "The Lion King" in the early 1970s. Elliard was featured as Officer Kevin Reynolds in several episodes of television's "The Wire" in 2003. He was also seen in episodes of "Hack", "All My Children", and "Law & Order". He was featured in the 2004 film "Dorian Blues" and the 2005 tele-film "Into Fire". Elliard was Jimmy James in the comedy television series "Barbershop" from 2005 to 2006.

Ellingson, Evan

Juvenile actor Evan Ellingson was found dead at his home in San Bernardino, California, on November 5, 2023. He was 35. Ellingson was born in Los Angeles County, California,

on July 1, 1988. He began his acting career in his early teens and was featured in such films as "The Gristle" (2001), "Time Changer" (2002), "Confession" (2005), "The Bondage" (2006), "Letters from Iowa Jima" (2006), "Walk the Talk" (2007), and "My Sister's Keeper" (2009) as Jesse Fitzgerald, the son of Cameron Diaz's character. Ellingson was seen on television in the tele-film "Living in Fear" (2001) and in episodes of "General Hospital", "Titus" in the recurring role of a young Christopher Titus from 2001 to 2002, "The Nick Cannon Show", "That Was Then", "Mad TV", "Complete Savages" as Kyle Savage from 2004 to 2005, "Bones", "Boys Life", "24" as Josh Bauer, the nephew of Kiefer Sutherland's Jack Bauer, in 2007, "State of Mind", and "CSI: Miami" in the recurring role of Kyle Harmon, the son of David Caruso's Horatio Caine, from 2007 to 2010. He largely retired from acting in the early 2010s. He reportedly suffered from drug abuse in his later years.

Ellsberg, Daniel

Military analyst and political activist Daniel Ellsberg, who was noted for leaking the Pentagon Papers to the press in 1971, died of pancreatic cancer at his home in Kensington, California, on June 16, 2023. He was 92. Ellsberg was born in Chicago, Illinois, on April 7, 1931, and was raised in Detroit, Michigan. He graduated from Harvard College in 1952 and studied at King's College, Cambridge, the following year. He served in the U.S. Marine Corps from 1954 until his discharge in 1957. He began working as a strategic analyst at the RAND Corporation in 1958 where he was involved in developing nuclear strategies for the U.S. National Security Council. He earned a PhD in economics from Harvard in 1962. Ellsberg  worked in the Pentagon as special assistant to Assistant Secretary of Defense for International Security Affairs John McNaughton in 1964. He then spent two years in South Vietnam, working for General Edward Lansdale as a member of the State Department. He returned to RAND in 1967 where he contributed to study on the conduct of the Vietnam War commissioned by Defense Secretary Robert McNamara. Ellsberg became an outspoken critic of the war by 1969. He made copies of many of the classified documents he had access to and they became known as the "Pentagon Papers". He leaked these documents to newspapers and several U.S. senators who opposed the war and many of them were published by "The New York Times" in June of 1971. The release of the documents proved an embarrassment to members of the Kennedy, Johnson, and Nixon administrations as they detailed the missteps and lies to the public about the war. The Nixon administration failed in a legal attempt to halt the publication and several White House staffers formed what became known as the White House Plumbers. G. Gordon Liddy and E. Howard Hunt carried out a burglary at the office of Ellsberg's psychiatrist in September of 1971 in an attempt to find potentially embarrassing information. Ellsberg was charged under the Espionage Act of 1917 in January of 1973, but governmental misconduct and illegal evidence-gathering led to all charges being dismissed the following May. He remained an anti-war activist and warned of the potential of a nuclear holocaust. He was author of several books including "Papers on the War" (1972), "Risk, Ambiguity, and Decision" (2001), "Secrets: A Memoir of Vietnam and the Pentagon Papers" (2003), and "The Doomsday Machine: Confessions of a Nuclear War Planner" (2017). Ellsberg was featured in numerous documentary films including "Hearts and Minds" (2003), "The Pentagon Papers" (2003), "The Most Dangerous Man in America: Daniel Ellsberg and the Pentagon Papers" (2009), "The Boys Who Said NO!" (2020), and "The Movement and the 'Madman'" (2023). Ellsberg appeared on television in episodes of "The Dick Cavett Show", "The Mike Douglas Show", "The Colbert Report", and "PoliticKING with Larry King". He also made a cameo appearance in an episode of "The Education of Max Bickford" in 2001. He was portrayed by James Spader in the 2003 tele-film "The Pentagon Papers" and by Matthew Rhys in the 2017 film "The Post". Ellsberg was married to Carol Cummings from 1952 until their divorce in 1966, and is survived by their two children, religious publisher Robert Ellsberg and epidemiologist Mary Ellsberg. He married Patricia Marx in 1970 and is also survived by her and their son, author Michael Ellsberg.

Ellsworth, Stan

Actor Stan Ellsworth, who was host of the history series "American Ride", died of complications of COVID-19 in  Lehi, Utah, on March 30, 2023. He was 63. Ellsworth was born in Salt Lake City, Utah, on June 20, 1959. He was a graduate of Brigham Young University, where he played football. He began coaching football after leaving college. He began acting in the early 2000s, appearing in the films "Clubhouse Detectives in Scavenger Hunt" (2003), "Church Ball" (2006), "Unaccompanied Minors" (2006), "Wieners" (2008), "Midnight Movie" (2008), "High School Musical 3: Senior Year" (2008), "Animals" (2009), and "The Do-Over" (2016), He was also seen on television in productions of "The Luck of the Irish" (2001),"True Caribbean Pirates" (2006), and "Dadnapped" (2009), and episodes of "Cover Me: Based on the True Life of an FBI Family", "American Experience", and "The Best of Studio C". He sat astride a Harley-Davidson motorcycle while serving as host of the BYUtv series "American Ride" from 2011 to 2016, recounting events from American history. Ellsworth was author of the 2018 book "Renegades and Rebels: Epic and True Stories of Our Revolutionary Heroes".

Emerson, Billy 'The Kid'

Singer and songwriter Billy 'The Kid' Emerson, who was noted for the hit song "Red Hot", died in a nursing home in Tarpon Springs, Florida, on April 25, 2023. He was 97.  Emerson was born in Tarpon Springs on December 21, 1925. He began playing piano in church in his youth and later performed with local bands. He joined the U.S. Navy during World War II in 1943. He resumed his musical career after the war performing in the Tampa area with such groups as the Billy Battle Band and Ivory Mitchell. He joined the U.S. Air Force during the Korean War in 1952. He soon joined Ike Turner's King of Rhythm. Turner assisted Emerson in securing a recording session with Sun Records and he released the 1954 single "No Teasing Around". He began playing with Phineas Newborn's band and wrote songs at Sun Records. He was best known for the songs "When It Rains, It Really Pours", which was recorded by Elvis Presley, and "Red Hot", which was a hit for Billy Lee Riley and Bob Luman. He joined Vee-Jay Records in Chicago in 1955 where he released the records "Every Woman I Know (Crazy 'Bout Automobiles)" and "Don't Start Me to Lying" with little success. Emerson soon became recording manager at Chess Records, where he recorded "Holy Mackerel Baby". He wrote songs for such artists as Buddy Guy, Junior Wells, Wynonie

Harris, and Willie Mabon. He formed his own label, Tarpon Records, in 1966. Emerson primarily worked in gospel music by the late 1970s.

Emes, Ian

British filmmaker and animator Ian Emes died of leukemia in London, England, on July 16, 2023. He was 73. Emes was born in Birmingham, England, on August 17, 1949.

He studied at the Birmingham College of Art and became a painter and sculptor. He worked on the experimental film "French Windows" in 1972 soon began creating moving images for Pink Floyd's concert tours. He also was involved with the band's music videos for "Time" (1972), "One of These Days" (1972), and "Dark Side of the Moon" (1973). Emes worked with other musicians including Mike Oldfield, Duran Duran, and Paul and Linda McCarthy's 1978 animated short "The Oriental Nightfish". He directed such television series as "The Comic Strip Presents", "How to Be Cool", "Streetwise", "Jim Tavare Pictures Presents", "Buddy Faro", "The Invisible Man", "Sir Gadabout, the Worst Knight in the Land", "Bookaboo" sharing a Daytime Emmy Award nomination, and "Queens of Mystery". He also directed television productions of "The Munsters' Scary Little Christmas" (1996), "Deadly Summer" (1997), and "Ice" (2001). Emes earned an Academy Award nomination and a BAFTA Award for the 1984 short film "Goodie-Two-Shoes" and directed and wrote the 1986 feature film "Knights & Emeralds".

Engelberg, Mort

Film producer Mort Engelberg, who produced "Smokey and the Bandit" in 1977, died of lung cancer in Los Angeles, California, on December 10, 2023. He was 86. Engelberg was born in Memphis, Tennessee, on August 20, 1937. He graduated from the University of Illinois and worked on a master's degree from the University of Missouri in the late 1950s. He was a journalist before moving to Washington, D.C., to work for Sargent Shriver at the Peace Corps and the Office of Economic Opportunity. Engelberg moved to New York City in 1967 to work at Metro-Goldwyn Mayer. He soon went to United Artists to serve as assistant to the president of productions. He was producer of such films as "Smokey and the Bandit" (1977) starring Burt Reynolds, "hot Stuff" (1979), "The Villain" (1979), "The Hunter" (1980), "Nobody's Perfekt" (1981), "Smokey and the Bandit Part 3" (1983), "The Heavenly Kid" (1985), "Three for the Road" (1987), "Maid to Order" (1987), "Pass the Ammo" (1987), and "Fright Night Part 2" (1988). Engelberg was

executive producer of "The Big Easy" (1986), "Dudes" (1987), "Russkies" (1987), "Remote Control" (1988), and "There Goes the Neighborhood" (1992). He became active in politics again as an advance man, handling publicity for unsuccessful presidential candidates Walter Mondale in 1984 and Michael Dukakis in 1988. He was advance man to Bill Clinton during the 1992 presidential campaign and his reelection campaign in 1996. Engelberg married Helaine Blatt in 2016 following a 26 year relationship and she survives him.

Engle, Debra

Actress Debra Engle died of complications from dementia in Los Angeles, California, on February 10, 2023. She was 69. Engle was born in Baltimore, Maryland, on July

4, 1954. She appeared frequently on television from the mid-1980s. She was seen in episodes of "Hometown", "Kay O'Brien", "Family Ties", "Beauty and the Beast", "Empty Nest", "The Fanelli Boys", "Blossom", "The Golden Girls" in the recurring role of Rebecca Devereaux, daughter of Rue McClanahan's Blanche DuBois, from 1989 to 1991, "Dream On", "The Golden Palace" reprising her role as Rebecca in 1993, "Married... with Children", "Dave's World", "Lost on Earth", "ER", "Home Improvement", "Sabrina the Teenage Witch", and "Crossing Jordan". Her other television credits include the mini-series "Kane & Abel" (1985) and the tele-films "Badlands 2005" (1988) and "Dark Avenger" (1990). She was also seen in small roles in the films "Key Exchange" (1985) and "Guinevere" (1999). Engle married producer Russell Smith in 1983 and he survives her.

Ennosuke, Ichikawa, III

Japanese kabuki actor Ichikawa Ennosuke III died from heart arrhythmia in Tokyo, Japan, on September 13, 2023.

He was 83. He was born Masahiko Kinoshi in Tokyo on December 9, 1939. He was the son of kabuki actor Danshiro III and actress Sanae Takasugi. He began performing on stage as a child under the name Ichikawa Danko III. He followed in the footsteps of his great-grandfather and grandfather, taking the name Ichikawa Ennosuke III in 1963. His kabuki performances were noted for their spectacular costumes and stage effects. He developed a more contemporary stagecraft which he dubbed Super Kabuki in 1986. Ennosuke suffered a stroke in 2003 and largely retired from the stage. He took the name Ichikawa En'no II in 2012 and his nephew, Takahiko Kioshi, previously known as Kamejiro II, adopted the name Ichikawa Ennosuke

IV. His son, Teruyuki Kagawa, also performed kabuki under the name Ichikawa Shusha IX. His younger brother, fellow kabuki actor Ichikawa Danshiro, died in a suspected suicide pact with his wife in May of 2023.

Enrich

Spanish cartoonist Enric de Manuel Gonzalez died in Spain on February 12, 2023. He was 93. Gonzalez was born in

Venissieux, France, on July 15, 1929. He began working in comics in 1950, creating the character "Ciriaco Majareto" for the "Trampolin" magazine. He also created "El Pirata Malapata" for the "Alex" magazine in the 1950s. He worked for the publisher Editorial Bruguera until 1957 when he joined the "Tio Vivo" magazine. He soon created the comic strips "El Caco Bonifacio", "El Doctor Perejil", and "Boliche". He helmed the short-lived "Rififi" magazine in 1961 before returning to Bruguera. He worked on such strips as "Tontainez", "Don Inocencio", "Pulgarcito", "Don Toribio, el Conserje", and "1x2 el Invasor" in the 1960s. Enrich worked on the series "Montse, la Amiga de los Animales" for "Gina" magazine in 1978.

Ernst, Donald W.

Film and television editor Donald W. Ernst, who was noted for his work in animation, died on April 9, 2023. He was 89. Ernst was born in Los Angeles, California, on January 25, 1934. He began his career in television in the 1950s as an editor

for such series as "Chevron Hall of Stars", "Hey, Jeannie!", "Karen", "The Wild Wild West", "Gilligan's Island", "Cimarron Strip", and "Gunsmoke". He was also editor of the 1972 tele-film "Rolling Man". He edited the films "Didn't You Hear?" (1970), "Le Mans" (1971), "The Only Way Home" (1972), "Thirty Dangerous Seconds" (1973), and "Easy to Be Free" (1973). He began working as an animation editor with Ralph Bakshi's "Heavy Traffic" (1973). He continued to edit such animated productions as "Coonskin" (1974), "Wizards" (1977), "The Lord of the Rings" (1978), "Hey Good Lookin'" (1982), "Starchaser: The Legend of Orin" (1985), "The Brave Little Toaster" (1987), "Back to Neverland" (1989), and Roger Rabbit's "Tummy Trouble" (1989). He was a sound or music editor for the films "The Killing Kind" (1973), "Electra Glide in Blue" (1973), "In Search of Noah's Ark" (1976), "She Came to the Valley" (1979), "Earthbound" (1981), "Early Warning" (1981), "Soggy Bottom, U.S.A." (1981), "Parasite" (1982), "A Time to Die" (1982), "Silent Rage" (1982), "Fire and Ice"

(1983), "The Lightship" (1985), "Stand Alone" (1985), "The Chipmunk Adventure" (1987), "The Hidden" (1987), and "Mind Games" (1989). He received Emmy Awards for his sound editing for "Raid on Entebbe" in 1977 and "Hill Street Blues" in 1983. Ernst earned addition Emmy nominations for sound editing for "The Plutonium Incident" (1980), "Attica" (1980), "The Women's Room" (1981), "Marian Rose White" (1982), "St. Elsewhere" (1983) and "L.A. Law" (1987). Ernst was also a sound or music editor for television productions of "A Summer Without Boys" (1973), "Dummy" (1979), "Survival of Dana" (1979), "The Boy Who Drank Too Much" (1980), "Knots Landing" (1980), "The Comeback Kid" (1980), "The Golden Moment: An Olympic Love Story" (1980), "A Time for Miracles" (1980), "Flamingo Road" (1981), "The Kid with the Broken Halo" (1982), "Seven Brides for Seven Brothers" (1982), "I Married Wyatt Earp" (1983), "If Tomorrow Comes" (1986), "Into the Homeland" (1987), "Once Upon a Texas Train" (1988), "Baby M" (1988), and "Dino-Riders" (1988). He worked with Disney from the early 1990s and served as producer for the animated films and shorts "Roller Coaster Rabbit" (1990), "Mickey's Audition" (1992), "Aladdin" (1992), "Homeward Bound: The Incredible Journey" (1993), "How to Haunt a House" (1999), and "Fantasia 2000" (1999). He was producer of the English language version of Hayao Miyazaki's "Spirited Away" (2002) and was story supervisor and co-producer of the Oscar-nominated animated short, "Destino", featuring work by Walt Disney and Salvador Dali.

Erwin, Steve

Comic book artist Steve Erwin, who was co-creator of the DC comics "Checkmate" and "Gunfire", died suddenly on October 25, 2023. He was 63. Erwin was born in Tulsa, Oklahoma, on January 16, 1960. He aspired to be a comic book artist from his youth and studied commercial art at Oklahoma

State University Institute of Technology at Okmulgee. He began his career in comics with First Comics in 1986 as an artist for the titles "Grimjack" with writer John Ostrander and "Shatter" with writer Steven Grant. He soon moved to DC where he worked on the final issues of the "Vigilante" series in 1987. He teamed with writer Paul Kupperberg to create the espionage series "Checkmate!" in 1988. He illustrated the "Deathstroke the Terminator" comic, working with writer Marv Wolfman, from 1991 to 1994. Erwin worked with writer Len Wein to create the new superhero character Gunfire in "Deathstroke the Terminator Annual" #3 (Oct. 1993) and illustrated the early issues of the short-lived "Gunfire" series in 1994. He was also an artist for the "Batman Returns" comic book adaptation, "Hawk and Dove", "New Gods", "The New Titans", "Superboy", and "Superman: The Man of Steel". He illustrated the mini-series "Star Trek: The Next Generation Shadowheart" in 1994 and the graphic novel adaptation of William Shatner's "The Ashes of Eden". He illustrated the comics "The Ferret", "Ultraforce", and "Star Trek: Deep Space Nine Worf Special" at Malibu and Marvel's "Star Trek: Operation Assimilation" and "ID4: Independence Day" in the mid-1990s. He left comics in the late 1990s to design toys for the fast-food industry's kid's meals. He was artist for historical graphic novels for children in the early 2000s including "The Wright Brothers and the Airplane" "The Lewis and Clark Expedition". He also worked on inflatable holiday decor for Gemmy Industries later in his career.

Evans, Andrea

Actress Andrea Evans, who starred as Tina Lord in the "One Life to Live" soap opera, died of breast cancer at her home in Pasadena, California, on July 9, 2023. She was 66. Evans was born in Aurora, Illinois, on June 18, 1957. She competed

in beauty pageants as a child and later appeared in commercials and regional theater. She attended the University of Illinois at Urbana-Champagne and was featured as an extra in Brian De Palma's 1978 horror film "The Fury" while a student. Evans appeared in the 1978 television mini-series "The Awakening Land" and the tele-films "Arch of Triumph" (1984), "Florence Nightingale" (1984), "Imaginary Friend" (2012), "I Know Where Lizzie Is" (2016), and "Joy & Hope" (2020). Her other television credits include episodes of "CHiPs", "Out of Control", "Jenny's War", "The $10,000 Pyramid", "Family Feud", "The New Hollywood Squares", and "Capital News". She was featured in several films including "The Opposite Sex and How to Live with Them" (1992), "A Low Down Dirty Shame" (1994), the horror film "Ice Cream Man" (1995), and "Hit List" (2011). Evans was best known for her work in soap operas, starring as Tina Lord in "One Life to Live" from 1978 to 1981, 1985 to 1990, 2008, and 2011. She received a Daytime Emmy nomination for her role in 1998. She was Patty Williams in "The Young and the Restless" from 1983 to 1984. She was featured as Tawny Moore in "The Bold and the Beautiful" from 1999 to 2000 and from 2010 to 2011 and starred as Rebecca Hotchkiss in "Passions" from 2000 to 2008. Evans appeared as Vivian Price in the web soap opera "DeVanity" in 2014, receiving another Daytime Emmy nomination, and was Patty Walker on "The Bay" from 2017 to 2020. Evans was married to actor and "One Life to Live" co-star Wayne Massey" from 1981 to 1984. She married Stephen Rodriguez in 1998 and is survived by him and their adopted daughter.

Evans, Joan

Actress Joan Evans died in Henderson, Nevada, on October 21, 2023. She was 89. She was born Joan Eunson in New York City on July 18, 1934. Her parents were writers Dale Eunson and Katherine Albert. They were close friends with actress Joan Crawford, who became Evans' godmother. She began acting on stage and made her film debut at the age of 14

in the title role of "Roseanna McCoy" (1949). Her parents had added two years to her age when Samuel Goldwyn selected her to replace Cathy O'Donnell to star opposite Farley Granger. She also appeared with Granger in the films "Our Very Own"

(1950) and "Edge of Doom" (1950). Evans' other films include "On the Loose" (1951), the MGM musical comedy "Skirts Ahoy!" (1952), Universal's "It Grows on Trees" (1952) as Irene Dunne's daughter, "Column South" (1953) opposite Audie Murphy, "The Outcast" (1954), "A Strange Adventure" (1956), "No Name on the Bullet" (1959) again with Audie Murphy, "The Flying Fontaines" (1959) as Jan Fontaine, and "The Walking Target" (1960). She was seen on television in episodes of "The Billy Rose Show", "General Electric Theater", "Climax!", "The Millionaire", "Schlitz Playhouse", "Cavalcade of America", "Lux Video Theatre", "Cheyenne", "77 Sunset Strip", "Wagon Train", "Zorro" as Leonar in several episodes in 1959, "The Chevy Mystery Show", "The Rebel", "Outlaws", "Tales of Wells Fargo", "The Brothers Brannagan", "Ripcord", "The Tall Man", and "Laramie". She retired from acting in the early 1960s. Evans began writing articles for "Photoplay" magazine in the 1950s. She became editor of "Hollywood Studio Magazine" in 1966. She became a teacher in the 1970s and was director of Carden Academy in Van Nuys, California. Evans had just turned 18 when she married car dealer Kirby Weatherly in July of 1952. She married at the home of Joan Crawford, who had encouraged the union. Her parents were against the marriage and their friendship with Crawford evaporated. She and her husband remained close with Crawford until the death of the actress in 1977. The two remained wed until Weatherly's death in January of 2023. She is survived by their son and daughter.

Ever, Ita

Estonian actress Ita Ever died in Tallinn, Estonia, on

August 9, 2023. Ever was born in Paidi, Estonia, on April 1, 1931. She was 92. She began her career on stage in the early 1950s. She was also seen in numerous Estonian and Russian films during her career. Her film credits include "Andruse Onn" (1955), "Tagahoovis" (1957), "Juunikuu Paevad" (1957), "Uhe Katuse All" (1963), "Mis Juhtus Andres Lapeteusega?" (1966), "Spring" (1969), "Vozvrashchenie k Zhizni" (1972), "Vaike Reekviem Suupillile" (1972), "Tuli Oos" (1973), "Minu Nainc Sai Vanaemaks" (1976), "Vremya Zhit, Vremya Lyubit" (1977), "Reigi Opetaja" (1978), "Kunksmoor Ja Kapten Trumm" (1978), "Naine Kutab Sauna" (1979), "Korboja

Peremees" (1979), "Nukitsamees" (1981), "Karge Meri" (1981), "Tayna Chyornykh Drozdov" (aka "Secret of the Blackbirds") (1983) as Agatha Christie's sleuth Miss Marple, "Kaks Paari Ja Uksindus" (1985), "Varastatud Kohtumine" (1989), "Doktor tockmann" (1989), "Regina" (1990), "Sugis" (1990), "Sputnik Planety Uran" (1990), "Luukas" (1992), "Lza Ksieia Ciemnosci" (1993), "Letters from the East" (1995), "Yantarnye Krylya" (2003), "Korini!" (2005), "Vana Daami Visiit" (2006), "Vedma" (2006), "A Lady in Paris" (2012), "Living Images" (2013), and "Salmonid. 25 Aastat Hiljem" (2020). Ever appeared onn television in productions of "Puha Susanna Ehk Meistrite Kool" (1983), "Tants Aurukatla Umber" (1987), "Gosudarstvennaya Granitsa: Solyonyy Veter" (1988), "Miss Marple'i Lood" (1990), "Nadja - Heimkehr in die Fremde" (1995), and "Armuke" (2000). She was also seen in episodes of "Kolm Rubiini", "Koige Suurem Sober", "Gosudarstvennaya Granitsa", and "Kelgukoerad" as Elviira from 2006 to 2011. Ever was married to actor Eino Baskin and was the mother of director and actor Roman Baskin who died in 2018.

Faber, Ron

Actor Ron Faber died of lung cancer in New York City on March 26, 2012. He was 90. Faber was born in Milwaukee, Wisconsin, on February 16, 1933. He began his career working in radio and trained at the Lucille Lortel White Barn Theater in Westport, Connecticut. He performed frequently on stage and

received an Obie Award for his role in the 1972 Off Broadway play "And They Put Handcuffs on Flowers". His other Off-Broadway productions include "Lucky Stiff", "Troilus and Cressida", and "Woyzeck". He made his film debut in 1972's "The Exorcist" in the role of Chuck, the assistant director for a film being made by Ellen Burstyn's character. He was noted for his small role of announcing the death of her film co-star, Burke Dennings, played by Jack MacGowran. Faber also provided some of the deep, guttural vocal sounds of the demon possessing Linda Blair's Regan MacNeil the supplement the work of Mercedes McCambridge, who was the primary voice of the demon. He was also seen in the films "L'Arbre de Guernica" (1975), "The Private Files of J. Edgar Hoover" (1977), "On the Yard" (1978), "Soup for One" (1982), "Navy Seals" (1990), "Romeo Is Bleeding" (1993), "Calling Bobcat" (2000), and the short "Back to Me" (2008). Faber appeared on television in the mini-series "The American Parade" (1976) and the tele-films "Hardhat and Legs" (1980), "Bill" (1981), and "Running Out" (1983). He was also seen in episodes of "Kojak", "The Edge of Night", "Law & Order", "Third Watch", and "Hope & Faith". He is survived by his wife, Kathleen Moore Faber, and four children. Another son, Eric, predeceased him.

Faichney, Stewart

Australian actor Stewart Faichney died in Melbourne, Victoria, Australia, on July 15, 2023. He was 77. Fiachney was born in Melbourne on April 15, 1946. He appeared frequently

in films from the 1970s with roles in "Raw Deal" (1977), "The Day After Halloween" (1979), "The Last of the Knucklemen" (1979), "Thirst" (1979), "Ground Zero" (1987), "Lex and Rory" (1994), "Muggers" (2000), "Lucky Day" (2002), "Till Human Voices Wake Us" (2002), "Rainbow Bird & Monster Man" (2002), "The Tender Hook" (2008), "Torn" (2010), and "That's Not My Dog!" (2018). He was also writer and casting director for the films "Strange Bedfellows" (2004), "Charlie & Boots" (2009), and "Little Johnny: The Movie" (2011). Faichney was seen on television in episodes of "Ryan", "Rush", "Homicide", "Division 4", "Matlock Police", "Bellbird", "Tandara", "Bluey", "Cop Shop", "Carson's Law", "Prisoner: Cell Block H", "Special Squad", "The Henderson Kids", "Neighbours", "A Country Practice", "The Flying Doctors", "Kelly", "Good Guys Bad Guys", "State Coroner", and "Blue Heelers". He also appeared in television productions of "Against the Wind" (1978), "The Last Outlaw" (1980), "The Dismissal" (1983), "Bodyline" (1984), "Glass Babies" (1985), "Flair" (1990), and "Dogwoman: The Legend of Dogwoman" (2001).

Failure, Care

Canadian singer and musician Care Failure, who was founder of the alternative rock band Die Mannequin, died of

complications from infections in Canada on March 30, 2023. She was 36. She was born Caroline Kawa in Toronto, Canada, on April 30, 1986. She began her career in rock with the four-piece band the Blood Mannequins. The band evolved into Die Mannequin in 2005 and Failure recorded her first EP "How to Kill" the following year. Die Mannequin released the EPs "Slaughter Daughter" (2007) and "Danceland" (2012) and the 2008 compilation album "Unicorn Steak". They recorded two albums, "Fino + Bleed" (2009) and "Neon Zero" (2014). The band opened for such artists as Guns N' Roses, Marilyn Manson, and Buckcherry. Die Mannequin was featured in the 2009 documentary series "City Sonic". Failure starred in the 2010 music mockumentary "Hard Core Logo 2".

Farina, Sandy

Singer and songwriter Sandy Farina, who was featured as Strawberry Fields in the 1978 musical film "Sergeant Pepper's Lonely Hearts Club Band", died in South Salem, New

York, on November 15, 2023. She was 68. She was born in Newark, New Jersey, on December 31, 1955. She was a singer

noted for her raspy voice when she was selected to star as Strawberry Fields in the musical "Sergeant Pepper's Lonely Hearts Club Band" in 1978. The movie was loosely based on the Beatles' hit album and starred Peter Frampton and the Bee Gees. Farina sang a version of the Beatles' song "Strawberry Fields Forever". She co-wrote Barbra Streisand's 1979 song "Kiss Me in the Rain" and released the 1980 album "All Alone in the Night". Farina was a contestant on the television talent series "Star Search" in 1985. She was co-lead vocalist for the charity single "Hands Across America" in 1986. She later did voice-overs and commercial jingles for such companies as Sears, Sara Lee, Ivory, Chevrolet, and Jif, and worked in real estate. She married Michael Farina in 1975 and is survived by him and two children.

Farkas, Jo

Actress Jo Farkas died in Studio City, California, on May 28, 2023. She was 96. Farkas was born in Boston, Massachusetts, on May 1, 1927. She earned a degree in school

counseling at Boston University. She worked in the Baltimore city schools system as a clinical psychologist. She retired in the early 1990s and moved to California to pursue an acting career. She worked as a school psychologist before becoming an actress after retiring in the early 1990s. She was featured in such films as "Meatballs 4" (1992),
"Hold Me thrill Me Kiss Me" (1992), "Tank Girl" (1995), "Forget Paris" (1995), "No Easy Way" (1996), "My Best Friend's Wedding" (1997), "Good Burger" (1997), "The Medicine Show" (2001), "Boxing Day" (2012), "Shock Value" (2014), "The Next Big Thing" (2016), and "Don't Mind Alice" (2017). Farkas was seen on television in productions of "Dead in the Water" (1991), "Out of Darkness" (1994), and "The Lake" (1998). Her other television credits include episodes of "Sisters", "Goode Behavior", "Tracey Takes On...", "Meego", "Ellen", "Chicago Hope", "Manhattan, AZ", "Weeds" in the recurring role of Bubbie in 2008, "Southland", "Family Tools", "Benched", "Getting On", "American Horror Story", "Angie Tribeca", "Superstore", "Shameless", "Legion", "Brooklyn Nine-Nine", "Tacoma FD", "The Kids Are Alright", "AJ and the Queen", and "Dream Corps LLC".

Farr, Judi

Australian actress Judi Farr died in Sydney, New South Wales, Australia, on June 30, 2023. She was 84. Farr was born in Cairns, Queensland, Australia, on October 5, 1938.

She began her career on television in the early 1960s and appeared in productions of "The Taming of the Shrew" (1962), "Split Level" (1964), "The Interpreters" (1966), "The Fourth

Wish" (1974), "Scales of Justice" (1983), "Who Killed Hannah Jane?" (1984), "Double Sculls" (1986), "Melba" (1988), "Australians" (1988), "Come in September" (1990), "Changi" (2001), "Go Big" (2004), "The Alice" (2004), "Farscape: The Peacekeeper Wars" (2004), "Fatal Contact: Bird Flu in America" (2006), and "Jack Irish: Bad Debts" (2012). Farr starred as Rita Stiller in the comedy series "My Name's McGooley, What's Yours?" from 1966 to 1968 and reprised the role in the spin-off series "Rita and Wally" in 1968. Her other television credits include episodes of "The Link Men", "Division 4", "A Nice Day at the Office", "Matlock Police", "The Evil Touch", "Mac and Merle", "Behind the Legend", "Number 96" as Alderman Mrs. April Bullock from 1974 to 1975, "Alvin Purple", "Tickled Pink", "Father, Dear Father in Australia", "Kingswood Country" as Thelma Bullpitt from 1980 to 1982, "Winners", "Mother and Son", "Rafferty's Rules", "Boys from the Bush", "A Country Practice", "G.P.", "Medivac", "Murder Call", "All Saints" as Kathleen O'Hara in 1999, "Stingers", "Water Rats", "Grass Roots" as Janice Corniglio from 2000 to 2003, "CrashBurn", "Laid", "Please Like Me" as Aunty Peg in 2013, "Twentysomething", "Camp", and "A Place to Call Home" in the recurring role of Peg Maloney from 2013 to 2015. Farr appeared in such films as "They're a Weird Mob" (1966), "Dawn!" (1979), "Just Out of Reach" (1979), "Fatty Finn" (1980), "For Love Alone" (1986), "The Year My Voice Broke" (1987), "Flirting" (1987), "Turning April" (1996), "Oscar and Lucinda" (1997), "Walking on Water" (2002), "Thunderstruck" (2004), and "December Boys" (2007). She performed frequently on stage throughout her career with roles in productions of "Death of a Salesman", "Lettice and Lovage", "Angels in America", "Women of Troy", and "Walking on Water". She retired from acting in 2015 following a battle with cancer.

Farrell, Judy

Actress Judy Farrell, who appeared in the recurring role of Nurse Able on the television series "M*A*S*H", died

from complications of a stroke at a hospital in Los Angeles, California, on April 2, 2023. She was 84. She was born Judy Hayden in Quapaw, Oklahoma, on May 11, 1938. She graduated from Oklahoma State University with a degree in theater and attended the University of California at Los Angeles, where she met actor Mike Farrell. The two married in 1963 and performed together on stage with the Laguna Playhouse. She also worked as a high school English and drama teacher. She appeared on television from the late 1960s with roles in episodes of "Judd for the Defense", "Get Smart", "The Interns", "Medical Center", "Emergency!", "Room 222", "The Rookies", "The Partridge Family", "Quincy", "Benson", "Tattletales", "The $10,000 Pyramid", "The Mike Douglas Show", "Fame" in the recurring role of Charlotte Miller from 1982 to 1983, "CBS Library", "ABC Afterschool Specials", and "Divorce Court". Her other television credits include the tele-films "Intimate Strangers" (1977) and "Fugitive Family" (1980). She appeared as Nurse Abel on eight episodes of the hit television series "M*A*S*H", where her then husband was starring as Captain B.J. Hunnicutt, from 1976 until the finale in 1983. Farrell appeared in a handful of films during her career including "The Andromeda Strain" (1971), "J W Coop" (1971), "Chapter Two" (1979), and "Long-Term Relationship" (2006). She wrote the 1982 tele-film "The Kid from Nowhere" and an episode of "Fame" in 1983. She was a writer for the television soap opera "Port Charles" from 1998 to 2003. She and Mike Farrell were married from 1963 until their divorce in 1984 and she is survived by their two children, Michael and Erin. She married actor Joe Bratcher in 1985 and he also survives her.

Farrell, Sharon

Actress Sharon Farrell, who starred in the cult horror film "It's Alive" in 1974, died in Orange County, California, on

May 15, 2023. She was 82. She was born Sharon Forsmoe in Sioux City, Iowa, on December 24, 1940. She studied ballet in high school and later toured with the American Ballet Theatre. She moved to New York where she pursued a career as an actress and model. She made her film debut in 1959's "Kiss Her Goodbye" and danced on Broadway in the

production of "There Was a Little Girl". She appeared frequently in films from the 1960s with roles in "40 Pound of Trouble" (1962), "The Man with My Face" (1965) an expanded version of "The Man from U.N.C.L.E." episode "The Double Affair", "Not with My Wife, You Don't!" (1966), "A Lovely Way to Die" (1968), "Marlowe" (1969) with James Garner, "The Reivers" (1969) with Steve McQueen, "The Love Machine" (1971), Larry Cohen's cult horror classic "It's Alive" (1974) as the Lenore Davis, the mother of a deformed carnivorous baby, the psychological horror "The Premonition" (1976) with Richard Lynch, "The Fifth Floor" (1978), "The Stunt Man" (1980) with Peter O'Toole and Steve Railsback, "Out of the Blue" (1980), "Separate Ways" (1981), the horror film "Sweet Sixteen" (1983), "Lone Wolf McQuade" (1983) with Chuck Norris, the cult science fiction film "Night of the Comet" (1984), "Can't Buy me Love" (1987), "One Man Force" (1989), "Lonely Hearts" (1991), "Arcade" (1993), "A Gift from Heaven" (1994), "Beyond Desire" (1995), "White Cargo"

(1996), "Timeless Obsession" (1996), and "Last Chance Love" (1997). Farrell was a familiar face on television with roles in episodes of "Naked City", "Alfred Hitchcock Presents", the short-lived newspaper series "Saints and Sinners" as Polly Holloran opposite Nick Adams from 1962 to 1963, "Empire", "My Favorite Martian", "Death Valley days", "Kraft Suspense Theatre", "The Lieutenant", "Arrest and Trial", "Wagon Train", "Bob Hope Presents the Chrysler Theatre", "Gunsmoke", "Burke's Law", "The Beverly Hillbillies", "The Alfred Hitchcock Hour", "The Fugitive", "Ben Casey", "Rawhide", "I Dream of Jeannie", "My Three Sons", "Dr. Kildare", "The Wackiest Ship in the Army", "Run for Your Life", "Iron Horse", "The Man from U.N.C.L.E.", "The Virginian", "The Wild Wild West", "Premiere", "Medical Center", "Men at Law", "The Name of the Game", "The Hollywood Squares", "the Merv Griffin Show", "The Tonight Show Starring Johnny Carson", "The D.A.", "Banyon", "Marcus Welby, M.D.", "The New Perry Mason", "Love, American Style", "The F.B.I.", "Chase", "This Is the Life", "Insight", "Match Game", "The Alan Hamel Show", "Police Surgeon", "Petrocelli", "The Six Million Dollar Man", "Harry O", "Kolchak: The Night Stalker", "Police Story", "McCloud", "Bronk", "Doc", "Police Woman", "Gibbsville", "Switch", "Man from Atlantis", "Mrs. Columbo", "Hawaii Five-O", "T.J. Hooker", "Small & Frye", "Rituals" as Cherry Lane from 1984 to 1985, "Freddy's Nightmares", "Matlock", the soap opera "The Young and the Restless" as Florence Webster from 1991 to 1997, and "J.A.G." Her other television credits include the tele-films "Quarantined" (1980), "The Eyes of Charles Sand" (1972), "A Little Bit Like Murder" (1973), "The Underground Man" (1974), "The Cloning of Clifford Swimmer" (1974), "The Young Runaways" (1978), "Confessions of the D.A. Man" (1978), "The Last Ride of the Dalton Gang" (1979), "Rage!" (1980), "Born to Be Sold" (1981), "Sworn to Vengeance" (1993), and "Yakuza Connection" (1995). Farrell largely retired from acting in the late 1990s but briefly returned to appear as Grandma Geraldine in a pair of episodes of the web series "Broken at Love" in 2013. Her memoir, "Hollywood Princess", was published in 2013. She was involved with producer Ron De Blasio, actor Andrew Prine, actor John Boyer, Steve Salkin, and director Dale Trevillion. She was reportedly married and divorced from all of them but her son denied that she had ever formally been wed. Her survivors include her son, actor Chance Boyer.

Faye, Stevie

British comedian Stevie Faye died in England on September 21, 2023. He was 95. Faye was born in Liverpool, England, in 1927. He was an amateur boxer and worked at various odd jobs before embarking on a career in comedy. He became a popular stand-up comic. He appeared frequently on the television series "The Comedians" from 1971 to 1985. He was also seen in the 1982

BBC2 drama mini-series "Boys from the Blackstuff". He announced his retirement from performing in 1997. Faye is survived by a son and daughter.

Ferreira, Patricia

Film director Patricia Ferreira died of a brain tumor in Madrid, Spain, on December 27, 2023. She was 65. Ferreira

was born in Madrid in 1958. She earned a degree at the Complutense University of Madrid, where she studied image sciences and journalism. She worked at TVE and RNE as a film journalist after graduation. She became involved in production in the late 1970s and served as an assistant director for the television series "Revista de Cine" (1977), "Que Usted lo Mate Bien" (1979), "Cervantes" (1981), and "La Celestina" (1983). Ferreira directed episodes of "Cronicas Urbanas" and "Paraisos Cercanos" in the late 1990s. She made feature directorial debut with 2000's "I Know Who You Are", earning a Goya Award nomination for Best New Director. She also directed and frequently wrote such films as "El Alquimista Impaciente" (2002), the short "El Secreto Mejor Guardado" (2004), "Para Que No Me Olvides" (2005), "Senora De" (2010), "The Wild Ones" (2012), "El Primer Dia" (2015), and "Thi Mai, Rumbo a Vietnam" (2017).

Ferro, Angie

Filipino actress Angie Ferro died of complications from a stroke in the Philippines on August 17, 2023. She was 86. She was born Angelica Caballero Ferro in Baleno, Philippines, on August 4, 1937. She began her career on stage in the late 1960s with the Philippine Educational Theater Association. She starred in a 1969 production of "The Trojan

Women" at the Manila Metropolitan Theater. Ferro was seen in numerous theatrical productions throughout her career. She also appeared frequently in films with roles in "Santiago!" (1970), "Dipped in Gold" (1970), "Now" (1971), "Lumuha Pati Mga Anghel" (1971), "Nora, Mahal Kita" (1972), "Hatinggabi Na Vilma" (1972), "Ta-Ra-Ra-Dyin Pot-Pot" (1972), "Lipad, Darna, Lipad!" (1973), "Zoom, Zoom, Superman!" (1973), "Bawai: Asawa Mo, Asawa Ko!" (1974), "Sunugin Ang Samar" (1974), "Patayin Mo Sa Sindak Si Barbara" (1974), "Psssst... Halika Babae" (1974), "Ine Night... Three Women!" (1974), "Anino Ng Araw" (1975), "Hindi Kami Damong Ligaw" (1976), "Bongbong" (1976), "Electgrika Kasi, Eh!" (1977), "Tutubing Kalabaw Tutubing Karayom" (1977), "Tisoy!" (1977), "Sudden Death" (1977), "Amorseko" (1976), "Pagputi Ng Uwak... Pag-itim Ng Tagak" (1978),

"Atsay" (1978), "Katawang Alabok" (1978), "Roberta" (1979), "High School Circa '65" (1979), "Bakit May Pag-ibit Pa?" (1979), "Diborsyada" (1979), "Pompa" (1980), "Darna at Ding" (1980), "Dormitoryo! Buhay Estudyante" (1982), "Gaano Kadalas Ang Minsan?" (1982), "Pedro Tunasan" (1983), "Saan Darating Ang Umaga?" (1983), "Isla" (1985), "Magdusa Ka!" (1986), "Kasalanan Bang Sambahin Ka?" (1990), "Apoy Sa Puso" (1992), "Kill Barbara with Panic" (1995), "Mananayaw" (1997), "Mother Ignacia - Ang Uliran" (1998), "Uod Sa Laman" (1998), "Sidhi" (1999), "La Vida Rosa" (2001), "Evolution of a Filipino Family" (2004), "Ang Anak Ni Broka" (2005), "Santa Mesa" (2008), "Bulong" (2011), "Graceland" (2012), "Bingoleras" (2013), "Ang Misis Ni Meyor" (2013), "Da Possessed" (2014), "The Trial" (2014), "Shake Rattle & Roll XV" (2014), "Etiquette for Mistresses" (2015), "The Achy Breaky Hearts" (2016), "Birdshot" (2016), "Moonlight Over Baler" (2016), "Lola Igna" (2019), the Irish psychological thriller "Nocebo" (2022) starring Eva Green and Mark Strong, and the horror film "Ang Mga Kaibigan Ni Mama Susan" (2023) as Mama Susan. Ferro appeared on television in productions of "Darating Ang Umaga" (2003), "Daisy Siete" (2005), "Amaya" as Hilway from 2011 to 2012, "Hiram No Puso" (2012), "Forever" (2013), "Luv U" (2015), "Magpakailanman" (2016), "Someone to Watch Over Me" (2016), and "Kambal, Karibal" as Edith in 2017.

Fiddler, Amp

Keyboardist and singer Joseph 'Amp' Fiddler, who performed with George Clinton's Parliament and Funkadelic groups, died of cancer in Detroit, Michigan, on December 18,

2023. He was 65. Fiddler was born in Detroit on May 17, 1958. He studied music in high school and continued his education at Wayne County Community College and Oakland University. He began singing with the R&B group Enchantment in the early 1980s and was heard on their final album, "Utopia", in 1983. He joined George Clinton's Parliament-Funkadelic bands in 1985. He continued to be a part of P-Funk through 1996. He and his brother, Thomas 'Bubz' Fiddler, formed the duo Mr. Fiddler in 1991 and recorded the album "With Respect". Fiddler's other albums include "Waltz of a Ghetto Fly (2004), "Afro Strut" (2006), "Inspiration Information" (2008), "Motor City Booty" (2016), "Kindred Live" (2017) with Will Sessions, "Amp Dog Knights" (2017), "The One" (2018), and "Basementality" (2021). Fiddler was instrumental in furthering the career of hip-hop producer J Dilla in the early 1990s. He is survived by his wife, Tombi Stewart, who he married earlier in 2023, and a son from a previous relationship.

Field, Shirley Anne

British actress Shirley Anne Field, who starred in the horror films "Horrors from the Black Museum" and "Peeping

Tom", died in England on December 10, 2023. She was 77. She was born Shirley Broomfield in Forest Gate, Essex, England, on June 27, 1936. She was abandoned as a child and raised in several children's homes.

She moved to London in her early teens where she became a photographic model. She was photographed for such pin-up magazines as "Reveille" and "Titbits". She began appearing in small roles in films in the mid-1950s including "Simon and Laura" (1955), "All for Mary" (1955), "Tears for Simon" (1956), "Yield to the Night" (1956), "It's Never Too Late" (1956), "It's a Wonderful World" (1956), "Loser Takes All" (1956), "The Weapon" (1956), "The Silken Affair" (1956), "Dry Rot" (1956), "The Good Companions" (1957), "The Flesh Is Weak" (1957), "The Beasts of Marseilles" (1957), "Upstairs and Downstairs" (1959), "Once More, with Feeling!" (1960), "And the Same to You" (1960), "Man in the Moon" (1960) with Kenneth More, "Jungle Street Girls" (1960), and "Wild for Kicks" (1960). Field starred as Angela Banks, the ill-fated girlfriend of mind-controlled Rick, played by Graham Curnow, who stabs her to death at a carnival's Tunnel of Love, on the orders of Michael Gough's homicidal Edmond Bancroft in 1959's "Horrors of the Black Museum". She was featured in the 1960 psychological horror film "Peeping Tom". Field starred as model Tina Lapford opposite Laurence Olivier in Tony Richardson's "The Entertainer" (1960) and was Doreen, the girlfriend of Albert Finney's Arthur Seaton in "Saturday Night and Sunday Morning" (1960). She starred with Steve McQueen in the 1962 World War II drama "The War Lover" and was Joan in the 1962 Hammer science fiction film "The Damned" (aka "These Are the Damned") with Macdonald Carey and Oliver Reed. Field was the Princess Ixchel in J. Lee Thompson's Mayan epic "Kings of the Sun" (1963) with Yul Brynner and George Chakiris. Her films also include "Lunch Hour" (1963), "The Wedding March" (1966), "Carnaby, M.D." (aka "Doctor in Clover") (1966), "Alfie" (1966) starring Michael Caine, "Hell Is Empty" (1967), "With Love in Mind" (1970), "A Touch of the Other" (1970), and the horror film "House of the Living Dead" (1974). She appeared more frequently in character roles by the 1980s with such credits as "My Beautiful Launderette" (1985), "Shag" (1988), "Getting It Right" (1989), "The Rachel Papers" (1989), "Hear My Song" (1991), the science fiction comedy "U.F.O." (1993) as the Supreme Commander, "At Risk" (1994), "Loving Deadly" (1994), the animated "A Monkey's Tale" (1999) as the voice of the Governess, "Christie Malry's Own Double-Entry" (2000), "The Kid" (2010), and "The Power of Three" (2011). She was seen frequently on television with roles in episodes of "The New Adventures of Martin Kane", "International Detective", "Five More", "Centre Play", "Shoestring", "Buccaneer" as Janet Blair in 1980, "Never the Twain", the soap opera "Santa Barbara" as Pamela Capwell Conrad in 1987, "El C.I.D.", "Murder, She Wrote", "Rumble", "Bramwell", "Barbara", "Madson" as Elaine Dews in 1996,

"Dalziel and Pascoe", "The Bill", "Where the Heart Is" as Linda in 2001, "Waking the Dead", "Monarch of the Glen", "Last of the Summer Wine", and "Doctors". Her other television credits include productions of "Two by Forsyth" (1984), "Anna Lee: Headcase" (1993), "Lady Chatterley" (1993), and "Taking Liberty" (1995). Her autobiography, "A Time for Love", was published in 1991. Field was married to race car driver Charles Crichton-Stuart from 1967 until their divorce in 1975, and is survived by their daughter, Nicola.

Fillieres, Sophie

French film director Sophie Fillieres died in France on July 13, 2023. She was 58. Fillieres was born in Paris, France,

on November 20, 1964. She attended La Femis film school, graduating in 1990. She directed her first short film, "Des Filles et des Chiens" ("Of Girls and Dogs") in 1991. She co-wrote such films as Xavier Beauvois' "Nord" (1991), Noemie Lvovsky's "Oubie-Moi" (1994), and Philippe Grandrieux's "Sombre" (1998). Fillieres helmed her debut feature, "Grande Petite", in 1994. She continued to direct such films as "Aie" (2000), "Gentille" (2005), "Pardn My French" (2009), "If You Don't, I Will" (2014), and "When Margaux Meets Margaux" (2018). She had recently completed filming of "Ma Vie Ma Gueule" at the time of her death. Fillieres appeared in several films including "Victoria" (2016), "Anatomy of a Fall" (2023), and "Super Drunk" (2023).

Finfer, David

Film editor David Finfer, who received an Oscar nomination for his work on the 1993 film "The Fugitive", died of a heart attack on April 3, 2023. He was 80. Finfer was born

in Brooklyn, New York, on June 7, 1942. He served in the U.S. Army before studying economics at Alfred University in New York. He worked as an agent with Creative Management Associates in New York before moving to Los Angeles. He studied film editing at the American Film Institute and edited the 1971 feature "You've Got to Walk It Like You Talk It or You'll Lose That Beat". Finfer worked on several films with director Albert Brooks including "Real Life" (1979), "Modern Romance" (1981), "Lost in America" (1985), and "Defending Your Life" (1991). He also edited the films "Defiance" (1980), "Soul Man" (1986), "Inside Out" (1986) also serving as second unit director, "Back to the Beach" (1987), "Warlock" (1989), "Heart Condition" (1990), "Bill & Ted's Bogus Journey" (1991), "Boxing Helena" (1993), "The Fugitive" (1993) sharing an

Academy Award nomination, "Exit to Eden" (1994), "Fair Game" (1995), "Romy and Michele's High School Reunion" (1997), "Kissing a Fool" (1998), "Simon Birch" (1998), "The Runner" (1999), "Snow Day" (2000), "Joe Somebody" (2001), "The Santa Clause 2" (2002), "Connie and Carla" (2004), "Waiting..." (2005), "The Last Time" (2006), "The Santa Clause 3: The Escape Clause" (2006), "Infestation" (2009), and "Tooth Fairy" (2010). Finfer is survived by his wife, Cinnia, and two children.

Finney, Shirley Jo

Actress and director Shirley Jo Finney died of cancer in Los Angeles, California, on October 10, 2023. She was 74. Finney was born in Meced, California, on July 14, 1949. She  attended the American Film Institute's Director Workshop for Women and earned a master's degree from the University of California at Los Angeles. She worked frequently on stage and directed numerous productions with the Fountain Theatre in Los Angeles. She also directed works at the Pasadena Playhouse, the Mark Taper Forum, the Goodman Theater in Chicago, the Kennedy Center for the Performing Arts in Washington, D.C., and the Crossroads Theatre Company in New Jersey. Finney was also an actress in films and television from the early 1970s. Her film credits include "Nashville Girl" (1976), "The River Niger" (1976), "Hey Good Lookin'" (1982) in a voice role, "Echo Park" (1985), "Nuts" (1987), "Moving" (1988), and "One Man Force". Finney was seen on television in episodes of "The New Temperatures Rising Show", "Police Woman", "Police Story", "The Blue Knight", "Snip", "Mork & Mindy", "Tenspeed and Brown Show", "Lou Grant", "Hill Street Blues" in the recurring role of Lynetta in 1985, "Amen", "Night Court", "CBS Schoolbreak Special", and "Where I Live". She starred as athlete Wilma Rudolph in the biographical tele-film "Wilma" in 1977. Her other television credits include the tele-films "Thornwell" (1981), "Uncle Tom's Cabin" (1987), and "Laker Girls" (1990). She directed several episodes of the comedy series "Moesha" in the late 1990s.

Fischer, Peter S.

Television writer Peter S. Fischer, who was co-creator  of the series "Murder, She Wrote", died at a care facility in Pacific Grove, California, on October 30, 2023. He was 88. Fischer was born on August 10, 1935. He graduated from Hofstra University in Hempstead, New York, in 1956. He worked at various jobs for over a decade before scripting the 1971 tele-film "The Last Child". He moved to

Los Angeles to further his career in screenwriting. He scripted episodes of such series as "Marcus Welby, M.D." "Owen Marshall, Counselor at Law", "Griff", "Kojak", "Baretta", and "McMillan & Wife", and the 1975 tele-film "A Cry for Help". He was a producer and writer for the series "Ellery Queen", "Richie Brockelman, Private Eye", "The Eddie Capra Mysteries", "Darkroom", "Blacke's Magic", "The Law and Harry McGraw", and "Columbo". Fischer also wrote and produced the tele-films and mini-series "Once an Eagle" (1976), "Charlie Cobb: Nice Night for a Hanging" (1977), "Black Beauty" (1978), and "Stranger at My Door" (1991). He scripted episodes of "Delvecchio", and "What Really Happened to the Class of '65?" and wrote the tele-films "The Case of the Biltmore Girls" (1978), "Donovan's Kid" (1979), "Hellinger's Law" (1981), "Tagget" (1991), "Coopersmith" (1992), and "Dead Man's Island" (1996). He was writer and executive producer for the 1995 film "Cops n Roberts". Fischer was co-creator of the hit mystery series "Murder, She Wrote" with Richard Levinson and Williams Link in 1984. He remained a writer and executive producer on the series starring Angela Lansbury as mystery writer and sleuth Jessica Fletcher through 1996. He was nominated for three Emmy Awards for his work on the series. He largely retired from television in the mid-1990s and began a series of novels, "The Hollywood Murder Mysteries", in 2010. The series includes "Jezebel in Blue Satin" (2010), "We Don't Need No Stinking Badges" (2011), "Love Has Nothing to Do with It" (2011), "Everybody Wants an Oscar" (2012), "The Unkindness of Strangers" (2012), "Nice Guys Finish Dead" (2013), "Pray for Us Sinners" (2013), "Has Anybody Here Seen Wyckham?" (2013), "Eyewitness to Murder" (2014), "A Deadly Shoot in Texas" (2016), "Everybody Let's Rock" (2016), "A Touch of Homicide" (2016), "Some Like Em Dead" (2016), "Dead Men Pay No Debts" (2016), "Apple Annie and the Dude" (2017), "Till Death Us Do Part" (2017), "Cue the Crows" (2017), "Murder Aboard the Highland Rose" (2018), "Ashes to Ashes" (2018), "The Case of the Shaggy Stalker" (2018), "Warner's Last Stand" (2018), and "The Man in the Raincoat" (2019). His other novels include "The Blood of Tyrants" (2009), 'The Terror of Tyrants" (2010), and "Expendable: A Tale of Love and War" (2015). He wrote the 2013 autobiography "Me and 'Murder, She Wrote'". Fischer was married to Lucille Warnock from 1957 until her death in 2017 and is survived by their three children.

Fisher, Guil

Actor Guil Fisher died at the Actors Fund Home in Englewood, New Jersey, on January 28, 2023. He was 93. Fisher was born in Philadelphia, Pennsylvania, on January 16, 1930. He attended the Philadelphia College of Art before moving to New York City. He studied acting under Sanford Meisner at the Neighborhood Playhouse. He worked in early television on such series as "Studio One", "Playhouse 90", "Lamp Unto My Feet", and "Omnibus". He performed frequently on stage from the late 1950s at such theaters as Palm Tree Playhouse in Sarasota, Florida, Bucks County Playhouse in Pennsylvania, Pasadena Playhouse and Pancake Playhouse in California, and Weathervane Theatre in New Hampshire. He

began his own theater company, Group Theatre East, in Philadelphia. Fisher also served as an actor and director for numerous local dinner theaters. He appeared in a handful of films including "Mystic Nights and Pirate Fights" (1998), "The Ding Light" (2006), and "100 Years of Evil" (2010). He was also featured in several short films including "Heavy Soul" (2005), "South of No North" (2009), "The Return Address" (2010), "The Hobo Menace" (2011) as the narrator, and "Tourists" (2015). Fisher was seen on television in the 1986 tele-films "George Washington II: The Forging of a Nation" and an episode of "Law & Order: Special Victims Unit" in 2010.

Fitzgerald, Nuala

Irish-Canadian actress Nuala Fitzgerald, who was featured in the 1979 horror film "The Brood", died in Toronto, Ontario, Canada, on July 31, 2023. She was 87. She was born Nuala Cassidy in Dublin, Ireland, on September 16, 1935. She

worked as a model in Dublin after graduating high school. She moved to Halifax, Canada, with her new husband, Royal Canadian Navy officer Michael Penrose-Fitzgerald, in 1954. She became involved in the children's television program "Randy Dandy" in Halifax, playing the Magic Lady. She and her husband separated, and she moved to Toronto, where she continued her acting career on stage. Fitzgerald was seen frequently on television with roles in episodes of "Festival", "The Wayne and Shuster Hour", "The Forest Rangers", "Paul Bernard, Psychiatrist", "Police Surgeon" as Nurse Louise Wynn from 1971 to 1972, "To See Ourselves", "The Starlost", "The Naked Mind", "High Hopes", "Mariah", and "Adderly. She appeared in the tele-films "Reckless Disregard" (1985) and "The Piano Man's Daughter" (2003), and the 1987 mini-series "Anne of Avonlea" as Mrs. Pringle. She was seen in the films "The Last Act of Martin Weston" (1970), "Deadly Harvest" (1977), "The Silent Partner" (1978), David Cronenberg's horror film "The Brood" (1979) as Juliana Kelly, the ill-fated mother of Samantha Eggar's character, "Obsession" (1981), "A Choice of Two" (1981), "Seeds of Doubt" (2998), the short "Tunnel" (2009), and "He Never Died" (2015). She continued to perform on stage, appearing with the Shaw Festival in Niagara-on-the-Lake and at venues throughout Canada. She and actor Larry Solway met while both were panelists on the quiz show "What's My Line?". They later opened the Marigold Dinner Theatre in Whitby and the two frequently starred together in productions there in the 1970s. She married Michael Penrose-Fitzgerald in 1954 and they had two sons, Brian and Timothy, before their divorce. Fitzgerald

married advertising executive Edgar Cowan in 1966 and is survived by him. Their son, producer Noah Cowan, died of brain cancer earlier in 2023.

Fitzhugh, Ellen

Lyricist Ellen Fitzhugh died on July 16, 2023. She was 81. Fitzhugh was born in Los Angeles, California, on July 5,

1942. She worked on numerous stage musicals writing lyrics for productions of "Paradise Found", "Johann Strauss", "Herringbone", "Big Blonde", "Paper Moon", "Muscle", "Diamonds", and "Los Otros". She shared a Tony Award nomination for Best Original Score for the 1985 Broadway musical "Grind". Fitzhugh wrote the lyrics for the MGM film musical "That's Dancing!" (1985). She also contributed song lyrics to the animated films "The Great Mouse Detective" (1986) also performing a voice role, and "The Brave Little Toaster to the Rescue" (1997).

Flynn, James

Irish television and film producer James Flynn, who was noted for such series as "The Tudors" and "Penny Dreadful", died in Dublin, Ireland, on February 11, 2023. He was 57. Flynn was born in Kilmacud, Ireland, on August 21, 1965. He began working in films as head of development of John Boorman's Merlin Films International. He was business

manager of the Irish Film board from 1993 to 1997. He founded Metropolitan Film Productions Limited in 1997 and Octagon Films in 2002. Flynn was producer of such films as "The General" (1998), "Sweety Barrett"(1998), "Sunset Heights" (1999), "Mal" (1999), "Angela's Ashes" (1999), "Nora"(2000), "An Everlasting Piece" (2000), "H3" (2001), "Not Afraid, Not Afraid" (2001), "The Count of Monte Cristo" (2002), "Reign of Fire" (2002), the short "What Miro Saw" (2002), "Veronica Guerin" (2003), "Cowboys & Angels" (2003), "Ella Enchanted" (2004), "King Arthur" (2004), "Rory O'Shea Was Here" (2004), "Tristan + Isolde" (2006), "The Front Line" (2006), "Becoming Jane" (2007), "Mister Lonely" (2007), "32A" (2007), "P.S. I Love You" (2007), the short "The Door" (2008) sharing an Academy Award nomination, "Dorothy Mills" (2008), the Oscar-nominated animated film "The Secret of Kells" (2009), "Cherrybomb" (2009), "A Shine of Rainbows" (2009), "Ondine" (2009), "Leap Year" (2010), "As If I Am Not There" (2010), "Asterix and Obelix: God Save Britannia" (2012), "Cavalry" (20140, "Love, Rosie" (2014), "Tomato Red: Blood Money" (2017), the short "Unforgotten"(2017), "Greta" (2018), Ridley Scott's "The Last Duel" (2021), the Oscar-nominated

"The Banshees of Inisherin" (2022), "Disenchanted"(2022), and "Silver and the Book of Dreams" (2023). Flynn produced numerous television productions including "Her Own Rules" (1998), "A Secret Affair" (1999), "St. Patrick: The Irish Legend" (2000), "Yesterday's Children" (2000), "Bobbie's Girl" (2002), "The Roman Spring of Mrs. Stone" (2003), "The Return" (2003), "Whatever Love Means" (2005), "Kitchen" (2007), "Northanger Abbey" (2007), "My Boy Jack" (2007), "Father & Son" (2009), "Ice Cream Girls" (2013), "Life of Crimc" (2013), "Cecilia Ahern: Ein Moment furs Lben" (2018), "Inspektor Jury: Der Tod des Harlekins" (2018), "Cecelia Ahern: Dich zu Lieben" (2018), "Redemption" (2022), and "Redemption" (2022). He was also producer for the television series "Mystic Nights of Tir Na Nog", "Raw", "The Tudors", "Camelot", "Foyle's War", "The Borgias", "Reign", "Love/Hate", "Clean Break", "Penny Dreadful", "Into the Badlands", "Vikings", "Moonhaven", "Kin", "Harry Wild", and "Vikings: Valhalla". Flynn is survived by his wife and business partner, Juanita Wilson, and two children.

Flynn, Michael

Science fiction writer Michael Flynn died at his home in Easton, Pennsylvania, on September 30, 2023. He was 75. Flynn was born in Easton on December 20, 1947. He graduated

from La Salle University in Easton and earned a master's degree in topology from Marquette University in Milwaukee, Wisconsin. He worked with Coors container Corporation and Stat-A-Matrix/Oriel as an industrial quality engineer and statistician before becoming an author. He was noted for writing hard science fiction stories for "Analog" magazine in the late 1980s. He received Hugo Award nominations for his novellas and novelettes "Eifelheim" (1987), "The Forest of Time" (1998), "Melodies of the Heart" (1995), "The Clapping Hands of God" (2005), "Dawn, and Sunset, and the Colours of the Earth" (2007), and "The Journeyman: In the Stone House" (2015). Much of his short fiction was published in the collections "The Nonotech Chronicles" (1991), "The Forest of Time and Other Stories" (1997), and "Captive Dreams" (2013). Flynn was author of the novels "In the Country of the Blind" (1990), "Fallen Angels" (1991) with Larry Niven and Jerry Pournelle, "The Wreck of the River of Stars" (2003), "Eifelheim" (2006) earning a Hugo nomination, and "In the Belly of the Whale" (2024). His "Firestar" series included the novels "Firestar" (1996), "Rogue Star" (1998), "Lodestar" (2000), and "Falling Stars" (2001). The related "Spiral Arm" series included "The January Dancer" (2008), "Up Jim River" (2010), "In the Lion's Mouth" (2012), and "On the Razor's Edge" (2013). Flynn was married to Margaret White from 1971 until her death in 2021 and is survived by their two children, Sara and Dennis.

Focas, Spiros

Greek actor Spiros died in Eleusis, Greece, on November 10, 2023. He was 86. He was born Spyridon Androutsopoulos in Patras, Greece, on August 17, 1937. He

made his film debut in the late 1950s starring in Andreas Labrinos' "Bloody Twilight" (aka "Matomeno Iliovasilemma") in 1959. He appeared in numerous Greek films over the next fifty years as well as productions in th United States and throughout Europe. His film credits include "Vacation in Kolopetinitsa" (1959), "Lyngos the Archbandit" (1959), "Messalina" (1960), "Morte di un Amico" (1960), Luchino Visconti's "Rocco and His Brothers" (1960), "Via Margutta" (1960), "Psycocissimo" (1961), "Apolytrosis" (1961), "Eighteen in the Sun" (1962), "A Man for Burning" (1962), "Egoismos" (1964), "Devil at My Heels" (1966), "The Fear" (1966), "Stefania" (1966), "Queen of Clubs" (1966), "Love on the Scorching Sand" (1966), "The Steps" (1966), "Psomi Gia ena Drapeti" (1967), "Odia il Prossimo Tuo" (1968), "Brosta Stin Aghoni" (1968), "Ekeinoi Pou Xeroun n' Agapoun" (1968), "I Zoi Enos Anthropou" (1968), "Zorro in the Court of England" (1969) as Zorro, "Corbari" (1970), "Basta Guardarla" (1970), "L'Amante dell'Orsa Maggiore" (1971), "Lui per Lei" (1972), "Baciamo le Mani" (1973), "Shaft in Africa" (1973) starring Richard Roundtree, the Italian-French exploitation film "Flavia, the Heretic" (1974), "Mark il Poliziotto Spara per Primo" (1975), Vincente Minnelli's musical fantasy "A Matter of Time" (1976), the horror film "Holocaust 2000" (aka "The Chosen") (1977) starring Kirk Douglas, "Souvliste Tous! Etsi tha Paroume to Kouradokastro" (1981), "Oi Tyhodiohtes" (1981), "Anametrisi" (1982), "I Parexigisi" (1983), "Fout Bol" (1985), "The Jewel of the Nile" (1985) starring Michael Douglas and Kathleen Turner, "Black Tunnel" (1986), "Rambo III" (1988) starring Sylvester Stallone, "The Serpent of Death" (1989), "Tre Colonne in Cronaca" (1990), "White Palace" (1990), "To Pethameno Liker" (1992), "Drapetis Tou Feggariou" (1994), "Biznes Sta Valkania" (1996), "Sonia" (1997), "Hill 33" (1998), "Vitsia Gynaikon" (2000), "Alexander and Aishe" (2001), "Sti Skia Tou Lemmy Kosion" (2002), "L'Ospite Segreto" (2003), "Death on the Prowl" (2003), "Min Pernas, Anavei Kokkino" (2003), "448 BC: Olympiad of Ancient Hellas" (2004), "A Simple Love Story" (2007), "Wild Night" (2009), "The Will of Father Jean Meslier" (2009), "Bring Them Back" (2010), "The First Line" (2014), "The Revenge of Dionysus" (2014), "To Mystiko" (2014), "Vakxes" (2014), "Raw Trip" (2016), "O Thisavros" (2017), "Outlanderss" (2019), and "Few Hours in Athens" (2019). Fokas appeared frequently on stage and was seen on television in productions of "Orlando Furioso" (1974), "Alle Origini della Mafia" (1976), "Mistress" (1987), "Errore Fatale" (1992), "Il Barone" (1995), and "Daiana, i Prigipissa Tou Laou" (1999). His other television credits include episodes of "O Oneiroparmenos", "Horis Anasa", "Ta Paidia Tou Zevedaiou",

"To Mythistorima Ton Tessaron", "Oi Klironomoi", "Il Ricatto", "Le Gorille", "Murder, She Wrote", "To Galazio Diamanti", "Happy Holiday", "Tolmires Istories", "Magiki Nyhta", "Anatomia Enos Eglimatos", "Elli Kai Anna", "Dipli Alitheia", "Nykterino Deltio", "Fili Zois", "Tis Agapis Mahairia" as Antonis Stamatakis from 2006 to 2007, and "Iatriko Aporitto" as Kimon Varnezis in 2008. Fokas married his fourth wife, actress Lilian Panagiotopoulou, in 2013 and is survived by her and his stepdaughter.

Forrest, Donald

Actor Donald Forrest died at his home in Humboldt County, California, on October 24, 2023. He was 74. Forrest was born in Detroit, Michigan, on June 18, 1950. He became

involved in theater while attending Eastern Michigan University. He performed on the stage in Boston and New York an became interested in the circus arts of acrobatics, clowning, and juggling. He moved to San Francisco in the early 1970s where he created the juggling group the Bay City Reds and the Pickle Family Circus. He joined the San Francisco Mime Troupe and moved to Humboldt County in 1978 to work with the Dell'Arte Company. He starred in numerous plays with Dell'Arte including "Whiteman Meets Bigfoot" (1980), the "Scar Tissue Mysteries" (1979-1991), "Performance Anxiety" (1981), "Malpractice" (1984), "Slapstick" (1989), the "Korbel Chronicles" (1993-2008) and "Mad Love" (1997). He also performed in regional theaters around the world. He was a theater and acrobatics teacher for the California State Summer School for the Arts at the CalArts campus in Santa Clarita for many years. He was featured in several films during his career including "Outbreak" (1995), "Remote Control Grandpa" (2008), and "A River of Skulls" (2010). Forrest was married to Nancy Stephenson from 1989 until their divorce in 2002 and is survived by the son, James, and his stepdaughter, Amelia. He is also survived by his companion, Alison Murray, who he met in 2014.

Forrest, Frederic

Actor Frederic Forrest, who received an Academy Award nomination for his role in the 1979 film "The Rose", died at his home in Santa Monica, California, on June 23, 2023. He was 86. Forrest was born in Waxahachie, Texas, on December 23, 1936. He attended Texas Christian University and trained as an actor under Sanford Meisner in New York city. He began performing on stage in the 1960s and appeared in an off-Broadway production of "Viet Rock" in 1966. He appeared in the low

budget films "The Filthy Five" (1968), a largely lost feature directed by Andy Milligan, and "Futz!" (1969), an adaptation of Tom O'Horgan's play. He appeared in the off-Broadway play "Silhouettes" in 1969 and accompanied the production to Los Angeles. He worked at a pizzeria while trying to break into films and attended classes at Actors Studio West. Forrest was featured in "When the Legends Die" (1972), "The Don Is Dead" (1973), Francis Ford Coppola's "The Conversation" (1974) as Mark, whose relationship with Cindy Williams' character is the subject of Gene Hackman's surveillance, "The Dion Brothers" (1974), "The Executioner" (1985), the off-beat western "The Missouri Breaks" (1976), Larry Cohen's horror sequel "It Lives Again" (1978), Coppola's Vietnam War epic "Apocalypse Now" (1979) as Jay 'Chef' Hicks, the river patrol boat engineman who is ambushed and beheaded by followers of Marlon Brando's Colonel Kurtz, the musical drama "The Rose" (1979) earning an Oscar nomination for his supporting role as Dyer, "One from the Heart" (1981), "Hammett" (1982) as mystery writer Dashiell Hammett, "Valley Girl" (1988), "The Stone Boy" (1984), "Return" (1985), "Where Are the Children?" (1986), "Stacking" (1987), "Tucker: The Man and His Dream" (1988), "Valentino Returns (1989), "Cat Chaser" (1989), "Music Box" (1989), "The Two Jakes" (1990), "Rain Without Thunder" (1992), "Double Obsession" (1992), "Twin Sisters" (1992), "Falling Down" (1993) as the racist Army surplus store owner who is dispatched by Michael Douglas' character, Dario Argento's horror film "Trauma" (1993), "Hidden Fears" (1993), "Chasers" (1994), "Lassie" (1994), "One Night Stand" (1995), "Crash Dive" (1996), "The Brave" (1997), "The End of Violence" (1997), "One of Our Own" (1997), "Boogie Boy" (1998), "Point Blank" (1998), "Whatever" (1998), "Black Thunder" (1998), "The First 9 1/2 Weeks" (1998), "Implicated" (1998), "Shadow Hours" (2000), "A Piece of Eden" (2000), "The Spreading Ground" (2000), "Militia" (2000), "The House Next Door" (2002), "The Quality of Light", and "All the King's Men" (2006) as the father of Sean Penn's Willie Stark. Forrest appeared on television in episodes of "Dark Shadows", "N.Y.P.D.", "Sweepstakes", "Mrs. Columbo", "21 Jump Street" as Captain Richard Jenko in 1987, "Die Kinder" as Lomax in 1990, "The Young Riders", and "Murphy Brown". He was also seen in television productions of "Larry" (1974), "Promise Him Anything" (1975), "Ruby and Oswald" (1978) as Lee Harvey Oswald, "Survival of Dana" (1979), "Who Will Love My Children?" (1983), "Saigon Year of the Cat" (1983), "The Parade" (1984), "calamity Jane" (1984) as Wild Bill Hickok, "Best Kept Secrets" (1984), "Quo Vadis?" (1985) as Petronius, "Right to Kill?" (1984), "Adventures of Huckleberry Finn" (1986) as Pap Finn, "The Deliberate Stranger" (1986), "Little Girl Lost" (1988), "Beryl Markham: A Shadow on the Sun" (1988), "Gotham" (1988), "Lonesome Dove" (1989) as Blue Duck, "Margaret Bourke-White" (1989) as Erskine Caldwell, "I Know My First Name Is Steven" (1989), "Citizen Cohn" (1992) as Dashiell Hammett, "The Habitation of Dragons" (1992), "Precious Victims" (1993), "Against the Wall" (1994), "Double Jeopardy" (1996), "Andersonville" (1996), "Alone" (1997), "Sweetwater" (1999), "Shadow Lake" (1999), and "Path to War" (2002) as General Earle G. Wheeler.

Forrest was married to Nancy Whitaker from 1960 until their divorce in 1963 and to actress Marilu Henner from 1980 until their divorce in 1983. He married British model and photographer Nina Dean in 1985, who was later diagnosed with paranoid schizophrenia before her suicide in 2003.

Forrest-Webb, Robert

British novelist Robert Forrest-Webb died at a hospital in Hereford, England, on April 23, 2023. He was 94. Forrest-Webb was born in Nottingham, England, on April 9, 1929. He

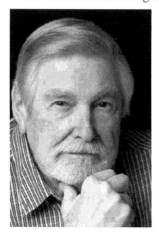

worked as a newspaper journalist and magazine editor. He and fellow journalist David Eliades wrote several books together in the late 1960s and early 1970s. They include "And to My Nephew Albert I Leave the Island What I Won Off Fatty Hagan in a Poker Game" (1969), "The Great Dinosaur Robbery" (1970) which was adapted for the 1975 Disney film "One of Our Dinosaurs Is Missing", "After Me, the Deluge" (1972) which became the Italian stage musical "Aggiungi un Posto a Tavola" and was known as "Beyond the Rainbow" for its English version, and the short-story collection "The Undertaker's Dozen" (1974). He wrote novels under various pseudonyms including "Brannigan's Leopard", "The Snowboys", "The Caviar Cruise", "The Sealing", "Chieftains", "Go for It", and "Circle of Raw" as Forrest Webb. He wrote the adventure series "Pendragon" series under the name Robert Trevelyan that included "Pendragon: Late of Prince Albert's Own", "His Highness Commands Pendragon", "Pendragon... The Montenegran Plot", and "Pendragon... Seeds of Mutiny". He took the female pseudonym Roberta Forrest to write the romance novels", "The Loshai Girl" and "When the Apricots Bloom".

Forster, Nora

German-British music promoter Nora Forster died of complications from Alzheimer's disease on April 6, 2023. She

was 80. She was born Nora Maier in Munich, Germany, on November 6, 1942. Her father owned a media company and was editor of the newspaper "Der Tagesspiegel". She went to work at her father's company after finishing school. Nora inherited much of his estate after his death. She began working as a music promoter in Munich before moving to London in the late 1960s. Her home became a meeting place for rock and punk musicians including Jimi Hendrix, Jon Anderson of Yes, and Joe Strummer of the Clash. She promoted and financially assisted the punk bands the Slits,

the Sex Pistols, and the Clash. Nora married John Lydon, the lead singer of the Sex Pistols, in 1979. She had a daughter from a previous marriage to West German singer Frank Forster. The daughter, Ariane, took the stage name of Ari Up as lead singer of the Slits until her death from breast cancer in 2010. She is survived by her husband, John Lydon.

Forsyth, Brigit

Scottish actress Brigit Forsyth, who was noted for her role as Thelma Ferris in the BBC comedy series "Whatever

Happened to the Likely Lads?", died in Great Britain on December 1, 2023. She was 83. Forsyth was born in Edinburgh, Scotland, on July 28, 1940. She worked as a secretary before training at the Royal Academy of Dramatic Art. She appeared frequently on television from the mid-1960s with roles in episodes of "R3", "The Wednesday Play", "Out of Town Theatre", "Doctor Who" as Ruth Maxtible in the 1967 serial "The Evil of the Daleks", "Boy Meets Girl", "Dr. Finlay's Casebook", "The Spanish Farm", "Thirty-Minute Theatre", "Love Story", "Who-Dun-It", ""Detective", "The Sinners", "Adam Smith" as Annie Smith in 1972, "Holly" as Holly Elliot in 1972, "Whatever Happened to the Likely Lads?" as Thelma Ferris from 1973 to 1974, "The Master of Ballantrae" as Alison Graeme in 1975, "Leave It to Charlie", "Graham's Gang", "Jackanory", "Can We Get on Now, Please?", "BBC2 Playhouse", "The Glamour Girls" as Veronica Haslett from 1980 to 1982, "Holding the Fort", "The Two Ronnies", "Tom, Dick and Harriet" as Harriet Maddison from 1982 to 1983, "Sharon and Elsie" as Elsie Beecroft from 1984 to 1985, "The Practice" as Dr. Judith Vincent from 1985 to 1986, "Cross Wits", "Poirot", "Running Wild" as Jenny in 1989, "Boon" as Helen Yeldham in 1989, "Dark Season" as Miss Maitland in 1991, "Wycliffe", "Dangerfield", "Murder Most Horrid", "In Suspicious Circumstances", "Omnibus", "Children's Ward", "Spark" as Mrs. Wells in 1997, "Harry Enfield and Chums", "Coronation Street", "Playing the Field" as Francine Pratt from 1998 to 2002, "This Is Your Life", "The Bill", "The Eustace Bros.", "Casualty", "Down to Earth", "Emmerdale", "Heartbeat", "The Street", "Jinx", "Waterloo Road", "The Alan Titchmarsh Show", "The Royal Today", "Midsomer Murders", "Mount Pleasant", "Doctors", "EastEnders", "Hollyoaks" as Cressida in 2013, "Holby City", "Unforgotten", "Pointless Celebrities", and "Still Open All Hours" as Madge from 2013 to 2019. Her other television credits include productions of "Bazaar and Rummage" (1983), "Nice Town" (1992), "Waiting" (1995), "The Outsiders" (2006), and "Rovers" (2016). Forsyth appeared in several films including "The Night Digger" (1971), the film version of "The Likely Lads" (1986) reprising her role as Thelma Ferris, "Crystalstone" (1987), and the short "Time & Again" (2019). She performed on radio in productions of "Sense and Sensibility" in 2013 and "Ed

Reardon's Week" in the recurring role of Pearl. Her stage credits include the plays "The Cello and the Nightingale" (2004), "Calendar Girls" (2008), "People" (2013), and "Now This Is Not the End" (2015). Forsythe was married to television director Brian Mills from 1975 until his death in 2006, though they separated in 1999. She is survived by their children, Zoe and Ben Mills.

Foskett, Jeffrey

Guitarist and music producer Jeffrey Foskett, who worked frequently with the Beach Boys, died of thyroid cancer on December 11, 2023. He was 67. Foskett was born in San

Jose, California, on February 17, 1956. He was the founder of the band Cherry in the 1970s. He formed the bands the Reverie Rhythm Rockers and the Pranks later in the decade while attending the University of California at Santa Barbara. He and Reverie were hired by singer Mike Love to tour with him in 1979 and became known as the Endless Summer Beach Band. Foskett replaced Carl Wilson in the Beach Boys in December of 1981 and remained with the band to perform falsetto parts after Wilson's return in May of 1982. He served as musical director for Brian Wilson during his tours in the late 1990s. He provided lead vocals on such Wilson songs as "Don't Worry Baby" and "Wouldn't It Be Nice". He joined the Beach Boys' live band for their 50th Anniversary Reunion Tour in 2012 and performed with them for the album "That's Why God Made the Radio". He subsequently resumed touring with Wilson and became a member of the Beach Boys touring band in May of 2014. He also performed on several of Mike Love's solo albums. Foskett recorded numerous solo albums including "Thru My Window" (1996), "Christmas at the Beach" (1997), "Cool and Gone" (1997), "Twelve and Twelve" (1998), "Love Songs" (2019), and "Voices" (2019). He left the Beach Boys in 2019 to have throat surgery and announced that he had been diagnosed with thyroid cancer.

Foster, Charles

British actor and television announcer Charles Foster died in England on February 27, 2023. He was 86. Foster was

born in the Wirral in North West England in 1936. He was featured in the 1977 tele-film "The Fighting Men" and was the ring announcer in the 1978 film "Blood & Guts". Foster also appeared on television in episodes of "Crown Court", "Coronation Street", "Brookside", "The Courtroom" as the court clerk in 2004, and "Emmerdale" as Judge David Connolly in 2008. He served as an

announcer for Granada Television from the mid-1970s until the early 1990s. He was heard on such television gameshows as "Cluedo", "Busman's Holiday", "Connections", "Catchprase", "Jeopardy!", "The Krypton Factor", "Raise the Roof", and "Spellbound". He provided the voiceover for the "Judge Rinder" series from 2014 to 2020. Foster was married to actress Meg Johnson from 1981 until his death. She died several months later in July of 2023.

Fournier, Claude

Canadian film director Claude Fournier died of complications from a heart attack at a hospice facility in Montreal, Quebec, Canada, on March 16, 2023. He was 91.

Fournier was born in Waterloo, Quebec, on July 23, 1931. He worked in journalism before becoming a news cameraman at Radio-Canada. He became a writer and director with the National Film Board of Canada in 1957. He directed and often wrote such films, documentaries, and shorts as "Telesphore Legare, Garde-Peche" (1959), "France on a Pebble" (1960), "Alfred Desrochers, Poete" (1960), "La Lutte" (1961), "Calgary Stampede" (1965), "Le Dossier Nelligan" (1969), "Coeurs Neufs" (1969), "Two Women in Gold" (1970), "Les Chats Bottes" (1971), "Alien Thunder" (1974) starring Donald Sutherland, "The Apple, the Stem and the Seeds!" (1974), "Je Suis Loin de Toi Mignonne" (1976), "Pump It Up" (1978), "Les Chiens Chauds" (1980), "Bonheur d'Occasion" (1983), "Heads or Tails" (1997), "The Book of Eve" (2002), and "Je n'Aime Que Toi" (2004). Fournier directed such television productions as "The Living Camera: Mooney vs. Fowle" (1962), "Tales of the Klondike" (1981), "Les Tisserands du Pouvoir" (1988), "Les Tisserands du Pouvoir II: La Revolte" (1988), "Golden Fiddles" (1991), "Juliette Pomerleau" (1999), and "Felix Leclerc" (2005). He also directed episodes of "Valerie et l'Aventure" and "The New Avengers". Fournier's autobiography, "A Force de Vivre", was published in 2009.

Foust, Mitch

Fantasy artist Jerry 'Mitch' Foust died in Memphis,

Tennessee, on August 25, 2023. He was 59. Foust was born in Memphis on January 26, 1964. He graduated from the University of Memphis and worked for Champion Awards as a graphic designer. He drew fantasy and comic art while in college and was a co-founder of Black Tie Studios in the 1980s. He worked with writer Bill Bryer and fellow artist David Porch on "The Last

Generation" comic book in 1984. He worked for Adventure Comics from the late 1980s on the comics "The Adventurers", "Warriors", "Sinbad", and "Badaxe". Foust provided cover art for Adventure's "Planet of the Apes" franchise including 1990's "Ape City". His other comic works include "Fugitive" for Caliber Comics and "Merlin" for Malibu. His illustrations have appeared on book covers, role playing games, and t-shirts. He published an annual compilation of his work in Yearbooks from 2009. Foust is survived by his wife of 36 years, Kathy, and children Daniel and Katie.

Frangione, Nancy

Actress Nancy Frangione, who was featured as Cecile de Poulignac on the daytime soap opera "Another World" in the 1980s and early 1990s, died in Barnstable, Massachusetts, on  August 18, 2023. She was 70. Frangione was born in Barnstable on July 10, 1953. He began her career on television in the late 1970s starring as Tara Martin Brent on the soap opera "All My Children" from 1977 to 1979. She was best known for her role as the villainess Cecile de Poulignac on "Another World" from 1981 to 1984. She returned to the role several times in 1986, 1989, 1993, and 1995 to 1996. Frangione was also seen in episodes of the series "The Mike Douglas Show", "Buck Rogers in the 25th Century", "Match Game/Hollywood Squares Hour", "Matlock", "One Life to Live", "Highway to Heaven", and "The Nanny" in the recurring role of Cousin Marsha from 1993 to 1994. Her other television credits include the tele-films "Sharing Richard" (1988) and "In the Line of Duty: A Cop for the Killing" (1990). She largely retired from the screen in the mid-1990s. Frangione was married to her "Another World" co-star Christopher Rich from 1982 until their divorce in 1996 and is survived by their daughter, Mariel.

Franklin, Richard

British actor Richard Franklin, who was featured as Captain Mike Yates in the "Doctor Who" series from 1971 to 1974, died in Islington, London, England, on December 24,  2023. He was 87. Franklin was born in Marylebone, London, England, on January 15, 1936. He was educated at Westminster School and Christ Church, Oxford. He served with Queen Victoria's Rifles during National Service. He worked at the Hobson and Grey advertising agency for several years before training as an actor at the Royal Academy of Dramatic Art. He began his career on stage in repertory theatre with the Century Theatre. He performed with the Birmingham Rep, the Bristol Old Vic, and the Ipswich Regent Theatre where

he was also an associate director. Franklin was featured in such West End productions as "As You Like It", "Same Time, Next Year", "Macbeth", "The Rocky Horror Show', "The Spider's Web", "Romeo and Juliet", and "The Woman in Black". He was also a playwright who penned such plays as "The Trial of Johnny Bull", "Dr. Weird and the Amazing Box", "The Cage", "Shakespeare Was a Hunchback", "Poison", "Luck of the Draw", and "Shakespeare by Shaggers". He appeared frequently on television from the late 1960s with roles in episodes of "Dixon of Dock Green", "The Saint", "Crossroads", "The Doctors", "From a Bird's Eye View", "Pathfinders", "Blake's 7", "Doctor Who" as UNIT Captain Mike Yates with Jon Pertwee's Third Doctor from 1971 to 1974, "Emmerdale" as Denis Rigg from 1988 to 1989, "Harry", and "Heartbeat". His other television credits include productions of "Little Women" (1970), "The Borgias" (1981), "Waving to a Train" (1984), and "The Gambling Man" (1995). Franklin was featured in the films "The Fiction-Makers" (1968), "Feedback" (2004), "Chemical Wedding" (2008), "The First Day of Spring" (2009), "Twilight of the Gods" (2013), and "Rogue One: A Star Wars Story" (2016). He reprised his role as Mike Yates in later "Doctor Who" productions including the 1983 twentieth anniversary special "The Five Doctors" and "Dimensions in Time" for the thirtieth anniversary. He also worked on several "Doctor Who" audio plays for Big Finish Productions and was a guest on podcasts devoted to the franchise. Franklin was also a political activist and unsuccessful candidate for the British Parliament in the 1990s and 2000s. He was author of the 2003 book "Forest Wisdom: Radical Reform of Democracy and the Welfare State".

Fred la Marmotte

Groundhog Fred la Marmotte, who predicted the coming of spring, was found dead on Groundhog's Day near his  home in Val-d'estoir, Quebec, Canada, on February 2, 2023. The original Fred, Gros Fred, was the official weather predictor in Quebec from 2010 to 2017 and again in 2019. Fred la Marmotte took over from his father in 2020 as official rodent prognosticator. He was found dead when he was called upon to again look for his shadow in February of 2023. It was believed he had died during hibernation several months earlier. His son, Fred Jr., took his place for the 2024 Groundhog's Day event.

Fried, Gerald

Film and television composer Gerald Fried, who worked on such series as "Star Trek" and "Gilligan's Island", died of pneumonia in Bridgeport, Connecticut, on February 17, 2023. He was 95. Fired was born in New York City on February 13, 1928. He graduated from New York's High School of Music and Art in 1945 and studied oboe at the Juilliard School of Music. He was first oboe with the Dallas

148

Symphony, Pittsburgh Symphony, and New York's Little Orchestra from 1948 to 1956. He moved to Los Angeles the following year and played for the Los Angeles Philharmonic. He was a childhood friend of director Stanley Kubrick and scored his first short film, "Day of the Fight", in 1951. He continued to work with Kubrick, scoring his early features including "Fear and Desire" (1952), "Killer's Kiss" (1955), "The Killing" (1956), and "Paths of Glory" (1957). Fried was a prolific film composer with such credits as "The Vampire" (1957), "Bayou" (1957), "Trooper Hook" (1957), "Dino" (1957), "The Flame Barrier" (1958), "The Return of Dracula" (1958), Roger Corman's "Machine-Gun Kelly" (1958), "I bury the Living" (1958), "Curse of the Faceless Man" (1958), "The Cry Baby Killer" (1958), "Terror in a Texas Town" (1958), "The Lost Missile" (1958), "Timbuktu" (1958), "I Mobster" (1959), "High School Big Shot" (1959), "Cast a Long Shadow" (1959), "A Cold Wind in August" (1961), "Twenty Plus Two" (1961), "The Second Time Around" (1961), "The Cabinet of Caligari" (1962), "Story of a Rodeo Cowboy" (1963), "The Great Rights" (1963), "To the Moon and Beyond" (1964), "One Potato, Two Potato" (1964), "Deathwatch" (1965), "The Killing of Sister George" (1968), "What Ever Happened to Aunt Alice?" (1969), "Too Late the Hero" (1970), "The Enchanted Years" (1971), "The Grissom Gang" (1971), "The Baby" (1973), "Soylent Green" (1973), the documentary "Birds Do It, Bees Do It" (1974) earning an Academy Award nomination for the score, "The Legacy of L.S.B. Leakey" (1975), "Survive!" (1976), "Vigilante Force" (1976), "The Bell Jar" (1979), and "Unbelievable!!!" (2016). He composed music for numerous television series from the 1950s including "M Squad", "Wagon Train", "Schlitz Playhouse", "Johnny Midnight", "Riverboat", "Whispering Smith", "Shotgun Slade", "Breaking Point", "Ben Casey", "Rawhide", "Gunsmoke", "The Felony Squad", "Jericho", "The Man Who Never Was", "T.H.E. Cat", "My Three Sons", "It's About Time", "Gilligan's Island", "Mr. Terrific", "The Man from U.N.C.L.E.", "Dundee and the Culhane", "Star Trek" and was noted for the underscore "The Ritual/Ancient Battle/2nd Kroykah" from the 1967 episode "Amok Time", "Iron Horse", "Lost in Space", "Family Affair", "Mission: Impossible", "Mannix", "The Sixth Sense", "Medical Story", "Police Story", "Police Woman", "The Chisholms", "Emergency!", "Number 96", "Flamingo Road", "National Geographic Specials", "Casablanca", "Dynasty", "World of Discovery", and "Square One Television". He also scored television productions of "The Mouse That Roared" (1966), "Danger Has Two Faces" (1967), "Gauguin in Tahiti: The Search for Paradise" (1967), "California" (1968), "Once Before I Die" (1970), "I Will Fight No More Forever" (1975), "Francis Gary Powers: The True Story of the U-2 Spy Incident" (1976), "Roots" (1977) earning an Emmy Award and a second nomination, "The Spell" (1977), "Testimony of Two Men"

(1977), "Sex and the Married Woman" (1977), "Roots: One Year Later" (1978), "Cruise Into Terror" (1978), "Maneaters Are Loose!" (1978), "The Beasts Are on the Streets" (1978), "Rescue from Gilligan's Island" (1978), "The Immigrants" (1978), "The Incredible Journey of Doctor Meg Laurel" (1979), "Roots: The Next Generation" (1979), "The Castaways on Gilligan's Island" (1979), "Son-Rise: A Miracle of Love" (1979), "The Rebels" (1979), "Breaking Up Is Hard to Do" (1979), "Disaster on the Coastliner" (1979), "Hong Kong: A Family Portrait" (1979), "The Seekers" (1979), "The Ordeal of Dr. Mudd" (1980), "Gauguin the Savage" (1980), "The Silent Lovers" (1980) earning another Emmy nomination, "Condominium" (1980), "The Wild and the Free" (1980), "The Harlem Globetrotters on Gilligan's Island" (1981), "Murder Is Easy" (1982), "For Us the Living: The Medgar Evers Story" (1983) for "American Playhouse", "The Return of the Man from U.N.C.L.E.: The Fifteen Years Later Affair" (1983), "A Killer in the Family" (1983), "The Mystic Warrior" (1984) earning another Emmy nomination, "Embassy" (1985), "Napoleon and Josephine: A Love Story" (1987) receiving another Emmy nomination, "Drop-Out Mother" (1988), and "Roots: The Gift" (1988). Fried and his second wife, Anna Belle Kaufman, lost their 5-year-old son, Zachary, to AIDS contracted from tainted blood supplied by a blood bank in December of 1987. He wrote the screenplay "Morningtime Train" based on his experiences. Fried is survived by four children from his second wife, Judith Pine, and his fourth wife, Anita.

Friedkin, William

Film director William Friedkin, who was noted for the films "The French Connection" and "The Exorcist", died of heart failure and pneumonia at his home in Los Angeles, California, on August 7, 2023. He was 87. Friedkin was born

in Chicago, Illinois, on August 29, 1935. He became interested in films during his teens and graduated from high school in the early 1950s. He soon began working in the mail room at the Chicago television station WGN-TV. He directed documentaries and live television shows including the 1962 true crime documentary "The People vs. Paul Crump". He subsequently moved to Los Angeles where he made documentaries for David L. Wolper including "The Bold Men" (1965), "Pro Football: Mayhem on a Sunday Afternoon" (1965), and "The Thin Blue Line" (1966). He also helmed a 1965 episode of "The Alfred Hitchcock Hour" and the unsold comedy pilot "The Pickle Brothers" in 1967. Friedkin helmed his first feature film, the musical comedy "Good Times" starring Sonny and Cher, in 1965. His subsequent films include "The Birthday Party" (1968), the burlesque comedy "The Night They Raided Minsky's" (1968), and "The Boys in the Band" (1970). He scored a major hit with his next film, 1971's "The French Connection", about a pair of unorthodox cops on the trail of a

French heroin smuggler. Gene Hackman and Roy Scheider starred as Detectives Jimmy 'Popeye' Doyle and Buddy 'Cloudy' Russo, and Fernando Rey was the French drug smuggler, Alain Charnier. The film earned five Academy Awards including Best Picture and a Best Director nod for Friedkin. He directed the 1973 adaptation of William Peter Blatty's best-selling novel "The Exorcist", starring Ellen Burstyn, Max von Sydow, Jason Miller, and the young Linda Blair as a demon-possessed Regan MacNeil. Friedkin earned another Oscar nomination for his direction. He had less success with his 1977 thriller "Sorcerer", about a quartet of truck drivers transporting dangerous explosives through dangerous terrain in South America. The film, based on the source novel for the 1953 French classic "The Wages of Fear", initially failed commercially and critically but has been frequently considered a 1970s classic in later reassessments. His 1978 film, "The Brink's Job", was also a commercial disappointment. He helmed the 1980 controversial crime thriller, "Cruising", starring Al Pacino as a police officer going undercover to find a serial killer targeting gay men. Friedkin's career was sidelined in 1981 after a heart attack from a genetic defect. He returned to filmmaking with the 1983 satire "Deal of the Century" starring Chevy Chase. He directed the music video for Barbra Streisand's rendition of the song "Somewhere" from "West Side Story" in 1985. He continued to direct and frequently write such films as "To Live and Die in L.A." (1985) starring William Petersen and Willem Dafoe, the crime drama "Rampage" (1987), the supernatural horror film "The Guardian" (1990) starring Jenny Seagrove, the basketball film "Blue Chips" (1994) starring Nick Nolte and Shaquille O'Neal, and the 1995 erotic thriller "Jade" starring Linda Fiorentino and David Caruso. He returned to television in the 1980s with the tele-films "C.A.T. Squad" (1986), "C.A.T. Squad: Python Wolf" (1988), "Jailbreakers" (1994), and an adaptation of "12 Angry Men" (1997) earning an Emmy Award nomination, and episodes of "The Twilight Zone", "Tales from the Crypt", "Rebel Highway", and "CSI: Crime Scene Investigation". He was director of numerous opera productions for the Los Angeles Opera, Teatro Regio Torino, Bavarian State Opera, and Maggio Musicale Fiorentino Theatre from the late 1990s. A re-edited and expanded version of "The Exorcist" was released in 2000 and again proved a success. His later films include "Rules of Engagement" (2000), "The Hunted" (2003), and 2006's psychological horror film "Bug" starring Ashley Judd. His black comedy, "Killer Joe" (2011), was based in a play by Terry Letts. Friedkin directed the exorcism documentary "The Devil and Father Amorth" in 2017. He had recently completed a film adaptation of "The Caine Mutiny Court-Martial" which is scheduled for a posthumous release later in 2023. His memoir, "The Friedkin Connection", was published in 2013. He provided a voice role in a 2017 episode of the animated television series "The Simpsons". Friedkin was involved with interior designer Kitty Hawks, the daughter of director Howard Hawks, for two years in the early 1970s. He had a relationship with Australian dancer Jennifer Nairn-Smith from 1972 to 1976 and is survived by their son, Cedric Nairn-Smith. He was married to French actress Jeanne Moreau from 1977 until their divorce in 1979. He was married to British actress Lesley-Anne Down from 1982 until their divorce in 1985 and is survived by their son Jack Friedkin. Friedkin was married to journalist Kelly Lange from 1987 until their divorce in 1990. He married film executive Sherry Lansing in 1991 and she also survives him.

Friedman, Andrea Fay

Actress Andrea Fay Friedman, who suffered from Down syndrome, died of complications from Alzheimer's disease in Santa Monica, California, on December 3, 2023. She was 53. Friedman was born in California on June 1, 1970. She graduated from Santa Monica College in the early 1990s. She made her television debut as Amanda Swanson, the girlfriend of Chris Burke's Corky Thatcher, on the television series "Life Goes On" from 1992 to 1993. She continued to appear in episodes of such series as "Baywatch", "Touched by an Angel", "Chicago Hope", "Walker, Texas Ranger", "7th Heaven", "Law & Order: Special Victims Unit", "ER", "The Division", and "Saving Grace". Friedman also appeared in the 1997 tele-film "Smudge" and as a voice actress in an episode of the animated "Family Guy". She was featured in a small role in the 1999 film "One Bad Day" and co-starred as Carol Harris in the 2019 drama "Carol of the Bells". She worked in the accounting department of a California law firm for two decades. She was the subject of the 2009 documentary "A Possible Dream: The Andrea Friedman Story".

Fuentes, Miguel Angel

Mexican actor Miguel Angel Fuentes, whose imposing size made him an impressive character in films in Mexico and the United States, died in Mexico City on December 28, 2023.

He was 70. Fuentes was born in Tlacotepec, Mexico, on September 29, 1953. He appeared frequently in films and television from the mid-1970s. His numerous film credits include "Mexico, Mexico, Ra Ra Ra" (19176), "The Bermuda Triangle" (1978), "Divinas Palabras" (1978), "Los de Abajo" (1978), "Rarotonga" (1978), "Milagro en el Circo" (1979), "El Vuelo de la Ciguena" (1979), "Manaos" (1979), the Italian super hero film "The Pumaman" (1980) as Vadinho the Aztec, "Las Tentadoras" (1980), "Las Grades Aguas" (1980), the prehistoric comedy "Caveman" (1981) starring Ringo Starr, "Green Ice" (1981), "Santo in the Border of Terror" (1981), Werner Herzog's epic "Fitzcarraldo" (1982), "Sorceress" (1982), the western "Triumphs of a Man Called Horse" (1983) starring Richard Harris, "The Evil That Men Do" (1984) with Charles Bronson, "Siempre en Domingo" (1984), the horror comedy

"Frankenstein's Great Aunt Tillie" (1984) ass the Monster, "In 'n Out" (1984) "Mission Kill" (1985), "Masacre en el Rio Tula" (1985), "Enemigos a Muerte" (1985), "Amenaza Roja" (1985), "Secuestro Sangriento" (1985), "Miracles" (1986), "Separate Vacations" (1986), "La Venganza del Rojo" (1986), "Firewalker" (1986) with Chuck Norris, "El Secuestro de Lola" (1986), "Hot Pursuit" (1987), the fantasy "Deathstalker and the Warriors from Hell" (1988), "Mi Pistola y Tus Esposas" (1989), "A Grande Arte" (1991), "Cordicia Mortal" (1991), "Gunmen" (1993), "Un Baul Lleno di Miedo" (1997), "Mookie" (1998), "Herod's Law" (1999), the short "Cerebro" (2000), "The Mexican" (2001), "Glow" (2001), "Hugoool" (2004), "Cansada de Besar Sapos" (2005), "El Garabato" (2008), "Al Acecho del Leopardo" (2011), and "La 4a Compania" (2016). Fuentes appeared on television in productions of "On Wings of Eagles" (1986), "Oceans of Fire" (1986), "Mercenary II: Thick & Thin" (1998), and "Texas Rising" (2015). His other television credits include episodes of "Seduccion", "Auf Achse", "Carrusel", "Clarisa", "Nazca", "Marisol" as Pulga in 1996, "Esmeralda", "Complices al Rescate", "Amor Real", "Rubi", "Rebelde", "Stepmother", "Peregrina", El Pantera", "Adictos", "Persons Unknown:, "Una Familia Con Suerte", "With or Without You", "Por Ella Soy Eva", "La Mujer del Vendaval", "Como Dice el Dicho", "Yago", "El Senor de los Cielos", "Nosotros los Guapos", "Run Coyote Run", and "Julia vs. Julia".

Fuller, Barry

Actor Barry Fuller, who was active on the local stage in Memphis, Tennessee, for over sixty years, died in Memphis on December 27, 2023. He was 95. Fuller was born in Wagga

Wagga, Australia, in 1928, and was raised in Sydney, Australia. He came to the United States in 1952 and attended the University of Iowa. He worked for various newspapers as a composing room printer. He came to Memphis and began performing on the local stage in the late 1950s with roles in Front Street Theatre. He was noted for his performance as Ebenezeer Scrooge in "A Christmas Carol" at Theatre Memphis 11 times between 1978 and 2013. He was Herr Drosselmeyer for 11 years with the Ballet Memphis and sang in such operas as "Die Fledermaus" and "La Traviata". He was featured as Gus the Theatre Cat at Theatre Memphis' production of "Cats". He made his final stage appearance in the musical "Hello, Dolly!" in 2021. Fuller worked in the travel industry and was a passenger service manager with American Airlines.

Fullmer, Randy

Animator Randy Fullmer, who was noted for his work with Walt Disney Animation Studios, died of cancer in Woodland Hills, California, on July 10, 2023. He was 73. Fullmer was born in Richland, Washington, on April 27, 1950. He attended Washington State University from 1968 to 1970,

where he studied architecture. He changed his interests to animation and transferred to the California Institute of the Arts,

where he graduated in 1974. He began his own animation business, working on educational films and commercials. He joined Don Bluth Studios in 1983 where he helped create special effects for the Laserdisc video games "Dragon's Lair" and "Space Ace". He soon moved to John Dykstra's Apogee and Filmation. Fullmer was part of the special effects crew for the 1985 science fiction film "Lifeforce" and was an effect animator for "The Brave Little Toaster" (1987) and "Pinocchio and the Emperor of the Night" (1987). He also worked in animation for the television cartoon series "She-Ra: Princess of Power", "Ghostbusters", and "BraveStarr". He was hired by Walt Disney Feature Animation to help animate the 1988 film "Who Framed Roger Rabbit". He continued to work at Disney in animation and effects for such films as "Oliver & Company" (1888), "Happily Ever After" (1989), "The Little Mermaid" (1989), "The Rescuers Down Under" (1990), "Beauty and the Beast" (1991), "Aladdin" (1992), "The Lion King" (1994), "Pocahontas" (1995), "Toy Story" (1995), and "The Hunchback of Notre Dame" (1996). He was producer of the animated films "The Emperor's New Groove" (2000) and "Chicken Little" (2005). Fullmer began building guitars in his early teens and left Disney to form Wyn Guitars in 2006. He crafted musical instruments for many musicians and his work was the subject of the 2014 documentary film "Restrung". Fullmer married Diana Kuriyama in 2017 and is survived by her and two stepchildren.

Funk, Terry

Professional wrestler Terry Funk, whose fifty-year career in the ring brought him championships from most major promotions, died at a hospital in Phoenix, Arizona, on August

23, 2023. He was 79. Funk was born in Hammond, Indiana, on June 20, 1944. He was the son of wrestler and promoter Dory Funk and younger brother of wrestler Dory Funk, Jr. He was raised in Amarillo, Texas, and attended West Texas State University in Canyon, Texas. He began his wrestling career with his father's Western States Sports promotion in Amarillo in 1965. He competed against such wrestlers as Sputnik Monroe, Ernie Ladd, and Hank James. He frequently teamed with his brother Dory in the Amarillo area and with All Japan Pro Wrestling from the early 1970s. Terry defeated Jack Brisco for the NWA World Heavyweight Championship in Miami in December of 1975. He had a reign of over a year defeating such challengers as

Brisco, Dusty Rhodes, Carlos Rocha, and Giant Baba. He was defeated by Harley Race for the belt in Toronto, Canada, in February of 1977. He and brother Dory captured the NWA Georgia Tag Team Title in December of 1978 and Terry also won the NWA Southern Championship in Florida. He wrestled with the Continental Wrestling Association in Memphis in 1981 where he engaged in a vicious feud with Jerry Lawler. He briefly wrestled with the American Wrestling Association (AWA) before making his debut with the World Wrestling Federation (WWF/now WWE) in June of 1985. He feuded with the Junkyard Dog and partnered with brother Dory, under the name Hoss Funk, and Jesse Barr, who wrestled as "brother" Jimmy Jack Funk. They were managed by Jimmy Hart in the promotion. Terry had several unsuccessful title matches against champion Hulk Hogan before leaving the promotion in April of 1986. He entered World Championship Wrestling (WCW) in 1989 where he had a feud with champion Ric Flair. He also served as a color commentator for the promotion had hosted the "Funk's Grill" segment on "NWA Power Hour". He returned to the WCW in May of 1999 and joined Colonel Robert Parker's Stud Stable. He feuded with Dusty and Dustin Rhodes and the Nasty Boys before leaving the promotion again in October of 1994. He joined the International Wrestling Association of Japan later in the year where he became noted for his hardcore extreme wrestling matches. He feuded with Cactus Jack, who was later known as Mick Foley, in a "No Ropes Barbed Wire Exploding Barbed Wire Boards & Exploding Ring Time Bomb Death Match". He also battled in hardcore matches with Extreme Championship Wrestling (ECW) where he feuded with Cactus Jack, Shane Douglas, Sabu, the Sandman, and Tommy Dreamer. He defeated Raven for the ECW World Heavyweight Championship in April of 1997. He lost the title to Sabu in August of 1997 in a barbed wire match. He returned to the WWF in 1997 at the promotion's "Royal Rumble". He soon began teaming with Cactus Jack while masked under the name Chainsaw Charlie. They engaged in a feud with the New Age Outlaws. The duo won the WWF Tag Team Championship at Wrestlemania XIV in March of 1998. They held the belts only one day, losing a rematch to the New Age Outlaws. Funk soon began wrestling under his own persona and had short-lived teams with 2 Cold Scorpio and Justin Bradshaw (JBL). He wrestled with ECW from 1998 to 1999, feuding with Tommy Dreamer. He returned to WCW in 2000 and was named Commissioner of the promotion. He feuded with the New World Order's Kevin Nash and lost the commissioner position to him. He also feuded with Ric Flair and Dusty Rhodes and won the WCW Hardcore Championship in April of 2000. He soon lost the belt to Shane Douglas the following month but regained it in a rematch. He was defeated for the title by Eric Bischoff in June of 2000. Funk defeated Lance Storm for the WCW United States Heavyweight Championship in September of 2000 but lost a rematch the following day. He recaptured the Hardcore Championship in December of 2000 in a match against Crowbar and lost the title in January of 2001 to Meng. He wrestled on the independent circuit in the early 2000s, battling C.M. Punk in Ring of Honor. He made brief appearances with Total Nonstop Action (TNA)

and returned to the WWE for a short period in 2006. He and his brother Dory were inducted into the WWE Hall of Fame in 2009. He continued to wrestle on the independent circuit despite a handful of retirement announcements, battling the likes of Jerry Lawler, Roddy Piper, Eddie Kingston, and Tommy Dreamer. His autobiography, "Terry Funk: More Than Just Hardcore", was published in 2005. He released a biographical self-titled comic book through Squared Circle Comics in 2022. Funk had an active acting career from the late 1970s, appearing as Frankie the Thumper in the Sylvester Stallone film "Paradise Alley". He was a stuntman in Stallone's "Rambo III" (1988) and "Rocky V" (1990). Funk was also seen in the films "Over the Top" (1987), "Road House" (1989) as Morgan the bouncer, Fred Olen Ray's "Mom, Can I Keep Her?" (1998) and "Active Stealth" (1999), "Friday Night Lights" (2004), and "The Ringer" (2005). He was featured as Prometheus Jones in the short-lived western science fiction series "Wildside" in 1985. His other television credits include the tele-film "Timestalkers" (1987), and episodes of "Swamp Thing", "Quantum Leap", "Good & Evil", "Tequila and Bonetti", "The Adventures of Brisco County, Jr.", "Thunder in Paradise", and "Beyond Belief: Fact or Fiction". He appeared in various wrestling documentaries including 1999's "Beyond the Mat". Funk was married to Vicky Ann from 1965 until her death in 2019 and is survived by their two daughters.

Fury, Ed

Actor and bodybuilder Ed Fury, who starred in several Italian peblum films in the 1960s, died at his home in Woodland Hills, California, on February 24, 2023. He was 94. He was born Rupert Holovchick in Long Island, New York, on June 6,

1928. He moved to Los Angeles, California, in the late 1940s where he began competing in bodybuilding competitions. He placed third in the 1951 Mr. Muscle Beach competition and was second in 1953. He also worked as a physique model for photographers Bob Mizer and Bruce Bellas and posed for the Athletic Model Guild and covers of "Muscles" magazine. He appeared in small roles in films from the early 1950s including "All Ashore" (1953), "Abbott and Costello Go to Mars" (1953), "Dangerous When Wet" (1953), "Gentlemen Prefer Blondes" (1953), "Island in the Sky" (1953), "The Actress" (1953), "The Eddie Cantor Story" (1953), "The Great Diamond Robbery" (1954), "Hell and High Water" (1954), "The Student Prince" (1954), "Demetrius and the Gladiators" (1954), "Athena" (1954), "The Country Girl" (1954), "Female on the Beach" (1955), "I Died a Thousand Times" (1955), "Raw Edge" (1956), "Bus Stop" (1956), "South Pacific" (1958), and the prehistoric adventure "The Wild Women of Wongo" (1959) as Gahbo. Fury went to Italy in the early 1960s to star in a handful of sword and sandal, or peblum, films including "Colossus and the Amazon Queen" (1960), "Ursus" (1961) in the title role, "The

Seven Revenges" (1961), "Ursus in the Valley of the Lions" (1961), "Maciste Against the Sheik" (1962), and "Ursus in the Land of Fire" (1963). Fury was seen on television in episodes of "My Little Margie", "Naked City", "Gilligan's Island", "Star Trek" in the uncredited role of a Yang drummer in the 1968 episode "The Omega Glory", "Mission: Impossible", "The Doris Day Show", "The Odd Couple", "The F.B.I.", "Barnaby Jones", "Police Story", "The Little People", "Columbo", "The Magician", "Medical Center", "Cannon", "Shazam!", "Desperate Women", and "Fantasy Island". He also appeared in the tele-films "Letters from Three Lovers" (1973) and "Desperate Women" (1978). He largely retired from the screen by the late 1970s but returned to appear in Donald F. Glut's prehistoric comedy "Dinosaur Valley Girls" as Ur-So in 1996. Fury married Marceline Yvette 'Sheri' Dubois in 1959.

Gadhvi, Sanjay

Indian film director Sanjay Gadhvi died of a heart attack in Mumbai, India, on November 19, 2023. He was 57. Gadhvi was born in Mumbai on November 22, 1965. He was the son of prominent Gujarati folk artist Manubhai Gadhvi. Sanjay began working in films as an assistant director for Anant Balani's 1991 film "Patthar Ke Phool". He made his debut as a director with 2001's "Tere Liye". He also directed "Mere Yaar Ki Shaadi Hai" in 2002 which he also scripted. He was noted for directing the hit action films "Dhoom" (2004) and "Dhoom 2" (2006). His other films include "Kidnap" (2008), "Ajab Gazabb Love" (2012), and "Operation Parindey" (2020). Gadhvi was featured as Balvinder Tondon in the 2017 comedy film "Patel Ki Punjabi Shaadi".

Galati, Frank

Theatrical director and screenwriter Frank Galati, who earned an Oscar nomination for scripting the 1988 film "The Accidental Tourist", died of cancer in Sarasota, Florida, on January 2, 2023. He was 79. Galati was born in Highland Park,

Illinois, on November 29, 1943. He attended Western Illinois University for a year before transferring to Northwestern University, where he graduated in 1965. He earned a master's degree the following year and a Ph.D. in interpretation in 1971. He directed and performed in numerous campus plays during his time at Northwestern. He became a leading figure on the Chicago state, earning nine Joseph Jefferson Awards. He was associate director of the Goodman Theatre from 1986 to 2008 and a member of the Steppenwolf Theatre Company. Galati directed and adapted the 1990 Broadway play based on John Steinbeck's "The Grapes of Wrath", earning Tony Awards for Best Play and Best Direction. He also directed Broadway productions of "The Glass Menagerie" (1994), "Ragtime" (1998) receiving another Tony nomination, "Seussical" (2000), and "The Pirate Queen" (2007). He was co-writer with Lawrence Kasdan of the 1988 film version of Anne Tyler's novel, "The Accidental Tourist", sharing an Academy Award nomination and a BAFTA Award. His adaptation of "The Grapes of Wrath" was performed on television's "American Playhouse" in 1991. He also scripted the 1993 tele-film "The American Clock". Galati married his longtime partner Peter Amster in 2017 and he survives him.

Gallinowski, Robert

German actor Robert Gallinowski died in Berlin, Germany, on March 28, 2023. He was 53. Gallinowski was born in Aachen, Germany, on October 3, 1969. He trained as an actor at the Ernst Busch School of Dramatic Arts in Berlin and began his career on stage with the Bonn Theatre. He was a member of the Deutsches Schauspielhaus in Hamburg during the 1990s and joined Berlin's Deutsches Theater in 1999. Gallinowski was seen on television in productions of "Kissenschlacht" (1995), "Und Alles Wegen Mama" (1998), "Mutter Courage und ihre Kinder" (2003), "Hans Christian Andersen: My Life as a Fairy Tale" (2003), "Vater Undercover - Im Auftrag der Familie" (2006), "Mordgestandnis" (2008), "Carlos" (2010), "Westflug - Entfuhrung aus Liebe" (2010), "Tod Einer Brieftaube" (2012), "Der Weihnachtsmuffel" (2012), "Mord Nach Zahlen" (2013), "Bornholmer Strasse" (2014), "Naked Among Wolves" (2015), "Schwarzach 23 und die Jagd Nach dem Mordsfinger" (2016), "Arthurs Gesetz" (2018), and "Das Quartett" (2019). His numerous television credits also include episodes of "Balko", "Wolffs Revier", "Einmal Bulle, Immer Bulle", "SK Kolsch", "Bella Block", "KDD - Kriminaldauerdienst", "Doppelter Einsatz", "Commissario Laurenti", "Deadline - Jede Sekunde Zahlt", "Schimanski", "In the Name of the Law", "Kommissarin Lucas", "A Case for Two", "Flemming", "Grosstadtrevier", "Stolberg", "Wilsberg", "Der Dicke", "Unter Andern Umstanden", "Crime Stories", "The Old Fox", "SOKO Stuttgart", "Cologne P.D.", "Letzte Spur Berlin", "In Aller Freundschaft", "Donna Leon", "Police Call 110", "Der Bozen Krimi", "Never Too Late for Justice", "Alarm fur Cobra 11 - Die Autobahnpolizei", "Heidt", "Stralsund", "Der Kriminalist", "Jenny: Echt Gerecht", "You Are Wanted", "Dogs of Berlin", "Der Bulle und das Biest", "Tatort", "Ein Starkes Team", "Kleo", "Baltic Crimes", "Die Kanzlei" as Commissioner Ole Hansen from 2015 to 2022, "Love Addicts", and "Leipzig Homicide". Gallinowski also appeared in a handful of films including "Null Uhr 12" (2001), "Gate to Heaven" (2003), "Frei

Nach Plan" (2007), "Berlin '36" (2009), "Der Preis" (2011), "Ein Morderisches Geschaft" (2011), "Back for Good" (2017), "Blind & Ugly" (2017), and "Gewalten" (2022). He produced a volume of poetry, "Between Heart and Beat", in 2012 and often gave readings of his verse. Gallinowski was also noted as an artist whose works were displayed in numerous exhibitions. He was married to actress Dagmar Manzel until 2016.

Gallo, Fred T.

Assistant director and film executive Fred T. Gallo, who worked frequently on Woody Allen's films, died after a long illness at his home in Santa Ynez Valley, California, on September 7, 2023. He was 78. Gallo was born in Queens,

New York, on November 8, 1944. He served in the U.S. military in Vietnam before entering the film industry in the mid-1960s. He served as a production assistant on the 1966 film "The Group" and the 1968 tele-film "The Thanksgiving Visitor". He was soon working as production manager on such films as "Paper Lion" (1968), "Stiletto" (1969), "Take the Money and

Run" (1969), "Where's Poppa?" (1970), "The Twelve Chairs" (1970), "The Bad News Bears in Breaking Training" (1977), "American Hot Wax" (1978), "Boulevard Nights" (1979), and "Hide in Plain Sight" (1980). Gallo was assistant director for the films "Jenny" (1970), "The Boys in the Band" (1970), "Bananas" (1971), "The Godfather" (1972), "Everything You Always Wanted to Know About Sex * But Were Afraid to Ask" (1972), Sleeper" (1973), "Murder by Death" (1976), "Annie Hall" (1977), and "September 30, 1955" (1977). He was also assistant director for the television series "Madigan" in 1972. Gallo was also an associate producer for the films "Love and Death" (1975), "Annie Hall" (1977), "The Bad News Bears in Breaking Training" (1977), "American Hot Wax" (1978), "Going in Style" (1979), "Hide in Plain Sight" (1980), "Body Heat" (1981), "Going Under" (1991), and "Aspen Extreme" (1993). He served as a production vice president at Warner Bros. before joining Paramount in 1993. He became executive vice president of feature production management in 1996 and was promoted to worldwide president of features production in 2001. He retired in 2005. Gallo was portrayed by Zack Schor in the 2022 Paramount_ mini-series "The Offer", about the making of "The Godfather". He is survived by his wife, Joan Bradshaw, and two children.

Gallucci, Victor

British actor Victor Gallucci died in England on May 14, 2023. He was 81. Gallucci was born in Islington, London, England, on November 30, 1942. He began appearing in small roles in film and television in 1967. He was a bit actor or stand-in for the films "The Dirty Dozen" (1967), "Carry on Henry VIII" (1971), "The Return of the Pink Panther" (1975), "Confessions of a Driving Instructor" (1976), "Star Wars" (1977) as a rebel pilot and a stormtrooper, "Why Not Stay for

Breakfast?" (1979), "Alien" (1979), "Blade Runner" (1982), "Top Secret!" (1984), "Legend" (1985) as a stand-in for Tom Cruise, "Jane and the Lost City" (1987), and "Mirrormask" (2005). Gallucci was listed in the Guinness Book of Records as the longest serving extra on a television series for his role as D.C. Tom Baker with over 1000 episodes from 1988 to 2002. He also appeared in episodes of "The Professionals", "Minder", and "Serious and Organised".

Gambon, Michael

Irish-English actor Michael Gambon, who was noted for is roles as Albus Dumbledore on the "Harry Potter" film

series from 2004 to 2011, died of pneumonia at his home in Wiltham, Essex, England, on September 27, 2023. He was 82. Gambon was born in Dublin, Ireland, on October 19, 1940. He moved to London with his family as a child. He attended St. Aloysius' College in Highgaten and Crayford Secondary School in North End, Kent. He worked as a

toolmaker for Vickers-Armstrongs engineering firm from his teens. He decided on an acting career in his early 20s and was accepted with Dublin's Gate Theatre after creating a fictional theatrical resume. He made his professional stage debut in a small role in a 1962 production of "Othello" at the Gate. He joined Laurence Olivier's newly formed National Theatre Company in 1963 and performed with the company for four seasons. Gambon starred in numerous productions of Shakespeare, appearing in such roles as Hamlet, Macbeth, Othello, and King Lear. He began performing in repertory in 1967 with the Birmingham Repertory Company. He appeared in the West End production of Alan Ayckbourn's comedy "The Norman Conquests" in 1974. He was recipient of the Olivier Award for his work in the plays "A Chorus of Disapproval" (1985), "A View from the Bridge" (1987), and "Man of the Moment" (1990). He earned an additional ten nominations for his roles in "Betrayal" (1979), "The life of Galileo" (1980), "Tales from Hollywood" (1983), "Skylight" (1997), "Tom and Clem" (1998), "The Unexpected Man" (1999), "The Caretaker" (2001), "A Number" (2003), "Endgame" (2005), and "No Man's Land" (2009). He appeared on Broadway in David Hare's "Skylight" in 1997 and received a Tony Award for best actor for his role as Tom Sergeant. He made his film debut in several small roles in Olivier's "Othello" in 1965. His other films include the horror film "Nothing But the Night" (1973) with Christopher Lee and Peter Cushing, the werewolf film "The Beast Must Die" (1974) as Jan Jarmokowski, "Turtle Diary" (1985), "Paris by Night" (1988), "Missing Link" (1988) as the Narrator, "The Rachel Papers" (1989), Peter Greenaway's off-beat crime drama "The Cook, the Thief, His Wife & Her Lover, as Albert, the thief, opposite Helen Mirren, "A Dry White Season" (1989), "Mobsters" (1991), Robin Williams' comic fantasy "Toys" (1992) as General Leland Zevo, "Clean Slate" (1994), "The Browning Version" (1994), "A Man of No Importance" (1994), "Squanto: A Warrior's Tale" (1994), "Nothing Personal" (1995), "Two Deaths" (1995), "The Innocent Sleep" (1995), the Jekyll & Hyde retelling "Mary Reilly" (1996) as the father of Julia Roberts' title character, "The Wings of the Dove" (1997), "The Gambler" (1997) as Fyodor Dostoyevsky, "Dancing at Lughnasa" (1998), "Plunkett & Macleane" (1999), "The Last September" (1999), "The Insider" (1999), Tim Burton's "Sleepy Hollow" (1999) as Baltus Van Tassel, the short "Shackleton's Antarctic Adventure" (2001) as the voice of Sir Ernest Shackleton, "High Heels and Low Lifes" (2001), the animated "Christmas Carol: The Movie" (2001) as the voice of the Ghost of Christmas Present, Robert Altman's "Gosford Park" (2001), "Charlotte Gray" (2001), "Ali G Indahouse" (2002), "The Actors" (2003), "Open Range" (2003), "Sylvia" (2003), the science fiction film

"Sky Captain and the World of Tomorrow" (2004) as Editor Paley, "Being Julia" (2004), "Layer Cake" (2004), Wes Anderson's "The Life Aquatic with Steve Zissou" (2004), the 2006 remake of the horror film "The Omen" (2006) as the archaeologist Bugenhagen, "Amazing Grace" (2006), "The Good Shepherd" (2006), "The Good Night" (2007), "The Baker" (2007), "Brideshead Revisited" (2008) as Lord Marchmain, the animated "Fantastic Mr. Fox" (2009) as the voice of Franklin Bean, "The Book of Eli" (2010), "The King's Speech" (2010) as King George V, "Quartet" (2012), "Paddington" (2014) as the voice of Uncle Pastuzo, "Hail, Caesar!" (2016) as the narrator, "Dad's Army" (2016), "Viceroy's House" (2018) as Lord Ismay, "Mad to Be Normal" (2017), "Victoria & Abdul" (2017) as Lord Salisbury, "Kingsman: The Golden Circle" (2017) as Arthur, "Paddington 2" (2017) reprising his voice role as Uncle Pastuzo, "The Last Witness" (2018), "Citizen Lane" (2018), "The Death & Life of John F. Donovan" (2018), "King of Thieves" (2018), "Johnny English Strikes Again" (2018) starring Rowan Atkinson, "Judy" (2019) starring Renee Zellweger as Judy Garland, and "Cordelia" (2019). He replaced the late Richard Harris in the role of Hogwart's headmaster Albus Dumbledore in the 2004 film "Harry Potter and the Prisoner of Azkaban". He continued in the role for the remainder of the series including "Harry Potter and the Goblet of Fire" (2005), "Harry Potter and the Order of the Phoenix" (2007), "Harry Potter and the Half-Blood Prince" (2009), "Harry Potter and the Deathly Hallows: Part 1" (2010), and "Harry Potter and the Deathly Hallows: Part 2" (2011). Gambon appeared on television in productions of "Much Ado About Nothing" (1967), "Romeo and Juliet" (1967), "A Midsummer Night's Dream" (1971), "Now Is Too

Late" (1976), "French Without Tears" (1976), "The Man Who Liked Elephants" (1977), "The Seagull" (1978), "La Ronde" (1982), "The Breadwinner" (1982), "Tropical Moon Over Dorking" (1985), "The Holy Experiment" (1985), "Absurd Person Singular" (1985), "The Singing Detective" (1986) winning a BAFTA Award for his role as Philip Marlow, "The Heat of the Day" (1989), "Blood Royal: William the Conqueror" (1990) as William I, "Mama's Back" (1993), "Faith" (1994), "Bullet to Beijing" (1995), "The Wind in the Willows" (1995) as the voice of Badger, "Midnight in Saint Petersburg" (1996), "Samson and Delilah" (1996), "The Willows in Winter" (1996) again as the voice of Badger, "Wives and Daughters" (1999) earning another BAFTA, "Longitude" (2000) winning another BAFTA, "Endgame" (2000), "Perfect Strangers" (2001) receiving his fourth BAFTA, "Path to War" (2002) receiving an Emmy Award nomination for his role as Lyndon B. Johnson, "The Post Prince" (2003) as Edward VII, "Angels in America" (2003), "Celebration" (2007), "Joe's Palace" (2007), "Emma" (2009) earning another Emmy Award nomination for his role as Mr. Woodhouse, "Page Eight" (2011), "Restless" (2012), "Fifty Years on Stage" (2013), "Lucan" (2013) as John Burke, "Quirke" (2014), "Common" (2014), "On Angel Wings" (2014), "The Casual Vacancy" (2015), "The Nightmare Worlds of H.G. Wells" (2016), "Churchill's Secret" (2016) as Winston Churchill, "Fearless" (2017), and "Little Women" (2017). His other television credits include episodes of "Softly Softly", "Public Eye", "Fraud Squad", "The Borderers" as Gavin Ker from 1968 to 1970, "Confessions", "Eyeless in Gaza" as Mark Staithes in 1971, "The Challengers" as John Killane in 1972, "The Man Outside", "Kate", "Softly Softly: Task Force", "Love Story", "Menace", "A Picture of Katherine Mansfield", "Special Branch", "Arthur of the Britons", "Six Days of Justice", "Play for Today", "Chalk and Cheese", "Play for Love", "Premiere", "The Other One" as Brian Bryant from 1977 to 1979, "Tales of the Unexpected", "Oscar" as Oscar Wilde in 1985, "Bergerac", "Theatre Night", "MuppeTelevision", "About Face", "The Storyteller: Greek Myths" as the Storyteller in 1991, "Minder", "Maigret" as Chief Inspector Jules Maigret from 1992 to 1993, "Performance", "Cranford", "Top Gear", "Krod Mandoon and the Flaming Sword of Fire", "Doctor Who" as Kazran Sardick in the 2010 special episode "A Christmas Carol", the short-lived horse-racing drama "Luck" starring Dustin Hoffman in 2012, "The Holly Crown", and the psychological horror thriller "Fortitude" as Henry Tyson from 2015 to 2018. Gambon married mathematician Anne Miller in 1962 and is survived by her and their son, "Antiques Roadshow" ceramics expert, Fergus. He was involved with Philippa Hart in the early 2000s and they had two sons before he reconciled with his wife.

Gangsta Boo

Rapper Lola Chantrelle Mitchell, who performed under the name Gangsta Boo with the group Three 6 Mafia, died of an accidental overdose of drugs and alcohol on the front porch of her mother's home in Memphis, Tennessee, on January 1, 2023. She was 43. Mitchell was born in Memphis on August 7, 1979. She began rapping in her early teens and became the only female member of the hip hop group Three 6 Mafia. She was featured of DJ Paul's 1994 mixtape "Volume 16: 4 Da

Summer Of '94" and Three 6 Mafia's debut album "Mystic Stylez" in 1995. She appeared on four subsequent albums before leaving the group to concentrate on her solo career in 2001. Gangsta Boo's solo album "Enquiring Minds" was released in 1998 and contained the hit single "Where Dem Dollas Att?". She recorded the albums "Both Worlds '69" (2001) and "Enquiring Minds II: The Soap Opera" (2003). She released the mixtape "Memphis Queen Is Bang (Still Gangsta Slowed & Throwed") (2007). She released other mixtapes over the next decade with such rap artists as DJ Drama, DJ Fletch, Trap-A-Holic, and Beatking". She was part of the spin-off group Da Mafia 6ix and worked on their 2013 mixtape "6ix Commandments".

Garcia, Andres

Mexican actor Andres Garcia died of hepatic cirrhosis in Acapulco, Mexico, on April 4, 2023. He was 81. Garcia was born in Santo Domingo, Dominican Republic, on May 24, 1941. He moved to Mexico in the 1960s to pursue an acting

career. He starred in the title role of the 1967 action-adventure film "Chanoc". Garcia's other films include "La Noche del Halcon" (1968), "Los Asesinos" (1968), the horror film "House of Evil" (aka "Macabre Serenade" & "Dance of Death" (1968) starring Boris Karloff, "Muchachas, Muchachas, Muchachas" (1968), "Pacto Diabolico" (1969), "Super Colt 38" (1969), "Tres Amigos" (1970), "Las Tres Magnificas" (1970), "Juan el Desalmado" (1970), "Los Juniors" (1970), "El Cinico" (1970), "La Rebelion de las Hijas" (1970), "Paraiso" (1970), "Siempre Hay Una Primera Vez" (1971), "Los Destrampados" (1971), "El Negocio del Odio" (1972), "Besos, Besos... y Mas Besos" (1973), "El Principio" (1973), "Moriras con el Sol (Motociclistas Suicidas)" (1973), "Adios, New York, Adios" (1973), "La Corona de un Campeon" (1974), "La Amargura de Mi Raza" (1974), "Aventuras de un Caballo Blanco y un Nino" (1975), "El Trinquetero" (1976), "Tintorera: Killer Shark" (1977), "La Llamada del Sexo" (1977), "The Bermuda Triangle" (1978), "Cuchillo" (1976), "El Cuatro Dedos" (1978), "Cave of Sharks" (1978), "Cyclone" (1978), "Suave, Carino, Muy Suave" (1978), "Encounters of the Deep" (1979), "Nora la Rebelde" (1979), "Midnight Dolls" (1979), "Manaos" (1979), "Day of the Assassin" (1979), "El Giro, el Pinto, y el Colorado" (1979), "Amigo" (1980), "Carlos el Terrorista" (1980), "Dos Hermanos Murieron" (1980), "El Sieta Vidas" (1980), "Carnada" (1980), "Las Tentadoras" (1980),

"Mirame Con Ojos Pornograficos" (1980), "Las Cabareteras" (1980), "Sexo Contra Sexo" (1980), "El Jinete de la Muerte" (1980), "The Sex Sense" (1981), "Bordello" (1981), "Mi Nombre es Sergio, Soy Alcoholico" (1981), "La Leyenda del Tambor" (1981), "D.F./Distrito Federal" (1981), "El Macho Bionico" (1981), "Una Gallina Muy Ponedora" (1982), "El Dia del Compadre" (1983), "Chile Picante" (1983), "Las Modelos de Desnudos" (1983), "Dos de Abajo" (1983), "Inseminacion Artificial" (1983), "La Venganza de Maria" (1983), "Pedro Navaja" (1984), "Hermelinda Linda" (1984), "El Embustero" (1985), "Tona Machetes" (1985), "Sangre en el Caribe" (1985), "La Risa Alarga la Vida y Algo Mas" (1985), "El Cafre" (1986), "Rio de Oro" (1986), "El Hijo de Pedro Navaja" (1986), "Lovers of the Lord of the Night" (1986), "El Nino y el Papa" (1987), "Demon Hunter" (1987), "Los Plomeros y las Ficheras" (1988), "Asesino Nocturno" (1988), "Mi Fantasma y Yo" (1988), "Solicito Marido Para Enganar" (1988), "Enter Compadres te Veas" (1989), "Programado Paa Morir" (1989), "Buscando la Muerte" (1989), "Deuda Saldada" (1989), "Perros de Presa" (1992), "El Dia de los Albaniles IV" (1993), "El Justiciero" (1994), "El Jinete de Acero" (1994), "Morir Mil Muertes" (1995), "El Tigre Murrieta" (1995), "Los Matones de Mi Pueblo" (1996), "Puppet" (1999), "Detras del Paraiso" (2002), "El Cristo de Plata" (2004), "La Ultima Noche" (2005), and "La Leyenda de los Chaneques" (2023). He appeared frequently on television with roles in such series as "I Spy", "Yo Se Que Nunca", "La Sonrisa del Diablo", "Velo de Novia", "El Carruaje", "Las Gemelas" as Leonardo Lobo in 1972, "Ana del Aire" as Jorge Romero in 1975, "Paloma" as Daniel in 1975, "Amame" as Rafael Alvarez in 1979, "Y Ahora Que?", "Tu o Nadie" as Antonnio Lombardo in 1985, "Escandalo", "Mi Nombre es Coraje" as Juan in 1988, "Herencia Maldita" as Gerardo Altamijra in 1990, "El Magnate" as Gonzalo in 1990, "Dark Justice", "La Mujer Prohibida" as Herman Gallardo in 1991, "Con Toda el Alma" as Daniel Linares from 1995 to 1996, "We Are Angels", "El Privilegio de Amar" as Andres Duval from 1998 to 1999, "Mujeres Enganadas" as Javier Duarte from 1999 to 2000, "La Hora Pico", "Al Filo de la Ley", the reality series "El Principle Azul" with his son, Leonardo, in 2005, "El Cuerpo del Deseo" as Pedro Jose Donoso from 2005 to 2006, "The Pretenders", "Hospital Central", "Cuentame Como Paso" as Victor Barquero from 2007 to 2008, "El Pantera" as Rubio Barrios from 2007 to 2008, and "Hay Alguien Ahi". Garcia was also seen in the tele-films "King of Texas" (2002) and "Sempere te Amare" (2004). Garcia was married to Sanda Vale from 1967 until their divorce in 1973 and is survived by their two sons, actors Andres Jr. and Leonardo. He married Maria Fernanda Ampudia in 1974 and they had a daughter, actress Andrea, before their subsequent divorce. Garcia was married to actress Sonia Infante from 1980 until their divorce in 1992. He married Margarita Portillo in the late 1990s and she also survives him.

Garcia Seijas, Ernesto

Argentine comic artist Ernesto Garcia Seijas died in Argentina on March 28, 2023. He was 81. Garcia was born in Ramos Mejia, Argentina, on June 1, 1941. He began working in comics in the late 1950s illustrating the "Bill y Boss" series for "Totem" magazine. He was artist for the title series of the  magazine "Bucaneros" from 1958. He frequently teamed with comic writer Hector G. Oesterheld in the 1960s and 1970s on such magazines as "Frontera", "Misterix", "Hora Cero", and "Rajo Rojo". He worked on romance titles at Editorial Columba including "Helena" with Robin Wood. Garcia Seijas as co-creator of such comic serials as "Black Soldier", "Skorpio", "Mandy Riley", "El Pequeno Rey", "La Estirpe de Josh", "Los Aventureros", and "El Hombre de Richmond". He created the "Kevin" serial with Robin Wood for "Nippur" magazine. He worked on Italian comics from the 1990s including "Radzel" and "Tex Willer".

Garcia, Lea

Brazilian actress Lea Garcia de Aguiar, who was noted for her role as Serafina in the 1959 film "Black Orpheus", died in Gramado, Brazil, on August 15, 2023. She was 90. Garcia was born in Rio de Janeiro, Brazil, on March 11, 1933. She  began her acting career on stage in the early 1950s with the Teatro Experimental do Negro-TEN (Black Experimental Theater). She was featured as Eurydice's cousin, Serafina, in Marcel Camus' Oscar-winning foreign language film "Black Orpheus" in 1959. She was seen in numerous films including "Os Bandeirantes" (1960), "Ganga Zumba" (1963), "O Santo Modico" (1964), "Compasso de Espera" (1969), "O Forte" (1974), "Feminino Plural" (1976), "Ladroes de Cinema" (1977), "A Noiva da Cidade" (1978), "A Deusa Negra" (1979), "Aguia Na Cabeca" (1984), "Quilombo" (1984), "Cruz e Sousa - O Poeta do Desterro" (1998), "Orfeu" (1999), "Viva Sapato!" (2003), "Filhas do Vento" (2004), "Mulheres do Brasil" (2006), "O Maior Amor do Mundo" (2006), "Nzinga" (2007), "Em Quadro" (2009), "Days Together" (2010), "Billi Pig" (2012), "Trinta" (2014), "Pacified" (2019), "Neighbors" (2019), "Golden Mouth" (2019), "Um Dia Com Jerusa" (2020), and "O Pai da Rita" (2021). Garcia was seen on television in productions of "Acorrentados" (1969), "Minha Doce Namorada" (1971), "O Homen Que Deve Morrer" (1971), "Meu Primeiro Baile" (1972), "Selva de Pedra" as Elza in 1972, "Os Ossos do Barao" (1973), "Feliz na Ilusao" (1974), "Fogo Sobre Terra" (1974), "A Moreninha" (1975), "Isaura: Slave Girl" (1976), "Maria, Maria" (1978), "A Morte E a Morte de Quincas Berro D'Agua" (1978), "Marina" (1980), "Bandidos da Falange" (1983) as Gladys, "Dona Beija" (1986), "Helena" (1987), "Abolicao" (1988), "Pacto de Sangue" (1989), "Araponga" (1990), "Desire" (1990) as Marianna, "August"

(1993), "A Viagem" (1994), "Evil Angel" as Aparecida 'Cida' Ribeiro in 1997, "Xicfa da Silva" as Bastiana from 1996 to 1998, "Mild Poison" (1999) as Selma, "The Clone" (2001), "Scars" (2006), "Sunshine" (2007) as Baba Edith, "The Law and the Crime" (2009) as Clara, "Mon Pere, Francis le Belge" (2010), "Lilyhammer" (2014), "The Good Side of Life!" (2016), "Rising Sun" (2017), "Mister Brau" (2017), "Harassment" (2018), "Under Pressure" (2018), "Jailers" (2018), "Baile de Mascaras" (2019), "Arcanja Renegado" (2020), and "IndependenciaS" (2022). Garcia was also a public servant at the Ministry of Health. She worked with National Department of Rural Endemics in the 1960s and later worked with the Psychiatric Hospital Philippe Pinel in Rio de Janeiro through the 1990s

Garland, N'Neka

Television producer N'Neka Garland died of a heart attack in Burbank, California, on March 29, 2023. She was 49.  Garland was born in Jersey City, New Jersey, on April 11, 1973. She was the half-sister of the late rapper Tupac Shakur. She graduated from Hampton University in Virginia in 1995. She began working for the ABC soap opera "General Hospital" as an executive assistant in 2001. She became associate producer of the soap in 2015 and later was coordinating producer. She shared a Daytime Emmy Award for her work on "General Hospital" in 2021 and two additional nominations in 2019 and 2020.

Gary, Pnina

Israeli actress and theatrical director Pnina Gary died in Tel Aviv, Israel, on August 2, 2023. She was 95. She was born Pnina Dromi in Nahalal, Palestine, on September 24, 1927.  She survived an ambush by Arabs at the Beit Keshet kibbutz in March of 1948, but her fiancee, Eli Ben-Zvi, was killed. Pnina volunteered to go to Munich later in the year to set up kindergartens at displaced person camps and work with Jewish children who survived the Holocaust. She met American journalist Robert Gary in Munich, and they married in late 1949. Pnina studied acting under Herbert Berghof and Lee Strasberg in New York from 1953 to 1957. She subsequently returned to Israel where she was co-founder of the Zavit Theater in 1959. She produced various plays and performed on stage there and at other venues in Tel Aviv. She worked with the HaBima Theatre from 1968 to 1980 and was artistic director of the Orna Porat Theater from 1981 to 1990. Pnina appeared in several films including

"Dreams" (1969), "Death Has No Friends" (1970), "Ariana" (1971), "Salomonico" (1972), and "A Dinner of Herbs" (1988). She wrote and directed the autobiographical one-woman show "An Israeli Love Story" in 2008. The play was adapted for a tele-film starring Adi Bielski in 2017. Her autobiographical novel of the same name was published in Hebrew in 2015. She and Robert Gary were married from 1949 until his death in 2017 and she is survived by their two daughters, Dorit and Meirav.

Gaylord, Jeff

Professional wrestler Jeff Gaylord was found dead at a bus stop in Englewood, Colorado, on March 15, 2023. He was 64. Gaylord was born in Columbus, Ohio, on October 15, 1958. He played football in high school and in college with the

Missouri Tigers at the University of Missouri. He was drafted by the Los Angeles Rams in 1982 but was let go during the summer. He was signed by the CFL's Toronto Argonauts later in the year but only played four games before being released. He played with the Boston Breakers of the United States Football League (USFL) from 1983 to 1984. He was trained to the San Antonio gunslingers in 1985 and the USFL folded the following year. He began his career as a wrestler with the Universal Wrestling Federation (UWF) in 1985. He joined World Class Wrestling (WCW) in 1988, competing as The Hood, where he feuded with Jeff Jarrett and Bill Dundee. He teamed with Jarrett to capture the USWA Tag Team Championship in September of 1990. He wrestled for the Global Wrestling Federation in Dallas, Texas, in 1991. He competed with the United States Wrestling Association (USWA) in the Memphis area where he feuded with Jerry Lawler later in 1991. He remained with the promotion for the next several years, competing against Tony Falk, Doug Gilbert, Reggie B. Fine, Koko B. Ware, the Moondogs, PG-13, the Spellbinder, and Spike Huber. He appeared in the World Wrestling Federation (now WWE) Survivor Series in 1993 and the Black Knight as part of Jerry Lawler's war against the Hart family. Gaylord left the USWA in 1995 and continued to wrestle with independence promotions over the next several years. He was arrested in 2002 on several charges of bank robbery in Aurora, Colorado, and was sentenced to prison. He again attempted a bank robbery in Monument, Colorado, in 2009, and was returned to prison. He was released in 2015. He was believed to be homeless at the time of his death.

Geddie, Bill

Television producer Bill Geddie, who was co-creator of television's "The View" with Barbara Walters, died at his home in Rancho Mirage, California, on July 20, 2023. He was 68. Geddie was born in San Antonia, Texas, on July 17, 1955. He graduated from the University of Texas at Austin in 1977. He began working in television at the local Oklahoma City station KOCO-TV where he was soon a camera operator for the

news. He was a cameraman at WSB-TV in Atlanta and WKYC-TV in Cleveland and was producer of "PM Magazine" in San Francisco and of ABC's

"Good Morning America" in the 1980s. He began working with Barbara Walters as producer of her ABC specials in 1988. He and Walters created the all-female talk show "The View" in 1997 and they served as executive producers of the daily series through Walters' BarWall Productions. Geddie would frequently appear on the show in various skits. He shared a Daytime Emmy Award for Outstanding Talk Show in 2003 and received an additional dozen nominations. He was recipient of a Lifetime Achievement Award from the Daytime Emmys in 2012. He remained with "The View" until 2014. Geddie was executive producer of the 2016 special "Megyn Kelly Presents" and the talk shows "The Preachers" in 2016 and "Tamron Hall" from 2019 to 2020. He also scripted the 1996 film "Unforgettable". Geddie married Barbara Pratt in 1979 and is survived by her and their two daughters, Allison and Lauren.

Geechy Guy

Comedian Michael Paul Cathers, who performed under the name Geechy Guy, was found dead at his home in Las Vegas, Nevada, on September 7, 2023. He was 59. Cathers

was born in Rochester, Michigan, on May 12, 1964. He began his career in comedy as a stand-up comic in the Detroit area in his late teens. He moved of San Francisco, California, in the late 1980s and was a contestant on the talent contest "Star Search" in 1990. He became noted for his rapid-fire joke telling abilities and performed at numerous venues in Las Vegas from the mid-1990s. He was a frequent opening act for comedian Ron White including 2014's "Ron White's Comedy Salute to the Troops". Geechy was a contestant in "America's Got Talent" in 2011 and was eliminated in the quarterfinals. He appeared on television in episodes of "The Tonight Show with Jay Leno", "An Evening at the Improv", "Make Me Laugh", "The Late Show with Craig Ferguson".

Geoffrey, Paul

British-American actor Paul Geoffrey died of cancer in Santa Fe, New Mexico, on June 3, 2023. He was 68. Geoffrey was born in Surrey, England, on February 12, 1955. He began his acting career in the late 1970s, appearing on television in productions of "Spaghetti Two-Step" (1977), "A Traveller in Time" (1978), "If Winter Comes" (1981), "Spyship" (1983), "The Jewel in the Crown" (1984), "Anna

Karenina" (1985), "Maggie" (1986), "Hold the Dream" (1987), "Napoleon and Josephine: A Love Story" (1987) as Murat, and "Some Other Spring" (1991). His other television credits include episodes of "Heartland", "Jackanory Playhouse", "The Man from Moscow", "Robin  Hood", "Florence ou La Vie de Chateau", "Inspector Morse", "Panique aux Caraibes", "Poirot", "The Manageress" as Simon Benson from 1989 to 1990, "Birds of a Feather", "The Paradise Club", and "Casualty". Geoffrey was seen in the films "At the Fountainhead (of German Strength)" (1980), "Excalibur" (1981) as Sir Perceval, "A Flame to the Phoenix" (1983), "Greystoke: The Legend of Tarzan, Lord of the Apes" (1984) as Lord Jack Clayton, "Zina" (1985), "Resurrected" (1989), and "Wuthering Heights" (1992) as Mr. Lockwood. He moved to the United States in the early 1990s and became a successful real estate agent in the Santa Fe area. He continued to act occasionally with roles in the films "The Thomas Crown Affair" (1999) and "Spells" (2012) and the tele-films "An Ungentlemanly Act" (1992) and "The Staircase" (1998). He also appeared in episodes of "The Good Guys", "Love Hurts", "Acapulco H.E.A.T.", "Better Call Caul", "Get Shorty", and "Perpetual Grace, LTD". Geoffrey was married and divorced from actress Belinda Sinclair. He is survived by his wife, Sue Taylor, and three children.

George, Butchie

Actor and artist William 'Butchie' George, who was featured in the 1978 horror film "Dawn of the Dead", died of  complication from injuries suffered in a motorcycle accident eight years earlier in Lone Pine, Pennsylvania, on August 10, 2023. He was 76. George was born in Washington County, Pennsylvania, on August 8, 1947. He was founder of the publication "Motorcycle Happenings Guide" from 1965 until his motorcycle accident. He was featured as the wild-haired bearded biker riding his own Harley-Davidson Panhead Motorcycle in George Romero's classic horror film "Dawn of the Dead" in 1978. He also served as motorcycle stuntman for Bruce McGill in 1978's "Animal House". George worked with Tom Savini in the art department for the 1990 remake of "Night of the Living Dead" and appeared as a biker. He had a small role in the 2003 film "Severe Injuries". George, who also had the nicknames Anteater and Crazy George, was noted as an artist and sculptor and frequently attended motorcycle rallies around the country.

Gessner, Nicolas

Hungarian-Swiss film director Nicolas Gessner, who helmed the 1976 thriller "The Little Girl Who Lives Down the Lane", died on August 22, 2023. He was 92. Gessner was born  in Szombathely, Hungary, on August 17, 1931. He began working in films in the late 1950s and directed the 1959 short "Auskunft im Cockpit". He was noted for directing and frequently writing European and Canadian co-productions featuring U.S. stars in the 1960s and 1970s. His films include "Diamonds Are Brittle" (1965) starring Jean Seberg, "The Blonde from Peking" (1967), the comedy "The Thirteen Chairs" (aka "12+1") (1969) starring Sharon Tate and Orson Welles, the psychological drama "Someone Behind the Door" (1971) starring Charles Bronson and Anthony Perkins, the off-beat thriller "The Little Girl Who Lives Down the Lane" (1976) starring Jodie Foster and Martin Sheen, and "It Rained All Night the Day I Left" (1980). Gessner worked frequently in television helming productions of "Der Gefangene der Botschaft" (1964), "Familienalbum der Weltgeschichte" (1965), "Herr Herr" (1982), "Le Tueur Triste" (1984), "Macho" (1986), "Des Andere Leben" (1987), "Le Chateau des Oliviers" (1993), "Cheques en Boite" (1994), and "Spaceship Earth" (1996). His later films include "Quicker Than the Eye (1988), "Tennessee Waltz" (1989), and "Swiss Faces" (1991).

Geyer, Renee

Australian singer Renee Geyer died of lung cancer in Geelong, Australia, on January 17, 2023. She was 69. Geyer  was born in Melbourne, Australia, on September 11, 1953. She began singing with the jazz-blues band Dry Red while still in high school in 1970. She left home soon after and joined the band Sun the following year. The group released a self-named album 1972 but Geyer had already departed to join Mother Earth. She was soon signed as a solo act by RCA Records and released a self-titled album in 1973. The title track for her 1974 album, "It's a Man's Man's World", became a hit. Her third album, "Ready to Deal", followed in 1975 and contained the hit single "Heading in the Right Direction". She moved to Los Angeles in mid-1976 and released the album "Moving Along" the following year. She worked as a session vocalist and made frequent return visits to Australia. Geyer was featured as Christine in Walter Murphy's 1978 album "Phantom of the Opera" and released the album "Winner" in 1978. She recorded numerous subsequent albums and released such popular songs as "Say I Love You", "Do You Know What I Mean", "All My Love", "I'm Gonna Make You Love Me", and "Baby, Please Don't Go". Her final studio album, "Swing", was released in 2013. She performed frequently on such television series as "GTK", "The Graham Kennedy Show", "The Ernie Sigley Show", "Countdown", "The Don Lane Show", "Funshine Show", "The Mike Walsh Show", "Hey Hey It's Saturday", "The Naked Vicar Show", "Nightmoves", "The Paul Hogan Show", "The Daryl Somers Show", "Late Night with Jono & Dano", "Tonight Live with Steve Vizard", "Midday with Kerri-Anne", "Good Morning Australia", "The Joint", "Laws", "Studio 22", "Denise", "Live at the Basement", "Spicks & Specks", and "Talking Heads". Geyer was featured as a barmaid in the 1984 film "My First Wife" and appeared as herself in the shorts "A Day and a Half" (1988) and "Sticktoitiveness" (1995). She provided the voice of Vera Lorraine Dinkle in the 2009 animated film "Mary and Max". Geyer's autobiography, "Confessions of a Difficult Woman", was published in 2000.

Gibbs, Matyelok

British actress Matyelok Gibbs died on August 14, 2023. She was 91. Gibbs was born in Leatherhead, Surrey, England, on August 1, 1932. She attended Queen's Gate school in South Kensington and trained as an actress at Webber Douglas Academy of Dramatic Art. She began working with

Caryl Jenner with his mobile touring theater for children in the early 1950s. It became known as the Unicorn theater in London, and she succeeded Jenner as artistic director from his death in 1973 to 1977. She performed in the West End in a 1978 production of Alan Ayckbourn's "Ten Times Table". She toured with the Royal Shakespeare Company from 1979 to 1980 in productions of "Much Ado About Nothing". She was seen on television in episodes of "Vision On", "Lady Killers", "BBC2 Playhouse", "The Agatha Christie Hour", "Grange Hill", "Chessgame", "Travelling Man", "Ladies in Charge", "Bergerac", "The New Statesman", "Screenplay", "Maigret", "Between the Lines", "Space Precinct", "Peak Practice", "Revelations", "The Vet", "Hetty Wainthropp Investigates", "All Quiet on the Preston Front" as Mrs. Ruddock from 1994 to 1997, "Kavanagh QC", "Heartbeat", "The Passion", "Midsommer Murders", "Fish", "A Touch of Frost", "The Residents", "Judge John Deed", "Casualty", "Doctors", "The Bill", "Rosemary & Thyme", and "Getting On". Her other television credits include productions of "The Bad Sister" (1983), "The Jewel in the Crown" (1984) as Sister Ludmila, "Hitler's S.S.: Portrait in Evil" (1985), "Blott on the Landscape" (1985) as Miss Percival, "A.D." (1985), "Past Caring" (1985), "This Is History, Gran" (1986), "The Deadly Recruits" (1986), "Heart of the Country" (1987), "The Perfect Spy" (1987), "Troubles" (1988), "Chelworth" (1989), "House of Glass" (1992), "A Masculine Ending" (1992), "Framed" (1992), "Seaforth" (1994), "Out of Hours" (1998), "The Cry" (2002), and "A Is for Acid" (2002). Gibbs was seen in numerous films including "Victor/Victoria" (1982),

"Secrets" (1983), "A Room with a View" (1985), "To Kill a Priest" (1988), Terry Jones' "Erik the Viking" (1989) as Erik's Mum, "Kafka" (1991), "Waterland" (1992), "When Pigs Fly" (1993), "Priest" (1994), "Jack & Sarah" (1995), "Crimetime" (1996), "Oscar and Lucinda" (1997), "Ever After: A Cinderella Story" (1998), "Just Visiting" (2001), "Superstition" (2001), "And Low Ladies & Gentlemen" (2002), "Fragile" (2005), "A Little Trip to Heaven" (2005), "Babel" (2006), "Copying Beethoven" (2006), "Pu-239" (2006), "Miss Potter" (2006), "Harry Potter and the Deathly Hallows: Part 1" (2010) as Auntie Muriel Weasley, "Your Highness" (2011), "Tinker Tailor Soldier Spy" (2011), and "The Hundred-Foot Journey" (2014). Shen was a long-time companion of actress and writer Ursula Jones from the late 1950s, and the later established a civil partnership. The couple moved to Toulouse, France, in the early 2000s where they operated a furniture shop. Gibbs is survived by Jones.

Gibson, Ian

British comic artist Ian Gibson, who was noted for his work on the series "Judge Dredd" and "The Ballad of Halo Jones", died of cancer in England on December 11, 2023. He

was 77. Gibson was born in England on February 20, 1946. He began producing illustrations for the British comic fanzines "Aspect" and "Orpheus" in the 1960s. He worked with "House of Hammer" in 1973 and did promotion art for record companies. He worked with writer John Wagner and others on numerous "Judge Dredd" stories for the comic magazine "2000 AD". He worked with Wagner and Alan Grant on the "Robo-Hunter" from 1979 series and with Alan Moore on "The Ballad of Halo Jones" from 1984. He illustrated stories for DC comics in the 1980s for such series as "Mister Miracle", "Millennium", "Green Lantern Corps". He also worked on "Meta-4" for First Comics, "Steed and Mrs. Peel" for Eclipse Comics, and "Star Wars: Droids" and "Star Wars: Boba Fett - Enemy of the Empire" for Dark Horse. Gibson was a production design consultant for the animated television series "ReBoot" in the 1990s. He returned to "2000 AD" to team with Alan Grant on the series "Samantha Slade Robo-Hunter" from 2003.

Gibson, Tarsha

Actress Tarsha Gibson died in Memphis, Tennessee, on February 8, 2023. She was 50. She was born on September 4, 1972. She was seen in the short films "The Game" (2017) and "One Man's Bed" (2017) and an episode of "Allies". Gibson also appeared in the films "Close Caption" (2021) and "The Reaper Man" (2023). She is survived by her husband, Marlon Gibson.

Giella, Joe

Comic book artist Joe Giella, who was noted for inking tales featuring Batman, the Flash, and Green Lantern, died in Long Island, New York, on March 21, 2023. He was  94. Giella was born in New York on June 27, 1928. He studied at the School of Industrial Art and the Art Students League in Manhattan. He made his comic debut in his teens on the humor feature "Captain Codfish" for Hillman's "Punch and Judy Comics" in 1946. He worked freelance inking C.C. Beck and Pete Costanza's "Captain Marvel" stories for Fawcett before joining the staff at Timely Comics, which later evolved into Marvel, in 1947. He did background work and inking and began assisting on comics featuring Captain America, Sub-Mariner, and the Human Torch. He worked with Mike Sekowsky and Stan Goldberg on the teen and romance titles "Patsy Walker" and "Millie the Model". He served for eight years in the United States Naval Reserve from the late 1940s. Giella joined DC Comics in 1949 where he was inker for tales featuring the Golden Age Flash, Green Lantern, and Black Canary. He also inked western and humor comics during the 1950s. He worked on science fiction tales featuring Adam Strange in "Showcase" and "Mystery in Space", and inked Carmine Infantino and Sheldon Moldoff's Batman stories for "Batman" and "Detective Comics" in the early 1960s. He served as inker for Carmine Infantino for the Silver Age version of the Flash and Gil Kane on Green Lantern. He pencilled and inked the "Batman" syndicated comic strip from 1966 to 1969. Giella inked for Dan Barry on the "Flash Gordon" syndicated comic strip in 1970 and inked for Sy Barry on "The Phantom" strip for nearly two decades. He was illustrator for the books "The Mighty Marvel Comics Strength and Fitness Book" and "The Mighty Marvel Superheroes' Cookbook" for Simon & Schuster in the 1970s. Giella worked primarily as a commercial artist in the 1980s, working on advertisements for McCann Erickson, Saatchi & Saatchi, and Doubleday Publishing. He served as artist on the "Mary Worth" comic strip from 1991 through his retirement in 2016. Giella married Shirley Pierrepoint in 1952 and is survived by her and their four children.

Giffen, Keith

Comic book artist and writer Keith Giffen, who was co-creators of the comic characters Rocket Raccoon, Lobo, and the Jaime Reyes version of the Blue Beetle, died of complications from a stroke at a hospital in Tampa, Florida, on October 9, 2023. He was 70. Giffen was born in Queens, New York, on November 30, 1952. He moved to Clifton, New Jersey, with his parents as a child. He graduated from high school in 1970 and aspired to a career in comics. He was working as a hazardous material handler before he began working at Marvel Comics in the mid-1970s. He co-created the character Rocket Raccoon with Bill Mantlo for "Marvel Preview" #7 in the summer of 1976. He also wrote "The Defenders" series from 1976 to 1977. He was writer for issues of "Claw the Unconquered" and "Challengers of the Unknown" in the late 1970s. Giffen was noted for his long tenure with the Legion of Super-Heroes, working with writer Paul Levitz during the 1980s. He wrote and illustrated the revamped "Legion of Super-Heroes" comic from 1989. Giffen became noted for his humorous approach to comics with his "Legion of  Substitute Heroes Special" in 1985. He teamed with Kevin Maguire and J.M. DeMatteis for the "Justice League International" series in 1987. He and DeMatteis continued with the spin-off series "Justice League Europe" from 1989 where he was co-creator of such characters as Crimson Fox, L-Ron, Lord Manga Khan, and Beefeater. He left the series in the early 1990s but reunited with DeMatteis for the 2003 mini-series "Formerly Known as the Justice League" and 2005's "I Can't Believe It's Not the Justice League" in "JLA Classified". He created the bizarre teleporting super-hero Ambush Bug in "DC Comics Presents" #52 (Dec. 1982) and was plotter and penciller for several mini-series and specials over the two decades. Giffen wrote the early issues of "The Omega Men" where he created the interstellar bounty hunter Lobo in issue #3 (June 1983). He was plotter for several of Lobo's subsequent mini-series. He was illustrator of a series of Doctor Fate stories written by Martin Pasko for "The Flash" comic in 1982 that were collected in the three-issue mini-series "The Immortal Dr. Fate" in 1985. He was writer or plotter for the DC Comics "Cosmic Boy" from 1986 to 1987, "Invasion" from 1988 to 1989, "Aquaman" in 1989, "L.E.G.I.O.N." in 1989, "Green Lantern: Emerald Dawn" from 1989 to 1990, "Green Lantern: Emerald Dawn II" in 1991, "Ragman" from 1991 to 1992, "Heckler" from 1992 to 1993, "Eclipso" from 1992 to 1993, and "Book of Fate" from 1997 to 1998. Giffen worked at Image Comics in the 1990s on the titles "Bloodstrike", "Super Patriot", "Trencher", and "Freak Force". He was writer at Valiant Comics on the series "Magnus, Robot Fighter" and "X-O Manowar" from 1995 to 1996. He was a writer for the "Annihilation" crossover storyline at Marvel in 2006 and the series "Drax the Destroyer" and "Nick Fury's Howling Commandos" from 2005 to 2006. Giffen worked in television in the early 2000s as a storyboard artist for the animated series "Spider-Man Unlimited", "Batman Beyond", and "Static Shock". He also wrote episodes of "Ed, Edd n Eddy" and "Hi Hi Puffy AmiYumi" in 2006. He returned to DC to work on the titles "Suicide Squad" from 2001 to 2002, "Reign of the Zodiac" from 2003 to 2004, "DC/Wildstorm: DreamWar" in 2008, "Reign in Hell" from 2008 to 2009, "Magog" from 2009 to 2010, "Doom Patrol" from 2009 to 2011, "Justice League: Generations Lost" in 2010, "O.M.A.C." from 2011 to 2012, "He-Man and the Masters of the Universe" from 2012 to 2013, "Larfleeze" from 2013 to 2014, and "Infinity-Man and the

Forever People" from 2014 to 2015. He teamed with writer John Rogers and artist Cully Hammer to create the character of Jaime Reyes, who became the new version of the Blue Beetle, in "Infinite Crisis" #3 (Feb. 2006), and wrote the first ten issues of his subsequent series. He co-created a short-lived new version of "The Inferior Five" in 2019. Giffen wife, Anna Jonasik Giffen, died in 2015. He is survived by two children, Melinda and Kyle.

Gilberto, Astrud

Brazilian singer Astrud Gilberto, who was noted for her rendition of the bossa nova song "The Girl from Ipanema", died in Philadelphia, Pennsylvania, on June 5, 2023. She was 83. She was born Astrud Evangelina Weinert in Salvador, Brazil, on March 29, 1940. She moved to Rio de Janeiro with her family in her teens. She became friends with singer and musician Joao Gilberto in her teens and they married in 1959. Astrud made her professional debut as vocalist for the bossa nova hit record "The Girl from Ipanema" in 1963. She also was singer for "Corcovado" and both songs were featured on the album "Getz/Gilberto". "The Girl from Ipanema" and the album both won Grammy Awards. She went on tour with jazz musician Stan Getz and sang on the 1964 album "Getz Au Go Go". Gilberto continued to record such solo albums as "The Astrud Gilberto Album" (1965) and "Look to the Rainbow" (1966) from Verve Records. She signed with CTI Records in 1971 and recorded with the James Last Orchestra in the 1980s. She sang a duet with George Michael, "Desafinado", for the "Red Hot + Rio" album in 1996. He final album, "Jungle". was released in 2002 and she subsequently retired. Gilberto was recipient of the Latin Grammy Award for Lifetime Achievement in 2008. She and Joao Gilberto were married from 1959 until their divorce in 1964. She was also married and divorced from Nicholas Lasorsa. She is survived by a son from each marriage, Marcelo Gilberto and Gregory Lasorsa, who both worked with her as musicians during her career.

Giles, Annabel

British actress and television host Annabel Giles died of brain cancer at a hospital in in Hove, England, on November 20, 2023. She was 64. Giles was born near Pontypool, Wales, on May 20, 1959. She was expelled from boarding school in her teens. She later worked as a secretary for advertising agencies. She soon began working as a model for Max Factor. Giles began appearing on television in the 1980s in such series as "Razzmatazz", "Through the Keyhole", "Going Live!", and "Help Squad". She was co-host of the series "Posh Frocks and New Trousers" in 1990. She continued to appear in variety series and gameshows including "Give Us a Clue", "Cluedo", "Have I Got News for You", "Come on Down & Out", "The Krypton Factor", "Pebble Mills at One", "Hit the Road", "Fist

of Fun", "You Bet!", "Shooting Stars", "Noel's House Party", "Win, Lose or Draw!", "It's Later Than You Think", "The Art Club", "The Vanessa Show", "Celebrity Eggheads", "Lorraine", "Daybreak", "Celebrity Chase", "The Wright Stuff", and "Pointless Celebrities". Giles appeared in the 1993 tele-film "Riders" and the 1997 film "Firelight". She was a contestant on the reality competition series "I'm a Celebrity... Get Me Out of Here!" in 2013. She wrote and performed in the one-woman show "Looking for Mr. Giles" in 1995 and "Anyone Can Be a TV Presenter" in 1996. She was the author of several books including "Birthday Girls" (2001), "Crossing the Paradise Line" (2003), and "The Defrosting of Charlotte Small" (2006). Giles was married to Midge Ure, the lead singer of the band Ultravox, from 1985 until their divorce in 1989. She is survived by their daughter, singer Molly Lorenne, leading singer of the pop punk group the Faders. She is also survived by a son, Ted Giles, from a later relationship.

Gilpin, Marc

Child actor Marc Gilpin, who was featured as young Sean Brody in the 1978 sequel "Jaws 2", died of glioblastoma in Dallas, Texas, on July 29, 2023. He was 56. Gilpin was born

in Austin, Texas, on September 26, 1966. He appeared in television commercials from an early age and was featured in a national spot for Exxon in 1970. He was featured in an episode of the Saturday morning juvenile series "Thunder" in 1977 and starred as boy genius Willie Wade in the 1978 family film "Where's Willie?". Gilpin was Sean Brody, the younger son of Police Chief Martin Brody, played by Roy Scheider, in the 1978 sequel "Jaws 2". He was also seen in such films as the science fiction "Earthbound" (1981) as the young alien Dalem, the western "The Legend of the Lone Ranger" (1981) as the young John Reid, and "She's Out of Control" (1989). Gilpin appeared on television in episodes of "CHiPs", "Fantasy Island", "Flying High", "CBS Afternoon Playhouse", "Silver Spoons", and "China Beach". His other television credits include the tele-films "License to Kill" (1984), "Surviving" (1985), and "Right to Kill?" (1985). Gilpin worked as a software engineer after ending his acting career in the late 1980s. He is survived by his wife of 24 years, Kaki, and two sons. He is also survived by his sister, actress Peri Gilpin, who was featured as Roz Doyle on the television comedy series "Frasier".

Gio, Frank

Actor Frank Gio died in New York City on May 5, 2023. He was 93. Gio was born in New York on August 2,

1929. He was a boxer before embarking on an acting career in the early 1960s. He appeared on television in episodes of "Car 54, Where Are You?", "The Lucie Arnaz Show", "The Equalizer", and "Leg Work". He was also seen in the tele-films "The Connection" (1973), "Honor Thy Father" (1973), and "A Question of Honor" (1982). Gio was frequently cast as gangsters and was featured in such films as "Hercules in New York" (1970), "Cauliflower Cupids" (1970), "The Valachi Papers" (1972), "Cops and Robbers" (1973), "Serpico" (1973), "Sorcerer" (1977), "From Corleone to Brooklyn" (1979), "Vigilante" (1982), "Once Upon a Time in America" (1984), "The Pick-Up Artist" (1987), "Weeds" (1987), "Moonstruck" (1987), "Married to the Mob" (1988), "Spike of Bensonhurst" (1988), "Cookie" (1989), "Catchfire" (1990), "King of New York" (1990), "My Blue Heaven" (1990), "Who Do I Gotta Kill?" (1994), "The Mouse" (1996), "One Tough Cop" (1998), "Intermezzo" (1998), "Assassination Tango" (2002), "Analyze That" (2002), "Dead Canaries" (2003), "The Signs of the Cross" (2005), "Frame of Mind" (2009), and "Once Upon a Time in Brooklyn" (2013).

Giuffre, Adriana

Italian actress Adriana Giuffre. who appeared in several spaghetti westerns in the 1960s, died in Tarquinia, Italy, on August 14, 2023. She was 84. Giuffre was born in Rome, Italy, on March 9, 1939. She began her career in films in the early 1960s. She appeared in numerous films over the next three decades including "Latin Lovers" (1961), "Un Alibi per Morire" (1962), "Il Lungo, il Corto, il Gatto" (1967), "Per Amore... per Magia..." (1967), the spaghetti western "Any Gun Can Play" (1967) with Gilbert Roland, "Django, Prepare a Coffin" (1968), "To Hell and Back" (1968), "Il Medico della Mutua" (1968), "The Great Silence" (1968), "Quel Giorno Dio Non c'era (Il Caso Defregger)" (1969), "Shango" (1970), "The Last Traitor" (1971), "Shoot the Living and Pray for the Dead" (1971), "Riuscira l'Avvocato Franco Benenato a Sconfiggere il Suo Acerrimo Nemico il Pretore Ciccio De Ingras?" (1971), "Il Clan Dei Due Borsalini" (1972), "I Sette Magnifici Cornuti" (1974), "Flying Sex" (1980), "L'Amante Tutta da Scoprire" (1981), "Fantasma d'Amore" (1981), "My Wife Gocs Back to School" (1981), "La Gatta da Pelare" (1981), "Chaste and Pure" (1981), "Erotic Flesh" (1981), "I Carabbimatti" (1981), "Teste di Quoio" (1981), "W la Foca" (1982), "Bello Mio Bellezza Mia" (1982), "Crazy Navy" (1982), "I Camionisti" (1982), "L'Ave Maria (L'artista)" (1982), "Sesso e Violentieri" (1982),

"Viuuulentemente Mia" (1982), "Dio Li Fa Pol Li Accoppia" (1982), "Vai Avanti Tu Che Mi Vien da Ridere" (1982), "Apocalisse di un Terremonto" (1982), "Pin il Monello" (1982), "Master of the World" (1983), "The Devil and Holy Water" (1983), the science fiction film "Raiders of Atlantis" (aka "The Atlantis Interceptors") (1983), "Razza Violenta" (1984), "Detenute Violente" (1984), "La Donna del Mare" (1984), "7, Hyden Park: La Casa Maledetta" (1985), "I Mercenari Raccontano" (1985), "Massimamente Folle" (1985), "L'Ultimo Giorno" (1985), "Detective School Dropouts" (1986), "Top Model" (1987), "La Lingua" (1987), "The Cello Teacher" (1989), "Strepitosamente... Flop" (1991), and "Ponte Milvio" (2000). Giuffre was also seen in television productions of "Nucleo Centrale Investigativo" (1974), "E Non Se Ne Vogliono Andare!" (1988), and "Una Lepre Con la Faccia di Bambina" (1988).

Gluck, Louise

Poet Louise Gluck, who received the Nobel Prize in Literature in 2020, died of cancer at her home in Cambridge, Massachusetts, on October 13, 2023. She was 80. Gluck was born in New York City on April 22, 1943. She took classes in poetry at Sarah Lawrence College and at Columbia University's School of General Studies. She wrote poetry and had her first publication in an issue of "Mademoiselle" in the mid-1960s. Her poetry was soon featured in the pages of "The Atlantic Monthly", "The New Yorker", and "The Nation". Gluck's first collection, "Firstborn", was published in 1968. She began teaching poetry at Goddard College in Vermont in 1971 and her second collection, "The House on Marshland", was published in 1975. Other collections followed including "Descending Figure" (1980), "The Triumph of Achilles" (1985), and "Ararat" (1990). Her book "The Wild Iris" earned her the Pulitzer Prize for Poetry in 1993. Her later works include "Proofs & Theories: Essays on Poetry" (1994), "Meadowlands" (1996), "Vita Nova" (1999), "The Seven Ages" (2001), the chapbook "October" (2004), "Averno" (2006), "A Village Life" (2009), and "Faithful and Virtuous Night" (2014) earning the National Book Award for Poetry. He collection of her poetry, "Poems: 1962-2012", was published in 2012 and a collection of essays, "American Originality", was released in 2017. Gluck served as Poet Laureate of the United States from 2003 to 2004 and received the National Humanities Medal in 2016. She was the recipient of the Nobel Prize in Literature in 2020. Her collection, "Winter Recipes from the Collective", was published in 2021. Her final book, "Marigold and Rose: A Fiction", was released in 2022. Gluck became a senior lecturer at Williams College in Massachusetts in 1984. She joined the faculty of Yale University in 2004 and was appointed a professor of English at Stanford University in 2023. She married Charles Hertz, Jr., in 1967 and they later divorced. She had a son, Noah, with her partner, Keith Monley, in 1973. She was married to John Dranow from 1977 until their divorce in 1996. She is survived by her son.

Gluck, Wolfgang

Austrian director Wolfgang Gluck, who earned an Academy Award nomination for Best Foreign Language Film for 1987's "'38 - Vienna Before the Fall", died in Austria on December 13, 2023. He was 94. Gluck was born in Vienna, Austria, on September 29, 1929. He began his career in films in the early 1950s. He was seen in a small role in the 1952 film "Abenteuer in Wien". Gluck served as an assistant director for "Viktoria und Ihr Husar" (1954), "Seine Tochter Ist der Peter" (195), "The Cowgirl of Saint Catherine" (1955), "Dunja" (1955), "Das Liebesleben des Schonen Franz" (1956), "Fuhrmann Henschel" (1956), "Ober Zahlen" (1957), "Dort in der Wachau" (1957) which he also scripted, and "Der Jungfrauenkrieg" (1957). He was directing films by the end of the decade with such credits as "Der Pfarrer von St. Michael" (1957), "Gafahrdete Madchen" (1958), "False Shame" (1958), "Das Nachtlokal zum Silbermond" (1959) which he also wrote, "Madchen fur die Mambo-Bar" (1959), "Denn das Weib Ist Schwach" (1961), "Der Graf von Luxemburg" (1972) which he also scripted, "Die Kleine Figur Meines Vaters" (1980), "'38 - Vienna Before the Fall" (1987) earning an Oscar nomination, and "Es War Doch Liebe?" (1997). Gluck worked frequently in television, directing and occasionally writing such productions as ""Kleines Bezirksgericht" (1961), "Staatsaffaren" (1961), "Nicht Zuhoren, Meine Damen!" (1962), "Die Mowe" (1963), "Eine Frau Ohne Bedeutung" (1964), "Ein Monat auf dem Lande" (1967), "Stellenangebote Weiblich" (1969), "Traumnovelle" (1969), "Die Turken Kommen" (1970), "Der Junge Baron Neuhaus" (1971), "Der Wald" (1971), "Literatur" (1975), "Das Gebell" (1976), "A Glass of Water" (1977), "Der Schuler Gerber" (1981), "Brigitta" (1982), and "Munchhausens Letzte Liebe" (1988). He appeared in the films "Red Sun" (1970) and "Funny Games" (1997) and was Dr. Kuno Brechtl in the 1993 television series "Familie Merian". He also taught classes at the Film Academy in Vienna and the Institute for Theatre-Sciences at Vienna University. Gluck was married to actress Christiane Horbiger from 1962 until their divorce in 1967. He married actress Claudia Sorbas in 1972 and is survived by her and two children.

Glynn, Carlin

Actress Carlin Glynn, who earned a Tony Award for her role as Madam Mona Stangley in the 1978 Broadway production of "The Best Little Whorehouse in Texas", died of complications from lung cancer and dementia, died at her home in upstate New York on July 13, 2023. She was 83. Glynn was born in Cleveland, Ohio, on February 19, 1940. She attended high school in Houston, Texas, and graduated from Newcomb College in New Orleans, Louisiana. She moved to New York City in 1959 where she studied acting with Stella Adler. She was featured in an off-Broadway production of "Waltz of the

Toreadors". She married actor and writer Peter Masterson in 1960. She made her film debut in the 1975 thriller "Three Days of the Condor" starring Robert Redford. Glynn worked with her husband at the Actors Studio in New York in the mid-1970s, where co-wrote the stage version of "The Best Little Whorehouse in Texas". She made her Broadway debut as Mona Stangley in the hit musical in June of 1978. She earned a Tony Award for her performance, which was taken over by Dolly Parton for the 1982 film version. She was also seen in the films "Resurrection" (1980), "Continental Divide" (1981), "The Escape Artist" (1982), "Sixteen Candles" (1984) as Brenda Baker, the mother of Molly Ringwald's character, "The Trip to Bountiful" (1984) the first of six of her films directed by her husband, Francis Ford Coppola's "Gardens of Stone" (1987) appearing with her husband and their daughter Mary Stuart Masterson, "Night Game" (1989), "Blood Red" (1989), "Convicts" (1991), "Blessing" (1994), "Judy Berlin" (1999), "West of Here" (2002) which she co-produced, "Lost Junction" (2003), and "Whiskey School" (2005). Glynn was seen on television in productions of "Johnny Garage" (1983), "A Woman Named Jackie" (1991) as Lady Bird Johnson, "Day-O" (1992), and "The Exonerated" (2005). She starred as First Lady Meg Tresch opposite George C. Scott in the short-lived comedy series "Mr. President" in 1987 and appeared in episodes of "Strange Luck" and "Law & Order: Criminal Intent". Glynn was married to Peter Masterson from 1960 until his death in 2018. She is survived by their three children, actress Mary Stuart Masterson, Alexandra Masterson, and Peter Masterson.

Gochnauer, Danny

Actor Danny Gochnauer, who was featured in the 1989 horror film "The Pit", died of a heart attack in

Harrisonville, Missouri, on June 26, 2023. He was 76. Gochnauer was born in Kansas City, Missouri, on September 26, 1946. He was active in theater while attending high school in Belton, Missouri, and graduated in 1964. He later moved to California, where he performed frequently on the local stage in the Carmel peninsula. He was featured as the resurrected mad scientist Dr. Colin Ramzi in the 1989 horror film "The Pit". Gochnauer returned to Belton in the 1990s where he worked for animal rescue and at Target before retiring in 2021.

Goddard, Mark

Actor Mark Goddard, who starred as Major Don West in the science fiction series "Lost in Space" in the 1960s, died from complications of pulmonary fibrosis in Hingham, Massachusetts, on October 10, 2023. He was 87. He was born Charles Harvey Goddard in Lowell, Massachusetts, on July 24, 1936. He was a leading athlete in high school, excelling at basketball and baseball. He attended the College of the Holy Cross after graduating before transferring to the American Academy of Dramatic Arts in New York City. He moved to Los Angeles in 1959 to embark on a career in acting. He was soon cast as Deputy Cully in the western television series "Johnny Ringo" starring Don Durant in the title role from 1959 to 1960. Goddard was also seen in episodes of "The DuPont Show with June Allyson", "The Chevy Mystery Show", "The Rebel", "Zane Grey Theatre", Robert Taylor's crime series "The Detectives" as Sgt. Chris Ballard from 1960 to 1962, "Fair Exchange", "The Rifleman", "Vacation Playhouse", "Burke's Law", "The Bill Dana Show", "The Beverly Hillbillies", "Channing", "The Virginian", "Gunsmoke", "Perry Mason", "The Fugitive", and the comedy series "Many Happy Returns" as Bob Randall from 1964 to 1965. He starred as Major Don West, the pilot of the spacecraft Jupiter 2, in Irwin Allen's science fiction series "Lost in Space" from 1965 to 1968. He and the Robinson family spent three seasons trying to find their way home while becoming increasingly overshadowed by the antics of Jonathan Harris' Dr. Zachary Smith, Bill Mumy's young Will Robinson, and the ever-present Robot. He appeared in a cameo role as a General in the 1998 film version of "Lost in Space" with Matt LeBlanc taking the part of Don West. Goddard continued his career on television with roles in episodes of "Mod Squad", "Dream Girl of '67", "Adam-12", "Switch", "Petrocelli", "The Streets of San Francisco", "Quincy", "Dog and Cat", "The Next Step Beyond", "Benson", B.J. and the Bear", "Barnaby Jones", "The Fall Guy", "The Master", and "Jake and the Fatman". He was seen in the soap operas "One Life to Live" as Ted Clayton in 1981, "The Doctors" as Lt. Paul Reed in 1982, and "General Hospital" as Derek Barrington from 1985 to 1986. His other television credits include the tele-films "The Death Squad" (1974), "The Centerfold Murders" (1975), and "A Reason to Live" (1985). Goddard appeared in a handful of films during his career including Disney's "The Monkey's Uncle" (1965), "A Rage to Live" (1965), "The Love Ins" (1967), "Play It Again, Sam" (1972), the horror film "Blue Sunshine" (1977), the disco film "Roller Boogie" (1979), "Strange Invaders" (1983), "Overnight Sensation" (2000), and "Soupernatural" (2010). He also performed on stage and was featured in the Broadway musical "The Act" in 1977. Goddard largely retired from acting by the late 1980s and returned to college to earn a master's degree in education from Bridgewater State College in Massachusetts. He taught special education and acting at the F.L. Chamberlain School in Middleboro, Massachusetts, from 1991 until 2009. His autobiography, "To Space and Back: A Memoir", was published in 2009. Goddard was married to Marcia Rogers from 1960 until their divorce in 1968 and is survived by their two children, Michael and producer Melissa. He was married to actress Susan Anspach from 1970 until their divorce in 1978 and he adopted her two children. He married Evelyn Pezzulich in 1990 and is also survived by their son, John.

Gold, Herbert

Novelist Herbert Gold died at his home in San Francisco, California, on November 19, 2023. He was 99. Gold was born in Lakewood, Ohio, on March 9, 1924. He moved to New York City in the early 1940s and studied at Columbia University. He served in the U.S. Army during World War II from 1943 to 1946. He graduated from Columbia in 1946 and received a master's degree in 1948. He moved to Paris on a Fulbright Scholarship and studied at the Sorbonne from 1948 to 1951. He wrote his first novel in Paris, "Birth of a Hero", which was published in 1951. He traveled around the world before settling in San Francisco, where he became a leading figure in the literary scene. Gold authored numerous books including "Room Clerk" (1955), "The Man Who Was Not With It" (1956), "The Optimist: A Novel" (1959), "Therefore Be Bold" (1960), "Salt: A Novel" (1963) which was adapted for the 1984 tele-film "Threesome", "Fathers: A Novel in the Form of a Memoir" (1966), "The Great American Jackpot" (1969), the autobiography "My Last Two Thousand Years" (1972), "The Young Prince and the Magic Cone" (1973), "Swiftie the Magician" (1974), "Waiting for Cordelia" (1977), "Slave Trade" (1979), "He/She" (1980), "Family: A Novel in the Form of a Memoir" (1981), "True Love" (1982), "Mister White Eyes: A Novel" (1984), "A Girl of Forty" (1986), "Best Nightmare on Earth: A Life in Haiti" (1991), "Bohemia: Digging the Roots of Cool" (1994), "She Took My Arm As If She Loved Me: A Novel" (2014), the memoir "Still Alive! A Temporary Condition" (2008), and "When a Psychopath Falls in Love" (2015). Gold was married to writer Edith Zubrin from 1948 until their divorce in 1956. He is survived by their daughter, Ann. Another daughter, Judith, died of cancer in 2016. He was married to Melissa Dilworth from 1968 until their divorce in 1975. He is survived by their daughter, Nina, and twin boys, filmmaker Ari and Ethan.

Goldberg, Daniel

Canadian film producer Daniel Goldberg, who was noted for such hit comedies as "Stripes" and "The Hangover" films, died in Los Angeles, California, on July 12, 2023. He was 74. Goldberg was born in Hamilton, Ontario, Canada, on

March 7, 1949. He attended McMaster University in Hamilton in the mid-1960s where he met Ivan Reitman. Goldberg starred in Reitman's 1968 short film "Orientation". The two produced  the 1969 film "Columbus of Sex" (aka "My Secret Life") and were arrested and convicted of making an obscene film. They received probation and a fine. Goldberg continued to work frequently with Reitman throughout his career as partners in Northern Lights Entertainment. He produced and co-wrote the horror comedy "Cannibal Girls" (1973), "Meatballs" (1979), and "Stripes" (1981). He was also producer for "Junior" (1994), "Space Jam" (1996), "Private Parts" (1997) starring Howard Stern, "Commandments" (1997), "Father's Day" (1997), "Six Days Seven Nights" (1998), "Road Trip" (2000), "Evolution" (2001), "Killing Me Softly" (2002), "Old School" (2003), "EuroTrip" (2004), "School for Scoundrels"(2006), "The Hangover" (2009), "Due Date" (2010), "The Hangover II" (2011), and "The Hangover Part III" (2013). Goldberg shared an Emmy Award nomination for the 1996 tele-film "The Late Shift". He was executive producer for the animated series "Beethoven", "Mummies Alive!", "Extreme Ghostbusters", and "Alienators: Evolution Continues". Goldberg co-wrote the films "Heavy Metal" (1981), "Spacehunter: Adventures in the Forbidden Zone" (1983), and "Feds" (1988) which he also directed. He is survived by his wife, fellow film producer Ilona Herzberg.

Goldman, Bo

Screenwriter Bo Goldman, who received Academy Awards for scripting "One Flew Over the Cuckoo's Nest" and "Melvin and Howard", died in Helendale, California, on July 25, 2023. He was 90. He was born Robert Spencer Goldman in New York City on September 10, 1932. He attended  Princeton University where he was president of the Princeton Triangle Club. He served in the U.S. Army for three years after graduation and was stationed on Eniwetok, an atoll in the Pacific Ocean used for nuclear bomb testing. He resumed working in theater after his discharge and was an assistant to composer Jule Styne. He was lyricist for the Broadway musical "First impressions" in 1959. He tried for several years without success to get his show "Hurray Boys Hurrah" produced. He worked as a writer and producer for such television series as "The Philco Television Playhouse", "The Seven Lively Arts", "Playhouse 90", "Theatre '62", "NBC Children's Theatre", and "The Defenders". He was involved in the productions of such "Playhouse 90" productions as "The

Plot to Kill Stalin" (1958), "Days of Wine and Roses" (1958), "Heart of Darkness" (1958), "Old Man" (1958), "The Grey Nurse Said Nothing" (1959), and "The Tunnel" (1959). He moved to Los Angeles in 1974, over a decade after his last script had been produced to pursue a career in films. He was selected by director Milos Forman to script the 1975 film "One Flew Over the Cuckoo's Nest", based on a novel by Ken Kesey. The film earned five Academy Awards including Best Picture, Forman for Best Director, Jack Nicholson for Best Actor, Louise Fletcher for Best Actress, and Goldman for Best Adapted Screenplay. Goldman scripted the 1979 film "The Rose" starring Bette Midler. He received another Oscar for his original screenplay for 1980's "Melvin and Howard" starring Paul LeMat and Jason Robards, Jr. His earlier script, "Shoot the Moon", was filmed by Alan Parker in 1982 and starred Diane Keaton and Albert Finney. He was an uncredited contributor on the scripts for the films "Ragtime" (1981), "The Flamingo Kid" (1984), "Swing Shift" (1984), and "Dick Tracy" (1990). He co-wrote the 1988 film "Little Nikita". He was again nominated for an Academy Award for his script for the 1992 film "Scent of a Woman" starring Al Pacino. He continued to write such films as "City Hall" (1996) and "Meet Joe Black" (1998) and provided an uncredited revision for 2000's "The Perfect Storm". He also worked on the script for Forman's "Goya's Ghost" (2006) and received a story credit for Warren Beatty's 2016 film "Rules Don't Apply". He received the Laurel Award for career achievement from the Writers Guild of America in 1998. Goldman was married to Mabel Rathbun Ashforth from 1954 until her death in 2017. He is survived by their five children, Mia, Amy, Diana, Justin, and Serena, who is married to director Todd Field. His oldest son, Jesse, was killed when he was struck by a car in a crosswalk in Santa Monica in 1981.

Goldoni, Lelia

Actress Lelia Goldoni died at the Lillian Booth Actors Home in Englewood, New Jersey, on July 22, 2023. She was 86. She was born Lelia Rizzuto in New York City on October  1, 1936, and was raised in Los Angeles. She appeared in films as a juvenile with small roles in "House of Strangers" (1949) and "We Were Strangers" (1949). She attended Los Angeles City College and performed with the Lester Horton Dancers in the 1950s. She returned to New York City later in the decade where she met John Cassavetes in an acting class. Goldoni starred in his 1959 debut film "Shadows". She was also seen on television in episodes of "Johnny Staccato" and "The Lloyd Bridges Show". She spent the next decade living in England where she continued her acting career in episodes of "First Night", "ITV Play of the Week", "Espionage", "Theatre 625:, "Blackmail", "Court Martial", "Secret Agent", "Felony Squad", "Thirty-Minute Theatre", "The Wednesday Play", "Omnibus", "Strange

Report", "Shirley's World", "Spyder's Web", and "Doctor in Charge". Goldoni also appeared in the Hammer psychological thriller "Hysteria" (1965), the horror film "Theatre of Death" (aka "Blood Fiend") (1967), and the crime caper film "The Italian Job" (1969). She returned to the United States in the early 1970s and was featured as Bea in the 1974 film "Alice Doesn't Live Here Anymore". She also appeared in the films "The Day of the Locust" (1975), "Baby Blue Marine" (1976), "Special Delivery" (1976), "Bloodbrothers" (1978), the science fiction remake "Invasion of the Body Snatchers" (1978) as Katherine, the horror film "The Unseen" (1980), "Choices" (1981), "Gangster Wars" (1981), "Rainy Day Friends" (1985), "Somebody to Love" (1994), "Chain Link" (2008), and "The Devil Inside" (2012). She appeared on television in episodes of "Doctors' Hospital", "Visions", "Vega$", "Cagney & Lacey", "Knots Landing" in the recurring role of Dr. Beauvais in 1983, "Santa Barbara", "The New Mike Hammer", "L.A. Law", "Homefront", "State of Mind", and "Cold Case". Her other television credits include the tele-films and mini-series "A Kiss Is Just a Kiss" (1971), "The Disappearance of Aimee" (1976), "The Spell" (1977), "Good Against Evil" (1977), "Nowhere to Hide" (1977), "Scruples" (1980), "Mistress of Paradise" (1981), "Anatomy of an Illness" (1984), "Victims for Victims: The Theresa Saldana Story" (1984), "The Computer Wore Tennis Shoes" (1995), "The Pacific" (2010), and "The Funeral Director" (2016). Goldoni produced and directed the 1993 documentary "Genius on the Wrong Coast" about Lester Horton. She also taught acting frequently during her career at the Lee Strasberg Theatre Institute, the University of California at Los Angeles, and Hampshire College. Goldoni was married to actor and "Shadows" co-star Ben Carruthers from 1957 until their divorce in 1960. She was also married to William B. Hale for several years in the 1960s. She was married to screenwriter and actor Robert Rudelson from 1968 until his death in 1997 and is survived by their son Aaron.

Golestan, Ebrahim
Iranian film director Ebrahim Golestan died in Sussex, England, on August 2, 2023. He was 100. He was born Ebrahim Taghavi Shirazi in Shiraz, Iran, on October 19, 1922.

He attended the University of Tehran but did not graduate. He began working in films in the late 1950s and formed Golestan Films in 1957. He made films, documentaries, and shorts including "From a Drop to the Sea" (1957), "A Fire" (1961), "Courtship" (1961), "Moj, Marjan, Khara" (1962), "The Hills of Marlik" (1963), "The Crown Jewels of Iran" (1965), "Harvest and the Seed" (1965), "Village Councils" (1965), "Brick and Mirror"(1966), "Kharab-Abad" (1966), and "Secrets of the Treasure of the Jinn Valley" (1974). Golestan left Iran following the Islamic Revolution in 1979 and settled in England. He was closely associated with poet Forough Farrokhzad from the late 1950s until her death in an automobile accident in 1967. He produced her 1963 short film "The House Is Black". Golestan was married to Fakhri Taghavi Shirazi from 1942 until her death in 2012. He is survived by their daughter, translator Lili Golestan. Their son, photojournalist Kaveh Golestan, was killed after stepping on a land mine while working for the BBC in Iraq in 2003.

Golubovich, Mikhail
Ukrainian actor Mikhail Golubovich died in Luhansk, an internationally unrecognized republic of Russia in the occupied parts of eastern Ukraine, on October 9, 2023. He was

79. Golbovich was born in Zolotonosha, Ukraine (then part of the Soviet Union), on November 21, 1943. He appeared on stage and screen from the late 1960s. His film credits include "Beginning of an Unknown Era" (1967), "I Byl Vecher, I Bylo Utro..." (1971), "Komisary" (1971), "Krasnaya Metel" (1971), "Propala Hramota" (1972), "Posledniy Gaiduk" (1973), "Svabda" (1973), "Duma o Kovpake: Nabat" (1974), "Husy-Lebedi Letyat" (1974), "Na Kray Sveta" (1975), "Mustang-Inokhodets" (1976), "Duma o Kovpake: Buran" (1976), "Vsego Odna Noch" (1976), "Duma o Kovpake: Karpaty, Karpaty..." (1978), "Biryuk" (1978), "Vragi" (1978), "Elodet Mokavshires" (1979), "More" (1979), "Gonka s Presledovaniem" (1980), "Mersedes Ukhodit ot Pogoni" (1980), "Koleso Istorii" (1981), "Night Is Short" (1982), "Rodnik" (1982), "Preodoleniye" (1982), "Legenda o Knyagine Olge" (1984), "Bereg" (1984), "Tikhiye Vody Gluboki" (1985), "Mama, Rodnaya, Lyubimaya..." (1987), "Obida" (1987), "Akseleratka" (1987), "Poka est Vremya" (1987), "Solomiani Dzvony" (1988), "Proshchay, Shpana Zamoskvoretskaya" (1988), "Navazhdenie" (1989), "Blagorodnyy Razboynik Vladimir Dubrovskiy" (1990), "Pod Severnym Siyaniyem" (1990), "Kozaki Ydut" (1991), "Luna Park" (1992), "Vyshnevi Nochi" (1992), "Deti Chugunnykh Bogov" (1993), "Zalozhniki Strakha" (1994), "Doroha Na Sich" (1995), "Lyublyu i Tochka 3D" (2011), "Brothel Lights" (2011), "Hetman" (2015), "The Traitor" (2017), and "Opolchenochka" (2019). Golubovich was seen on television in productions of "Uzniki Bomona" (1971), "How the Steel Was Tempered" (1973), "Kortik" (1974), "Yurkiny Rassvety" (1974), "Khozhdenie Po Mukam" (1977), "Patyat Kam Sofia" (1978), "Mozhestvo" (1981), "Dolgiy Put v Labirinte" (1981), "Na Krutizne" (1985), "Gde-to Gremit Voyna" (1986), "Shtormovoe Preduprezhdenie" (1988), "Vuyna" (1990), and "And Quiet Flows the Don" (2006). Golubovich served on the People's Council of the Luhansk People's Republic, a position that resulted in sanctions from the European Union following Russia's invasion of Ukraine in April of 2022.

Gomez-Lacueva, Laura

Spanish actress Laura Gomez-Lacueva died of cancer in Zaragoza, Spain, on March 30, 2023. She was 48. Gomez-Lacueva was born in Zaragoza on February 24, 1975. She trained as an actress at the Escuela Municipal de Teatro de Zaragoza from 1994 to 1997. She

performed frequently on stage and was co-founder of the theatrical companies Muac Teatro, Nueve de Nueve Teatro, and La Extinta Poetica. She appeared in the films "De Tu Ventana a la Mia" (2011), "El Encamado" (2012), "Justi&Cia" (2014), "The Bride" (2015), "Bendita Calamidad" (2015), "Refugios" (2015), "Uncertain Glory" (2017), "La Tierra Muerta" (2018), "Becquer and the Witches" (2018), "The Footballest" (2018), "The Candidate" (2018), "Miau" (2018), "Schoolgirls" (2020), "Marcelino, el Mejor Payaso del Mundo" (2020), "Historias Lamentables" (2020), and "Alumbramiento" (2024). She was also seen in the shorts "Parresia" (2021) and "Plastic Killer" (2022). Gomez-Lacueva appeared on television in the series "Vaya Comunidad!", "Aida", "The Zone", "El Ultimo Show", "Cuentame Como Paso", "La Que se Avecena", and "The Countryside" as Mariajo from 2021 to 2023.

Gonzales Falcon, Peter

Actor Peter Gonzales Falcon was found dead at his home in La Pryor, Texas, on August 22, 2023. He was 75.

Gonzales was born in La Pryor on December 26, 1948. He was attending Texas State University when he was cast in a small role in the 1969 film "Viva Max". He was cast by director Federico Fellini to portray a younger version of Fellini in the 1972 Italian film "Roma". He also starred in Liliana Cavani's "L'Ospite" (1971). Gonzales soon left Europe and appeared in the 1974 Mexican film "The Holy Inquisition". He appeared on television in an episode of "Police Woman" and in the tele-films "Secrets" (1977) and "Houston: The Legend of Texas" (1986). His other films include Burt Reynolds' "The End" (1978), "Heartbreaker" (1983), "Bordertown" (2007), "Tiramisu for Two" (2016), and "Dis" (2018).

Goode, Joanna

Actress and model Joanna Goode died at her home in Santa Monica, California, on January 14, 2023. She was 53. Goode was born in St. Louis, Missouri, on December 19, 1969. She moved to California in 1985 and graduated from California State University at Long Beach. She

worked as a model and was a singer and songwriter. She was featured as Incense Berkowitz, a model and rival of Christina Applegate's Kelly Bundy, in a 1990 episode of "Married... with Children". She starred as Kayla MacIntyre in the 2009 western film "Palo Pinto Gold".

Goodman, Len

Dancer and television personality Len Goodman, who was a judge on the reality television series "Strictly Come

Dancing" and "Dancing with the Stars", died of prostate and bone cancer in Royal Tunbridge Wells, Kent, England, on April 23, 2023. He was 78. Goodman was born in Farnborough, Kent, on April 25, 1944. He moved to Blackfen with his family as a child. He worked as an apprentice welder in Woolwich and began dancing in the early 1960s as therapy for a foot injury. Goodman was a successful ballroom dancer winning numerous competitions over the next decade. He retired from competitive dancing in the early 1970s and opened a dance school in Dartford. He became head judge of the BBC dance competition series "Strictly Come Dancing" in 2004. He remained with the series through 2016. Goodman became head judge of the American adaptation, "Dancing with the Stars", in 2005. He led the judges panel with Ann Inaba and Bruno Tonioli with occasional guest judges. He was absent for several later seasons due to conflict with his work in Great Britain. He announced his retirement from the show during the 31st season in 2022. The award given to the show's winners was renamed the Len Goodman Mirrorball Trophy following his death. Goodman provided the voice of the Professor in the animated series for preschoolers, "Auto-B-Good", from 2005 to 2006. He was host of the documentary mini-series "Titanic with Len Goodman" and "Len Goodman's Dancing Feet: The British Ballroom Story" in 2012. He also hosted "Len Goodman's Dance Band Days" (2013), "Dancing Cheek to Cheek: An Intimate History of Dance" (2014), "Len Goodman's Big Band Bonanza" (2014), "Len and Ainsley's Big Food Adventure" (2015) with Ainsley Harriott, "Holiday of My Lifetime with Len Goodman" (2014-2016), "Dancing Through the Blitz: Blackpool's Big Band Story" (2015), and "Strictly Len Goodman" (2016). He was also a guest on such talk and variety shows as "The Weakest Link", "Rachael Ray", "The Morning Show with Mike & Juliet", "Friday Night with Jonathan Ross", "What Are You Like?", "The View", "Piers Morgan's Life Stories", "Who Do You Think You Are?", "Katie", "The Graham Norton Show", "Jimmy Kimmel Live!", "Partners in Rhyme", "Loose Women", "The Alan Titchmarsh Show", "Good Morning America", "Lorraine", "Good Morning Britain", and "Celebrity Chase". His autobiography, "Better Late Than Never", was published in 2008. Goodman was married to dancing partner Cherry Kingston from 1972 until their divorce in 1987. He was subsequently involved with a woman named Lesley and they had a son, James, prior to their separation. He married longtime companion Sue Barrett in 2012 and she also survives him.

Goodwyn, Myles

Canadian musician Myles Goodwyn, who was lead singer and guitarist for the band April Wine, died of complications from diabetes in Halifax, Nova Scotia, Canada, on December 3, 2023. He was 75. He was born Miles Goodwin in Woodstock, New Brunswick, Canada, on June 23, 1948, and was raised in Waverley, Nova Scotia. He played with bassist Jim Henman in the band the Termites. They teamed with Henman's cousins, David Henman on guitar and Ritchie Henman on drums, to form the band April Wine in 1969. They signed with Aquarius Records in Montreal and recorded their self-named debut album in 1971. Goodwyn was the primary songwriter for the group, which had a minor hit with the single "Fast Train". Jim Henman was soon replaced on bass by Jim Clench and had success with their 1972 album "On Record". They had hits with their covers of the songs "You Could Have Been a Lady" and "Bad Side of the Moon". The Henman brothers left April Wine while recording the 1973 album "Electric Jewels" and drummer Jerry Mercer and guitarist Gary Moffet took their place. Goodwyn remained a constant in the bands shifting lineup. They continued to record the albums "April Wine Live" (1974), "Stand Back" (1975), "The Whole World's Goin' Crazy" (1976), "Forever for Now" (1977), "First Glance" (1978), "Harder... Faster" (1970), "The Nature of the Beast" (1981), "Power Play" (1982), "Animal Grace" (1984), "One for the Road" (1984), and "Walking Through Fire" (1985). Goodwyn moved to the Bahamas and April Wine disbanded in 1986. He recorded a self-named solo album in 1988. He returned to Canada in 1992 and reunited with Brian Greenway, who had joined April Wine as a guitarist and singer in 1977. Jim Mercer returned on drums and Jim Clench on bass, with Steve Segal added to the mix as a guitarist for a new version of "April Wine". The revived band recorded the albums "Altitude" (1993), "Frigate" (1994), "Back to the Mansion" (2001), and "Roughly Speaking" (2006). His memoir, "Just Between You and Me", was published in 2016 and he also wrote the 2018 novel "Elvis and Tiger". Goodwyn retired from touring in late 2022 due to reasons of health. He was inducted into the Canadian Songwriters Hall of Fame in 2023. His survivors include his wife, Kim Goodwyne, and their two children, and another child from a previous relationship.

Goody, Bob

British actor Bob Goody died of cancer in England on March 5, 2023. He was 71. Goody was born in Brighton, Sussex, England, on April 16, 1951. He attended Brighton Technical College and trained at the Royal Academy of Dramatic Art from 1973 to 1975. He began his career on stage

and was a founding member of the Shared Experience theatrical company. He performed in numerous productions with the company and appeared on stage in "The Comedy of Errors" and "Hamlet" for the Royal Shakespeare Company in 1987. He was featured in a production of "The Wind in the Willows" at the Old Vic for the National Theatre in 1991. He appeared in the role of Lucky in a 2015 production of Samuel Beckett's "Waiting for Godot" at the Crucible Theatre in Scotland. He worked often with comic Mel Smith and co-wrote the musical black comedies "'Ave You 'Eard the One About Joey Baker?", "Irony in Dorking", and "The Gambler". They co-hosted the children's comedy sketch show "Smith and Goody" in 1980. He also co-wrote the comedy series "Wilderness Road" with Richard Cottan in 1986. Goody was seen frequently on television with roles in episodes of "The Devil's Crown", "A Soft Touch", "Sherlock Holmes and Doctor Watson", "Robin's Nest", "The History of Mr. Polly", "Dear Heart", "Luna", "The Kenny Everett Television Show", "Bunch of Five", "Screen Two", "Lovejoy", "Paul Merton's Life of Comedy", "McCallum", "Crime Traveller" as Danny the caretaker in 1997, "The Queen's Nose", "Lock, Stock...", "The Ghost Hunter" as Mr. Povey in 2001, "Dark Realm", "Doctors", "The Bill", "Hotel Babylon", "Crusoe", "EastEnders", "X Company", "Fleabag", and "Queens of Mystery". His other television credits include productions of "Those Glory Glory Days" (1983), "Bleak House" (1985), "Porterhouse Blue" (1987), "My Family and Other Animals" (1987), "The Stone Age" (1989), "Selling Hitler" (1991), "The Blackheath Poisonings" (1992), "Buskers Odyssey" (1994), "Treasure Island" (1995), "That Summer Day" (2006), "Cider with Rosie" (2015), "The Last Dragonslayer" (2016), "Vanity Fair" (2018), and "Why Didn't They Ask Evans?" (2022). Goody was seen in the films "Flash Gordon" (1980), "Lifeforce" (1985), "The Cook, the Thief, His Wife & Her Lover" (1989), "Feuer, Eis & Dynamit" (1990), "Gentlemen Don't Eat Poets" (1995), "The Borrowers" (1997), "Lighthouse" (1999), "The Thief Lord" (2006), "Low Tide" (2008), "The Great Ghost Rescue" (2011), "Late September" (2012), "Back to the Garden" (2013), "Mr. Turner" (2014), "A Change in the Weather" (2017), "Peterloo" (2018), "Intrigo: Samaria" (2019), "23 Walks" (2020), and "A Clever Woman" (2023). He also appeared in the short films "In the Doghouse" (2002), "Curtains" (2009), "Skyborn" (2012), "Orbit Ever After" (2013), and "Make Aliens Dance" (2017). He wrote the libretto for the opera "The Fashion" for the Deutsche Oper am Rhein in 2008 and his book of verse, "War & Paracetamol", was published in 2021. Goody married Gina Donovan in 1978 and is survived by her and their three daughters.

Goraguer, Alain

French jazz pianist and composer Alain Goraguer died in Paris, France, on February 13, 2023. He was 91. Goraguer was born in Rosny-sous-Bois, France, on August 20, 1931. He moved to Nice with his family as a child where he studied piano and violin. He later moved to Paris where he performed with  jazz bands and began co-writing songs with Boris Vian. He also collaborated with singers Serge Gainsbourg, Boby Lapointe, and France Gall. He also worked with such artists as Nana Mouskouri, Juliette Greco, Brigitte Bardo, Jean Ferrat, Georges Moustaki, and Regine. Goraguer was composer for numerous films from the late 1950s and used the pseudonym Paul Vernon when scoring adult films in the 1970s and 1980s. His films include "Girl in His Pocket" (1957), "Le Corbusier, l'Architecte du Bonheur" (1957), "No Escape" (1958), "I Spit on Your Grave" (1959), "Les Loups Dans la Bergerie" (1960), "Le Bel Age" (1960), "Les Heritiers" (1960), "Le Sahara Brule" (1961), "Sweet Skin" (1963), "Blague Dans le Coin" (1963), "Mission to Venice" (1965), "Les Longues Annees" (1964), "Paris Secret" (1965), "Nick Carter et le Trefle Rouge" (1965), "L'Homme de Marrakech" (1966), "Un Garcon, Une Fille. Le Dix-Septieme Ciel" (1966), "Un Choix d'Assassins" (1967), "La Servante" (1970), "Sur un Arbre Perche" (1971), "Les Portes de Feu" (1972), "Escape to Nowhere" (1973), "L'Affaire Domiici" (1973), the animated science fiction film "Fantastic Planet" (aka "La Planete Sauvage") (1973), "Ursule et Grelu" (1974), "Sex Rally" (1974), "Les Noces de Porelaine" (1975), "Au-Dela de la Peur" (1975), "La Villa" (1975), "Hard Love" (1975), "Indecences" (1975), "Safari Porno" (1976), "P... Comme Penetration" (1976), "Hurlements de Plaisir" (1976), "L'Essayeuse" (1976), "De Cote des Tennis" (1976), "Le Fessee ou Les Memoires de Monsieur Leon Maitre-Fesseur" (1976), "L'Aigle et la Colombe" (1977), "Cailles Sur Canape" (1977), "Stella" (1977), "Esclaves Sexuelles Sur Catalogue" (1977), "Pornotissimo" (1977), "La Rabatteuse" (1978), "Les Grabdes Hiyusseyses" (1978), "Salopes et Vicieuses" (1978), "Cuisses Infernales" (1978), "Veuves en Chaleur" (1978), "The Wives of Others" (1978), "La Perversion d'Une Jeune Mariee" (1978), "Je Cris... Je Jouis" (1978), "Les Filles du Regiment" (1978), "Miss Partouze" (1978), "La Grande Leche" (1979), "Caresses" (1979), "Auto-Stoppeuses en Chaleur" (1979), "Soumission" (1979), "Hot and Horny" (1979), "Les Seceuses" (1979), "Le Droit de Cuissage" (1980), "Parties Carrees Campagnardes" (1980), "Take Me Down" (1980), "Croisieres Pour Couples en Chaleur" (1980), "Charlie Bravo" (1980), "Les Nymphomane" (1980), "Secretariat Prive" (1980), "Les Bas de Soie Noire" (1981), "Garconnieres Tres Speciales" (1981), "Couple Seeking Liberated Girl" (1982), "Dames de Compagnie" (1982), "Chambres d'Amis Tres Particulieres" (1983), "L'Initiation d'Une Femme Mariee" (1983), "A Notre Regrettable Epoux" (1988), "Adieu Je t'Aime" (1988), "L'Oeil Ecarlate" (1993), and "Love Me No More" (2008). Goraguer scored television productions of "La Megere Apprivoisee" (1964),

"Sheherazade" (1971), "Michel, l'Enfant-Roi" (1972), "La Porte du Large" (1975), "Les Monte-en-l'Air" (1976), "Faits Divers" (1976), "Histoires Etranges" (1980), "Adieu" (1982), "Jakob und Adele" (1982), "Merci Sylvestre" (1983), "Ich Heirate Eine Familie..." (1983-1985), "The Adventures of Dr. Bayer" (1985-1989), "Florence ou La Vie de Chateau" (1987), "Panique Aux Caraibes" (1989), "Marie Perenche" (1989-1991), "L'Ordinateur Amoureux" (1991), "Bebe Express" (1991), "Quiproquos!" (1991), "Le Reveillon, c'Est a Quel Etage?" (1993), "Le Galopin" (1993), "Au Beau Rivage" (1994), "Le Raisin d'Or" (1994), and "L'Aigle et le Cheval" (1994).

Gordon, Bert I.

Film director Bert I. Gordon, who was known for such cult science fiction films as "The Amazing Colossal Man" and "Attack of the Puppet People", died at a hospital in Los  Angeles, California, after collapsing at his home on March 8, 2023. He was 100. Gordon was born in Kenosha, Wisconsin, on September 24, 1922. He became interested in making films when he was given his first camera in his youth. He attended the University of Wisconsin at Madison but dropped out to serve in the U.S. Army Air Forces during World War II. He began making television commercials after his discharge. He served as a production assistant on the television series "Racket Squad" in the early 1950s. Gordon was producer and cinematographer for the 1954 adventure film "Serpent Island". He made his first feature film, "King Dinosaur", about astronauts visiting an alien planet inhabited by prehistoric beasts, in 1955. He made numerous films featuring radioactive mutants and monsters over the next sixty years, often serving as producer, director, screenwriter, and special effects designer. His 1957 film, "Beginning of the End", featured Peter Graves battling an army of huge grasshoppers. "The Cyclops" (1957) featured Dean Parkin as a human who grows to giant size in a radioactive valley and co-starred James Craig, Lon Chaney, Jr., and Gloria Talbott. Gordon continued his theme of radioactively enlarged humans in 1957's "The Amazing Colossal Men" starring Glenn Langan in the title role, and the 1958 sequel "War of the Colossal Beast" starring Dean Parkin. His penchant for huge men and creatures earned him the nickname of Mr. B.I.G., referencing his initials. He reversed his formula from the large to the small for the 1958 film "Attack of the Puppet People" starring John Agar and John Hoyt. An arachnid received the growing treatment in the 1958 film "Earth vs. the Spider". He helmed the adventure film "The Boy and the Pirates" (1960) starring juvenile star Charles Herbert opposite his daughter, Susan Gordon. He made the 1960 ghost story "Tormented" starring Richard Carlson. His 1962 fantasy classic "The Magic Sword", starred Basil Rathbone, Gary Lockwood, and Anne Helm and featured an array of ogres, pinheads, dwarves, and a two-headed dragon.

Gordon also made the unsold television pilots "Famous Ghost Stories" (1961) and "Take Me to Your Leader" (1964). He made the 1965 film "Village of the Giants", loosely based on H.G. Wells' book "The Food of the Gods", about a group of rebellious teenagers who grown to gigantic size and terrorize a small town. It featured such young stars as Tommy Kirk,

Johnny Crawford, Beau Bridges, and Ron Howard. His 1966 film "Picture Mommy Dead" as a psychological thriller starring Don Ameche, Martha Hyer, Zsa Zsa Gabor, and his daughter Susan. He directed and wrote the 1970 comedy "How to Succeed with Sex" and the 1972 horror film "Necromancy" (aka "The Witching") starring Orson Welles. He made the 1972 crime film "The Mad Bomber" starring Chuck Connors and Vince Edwards. Gordon revisited the H.G. Wells book for 1976's "The Food of the Gods", with a cast including Marjoe Gortner, Ida Lupino, Pamela Franklin, and Ralph Meeker pitted against giant rats, wasps, and grubs. His 1977 film "Empire of the Ants" was also loosely based on an H.G. Wells story and starred Joan Collins and Robert Lansing. He returned to horror with the 1981 film "The Coming" (aka "Burned at the Stake") about a resurrected witch in Salem. He directed and wrote the teen comedy films "Let's Do It!" (1982) and "The Big Bet" (1985). His 1990 horror film "Satan's Princess" starred Robert Forster and Lydie Denier. He returned to filmmaking after a 25-year hiatus, writing and directed the 2015 horror film "Secrets of a Psychopath". His autobiography, "The Amazing Colossal World of Mr. B.I.G.", was published in 2012. Gordon was married to Flora Lang from 1945 until their divorce in 1979 and is survived by two of their daughters, Carol and Patricia. Another daughter, actress Susan Gordon, who appeared in several of his films, died in 2011. Flora worked on many of Gordon's films as a production manager and visual effects artist and died in 2016. He married Eva Marie Marklstorfer in 1980 and is also survived by her and their daughter, Christina.

Gordon, Jim

Musician and songwriter Jim Gordon, who was drummer for the group Derek and the Dominos, died at a medical prison in Vacaville, California, on March 13, 2023. He was 77. Gordon was born in Los Angeles, California, on July 14, 1945. He began his career in music in his late teens backing the Everly Brothers in 1963. He became one of the leading sessions drummers in the 1960s, recording with the Beach Boys, Paul Revere and the Raiders, the Byrds, and Mason Williams on his 1968 hit "Classical Gas". He toured with Delaney & Bonnie's backing band in 1969 and 1970. He was a founding member of the blues rock band Derek and the

Dominos in 1970 with Eric Clapton, Bobby Whitlock, and Carl Radle. They were best known for their hit song "Layla" and recorded one album before

splitting up in 1971. Gordon also toured with Joe Cocker's "Mad Dogs & Englishmen" and was featured in two songs for the Traffic album "The Low Spark of High Heeled Boys". He also recorded with Harry Nilsson, the Incredible Bongo Band, Frank Zappa, Helen Reddy, Johnny Rivers, Art Garfunkel, Steely Dan, and Alice Cooper. Gordon developed schizophrenia in the early 1970s claiming to hear voices. He used a hammer and butcher knife to kill his mother, Osa Beck Gordon, in June of 1983, claiming the voices and compelled him. He was only then diagnosed with acute schizophrenia but was denied the use of an insanity defense due to changes in California law. He was sentenced to sixteen years to life in prison in 1984. He was denied parole on multiple occasions and was incarcerated at the California Medical Facility, a medical and psychiatric prison, at the time of his death. Gordon was married and divorced from singer Renee Armand and dancer Jill Barabe, and is survived by a daughter, Amy.

Gordon, Pamela Anne

Canadian model Pamela Anne Gordon, who was Playboy Playmate of the Month in March of 1962, died of

complications from pneumonia and a heart attack in Abbotsford, British Columbia, Canada, on January 25, 2023. She was 79. Gordon was born in British Columbia on February 10, 1943. She became the first Canadian to become a Playboy Playmate when she was the centerfold for the March 1962 issue of the magazine. She moved to Chicago where she was a Playboy bunny at the Playboy mansion. She later returned to Canada and worked as a go-go dancer in Montreal in the 1960s. She also appeared in a small role in the television series "The Littlest Hobo". Gordon was married and divorced three times and is survived by a daughter from an earlier relationship, Indira Gordon. She is also survived by a son, Robin, from her second marriage to Bob Johnson.

Gorgatti, Guido

Italian-Argentine actor Guido Gorgatti died in Buenos Aires, Argentina, on May 11, 2023. He was 103. Gorgatti was born in Rovigo, Italy, on December 5, 1919. He moved to Argentina with his family in 1929. He made his film debut as a juvenile in 1935's "Pibelandia". He continued to perform frequently on radio in his youth. He began his film career in earnest in the early 1950s with roles in "Una Noche en El

Relampago" (1950), "Barbara Atomica" (1952), "Romeo y Julita" (1953), "Somos Todos Inquillinos" (1954), "Una

Americana en Buenos Aires" (1961), "Il Gaucho" (1964), "Disloque en el Presidio" (1965), "La Pergola de las Flores" (1965), "Ritmo Nuevo y Vieja Ola" (1965), "De Profesion, Sospechosos" (1966), "La Cigarra Esta Que Arde" (1967), "Quiere Casarse Conmigo...?!" (1967), "Villa Carino Esta Que Arde" (1968), "El Caradura y la Millonaria" (1971), "Hoy le Toca a Mi Mujer" (1973), "La Super, Super Aventura" (1975), "Los Chicos Crecen" (1976), "Millonarios a la Fuerza" (1979), "Vivir Con Alegria" (1979), "Los Fierecillos se Divierten" (1983), "Mingo y Anibal Contra los Fantasmas" (1985), "Las Aventuras de Tremendo" (1986), "Two Crazy Privates II" (1986), "Mingo y Anibal en la Mansion Embrujada" (1986), and "Delito de Corrupcion" (1991). Gorgatti appeared television in productions of "La Revista de Dringue" (1967), "El Mundo del Espectaculo" (1968), "Atras en la Via" (1970), "El Chinchorro" (1971), "Rolando Rivas, Taxista" (1972), "Revista de Revistas" (1972), "Una Mujer en la Multitud" (1974), "No Hace Falta Querete" (1975) as Belisario, "Vos y Yo, Toda la Vida" (1978) as Don Dimas, "Agui Llegan los Manfredi" (1980), "El Ciclo de Guillermo Bradeston y Nora Carpena" (1981), "La Tuerca" (1981), "La Torre en Jaque" (1981), "Sabado de Todos" (1982), "Esos Que Dicen Amarse" (1993) as Aroldo, "Como Pan Caliente" (1996), "Ricos y Famosos" (1997), "La Condena de Gabriel Doyle" (1998), "Tiempofinal" (2001), "Un Cortado" (2001), "Resistire" (2003), "Son Amores" (2004), "Los de la Esquina" (2004), "Un Cortado Historias de Cafe" (2006), and "El Tabaris, Lleno de Estrellas" (2012).

Gottlieb, Robert

Writer and editor Robert Gottlieb died at a hospital in New York City on June 14, 2023. He was 92. Gottlieb was born in New York City on April 29, 1931. He graduated from

Columbia University in 1952 and earned a graduate degree from Cambridge University in 1954. He began working at Simon & Schuster as an editorial assistant to editor Jack Goodman in 1955. He was instrumental in the publication of Joseph Heller's "Catch-22" and Leon Uris' "Mila 18" in the early 1960s. Gottlieb rose to the position of editor-and-chief before moving to Alfred A. Knopf to occupy the same position in 1968. He became president of Knopf before succeeding William Shawn as editor of "The New Yorker" from 1987 to 1992. He subsequently returned to Knopf. He served as the dance critic for "The New

York Observer" from 1999. He estimated that he had edited between 600 to 700 books during his career and worked with such authors as John Cheever, Toni Morrison, Chaim Potok, Doris Lessing, Salman Rushdie, John le Carre, Ray Bradbury, Michael Crichton, Bill Clinton, Bob Dylan, Katharine Hepburn, Katharine Graham, Robert Caro, Lauren Bacall, Liv Ullman, Paul Simon, and Jessica Mitford. Gottlieb was author of various non-fiction works including "A Certain Style: The Art of the Plastic Handbag" (1988), "Forcing the Spring: The Transformation of the American Environmental Movement" (1993), "Reading Jazz: A Gathering of Autobiography, Reportage, and Criticism from 1919 to Now" (1996), "George Balanchine: The Ballet Maker" (2004), "Sarah: The Life of Sarah Bernhardt" (2010), "Food Justice" (2010), "Lives and Letters" (2011), "Great Expectations: The Sons and Daughters of Charles Dickens" (2012), "Avid Reader: A Life" (2016), "Near-Death Experiences...and Others" (2018), and "Garbo" (2021). His work with writer Robert Caro was the subject of the 2022 documentary film "Turn Every Page". Gottlieb married Muriel Higgins in 1952 and they had a son, Roger, before their divorce. He married actress Maria Tucci in 1969 and is also survived by her and their two children, director Lizzie Gottlieb and Nicky Gottlieb.

Govedarica, Vojislav

Serbian-American actor Vojislav Govedarica, who was sometimes billed as Vojo Goric and Voja Krstarica, died at

his home in Los Angeles, California, on December 5, 2023. He was 83. Govedarica was born in Gacko, Bosnia and Herzegovina, Yugoslavia, in 1940. He settled in Belgrade, where he worked as a lifeguard and nightclub bouncer. He began working in films with the Yugoslav film industry in the mid-1960s. He was featured in "Die Goldsucher von Arkansas" (1964), "Praznik" (1967), "Jutro" (1967), "The Hell Before Death" (1968), "Podne" (1968), "Operacija Beograd" (1968), "The Valley of Death" (1968), "Murder Commited in a Sly and Cruel Manner and from Low Motives" (1969), "Girl from the Mountains" (1972), "I Bog Stvori Kafansku Pevacicu" (1972), "Zuta" (1973), "Die Blutigen Geier von Alaska" (1973), and "The Coach" (1978). He was seen on television in an episode of "Muzikanti" and the 1968 mini-series "Odissea". Govedarica emigrated to the United States in the early 1980s. He worked as a bodyguard to Sylvester Stallone, who was instrumental in casting him his 1985 film "Rambo: First Blood Part II". He became noted for his roles as muscular thugs and military men. He was seen in the films "Modern Girls" (1986), "Code Name Zebra" (1987), "Russkies" (1987), "Lottle Nikita" (1988), "Lionheart" (1990), "Alligator II: The Mutation" (1991), "Universal Soldier" (1992), "Nowhere to Run" (1993), "The Evil Inside Me" (1993), "Balance of Power" (1996), "Mars" (1997), and "Hostile

Environment" (1999). He also appeared in television episodes of "Scarecrow and Mrs. King", "Cover Up", "Hunter", and "The Fifth Corner".

Gowers, Bruce

British television and music video director Bruce Gowers, who helmed the live episodes of "American Idol" from 2001 to 2010, died of an acute respiratory infection in Santa Monica, California, on January 15, 2023. He was 82. Gowers was born in West Kilbride, Scotland, on December 21, 1940. He graduated from the Latymer School and studied at the BBC Training College. He began his career at the BBC where he worked as a cameraman and production manager. He also directed such series as "The Kenny Everett Explosion", "Ev", "The Frost Programme", "Russell Harty Plus", "The Rolf Harris Show", "Opportunity Knocks", "The Top Secret Life of Edgar Briggs", "Aquarius" earning a BAFTA nomination in 1974 for the episode "Hello Dali", "This Week", "The Sweepstakes Game", "Hi! Summer", "The South Bank Show", "Larry Grayson", "Twiggy's Jokebox", "Headliners with David Frost", and the 1976 tele-film "Christmas Box". Gowers began directing music videos in the early 1970s for such artists as Queen (notably "Bohemian Rhapsody"), Mike Oldfield, Rod Stewart, Genesis, the Bee Gees, and the Rolling Stones. He moved to the United States in the late 1980s where he continued to direct music videos for Journey, Michael Jackson, Supertramp, John Cougar Mellencamp, the Tubes, REO Speedwagon, Toto, Rush, Prince, Van Halen, Santana, Leo Sayer, Whitney Houston, Fleetwood Mac, and Jennifer Lopez. Gowers received a Grammy Award for Best Music Video in 1986 for "The Heart of Rock 'n' Roll" by Huey Lewis & the News. He and his future wife, Carol Rosenstein, founded Together Again Video Productions (TAVP) co-created the "Kidsongs" sing-along videos for Warner Bros. Records in the mid-1980s and the television series that aired from 1987 to 1997. Gowers directed numerous variety programs and specials including "The Toni Tennille Show" (1979), "This Is Your Life: 30th Anniversary Special" (1981), "All-Star Salute to Mother's Day" (1981), "Rod Stewart: Tonight He's Yours" (1981), "Bob Welch and Friends: Live from the Roxy" (1981), "Doobie Brothers: Live at the Greek Theatre" (1982), "Eddie Murphy: Delirious" (1983), "Billy Crystal: A Comic's Line" (1984), "Greater Tuna" (1984), "The Fifth International Guinness Book of World Records" receiving an Emmy Award nomination in 1985, "That Was the Week That Was" (1985), "Harry Belafonte in Concert" (1985), "Solid Gold" (1985), "Robin Williams: An Evening at the Met" (1986), "Jerry Seinfeld: Stand-Up Confidential" (1987), "Harry Anderson's Sideshow" (1987), "George Carlin: What Am I Doing in New Jersey?" (1988), "The I'm Exhausted Concert" (1988), "Live! Dick Clark Presents" (1988), "L.A. Friday"

(1989), "Vh1 Salutes" (1990), "MTV Headbangers Ball - Decade of Metal Marathon" (1990), "Richard Lewis: I'm Doomed" (1990), "Vh1 to One: Bee Gees" (1990), "Live at Knebworth" (1990), "Paula Poundstone: Cats, Cops and Stuff" (1990), "That's What Friends Are For: Arista's 15th Anniversary Concert" (1994), "Dame Edna's Hollywood" (1992), "The Paula Poundstone Show" (1992), "Roundhouse" (1992), "An American Revolution: The People's Inaugural Celebration" (1993), "Barney and Friends Family Marathon" (1993), "TV's All Time Classic Comedy" (1994), "Woodstock '94" (1994), "Fleetwood Mac: The Dance" (1997) earning another Emmy nomination, "The Rolling Stones: Bridges to Babylon Tour '97-98" (1997), "Rodney Dangerfield's 75th Birthday Toast" (1997), "Explosion!" (1997), "Three Cats from Miami and Other Pet Practitioners" (1998), "Ricky Martin: One Night Only" (1999), "Radio City Music Hall's Grand Re-Opening Gala" (1999), "All That" (1999), "The Amanda Show" (1999), "Britney Spears: There's No Place Like Home" (2000), "Women Rock! Girls and Guitars" (2000), "Backstreet Boys: Larger Than Life" (2001), "An All-Star Tribute to Brian Wilson" (2001), "Michael Jackson: 30th Anniversary Celebration" (2001), "'N Sync: The Atlantis Concert" (2001), "Muhammad Ali's All-Star 60th Birthday Celebration!" (2002), "Ultimate Manilow!", "Classics: The Best of Sarah Brightman" (2002), "The Challenge" (2003), "American Juniors" (2003), "Harry for the Holidays" (2003), "Justin Timberlake: Down Home in Memphis - One Night Only" (2003), "Genius: A Night for Ray Charles" (2004), "An All-Star Salute to Patti LaBelle: Live from Atlantis" (2005), "Celebrity Duets" (2006), and "Live Earth" (2007). He directed numerous presentations of the "MTV Video Music Awards", "MTV Movie Awards", "Essence Awards, Blockbuster Entertainment Awards", "Billboard Music Awards", "VH1 Fashion Awards", "American Comedy Awards", "AFI Life Achievement Awards", "GQ Men of the Year Awards", "Academy of Country Music Awards", "ESPYs", "Teen Choice Awards", "Nickelodeon Kids' Choice Awards", and "Primetime Emmy Awards". He directed the comedy series "Whose Line Is It Anyway?" from 1998 to 2007. He was director of "American Idol" from 2002 to 2011, winning an Emmy Award in 2009 and additional nominations in 2003, 2005, 2006, and 2007. Gowers married Carol Rosenstein in 1999 and is survived by her. He is also survived by a son and a daughter from a previous marriage.

Grable, Joyce

Professional wrestler Joyce Grable died of leukemia on September 29, 2023. She was 70. She was born Betty Wade in LaGrange, Georgia, on November 9, 1952. She was trained by Judy Grable and made her wrestling debut in the early 1970s. She became the second female wrestler to use the name Joyce Grable, following Joyce Fowler who competed in the 1960s. She teamed with Vicki Williams to capture the NWA Women's World Tag Team Championship in October of 1973 and maintained the belts until October of 1975. Grable defeated Ann Casey to win the NWA United States Women's Championship in 1978. She reunited with Vicki Williams to become NWA tag champions in 1978 and again in 1980. She

also competed with the World Wrestling Federation (now WWE) where she feuded with WWF Women's Champion the Fabulous Moolah. Grable began teaming with Wendi Richter in 1982 and competed with Stampede Wrestling in Canada, the World Wrestling Council in Puerto Rico, and the American Wrestling Association (AWA). Their frequent opponents were the team of Velvet McIntyre and Judy Martin. Grable underwent back surgery in 1991 and retired from the ring. She continued to make appearances at wrestling reunions and independent shows, sometimes acting as a manager.

Gracie, James
    see Alexander, James

Graham, Superstar Billy
        Professional wrestler Eldridge Wayne Coleman, Jr., who was a wrestling champion under the name Superstar Billy

Graham, died of sepsis and multiple organ failure in a hospital in Phoenix, Arizona, on May 17, 2023. He was 79. Coleman was born in Phoenix on June 7, 1943. He became a weightlifter and body builder at an early age. He was an athlete and boxer in his teens. He was winner of the Mr. Teenage America West Coast division bodybuilding title in 1961. He trained at Gold's Gym in Santa Monica, California, in the late 1960s where he worked out with Arnold Schwarzenegger and Franco Columbo. He appeared in the pages of such magazines as "Strength and Fitness" and "Muscle Fitness". He began training as a professional wrestler at Stu Hart's Stampede Wrestling promotion in 1969. He began wrestling under his own name until teaming with Dr. Jerry Graham with the National Wrestling Alliance (NWA) Los Angeles promotion in 1970. He dyed his hair blonde and was billed as Superstar Billy Graham, the "brother" of Jerry, Eddie, and Luke Graham, when he competed with Championship Wrestling in Florida. He moved to the NWA's San Francisco promotion later in the year where he worked with such stars as Pat Patterson, Ray Stevens, and Peter Maivia. He joined the American Wrestling Association (AWA) in 1972 where he feuded with Verne Gagne, the Crusher, the Bruiser, Billy Robinson, Ken Patera, and Wahoo McDaniel. He incorporated arm wrestling contests and weight-lifting challenges during his time with the AWA. Graham wrestled with the NWA in Dallas for several months in mid-1975 and with the Mid Atlantic promotion later in the year. He joined the World Wide Wrestling Federation (WWWF/now WWE) in October of 1975

where he teamed with Spiros Arios and was managed by the Grand Wizard. He made several tours of Japan where he feuded with Antonio Inoki. He captured the NWA Florida heavyweight championship from Dusty Rhodes in November of 1976. He also held the Florida tag titles with Ox Baker. Graham returned to the WWWF where he defeated Bruno Sammartino for the promotion's heavyweight championship in April of 1977. He defeated such challengers as Jack Brisco, Dusty Rhodes, Pedro Morales, Mil Mascaras, Riki Choshu, and Harley Race in a WWWF vs. NWA championship match that ended in a draw. He was defeated for the belt by Bob Backlund in February of 1978. He subsequently rejoined the NWA and made another tour of Japan. He became heavyweight champion of the Continental Wrestling Association (CWA) in October of 1978 after defeating Pat McGuinness. He lost the title to Jerry Lawler the following month. He continued to wrestler throughout the United States, Canada, and Japan over the next several years. He returned to the WWF in August of 1982 and lost a championship bout against Backlund. He wrestled with the AWA in 1983 and returned to the NWA in Florida in April of 1985. He was initially a member of Kevin Sullivan's Army of Darkness before turning against the heel faction. He joined Jim Crockett Promotions in North Carolina later in the year and worked with Paul Jones in a feud with Jimmy Valiant. He again worked at the WWF in 1986 before requiring hip replacement surgery. He largely ended career in the ring in late 1987 but continued to work for the promotion as a manager for Don Muraco and a commentator. He was inducted into the WWE Hall of Fame in 2004 and made appearances at various television tapings and events through the end of the decade. He appeared in cameo roles in the films "The Wrestler" (1974) and "Fist Fighter" (1988) as an arm wrestler. His autobiography, "Superstar Billy Graham: Tangled Ropes", was published in 2006. Graham was an admitted steroid user and blamed many of his later health issues on steroid abuse. He made various accusations towards the WWF and Vince McMahon that he later admitted were false. He was diagnosed with hepatitis C and received a liver transplant in 2002. He continued to suffer from liver disease, cirrhosis, and bouts of pneumonia and heart problems over the next two decades. Graham was married to Madelyn Miluso from 1971 until their divorce in 1978, and is survived by their two children, Capella and Joey. He was also married and divorced from Shirley Potts. He married Valerie Belkas in 1978 and she also survives him.

Grant, Paul
        British actor Paul Grant, who played an Ewok in the

1983 "Star Wars" film "Return of the Jedi", died at a hospital in London, England, on March 20, 2023. He was 56. Grant was born in Peterborough, Cambridgeshire, England, on February 3, 1967. The diminutive (4'4") performer began his career in his teens as an Ewok in 1983's "Return of the Jedi". He was a stunt double in the films "Legend"

(1985), "Labyrinth" (1986) also playing a member of the Goblin corps, and "Willow" (1988). He was featured in the 1987 film "The Dead". He returned to the screen to portray a Goblin in the 2001 film "Harry Potter and the Philosopher's Stone". Grant collapsed outside a railway station in London on March 16, 2023, and was taken to a hospital. He was pronounced dead at the scene and was taken off life support four days later. He married Janet Crowson in 1989 and they later divorced. His survivors include two daughters and a son.

Green, Dan

Comic book artist Dan Green died in New York on August 19, 2023. Green was born in Detroit, Michigan, on November 26, 1952. He was 70.

He began his career in comics as an inker in the early 1970s. He worked with such artists as Jack Kirby, Steve Ditko, Sal Buscema, John Romita, Sr. & Jr., Carmine Infantino, Bernie Wrightson, and George Perez during his career. He was inker at Marvel Comics for issues of "Uncanny X-Men", "Wolverine", "The Defenders", and "The New Mutants". His work at DC includes the titles "Animal Man", "The Weird", "Tarzan", "Weird Worlds", "G.I. Combat", "Detective Comics", "House of Mystery", "Jack of Fables", and "Hellblazer: Papa Midnite". Green was co-writer and watercolor illustrator for the 1986 graphic novel "Doctor Strange: Into Shamballa". He also painted covers for "Amazing High Adventure" and "Gargoyle" for Marvel. He provided pencil illustrations for "The Raven & Other Poems & Tales", a collection of Edgar Allan Poe's works, in 2001. He returned to DC in recent years as inker for the titles "The New 52: Futures End", "Convergence: Batgirl", and "Convergence: Batman: Shadow of the Bat".

Green, Gigi

Actress Gigi Green died at a hospital in New Orleans, Louisiana, on March 31, 2023.

She was 75. She was born Geraldine Bean in New Orleans on March 3, 1948. She performed on stage as an actress and singer. Green was featured in small roles in the films "The Baltimore Bullet" (1980) and "Dixie: Changing Habits" (1983). She played Ma Fenster in the 1987 science fiction action film "R.O.T.O.R." Green interviewed various celebrities on her YouTube Channel "In-Home On-Line Live I'm the New Set Show". She is survived by a son and daughter, Tina and Gerald Fields. She was predeceased by another son, James Fields, Jr.

Greenan, Russell H.

Novelist Russell H. Greenan, who was noted for his works of crime fiction, died in Providence, Rhode Island, on July 22, 2023. He was 97. Greenan was born in the Bronx,

New York, on September 17, 1925. He served in the U.S. Navy in the 1940s and attended Long Island University. He worked as a traveling salesman out of Boston and spent a year in Nice, France, where he began to write. He returned to Boston where he married Flora Bratko and opened an antique store called the Cat and Racquet. He worked at various jobs before returning to Nice in 1966 where he completed a novel. It was titled "It Happened in Boston?" and was published by Random House in 1968. He wrote a dozen subsequent novels, primarily crime or horror fiction. His works include "Nightmare" (1970), "The Queen of America" (1972), "The Secret Life of Algernon Pendleton" (1973) which was adapted for a 1998 film starring John Cullum, "Heart of Gold" (1975), "The Bric-a-Brac Man" (1976), "Keepers" (1978), "Can of Worms" (1987), "Dread of Night" (2010), "Glamour Doom" (2012), "Nether Netherland" (2013), "Sealed Fate" (2013), and A Tangled Web" (2022). He is survived by his wife, Flora Bratko, and they had three children.

Greenburg, Dan

Author and humorist Dan Greenburg died of complications from a stroke in the Bronx, New York, on December 18, 2023. He was 87. Greenburg was born in

Chicago, Illinois, on August 7, 1933. He graduated from the University of Illinois. His first published work was a parody of "Goldilocks and the Three Bears" written in the style of J.D. Salinger, James Joyce, and Ernest Hemingway. It was published in "Esquire" in 1958. He followed with a version of "Hansel and Gretel" if written by Samuel Beckett, Jack Kerouac, and Vladimir Nabokov. He earned a master's degree from the University of California at Los Angeles in 1960 and worked as an advertising copywriter. Greenburg moved to New York City in 1962 where he was managing editor of the sexually oriented literary quarterly "Eros". His first book, the satirical "How to Be a Jewish Mother: A Very Lovely Training Manual", was published in 1964. Gertrude Berg recorded a successful comedy album from the book in 1965 and it was adapted for a play that appeared on Broadway in 1967. He wrote the short-lived off-Broadway play "Arf" and contributed to the hit Broadway play "Oh! Calcutta!" in 1969. He continued to write such books as "Kiss My Firm But Pliant Lips" (1965) which was adapted for the 1968 film "Live a Little, Love a Little" starring Elvis Presley, "How to

Make Yourself Miserable: Another Vital Training Manual" (1966), "Chewsday" (1968) which was adapted for the 1973 film "I Could Never Have Sex with Any Man Who Has So Little Regard for My Husband" featuring Greenburg in a small role, "Philly" (1969) which was adapted for the 1981 film "Private Lessons", "Porno-Graphics: The Shame of Our Art Museums" (1969), "Scoring" (1972), "Something's There: My Adventures in the Occult" (1976), "Love Kills" (1978) which was adapted for the 1997 tele-film "A Deadly Vision", "What Do Women Want?" (1982), "How to Avoid Love and Marriage" (1983), "True Adventures" (1985), "Confessions of a Pregnant Father" (1986), "The Nanny" (1987) which was adapted for the 1990 supernatural horror film "The Guardian which he also co-produced, "Exes" (1990), and "Moses Supposes: The Bible As Told to Dan Greenburg" (1997). He was featured as Clum in the 1971 film "Doc". He wrote the "Norman and the Polish Doll" segment of the 1975 anthology film "Fore Play". He and his wife, Suzanne O'Malley, scripted the 1983 teen comedy "Private School". He was credited with stories for the 1974 tele-film "Free to Be... You & Me" and episodes of "Adam's Rib", "Steambath", and "Mad About You". Greenburg was a guest on such shows as "The David Susskind Show", "The David Frost Show", "Saturday Night Live", "The Mike Douglas Show", "The Irv Kupcinet Show", and "Late Night with David Letterman". He was author of several series of children's books including "The Zack Files" named after his son, "Secrets of Dripping Fang", "Maximum Boy", and "Weird Planet". "The Zack Files" was the basis of a Canadian syndicated paranormal series of the same name that aired from 2000 to 2002. Greenburg was married to film director and author Nora Ephron from 1967 until their divorce in 1973. He was married to writer Suzanne O'Malley from 1980 until their divorce in 1998 and is survived by their son, writer Zack O'Malley Greenburg. He married children's book writer Judith Wilson in 1998 and she also survives him.

Greene, Shecky

Comedian and actor Shecky Greene died at his home in Las Vegas, Nevada, on December 31, 2023. He was 97. He was born Fred Sheldon Greenfield in Chicago, Illinois, on April

8, 1926. He was a singer and formed a drama club while attending high school. He served in the U.S. Navy for three years during World War II. Greene briefly attended Wright Junior College and began performing as a stand-up comic in Chicago nightclubs after his discharge in 1944. He soon moved to New Orleans where he performed at the Prevue Lounge for several years. He worked at various venues before becoming the opening act for Dorothy Shay in Las Vegas in 1954. He was a headliner at the Tropicana Hotel in Vegas from 1957 through the early 1960s. Greene appeared frequently on television variety series and game shows from the late 1950s including "The NBC Comedy Hour", "The Vic

Damone Show", "The Tonight Show Starring Jack Paar", "The Dinah Shore Chevy Show", "The Ed Sullivan Show", "The Joey Bishop Show", "The Steve Allen Playhouse", "Bob Hope Presents the Chrysler Theatre", "Pat Boone in Hollywood", "The Joan Rivers Show", "Playboy After Dark", "The Hollywood Palace", "This Is Tom Jones", "The Dean Martin Show", "The Kraft Music Hall", "The Irv Kupcinet Show", "The Carol Burnett Show", "The Glen Campbell Goodtime Hour", "The ABC Comedy Hour", "The Bob Hope Show", "Tattletales", "Match Game", "Celebrity Showcase", "The Merv Griffin Show", "Dinah!", "The Tonight Starring Johnny Carson" appearing in over sixty episodes as a comic and guest host from 1963 to 1979, "The Mike Douglas Show", "The Alan Hamel Show", "The Hollywood Squares", "The Toni Tennille Show", "An Evening at the Improv", "Super Bloopers and Practical Jokes", and "The Real Las Vegas". He also appeared in episodes of such television series as "Whirlybirds", "Combat!" as Private Braddock from 1962 to 1963, "Love, American Style", "The Love Boat", "Fantasy Island", "Laverne & Shirley", "The Fall Guy", "The A-Team", "Trapper John, M.D.", "The Law & Harry McGraw", "Northern Exposure", "Roseanne", and "Mad About You". He was also seen in the 1981 tele-film "Midnight Lace". Greene was featured in a handful for films including "Tony Rome" (1967) starring Frank Sinatra, "The Love Machine" (1971), "Won Ton Ton: The Dog Who Saved Hollywood" (1976), Mel Brooks' "History of the World: Part I" (1981) as Marcus Vindictus, "Splash" (1983) starring Tom Hanks and Darryl Hannah, "Lovelines" (1984), "Beverly Hills Pizza Girls" (1997), and "The Last Producer" (2000). Greene suffered from bipolar disorder and depression and had anxiety attacks and stage fright. He also battled alcohol, prescription drug, and gambling addictions. He was married to nightclub performer Nalani Kele from 1972 until their divorce in 1982. He married Marie Musso in 1985 and she survives him.

Gregorio, Rose

Actress Rose Gregorio died of pneumonia at her home in Greenwich Village, New York, on August 17, 2023. She was 97. Gregorio was born in Chicago, Illinois, on October 17,

1925. She attended the School of Speech at Northwestern and the School of Drama at Yale University. She began her career performing on the Chicago stage in the 1950s. She moved to New York City in the early 1960s where she appeared in the off-Broadway drama "The Days and Nights of Beebee Fenstermaker, directed by her future husband, Ulu Grosbard. She appeared on Broadway in productions of "The Owl and the Pussycat" (1964), "The Investigation" (1966), "Daphne in Cottage D" (1967), "The Cuban Thing" (1968), "Jimmy Shine" (1968), "The Shadow Box" (1977) earning a Tony Award nomination for her role as Agnes, "A View from the Bridge" (1983), and "M. Butterfly"

(1988). Gregorio was also seen frequently on television from the early 1960s with roles in episodes of "Armstrong Circle Theatre", "Naked City", "The Doctors and the Nurses", "East Side/West Side" (1963), "Route 66", "The Reporter", "New York Television Theatre", "Great Performances", "The Doctors" as Lorraine Jarrett in 1972, "The Bob Newhart Show", "Medical Center", "The Rookies", "Harry O", "Mary Hartman, Mary Hartman" in the recurring role of Florence Baedecker in 1976, "Jigsaw John", "The Rockford Files", "Charlie's Angels", "Another World" as Dr. Doris Wagner in 1981, "Falcon Crest", "Hothouse", "Doogie Howser, M.D.", "Against the Law", "Murder, She Wrote", "The Practice", "ER" in the recurring role of Helen Hathaway, mother of Julianna Margulies' character, from 1996 to 1999, and "Law & Order: Criminal Intent". She also appeared in such tele-films as "Tell Me Where It Hurts" (1974), "Miles to Go Before I Sleep" (1975), "One of Our Own" (1975), "The Death of Richie" (1977), "Sharon: Portrait of a Mistress" (1977), "The Storyteller" (1977), "Dummy" (1979), "Do You Remember Love" (1985), "The Last Innocent Man" (1987), and "The Brotherhood" (1991). Gregorio made her film debut as Sylvia Finney in Frank and Eleanor Perry's off-beat drama "The Swimmer" starring Burt Lancaster. Her other films include Grosbard's "Who Is Harry Kellerman and Why Is He Saying Those Terrible Things About Me?" (1971) with Dustin Hoffman, "Desperate Characters" (1971), "Mr. Ricco" (1975) with Dean Martin, the slasher film "Eyes of Laura Mars" (1978) starring Faye Dunaway, the crime drama "True Confessions" (1981) again directed by her husband Grosbard, "Five Corners" (1987), "City of Hope" (1991), "Tarantella" (1995), "The Deep End of the Ocean" (1999), "Maze" (2000), the short "Irene & Marie" (2015), and "Good Time" (2017). Gregorio was married to stage and film director Ulu Grosbard from 1965 until his death in 2012.

Griesser, Matt

Comedian and actor Matt Griesser died in McKeesport, Pennsylvania, on September 2, 2023. He was 53. Griesser was born in Pittsburgh, Pennsylvania, on May 5, 1970.

 He graduated from Chapman University in Orange, California, in 1992. He subsequently moved to Los Angeles to pursue a career in show business. He was noted for his appearances in national advertising campaigns, serving as Sign Boy for Footjoy golf shoes and providing the voice of a wheel of cheese for Cheez-It Crackers commercials. Griesser appeared on television in episodes of "Love & War", "Grace Under Fire", "Coach", "Murphy Brown", "USA High", "Hang Time", "The King of Queens", "10 Items or Less", "Hawthorne", "'Til Death", "Rules of Engagement", and "Family Tree" in the recurring role of Rick Tillman in 2013. He was seen in the films "The Flintstones in Viva Rock Vegas" (2000), "Almost Famous" (2000), "Merry Ex Mas" (2014),

"November Rule" (2015), "Mascots" (2016), and "Rules Don't Apply" (2016).

Gross, Daerick

Comic artist Daerick Gross died of gall bladder cancer in Simi Valley, California, on December 9, 2023. He was 76. Gross was born in Kettering, Ohio, on January 28, 1947. He

 studied art and theater at Ohio University from 1965 to 1967. He attended the Central Academy of Commercial Art in Cincinnati, Ohio, in 1969. He began working as a set designer for WCPO-TV in Cincinnati after graduation. He was also a staff artist and cartoonist for the "Cincinnati Post". He began working in comics in 1988, creating the mutant "Murcielaga She-Bat". The character was published by Heroic Publishing and Revolutionary Comics from the early 1990s. Gross painted the interior art for "Anne Rice's "The Vampire Lestat" from Innovation Comics in 1990. He was cover artist for Innovation's "Forbidden Planet" series in 1992. He worked on several Marvel Comics titles including "Excalibur", "Midnight Sons", "Captain Marvel", "Cable", "X-Men: Domino", and "Cable & X-Force: Onslaught Rising". He also illustrated "Neuroscope" for Malibu in 1992 and the "Bloodwulf" series for Image in 1995. He illustrated "Batman: Two-Face Twice" for DC Comics in 1993. He drew several adult comics for Carnal Comics in the mid-1990s including "Brittany O'Connell", "Porn Star Fantasies", and "Women of Porn: A Cartoon History". He illustrated psychoanalyst Paulo Joannides education sex manual "The Guide to Getting It On" for Goofy Foot Press in 1996. Gross created the satirical political comic "Trumpy" in 2019.

Gross, Sam

Cartoonist Sam Gross died of complications from heart failure at his home in Manhattan, New York, on May 6,

 2023. He was 89. Gross was born in the Bronx, New York, on August 7, 1933. He graduated from City College in New York. His first cartoon was published in "Saturday Review" in 1953. He subsequently served in the U.S. Army in Germany. He worked as an accountant after his discharge. He began submitting cartoons to various magazines in the early 1960s and was soon appearing in the pages of "The New Yorker", "Saturday Evening Post", "Parents Magazine", "Esquire", "Cosmopolitan", "Good Housekeeping", and several men's magazines. He served as cartoon editor at "National Lampoon" in the 1970s. Gross estimated that he drew over 33,000

177

cartoons in his lifetime. He created the "Cigarman" comic strip with artist Randy Jones for "Smoke Magazine" from 1997 to 1998. Many of his cartoons were featured in the collections "How Gross!: The Collected Craziness of S. Gross (1973), "I Am Blind and My Dog Is Dead" (1978), "An Elephant Is Soft and Mushy" (1982), "More Gross" (1982), "Totally Gross" (1984), "Love Me, Love My Teddy Bear" (1986), "No More Mr. Nice Guy" (1987), "Your Mother Is a Remarkable Woman" (1992), "Catss by Gross" (1995), and "We Have Ways of Making You Laugh: 120 Funny Swastika Cartoons" (2008). Gross married Isabelle Jaffe in 1959 and is survived by her and their daughter, Michelle.

Grove, Wilfred

British actor Wilfred Grove died in hospice near Cambridge, England, on June 15, 2023. He was 92. Grove was born in Nottinghamshire, England, on May 13, 1931. He appeared frequently on television from the late 1950s with roles

in productions of "The Rough and Ready Lot" (1959), "The Three Princes" (1959), "The Secret Kingdom" (1960), "Nicholas Nickleby" (1968), "The O'Hooligan File" (1978), "On Giant's Shoulders" (1979), "Flickers" (1980), "A Tale of Two Cities" (1980), "Sons and Lovers" (1981), "Witness for the Prosecution" (1982), "Enemies of the State" (1983), "Anna of the Five Towns" (1985), "The Daughter-in-Law" (1985), "Hold the Back Page" (1985), "All Passion Spent" (1986), "Intimate Contact" (1987), "Christabel" (1988), "The Sharp End" (1991), and "My Friend Walter" (1992). Grove also was seen in episodes of "Maigret", "Man of the World", "The Avengers", "The Sentimental Agent", "Festival", "A Tale of Two Cities", "Secret Agent", "Theatre 625", "Virgin of the Secret Service", "The Expert", "Fraud Squad", "Please Sir!", "The Flaxton Boys", "Couples", "Killers", "Star Maidens", "Striker", "Play for Today", "Van der Valk", "Premiere", "Dick Turpin", "Dick Barton: Special Agent", "Fox", "A Question of Guilt", "Sounding Brass", "Born and Bred", "Sorry!, "The Gentle Touch", "By the Sword Divided" as John Moresby in 1983, "All Creatures Great and Small", "Tales of the Unexpected", "Big Deal", "Emmerdale", "Brookside", "EastEnders", "London's Burning", "Screen Two", "Casualty", "Doctor at the Top", "Minder", and "Lovejoy". He was featured in several films including "The Adventures of Barry McKenzie" (1972), "Side by Side" (1975), "Take It or Leave It" (1981), and "The Thompsons" (2012).

Gudgeon, Mac

Australian screenwriter Mac Gudgeon died in Australia on May 25, 2023. He was 74. Gudgeon was born in Wollongong, New South Wales, Australia, on March 2, 1949. He was a painter and dock worker before entering television as a writer and producer for the 1984 mini-series "Waterfront". He also scripted the tele-films and mini-series "The Petrov Affair"

(1987), "Snowy" (1993), "Dogwoman: A Grrrl's Best Friend" (2000), "Monash: The Forgotten Anzac" (2008), "Killing Tine" (2011), "Fatal Honeymoon" (2012), and "The Secret River" (2015). His other television credits include episodes of "Skirts", "Sky Trackers", "Stingers", "Good Guys Bad Guys", "Halifax f.p.", and "Captain Cook: Obsession and Discovery". Gudgeon wrote the original story for the 1988 film "Georgia". He scripted the films "Ground Zero" (1987), "The Delinquents" (1989), "Wind" (1992), and "Last Ride" (2009). He was script editor for the horror film "Wolf Creek" (2005) and "The Snowtown Murders" (2011), and the television mini-series "Devil's Dust" (2012).

Gunning, Christopher

British composer Christopher Gunning, who scored numerous film and television productions, died of kidney cancer at his home in Hertfordshire, England, on March 25, 2023. He was 89. Gunning was born in Cheltenham, Gloucestershire, England, on August 4, 1944. He studied at the

Guildhall School of Music and Drama. He began working as an assistant to Richard Rodney Bennett and Dudley Moore in his early twenties. He composed scores for several documentary films and was soon working with such artists as Mel Torme, Cilla Black, Shirley Bassey, and Cilla Black. He collaborated with Colin Blunstone on his 1972 hit recording of "Say You Don't Mind" and worked on Lynsey De Paul's recordings of "Won't Somebody Dance with Me" and "My Man and Me". Gunning provided music for advertising campaigns as Martini (It's the Right One) and Black Magic. He was noted for his work in film and television from the early 1970s. He was orchestrator and arranger for the films "The Best House in London" (1969), "The Buttercup Chain" (1970), and "Nicholas and Alexandra" (1971). He scored the films "Goodbye Gemini" (1970), "Hands of the Ripper" (1971), "Get Charlie Tully" (1972), "Man About the House" (1974), "In Celebration" (1975), "Amin: The Rise and Fall" (1981), "When the Whales Came" (1989), "Under Suspicion" (1991), "Firelight" (1997), "Lighthouse Hill" (2004), "La Vir En Rose" (2007) earning a BAFTA Award, "Bloom" (2011), and "Grace of Monaco" (2014). Gunning also earned BAFTA Awards for his work on television productions of "Porterhouse Blue" (1988), "Poirot" (1990), and "Middlemarch" (1995), and additional nominations for "The Big Battalions" in 1992 and 1993. His other television credits include such series and tele-films as "The Man from Haven" (1972), "Intimate Strangers" (1974), "Dangerous Knowledge" (1976), "Rogue Male" (1976), "Running Blind" (1979), "A

Deadly Game" (1979), "The Day off the Triffids" (1981), "Wilfred and Eileen" (1981), "The Brack Report" (1982), "East Lynne" (1982), "Chessgame" (1983), "Helen: A Woman of Today" (1973), "The Alamut Ambush" (1986), "Cold War Killers" (1986), "The Deadly Recruits" (1986), "Knights of God" (1987), "Starting Out" (1989), "All or Nothing at All" (1993), "Wings Over the Serengeti" (1994), "The Glass Virgin" (1995), "The Affair" (1995), "Karaoke" (1996), "Cold Lazarus" (1996), "Family Money" (1996), "Reckless" (1997), "Rebecca" (1997), "The Life and Crimes of William Palmer" (1998), "The Cater Street Hangman" (1998), "The Last Train" (1999), "Nova" (1999), "The Innocent" (2001), "Wild Africa" (2001), "Pollyanna" (2003), and "Rosemary & Thyme" (2003). He composed 13 symphonies, numerous concertos and other concert works, including "Concerto for Saxophone and Orchestra" and "The Lobster". He was the subject of the 2016 documentary film "Christopher's Music". Gunning was married to Annie Farrow from 1974 until their divorce in 1999 and is survived by their four daughters. He married Svitlana Salenko in 2004 and she also survives him.

Guzman, Jesus

Spanish actor Jesus Guzman died in Madrid, Spain, on October 16, 2023. He was 97. Guzman was born in Madrid on June 15, 1926. He was the son of actors Rafael Guzman and Aurora Greta. His parents operated a theatrical company, and

he appeared on stage as a child. He appeared frequently in films from the mid-1950s with roles in numerous Euro-westerns. His films include "Manolo Guardia Urbano" (1956), "El Hombre Que Viajaba Despacito" (1957), "091 Poliia al Habla" (1960), "Festival" (1961), "Usted Puede Ser un Asesino" (1961), "Siempre es Domingo" (1961), "Tres de la Cruz Roja" (1961), "Accidente 703" (1962), "Vuelve San Valentin" (1962), "Robbery at 3 O'Clock" (1962), "La Gran Familia" (1962), "Operacion Embajada"(1963), "El Turista" (1963), "Implacable Three" (1963), "El Juego de la Verdad" (1963), "Marisol Rumbo a Rio" (1963), "Como dos Gotas de Agua" (1964), "La Historia de Bienvenido" (1964), "La Nueva Cenicienta" (1964), "Busqueme a esa Chica" (1964), "Historias de la Television" (1965), "Mas Bonita Que Ninguna" (1965), "Whisky y Vodka" (1965), "La Familia y... Uno Mas" (1965), "Gunman's Hands" (1965), "For a Few Dollars More" (1965), "Every Day Is a Holiday" (1965), "Operacion Plus Ultra" (1966), "Las Viudas" (1966), "The Good, the Bad and the Ugly" (1966), "Las Salvajes en Puente San Gil" (1966), "Tres Perros Locos, Locos" (1966), "Sor Citroen" (1967), "Buenos Dias, Condesita" (1967), "Los Guardiamarinas" (1967), "Un Millon en la Basura" (1967), "Up the MacGregors" (1967), "El Padre Manolo" (1967), "Que Hacemos Con los Hijos?" (1967), "Dakota Joe" (1967), "Los Chicos del Preu" (1967), "Escuela de Enfermeras" (1968), "El Turismo es un Gran Invento" (1968), "No Desearas la Mujer de tu Projimo" (1968), "One

Dollar Too Many" (1968), "Pistol for a Hundred Coffins" (1968), "Cuidado Con las Senoras" (1968), "Dead Men Don't Count" (1968), "Death on High Mountain" (1969), "Juicio de Faldas" (1969), "Viva Cangaceiro" (1969), "Se Armo el Belen!!" (1969), "Amor y Medias" (1969), "El Relicario" (1970), "Por Que Pecamos a los Cuarenta?" (1970), "An Imperfect Crime" (1970), "Sartana Kills Them All" (1970), "Don Erre Que Erre" (1970), "Bastard, Go and Kill" (1971), "El Apartamento de la Tentacion" (1971), "Prestame Quince Dias" (1971), "Las Ibericas F.C." (1971), "Los Dias de Cabirio" (1971), "Me Debes un Muerto" (1972), "Ben and Charlie" (1972), "Nada Menos Que Todo un Hombre" (1972), "Las Piernas de la Serpiente" (1972), "Travels with My Aunt" (1972), "Lo Verde Empieza en los Pirineos" (1973), "Bienvenido, Mister Krif" (1975), "Zorrita Martinez" (1975), "El Senor Esta Servido" (1976), "Las Delicias de los Verdes Anos" (1976), "Una Prime en la Banera" (1976), "Der Tiefstapler" (1978), "Mi Adultero Esposo ('In Situ')" (1979), "...Y al Tercer Ano, Resucito" (1980), "Despido Improcedente" (1980), "Buddy Goes West" (1981), "Victoria! La Gran Aventura d'un Poble" (1983), "Victoria! 2: La Disbauxa del 17" (1983), "Victoria! 3: El Seny i la Rauxa" (1984), "The Rogues" (1987), "Tahiti's Girl" (1990), "Maestros" (2000), "Cachimba" (2004), "8 Citas" (2008), "The Great Vazquez" (2010), "Un Dios Prohibido" (2013), "Blockbuster" (2013), "The Tunnel" (2016), and "Amalia en el Otono" (2020). Guzman appeared on television in such series as "La Familia Colon", "Tele-Club", "Los Paladines", "Cronicas de un Pueblo" as Postman Braulio from 1971 to 1974, "Im Auftrag von Madame", "Este Senor de Negro", "Estudio 1", "Que Usted lo Mate Bien", "Teatro Breve", "Un, Dos, Tres... Responda Otra Vez", "Anillos de Oro", "Turno de Oficio", "Lorca, Muerte de un Poeta", "Del Mino al Bidasoa", "La Huella del Crimen", "Cronicas del Mal", "Lleno, Por Favor", "Habitacion 503", "Los Ladrones Van a la Oficina", "Farmacia de Guardia", "Aqui Hay Negocio!", "Ay, Senor, Senor!", "Hostal Royal Manzanares", "Colegio Mayor", "Kety No Para", "La Casa de los Lios", "Medico de Familia", "Cafe con Leche", "Ala... Dina!", "Manos a la Obra", "Se Puede?", "El Comisario", "Manolo & Benito Corporeision", "Aida", "Countdown", and "La Hora de Jose Mota". Guzman married Elena Graci in 1951 and they had four children.

Gwynne, Haydn

British actress Haydn Gwynne, who starred as Camilla in the comedy series "The Windsors" since 2016, died of cancer in London, England, on October 20, 2023. She was 66. Gwynne was born in Hurstpierpoint, West Sussex, England, on March 21, 1957. She studied at the University of Nottingham and taught English as a foreign language at the University of Rome La Sapienze in Italy for five years. She began acting in the mid-1980s and appeared frequently on television. She was seen in episodes of "Lovejoy", "A Very Peculiar Practice", "Call Me Mister" as Bridget Bartholomew in 1986, "Ten Great Writers of the Modern World", "Drop the Dead Donkey" as Alex Pates in 1990, the ITV juvenile science fiction series "Time Riders" as Dr. B.B. Miller in 1991, "Kavanagh QC", "Verdict", "Dangerfield", "The Canterbury Tales", "Peak

Practice" as Dr. Joanna Graham from 1999 to 2000, "The Secret", "Merseybeat" as Superintendent Susan Blake from 2001 to 2002, "Dalziel and Pascoe", "Absolute Power", "Rome" as Julius Caesar's wife, Calpurnia, from 2005 to 2007, "Inspector Lewis", "Poirot", "Masterpiece Mystery", "Sherlock", "New Tricks", "Midsomer Murders", "Silent

Witness", "Uncle", "Death in Paradise", "Law & Order: UK", "Ripper Street", "Father Brown", "Urban Myths", "The Canterville Ghost", "The Suspect", and "The Crown". She starred as Camilla in "The Windsors", a parody version of the British royal family, from 2016 until her death. Her other television credits include productions of "What Mad Pursuit?" (1984), "After the War" (1989), "Nice Work" (1989), "The Merchant of Venice" (1996), "Hospital!" (1997), "Human, All Too Human" (1999), "Consenting Adults" (2007), "The C Word" (2015), and "The Midnight Gang" (2018). She performed frequently on stage, appearing in regional theater and in London's West End. She starred as Billie Burke in a West End production of "Ziegfeld" (1988) and earned Laurence Olivier Award nominations for her work in "City of Angels" (1994), "Billy Elliot the Musical" (2006), "Women on the Verge of a Nervous Breakdown" (2015), and "The Threepenny Opera" (2017). Gwynne received a Drama Desk Award and a Tony nomination for her featured role as Mrs. Wilkinson in the Broadway production of "Billy Elliot: The Musical" (2008). She was featured as Pam Lee in "The Great British Bake Off Musical" in 2023. She appeared in a handful of films during her career including "Car Trouble" (1986), "The Pleasure Principle" (1991), "Remember Me?" (1997), "These Foolish Things" (2006), "Hunky Dory" (2011), "The Audience" (2013) as Margaret Thatcher, Disney's live-action "Beauty and the Beast" (2017) as Clothilde, and "Coriolanus" (2018). Gwynne is survived by her long-time partner Jason Phipps and two sons.

Hadji-Lazaro, Francois

French actor and musician Francois Hadji-Lazaro died of septicemia in Paris, France, on February 25, 2023. He was

66. Hadji-Lazaro was born in Paris on June 22, 1956. He taught himself to play the acoustic guitar and added numerous other instruments to his repertoire including the banjo, fiddle, dulcimer, accordion, mandolin, flute, and bagpipes. He performed with the band Penelope from the late 1970s through early 1980s and teamed with bassist Daniel Hennion to launch the band Pigalle in 1982. He formed a new group, the Garcons Bouchers, in 1987. He was featured in numerous films including "Beatrice" (1987), "Le Brasier"

(1991), "The Jackpot!" (1991), "Room Service" (1992), "Les Mamies" (1992), "La Cavale des Fous" (1993), the horror comedy "Cemetery Man" ("Dellamorte Dellamore") (1994) as Gnaghi, the disabled assistant of Rupert Everett's title character, "The City of Lost Children" (1995) as the Killer, "Rainbow for Rimbaud" (1996), "Black Dju" (1997), "Charite Biz'ness" (1998), "Brotherhood of the Wolf" (2001), "Nha Fala" (2001), "Lucky Luke and the Daltons" (2004), "J'ai Vu Tuer Ben Barka" (2005), "Dante 01" (2008), "Chubby" (2014), and "Le Cabanon Rose" (2016). Hadji-Lazaro was seen on television in productions of "Le Gang des Trations" (1991), "Le Voyage d'Eva" (1992), "Les Miserables" (2000), "Milady and the Three Musketeers" (2004), and "Capitain Marleau" (2021).

Hadley, Brett

Actor Brett Hadley, who starred as Detective Carl Williams on the soap opera "The Young and the Restless" for nearly twenty years, died of sepsis at the Motion Picture &

Television Country House and Hospital in Woodland Hills, California, on June 15, 2023. He was 92. Hadley was born in Louisville, Kentucky, on September 25, 1930. He studied drama at the University of New Mexico. He began his career on stage at the Goodman Theatre in Chicago. He appeared in films and television from the late 1960s. Hadley was seen in episodes of "The Name of the Game", "The Bold Ones: The Lawyers", "Room 222", "The F.B.I.", "Lucas Tanner", "Ironside", "Police Story" "The Waltons", "Kojak", "McMillan & Wife", "The Invisible Man", "Marcus Welby, M.D.", "The Rockford Files", "The Incredible Hulk", "The New Mike Hammer", "The Colbys", "Highway to Heaven", and "Beauty and the Beast". He joined the cast of the soap opera "The Young and the Restless" as Genoa City police detective Carl Williams in 1980. He remained in the role through 1990, when his character disappeared. He was gone for nearly a decade when he resurfaced in 1998 under the name Jim Bradley. He suffered from amnesia from a beating and didn't remember his previous life. Hadley left the series in 1999. His other television credits include the tele-films "The Footloose Goose" (1975) and "The Courage and the Passion" (1978). Hadley was featured in a handful of films including "The Mad Bomber" (1973), "Funny Lady" (1975), "Maid to Order" (1987), "Next of Kin" (1989), "The Babe" (1992), and "Schooled" (2007). He was seen in the short films "Mush" (2005), "Lucy's Piano" (2006), "1045 Mercy Street" (2009), "The Lottery" (2014), "Entanglement" (2014), and "Dreamcatchers" (2015). Hadley also worked as a bartender at the country music nightclub the Palomino in North Hollywood.

Hadrbolcova, Zdena

Czech actress Zdena Hadrbolcova died after a long illness in the Czech Republic on November 20, 2023. She was

180

86. Hadrbolcova was born in Prague, Czechoslovakia, on July 13, 1937. She attended the French lycee in Prague and trained at the Academy of Performing Arts in Prague. She began her career on stage, working with the Palmovka Theatre, Theatre on the Edge, and Theatre on the Balustrade. She appeared frequently in films and television from the early 1960s. Her film credits include "Probuzeni" (1960), "Cerna Sobota" (1961), "Blbec z Xeenemunde" (1963), "The Death of Tarzan" (1963), "Vanoce s Alzbetou" (1968), "Jumping Over Puddles" (1971), "Zeny v Ofsajdu" (1971), "Sklameny Klobouk" (1972), "O Snehurce" (1972), "Zlata Svatba" (1972), "Cesty Muzu" (1972), "Three Men Travelling" (1973), "Hroch" (1973), "Prijela k Nam Pout" (1973), "Televize v Bublicich Aneb Bublice v Televizi" (1974), "Anna, Sestra Jany" (1976), "Gentlemen, Boys" (1976), "Monkey's Playtime" (1978), "Podivny Vylet" (1978), "Jak Se Toci Rozmaryny" (1978), "Solo Pro Starou Damu" (1978), "Friday Is No Holiday" (1980), "Svitalo Celou Noc" (1980), "Neco Je Ve Vzduchu" (1981), "Kopretiny Pro Zameckou Pani" (1981), "Hodina Zivota" (1981), "Vikend Bez Rodicu" (1982), "Zelenaz Vlna" (1982), "Jak Svet Prichazi o Basniky" (1982), "Ma Laska s Jakubem" (1982), "The Snowdrop Festivities" (1984), "Vsichni Maji Talent" (1984), "Rumburak" (1985), "Do Zubu a Do Srdicka" (1986), "Ja Nejsem Ja" (1986), "The Great Movie Robbery" (1986), "Muj Hrisny Muz" (1987), "Narozeniny Rezisera Z.K." (1987), "Dva Lidi v Zoo" (1989), "Skrivanci Ticho" (1990), "The Idiot Returns" (1999), "Archa Pro Vojtu" (2000), "Chytte Doktora" (2007), "Frantisek Je Devkar" (2008), "I Wake Up Yesterday" (2012), "Wings of Christmas" (2013), "Celebrity Ltd." (2015), and "Over Fingers" (2019). Hadrbolcova appeared on television in productions of "Neprovdana Pani Rosita" (1960), "Nepokojne Hody Svate Kateriny" (1960), "Aristokrati" (1961), "Zitra a Pozitri" (1961), "Zly Jelen" (1962), "Zapomenuty Cert" (1964), "Zla Minuta" (1965), "Odchazeti s Podzimem" (1966), "Kdyz Se Certi Rojili" (1966), "Pan Vetrovsky z Vetrova a Pani Destina z Destova" (1969), "Romeo a Julie Na Konci Listopadu" (1972), "Sedm Pater Pro Tisic Prani" (1976), "Co Je s Tebou, Lenko?" (1977), "Kam Uhnout Ocima" (1977), "Tri Musketyri Po Triceti Letech" (1978), "Jak Je Dulezite Miti Filipa" (1979), "Neboztici Na Bale" (1979), "Holubnik" (1980), "Jak Namalovat Ptacka" (1980), "Porucik Petr" (1981), "Pocitani Ovecek" (1982), "Kvuli Mne Prestane" (1982), "Restaurace" (1983), "Letajici Cestmir" (1983), "Byt Je Vykraden, Maminko" (1983), "Cizi Hoklka" (1984), "Kolobezka Prvni" (1984), "O Nosate Carodejnici" (1984), "Slecna Mary" (1984), "Logaritmus Lasky" (1985), "Cekani Na Stribrne Zvonky" (1985), "Draha Teticko" (1986), "Hvezdy Nad Syslim Udolim" (1986), "O Stesti a Krase" (1986), "Sardinky Aneb Zivot Jedne Rodinky" (1986), "Zazracne Dite" (1986), "Vysoka Hra" (1987), "Arabesky" (1987), "Pan Pickwick" (1987), "Moudry Tata" (1988), "Lek Pod Kuzi" (1988), "Prejdete Na Druhou Stranu"

(1988), "Pani Liska" (1988), "Nejlepsi Kseft Myho Zivota" (1988), "Nanecisto" (1988), "O Kouzelnici Klotynce" (1988), "Prizraky" (1988), "Krecek v Nocni Kosili" (1988), "Kdo Probudi Pindruse...?" (1989), "Sedm Bilych Plastu" (1989), "Koho Ofoukne Vetricek" (1990), "Pritelkyne z Domu Smutku" (1992), "Okno" (1997), "Inzerat" (1997), "Navrat Zbloudileho Pastyre" (2004), "Modry Mauritius" (2004), "Pohadkove Pocasi" (2008), "Mejdan Roku z Obyvaku" (2009), "Nespavost" (2010), "Skola Princu" (2010), "Sraci" (2011), and "Pustina" (2016). Her other television credits include episdoes of "The Phantom of the Operetta", "Kodytkova Detektivni Kancelar", "My z Konce Sveta" as Matka in 1975, "Pau Tau" as Malkova from 1977 to 1978, "Bakalari", "Tri Spory", "Sanitka", "My Vsichni Skolou Povinni" as Alzbeta Gajdosova in 1984, "Povidky Malostranske", "Rozpaky Kuchare Svatopluka", "Chlapci a Chalpi" as Ctibor's Mother in 1988, "Redakce" as Emilie from 2004 to 2005, "Trapasy", "PanMama" as Vera in 2013, and "The Zodiac Murders" (2015). Hadrbolcova starred as Ruzena Habartova in the soap opera Ulice from 2005 to 2016.

Haggard, Piers

British director Piers Haggard, who directed the horror films "Blood on Satan's Claw" and "Venom", died in England on January 11, 2023. He was 83. Haggard was born in London, England, on March 18, 1939. He was largely raised in Clackmannanshire, Scotland, and attended Edinburgh

University from 1956 to 1960. He began his career working at the Royal Court theater as an assistant director in 1960. He began directing productions at the Dundee Rep the following year and moved to the Glasgow Citizens in 1962. He directed for the National Theatre company from 1963 until joining BBC Television in 1965. Haggard directed episodes of such series as "Thirty-Minute Theatre", "The Newcomers", "Sir Arthur Conan Doyle", "The Jazz Age", "The Wednesday Play", "Callan", "Man at the Top", "Public Eye", "The Rivals of Sherlock Holmes", "Six Days of Justice", "Armchair Theatre", "Love Story", "Zodiac", "The Love School", "Churchill's People", "Against the Crowd", "The Velvet Glove", "Romance", "Love for Lydia", "BBC2 Playhouse", "Objects of Affection", "Play for Today", "Screen Two", "Space Precinct", "Ruth Rendell Mysteries", and "McCready and Daughter". His other television credits include productions of "Neutral Ground" (1968), "Murder: Identikit" (1969), "The Patriot Game" (1969), "Marvelous Party!" (1969), "Trilby" (1976), "Chester Mystery Cycle" (1976), "A Divorce" (1976), "Lucia di Lammermoor" (1977), Dennis Potter's "Pennies from Heaven" (1978) earning a BAFTA Award, "Quatermass" (aka "The Quatermass Conclusion") (1979), "Waters of the Moon" (1983), "Return to Treasure Island" (1986), "Sam Found Out: A Triple Play" (1988), "The Fulfillment of Mary Gray" (1989), "Back Home" (1989)

earning a Daytime Emmy Award nomination, "Centrepoint" (1990), "She'll Take Romance" (1990), "Four Eyes and Six-Guns" (1992), "The Lifeforce Experiment" (1994), "Interview Day" (1996), "Cold Enough for Snow" (1997), "Big Bad World" (1999), "The Hunt" (2001), and "The Shell Seekers" (2006). Haggard worked as a dialogue assistant on Michelangelo Antonioni's 1966 film "Blowup". He directed several films during his career including "Wedding Night" (1969), the horror film "The Blood on Satan's Claw" (1971), "The Fiendish Plot of Dr. Fu Manchu" (1980), "Venom" (1981), "A Summer Story" (1988), and "Conquest" (1998). Haggard married Christiane Stokes in 1960 and they had four children before their subsequent divorce. He married stained glass artist Anna Sklovsky in 1972 and is also survived by her their two children, including actress Daisy Haggard.

Haitkin, Jacques

Cinematographer Jacques Haitkin, who was noted for his work on Wes Craven's horror film classic "A Nightmare on Elm Street", died of complications from amyotrophic lateral sclerosis and leukemia in San Francisco, California, on March 21, 2023. He was 72. Haitkin was born in Brooklyn, New

York, on August 29, 1950. He attended New York University's Tisch School of the Arts, where he made the 1972 short film "Hot Dogs for Gauguin". He continued his studies in Los Angeles with the American Film Institute. He began working in films in the late 1970s as a gaffer on "The Van" (1977) and "The Billion Dollar Hobo" (1977). He worked as a camera operator or second unit cinematographer for the films "Supervan" (1977), "Jennifer" (1978), "America's Sweetheart: The Mary Pickford Story" (1978), "Young Warriors" (1983), "The Osterman Weekend" (1983), "Breakin' 2: Electric Boogaloo" (1984), "Too Much Sun" (1990), "Ticks" (1993), "Last Man Standing" (1995), "Top of the World" (1997), "Hot Boyz" (2000), "Beeper" (2002), "Herbie Fully Loaded" (2005), "Survival Island" (2005), "Talladega Nights: The Ballad of Ricky Bobby" (2006), "Amelia" (2009), "Kites" (2010), "The Expendables" (2010), "Fast Five" (2011), "X-Men: First Class" (2011), "The Last Stand" (2013), "Captain Phillips" (2013), "Captain America: The Winter Soldier" (2014), "Unfinished Business"(2015), "Furious 7" (2015), "Captain America: Civil War" (2016), "Teenage Mutant Ninja Turtles: Out of the Shadows" (2016), "Kong: Skull Island" (2017), "The Fate of the Furious" (2017), "Black Panther" (2018), "Venom" (2018), and "21 Bridges" (2019). Haitkin was director of photography or cinematographer for numerous films including "Hot Tomorrows" (1977), "The Hitter" (1978), "They Went That-A-Way & That-A-Way" (1978), "Swap Meet" (1979), "The Prize Fighter" (1979), "The Private Eyes" (1980), "St. Helens" (1981), Roger Corman's cult science fiction film "Galaxy of Terror" (1981), "Longshot" (1981), "The House Where Evil Dwells" (1982), "Angel of H.E.A.T." (1983), "Last Plane Out"

(1983), "Making the Grade" (1984), "The Lost Empire" (1984), Wes Craven's "A Nightmare on Elm Street" (1984) and the sequel "A Nightmare on Elm Street 2: Freddy's Revenge" (1985), "The Imagemaker" (1986), "Quiet Cook" (1986), "My Demon Lover" (1987), "The Hidden" (1987), "Cherry 2000" (1987), "Lucky Stiff" (1988), "To Die For" (1988), "Cage" (1989), "Shocker" (1989), "The Ambulance" (1990), "Fast Getaway" (1991), "We're Talkin' Serious Money" (1992), "Mom and Dad Save the World" (1992), "Maniac Cop 3: Badge of Silence" (1992), "Relentless 3" (1993), "Scanner Cop" (1994), "The Force" (1994), "The Silence of the Hams" (1994), "Evolver" (1995), "Fist of the North Star" (1995), "Two-Bits & Pepper" (1995), "Bloodsport 2" (1996), "One Good Turn" (1996), "The Big Squeeze" (1996), "Wishmaster" (1997), "Assignment Berlin" (1998), "The Glass Jar" (1999), "The Base" (1999), "The Chaos Factor" (2000), "Faust" (2000), "Rockets' Red Glare" (2000), "The Elite" (2001), "Layover" (2001), "A Month of Sundays" (2001), "Bad Karma" (2001), "Instinct to Kill" (2001), "Storm Watch" (2002), "Global Effect" (2002), "Face of Terror" (2004), "Shut Up and Kiss Me!" (2004), "Art Heist" (2004), "The Curse of El Charro" (2005), "The Haunting Hour: Don't Think About It" (2007), "The Deal" (2007), "Unnatural Causes" (2008), "Reflections" (2008), "Visible Scars" (2012), and "Forgotten" (2022). Haitkin worked in television as cinematographer for productions of "The Olympiad" (1976), "The Girl, the Gold Watch & Everything" (1980), "Save the Dog!" (1988), "Buried Alive" (1990), "Strays" (1991), "Rattled" (1996), "Buried Alive II" (1997), "Inferno" (19978), "The Last Man on Planet Earth" (1999), "The Apartment Complex" (1999), "12 Days of Terror" (2004), "Crusader" (2005), "Hidden Camera" (2007), "Stevie" (2008), and "The Lost" (2009). His other television credits include episodes of "ABC Afterschool Specials", "Team Knight Rider" also appeared onscreen in an episode as a director, "The Player", and "Son of the Beach". Haitkin was married to camera operator Anne Coffey until her death in 2013 and is survived by their two sons, Zak and Harry.

Hall, Ginger

Actress Ginger Hall died in Napa, California, on March 27, 2023. She was 92. Hall was born in Larchmont, New York, on August 15, 1930. She moved to Los Angeles in the late 1940s and was part of Paramount's Golden Circle Stars of Tomorrow campaign in 1951. She appeared on television in episodes of "The Scarlet Pimpernel", "Four Star Playhouse",

and "Harbor Command". She performed as a singer in Las Vegas and joined one of Bob Hope's USO tours. She remained in Paris for over a decade and appeared in the films "Deux Hommes dans Manhattan" (aka "Two Men in Manhattan") (1959), "Les Ennemis" (aka "A Touch of Treason") (1962), "L'Aine des Ferchaux" (aka "Magnet of Doom") (1963), "The Sandpiper" (1965), and the animated

"Asterix and Cleopatra" (1968) as the English voice of Cleopatra. She was also a founding member of the Studio Thater of Paris where she appeared in numerous plays. Hall continued to perform as a cabaret singer and became co-owner of an antiques shop. She returned to California in the 1970s. Hall wrote the 1995 book "European Designer Jewelry". She was married to actor Russ Moro until their divorce in 1975 and is survived by their son, Sandro Moro.

Halliwell, Steve

British actor Steve Halliwell, who played Zak Dingle on the ITV soap opera "Emmerdale", died in Leeds, West Yorkshire, England, on December 15, 2023. He was 77. Halliwell was born in Bury, Lancashire, England, on March 21,

1946. He worked as an apprentice engineer before training as an actor at the Mountview Theatre School. he began performing on stage and was a founding member of the Interchange Theatre in Bury. Halliwell appeared frequently on television from the late 1970s with roles in episodes of "Second City Firsts", "Here I Stand...", "Pickersgill People", "Crown Court", "The Practice" as Peter Bishop from 1985 to 1986, "Children's Ward", "Stay Lucky", "All Creatures Great and Small", "Three Seven Eleven", "Heartbeat", "Screenplay", "Cracker", "Comic Timing", "Coronation Street", "Elidor", and "Ant & Dec's Saturday Night Takeaway". He starred as Zak Dingle on the ITV soap opera "Emmerdale Farm" for nearly thirty years between 1994 and 2023. His other television credits include productions of "Threads" (1984), "Wipe Out" (1988), "First and Last" (1989), "Shoot to Kill" (1990), "G.B.H." (1991), and "Fair Game" (1994). Halliwell married Susan Woods in 1972 and they later divorced. He married Valerie Kirby in 1984 and is survived by her and their daughter, Charlotte.

Hamilton, Patricia

Canadian actress Patricia Hamilton, who was featured as the ill-fated Mabel Osbourne in the 1981 horror film "My Bloody Valentine" and was Rachel Lynde in the "Anne of Green Gables" television series,

died in Stratford, Ontario, Canada, on April 30, 2023. She was 86. Hamilton was born in Regina, Saskatchewan, Canada, on April 27, 1937. She attended Carnegie Tech in Pittsburgh. She began her acting career on stage and performed with the Tarragon Theatre in Toronto during its inaugural season in 1971, with roles in productions of "See No Evil, Hear No Evil" and "Forever Yours, Marie-Lou". She appeared frequently on stage throughout her career, working with CanStage, the Harold

Green Jewish Theatre, Soulpepper, and the Shaw Festival. Hamilton appeared in the films "A Bird in the House" (1973), "The Last Detail" (1973), "Why Rock the Boat?" (1974), "Goldenrod" (1976), "Age of Innocence" (1977), "Who Has Seen the Wind" (1977), "The Case for Barbara Parsons" (1978), "Middle Age Crazy" (1980), "My Bloody Valentine" (1981) as launderette owner Mabel Osbourne, who has her heart removed by the killer miner and her body stuffed in a clothes dryer, "Changes of Heart" (1985), the short "Connection" (1986), "Screwball Hotel" (1988), "Little Brother of War" (2003), and the short "Lira's Forest" (2017). She appeared on television in productions of "The House Without a Christmas Tree" (1972) as the narrator, "Ticket-of-Leave Man" (1972) for "Purple Playhouse, "The Thanksgiving Treasure" (1973), "Other People's Children" (1980), "When We First Met" (1984), "Heartsounds" (1984), "The Last Polka" (1985), "Love & Larceny" (1985), "The Lawrenceville Stories" (1987), "Really Weird Tales" (1987), "The Prodigious Hickey" (1987) for "American Playhouse", "Fight for Life" (1987), "Echoes in the Darkness" (1987), "The Christmas Wife" (1988), "Blades of Courage" (1988), "Chasing Rainbows" (1988), "Bridge to Silence" (1989), "In Defense of a Married Man" (1980), "Holiday Affair" (1996), "When Secrets Kill" (1997), "Happy Christmas, Miss King" (1998), and the animated "A Miser Brothers' Christmas" (2008), Hamilton starred as Rachel Lynde in the television mini-series "Anne of Green Gables" in 1985 and reprised the role in "Anne of Avonlea" (1987), the series "Avonlea" from 1990 to 1996, the mini-series "Anne of Green Gables: The Continuing Story" (2000), the animated series "Anne of Green Gables: The Animated Series" from 2001 to 2002, and the tele-film "Anne of Green Gables: A New Beginning" (2008). Her other television credits include episodes of "Police Surgeon", "The ABC Afternoon Playbreak", "Performance", "Teleplay", "The Great Detective", "For the Record", "Hangin' In", "Night Heat", "Alfred Hitchcock Presents", "Air Waves", "Friday the 13th: The Series", "Check It Out", "Street Legal", and "Traders". She was given a lifetime achievement award from the Toronto Alliance for the Performing Art in 1995. Hamilton was married to actor Leslie Carlson from 1966 until their divorce in 1973 and is survived by their son, actor Ben Carlson.

Hamilton, Ron

Christian musician and radio personality Ron Hamilton, who was known as Patch the Pirate, died at his home in Harrisburg, Pennsylvania, on April 19, 2023. He was 72. Hamilton was born in Indiana on November 9, 1950. He learned to play several musical instruments as a child including the piano and guitar. He graduated with a degree in church music from Bob Jones University in 1973. He married Shelley Garlock in 1975 and they began working with her father, Dr. Frank Garlock, and Majesty Music. Dr. Garlock was a speaker at evangelical Baptist churches and Hamilton began accompanying him. He had lost an eye to cancer in 1978 and children began calling him Patch. He released an album of children's church songs, "Rejoice i the Lord", in 1978. He incorporated his Patch persona in a subsequent children's album

"Patch the Pirate Goes to Space" in 1982. Hamilton, who was frequently accompanied by his wife and children, wrote and recorded over forty subsequent "Patch the Pirate" albums  including "Patch the Pirate Goes West" (1983), "Kidnapped on I-Land" (1985), "The Great American Time Machine" (1986), "The Calliope Caper" (1988), "The Custard's Last Stand" (1990), "Peanut Butter Christmas" (1991), "The Friend Ship Mutiny" (1991), "Once Upon a Starry Knight" (1992), "Harold the King" (1993), "The Evolution Revolution" (1994), "Mount Zion Marathon" (1995), "Giant Killer" (1996), "Polecat's Poison" (1997), "The Sneaky Sheik" (1998), "Afraidika Fever" (1999), "The Tumbleweed Opera" (2001), "Limerick the Leprechaun" (2003), "The Kashmir Kid" (2005), "The Villain of Venice" (2006), "The Colonel's Colossal Character Quest" (2007), "Armadillo Amigos" (2008), "Kung Phooey Kid" (2009), "The Legend of Stickyfoot" (2010), "Incrediworld" (2011), "International Spy Academy" (2013), "Kilimanjaro" (2014), "Ocean commotion" (2015), "Time Twisters" (2017), "The Incredible Race" (2018), "Mystery Island" (2020), and "A Whale of a Tale" (2021). Patches was featured in the 2018 animated film "Operation Arctic: Viking Invasion". Hamilton was music pastor at Cavalry Baptist Church in Simpsonville, South Carolina, for over twenty years. He continued to travel to churches around the country and was director of Majesty MusiColleges until 2018, after being diagnosed with early onset dementia. He is survived by his wife and five children.

Hammatt, Richard

British stuntman Richard Hammatt, who worked on such films as "Star Wars" and "Batman", died in England on March 24, 2023. He was 75. Hammatt was born in England on  June 30, 1947. He was a stuntman, stunt coordinator, and occasional actor for numerous films and television productions from the mid-1970s. His numerous film credits include "The Eagle Has Landed" (1976), "Star Wars" (1977), "The Empire Strikes Back" (1980), "Flash Gordon" (1980), "Outland" (1981), "The Great Muppet Caper" (1981), "The Appointment" (1982), "Superman III" (1983), "D.A.R.Y.L." (1985), "Superman IV: The Quest for Peace" (1987), "Willow" (1988), "Red Scorpion" (1988), "The Tall Guy" (1989), "Batman" (1989), "Nightbreed" (1990), "A Killer's Romance" (1990), "Blue Ice" (1992), "Shopping" (1994), "The Steal" (1995), "I.D." (1995), "GoldenEye" (1995), "Trainspotting" (1996), "The Man Who Knew Too Little" (1997), "Tomorrow Never Dies" (1997), "Among Giants" (1998), "Divorcing Jack"

(1998), "The Theory of Flight" (1998), "Waking Ned Devine" (1998), "Women Talking Dirty" (1999), "Dreaming of Joseph Lees" (1999), "The World Is Not Enough" (1999), "Guest House Paradiso" (1999), "Billy Eliot" (2000), "Quills" (2000), "Five Seconds to Spare" (2000), "Chocolat" (2000), "Enigma" (2001), "Chica de Rio" (2001), "Dreams" (2001), "Sweet Sixteen" (2002), "The Gathering" (2002), "The Wedding Date" (2005), "Ramji Londonwaley" (2005), "Stormbreaker" (2006), "The Walker" (2007), "In Your Dreams" (2008), "Harry Potter and the Deathly Hallows: Part 1" (2010), and "Harry Potter and the Deathly Hallows: Part 2" (2011). Hammatt worked on such television series as "Tales of the Unexpected", "Turtle's Progress", "Mitch", "Dempsey and Makepeace", "Bergerac", "Boon", "Civvies", "Kinsey", "Emmerdale", "Pie in the Sky", "Harry", "Common as Muck", "Wokenwell", "An Unsuitable Job for a Woman", "The Jump", "Bugs", "Poirot", "Down to Earth", "North Square", "London's Burning", "The Bill", "Taggart", "Murder in Mind", "Cold Feet", "Dalziel and Pascoe", "Steel River Blues", "Monarch of the Glen", "New Tricks", "Waking the Deade", "The Worst Week of My Life", "Doctor Who", "Silent Witness", "Trial & Retribution", "The Royal", "Primeval", "Coronation Street", "Midsomer Murders", "The Indian Doctor", "Shameless", "Law & Order: UK", "Vera", "Warren", and "The End of the F***ing World". He also arranged stunts for television productions of "Scoop" (1987), "The Face of Trespass" (1988), "She's Out" (1995), "The Crow Road" (1996), "Hospital!" (1997), "Our Boy" (1997), "Into the Blue" (1997), "The Woman in White" (1997), "The Scold's Bridle" (1998), "Little White Lies" (1998), "RKO 281" (1999), "Madame Bovary" (2000), "Blind Ambition" (2000), "The Sight" (2000), "NCS: Manhunt" (2001), "Come Together" (2002), "Sirens" (2002), "The Planman" (2003), "Lucky Jim" (2003), "Second Nature" (2003), "After Thomas" (2006), "Mobile" (2007), "The Commander: The Fraudster" (2007), "Boy Meets Girl" (2009), and "Pluen Eira" (2018).

Handler, Carole

Entertainment lawyer Carole Handler, who instrumental in restoring the rights of Spider-Man and other characters to Marvel Comics, died at a senior living facility in  Knoxville, Tennessee, on October 22, 2023. She was 87. Handler was born on December 23, 1935. Her father, Milton Handler, was a professor at Columbia Law School. Carole graduated from Radcliffe in 1957 and earned a master's degree in city planning from the University of Pennsylvania in 1963. She received a law degree from the University of Pennsylvania Law School in 1975. She specialized in intellectual property litigation focusing on trademark and copyright laws. She practiced in Philadelphia before moving to Los Angeles to work in the entertainment industry. Her best-known work was for Marvel Comics, who had optioned the

Spider-Man property to Cannon Films for $225,000 for a five-year period. Cannon's Menahem Golan oversaw the writing of various scripts during the next decade, but the budget for a proposed film kept decreasing due to the company's film failures. The rights to the character had shifted from Cannon, to 21st Century, to Carolco, before landing with MGM. Handler discovered that the rights to Spider-Man were never registered with the United States Copyright Office. That revelation led to the rights reverting to Marvel, which was bought by Avi Arad and Ike Perlmutter. The result was the production of a popular trilogy of films from Columbia beginning in 2002. She also worked with the National Basketball Association (NBA) and several film studios on antitrust work, where she defended block booking of movies. Handler was an adjunct professor at the University of Southern California law school for thirteen years. She moved to Knoxville in 2019 to be close to her family. She was married to Peter Schoenbach from 1965 until their divorce in 1978 and is survived by their two daughters, Alisa and Ilana.

Hardaway, Lynnette

Political commentator Lynnette Hardaway, who was half of the Black conservative duo Diamond and Silk, died of heart disease in North Carolina on January 8, 2023. She was 51. Hardaway was born in Detroit, Michigan, on November 25, 1971. She was the daughter of Freeman and Betty Willis

Hardaway, a pair of televangelists from Fayetteville, North Carolina. She and her sister, Rochelle Hardaway Richardson, began posting videos on YouTube in 2012. Their earlier vlogging was in opposition of police brutality to blacks. Their audience began to grow when the two began making videos in support of Donald Trump's presidential aspirations in 2015. The became known as Diamond and Silk and appeared frequently on the campaign trail with Trump and his family. They were seen on such Fox News shows as "Hannity", "Fox News Sunday", "The Ingrahan Angle", "Watters' World", and "Fox & Friends". The sisters made the 2018 documentary film "Dummycrats" and had a weekly show on the Fox News' streaming service. Fox and the sisters parted ways in 2020 over Diamond and Silk's propagation of misinformation regarding the COVID-19 pandemic. They moved to Newsmax TV where they hosted "Diamond and Silk Crystal Clear". Their book, "Uprising: Who the Hell Said You Can't Ditch and Switch? — The Awakening of Diamond and Silk", was published in 2020.

Hardcore, Max

Adult actor Paul F. Little, who was known by the stage name Max Hardcore, died of complications from septic shock and thyroid cancer in Los Angeles, California, on March 27, 2023. He was 66. Little was born in Racine, Wisconsin, on August 10, 1956. He began working in the adult entertainment

industry in the early 1990s and was noted for his 1992 film "The Anal Adventures of Max Hardcore". He became a controversial figure even in the porn community. He directed and starred in numerous pornographic productions, often humiliating and

torturing his female co-stars. His numerous films included such series as "Anal Vision", "Casting Call:", "Cherry Poppers", "Max World", "Hardcore Schoolgirls", "Planet Max", "Pure Max", and "Max Faktor". He was arrested on charges of obscenity in 1998 regarding his film "Max Extreme 4". A trial in 2002 resulted in the jury failing to reach a verdict. His offices at Max World Entertainment were raided by the FBI in October of 2005. His extremely graphic and hardcore films led to an indictment on charges of obscenity in 2007. He was found guilty on all counts and sentenced to 46 months in prison. He began serving his sentence in January of 2009 after losing an appeal. He was originally incarcerated at the Federal Metropolitan Correctional Facility in Los Angeles, and then transferred to Federal Correctional Institution, La Tuna, in Anthony, Texas. He served his final months under house arrest before his release in 2011.

Hardiman, Terrence

British actor Terrence Hardiman, who starred in the title role in the children's series "Demon Headmaster" in the late 1990s, died in England on May 8, 2023. He was 86. Hardiman

was born in Forest Gate, London, England, on April 6, 1937. He began acting on stage while attending Fitzwilliam College, Cambridge, performing with the Cambridge University Amateur Dramatic Club. He later toured with the Royal Shakespeare Company from 1966 to 1970, appearing in productions of "Doctor Faustus" and "A Midsummer Night's Dream". Hardiman was noted for his role as Stephen Harvesty in the television series "Crown Court" from 1972 to 1983. He was also seen in television productions of "Love's Labour's Lost" (1965), "Caucasian Chalk Circle" (1973), "Edward the King (1975), "The Story of David" (1976), "The Sinking of HMS Victoria" (1977), "Rebecca" (1979), "Oresteia" (1979), "The Bunker" (1981), "My Father's House" (1981), "Rules of Justice" (1981), "Inside the Third Reich" (1982), "Skorpion" (1983), "Miss Marple: Sleeping Murder" (1987), "The Charmer" (1987), "Detonator" (1993), "Prime Suspect 3" (1993), "Circles of Deceit: Kalon" (1996), "The Moonstone" (1996), "McLibel!" (1997), "The Slavery Business" (2005), "Into the Storm" (2009), "The Fairy Queen" (2009), and "Ein Sommer in Oxford" (2018). His other television credits include episodes of "Thursday Theatre", "Softly Softly: Task Force", "A Family at War", "Colditz",

"Dead of Night", "Justice", "Late Night Theatre", "The Carnforth Practice", "Horizon", "Churchill's People", "When the Boat Comes In", "BBC2 Playhouse", "Second Verdict", "Wings", "Everyman", "Out of the Past", "Enemy at the Door", "Angels", "Diary of a Nobody" as Charles Pooter in 1979, "Secret Army" as Major Hans Dietrich Reinhardt in 1979, "Lady Killers", "Juliet Bravo", "Natural World", "Fresh Fields", "Late Starter", "Storyboard", "Bergerac", "All in Good Faith", "Home to Roost", "The Bretts", "Hannay", "Inspector Morse", the anime "Crying Freeman" in a voice role, "Wish Me Luck" as Superintendent Carter in 1990, "This Is David Harper", "Minder", "Moon and Son", "The Brittas Empire", "Poirot", "Grange Hill", "Surgical Spirit", "The Young Indiana Jones Chronicles", "Keeping Up Appearances", "Casualty", "True Crimes", "Law and Disorder", "Magic Grandad", "Goodnight Sweetheart", "Ruth Rendell Mysteries", "An Independent Man", "Ellington", "Beck", "Crime Traveller", "Strange But True?", "Heartbeat", "Wogan's Web", "Verdict", "Cadfael", "ChuckleVision", "Jonathan Creek", "The Worst Witch" in the recurring role of Grand Wizard Hellibore from 1998 to 2001, "Urban Gothic", "The Bill", "Midsomer Murders", "The Courtroom" as Judge Garrett Warburton James in 2004, "The Royal", "The Worst Week of My Life" as Gerard in 2005, "Doctor Who" as Hawthorne in the 2010 episode "The Beast Below", "The Bleak Shop of Old Stuff", "Doctors", "Holby City", "Wallander", "Agatha Raisin", "Genius", and "The Crown". Hardiman starred in the title role in the juvenile horror series "The Demon Headmaster" from 1996 to 1998 and reprised his role in an episode of the 2019 reboot. He was also seen in such films as "Running Scared" (1972), "Pope Joan" (1972), "Loophole" (1981), "Gandhi" (1982) as Ramsay MacDonald, "Sahara" (1983), "God's Outlaw" (1986), "Mask of Murder" (1988), "A Demon in My View" (1991), "Lethal Impact" (1991), "Distant Shadow" (2000), "Fishtales" (2007), the short "For George" (2012), and "Mr. Turner" (2014). He provided voice-overs and narration for numerous audio books by such authors as Roald Dahl, Ken Follett, and Wilkie Collins. Hardiman married actress Rowena Cooper in 1964 and is survived by her and their two children.

Hardwick, Johnny

Actor and comedian Johnny Hardwick, who was best known as the voice of Dale Dribble on the animated television series "King of the Hill", was found dead at his home in Austin, Texas, on August 8, 2023. He was 64. It was later reported that

his body was badly decomposed when it was discovered, and the time and cause of death could not be determined. Hardwick was born in Austin on December 31, 1958. He graduated from Texas Tech University in Lubbock with a degree in journalism. He worked as a bartender in the Dallas and Austin areas for over a decade. He began performing stand-up comedy routines in 1990, appearing at the Dallas Improv and the Velveeta Room in Austin. He was also seen on television in episodes of "Evening at the Improv", "Caroline's Comedy Hour", and "The Jon Stewart Show". Hardwick appeared at the Laugh Factory in Los Angeles where he was seen by television writers Greg Daniels and Mike Judge. He was offered the voice role of Hank Hill's eccentric neighbor, Dale Gribble, in the animated series "King of the Hill". He performed the role from 1997 to 2010 and served as a producer, writer, and story editor. He shared an Emmy Award when "King of the Hill" was named Outstanding Animated Program in 1999 and received additional nominations in 2001 and 2002. He uploaded song parodies and monologues to a YouTube channel from 2015. Hardwick planned to resume voicing Dale Dribble in an upcoming revival of "King of the Hill" and had reportedly recorded several episodes prior to his death.

Hardy, Peter

Australian actor Peter Hardy died from drowning while snorkeling at South Beach in Fremantle, Western Australia, on March 16, 2023. He was 66. Hardy was born in

Perth, Western Australia, on January 11, 1957. He performed on stage and screen from the 1980s. He was seen on television in episodes off "A Country Practice", "Prisoner: Cell Block H", "Phoenix", "Time Trax", "Janus", "Snowy River: The McGregor Saga", "Naked: Stories of Men", "Halifax f.p.", "Sweat" as Sid O'Reilly in 1996, "Good Guys Bad Guys", "State Coroner", "Neighbours", "Wildside", "Stingers", "Eugenie Sandler P.I.", "Blue Heelers", "The Strip", "McLeod's Daughters" as Phil Rakich from 2006 to 2009, "East West 101", "Rush" as Doug Rainey in 2011, "Underbelly", "It's a Date", and "The Doctor Blake Mysteries". His other television credits include productions of "Jackaroo" (1990), "Snowy" (1993), "Desperate Journey: The Allison Wilcox Story" (1993), "Stark" (1993), "Baby Bath Massacre" (1994), "The Feds: Terror" (1995), "The Bite" (1996), "The Last of the Ryans" (1997), "Fable" (1997), "The Ripper" (1997), "Tales of the South Seas" (2000), "Dangerous Remedy" (2012), and "The Engineering That Built the World" (2021). Hardy appeared frequently in films during his career with roles in "The Pursuit of Happiness" (1988), "Daisy and Simon" (1989), "Dingo" (1991), "Dead End" (1999), "Chopper" (2000), "Is This the Real World" (2015), the short "Waste of Time" (2016), "Hard Target 2" (2016), and "The King's Man" (2021). He was seen in numerous stage productions including "Priscilla Queen of the Desert", "The Boy from Oz", and over 1,500 performances of "Mamma Mia!" as Bill Austin.

Harmony, Dotty

Actress Dotty Harmony died in Los Angeles, California, on April 4, 2023. She was 90. Harmony was born

in Brooklyn, New York, on February 14, 1933. She attended the High School of Performing Arts in New York. She moved to Florida after graduation and joined the June Taylor Dancers. She then worked in Las Vegas where she met and dated singing legend Elvis Presley. Harmony moved to Los Angeles in 1960 and appeared on television in episodes of "Hawaiian Eye" and "Tallahassee 7000". Harmony married actor Robert Colbert in 1961 and had a son and daughter, Cami and Clayton, before their divorce in 1976. She and Colbert remarried in April of 2022, and is survived by him and their two children.

Harnick, Sheldon

Songwriter Sheldon Harnick, who worked with Jerry Bock on such hit Broadway musicals as "Fiorello!" and "Fiddler on the Roof", died at his apartment in Manhattan, New

York, on June 23, 2023. He was 99. Harnick was born in Chicago, Illinois, on April 30, 1924. He played violin as a child and started writing music while in high school. He served in the U.S. Army and attended the Northwestern University School of Music from 1946 to 1949. He performed with several orchestras in the Chicago area before moving to New York City. He began writing songs for revues and for such Broadway musicals as "Leonard Sillman's New Faces of 1952" (1952), "Two's Company" (1952), "John Murray Anderson's Almanac" (1953), and "The Littlest Revue" (1956). His song "The Merry Minuet" became a hit recording by the Kingston Trio. Harnick began working with composer Jerry Bock on the 1958 Broadway musical "The Body Beautiful", though it proved unsuccessful. He and Bock scored a major hit with their next collaboration, the 1959 Broadway musical "Fiorello!". They shared the Pulitzer Prize for Drama, the Tony Award, and the New York Drama Critics Award. They also wrote music and lyrics for the Broadway productions "Tenderloin" (1960) and "She Loves Me" (1963) and had another major hit with 1964's "Fiddler on the Roof". The musical about the poor Russian Jewish milkman Tevye and his family included such popular songs as "If I Were a Rich Man", "Tradition", "Matchmaker, Matchmaker", and "Sunrise, Sunset". The show earned nine Tony Awards and had an extraordinary eight year run on Broadway. It was adapted for an Oscar-nominated film in 1971 and had five Broadway revivals, most recently in 2015. Bock and Harnick also earned Tony nominations for their work on the musicals "The Apple Tree" (1966) and "The Rothschilds" (1970), which proved their last production together after they had an artistic dispute about

the play's director. Harnick continued to work with other composers including Mary Rodgers on the 1973 version of "Pinocchio", Richard Rodgers for "Rex" in 1976, and Michel Legrand for a stage version of the film "The Umbrellas of Cherbourg" in 1979 and a new adaptation of "A Christmas Carol" in 1982. His other Broadway credits include "The Madwoman of Central Park West" (1979), "Barbara Cook: A Concert for the Theatre" (1987), "Jerome Robbins' Broadway" (1989), "Cyrano - The Musical" (1993) receiving another Tony nomination, "Mostly Sondheim" (2002), "Barbara Cook's Broadway" (2004), "Chita Rivera: The Dancer's Life" (2005), and "Prince of Broadway" (2017). Harnick was also noted as an opera translator, providing English librettos for Bizet's "Carmen", Stravinsky's "The Soldier's Tale", and Lehar's "The Merry Widow". He teamed with Joe Raposo for a musical version of "A Wonderful Life" in 1986. He wrote the original libretto for Henry Mollicone's opera "Coyote Tales" in 1988. He wrote the book, lyrics, and music for the 2003 musical "Dragons". He supplied the lyrics and co-wrote the book with Norton Juster for the 2007 musical "The Phantom Tollbooth". He was inducted into the Songwriters Hall of Fame in 1972 and was the recipient of a Special Tony Award for Lifetime Achievement in 2016. Harnick was married to Mary Boatner from 1950 until their annulment in 1957. He was briefly married to comedian and playwright Elaine May from 1962 until their divorce in 1963. He married actress and artist Margery Grey in 1965 and is survived by her, their son Matthew, and daughter Beth.

Harper, Toni

Singer Toni Harper died in Palm Desert, California, on February 10, 2023. She was 85. Harper was born in Los Angeles, California, on June 8, 1937. She learned dancing as a

child under Maceo Anderson and made her stage debut in a production of "Christmas Follies" in 1945. She performed at the Cavalcade of Jazz concert in 1947 and again in 1952. She was noted for recording the hit 1946 song "Candy Store Blues" and made several appearances on Ed Sullivan's "Toast of the Town". She was also seen in the films "Manhattan Angel" (1948) and "Make Believe Ballroom" (1949). Harper also sang on episodes of "The Frank Sinatra Show" and "Hollywood a Go Go". She recorded the 1956 album "Toni" with the Oscar Peterson trio. She made the albums "Lady Lonely" (1959) and "Night Mood" (1960) with Marty Paich and his Orchestra. Harper toured Japan with Cannonball Adderley in 1963 and made her final film appearance in the 1965 beach party film "How to Stuff a Wild Bikini". She retired from performing in the mid-1960s to work for the U.S. Postal Service in the Los Angeles region until her retirement in the early 1990s. She was predeceased by her husband, Ron Dunlap.

Harrell, Dickie

Drummer Dickie Harrell, who played with Gene Vincent's band the Blue Caps, died in Portsmouth, Virginia, on

May 31, 2023. He was 82. Harrell was born in Portsmouth on August 27, 1940. He was the original drummer for the Blue Caps when he was fifteen years old. His drum brushing and background screams were featured on Vincent's 1955 hit record "Be-Bob-A-Lula". Vincent and the Blue Caps appeared in a cameo role performing the song in the 1956 film "The Girl Can't Help It". Harrell tired of touring and left the band after little over a year. Vincent disbanded the Blue Caps by the end of the 1950s. Harrell later worked with hazardous materials for the government for nearly forty years. He occasionally reunited with fellow surviving Blue Caps in his later years performing at nostalgia festivals. Harrell and the Blue Caps were inducted into the Rock and Roll Hall of Fame in 2012.

Harris, C.J.

Singer C.J. Harris, who was a contestant on the 13th season of the television talent competition "American Idol" in

2014, died of a heart attack at a hospital in Jasper, Alabama, on January 15, 2023. He was 31. Harris was born in Jasper on January 28, 1991. He began singing and playing the guitar from an early age. He made his first audition for "American Idol" in 2010. He also tried out for other singing competition shows including "The X-Factor" and "The Voice". He was selected as a finalist for "American Idol" in 2014 following his rendition of the Allman Brothers' "Soulshine". He progressed through the series, finishing in sixth place. Harris released his debut single, "In Love", in 2019.

Harris, Pat Vern

Actress Pat Vern Harris died in Chicago, Illinois, on December 19, 2023. She was 83. Harris was born in Memphis,

Tennessee, on March 23, 1940. She attended the University of Iowa and completed her education at Truman State University in Kirksville, Missouri. She performed frequently in regional and community theater and appeared on Broadway in the 1996 revival of the musical "Show Boat". Harris was featured as Sheila Portnadi in the television series "Detroiters" from 2017 to 2018 and was Nana in "Joe Pera Talks with You" from 2019 to 2020. She was also seen in

the tele-film "Two Fathers: Justice for the Innocent" (1994) and episodes of "Shameless", "Underemployed", "Sirens", "South Side", and "Night Sky". Harris was featured in the 2022 film "Angry Neighbors". She was predeceased by her husband, Dr. James G. Severns, and is survived by their three children.

Harris, Rolf

Australian musician and actor Rolf Harris, who recorded the hit song "Tie Me Kangaroo Down, Sport", died of complications from cancer at his home in Bray, Berkshire, England, on May 10, 2023. He was 93. Harris was born in Bassendean, Western Australia, on March 30, 1930. He

graduated from the University of Western Australia and Claremont Teachers' College. Harris moved to England in 1952 to attend the City and Guilds of London Art School. He began working for the BBC the following year drawing cartoons for the children's series "Jigsaw". He appeared regularly as an artist on the BBC children's series "Whirligig" from 1955 to

1956 and was host of the ITV series "Small Time" in 1955. He appeared in several films in the 1950s including "You Lucky People!" (1955), "Web of Suspicion" (1959), and "Crash Drive" (1959). He was also an actor in episodes of "The Vise" and "Man from Interpol". He also began performing the piano accordion at the Down Under nightclub, where he wrote the popular song "Tie Me Kangaroo Down, Sport". The song became a popular hit novelty recording in 1959. He also recorded the hit songs "Jake the Peg" and "Two Little Boys" in the 1960s. Harris became a popular figure on television, appearing in such series as "Studio E", "Spotlight", "Musical Box", "Blue Peter", "The Andy Stewart Show", "The Tonight Show Starring Johnny Carson", "To Tell the Truth", "Hi There! It's Rolf Harris" which he hosted in 1964, "A Swingin' Time", "Ring-a-Ding-Ding", "Comedy Bandbox", "The Mike Douglas Show", "Thank Your Lucky Stars", "Tich & Quackers", "David Nixon's Comedy Bandbox", "The Dickie Valentine Show", "Hey Presto! It's Rolf" serving as host from 1965 to 1966, "Billy Cotton Band Show", "The Norman Vaughan Show", "Juke Box Jury", "Something Special", "Carnival Time", "The Val Doonican Show", "Dee Time", "Lulu's Back in Town", "BBC Show of the Week", "The Talk of the Town", "The Eamonn Andrews Show", "Jokers Wild", "The Liberace Show", "The Tommy Leonetti Show", "Vera Lynn", "The Harry Secombe Show", "The Rolf Harris Show" hosting from 1967 to 1974, "Crackerjack!", "Rolf's Walkabout" hosting in 1969, "Frost on Sunday", "The Young Generation", "The Mike Neun Show", "He Said, She Said", "The David Frost Show", "Saturday Variety", "Quick on the Draw", "Stars on Sunday", "The Norman Gunston Show", "Celebrity Squares", "Shirley", "The Basil Brush Show", "Rolf on Saturday O.K.?" hosting from 1977 to 1980, "This Is Your Life", "The David Nixon Show", "The Alan Hamel Show", "The Rolf Harris Show" hosting in 1979, "Star Games", "The Alan Thicke Show", "The Don Lane

Show", "Rolf's Here! - OK?" hosting from 1981 to 1982, "Give Us a Clue", "The Paul Daniels Magic Show", "Emu's All Live Pink Windmill Show", "On Safari", "The Keith Harris Show", "Blankety Blank", "Wogan", "The Last Resort with Jonathan Ross", "It's a Knockout", "Rolf Harris' Cartoon Time", "Rolf's Cartoon Club" from 1989 to 1990, "Surprise! Surprise!", "Phil Cool", "Top of the Pops", "Bruce Forsyth and the Generation Game", "Noel's House Party", "The Mrs. Merton Show", "Smillie's People", "Night Fever", "Shooting Stars", "Des O'Connor Tonight", "The Zig and Zag Show", "Goodnight Sweetheart", "Richard and Judy", "The South Bank Show", "Piers Morgan's Life Stories", and numerous specials. Harris recorded a cover of Led Zeppelin's "Stairway to Heaven" in the late 1980s and was a featured guest at seven Glastonbury Festivals in the 1990s and early 2000s. He was host of the reality television programs "Animal Hospital" from 1994 to 2003 and "Rolf's Animal Clinic" in 2012. He remained a talented artist and hosted the art series "Rolf on Art" and "Star Portraits with Rolf Harris" in the 2000s. He was commissioned to paint a portrait of Queen Elizabeth II for her 80th birthday in 2005. He was the subject of the 2007 television documentary "A Lifetime in Paint". He was featured as a busker in the 2012 film "Run for Your Wife". Harris was arrested in March of 2013 on allegations of indecent assault and making indecent images of children. He entered a plea of not guilty to all charges relating to events that were alleged to have occurred from the 1960s through the 1990s. He was found guilty of indecent assault and was sentenced to over five years in prison in July of 2014. He served three years in prison before his release in May of 2017. He was subsequently charged with other incidents of indecent assault. He again entered a not guilty plea and the prosecution eventually announced they would not pursue a retrial when a jury was unable to reach a verdict. A documentary about the allegations, "Rolf Harris: Hiding in Plain Sight", was released in May of 2023. He received numerous awards and honors including Member of the Order of the British Empire (MBE) in 1968, Officer (OBE) in 1977, and Commander (CBE) in 2006. These honors were revoked after his criminal convictions. He was named to the Australian Recording Industry Association's Hall of Fame in 2008, which was also later revoked. Harris married sculptor Alwen Hughes in 1958 and is survived by her and their daughter, Bindi Harris.

Hart, Anne

British actress Anne Hart, who was the widow of comedian Ronnie Corbett, died in Scotland on November 5, 2023. He was 90. Hart was born in Lambeth, London, England, on April 26, 1933. She began her career on stage as a child appearing in the West End Christmas production "Where the Rainbow Ends". She starred with the Crazy Gang comedy troupe in the 1950s in productions of "Clown Jewels" and "Young at Heart". Hart met comedian

Ronnie Corbett while performing at Danny La Rue's club in the late 1950s. The two were married in 1965 and the two worked together frequently. Hart appeared on television in episodes of "Sherlock Holmes", "Z Cars", "Hope and Keen", "The Corbett Follies", "The Two Ronnies", "The Good Old Days", "Seaside Special", "The Keith Barret Show", "Ronnie's Animal Crackers", and "The Man Faces of..." She was featured in the 1965 television production "Solo for the Banker" and had a small role in the 1967 film "Cop-Out". Hart was married to Ronnie Corbett from 1965 until his death in 2016. Their son, Andrews, died in infancy in 1966. She is survived by their two daughters, Emma and Sophie.

Hartner, Rona

Romanian actress and singer Rona Hartner died of lung and brain cancer in Toulon, France, on November 23, 2023. She was 50. Hartner was born in Bucharest, Romania, on March 9, 1973. She began her film career as Tessa in the Full Moon Entertainment science fiction films "Trancers 4: Jack of Swords" (1994) and "Trancers 5: Sudden Deth" (1994) which were filmed in Romania. She continued to appear in numerous films, including many French productions. Hartner's films include "Terente - Reele Baltilor" (1995), "Asphalt Tango" (1996), "Semne in Pustiu" (1996), "The Crazy Stranger" (1997), "Nekro" (1997), "Dublu Extaz" (1998), "Doggy Bag" (1999), "Children of the Stork" (1999), "Cours Toujurs" (2000), "Sauve-moi" (2000), "Sexy Harem Ada-Kaleh" (2001), "Mischka" (2002), "Time of the Wolf" (2003), "The Divorce" (2003), "Maria" (2003), "Visions of Europe" (2004), "Housewarming" (2005), "Madame Irma" (2006), "Tombe d'Une Etoile" (2007), "Chicken with Plums" (2011), "Des Milliards de Toi Mon Poussin" (2015), "Ce Qui Reste" (2015), "Nelly's Adventure" (2016), "Le Correspondant" (2016), and "Le Petit Blond de la Casbah" (2023). She was seen on television in the 1998 production of "Les Grands Enfants" and episodes of "Un Flic" and "Grown Ups". Hartner was also a singer and musician who specialized in Gypsy music.

Harvey, James

Musician James Harvey, who was bassist for the band Goatwhore, died on July 26, 2023. He was 35. Harvey was born in Pensacola, Florida, on May 18, 1988. He began his career in music with the band Driven by Suffering from 2003 to 2004. He played with the bands Ritual Killer and Psychon Vex before joining Goatwhore in 2009. He was bassist on the albums "Blood for the Master" (2012), "Constricting Rage of the

Merciless" (2014), and "Vengeful Ascension" (2017). He quit touring after the birth of his son and left the band in 2017. Harvey is survived by his wife and two sons.

Harwell, Steve

Rock musician Steve Harwell, who was lead singer for the band Smash Mouth, died of liver failure at his home in Boise, Idaho, on September 4, 2023. He was 56. Harwell was born in Santa Clara, California, on January 9, 1967. He began his career in the late 1980s as a rapper with the group F.O.S. (Freedom of Speech). He joined Kevin Coleman on drums, Greg Camp on guitar, and Paul De Lisle on bass to form the rock band Smash Mouth in 1994. They had a hit with the songs "Walkin' on the Sun" and the cover of "Why Can't We Be Friends?" from their first album "Fush Yu Mang" in 1997. Smash Mouth's 1999 album "Astro Lounge" contained the hits "All Star" and "Then the Morning Comes". He was lead singer on the albums "Smash Mouth" (2001), "Get the Picture?" (2003), "The Gift of Rock" (2005), "Summer Girl" (2006), and "Magic"(2012). Harwell was featured in the VH1 reality series "The Surreal Life" in 2006. He was featured in a cameo role in the 2001 film "Rat Race" and was a voice performer in the animated series "Kim Possible", "What's New, Scooby-Doo?", and "We Bare Bears". He suffered from alcoholism and other health diseases including cardiomyopathy and Wernicke encephalopathy. He retired in 2021 as his ability to perform became impaired. Harwell was married and divorced from Michelle Laroque and their son, Presley, died of leukemia in July of 2001 at the age of six months.

Haskins, Fuzzy

Singer Clarence 'Fuzzy' Haskins, who performed with Parliament-Funkadelic, died of complications from diabetes in Grosse Pointe Woods, Michigan, on March 16, 2023. He was

81. Haskins was born in Elkhorn, West Virginia, on June 8, 1941, and was raised in New Jersey. He was a founding member of George Clinton's vocal group the Parliaments in the late 1950s. The group began performing and recording in Detroit and scored their first hit with "(I Wanna) Testify" in 1967. The Parliaments had several membership changes but solidified with the quintet of Haskins, Clinton, Ray Davis, Calvin Simon, and Grady Thomas. They began touring with a group of five backing musicians who were known as Funkadelic. They groups released their first album as "Funkadelic" in 1970 and they became collectively known as Parliament-Funkadelic (or P-

Funk). Haskins and several other original members of the group left Clinton over financial disputes in 1977. He released the 1976 solo album "A Whole Nother Thing". He joined Simon and Thomas as a new band using the name Funkadelic in 1981. They performed on "Soul Train" and released the album "Connections & Disconnections". He toured with other former members of the Parliaments as the Original P in the 1990s. He was inducted into the Rock and Roll Hall of Fame with Parliament-Funkadelic in 1997 and received a Grammy Lifetime Achievement Award with the group in 2019.Haskins was married and divorced from Estelle James and Lorraine Debney. He was predeceased by two children and is survived by three others.

Hata, Masanori

Japanese zoologist and filmmaker Masanori Hata, who directed the film "The Adventures of Milo and Otis", died of a heart attack in Hokkaido, Japan, on April 5, 2023. He was 87. Hata was born in Fukoaka, Japan, on April 17, 1935. He graduated with a degree in biology from Tokyo University in 1958 and earned a master's degree in the following year. He trained as a zoologist and wrote numerous books and essays under the name Mutsugoro. His books include "All of Us Animals Are Brothers and Sisters" (1967) and "Mutsugor's Natural History" (1975). He established the nature preserve Mutsugoro Animal Kingdom in Hokkaido where he and his family lived with over 300 animals. He was the director and shot much footage at the preserve, including the story of an orange tabby cat and a pug. The film was released by Toho in 1986 as "Koneko Monogatari". It was edited and given an English narration by Dudley Moore for its U.S. release under the title "The Adventures of Milo and Otis" in 1989.

Hayne, Murray

British actor Murray Hayne died in England on April 13, 2023. He was 91. Hayne was born in India on October 18, 1931. He appeared frequently on television with roles in episodes of "Shadow Squad", "Sword of Freedom", "Mary Britten, M.D.", "Murder Bag", "All Aboard", "Knight Errant Limited", "International Detective", "Emergency-Ward 10" as Nigel Harcourt in 1960, "Out of This World", "It Happened Like This", "Secret Beneath the Sea" as Sanders in 1963, "Moonstrike", "The Edgar Wallace Mystery Theatre", "The Odd Man", "No Hiding Place", "The Plane Makers", "Secret Agent", "A Game of Murder", "Redcap", "Conflict", "Armchair Theatre", "Boy Meets Girl", "The Wednesday Play", "Z Cars", "The Avengers", "Dixon of Dock

Green", "Love Story", "W. Somerset Maugham", "Mystery and Imagination", "Special Branch", "Brett", "Crown Court", "The Brothers" as Martin Farrell from 1974 to 1975, "Survivors", "The Expert", and "When the Boat Comes In" as Hodges in 1977. His other television credits include productions of "When We Are Married" (1957), "The Long Wait" (1957), "2000 Minus 60" (1958), "Twelfth Night" (1959), "Triangle" (1964), "The Colonel and the Naturalist" (1969), "Follow Me..." (1977), and "Smuggler" (1981). Hayne was seen in small roles in several films including "Foxhole in Cairo" (1960), "Death Trap" (1962), "The Rivals" (1963), and "The Vulture" (1966). He wrote "The Trial and Error of Colonel Winchip" in 1967 for "ITV Play of the Week" and penned an episode of "Love Story" in 1969 under the name Manus Hardy. Hayne married actress Gillian Muir in 1958 and they had four children.

Haynes, Linda

Actress Linda Haynes who was noted for her role in the 1970s films "Rolling Thunder" and "Human Experiments", died in Summerville, South Carolina, on July 17, 2023. She was 75. She was born Linda Lee Sylvander in Miami, Florida, on Nov. 4, 1947. She trained at  the Ivor Francis Acting Workshop in West Hollywood and became a life member of the Actors Studio. She made her film debut in a small role in the 1967 spy spoof "In Like Flint" and starred as Dr. Anne Barton in the 1969 science fiction film "Latitude Zero". Her other films include the blaxploitation film "Coffy" (1973) starring Pam Grier, Robert Mulligan's crime film "The Nickel Ride" (1974), "The Drowning Pool" (1975) starring Paul Newman, the psychological thriller "Rolling Thunder" (1977) as Linda Forchet, the 1979 exploitation horror film "Human Experiments" (1979) as Rachel Foster, and the prison film "Brubaker" (1980) starring Robert Redford. Haynes was seen on television in episodes of "Room 222", "Owen Marshall, Counselor at Law", "This Is the Life", "My Three Sons", and "Paper Moon" as outlaw Bonnie Parker in a 1974 episode. Her other television credits include the tele-films "Judgment: The Court Martial of Lieutenant William Calley" (1975) and "Guyana Tragedy: The Story of Jim Jones" (1980). Haynes left acting in the early 1980s and worked as a legal secretary at a law firm in Florida. Tom Graves profiled the actress in his essay "Blonde Shadow: The Brief Career and Mysterious Disappearance of Actress Linda Haynes" that is included in his 2015 anthology "Louise Brooks, Frank Zappa, & Other Charmers & Dreamers". She is survived by two grandchildren.

Haze, Doktor

British circus owner John Hayes Mabley, who was known as Doktor Haze and was ringmaster of the Circus of Horrors, died of esophageal cancer in England on April 15, 2023. He was 66. Mabley was born in Preston, Lancashire, England, on December 22, 1956. His parents were circus performers, and he joined his father as a fire eater at a circus in Ireland at age 12. He learned to play the guitar several years  later and began performer with the rock band Flash Harry in the late 1970s. He formed the band Haze Vs The X Factor in the 1980s that incorporated illusions and circus motifs in their stage shows. They performed frequently at the Marquee Club in London. Haze and circus owner Gerry Cottle created The Circus of Horrors in 1994 which made its first appearance at the Glastonbury Festival the following year. Haze supplied the rock score to the blend of circus, cabaret, and horror. He was ringmaster of The Circus of Horrors which appeared on such television series as "Britain's Got Talent". He released his autobiography "Dr. Haze: Mud, Blood and Glitter" in 2011. He was also co-owner of Circus Extreme, Circus Ukraine, and Continental Circus Berlin. Haze remained ringmaster of The Circus of Horrors until 2021. He is survived by his partner of 16 years, Stephanie Bates.

Hazelton, Ron

Television host Ron Hazelton, who was noted for his work on the "Home Improvement" series, died at his home in Fairfield, Connecticut, on April 30, 2023. He was 81. Hazelton  was born in Binghampton, New York, on May 29, 1942. He graduated from the Florida State University College of Business in 1965. He served in the U.S. Navy for four years during the Vietnam War. He began working in marketing and advertising in Boston after his discharge. He quit and moved to San Francisco in 1978 where he opened a restoration workshop called Cow Hollow Woodworks. He created and hosted the home improvement television series "The House Doctor for KGO-TV, the local ABC affiliate in San Francisco, in 1989. It aired until 1997 and was seen on the HGTV Network until 2001. He also served as home improvement editor for ABC's "Good Morning America" from 1997 to 2007. He was featured as a home improvement expert on various other series including "The Oprah Winfrey Show", "Inside Edition", Lifetime's "Our Home", "Modern Marvels" on the History Channel. He hosted the traveling home improvement series "Ron Hazelton's Housecalls". He married television producer Lynn Drasin in 1997 and is survived by her and their two children.

He Ping

Chinese film director He Ping died in Beijing, China, on January 10, 2023. He was 65. He was born in Shanxi,

China, on May 7, 1957. He began working as a director for stage productions and documentary films in the early 1980s. He

joined Xi'an Film Studio later in the decade where he began directing feature films. He helmed the films "We Are the World" (1988), "Kawashima Yoshiko" (1989), the Chinese western "Swordsmen in Double Flag Town" (1991), the historical drama "Red Firecracker, Green Firecracker" (1994), "Sun Valley" (1995), the adventure film "Warriors of Heaven and Earth" (2004), the historical action film "Wheat" (2009), and the drama "The Promised Land" (2015).

Heath, Dodie

Actress Dodie Heath, who was noted for her roles on the Broadway stage, died in Beverly Hills, California, on June 24, 2023. She was born Rowena Dolores Heath in Seattle, Washington, on August 3, 1926. She graduated from the University of Washington School and moved to Manhattan in

1949 to pursue a career in acting. She made her Broadway debut as a replacement for the role of Ensign Sue Yaeger in the musical "South Pacific" in 1950. She was featured as Hildy in the 1951 Broadway production of "A Tree Grows in Brooklyn". She appeared in the comedy play "A Girl Can Tell" in 1954 and made her film debut in the 1954 musical "Brigadoon" as Meg Brockie. Heath returned to Broadway for the 1954 play "Oh, Men! Oh, Women!". She appeared frequently on television in the late 1950s and early 1960s with roles in episodes of "The Web", "Alfred Hitchcock Presents", "Colt .45", "Lawman", "The Untouchables", "Overland Trail", "The Twilight Zone" as Susanna Kittridge in the 1960 episode "Long Live Walter Jameson", "The DuPont Show Starring June Allyson", "Riverboat", "Tales of Wells Fargo", "Outlaws", "Stagecoach West", the 1962 "Hallmark Hall of Fame" production of "Arsenic and Old Lace" with Boris Karloff and Tony Randall, and "The Alfred Hitchcock Hour". Heath was featured as Miep Gies in the 1959 film "The Diary of Anne Frank". Her other films include "Ask Any Girl" (1959), the West German crime drama "Dog Eat Dog" (1964), "Seconds" (1966), "The Fortune Cookie" (1966), and the horror film "Welcome to Arrow Beach" (1973). She largely retired from acting in the mid-1970s. Heath had a long relationship with circus owner John Ringling North in the 1950s. She was married to agent and producer Jack Cunningham from 1962 until his death in 1984. She was later married and divorced from British producer Richard Soames.

Hedrick, Jim Tom

Reality television personality Marvin 'Jim Tim' Hedrick, who starred in the Discovery Channel series

"Moonshiners" from 2012, died of kidney cancer in Tennessee on September 6, 2023. He was 72. Hedrick was born in Graham County, North Carolina, on December 25, 1940. He was a leading moonshiner in the Appalachia area. He joined the cast of the "Moonshiners" series in Season Two in 2012 and remained with the show through Season Six in 2017. He made occasional returns to the series through 2021 and was also a guest judge on the "Master Distiller" series in 2019. Hedrick quit making moonshine to become a legitimate distiller, helping to start the distillery Sugarland Shine in Gatlinburg, Tennessee.

Heklina

Drag queen and actor Stefan Grygelko, who performed under the name Heklina, died in London, England, on April 3, 2023. She was 55. Grygelko was born in Hennepin,

Minnesota, on June 17, 1967. She lived in his mother's native Iceland before moving to San Francisco. He created the drag character Heklina, which was named after an Icelandic volcano. He became active in the local drag community where he hosted the weekly event "Trannyshack" from 1996. "Trannyshack" was renamed "Mother" in 2015. Heklina appeared frequently in local theatrical productions with the S.F. Golden Girls and the Folsom Street Fair. She and several partners bought the Oasis theater and cabaret nightclub in 2015 She was seen in various films and sorts including "Season of the Troll" (2001), "A Nightmare on Castro Street" (2002), "Whatever Happened to Peaches Christ?" (2004), "All About Evil" (2010), "Baby Jane?" (2010), "Read the Signs" (2014), "Hush Up Sweet Charlotte" (2015), "Here Comes Helen!" (2016), "Shit & Champagne" (2020), and "Anti-Venom for a Snake" (2022). She was host of the podcast series "Drag Time with Heklina" from 2020 to 2021. Heklina and Peaches Christ performed on stage in the drag parody "Mommie Queerest" in Palm Springs and in Seattle and were in London for a production at the time of her death.

Helmrich, Leonard Retel

Dutch film director and cinematographer Leonard Retel Helmrich died after a long illness in the Netherlands on July 15, 2023. He was 63. Helmrich was born in Tilburg, Netherlands, on August 16, 1959. He moved to Amsterdam in 1982 and graduated from the Dutch Film and Television Academy in 1986. He soon began directing, writing, and

photographing such films as "Het Phoenix Mysterie" (1990), the documentary "Moving Objects" (1991), "De Stand van de Zon" ("Eye of the Day") (2001), "Stand van de Maan" ("Shape of the Moon") (2004), "Promised Paradise" (2007), "Position Among the Stars" (2010), "Raw Herring" (2013), and "The Long Season" (2017). He was noted for his "single shot" or long take filming method. Helmrich also served as cinematographer for the films "Promised Paradise" (2007), "Contractpensions - Djangan Loepah!" (2008), "Luan Qing Chun" ("Beautiful Crazy") (2008), "The Burning Season" (2008), "In My Father's Country" (2008), "Containment" (2015), "Tagore's Natir Puja: The Court Dancer" (2016), and "Klanken van Oorsprong" (2018). He was a jury member for numerous film festivals around the world.

Hem, Narie

Cambodian actress Narie Hem, who starred in the 1962 French film "Bird of Paradise", died in Paris, France, on September 13, 2023. She was 86. Hem was born in Cambodia

on February 13, 1937. She competed in the 1960 Miss Cambodia contest and was a runner up. She was noted for her role as Dara, a beautiful Khmer dancer in Marcel Camus' 1962 French film "L'Oiseau de Paradis" ("Bird of Paradise"). Heim and her family formed the Baksey Thaansuo (Bird of Paradise) production company which produced three films between 1963 and 1965, "Rosat Tam Khyol", "Sekkarak Bopha", and "Khmer Ler Lady". The films were believed to have been destroyed during the Khmer Rouge regime of the 1970s. She and her first husband, Armand Gaston Gerbie, and two children before his death in the early 1960s. She later remarried and moved to France in 1967.

Hendryx, Shirl

Playwright and screenwriter Shirl Hendryx died on July 15, 2023. He was 99. Hendryx was born in Indianapolis,

Indiana, on December 27, 1923. He wrote frequently for television from the late 1940s, penning episodes of "The Chevrolet Tele-Theatre", "Suspense", "Shadow of the Cloak", "The Adventures of Robin Hood", "Climax!", "Ivanhoe", "Johnny Staccato", "Zane Grey Theatre", "The Roaring 20's", "Bonanza", "The Travels of Jaimie McPheeters", "The Virginian", "Combat!", "Run

for Your Life", "The Outsider", "Hawaii Five-O", "The Wild Wild West", "Mannix", "Land of the Giants", "The F.B.I.", "Mod Squad", "Monty Nash", "Mission Impossible", "Banacek", "Columbo", "Barnaby Jones", "Cannon", "The Streets of San Francisco", "Switch", and "Eight Is Enough". Hendryx also wrote the 1983 film "Running Brave" and the 1985 tele-film "Final Jeopardy". He was author of the comedy play "The Last of Jane Austen" which was adapted for the television production "Ladies and the Champ" for "The Wonderful World of Disney" in 2001.

Henry, David

South African-British actor David Henry died of a

heart attack at Denville Hall, Northwood, London, England, on August 9, 2023. He was 83. Henry was born in Durban, South Africa, on May 14, 1940. He moved to Australia with his family in 1954. He trained as an actor in Sydney with the Ensemble Theatre. He pursued an acting career in England and was seen on such television series as "New Scotland Yard", "Play for Today", "Crossroads", "The Legend of King Arthur", "The Professionals", "Tenko", "Shine on Harvey Moon", "The Manageress", "Victoria Wood", "Tygo Road", "The Bill", "Poirot", "For the Greater Good", "Casualty", "The Piglet Files", "EastEnders", "Between the Lines", "Absolutely Fabulous", "Murder Most Horrid", "Alleyn Mysteries", "Chandler & Co", "Chalk", "Touching Evil", "Mosley", "The Unknown Soldier", "Kavanagh QC", "Bad Girls", "Waking the Dead", "Midsomer Murders", "Doctors", "Sharpe", and "Hustle". He also appeared in television productions of "Bill Brand" (1976), "The Voyage of the Charles Darwin" (1978), "The Mill on the Floss" (1979), "Julius Caesar" (1979), "Hamlet, Prince of Denmark" (1980), "Being Normal" (1983), "Death Is Part of the Process" (1986), "Noble House" (1988), "Sir Norbert Smith, a Life" (1989), "Devices and Desires" (1991), "The Final Cut" (1995), "20,000 Leagues Under the Sea" (1997), "Have Your Cake and Eat It" (1997), and "The Life and Adventures of Nick Nickleby" (2012) as Mr. Cheerybles. Henry appeared in the films "The Killing Fields" (1984), "Cry Freedom" (1987), "The March" (1990), "The Russia House" (1990), "Gentlemen Don't Eat Poets" (1995), "Evita" (1996), "Tale of the Mummy" (1998), "Still Crazy" (1998), "Ali G Indahouse" (2002), "Rabbit Fever" (2006), "Flawless" (2007), and "Endgame" (2009).

Herbert, Diana

Actress Diana Herbert died in Los Angeles, California, on May 3, 2023. She was 94. Herbert was born in Hollywood, California, on December 25, 1928. She was the daughter of playwright F. Hugh Herbert. She studied at the University of California at Los Angeles for two years. She began her career on stage in the late 1940s. Herbert was seen in Broadway productions of "For Love or Money" (1947), "The Humber" (1951), "Wonderful Town" (1953), and "Men of Distinction"

(1953). Herbert was seen on television in episodes of "I Cover Times Square", "Broadway Television Theatre", "Dark of Night", "The Doctor", "Man Against Crime", "The Web", "The Second Hundred Years", "The Ghost and Mrs. Muir", "The Flying Nun", "That Girl", "Bracken's World", "Here We Go Again", "This Is the Life", "Matt Helm", "Police Woman", "Three's Company", and "Head Cases". She also appeared in the tele-film "Guess Who's Been Sleeping in My Bed?" (1973). Herbert was featured in a handful of films during her career including "Four Boys and a Gun" (1957), "Frasier, the Sensuous Lion" (1973), "Earthquake" (1974), "Malibu Beach" (1978), "The Invisible Maniac" (1990), and "Welcome to Hollywood" (1998). She was seen in various shorts in her later years including "Shooting Puppies" (2009), "It Could Be Worse" (2010), "In 30 Minutes" (2010), "In Sight" (2010), "To Grandmother's House We Go" (2010), and "Psychosis" (2011). Herbert was a friend of actress Marilyn Monroe and was interviewed for the 2022 documentary film "Dream Girl: The Making of Marilyn Monroe". She was married to singer Lawrence W. Markes from 1956 until their divorce in 1978 and to television writer Gene Levitt from 1985 until his death in 1999.

Heriban, Dano

Slovak actor Dano Heriban died of a heart attack in Svaty Jur, Slovakia, on May 24, 2023. He was 43. Heriban was born in Trnava, Czechoslovakia, on March 25, 1980. He

graduated from the Academy of Performing Arts in Bratislava in 2004. He began his career on stage performing with the Theatre in Martin. He performed with the Slovak National Theatre from 2014. Heriban appeared in the films "After..." (2006), the short "Oslava" (2014), "Unos"(2017), "Parralel" (2018), "Scumbag" (2020), and "The Man Who Stood in the Way" (2023) as Alexander Dubcek. He was seen on television in such series as "Kvet Stasia" (2002), "Kredenc" (2014), "Horna Dolna" (2015), "Hniezdo" as Roman in 2020, "Druha Sanca" (20220, and "Metoda Merkovic: Hojer" (2024). He was married to actress Slavka Halcakova from 2005 until their divorce in 2007. He married actress Kamila Heribanova in 2016 and is survived by her and their two sons. He is also survived by another son from a previous relationship.

Hesketh-Harvey, Kit

British comedian and screenwriter Kit Hesketh-Harvey died in England on February 1, 2023. He was 65. Hesketh-Harvey was born in Zomba, Nyasaland (now Malawi), on April 30, 1957, where his father worked in the Foreign

Office. He returned with his family to England in his youth and sang with the choir at Canterbury Cathedral. He attended Clare College, Cambridge, where he performed with the student sketch comedy troupe the Footlights. He joined the BBC in 1980 where he was a staff producer for the Music and Arts Department. He performed with pianist Richard Sisson as the double act Kit and The Widow from 1982 to 2012. They performed together on the West End and at the Edinburgh Fringe and were featured in the 1989 television special "Hysteria 2!". They received acclaim for their 1993 show "Lavishly Mounted" and hosted the BBC Radio 4 series "Kit and the Widow Cocktails" in 2005. Hesketh-Harvey scripted the 1987 Merchant Ivory film "Maurice" and the tele-films "Camp Christmas" (1993), "Full Throttle" (1995), and "Hans Christian Andersen: My Life as a Fairy Tale" (2003). He also scripted an episode of television's "The Vicar of Dibley". He appeared in episodes of the series "Chelmsford 123" and "A Word in Your Era". Hesketh-Harvey performed frequently in stage productions of "Putting It Together" (1992), "Salad Days" (1996), and "Cowardly Custard" (2011). He wrote several musicals including "Writing Orlando" (1988) with composer James McConnel, "The Beautiful and the Damned" (2003), and the English version of Jacques Offenbach's "La Belle Helene" (2006). He wrote numerous opera translations including "The Daughter of the Regiment", "The Turk in Italy", "La Belle Helene", "The Bartered Bride", "The Magic Flute", "The Marriage of Figaro", "Bluebeard", and "Le Roi Malgre Lui". He was also a regular panelist on the Radio 4 series "Just a Minute". His detective novel, "For the Shooting", was published in 2017. Hesketh-Harvey was married to actress Catherine Rabett from 1986 until their divorce in 2021 and is survived by their two children.

Heywood, Anne

British actress Anne Heywood, who starred in the 1967 film "The Fox", died of cancer in Houston, Texas, on October 27, 2023. She was 91. She was born Violet Pretty in Handsworth, Birmingham, England, on December 11, 1931. She began performing on stage in her teens with the Highbury Little Theatre in Sutton Coldfield in 1947. She won the Birmingham University Carnival Queen and National Bathing Beauty Contest before being crowned Miss Great Britain in 1950. She was featured in a small role in the 1951 film "Lady Godiva Rides Again" (aka "Bikini Baby") in 1951. She was soon signed by the Rank Organisation and her name was changed to Anne Heywood. She was seen in supporting roles in the films "Checkpoint" (1956), "Find the Lady" (1956), and "Doctor at Large" (1957) and starred as Laura Wilton in the 1957 film noir "The Depraved". She continued to star in such films as "Dangerous Exile" (1957) with Stanley Baker, "Violent Playground" (1958), "Floods of Fear" (1958), "The Heart of a Man" (1959), "Upstairs and Downstairs" (1959), the Italian historical drama "Carthage in Flames" (1960), the war films "The Night Fighters" (aka "A Terrible Beauty") (1960) with Robert Mitchum, "Petticoat Pirates" (1961), "Stork Talk"

(1962), the science fiction "The Brain" (1962) opposite Peter Van Eyck, "The Very Edge" (1963), and "90 Degrees in the Shade" (1965). She was filming "High Jungle" for MGM in 1966 when star Eric Fleming drowned while on location in Peru and the film was cancelled. Heywood starred as Ellen March in the controversial 1967 film "The Fox", based on the novella by D.H. Lawrence. It was produced by her husband, Raymond Stross, and co-starred Sandy Dennis and Keir Dullea. She starred as Virginia de Leyva in the 1969 historical drama, "The Lady of Monza". She was seen in the 1969 comedy "Midas Run" and had a small role in the espionage film "The Chairman" (1969) starring Gregory Peck. She continued to appear in such films as "I Want What I Want" (1962), the Italian giallo "The Killer Is on the Phone" (1972), "The Nun and the Devil" (1973) as Mother Giulia, "Trader Horn" (1973) opposite Rod Taylor, "Love Under the Elms" (1975), "Good Luck, Miss Wyckoff" (1979), the Italian horror film "Ring of Darkness" (1979), and the science fiction film "What Waits Below" (1984). Heywood was featured in the 1983 television mini-series "Sadat" and in episodes of "The Equalizer" and "Ohara". She retired from the screen following the death of her husband. She was married to Raymond Stross, who produced many of her films, from 1960 until his death in 1988, and is survived by their son, Mark Stross. She was married to George Danzig Druke, a former Assistant Attorney General for New York State, from 1990 until his death in 2021.

Hickox, Anthony

British film director Anthony Hickox, who helmed

such horror films as "Waxwork", "Sundown: The Vampire in Retreat", and "Hellraiser III: Hell on Earth", was found dead at his home in Bucharest, Romania, on October 9, 2023. He was 64. His friends reported that they had not seen him for some time. Hickox was born in London, England, on January 30, 1959. His father was director Douglas Hickox, and his mother was Oscar-winning film editor Anne V. Coates. He attended Algion College in

Switzerland before working in London as a club promoter. Hickox moved to Los Angeles in 1986 where he wrote, directed, and appeared in a small role in the cult horror film "Waxwork" (1988). He directed and wrote the comedy horror film "Sundown: The Vampire in Retreat" (1989) starring David Carradine and Bruce Campbell, and the sequel "Waxwork II: Lost in Time" (1992). He continued to director, and often write, such films as "Hellraiser III: Hell on Earth" (1992), "Warlock: The Armageddon" (1993), "Payback" (1995), "Invasion of Privacy" (1996), "Prince Valiant" (1997), "Storm Catcher" (1999), "Jill Rips" (2000), "The Contaminated Man" (2000), "Last Run" (2001), "Consequence" (2003), "Blast" (2004), "Submerged" (2005), "Knife Edge" (2009), "Exodus to Shanghai" (2015), and "Infamous Six" (2020). Hickox directed the tele-films "Full Eclipse" (1993), "Martial Law" (1998), and "Federal Protection" (2002), and episodes of "New York Undercover", "Extreme", "Two", "Pensacola: Wings of Gold", and "Shoot Me!". He continued to appear in small roles in films directed by himself and others including "Lobster Man from Mars" (1989), "Waxwork II: Lost in Time" (1992), "Hellraiser III: Hell on Earth" (1992), "Warlock: The Armageddon" (1993), "Return of the Living Dead III" (1993), "Deadly Exposure" (1993), "The Granny" (1995), "Children of the Corn III: Urban Harvest" (1996), "Invasion of Privacy" (1996), "Prince Valiant" (1997) as Prince Gawain, "The Gardener" (1998), "Storm Catcher" (1999), "Last Run" (2001), "Blast" (2004), and "Exodus to Shanghai" (2015). He was seen in the tele-films "Hollywood Confidential" (1997), "Federal Protection" (2002), "Love by Design" (2014), and "Last Tango in Constanta" (2022). Hickox was married to Romanian actress Madalina Anea.

Hight, Ahmo

Actress and fitness model Ahmo Hight died of complications from a fall on August 29, 2023. She was 49. Hight was born in Chicago, Illinois, on September 18, 1973.

She began competing in fitness competitions and was crowned Ms. Ft Body Bay Area in 1994. She posed for fitness and muscle magazines. She soon began acting, appearing in an episode of the television series "Pacific Blue" in 1997. She was featured in numerous softcore erotic films and videos over the next several years including "Playboy: Hard Bodies" (1996), "Anna Nicole Smith: Exposed" (1998), "Erotic Confessions" (1998), "Restless Souls" (1998), "Hotel Exotica" (1998), "Inside Club Wild Side" (1998), "Passion's Desire" (2000), "Insatiable Wives" (2000), and "Secret Pleasures" (2002). She was a contestant on the reality dating television series "Real Chance of Love" from 2008 to 2009 under the nickname Milf. She also competed in the reality series "I Love Money" in 2009. Hight was charged with domestic assault after stabbing a man with a pair of scissors in March of 2015. She is survived by a son she had with bodybuilder Chris Cormier.

Hildebrand, Ray

Singer Ray Hildebrand, who was half of the duet Paul and Paula, died at his home in Overland Park, Kansas, on August 18, 2023. He was 82. Hildebrand was born in Joshua,

Texas, on November 21, 1940. He attended Howard Payne College in Brownwood, Texas, where he met his future singing partner, Jill Jackson. Hildebrand wrote the song "Hey Paula" which he and Jackson sang on a local radio show in 1962. They soon recorded the song after changing their stage names to Paul and Paula and had a major hit. They also had success with their second single "Young Lovers". They recorded the albums "Paul & Paula Sing for Young Lovers", "We'll Go Together", and "Holiday for Teens" in 1963. They toured with Dick Clark's Caravan of Stars and appeared on television in episodes of "American Bandstand", "Thank Your Lucky Stars", and "Celebrity Party". Hildebrand left the duo in 1965 to finish college. He later recorded the 1967 Christian music album "He's Everything to Me". He had a hit with the song "Anybody Here Wanna Live Forever?" in the 1970s and toured with fellow Christian performer Paul Land as Land & Hildebrand in the 1980s and 1990s. He and Jackson occasionally reunited as Paul & Paula in later years for nostalgia shows. Hildebrand's wife, Judy, died in 1999 and he is survived by their two children.

Hill, Mike

Film editor Mike Hill, who shared an Academy Award for his work on the 1995 film "Apollo 13", died of cryptogenic organizing pneumonia at his home in Omaha, Nebraska, on January 5, 2023. He was 73. Hill was born in Omaha on March

24, 1949. He worked as an assistant editor for a local Omaha television station before moving to Hollywood. He was an apprentice editor at Paramount for the 1976 film "Bound for Glory" and was an assistant editor for the film "Sunnyside" (1979) and the tele-film "The Gathering, Part II" (1979). He worked in television as an editor for episodes of "Cagney & Lacey" and the tele-films "The First Time"(1982), "Baby Sister" (1983), "Obsessive Love" (1984), and "Combat High" (1986). He began working in films with Dan Hanley on Ron Howard's 1982 feature "Night Shift". They continued to work with Howard on most of his subsequent films. They received an Academy Award for editing 1995's "Apollo 13" and earned subsequent nominations for the films "A Beautiful Mind" (2001), "Cinderella Man" (2005), and "Frost/Nixon" (2008). His other film credits include "Splash" (1984), "Cocoon" (1985), "Gung Ho" (1986),

"Armed and Dangerous" (1986), "Willow" (1988), "Pet Sematary" (1989), "Parenthood" (1989), "Problem Child" (1990), "Backdraft" (1991), "Far and Away" (1992), "The Paper" (1994), "Ransom" (1996), "Edtv" (1999), "How the Grinch Stole Christmas" (2000), "Full Ride" (2002), "The Missing" (2003), "The Da Vinci Code" (2006), "Angels & Demons" (2009), "The Dilemma" (2011), "Rush" (2013), and "In the Heart of the Sea" (2015). Hill is survived by his wife, LeAnne, and daughter, Jesica.

Hill, Trevor

British television writer and director Trevor Hill died in England on October 29, 2023. He was 98. Hill was born in Southampton, Hampshire, England, on October 28, 1925. He

began working for the BBC in his teens in 1942, serving as a sound effects assistant for the radio comedy "It's That Man Again". He was attached with the British Forces Network from 1945 to 1949. He appeared in small roles in several BBC television productions including "The Case of Thomas Pyke" (1949), "Portrait by Rembrandt" (1952), and "The Thief, the Gang and Jeremiah" (1953). He and his wife, Margaret Potter, produced and wrote the radio series "Children's Hour" in the 1950s. He was also producer of the programs "Round Britain Quiz" and "Transatlantic Quiz". He produced the children's television series "Sooty" from 1955 to 1967. He produced the television series "Pinky and Perky" in 1963 and "Jackanory" from 1969 to 1970. He was assistant head of BBC Radio when he retired in 1984. His memoir, "Over the Airwaves", was published in 2005. Hill was married to BBC producer and writer Margaret Potter from 1952 until her death in 1993.

Hill, Vince

British singer Vince Hill, who was noted for his rendition of the song "Edelweiss", died at his home in Henley-on-Thames, Oxfordshire, England, on July 22, 2023. He was

89. Hill was born in Holbrooks, Coventry, England, on April 16, 1934. He began singing in his teens and worked at various jobs before embarking on a career as an entertainer. He joined the Band of the Royal Corps of Signals as a vocalist, where he completed his National Service. He then performed with Teddy Foster's Bad in London in the late 1950s. He joined the vocal group the Raindrops in 1960 and began a solo career the following year. He had minor hits with his recordings of "The River's Run Dry" and "A Day at the Seaside". Hill signed a recording contract with EMI in 1965

196

and had hits with his renditions of "La Vie En Rose", "Roses of Picardy", "Heartaches", "Mercie Cherie", "Love Letters in the Sand", and "Look Around (And You'll Find Me There)". He had his biggest hit with his cover recording of "Edelweiss" from the Rodgers and Hammerstein musical "The Sound of Music" in 1967. He released 14 studio albums and numerous singles before his contract with EMI ended in 1974. He continued to record with CBS Records. Hill was featured as Prince Charming in a 1970 television production of "Cinderella" on "The ITV Play". He was also seen in episodes of "Stars and Garters", "Thank Your Lucky Stars", "The Des O'Connor Show", "Juke Box Jury", "The Benny Hill Show", "The Billy Cotton Band Show", "The Val Doonican Show", "Will the Real Mike Yarwood Stand Up?", "They Sold a Million" as host in 1973, "The Ken Dodd Show", "The Morecambe and Wise Show", "The Roy Castle Show", "The Leslie Crowther Show", "It's Lulu", "Vera Lynn", "The Rolf Harris Show", "The Harry Secombe Show", "Cilla", "The Tommy Cooper Show", "Celebrity Squares", "Who Do You Do", "Rainbow", "The Good Old Days", "3-2-1", "The Little and Large Show", "Blankety Blank", "This Is Your Life", and "Good Morning Britain". He was co-host of the ITV talk show "Gas Street" in 1988. He continued to perform frequently on stage at venues around the world. His autobiography, "Another Hill to Climb", was published in 2010. Hill was married to Annie Davidson from 1959 until her death in 2016. Their son, Athol, was found dead in 2014.

Himu, Humaira

Bangladeshi actress Humairaz Himu died of a suicide by hanging in Dhaka, Bangladesh, on November 2, 2023. Himu

was born in Lakshmipur, Bangladesh, on November 23, 1985. She began performing on stage in her youth. She moved to Dhaka in 1999 where she continued her career in theater. Himu also began working as a model for advertising agencies. She appeared frequently on television from the early 2000s, appearing in such series as "PI", "Shonaghat", "Chairman Bari", "Batighar", "Shone Na Se Shone Na", "Comedy-420", "Chapabaaz", "Action Detective", "Chayabibi", "Ek Cup Cha", "E Kemon Protidan", "Hulo Biral", "Chonnochara 420", "Ambulance Doctor", and "Crazy Lover". She was featured in the 2010 tele-film "Arman Bhaier Godisait". Himu made her film debut as Toru Apa in the 2011 film "Amar Bondhu Rashed" and was Rosy in 2014's "Ek Cup Cha".

Hines, Maurice

Dancer and actor Maurice Hines died at the Actors Fund Home in Englewood, New Jersey, on December 29, 2023. He was 80. Hines was born in New York City on December 13, 1943. He studied tap dance at the Henry LeTang Dance Studio in Manhattan from an early age. He and his younger

brother, Gregory Hines, began performing together and appeared in the 1954 Broadway musical "The Girl in Pink Tights". They began touring as the opening act for such stars

as Gypsy Rose Lee and Lionel Hampton. They were joined by their father, Maurice Sr., as Hines, Hines & Dad, and they performed frequently at New York's Apollo Theater. They also appeared on television in the variety series "The Pearl Bailey Show", "The Ed Sullivan Show", "The Clay Cole Show", "Away We Go", "The Hollywood Palace", "The Kraft Music Hall", "The Joey Bishop Show", "Jimmy Durante Presents the Lennon Sisters", "The Pearl Bailey Show", "The New Bill Cosby Show", "The David Frost Show", and "The Tonight Show with Johnny Carson". Maurice began a solo career in the 1970s and starred as Nathan Detroit in the national tour of "Guys and Dolls". He returned to Broadway to appear in the musicals "Eubie!" (1978), "Sophisticated Ladies" (1981), and "Bring Back Birdie" (1981). He was director, choreographer, and performer for the 1986 musical revue "Uptown... It's Hot!" receiving a Tony Award nomination for Best Actor in a Musical. He was also director and choreographer for the 2006 production of "Hot Feet". He and brother Gregory starred as the Williams Brothers in Francis Ford Coppola's 1984 film "The Cotton Club". He was seen on television in episodes of "The Mike Douglas Show", "Sesame Street", "The Pat Sajak Show", "The Mo'Nique Show", and "Tavis Smiley". Hines also appeared in television productions of "Eubie!" (1981) and episodes of "Love, Sidney", "The Equalizer" in the recurring role of Billy Bump in 1987, and "Cosby". He was co-director and choreographer for the national tour of the Louis Armstrong biography "Satchmo" and starred in the national tour of "Harlem Suite". He was the subject of the 2019 documentary film "Maurice Hines: Bring Them Back". Maurice and Gregory had a long period where they did not speak to each other for reasons neither discussed. They reconciled before Gregory's death in 2003. His father, Maurice Hines, Sr., died in 2010.

Hirdwall, Ingvar

Swedish actor Ingvar Hirdwall died in Stockholm, Sweden, on April 6, 2023. He was 88. Hirdwall was born in Stockholm on December 5, 1934. He trained with the Gothenburg City Theatre stage school from 1957 to 1960. He performed frequently on stage throughout his career with roles at the Oscarsteatern in Stockholm. He was seen in such films as "Raven's End" (1963), "Min Kara ar en Ros" (1963), "...for Vanskaps Skull..." (1965), Bo Widerberg's "The Man on the Roof" (1976) as the killer Ake Eriksson, "Children's Island" (1976), "Berget Pa Manens Baksida" (1983), "The Man from Majorca" (1984), "Miraklet i Valby" (1989), "1939" (1989), "Honungsvvargar" (1990), "Like It Never Was Before" (1995), "Juloratoriet" (1996), "En Kvinnas Huvud"(1997),"Miffo" (2003), "Mamma Pappa Barn" (2003), "Daybreak" (2003),

"Mun Mot Mun" (2005), "Offside" (2006), "Den Ensiklde Medborgaren" (2006), "The Girl with the Dragon Tattoo"

(2009) as the lawyer Dirch Frode, and "Miraklet i Viskan" (2015). Hirdwall appeared frequently on television with roles in productions of "Trangningen" (1962), "Mannen Som Vaxte i Ett Sommartrad" (1965), "Farlig Kurs" (1965), "Huset Vid Gransen" (1968), "Berndt & Anita" (1970), "Kommissarie Migran Leker Med Doden" (1971), "Spelaren" (1971), "Fosterbarn" (1971), "Ostindiefarare" (1971), "Flotten" (1972), "Snapphanepojken" (1972), "Hemmet" (1972), "Et Nytt Liv" (1972), "Sandladan" (1972), "Foklorarna" (1972), "Gustav III" (1974), "Agnes" (1974), "Engeln II" (1976), "Har du Inga Moderskanslor?" (1976), "Hammarstads BK" (1977), "Rikedom" (1978), "Jackpot" (1980), "Nattvandraren" (1980), "Ett Dromspel" (1980), "Babels Hus" (1981), "Som Enda Narvarande" (1981), "Drottning Christina" (1981), "Dom Unga Ornarna" (1982), "Peoikanen" (1982), "Master Olof" (1983), "Savannen" (1983), "Midvinterduell" (1983), "August Strindberg: Ett Liv" (1985), "Korset" (1985), "Det Ar Manskligt Att Fela" (1985), "Flaskfarmen" (1986), "Sammansvarjningen" (1986), "Kunglig Toilette" (1986), "Ondskans Ar" (1987), "Kejsarn Av Portugallien" (1992), "Onkel Vanja" (1994), "Zonen" (1996), "Potatishandlaren" (1996), "Torntuppen" (1996), "Ett Sorts Hades" (1996), "Tartuffe, or The Hypocrite" (1997), "Den Tatuerade Ankan" (1998), "Ivar Kreuger" (1998), "Anderssons Alskarinna" (2001), "Fastighetsskotaren" (2004), "Deadline Torp" (2005), "Mobelhandlarens Dotter" (2006), "Stormen" (2009), and "Millennium" (2010) as Dirch Frode. He was seen in episodes of "Hedebyborna" as Skomakar-Ludde in 1978, "Godnatt, Jord" as Sackeus in 1979, "Tre Karlekar" as Egon Nilsson from 1989 to 1991, "Kvallspressen" as Sockander in 1992, "Tomtemaskinen" as Pettson in 1993, "Emma Aklagare" as Ivan Josefsson in 1997, "Skargardsdoktorn", and "Wallander". He was featured as the eccentric neighbor in the long-running crime series "Beck" from 1997 to 2023. Hirdwall married actress Marika Lindstrom in 1975 and is survived by her and their two children, director Jacob Hirdwall and actress Agnes Hirdwall.

Hitchcock, Stan

Country singer Stan Hitchcock died of cancer in Gallatin, Tennessee, on January 4, 2023. He was 86. Hitchcock was born in Pleasant Hope, Missouri, on March 22, 1936. He began playing the guitar in his youth and appeared frequently on local radio during his teens. He finished high school in 1954 and joined the U.S. Navy. He was stationed on the USS Bryce Canyon in Long Beach, California, from 1955 to 1957 where he was leader of the ship's band. He left the Navy in 1958 and pursued a career in music. He signed with Columbia and had little success with his early recordings. He switched to the Epic

Records' label in 1961 and moved to Nashville. He had a hit with his recording of "Honey I'm Home" in 1969. He released

twelve albums during his career and performed regularly on the local programs "The Eddie Hill Show" and "The Ralph Emory Show". He had his own morning show in Nashville, Tennessee, "The Stan Hitchcock Show", from 1964 to 1970. He appeared on an episode of "Hee Haw" in 1970 and was host of "Stan Hitchcock from the Ozarks" in 1979. He was a founder of the Country Music Television network in 1982. He hosted the station's interview program "Heart to Heart" until leaving Nashville in 1991. He returned to Missouri, settling in Branson where he founded the Americana Television Network. His memoir, "Corner of Music Row & Memory Lane", was published in 2009. He married Denise T. Hitchcock in 1985 and she survives him. He is also survived by five children. A son and daughter predeceased him.

Hitchon, Nick

British scientist Nick Hitchon, who was featured in the long-running documentary film series "Seven Up!" since 1964, died of throat cancer in Wisconsin on July 23, 2023. He was 65.

Hitchon was born in Littondale, North Yorkshire, England, on October 22, 1957. He was a 7-year-old child from a farming family when he was featured in the 1964 documentary film "Seven Up!". The film dealt with ten males and four females from England, all at the age of seven. The children were chosen to represent the various social classes at the time, with Hitchon representing the rural community. Director Michael Apted continued to interview the participants at seven-year intervals, most of which were aired on ITV. Hitchon, and most of his fellow subjects, appeared in "7 Plus Seven" (1970), "21 Up" (1977), "28 Up" (1977), "28 Up" (1984), "35 Up" (1991), "42 Up" (1998), "49 Up" (2005), "56 Up" (2012), and "63 Up" (2019). Hitchon received a Ph.D. in engineering science from Oxford University in 1981 and joined the faculty of the Department of Electrical and Computer Engineering at the University of Wisconsin-Madison the following year. He was diagnosed with throat cancer and mentioned in his last appearance in the series that he would likely not be alive for a possible "70 Up" edition. He retired from the University of Wisconsin-Madison in the Spring of 2022. Hitchon married Jacqueline Bush in 1974 and she was featured with him in several of the documentaries before their divorce in 1999. He is survived by their son, Adam. He married C. Cryss Brunner in 2001 and she also survives him.

Hoffman, Elizabeth

Actress Elizabeth Hoffman, who starred as Bea Ventnor, matriarch of "Sisters", from 1991 to 1996, died at her home in Malibu, California, on August 21, 2023. She was 97.

Hoffman was born in Corvallis, Oregon, on February 8, 1926. She appeared frequently on stage in the San Fernando Valley before appearing in films and television from the early 1980s. She made her film debut as Margaret Buchanan in the 1981 horror film "Fear No Evil". Her other films include "Nuts" (1987), "Born on the Fourth of July" (1989), "Silent Night, Deadly Night 3: Better Watch Out!" (1989), "The River Wild" (1994), and "Dante's Peak" (1997) as Grandma Ruth. She was featured as Miss Mason in several episodes of the television series "Little House on the Prairie" from 1980 to 1981. Hoffman was also seen in episodes of "The Greatest American Hero", "The A-Team", "Cutter to Houston", "Blue Thunder", "Hunter", "L.A. Law", "Star Trek: The Next Generation" as Premier Bhavani in the 1989 episode "The Price", "Matlock", "thirtysomething" in the recurring role of Eleanor Krieger from 1989 to 1991, and "Stargate SG-1" in the recurring role of Dr. Catherine Langford from 1997 to 1998. She starred as Beatrice 'Bea' Reed Ventnor, mother of the title characters played by Swoosie Kurtz, Sela Ward, Patricia Kalember, and Julianne Phillips, in "Sisters" from 1991 to 1996. Her other television credits include productions of "The Winds of War" (1983) as Eleanor Roosevelt, "Do You Remember Love" (1985), "Elvis and Me" (1988), "War and Remembrance" (1988) reprising her role as Eleanor Roosevelt, and "The Great Pretender" (1991). She largely retired from the screen in the late 1990s. Hoffman is survived by two sons, Chris and Paul.

Hogan, Jack

Actor Jack Hogan, who starred as Private William Kirby in the television series "Combat!" in the 1960s, died on Bainbridge Island, Washington, on December 6, 2023. He was

94. He was born Richard Roland Benson, Jr., in Chapel Hill, North Carolina, on November 24, 1929. He studied architecture in college before joining the U.S. Air Force during the Korean War. He trained as an actor at the Pasadena Playhouse after his discharge. He also studied at the American Theatre Wing in New York in 1955. He was featured in several films from the mid-1950s including "Man from Del Rio" (1956), "The Bonnie Parker Story" (1958), "Paratroop Command" (1959), "The Legend of Tom Dooley" (1959), and "The Cat Burglar" (1961). Hogan was a prolific television actor with roles in episodes of "State Trooper", "The Sheriff of Cochise", "The Adventures of McGraw", "Dr. Christian",

"Official Detective", "Harbor Command", "Broken Arrow", "The Rough Riders", "Have Gun - Will Travel", "Steve Canyon", "Target", "Men of Annapolis", "Sea Hunt", "Tombstone Territory", "Mackenzie's Raiders", "Mike Hammer", "Laramie", "Lock Up", "Tightrope", "Colt .45", "U.S. Marshal", "The Rebel", "Men Into Space", "The Deputy", "Tate", "Riverboat", "The Best of the Post", "Peter Gunn", "The Tall Man", "Bat Masterson", "Bonanza", "Cheyenne", "Ben Casey", "Bronco", "Ripcord", "Cain's Hundred", "The Rifleman", "Lawman", "87th Precinct", "The New Breed", "Death Valley Days", "G.E. True", "Hawaiian Eye", the World War II series "Combat!" as Private William G. Kirby from 1962 to 1967, "Custer", "The Felony Squad", "Garrison's Gorillas", "Tarzan", "Ironside", "The Outsider", "The Name of the Game", "The Little People", "Emergency!", "Marcus Welby, M.D.", "Chase", "The Six Million Dollar Man", "Adam-12", "Sierra" as Chief Ranger Jack Moore in 1974, "S.W.A.T.", "Medical Center", "Hawaii Five-O", "The Quest", "Insight", "Switch", "The Oregon Trail", "Kojak", "The Hardy Boys/Nancy Drew Mysteries", "Project U.F.O.", "Quincy", "Magnum, P.I.", "Scarecrow and Mrs. King", "Matt Houston", "Riptide", "Berrenger's" in the recurring role of Jacob Ludwig in 1985, "Airwolf", "Outlaws", "Jack and the Fatman" in the recurring role of Judge Smithwood from 1989 to 1990, and "Raven". His other television credits include the tele-films "Houston, We've Got a Problem" (1974) as astronaut Joseph Kerwin, "The Specialists" (1975), and "Mobile Two" (1975). Hogan moved to California in the early 1980s where he continued his acting career. He also served as a casting director for "Magnum, P.I." He was married to actress Joyce Nizzari from 1967 until their divorce in 1980 and is survived by their son and daughter.

Holland, Byrd

Actor and makeup artist Byrd Holland, who was featured as the Sheriff in the notorious 1964 horror classic "The Creeping Terror", died in Palm Springs, California, on March 7, 2023. He was 95. Holland was born in Marietta, Georgia,

on July 20, 1927. He served in the U.S. Navy near the end of World War II. He subsequently moved to New York City where he studied under Sanford Meisner at the Neighborhood Playhouse. He performed on stage in off-Broadway and summer stock productions. Holland moved to Hollywood in the early 1950s and was featured in such films as "The Fast and the Furious" (1954), "Stakeout on Dope Street" (1958), "Get Outta Town" (1960), "Five Minutes to Live" (1961) with Johnny Cash, "Vengeance" (1964), the cult classic "The Creeping Terror" (1964) as the Sheriff, "Madame X" (1966), "The Black Klansman" (1966), "The Last Moment" (1966), "The Money Jungle" (1967), "The Road Hustlers" (1968), "Terror in the Jungle" (1968), "Wild Wheels" (1969), "The Red, White, and Black" (1970), "Swamp Girl" (1971), "Doomsday

Voyage" (1972), "Journey Through Rosebud" (1972), and "Terror Circus" (1973). Holland began working as a makeup artist and visual effects creator for films in the mid-1960s. He worked on numerous exploitation and horror films including "The Black Klansman" (1966), "The Undertaker and His Pals" (1966) under the name John De Heven, "Journey to the Center of Time" (1967), "The Road Hustlers" (1968), "Terror in the Jungle" (1968), "The Mummy and the Curse of the Jackals" (1969), "Cain's Cutthroats" (1970), "Glen and Randa" (1971), "Jud" (1971), "Swamp Girl" (1971), "Journey Through Rosebud" (1972), "Irish Whiskey Rebellion" (1972), "Doomsday Voyage" (1972), "The Baby" (1973), "The Legendary Curse of Lemora" (1973), "Terror Circus" (1973), "Executive Action" (1973), "When the Line Goes Through" (1973), "The Spectre of Edgar Allan Poe" (1974), David Cronenberg's "Rabid" (1977), "Human Highway" (1982), "The Man with One Red Shoe" (1985), "Say Yes" (1986), and "Dead Men Don't Die" (1990). He was also a makeup artist for the television series "Barney Miller" and productions of "Good Old Days" (1977), "To Race the Wind" (1980), "The Alamo: Thirteen Days to Glory" (1987), "Six Against the Rock" (1987), and "Gunsmoke: Return to Dodge" (1987). Holland was featured in the 2014 documentary "The Creep Behind the Camera", about director Art Nelson (aka Vic Savage), and the making of "The Creeping Terror". He was married to Patricia Ann Masters from 1962 until her death in 2011 and is survived by two children.

Holland, Kristina

Actress Kristina Holland died in Berkley, California, on February 22, 2023. She was 78. She was born Kristina Jane Hermanson in Fayetteville, North Carolina, on February 25, 1944.

She appeared frequently in television from the 1960s with roles in episodes of "The Loner", "Laredo", "Here Come the Brides", "Mr. Deeds Goes to Town", "The Doris Day Show", "Make Room for Granddaddy", "The Courtship of Eddie's Father" as Tina Rickles, the secretary for Bill Bixby's Tom Corbett, "Love, American Style", "Banyon", "Mod Squad", "Marcus Welby, M.D.", "Owen Marshall, Counselor at Law", "The Magician", "Love Story", "The Girl with Something Extra", "Medical Center", "Insight", "Barnaby Jones", "Kolchak: The Night Stalker", "Harry O", "The Bob Newhart Show", and "Good Heavens". She was also seen in the tele-film "Jamison's Kids" (1971). Holland was also a prolific voice actress for such animated series as "The Funky Phantom" as April Stewart from 1971 to 1972, ""Jeannie", "Butch Cassidy" as Steffy in 1973, "Wait Till Your Father Gets Home" as Alice Boyle from 1972 to 1973, and the 1975 animated tele-film "The Last of the Mohicans". She appeared in several films in the early 1970s including "The Strawberry Statement" (1970), "Doctors' Wives" (1971), "Win, Place or Steal" (1974), and "Goodnight Jackie" (1974). Holland largely retired from acting in the 1970s and later worked as a professional psychotherapist.

Holley, Levi

New Zealand actor Jason 'Levi' Holley, who was featured as Lock in the television series "Shortland Street" in

2022, died from an inoperable brain tumor in New Zealand on December 20, 2023. He was 48. He was a body builder and competitive arm wrestler before working in films and television from the early 2000s. He was featured in the short films "Bigger Fish" (2004), "Sounds Perfect" (2013), "Blind Mice" (2013), "Help" (2014), "If You Can Get Blood" (2014), and "Stick to Your Gun" (2016). He was also seen in the 2015 feature film "Not for Children". Holley appeared on television in episodes of "Spartacus" in the recurring role of Leviticus from 2010 to 2012, "Power Rangers Ninja Steel", "800 Words", "James Patterson's Murder Is Forever", "Straight Forward" as Zoran in 2019, "Westside", the medical soap opera "Shortland Street" as Lock in 2022, and "One of Us Is Lying". Holley was diagnosed with an inoperable brain tumor and sold nearly all his belongings to raise money to pay for additional medical treatments in the hopes of prolonging his life.

Hollis, Dave

Film executive Dave Hollis, who worked with Walt Disney Studios, was found dead of an accidental drug overdose at his home in Austin, Texas, on February 11, 2023. He was

47. Hollis was born in Orange County. California, on February 14, 1975. He was a graduate of the Frank R. Seaver College of Letters, Arts, and Sciences in 1977. He began working for Disney in 2002 and served as head of worldwide theatrical distribution from 2011 to 2018. He oversaw the release of "Star Wars" films and Marvel's "The Avengers" and "Black Panther" franchises. His wife, Rachel Hollis, was author of the 2018 self-help book "Girl, Wash Your Face" and Dave left Disney to run The Hollis Company and the Chic Medea lifestyle empire. He was the author of the motivational books "Get Out of Your Own Way" (2020) and "Built Through Courage: Face Your Fears to Live the Life You Were Meant For" (2021), and the children's book "Here's to Your Dreams" (2022). He and his wife were also hosts of the podcast "Rise Together". Hollis had a history of drug and alcohol abuse as well as heart disease. He and his wife, author Rachel Hollis, were married 16 years before their divorce in 2020. He is survived by their three sons, Jackson, Sawyer, and Ford, and daughter Noah.

200

Holly, Ellen

Actress Ellen Holly, who was featured as Carla Gray-Hall on the ABC soap opera "One Life to Live" for nearly twenty years, die at a hospital in the Bronx, New York, on December 6, 2023. She was 92. Holly was born in New York City on January 16, 1931. She graduated from Hunter College, where she appeared in theatrical productions. She trained at the Actors Studio and began her career on stage in the 1950s. She was seen on Broadway in productions of "Too Late the Phalarope" (1956), "Face of a Hero" (1960), "Tiger, Tiger, Burning Bright" (1962), and "A Hand Is on the Gate" (1966). Holly appeared on television in episodes of "The Big Story", "The Defenders", "Sam Benedict", "Dr. Kildare", and "The Doctors and the Nurses". She became the first black actress to a leading role on a daytime soap opera, playing Carla Gray-Hall on "One Life to Live" from 1968 to 1980 and from 1983 to 1985. She appeared in television productions of "King Lear" for "Great Performances" in 1974 and "Sergeant Matlovich vs. the U.S. Air Force" in 1978. Her other television credits include episodes of "ABC Afterschool Specials", "Family Feud", "The Mike Douglas Show", "Spenser: For Hire", and "In the Heat of the Night" in the recurring role of Ruth Peterson from 1989 to 1990. Holly was featured as Judge Frances Collier on the soap opera "Guiding Light" from 1988 to 1993. She also starred in the 2002 tele-film "10,000 Black Men Named George". Her autobiography, "One Life: The Autobiography of an African American Actress", was published in 1996. She was featured in several films during her career including "Take a Giant Step" (1959), "Cops and Robbers" (1973), and Spike Lee's "School Daze" (1988).

Holt, Redd

Jazz drummer Isaac 'Redd' Holt, who played with the Ramsey Lewis Trio, died of lung cancer in Chicago, Illinois, on May 23, 2023. He was 99. Holt was born in Rosedale,

Mississippi, on May 16, 1932, and was raised in Chicago. He began playing drums while in high school and later studied at the Chicago Music College and Kennedy-King College. He joined the U.S. Army in 1954 and played with the military band. He joined with pianist Ramsey Lewis and double-bassist Eldee Young as the Ramsey Lewis Trio from 1956 to 1966. He was drummer for the group's 1965 album "The In Crowd", which earned a Grammy Award for Best Jazz Performance. He and Young left Lewis in 1966 to form Young-Hold Unlimited and produced such soul hits as 1968's "Soulful Strut". He formed the Redd Holt Unlimited in 1974 and continued to perform and record under that name through the 1990s. He occasionally played reunion shows with the Ramsey Lewis Trio until Young's death in 2007 and Lewis' in 2022. Holt married Marylean Green in 1954 and is survived by her and their three sons.

Hooper, Ewan

Scottish actor Ewan Hopper, who was noted for his role in the 1968 Hammer horror film "Dracula Has Risen from the Grave", died in England in April of 2023. He was 87.

Hooper was born in Dundee, Scotland, on October 23, 1935. He trained at the Royal Academy of Dramatic Art for a year after graduating high school in Dundee in 1952. He served in the army for national service then resumed his training at the Royal Academy. He performed frequently on stage during his career and was instrumental in setting up the Greenwich Theatre in London in 1969. Hooper was seen on television in episodes of "Undermind", "A Poor Gentleman", "The Power Game", "Theatre 625" (1966), "The Avengers", "Knock on Any Door", "No Hiding Place", "Redcap", "Sergeant Cork", "Love Story", "This Man Craig", "Armchair Theatre", "Half Hour Story", "Sanctuary", "Public Eye", "Packers End", "The Revenue Man", "Man in a Suitcase", "Detective", "ITV Playhouse", "The Expert", "Dixon of Dock Green", "Dr. Finlay's Casebook", "Softly Softly", "Strange Report", "Thirty-Minute Theatre", "Hunters Walk" as Detective Sgt. Smith from 1973 to 1976, "General Hospital", "Play for Today", "Minder", "Life from Pebble Mill", "Crown Court", "The Theban Plays of Sophocles", "Hi-de-Hi!" in the recurring role of Alec Foster from 1986 to 1988, "Tickets for the Titanic", "Gentlemen and Players", "Boon", "Poirot", "Performance", "Growing Pains", "Coronation Street", "Peak Practice", "Casualty", "Wire in the Blood", "Heartbeat", and "Doc Martin". His other television credits include productions of "Double Stakes" (1963), "The Life of Galileo" (1964), "Find Yourself a Mug" (1964), "The Rules That Jake Made" (1964), "Drill Pig" (1964), "The Misunderstanding" (1965), "Double Image" (1966), "The Cabbage Tree Hat Boys" (1965), "A Brand New Scrubbing Brush" (1967), "The Distracted Preacher" (1969), "King Lear" (1975), "Invasion" (1980), "The Crucible" (1981), "Partners in Crime" (1984), "Moonfleet" (1984), "This Office Life" (1984), "Across the Lake" (1988), "The Most Dangerous Man in the World" (1988), "Winners and Losers" (1989), "Act of Will" (1989), and "In Denial of Murder" (2004). Hooper was seen in several films including "How I Won the War" (1967), "Dracula Has Risen from the Grave" (1968) as a priest who becomes the slave of Christopher Lee's Count Dracula, "Julius Caesar" (1970), "Yesterday's Hero" (1979), "Personal Service" (1987), and "Kinky Boots" (2005) as George. He married actress Marion Fiddick in 1961 and they had three children.

Hope, Teri

Actress and model Teri Hope, who was Playboy Playmate of the Month in September of 1958, died in Albuquerque, New Mexico, on September 19, 2023. She was 85. She was born Natalie Hope Reisberg on February 19, 1938. She attended college at Carnegie Tech in Pittsburgh, Pennsylvania, when she was chosen as Party Playmate while attending a Playboy-themed fraternity party. Her photos were sent to "Playboy" magazine, who selected her for their centerfold in September of 1958. Hope continued to model and was featured in several films from the early 1960s including "Force of Impulse" (1961), "Gypsy" (1962), "Fun in Acapulco" (1963) with Elvis Presley, and "Roustabout" (1964). She appeared on television in episodes of "The Gertrude Berg Show", "Hennesey", and "Shannon". Hope returned to the screen for a small role in the 1978 comedy film "Rabbit Test" written by her husband, Jay Redack.

Houghton, Tom

Cinematographer Tom Houghton died on May 3, 2023. He was 75. Houghton was born in San Rafael, California, on July 23, 1947. He began working as a

cameraman and editor at a local television station in Redding, California, in his early teens. He studied at the Slade School of Fine Art in England and graduated from the New York University Tisch School of the Arts in the early 1970s. He worked as a lighting assistant on the 1974 film "A Very Natural Thing" and was a gaffer for "Happiness Is..." (1975), "Sammy" (1977), "Sketches of a Strangler" (1978), "Nite Song" (1978), and "Something Short of Paradise" (1979). He also served as a gaffer on the television productions "Too Far to Go" (1979), "The Man That Corrupted Hadleyburg" (1980), "Rappaccini's Daughter" (1980), "The Jilting of Granny Weatherall" (1980), "The Private History of a Campaign That Failed" (1981), "Mystery at Fire Island" (1981), and "Bill" (1981). Houghton was cinematographer for industrial films and commercials. He worked frequently in television as cinematographer for episodes of "American Playhouse", "30 Rock", "Love Monkey", "Canterbury's Law", "Rescue Me" earning an Emmy Award nomination in 2008, "I Just Want My Pants Back", "Person of Interest", "Spotlight on Broadway", "Saturday Night Live", "American Horror Story", and "Elementary". He was also director of photography for the tele-films "My First Love" (1988) and "Gaffigan" (2013). Houghton was cinematographer for numerous films and shorts including "We Are the Guinea Pigs" (1980), "Close Harmony" (1981), "Supervisors" (1982), "The Beat Generation: An American Dream" (1988), "Fire Down Below" (1997), "Who Was That Man" (1999), "Forever Fabulous" (1999), "Jazz Night" (1999), "Barstow 2008" (2001), "By Courier" (2001), "Gully" (2002), "Another Bobby O'Hara Story..." (2002), "Hung-Up" (2002), "What Adam Knows" (2004), "The Crux" (2004), "Stone Mansion" (2004), "The Cookout" (2004), "State Property: Blood on the Streets" (2005), "Finding Amanda" (2008), "Montauk" (2011), and "They Came Together" (2014). He served as second unit director of photography or cameraman for the films "Major League II" (1994), "I Love Trouble" (1994), "Trial by Jury" (1994), "Highlander: The Final Dimension" (1994), "I.Q." (1994), "Reckless" (1995), "The Empty Mirror" (1996), "American Psycho" (2000), "Meet the Parents" (2000), "Down to Earth" (2001), "Spider-Man" (2002), "American Gun" (2002), "Mr. Deeds" (2002), "Stuart Little 2" (2002), "Godsend" (2004), and "The Amazing Spider-Man" (2012). Houghton is survived by his wife, Janet Forman.

Hovde, Ellen

Documentary filmmaker Ellen Hovde, who was noted for the 1975 film "Grey Gardens", died of complications from

Alzheimer's disease in Brooklyn, New York, on February 16, 2023. She was 97. Hovde was born in Meadville, Pennsylvania, on March 9, 1925. She attended the Carnegie Institute of Technology and received a degree in theater in 1947. She also studied at the University of Oslo. She worked with Albert and David Maysles as an editor for the Rolling Stones musical documentary "Gimme Shelter" (1970) and was co-director of the 1974 documentary short "Christo's Valley Curtain". Hovde was best known for co-directing the 1975 documentary "Grey Gardens" with the Maysles brothers. The film was about a reclusive upper-class mother and daughter, Big Edie and Little Edie Bouvier Beale, who were the aunt and cousin of Jacqueline Kennedy Onassis. They lived in a derelict mansion in East Hampton, New York, called Grey Gardens which was filled with garbage, fleas, cats, and raccoons. The documentary was adapted for a musical which was performed on Broadway in 2006. "Grey Gardens" was also adapted as an HBO film starring Jessica Lange and Drew Barrymore in 2009. Hovde was also co-director of "The Burks of Georgia" for television's "Six American Families" in 1976 and the 1983 film "Enormous Changes at the Last Minute". She also directed television productions of "Behind the Scenes" (1992), "Discovering Women" (1994), "Liberty! The American Revolution" (1997), and "American Photography: A Century of Images" (1999), and episodes of "Nature" and "Nova". She shared an Emmy Award for directing the 2002 mini-series "Benjamin Franklin". Hovde was married to Matthew Huxley from 1950 until their divorce in 1961 and is survived by their son and daughter. She married cinematographer Adam Giffard in 1963 and they also divorced.

Howard, David S.

Actor David S. Howard died of complications from Parkinson's disease in Sarasota, Florida, on January 10, 2023. He was 94. Howard was born in Mount Kisco, New York, on September 10, 1928. He received a master's degree from Brandeis University and later worked there as an acting teacher from 1967 to 1975. He performed on stage at the Asolo Repertory Theatre in Sarasota, Florida, for many years. Howard was featured in the films "Moonstruck" (1987), "Crimes and Misdemeanors" (1989), "The Substance of Fire" (1996), "No Way Home" (1996), "Deconstructing Harry" (1997), and "Meet Joe Black" (1998). He also appeared in the 1976 tele-film "The Phantom of the Open Hearth" and episodes of "Guiding Light", "The Street", and "Law & Order". He is survived by his wife, Anne, two daughters, a stepson, and stepdaughter.

Howard, Gregory Allen

Screenwriter Gregory Allen Howard, who was noted for the 2000 film "Remember the Titans", died of heart failure in Miami, Florida, on January 27, 2023. He was 70. Howard was born in Norfolk, Virginia, on January 28, 1952. His parents divorced when he was a child, and his mother remarried a sailor with the U.S. Navy. He lived in numerous places around the country over the next decade as the family accompanied his stepfather at different bases. He attended high school in Vallejo, California, and graduated from Princeton University with a degree in history. He briefly worked on Wall Street before settling in Los Angeles to pursue a career in writing. Howard worked as a story editor for the television series "Where I Live" and "True Colors". He also wrote the stage play "Tinseltown Trilogy". He was writer for 2001's "Ali", a biographical film about boxer Muhammad Ali. He wrote the 2000 sports film "Remember the Titans", which was based on the true story of coach Herman Boone, played by Denzel Washington, and his attempts to integrate T.C. Williams High School in Alexandria, Virginia, in the early 1970s. Howard co-wrote and co-produced the 2019 biographical film "Harriet" about Harriet Tubman. He was writer of several uncompleted projects including "Night Witches" about Soviet female pilots during World War II, "Misty", the story of ballerina Misty Copeland, "This Little Light" about civil rights leader Fannie Lou Hamer, and "Power to the People" about the civil right movement.

Howe, Tina

Playwright Tina Howe died of complications from a hip fracture in Manhattan, New York, on August 24, 2023. She was 85. Howe was born in New York City on November 21, 1937. Her father, Quincy Howe, was a historian and newscaster. She graduated from Sarah Lawrence College in New York, in 1959. She wrote her first play, "Closing Time", while in college. She studied philosophy at the Sorbonne in Paris after graduation and continued her education at Columbia University Teacher's College and Chicago Teachers College. She subsequently taught high school in Monona Grove, Wisconsin, and Bath, Maine. Her play, "The Next", was produced off-Broadway in 1970, and was followed by "Museum" (1976) and "The Art of Dining" (1979). She was noted for her 1983 play "Painting Churches" and received an Obie Award. The play was adapted for television by "American Playhouse" in 1986 and became the tele-film "The Portrait" in 1993. Howe's play "Coastal Disturbances" was performed on Broadway in 1987 and received a Tony Award for Best Play. Her other plays include "Approaching Zanzibar" (1989), "One Shoe Off" (1993), "East of the Sun and West of the Moon" (1994), "Pride's Crossing" (1997), "Rembrandt's Gift" (2002), "Chasing Manet" (2009), "Cheri" (2013), "Breaking the Spell" (2013), "Singing Beach" (2017), and "Where Women Go" (2023). She also wrote English translations of Eugene Ionesco's "The Bald Soprano" and "The Lesson" in 2004. She was the subject of Judith Barlow's 2014 book "Howe in an Hour". She was inducted into the American Theater Hall of Fame in 2017. Howe was married to historian Norman Levy from 1961 until his death in 2022 and is survived by their two children, Eben and Dara.

Hubbard, Elizabeth

Actress Elizabeth Hubbard, who starred as Lucinda Walsh on the television soap opera "As the World Turns", died of cancer at her home in Roxbury, Connecticut, on April 8, 2023. She was 89. Hubbard was born in New York City on December 22, 1933. She graduated with honors from Radcliffe College in Cambridge, Massachusetts, in 1955. She subsequently studied acting at the Royal Academy of Dramatic Art in London, graduating in 1957. She began her career on stage and made her Broadway debut as a replacement in the 1955 revival of "Threepenny Opera". Her other Broadway credits include "Compulsion" (1957), "The Fighting Cock" (1959), "Kwamina" (1961), "The Affair" (1962), "The Passion of Josef D." (1964), "The Physicists" (1964), "A Time for Singing" (1966), "A Day in the Death of Joe Egg" (1968), "Children!

Children!" (1972), "I Remember Mama" (1979), "John Gabriel Borkman" (1980), "Present Laughter" (1982), and "Dance a Little Closer" (1983). Hubbard appeared in several films including "I Never Sang for My Father" (1970), "The Bell Jar" (1979), "Ordinary People" (1980), "Cold River" (1982), "Center Stage" (2000), and "The Treatment" (2006). She was best known for her roles in daytime soap operas, appearing as Anne Benedict Fletcher on "Guiding Light" in 1962 and Carol Kramer on "The Edge of Night" in 1963. She starred as Dr. Althea Davis on "The Doctors" from 1964 to 1982, earning a Daytime Emmy Award in 1974, and was Estelle Chadwick on "One Life to Live" from 1983 to 1984. Hubbard starred as wealthy businesswoman Lucinda Walsh on "As the World Turns" from 1975 to 2010 and earned eight Emmy Award nominations for the role. She appeared in the recurring role of Sair Poindexter in the Dutch soap opera "Goede Tijden, Slechte Tijden" in 2009. She was featured as Eva Montgomery on the web series soap opera "Anacostia" from 2015 to 2018, earning another Daytime Emmy nomination. Hubbard was also seen in episodes of "The Virginian", "Marcus Welby, M.D.", "The Merv Griffin Show", "The Tonight Show Starring Johnny Carson", "The Mike Douglas Show", "Law & Order", "The Job", "Hope & Faith", "The Talk", and "Life on Mars". Her other television credits include productions of "The Ceremony of Innocence" (1970) for "NET Playhouse" and "First Ladies Diaries: Edith Wilson" (1976) earning a Daytime Emmy Award for her title role. Hubbard was married to David Bennett from 1968 until their divorce in 1973, and is survived by their son, Jeremy Bennett.

Hudson, Hugh

British film director Hugh Hudson, who helmed such features as "Chariots of Fire" and "Greystoke: Legend of Tarzan, Lord of the Apes", died at a hospital in London, England, on February 10, 2023. He was 86. Hudson was born  in London on August 25, 1936. He attended Eton College and served in the Dragoon Guards for National Service from 1956 to 1960. He edited documentaries in Paris for several years in the early 1960s. He subsequently teamed with Robert Brownjohn and David Cammell to form a documentary film company. He produced or directed such documentary shorts as "A... Is for Apple" (1963), "Boxes for Eggs" (1965), "Design for Today" (1965), "The Tortoise and the Hare" (1966), "Birds and Planes" (1967), "Irresistible" (1971), and "12 Squadron Buccaneers" (1978). He worked frequently in advertising for Ridley Scott Associates from the late 1960s. He was noted for his commercials for British Rail, British Airways, Benson & Hedges, and Fiat Strada. Hudson served as a second-unit director for Alan Parker's 1978 film "Midnight Express". He produced and directed the 1981 racing documentary "Fangio: Una Vita a 300 all'Ora". He directed the 1981 film "Chariots of Fire", which

earned four Academy Awards including Best Picture and gained Hudson a nomination for Best Director. He produced and directed the 1984 film "Greystoke: The Legend of Tarzan, Lord of the Apes", starring Christopher Lambert, Andie MacDowell, and Sir Ralph Richardson in his final role. His film, "Revolution" (1985), about the American War of Independence, was a commercial and critical failure. He continued to helm such features as "Lost Angels" (1989), "Lumiere and Company" (1985), "My Life So Far" (1999), "I Dreamed of Africa" (2000), "Rupture: A Matter of Life OR Death" (2011) which he also produced, and "Finding Altamira" (2016). He co-wrote the films "The Journey Home" (2014) and "The Tiger's Nest" (2022). He directed Robert Ward's opera "The Crucible" at the Staatstheater Braunschweig in 2016. Hudson married painter Susan Michie in 1977 and they had a son before their subsequent divorce. He married actress Maryam d'Abo in 2003 and she also survives him.

Hughes, Leon

Singer Leon Hughes, who was a founding member of the vocal group the Coasters, died at his home in Los Angeles, California, on March 1, 2023. He was 92. Hughes was born in  Dallas, Texas, on May 6, 1930. He sang with the doo wop groups the Lamplighters, the Hollywood Flames, the Celebritys, and the Signals in the early 1950s. He teamed with Carl Gardner, Bobby Nunn, and Billy Guy to sing second tenor as part of the vocal group the Coasters in 1955. The group recorded several hits written by Jerry Leiber and Mike Stoller including "Down in Mexico", "Searchin'", and "Young Blood". Hughes appeared with the Coasters on television's "The Tonight Show" and "American Bandstand" before leaving the group in 1957. He reunited with Bobby Nunn to release the song "Looking for You" as the Dukes in 1959. He performed with several groups using the Coasters name from the 1970s including his own Leon Hughes and His Original Coasters in recent years.

Hulin, Dominique

French actor Dominique Hulin died in Ploermel, France, on August 7, 2023. He was 71. Hulin was born in Kerrata, Algeria, on June 11, 1952. The hulking (6 ft. 8.75 in.) performer began his career in the early 1970s. He worked on such films as "Les Quatre Charlots Mousquetaires" (1974), "Clockwork Bananas" (1974), "Bons Baisers de Hong-Kong" (1975), "Le Roi des Bricoleurs" (1977), "Moonraker" (1979) as stunt double for Richard Kiel's Jaws, "Les Sous-Doues" (1980), "Inspector Blunder" (1980), "Rends-Moi la Cle!" (1981), "Les Sous-Doues en Vacances" (1982), "Zig Zag Story" (1983), "Le Fou du Roi" (1984), "J'ai Rencontre le Pere Noel" (1984), "Police des Moeurs: Les Filles de Saint Tropez" (1987), "Street of No Return" (1989), "Le Moulin de Daudet" (1992), "The Visitors" (1993), "L'Histoire du Garcon Qui Voulait Qu'on

l'Embrasse" (1994), "Francorusse" (1998), "Tom Thumb" (2001) as the Ogre, "Narco" (2004), "Le Jour du Festin" (2006), "Les Deux Mondes" (2007), and "I'm Glad My Mother Is Alive" (2009). Hulin was seen on television in productions of "Napoleon and Josephine: A Love Story" (1987), "Does This Mean We're Married?" (1991), "A Year in Provence" (1993), "De Gre ou de Force" (1998), "Il Cuore e la Spada" (1998), and "The Sleeping Beauty" (2010). His other television credits include episodes of "Mini-Chroniques", "Histoires de Voyous", "Crossbow", "Helene et les Garcons", "Salut les Muscles", "Highlander", "Les Vacances de l'Amour", and "Relic Hunter".

Hume, Edward

Screenwriter Edward Hume, who scripted the 1983 tele-film "The Day After", died on July 13, 2023. He was 87. Hume was born in Chicago, Illinois, on May 18, 1936. He

began writing for television in the late 1960s, penning an episode of "The Fugitive". He wrote the pilot episodes for the detective series "Cannon", "Barnaby Jones", "The Streets of San Francisco", and "Toma" in the early 1970s. Hume scripted the tele-films "The Face of Fear" (9171), "The Harness" (1971), "The Abduction of Saint Anne" (1975), "Sweet Hostage" (1975), "21 Hours at Munich" (1976), "Parole" (1982), "Parole" (1982), "The Terry Fox Story" (1983), "John and Yoko: A Love Story" (1985), "Stranger on My Land" (1988), and "Common Ground" (1990). He was best known for scripting the landmark 1983 ABC tele-film "The Day After", featuring the horrific aftermath of a nuclear exchange between the United States and the Soviet Union. Hume earned an Emmy Award nomination for his work. He wrote several films including "Summertree" (1971), the psychological thriller "A Reflection of Fear" (1972) starring Robert Shaw and Sondra Locke, "Two-Minute Warning" (1976), and "Deceptions" (1992). Hume is survived by three children.

Humphries, Barry

Australian comedian and actor Barry Humphries, who was noted for such satirical alter egos as Dame Edna Everage and Sir Les Patterson, died of complications from hip surgery at a hospital in Sydney, Australia, on April 22, 2023. He was 89. Humphries was born in Melbourne, Australia, on February 17, 1934. He began dressing up as various characters to entertain family and friends as a child. He studied English and art in grammar school and attended the University of Melbourne for two years. He became involved in the satirical

Dada art movement and wrote and performed songs and sketches while attending university. He joined the newly formed Melbourne Theatre Company after leaving school. He first performed the character who became Dame Edna Everage while performing at Melbourne University's Union Theatre in 1955. Humphries moved to Sydney in 1957 where he joined the Phillip Street Theatre. He became the star of numerous

satirical revues where he revived Edna in the productions "Two to One" and "Around the Loop". He soon added the character of Sandy Stone, a grandfatherly suburban man, to his repertoire. Humphries was featured as Estragon in the 1957 production of Samuel Beckett's "Waiting for Godot" at the Arrow Theatre in Melbourne. He teamed with director Peter O'Shaugnessy for the "Rock'n'Reel Revue" at Melbourne's New Theatre in 1958 where Edna Everage and Sandy Stone were introduced to a larger audience. Humphries moved to London in 1959 and was a contributor to Peter Cook's satirical magazine "Private Eye". He created the cartoon strip "The Wonderful World of Barry McKenzie" with artist Nicholas Garland. He appeared on the West End stage in the 1960 production of "Oliver!" and reprised the role on Broadway in 1963. He was also seen in West End productions of "Maggie May", "The Bed-Sitting Room", and "Treasure Island" as Long John Silver in 1968. Humphries made his film debut as Envy in Peter Cook and Dudley Moore's comedy classic "Bedazzled". He was featured as Mr. Wainwright in the film "The Bliss of Mrs. Blossom" starring Shirley MacLaine in 1968. He was best known for his one-man revues, portraying such characters as Edna, Sandy Stone, trade union official Lance Boyle, art salesman Morrie O'Connor, socialist educator Neil Singleton, underground filmmaker Martin Agrippa, and Australian bloke Barry McKenzie. He returned to Australia to bring Edna Everage to the screen in the 1970 film "The Naked Bunyip". He portrayed Edna and other characters in the films "The Adventures of Barry McKenzie" (1972) and "Barry McKenzie Holds His Own" (1974) where Edna was made a dame by Australian prime minister Gough Whitlam. Humphries' other films include "It's Not the Size That Counts", "The Great MacArthy" (1975), "Side by Side" (1975), "The Getting of Wisdom" (1977), "Sgt. Pepper's Lonely Hearts Club Band" (1978), "Shock Treatment" (1981), "The Secret Policeman's Other Ball" (1982), "Les Patterson Saves the World" (1987) in the joint role of Patterson and Dame Edna, "Howling III" (1987) in a cameo role as Dame Edna, "Immortal Beloved" (1994) as Count Metternich, the animated "Napoleon" (1995) as the voice of the Kangaroo, "Pterodactyl Woman from Beverly Hills" (1996), "The Leading Man" (1996), "Welcome to Woop Woop" (1997), "Spice World"

(1997), "Nicholas Nickleby" (2002), the animated "Finding Nemo" (2003) as the voice of Bruce the shark, "Salvation" (2008), "Kath & Kimderella" (2012), "The Hobbit: An Unexpected Journey" (2012) as the Great Goblin, "Justin and the Knights of Valour" (2013) as the voice of Braulio, the animated "Blinky Bill the Movie" (2015) as the voice of Wombo the Wombat, and "Absolutely Fabulous: The Movie" (2016). Humphries appeared in television productions of "Strangers in the Night" (1969), "Barry McKenzie: Ogre or Ocker" (1974), "Pleasure at Her Majesty's" (1976), "An Audience with Dame Edna Everage" (1980), "Dr. Fischer of Geneva" (1984), "Another Audience with Dame Edna" (1986), "An Aussie Audience with Dame Edna" (1986), "A Day in the Life of Barry Humphries" (1987), "One More Audience with Dame Edna Everage" (1988), "A Night on Mount Edna" (1990), "Selling Hitler" (1991) as Rupert Murdoch, "A Late Lunch with Les" (1991), "Python Night: 30 Years of Monty Python" (1999), "The Jubilee Girl" (2002), "Dame Edna Live at the Palace" (2003), "Avenue of the Stars: 50 Years of ITV" (2005), "Da Kath & Kim Code" (2005), "Little Britain Down Under" (2007), "The Man Inside Dame Edna" (2008), and "Jack Irish: Dead Point" (2014). His numerous television appearances, portraying Edna and various other characters, include such series as "Startime", "The Late Show", "Barry Humphries' Scandals", "Not Only... But Also", "Saturday Night Live", "The Barry Humphries Show", "Frost on Saturday", "Omnibus", "The Don Lane Show", "Arena", "Saturday Night at the Mill", "Top of the Pops", "Friday Night, Saturday Morning", "Comic Relief", "Motormouth", "The Russell Harty Show", "Time with Betjeman", "Single Voices", "The Life and Death of Sandy Stone", "Dame Edna's Hollywood", "Edna Time", "Dame Edna's Neighbourhood Watch", "Joan Rivers: Can We Talk?", "The Late Show", "The Last Resort with Jonathan Ross:, "Talkshowet", "The Dame Edna Experience", "Wogan", "Tonight Live with Steve Vizard", "Aspel & Company", "The South Bank Show", "The Tonight Show Starring Johnny Carson", "Lateline", "Vicki!", "The Dennis Miller Show", "Clive Anderson Talks Back", "The Big Breakfast", "Des O'Connor Tonight", "Esther", "The Roseanne Show", "Flashbacks with Barry Humphries", "The Rosie O'Donnell Show", "This Is Your Life", "Hollywood Squares", "Dame Edna Kisses It Better", "Tracey Ullman's Visible Panty Lines", "Ally McBeal" in the recurring role of Claire Otoms (as played by Edna Everage) from 2001 to 2002, "Late Night with Conan O'Brien", "Who Wants to Be a Millionaire", "The Sharon Osbourne Show", "The Tony Danza Show", "This Morning", "The Dame Edna Treatment", "Parkinson", "The Graham Norton Show", "The Late Late Show with Craig Ferguson", "The View", "Loose Women", "Comedy Rocks with Jason Manford", "Live with Kelly and Mark", "The Crocodile Hunter Diaries", "The Osbournes", "The Tonight Show with Jay Leno", "The Dame Edna Treatment", "The Rob Brydon Show", "The Project", "Chickens", "BBC Proms", "Bubble Guppies", "To Do Anything", "The Paul O'Grady Show", "Rove Live", "Piers Moran Live", "Dancing with the Stars", "The Alan Titchmarsh Show", "The Talk", "Today", "The Great Comic Relief Bake Off", and "Michael McIntyre's Big Show". He brought Dame Edna to the Broadway stage in productions of "Dame Edna: The Royal Tour" (1999), "Dave Edna: Back with a Vengeance" (2004), and "All About Me" (2010). Humphries was author of the autobiographies "More Please" (1992) and "My Life As Me: A Memoir" (2002). He also penned various books in the guise of Dame Edna, Sandy Stone, and Les Patterson. He was married to Brenda Wright from 1955 until their divorce in 1957. He was married to Rosalind Tong from 1959 until their divorce in 1970 and is survived by their two children. He was married to Diane Millstead from 1979 until their divorce in 1989 and is survived by their two children. He married actress Elizabeth Spender in 1990 and she also survives him.

Hunnicutt, Gayle

Actress Gayle Hunnicutt, who starred in the horror films "Eye of the Cat" and "The Legend of Hell House", died in London, England, on August 31, 2023. She was 80. Hunnicutt was born in Fort Worth, Texas, on February 6, 1943.

 She graduated from the University of California at Los Angeles in 1965 where she studied theater arts. She performed on stage in local theaters, where she was discovered by a talent scout. She made her film debut in Roger Corman's 1966 biker film "The Wild Angels". Hunnicutt also appeared in the films "P.J." (1967), the feline horror film "Eye of the Cat" (1969), and the film noir "Marlowe" (1969) starring James Garner. She was seen on television in episodes of "Mister Roberts", "The Beverly Hillbillies" as beautiful con artist Emaline Fetty in a pair of 1966 episodes, "Hey, Landlord", "Love on a Rooftop", "Get Smart", and "Love, American Style", and the 1968 tele-film "The Smugglers". Hunnicutt married British actor David Hemmings in 1968 and moved to England with him in 1970. The couple starred together in the horror thriller "Fragment of Fear" (1970) and "Voices" (1973) and she was directed by Hemmings in the 1972 drama "Running Scared" before their divorce in 1975. Hunnicutt was married to newspaper editor Simon Jenkins from 1978 until their divorce in 2009. She largely continued her acting career in England, appearing in the films "Freelance" (1970), "The Love Machine" (1971), "Scorpio" (1973), the classic horror film "The Legend of Hell House" (1973) as Ann Barrett, Georges Franju's crime thriller "Shadowman" (aka "Nuits Rouges") as La Femme, the 1975 mystery thriller remake "The Spiral Staircase", the Italian action thriller "Strange Shadows in an Empty Room" (1976) with Stuart Whitman, "The Sell-Out" (1976), "Once in Paris..." (1978), "The Saint and the Brave Goose" (1979), "A Man Called Intrepid" (1980), "Flashpoint Africa" (1980), "Target" (1985), the horror thriller "Dream Lover" (1986), "Turnaround" (1987) "Silence Like Glass" (1989), and the European science fiction co-production "Hard to Be a God" (1989) based on Arkady and Boris Strugatsky's novel. Hunnicutt was seen on television in productions of "Man and Boy" (1971), "The Golden Bowl"

(1972), "Fall of Eagles" (1974) as Russian Tsarina Alexandra, "Color Him Dead" (1974), "The Man Without a Face" (1975), "The Ambassadors" (1977), "Dylan" (1978), "A Man Called Intrepid" (1979), the 1979 French mini-series "Fantomas" directed by Claude Chabrol and Jean-Luis Bunuel, "The Martian Chronicles" (1980) mini-series based on Ray Bradbury's science fiction classic, "The Million Dollar Face" (1981), "The Return of the Man from U.N.C.L.E.: The Fifteen Years Later Affair" (1983), "Savage in the Orient" (1983), "Two by Forsyth" (1984), "The First Olympics: Athens 1896" (1984), "A Woman of Substance" (1985), "Dream West" (1986), "Strong Medicine" (1986), and "The Saint: The Brazilian Connection" (1989). Her other television credits include episodes of "Away for It All", "Affairs of the Heart", "Switch", "2nd House", "Return of the Saint", "The Love Boat", "Lady Killers", "Matt Houston", "Taxi", "Fantasy Island", "Philip Marlowe, Private Eye", "Tales of the Unexpected", "The Adventures of Sherlock Holmes" as actress Irene Adler opposite Jeremy Brett's Sherlock Holmes in the 1984 premiere episode "A Scandal in Bohemia", "Lime Street", "Dallas" in the recurring role of Vanessa Beaumont from 1989 to 1991, "Screen Two", "Tales from the Crypt", and "CI5: The New Professionals". Hunnicutt was author of the 1984 self-help book "Health and Beauty in Motherhood" and 2004's "Dearest Virginia, Love Letters from a Calvary Officer in the South Pacific", containing love letters between her parents during World War II. Hunnicutt is survived by her son, actor Nolan Hemmings, with her first husband. She is also survived by her son Edward Jenkins with her second husband.

Hunt, Bernadette

British television personality Bernadette Hunt, who was featured as Falcon on the British version of "Gladiators" in

the 1990s, died of cancer in England on March 14, 2023. She was 59. Hunt was born in Brighton, England, on November 6, 1963. She joined the ITV series "Gladiators" as Falcon in its second season in 1993 and remained with the show until it ended in 1999. She also participated in two seasons of the spinoff series "International Gladiators". Hunt later worked as a fitness instructor in Basingstoke. She is survived by two children.

Hunt, Ruth

Actress Ruth Hunt died of complications from an intestinal obstruction in Manhattan, New York, on April 24, 2023. She was 87. She was born Ruth Saxton in Kansas City, Missouri, on December 26, 1935, and was raised in Kansas following her adoption. She studied at the Yale School of Drama and earned a master's degree from Stanford University. She began her career on stage and performed with the California Shakespeare Festival in 1969. She toured in productions of "Hamlet" starring Judith Anderson and "Jesus Christ

Superstar". Hunt appeared on Broadway in the plays "Emperor

Henry IV" (1973), "Crown Matrimonial" (1973), and "Dogg's Hamlet, Cahoot's Macbeth" (1979). She was featured as Ms. Chaeffer in the soap opera "Another World" in 1981 and was Major Lisa Aligueri in "The Edge of Night" (1984). She appeared as Florence in the 1981 horror film "Ghost Story". Hunt was married and divorced from William England and Derek Hunt. She is survived by her third husband, actor Stephen D. Newman, who performed with her on stage with the British American Repertory Company.

Hunter, Lew

Screenwriter Lew Hunter died of complications from COVID-19 in Tucson, Arizona, on January 6, 2023. He was 87. Hunter was born in Guide Rock, Nebraska, on July 18,

1935. He graduated from Nebraska Wesleyan University and earned master's degrees from Northwestern University and the University of California at Los Angeles. He began working in production and programming for television in the 1960s. He began writing scripts in the early 1970s with such tele-films as "If Tomorrow Comes" (1971), "The Sound of Love" (1978), and "Goldie and the Boxer Go to Hollywood" (1981). He wrote and produced the tele-films "Fallen Angel" (1981), "Desperate Lives" (1982), and "Playing with Fire" (1985). Hunter also scripted episodes of "240-Robert", "The Littlest Hobo", "Code Red", and "The Yellow Rose", and produced the science fiction series "Otherworld" in 1985. He was a founder of the American Screenwriters Association and was inducted into its Hall of Fame in 2015. He began teaching screenwriter at UCLA in 1979 and became chairman of the department in 1988. He retired in 2000 but continued to teach one class each winter semester through 2015. He returned to Nebraska in 2003 and continued to hold seminars for aspiring screenwriters through 2014. He was author of the book "Lew Hunter's Screenwriting 434" in 1993. He was the subject of the 2015 documentary "Once in a Lew Moon". Hunter is survived by his second wife, Pamela, and four children from his first marriage.

Hurt, Dakota Fred

Television personality Dakota Fred Hurt, who starred in the reality television franchise "Gold Rush", died of brain cancer in Glendale, Oregon, on July 11, 2023. He was 80. Hurt was born in Minot, North Dakota, on July 10, 1943. He began appearing on the Discovery Channel realty television series

"Gold Rush" in 2011. He was also seen in spin-off series "Gold Rush: South America" and "Gold Rush: The Dirt", and the 2020 tele-film "Gold Rush: The Legend of Porcupine Creek". He and his son, Dustin, were stars of "Gold Rush: White Water" from 2018. The series featured the two, known as the Dakota Boys, as they mine McKinley and Cahoon Creeks in Haines Borough, Alaska.

Husband, Tony

British cartoonist Tony Husband died of a heart attack in London, England, on October 18, 2023. He was 73. Husband was born in Blackpool, England, on August 28, 1950.

He left school in his early teens and worked for a jeweler for over a decade. He began drawing cartoons that he submitted to the satire magazine "Public Eye". He frequently featured skinhead characters in is cartoons which led to a regular strip, "The Yobs", in 1985. He also drew "The Oldies" strip in the 1990s. Husband was co-founder and editor of "Oink!" comic magazine from 1986 to 1988. He created the children's television series "Round the Bend" which aired from 1989 to 1991. He also worked on the children's series "Hangar 17" from 1992 to 1994. He married Carol Garner in 1976 and she survives him. He is also survived by their son, photographer Paul Husband.

Hywel, Dafydd

Welsh actor Dafydd Hywel died in Garnet, Wales, on March 23, 2023. He was 77.

Hywel was born in Garnet on December 4, 1945. He appeared frequently in stage, film, and television productions in Welsh an English from the 1960s. His film credits include "Gwaed ar y Ser" (1975), "The Mouse and the Woman" (1980), "Yr Alcoholig Lion" (1984), "Coming Up Roses" (1986), "Milwr Bychan" (1987), "The Angry Earth" (1989), "Rebecca's Daughters" (1992), "Arthur'd Dyke" (2001), "Undertaking Betty" (2002), "One Chance" (2013), and "Miss Peregrine's Home for Peculiar Children" (2016). He was seen on television in episodes of "Armchair Thriller", "Off to Philadelphia in the Morning", "The Dawson Watch", "Pobol y Cwm", "Brendon Chase" as Jack Welsh in 1981, "Taff Acre" as Johnny Owen in 1981, "Screenplay", "We Are Seven" as

Jamesy James from 1989 to 1991, "Wales Playhouse", "Halen yn y Gwaed" as Captain Tom Francis in 1994, "Tair Chwaer", "Mortimer's Law", "The Unknown Soldier" as Dr. Ewan Thomas in 1998, "The Bill", "Dangerfield", "Peak Practice", "Other People's Children", "Darn o Dir", "A Mind to Kill", "The Bench" as Wynford Thomas" from 2001 to 2002, "Holby City", "High Hopes", "Y Pris" as Clive Owen in 2007, "Pen Talar", "Doctors", "The Indian Doctor", "Hinterland", "35 Diwrnod", "Keeping Faith", "The Crown", and "The Tuckers". Hywel was known for his role as Glen Brennig in the series "Stella" from 2012 to 2017. His other television credits include productions of "The Life and Times of David Lloyd George" (1981), "The Mimosa Boys" (1985), "I Fro Breuddwydion" (1987), "Come Home Charlie and Face Them" (1990), "Stanley and the Women" (1991), "Richard Burton's Christmas Story" (1991), "The Blackheath Poisonings" (1992), "The Christmas Stallion" (1992), "Rhag Pob Brad" (1993), "Harpur and Iles" (1996), "Forbidden Territory: Stanley's Search for Livingstone" (1997), "In the Company of Strangers" (1999), "Rhinoceros" (1999), "Border Cafe" (2000), "Dirty Tricks" (2000), "Stopping Distance" (2003), "Perfect Day: The Millennium" (2006), "Cwpan Caerdydd" (2008), and "Burton: Y Gyfrinach" (2011). Hywel's autobiography, "Hunangofiant Alff Garnant", was published in 2013.

Iacovelli, John

Production designer John Iacovelli died of cancer in Los Angeles, California, on April 14, 2023. He was 64. Iacovelli was born on February 25, 1959. He formed a theater

troupe with friends during his childhood and studied scenic design at the University of Nevada at Las Vegas. He earned his master's degree from New York University. He worked frequently on stage as a scenic designer for hundreds of productions including national tours and regional theaters. He worked frequently with the Pasadena Playhouse in California and designed Broadway productions of "The Twilight of the Golds" (1993) and "Peter Pan" (1998). He was also scenic designer for the touring production of "Camelot" in 2007. Iacovelli was production designer for the films "Honey, I Shrunk the Kids" (1989), "Keaton's Cop" (1990), "Public Enemy" (1991), "Ruby in Paradise" (1993), "A Question of Faith" (2000), and "The Cat That Looked at a King" (2004). Iacovelli was designer for such television productions as "See Dick and Jane... Lie, Cheat and Steal: Teaching Morality to Kids" (1989), "Becket Directs Beckett: Endgame by Samuel Beckett" (1991), "The Wild West" (1993), "Siringo" (1995), "Favorite Deadly Sins" (1995), "Babylon 5: In the Beginning" (1998), "Babylon 5: Thirdspace" (1998), "Babylon 5: The River of Souls" (1998), "Titanic: Secrets Revealed" (1998), "Babylon 5: A Call to Arms" (1999), "Peter Pan" (2000) sharing an Emmy Award, "War Games" (2001), "The Old Settler" (2001), "The Gin Game" (2003), and

"Play or Be Played" (2008). His other television credits include episodes of "Captain Power and the Soldiers of the Future", "Trying Times", "Babylon 5", "Crusade", "Resurrection Blvd.", "Ed", ""Worst Case Scenarios", "Ripley's Believe It or Not!", "Te Amare en Silencio", "The Book of Daniel", "The Knights of Prosperity", "Lincoln Heights", and "Los Americans".

Ibanez Talavera, Francisco

Spanish cartoonist Francisco Ibanez Talavera died in Barcelona, Spain, on July 15, 2023. He was 87. Ibanez was born in Barcelona on March 15, 1936. He was fascinated with

comics and cartoons as a child but studied banking and accounting after his primary education. He worked at various jobs including bellhop and risk assistant at the Banco Espanol de Credito during the 1950s. He continued to draw humor comic strips and his drawings began appearing in such magazines as "Nicolas", "Chicolino" "Alex", "Liliput", "La Risa", and "Hipo, Minoti y Fifi". He created the series "Kokolo", "Melenas", "Don Usura", and "Haciendo el Indio". He left his job in banking to work full time as a cartoonist in 1957. He created the series "Pepe Rona" for the magazine "Paseo Infantil". He soon began working with the publisher Editorial Bruguera where he created a pair of bumbling detectives who starred in the comic "Mortadelo y Filemon" ("Mort & Phil) from 1958 through 2023. The characters, who transformed from detectives to spies in the late 1960s, were adapted for a series of animated shorts from 1965 to 1970 and an animated series in 1994. They were also featured in the live-action films "Mortadelo & Filemon: The Big Adventure" (2003), "Mortadelo y Filemon. Mision: Salvar la Tierra" (2008), and "Mortadelo and Filemon: Mission Implausible" (2014). Ibanez also created such comics and characters as "Don Adelfo" (1958), "Celestino" (1958-1959), "The Brawl Family" (1958-1968), "La Historia Esa, Vista por Hollywood" (1959-1960), "El Capitan Trueno Extra" (1960-1968), "Polito, Tipo Duro" (1961), "Go Laugh with Noah's Ark" (1961), "13. Rue del Percebe" (1961-1968), "Cabeza de Ajo, El Penultimo Navajo" (1962), "Los Perez" (1963), and "Bellhop Sacarino of the Evening Howl" (1963-1982). He was featured in his own magazines from Bruguera, "Sacarino" from 1975 to 1977 and "Super Sacarino" from 1975 to 1985. His comic "Rompetechos" was published from 1964 to 1978 and again from 2003 to 2009. His other cartoons include "Doctor Esparadrapo and his Assistant Gazapo" (1964-1965), "Don Pedrito" (1964-1967), and "Pepe Leak and Otilio, Botched Jobs Home Delivered" (1966-1970). He continued to produce comics featuring Mortadel y Filemon throughout his life with his final album released in June of 2023. Ibanez married Remedios Solera Sanchez in 1966 and is survived by her and two daughters.

Ichaso, Leon

Cuban-American film and television director Leon Ichaso died of a heart attack in Santa Monica, California, on May 21, 2023. He was 74. Ichaso was born in Havannah, Cuba, on August 3, 1948. He moved to Mexico with his family in the early 1960s before settling in the United States. He was raised in Miami and moved to New York, where he made television commercials and wrote advertising copy. He made his film

debut with the 1979 Spanish-language feature "El Super", which he produced, directed, and wrote. Ichaso worked frequently on television, directing episodes of "Saturday Night Live", "Crime Story", "The Equalizer", "Miami Vice", "Veronica Clare", "Sins of the City", "The Division", "The Handler", "Sleeper Cell", "Cane", "Medium", "The Cleaner", "Persons Unknown", "Criminal Minds", "Criminal Minds: Beyond Borders", "Chicago Med", "Prodigal Son", and "Queen of the South". He also helmed television productions of "Tales from the Hollywood Hills: A Table at Ciro's" (1987), "The Take" (1990), "The Fear Inside" (1992), "A Kiss to Die For" (1993), "Zooman" (1995), "Free of Eden" (1998), "Execution of Justice" (1999), "Ali: An American Hero" (2000), "Hendrix" (2000), and "Left to Die" (2012). Ichaso directed, and frequently wrote, the films "Crossover Dreams" (1985), "Sugar Hill" (1993) starring Wesley Snipes, "Bitter Sugar" (1996), "Pinero" (2001), "El Cantante" (2006) starring Marc Anthony and Jennifer Lopez, and "Paraiso" (2009). He was married and divorced from Karen Willinger and Amanda Barber.

Ichijo, Miyuki

Japanese actress Miyuki Ichijo, who was noted for her voice role as Jodie Starling in the "Detective Conan" anime franchise, died of multiple organ failure in Japan on October 24,

2023. She was 74. She was born Hiroko Okamoto in Oshu, Iwate, Japan, on August 23, 1949. She began working in anime as a voice actress in the late 1970s. She began best known for her role as Jodie Starling in numerous film and television productions from the "Detective Conan" franchise from the mid-1990s. Ichijo also voiced roles in "Galaxy Express 999" as Kufuremu, "Super Dimension Century Orguss" as Manisha, "Nekusuto Senki Eagaitsu" as Akane, "Cowboy Bebop" as Anastasia, "Project ARMS" as Misa Takatsuki, "Pecola" as Grandma Yokusha, "Blue Drop" as Maiyama Kyomu Shunin, "Minami Kamakura High School Girls Cycling Club" as Ryuko Kamikura, and "Golden Kamuy" as Huci. Her other anime credits include episodes of "Nobara no Julie", "The New Adventures of Gigantor", "Space Cobra", "The Vision of Escaflowne",

"Martian Successor Nadesico", "The Big O", "Rumiko Takahashi Anthology", "Mars Daybreak", "Doki Doki School Hours", "Monster", "Gallery Fake", "Blood+", "Roketto Garu", ""Phantom: Requiem for the Phantom", "Stitch!", "Space Dandy", "Maria the Virgin Witch", "Is the Order a Rabbit?", "Mobile Suit Gundam",. "BNA", and "Akebi's Sailor Uniform". She provided the Japanese dubbing voice for numerous films and television shows including Dr. Beverly Crusher for "Star Trek: The Next Generation". She also was the Japanese voice for such animated characters as Marge Simpson in "The Simpsons", Jessica Rabbit in "Who Framed Roger Rabbit", Lucy Van Pelt in "Peanuts", and the Blue Fairy in "Pinocchio". Ichijo was the voice of over 500 early childhood education recordings that were frequently used in Japan.

Iglesias, Eugene

Puerto Rican actor Eugene Iglesias, who appeared frequently in character roles in the 1950s and 1960s, died of a heart attack in Lamesa, Texas, on February 4, 2023. He was 96. Iglesias was born in San Juan, Puerto Rico, on December 3, 1926. He came to California to attend school in the late

1940s. He made his film debut in 1951's "The Brave Bulls" and the younger brother of Mel Ferrer's character. He appeared in film and television over the next two years, often playing Spanish, Italian, or Native American characters. Iglesias' films include "Mask of the Avengers" (1951), "Indian Uprising" (1952), "California Conquest" (1952), "The Duel at Silver Creek" (1952), "Hiawatha" (1952), "Jack McCall, Desperado" (1953), "East of Sumatra" (1953), "Tumbleweed" (1953), "Taza, Son of Cochise" (1954) starring Rock Hudson, "They Rode West" (1954), "Underwater!" (1955), "The Naked Dawn" (1955), "Walk the Proud Land" (1956), "Domino Kid" (1957), "Cowboy" (1958), "Rio Bravo" (1959), "Key Witness" (1960), "Frontier Uprising" (1961), "Safe at Home!" (1962), "Apache Rifles" (1964), "The Money Trap" (1965), and "Harper" (1966). He was seen on television in episodes of "Cavalcade of America", "Dragnet", "My Little Margie", "The Donald O'Connor Show", "Waterfront", "Cheyenne", "General Electric Theater", "The Loretta Young Show", "Crossroads", "Tales of the 77th Bengal Lancers", "Circus Boy", "Climax!", "The Silent Service", "Broken Arrow", "Zorro", "The Adventures of Jim Bowie", "Maverick", "Schlitz Playhouse", "Sea Hunt", "Flight", "Lawman", "The Third Man", "Frontier Doctor", "Playhouse 90", "Adventure Showcase", "Alcoa Theatre", "Sugarfoot", "Outlaws", "The Deputy", "Peter Gunn", "Coronado 9", "The Rebel", "One Step Beyond", "Laramie", "The Untouchables", "Cain's Hundred", "Rawhide", "The DuPont Show of the Week" production of "The Richest Man in Bogota" in 1962, "The Real McCoys", "The Dakotas", "The Alfred Hitchcock Hour", "Death Valley Days", "Bonanza", "The Fugitive", "Combat!", and "Hondo". Iglesias largely retired from acting in the early 1970s.

Iizuka, Shozo

Japanese voice actor Shozo Iizuka died of heart failure in Japan on February 15, 2023. He was 89. Iizuka was born in Fukushima, Japan, on May 23, 1933. He graduated from Nihon University and began working as a voice actor for anime series

in the 1960s. He was heard on such cartoons as "Astro Boy", "Gigantor", "Wolf Boy Ken", "Tomorrow's Joe" as Tiger Ozaki, "Brave Raideen" as Gekido Kyoretsu, "Daimos", "Mobile Suit Gundam" as Ryu Jose, "Urusei Yatsura", "Space Adventure Cobra", "Space Sheriff Shaider" as Great Emperor Kuilai, "Fist of the North Star" as Fudo, "Mobile Sheriff Jiban" as Dr. Giba, "Sherlock Hound" as Inspector Lestrade, "Metal Armor Dragonar", "Dragon Ball Z" as Nappa, "Brae Exkaiser", "Tekkaman Blade" as Honda, "Crying Freeman", "Ghost Sweeper Mikami", "YuYu Hakusho", "Street Fighter II", "Detective Conan", "Kindaichi Case Files", "Lost Universe", "Yu-Gi-Oh!", "Pokemon", "Monkey Typhoon", "Planetes", "Monster", "Paranoia Agent", "Damurai Champloo", "Black Jack", "Gun X Sword", "Oban Star-Racers", "Deltora Quest", "Devil May Cry", "Doraemon", "Soul Eater", "Bleach", "Fullmetal Alchemist: Brotherhood", "K: Return of Kings", "Little Witch Academia", "Time Bokan 24", "Stitch" as Dr. Jumba, "Puzzle & Dragons X", and "White Cat Project: Zero Chronicle". Iizuka was a voice actor for numerous characters in the "Super Sentai" series, which was reedited in the United States to form the "Power Rangers" series. He provided the voice for members of the cyborg Black Cross Army for "Himitsu Sentai Gorenger" in 1977 and for most of the Vader Monsters in "Denshi Senai Denjiman" in 1980. He was the voice of High Priest Darom on "Kamen Rider Black" from 1987 to 1988. Iizuka was also a dubbing actor, supplying Mr. T's voice for "The A-Team" and "Rocky III" and John Rhys-Davies for "Indiana Jones and the Last Crusade" and "The Living Daylights". He was also the demon voice for "The Exorcist" and High Priest Imhotep in "The Mummy Returns".

Ingram, Michael H.

Actor Michael H. Ingram died in Yonkers, New York, on September 20, 2023. He was 85. Ingram was born in Crown Heights, Brooklyn, New York, on May 26, 1938. He attended Hofstra University on a music scholarship, graduating in 1960. He later earned a master's degree from Stony Brook University. He toured with the Robert Shaw Chorale before becoming a high school music teacher in Lake Ronkonkoma, New York. He also directed various student productions and performed on stage in summer stock. He began pursuing an acting career in the 1970s. He performed on Broadway in productions of "Sarava" (1979), "Sweet Charity" (1986), "Chu Chem" (1989), and "Jekyll & Hyde" (1997). Ingram was featured as Lt. Vince Wolek on the television soap opera "One Life to Live" from

1978 to 1981. He was also seen in episodes of "Guiding Light", "Sex and the City", "Law & Order", "Law & Order: Special Victims Unit", "Law & Order: Criminal Intent", "Third Watch" in the recurring role of Dr. Case from 2001 to 2002, "The Sopranos", "Louie", "Unforgettable", and "Orange Is the New

Black". His other television credits include the tele-films "Muggable Mary, Street Cop" (1982) and "You Don't Know Jack" (2010). Ingram was featured in several films including "The First Deadly Sin" (1980), "Lock 'n' Load" (1990), "A Perfet Murder" (1998), "Prison Song" (2001), "Mergers & Acquisitions" (2001), "Fortunes" (2005), and "Every Day" (2010). He married Donna Ingram in 1982 and is survived by her and their son and daughter. He is also survived by a daughter from his first marriage.

Inuzuka, Hiroshi

Japanese actor Hiroshi Inuzuka, who starred in the 1972 kaiju fantasy film "Daigoro vs. Goliath", died in Japan on October 7, 2023. He was 94. Inuzuka was born in Tokyo,

Japan, on March 23, 1929. He began performing with the comedy jazz band the Crazy Cats in the mid-1950s. He played bass with the group and appeared with them in such films as "Nippon Musekinin Jidai" (1962), "Let's Meet in Our Dreams" (1962), "Strategy First Win" (1963), "Irresponsible Crushed!" (1963), "Crazy Cats Go to Hong Kong" (1963), "Irresponsible Yuden" (1964), "Crazy Adventure" (1965), "It's a Strange Heaven" (1966), "Operation Crazy" (1966), "Industrial Spy Free for All" (1967), "Las Vegas Free for All" (1967), "Monsieur Zivaco" (1967), "Mexican Free for All" (1968), "The Great Discovery" (1969), "The Big Explosion" (1969), and "Be Deceived!" (1971). Inuzuka was also seen in the films "Ten Dark Women" (1961), "When Spring Comes Late" (1970), "Tora-san, the Good Samaritan" (1971), "Daigoro vs. Goliath" (1972) as Ojisan, "Stage-Struck Tora-san" (1978), "Tora-san, the Matchmaker" (1979), "Tora-san's Dream of Spring" (1979), "Tora-san's Promise" (1981), "Eijanaika" (1981), "Samurai Reincarnation" (1981), "Aiko 16 Sai" (1983), "Kaisha Monogatari: Memories of You" (1988), "Door II: Tokyo Diary" (1991), "Kamen Rider ZO" (1993), "Tora-san to the Rescue" (1995), "Women in the Mirror" (2003), "Goodbye Me" (2007), "Chameleon" (2008), "Brass Knuckle Boys" (2008), "Tsure Ga Utsu Ni Narimashite" (2011), "Casting Blossoms to the Sky" (2012), "Giovanni's Island" (2014) in a voice role, and "Labyrinth of Cinema" (2019). He was seen on television in productions of "Shin Hissatsu Shiokinin", "Hattori Hanzo:

Kage no Gundan", "Onihei Hankacho Ryusei", "Kokoro", "Ultraman Max", and "Ohisama".

Iosseliani, Otar

Georgian actor Otar Iosseliani died in Tbilisi, Georgia, on December 17, 2023. He was 89. Iosseliani was born in Tbilisi (then part of the Soviet Union), on February 2, 1934. He studied mathematics at the University of Moscow for two years

before transferring to the Gerasimov Institute of Cinematography. He also began working as an assistant director and editor at the Georgian Film Studio (Gruziafilm). He directed his first short film for television, "Akvarel" in 1958, prior to his graduation in 1961. He directed the short film, "Sapovnela" (1959), and "Aprili" which was filmed in 1961 but was denied distribution until 1972. He left filmmaking for several years before returning to direct and write the short "Tudzhi" (1964) and the feature "Falling Leaves" (1966). He also directed the 1969 short "Dzveli Qartuli Simgera" (1969) and the features "Once Upon a Time There Was a Singing Blackbird" (1970) and "Pastorale" (1975). Iosseliani left the Soviet Union for France in 1982 due to the government's continued interference with his films. He continued to direct, write, and often appear in such critically acclaimed films as "Favourites of the moon" (1984), "A Little Monastery in Tuscany" (1988), "Et la Lumiere Fut" (1989), "La Chasse aux Papillons" (1992), "Georgia, Alone" (1994), "Brigands-Chapter VII" (1996), "Farewell, Home Sweet Home" (1999), "Monday Morning" (2002), "Jardins en Automne" (2006), "Chantrapas" (2010), and "Winter Song" (2015). He also appeared in small roles in several of his later films. He was given the CineMerit Awarde, a lifetime achievement honor, at the Munich International Film Festival in 2011.

Iron Sheik

Iranian professional wrestler Hossein Khosrow Ali Vaziri, who competed in the World Wrestling Federation under the name the Iron Sheik, died of heart failure at his home in Fayetteville, Georgia, on June 7, 2023. He was 81. Khosrow was born in Damgham, Iran, on March 15, 1942. He was a leading amateur wrestler and served as a bodyguard for the Shah of Iran's family. He left Iran in 1968 after the mysterious death of Olympic wrestling champion Gholamreza Takhti. He settled in Minnesota where he competed with an amateur wrestling group. He served as an assistant coach for the U.S. Olympic wrestling team in 1972. He trained to become a professional wrestler with Verne Gagne and Billy Robinson. He began his career with Gagne's American Wrestling Association (AWA). He soon adopted the name the Great Hossein Arab, shaving his head bald, growing a bushy mustache, and wearing wrestling boots with curled toes. He became a notorious ring villain, particularly after the Iranian

Revolution and hostage crisis in 1979. He competed with the World Wrestling Federation (WWF/now WWE) from 1979 to 1980, losing a championship match to Bob Backlund and feuding with Chief Jay Strongbow and Bruno Sammartino. He became known as the Iron Sheik while wrestling with Jim  Crockett Promotions from 1980 to 1981. He defeated Jim Brunzell for the NWA Mid-Atlantic Heavyweight Championship in May of 1980 and lost the title to Ricky Steamboat the following November. He also had a lengthy feud with Blackjack Mulligan and failed in a challenge for the NWA World Heavyweight Championship against Dusty Rhodes in July of 1981. He wrestled in Florida and Georgia over the next two years, holding the NWA National Television Championship from May to July of 1983. He returned to the WWF in 1983 and again challenged Bob Backlund for the heavyweight championship. He captured the title when Backlund's manager forfeited the match when the champion was locked in the Iron Sheik's signature camel Clutch chin lock hold in December of 1983. He had matched with Backlund, Chief Jay Strongbow, and Pat Patterson over the next month. He lost the title when Hulk Hogan entered the promotion and defeated him in a match in January of 1984. The Iron Sheik subsequently embarked on a lengthy feud with wrestling hero Sgt. Slaughter. He teamed with Nikolai Volkoff under the management of Freddie Blassie to capture the WWF World Tag Team Championship from Barry Windham and Mike Rotundo at the first WrestleMania in March of 1985. They were defeated in a rematch the following June. Slick replaced Blassie as the Iron Sheik's manager in 1986. He feuded with Hacksaw Jim Duggan until May of 1987 when the two men were traveling together in New Jersey for a WWF event. They were arrested when it was determined that Duggan, the driver, was using marijuana and that the Iron Sheik had cocaine. The arrest was particularly embarrassing for the WWF as two in-ring enemies had been traveling and partying together. He was sentenced to a year's probation and was released from the WWF in October of 1987. He continued to suffer from drug addiction for the next two decades until quitting cocaine in 2009. He briefly feuded with Matt Borne in Dallas' World Class Championship Wrestling (WCCW) later in the year. He also wrestled in Puerto Rico with the World Wrestling Council. He returned to the WWF from February to July of 1988, competing in matches against Lanny Poffo, Kent Patera, and Scott Casey. The Iron Sheik appeared at World Championship Wrestling (WCW) in February of 1989 and failed to defeat Sting for the promotion's TV championship the following May. He competed against Brian Pillman, Terry Taylor, Big Van Vader, and the Junkyard Dog before leaving WCW in January of 1991. He reemerged in the WWF in March of 1991 under the name Colonel Mustafa. He teamed with former foe Sgt. Slaughter, who was now anti-American and pro-Iraqi during the Gulf War. They were accompanied by

Iraqi General Adnan (Al-Kaissey) and feuded with Hulk Hogan and the Ultimate Warrior. Slaughter resumed his good guy persona and turned on Mustafa in August of 1991. Mustafa wrestled Slaughter and other competitors including the British Bulldog, Ricky Steamboat, Hacksaw Jim Duggan, Kerry von Erich, and Tatanka before leaving the WWF in May of 1992. He made occasional returns to the WWF/WWE including co-managing the Sultan (later known as Rikishi) with former foe Bob Backlund in 1997. He won the Gimmick Battle Royal at WrestleMania X-Seven in April of 2001 and was inducted into the WWE Hall of Fame in 2005. He retired from the ring later in the decade. He was featured in Cyndi Lauper's 1985 music video for "The Goonies 'R' Good Enough". He appeared in several films including "The Tale of 3 Mohammads" (2005), "Operation Belvis Bash" (2011), and "Killing Hasselhoff" (2017). He was seen on television in episodes of "Hogan Knows Best", "Kenny vs. Spenny", and "The Eric Andre Show", and had a voice role in "Robot Chicken". He was also a frequent guest on Howard Stern's radio show and was noted for his controversial diatribes on social media in his later years. He was the subject of the 2014 documentary film "The Sheik". He was voiced by Aron Kincaid for the animated television series "Hulk Hogan's Rock 'n' Wrestling from 1985 to 1986. Brett Azar played the Iron Sheik in a recurring role on the television series "Young Rock". Iron Sheik married Caryl Peterson in 1976 and is survived by her and their daughters, Nicole and Tanya. Another daughter, Marissa, was murdered by her boyfriend in 2003.

Isley, Rudolph

Singer Rudolph Isley, who was a founding member of the musical group the Isley Brothers, died of a heart attack at his home in Olympia Fields, Illinois, on October 11, 2023. He  was 84. Isley was born in Cincinnati, Ohio, on April 1, 1939. He sang in the church choir in his youth and formed a vocal trio with his brothers Ronald and O'Kelley. They were joined by brother Vernon and performed as the Isley Brothers from 1954. Vernon died after being struck by a car soon after and the three surviving brothers moved to New York City in 1957. They signed with RCA Records in 1959 and wrote and recorded the hit song "Shout". They continued to record such popular songs as "Twist and Shout", "This Old Heart of Mine (Is Weak for You)", and the Grammy Award-winning "It's Your Thing" in the 1960s. They were joined by younger brothers Ernie Isley on lead guitar and drums and Marvin Isley on bass guitar, and Rudolph's brother-in-law Chris Jasper on keyboards in the early 1970s. Rudolph performed lead vocals on the songs "Fight the Power", "Livin' in the Life", "You Still Feel the Need", and "It's a Disco Night (Rock Don't Stop)". The brothers recorded the hit albums "3+3", "Between the Sheets", and "The Heat Is On" before Ernie, Marvin, and Chris Jasper left the group in 1983. O'Kelly died in 1986 after the release of the album "Masterpiece". Rudolph and Ronald recorded the albums "Smooth Sailin'" and "Spend the Night" as a duo before Rudolph retired from performing to become a Christian minister in 1989. He continued to sing in church and recorded some gospel songs. He released a religious album, "Shouting for Jesus: A Loud Joyful Noise", in 1996. The Isley Brothers were inducted into the Rock and Roll Hall of Fame in 1992 and the Vocal Hall of Fame in 2003. Rudolph reunited in a performance with his brothers for one night when they were given a lifetime achievement honor at the BET Awards in 2004. Isley married Elaine Jasper in 1958 and is survived by her and their children, Rudy Jr., Elizabeth, Valerie, and Elaine.

Jackson, Chuck

Singer Chuck Jackson died in Atlanta, Georgia, on February 16, 2023. He was 85. Jackson was born in Winston-

Salem, North Carolina, on July 22, 1937. He sang with a gospel group in his youth and moved to Pittsburgh, Pennsylvania, in his early teens. He performed with the vocal group the Del-Vikings from 1957 to 1959 and was lead singer on their song "Willette". He signed a solo recording contract with Scepter Records and co-wrote and recorded the 1961 single "I Don't Want to Cry". He scored a major hit with his 1962 rendition of the Burt Bacharach and Bob Hilliard song "Any Day Now". He subsequently moved to Motown where he recorded "Honey Come Back" in 1969. He recorded with various labels through the 1970s with minor success. He teamed with Dionne Warwick on the song "If I Let Myself Go" in 1997, and his final single, "I Only Get This Feeling", was released in 2010. Jackson's wife, Helen Cash, died in 2013, and a daughter died in 2021. He is survived by two children.

Jackson, Glenda

British actress Glenda Jackson, who received Academy Awards for her roles in the films "Women in Love" and "A Touch of Class", died at her home in Blackheath, London, England, on June 15, 2023. She was 87. Jackson was

born in Birkenhead, England, on May 9, 1936. She performed in local amateur theater in her teens. She worked for two years at the Boots pharmacy chain before earning a scholarship to the Royal Academy of Dramatic Art in London in 1954. She made her professional debut in a production of "Doctor in the House" at Worthing's Cannaught Theatre in 1957 while still a student. She worked at various odd jobs including waitressing and clerical work while trying to pursue an acting career after her graduation in 1958. She was featured in a small role in the 1963 film "This Sporting Life". Jackson

worked in repertory as an actress and stage manager and joined the Royal Shakespeare Company for four years in 1973. She was featured as an asylum inmate portraying Charlotte Corday in the 1965 production of Peter Weiss' "The Persecution and Assassination of Marat as Performed by the Inmates of the Asylum of Charenton Under the Direction of the Marquis de Sade" and accompanied the play to Broadway, where she received a Tony Award nomination. She reprised the role in the 1967 film version of "Marat/Sade". She starred as Ophelia in Peter Hall's 1965 production of "Hamlet" and appeared in the 1966 anti-Vietnam War play "US". She returned to the screen in Peter Medak's psychological drama "Negatives" (1968). She starred as Gudrun Brangwen in Ken Russell's 1969 adaptation of D.H. Lawrence's "Women in Love" and earned an Academy Award for Best Actress. She starred in Russell's 1970 feature "The Music Lovers" opposite Richard Chamberlain as Tchaikovsky. She received an Academy Award nomination and a BAFTA Award for her role as Alex Greville in John Schlesinger's 1971 film "Sunday Bloody Sunday". Her other films include "The Boy Friend" (1971), "Mary, Queen of Scots" (1971) as Queen Elizabeth I, "The Triple Echo" (1972), "The Nelson Affair" (1973) as Lady Hamilton, "A Touch of Class" earning another Oscar for Best Actress for her role as Vickie Allessio, "The Devil Is a Woman" (1974), "The Maids" (1975), "The Romantic Englishwoman" (1975) with Michael Caine, "Hedda" (1975) receiving another Oscar nomination for her title role, "The Incredible Sarah" (1976) as Sarah Bernhardt, "Nasty Habits" (1977), the comedy "House Calls" (1978) opposite Walter Matthau, "Stevie" (1978) and poet Stevie Smith, "The Class of Miss MacMichael" (1978), "Lost and Found" (1979), "HealtH" (1980), "Hopscotch" (1980) again with Matthau, "The Return of the Soldier" (1982), "Giro City" (1982), "Turtle Diary: (1985), "Beyond Therapy" (1987), "Business as Usual" (1988), "Salome's Last Dance" (1988), "The Rainbow" (1989), "Doombeach" (1989), and "King of the Wind" (1990). Jackson returned to Broadway in the 1981 production of "Rose" and was also seen in "Strange Interlude" (1985), and "Macbeth" (1988), earning Tony Award nominations for all three plays. Jackson was seen on television in episodes of "Z Cars", "Half Hour Story", "The Wednesday Play", "Armchair Theatre", "The Morecambe & Wise Show", "The Muppet Show", and "Carol & Company". She also appeared in television productions of "A Voice in Vision" (1957), "Doctor Everyman's Hour" (1961), "Salve Regina" (1969), "Howards End" (1970), "Elizabeth R" (1971) winning an Emmy Award for her role as Queen Elizabeth I, "The Patricia Neal Story" (1981) receiving an Emmy nomination for her role as actress Patricia Neal, "Sakharov" (1984) as Yelena Bonner, "Strange Interlude" (1988), "T. Bag's Christmas Ding Dong" (1990), "A Murder of Quality" (1991), "The House of Bernarda Alba" (1991), and "The Secret Life of Arnold Bax" (1992). She was a guest on such series as "The Dick Cavett Show", "The David Frost Show", "The Merv Griffin Show", "Dinah!", "The Mike Douglas Show", "The Talk Show with Clive James", "Wogan", "So Graham Norton", "The Late Show with Stephen Colbert", "Late Night with Seth Meyers", "Today", and "The Jonathan Ross Show". Jackson was active in leftist political and social issues for many years. She assisted with the campaign to fight famine in Ethiopia and campaigned against apartheid in South Africa. She put her acting career on hold after being elected a Member of Parliament for Hamstead and Highgate in 1992 as a candidate for the Labour Party. She served as Parliamentary Under-Secretary of State for Transport in the government of

Tony Blair from 1997 to 1999. She remained in Parliament as a member from Hampstead and Kilburn from 2010 to 2015. Jackson returned to acting after retiring from politics and starred in "Blood, Sex and Money", based on novels by Emile Zola. She starred as "King Lear" in a 2018 production of Shakespeare's play at the Old Vic Theater in London and repeated the role on Broadway the following year. She received a Tony Award for Best Actress for the 2018 Broadway revival of Edward Albee's "Three Tall Women". She returned to television in the role of Maud, an elderly woman suffering from Alzheimer's, in the 2019 production of "Elizabeth Is Missing", receiving a BAFTA and an International Emmy Award. She was featured in the 2021 film "Mothering Sunday" and starred with Michael Caine in "The Great Escaper" which was completed before her death and scheduled for release later in 2023. Jackson married actor and stage manager Roy Hodges while working in repertory in 1958. She and Hodges divorced in 1976 and are survived by their son, Daniel Hodges.

Jackson, Nathan Louis

Playwright and television writer Nathan Louis Jackson, who wrote and produced Netflix's "Luke Cage" series,

died in Lenexa, Kansas, on August 22, 2023. He was 44. Jackson was born in Lawrence, Kansas, on December 4, 1978. He began writing plays while attending Kansas State University. He later earned a master's degree in playwriting from Juilliard School in New York City. He was noted for the 2008 play "Broke-ology". He also wrote the plays "The Last Black Play", "The Mancherios", "Sticky Traps", "Brother Toad", and "When I Come to Die". Jackson was a writer for the television series "Southland", "Lights Out", "Shameless", and "Resurrection". He wrote and produced episodes of "13 Reasons Why", "Luke Cage", "Genius", and "S.W.A.T." His survivors include his wife, Megan Mascorro, and children Amaya and Savion.

Jacobs, Abe

New Zealand professional wrestler Abe Jacobs died in Charlotte, North Carolina, on August 21, 2023. He was 95. Jacobs was born in the Chatham Islands, New Zealand, on June 18, 1928. He worked at his family's ranch and began

weightlifting at an early age. He trained as an amateur wrestler in his teens. He held several amateur titles and captured the New Zealand Championship in 1953. He failed to make the team for the 1956 Olympics and began training to be a professional wrestler. He trained with the Zebra Kid and Al Costello and made his ring debut in 1958. He became noted for his "Kiwi Roll" submission hold. He began wrestling in the United States later in the year and competed for a year for Capitol Sports, run by Vince McMahon, Sr., in Washington, D.C. He feuded with NWA Heavyweight Champion Buddy Rogers and Karl Von Hess. Jacobs also had bouts with Johnny Valentine, the Sheik, Wild Bull Curry, Dr. Jerry Graham, and Bruno Sammartino. He traveled to other promotions and challenged fellow New Zealander Pat O'Connor for the NWA World Heavyweight Championship in 1961. He entered Jim Crockett Promotions in 1961 where he feuded with Swede Hanson. He also fought in tag team bouts with such partners as George Becker, Haystack Calhoun, and Sailor Art Thomas. He and Calhoun won the NWA Los Angeles International Television Tag Team Championship in October of 1962. He teamed with Don Curtis to capture the NWA World Tag Team Championship in Flora in May of 1964. He had several prominent matches with Lou Thesz in 1965. Jacobs competed under a mask as the Red Pimpernel when he fought in Japan in 1966, where he fought Antonio Inoki. He continued to wrestle in the United States and Canada, where he faced Big Bill Miller, Dick the Bruiser, Ray Stevens, Whipper Billy Watson, Wilbur Snyder, Gene Kiniski, and Dory Funk, Jr., during the 1960s. He frequently teamed with Luther Lindsay, challenging the Infernos and Gene & Ole Anderson. He largely settled in North Carolina in the early 1970s where he became an early opponent for Ric Flair. He teamed with Pistol Pez Whatley to capture the NWA Western States tag belts in Amarillo, Texas, in 1976. His later opponents include Randy Savage, the Masked Superstar, Iron Mike Sharpe, Jimmy Snuka, Terry Gordy, and David Von Erich before retiring in 1981. He emerged from retirement for several months in 1983. Jacobs later managed Ricky Steamboat's gym in the Charlotte area. He also appeared as a guest at various promotions and wrestling reunions.

Jacobs, David

Television producer and writer David Jacobs, who was a creator of the prime-time soap operas "Dallas" and Knots Landing", died of complications from Alzheimer's disease in Burbank, California, on August 20, 2023. He was 84. Jacobs was born in Baltimore, Maryland, on August 12, 1939. He graduated from the Maryland Institute College of Art and moved to New York City. He aspired to be an artist but soon began writing. He received a master's degree in art history from Hunter College. He wrote biographies for "The Book of Knowledge" and articles about architecture for the magazines

"Esquire", "Holiday", and "The New York Times Magazine". He also wrote for "Newsweek" and was a story editor for "American Heritage". His first book, "Master Painters of the Renaissance", was published in 1968. He wrote the film book "Chaplin, the Movies & Charlie" in 1975. Jacobs wrote short stories for the magazines "Cosmopolitan" and "Redbooks". He

moved to Los Angeles in the mid-1970s where he began writing for television. He scripted episodes of the series "Kingston: Confidential", "Family", "Kaz", and "The Lazarus Syndrome". He was a writer and executive producer for the series "Married: The First Year", "Secrets of Midland Heights", and "Behind the Screen". Jacobs created the hit series "Dallas" in 1978 and the spin-off series "Knots Landing" in 1979. He also directed a handful of the episodes. He wrote and produced the 1986 tele-film "Dallas: The Early Years". He created the western series "Paradise" in 1988 which he also produced. He served as a producer for the 1984 mini-series "Lace" and episodes of "Berrenger's", "Bodies of Evidence", "Homefront" sharing Emmy Award nominations in 1992 and 1993, "Lois & Clark: The New Adventures of Superman", "Four Corners", and "Family Feud". He also produced the television productions "The Knots Landing Block Party" (1993), "Knots Landing: Back to the Cul-de-Sac" (1997), and "Knots Landing Reunion: Together Again" (2005). Jacobs was married to Lynn Oliansky from 1963 until their divorce in the early 1970s and is survived by their daughter, Albyn. He married Diana Jacobs in 1977 and is survived by her and their two children, Aaron and Molly.

Jacobs, Kyle

Country music singer and songwriter Kyle Jacobs, who starred with his wife on the reality series "I Love Kellie

Pickler", died from a self-inflicted gunshot wound in Nashville, Tennessee, on February 17, 2023. He was 49. Jacobs was born in Bloomington, Minnesota, on June 26, 1973. He began writing songs for Curb Music in 2003. He wrote songs on piano and guitar and was noted for co-writing Garth Brooks' 2007 hit "More Than a Memory". His songs were also recorded by such artists as Trace Adkins, Jo Dee Messina, Craig Morgan, Tim McGraw, Kelly Clarkson, and Scotty McCreery. Jacobs married country singer and American Idol contestant Kellie Pickler in January of 2011 after dating for two and a half years. He co-starred with his wife in the CMT reality show "I Love Kellie Pickler" in 2015. He is survived by Pickler.

Jaffee, Al

Cartoonist Al Jaffee, who contributed to "Mad" magazine for over 60 years, died in New York City on April 10, 2023. He was 102. He was born Abraham Jaffee in Savannah, Georgia, on March 13, 1921. He divided his time between the

United States and his parents' native Lithuania in his youth. He settled with his father in Queens, New York, in 1933. He studied at the High School of Music & Art in New York City later in the decade. He began working as an artist in comic books in 1942 for such publications as "Joker Comics". He worked at Timely Comics under Stan Lee, creating the humor features "Inferior Man" and "Ziggy Pig and Silly Seal". He served in the U.S. Army Air Force during World War II where he often served as an artist for the military. He was discharged in 1946 and returned to Timely, where he served as an editor of the label's humor and teen comics. He illustrated the "Patsy Walker" comic from 1944 to 1949. Jaffee began working for Harvey Kurtzman's "Mad" comic magazine in 1955. He followed Kurtzman to the magazines "Trump" and "Humbug" before returning to "Mad", where he remained for over half a century. He worked primarily as a writer until the early 1960s. He created the magazine's parody back cover Fold-Ins in 1964. He continued to write and draw the Fold-In features until his retirement in 2020. Jaffee created the features "Snappy Answers to Stupid Questions" in 1965, which he continued through 2015, "Don't You Hate...?" from 1967 to 1973, and "Hawks & Doves" from 1970 to 1972. His other contributions to "Mad" include parody advertisements and step-by-step guides to absurd inventions. He wrote several film and television parodies and designed a handful of covers during his career. Jaffee wrote the syndicated pantomime comic "Tall Tales" from 1957 to 1963 and scripted the newspaper comic strip "Debbie Deere" from 1966 to 1969. He created the humorous adventure comic about a Jewish inspector, "The Shpy", for "The Moshiach Times" which ran from 1984 to 2020. Jaffee received the Reuben Award for Cartoonist of the Year and Inkpot Award in 2008. He was inducted into the Will Eisner Hall of Fame in 2013 and the Society of Illustrators' Hall of Fame in 2014. He was the subject of the 2010 biography "Al Jaffee's Mad Life" by Mary-Lou Weisman, and he added illustrations for the book. Much of his work was published in collections including "Mad's Vastly Overrated Al Jaffee" (1976), "Al Jaffee's Mad Inventions" (1978), "Al Jaffee Draws a Crowd" (1978), "Good Lord! Not Another Book of Snappy Answers to Stupid Questions" (1980), "Al Jaffee Fowls His Nest" (1981), "Al Jaffee Meets Willie Weirdie" (1981), "Al Jaffee Goes Bananas" (1982), "Once Again Mad's Al Jaffee Spews Out Snappy Answers to Stupid Questions" (1987), "Al Jaffee's Mad (Yeech!) Rejects" (1990), and the four-volume "The Mad Fold-In Collection: 1964–2010" in 2011. Jaffee was married to Ruth Ahlquist from 1945 until their divorce in 1967, and is survived by their children, Richard and Debbie. He was married to Joyce Revenson from 1977 until her death in 2020.

Jakes, John

Novelist John Jakes, who was noted for the civil war trilogy "North and South", died in Sarasota, Florida, on March 11, 2023. He was 90. Jakes was born in Chicago, Illinois, on March 31, 1932. He graduated from DePauw University in Greencastle, Indiana, in 1953, and earned a master's degree from Ohio State University. He worked as a copywriter for a pharmaceutical company and advertising agencies for over a decade. He began writing stories for science fiction digests while still in college including "The Dreaming Trees" for "Fantastic Adventures" and "Your Number Is Up!" for "Amazing Stories" in 1950. He wrote numerous other science fiction short stories in the early 1950s. He was also the author of many novels, some under the pseudonyms Jay Scotland and Alan Payne, including "The Texans Ride North" (1952), "A Night for Treason" (1956), "Wear A Fast Gun" (1956), "The Devil Has Four Faces" (1958), "Murder He Says" (1958), "This'll Slay You" (1958), The Seventh Man" (1958), "I, Barbarian" (1959), "Johnny Havoc" (1960), "Strike the Black Flag" (1961), Sir Scoundrel" (1962), "Veils of Salome" (1962), "Arena" (1963), "G.I. Girls" (1963), Making It Big" (aka "Johnny Havoc and the Siren in Red") (1968), "Fortune's Whirlwind" (1975), "To an Unknown Shore" (1975), "King's Crusader" (1977), "The Man from Cannae" (1977), "Susanna of the Alamo" (1986), "California Gold" (1989), "In The Big Country" (1993), "On Secret Service" (2000), "Charleston" (2002), "Savannah or a Gift for Mr. Lincoln" (2004), "Funeral for Tanner Moody" with Elmer Kelton and Robert Randish (2004), and "The Gods of Newport" (2006). He wrote several works of non-fiction including "Famous Firsts in Sports" (1967), "Great War Correspondents" (1967), "Great Women Reporters" (1969), and "Mohawk: The Life of Joseph Brant" (1969). He wrote numerous works of fantasy and science fiction including the "Dragonard" trilogy consisting of "When the Star Kings Die" (1967), "The Planet Wizard" (1969), and "Tonight We Steal the Stars" (1969). He wrote the 1968 sword and sorcery novel "Brak the Barbarian" and the sequels "Brak vs. the Sorceress" (1969), "The Mark of the Demons" (1969), "When the Idols Walked" (1978), and "The Fortunes of Brak" (1980). The character of Gavin Black was featured in his novels "Master of the Dark Gate" (1970) and "Witch of the Dark Gate" (1972). He wrote the novelization for the film "Conquest of the Planet of the Apes" in 1972. His other science fiction and fantasy novels include "Secrets of Stardeep" (1969), "The Hybrid" (1969), "The Last Magicians" (1969), "The Asylum World" (1969), "Mask of Chaos" (1970), "Monte Cristo #99" (1970), "Six-Gun Planet" (1970), "Black in Time" (1970), "Time Gate" (1972), "Mention My Name in Atlantis" (1972), "On Wheels" (1973), and the graphic novel "Excalibur" (1980)

with artist Gil Kane. Some of his short fiction was collected in 1977's "The Best of John Jakes". He was noted for his best-selling "Kent Family Chronicles" including "The Bastard" (1974), "The Rebels" (1975), "The Seekers" (1975), "The Furies" (1976), "The Titans" (1976), "The Warriors" (1977), "The Lawless" (1978), and "The Americans" (1980). "The Bastard" and "The Rebels" were adapted for tele-films in 1978 and 1979 and starred Andrew Stevens as Philip Kent. "The Seekers" was adapted for a tele-film in 1979 and starred Randolph Mantooth as Abraham Kent. He was best known for his Civil War trilogy about two families on opposite sides that commenced with "North and South" (1982). It was adapted into a television mini-series on ABC in 1985. The sequel, "Love and War" (1984), became a mini-series in 1986, and the concluding volume, "Heaven and Hell" (1987), was adapted for a mini-series in 1994. Patrick Swayze starred as Orry Main, Kirstie Alley played Virgilia Hazard, and James Read was George Hazard. "The Crown Family Saga" consisted of a pair of books, "Homeland" (1993) and "American Dreams" (1998). He also wrote a stage adaptation of Charles Dickens' "A Christmas Carol", the was first produced in 1988. Jakes married Rachel Jakes in 1951 and is survived by her and their four children.

Jakubisko, Juraj

Slovak film director Juraj Jakubisko died in Prague, Czech Republic, on February 24, 2023. He was 84. Jakubisko was born in Kojsov, Czechoslovakia (now Slovakia), on April 30, 1938. He studied still photography in Bratislava and worked for a television company in Kosice before pursuing a film career. He moved to Prague in 1960 and attended the Film and TV School of the Academy of Performing Arts (FAMU). He began working with the Laterna Magika theatre in Prague after graduating in 1965. He directed several experimental short films in the early 1960s including "Last Attack" (1960), "Every Day Has a Name" (1960), "Silver Wind" (1961), "First Class" (1962), "Silence" (1963), "Rain" (1965), and "Waiting for Godot" (1965). He made his feature debut in 1967 with "Crucial Years" ("Kristove Roky"). He followed with the films "The Deserters and the Nomads" (1968), "Birds, Orphans and Fools" (1969), and "See You in Hell, Friends" (1970) which remained unreleased until 1990. His career was interrupted following the Warsaw Pact invasion of Czechoslovakia in 1969 to halt the liberal reforms initiated by Alexander Dubcek. Jakubisko primarily made documentaries in the 1970s including "The Construction of the Century" (1972), "Slovakia - A Country Under the Tatras" (1975), "The Red Cross Drummer" (1977), and "Three Bags of Cement and a Live Rooster" (1979). He directed the children's fantasy "Painted on Wood" for television in 1979. He resumed making feature films with 1980's "Build a House, Plant a Tree". He earned international acclaim for his 1983 film "The Millennial

Bee". He continued to direct and often write such films as "The Feather Fairy" (1985), "Freckled Max and the Spooks" (1987), "Frankenstein's Aunt" (1987), "Sitting on a Branch, Enjoying Myself" (1989), "It's Better to Be Wealthy and Healthy Than Poor and Ill" (1992), "An Ambiguous Report About the End of the Worl" (1997), "Post Coitum" (2004), "Bathory: Countess of Blood" (2008), and "Perinbaba 2 A Dva Svety" (2023). He also began teaching at FAMU in 2001. Jakubisko's autobiography, "Zive Stribro", was published in 2013. He married actress Deana Horvathova in 1985 and she survives him.

Jamal, Ahmad

Jazz pianist and composer Ahmad Jamal died from complications of prostate cancer at his home in Ashley Falls, Massachusetts, on April 16, 2023. He was 92. He was born Frederick Russell Jones in Pittsburgh, Pennsylvania, on July 2, 1930.

He began playing piano as a child and performed professionally from his early teens. He began touring with George Hudson's Orchestra after graduating high school in 1948. He also performed with the Four Strings until moving to Chicago in 1950. He converted to Islam and changed his name to Ahmad Jamal. He performed at local venues and made his recording debut 1951 with the Ahmad Jamal Trio, who were also known as the Three Strings. The trio included Jamal, guitarist Ray Crawford, and a changing lineup of bassists including Eddie Calhoun, Richard Davis, and Israel Crosby. Crawford was replaced by drummer Vernel Fournier in 1957 and the new trio had success with the jazz album "At the Pershing: But Not for Me" in 1958, featuring the hit song "Poinciana". The trio disbanded in 1962 and Jamal recorded the album "Macanudo" with a full orchestra. He moved to New York in 1964 where he performed and recorded with bassist Jamil S. Nasser. He released an instrumental recording of the song "Suicide Is Painless" from the 1970 film "MASH". He continued to perform with various trios over the next two decades. His later recordings include "Saturday Morning" (2013), "Ahmad Jamal Featuring Yusef Lateef Live at L'Olympia" (2014), "Marseille" (2017), and "Ballades" (2019). He received the Grammy Lifetime Achievement Award in 2017. He was married to Virginia Wilkins (Maryam Jamal) from 1947 until their divorce in 1962. Their daughter, Mumeenah, predeceased him in 1979. He married Sharifah Frazier in the early 1960s and they divorced in 1982. He is survived by their daughter, Sumayah Jamal. He was briefly married to his manager, Laura Hess-Hay, from 1982 until their divorce in 1984.

James, Judith

Producer Judith James, who worked frequently with actor Richard Dreyfuss, died of cancer at her home in Santa Barbara, California, on July 14, 2023. She was 86. She was born Judith Rutherford in Worcester, Massachusetts, in 1937.

She graduated from Vassar College in 1959 and moved to New York City to pursue a career in acting. She was producer of the pioneering interracial off-Broadway play "In White America" in 1963 and earned a Drama Desk award. She worked with Richard Dreyfuss on the 1987 television special "Funny, You Don't Look 200: A Constitutional Vaudeville". They worked

together frequently over the next 35 years. James produced Lee Remick's one-woman show about Eleanor Roosevelt, "Eleanor: In Her Own Words", for American Playhouse in 1987. She was also a producer for the tele-films "The Brotherhood of Justice" (1986), "Daniel and the Towers" (1987), "Prisoner of Honor" (1991), and "Kissinger and Nixon" (1995). She worked with Dreyfuss on the films "Quiz Show" (1994), "Mr. Holland's Opus" (1995), "Mad Dog Time" (1996), and "The Lightkeepers" (2009). She co-produced the play "Having Our Say: The Delaney Sisters' First 100 Years", which was adapted for a tele-film in 1999. James was married to personal manager and music publicist Billy James from the 1960s until their divorce in 1982, and is survived by their son, Jackson James.

James, Stu

Singer Stu James, who performed with the band the Mojos in the 1960s, died in England on May 10, 2023. He was 77. He was born Stuart Slater in Liverpool, England, on July 14, 1945. He attended the Liverpool Institute of Performing

Arts in the early 1960s and formed his own band, Penny Lane. He joined Keith Karlson and John 'Bob' Conrad in the Nomads, serving as pianist and lead singer in 1962. Guitarist and vocalist Adrian Lord and pianist Terry O'Toole also joined the band, which became known as the Mojos in 1963. He co-wrote the Mojos 1964 hit song "Everything's Alright" and the band had success with the singles "Why Not Tonight" and "Seven Daffodils". The Mojos underwent lineup changes with James leading several subsequent variations of the band until 1967. James resumed his education after leaving the Mojos, earning a law degree from London University. He began working at the CBS record label in London before becoming general manager at Bradley's Records in Mayfair. He also worked at ATV Music in A&R (artists and repertoire) and publishing and joined Chrysalis in 1978. He signed such artists as Spandau Ballet, the Proclaimers, and Living in a Box. He joined Mega Records, a Danish independent dance label, in 1994 and lead their London operation. He later headed up Virgin Publishing. James married Jeanette Ross in 1965 and they later divorced. He is survived by their daughter Tracy. He lived with singer Stephanie De Sykes in the 1970s and is survived by their son, Barnaby. Another son, Toby, died in 2021. He married Andrea Witty in 1986 and she also survives him.

Jarrett, Jerry

Professional wrestler and promoter Jerry Jarrett died of a heart attack and complications of esophageal cancer in Tennessee on February 14, 2023. He was 80. Jarrett was born in Nashville, Tennessee, on September 4, 1942. His mother,

Christine 'Teeny' Jarrett, began working for the NWA Mid-America wrestling promotion in Nashville as a ticket seller when Jerry was a child. She was given more responsibility by promoters Nick Gulas and Roy Welch and was promoting shows herself in Indiana and Kentucky by the early 1970s. Jerry worked with his mother selling programs for wrestling events at the age of seven. He worked as a promoter for the company in his teens before going to Peabody College. He graduated in 1963 and worked as a purchasing agent at the Murray Ohio Manufacturing Company for four years. He returned to work as an office assistant and referee for Welch and Gulas in the mid-1960s. He was trained by Tojo Yamamoto and Sailor Moran to wrestle himself and made his ring debut in 1965. He soon began teaming with Yamamoto. They held the NWA Southern Tag Team Championship seven times with Yamamoto and eight times with Jackie Fargo. Jarrett broke with Gulas, who was based in Nashville, in 1977, and began a rival promotion, Continental (later Championship) Wrestling Association (CWA) for the Memphis area. He was partnered with the wrestling headliner, Jerry Lawler, in his endeavor. Gulas folded his remaining territory in 1980 and Jarrett took over much of the Nashville area. He continued to wrestle and held the first CWA World Tag Team Championship with Yamamoto in July of 1980. They lost the belts the following month to Austin Idol and Dutch Mantel. He retired from the ring in 1988 but made occasional returns in the mid-1990s. Jarrett merged the CWA with World Class Championship Wrestling (WCCW) to form the United States Wrestling Association (USWA) in 1989. The WCCW withdrew the following year and the USWA worked with the World Wrestling Federation (WWF/now WWE) with a talent exchange program in 1992. The promotion began a decline and Jarrett sold his part of the USWA to Jerry Lawler and Larry Burton before it folded in 1997. Jarrett served as a consultant with World Championship Wrestling (WCW) and the WWF through the early 2000s. He and his son, leading wrestler Jeff Jarrett, formed a new professional wrestling promotion, Total Nonstop Action Wrestling (TNA), in 2002. TNA was soon sold to Panda Energy with Dixie Carter becoming president of the organization. Jarrett remained involved in management until leaving the promotion in late-2005. He later owned a construction company and a television distribution company. Jarrett is survived by his wife of 51 years, Deborah Marlin, the son of wrestler and promoter Eddie Marlin. He is also survived by sons Jerry Jr., Jeff, and Jason. He was predeceased by daughter Jennifer Jarrett Anderson in 2021.

Jarvi-Laturi, Ilkka

Finnish film director Ilkka Jarvi-Laturi died in Padasjoki, Finland, on March 5, 2023. He was 61. Jarvi-Laturi was born in Valkeakoski, Finland, on November 28, 1961. He began writing and directing short films in the 1980s including

"Arsenic and Old Penises" (1983), "Papa and the Radio" (1985), "Come with Us" (1986), "Kenkaa Korjaamassa" (1986), "Muuan Yo" (1986), and "Kaasari" (1989). He was an actor in several films including "Angela's War" (1984), "The Unknown Soldier" (1985) also serving as assistant director, "The Last Season" (1986), "Lumberjacking" (1988), and "The Winter War" (1989). Jarvi-Laturi helmed the features "Kotia Pain" ("Homebound") (1989) and "Darkness in Tallinn" (1993). He was best known for directing the 1999 thriller "Spy Games" (aka "History Is Made at Night") starring Bill Pullman.

Jasper, Zina

Actress Zina Jasper died in New York City on June 8, 2023. She was 84. Jasper was born in the Bronx, New York,

on January 29, 1939. She trained as an actress under Stella Adler and Harold Clurman and began her career on the New York stage. She appeared on Broadway in productions of "Something Different" (1967), "Paris Is Out!" (1970), and "A Doll's House" (1975). Jasper appeared in several films including "Death Play" (1976) and Woody Allen's "Crimes and Misdemeanors" (1989). She was seen on television in episodes of "Visions" and "Law & Order". She began teaching acting in 1983 and remained an acting coach throughout her career. Jasper was married to actor and director Burt Brinckerhoff from 1959 until their divorce in 1986.

Jay, Kenny

Professional wrestler Kenneth John Benkowski, who competed in the ring under the name Kenny Jay, died in Bloomington, Minnesota, on February 2, 2023. He was 85. Benkowski was born in Holdingford, Minnesota, on March 27, 1937. He graduated from high school in 1955 and moved to Milwaukee, Wisconsin, to work in a factory. He made his wrestling debut in 1958 and was soon competing in the Chicago area. He spent two years in the U.S. Army before resuming his wrestling career with the American Wrestling Association (AWA). He was primarily used as a jobber, losing matches to wrestlers when they came into the area. His opponents included Jesse Ventura, Mad Dog Vachon, Jerry Blackwell, and Bruiser Brody. He lost a boxer vs. wrestler match against Muhammad

Ali in 1976. He owned and operated a landscaping business when not wrestling and became known as the Sodbuster. He teamed with wrestlers George Gadaski and Baron Von Raschke in the late 1970s and early 1980s. He remained with the AWA until they went out of business in 1991. He continued to make occasional ring appearances with independent promotions in the Midwest until his retirement in 2012. Jay is survived by his wife of 59 years, Diane, and three children.

Jefferson, Keith

Actor Keith Jefferson, who was featured in Quentin Tarantino's films "Django Unchained" and "The Hateful Eight", died of cancer at a hospital in Santa Monica, California, on

October 5, 2023. He was 53. Jefferson was born in Houston, Texas, on April 7, 1970. He studied musical theater at U.S. International in San Diego and earned a master's degree in acting from the University of Arizona. He made his film debut in 1995's "Boys on the Side". He was friends with actor Jamie Foxx from college and appeared in several episodes of "The Jamie Foxx Show" on television in 1998 and 1999. Jefferson was also seen in the tele-films "Buffalo Soldiers" (1997), "Murder, She Wrote: The Last Free Man" (2001), and "Hip Hop Family Christmas Wedding" (2022), and episodes of "Relative Opposites", "Dad Stop Embarrassing Me!", and "Bosch: Legacy". He appeared in small roles in the films "Tank Girl" (1995) and "The Fantasticks" (2000). He was featured as Pudby Ralph in Quentin Tarantino's western "Django Unchained" starring Jamie Foxx in 2012. He was also seen in Tarantino's films "The Hateful Eight" (2015) and "Once Upon a Time in Hollywood" (2019). Jefferson's later films include "Day Shift" (2022), "Hot Take: The Depp/Heard Trial" (2022), and "The Burial" (2023) again reuniting with Foxx. He performed frequently on stage with touring and regional theaters.

Jivkov, Christo

Bulgarian actor Christo Jivkov (Hristo Zhivkov), who was featured as John the Apostle in Mel Gibson's 2004 biblical epic "The Passion of the Christ", died of cancer in Los Angeles, California, on April 1, 2023. He was 48. Jivkov was born in Sofia, Bulgaria, on February 18, 1975. He studied film directing at the Bulgarian Film and Theater Academy. He began his film career as an actor in the late 1990s with roles in "Sulamit" (1997), the Italian historical drama "The Profession

of Arms" (2001) as Giovanni de Medici, "Pechalbata" (2001), "The Good War" (2002), Mel Gibson's "The Passion of the

Christ" (2004) as John, "Occhi di Cristallo" (2004), "The Final Inquiry" (2006), "In Memory of Me" (2007), "La Masseria Delle Allodole" (2007), "The Counting House" (2007), "David's Birthday" (2009), "Sword of War" (2009), "Fly Light" (2009), "La Soluzione Migliore" (2011), "The Invisible Boy" (2014), "Lucania" (2019), and "De Sable et de Feu" (2019). Zhivkov appeared on television in productions of "Ostatazi" (1999), "Mafalda of Savoy" (2006), "Fuga per la Liberta - L'Aviatore" (2008), "Bread and Freedom" (2009), "La Figlia del Capitano" (2012), and "Segreti del Mestiere" (2019). He served as an assistant director for the films "Druids" (2001) and "Pechalbata" (2001) and the 2002 television mini-series "Caesar".

Joaquin, Jaymee

Filipino actress and model Jaymee Joaquin died of cancer in California on October 18, 2023. She was 44. She was born Jaymee Geronimo Tapacio in San Juan, Philippines, on July 27, 1979. She began her career as a model before

appearing in films and television in the early 2000s. She became game show anchor of the daily series "Games Uplate Live" in 2006. she was also seen on television in the series "Bora: Sons of the Beach", "Super Ingggo 1.5: Ang Bagong Bangis", "Ligaw No Bulaklak", and "Parekoy". Joaquin appeared in the films "Kutob" (2005), "A Love Story" (2007), "Shake, Rattle & Roll 9" (2007), "My Big Love" (2008), "Walong Linggo" (2008), and "The Only Mother to You All" (2008). She left acting to teach communications in Sydney, Australia, for two years from 2010. She taught English in Madrid, Spain, for four years. Joaquin moved to San Diego, California in 2015 to work in the hotel industry. She was diagnosed with breast cancer in 2016 and documented her treatment on social media as "Jaymee Wins". She began the podcast "WIN Your Daily Battles" in 2020 and published the book "That Sh*t Called Cancer. She released the children's picture book "No-Hair Mama, Don't Care" in 2022 to help mothers explain chemotherapy treatments to their children.

Joassin, Pierre

Belgian film director Pierre Joassin died in Belgium on January 4, 2023. He was 74. Joassin was born in Amay, Belgium, on August 6, 1948. He began working in films in the early 1970s as an assistant editor on the horror film "Devil's Nightmare" (1971). He was editor for "La Chambre Rouge"

(1972), "Belle" (1973), and "Isabelle and Lust" (1975). He wrote Jean-Marie Degesves' 1976 film "Du Bout des Levres"

and wrote and directed "Gros Coeurs" (1987). Joassin worked frequently in television, directing productions of "Minitrip" (1981), "Une Folie" (1995), "Folle de Moi" (1996), "Un Fille a Papas" (1986), "Mon Amour" (1997), "Un Amour de Cousine" (1998), "La Tribu de Zoe" (2000), "A Taxi Romance" (2005), "8 on a Beach Chair" (2006), "Une Ombre Derriere la Porte" (2008), "Mother at 40" (2010), and "Who's the Boss Now?" (2011). His other television credits include episodes of "C'est Mon Histoire", "Cordier and Son: Judge and Cop", "Josephine, Ange Gardien", "Crimes en Serie", "Maigret", "A Tort ou a Raison", and "Sauveur Giordano".

Johnson, Coslough

Television writer and producer Coslough Johnson, who worked with his brother Artie Johnson on "Rowan & Martin's Laugh-In", died of prostate cancer in Thousand Oaks,

California, on March 23, 2023. He was 94. Johnson was born in Chicago, Illinois, on November 8, 1931. He attended the University of Illinois and served in the U.S. Air Force during the Korean War. He joined his older brother, Arte Johnson, in New York City where he wrote jokes for nightclub comics. He subsequently moved to Los Angeles where he worked on industrial films for Hughes Aircraft and Douglas Aircraft. He began writing for television in 1966, penning episodes of "Bewitched", "The Monkees", and "That Girl". He also wrote television specials for such stars as Dinah Shore, Jerry Reed, Ben Vereen, Monty Hall, and John Byner. He worked with his brother as a writer for "Rowan & Martin's Laugh-In" from 1968 to 1970. He also wrote for "The Sonny & Cher Comedy Hour" from 1971 to 1974 and "The Sonny and Cher Show" from 1976 to 1977. He wrote the 1971 film "Bunny O'Hare" starring Bette Davis. Johnson wrote the 1971 tele-film "Li'l Abner" (1971) and scripted episodes of "The Partridge Family", "The Glen Campbell Goodtime Hour", "The Hudson Brothers Razzle Dazzle Show" which he also produced in 1974, "Good Times", "CPO Sharkey", "Operation Petticoat", "The Mary Tyler Moore Hour", "Flo", and "Rocky Road". He worked primarily in cartoons from the late 1970s, writing for "The New Adventures of Mighty Mouse and Heckle and Jeckle", "Sport Billy", "The Tom and Jerry Comedy Show", "Hero High", "The Kid Super Power Hour with Shazam!", "He-Man and the Masters of the Universe", "Voltron: Defenders of the Universe", "The Flintstone Kids", "She-Ra: Princess of Power", and "BraveStarr". Johnson co-wrote the 1986 children's book

"American Rabbit: The Case of the Missing Moose". He married Mary Jane Ferguson in 1975 and she survives him.

Johnson, Meg

British actress Meg Johnson, who starred as Pearl Ladderbanks on the ITV television soap opera "Emmerdale" from 2003 to 2020, died of complications from dementia in Lancashire, England, on July 1, 2023. She was 86. Johnson was born in Manchester, Lancashire, on September 30, 1936.

She began her career on television in the early 1960s. She was seen in episodes of such series as "Family Solicitor" as Mary Carslake in 1961, "Comedy Playhouse", "Here's Harry", "Country Matters", "Nearest and Dearest", "How's Your Father?", "The Life of Riley", "Play for Today", "Yanks Go Home", "Two Up, Two Down", "Mother Nature's Bloomers", "Empire Road" as Mrs. Ridley from 1978 to 1979, "Watch All Night", "Strangers", "The Good Companions", "The Olympian Way", "The Practice", "Victoria Wood: As Seen on TV", "Split Ends", "Victoria Wood", "Taggart", "Lovejoy", "Chris Cross", "The Wild House", "Rab C. Nesbitt", "Peak Practice", and "The Thing About Vince", Johnson was best known for her roles on soap operas. She was featured as Brenda Holden in "Coronation Street" in 1976 and was Eunice Nuttall Gee from 1981 to 1982 and again in 1999. She starred as Brigid McKenna on "Brookside" from 2000 to 2003 and was Pearl Ladderbanks" on "Emmerdale" from 2003 to 2020. Johnson was married to actor and television host Charles Foster from 1981 until his death in February of 2023.

Johnson, Pat E.

Martial artist and stuntman Pat E. Johnson died in Los Angeles, California, on November 5, 2023. He was 84. Johnson was born in Niagara Falls, New York, in 1939. He served as a chaplain in the U.S. Army and was stationed in

South Korea in the early 1960s. He began studying the Korean martial art Tang Soo Do, earning a black belt. He began working with Chuck Norris after his discharge and became an instructor at his Tang Soo Do school in Sherman Oaks, California, in 1968. He was captain of Norris' black belt competition team from 1968 to 1973 and earned 33 national and international titles. He originated the penalty point system used in karate tournaments in 1968. He was National Tang Soo Do Champion in 1971. He became executive vice president of chief instructor of the National Tang Soo Do Congress (NTC), which was founded by Norris in 1973. Norris created the United Fighting Arts Federation (UFAF) in 1979 with Johnson remaining executive vice president. He left the UFAF in 1986 and reformed the National Tang So Do Congress. He worked frequently in films from the early 1970s, serving as a stuntman, fight choreographer, and actor in small roles. Johnson's films include "Enter the Dragon" (1973), "Golden Needles" (1974), "Black Belt Jones" (1974), "The Ultimate Warrior" (1975), "Hot Potato" (1976), "Good Guys Wear Black" (1978), "Teheran Incident" (1979), "A Force of One" (1979) which he also wrote, "The Little Dragons" (1979), "Tom Horn" (1980), "The Hunter" (1980), "Battle Creek Brawl" (1980), "Force: Five" (1981), and "To Live and Die in L.A." (1985). He was featured as a referee in the films "The Karate Kid" (1984), "The Karate Kid Part II" (1986), "The Karate Kid Part III" (1989). His other films include "Teenage Mutant Ninja Turtles" (1990), "Teenage Mutant Ninja Turtles II: The Secret of the Ooze" (1991), "Showdown in Little Tokyo" (1991), "Buffy the Vampire Slayer" (1992), "Shootfighter: Fight to the Death" (1993), "Teenage Mutant Ninja Turtles III" (1993), "The Next Karate Kid" (1994), "Mortal Kombat" (1995), "Batman & Robin" (1997), "Mortal Kombat: Annihilation" (1997) also serving as second unit director, "Wild Wild West" (1999), "Militia" (2000), "Impostor" (2001), "They Crawl" (2001), the short "Johnny Flynton" (2002), "Scorcher" (2002), "Green Street Hooligans" (2005), "Wheelman" (2005), and "Punisher: War Zone" (2008). Johnson worked on television in the tele-films "The Last Ninja" (1983), "C.A.T. Squad" (1986), "C.A.T. Squad: Python Wolf" (1988), and "Project Viper" (2002), and episodes of "La Femme Musketeer" and "Rush Hour" (2016). He is survived by his wife of over fifty years, Sue, and four sons.

Johnson, Tom

Film historian Tom Johnson died of a stroke in Hershey, Pennsylvania, on July 11, 2023. He was 75. Johnson  was born in West Reading, Pennsylvania, on November 22, 1947. Johnson wrote the books "Peter Cushing: The Gentle Man of Horror and His 91 Films" (1992), "Hammer Films: An Exhaustive Filmography" (1996), and "Censored Screams: The British Ban on Hollywood Horror in the Thirties" (1997) for McFarland & Co. He co-wrote 1996's "The Christopher Lee Filmography" with Mark A. Miller, and the books "The Mummy in Fact, Fiction and Film" (2002) and "The Films of Oliver Reed" (2011) with Susan D. Cowie. Johnson appeared in the 2012 video documentary "Christopher Lee: A Legacy of Horror and Terror". His articles about film were also seen in numerous magazines and fanzines. Johnson also worked as a high school track coach in Pennsylvania.

Johnstone, Iain

British television producer and author Iain Johnstone died in England on May 4, 2023. He was 80. Johnstone was born in Reading, Berkshire, England, on April 8, 1943. He was educated at Campbell College, Belfast, and Bristol University, where he studied law and graduated in 1965. He was the film critic for "The Sunday Times" for over a decade. He was a  regular host on the series "Film '82" through "Film '84". He produced such television series as "Ask Aspel", "Points of View", "On Location", and "The Frost Interview". He hosted the BBC Radio 4 quiz show "Screenplay" from the late 1980s to the early 1990s. He directed numerous documentaries about film including "Jaws: From the Set" (1974), "The Making of Superman: The Movie" (1980), "Snowdon on Camera" (1981), "The Making of Superman II" (1982), "The Meaning of Monty Python's Meaning of Life" (1983), "The Making of Superman III" (1984), "Santa Claus: The Making of the Movie" (1985), and "Waging the War of the Worlds: From H.G. Wells to Steven Spielberg" (2005). Johnston co-wrote the 1997 film "Fierce Creatures" with John Cleese. He also wrote over a dozen books about films and filmmakers including "The Arnhem Report: The Story Behind A Bridge Too Far" (1977), "The Man with No Name: Clint Eastwood" (1981), "Dustin Hoffman" (1984), "The World Is Not Enough: A Companion" (1999), "Streep: A Life in Film" (2011), "Tom Cruise: All the World's a Stage" (2014), and "Close Encounters: A Media Memoir" (2015). He penned several novels including "Cannes: The Novel" (1990), the thriller "Wimbledon" (2000), and "Pirates of the Mediterranean" (2010). He was briefly married to Renate Kohler. Johnstone married script supervisor Maureen Watson in 1980 and is survived by her and three children.

Jolicoeur, David

Rapper David 'Trugoy the Dove' Jolicoeur, who performed with the hip hop trio De La Soul, died of congestive heart failure on February 12, 2023. He was 54. Jolicoeur was  born in New York City on September 21, 1968, and was raised in East Massapequa on Long Island. He and high school friends Kelvin 'Posdnuos' Mercer and Vincent 'Maseo' Mason formed the hip hop group De La Soul in 1988. They recorded their debut album, "3 Feet High and Rising", in 1989. They became part of the Native Tongues Posse and had a hit with the single "Me Myself and I". Their next album, "De La Soul Is Dead" (1991), featured the singles "Millie Pulled a Pistol on Santa" and "Ring Ring Ring (Ha Ha Hey)". De La Soul continued to record such albums as "Buhloone Mindstate" (1993), "Stakes Is High" (1996), "Art Official Intelligence: Mosaic Thump" (2000), "AOI: Bionic" (2001), and "The Grand Date" (2004). They received a Grammy Award for Best Pop Collaboration for the song "Feel Good Inc." with Gorillaz in 2006. They performed on television in such series as "House of Style", "Unplugged", "Top of the Pops", "Soul Train", "Late Night with Conan O'Brien", "Last Call with Carson Daly", "Chappelle's Show", "Tavis Smiley", "Late Night with Jimmy Fallon", "The One Show", "Jimmy Kimmel Live", "The Tonight Show Starring Jimmy Fallon", and "The Late Show with Stephen Colbert". Their later albums include "Plug 1 & Plug 2 Present... First Serve" (2012) and "And the Anonymous Nobody..." (2016). Jolicoeur and his bandmates voiced animated versions of themselves in the "Teen Titans Go!" episode "Don't Press Play" in 2021. He revealed that he suffered from congestive heart failure in November of 2017 which limited his touring and performing with the trio.

Jolls, Tom

Television personality Tom Jolls, who was host of the New York children's series "The Commander Tom Show", died at his home in Cheektowaga, New York, on June 7, 2023.

He was 89. Jolls was born in Newfane, New York, on August 16, 1933. He worked at WUSJ radio in Lockport, New York, from 1951 to 1962. He briefly appeared on WBES-TV in 1953 and later moved to Buffalo to work at WBEN-TV. He moved to WKBW-TV in 1965 where he became the evening weatherman. He also became known as Captain Tom while hosting the local airing of "Adventures of Superman" on weekday afternoons. He soon gained a promotion and his own show, "The Commander Tom Show", in December of 1965. He introduced his own puppets to the show including Dustmop the dog, alligator Matty the Mod, and Cecily Fripple. Superman was replaced of other series in the early 1970s including "Little Rascals", "Batman", "The Three Stooges", and "The Munsters". Commander Tom also introduced cartoons including "Merrie Melodies", "Looney Tunes", "Touche Turtle", "Peter Potamus", and "Davey and Goliath". Jolls' series became known as "Commander Tom's World" and aired on the weekends before its cancellation in 1991. He briefly resurrected Commander Tom in a recurring role in the morning children's show "Rocketship 7" in 1992. He remained WKBW's weatherman until his retirement in 1998. Jolls was inducted into the New York State Broadcasters Association Hall of Fame in 2019. He is survived by his wife of 68 years, Janice Cronkhite, three daughters, and three sons.

Jones, Andrew

Welsh filmmaker Andrew Jones, whose low-budget horror films include "Werewolves of the Third Reich" and the "Robert the Doll" series, died in Wales on January 15, 2023. He was 39. Jones was born in Swansea, Wales, on October 6, 1983. He attended the University of Glamorgan. He began making low-budget independent films in the early 2000s. He was founder of the British production company North Bank Entertainment. Jones produced, directed, and wrote such horror

films as "Teenage Wasteland" (2006), "The Feral Generation" (2007), "The Amityville Asylum" (2013), "The Midnight Horror Show" (2014), "Valley of the Witch" (2014), "The Last House on Cemetery Lane" (2015), "A Haunting at the Rectory" (2015), "Poltergeist Activity" (2015), "The Exorcism of Anna Ecklund" (2016), "Cabin 28" (2017), "Werewolves of the Third Reich" (2017), "Jurassic Predator" (2018), "The Legend of Halloween Jack" (2018), "Alcatraz" (2018), "D-Day Assassins" (2019), "Bundy and the Green River Killer" (2019), "The Manson Family Massacre" (2019), "The Utah Cabin Murders" (2019), "The Curse of Halloween Jack" (2019), "The Jonestown Haunting" (2020), "A Killer Next Door" (2020), "The Haunting of Margam Castle" (2020), and "Alien: Battlefield Earth" (2021). He was best known for his "Robert the Doll" film series that began with 2015's "Robert" and includes "The Curse of Robert the Doll" (2016), "Robert and the Toymaker" (2017), "The Revenge of Robert the Doll" (2018), and "Robert Reborn" (2019). Jones also produced and wrote the films "Night of the Living Dead: Resurrection" (2012), "Silent Night, Bloody Night: The Homecoming" (2013), "Kill Kane" (2016), "Horror Express" (2022), and "Ed Gein: American Psycho" (2022). He married artist and filmmaker Sharron Jones in 2012 and she survives him.

Jones, Cedric D.

Actor Cedric D. Jones died in California on October 16, 2023. He was 46. Jones was homeless in Compton,

California, before making his mark in Hollywood as a personal trainer and actor. He became friends with actor Chris Pratt and appeared with him in the films "The Magnificent Seven" (2016) and "The Terminal List" (2023). He was also seen in the short films "Marshall County" (2013) and "Hold'em" (2017) and the features "Southpaw" (2015), "Fight Your Way Out" (2017), "Princess of the Row" (2019), and "Emancipation" (2022). Jones was founder of the Beastie Boxing gym and the BMoved Foundation, which was designed to help people in need. He is survived by his wife and three children.

Jones, Evan

Jamaican-British screenwriter Evan Jones, who scripted the films "These Are the Damned" and "Modesty Blaise", died in England on April 18, 2023. He was 95. Jones was born in Portland, Jamaica, on December 29, 1927. He attended boarding school at Munro College in St. Elizabeth and attended Haverford College in Pennsylvania. He went to the Gaza Strip in Palestine in 1949 to help organize refugee camps with the American Friends Service Committee. He graduated

from Wadham College, Oxford, in England in 1952 and taught at the George School in Pennsylvania and Wesleyan University in Connecticut. He settled in England in 1956 where he began working in films and television. His first teleplay, "The Widows of Jaffa", aired on the BBC and was inspired by his work in Gaza. He also wrote such television productions as "In a Backward Country" (1958), "Madhouse on Castle Street" (1963), "Old Man's Fancy" (1965), "Go Tell It on Table Mountain" (1967), the mini-series "The Fight Against Slavery" (1975), "The Mind Beyond: The Man with the Power" (1976), "Rehearsal" (1977), "The Dick Francis Thriller: Gambling Lady" (1979), and "A Curious Suicide" for "Chillers" in 1990. He also scripted episodes of "Jezebel ex UK", "Full House", and "Away from It All". Jones wrote several films for director Joseph Losey including "Eva" (1962), "The Damned" (aka "These Are the Damned") (1963), "King & Country" (1964), and cult classic "Modesty Blaise" (1966). His other films include the spy thriller "Funeral in Berlin" (1966), "Two Gentlemen Sharing" (1969), "Wake in Fright" (1971), "Night Watch" (1973), "Ghost in the Noonday Sun" (1974), "Victory" (1981), "The Killing of Angel Street" (1981), "Champions" (1984), "Kangaroo" (1986), "A Show of Force" (1990), and "Shadow of the Wolf" (1992). Jones was noted for his poems, "The Song of the Banana Man" (1956) and "Lament of the Banana Man" (1956). He also wrote text books and novels for children including "Protector of the Indians" (1958), "Tales of the Caribbean: Anansi Stories" (1984), Tales of the Caribbean: Witches and Duppies" (1984), "Tales of the Caribbean: The Beginning of Things" (1984), "Skylarking" (1993), "Stonehaven" (1993), "Alonso and the Drug Barron" (2006), and A Poem For Every Day of the Year" (2017). He is survived by his wife, actress Joanna Vogel, and two daughters, novelists Melissa and Sadie.

Jones, Ron Cephus

Actor Ron Cephus Jones, who received two Emmy Awards for his role as William Hill in the drama series "This Is Us", died after a long battle with chronic obstructive pulmonary disease (COPD) in Los Angeles, California, on August 19, 2023. He was 66. Jones was born in Paterson, New Jersey, on January 8, 1957. He graduated from Ramapo College in 1978 where he studied on stage and performed on stage. He moved to subsequently moved to Los Angeles where he worked as a bus driver. His acting career became stalled after developing a heroin addiction. He traveled around before returning to New York City in 1985. He overcame his addiction and starred in his first play, "Don't Explain", at the Nuyorican Poets Cafe in Manhattan in 1990. He appeared in the starring role in

Shakespeare's "Richard III" at the Public Theater and was acted in productions with the Steppenwolf Theatre Company in Chicago. He was seen in several other Off-Broadway plays and was an understudy for Broadway productions of "Gem of the Ocean" (2004) and "The Motherfucker with the Hat" (2011). He was seen in the Broadway plays "Of Mice and Men" (2014) and "Clyde's" (2021) receiving a Tony Award nomination for his role as Montrellous. Jones appeared in such films as "Murder Magic" (1994), "Naked Acts" (1996), "He Got Game" (1998), "A Day in Black and White" (199), "Sweet and Lowdown" (1999), "Little Senegal" (2000), "Paid in Full"

(2002), "Carlito's Way: Rise to Power" (2005), "Preaching to the Choir" (2005), "Half Nelson" (2006), "Across the Universe" (2007), "Ashes" (2010), "Watching TV with the Red Chinese" (2012), "Titus" (2013), "Of Mice and Men" (2014), "Glass Chin" (2014), "Dog Days" (2018), "Venom" (2018), "The Holiday Calendar" (2018), and "Dolemite Is My Name" (2019). He was seen on television in episodes of "New York Undercover", "Law & Order", "NYPD Blue", "Law & Order: Criminal Intent", "NYC 22", "Low Winter Sun" as Reverend Lowdown in 2013, "The Blacklist", "Banshee", the animated "Amphibia", "Better Things", and "Law & Order: Organized Crime". He also appeared in the tele-films "Double Platinum" (1999), "Word of Honor" (2003), and "A Raisin in the Sun" (2008). Jones was featured as Romero on the television series "Mr. Robot" from 2015 to 2016 and was Winston Kipling in "The Get Down" from 2016 to 2017. He was chess-playing Bobby Fish in the Netflix Marvel superhero series "Luke Cage" from 2016 to 2018 and was featured in the mini-series "Looking for Alaska" (2019) and "Lisey's Story" (2021). He appeared as William Hill, a former drug addict with terminal cancer, on the NBC series "This Is Us", receiving four Emmy Award nominations and winning for his guest performances in 2018 and 2020. Jones was featured as Leander 'Shreve' Scoville in "Truth Be Told" from 2019 to 2023 and completed the role of Elijah Muhammad in the upcoming series "Genius: MLK/X". He suffered with COPD for many years and underwent a double-lung transplant in 2020. His survivors include a daughter with jazz singer Kim Lesley, Emmy Award-winning actress Jasmine Cephas Jones.

Jones, Tom

Lyricist Tom Jones, who was noted for the hit Off-Broadway musical "The Fantasticks", died of cancer in Sharon, Connecticut, on August 11, 2023. He was 95. Jones was born in Littlefield, Texas, on February 17, 1928. He attended the University of Texas at Austin, graduating in 1951, and was active in the theater department. Jones moved to New York after serving in the military during the Korean War. He was contributor to several Julius Monk revues including "Shoestring '57" (1957) and "Demi-Dozen" (1958). He and his longtime collaborator, composer Harvey Shmidt, who he had met in college created the musical allegory "The Fantasticks". The musical opened in Greenwich Village in 1962 and ran off-Broadway for 42 years until 2002, with over 17,000  performances. It was the longest-running musical in U.S. history and included such popular songs as "Try to Remember" and "Soon It's Gonna Rain". Jones appeared in the play as Henry, the Old Actor. He and Schmidt won the Drama Desk Vernon Rice Award for "The Fantasticks" in 1961. The musical was aired on television on "Hallmark Hall of Fame" in 1964 and Michael Ritchie directed a film version in 1995. A revival of "The Fantasticks" ran off-Broadway from 1006 until 2017, with Jones reprising his role as the Old Actor. He and Schmidt also worked together on the Broadway musicals "110 in the Shade" (1963) and "I Do! I Do!" (1966) sharing Tony Award nominations for both. He wrote and directed the 1969 Broadway musical "Celebration". He also worked on the musicals "Colette" (1970), "Philemon" (1973), "Grover's Corners" (1987), "Mirette" (1996), "Roadside" (2001), "Harold and Maude" (2004), and "The Game of Love" (2012). He was author of the 1998 book "Making Musicals: An Informal Introduction to the World of Musical Theater". Jones married Elinor Wright in 1963 and they later divorced. He was married to choreographer Janet Watson from 1984 until her death in 2016 and is survived by their two sons, Michael and Sam.

Jossa, Marisa

Italian actress and model Marisa Jossa, who was crowned Miss Italia in 1959, died in Italy on November 19, 2023. She was 85. Jossa was born  in Naples, Italy, on August 30, 1959. She won the title Miss Italian in August of 1959 during Enzo Mirigliani's first year as head of the pageant. She later had an acting career, appearing in the films "Shirley Temple Story" (1976), "Una Dona al Meu Jardi" (1989), "Sai" (1998), and the short "Darrera la Porta" (2007). She was seen on television in episodes of "Estacio d'Enllac" as Roser from 1995 to 1996, "Croniques de la Veritat Oculta", "Des del Balco" as Cinta from 2001 to 2002, "La Mari", "Lo Cartanya" as Maria Munt from 2005 to 2007, and "La Sagrada Familia". Jossa's daughter, Roberta Capua, became Miss Italia in 1986.

Jove, Angel

Spanish actor Angel Jove died of a stroke in Girona, Spain, on October 18, 2023. He was 83. Jove was born in Lleida, Spain, in 1940. He studied architecture there, graduating in 1964. He became involved in the pop art

movement as founder of the Cogul group. He was a pioneer in the Catalan conceptual art movement and utilized photographic printing on canvas and photomontages. He published several  books of poetry in the 1970s including "Verbo Ser" (1970) and "Tratado de los Ordenes Arquitectonicos" (1971). He became involved in cinema later in the decade and appeared in "Bilbao" (1978) also providing graphic design, "Caniche" (1979), "Reborn" (1981) which he also wrote and designed, "Barcelona Sur" (1981), "Ultimas Tardes con Teresa" (1984), "Far Passion" (1986), Bigas Luna's horror film "Anguish" (1987), "La Banyera" (1989), "Boom Boom" (1990), "The Ages of Lulu" (1990), and "La Febre d'Or" (1993).

Jung Chae-yul

South Korean actress Jung Chae-yul, who starred in the television series "Zombie Detective", was found dead at her  home in Seoul, South Korea, on April 11, 2023. She was 26. Jung was born in South Korea on September 4, 1996. She began her career as a fashion model and appeared in the 2016 television reality series "Devil's Runway". She was featured in the 2018 film "Deep". Jung starred as Bae Yoon Mi on the fantasy comedy series "Zombie Detective" in 2020. She was filming the Korean television series "Wedding Impossible" at the time of her death.

Kalb, Bernard

Broadcast journalist and reporter Bernard Kalb died of injuries he received in a fall at his home in North Bethesda, Maryland, on January 8, 2023. He was 100. Kalb was born in  New York City on February 4, 1922. He graduated from the City College of New York in 1942 and later earned a master's degree from Harvard University. He served in the U.S. Army for two years working on a newspaper in Alaska's Aleutian Islands. He began writing for radio station WQXR after his discharge. The station was owned by "The New York Times" and he joined the newspaper's staff in 1946. He was initially a metropolitan reporter before becoming an overseas correspondent. He accompanied Admiral Richard E. Byrd on his mission to Antarctica in 1955. He reported from Southeast Asia before leaving the Times for CBS in 1962. He operated out of Hong Kong and often covered the Vietnam War. He became Washington anchorman for the "CBS Morning News" in 1970. He was CBS correspondent for President Richard Nixon's trip to China in 1972. He covered the State Department for CBS from 1975 to 1980 when he joined NBC in the same capacity. He was appointed Assistant Secretary of State for Public Affairs and spokesman for the U.S. State Department in the administration of President Ronald Reagan in 1984. Kalb resigned in 1986 in protest of a "reported disinformation program" by the administration regarding Libyan leader Muammar al-Qaddafi. He and his younger brothers, journalist Marvin Kalb, frequently traveled with Henry Kissinger on diplomatic missions. They co-wrote the 1974 book "Kissinger". The brothers also collaborated on the 1981 novel "The Last Ambassador" set during the fall of Saigon in 1975. He was anchor and a panelist on the CNN program "Reliable Sources" from 1993 to 1998. Kalb is survived by his wife of 64 years, Phyllis Bernstein, and four daughters.

Kaleikini, Danny

Singer and actor Danny 'Kaniela' Kaleikini, who was known as the Ambassador of Aloha after a long career performing at the Kahala Hilton in Hawaii, died at a hospice facility in Nuuanu, Hawaii, on January 6, 2023. He was 85.

Kaleikini was born in Honolulu on October 10, 1937. He learned to sing and play musical instruments from an early age and sang in the choir during high school. He studied music at the University of Hawai'i at Manoa. He also began working as a busboy at the Waikiki Sands hotel and was soon performing with bandleader Ray Kinney and singer Haunani Kahalewai. He was headlining shows at the Tapa Room at the Hilton Hawaiian Village in the 1960s and worked at the Hala Terrace at the Kahala Hilton from 1967. He performed there for nearly thirty years until retiring in 1994. Kaleikini appeared in a small role in the 1970 film "The Hawaiians" and was featured in episodes of "Hawaii Five-O" and "The Little People". He also performed on the talk shows "The Merv Griffin Show", "The Mike Douglas Show", and "Dolly". He was host of the WKVH radio show "Hawaii Calls" in the early 1970s. He was an unsuccessful candidate of lieutenant governor of Hawaii in 1994, running second on an independent ticket. Kaleikini was married to Jacqueline Wong and they had two children together. Both children performed with their father from an early age. He is survived by his wife and daughter, Leonn. His son, Danjacques, died in 1992.

Kanakis, Anna

Italian actress and model Anna Kanakis, who was crowned Miss Italy in 1977, died in Rome, Italy, on November 19, 2023. She was 61. Kanakis was born in Messina, Italy, on February 1, 1962. She competed in the Miss Italy pageant in her early teens and won the crown in 1977. She competed in the subsequent Miss World pageant. She was also a contestant

in Miss Universe in 1981 and Miss Europe in 1981 where she was second runner-up. Kanakis began a film career in the early 1980s with roles in "Zucchero, Miele e Peperonchino" (1980),

"Bello di Mamma" (1980), "Attili Flagello di Dio" (1982), "Acapulco, Prima Spiaggia... a Sinistra" (1983), the post-apocalyptic action thrillers "Warriors of the Wasteland" (aka "The New Barbarians") (1983) and "2019: After the Fall of New York" (1983), "Occhio, Malocchio, Prezzemolo e Finocchio" (1983), "Segni Particolari: Bellissimo" (1983), "'O re" (1989), "L'Avaro" (1990), "Money" (1991), "Riflessi in un Cielo Scuro" (1991), "Coma" (1993), "Gli Inaffidabili" (1997), and "The Final Inquiry" (2006). Kanakis was seen on television in productions of "Ocean" (1989), "A Season of Giants" (1990), "Young Catherine" (1991), "Princesse Alexandra" (1992), "Due Vite, un Destino" (1993), "La Famiglia Ricordi" (1995), "La Tenda Nera" (1996), "Il Maresciallo Rocca" (1996), "Turn of the Century" (1999), "Una Sola Debole Voce 2" (2001), "O la Va, o la Spacca" (2004), and "La Terza Verita" (2007). She starred as Paola Ghiglione in the series "Vento di Ponente" from 2002 to 2004. Kanakis was briefly married to composer Carlo Simonetti in the early 1980s. She married Marco Merati Foscarini in 2004 who survives her.

Kandel, Stephen

Film and television writer Stephen Kandel died at his home in Boston, Massachusetts, on October 21, 2023. He was 96. Kandel was born in New York City on April 30, 1927, and was raised in Pennsylvania. His father, Aben Kandel, was also

a leading screenwriter. He graduated from high school in 1943 and briefly attended college before serving in the U.S. Army in Germany during World War II. He resumed his education after his discharge, graduating from Dartmouth College in 1950. He began his career in films in the mid-1950s, scripting "Singing in the Dark" (1956) which he co-wrote with his father Aben Kandel, "Magnificent Roughnecks" (1956), "Frontier Gun" (1958), "Battle of the Coral Sea" (1959), "The Walking Target" (1960), the horror film "Chamber of Horrors" (1966), and "Cannon for Cordoba" (1970). Kandel worked frequently in television, penning episodes of "Steve Randall", "State Trooper", "Tombstone Territory", "The Man and the Challenge", "77 Sunset Strip", "The Millionaire", "Johnny Midnight", "The Chevy Mystery Show", "The Brothers Brannagan", "Sea Hunt", "Everglades!", "Ripcord", "Empire", "The Littlest Hobo", "Burke's Law", "The Rogues", "Daktari", "Gidget", "The Wackiest Ship in the Army", "Batman", "Star Trek" penning the episodes "Mudd's Women" and "I, Mudd" in the mid-1960s, "Cimarron Strip", "Iron Horse", "I Spy", "Ironside", "The Wild Wild West", "Mod Squad", "The Outcasts", "It Takes a Thief", "The New People", "Bracken's World", "The Bold Ones: The Lawyers", "The Immortal", "Alias Smith and Jones", "The Young Lawyers", "Dan August", "Men at Law", "Cade's County", "Longstreet", "Bearcats!", "The Bold Ones: The New Doctors", "Banacek", "Mission: Impossible", "Room 222", "Mannix", "The Magician", "Star Trek: The Animated Series", "Marcus Welby, M.D.", "The Manhunter", "Movin' On", "Caribe", "Barnaby Jones", "Medical Center", "Bronk", "Harry O", "Cannon", "The Bionic Woman", "Bert D'Angelo/Superstar", "Hawaii Five-O", "Most Wanted", "Switch", "Wonder Woman", "Man from Atlantis", "The Six Million Dollar Man", "Charlie's Angels", "The Paper Chase", "The Amazing Spider-Man", "Supertrain", "Time Express", "The Dukes of Hazzard", "A Man Called Sloane", "CHiPs", "When the Whistle Blows", "The Love Boat", "Vega$", "Nero Wolfe", "Jessica Novak", "Dynasty", "Lottery!", "For Love and Honor", "Hart to Hart", "The New Mike Hammer", "Cover Up", and "MacGyver". Kandel also served as a producer for the series "Iron Horse", "The New Mike Hammer", and "MacGyver". His other television credits include the tele-films and mini-series "Scalplock" (1966), "Winchester '73" (1967), "Death Stalk" (1975), "McNaughton's Daughter" (1976), "Son-Rise: A Miracle of Love" (1979), "California Fever" (1979), "Dallas Cowboys Cheerleaders II" (1980), "Broken Promise" (1981), "Shocktrauma" (1982), and "Living Proof: The Hank Williams, Jr. Story" (1983). He retired from films and television in the early 1990s and settled on the East Coast with his family. He is survived by his wife, Anne Kandel, and their four children.

Kane, Howie

Singer Howie Kane, who performed with the band Jay and the Americans, died on March 27, 2023. He was 81. He was born Howard Kirschenbaum in Brooklyn, New York, on

June 6, 1941. He joined John 'Jay' Traynor, Kenny Vance, and Sandy Deanne in the rock band Jay and the Americans in 1960. They signed with United Artists and had a hit with the 1962 single "She Cried". Jay Black replaced Traynor as lead singer in 1962 and they had such hits as "Come a Little Bit Closer", "Cara Mia", "This Magic Moment", and "No Other Love" over the next several years. The band was featured in the 1966 film "Wild Wild Winter" where they sang "Two of a Kind". Jay and the American disbanded in 1973 and Kane continued as a solo artist. He was inducted with the band in the Vocal Group Hall of Fame in 2002. Kane rejoined with former members Sandy Deanne and Marty Sanders and added vocalist John 'Jay' Reincke to resume playing under the name Jay and the Americans in 2006.

Kapp, Joe

Football player and actor Joe Kapp died of complications from Alzheimer's disease at a care facility in San Jose, California, on May 8, 2023. He was 85. Kapp was born in Santa Fe, New Mexico, on March 19, 1938, and was raised

in California. He attended the University of California at Berkeley where he played football and basketball. He led the California Golden Bears football team to the Pacific Coast Conference championship and an appearance at the Rose Bowl in 1958. He graduated the following year and was drafted by the Washington Redskins. He was not called up to play for Washington and joined the Calgary Stampeders with the Canadian Football League from 1959 to 1960. He was quarterback with the British Columbia Lions from 1961 to 1966. He returned to the United States in 1967 and played with the NFL's Minnesota Vikings for two years. He ended his football career with a season for the New England Patriots in 1970. Kapp had an acting career in films and television in the 1970s and early 1980s with roles in the films "M*A*S*H" (1970), "The World's Greatest Athlete" (1973), "The Longest Yard" (1974), "Breakheart Pass" (1975), "Two-Minute Warning" (1976), "Semi-Tough" (1977), "The Choirboys" (1977), and "The Frisco Kid" (1979). He appeared on television in episodes of "The Rookies", "Medical Center", "Ironside", "Adam-12", "Chase", "Nakia", "Lucas Tanner", "Marcus Welby, M.D.", "Emergency!", "Movin' On", "The Six Million Dollar Man", "Police Woman", "Police Story", "Vega$", "Trapper John, M.D.", and "Dynasty". He was also seen in the tele-films and mini-series "Climb an Angry Mountain" (1972), "Captains and the Kings" (1976), "Smash-Up on Interstate 5" (1976), and "Pigs vs. Freaks" (1982). Kapp served as head football coach for the University of California at Berkley from 1982 to 1986. He was general manager for British Columbia Lions in 1990 and served as head coach of the Arena Football League's Sacramento Attack in 1992. He was inducted into the Canadian Football Hall of Fame in 1984 and the College Football Hall of Fame in 2004. Kapp was married to Marcia Day from 1962 until her death in 2005 and is survived by their son. He subsequently married Jennifer Adams and is also survived by her, their two daughters, and a son.

Karwanski, Edmund

Polish actor Edmund Karwanski died in Poland on April 22, 2023. He was 94. Karwanski was born in Warsaw, Poland, on February 20, 1929. He graduated from the Warsaw Theater Academy in 1952. He performed on stage throughout his career acting with the theaters Powszechny, National, and Rozmaitosci. He worked frequently with the Kwadrat Theater in Warsaw and served as director from 1986 to 2010. He was featured in such films as "Skazany" (1976), "Man of Marble" (1977), "Death of a President" (1977), "Romans Teresy

Hennert" (1978), "Olciec Krolowej" (1980), and "Experiment Eva" (1985). Karwanski appeared on television in productions of "Gniewko, Syn Rybaka" (1969),"Romans Prowincjonalny" (1977), "Doktor Murek" (1979), of "Temida: Strzaly o Swicie" (1987). His other television credits include episodes of "Zywot Czlowieka Rozbrojonego", "Zlotopolscy", "Magda M", and "Barwy Szczescia" as Remigiusz Jarzebski from 2009 to 2015.

Kasabian, Linda

Linda Kasabian, a former Manson Family member who was a key witness for the prosecution in the trial of Charles Manson and his followers for a

series of brutal murders in 1969, died in Tacoma, Washington, on January 21, 2023. She was 73. She was born Linda Drouin in Biddeford, Maine, on June 21, 1949, and was raised in Milford, New Hampshire. She left high school and ran away from home at age sixteen. She soon married Robert Peasley but they divorced after a brief time. She subsequently married Robert Kasabian and they had a daughter, Tanya, in 1968. She moved with him to California before he left for South America. Linda became involved with a hippie commune at Spahn Ranch in Death Falley, where she met Charles Manson and the other members of the Manson Family. She participated in several criminal exploits including robbing homes with the family. Manson decided in August of 1969 to escalate the Family's violent proclivities. He instructed Kasabian to drive family members Tex Watson, Susan Atkins, and Patricia Krenwinkel to the home of film director Roman Polanski and his pregnant wife, actress Sharon Tate. Kasabian remained outside and did not participate in the subsequent murders of the people there including Tate, Jay Sebring, Wojciech Frykowski, Abigail Folger, and Steven Parent. She claimed she attempted to stop the killings but was unable. The following night she drove Watson, Krenwinkel, and Leslie Van Houten to the home of Leno and Rosemary LaBianca where they were brutally murdered. Kasabian fled the ranch with her daughter and went to New Hampshire. When suspicion of the murders fell on the Manson Family an arrest warrant was issued for Kasabian. She turned herself in to the police in New Hampshire and was offered immunity from prosecution for turning state's evidence and testifying against Manson and company. Kasabian had a second daughter, Quanu, while she was in police custody. She was the star prosecution witness in the subsequent trial that resulted in death penalties for Mason, Watson, Atkins, Krenwinkel, and Van Houten. The sentence was commuted to

life in prison after California repealed the death penalty. She largely lived outside of the public eye after the Manson trials including a stint at a hippie commune. She moved to the Tacoma, Washington, area in the late 1980s. She was the subject of a rare interview for the television program "A Current Affair" in 1988. She was featured in the 2009 docu-drama "Manson" and was a live interview subject for "Larry King Live" in 2009. Kasabian was portrayed in numerous film and television productions about the Manson Family including "Helter Skelter" (1976) by Marilyn Burns, "The Manson Family" (1997) by Michelle Briggs, "Helter Skelter" (2004) by Clea DuVall, "The Family: Inside the Manson Cult" (2009) by Tamara Hope, "House of Manson" (2014) by Erin Marie Hogan, "Manson's Lost Girls" (2016) by Mackenzie Mauzy, "Prettyface" (2016) by Lulu Miller, "Charles Manson: The Final Words" (2017) by Amanda Barnum, "Charlie Says" (2018) by India Ennenga, and Quentin Tarantino's "Once Upon a Time in Hollywood" (2019) by Maya Hawke as the Kasabian character Flowerchild.

Kastel, Roger

Artist Roger Kastel, who was noted for designing posters for such films as "Jaws", and "The Empire Strikes Back", died of kidney and heart failure at a hospice facility in Worcester, Massachusetts, on November 8, 2023. He was 92.

Kastel was born in White Plains, New York, in 1931. He attended classes at the Art Students League of New York in Manhattan. He served in the U.S. Navy during the Korean War in the 1950s. He worked as an artist for ad agencies and movie studios. Kastel designed the painting used for the paperback version of Peter Benchley's "Jaws" that was used for the film poster for Steven Spielberg's 1975 adaptation. He also designed posters for "Doctor Faustus" (1967), "Doc Savage: The Man of Bronze" (1975), "The Great Train Robbery" (1978), and the "Star Wars" sequel "The Empire Strikes Back" (1980). Kastel painted the covers for paperback editions of "50 Great Horror Stories", H.G. Wells' "The Invisible Man", Franz Kafka's "The Metamorphosis", Nancy Garden's "Werewolves", John Steinbeck's "East of Eden", Richard Price's "The Wanderers", Betina Krahn's "Behind Closed Doors", and Jackie Collins "Hollywood Wives", He was interviewed in the 2007 documentary film "The Shark Is Still Working: The Impact & Legacy of 'Jaws'". Kastel is survived by his wife of 66 years, Grace Trowbridge, and their son and daughter.

Katz, Gene

Actor Gene Katz died at his home in Memphis, Tennessee, on March 14, 2023. He was 92. Katz was born in Chicago, Illinois, on September 10, 1930. He moved to Memphis with his family in 1943. He graduated from Tulane University in 1951 and began performing on stage in New Orleans while attending college. He went to New York after

graduation where he pursued a career on stage. He soon returned to Memphis where he became a leading performer on the local stage. He appeared in productions at Front Street Theatre, Circuit Playhouse, Little Theater (now Theatre Memphis), McCoy Theatre, and Playhouse on the Square. His numerous roles include Tevye in "Fiddler on the Roof" and Oscar in "The Odd Couple". He was seen in several films shot in Memphis and the 1990 tele-film "Blind Vengeance". Katz appeared in over 50 local commercials and was narrator for several "Memphis Memoirs" for WKNO. He also worked as a stockbroker for over forty years until his retirement in 2012. Katz is survived by his wife of 45 years, Carol, and daughter Kathryn.

Kayaalp, Merve

Turkish actress Merve Kayaalp died of a suicide by shooting herself in the head at her apartment in the Dalaman

district of Mugla, Turkey, on September 18, 2023. She was 36. She graduated from Isparta Suleyman Demirel University and began her career with the Istanbul State Theater. She was seen frequently on television over the last decade with roles in productions of "Sakarya Firat", "Kucuk Kiyamet", "Dusler ve Umutlar", "Elif" as Gilay from 2016 to 2017, "Seref Meselesi", and "Savasci" as Gulten in 2018.

Keane, Sean

Irish musician Sean Keane, who performed with the Irish folk band the Chieftains, died in Ireland on May 7, 2023. He was 76. Keane was born in Drimnagh, Ireland, on July 12,

1946. His parents were traditional Irish musicians and Sean began playing the fiddle at an early age. He was a member of the band Ceoltoiri Chualann before joining the Chieftains in 1968. He performed with the band on the Oscar-winning soundtrack for Stanley Kubrick's 1975 film "Barry Lyndon". The Chieftains became popular in the United States and recorded the album "Irish Heartbeat" with Van Morrison in 1988. Keane also recorded the solo albums "Gusty's Frolics" (1975), "Sean Keane" (1982), and "Jig It in Style" (1990). He remained a member of the Chieftains until 2002 but continued to make appearances with the group. He was married to Virginia Keane

until her death in 2010 and is survived by three children. Most of his children and grandchildren also became musicians.

Kedar, Dvora

Israeli actress Dvora Kedar died in Tel Aviv, Israel, on May 17, 2023. She was 98. Kedar was born in Wilno, Poland

(now Vilnius, Lithuania), on June 8, 1924. She came to Israel as a child and studied acting at the Habima Theater. She joined the Cameri Theater in 1949 where she was seen in such plays as Garcia Lorca's "Blood Wedding" and Arthur Miller's "After the Fall". She was seen in the films "Dreamboat" (1964), "The Prodigal Son" (1968), "The Dreamer" (1970), "A Gift from Heaven" (1973), and Menahem Golan's "Operation Thunderbolt" (1977) which was nominated for the Academy Award for Best Foreign Language Film. Kedar was best known for her role as Sonja, Benzi's mother, in the teen comedy film "Lemon Popsicle" ("Eskimo Limon") (1978). She reprised her role in the sequels "Going Steady" (1979), ""Hot Bubblegum" (1981), "Private Popsicle" (1982), "Baby Love" (1983), "Up Your Anchor" (1985), and "Summertime Blues" (1988). Her other films include "The Revenge of Itzik Finkelstein" (1993) and "Fire Birds" (2015). Kedar appeared on television in episodes of "Itche" and "Zaguri". She continued to perform on stage with the Habima Theater through the 2000s.

Kelly, Jody

Josephine 'Jody' Kelly, who was a contestant on the television reality competition show "The Amazing Race" in 2010, died visiting Bemidji, Minnesota, on September 5, 2023.

She was 85. Kelly was born in Opelika, Alabama, on January 21, 1938, and was raised in Gainesville, Florida. She earned a PhD in English literature from Duke University in 1974. She was a professor of English at the University of Louisiana for sixteen years and later taught writing at Austin Community College. Kelly was the oldest female to ever compete on the series when, at 71, she and her granddaughter, Shannon Foster, were contestants on Season 16 of CBS's "The Amazing Race" in 2010. They were eliminated during following the second round, coming in tenth. She was founder of StrengthMobile, providing physical training for the elderly, following the show. She competed in triathlons and represented Team USA at several international competitions throughout the 2010s. She also wrote books about lifestyle topics including "Feeling Good: Strength Training with Your Significant Elder". Kelly's survivors include four children and eleven grandchildren, including her teammate Shannon.

Kelsch, Ken

Cinematographer Ken Kelsch died of complications from COVID-19 and pneumonia at a hospital in Hackettstown, New Jersey, on December 11, 2023. He was 76. Kelsch was born in Brooklyn, New York, on July 8, 1947. He attended Rutgers University before serving in the U.S. Army during the Vietnam War. He worked in films from the early 1970s and served as a gaffer for Wes Craven's horror film "The Last House on the Left" (1972). He was key grip for 1978's "The Fox Affair" and worked in the electrical department for 1979's "Don't Go in the House", also appearing on screen in a small role. Kelsch graduated from the New York University Tisch School of the Arts in 1997. He was director of photography for Abel Ferrara's 1979 slasher film "The Driller Killer". He also served as cinematographer for the films "In Our Water" (1982), "Spookies" (1986), Ferrara's "Bad Lieutenant" (1992) among nearly a dozen other films with the director, "Killer Dead" (1992), "Dangerous Game" (1993), "Drop Squad" (1994), "The Addiction" (1995), "Condition Red" (1995), "Killer: A Journal of Murder" (1996), Stanley Tucci's "Big Night" (1996), "The Funeral" (1996), "The Blackout" (1997), "Montana" (1998), "A Brooklyn State of Mind" (1998), "The Impostors" (1998), "New Rose Hotel" (1998), "Susan's Plan" (1998), "It Had to Be You" (2000), "'R Xmas" (2001), "Testosterone" (2003), "Asmali Konak: Jayat" (2003), "Happy End" (2003), "Missing in America" (2005), "Before It Had a Name" (2005), "Chelsea on the Rocks" (2008), "Return to Sleepaway Camp" (2009), "100 Feet" (2008), "Sicak" (2008), "Desert Flower" (2009), "Lily of the Feast" (2010), "Keep Your Enemies Closer" (2011), "4:44 Last Day on Earth" (2011), "House of Last Things" (2013), "Welcome to New York" (2014), "the 2015 short "The Cask of Amontillado", "The Brooklyn Banker" (2016), and the documentary "The Projectionist" (2019). He also appeared in small roles in "Dangerous Game" (1993), "New Rose Hotel" (1998), "Susan's Plan" (1998), and "100 Feet" (2008). Kelsch was cinematographer for television productions of "Assault at West Point: The Court-Martial of Johnson Whittaker" (1994), "The Prosecutors" (1996), "Backroads to Vegas" (1996), "SUBWAYStories: Tales from the Underground" (1997), "Every 9 Seconds" (1997), "Rear Window" (1999), "Invisible Child" (1999), and "Private Lies" (2001). He also worked on episodes of such series as "Now and Again", "The $treet", "Fling", "Hack", and "Medium". He was married and divorced from camera operator Dale K. Denning, who died in 2016. Kelsch is survived by a son and two daughters and was predeceased by a son, Scot, in 1984.

Kemble, Mark

Actor and screenwriter Mark Kemble died of cancer in Los Angeles, California, on August 14, 2023. He was 69. Kemble was born in Providence, Rhode Island, on August 21,

1953. He served in the U.S. Navy in the Philippines after graduating high school. He moved to Los Angeles in 1977 where he studied acting at the Beverly Hills Playhouse. Kemble performed frequently on stage and was featured in several films including "The Hanoi Hilton" (1987), "Penitentiary III" (1987), "The Arrival" (1991), the Full Moon horror film "Netherworld" (1992), and "Forget Me Not" (2009). He appeared on television in episodes of "The Young and the Restless", "Quantum Leap", and "Silk Stalkings", and the tele-films "Police Story: The Freeway Killings" (1987), "Fatal Judgement" (1988), "The Girl Who Came Between Them" (1990), and "A Quiet Little Neighborhood, a Perfect Little Murder" (1990). Kemble also began writing stage productions including "Names", which was performed Off-Broadway in 1997. He co-wrote the 1998 film "Race" for HBO and 2000's "Flight of Fancy" (aka "Facing Fear"). He wrote and directed the 2015 film "Bad Hurt", based on his play "Bad Hurt on Cedar Street".

Kemper, Victor J.

Cinematographer Victor J. Kemper died in Sherman Oaks, California, on November 27, 2023. He was 96. Kemper was born in Newark, New Jersey, on April 14, 1927. He graduated from Seton Hall University in South Orange, New

Jersey. He began his career working at a local television station, recording and mixing sound and serving as a technical director. He traveled to California in 1953 to learn how to show productions on the newly developed videotape systems. He returned to New York to train cinematographers on the East Coast to shoot videos. He briefly owned his own video production company before it was forced to close. Kemper served as a camera operator for the films "The Tiger Makes Out" (1967) and "Alice's Restaurant" (1969). He was named cinematographer for John Cassavetes' 1970 film "Husbands". Kemper continued to serve as cinematographer or director of photography for such films as "The Magic Garden of Stanley Sweetheart" (1970), "They Might Be Giants" (1978), "Who Is Harry Kellerman and Why Is He Saying Those Terrible Things About Me?" (1971), Arthur Hiller's medical black comedy "The Hospital" (1971), Michael Ritchie's political satire "The Candidate" (1972), "Last of the Red Hot Lovers" (1972), "Shamus" (1973), "The Friends of Eddie Coyle" (1973), "Gordon's War" (1973), "From the Mixed-Up Files of Mrs. Basil E. Frankweiler" (1973), "The Gambler" (1974), "The Reincarnation of Peter Proud" (1975), Sidney Lumet's "Dog Day Afternoon" (1976), "Stay Hungry" (1976), "The Last Tycoon" (1976), "Mikey and Nicky" (1976), George Roy Hill's "Slap Shot" (1977), "Audrey Rose" (1977), "Oh,

God!" (1977), "Coma" (1978), "The One and Only" (1978), "Eyes of Laura Mars" (1978), Richard Attenborough's psychological horror film "Magic" (1978), "And Justice for All" (1979), "The Jerk" (1979), "Night of the Juggler" (1980), "The Final Countdown" (1980), the musical fantasy "Xanadu" (1980), "The Four Seasons" (1981), "Chu Chu and the Philly Flash" (1981), "Partners" (1982), "Author! Author!" (1982), "Mr. Mom" (1983), "National Lampoon's Vacation" (1983), "The Lonely Guy" (1984), "National Lampoon's European Vacation" (1985), "Cloak & Dagger" (1984), "Secret Admirer" (1985), "Pee-wee's Big Adventure" (1985), "Clue" (1985), "Walk Like a Man" (1987), "Hot to Trot" (1988), "Cohen and Tate" (1988), "See No Evil, Hear No Evil" (1989), "Crazy People" (1990), "F/X2" (1991), "Another You" (1991), "Married to It" (1991), "Beethoven" (1992), "Tommy Boy" (1995), "Eddie" (1996), "Jingle All the Way" (1996), "American Pie Presents: Bad Camp" (2005), and "Bring It On: All or Nothing" (2006). Kemper was cinematographer for television productions of "The Prince of Central Park" (1977), "The Atlanta Child Murders" (1985), "Kojak: The Price of Justice" (1987) earning an Emmy Award nomination, "Too Rich: The Secret Life of Doris Duke" (1999), and "On Golden Pond" (2001). He served as president of the American Society of Cinematographers from 1993 to 1996 and from 1999 to 2001. He was recipient of their Lifetime Achievement Award in 1998. Kemper married Claire Kellerman in 1953 and is survived by her and their three children.

Kempinski, Tom

British actor and playwright Tom Kempinski died in England on August 2, 2023. He was 85. Kempinski was born

in Hendon, England, on March 24, 1938. He earned a scholarship to Gonville and Caius College, Cambridge, in 1957 but withdrew after suffering a breakdown several months later. He began working as an actor in the early 1960s and was seen in such films as "These Are the Damned" (1962), "Othello" (1965), "Cop-Out" (1967), "The Whisperers" (1967), "Mrs. Brown, You've Got a Lovely Daughter" (1968), "The Committee" (1968), "Moon Zero Two" (1969), "Taste of Excitement" (1969), "The Reckoning" (1970), "Praise Marx and Pass the Ammunition" (1970), "Doctor in Trouble" (1970), "The McKenzie Break" (1970), "Gumshoe" (1971), and "Adult Fun" (1972). Kempinski was seen on television in episodes of "Sir Francis Drake", "The Power Game", "No Hiding Place", "Callan", "Love Story", "The Queen's Traitor", "Public Eye", "Virgin of the Secret Service", "The Avengers", "Dixon of Dock Green", "Counterstrike", "The Root of All Evil?", "Kate", "The Main Chance", "Clochemerle", "Pretenders", "Z Cars", "Spy Trap", "Crown Court", "Softly Softly: Task Force", "Play for Today", and "Life at Stake". His other television credits include productions of "Big Brother" (1970), "A.D.A.M."

(1973), "Moonbase 3" (1973) as Dr. Stephen Partness, and "Fall of Eagles" (1974). Kempinski was noted for writing the 1980 play "Duet for One" which starred his wife, actress Frances de la Tour, during its original London run. He also wrote the 1985 television adaptation and the 1986 screen version, which starred Julie Andrews. Kempinski was married to actress Margaret Nolan from 1967 until their divorce in 1972 and to Frances de la Tour from 1972 until their divorce in 1982.

Kennedy, Don

Radio and television personality Don Kennedy, who hosted the children's series "The Popeye Club" in Atlanta under the name Officer Don, died of complications from dementia and

a stroke in Atlanta, Georgia, on June 29, 2023. He was 93. Kennedy was born in Beaver, Pennsylvania, on March 2, 1930. He graduated from Geneva College in 1953 and served in the U.S. military for several years. He began working in broadcasting for the weekend radio show "Monitor" on NBC in the mid-1950s. He was the host of the Atlanta children's television show "The Popeye Club" as Officer Don on WSB-TV from 1956 to 1970. Kennedy was later a voice actor on such animated shows as "Space Ghost Coast to Coast", "The Brak Show", and "Aqua Teen Hunger Force". He became host of the radio programs "Big Band Jump" and "The Don Kennedy Show" in the mid-1980s and remained with them until retiring from radio in 2013.

Kent, Darren

British actor Darren Kent, who starred as the Scholar in the cult horror series "Blood Drive" in 2017, died of multiple health issues including osteoporosis, arthritis, and a rare skin disorder in England on August 11, 2023. He was 36. Kent was born in Essex, England, on March 30, 1987. He trained as an

actor at the Italia Conti Academy of Theatre Arts in Woking, England. He was noted for his unique appearance and Cockney accent. Kent appeared on television in episodes of "Marshal's Law", "Game of Thrones" as a Slavers' Bay goatherd in a 2014 episode, "Bloody Cuts", "The Frankenstein Chronicles", the off-beat science fiction television series "Blood Drive" as the Scholar in 2017, "Green Fingers", "EastEnders", "Happy Hours", and "Malpractice". He was featured as Chenildieu in the 2018 mini-series "Les Miserables". Kent was seen in the films "Mirrors" (2008), "Asylum Blackout" (2011), "Snow White and the Huntsman" (2012), "Community" (2012), "Abusing Protocol" (2015), "My Feral Heart" (2016), "The Little Stranger" (2018), "Jeepers Creepers: Reborn" (2022), "A Beautiful Debt" (2022), "Dungeons & Dragons: Honor Among

Theives" (2023) as a reanimated corpse, and "Love Without Walls" (2023). He appeared in numerous short films including "Sunny Boy" (2011), "Twitcher" (2014), "1-0-8-0" (2014), "Infected" (2015), "The Outer Darkness" (2015), "Boris in the Forest" (2015), "Catford Jesus" (2017), "In Two Minds" (2019), "Lockdown Lowdown: Global Glance" (2020), "The Man Who Wouldn't Die" (2020), "Back Up" (2021), "Rise of Fizzy Pop" (2022), "Driver" (2022), "Ties That Bind Us" (2022), "Love Without Walls" (2023), "The Monster" (2023), "Alleviate" (2023), and "The Stainless Steel Soul" (2023). Kent produced and directed the shorts "Abusing Protocol" (2015), "Meadow Lane" (2016), and "You Know Me" (2021), and directed episodes of "The Break" and "Happy Hours".

Kent, Gary

Actor and stuntman Gary Kent died in Austin, Texas, on May 25, 2023. Kent was born in Walla Walla, Washington, on June 7, 1933. He was 89. He briefly attended the University of Washington before dropping out to join the U.S. Navy in 1952. He was stationed in Texas for two years where he wrote publicity releases for the Blue Angels elite flying team. He worked on local theatrical productions in the Houston area as an actor and director. He moved to Hollywood later in the 1950s to pursue a career in films. He was soon performing stunts and appearing in small roles in such films as "Legion of the Doomed" (1958), "King of the Wild Stallions" (1959), "Battle Flame" (1959), "The Thrill Killers" (1964), "One Shocking Moment" (1965), and "Run Home, Slow" (1965). Kent was stunt coordinator and served as stunt double for Jack Nicholson in Monte Hellman's off-beat western films "The Shooting" and "Ride in the Whirlwind" in 1966. He continued to work in such action and exploitation films as "The Black Klansman" (1966), "Suburbia Confidential" (1966), "Journey to the Center of Time" (1967), "Hells Angels on Wheels" (1967), "Hells Chosen Few" (1968), "A Man Called Dagger" (1968) as Paul Mantee's stunt double, "Psych-Out" (1968), "The Savage Seven" (1968), "Nymphs (Anonymous)" (1968), Peter Bogdanovich's "Targets" (1968) starring Boris Karloff, "Sappho Darling" (1968), "The Angry Breed" (1968), "The Kiss Off" (1968), "Voyage to the Planet of Prehistoric Women" (1968) providing special effects, "The Mighty Gorga" (1969), "Satan's Sadists" (1969), "The Fabulous Bastard from Chicago" (1969), "One Million AC/DC" (1969), "Body Fever" (1969), "The Girls from Thunder Strip" (1970), "Hell's Bloody Devils" (1970), "Sinthia: The Devil's Doll" (1970), "The Incredible 2-Headed Transplant" (1971), "Machismo: 40 Graves for 40 Guns" (1971), "How's Your Love Life?" (1971), "The Return of Count Yorga" (1971), "Angels' Wild Women" (1971), Al Adamson's cult classic "Dracula vs. Frankenstein" (1971) also serving as assistant director, "Lash of Lust" (1972), "Blue Money" (1972), "The Hard Road" (1973), "Schoolgirls in Chains" (1973),

"Inside Amy" (1974), "Freebie and the Bean" (1974), "The Forest" (1982), "Lost" (1983), "Rainy Day Friends" (1985), "Lethal Pursuit" (1988), "Warbirds" (1988), "Color of Night" (1994), "Flipping" (1996), "Street Corner Justice" (1996) which he also scripted, "Bubba Ho-Tep" (2002), "Groom Lake" (2002), "Forest of the Vampire" (2016), "Frame Switch" (2016), "Bonehill Road" (2017), "Aghora: The Deadliest Blackmagic" (2018), "Virgin Cheerleaders in Chains" (2018), "Sex Terrorists on Wheels" (2019), and "Rondo and Bob" (2020). He also served as an actor or stuntman for the television series "The Man from U.N.C.L.E.", "The Green Hornet", "Daniel Boone", and "The New Adam-12", and the 1991 telefilm "Flight of the Black Angel". Kent was production manager for the films "The Psycho Lover" (1970), "Sandra: The Making of a Woman" (1970), "Blood Mania" (1970), "The Blue Hour" (1971), "The Hard Road" (1973), "Schoolgirls in Chains" (1973), "The House of Seven Corpses" (1974) also serving as associate producer, and Brian De Palma's "Phantom of the Paradise" (1974). He directed, produced, and wrote the films "Secret Places, Secret Things" (1971), "The Pyramid" (1976), and "Rainy Day Friends" (1985). Kent was featured in several documentaries about his work in films including "Danger God" (2018), "Blood & Flesh: The Reel Life & Ghastly Death of Al Adamson" (2019), and "Masters of the Grind" (2023). His memoir, "Shadows & Light: Journeys with Outlaws in Revolutionary Hollywood", was published in 2009. Kent served as an inspiration for Brad Pitt's character, stuntman Cliff Booth, in Quentin Tarantino's 2019 film "Once Upon a Time in Hollywood". He was married to Joyce Peacock from 1953 until their divorce in 1964 and is survived by their three children. He was married to Rosemary Galleghly from 1961 until their divorce in 1968 and is also survived by their three children. Kent was briefly married to Sherry Lee Tilley in 1973. He was married to actress Shirley Willeford (aka Tomi Barrett) from 1977 until her death in 2005.

Kenwright, Bill

British stage and film producer Bill Kenwright died of liver cancer in London, England, on October 23, 2023. He was 78. Kenwright was born in Liverpool, England, on September 4, 1945. He graduated from Liverpool Institute High School for Boys in 1964. He began his career as an actor appearing in television productions of "Julius Caesar" (1964), "St. Patrick" (1966), and "Strike Pay" (1967). He was also seen in episodes of "The Villains", "King of the River", "Softly Softly", "The Fellows", "City '68", "The Doctors", "Rules, Rules, Rules", "Z Cars", "The Liver Birds", "Dixon of Dock Green", "Thirty Minutes Worth", "The Zoo Gang", "The ITV Play", and "Dream Team". Kenwright was featured as Gordon Clegg on the television soap opera "Coronation Street" from 1968 to 1969. He made occasional cameo returns to the show over the next four decades with his last performance as Clegg in 2012. He had a small role in the 1972 film "Carry on Matron". He began best known as a theatrical producer, overseeing West End productions including "Blood Brothers" which he also directed, "Joseph and the Amazing Technicolor Dreamcoat", "Whistle Down the Wind" which he also directed, "Festen", "The Big Life", "Elmina's Kitchen", "Scrooge - The Musical", "The Night of the Iguana", "A Few Good Men", "The Wizard of Oz", "A Man for All Seasons". Kenwright also produced touring productions of "Jesus Christ Superstar", "Tommy", "Tell Me on Sunday", "Jekyll & Hyde", "Evita", "Cabaret", and "This Is Elvis". Many of his theatrical productions reached Broadway and he earned Tony Awards as producer of "Dancing at Lughnasa" (1992) and "A Doll's House" (1997). He received nominations for "Blood Brothers" in 1993 for producing and directing. His other Tony producing nominations include "Medea" (1994), "An Ideal Husband" (1996), "The Chairs" (1998), "Passing Strange" (2008), and "Guys and Dolls" (2009). Kenwright was producer of such films as "The Day After the Fair" (1986), "Stepping Out" (1991), "Don't Go Breaking My Heart" (1999), "Zoe" (2001), "Die, Mommie, Die!" (2003), "The Boys from County Clare" (2003), "The Purifiers" (2004), "Cheri" (2009), "Dixie: The People's Legend" (2011), "Broken" (2012), "My Pure Land" (2017), "Burden" (2018), "Peripheral" (2018), "The Fanatic" (2019), "My Night with Reg" (2021), "Off the Rails" (2021), "The Runner" (2021), "Heathers: The Musical" (2022), "The Shepherd" (2023), "The Critic" (2023), and "The Kill Room" (2023). He served as a judge on the BBC One television competition series "Any Dream Will Do" in 2007. He served on the board of the Everton Football Club from 1989 until his death. He became the largest stakeholder and chairman of the soccer club in 2004. Kenwright was married to actress Anouska Hempel from 1978 until their divorce in 1980. He is survived by a daughter from his relationship with actress Virginia Stride. He was involved in a long-term relationship with actress Jenny Seagrove from 1994 until his death.

Kepros, Nicholas

Actor Nicholas Kepros died of complications from a stroke in Manhattan, New York, on January 26, 2023. He was 90. Kepros was born in Salt Lake City, Utah, on November 8, 1932. He attended medical school at the University of Utah

before pursuing a career in theater. He trained in London at the Royal Academy of Dramatic Art. He returned to the United States and appeared frequently on Broadway from the early 1960s. He was seen in the plays "Peer Gynt" (1960), "Henry IV, Part II" (1960) and "Henry IV, Part II" (1960) as Prince John of Lancaster, "She Stoops to Conquer" (1960), "The Plough and the Stars" (1960), "The Octoroon" (1961), "Hamlet" (1961), "Saint Joan" (1968), "Amadeus" (1980) as Emperor Joseph II, "Execution of Justice"

(1986), "Saint Joan" (1993), "Timon of Athens" (1993), "The Government Inspector" (1994), and "The Rehearsal" (1996). Kepros was seen on television in productions of "Henry IV" (1960), "Particular Men" (1972), "School for Scandal" (1975), "Equal Justice Under the Law" (1977) as Aaron Burr, "Bartleby the Scrivener" (1977), "Yulya's Diary" (1980), "Thornywell" (1981), "Guests of the Nation" (1981), "Pardon Me for Living" (1982), "Apology" (1986), "George Washington II: The Forging of a Nation" (1986), "Blood Ties" (1991), and "Witness to the Mob" (1998). His other television credits include episodes of "Chronicle", "Search for Tomorrow", "Spenser: For Hire", "Gideon Oliver", "Starting from Scratch", "Loving", "Equal Justice", "The Antagonists", "Baby Talk", "Star Trek: The Next Generation" as General Movar in the two-part episode "Redemption" in 1991, "The Golden Girls", and "Ed". He was the voice of Captain Needa in the 1983 radio drama "Star Wars: The Empire Strikes Back". Kepros appeared in a handful of films including "Amadeus" (1984) as Archbishop Hieronymus von Colloredo, "Grace Quigley" (1984), "The Sicilian" (1987), "Identity Crisis" (1989), "Quiz Show" (1994), "The Associate" (1996), "Hit and Runway" (1999), and "Carlito's Way: Rise to Power" (2005).

Kernan, David

British actor and singer David Kernan died of complications from pneumonia in England on December 26, 2023. He was 85. Kernan was born in London, England, on

June 23, 1938. He began his career on stage in the late 1950s with the Huddersfield Repertory Company. He was featured as Edward Rutledge in the original London production of the musical "1776" in 1970 and starred as Count Malcolm in Stephen Sondheim's "A Little Night Music" in London in 1975. He was a leading performer in stage musicals and was noted for his interpretations of Stephen Sondheim songs. He starred in the original Broadway revue "Side by Side by Sondheim" in 1977, earning a Tony Award nomination for best actor. He conceived and directed the musical "Jerome Kern Goes to Hollywood" in 1986. Kernan was seen on television from the late 1950s with roles in episodes of "On the Bright Side", "On the Brighter Side", "The Friday Show", "Dixon of Dock Green", "Raise Your Glasses", "Bold as Brass", "That Was the Week That Was" as a regular performer from 1962 to 1963, "Knock on Any Door", "The Avengers", "Dr. Finlay's Casebook", "No - That's Me Over Here!", "Up Pompeii!", "Brett", "Upstairs, Downstairs", "Omnibus", "Churchill's People", "Saturday Night at the Mill", "The Lively Arts", "The Good Old Days", "Let's Face the Music", and "The Chief". His other television credits include productions of "Steam, Sanctity and Song" (1963), "Man O'Brass" (1963), "So Much to Remember" (1964), "The Man in the Panama Hat" (1964), "Stiff Upper Lip" (1967), "The Merry Widow" (1968), "Traces of Love" (1979),

"She Loves Me" (1979), "The Sorcerer" (1982), "Treasure Island" (1982), and "A Swell Party" (1992). Kernan was also seen in the films "Jailbreak" (1962), "Mix Me a Person" (1962), "Farewell Performance" (1963), "Zulu" (1964) as Private Hitch, "Otley" (1969), "Der Porno-Graf von Schweden" (1969), "The Chastity Belt" (1972), "Carry on Abroad" (1972), "The Day of the Jackal" (1973), and "The Education of Sonny Carson" (1974). His autobiography, "From Eastham to Broadway", was published in 2019.

Kerr, Richard

British songwriter Richard Kerr, who co-wrote Barry Manilow's hit songs "Mandy" and "Looks Like We Made It", died in England on December 8, 2023. He was 78. Kerr was

born in Bedford, Bedfordshire, England, on December 14, 1944. He became interested in music while attending Bedford School in the 1950s. He became a songwriter and was collaborating with such musicians as Peter Green, Don Partridge, and Scott English by the late 1960s. He co-wrote the song "Brandy" which was recorded by English in 1971. It became a major hit when retitled "Mandy" for a recording by Barry Manilow in 1974. Kerr and Partridge also had a hit with "Blue Eyes" in 1974. He recorded a solo album, "Richard Kerr", in 1976. He and lyricist Will Jennings wrote the songs "Looks Like We Made It" for Manilow, "Somewhere in the Night" for Helen Reddy, and "I'll Never Love This Way Again" and "No Night So Long" for Dionne Warwick. Kerr's numerous songwriting credits also include "Shine On", "I'm Dreaming", "Where Did We Go Wrong", "A Little Bit of Heaven", "Don't Close Your Eyes Tonight", and "I Am What I Am".

Kerwin, Lance

Juvenile actor Lance Kerwin, who starred in the 1977 television series "James at 15", died in San Clemente,

California, on January 24, 2023. He was 62. Kerwin was born in Newport Beach, California, on November 6, 1960. His father was an acting coach, and his mother was a talent agent. He began his career as a juvenile actor in the mid-1970s. He appeared in episodes of "Emergency!", "Shazam!", "Little House on the Prairie", "Police Story", "Cannon", "Gunsmoke", "The Family Holvak" as Ramey Holvak in 1975, "Sara", "Good Heavens", "NBC Special Treat", "The Quest", "ABC Afterschool Specials", "Wonder Woman", "The Bionic Woman", "James at 15" (later "James at 16") as James Hunter from 1977 to 1978, "Family", "CBS Library", "Hagen", "CBS

Afternoon Playhouse", "Hotel", "Insight", "Buchanan High", "Trapper John, M.D.", "Finders of Lost Loves", "Faerie Tale Theatre" in a 1985 production of "The Snow Queen", "Simon & Simon", "Houston Knights", "Murder, She Wrote", "The New Adam-12", "The New Lassie", and "FBI: The Untold Stories". Kerwin also appeared in the tele-films "The Healers" (1974), "The Cloning of Clifford Swimmer" (1974), "The Greatest Gift" (1974), "Reflections of Murder" (1974), "Long Way Home" (1975), "Amelia Earhart" (1976), "The Loneliest Runner" (1976), "The Death of Richie" (1977), "Young Joe, the Forgotten Kennedy" (1977) as Joe Kennedy, Jr., at age 14, Stephen King's horror mini-series "Salem's Lot" as Mark Petrie, the youthful vampire hunting protege of David Soul's Ben Mears, "The Boy Who Drank Too Much" (1980), "Children of Divorce" (1980), "Side Show" (1981), "Advice to the Lovelorn" (1981), "The Mysterious Stranger" (1982), "A Killer in the Family" (1983), "The Fourth Wise Man" (1985), "Challenger" (1990), and "Final Verdict" (1991). Kerwin appeared in occasional films during his career including "Escape to Witch Mountain" (1975), "Cheering Section" (1977), "Enemy Mine" (1985), "Outbreak" (1995). Kerwin largely retired from acting in the mid-1990s after suffering from alcohol and drug addiction. He was able to rehabilitate himself through a faith-based program and worked with U-Turn for Christ, becoming a minister and youth pastor in the early 2000s. He returned to the screen to appear in the Hawaiian historical drama "The Wind & the Reckoning" in 2022. He was married and divorced from Kristen Lansdale and is survived by their daughter, Savanah Paige. He married Yvonne Kerwin in 1998 and is also survived by her and their four children.

Killer Khan

Japanese professional wrestler Masashi Ozawa, who was known in the ring as the Mongolian giant Killer Khan, died from an aortic dissection in Tokyo, Japan, on December 29, 2023.

He was 76. Ozawa was born in Tsubame, Japan, on March 6, 1947. He was a sumo wrestler with the Kasugano stable, competing under the name Koshinishiki from 1963 to 1970. He began wrestling in Japan under his real name in 1971. He was known as Kim Chang when he wrestled in Toronto, Canada, in 1977 and was Temojin El Mongol in Mexico in 1978. He became known as Killer Khan, the Mongolian giant, later in the decade. He teamed with Pak Song to win the NWA United States Tag Team Championship in Florida in March of 1979. He first wrestled Andre the Giant in a tag team match in Georgia in 1980 and joined the World Wrestling Federation (WWF/now WWE) shortly after. He feuded with Bob Backlund and Pedro Morales, and competed in a series of high profile matches against Andre the Giant. Killer Khan wrestled with Canada's Stampede Wrestling in 1984, where he won the Stampede North American Heavyweight Championship from Archie 'The Stomper'

Gouldie. He dropped the title to the Dynamite Kid two months later. He was managed by Skandor Akbar in Mid-South Wrestling and World Class Championship Wrestling. He also competed in Japan with New Japan Pro Wrestling. He briefly returned to the WWF in 1987 where he was managed by Mr. Fuji in feuds with Outback Jack, Hulk Hogan, and Randy Savage. He retired from the ring later in the year. Khan was featured in several films including "Funky Monkey Teacher 2" (1992), "3 Ninjas Kick Back" (1994), and "Maju Toshi 9-1 II" (1994). He ran restaurants and bars in Tokyo in his later years. He married Cindy Ozawa in 1975 and is survived by her and three children.

Khan, Sajid

Indian actor Sajid Khan, who co-starred with Jay North in the 1966 film "Maya" and the subsequently television series of the same name, died of cancer in Kayamkulam, India, on December 22, 2023. He was 71. He was born in Bombay,

India, on December 28, 1951. He was raised in the slums and made his film debut under the name Master Sajid as the young Birju in Mehboob Khan's 1957 Oscar-nominated Hindi language film "Mother India". He became the adopted son of Mehboob Khan and his wife, actress Sardar Akhtar, and became known as Sayid Khan. He starred as Gopal in his father's 1962 sequel "Son of India". Sajid moved to the United States after Mehboob's death in 1964. He co-starred as Raji in the 1966 adventure film "Maya" with Jay North. He and North starred in the subsequent television series from 1967 to 1968. He was also featured in a 1969 episode of "The Big Valley". He released an album, "Sajid", in 1969 and was a guest on the series "The Merv Griffin Show", "American Bandstand", and "It's Happening". Khan appeared in several films in the Philippines in the early 1970s including "The Singing Filipina" (1971), "The Prince and I" (1971), and "My Funny Girl" (1971). He subsequently returned to India where he attempted to reestablish a career in Hindi films with little success. He was seen in a handful of films over the next decade including "Savera" (1972), the short "Mahatma and thed Mad Boy" (1974), "Do Nambar Ke Amir" (1974), "Zindagi Aur Toofan" (1975), "Mandir Masjid" (1977), "Daku Aur Jawan" (1978), "Abdullah" (1980), "Dahshat" (1981), and "Heat and Dust" (1983). Khan left the film industry to become a jewelry maker and was involved in the import-export business.

Khorvash, Fakhri

Iranian actress Fakhri Khorvash died in Los Angeles, California, on June 10, 2023. She was 94. Khorvash was born in Kermanshah, Iran, on May 31, 1929. She became a teacher in Tehran after attending university. She began her acting career on stage in 1948. She made her film debut nearly a decade later with "Mostashare Jazireh" in 1956. She continued

to appear in such films as "Bohloul" (1958), "Chivalrous and Villain" (1958), "South of the City" (1958), "The Nobody" (1960), "Serpant's Skin" (1963), "Whisper of Love" (1965), "Sunrise" (1970), "Mr. Gullible" (1970), "Hasan Siah" (1972),

"Shir-Too-Shir" (1972), "The Curse" (1973), "The Sun in the Swamp" (1973), "Bi-Gharar" (1973), "Prince Ehtejab" (1974), "Chess of the Wind" (1976), "When the Sky Splits" (1976), "The City of Wine" (1976), "Mr. Mostafa's Mother" (1976), "Desiderium" (1978), "Dust-Dwellers" (1978), "Flight in the Cage" (1980), "Destiny's 5th Rider" (1980), "Whirlpool" (1981), "Quarantine" (1982), "Dada" (1983), "The Mallet" (1984), "The Scarecrow" (1984), "Locusts" (1984), "The Invasion" (1985), "Thunderbolt" (1985), "Shooting Star" (1985), "Let Me Live" (1986), "The Broken Gun" (1986), "Shirin and Farhad" (1996), "Crystal Man" (1999), "Mahboubeh" (1999), "Homa" (2001), "Tara and the Strawberry Fever" (2004), and "A Little Kiss" (2005). Khorvash was seen on television in productions of "Amirkabir" (1985), "Baghe Gilas" (1994), "The Martyr of Kufa" (1997), "Hame-Ye Farzandan-e Man" (1997), "Matic Coat" (1998), "Commandment" (2002), "Dayere-ye Tardid" (2003), "Roshantar Az Khamooshi" (2003), and "A House in Darkness" (2004). She moved to the United States in 2010 to be closer to her children.

Kido, Osamu

Japanese professional wrestler Osamu Kido died of cancer in Yokosuka, Japan, on December 11, 2023. He was 73.

Kido was born in Kawasaki, Japan, on February 2, 1950. He made his wrestling debut with the Japanese Wrestling Association (JWA) in February of 1969. He left the JWA with Antonio Inoki in 1971 and assisted him in forming New Japan Pro-Wrestling (NJPW) the following year. Kido went to Europe in 1975 and then to the United States, where he trained with Karl Gotch. He returned to Japan and NJPW in early 1976. Kido joined the Universal Wrestling Federation (UWF) in 1984. He resumed competing with NJPW when the UWF folded in 1986. He soon teamed with Akira Maeda to capture the IWGP Tag Team Championship. He teamed with such wrestlers as Tatsumi Fujinami, Scott Norton, Kazuo Yamazaki, and Riki Choshu over the next decade. Kido retired from the ring in May of 2003. He resumed wrestling several years later for independent promotions until again retiring in 2010.

234

Kim Soo-yong

South Korean film director Kim Soo-yong, who helmed over 100 films since the late 1950s, died in South Korea on December 3, 2023. He was 94. Kim was born in Anseong, Korea, on September 23, 1929. He began working in films as a director with 1958's "A Henpecked Husband". Many of his later films were based on popular Korean novels. Kim's numerous film credits also include "Three Brides" (1959), "Delivery of Youths" (1959), "A Grief" (1959), "A Band for Proposal" (1959), "A Love Front" (1960), "A Returned Man" (1960), "A Deserted Angel" (1960), "How to Become Man and Wife" (1961), "An Upstart" (1961), "My Only Love" (1961), "Bravo, Young Ones!" (1962), "Son Ogong" (1962), "Farewell to My Adolescence" (1962), "The Fiancee" (1963), "Flyboy's Penniless Trip" (1963)," Dried Yellow Croaker Fish" (1963), "My Wife Is Best" (1963), "The Classroom of Youth" (1963), "Bloodline" (aka "Kinship") (1963), "An Aristocrat's Love Affair" (1963), "The Opium War" (1964), "Are You Really a Beauty?" (1964), "The Dangerous Flesh" (1964), "The Pay Envelope" (1964), "The Student Couple" (1964), "The Girl Is Nineteen" (1964), "The Life in the Red Figures" (1965), "The Youngest Daughter" (1965), "The Seashore Village" (1965), "The Heir" (1965), "Sad Story of Self Supporting Child" (aka Sorrow in the Heavens") (1965), "Madam Wing" (1965), "The Legal Wife" (1965), "The Sea Village" (1965), "The Third Doom" (1965), "Affection" (1966), "A Gisaeng with a Bachelor's Degree" (1966), "Nostalgia" (1966), "Love Detective" (1966), "Goodbye, Japan" (1966), "Full Ship" (1967), "Confession of an Actress" (1967), "Lost Migrant" (1967), "Lovers" (1967), "Flame in the Valley" (1967), "The Freezing Point" (1967), "Accusation" (1967), "Mist" (1967), "Children in the Firing Range" (1967), "Sound of Magpies" (1967), "Chunhyang" (1968), "A Devoted Love" (1968), "Glory of Barefoot" (1968), "Salt Pond" (1968), "A Japanese" (1968), "Correspondent in Tokyo" (1968), "Bun-nyeo" (1968), "Starting Point" (1969), "Rejected First Love" (1969), "Spring, Spring" (1969), "Parking Lot" (1969), "Chaser" (1969) "A Barren Woman" (1969), "Mi-ae" (1970), "The Bride's Diary" (1970), "The Pagoda of No Shadow" (1970), "Agony of Man" (1970), "That Is the Sky Over Seoul" (1970), "Love in the Snowfield" (1970), "The Alimony" (1971), "When a Woman Breaks Her Jewel Box" (1971), "His Double Life" (1971), "The Merry Wife" (1972), "When a Little Dream Blooms" (1972), "Flower in the Rain" (1972), "A Family with Many Daughters" (1973), "Guests on Sunday" (1973), "The Land" (1974), "The Instinct" (1975), "Bird of Paradise" (1975), "Truth of Tomorrow" (1975) "Wasteland" (1975), "Windmill of My Mind" (1976), "Hot Wind in Arabia" (1976), "Similar Toes" (1976), "My Love, Elena" (1977), "Night Journey" (1977), "Scissors, Rock, and Wrap" (1977), "Forest Fire" (1977), "Two Decades as a Woman Journalist" (1977), "A Splendid Outing" (1978), "The Swamp of Exile" (1978), "The Sound of Laughter" (1978), "Yeosu (The Loneliness of the Journey)" (1979), "The Terms of Love" (1979), "Flowers and Birds" (1979), "Man-suk, Run!" (1980), "Rainbow" (1980), "White Smile" (1980), "Water Spray" (1980), "The Maiden Who Went to the City" (1981), "Late Autumn" (1982), "Bird That Cries At Night" (1982), "The Chrysanthemum and the Clown" (1982), "Sadness Even in the Sky" (1984), "Jung-kwang's Nonsense" (1986), The Apocalypse of Love" (1995), and "Scent of Love" (2000). He was instrumental in relaxing film censorship as chairman of the Korea Media Rating Board from 1998 to 2004.

Kimbrough, Charles

Actor Charles Kimbrough, who starred as anchorman Jim Dial on the "Murphy Brown" sitcom, died in Culver City, California, on January 11, 2023. He was 86. Kimbrough was born in St. Paul, Minnesota, on May 23, 1936. His aunt, Emily Kimbrough, was co-author of the memoir "Our Hearts Were Young and Gay" with Cornelia Otis Skinner. He graduated from Indiana University Bloomington in 1959 and received a Master of Fine Arts degree from Yale University's School of Drama. He and his first wife, actress Mary Jane Wilson, performed frequently with the Milwaukee Repertory Theatre in the late 1960s and early 1970s. He appeared frequently on Broadway throughout his career with roles in "Cop-Out" (1969), "Company" (1970) earning a Tony Award nomination for his role as Harry, "Candide" (1974), "Love for Love" (1974), "The Rules of the Game" (1974), "Same Time, Next Year" (1975), "Secret Service" (1976), "Boy Mets Girl" (1976), "The Water Engine/Mr. Happiness" (1978), "One Night Stand" (1980), the Stephen Sondheim musical "Sunday in the Park with George" (1984), "Hay Fever" (1985), "Accent on Youth" (2009), "The Merchant of Venice" (2010), and the 2012 revival of "Harvey" with Jim Parsons. He starred in the original off-Broadway production of A.R. Gurney's comedy "Sylvia" in 1995. Kimbrough began his career on television in the mid-1970s with roles in episodes "Kojak", "All My Children", "Tales of the Unexpected", "Spenser: For Hire", "Hothouse", "Love Boat: The Next Wave", "The Pat Sajak Show", "The Tonight Show Starring Johnny Carson", "Katie", and "Ally McBeal". He was also seen in television productions of "The Rules of the Game" (1975), "Secret Service" (1977), "For Ladies Only" (1981), "The Innocents Abroad" (1983), "A Doctor's Story" (1984), "Concealed Enemies" (1984), "The Recovery Room" (1985), "Sunday in the Park with George" (1986), "Weekend War" (1988), and "Cast the First Stone" (1989). Kimbrough was a voice actor in episodes of the animated series "Dinosaurs", "Mighty Max", "Pinky and the Brain", "Hercules", "Recess", "Family Guy", "The Angry Beavers", "Batman Beyond", and "The Zeta Project". He also voiced roles in the films and videos "Whisper of the Heart" (1995), "The Hunchback of Notre

Dame" (1996) as Victor, "Buzz Lightyear of Star Command: The Adventure Begins" (2000), "The Land Before Time VII: The Stone of Cold Fire" (2000), "Recess: School's Out" (2001) as Mort Chalk, "The Hunchback of Notre Dame II" (2002), and "Recess: Taking the Fifth Grade" (2003). He appeared in several films during his career including "The Front" (1976), "The Sentinel" (1977), "The Seduction of Joe Tynan" (1979), "Starting Over" (1979), "It's My Turn" (1980), "Switching Channels" (1988), "The Good Mother" (1988), "The Wedding Planner" (2001), and "Marci X" (2003). Kimbrough was best known for his role as veteran anchorman Jim Dial on the "Murphy Brown" comedy series "Murphy Brown" from 1988 to 1998. He earned an Emmy Award nomination in 1990 and reprised the role of Jim Dial in the 2018 reboot of "Murphy Brown". Kimbrough was married to Mary Jane Wilson from 1961 until their divorce in 1991, and is survived by their son, singer and musician John. He was married to actress Beth Howland, who co-starred as Vera in the television comedy series "Alice", from 2002 until her death in 2015.

Kirkman, Terry

Singer and songwriter Terry Kirkman, who performed with the band The Association, died of congestive heart failure in Montclair, California, on September 23, 2023. He was 83. Kirkman was born in Salina, Kansas, on December 12, 1939, and was raised in Chino, California. He studied music in his youth and was a music major at Chaffey College. He met Frank Zappa while a student and they performed together at coffeehouses in the late 1950s and early 1960s. Kirkman was working as a salesman when he met Jules Alexander in 1962. They soon joined with Doug Dillard to form the group the Inner Tubes in Los Angeles in 1964. They were joined by a rotating lineup of other musicians and singers including David Crosby and Cass Elliot. The group evolved into the folk-rock band the Men later in the year. The Association was put together in February of 1965 including Kirkman on vocals and a variety of other instruments, Alexander on vocals and lead guitar, Brian Cole on vocals, bass and woodwinds, Ted Bluechel, Jr., on drums, guitar, and bass, and Bob Page on guitar and banjo. Page was soon replaced by Jim Yester before the Association began performing publicly. They recorded their debut album "And Then... Along Comes the Association" in 1966, which included the hit songs "Cherish", which Kirkman wrote, and "Along Comes Mary". Kirkman also provided vocals on the songs "Never My Love", "Windy", and "Everything That Touches You". The Association performed at the Monterey Pop Festival in 1967 and released the albums "Renaissance" (1966), "Insight Out" (1967), "Birthday" (1968), "The Association" (1969), "Stop Your Motor" (1971), and "Waterbeds in Trinidad!" (1972). They earned six Grammy Award nominations in 1967 and 1968. They band performed on such television series as

"Hollywood a Go Go", "The Lloyd Thaxton Show", "Shivaree", "Where the Action Is", "The Andy Williams Show", "The Clay Cole Show", "The Steve Allen Comedy Hour", "The Hollywood Palace". "The Smothers Brothers Comedy Hour", "The Red Skelton Hour", "The Jonathan Winters Show", "The Glen Campbell Goodtime Hour", "The Joey Bishop Show", "Della", "The Ed Sullivan Show", "The Merv Griffin Show", "American Bandstand", and "The Don Knotts Show". They recorded four songs, including the title track, for the 1969 film "Goodbye, Columbus". Kirkman left the Association in 1972 but returned to perform with the band from 1979 to 1984. He and other members of the band were inducted into the Vocal Group Hall of Fame in 2003. He worked as an addiction counselor after leaving the music business. He is survived by his wife of thirty years, Heidi, and a daughter Alixandra, from his first marriage.

Kirksey, Iris

Actress and dancer Iris Kirksey died in Santa Rosa, California, on June 20, 2023. She was 96. Kirksey was born in Los Angeles, California, on October 13, 1926. She appeared in

a handful of films from the late 1930s including "The Under-Pup" (1939), "Top Man" (1943), "Chip Off the Old Block" (1944) as part of the Jivin' Jacks and Jills, and "National Velvet" (1944). She entertained as a singer and dancer at military bases throughout California as part of the USO during World War II. She retired from performing and married Wesley Rued in 1946. They settled in Santa Rosa where she was active in church and community affairs. She and Rued had four sons and two daughters before their divorce and she is survived by their children.

Kissinger, Henry

Diplomat and Nobel Peace Prize winner Henry Kissinger, who served as U.S. Secretary of State from 1973 to 1977, died of heart failure at his home in Kent, Connecticut, on November 29, 2023. He was 100. Kissinger was born to a Jewish family in Furth, Germany, on May 27, 1923. He fled Germany with his family to escape Nazi persecution in August of 1938. They stopped briefly in London before settling in New York City. He studied accounting at the City College of New York before being drafted into the U.S. Army in 1943. He became a naturalized citizen and was assigned to the 84th Infantry Division in Europe. He served in the military intelligence division and participated in the Battle of the Bulge. He was reassigned to the Counterintelligence Corps in 1945 and helped track down former Gestapo officers. He earned a Bronze Star for his service and took charge of the denazification of the Bergstrasse district of Hesse. He taught at the European Command Intelligence School at Camp King in Oberisel, Germany, in 1946. He returned to the United States after his discharge and earned a degree in political science from Harvard

University in 1950. He earned a master's degree in 1951 and a Doctor of Philosophy in 1954. He subsequently began teaching at Harvard and became a professor of government in 1962. He also served as director of the Defense Studies Program from 1959 to 1969. Kissinger was author of the book "Nuclear Weapons and Foreign Policy" in 1957. He was a consultant on security matters to various U.S. Agency during the administrations of Dwight Eisenhower, John Kennedy, and Lyndon B. Johnson. His 1960 book "The Necessity of Choice" supported a flexible response to possible attacks by the Soviet Union. He became an adviser to New York Governor Nelson Rockefeller during his unsuccessful campaigns for the Republican presidential nomination during the 1960s. He was named head of the National Security Council by President Richard Nixon in 1969 and became U.S. Secretary of State in 1973. Kissinger became the leading architect of Nixon's foreign policy toward Vietnam, China, the Soviet Union, and the Middle East. He helped establish a detente with the Soviet Union that led to the Strategic Arms Limitation Talks (SALT) in 1969. He was instrumental in bringing the United States and the People's Republic of China together diplomatically in the early 1970s. This resulted in a summit between Nixon and Chinese Communist Party Chairman Mao Tse-tung that established diplomatic relations between the two nations for the first time. Kissinger originally advocated increased military

action during the Vietnam War including the U.S. bombing of Cambodia. He soon became a supporter of the Vietnamization policy and the removal of U.S. troops from South Vietnam. He engaged in peace negotiations with North Vietnamese diplomat Le Duc Tho that resulted a cease-fire agreement at the Paris Peace Talks in 1973. Kissinger and Le Duc Tho were jointly awarded the Nobel Prize for Peace for the resolution of the Vietnam conflict later in 1973. Le Duc Tho declined the award and fighting continued between the north and south without American support and resulted in the fall of Saigon in 1975. He exercised what was described as shuttle diplomacy regarding the Middle East after the 1973 Arab-Israeli war. He helped reestablish diplomatic relations between the United States and Egypt. He advocated support for Pakistan against India in the Bangladesh War of Independence and for Indonesia in its invasion of East Timor. He was also the main architect of the Nixon administration's policies in South American, supporting brutal military coups in Chile and Argentina. Kissinger remained in office after the resignation of Nixon in 1974. President Gerald Ford replaced him as National Security Advisor with Brent Scowcroft in November of 1975. He remained as Secretary of State until Ford was replaced by President Jimmy Carter in January of 1977. He continued to participate in world affairs and was a critic of President Carter's foreign policy. He accepted a position at Georgetown University's Center for Strategic and

International Studies in the late 1970s. He formed the consulting firm of Kissinger Associated in 1982 and was a partner in Kissinger McLarty Associates. He served on the boards of numerous corporations and was an advisor to political leaders, foreign and domestic. He served as ceremonial Chancellor of the College of William and Mary from 2000 to 2005. He briefly served as chairman of President George W. Bush's National Commission on Terrorist Attack Upon the United States following the September 11, 2002, attacks. He stepped down soon after rather than release a list of his business clients who might cause a conflict of interest. He reportedly was an advisor to the Bush Administration during the Iraq War in 2006. He continued to give his opinion on matters ranging from Iran's nuclear potential to the Russian invasion of Ukraine. Kissinger remained a controversial figure throughout his career both at home and abroad. He was revered by some and reviled by others but left an unmistakable mark on American foreign policy from the 1960s. He was awarded the Presidential Medal of Freedom from President Ford in 1977. His first volume of memoirs, "The White House Years", earned the National Book Award in History in 1980. The subsequent volumes of his memoirs were "Years of Upheaval" (1982) and "Years of Renewal" (1999). He was a recipient of the Medal of Liberty from President Ronald Reagan in 1986. His other books include "Observations: Selected speeches and essays 1982-1984" (1985), "Diplomacy" (1994), "Does America Need a Foreign Policy? Toward a Diplomacy for the 21st Century" (2001), "Vietnam: A Personal History of America's Involvement in and Extrication from the Vietnam War" (2002), "On China" (2011), and "World Order" (2014). Kissinger was played by Roger Bowen in the comedy spoof film "Tunnelvision" in 1976 and Peter Jurasik had the role in the 1978 film "Born Again". Theodore Bikel was Kissinger in the 1989 tele-film "The Final Days". Paul Sorvino played the role opposite Anthony Hopkins' Richard Nixon in the 1994 film "Nixon", and Ron Silver was Kissinger to Beau Bridges' Nixon in the 1995 tele-film "Kissinger and Nixon". He was he played by Saul Rubinek in the 1999 comedy film "Dick". He was played by Henry Goodman in the 2012 British tele-film "Nixon's the One" and by Kirk Bovill in 2018's "Vice" starring Christian Bale as Dick Cheney. Liev Schreiber starred as Kissinger opposite Helen Mirren's Golda Meir in the 2023 film "Golda". He appeared in cameo roles in episodes of the television series "Dynasty" in 1983 and "Brother's Keeper" in 1999. He supplied the voice of Ducky Daddles in an episode of the animated series "Happily Ever After: Fairy Tales for Every Child" in 1999. He was a consultant for the 1997 James Bond film "Tomorrow Never Dies". He was a guest on various talk shows including "The Dick Cavett Show", "Today", "Late Show with David Letterman", "The Oprah Winfrey Show", "The Tonight Show with Jay Leno", "The Daily Show", "Breakfast with Frost", "Tavis Smiley", "The Colbert Report", and "Charlie Rose". Kissinger was married to Ann Fleischer from 1949 until their divorce in 1964 and is survived by two children, Elizabeth and David. He married philanthropist Nancy Maginnes in 1974 and she also survives him.

Kitman, Marvin

Television critic and humorist Marvin Kitman died of cancer at the Lillian Booth Actors Home in Englewood, New Jersey, on June 29, 2023. He was 93. Kitman was born in Pittsburg, Pennsylvania, on November 24, 1929, and moved to Brooklyn, New York, with his family as a child. He attended Baruch College before switching to the City College of New York, where he graduated in 1953. He served in the U.S. Army at Fort Dix in New Jersey from 1953 to 1955. He was a sportswriter for the base newspaper during his service. He began writing articles for the horse-racing sheet "The Armstrong Daily" after his discharge and penned satirical consumer advocacy columns for "The Realist". Kitman became editor of the satire magazine "Monocle" in 1963. He briefly staged a campaign for the Republican presidential nomination in the New Hampshire primary in 1964. He was a staff writer for "The Saturday Evening Post" from 1965 to 1966. He subsequently worked in advertising for several years before becoming a television critic. He joined "The New Leader" in 1967 and "Newsday" in 1969. His column at "Newsday", "The Marvin Kitman Show", frequently bashed the television content of the time, and continued until 2005. Kitman also appeared on the New York local news as a critic in the 1970s and 1980s and was panelist on the "All About TV" show. He was co-creator and writer of the short-lived 1976 television comedy series "Ball Four" with Jim Bouton and Vic Ziegel. Kitman was the author of the books "The Number One Best Seller: The True Adventures of Marvin Kitman" (1966), "The Red Chinese Air Force Exercise, Diet, and Sex Book" (1968), "You Can't Judge a Book By Its Cover" (1969), "George Washington's Expense Account" (1970), "The Marvin Kitman Show: An Encyclopedia Televisiana" (1973), "The Coward's Almanac" (1975), "I Am a VCR: The Kitman Tapes" (1988), "The Making of the President 1789: The Unauthorized Campaign Biography" (1989), "The Man Who Would Not Shut Up: The Rise of Bill O'Reilly" (2020), and "Gullible's Travels: A Comical History of the Trump Era" (2020). Kitman was a guest on several talk shows including "The Tonight Show Starring Johnny Carson" and "The Dick Cavett Show". He wrote columns and criticisms for various internet sites during his later years. Kitman married photographer Carol Sibushnick in 1951 and is survived by her and their son and two daughters.

Klane, Robert

Screenwriter Robert Klane, who was best known for scripting the 1989 comedy "Weekend at Bernie's", died of kidney failure in Woodland Hills, California, on August 29, 2023. He was 81. Klane was born in Port Jefferson, New York, on October 17, 1941. He graduated from the University of North Carolina at Chapel Hill in 1963. He worked in New York City as an advertising copywriter after his graduation, and later directed television commercials. His first novel, "The Horse Is Dead", was published in 1968. His second novel, "Where's Poppa?", was published in 1970 and Klane scripted the film adaptation for a feature directed by Carl Reiner later in the year.

He was executive producer of a 1979 tele-film version. He adapted his 1975 novel, "Fire Sale", for a 1977 film of the same name. Klane co-scripted the 1972 film "Every Little Crook and Nanny" and directed and wrote the 1978 comedy film "Thank God It's Friday". He scripted the films "Unfaithfully Yours" (1984), "The Man with One Red Shoe" (1985), "National Lampoon's European Vacation" (1985), and "Folks!" (1992). He was writer and executive producer for the films "Walk Like a Man" (1987) and the cult comedy "Weekend at Bernie's" (1989). He directed and wrote the 1993 sequel "Weekend at Bernie's II". Klane wrote and sometimes produced such tele-films as "Aces Up" (1974), "Rosenthal and Jones" (1975), "The Banana Company" (1977), "Camp Grizzly" (1980), "The Ladies" (1987), "The Odd Couple: Together Again" (1993) which he also directed, and "Kidz in the Wood" (1995). He scripted episodes of "The Michele Lee Show", "M*A*S*H", "Mr. & Mrs. Dracula", and "Tracey Takes On..." winning an Emmy Award in 1997 and directed an episode of "Baby Boom". Klane was married to Linda Tesh from 1962 until their divorce in 1975 and is survived by their two sons, David and Jon. A daughter, Tracy, died in 2011. He was married to actress Anjanette Comer from 1976 until their divorce in 1983. He married J.C. Scott in 1984 and is survived by her and their daughter Caitlin.

Klenman, Norman

Canadian screenwriter Norman Klenman died in Vancouver, British Columbia, Canada, on June 8, 2023. He was 99. Klenman was born in Brandon, Manitoba, Canada, on August 2, 1923, and was raised in Vancouver. He graduated

from the University of British Columbia with a degree in journalism. He served in the Royal Canadian Air Force during World War II. Klenman worked as a sportswriter for the "Vancouver Sun" and Reuters after the war. He joined the National Film Board of Canada in the early 1950s where he wrote such short films as "Shadow on the Prairie: A Canadian Ballet" (1953), "Tempest in Town" (1953), "Security Depends on You" (1953), "The Photographer" (1953), "Each Man's Son" (1954), "The Magnificent" (1954), "Le Voleurs de Reves" (1954), "Grain Handling in Canada" (1955), "L'Avocat de la Defense" (1955), "Problem Clinic" (1955), "The Hoax" (1955), and "The Curlers" (1955). He produced and write the feature films "Now

That April's Here" (1958) and "Ivy League Killers" (1959). Klenman worked frequently in television from the 1960s and scripted episodes of "The Steve Allen Plymouth Show", "On the Road", "Quest", "ABC's Nightlife", "Seaway", "Iron Horse", "The Invaders", "The Danny Thomas Hour", "The Felony Squad", "The Survivors", and "Performance". He was story editor for the science fiction series "The Starlost" from 1973 to 1974. He also scripted the tele-film "Our Man Flint: Dead on Target" (1976) and the feature "The Swiss Conspiracy" (1976). Klenman was married to Daphne Dagmar Joy Timmins from 1951 until her death in 1995. He was predeceased by their daughter, Anna, and is survived by their son, Alex.

Klibingaitis, Maxine

Australian actress Maxine Klibingaitis died in Melbourne, Australia, on April 17, 2023. She was 58. Klibingaitis was born in Ballarat, Australia, on May 17, 1964.

She began her career on television in the early 1980s and starred as teen punk Bobbie Mitchell on the series "Prisoner: Cell Block H" from 1983 to 1985. She starred as Terry Inglis Robinson in the soap opera "Neighbours" in 1985. Klibingaitis also appeared in episodes of "Home", "Special Squad", "The Flying Doctors", "Home and Away", "Family and Friends", the short-lived comedy "Hampton Court" as Sophie Verstak in 1991, "Col'n Carpenter", "All Together Now", "Blue Heelers", "Round the Twist", "MDA", "Celebrity House Cleaner, "Five Bedrooms", an "Mondo Maniacs". Her other television credits include the mini-series "Fields of Fire" (1987) and "Marshall Law" (2002). She was featured in several films including "Kiss the Night" (aka "Candy Regentag") (1989), "Prisoner Queen - Mindless Music & Mirrorballs" (2003), "Moonlight & Magic" (2007), the short "Miss Mouskouri" (2007), "Boronia Boys" (2009), "Boronia Backpackers" (2011), and "The House Cleaner" (2013). Klibingaitis married director Andrew Friedman in 1987 and is survived by him and their son, Zane.

Kluck, Tony

Dutch director and animator Tony Kluck died in Amsterdam, Netherlands, on April 24, 2023. He was 75. Kluck was born in the Netherlands on August 16, 1947. He began his career at Toonder Studio in Amsterdam working on such animated productions as "Gnomes" (1980), "Als Je Begrijpt Wat Ik Bedoel" (aka "The Dragon That Wasn't") (1983), "Kinderen Voor Kinderen" (1984), and "Peterchens Mondfahrt" (1990). Kluck came to the United States in the 1990s where he was an artist and animator on such series as "Beavis and Butt-Head", "KaBlam!", "Cartoon Sushi", "CatDog", "Downtown" earning an Emmy Award nomination in 2000, "Sheep in the Big City", "Celebrity Deathmatch", "Daria", "The Adventures of Captain Cross Dresser, "Maya & Miguel", "Bob's Burgers", and "King of the Hill" earning another Emmy nomination in 2008. He also was storyboard artist and animator for the animated films "Beavis and Butt-Head Do America" (1996), "Ice Age" (2002), "Daria in Is It College Yet?" (2002), "The Lizzie McGuire Movie" (2003), and "Duplex" (2003). Kluck is survived by his wife, Cynthia, and two sons.

Klunis, Tom

Actor Tom Klunis died in Los Angeles, California, on October 23, 2023. He was 93. Klunis was born in San Francisco, California, on April 29, 1930. He attended San

Francisco State College where he began performing on stage. He continued his training with the San Francisco Actor's Workshop for two years before moving to New York City in 1957. He continued to perform on stage and appeared on Broadway in productions of "Gideon" (1961), "The Devils" (1965), "Ivanov" (1966), "King Henry V" (1969), "Romeo and Juliet" (1977), "Saint Joan" (1977), "Hide and Seek" (1980), "The Bacchae" (1980), "Ghosts" (1982), "Plenty" (1983), and "M. Butterfly" (1988). Klunis was seen in several films during his career including "Hamlet" (1964), "The Day the Fish Came Out" (1967), "Assignment Skyboldt" (1968), "Towers of Silence" (1975), "The Next Man" (1976), and "Taps" (1981). He appeared frequently on television with roles in episodes of "Guiding Light", "Salty", "Search for Tomorrow", "Ryan's Hope" as Ivan Reese in 1981, "Little House on the Prairie", "Crossboy", "The Equalizer", "Great Performances" in "Hamlet" in 1990, "thirtysomething", "Cheers", "Wings", "Star Trek: Deep Space Nine", and "Reasonable Doubts". His other television credits include the tele-films "Kojak: Fatal Flaw" (1989), "Michigan Melodie" (1990), and "Her Wicked Ways" (1991).

Knievel, Robbie

Motorcycle stunt performer Robbie Knievel, who was the son of daredevil Evel Knievel, died of pancreatic cancer in

Reno, Nevada, on January 13, 2023. He was 60. He was born Robert Edward Knievel II in Butte, Montana, on May 7, 1962. He began riding a motorcycle from an early age and performed in pre-jump shows with his father from the age of twelve. He left high school in 1976 and began his own motorcycle jumping career. He used a Honda CR5000

motocross bike during most of his jumps which included many from his father's career. He completed over 340 jumps and set 20 world records during his career. Many of his jumps were televised including "Robbie Knievel: Grand Canyon Death Jump" (1999) and "Robbie Knievel's Head-On Train Jump Live" (2000). He was featured in episodes of television's "CHiPs" and "Hawaii Five-O", and on the series "The Tonight Show with Jay Leno", "Howard Stern", "Late Night with Conan O'Brien", "The Great Ride", and "Top Gear". He was a stunt performer for the 1984 film "Ninja III: The Domination" and appeared in the films "The Last of the Gladiators" (1988), "I Am Evel Knievel" (2014), "Chasing Evel: The Robbie Knievel Story" (2017), and "Evelution" (2019). He starred in the 2005 A&E reality series "Knievel's Wild Ride" and performed his final stunt, clearing a series of tractor-trailers at a Coachella casino, in 2011. His father died in November of 2007. Robbie is survived by three daughters.

Knight, Bobby

College basketball coach Bobby Knight, who was head coach for the Indiana Hoosiers from 1971 to 2000, died in Bloomington, Indiana, on November 1, 2023. He was 83.

Knight was born in Massillon, Ohio, on October 25, 1940. He began playing basketball in high school and continued with the Ohio State Buckeyes from 1959 to 1962. He coached at Cuyahoga Falls High School in Ohio after graduating in 1962. Knight served in the U.S. Army from 1963 to 1965 and remained in the U.S. Army Reserves from 1965 to 1969. He was assistant coach of the Army Black Knights basketball team at West Point from 1963 to 1965 and served as head coach from 1965 to 1971. He joined Indiana University as head coach for the Indiana Hoosiers in 1971. The team won 662 and lost 239 games under Knight, and won titles in 1976, 1981, and 1987. He had numerous controversies, frequently regarding his volatile temper, during his time at Indiana. Despite his winning record he was asked to resign in September of 2000 following allegations he choked and manhandled students. He subsequently joined Texas Tech University in Lubbock, Texas, as head coach of the Red Raiders from 2001 until his retirement in 2008. He was a studio analyst for ESPN basketball coverage from 2008 until 2015. Knight appeared as himself, an opposing coach to Nick Nolte's Pete Bell, in the basketball film "Blue Chips" in 1994. He was portrayed by Brian Dennehy in the 2002 ESPN tele-film adaptation of John Feinstein's "A Season on the Brink" and made a cameo appearance in the 2003 film "Anger Management". He starred in the ESPN reality series "Knight School with Coach Bobby Knight" in 2006. He was a guest on the television talk shows "Late Night with David Letterman", "Late Show with David Letterman", "Quite Frankly with Stephen A. Smith", "The Tonight Show with Jay Leno", "Charlie Rose", and "Mike & Mike". He also appeared in television commercials for Volkswagen and Guitar Hero: Metallica. He was the subject of various books including Joan Mellen's "Bob Knight: His Own Man" (1988), Robert P. Sulek's "Hoosier Honor: Bob Knight and Academic Success at Indiana University" (1990), Steve Alford's "Playing for Knight: My Six Seasons with Bobby Knight", and Kirk Haston's "Days of Knight: How the General Changed My Life" (2016). He co-wrote his autobiography, "Knight: My Story", with Bob Hammel in 2003. He and Hammel also co-authored the 2013 book "The Power of Negative Thinking: An Unconventional Approach to Achieving Positive Results". Knight was married to Nancy Falk from 1963 until their divorce in 1985 and is survived by their two sons. He married Karen Vieth Edgar in 1988 and she also survives him.

Knight, Charles T.

Film sound engineer Charles T. Knight died on June 29, 2023. He was 91. Knight was born on October 18, 1931. He began working in films in the sound department for the 1963 horror film "Monstrosity" (aka "The Atomic Brain"). His other

films as a sound mixer and engineer include "The Dunwich Horror" (1970), "How Did a Nice Girl Like You..." (1970), "Bloody Mama" (1970), "Five Easy Pieces" (1970), "Drive, He Said" (1971), "Two-Lane Blacktop" (1971), "The Late Liz" (1971), "Deadhead Miles" (1972), "Silent Running" (1972), "Butterflies Are Free" (1972) earning an Academy Award nomination, "Blacula" (1972), "Oklahoma Crude" (1973), "Zandy's Bride" (1974), "Harrad Summer" (1974), "Framed" (1975), "Futureworld" (1976), "Airport '77" (1977), "Bloodbrothers" (1978), "Jimmy the Kid" (1982), "Last Time Out" (1994), and the 1994 short "Tuesday Morning Ride". Knight worked frequently in television, serving as a sound mixer for productions of "Don't Be Afraid of the Dark" (1973), "The Autobiography of Miss Jane Pittman" (1974), "It's Good to Be Alive" (1974), "Betrayal" (1974), "The Loneliest Runner" (1976), "Murder by Natural Causes" (1979), "The Child Stealer" (1979), "The Billion Dollar Threat" (1979), "Topper" (1979), "This House Possessed" (1981), "Stand By Your Man" (1981), "Bitter Harvest" (1981), "The Two Lives of Carol Letner" (1981), "Rehearsal for Murder" (1982), "Callahan" (1982), "Intimate Agony" (1983), "Sunset Limousine" (1983), "The Day After" (1983), "For Love or Money" (1984), "A Reason to Live" (1985), "The Rape of Richard Beck" (1985), "Promises to Keep" (1985), "Beverly Hills Madam" (1986), "North & South: Book 2, Love & War" (1986), "Kate's Secret" (1986), "Love Among Thieves" (1987), "Weekend War" (1988), "The Karen Carpenter Story" (1989), "The Hollywood Detective" (1989), "A Killer Among Us" (1990), and "Crazy from the Heart" (1991). His other television credits include episodes of "Harry O", "Little House on the Prairie" serving as sound recordist from 1974 to 1977, "Gideon Oliver", "A Brand New Life", and "CBS Schoolbreak Special".

Knight, Jean

Singer Jean Knight, who was noted for the 1971 hit "Mr. Big Stuff", died at a hospital in Tampa, Florida, on November 22, 2023. She was 80. She was born Jean Caliste in New Orleans, Louisiana, on January 26, 1943. She began singing at a local bar after graduating high school. She was soon being accompanied by various bands and took the stage name Jean Knight. She was signed by the Jet Star/Tribe record labels in the mid-1960s. She released several singles including "The Man That Left Me", "Lonesome Tonight", and "Anyone Can Love Him", but achieved little success. She left music by the end of the decade and worked as a baker's assistant in the cafeteria of a New Orleans' college. She was encouraged to revive her career by songwriter Ralph Williams in the early 1970s. Her recording of "Mr. Big Stuff" from Stax Records became a major hit and earned a Grammy Award nomination. She performed the song on "Soul Train" and recorded an album of the same name. She left Stax later in the decade and was signed to the Soulin' label in 1981. She recorded the song "You Got the Papers But I Got the Man" and covered the zydeco hit "My Toot Toot" in 1985, which she performed on "Solid Gold". She continued to release occasional records over the next decade with her later songs including "Mama's Baby" and "Bill". She graduated from nursing school in the 1980s and was a practical nurse for over a decade. She continued to perform at local venues in the New Orleans area and was a regular guest at the New Orleans Jazz & Heritage Festival until 2016. Knight was married and divorced from Thomas Commedore and Earl Harris. She is survived by her son, Emile Commedore.

Knight, Tonya

Bodybuilder Tonya Knight, who was featured as Gold on "American Gladiators" from 1989 to 1992, died of cancer in Kansas City, Missouri, on February 7, 2023. She was 56.

Knight was born in Peculiar, Missouri, on March 24, 1966. She began bodybuilding in her teens and participated in competitions with the National Physique Committee in the mid-1980s. She placed fourth in the International Federation of BodyBuilding and Fitness (IFBB) Ms. Olympia competition in 1988 and was crowned Ms. International in 1989. She was stripped of her title later in the year when she acknowledged avoiding the mandatory drug test for the event. She later returned to claim the Ms. International title in 1991 and placed sixth in 1992. She appeared as Gold on the competition series "American Gladiators" from 1989 to 1992. Knight was married and divorced from fellow bodybuilder and actor John Poteat, who died in 2016. She is survived by her son, Malachi.

Knode, Charles

British costume designer Charles Knode, who received an Academy Award nomination for his work on "Braveheart", died in West Sussex, England, on February 16, 2023. He was 80. Knode was

born in Alcester, Warwickshire, England, in 1942. He began working in costume design with the BBC in the 1960s on such series as "Sir Arthur Conan Doyle", "The Big M", "The Jazz Age", 'Out of the Unknown", "The Way We Live Now", "Solo", "Music on 2", "W. Somerset Maugham", "Sense and Sensibility", "War & Peace" earning an Emmy Award nomination in 1974, and "Operation Patch". He was also costume designer for television productions of "The Three Princes" (1968), "The Marquise" (1969), "The Rivals" (1970), "Owen Wingrave" (1971), "Miss Nightingale" (1974), "Hedda Gabler" (1981), "Death in Venice" (1981), "Spymaker: The Secret Life of Ian Fleming" (1990), "The Odyssey" (1997), "Snow White: A Tale of Terror" (1997) earning an Emmy nomination for Sigourney Weaver's wardrobe, "Frenchmans Creek" (1998), "Alice in Wonderland" (1999) sharing an Emmy Award, "A Christmas Carol" (1999), "Don Quixote" (2000) sharing an Emmy nomination, and "Dinotopia" receiving an Emmy nomination in 2002. He made his film debut as costume designer for "Monty Python and the Holy Grail" (1975) and was featured onscreen as Robin's Minstrel. He also designed costumes for the films "Jabberwocky" (1977), "The Hound of the Baskervilles" (1978), "Life of Brian" (1979), the short "Black Angel" (1980), Ridley Scott's "Blade Runner" (1982) receiving a BAFTA Award, the 1983 James Bond film "Never Say Never Again", "Legend" (1985), "Love Potion" (1987), "A Dry White Season" (1989), "1493: Conquest of Paradise" (1992), and Mel Gibson's "Braveheart" (1995) receiving a BAFTA Award and an Academy Award nomination.

Kochanova, Gergana

Bulgarian model Gergana Kochanova, who was Miss

Bulgaria in 2007, was shot to death at her home in South Africa along with her husband and two others on May 25, 2023. She was 38. Kochanova was born in Sofia, Bulgaria, on January 24, 1985. She was a model and was crowned Miss Bulgaria in 2007. She represented Bulgaria in the Miss Universe competition in Mexico City later in the year. She became involved with Bulgarian crime figure Krasimir 'Kuro' Kamenov in 2015. He had settled in

South Africa in a mansion in the wealth Cape Town suburb of Constantia. Kamenov was believed to be the target of a hit squad that killed him, Kochanova, and two housekeepers.

Koenig, Laird

Author and screenwriter Laird Koenig, who wrote the 1974 novel "The Little Girl Who Lives Down the Lane", died in Santa Barbara, California, on June 30, 2023. He was 95. Koenig was born in Seattle, Washington, on September 24, 1927. He attended the University of Washington and worked in advertising in New York City. He moved to Los Angeles in the mid-1960s where he teamed with frequent writing partner Peter L. Dixon to script episodes of the television series "Flipper" and "The High Chaparral". He wrote the 1966 film "The Cat" and the 1969 short-lived Broadway play "The Dozens". He and Dixon co-wrote the 1970 novel "The Children Are Watching". It was adapted for the French film "Attention Les Enfants Regardent" in 1978 starring Alain Delon. Koenig's best-known novel, the psychological thriller "The Little Girl Who Lives Down the Lane", was published in 1974. He scripted a film version of the same name starring Jodie Foster and Martin Sheen in 1976. He adapted it for a play in 1997. His 1978 novel "The Neighbor" was filmed as "Killing 'em Softly" in 1982. His other novels include "Islands" (1980), "Rockabye" (1981) which he adapted for a tele-film 1986, "The Disciple" (1983), "The Sea Wife" (1986), "Rising Sun" (1986), and "Morning Sun: The Story of Madam Butterfly's Boy" (2012). He was a writer of three films by director Terence Young, "Red Sun" (1971), "Bloodline" (1979), and "Inchon" (1981). Koenig scripted the 1979 film "Bloodline" based on a novel by Sydney Sheldon and "Tennessee Waltz" in 1989. He wrote episodes of the series "Flipper", "The High Chaparral", and "Intrigues", and the tele-films "Macho" (1986), "Stillwatch" (1987), "The Fulfillment of Mary Gray" (1989), and "Lady Against the Odds" (1992).

Kolesnikov, Sergei

Russian actor Sergei Kolesnikov died in Moscow, Russia, on April 29, 2023. He was 68. Kolesnikov was born in

Moscow on January 4, 1955. He graduated from the Moscow Art Theatre School in 1978 and began his career on stage. He later worked at the Gorky Moscow Art Theatre and performed with the Chekhov Moscow Art Theatre from 1990 to 2011. Kolesnikov was seen in the films "Tolko Vdvoyom" (1976), "Dolgi Nashi" (1977), "Ballada o Pesne" (1981), "Man with an Accordion" (1985), "Tsar Ivan the Terrible"

(1991), "Vovochka" (2002), "Cold Souls" (2009), "Shapito-Shou: Lyubov i Druzhba" (2011), "A Good Day to Die Hard" (2013) starring Bruce Willis, "Black Sea" (2014), "Crazy Alien" (2019), and the historical fantasy "Land of Legends" (2022). He was seen on television in productions of "Seredina Zhizni" (1976), "Vizhu Tsel" (1978), "Svoyo Schastye" (1979), "Kvartira" (1992), "Melochi Zhizni" from 1992 to 1996, "Peterburgskie Tayny" as the Investigator in 1996, "MUR est MUR" as Toropov in 2004, "Delo o Myortvykh Dushakh" (2005), "Serdtsu Ne Prikazhesh" as Oleg Matetsky in 2007, "McMafia" (2018), and "Doktor Krasnov" (2023). Kolesnikov was married to actress Maria Velikanova Kolesnikova and is survived by her and sons.

Konuma, Masaru

Japanese film director Masaru Konuma died in Japan on January 22, 2023. He was 85. Konuma was born in Otaro, Hokkaido, Japan, on December 30, 1937. He was sent to live

in Tokyo in his teens. He attended Nihon University where he majored in film studies. He began working at Nikkatsu Studios shortly after graduating in 1961. He served as an assistant director on the 1967 film "Daikyoju Gappa" (aka "Monster from a Prehistoric Planet"). He was also an assistant director for the films "Harenchi Gakuen: Takkuru Kissu No Maki" (1970), "Shin Harenchi Gakuen" (1971), "The House of Beasts" (1973), and "Mitsu No Shitatari" (1973). Konumu began directing for Nikkatsu in the early 1970s and became noted for his Roman Porno, or softcore pornographic, films. He helmed numerous such features including "Call of the Pistil" (1971), "Love Hunter: Hot Skin" (1972), "Headlights in the Rain" (1972), "Secret Wife" (1972), "Three Wives: Wild Nights" (1972), "Afternoon Affair: Kyoto Holy Tapestry" (1973), "Erotic Journey: Love Affair in Hong Kong" (1973), "Female Teacher: Sweet Life" (1973), "Koi No Karyudo: Atsui Hada" (1973), "Kashin No Takamari" (1974), "Flower and Snake" (1974), "Wife to Be Sacrificed" (1974), "Lost Love: Oil Hell" (1974), "Lesbian World: Ecstasy" (1975), "Female Teacher: Boy Hunt" (1975), "Great Edo: Secret Story of a Female Doctor in Trouble" (1975), "Cloistered Nun: Runa's Confession" (1976), "Nureta Tsubo" (1976), "Getting Raped" (1976), "Tattooed Flower Vase" (1976), "Erotic Diary of an Office Lady" (1977), "In the Realm of Sex" (1977), "Yumeno Kyusaku's Girl Hell" (1977), "Kifujin Shibari Tsubo" (1977), "Wandering Lovers: Dizziness" (1978), "Friday Bedroom" (1978), "Sometimes... Like a Prostitute" (1978), "College Girls on Friday" (1979), "Mr. Dilemma Man: Lunatic for Lust" (1979), "Uptown Lady: Days of Eros" (1980), "Wife's Sexual Fantasy Before Husband's Eyes" (1980), "Image of a Bound Girl" (1980), "Woman Who Exposes Herself" (1981), "Woman Who Is Used" (1981), "Fallen Angel Gang" (1981), "Slave Contract" (1982), "Lady Karuizawa" (1982), "Rope and Breasts" (1983), "Blue Rain Osaka" (1983), "Joshu Ori" (1983), "Madam Scandal - Final

Scandal: Madam Likes It Hard" (1983), "Flight Attendant: Scandal" (1984), "Yawaharda Iro-kurabe" (1984), "Tsuma Toiu Na No Tanin" (1984), "Woman in a Box: Virgin Sacrifice" (1985), "Inko" (1986), "Bed-In" (1986), "La Ronde" (1988), "Woman in a Box 2" (1988), "Ten To Chi To: Reimei-hen" (1990), "XX: Utsukushiki Karyuudo" (1994), "Lustful Revenge" (1996), "Kairakusatsujin: Onna Sousakan" (1996), "Beach" (2000), and "Onna Wa Basutei de Fuku o Kigaeta" (2002). Konuma was the subject of Hideo Nakata's 2000 documentary film "Sadistic and Masochistic".

Koo, Joseph

Hong Kong composer Joseph Koo (aka Ku Chia-hui), who was noted for his film scores, died of complications of Covid-19 at a hospital in Richmond, Canada, on January 3, 2023. He was 91. He was born Koo Kar-Fai in Canton, China,

on February 25, 1931. He moved to Hong Kong with his family in 1948. He began training on the piano in his teens and composed his first song, "Dreams", in 1961. His early songs were performed by his sister, Koo Mei, who was a popular recording artist. He attended the Berklee College of Music in Boston in the early 1960s. He returned to Hong Kong after graduation and worked for

the film studios the Shaw Brothers and Golden Harvest. He scored and wrote songs for numerous films throughout his career including "The Grand Substitution" (1964), "Hong Kong, Manila, Singapore" (1965), "Inside the Forbidden City" (9165), "Chun Can" (1969), "The Singing Escort" (1969), "Four Moods" (1970), "Jian Nu You Hun" (1970), "Wu Di Tie Sha Zhang" (1971), "Fist of Fury" (1972), "Lady Whirlwind" (1972), "Kung Fu-ry" (1972), "The Way of the Dragon" (1972), "Shitu Lao Ma" (1972), "A Man Called Tiger" (1973), "Seven Magnificent Fights" (1973), "Attack of the Kung Fu Girls" (1973), "Deadly China Doll" (1973), "The Fate of Lee Khan" (1973), "Tattooed Dragon" (1973), "The Story of Mother" (1973), "The Skyhawk" (1974), "Yellow-Faced Tiger" (1974), "Games Gamblers Play" (1974), "Hard as a Dragon" (1974), "Snake Girl" (1974), "Ghost of the Mirror" (1974), "The Bedeviled" (1975), "The Dragon Tamers" (1975), "My Wacky, Wacky World" (1975), "The Last Message" (1975), "Bruce Lee and I" (1976), "Princess Chang Ping" (1976), "The Girlie Bar" (1976), "The Last Tempest" (1976), "Gonna Get You" (1976), "The Hand of Death" (1976), "Chelsia My Love" (1976), "H-Bomb" (1976), "Innocent Lust" (1977), "Heaven Sword and Dragon Sabre 2" (1978), "Fly Up with Love" (1978), "Full Moon Scimitar" (1979), "Money Trip" (1979), "The Deadly Breaking Sword" (1979), "Law Don" (1979), "The Sword" (1980), "Heroes Shed No Tears" (1980), "Man on the Brink" (1981), "Older Master Cute Part II" (1982), "Tou Shou Zai" (1982), "Crazy Kung Fu Master" (1984), "Be Careful Sweetheart" (1984), "Beloved Daddy" (984), "Holy Robe of the Shaolin Temple" (1985), "Happy Ghost III" (1986), John Woo's

"A Better Tomorrow" (1986), "Mirage" (1987), "A Better Tomorrow II" (1987), "Paper Marriage" (1988), "A Terra-Cotta Warrior" (1989), "King of Beggars" (1992), and "Fist of Legend" (1994). Koo composed over 1200 songs during his career and worked with lyricist Wong Jim on numerous television theme songs and Cantopop hits. He moved to Canada in the 1990s but continue to work on music for Hong Kong films and television. He largely retired as a conductor in 2015 and made limited compositions. Koo is survived by his wife Ella Tsang Noi Koo, son Ken, and daughter Sally.

Korthaze, Richard

Actor Richard Korthaze, who was best known for his roles on the Broadway stage, died in Connecticut on January 1,

2023. He was 94. Korthaze was born in Chicago, Illinois, on February 11, 1928. He began his career on stage and made his Broadway debut in the chorus of the 1951 revival of "Pal Joey". He was an actor and dancer in numerous Broadway shows including "Phoenix '55" (1955), "Happy Hunting" (1956), "The Conquering Hero" (1961), "How to Succeed in Business Without Really Trying" (1961),

"Skyscraper" (1965), "Walking Happy" (1966), "Promises, Promises" (1968), "Pippin" (1972), "Chicago" (1975), "Dancin'" (1978), "The American Dance Machine" (1978), "Take Me Along" (1985), and "Anything Goes" (1987). Korthaze appeared in several films during his career including "Sweet Charity" (1969), "Magic Sticks" (1987), "The Addams Family" (1991) as Slosh Addams, and "I'm Not Rappaport" (1996).

Kozachik, Pete

Cinematographer and special effects artist Pete Kozachik died of complications from primary progressive aphasia at his home in Carmel, California, on September 12,

2023. He was 72. Kozachik was born in Michigan on March 28, 1951. He began making stop-motion animation films while in grade school. He moved to Tucson, Arizona, in high school and attended the University of Arizona. He subsequently taught school and directed shows for a local television station. He moved to Hollywood in the late 1970s and began working at Coast Special Effects. He soon joined Industrial Light & Magic (ILM)

where he worked on stop-motion effects for numerous films. He worked frequently with effects artist Phil Tippett and directors Henry Selick and Tim Burton. Kozachik's films include "Dreamscape" (1984), "Howard the Duck" (1986), "Star Trek IV: The Voyage Home" (1986), "Innerspace" (1987), "Willow" (1988), "Ghostbusters II" (1989), "Spaced Invaders" (1990), "RoboCop 2" (1990), "Hudson Hawk" (1991), "RoboCop 3" (1993), "The Nightmare Before Christmas" (1993) sharing an Academy Award nomination for Best Visual Effects, "James and the Giant Peach" (1996), "Starship Troopers" (1997), "Monkeybone" (2001), "Evolution" (2001), "Star Wars: Episode II - Attack of the Clones" (2002), "Corpse Bride" (2005), "Coraline" (2009), "The Flying Machine" (2010), and Tippett's animated horror film "Mad God" (2021). His memoir, "Tales from the Pumpkin King's Cameraman", was published in 2021. Kozachik married scenic artist Kate Moore in 2002 and she survives him.

Kramer, Casey

Actress Casey Kramer died at her home in Chicago, Illinois, on December 24, 2023. She was 67. Kramer was born in Los Angeles, California, on December 28, 1955. She was

the daughter of acclaimed director Stanley Kramer. Casey made her film debut in her father's 1979 feature "The Runner Stumbles". She trained as an actress at the Actor's Studio and performed on stage. She continued to appear in various independent films and shorts including "The Lone Star Letters" (1996), "Venus Envy" (1997), "Such Great Joy" (2005), "Broken" (2005), "Heart of the Beholder" (2005), "Young, Single & Angry" (2006), "The Substance of Things Hoped For" (2006), "The Counter" (2006), "Solid Gold" (2007), "On the Revolution of Heavenly Spheres" (2007), "The Wrath" (2007), "Watercolors" (2008), "Rock Bottom" (2010), "Mama, No!" (2010), "The Whisperer in Darkness" (2011), "Fix Me: The Trainer" (2012), "Behind the Candelabra" (2013) as Dora Liberace, "Gefilte Fish" (2014), "About Scout" (2015), "Boned" (2015), "Little Old Cat Lady from Rancho Cucamonga" (2015), "Family Unit" (2016), "Karen" (2016), "Owen" (2016), "Tiff" (2017), "In Vino" (2017), "Awaken the Shadowman" (2017), "Mississippi Requiem" (2018), "Thrasher Road" (2018), "A Rose for Emily" (2018), "Someone Somewhere" (2019), and the horror thrillers "Blood of Drago" (2019) and "Darkness in Tenement 45" (2020). Kramer was seen on television in episodes of "Falcon Crest", "Family Medical Center", "Criminal Minds", "The Tonight Show with Jay Leno", "The Event", "Dexter", "Awake", "Southland", "The Young and the Restless", "30, Debt-Free & Far from Happy", "Transparent", "Lethal Weapon", and "Baskets". Her other television credits include the tele-films "McBride: Murder Past Midnight" (2005) and "Monster Girls" (2015).

Krebs, Michael

Actor Michael Krebs, who often portrayed Abraham Lincoln on stage and screen, died at his home in Chicago, Illinois, on January 29, 2023. He was 66. Krebs was born in

Freeport, Illinois, on February 20, 1956. He graduated from Western Illinois University where he studied theater. He began his career on stage and performed with the New American Theater in Rockford, Illinois. He began a long association performing the role of Abraham Lincoln in 1995. He appeared at the Abraham Lincoln Presidential Library and Museum, the Gerald Ford Presidential Library, Hoover Presidential Library, Chicago History Museum, and Gettysburg. He delivered a live broadcast of the Lincoln-Douglas Galesburg Debate" on C-SPAN in 1994 and appeared at the Library of Congress' "Lincoln's Virtual Library" in 1998. Krebs was seen as Lincoln in episodes of "Conspiracy?", "The Rachel Maddow Show", and "Timeless". He also delivered "President Lincoln's Inauguration Re-enactment" in 2011 and "President Lincoln's Second Inaugural Address 150th Anniversary" in 2015. He was featured as a vampire Abraham Lincoln in the 2008 short film "The Transient" and again played Lincoln in the 2015 Civil War drama "Field of Lost Shoes".

Kreke, Lotti

German actress Lotti Krekel died in Cologne, Germany, on April 11, 2023. She was 81. Krekel was born in

Roetgen, Germany, on August 23, 1941. She began working on radio as a play announcer as a child. She later took acting lessons and made her stage debut at the Millowitsch Theater in Cologne in 1958. She was seen frequently on television with roles in productions of "Die Spanische Fliege" (1958), "Der Mude Theodor" (1959), "Der Frohliche Weinberg" (1961), "Im Nachtjackenviertel" (1961), "Schweinefleisch in Dosen" (1961), "Bubusch" (1962), "Tevye and His Seven Daughters" (1962), "Tante Jutta aus Kalkutta" (1962), "Schones Wochenende" (1962), "Was Soll Werden, Harry?" (1963), "Eine Dumme Sache" (1963), "Waidmannsheil" (1963), "Der Pedell" (1964), "Hofloge" (1964), "Zwangseinquartierung" (1964), "Drei Kolsche Jungen" (1965), "Leutnant Nant" (1965), "Zwei Dickkopfe" (1965), "Das Rote Tuch" (1966), "Der Doppelte Moritz" (1966), "Der Unglaubige Thomas" (1967), "Gemuse und Liebe Engros" (1967), "Der Kuhne Schwimmer" (1967), "Der Meisterboxer" (1968), "Der Saisongockl" (1968), "Pension Scholler" (1968), "Der Etappenhase" (1969), "Vier Tage Unentschuldigt" (1971), "The Catamount Killing" (1974), "Ein Frohliches Dasein" (1974), "Um Zwei Erfahrungen Reicher" (1976), "Rosenmontag Ist Kein Feiertag" (1978), "Affare Nachtfrost" (1989), "Der Gartenkrieg" (1993),

"Sommerliebe" (1993), and "Schrage Vogel" (1995). Her other television credits include episodes of "Sonny-Boyd", "Tim Frazer", "Aus dem Bucherschrank Geholt", "Donaug'schichten" as Elke Muller in 1965, "Der Dritte Handschuh", "Die Drehscheibe", "Dem Tater Auf der Spur", "Die Rudi Carrell Show", "Express", "MS Franziska", "Felix und Oskar", "Der Schiedsmann" as Wahrsagerin Tilla Schranz from 1983 to 1985, "Der Paragraphenwirt", "Weissblaue Geschichten", "Locker vom Hocker", "Hafendetektiv", "Geschichten aus der Heimat", "Drei Dschungeldetektive", "Die Dirk Bach Show", "Die Weltings vom Hauptbahnhoff - Scheidung auf Kolsch" as Dr. Hanna Welting in 1994, "Zum Stanglwirt", "Sylter Geschichten", "Mit Einem Bein im Grab", "Familie Heinz Becker", "SK Kolsch", "Tatort", "Das Amt", "Der Bulle von Tolz", "Cologne P.D.", and "Ein Fall fur die Anrheiner" as Trudi Fritsch from 2011 to 2013. Krekel appeared in a handful of films during her career including "Der Wahre Jakob" (1960), "Willy, der Privatdetektiv" (1960), "Der Hochtourist" (1961), "Robert und Bertram" (1961), and "Geld Oder Leber!" (1986). She was featured in numerous radio plays throughout her career. She also became a popular singer in the late 1960s and recorded numerous albums over the next decade. Krekel married her longtime companion, actor Ernst H. Hilbich, in 2003 and he survives her.

Kristi, Rhonda

Canadian actress Rhonda Kristi died of abdominal cancer in Toronto, Ontario, Canada, on March 31, 2023. She

was 69. She was born Rhonda Feduck in Port Colborne, Ontario, Canada, on October 20, 1953. She worked as an actress on stage and screen and was featured in the 1987 short film "Danger Keep Out!". She was best known for her role as Mrs. Nelson, Spike's mother, on the television series "Degrassi High" from 1987 to 1989. Kristi was married and divorced from Peter Dick and is survived by their two sons. She is also survived by her partner, Dan Smith.

Krofft, Marty

Television producer Marty Krofft, who teamed with his brother Sid to create such children's series as "H.R. Pufnstuf" and "Land of the Lost", died of kidney failure in Los Angeles, California, on November 25, 2023. He was 86. He was born Moshopopoulos Yolas in Montreal, Quebec, Canada, on April 9, 1937. Sid Krofft began working in puppeteering in his teens and joined the Ringling Bros. and Barnum & Bailey Circus. Marty joined his brother in 1958 and they created the adult burlesque puppet show "Les Poupees de Paris" for a dinner theater in the San Fernando Valley. The show proved successful and was performed at the World's Fair in Seattle in 1962 and New York in 1964. The brothers were soon creating puppet shows for the Six Flags amusement parks and television's "The Dean Martin Show" in 1965. The Kroffts

were hired by NBC to create the costumes for the live-action segments for "The Banana Splits Adventure Hour", featuring the furry animal rock band consisting of Fleegle, Bingo, Drooper, and Snorky. The popular Saturday morning show ran from 1968 to 1970. They created the series "H.R. Pufnstuf" in

1969 featuring life-size puppets and psychedelic sets. The series starred English actor Jack Wild as Jimmy, who has a talking magic flute, and featured Billie Hayes, under heavy makeup, and the villainous Wilhelmina W. Witchiepoo. The original series ran from 1969 to 1970, though it continued in reruns for years. They produced a film version, "Pufnstuf" in 1970. The brothers sued the McDonald's fast-food chain for plagiarizing "H.R. Pufnstuf" for the McDonaldland advertising campaign and received a settlement for copyright infringement. The Kroffts continued making a wide assortment of off-beat television programs for younger audiences including "The Bugaloos" (1970-1971), "Lidsville" (1971-1972), "Sigmund and the Sea Monsters" (1973-1974), "Land of the Lost" (1974-1976), "Far Out Space Nuts" (1975), and "The Lost Saucer" (1976). "The Krofft Supershow" aired from 1976 to 1977 and featured the segments "Kaptain Kool and the Kongs", "Dr. Shrinker", "Electra Woman and Dyna Girl", "Wonderbug", "Magic Mongo", and "Bigfoot and Wildboy". A similar showcase, "The Krofft Superstar Hour", starring the Bay City Rollers as hosts, featured "Horror Hotel" and "The Lost Island". The brothers opened a vertical theme park, The World of Sid & Marty Krofft", in Atlanta's Omni Complex in 1976, which closed after six months. The Kroffts produced several variety series including "Donny & Marie" (aka "The Osmond Family Show") (1975-1977), "The Brady Bunch Hour" (1976-1977), "Pink Lady and Jeff" (1980), "Barbara Mandrell & the Mandrell Sisters" (1980-1982), "Pryor's Place" (1984) starring Richard Pryor, "All Star Rock 'n' Wrestling Saturday Spectacular" (1985), and the puppet political satire "D.C. Follies" (1987-1989). The Kroffts were executive producers of the films "Middle Age Crazy" (1980) and "Harry Tracy: The Last of the Wild Bunch" (1982), and the tele-film "Side Show" (1981). They were executive producers of television reboots of "Land of the Lost" (1991-1992), "Electra Woman and Dyna Girl" (2016), and "Sigmund and the Sea Monsters" (2016-2017), and producers of the 2009 "Land of the Lost" film starring Will Ferrell. They also created the Nickelodeon children's series "Mutt & Stuff", which aired from 2015 to 2017. The Kroffts received the Lifetime Achievement Award from the Daytime Emmys in 2018 and were given a star on the Hollywood Walk of Fame in 2020. He was married to Christa Rogalski, who was known was Christa Speck when she was Playboy Playmate of the Year in 1962, from 1965 until her death in 2013, and is survived by their three daughters. He is also survived by his brothers, Sid and Harry.

Kundera, Milan

Czech-French novelist Milan Kundera, who was noted for his 1984 book "The Unbearable Lightness of Being", died in Paris, France, on July 11, 2023. He was 94. Kundera was born in Brno, Czechoslovakia, on April 1, 1929. His father was  musicologist and pianist Ludvik Kundera and Milan learned to play the instrument as a child. He later studied musical composition at Charles University in Prague. He soon changed his interests to film and attended Film and TV School of the Academy of Performing Arts in Prague (FAMU), graduating in 1952. He subsequently became a lecturer in world literature. He published several poetry collections including "The Last May" (1955) and "Monologues" (1957). He also published several volumes of short stories and wrote the popular one-act play, "The Owners of the Keys", in 1962. Kundera's debut novel, "The Joke", was published in 1967. His 1969 novel, "Life Is Elsewhere", was unpublished in Czechoslovakia and his earlier works were banned due to his support for Alexander Dubcek's liberal reforms that were crushed by the Warsaw Pact invasion in August of 1968. He left Czechoslovakia in 1975 to teach at the University of Rennes in France, and he was stripped of Czech citizenship in 1979. His novels written in France include "The Farewell Party" (1976), "The Book of Laughter and Forgetting" (1979), "The Unbearable Lightness of Being" (1984) which was adapted for a 1988 film starring Daniel Day-Lewis, "Immortality" (1990), "Slowness" (1994), "Identity" (1997), "Ignorance" (2000), and "The Festival of Insignificance" (2013). His other works include "The Art of the Novel" (1986), "Testaments Betrayed" (1993), "The Curtain" (2005), and "Encounter" (2009). Kundera married singer Olga Haasova-Smrckova in 1956 and they later divorced. He married Vera Hrabankova in 1967 and she survives him.

Kuri, Ippei

Japanese manga artist and animator Ippei Kuri died in Japan on July 1, 2023. He was 83. He was born Toyoharu  Yoshida in Kyoto, Japan, on January 1, 1940. He left high school in 1958 to work with his brothers, Tatsuo and Kenji Yoshida, as a manga artist in Tokyo. Kuri made his debut on the manga "Abare Tengu" ("Raging Crow Goblin") in the "Z-Boy" magazine in 1959. He worked with Minoru Kume on the "Mach Sanshiro" manga from 1960 to 1961. He co-created the manga "Kurenai Sanshiro" ("Judo Boy") in 1962. He and his brothers co-founded the animation production company Tatsunoko Productions in 1962. He served as managing director of the company's subsidiary Anime Friend from 1977 to 1990. He replaced his brother, Kejnji, as president of Tatsunoko in 1987 until the company as sold to the toy manufacturer Takara in 2005. Kuri was involved with the production of numerous animes including "Space Ace", "Speed Racer", "Judo Boy", "The Adventures of Hutch the Honeybee", "Pinocchio: The Series", "Science Ninja Team Gatchaman", "Demetan Croaker, the Boy Frog", "Casshan", "New Honeybee Hutch", "Tekkaman: The Space Knight", "Time Bokan", "Gowappa 5 Godam", "Paul's Miraculous Adventure", "Temple the Balloonist", "Yatterman", "Gatchaman II", "Gatchaman Fighter", "Zenderman", "Gordian Warrior", "Muteking, the Dashing Warrior", "Rescueman", "Dash Kappei", "Golden Warrior Gold Lightan", "Yattodetaman", "Gyakuten! Ippatsuman", "Itadakiman", "Mirai Keisatsu Urashiman", "Doteraman", "Zillion", "Oraa Guzura Dado", "Legend of the Heavenly Sphere Shurato", "Kyatto Ninden Teyandee", "Tekkaman Blade", and "Time Bikan: Royal Revival". His brother, Tatsuo, died in 1977, and he is survived by brother Kenji.

Lachens, Catherine

French actress Catherine Lachens died in France on September 27, 2023. She was 78. Lachens was born in 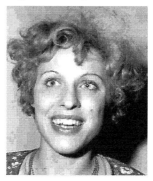 Boulogne-Billancourt, France, on September 2, 1945. She studied acting with Jean Perimony and Jean-Laurent Cochet and attended the National Conservatory of Paris in the early 1970s. She soon embarked on a lengthy career on stage and screen. Lachens' film credits include "What a Flash!" (1972), "The Edifying and Joyous Story of Colinot" (1973), "Ariane" (1974), "Flic Story" (1975), "Incorrigible" (1975), "Let's Make a Dirty Movie" (1976), "Monsieur Albert" (1976), "Silence... on Tourne" (1976), "The Arrest" (1976), "Le Gang" (1977), "Violette & Francois" (1977), "Dis Bonjour a la Dame!.." (1977), "Monsieur Papa" (1977), "Death of a Corrupt Man" (1977), "Dirty Dishes" (1978), "The Last Romantic Lover" (1978), "Ils Sont Fous Ces Sorciers" (1978), "I'm Shy, But I'll Heal" (1978), "L'Honorable Societe" (1978), "Cop or Hood" (1979), "I've Got You, You've Got Me by the Chin Haris" (1979), "Le Divorcement" (1979), "Bete, Mais Discipline" (1979), "The Medic" (1979), "La Gueule de l'Autre" (1979), "La Banquiere" (1980), "Deux Lions au Soleil" (1980), "T'es Folle ou Quoi?" (1982), "On s'en Fout... Nous on s'Aime" (1982), Yves Boisset's science fiction film "The Prize of Peril" (1983), "Ca Va Pas Estre Triste" (1983), "Flics de Choc" (1983), Volker Schlondorff's "Swann in Love" (1984) starring Jeremy Irons, "Aldo et Junior" (1984), "Rosa la Rose, Fille Publique" (1986), "La Vie Dissolue de Gerard Floque" (1986), the comedy "Les Deux Crocodiles" (1987), "In Extremis" (1988), "Rouge Venise" (1989), "Le Sixieme Doigt" (1990), "Le Cri du Cochon" (1991), "La belle Histoire" (1992), "French Twist" (1995), "Les Bidochon" (1996), "It's Hard Killing

Someone Even on a Monday" (2001), "Confessions d'un Dragueur" (2001), "One Fine Day, a Hairdresser" (2004), "A Vot' Bon Coeur" (2004), "Bright Days Ahead" (2013), and "French Cuisine" (2015). She was seen on television in productions of "Opera Pour Baudelaire" (1974), "Un Professeur d'Americain" (1978), "Le Fleuve Rouge" (1981), "Quatre Acteurs a Bout de Souffle" (1982), "L'Amour Fugitif" (1983), "Pauvre Eros" (1983), "The Blood of Others" (1984), "Tendre Comme le Rock" (1985), "La Derapade" (1985), "Chahut-Bahut" (1987), "Un Coeur de Marbre" (1988), "Personne ne M'Aime" (1989), and "The Maid" (1990). Lachens' other television credits include episodes of "Docteur Erika Werner", "Les Grandes Conjurations", "Les Amours des Annees Grises", "Le Petit Theatre d'Antenne 2", "Au Gui l'an Neuf", "Emmenez-Moi au Theatre", "Hello Beatrice", "Les Bargeot", "Le Vent du Large", "Cinema 16", "Softly from Paris", "L'Agence", "Le Retour d'Arsene Lupin", "Marc et Sophie", "Place en Garde a Vue", "Quatre Pour un Loyer", "Navarro", "Jamais 2 Sans Toi", "Mes Pires Potes", "France Truc", "Sous le Soleil", "Venus and Apollo", and "Scenes de Menages".

Lado, Aldo

Italian film director and writer Aldo Lado died at his home in Rome, Italy, on November 25, 2023. He was 88. Lado was born in Fiume, Italy (now Rijeka, Croatia), on December 5, 1934. He began working in films in the late 1960s as an

assistant director on "Pecos Cleans Up" (1967), "Halleluja for Django" (1967), "Colt in the Hand of the Devil" (1967), "May God Forgive You... But I Won't" (1968), "Five Days in Sinai" (1968), "Probabilita Zero" (1969), Bernardo Bertolucci's "The Conformist" (1970), "Diamond Bikini" (1971), the giallo "The Designated Victim" (1971) which he also scripted, and "Un'anguilla da 300 Millioni" (1971). He made his directorial debut with the giallo "Short Night of Glass Dolls" (1971). He continued to direct and frequently write such films as "La Cosa Buffa" (1972), "Who Saw Her Die?" (1972), "Sepolta Viva" (1973), "The Cousin" (1974), "Last Stop on the Night Train" (1975), "Born Winner" (1976), the science fiction film "The Humanoid" (1979) under the name George B. Lewis, "La Disubbidienza" (1981), "Sahara Heat" (1978), "Love Ritual" (1989), "Alibi Perfetto" (1992), "Dark Friday" (1993), and "Power and Lovers" (1994). Lado directed television productions of "Il Prigioniero" (1978), "Delitto in Via Teulada" (1980), "La Citta di Miriam" (1983), and "I Figli dell'Ispettore" (1986). He also helmed episodes of "Il Etait un Musicien", "La Pietra di Marco Polo", and "La Stella del Parco". He returned to directing for films after a twenty-year hiatus with "Il Notturno di Chopin" in 2013. Lado published a book containing his unfilmed screenplays, "The Films You Will Never See" ("I Film Che Non Vedrete Mai") in 2017.

Laffan, Adriana

Mexican actress Adriana Graciela Laffan Lara died of pneumonia in Ciudad de Mexico, Mexico, on November 1, 2023. She was 63. Laffan was born in Ciudad de Mexico on

September 4, 1960. She began her acting career in the mid-1970s and was seen in the films "Las Fuerzas Vivas" (1975), "Cuartelazo" (1977), "Pasajeros en Transito" (1978), "Mary My Dearest" (1981), "Un Mundo Raro" (2001), and "The Last Death" (2011). Laffan appeared frequently on television with roles in productions of "El Combate" (1980), "El Hogar Que Yo Robe" (1981), "El Derecho de Nacer" (1981), "Cachun Cachun Ra Ra!!" (1981) as Tina, "La Pobre Senorita Limantour" (1987), "Carrusel" as Luisa from 1989 to 1990, "La Sombra del Otro" as Betsy in 1996, "First Love" (2000), "Complices al Rescate" (2002), "Alegrijes y Rebujos" (2004), "Wooden Woman" as Jemena in 2004, "Barrera de Amor" (2005), "Destilando Amor" as Ofelia de Quijano in 2007, "Vecinos" (2008), "Mujeres Asesinas" (2008), "Soy Tu Duena" (2010), "A Shelter for Love" (2012), "Porque el Amor Manda" as Begona de Godinez from 2012 to 2013, "Gossip Girl: Acapulco" (2013), and "Lady of Steel" (2014) as Visitacion Godinez. Laffan was also seen in episodes of "Maria Belen", "Guereja de Mi Vida", "Clase 406", "Mujer, Casos de la Vida Real", "La Rosa de Guadalupe", and "Como Dice el Dicho".

Laine, Denny

British singer and musician Denny Laine, who was a founding member of the rock bands the Moody Blues and Wings, died of interstitial lung disease in Naples, Florida, on

December 5, 2023. He was 79. He was born Brian Frederick Hines in Tyseley, Birmingham, England, on October 29, 1944. He played the guitar from his youth and formed the band Denny Laine and the Diplomats in his early teens. He joined Mike Pinder and Ray Thomas in a new band, M&B 5, in May of 1964. They were joined by Graeme Edge and Clint Warwick and the band became known as the Moody Blues. Laine was the lead vocalist on their first hit, "Go Now". He also sang "I Don't Want to Go on Without You", "Can't Nobody Love You", and "Bye Bye Bird". He and Pinder wrote many of the band's songs including "You Don't (All the Time)", "And My Baby's Gone", and "This Is My House". The album "The Magnificent Moodies" was released in 1965 and Laine left the band in October of the following year. He soon formed the short-lived band the Electric String Band with Trevor Burton on guitar, Viv Prince on drums, and Binky McKenzie on bass Guitar. Laine recorded the solo releases

"Say You Don't Mind" and "Too Much in Love" in 1967. He and Burton played with the band Balls from 1969 to 1971 and performed with Ginger Baker's Air Force in 1970. Laine formed the band Wings with Paul McCartney and his wife Linda in 1971. They toured and recorded with a rotating group of fellow bandmates. He remained with Wings through 1981 and was featured on the albums "Wild Life" (1971), "Red Rose Speedway" (1973), "Band on the Run" (1973) co-writing many songs on the hit album, "Venus and Mars" (1975), "Wings at the Speed of Sound" (1976), "London Town" (1978), and "Back to the Egg" (1979). Laine also released the solo albums "Ahh... Laine" (1973), "Holly Days" (1976), "Japanese Tears" (1980), "Anyone Can Fly" (1982), "Wings on My Feet" (1987), "Lonely Road" (1988), "Master Suite" (1988), "All I Want Is Freedom" (1990), and "Reborn" (1996). He worked with Paul McCartney on the albums "Tug of War" (1982) and "Pipes of Peace" (1983), and with Linda McCarthy on "Wide Prairie" (1998). He toured with the World Classic Rockers from 1997 to 2002 and the Denny Laine Band. His final solo album, "The Blue Musician", was released in 2008. He was inducted with the Moody Blues in the Rock and Roll Hall of Fame in 2018. Laine was married to Joanne Patrie from 1978 until their divorce in 1981 and is survived by their two children, Heidi and Laine. He married Rosha Kasravi in 2003. They later separated and divorced in 2021. He married Elizabeth Mele in July of 2023, and she also survives him. He is also survived by three children from other relationships, Damian James, Ainsley Adams, and Lucy Grant.

Lakin, Rita

Television writer Rita Lakin died in Novato, California, on March 23, 2023. She was 93. She was born Rita Weisinger in New York City on January 24, 1930. She attended Hunter College in New York and began writing adventure

stories for magazines under the name R.W. Lakin. She moved to Simi Valley, California, with her family and began working as a secretary at Universal after her husband's death in 1961. She made her debut as a script writer in 1964 with an episode of "Dr. Kildare". She continued to write episodes of such series as "Bob Hope Presents the Chrysler Theatre", "Daniel Boone", and "The Virginian". Lakin served as a staff writer for the prime-time soap opera "Peyton Place" from 1965 to 1966. She wrote episodes of "Run for Your Life", "The Invaders", "The Outsider", and "Family Affair", and was head writer for the soap opera "The Doctors" from 1967 to 1969. She worked as story editor and writer for producer Aaron Spelling's "Mod Squad" from 1969 to 1971. She was credited as creator of Spelling's subsequent series "The Rookies" which aired from 1972 to 1976. She was executive producer of the series "Executive Suite" from 1976 to 1977. She created the series "Flamingo Road" and served as supervising producer from 1980 to 1982 and was writer and creative consultant for

"Emerald Point N.A.S." in 1984. Lakin scripted numerous telefilms including "The Forty-Eight Hour Mile" (1970), "Death Takes a Holiday" (1971), "Women in Chains" (1972), "A Summer Without Boys" (1973), "Message to My Daughter" (1973), "Hey, I'm Alive" (1975), "A Sensitive, Passionate Man" (1977), "Torn Between Two Lovers" (1979), "Peyton Place: The Next Generation" (1985), "Strong Medicine" (1986), and "Nightingales" (1988). Her other television credits include episodes of "The ABC Afternoon Playbreak", "Medical Center", "Medical Story", "Executive Suite", "Dynasty", and "Voice of the Heart". She wrote the "Gladdy Gold Mystery" novel series that include "Getting Old Is Murder" (2005), "Getting Old Is the Best Revenge" (2006), "Getting Old Is Criminal" (2007), "Getting Old Is to Die For" (2007), "Getting Old Is a Disaster" (2009), "Getting Old Is Tres Dangereux" (2010), and "Getting Old Can Kill You" (2011). Her autobiography, "The Only Woman in the Room", was published in 2015. She was married to atomic physicist Hank Lankin from the early 1950s until his death in 1961. She is survived by three children, writer and director Howard, Susan, and Gavin. Lakin was married to Robert Michael Lewis, a producer and director of "Mod Squad", from 1972 until his death in 1980.

Lally, Ken

Stuntman Ken Lally, who was a voice and motion capture actor for numerous video games, died from an accident at his home in Los Angeles, California, on October 20, 2023. He was 52. Lally was born on August 11, 1971. He studied

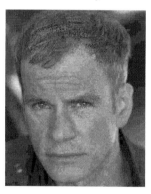

theater at St. Lawrence University and trained with the National Shakespeare Conservatory and the London Classic Theatre School. He joined Benny 'The Jet' Urquidez Action/Stunt team in 2002. He performed stunts and appeared in small roles in the films "Shelter Island" (2003), "Timecop: The Berlin Decision" (2003), "Pirates of the Caribbean: Dead Man's Chest" (2006), "Street Dreams" (2009), "Ambushed" (2013), "Resident Evil: Vengeance" (2013), "Blood of Redemption" (2013), "Puncture Wounds" (2014), "3 Hikers" (2015), "The Hopping Dead" (2016), "I Am You Are Everyone" (2016), and "Happy Hunting" (2017). He also worked on such television series as "Alias", "General Hospital", "Star Trek: Enterprise", "Big Love", "CSI: Miami", "Heroes" in the recurring role of the villain The German in 2008, "Terminator: The Sarah Connor Chronicles", "Criminal Minds", "How I Met Your Mother", "Zero Hour", "The Young and the Restless", "Revenge", and "Baker & Dunn". Lally provided voices and worked in motion capture for such video games as ""Star Ocean: Till the End of Time" (2003), "Joint Operations" (2004), "World of Warcraft: Mists of Pandaria" (2005), "Castlevania: Curse of Darkness" (2005) as Zead, "The Darkness" (2007), "Red Faction: Guerrilla" (2009), "Dragon Age: Origins" (2009), "Call of

Duty: Modern Warfare 2" (2009), "Resident Evil 5" (2009), "Tron: Evolution" (2010), "Red Dead Redemption" (2010) as Floyd Brogles, "Mortal Kombat" (2011) as Goro and Smoke, "Syndicate" (2012), "Call of Duty: Black Ops II" (2012), "BioShock Infinite" (2013), "Armored Core: Verdict Day" (2013), "Battlefield 4" (2013), "Dead Rising 3" (2013), "Wolfenstein: The New Order" (2014), "The Order: 1886" (2015), "Mirror's Edge: Catalyst" (2016), "World of Warcraft: Legion" (2016), "Call of Duty: Infinite Warfare" (2016), "Wolfenstein II: The New Colossus" (2017), "Final Fantasy XV: Comrades" (2017), "Far Cry 5" (2018), "Resident Evil 2" (2019) as Robert Kendo, "Far Cry New Dawn" (2019), "Star Wars Jedi: Fallen Order" (2019), "Resident Evil 3" (2020), "Star Wars: Squadrons" (2020), and "Spider-Man: Miles Morales" (2020).

Lambert, Steven

Actor and stuntman Steven Lambert died on August 18, 2023. He was 68. Lambert was born in Brooklyn, New York, on October 28, 1954. He began training in martial arts in his childhood. He moved to California in his early teens where he continued to study various martial art including kung fu. He

competed in various tournaments and began working in films as a stuntman in the early 1970s. Lambert performed stunts and appeared in small roles in numerous films including "Good Guys Wear Black" (1978), "Do It in the Dirt" (1979), "The Incredible Shrinking Woman" (1981), "The Sword and the Sorcerer" (1982), "They Call Me Bruce" (1982), "One Down, Two to Go" (1982), "Lone Wolf McQuade" (1983), "Revenge of the Ninja" (1983), "Racing with the Moon" (1984), "Ninja III: The Domination" (1984), "City Limits" (1984), "Tuff Turf" (1985), "Friday the 13th: A New Beginning" (1985), "Pee-wee's Big Adventure" (1985), "My Science Project" (1985), "American Ninja" (1985), "Remo Williams: The Adventure Begins" (1985) as Fred Ward's stunt double, "P.O.W. the Escape" (1986), "Critters" (1986), "Raw Deal" (1986), "Invaders from Mars" (1986), "Firewalker" (1986), "Big Trouble" (1986), "Eye of the Tiger" (1986), "Barfly" (1987), "Innerspace" (1987), "Best Seller" (1987), "Cop" (1988), "Aloha Summer" (1988), "Two Moon Junction" (1988), "Rambo III" (1988), "Out of the Dark" (1988), "Traxx" (1988), "Slipping Into Darkness" (1988), "Twins" (1988), "Collision Course" (1989), "Indiana Jones and the Last Crusade" (1989), "Ghostbusters II" (1989), "Blind Fury" (1989), "Ninja Academy" (1989), "An Innocent Man" (1989), "Always" (1989), "Delta Force 2: The Colombian Connection" (1990), "Total Recall" (1990), "Solar Crisis" (1990), "Air America" (1990), "Marked for Death" (1990), "Eve of Destruction" (1991), "The Hard Way" (1991), "Out for Justice" (1991), "Past Midnight" (1991), "Sweet Justice" (1991), "Straight Talk" (1992), "Deep Cover" (1992), "Live Wire"

(1992), "Diggstown" (1992), "Army of Darkness" (1992), "Dead On: Relentless II" (1992), "Hoffa" (1992), "Fear of a Black Hat" (1993), "Falling Down" (1993), "Bounty Tracker" (1993), "Best of the Best II" (1993), "RoboCop 3" (1993), "Dragon: The Bruce Lee Story" (1993), "Another Stakeout" (1993), "Ed and His Dead Mother" (1993), "Sister Act 2: Back in the Habit" (1993), "The Getaway" (1994), "The Silence of the Hams" (1994), "Timecop" (1994), "Surviving the Game" (1994), "Beverly Hills Cop III" (1995), "The Specialist" (1994), "Houseguest" (1995), "For Better or Worse" (1995), "Jury Duty" (1995), "A Walk in the Clouds" (1995), "The Tie That Binds" (1995), "Killer: A Journal of Murder" (1995), "Cover Me" (1995), "Casino" (1995), "Escape from L.A." (1996), "The Quest" (1996), "Fox Hunt" (1996), "The Beautician and the Beast" (1997), "Conspiracy Theory" (1997), "Still Breathing" (1997), "L.A. Confidential" (1997), "The Alarmist" (1997), "Best Men" (1997), "Titanic" (1997), "Boogie Boys" (1998), "Vampires' (1998), "Another Day in Paradise" (1998), "The Negotiator" (1998), "Star Trek: Insurrection" (1998), "Interceptor Force" (1999), "Scream 3" (2000), "Traffic" (2000), "What Planet Are You From?" (2000), "Spanish Judges" (2000), "The Alternate" (2000), "Double Bang" (2001), "Joy Ride" (2001), "The One" (2001), "Ocean's Eleven" (2001), "Panic Room" (2002), "The First $20 Million Is Always the Hardest" (2002), "Angels Don't Sleep Here" (2002), "Red Dragon" (2002), "Holes" (2003), "11:14" (2003), "Along Came Polly" (2004), "Dodgeball: A True Underdog Story" (2004), "Lost" (2004), "Ocean's Twelve" (2004), "Me and You and Everyone We Know" (2005), "Payback" (2007), "Ocean's Thirteen" (2007), "Alvin and the Chipmunks: The Squeakquel" (2009), "Let Me In" (2010), "The Green Hornet" (2011), "Repentance" (2013), "White House Down" (2013), "Jamesy Boy" (2014), "The Horde" (2016), and "Havenhurst" (2016). He worked in television on the tele-films "The Fantastic World of D.C. Collins" (1984), "Steal the Sky" (1988), "Full Exposure: The Sex Tape Scandals" (1989), "Cast a Deadly Spell" (1991), "State of Emergency" (1994), "Next Door" (1994), "Don't Look Back" (1996), "Brave New World" (1998), and "A Painted House" (2003). His other television credits include episodes of "Fantasy Island", "Red Shoe Diaries", "The Colbys", "Unsolved Mysteries", "Days of Our Lives", "Silk Stalkings", "Murder, She Wrote", "Walker, Texas Ranger", "Babylon 5", "Eleventh Hour", and "Shark" as James Woods stunt double from 2006 to 2008. Lambert was inducted into the Stuntman's Hall of Fame in 1986. He was author of the 2019 autobiography "Steven Lambert: From the Streets of Brooklyn to the Halls of Hollywood".

Lamtiugina, Asja

Polish actress Asja Lamtiugina died in Poland on March 31, 2023. She was 82. Lamtiugina was born in Zary, Poland, on November 8, 1940. She began her career on stage with the Osterwa Theatre in Gorzow. She remained a leading stage actress throughout her career and also began directing in 1995. She appeared in occasional films including "Awans" (1975), "The Scar" (1976), "Life for Life: Maximilian Kolbe" (1991), "Sztos" (1997), "Pan Tadeusz" (1999), "Boys Don't

Cry" (2000), "Zloty Srodek" (2009), and "Polish Roulette" (2012). Lamtiugina was seen on television in productions of "Odejscia, Powroty" (1973), "Lasst Uns Frei Fliegen Uber den Garten" (1974), "Wielkanoc" (1975), and "Meta" (1980), and episodes of "Pogranicze w Ogniu" and "M Jak Milosc". She was divorced from actor Edward Linde-Lubaszenko and is survived by their son, actor and director Olaf Lubaszenko.

Landgard, Janet

Actress Janet Landgard, who starred with Burt Lancaster in the 1968 film "The Swimmer", died of brain cancer on November 6, 2023. She was 75. Landgard was born in Pasadena, California, on December 2, 1947. She began

working with the William Adrian Modeling Agency while in high school. She made her acting debut as Sabrina in an episode of "The Donna Reed Show" during its fifth season in 1963. She joined the cast on a semi-regular basis the following season playing Karen, the girlfriend of Paul Petersen's Jeff Stone, through 1965. She also appeared in the 1965 special "The Hollywood Deb Stars of 1965" and in episodes of "My Three Sons" and "Dream Girl of '67". Landgard was featured as Julie Ann Hooper, the former babysitter for Burt Lancaster's Ned Merrill who later briefly accompanies him on his bizarre quest to swim home from pool to pool in his suburban neighborhood in the 1968 film "The Swimmer". He other films include the 1970 western "Land Raiders", the 1971 tele-films "The Deadly Dream" starring Lloyd Bridges, and the 1972 horror film "Moonchild" starring Victor Buono and John Carradine. She largely retired from the screen in the early 1970s. Landgard was interviewed for the 2014 documentary "The Story of the Swimmer", which was included with the film's DVD restoration.

Landgre, Inga

Swedish actress Inga Landgre died in Norberg, Sweden, on July 31, 2023. She was 95. She was born Inga Linnea Lundgren in Stockholm, Sweden, on August 6, 1927. She trained as an actress at the Calle Flygare Teaterskola. She made her acting debut on stage with the Blanch Theatre in a production of "The Cherry Orchard" in 1944. She was seen in numerous films from the early 1940s including "Ordet" (1943), "The Old Clock at Ronneberga" (1944), "Rosen Pa Tistelon" (1945), "Pengar - En Tragikomisk Saga" (1946), "Crisis" (1946), "Ballongen" (1946), "Sunshine Follows Rain" (1946), "Medan Porten Var Stangd" (1946), "Brollopsnatten" (1947), "Maj Pa Malo" (1947), "Railroad Workers" (1947),

"Hammarforsens Brus" (1948), "Soldat Bom" (1948), "Eva" (1948), "Farlig Var" (1949), "While the City Sleeps" (1950), "Kvartetten Som Sprangdes" (1950), "Tull-Bom" (1951), "Flyg-Bom" (1952), "Dansa, Min Docka..." (1953), "Dum-Bom" (1953), "Mord, Lilla van" (1955), "Dreams" (1955), "Det Ar Aldrig For Sent" (1956), Ingmar Bergman's "The Seventh Seal" (1957), "En Drommares Vandring" (1957), "Brink of

Life" (1958), "Playing on the Rainbow" (1958), "V Pa Vaddo" (1958), "Det Ar Hos Mig Han Har Varit" (1963), "Loving Couples" (1964), "Stimulantia" (1967), "Hugo and Josephine" (1967), "Korridoren" (1968), "Langt Borta Och Nara" (1976), "Paradistorg" (1977), "Mamma" (1982), "Broderna Mozart" (1986), "Amorosa" (1986), "The Best Intentions" (1992), "Dodlig Drift" (1999), "Paradiset" (2003), "Tur & Retur" (2003), "Nina Frisk" (2007), "God, Smell and Her" (2008), "Bella & Real, the Movie" (2010), "The Girl with the Dragon Tattoo" (2011), "The Hidden Child" (2013), "Lamento" (2014), "Holy Mess" (2015), and "King of Atlantis" (2019). Landgre was seen often on television in productions of "Ovader Pa Sycamore Street" (1959), "Hans Brinker of the Silver Skates" (1962), "Familjen Ekbladh" (1971), "Brod for Dagen" (1973), "Ambassaden" (1974), "Meningen Med Foreningen" (1976), "Det Kom Ett Brev" (1977), "Distrikt 5" (1983), "Ester: Om John Bauers Hustru" (1986), "The Best Intentions" (1991), "Kejsarn Av Portugallien" (1992), "Skuggornas Hus" (1996), "In the Presence of a Clown" (1997), "Den Tatuerade Ankan" (1998), "Solbacken: Avd. E" (2003), "Mobelhandlarens Dotter"(2006), and "Crimes of Passion: King Lily of the Valley" (2013). Her other television credits include episodes of "Foreign Intrigue", "Greta Och Albert", "De Lyckligt Lottade", "Radda Joppe -Dod Eller Levande", "Flickan Vid Stenbanken", "Rosenbaum", "Skargardsdoktorn", "OP: 7", "Belinder Auktioner", "Irene Huss", "Wallander", "Akta Manniskor", "Syrror", and "Grotesco". Landgre was married to actor Nils Poppe from 1949 until their divorce in 1959 and is survived by their two children, actress Anja Landgre and Don Landgre. She was married to Roger Bjornstjerna from 1982 until his death in 2006.

Lane, Sara

Actress Sara Lane, who starred as Elizabeth Grainger on the television western series "The Virginian", died of breast cancer in Napa, California, on March 3, 2023. She was 73. Lane was born in New York City on March 12, 1949, the daughter of actors Russell Lane and Sara Anderson. She appeared in a television soap commercial and an educational film as a baby. He later appeared in a vitamin commercial at age 12. She subsequently moved to Los Angeles where was a semi-finalist in the Miss Los Angeles Teen beauty contest. She was cast as Kit Austin, one of two imperiled teenagers, in William Castle's psychological thriller film "I Saw What You

Did" (1965) starring Joan Crawford. She was featured as Elizabeth Grainger, the orphaned granddaughter of Charles

Bickford's John Grainger on television's "The Virginian" from 1966 to 1970 with James Drury and Doug McClure. Her experience as an equestrian enabled her to perform many of her on stunts on the western. She also appeared in episodes of the television game show "The Hollywood Squares" and was billed as Russell Lane in the films "Schoolgirls in Chains" (1973), "The Trial of Billy Jack" (1974), and "Billy Jack Goes to Washington" (1977). Lane subsequently retired from acting and married Jon Scott in 1979. They were later the co-founders of the Havens Winery in Napa Valley. Their winery was acquired by the Smith-Anderson Wine Group in 2010. She is survived by her husband and their son and daughter.

Lara, Christian

Guadeloupean film director Christian Lara died in Fort-de-France, Martinique, on September 9, 2023. He was 84.

Lara was born in Pointe-a-Pitre, Guadeloupe, a French-governed archipelago in the Caribbean, on January 25, 1939. He worked in Paris, France, as a journalist for "Le Figaro" newspaper. He began his career in films in the early 1970s directing "Jeu de Dames" in 1973. He helmed the 1973 French erotic film "Les Infideles". He directed the films "Corps Brulants" (1976), "Dechainements Charnels" (1977), and "Jeux de Minettes" (1978) under the pseudonym Bart Carral. He also helmed the 1977 film "Un Amour de Sable" starring Jacques Weber and Anne Parillaud. Lara began a series of Guadeloupean films with 1979's "Coco la Fleur, Candidate". He was soon acknowledged by many as the father of French Antilles cinema. He continued his career directing and frequently writing such films as "Mamito" (1980), "Chap'la" (1980), "Vivre Libre ou Mourir" (1980), "Une Glace Avec Deux Boules..." (1982), "Adieu Foulards" (1983), "Black" (1987), "Une Sacree Chabine" (1993), "Bitter Sugar" (1998), "1802, l'Epopee Guadeloupeenne" (2004), the tele-film "Le Mystere Josephine" (2009), "Heritage Perdu" (2010), "Tout est Encore Possible" (2011), "Pani Pwoblem" (2011), "Summer in Provence" (2012), "The Legend" (2012), and "Esclave et Courtisane" (2016).

Larsen, Milt

Magician Milt Larsen, who was co-creator of the Magic Castle, a clubhouse for magicians, died in Hollywood, California, on May 28, 2023. He was 92. Larsen was born in Pasadena, California, on April 9, 1931. He was the son of

magician and defense attorney William Larsen, Sr., and children's television pioneer Geraldine Larsen, who was known as the Magic Lady. His parents began publishing "Genii, the Conjurors Magazine" in 1936. Milt began appearing on radio in his teens and was noted for his musical expertise. She soon began writing for a radio audience participation show. He worked with Ralph Edwards on the television programs "This Is Your Life" and "Truth or Consequences" in the 1950s. He

later wrote for the television series "Malibu U." and "The Jim Nabors Show". Larsen produced the magic revue "It's Magic!" in 1956 and various editions of the show were staged over the next sixty years. He and Richard M. Sherman wrote the musical revue "Whoopee Kid" in 1957. They also created the satirical record albums "Smash Flops" and "Banned Barbershop Ballads" the included such songs as "Bon Voyage, Titanic", "General Custer", and "Congratulations Tom Dewey". Larsen and his brother, Bill Jr., founded the Magic Castle in 1963 to be a nightclub for magicians and headquarters of the Academy of Magical Arts. He co-wrote the musical "Victory Canteen" (1971) with Bobby Lauher. He and Richard Sherman wrote the words and music for the musical comedy "Pazzazz!", which was staged in 2008. Larsen was a technical consultant for the 1971 Disney film "Bedknobs and Broomsticks". He was featured as a magician on an episode of the "Hart to Hart" television series in 1981. He wrote the books "Milt Larsen's Magical Mystery Tour of Hollywood's Most Amazing Landmark: The Magic Castle" (1997), "Hockmann, the Great Exposes Himself! and Other Phony Magicians and Vaudevillians" (1998), "Hollywood Illusion: The Magic Castle" (2000), and the autobiography "My Magical Journey – The First 30,000 Days: It's Magic!" (2012). He was founder of the Society for the Preservation of Variety Arts and served as president from 1975 to 1990. He remained president of the Academy of Magical Arts until his death. Larsen is survived by his wife, Arlene.

Lauren, Ava

Adult film actress Dorian Tardiff, who was frequently billed as Ava Lauren, died in Idaho Falls, Idaho, on September

7, 2023. She was 51. Tardiff was born in Burbank, California, on December 20, 1971. The buxom actress began appearing in porn films in the early 2000s. She was seen in productions of "Busty Bombshells" (2003), "All Ditz and Jumbo Tits" (2006), The MILF Chronicles" (2007), "Soccer Mommies" (2007), "Cougars in Heat" (2007), "Boy Meats MILF" (2007), "Dirty Sexy Mommys" (2017), "Big Tits at School"

(2008), "The Chauffeur's Daughter" (2008), and "MILFwood USA" (2008). She largely retired from the screen by the end of the decade.

Laurie, Piper

Actress Piper Laurie, who received Academy Award nominations for her roles in films "Hustler", "Carrie", and "Children of a Lesser God", died in Los Angeles, California on October 14, 2023. She was 91. She was born Rosetta Jacobs  in Detroit, Michigan, on January 22, 1932. She moved to Los Angeles with her family as a child. She studied elocution and performed in talent contests while in grade school. She signed a contract with Universal Studios in 1949 and took the screen name Piper Laurie. She made her film debut opposite Ronald Reagan in 1950's "Louisa". She continued to appear in such films as "The Milkman" (1950), "Francis Goes to the Races" (1951), "The Prince Who Was a Thief" (1951), "No Room for the Groom" (1952), "Has Anybody Seen My Gal" (1952) opposite Rock Hudson, "Son of Ali Baba" (1952), "The Mississippi Gambler" (1953), "The Golden Blade" (1953), "Dangerous Mission" (1954), "Johnny Dark" (1954), "Dawn at Socorro" (1954), "Smoke Signal" (1955), "Ain't Misbehavin'" (1955), "Kelly and Me" (1956), and "Until They Sail" (1957). She subsequently moved to New York to study acting and perform on stage and television. She appeared on television in productions of "Winter Dreams" (1956) on "Front Row Center", "The Ninth Day" (1957) and "Days of Wine and Roses" (1958) on "Playhouse 90", "Legends of Lovers" (1960) as Eurydice on "Play of the Week", "Winterset" (1959) on "Hallmark Hall of Fame", and "Come Again to Carthage" (1961) on "Westinghouse Presents". Laurie was also seen in episodes of "The Best of Broadway", "Robert Montgomery Presents", "Studio One", "The Seven Lively Arts", "Westinghouse Desilu Playhouse", "General Electric Theater", "Naked City", "The United States Steel Hour", "What's My Line?", "Bob Hope Presents the Chrysler Theatre", "Ben Casey", "Password", "The Tonight Show", "The Eleventh Hour", "Breaking Point", and the 1965 unsold western pilot "The Long Hunt of April Savage". Laurie returned to Hollywood to co-star with Paul Newman as his girlfriend, Sarah Packard, in the pool drama "The Hustler" in 1961. She received an Academy Award nomination as Best Actress for her work. She was disappointed in subsequent film offers and again returned to New York. She appeared on Broadway in a revival of Tennessee Williams' "The Glass Menagerie" in 1965. Laurie returned to the screen over a decade later to appear as religious fanatic Margaret White, mother of Sissy Spacek's powerful telekinetic Carrie White, in Brian DePalma's 1976 adaptation of Stephen King's horror novel "Carrie". She received an Oscar nomination for Best Supporting Actress for her role. She continued to appear in such films as "The Woman Rebel" (1976) as Margaret

Sanger, the horror film "Ruby" (1977) as Ruby Claire, "The Boss' Son" (1978), the Australian romantic drama "Tim" (1979) opposite Mel Gibson, "Return to Oz" (1985) as Aunt Em to Fairuza Balk's Dorothy, "Children of a Lesser God" (1986) earning another nomination for Best Supporting Actress for her role as the mother of Marlee Matlin's Sarah Norman, "Appointment with Death" (1988), "Tiger Warsaw" (1988), the romantic fantasy "Dream a Little Dream" (1989), "Other People's Money" (1991), "Storyville" (1992), "Rich in Love"  (1992), Dario Argento's Italian horror film "Trauma" (1993), "Wrestling Ernest Hemingway" (1993), "The Crossing Guard" (1995), "The Grass Harp" (1995), "St. Patrick's Day" (1997), the sci-fi horror "The Faculty" (1998), "Palmer's Pick-Up" (1999), "The Mao Game" (1999), "Eulogy" (2004), "The Dead Girl" (2006), "Hounddog" (2007), "Saving Grace B. Jones" (2009), "Hesher" (2010), "Another Harvest Moon" (2010), "Bad Blood" (2012), "Snapshots" (2018), and "White Boy Rick" (2018). Laurie continued to appear frequently on television with roles in episodes of the short-lived drama "Skag" as Jo Skagska in 1980, "The Mike Douglas Show", "St. Elsewhere" receiving an Emmy Award nomination for her role as Fran Singleton in 1984, "Hotel", "Murder, She Wrote", "The Twilight Zone", "Matlock", "Donahue", and "Beauty and the Beast". She starred as wealthy businesswoman Catherine Martell in David Lynch's off-beat thriller "Twin Peaks" in 1989. Her character is presumed killed in a lumber mill fire at the end of the first season but makes a surprise return in the second season under a disguise as Japanese businessman Mr. Tojamura. She received Emmy Awards for her work on "Twin Peaks" in 1990 and 1991. She was also featured in episodes of the short-lived police drama "Traps" as Cora Trapchek in 1994, "ER", "Diagnosis Murder", "Touched by an Angel", "Brother's Keeper", "Frasier" receiving an Emmy nomination for her guest role as Mr. Mulhern in the episode "Dr. Nora" in 1999, "Partners", "Will & Grace", "Law & Order: Special Victims Unit", "State of Grace", "Dead Like Me", "Cold Case", and "MacGyver". Her other television credits include the tele-films and mini-series "In the Matter of Karen Ann Quinlan" (1977), "Rainbow" (1978) as Ethel Gumm, "The Bunker" (1981) as Magda Goebbels, "Mae West" (1982) as Matilda West, "The Thorn Birds" (1983), "Tender Is the Night" (1985), "Love, Mary" (1985), "Toughlove" (1985), "Promise" (1986) earning an Emmy Award for her role as Annie Gilbert, "Go Toward the Light" (1988), "Rising Son" (1990), "Love, Lies & Lullabies" (1993), "Shadows of Desire" (1994), "Fighting for My Daughter" (1995), "The Road to Galveston" (1996), "In the Blink of an Eye" (1996), "Wolf Pack" (1996), "Alone" (1997), "Intensity" (1997), "A Christmas Memory" (1997), "Inherit the Wind" (1999), "Possessed" (2000), "Midwives" (2001), and "The Last Brickmaker in America" (2001). Laurie returned to the New York stage for the Off-Broadway production of "The Destiny of Me" in 1992 and portrayed Esther Crampton in the 2002 comedy revival of "Morning's at Seven" on Broadway. She directed Jim Brochu's one-man show "Zero Hour" Off-Broadway in 2010. Her autobiography, "Learning to Live Out Loud", was published in 2011. Laurie was married to entertainment writer and critic Joe Morgenstern from 1962 until their divorce in 1982. She is survived by their daughter, Anna.

Lavat, Queta

Mexican actress Queta Lavat died in Mexico City, Mexico, on December 4, 2023. She was 94. She was born Enriqueta Margarita Lavat Bayona in Mexico City on February 23, 1929.

Her two brothers, Jorge Lavat and Jose Lavat, also became noted actors. Queta studied dance at La Academia Shirley. She began her acting career in the mid-1940s and was featured in over 100 films during her sixty-year career. Her numerous film credits include "Las Colegialas" (1946), "La Noche y Tu" (1946), "El Pasajero Diez Mil" (1946), "Se Acabaron las Mujeres" (1946), "Angelo o Demonio" (1947), "Los Tres Garcia" (1947), "La Mujer del Otro" (1948), "Matrimonio Sintetico" (1948), "La Novia del Mar" (1948), "Comisario en Turno" (1949), "Tuya Para Siempre" (1949), "El Mago" (1949), "Tres Hobres Malos" (1949), "La Panchita" (1949), "Soy Charro de Levita" (1949), "Las Tandas del Principal" (1949), "Al Caer la Tarde..." (1949), "Escuela Para Casadas" (1949), "Arriba el Norte" (1949), "Conozco a las Dos" (1949), "Yo Quiero Ser Mala" (1950), "Lluvia Roja" (1950), "La Dama del Alba" (1950), "Nuestras Vidas" (1950), "Pina Maduraz" (1950), "El Hombre Sin Rostro" (1950), "Si Me Viera Don Porfirio" (1950), "Azahares Para Tu Boda" (1950), "Medico de Guardia" (1950), "Para Que la Cuna Apriete" (1950), "Casa de Vecindad" (1951), "Tierra Baja" (1951), "Entre Abogados te Veas" (1951), "Vivillo Desde Chiquillo" (1951), "Menores de Edad" (1951), "Aca las Tortas" (1951), "Perdicion de Mujeres" (1951), "Hombres Sin Alma" (1951), "Chucho el Remendado" (1952), "El Derecho de Nacer" (1952), "Un Gallo en Corral Ajeno" (1952), "Se la Paso le Mano" (1952), "Tal Para Cual" (1953), "Cancion de Cuna" (1953),

"Siete Mujeres" (1953), "El Jugador" (1953), "Dos Tipos de Cuidado" (1953), "Reportaje" (1953), "The Price of Living" (1954), "Retorno a la Juventud" (1954), "La Ladrona" (1954), "Spring in the Heart" (1956), "Los Hijos de Rancdho Grande" (1956), the fantasy classic "Santa Claus" (1959), "El Proceso de las Senoritas Vivanco" (1961), "Memorias de Mi General" (1961), "Estrageia Matrimonio" (1966), "Don Juan 67" (1967), "Maria Isabel" (1968), "No Se Mande, Profe" (1969), "Modisto de Senoras" (1969), "El Aviso Inoportuno"

(1969), "La Hermana Trinquete" (1970), "Cruz de Amor" (1970), "La Mujer de Oro" (1970), "Ya Somos Hombres" (1971), "El Idolo" (1971), "Yesenia" (1971), "El Arte de Enganar" (1972), "El Deseo en Otono" (1972), "Me He de Comer Esa Tuna" (1972), "La Gatita" (1972), "El Festin de la Loba" (1972), "Peluquero de Senoras" (1973), "San Simon de los Magueyes" (1973), "Quiero Vivir Mi Vida!" (1973), "Chronica de un Amor" (1974), "Los Perros de Dios" (1974), "La Recogida" (1974), "La Trenza" (1975), "Acapulco 12-22" (1975), "Carita de Primavera" (1977), "Sor Tequila" (1977), "Duro Pero Seguro" (1978), "La Hora del Jaguar" (1978), "Las Noches de Paloma" (1978), "Los Hijos del Diablo" (1978), "El Perdon de la Hija de Nadie" (1980), "Lagunilla, Mi Barrio" (1981), "La Jorobada" (1981), "Aborto: Canto a la Vida" (1983), "Hermelinda Linda" (1984), "El Monje Loco" (1984), "Mas Vale Pajaro en Mano" (1985), "Cinco Nacos Asaltan Las Vegas" (1987), "La Bruja de la Vecindad" (1987), "Terror en los Barrios" (1988), "Central Camionera" (1988), "A Gozar, a Gozar, Que el Mundo se va Acabar" (1990), "Un Corazon Para Dos" (1990), "El Secuestro de un Policia" (1991), "Amargo Destino" (1993), "La Pura" (1994), and the short "Pata de Gallo" (2004). Lavat appeared on television in episodes of "Un Paso al Abismo", "Un Largo Amor", "Vertigo", "Angustia del Pasado", "Encrucijada" as Christian Bruce in 1970, "La Recogida", "El Edificio de Enfrente", "Mi Primer Amor", "Telemecanica Nacional", "Rina", "Extranos Caminos del Amor", "Nosotras las Mujeres", "Herencia Maldita", "La Pobre Senorita Limantour", "Yo Compro Esa Mujer", "Angeles Blancos", "Corazon Salvaje" as Mother Superior in 1993, "Alondra", "Tres Mujeres", "Rosalinda", "Atrevete a Olvidarme", "The Outsider" as Rosalia de Limantur in 2001, "El Gran Carnal 2", "Clase 406", "Velo de Novia", "Corazones al Limite", "Rebelde", "Sexo y Otros Secretos", "In the Name of Love", "Camaleones" as Graciela in 2009, "Curse by the Sea" as Alfonsina Zapata from 2009 to 2010, "Como Dice el Dicho", "The Power of Destiny", "Nueva Vida", "Mentir Para Vivir", "Corazon Indomable" as Lucrecia in 2013, "La Vida es Como el Cine" as Abuela in 2014, "Que Pobres Tan Ricos" as Matilde Alvarez de Ruizpalacios" from 2013 to 2014, "La Rosa de Guadalupe", "Love from the Hood" as Zelma in 2015, "El Hotel de los Secretos" as Senora Limantour in 2016, "La Usurpada" as Piedad de Bernal in 2019, "Esta Historia Me Suena", and "SOS Me Estoy Enamorando". Lavat was married to Armando Carrillo Ruiz from 1952 until his death in 1994. They had four children together including sportscaster Pablo Carrillo.

Lawson, Sarah

British actress Sarah Lawson, who was featured in the Hammer horror film "The Devil Rides Out", died in England on August 18, 2023. She was 95. Lawson was born in Wandsworth, London, England, on August 8, 1928. She trained for the stage at the Webber Douglas Academy of Dramatic Art and began her career in repertory in the late 1940s. She performed on the West End stage in Jean Cocteau's "Intimate Relations" in 1961. She made her film debut at Betty Carstairs in 1951's "The Browning Version". Her other films include "The Night Won't Talk" (1952), "Both Sides of the Law"

(1953), "Three Steps in the Dark" (1953), "Meet Mr. Malcolm" (1954), "You Know What Sailors Are" (1954), "Navy Heroes" (1955), "It's Never Too Late" (1956), "Links of Justice" (1958), "The Solitary Child: (1958), "Three Crooked Men" (1959),

"Night Without Pity" (1961), "The World Ten Times Over" (1961), the science fiction film "Night of the Big Heat" (aka "Island of the Burning Damned") (1967) opposite her husband, Patrick Allen, and co-starring Peter Cushing and Christopher Lee, the Hammer horror film "The Devil Rides Out" (aka "The Devil's Bride") (1968) with Christopher Lee and Charles Gray, "The Battle of Britain" (1969), and "The Stud" (1978). Lawson was seen on television in productions of "Face to Face" (1951), "The Lady from the Sea" (1953), "Caste" (1954), "The River Line" (1955), "The Happy Prisoner" (1955), "The Whole Truth" (1955), "Arrow to the Heart" (1956), "The Silver Cord" (1956), "Mrs. Moonlight" (1956), "Siding 273" (1956), the science fiction serial "The Trollenberg Terror" (1956) as Sarah Pilgrim, "Busman's Honeymoon" (1957), "Rupert of Hentzau" (1957), "Time and the Conways" (1957), "An Ideal Husband" (1958), "The Rossiters" (1958), "The Young May Moon" (1958), "The White Guard" (1960), "Death of a Guest" (1960), "Haven in Sunset" (1962), "Legend of Death" (1965) as Myra Gargan, "Corridors of Power" (1966), "The Innocent Ceremony" (1969), "The Midsummer Dream of Chief Inspector Blossom" (1972), "The Rose Garden" (1972), and "Severe Chill" (1972). Her other television credits include episodes of "Rheingold Theatre", "The Buccaneers", "Hour of Mystery", "White Hunter", "The World Our Stage", "O.S.S.", "Boyd Q.C." (1958), "ITV Television Playhouse", "Armchair Theatre", "The Invisible Man", "Danger Man", "The Vise", "Silent Evidence", "Suspense", "Thirty Minute Theatre", "The Edgar Wallace Mystery Theatre", "Zero One", "The Odd Man" as Judy Gardiner in 1962 and as twin sister Anne Braithwaite in 1963, "No Hiding Place", "Gideon C.I.D.", "Drama 65", "The Saint", "Thirty-Minute Theatre", "The Avengers", "The Wednesday Play", "Theatre 625", "Detective", "Journey to the Unknown", "Department S", "The Expert", "Trial", "The Persuaders!", "Jason King", "Callan", "Crime of Passion", "Full House", "Crown Court", "Father Brown", "Within These Walls" as Prison Governess Sarah Marshall in 1978, "The Standard", "ITV Playhouse", "The Professionals", "Cuffy", "Lovejoy", and "Bergerac". She largely retired from acting by the late 1980s. Lawson was married to actor Patrick Allen from 1960 until his death in 2006 and is survived by their two sons, Stephen and Stuart.

Leadon, Tom

Guitarist Tom Leadon, who was a founding member of Tom Petty's first band, Mudcrutch, died on March 22, 2023. He was 70. Leadon was born in Rosemount, Minnesota, on September 16, 1952, and was raised in San Diego, California. He played with the band the Epic while in high school in Gainesville, Florida. He joined Tom Petty, Jim Lenahan, Randall Marsh, and Mike Campbell to form the band

Mudcrutch in 1970. Leadon was originally the lead singer for the band but Petty soon took over. Leadon left the band in 1972 and moved to Los Angeles. He played with Linda Ronstandt's backing band and joined the country rock band Silver in 1976. He later moved to Nashville to work as a music teacher. Leadon rejoined Petty, Campbell, and Marsh, along with Benmont Tench, to reform Mudcrutch in 2007. They released two albums, "Mudcrutch" (2008) and "Mudcrutch 2" (2016). The band largely ended following the death of Petty in 2017. Leadon wrote and recorded a tribute to Petty, "My Best Old Friend", shortly after his death.

Lear, Norman

Television writer and producer Norman Lear, who was noted for such hit series as "All in the Family" and Sanford and Son", died at his home in Los Angeles, California, on December 5, 2023. He was 101. Lear was born in New Haven, Connecticut, on July 27, 1922. He graduated from high school

in Hartford, Connecticut, in 1940. He attended Emerson College in Boston but dropped out to join the U.S. Army Air Force in 1942. He was a radio operator and gunner on a bomber and flew 52 combat missions during the war. He began working in public relations after his discharge in 1945. He soon moved to Los Angeles where he worked in door-to-door sales with Ed Simmons. He and Simmons also began writing comedy sketches for Jerry Lewis and Dean Martin's "The Martin and Lewis Show" on radio and their appearances on television's "Colgate Comedy Hour" in the early 1950s. He also wrote additional dialogue for their 1953 film "Scared Stiff". Lear was a writer and producer for "The Martha Raye Show" from 1954 to 1956. He also wrote for the series "Ford Star Revue", "The Tennessee Ernie Ford Show", and "The George Gobel Show" which he also directed, wrote and produced the 1961 special "Bobby Darin and Friends". Lear created the western series "The Deputy" which starred Henry Fonda from 1959 to 1961. Lear scripted and produced several films including "Come Blow Your Horn" (1963) also appearing in a small role, "Divorce American Style" (1967) sharing an Academy Award nomination, "The Night They Raided Minsky's" (1968), and "Cold Turkey" (1971) which he also directed and appeared in a small role. Lear and his frequently producing partner Bud Yorkin pitched a comedy series about a blue-collar family to ABC, which was rejected after two pilots were taped, "Justice for All" in 1968 and "Those

Were the Days" in 1969. CBS picked up the series, now known as "All in the Family", in 1971. The popular series, loosely based on the British series "Till Death Us Do Part", starred Carroll O'Connor as conservative bigot Archie Bunker and Jean Stapleton as his wife, Edith. Sally Struthers and Rob Reiner were his daughter and liberal son-in-law. The groundbreaking series dealt with such issues as racism, antisemitism, women's lib, homosexuality, rape, abortion, and the Vietnam War. It proved highly popular and aired from 1971 to 1979. It was continued with the sequel series "Archie Bunker's Place" from 1979 to 1983. Lear received four Emmy Awards and an additional five nominations for his work on the series. His series "Sanford and Son", starring comedian Redd Foxx, was based on the British series "Steptoe and Son". It aired on NBC from 1972 to 1977 and spawned the spin-off shows "Grady" starring Whitman Mayor as Fred Sanford's friend from 1975 to 1976, "Sanford Arms" in 1977, and "Sanford" from 1980 and 1981. "All in the Family" spawned several spin-offs including "Maude", starring Bea Arthur as Edith Bunker's cousin, Maude Findlay". The series ran from 1972 to 1978 and Lear received two Emmy nominations for his work on the series. "Maude" spawned the spinoff "Good Times", starring Esther Rolle as Maude's maid, Florida Evans. It aired from 1974 to 1979. Sally Struthers returned to her role as Gloria Spivak, Archie Bunker's daughter, for the comedy series "Gloria" from 1982 to 1983. Another groundbreaking series, "The Jeffersons", starring Sherman Hemsley and Isabel Sanford as prosperous black couple George and Louise Jefferson, who were originally introduced on "All in the Family", aired from 1975 to 1985. A short-lived spin-off, "Checking In", starred Marla Gibbs as the Jeffersons' maid Florence Johnson, taking a new job as a hotel housekeeper. It lasted for four episodes in 1981. Another short-lived spin-off of "All in the Family", "704 Hauser", featured John Amos as Ernie Cumberbatch, who moves into Archie Bunker's old house. It aired from April to May of 1994. Lear's off-beat comedy series "Mary Hartman, Mary Hartman" aired from 1976 to 1977 and earned him another Emmy nomination. Sequel series "Forever Fernwood aired from 1977 to 1978, the parody talk show "Fernwood 2 Night" starring Martin Mull as Barth Gimble aired in 1977, and "American 2-Night" appeared in 1978. He also produced and frequently wrote for such series as "Hot l Baltimore" in 1975, "One Day at a Time" from 1975 to 1984, "The Dumplings" (1976), "The Nancy Walker Show" from 1976 to 1977, "All's Fair" from 1976 to 1977, "All That Glitters" in 1977, "A Year at the Top" in 1977, "Apple Pie" in 1978, "Mr. Dugan" in 1979, "The Baxters" in 1979, "Palmerstown, U.S.A." from 1980 to 1981, "Square Pegs" from 1982 to 1983, "Silver Spoons" from 1982 to 1987, "a.k.a. Pablo" in 1984, "Mama Malone" in 1984, "227" from 1985 to 1990, "Sunday Dinner" in 1991, "The Powers That Be" from 1992 to 1993, the children's cartoon "Channel Umptee-3" from 1997 to 1998, "America Divided" in 2018, the reboot of "One Day at a Time" from 2017 to 2020, and "Gamergate" in 2023. He produced the tele-films and specials "Justice for All" (1968), "Three to Get Ready" (1975), "The Little Rascals" (1977), "King of the Road" (1978), "I Love Liberty" (1982) earning an Emmy nomination, "Good Evening, He Lied" (1984), "P.O.P."

(1984), "Heartsounds" (1984) earning an Emmy nomination, "All in the Family" 20th Anniversary Special" (1991) receiving an Emmy nomination, "Those Were the Days" (1998), "Maggie Bloom" (2000) which he also directed, "Independence Day 2001" (2001), "Chappelle's Show" from 2003 to 2006, and "Guess Who Died" (2018). He received Emmy Awards for "Live in Front of a Studio Audience: Norman Lear's 'All in the Family' and 'The Jeffersons'" (2019) and "Live in Front of a

Studio Audience: 'All in the Family' and 'Good Times'" (2019) and received an Emmy nomination for "Live in Front of a Studio Audience: 'The Facts of Life' and 'Diff'rent Strokes'" (2021). Lear was executive producer of the films "The Princess Bride" (1991), "Fried Green Tomatoes" (1991), "Way Past Cool" (2000), "Pete Seeger: The Power of Song" (2007), "El Superstar: The Unlikely Rise of Juan Frances" (2008), "I Carry You with Me" (2020), "Rita Moreno: Just a Girl Who Decided to Go for It" (2021), and "I Got a Monster" (2023). Lear provided the voice of Benjamin Franklin in an episode of the animated series "South Park" in 2003 and voiced himself in a 2017 episode of "The Simpsons". He was seen in episodes of "Jack & Bobby" and "Dem Tinseltown Homiez, the Hollywood Guys". He was co-founder of the production company T.A.T. Communications with Jerry Perenchio. They bought Avco Embassy Pictures in 1982 and merged to two companies as Embassy Communications, Inc. They sold Embassy to Columbia Pictures in 1985. Lear was active in liberal causes and was founded of People for the American Way in 1980 to help combat the Christian right Moral Majority. He was host of the revival of the game show "Quiz Kids" for the CBS Cable Network from 1981 to 1982. He was founder of Act III Communications in 1987. His memoir, "Even This I Get to Experience", was published in 2014 and he was subject of the 2016 documentary "Norman Lear: Just Another Version of You". He was inducted into the Television Academy Hall of Fame in 1984 and received the Peabody Awards Lifetime Achievement Award in 2017. Lear was awarded the National Medal of Arts by President Bill Clinton in 1999 and was recipient of the Kennedy Center Honors in 2018. Lear was married to Charlotte Rosen from 1943 until their divorce in 1956 and is survived by their daughter Ellen. He was married to magazine publisher Frances Loeb from 1956 until their divorce in 1985 and is survived by their daughters Kate and Maggie. He married producer Lyn Davis in 1987 and is also survived by her and their son, Benjamin, and daughters, Brianna and Madeline.

Leather, Peggy Lee

Professional wrestler Peggy Lee Fowler, who competed under the name Peggy Lee Leather, died on May 22, 2023. She was 64. Fowler was born in Reynolds, Georgia, on January 19, 1959. She was trained by the Fabulous Moolah and

Joyce Grable in 1980. She was originally billed as Peggy Lee before adding Leather to her name. She and Wendi Richter

formed a tag team in 1984 and challenged unsuccessfully for the World Wrestling Federation (WWF) Tag Team Championship. Richter left the team to become WWF Women's Champion in 1985 and Leather lost a championship bout to her. She briefly worked in Montreal before entering Florida Championship Wrestling as Peggy Lee Pringle in 1986. She engaged in a feud with Mad Maxine as the "sister" of Percy Pringle. She challenged Madusa Miceli for the AWA World Women's Championship in 1988. Leather worked in David McLane's Powerful Women of Wrestling (POWW) in the late 1980s where she feuded with Wendi Richter and Bambi. She competed in the Ladies Professional Wrestling Association (LPWA) under the name Lady X and won the title from Susan Sexton of January of 1991. She made several appearances with World Championship Wrestling (WCW) in the 1990s. She reunited with McLane for the Women of Wrestling (WOW) promotion from 2000 to 2001 under the name Thug. She continued to make appearances on the independent circuit until her retirement in 2013.

LeBlanc, Whitney J.

Television director Whitney J. LeBlanc died in St. Helena, California, on February 9, 2023. He was 91. LeBlanc was born in Memphis, Tennessee, on June 20, 1931. He was

raised in Louisiana and attended Xavier University in New Orleans in 1950. He earned a degree in education from Southern University. He served in the U.S. Army in the mid-1950s. He later studied theater productions, earning a master's degree, at the University of Iowa in 1958. He began teaching at Antioch College in Ohio in the early 1960s. He taught at numerous colleges and

universities during his career including Howard University, Lincoln University, and the University of Texas at Austin. He was also involved in designing and producing numerous theatrical productions. He began working in television in 1969 when he joined the Maryland Center for Public Broadcasting in Baltimore. He served as producer for the local series "Our Street". He subsequently moved to Hollywood where he served as associate producer for the "Good Times" series in the mid-1970s. He was also stage manager for "The Jim Nabors Show" in 1978. LeBlanc directed episodes of such series as "Benson", "The Young and the Restless", "Me & Mrs. C", "Marblehead Manor", "227", "Generations", and "The Robert Guillaume Show" in the 1980s. He retired from television in the mid-1990s and settled in Napa Valley. He became noted for creating

stained glass windows. He was author of a trilogy of historical fiction novels including "Blues in the Wind" (2001), "Shadows of the Blues" (2007), and "Bodacious Blues" (2011). LeBlanc was married and divorced from Audrey Daste and is survived by their daughter. He was also married and divorced from dancer Elizabeth Walton and is survived by their son and daughter. He married Dr. Diane Hambrick in 1978 and is also survived by her and his stepson.

Lee, Bill

Jazz musician Bill Lee, the father of director Spike Lee who worked on the soundtracks for several of his films, died in New York City on May 24, 2023. He was 94. Lee was born in Snow Hill, Alabama, on July 23, 1928. His parents were both

musicians and he learned music from an early age. He graduated from Morehouse College in Atlanta in 1951. He played the double bass with small jazz groups in Atlanta and Chicago before moving to New York City in 1959. He collaborated with numerous artists during his career including Duke Ellington, Billie Holiday, Harry Belafonte, Woody Guthrie, Pete Seeger, Aretha Franklin, Bob

Dylan, Odetta, Simon & Garfunkel, Gordon Lightfoot, John Lee Hooker, Judy Collins, Cat Stevens, and the Chad Mitchell Trio. He recorded a trio of records for the independent label Strata-East Records including "The Descendants of Mike and Phoebe: A Spirit Speaks", "The Brass Company", "The New York Bass Violin Choir". His son, Spike Lee, became a leading director in the 1980s and Bill composed the scores for his films "She's Gotta Have It" (1986), "School Daze" (1988), "Do the Right Thing" (1989), and "Mo' Better Blues" (1990). Lee appeared in small roles in his son's films and in 1993's "Rage of Vengeance". He also scored Stephen Kijak's 1996 film "Never Met Picasso" and the 2010 science fiction film "Window on Your Present", written and directed by his son, Cinque Lee. Lee was married to Jackie Shelton from 1954 until her death in 1976. He is survived by four of their children, director Spike Lee, photographer David Lee, actress and screenwriter Joie Lee, and filmmaker Cinque Lee. Another son, Christopher, died in 2014. He married Susan Kaplan in 1977 and is also survived by her and their son, saxophone player Arnold 'T@NE' Lee.

Lee. Coco

Chinese singer Ferren 'Coco' Lee died of a suspected drug overdose at a hospital in Hong Kong on July 5, 2023. She was 48. Lee was born in Wuhan, China, on January 17, 1975. She was raised in Hong Kong and moved to San Francisco, California, with her family at age ten. She was crowned Miss Teen Chinatown San Francisco in 1991. She won local singing competitions and graduated high school in 1993. She attended the University of California in Irvine to study medicine but left after a year to concentrate on her singing career in Hong Kong.

She released the 1994 albums "Love from Now On" and "Promise Me" in Taiwan. Her first English-language album, "Brave Enough to Love", was released in 1995 and the  Mandarin album "Woman in Love" soon followed. She continued to record in Mandarin, English, and Cantonese with such albums as "CoCo Lee" (1996), "Sincere" (1997), and "Di Da Di" (1998). She was the voice of Fa Mulan in the Mandarin version of the Disney animated film "Mulan" in 1998 and sang the theme song "Reflection". She also sang "Missing You in 365 Days", the theme for the Chinese animated film "Lotus Lantern", in 1998. Her other albums include "Sunny Day" (1998), "From Today Till Forever" (1999), "Just No Other Way" (1999), "True Lover You & Me" (2000), "Promise CoCo" (2001), "Exposed" (2005), "Just Want You" (2006), "East to West" (2009), and "Illuminate" (2013). She appeared in the films "No Tobacco" (2002), "Master of Everything" (2004), and "Forever Young" (2015). She was seen frequently on television, serving as a judge for "Chinese Idol" in 2013, "Dancing with the Stars China" in 2015, "Super Idol" in 2015, and "World's Got Talent" in 2019. She was also seen in such series as "Kangsi Coming", "Talented Singer", "I Am a Singer", "Come Sing with Me", "The Jin Xing Show", "Sing Out!", "Jungle Voice", "Infinity and Beyond", and "Sing! China". She had suffered from health problems throughout her life and was diagnosed with breast cancer in 2022. She was also reportedly diagnosed with depression. She had been hospitalized for taking an overdose of sleeping pills in June of 2023. She was again taken to the hospital on July 2, 2023, after a suicide attempt and died three days later. Lee married Canadian businessman Bruce Rockowitz in 2011 and is survived by him and two stepdaughters.

Lee, Eugene

Set designer Eugene Lee, who was production designer for "Saturday Night Live" for over four decades, died in Providence, Rhode Island, on February 6, 2023. He was 83.  Lee was born in Beloit, Wisconsin, on March 9, 1939. He attended the University of Wisconsin, the Goodman School of Drama at the Art Institute of Chicago, Carnegie Mellon University, and the Yale School of Drama where he later received a master's degree. He began working in theater from the late 1960s and served as resident designer for the Trinity Repertory Company in Providence, Rhode Island. He made his Broadway debut as scenic designer for 1970's "Wilson in the Promised Land". He worked frequently with his partner, Franne Lee,

throughout the 1970s. He received Tony Awards for his work on the plays "Candide" (1974), "Sweeney Todd" (1979), and "Wicked" (2003), and an additional nomination for 1998's "Ragtime". His numerous Broadway credits also include "Dude" (1972), "The Skin of Our Teeth" (1975), "Some of My Best Friends" (1977), "Gilda Radner - Live from New York" (1979), "Merrily We Roll Along" (1981), "The Little Prince and the Aviator" (1982), "Agnes of God" (1982), "The Hothouse" (1982), "Show Boat" (1994), "On the Waterfront" (1998), "Colin Quinn - An Irish Wake" (1998), "A Moon for the Misbegotten" (2000), "Seussical" (2000), "The Pirate Queen" (2007), "The Homecoming" (2007), "You're Welcome America" (2009), "A Streetcar Named Desire" (2012), "Glengarry Glen Ross" (2012), "The Other Place" (2013), "The Velocity of Autumn" (2014), "Amazing Grace" (2015), and "Bright Star" (2016). Lee was noted as the long-running production designer for "Saturday Night Life" from its start in 1975 through 1980, and again from 1985 until his death. He received six Emmy Awards and an additional twelve nominations for his work on the series. He was also designer for television productions of "Steve Martin's Best Show Ever" (1981), "The Concert in the Park" (1982), "Sweeney Todd: The Demon Barber of Fleet Street" (1982), "Some Men Need Help" (1985), "Paul Simon, Graceland: The African Concert" (1987), "The 40th Annual Primetime Emmy Awards" (1988), "The Kids in the Hall" (1988-1989), "A Marriage: Georgia O'Keeffe and Alfred Stieglitz" (1991), "On Golden Pond" (2001), "Night of Too Many Stars" (2003), and "Goodnight, Sweet Prince" (2016). He was set designer for "Late Night with Conan O'Brien" from 1993 to 1994 and for "Late Night with Seth Meyers" from 2014 to 2016. Lee was production designer for "The Tonight Show Starring Jimmy Fallon" from 2014 to 2018. He was production designer for the films "Mr. Mike's Mondo Video" (1979), "Gilda Live" (1980), "Hammett" (1982), "Easy Money" (1983), "Mr. North" (1988), "Vanya on 42nd Street" (1994), and "A Master Builder" (2013). Lee had a relationship with fellow designer Franne Newman Lee in the 1970s and is survived by their son, Willie. He married Brooke Lutz in 1981 and is also survived by her and their son, Ted.

Lee, Franne

Costume and production designer Franne Lee died in Atlantis, Florida, on August 27, 2023. She was 81. She was  born Frances Newman in the Bronx, New York, on December 30, 1941. She studied painting at the University of Wisconsin and developed an interest in stage and costume design. She moved to New York after the end of her first marriage in 1967 where she worked for the Manhattan nightclub Cerebrum. He became involved with production designer Eugene Lee in 1970 and they worked frequently together throughout the decade. She won Tony Awards for Scenic Design and Costume Design for the

1974 Broadway production of "Candide" and received another Tony for her costumes for 1979's "Sweeney Todd". She worked on other Broadway plays, usually with Eugene Lee, including "Dude" (1972), "Love for Love" (1974), "The Skin of Our Teeth" (1975), "Some of My Bet Friends" (1977), and "Gilda Radner - Live from New York" (1979). Franne and Eugene worked together on "Saturday Night Live" from 1975 to 1980, and she served as a costume designer and production designer. She was noted for outfitting John Belushi and Dan Aykroyd in black to become the Blues Brothers, creating the Killer Bee costumes, and making the outsized heads for the Coneheads. She earned Emmy nominations for her work on the show in 1977 and 1978. She was a costume designer or productions designer for the films "Mr. Mike's Mondo Video" (1979), "Gilda Live" (1980), "Dead Ringer" (1982), "Baby It's You" (1983), "Emo Philips Live" (1987), "The Local Stigmatic" (1990), "Sweet Nothing" (1995), "Total Stranger" (1999), "Chinese Coffee" (2000), and "Sam the Man" (2001). She continued to design costumes for such short-lived Broadway productions "The Moony Shapiro Songbook" (1981), "Rock 'N Roll! The First 5,000 Years" (1982), and "Camelot" (1993). She was also costume designer for the tele-films "Runaway" (1989), "Gryphon" (1990), and "Runaway Car" (1997). She moved to Nashville, Tennessee, in 2001 where she was involved with Plowhaus, a gallery and artists' cooperative. She subsequently lived in Wisconsin and moved to Florida in 2017. She was married to Ralph Sandler from 1962 until their divorce in 1962 and is survived by their son and daughter. She maintained a personal and professional partnership with production designer Eugene Lee throughout the 1970s, though they reportedly never married. She is also survived by their son.

Lee, Ralph

Puppeteer Ralph Lee died in Manhattan, New York, on May 12, 2023. He was 87. Lee was born in Middlebury, Vermont, on July 9, 1935. He began making puppets in his youth. He graduated from Amherst College in Massachusetts in 1957 and studied theater and dance in Europe for two years.

He began his career on stage in regional theater and off-Broadway productions after settling in New York City. He appeared on Broadway in the plays "Caligula" (1960), "A Passage to India" (1962), and "The Royal Hunt of the Sun" (1965). He worked with the La MaMa Experimental Theatre Club with off-off-Broadway productions later in the decade. He designed sets for "Niagara Falls" in 1967 and appeared in the plays "A Vietnamese Wedding" and "The Red Burning Light of the American Way of Life" in 1969. Lee directed and designed Nancy Fales' play "Ark" in 1974 and made the props and masks for Adrienne Kennedy's A Rat's Mass" in 1976. He became adept at creating puppets, props, and masks for theatrical productions. He organized the Greenwich Village Halloween Parade in 1974 and directed the parade until 1985. He became artistic director of the Mettawee River Theatre Company in 1976 and was artist-in-residence at the Cathedral of St. John the Divine from 1984. Lee also created giant figures for numerous parades and celebrations including Central Park's New Year's Eve celebrations from 1974 to 1980 and the Bronx Zoo's Easter events from 1980 to 1984. His work was featured at the New York Botanical Garden events "Halloween on Haunted Walk" from 1993 to 2005 and "The Little Engine That Could" from 1995. He designed the Land Shark for television's "Saturday Night Live" in 1975. His masks and figures were seen in productions of the Metropolitan Opera, the New York Shakespeare Festival, New York City Opera, and Theater for the New City. He taught and various colleges and served on the faculty of New York University from 1988. Lee was married to Stephanie Lawrence Ratner from 1959 until their divorce in 1973 and is survived by their three children. He married Casey Compton in 1982 and is also survived by her and their daughter.

Lee Sun-Kyun

South Korean actor Lee Sun-Kyun, who starred in Bong Joon-ho's Oscar-winning 2019 film "Parasite", died of a suicide by carbon monoxide poisoning inside his car at a

parking lot by Waryong Park in central Seoul, South Korea, on December 27, 2023. Lee was born in Seoul on March 2, 1975. He graduated from the Korea National University of Arts School of Drama in the late 1990s. He began his career on stage in the role of Brad Majors in the musical "The Rocky Horror Show" in 2001. He appeared frequently on television with roles in such series as "Loveholic" as Kim Tae-Hyun in 2005, the medical drama "Behind the White Tower" as CDhoi Do-youn in 2007, "The 1st Shop of Coffee Prince" as Choi Han Sung in 2007, "Dal-kom-han Na-eui Do-si", "Teuripeul" as Jo Hae-yoon in 2009, "Pasta" as Choi Hyun Wook in 2010, "Golden Time" as Lee Min-woo in 2012, "Miss Korea" as Kim Hyung Joon from 2013 to 2014, "My Wife's Having an Affair This Week" as Do Hyun-woo in 2016, "My Mister" as Park Dong-hoon in 2018, "Diary of a Prosecutor" as Lee Seon-woong from 2019 to 2020, the science fiction web thriller "Dr. Brain" earning an International Emmy Award nomination for his role as Sewon Koh in 2022, and "Payback" as Eun Yong in 2023. Lee was seen in numerous films from the early 2000s including the short "Psycho Drama" (2000), the comedy "Make It Big" (2002), "Surprise Party" (2002), "A Perfect Match" (2002), "Boss X-File" (2002), "Scent of Love" (2003), "Show Show Show" (2003), the fantasy "My Mother, the Mermaid" (2005), "Love, So Divine" (2004), the psychological horror film "R-Point" (2004), "The Customer Is Always Right" (2006), "A Cruel Attendance" (2006), "Our Town" (2007), "Night and Day" (2008), "Sa-kwa" (2008), "Romantic Island" (2008), "Paju" (2009), "Oki's Movie" (2010), "Petty Romance" (2010), "Officer of the Year" (2011),

"Helpless" (2012), "All About My Wife" (2012), "Nobody's Daughter Haewon" (2013), "Our Sunhi" (2013), "A Hard Day" (2014), "The Advocate: A Missing Body" (2015), "A King's Case Note" (2017), "Man of Will" (2017), "A Special Lady" (2017), "Take Point" (2018), "Jo Pil-ho: The Dawning Rage" (2019), Bong Joon-ho's Academy Award winning black comedy thriller "Parasite" (2019) as the Park family patriarch Dong-ik/Nathan, "Mr. Zoo: The Missing VIP" (2020) as the voice of the Black Goat, the political drama "Kingmaker" (2022), "Killing Romance" (2023), the horror comedy "Sleep" (2023), and "Project Silence" (2023). Lee was charged by the South Korean police on suspicion of using cannabis and psychoactive drugs. He was summoned for questioning and was reportedly interrogated for over 19 hours. Test results of a hair sample tested negative for drugs. He had voluntarily dropped out of the cast for the television thriller series "No Way Out" due to the allegations. Lee married actress Jeon Hye-jin in 2009 and is survived by her and their two sons.

Leger, Viola

American-Canadian actress Viola Leger died in Dieppe, New Brunswick, Canada, on January 28, 2023. She was 92. Leger was born in Fitchburg, Massachusetts, on June 29, 1930. She graduated from the Universite de Moncton in New Brunswick and earned a master's degree in theater from Boston University. She began her career on stage and was noted for starring in the title role of Antonine Maillet's play "La Sagouine" in over 3,000 performances. She also starred in television productions of "La Sagouine" in 1975, 2006, and 2017. Leger was featured in the 1994 film "Le Secret de Jerome". She was seen on television in an episode of "Bouscotte" in 1998 and the mini-series "Les Couleurs de Mon Accent" in 2003. Leger received the Governor General's Performing Arts Award for her acting career in 2013.

Leitch, Maurice

Northern Irish author Maurice Leitch died in Canterbury, Kent, England, on September 26, 2023. He was 90. Leitch was born in Muckamore, Northern Ireland, on July 5, 1933. He attended Methodist College Belfast and Stranmillis College. He began teaching primary school in Antrim before he began writing about the local countryside. He began writing radio plays for the BBC Northern Ireland and "The Old House" was produced in 1960. His first novel, "The Liberty Lad", as published in 1965 and was followed by "Poor Lazarus" in 1969. Leitch's works also include "Stamping Ground"(1975), "Silver's City" (1981)

which won the Whitbread Prize, "Chinese Whispers" (1987), "The Hands of Cheryl Boyd and Other Stories" (1987), "Burning Bridges" (1989), "Gilchrist" (1994), "The Smoke King" (1998), "The Eggman's Apprentice" (2001), "Tell Me About It" (2007), "Dining at the Dunbar" (2009), "A Far Cry" (2013), "Seeking Mr. Hare" (2013), and "Gone to Earth" (2019). Leitch wrote numerous tele-plays including "Rifleman" (1980), "Guests of the Nation" (1983), "Gates of Gold" (1983), and "Chinese Whispers" (1989). He also served as a producer for the BBC Radio drama department in London from 1970 and was editor of Radio Four's "Book at Bedtime" from 1977 to 1989. He married Isobel Scott in 1955 and they later divorced. He is survived by their two children. Leitch was married to Sandra Hill from 1972 until her death in 2020 and is also survived by their son.

Leland, David

British film director and actor David Leland died in England on December 24, 2023. He was 82. Leland was born in Cambridge, England, on April 20, 1941. He trained at the Central School of Speech and Drama before becoming a founding member of Drama Centre London in 1963. He began his career on television as an actor and appeared in productions of "Four People" (1966), "The Last of the Mohicans" (1971), "The Love-Girl and the Innocent" (1973), "Bull Week" (1980), "The Hitchhiker's Guide to the Galaxy" (1981), "Miss Morison's Ghosts" (1981), and "The Jewel in the Crown" (1984). He as also seen in episodes of "Sat'day While Sunday", "The Queen Street Gang" as Franco in 1968, "Sherlock Holmes", "Callan", "Big Breadwinner Hogg" as Grange in 1969, "Parkin's Patch", "Van der Valk", "Barlow at Large", "Warrior Queen" as Agricola in 1978, "The Devils Crown", "Target", "Ripping Yarns", "Arena", and "The Young Indiana Jones Chronicles". He appeared in the films "Julius Caesar" (1970), "Underground" (1970), "Scars of Dracula" (1970), "One Brief Summer" (1971), "The Pied Piper" (1972), "Gawain and the Green Knight" (1973), "Time Bandits" (1981), and "The Missionary" (1982). He wrote the 1981 tele-film "Made in Britain" for director Alan Clarke. Leland also wrote the television productions "Birth of a Nation" (1983), "Flying Into the Wind" (1983), and "R.H.I.N.O.: Really Here in Name Only" (1983). He co-wrote the 1986 film "Mona Lisa" with director Neil Jordan". He scripted the 1987 film "Personal Services" which received a BAFTA Award for best screenplay. He also appeared in the film in a small role. Leland made his directorial debut with 1988's "Checking Out. He helmed the stage musical "A Tribute to the Blue Brothers" in 1991, which was performed in London's West End. He also directed, and frequently wrote and appeared in, the films "Crossing the Line" (1990), "The Land Girls" (1998), and "Virgin Territory" (2007). He scripted and appeared in the 1999 film "The White River Kid". He directed music videos for the Traveling Wilburys, Tom Petty, and Paul McCartney. Leland directed an episode of the 2001 mini-series "Band of Brothers", sharing an Emmy Award, and the 2003 television tribute to George Harrison, "Concert for George", which received a Grammy Award. He was director and executive producer for the Showtime series "The Borgias" from 2012 to 2013. Leland is survived by his wife, Sabrina Canale, four daughters, and a son.

LePere, Ray

Actor Ray LePere died of complications from Alzheimer's disease on January 2, 2023. He was 88. LePere was born in Dallas, Texas, on September 19, 1934. He attended Southern Methodist University in Dallas and served three years in the U.S. Army. He was an actor and model for television and radio ads before becoming a licensed mortician. He later moved into radio serving as a traffic reporter and police reporter. LePere's final career move was as a deputy sheriff with the Dallas County Sheriff's Department for thirty years. He was featured in several films during his career including "The Seniors" (1978), "Tender Mercies" (1983), "Perfect Profile" (1989), "Caged Fear" (1991), and "JFK" (1991) as Zapruder. LePere appeared on television in the tele-films "The Trial of Lee Harvey Oswald" (1977), "Cotton Candy" (1978), "Crisis at Central High" (1981), "Time Bomb" (1984), and "Stormin' Home" (1985), and several episodes of "Dallas".

Lerner, Michael

Actor Michael Lerner, who received an Academy Award nomination for Best Supporting Actor for his role in the 1991 film "Barton Fink", died of complications from brain seizures at a hospital in Burbank, California, on April 8, 2023. He was 81. Lerner was born in Brooklyn, New York, on June 22, 1941. He attended Brooklyn College where he studied acting and performed on stage. He earned a master's degree in English drama from the University of California at Berkeley and continued training at the London Academy of Music and Dramatic Art. He shared a flat in London with John Lennon and Yoko Ono and appeared in Yoko's 1968 experimental short film "Smile". He moved to the San Francisco Bay area in 1968 and appeared on stage with the American Conservatory Theater. Lerner moved to Los Angeles the following year. He was a familiar face on television with roles in episodes of "Dr. Kildare", "The Good Guys", "Three's a Crowd", "The Brady Bunch", "The Doris Day Show", "The Young Lawyers", "That Girl", "The D.A.", "Banacek", "The Bold Ones: The New Doctors", "Ironside", "Night Gallery", "The Streets of San Francisco", "The Delphi Bureau", "The Bob Newhart Show", "Emergency!", "Love Story", "The New Perry Mason", "Bob & Carol & Ted & Alice", "Love, American Style", "M*A*S*H", "Chase", "The Odd Couple", "Lucas Tanner", "Starsky and Hutch", "Rhoda", "Jigsaw John", "Harry O", "Police Woman", "The Rockford Files", "Kojak", "Vega$", "Wonder Woman", "Barnaby Jones", "B.A.D. Cats", "Today's F.B.I.", "Hart to Hart", "I Gave at the Office", "Hollywood Beat", "MacGyver", "The A-Team", "Hill Street Blues" in the recurring role of Rollie Simone in 1983, "Amazing Stories", "The Equalizer", "The Boys", "Tales from the Crypt", "Picture Windows", "Courthouse" as Judge Myron Winkleman in 1995, "Clueless" as Mel Horowitz from 1996 to 1997, "Third Watch", "Kingdom Hospital" in the recurring role of Sheldon Fleischer in 2004, "Law & Order: Special Victims Unit", "Entourage", "Dirty Sexy Money", "Saving Grace", "Matumbo Goldberg" as the Rabbi in 2011, "The Good Wife", "Suburgatory", "Glee" in the recurring role of Broadway producer Sidney Greene from 2013 to 2014, "Comedy Bang! Bang!", "Recorded Lives", "Childrens Hospital", and "Maron". His other television credits include the tele-films "Thief" (1971), "Marriage: Year One" (1971), "What's a Nice Girl Like You...?" (1971), "Magic Carpet" (1972), "Firehouse" (1973), "Reflections of Murder" (1974), "The Missiles of October" (1974) as Pierre Salinger, "The Dream Makers" (1975), "Sarah T. - Portrait of a Teenage Alcoholic" (1975), "A Cry for Help" (1975), "Grandpa Max" (1975), "F. Scott Fitzgerald in Hollywood" (1975), "Dark Victory" (1976), "Scott Free" (1976), "A Love Affair: The Eleanor and Lou Gehrig Story" (1977), "Killer on Board" (1977), "Confessions of the D.A. Man" (1978), "Ruby and Oswald" (1978) as Jack Ruby, "Diary of a Young Comic" (1979), "This Year's Blonde" (1980) as Jack Warner, "Gridlock" (1980), "Blood Feud" (1983), "Rita Hayworth: The Love Goddess" (1983) as Harry Cohn, "The Execution" (1985), "This Child Is Mine" (1985), "That Secret Sunday" (1986), "Hands of a Stranger" (1987), "The King of Love" (1987), the mini-series "Melba" (1988) as Oscar Hammerstein, "Framed" (1990), "Made in Hollywood" (1990), "Omen IV: The Awakening" (1991), "The Comrades of Summer" (1992), "Murder at the Cannes Film Festival" (2000), and the short film "Frankenstein's Monster's Monster, Frankenstein" (2019). Lerner appeared frequently in films with roles in "Alex in Wonderland" (1970), "The Ski Bum" (1971), "The Candidate" (1972) with Robert Redford, "Busting" (1974), "Newman's Law" (1974), "Hangup" (1974), "St. Ives" (1976), "The Other Side of Midnight" (1977), "Outlaw Blues" (1977), "Goldengirl" (1979), "The Baltimore Bullet" (1980), "Borderline" (1980), "Coast to Coast" (1980), "The Postman Always Rings Twice" (1981), "Threshold" (1981), "Class Reunion" (1982), the science fiction film "Strange Invaders" (1983), "Movers & Shakers" (1985), the Spanish horror film "Anguish" (1987), "Vibes" (1988), "Eight Men Out" (1988) as Arnold Rothstein, "Harlem Nights" (1989) as gangster Bugsy Calhoune, "Any Man's Death" (1990), the horror film "Maniac Cop 2" (1990), "The Closer" (1990), the Coen Brothers' "Barton Fink" (1991)

earning an Oscar nomination for his role as film producer Jack Lipnick, "Newsies" (1992), "Amos & Andrew" (1993), "Blank Check" (1994), "No Escape" (1994), "Radioland Murders" (1994), "The Road to Wellville" (1994), "A Pyromaniac's Love Story" (1995), "No Way Back" (1995), "Girl in the Cadillac" (1995), "The Beautician and the Beast" (1997), "For Richer or Poorer" (1997), "Tales of the Mummy" (1998), "Godzilla" (1998) as Mayor Ebert, "Safe Men" (1998), "Celebrity" (1998), "Desperation Boulevard" (1998), "The Mod Squad" (1999), "My Favorite Martian" (1999), "Attention Shoppers" (2000), "Mockingbirds Don't Sing" (2001), the animated "101 Dalmatians 2: Patch's London Adventure" (2002), "29 Palms" (2002), the Christmas comedy "Elf" (2003) as book publisher Fulton Greenway, "Nobody Knows Anything!" (2003), "Larceny" (2004), "The Calcium Kid" (2004), "Poster Boy" (2004), "When Do We Eat?" (2005), "Art School Confidential" (2006), "Love and Other Disasters" (2006), "The Last Time" (2006), "Slipstream" (2007), "A Dennis the Menace Christmas" (2007), "Yonkers Joe" (2008), "Life During Wartime" (2009), "A Serious Man" (2009), "The Bannen Way" (2009), "Pete Smalls Is Dead" (2010), "Atlas Shrugged: Part 1" (2011), "Mirror Mirror" (2012), "Somebody Marry Me" (2013), "Brahmin Bulls" (2013), "Immigrant" (2013), "2 Dead 2 Kill" (2013), "1000 to 1: The Cory Weissman Story" (2014), "X-Men: Days of Future Past" (2014) as Senator Brickman, "Ashby" (2015), "Switching Lanes" (2015), "The Shickles" (2016), "American Bred" (2016), "Internet Famous" (2016), "Drive Me to Vegas and Mars" (2018), and "First Oscar" (2022) as Louis B. Mayer. He continued to perform on stage, appearing in a West End production of "Up for Grabs" with Madonna in 2002. Lerner was also a noted collector of rare books. His survivors include his younger brother, actor Ken Lerner.

Lester, Heddy

Dutch singer and actress Heddy Lester died of bladder cancer in Amsterdam, Netherlands, on January 29, 2023. She was 72. She was born Heddy Affolter in Leeuwarden, Netherlands, on June 15, 1950. She began her career as a singer as part of the duo April Shower with Gert Balke. They had a minor hit with 1971's "Railroad Song". She soon began touring with singer Ramses Shaffy and began a solo career in 1974. She was the Dutch contestant in the Eurovision Song Contest in 1977 with the song "De Mallemolen" ("The Merry-Go-Round"). She placed twelfth in the competition. She continued to perform and appeared on stage in musicals and dramas. She appeared on television in a 1984 episode of "Zeg 'ns Aaa" and the tele-film "Maria Magdalena" in 1985. She was also seen in the short films "De Tranen van Maria Machita" (1991) and "Kras Lot" (2018), and the 2020 comedy feature "Groeten van Gerri".

Levenduski, Nick

Special effects designer Nick Levendiski died suddenly in Los Angeles, California, on April 6, 2023. He was 41. Levenduski was born in Harrisburg, Pennsylvania, on April 12, 1981. He graduated from the Thompson Institute, where he studied digital arts and computer animation. He began working in films in the early 2000s for such companies as Digital Domain, Disney, Scanline, and DreamWorks. His film effects credits include "Music and Lyrics" (2007), "The Golden Compass" (2007), "The Mummy: Tomb of the Dragon Emperor" (2008), "2012" (2009), "Tron: Legacy" (2010), "Puss in Boots" (2011), "Rise of the Guardians" (2012), "Turbo" (2013), "How to Train Your Dragon 2" (2014), "Penguins of Madagascar" (2014), "Home" (2015), "Black Panther" (2018), "The Meg" (2018), "Aquaman" (2018), "Dark Phoenix" (2019), "Spies in Disguise" (2019), "Encanto" (2021), and "Ruby Gillman: Teenage Kraken" (2023). Levenduski also worked on the television series "Fear the Walking Dead", "Blood Drive", and "Game of Thrones".

Levin, Michael

Actor Michael Levin, who starred as Jack Fenelli in the television soap opera "Ryan's Hope" for over a decade, died in Mount Kisco, New York, on January 6, 2023. He was 90. Levin was born in Minneapolis, Minnesota, on December 8, 1932. He served in the U.S. Navy for two years before attending the University of Minnesota. He began his career on stage at Minneapolis' Guthrie Theater in the early 1960s. He continued to perform on stage after moving to New York City and was seen in Broadway productions of "The Royal Hunt of the Sun" (1965), "Camino Real" (1970), "Operation Sidewinder" (1970), and "The Good Woman of Setzuan" (1970). He was best known for his role as reporter Jack Fenelli on the soap opera "Ryan's Hope" for its entire run from 1975 to 1989. He was featured as John Eldridge in "As the World Turns" from 1991 to 1992 and Dr. Gould on "All My Children" in 1993. Levin also appeared in episodes of the series "N.Y.P.D.", "The Equalizer", "Law & Order", and "New York News". He married Loretta Chiljian in 1960 until their divorce several years later and is survived by their son. He married soap opera writer Elizabeth Levin in 1965 and is also survived by her and their son.

Levinson, Madge

Actress Madge Levinson died of lung cancer in Toledo, Ohio, on March 22, 2023. She was 98. She was born Madeline Weiner in Beaver Falls, Pennsylvania, on April 14,

1924. She graduated from the University of Chicago where she received a degree in chemistry. She and her family moved to Toledo in the late 1960s. She became involved in local theater and performed in numerous local productions over the next fifty years. Levinson appeared frequently in television commercials and industrial films. She became  a character actress in feature films later in life with such credits as "All of It" (1998), "In the Company of Strangers" (2001), "Nevermore" (2007), "Whip It" (2009), "Puzzled" (2010), "This Must Be the Place" (2011), "The Five-Year Engagement" (2012), "Grave" (2013), "Highland Park" (2013), "A Grain of Sand" (2013), "Max Anderson, Private Eye" (2013), "The Funeral Guest" (2015), "Adam" (2020), and "Chasing the Rain" (2020). She was also seen in the 2009 tele-film "Prayers for Bobby" and an episode of "Baldwin Cafe". Levinson continued to appear on the local stage through 2021. She was married to Al Levinson from 1946 until his death in 2011 and is survived by their son and daughter.

Lewis, Greg

Actor and comedian Greg Lewis died of heart failure in Los Angeles, California, on September 18, 2023. He was 88. Lewis was born in Chicago, Illinois, on April 21, 1935. He began performing with the musical comedy groups Jerry Murads Harmonicats and Little Johnny Puleo's Harmonica Rascals while in his teens. He  performed on such variety series as "The Ed Sullivan Show", "The Hollywood Palace", "The Merv Griffin Show", and "The Mike Douglas Show". He teamed with Gus Christy in the comedy act the Mad Greeks. He continued to perform as a solo stand-up comedian after they broke up. Lewis was a character actor in television and films from the 1970s, appearing in episodes of "Laverne & Shirley", "The Bob Newhart Show", "The Tony Randall Show", "In the Beginning", "Beyond Westworld", "Ace Crawford... Private Eye", "Scarecrow and Mrs. King", "Simon & Simon", "Riptide", "Who's the Boss?", "Hill Street Blues", "The Love Boat", "Silver Spoons", "Misfits of Science", "Fresno", "Night Court", "Falcon Crest", "Out of This World", "Punky Brewster", "It's a Living", "Good Grief", "Married... with Children", "The Munsters Today", "Dragnet", "Top of the Heap", "Days of Our Lives", "Reasonable Doubts", "Johnny Bago", "Phenom", "Murder, She Wrote", "Murphy Brown", "Renegade", "Baywatch Nights", "Malcolm & Eddie", "The Pretender", "Sabrina the Teenage Witch", "Everybody Loves Raymond", "Power Rangers Lightspeed Rescue", "As Told by Ginger" in a voice role, "Three Sisters", "Gilmore Girls",

"Desperate Housewives", "How I Met Your Mother", "2 Broke Girls", "Bunheads", and "Workaholics". He was also seen in the tele-films "Sporting Chance" (1990), "Marilyn & Bobby: Her Final Affair" (1993), and "Motorcycle Gang" (1994). Lewis appeared in the films "Angel" (1983), "Vamp" (1986), "The Running Man" (1987), "Club Fed" (1990), "Repossessed" (1990), "Frankie and Johnny" (1991), "American Kickboxer 2" (1993), "Prehysteria! 2" (1994), "The Takeover" (1994), "Save Me" (1994), "For Better or Worse" (1995), "Guns & Lipstick" (1995), "Larger Than Life" (1996), "White Cargo" (1996), "Dear God" (1996), "No Easy Way" (1996), "Centurion Force" (1998), "Eating L.A." (1999), "Carlo's Wake" (1999), "Gentleman B." (2000), the short "Mars and Beyond" (2000), "Spin Cycle" (2000), "The Princess Diaries" (2001) as Baron Siegfried von Troken, "Max Keeble's Big Move" (2001), "K-PAX" (2001), "Backgammon" (2001), "Driving Me Crazy" (2001), "Love and a Bullet" (2002), "The Princess Diaries 2: Royal Engagement" (2004), and "Hop" (2011). He toured with the autobiographical one-man show "Some Greeks Are Not in the Restaurant Business" later in his career. Lewis is survived by his wife, Roberta, and daughter Anastasia. He was predeceased by two sons, Montgomery and Gregory.

Lewis, James

Singer James Lewis, who performed with the Trans-Siberian Orchestra (TS0), died of cancer in Pittsburgh, Pennsylvania, on May 22, 2023. He was 63. He was born in Cranberry Township, Pennsylvania, in 1960. He moved to New  York City after high school to pursue a career in music. He became a member of the bands BlueHouse and ROY-G-BIV and provided voice-overs for commercials for G.I. Joe, Campbells Soup, and other products. Lewis joined the Trans-Siberian Orchestra as a lead singer in 2004. He toured and performed with TSO until failing health forced his retirement in 2023.

Lewis, Linda

British singer and songwriter Linda Lewis died at her home in Waltham Abbey, Essex, England, on May 3, 2023. She was 72. She was born Linda Fredericks in Custom House,  Essex, on September 27, 1950. She studied acting as a child and appeared in small roles in the films "The Wreck of the Mary Deare" (1959), "A Taste of Honey" (1961), and the Beatles' "A Hard Day's Night" (1964). She joined the Jamaican-style music band the Q Set in the mid-1960s and made her recording debut on the single "You Turned My Bitter into Sweet" in 1967. She and Junior Kerr teamed as White Rabbit in 1967 and she toured with the soul rock band the Ferris Wheel in 1970. Lewis sang on their self-named album and the single "Can't Stop Now". She was a session singer for such artists as David Bowie, Cat Stevens, Al Koper, and Hummingbird. She became noted for her five-octave vocal range. She had a hit with her 1973 single "Rock-a-Doodle-Doo" and the subsequent album, "Fathoms Deep". She performed on television in such variety series as "In Concert", "Twiggy", "Shang-a-Lang", "Pop at the Mill", "Top of the Pops", "Juke Box Jury", "The Basil Brush Show", "Roadshow Disco" which she hosted in 1979, "The Marti Caine Show", "The Jim Davidson Show", "Good Time George", and "The Lenny Henry Show". Lewis had a major hit with the 1975 album "Not a Little Girl Anymore" and the single "It's in His Kiss". She continued to record and perform over the next decade and teamed with sisters Dee and Shirley as the Lewis Sisters. She moved to Los Angeles in the 1980s and was a backing singer for Joan Armatrading. Her 1995 album "Second Nature" was a hit in Japan and resulted in a tour. Her later singles include "Reach Out" with Midfield General in 2000 and "Earthling" with the Paracosmos in 2023. Lewis was married to musician Jim Cregan from 1977 until their divorce in 1980. She married music agent Neil Warnock in 2004 and he survives her.

Leyson, Johan

Belgian actor Johan Leysen died of cardiac arrest in France on March 30, 2023. He was 73. Leysen was born in Hasselt, Belgium, on February 19, 1950. He graduated from Studio Herman Teirlinck in 1974 and began performing on the

Dutch and Belgian stage in the 1970s. He was seen in numerous films from the mid-1970s including "Agamemnoon" (1975), "Rubens, Schilder en Diplomaat" (1977), "In Alle Stilte" (1978), "The Girl with the Red Hair" (1981), "Come Back" (1981), "Le Lit" (1982), "De Stille Oceaan" (1984), "De Grens" (1984), "Broken Mirrors" (1984), "Parfait Amour" (1985), "Hail Mary" (1985), "De Prooi" (1985), "De Deur van Het Huis" (1985), "Desiderando Giulia" (1986), "Requiem" (1986), "Macbeth" (1987), "L'Oeuvre au Noir" (1988), "Ei" (1988), "The Music Teacher" (1988), "Sailors Don't Cry" (1990), "Romeo" (1990), "Dilemma" (1990), "Rosa Rosa" (1990), "Alissa in Concert" (1990), "Schrodingers Kat" (1990), "Eline Vere" (1991), "Openbaringen van een Slapeloze" (1991), "De Laasten der Mohikanen" (1991), "Boven de Bergen" (1992), "The Johnsons" (1992), "Between Heaven and Hell" (1992), "Daens" (1992), "Rooksporen" (1992), "Swing Kids" (1993), "L'Ordre du Jour" (1993), "Trahir" (1993), "Queen Margot" (1994), "Moon Shadow" (1995), "Un Samedi Sur la Terre" (1996), "True Blue" (1996), the science fiction film "Tykho Moon" (1996), "The Gambler" (1997), "Felice... Felice..." (1998), "The Commissioner" (1998), "L'Inconnu de Strasbourg" (1998), "Train of Life"

(1998), "Missing Link" (1999), "The Crossing" (1999), "Nag la Bombe" (1999), "Le Pique-nique de Lulu Kreutz" (1999), "Faites Comme Si Je n'Etais Pas La" (2000), "Princesses" (2000), "Le Roi Danse" (2000), "Lisa" (2001), the horror film "Brotherhood of the Wolf" (2001), "Savage Souls" (2001), "Tattoo" (2002), "The Red Siren" (2002), "Moonlight" (2002), "Gun-Shy" (2003), "Grimm" (2003), "Gli Occhi dell'Altro" (2005), "Miss Montigny" (2005), "Someone Else's Happiness" (2005), "Le Lievre de Vatanen"(2006), "L'ete Indien" (2007), "West Point" (2007), "Zomerhitte" (2008), "Private Lessons" (2008), "Sister Smile" (2009), the action thriller "The American (2010) starring George Clooney, "Sea of Tranquility" (2010), "Requiem for a Killer" (2011), "The Silence of Joan" (2011), "Photo (2012), "Young & Beautiful" (2013), "Het Vonnis" (2013), "Obsessive Rhythms" (2013), "2/11 Het Spel van de Wolf" (2014) "Son of Mine" (2015), the dark fantasy "The Brand New Testament" (2015), "The Assistant" (2015), "Despite the Night" (2015), "Louis-Ferdinand Celine" (2016), "Souvenir" (2016), "Waldstille" (2016), "Back to Utopia" (2016), "Past Imperfect" (2017), "Tueurs" (2017), "Resurrection" (2017), "Around Luisa" (2017), "Facades" (2017), "Alone at My Wedding" (2018), "Claire Darling" (2018), "A Hidden Life" (2019), "Pink Moon" (2022), "Temps Mort" (2023), "Noise" (2023), "Onder de Blote Hemel" (2023), and "Bijt" (2024). Leysen appeared frequently on television with roles in productions of "Maya" (1982), "Titaantjes" (1983), "Jacht Op Het Verleden" (1985), "Zondag Weet Je Alles" (1985), "Minj Idee: Het Schilderij" (1986), "Tourbillons" (1988), "'t Bolleken" (1988), "Het Europa van Het Gulden Vlies" (1989), "Braindrain" (1989), "Niemand Mag Dit Weten" (1991), "Hoffman's Honger" (1993), "Kuchnia Polska" (1993), "La Rage au Coeur" (1994), "Abus de Confiance" (1994), "Tralievader" (1995), 'Poezie is Woordkunst: Paul Van Ostaijen 1896-1928" (1996), "Les Steenfort, Maitres de l'Orge" (1996), "De Langste Reis" (1996), "Maten" (1999), "Le Destin des Steenfort" (1999), "L'enfant des Lumieres" (2002), "De Enclave" (2002), "Retour aa Locmaria" (2003), "Les Thibault" (2003), "Carmen" (2005), "La Derive des Continents" (2006), and "Goldman" (2011). His other television credits include episodes of "Les Enquetes du Commissaire Maigret", "Vijf Minuten Bedenktijd", "Het Bloed Kruipt", "Les Cinq Dernieres Minutes", "Hoe Voelen Wij Ons Vandaag", "Op Leven en Dood", "Oog in Oog", "Maigret", "Le Cascadeur", "Regards d'Enfance", "Pleidooi", "La Grande Collection", "L'Histoire du Samedi", "Madame le Consul", "Vertiges", "The Squad", "Schimanski", "De 9 Dagen van de Gier" as Martin Jonker from 2001 to 2002, "Tatort", "De Sole et de Cendre", "Boulevard du Palais", "Matinee", "Clara Sheller", "Enneagram", "The Emperor of Taste", "Collection Fred Vargas", "The Spiral" as Victor Detta and Arturo in 2012, "The Missing", "Vechtershart" as John Roest from 2015 to 2017, "Ik Weet Wie Je Bent" as Herman Kasteel in 2018, "Lockdown", "Pandore" as Simon Delval in 2022, and "Before We Die". Leysen was married and divorced from filmmaker Rita Horst and is survived by their daughter, director and screenwriter Eva.

Licata, Richard V.

Actor Richard V. Licata died in Brooklyn, New York, on November 3, 2023. He was 74. Licata was born in Brooklyn on November 23, 1948. He graduated from Catholic University in the late 1960s and earned a degree in law from St. John's University. He began practicing law in New York with various firms before opening his own specializing in personal injury law in Rockland County in the early 1980s. He also began performing on the local stage in community productions. Licata began appearing in films and television in the late 1990s and moved to Los Angeles. He was featured in such films as "A Killing" (1998), "Just Looking" (1999), "Two Family House" (2000), "Dregs of Society" (2001), "A Tale of Two Pizzas" (2003), "The Island" (2005), "Johnny Virus" (2005), "Get Smart" (2008), "Spy" (2011), "Excuse Me for Living" (2012), and Martin Scorsese's "The Irishman" (2019). He also appeared in the shorts "The Shift" (2006), "Mr. Fisher" (2007), "The Man Under the Tere" (2007), "Expendable" (2007), "The Hit" (2007), "Twins" (2007), "The Golden Egg" (2008), "The Sit Down" (2008), and "Regulars" (2010). Licata was seen on television in episodes of "Third Watch", "Guiding Light", "Law & Order", "Law & Order: Special Victims Unit", "Queens Supreme", "100 Centre Street", "The Division", "The West Wing" in the recurring role of Congressman Lackey in 2004, "Threshold", "Malcolm in the Middle", "That '70s Show", "Boston Legal", "State of Mind", "Two and a Half Men", "CSI: NY", "Without a Trace",, "Bones", "Criminal Minds", "Law & Order: Criminal Intent", "Person of Interest", "House of Cards", "Prodigal Son", and "For Life" in the recurring role of Judge Thomas Lassaro in 2021. He returned to Brooklyn in 2010, where he continued to act and practice law. Licata was predeceased by his wife, Maria, in 1992, and is survived by their son and daughter.

Lieberman, Robert

Film and television director Robert Lieberman died of cancer in Los Angeles, California, on July 1, 2023. He was 75. Lieberman was born in Buffalo, New York, on July 16, 1947. He graduated from the University of Buffalo where he was instrumental in founding the school's film department. He worked for the National Football League's Buffalo Bills as a video assistant in the 1970s. He moved to Los Angeles later in the decade and made his television debut directing episodes for "ABC Afterschool Specials" in 1978. He was noted for his work in television commercials, filming spots for McDonald's, Budweiser, Coca-Cola, Sprint, Oreo, and Hallmark. He was recipient of 29 Clio Awards and received the first Director's Guild of America Award for commercials in 1979. Lieberman worked frequently in television, directing the tele-films and mini-series "Fighting Back: The Story of Rocky Bleier" (1980), "Will: The Autobiography of G. Gordon Liddy" (1982), "To Save a Child" (1991), "Titanic" (1996), "NetForce" (1999), "Red Skies" (2002), "Second String" (2002), "Earthsea" (2005), "Final Days of Planet Earth" (2006), "A.M.P.E.D." (2007), "Eve of Destruction" (2013), "Ascension" (204), "Love Stories in Sunflower Valley" (2021), "Love on the Road" (2021), and "Christmas in Tahoe" (2021). He was also director and often producer for episodes of such series as "thirtysomething", "Dream Street", "The Young Riders", "Gabriel's Fire", "Harts of the West", "Under Suspicion", "Medicine Ball", "Moloney", "Once and Again", "The X-Files", "Strong Medicine", "The Dead Zone", "Jake 2.0", "Killer Instinct", "Dexter", "Shark", "Eureka", "Brothers & Sisters", "Republic of Doyle", "Nikita", "Lost Girl", "Arctic Air", "King", "XIII: The Series", "The Listener", "Criminal Minds", "Haven", "Falling Skies", "Houdini and Doyle", "The Art of More", "Eyewitness", "The Expanse", "Rogue", "Private Eyes", and "Take Two". He was co-founder of Harmony Pictures with Stuart Gross. Lieberman directed several films including "Table for Five" (1983) starring Jon Voight, "All I What for Christmas" (1991), the science fiction film "Fire in the Sky" (1993), Disney's "D3: The Mighty Ducks" (1996), "The Stranger" (2010), "The Tortured" (2010), and "Breakaway" (2011). He was married to Myrna Narad from 1969 until their divorce in 1979 and is survived by their children, Erin and Lorne. Lieberman was married to actress Marilu Henner from 1990 until their divorce in 2001 and is survived by their children, Nick and Joseph. He married Vicky Peters in 2010 and she also survives him.

Lightfoot, Gordon

Canadian singer and songwriter Gordon Lightfoot, who was best known for the songs "The Wreck of the Edmund Fitzgerald" and "If You Could Read My Mind", died in Toronto, Ontario, Canada, on May 1, 2023. He was 84. Lightfoot was born in Orillia, Ontario, on November 17, 1938. He began performing as a child and sang with the local church choir. He was featured on local radio and sang in operettas. He learned to play the piano, drums, and guitar in his early teens and continued to perform in concerts during high school. Lightfoot went to Los Angeles in 1958 and attended Westlake College of Music. He wrote and produced commercial jingles while in Los Angeles and sang on record demos. He returned to Canada in 1960, where he joined the musical group the Singin' Swingin' Eight. He performed on television with CBC TV's "Country Hoedown". He sang folk music at coffee houses in Toronto and soon began recording such singles as "(Remember Me) I'm the

One)" and "Negotiations"/"It's Too Late, He Wins". He and Terry Whelan formed a singing duo and released the album "Two-Tones at the Village Corner" in 1962. He spent a year in Europe in 1963 and hosted BBC TV's "Country and Western Show" in England. He returned to Canada the following year and wrote the songs "Early Mornin' Rain", "For Lovin' Me", "I Can't Make It Anymore", and "Ribbon of Darkness". His songs were performed and recorded by such artists as Peter, Paul and Mary, Elvis Presley, Bob Dylan, Marty Robbins, Judy Collins, and the Kingston Trio. He appeared on television's "The Tonight Show Starring Johnny Carson" in 1965 and signed a recording contract with United Artists. His first solo album, "Lightfoot!", was released in 1966 and included many of the popular songs he had written. He wrote and sang the "Canadian Railroad Trilogy", a story song commissioned by the CBC in honor of Canada's Centennial. He recorded the albums "The Way I Feel" (1967), "Did She Mention My Name?" (1968), "Back Here on Earth" (1968), and the live album "Sunday Concert" (1969). He had hit singles with "Go-Go Round", "Spin, Spin", "The Way I Feel", and a cover of Bob Dylan's "Just Like Tom Thumb's Blues". Lightfoot moved to Warner Bros. Records in 1970 and had a major hit with 1971's "If You Could Read My Mind". He continued to record such albums as "Summer Side of Life" (1971) which included the songs "Ten Degrees and Getting Colder" and "Cabaret", "Don Quixote" (1972), "Old Dan's Records" (1972), "Sundown" (1974), "Cold on the Shoulder" (1975), the double compilation album "Gord's Gold" (1975), "Summertime Dream" (1976) which contained his major hit "The Wreck of the Edmund Fitzgerald", and "Endless Wire" (1978). He had another hit with his 1978 recording of "The Circle Is Small (I Can See It in Your Eyes)". Lightfoot was seen on television in such variety and talk shows as "The Rolf Harris show", "Dee Time", "The David Frost Show", "The Johnny Cash Show", "Top of the Pops", "The Midnight Special", "Saturday Night Live" as the musical guest in 1976, "The Alan Thicke Show", and "Late Night with Jimmy Fallon". He was featured in the 1982 film "Harry Tracy: The Last of the Wild Bunch" and a 1988 episode of the television series "Hotel". His albums over the next two decades include "Dream Street Rose" (1980) with the songs "Ghosts of Cape Horn" and "On the High Seas", "Shadows" (1982), "Salute" (1983), "East of Midnight" (1986), the compilation "Gord's Gold Volume II" (1988), "Waiting for You" (1993), and "A Painter Passing Through" (1998). His 2000 concert in Reno, Nevada, was released as a television special in CBC in Canada and PBS in the United States. Lightfoot suffered a ruptured abdominal aortic aneurysm in early 2002. He underwent emergency surgery and spent several months at a hospital in Hamilton, Canada. He recovered sufficiently to record a new album from Linus Entertainment, "Harmony", which was released in 2004. He returned to the concert stage and appeared in an episode of television's "Canadian Idol" in 2005. His career was sidetracked by health issues again in 2006 when he suffered a minor stroke. He resumed touring several years later and performed in Canada and the United States through the 2010s. His concert schedule was halted in early 2020 due to the coronavirus pandemic. He returned to Warner Music for the release of his 2020 album "Solo". He made his final concert appearance in Winnipeg in October of 2022. Lightfoot was inducted into the Canadian Music Hall of Fame in 1986 and the Canadian Country Music Hall of Fame in 2001. He received Canada's Governor General's Performing Arts Award in 1997 and was inducted into the Songwriters Hall of Fame in 2012. He was the subject of the 2019 documentary film "Gordon Lightfoot: If You Could Read My Mind". Lightfoot was married to Brita Ingegerd Olaisson from 1963 until their divorce in 1973, and is survived by their children, Fred and Ingrid. He had two children from other relationships, Gaylen McGee and Eric Lightfoot, before marrying Elizabeth Moon in 1989. They had two children, Miles and Meredith, before separating in the early 2000s and divorcing in 2011. He married Kim Hasse in 2014 and she also survives him.

Lim Ji-hye

South Korean model and internet personality Lim Ji-hye died of a suicide in Seoul, South Korea, on June 12, 2023. She was 37. Lim was born in Seoul on February 14, 1986. She  began working as a model and appeared in the pages of "Maxim" magazine in 2006. She appeared in a small role in the 2006 film "Sunflowers". She was also a racing model and was a ring girl for the mixed martial arts promotion Road FC in 2012. Lim retired after her marriage in 2014 but resumed modeling following her divorce in 2018. She became a life streamer on YouTube and AfreecaTV using the name BJ Imvely. She left a gathering with fellow internet streamers earlier in the evening of June 13, 2024, and was reportedly intoxicated. She began live streaming on her YouTube channel after arriving home and tearfully talked about how she was feeling. She displayed her will on camera and apologized to her family before walking off-screen. Concerned friends called her repeatedly without success and alerted the authorities. She was found in critical condition after a suicide attempt when paramedics arrived. She was taken to the hospital and was pronounced dead the following day. Lim is survived by two daughters.

Lindley, David

Rock musician David Lindley died of complications of long Covid-19 and chronic kidney damage in Claremont, California, on March 3, 2023. He was 78. Lindley was born in Los Angeles, California, on March 21, 1944. He began playing the violin as a child and moved to the ukulele in his early teens. He began playing the banjo in high school and won several talent contests. He performed with the Dry City Scat Band and became involved with the folk music scene in Los Angeles in the 1960s. He became friends with musician Ry Cooder and they experimented with folk and exotic music. Lindley was a founding member of the psychedelic band Kaleidoscope in 1966. They recorded four albums for Epic Records until breaking up in 1970. He moved to England and played with Terry Reid's band for two years before returning to the United

States. He played in Jackson Browne's band from 1972 to 1980 and was part of the backing bands for David Crosby, Graham Nash, Linda Ronstadt, and James Taylor. Lindley formed the band El Rayo-X in 1981 and they toured and recorded through 1989. He continued to perform as a solo artist and worked as a session musician. He toured or recorded with such artists as Warren Zevon, Dolly Parton, Maria Muldaur, Bonnie Raitt, and Curtis Mayfield. He was a multi-instrumentalist playing primarily string instruments including violin, guitar, bass, banjo, mandolin, hardingfele, dobro, bouzouki, baglama, cumbus, oud, zither, and lap steel guitar. He was heard on the soundtracks of such films as "The Long Riders" (1980), "The Right Stuff" (1983), "Streets of Fire" (1984), "The Beverly Hillbillies" (1993), "Blue Sky" (1994), and "Encounters at the End of the World" (2007). Lindley married Nancy Jolly in 1967 and they later divorced. He married Joan Darrow in 1976 and is survived by her and their daughter, folk singer Rosanne.

Lindsay, Helen

British actress Helen Lindsay died in London, England, on March 15, 2023. She was 93. She was born to British parents in Coimbatore, India, on July 22, 1929. She

made her debut on stage with the Library Theatre in Manchester in 1952. She appeared frequently on television from the early 1950s with roles in such productions as "The Noble Spaniard" (1953), "Robert's Wife" (1955), "The Assassin" (1957), "Not Proven" (1957), "Test of Truth" (1958), "The Land of Promise" (1958), "The Trial of Admiral Byng" (1958), "The Clandestine Marriage" (1958), "Great Expectations" (1959), "By Invitation Only" (1961), "I'll Die for You" (1962), "Dangerous Corner" (1963), "Valentina" (1964), "The Piano Tuner" (1969), "Jane Eyre" (1970), "Seven Days in the Life of Andrew Pelham" (1971), "The Pallisers" (1974), "A Journey to London" (1975), "Love Among the Artists" (1979), "Frost in May" (1982), "The Gourmet" (1984), "The Disputation" (1986), "Scoop" (1987), "A Murder of Quality" (1991), "Little Lord Fauntleroy" (1995), "Confessions of an Ugly Stepsister" (2002), and "Ella and the Mothers" (2002). Lindsay's other television credits include episodes of "Spy-Catcher", "Don't Do It Dempsey", "Police Surgeon", "The World of Tim Frazer" as Rita Coleman in 1961, "Storyboard", "Top Secret", "You Can't Win", "Playbox", "The Odd Man, "Tales of Mystery", "The Monsters" as Esmee Pulford in 1962, "It Happened Like This",

"Suspense", "Jezebel ex UK", "The Avengers", "The Edgar Wallace Mystery Theatre", "No Hiding Place", "Crane", "Detective", "The Walrus and the Carpenter", "The Sullavan Brothers", "Riviera Police", "Out of the Unknown", "Barney Is My Darling", "Public Eye", "Sexton Blake", "The Wednesday Play", "The Inside Man", "ITV Playhouse", "Strange Report", "Kate", "Armchair Theatre", "Menace", "Dr. Finlay's Casebook", "Thirty-Minute Theatre", "Spyder's Web", "Boney", "Between the Wars", "New Scotland Yard", "Upstairs, Downstairs", "Masquerade", "Justice", "Warship", "Churchill's People", "Within These Walls", "When the Boat Comes In", "Thomas and Sarah", "Play for Today", "Spearhead", "The Agatha Christie Hour", "Morgan's Boy", "Don't Wait Up", "Shades of Darkness", "The Storyteller" as the Queen in the "Hans My Hedgehog" segment in 1987, "The Bill", "Streets Apart", "All Creatures Great and Small", "Boon", "T. Bag and the Rings of Olympus", "Screen One", "Ruth Rendell Mysteries", "Annie's Bar", "Midsomer Murders", "Foyle's War", "doctors", and "Poirot". She was featured in a handful of films during her career including "Dublin Nightmare" (1958), "The Partner" (1963), "Darling" (1965), "One Brief Summer" (1971), "Sunday Bloody Sunday" (1971), "Secrets" (1983), "Playing Away" (1987), "Strapless" (1989), "Mission: Impossible" (1996), "The Tribe" (1998), "AKA" (2002), and "The Wedding Date" (2005). Lindsay was married to production designer Alan Picford until his death in 2002.

Lindsay, Lara

Actress Lara Lindsay died in California on January 17, 2023. She was 81. She was born Gladys Jacobs in Chicago, Illinois, on January 1, 1942. She began ice skating as a child and performed with the Icecapades while in her teens. She was

married for several years in the early 1960s and began working in television commercials in Tucson, Arizona, after her marriage ended. She served as a stand-in for the 1966 western film "El Dorado" before heading to Hollywood. She was trained at the 20th Century Fox school and appeared in small roles in the films "In Like Flint" (1967), "The Sweet Ride" (1968), and "The Boston Strangler" (1968) as victim Bobbie Eden. She also appeared on television in the 1968 unsold "Braddock" pilot and episodes of "The Felony Squad" and "Judd for the Defense". She began working behind the scenes and served as an assistant for producer Saul David. Lindsay made her last onscreen appearance as a runner in the 1976 science fiction film "Logan's Run".

Lister, Robert

British actor Robert Lister died at a nursing home in Stratford-upon-Avon, England, on July 21, 2023. He was 79. He appeared frequently on the London stage and appeared on television in episodes of "New Scotland Yard", "Between the

Wars", "Play for Today", "Dial M for Murder, "Affairs of the Heart", "Within These Walls", "Blood Money", "Dempsey and Makepeace", "Wish Me Luck" as Sgt. Supervisor in 1988, "Storyboard", "Peak Practice", "The Bill", and "Hustle". Lister was also seen in television productions of "Lillie" (1978), and "Broken Glass" (1982). He was featured in several films including "All the Fun of the Fair" (1979) and "The Casebook of Eddie Brewer" (2012). Lister is survived by his wife, Patricia.

Littlewood, Yvonne

British television director Yvonne Littlewood died in London, England, on July 7, 2023. She was 95. Littlewood was born in Maidstone, Kent, England, on July 22, 1927. She

was educated in Ross-on-Wye, Herefordshire, where her parents were active in local dramatics. She later studied dance and attended the Royal Academy of Arts. She began working as a typist at the BBC in 1944 and soon became the secretary for a producer. She became the first female producer for BBC light entertainment. She directed episodes of "The Friday Show" and "This Is Your Life" in the early 1960s. She directed "A Song for Europe" specials in 1963 and 1964 and the 1963 "Eurovision Song Contest". She worked extensively with singer Petula Clark from the 1960s to the 1980s. Littlewood directed television "A Christmas Night with the Stars" specials in 1962, 1963, and 1969, and productions of "Nana International" (1971), "Keith Michell at Her Majesty's" (1972), "The Sound of Petula" (1974), "The Carpenters Concert: Live at the New London Theatre" (1976), "Royal Variety Performance" (1980), "Christmas Carol" (1986), and "The Children's Royal Variety Performance" (1987). She produced such series and specials as "An Evening with Nat King Cole" (1963), "Jazz 625" (1964), "Presenting Johnny Mathis" (1965), "Presenting Peter Nero" (1965), "Tonight in Person" (1965-1967), "A Song for Everyone" (1965-1969), "Something Special" (1967), "This Is Petula Clark" (1966-1968), "Tony Bennett Meets Robert Farnon" (1967), "Hey Riddle Diddle" (1967), "It's Topol" (1968), "Just Esther" (1968), "Presenting Nana Mouskouri" (1968-1970), "Portrait of Petula" (1969), "Just Pet" (1969), "It's Nice to Remember" (1970), "Presenting Keith Michell" (1971), "Tony Bennett Sings..." (1971), "Michele Legrand" (1974), "Max Bygraves Says I Wanna Tell You a Story" (1975), "A World of Music" (1976-1978), "The Val Doonican Music Show" (1976-1986), "Only Olivia" (1977), "Perry Como's Olde English Christmas" (1977), "The King's Singers" (1978-1981), "Billy Jo Spears" (1981), "Gladys Knight and the Pips" (1981), "Tommy Steele: A Handful of Sons" (1981), "A Dream of

Alice" (1982), "John Denver: His Guitar and His Music" (1982), "Royal Variety Performance" (1984), and "A Royal Birthday Gala" (1990).

Lloyd Webber, Nick

British composer Nick Lloyd Webber, who was the son of famed composer Andrew Lloyd Webber, died of gastric cancer at a hospital in Basingstoke, Hampshire, England, on

March 25, 2023. He as 43. Lloyd Webber was born in England on July 22, 1979. He was the son of Andrew Lloyd Webber and his first wife, Sarah Hugill. Nick worked with his father from his early teens and served as the tape operator for the 1993 album "Sunset Boulevard: World Premiere Recording" of his father's musical. He composed the score for the short films "Mon Amour Mon Parapluie" (2001), "Homecoming" (2003), and "Mr. Invisible" (2013), and the 2012 television documentary "56 Up". He scored the theatrical productions "The Little Prince" (2016) and "Fat Friend: The Musical" (2017). He also composed for the series "Love, Lies and Records", "Monarca", and "Control Z", and the 2021 film "The Last Bus". Lloyd Webber and his father collaborated on the original cast album for the 2021 stage production "Bad Cinderella". He married theatrical producer and designer Charlotte Windmill and they later divorced. He married viola player Polly Wiltshire in 2018 and she survives him.

Locatell, Carol

Actress Carol Locatell, who originally performed under the name Carol Lawson, died of cancer at her home in Sherman Oaks, California, on April 11, 2023. She was 82. Locatell was born in Atlanta, Georgia, on December 13, 1940,

and was raised in San Mateo, California. She attended San Francisco State University but left school to perform on stage with a touring production of "The Odd Couple". She appeared on stage throughout her career, starring as Fonsia Dorsey in the original Los Angeles production of "The Gin Game" in 1976. She was seen on Broadway in the plays "Broadway Bound" (1986), "The Shadow Box" (1994), and "The Rose Tattoo" (1995). She appeared frequently in films and television from the late 1960s, originally being billed as Carol Lawson. She was seen in episodes of "The Flying Nun", "It Takes a Thief", "Medical Center", "McCloud", "Sarge", "The Smith Family", "The Bold Ones: The New Doctors", "Bonanza", "The Streets of San Francisco", "Mannix", "Barnaby Jones", "Emergency!", "Lucas Tanner", "Bronx", "M*A*S*H", "This Is the Life", "Police Woman", "Brothers", "Dynasty", "Growing

Pains", "Mathnet", "Life Goes On", "ER", "7th Heaven", "The Pretender", "Saved by the Bell: The New Class", "Ally McBeal", "Caroline in the City", "The Practice", "Family Law", "Touched by an Angel", "The Division", "NYPD Blue", "Without a Trace", "Numb3rs", "Grey's Anatomy", "Mad Men", "Sonny with a Chance", "Scandal", "I Didn't Do It", "Battle Creek", "JoJoHead", "NCIS", "Station 19", and "Shameless". Her other television credits include the tele-films "Cry Rape" (1973), "The Death of Richie" (1977), "Yesterday's Child" (1977), "Games Mother Never Taught You" (1982), "Happy" (1983), "The Bad Seed" (1985), "The Flamingo Kid" (1989), "Unauthorized: The Mary Kay Letourneau Story" (2000), "Bound by a Secret" (2009), and "Parole Officers" (2013). She was seen in the films "The No Mercy Man" (1973), "Coffy" (1973), "This Is a Hijack" (1973), "Thunder County" (1974), "Sammy" (1977), "Paternity" (1981), "Sharky's Machine" (1981), "Best Friends" (1982), "Friday the 13th: A New Beginning" (1985) as the ill-fated neighbor Ethel Hubbard, "The Daytrippers" (1996), "Bug" (2002), "BachelorMan" (2003), "The Family Stone" (2005), "Reality" (2014), "Fishes 'n Loaves: Heaven Sent" (2016), "Dove" (2018), "The Way You Look Tonight" (2019), and "13 Fanboy" (2021). Locatell is survived by her husband of fifty years, musician and songwriter Gregory Prestopino.

Loeckx, Joseph

Belgian comic book artist Joseph Loeckx, who often worked under the pseudonym Jo-El Azara, died in Montegut, France, on February 7, 2023. He was 85. Loeckx was born in Drogenbos, Belgium, on May 4, 1937. He studied art at the Institute Saint-Luc in Brussels. He began his career in comics working with artist Willy Vandersteen at his studio in 1953. He worked at Studio Herge from 1954 to 1961 where he helped produce the "Tintin et Milou" comic albums. He began using the pseudonyms Jo-El and Ernest before settling on Jo-El Azara. His work appeared in the comic magazines "Caravane" and "Spirou" and he worked with Will (Willy Maltaite) on the "Peyo" series "Jacky et Celestin" for "Le Soir Illustre" in the early 1960s. He produced numerous humorous comics for "Tintin" magazine and teamed with writer Vicq for the series "Taka Takata" in 1965. Ht worked on the series throughout the 1970s. He also worked for other comics including "Bonnedague" for "Record from 1962 to 1966, "Pauvre Icare" for "Chouchou" in 1965, and "Mayflower", "La Campagne de Grece", and "Monsieur Chapornou" for "Pilote from 1963 to 1966. He and Vicq created the samurai comic "Haddadaa Surmamoto" for "Spirou" from 1967 to 1968. Loeckx worked in advertising and was artist for several books including "L'Histoire Mondiale du Transport et de la Logistique" (1989) and "L'Heure de l'Euro" (1999). He began his own label, Azeko, after settling in Southwest France in 1994

and reprinted his "Taka Takata" albums. He was the longtime companion of fellow comic artist Josette Baujot from the 1950s until her death in 2009.

Logan, George

British comedian George Logan, who was best known as half of the drag duo Hinge and Bracket, died in Le Dorat, France, on May 21, 2023. He was 78. Logan was born in Rutherglen, Scotland, on July 7, 1944. He studied piano at the Royal Scottish Academy of Music in his teens and continued to study music at Rutherglen Academy and the University of Glasgow. He became involved in the homosexual scene later

in his teens and moved to London in 1965. He worked as a computer programmer and began playing piano to accompany a drag act at a local pub. He soon created his own drag piano act and was joined by Patrick Fyffe in 1970. They created the dual drag act of Hinge and Bracket with both portraying eccentric older ladies performing songs by Gilbert and Sullivan and Noel Coward. Logan played the piano as Dr. Evadne Hinge and Fyffe was retired opera singer Dame Hilda Backet. They appeared at gay clubs throughout London in the early 1970s and were featured at the Edinburgh Festival Fringe in 1974. They were soon appearing at clubs around the country and starred in the BBC Radio series "The Random Jottings of Hinge and Bracket". They starred in the BBC television program "Dear Ladies" from 1983 to 1984. Logan appeared frequently on television, usually in his drag persona, in such series as "Aquarius", "The Good Old Days", "Celebrity Squares", ""What's on Next?", "Ronnie Corbett's Saturday Special", "Dawson and Friends", "The King's Singers", "The Marti Caine Show", "Wogan", "The Ronnie Corbett Show", "The Krypton Factor", "Jameson Tonight", "You Bet!", and "What a Performance!". He also appeared in television productions of "At Home with Dr. Evadne Hinge and Dame Hilda Bracket" (1977), "Night of One Hundred Stars" (1980), and "Die Fledermaus" (1983). Hinge and Bracket continued to perform together until Fyffe's death in 2002. Logan wrote a fictional autobiographical account of Dr Evadne Hinge for the 2014 book "The Naked Doctor", and his own memoirs, "A Boy Called Audrey", were published in 2015. Logan was in a longtime relationship with Louie Perone. They married in 2019 and settled in France. He is survived by his husband.

Lolita

Lolita the orca, a popular attraction at the Miami Seaquarium, died of renal failure in Miami, Florida, on August 18, 2023. She was 57. Lolita (also known as Tokitae) was born in the Northeast Pacific Ocean in 1966 and was captured in Puget Sound, Washington, in August of 1970. At the age of

four she was torn away from her family and ocean home during the largest capture of wild orcas in history and would spend the rest of her life in captivity. She was the survivor of that horrifying capture and has spent the rest of her life in the smallest, oldest water tank in the world, one that didn't even meet the federal Animal Welfare Act's minimum size requirement and that failed to provide her with any shelter from the blistering Florida sun. Orcas in nature spend 90 percent of their time underwater and dive to depths of thousands of feet, but Lolita's tank was just 20 feet at its deepest point, which was the same length as her body. Her tankmate, Hank, died in 1980 after repeatedly ramming his head into the tank wall. She had been alone ever since. Lolita's family, the Southern Resident orca population, is now endangered and have been placed on the Endangered Species Act for protection. After a lengthy petition, Lolita was also granted the same protection on paper but remained in captivity until her death, nonetheless. She was retired in 2022, though remained in her 20-foot deep, by 35-foot-wide, by 80-foot-long enclosure with her dolphin companion, Li'i. Miami Seaquarium had been promising to build Lolita a new tank since 1978 and has a long list of animal violations and deaths throughout the years.

Lollobrigida, Gina

Italian actress Gina Lollobrigida, who was an international sex symbol in the 1950s and starred as Esmeralda in the 1956 version of "The Hunchback of Notre Dame", died

in Rome, Italy, on January 16, 2023. She was 95. Lollobrigida was born in Subiaco, Italy, on July 4, 1927. She moved to Rome with her family after the end of World War II. She began taking singing lessons and worked as a model while studying sculpture and art. She competed in the Miss Italy beauty contest in 1947, placing third. Lollobrigida began appearing in small roles in films in the mid-1940s including "Return of the Black Eagle" (1946), "Elixir of Love" (1947), "Flesh Will Surrender" (1947), "A Man About the House" (1947), "When Love Calls" (1947), "Mad About Opera" (1948), "Love of a Clown - Pagliacci" (1948), "Campane a Martello" (1949), "La Sposa Non Puo Attendere" (1949), "Miss Italia" (1950), "Alina" (1950), "The White Line" (1950), and "A Dog's Life" (1950). She initially signed a seven-year contract with Howard Hughes at RKO Pictures in 1950. She traveled to the United States where she rejected his romantic advances. She soon returned to Europe and refused to work with him. Lollobrigida continued to star in such films as "A Tale of Five Women" (1951), "Four Ways Out" (1951), "The Young Caruso" (1951), "Achtung! Banditi!" (1951), "Amor Non Ho! Pero, Pero..." (1951), "Fanan la Tulipe" (1952), "Wife for a Night" (1952), "Times Gone By" (1952), "Beauties of the Night" (1952), "The Unfaithfuls" (1953), and "The Wayward Wife" (1953). She received a BAFTA Award nomination for her role as La Bersagliera in the 1953 film "Bread, Love and Dreams", and starred as Maria Dannreuther, the wife of Humphrey Bogart's character, in "Beat the Devil" (1953). Her other films include "Flesh and the Woman" (1954), "Crossed Swords" (1954) opposite Errol Flynn, "Woman of Rome" (1954), "Frisky" (1954), "Beautiful But Dangerous" (1955) earning Italy's first David di Donatello Award for Best

Actress for her role as soprano Lina Cavalieri, "Trapeze" (1956) as high-wire artist Lola in a love triangle with Burt Lancaster and Tony Curtis, "The Hunchback of Notre Dame" (1956) as the Gypsy girl Esmeralda opposite Anthony Quinn's Quasimodo, "Fast and Sexy" (1958), "The Law" (1959), "Solomon and Sheba" (1959) as Sheba to Yul Brynner's Solomon (taking over the role when Tyrone Power died during production), "Never So Few" (1959) with Frank Sinatra, "Go Naked in the World" (1961), the romantic comedy "Come September" (1961) opposite Rock Hudson, "La Bellezza d'Ippolita" (1962), "Imperial Venus" (1962) receiving another David di Donatello Award, "Mare Matto" (1963), "Woman of Straw" (1964) opposite Sean Connery, "The Dolls" (1965), "Strange Bedfellows" (1965) again with Rock Hudson, "Me, Me, Me... and the Others" (1966), "Les Sultans" (1966), "Le Piacevoli Notti" (1966), "Hotel Paradiso" (1966) starring Alec Guinness, "The Young Rebel" (1967), "Plucked" (1968), "The Private Navy of Sgt. O'Farrell" (1968) co-starring with Bob Hope, the comedy "Buona Sera, Mrs. Campbell" (1968) earning another David di Donatello Award, "Stuntman" (1968), "That Splendid November" (1969), "Bad Man's River" (1971), "King, Queen, Knave" (1972) with David Niven, and "The Lonely Woman" (1973). Lollobrigida made occasional appearances on television with roles in episodes of "The Jimmy Durante Show", "Perry Como's Kraft Music Hall", "Person to Person", "The Pat Boone-Chevy Showroom", "The Les Crane Show", "The Bob Hope Show", "What's My Line?", "The Ed Sullivan Show", "The Dean Martin Show", "Rowan & Martin's Laugh-In", "The Engelbert Humperdinck Show", "The Dick Cavett Show", "Flip", "The Don Knotts Show", "V.I.P.-Schaukel", "The Merv Griffin Show", "The Mike Douglas Show", "The Tonight Show Starring Johnny Carson", "Jerry Lewis MDA Labor Day Telethon", "Night of 100 Stars", "Falcon Crest" as Francesca Gioberti in 1984, "The Love Boat",

"Wogan", "The Tonight Show with Jay Leno", "Fata Morgana", and "Maurizio Costanzo Show". She was also seen in television productions of "La Avventura di Pinocchio" (1972), the 1982 special "Lola, Lola y Lollo", "Deceptions" (1985), "La Romana" (1988), and "Una Donna in Fuga" (1996). Lollobrigida largely retired from acting after returning to the big screen for the films "One Hundred and One Nights" (1995), and "XXL" (1997). She was an unsuccessful candidate for the European Parliament in 1999 and lost an election for the Italian Senate in 2022 at age 95. She sold her collection of jewelry and gems in 2013 and donated the proceeds, nearly $5 million, to stem cell research. She was also noted for her photographs which were collected in such books as "Italia Mia" (1973), "The Philippines" (1976), "Wonder of Innocence" (1994), and "Gina Lollobrigida Photographer" (2009). Lollobrigida married Slovenian physician Milko Skofic in 1949 and he became her manager. They divorced in 1971 and she is survived by their son. She married Spanish businessman Javier Rigau y Rafols in 2010 and began legal proceedings to end the marriage in 2013. The marriage was annulled in 2019.

Lo Monaco, Sebastiano

Italian actor Sebastiano Lo Monaco died in Rome, Italy, on December 16, 2023. He was 65. Lo Monaco was born in Floridia, Sicily, Italy, on September 18, 1958. He trained at the Silvio d'Amico National Academy of Dramatic Arts. He

performed frequently on stage throughout his career and served as an artistic director from 1989. Lo Monaco was featured in such films as "Il Petomane" (1983), "Festa di Laurea" (1985), "Jealous Eyes" (1989), "Panama Sugar" (1990), "Cellini: A Violent Life" (1990), Lamberto Bava's horror thriller "Body Puzzle" (1992), "Dove Siete? Io Sono Qui" (1993), "Prima del Tramonto" (1999), "Maestrale" (2000), "Body Guards - Guardie del Corpo" (2000), "Storia di Guerra e d'Amicizia" (2002), "Gli Angeli di Borsellino" (2003), "Se Sara Luce Sara Bellissimo - Moro: Un'altra Storia" (2004), "I Vicere" (2007), "Baaria" (2009), "Io, Don Giovanni" (2009), "Life Is a Wonderful Thing" (2010), "Napoletans" (2011), the horror film "Lilith's Hell" (2017) starring Ruggero Deodato, and "Caravaggio's Shadow" (2022). He was seen on television in productions of "Vita di Antonio Gramsci" (1981), "Saro il Tuo Giudice" (2001), "Joe Petrosino" (2006), "Saint Philip Neri: I Prefer Heaven" (2010), and "Il Delitto di Via Poma" (2011). His other television credits include episodes of "La Piovra" as Torrisi the Lawyer from 1997 to 1998, "Un Prete Tra Noi" as Walter in 1999, "Don Matteo", "Boris Giuliano: Un Poliziotto a Palermo", and "Detective Montalbano".

Lombardo Radice, Giovanni

Italian actor Giovanni Lombardo Radice, who was sometimes billed as John Morghen and starred in such horror

films as "Cannibal Apocalypse" and "The House on the Edge of the Park", died in Rome, Italy, on April 27, 2023. He was 68. Lombardo Radice was born in Rome on September 23, 1954. He began his acting career on stage and founded The Swan Company to stage Shakespearean works in 1973. He

became acquainted with director Ruggero Deodato who cast him as Ricky, the drug addict, in the 1980 horror film "The House on the Edge of the Park". He became noted for his often-villainous roles in horror films, sometimes using the stage name John Morghen to spare his family embarrassment for his frequently gruesome credits. His films include Antonio Margheriti's horror film "Cannibal Apocalypse" (aka "Apocalypse Domani", 'Invasion of the Flesh Hunters", "Cannibals in the Streets") (1980) as former POW Charlie Bukowski whose virulent bites initiates a cannibal virus, Lucio Fulci's "City of the Living Dead" (aka "The Gates of Hell") (1980) as the deranged derelict Bob who meets a gruesome end with a drill through his head, Umberto Lenzi's controversial cannibal exploitation film "Make Them Die Slowly") (aka "Cannibal Ferox") (1981) as Mike Logan, whose actions in the Colombian jungle provoke a tribe of cannibals result in the top of skull being removed so his brain can be devoured by the tribe, Joe D'Amato's "Cannibal Love" (1982), "Deadly Impact" (1984), "Big Deal After 20 Years" (1985), "The American Bride" (1986), Michele Soavi's slasher film "Stage Fright" (aka "Aquarius") (1987), D'Amato's erotic drama "Eleven Days, Eleven Nights" (1987), Deodato's "Phantom of Death" (1988) with Michael York and Donald Pleasence, "La Parola Segreta" (1988), Soavi's "The Church" (aka "La Chiesa") (1989) as Reverend Dominic, Dario Argento's "The Sect" (aka "The Devil's Daughter") (1991), Lamberto Bava's horror thriller "Body Puzzle" (1992) starring Joanna Pacula, the comedy "Ricky & Barabba" (1992), "Honolulu Baby" (2001), "The Soul Keeper" (2002), Martin Scorsese's historical epic "Gangs of New York" (2002) as Mr. Legree, "The Omen" (2006) as Father Spiletto, "Il Nascondiglio" (2007), "House of Flesh Mannequins" (2009), "A Day of Violence" (2010), "The Reverend" (2011), "The Inflicted" (2012), "Long Live Freedom" (2013), "3 Sisters" (2015), "Violent Shit: The Movie" (2015), "Moderation" (2016), "Una Gita a Roma" (2017), "Dogman's Rabies" (2017), "Beyond Fury" (2019), "Crucified" (2019), "Baphomet" (2021), and "The Well" (2023). Lombardo Radice was seen on television in productions of "Greggio e Pericoloso" (1981), "The Scarlet and the Black" (1983), "Flipper" (1984), "Nata d'Amore" (1984), "Progetto Atlantide" (1984), "Majakowski" (1984), "L'Armata Sagapo" (1985), "Quando Arriva i Giudice" (1986), "Treasure Island in Outer Space" (1987), "sei Delitti per Padre Brown" (1986), "Un Posto Freddo in Fondo al Cuore" (1992), "Il Cuore e la Spada" (1998), "Michele Strogoff - Il Corriere dello Zar" (1999), "Padre Pio: Tra Cielo e Terra" (2000) as Pope Leo XII, "St. Paul" (2000) as King Herod, "Don

Matteo" (2002), and "La Notte di Pasquino" (2003). His other television credits include episodes of "Aeroporto Internazionle" and "Caccia al Ladro d'Autore". He married actress Alessandra Panelli in 1989 and is survived by her and their child.

Longmore, Wyllie

Jamaican-British actor Wyllie Longmore died of cancer in Manchester, England, on January 4, 2023. He was 82. Longmore was born in Stirling, St. Ann, Jamaica, on November 2, 1940. He moved to England in 1961 and trained at the Rose Bruford College of Speech and Drama in Sidcup. He began performing on stage with the Leeds Theatre-in-Education Company. He appeared frequently on the Manchester stage

with roles in productions of "Ma Rainey's Black Bottom", "The Merchant of Venice", "My Children! My Africa!", and "I Just Stopped by to See the Man". He appeared as Dr. McKinnon in the television soap opera "Coronation Street" in 1992. Longmore was also seen in episodes of "Screen Two", "How We Used to Live", "Floodtide", "Hard Cases", "Kinsey", "Between the Lines", "The Bill", "Cardiac Arrest", "New Voices", "Deep Secrets", "Casualty", "Wing and a Prayer", "Merseybeat", "Cold Feet", "Blue Murder", and "Waking the Dead". He appeared in the 2003 tele-film "On the Out" and was featured as Jeremy, an associate of Hugh Grant's Prime Minister, in romantic comedy film "Love Actually" (2003).

Longo, Cody

Actor Cody Longo, who was featured in the 2010 cult film "Piranha 3D", was found dead of alcohol poisoning at his home in Austin, Texas, on February 8, 2023. He was 34. Longo was born in Littleton, Colorado, on March 4, 1988. He studied

acting from his youth and performed in productions at the Denver Performing Arts Academy. He moved to Los Angeles after graduating high school to pursue an acting career. He studied psychology and film at the University of California at Los Angeles. He appeared in a pair of music videos for JoJo and was featured in the video film "Hip Hop Kidz: It's a Beautiful Thing" in 2006. Longo continued to appear in such films as "Ball Don't Lie" (2008), the 2009 remake of "Fame", "Bring It On: Fight to the Finish" (2009), "High School" (2010), the horror comedy "Piranha 3D" (2010) as Todd Dupree, "The Silent Thief" (2012), "For the Love of Money" (2012), "Not Today" (2013), "Wildflower" (2014), "Promoted" (2015), "48 Hours to Live" (2016), "The Last

Movie Star" (2017), "Death House" (2017), and "Rich Boy, Rich Girl" (2018). He appeared on television in episodes of "Medium", "Three Rivers", and "Brothers & Sisters", and starred as Nicky Russo in the ABC Family series "Make It or Break It" from 2009 to 2010. He and co-star Johnny Pacar formed a band, Forever The Day, and released the EP "Under the Afterglow" in 2010. Longo was featured as Nicholas Alamain in the soap opera "Days of Our Lives" in 2011. He also appeared in episodes of "CSI: Crime Scene Investigation", "CSI: NY", "Nashville", "The Catch", "Secrets and Lies", and "High School Crimes & Misdemeanors". He starred as Eddie Duran in the Nick at Nite drama series "Hollywood Heights" in 2012. His other television credits include the tele-films "Lovelives" (2011) and "Starting Up Love" (2019). Longo moved to Nashville in 2015 to further his music career and released such singles as "What Up Tho", "Scream", "'Til Tomorrow", and "Loud". Longo married Stephanie Clark in 2015 and is survived by her and their three children.

Lopes-Curval, Philippe

French film director and screenwriter Philippe Lopes-Curval died in Bayeux, France, on February 13, 2023. He was 71. Lopes-Curval was born in Bayeux on June 9, 1951. He

began working in films as an assistant director in the early 1970s. His credits include Alain Resnais' "Stavisky" (1973), "L'Alpagueur" (1976), "A Young Emmanuelle" (1976), "Violette and Franois" (1977), "Sale Reveur" (1978), "See Here My Love" (1978), "Le Sucre" (1978), "Ils Sont Grands Ces Petits" (1976), "I... For Icarus" (1979), and "Rends-Moi la Cle!" (1981). Lopes-Curval directed several short films in the earlyl 1980s including "Le Drapeau Tricolore" (1982), "A Pic" (1982), and "Rohner Peintre" (1983). He wrote and directed the 1986 feature film "Trop Tard Balthazar". He scripted numerous films including "Une Epoque Formidable..." (1991), "Blue Helmet" (1994), Fallait Pas!..." (1996), "Monsieur Batignole" (2002), "The Chorus" (2004), "Boudu (2005), "Fashion Victim" (2009), and "War of the Buttons" (2011). Lopes-Curval wrote the television productions "Adorable Petite Bombe" (1996), "Le Surdoue" (1997), "Maintenant ou Jamais" (1997), and "Maintenant et Pour Toujours" (1998). He is survived by his wife, painter Catherine Lopes-Curval, and daughter, director Julie Lopes-Curval.

Lopez Tarso, Ignacio

Mexican actor Ignacio Lopez Tarso died of complications from pneumonia and an intestinal obstruction at a hospital in Mexico City on March 11, 2023. He was 88. He was born Ignacio Lopez Lopez in Mexico City on January 15, 1925. He became interested in acting as a child and performed in plays while in his teens. He served in the military in the mid-1940s and worked in sales for a clothing company in Mexico

City after his discharge. He trained as an actor under Xavier Villarrutia at the Palacio de Bellas Artes later in the decade. He began his professional career on stage in a production of "Born Yesterday" in 1951. He appeared in over 100 plays throughout his career including "Macbeth", "Othelo", "The Crucible", "King Lear", "Cyrano de Bergerac", "The Miser", "Exit the King", and "Equus". Lopez made his film debut in a small role in Chano Urueta's "La Desconcida" in 1954. He appeared in numerous films over the next seven decades including "Chilam Balam" (1955), "Feliz Ano, Amor Mio" (1957), "Vainilla, Bronce y Morir (Una Mujer Mas)" (1957), "Ama a Tu Projimo" (1958), "Nazarin" (1959), "Sonatas" (1959), "El Hambre Nuestra de Cada Dia" (1959), "The Soldiers of Pancho Villa" (1959), "La Estrella Vacia"

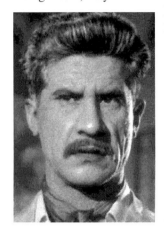

(1960), "Macario" (1960), La Sombra del Caudillo" (1960), "Ellas Tambien Son Rebeldes" (1961), "The Guns of Juana Gallo" (1961), "My Son, the Hero" (1961), "Y Dios la Llamo Tierra" (1961), "Rosa Blanca" (1961), "La Bandida" (1962), "Corazon de Nino" (1962), "The Paper Man" (1963),, "Dias de Otono" (1963), "Cri Cri el Grillito Cantor" (1963), "Furia en el Eden" (1964), "The Golden Cockerel" (1964), "Un Hombre en la Trampa" (1965), "Tarahumara (Cada Vez Mas Lejos)" (1965), "Pedro Paramo" (1967), "Un Largo Viaje Hacia la Muerte" (1968), "Les Visitaciones del Diablo" (1968), "La Puerta y la Mujer del Carnicro" (1969), "La Trinchera" (1969), "La Vida Inutil de Pito Perez" (1970), "La Generala" (1971), "Cayo de la Gloria el Diablo" (1972), "El Profeta Mimi" (1973), "En Busca de un Muro" (1974), "Rapina" (1975), "Renuncia por Motivos de Salud" (1976), "Los Albaniles" (1976), "La Casta Divia" (1977), "Y Ahora Que, Senor Fiscal?" (1977), "Los Amantes Frios" (1978), "The Children of Sanchez (1978), "Corrupcion Oficial" (1980), "Antonieta" (1982), John Huston's "Under the Volcano" (1984) as Dr. Vigil, "El Otro" (1984), "Tona Machetes" (1985), "Astucia" (1986), "Muelle Rojo" (1987), "Codicia Mortal" (1991), "Tirano Banderas" (1993), "Santo Luzbel" (1996), "Santo Luzbel" (1996), "Reclusorio" (1997), Virgingate" (2008), "Mas Sabe el Diablo Por Viejo" (2018), "Identidad Tomada" (2020), and "Buenos Dias, Ignacio" (2021). Lopez appeared frequently in television with roles in episodes of "Noches de Angustia", "Cuatro en la Trampa", "Gran Teatro", "Amor y Orgull", "La Tormenta" as Gabriel in 1967, "La Constitucion", "Rosas Para Veronica", "El Edificio de Enfrente" as Arturo in 1972, "El Carruaje" as Cura in 1972, "El Honorable Senor Valdez" as Humberto Valdez in 1973, "La Trampa" as Henry Morell in 1978, "Amor Prohibido" as Arturo Galvan in 1979, "El Combate", "El Periquillo Sangriento", "El Derencho de Nacer" as Rafael from 1981 to 19892, "El Gran Mundo del Teatro", "Senda de Gloria" as General Eduardo Alvarez in 1987, "Angeles Blancos" as Perfecto from 1990 to 1991, "Bajo un Mismo Rostro", "Imperio de Cristal" as Cesar Lombardo from 1994 to 1995, "Esmeralda"

as Melesio in 1997, "Camila" as Genaro in 1998, "Angela" as Feliciano Villanueva from 1998 to 1999, "The Beach House" as Don Angel Villarreal Cueto in 2000, "Atrevete a Olvidarme" as Gonzalo Rivas in 2001, "Nividad Sin Fin" as Rodito in 2001, "Vivan los Nonos!" as Don Ignacio Robles in 2002, "De Pocas, Pocas Pulgas" as Don Julian Montes in 2003, Peregrina" as Don Baltazar in 2005, "La Esposa Virgen" as General Francisco Ortiz in 2005, "Amor Sin Maquillaje" as Ignacio in 2007, "Manana ess Para Siempre", "El Pantera" as General Porfirio Ayala from 2007 to 2009, "Curse by the Sea" as El Mojarras from 2009 to 2010, "The Power of Destiny", "El Encanto del Aguila" as Porfirio Diaz in 2011, "The One Who Couldn't Love" as Don Fermin in 2011, "Corazon Indomable" as Don Ramiro in 2013, "La Malquerida" as Juan Carlos in 2014, "Amores con Trampa" as Porfirio in 2015, "Como Dice el Dicho", "Cien Anos Con Juan Rulfo", "Medicos, Linea de Vida", "Here on Earth",. "Vecinos" as Don Lorenzo" from 2022 to 2023, and "Gloria Trei: Ellas Soy Yo". Lopez was married to Clara Aranda until her death in 2000. He is survived by three children, actor Juan Ignacio Aranda, Susana, and Gabriela.

Lorayne, Harry

Magician Harry Lorayne, who was noted for his mastery of memory recall, died at a hospital in Newburyport, Massachusetts, on April 7, 2023. He was 96. He was born Harry Ratzer in New York City on May 4, 1926. He became interested in card tricks as a child and developed memory

techniques to help overcome his dyslexia. He left school in his early teens to work at odd jobs. He began performing sleight of hand magic and adopted the stage name Harry Lorayne in the early 1940s. Actor Victor Jory became fascinated by his abilities to memorize the location of every card in an entire deck. He began using memory tricks in his act. He developed a mnemonic system that allowed him to recall the names of hundreds of people after a single meeting. He first became nationally known by exhibiting his talent on an episode of "I've Got a Secret" in 1958. He was a guest on such television series as "The Tonight Show Starring Jack Paar", "The Ed Sullivan Show", "The Joe Franklin Show", "McLean and Company", "The David Frost Show, "The Mike Douglas Show", "The Tonight Show Starring Johnny Carson", "The Bob Braun Show", "The Merv Griffin Show", "Dinah!", "Good Morning America", "The Paul Daniels Magic Show", "Beyond Vaudeville", and "The Dick Cavett Show". He traveled the country performing his memory talents on stage and trade shows. He operated a memory-training school in New York in the 1960s. He later starred in infomercials selling his home memory-improvement system. Lorayne wrote numerous books about memory and magic including "How to Develop a Super Power Memory" (1957), "Harry Lorayne's Secrets of Mind Power" (1961), "Close-Up Card Magic" (1962), "My Favorite

Card Tricks" (1965), "The Harry Lorayne Memory Isometrics Course" (1968), "The Great Divide" (1972), "The Memory Book: The Classic Guide to Improving Your Memory at Work, at School, and at Play" (1974) with Jerry Lucas), "Remembering People (The Key to Success)" (1976), "The Magic Book" (1977), "Memory Makes Money" (1985), "Page-a-Minute Memory Book" (1987), "Complete Guide to Memory Mastery" (1998), "How to Get Rich Using the Power of Your Mind" (2003), "Jaw Droppers" (2015), "Jaw Droppers Two" (2017), and "And Finally!" (2018). He also wrote and published the monthly magazine "Apocalypse" from 1978 to 1997. Lorayne was married to Renee Lorraine Lefkowitz from 1948 until her death in 2014, and she frequently assisted in his act. He is survived by their son Robert.

Loring, Lisa

Child actress Lisa Loring, who starred as Wednesday Addams in the television series "The Addams Family" in the mid-1960s, died from complications of a stroke at a hospital in Burbank, California, on January 28, 2023. She was 64. She

was born Lisa Ann DeCinces on Kwajalein Atoll, in the Marshall Islands, on February 16, 1958, while her parents were serving in the U.S. Navy. She moved to Los Angeles with her mother as a child and began modeling at the age of three. She made her television debut in an episode of "Dr. Kildare" in 1964. Loring was the precocious Wednesday Addams on the ABC series "The Addams Family" from 1964 to 1966, with John Astin and Carolyn Jones as her comically macabre parents Gomez and Morticia Addams. Loring starred as Suzy Pruitt in the short-lived comedy series "The Pruitts of Southampton" with Astin and Phyllis Diller in 1966. She also appeared in an episode of "The Girl from U.N.C.L.E." She took a hiatus from acting for a decade before reprising her role as Wednesday in the 1977 tele-film "Halloween with the New Addams Family". She also appeared in the tele-films "Annie Flynn" (1978) and "Gabe and Walker" (1981), and episodes of "Fantasy Island"

and "Barnaby Jones". She was featured as Cricket Montgomery on episodes of the daytime soap opera "As the World Turns" from 1980 to 1983. Loring worked as a makeup artist on several adult films including "Bi-Coastal" (1985), "Traci's Big Trick" (1986), and "Blowing in Style" (1989). She appeared in several horror films in the late 1980s including "Blood Frenzy" (1987), "Savage Harbor" (1987), and "Iced" (1989). Loring suffered from drug addiction in the early 1990s before going into rehab. She returned to the screen for the low budget chillers "Way

Down in Chinatown" (2014) and "Doctor Spine" (2015). Loring was married to Farrell Foumberg from 1973 until their divorce in 1974 and is survived by their daughter, Vanessa. She was married to actor Doug Stevenson from 1981 until their divorce in 1983, and is survived by their daughter, Marianne. She married adult film actor Jerry Butler in 1987 and the couple appeared together on an episode of the "Sally Jessy Raphael Show" where they discussed the damage his porn career was causing their marriage. They divorced in 1992. Loring married Graham Rich in 2003. They separated in 2008 and divorced in 2014.

Loring, Lynn

Actress Lynn Loring died at a hospital in Tarzana, California, on December 23, 2023. She was 80. She was born Lynn Eileen Zimring in Manhattan, New York, on July 14, 1943. She began modeling at the age of three and appeared in commercials for RCA Victor as a child. She starred as young

Patti Barron on the television soap opera "Search for Tomorrow" from 1951 to 1961. She was also seen on television in episodes of "The Web", "The Colgate Comedy Hour", "Starlight Theatre", "Hands of Mystery", "Robert Montgomery Presents", "The Jean Carroll Show" as the daughter from 1953 to 1954, "Studio One", "The Man Behind the Badge", "The Stranger", "Omnibus" as Eva in a production of "Uncle Tom's Cabin" in 1955, "Frontiers of Faith", "Lamp Unto My Feet", "Kraft Theatre", and "Armstrong Circle Theatre". She had graduated to more mature roles when she made her film debut in "Splendor in the Grass" in 1961. She also appeared in the films "Pressure Point" (1962) and the science fiction thriller "Journey to the Far Side of the Sun" (aka "Doppelganger") (1969) with her then husband Roy Thinnes. She appeared on television in productions of "The Brick and the Rose" for "CBS Repertoire Workshop" in 1960, "Climate of Eden" for "Play of the Week" in 1960, and 1962's "Special for Women: Mother and Daughter". Her other television credits include episodes of "Bus Stop", "Wagon Train", "Target: The Corruptors", "The Many Loves of Dobie Gillis", "The Eleventh Hour", the comedy series "Fair Exchange" as Patty Walker from 1962 to 1963, "Gunsmoke", "The Defenders", "The Greatest Show on Earth", "Daniel Boone", "Perry Mason", "Mr. Novak", "The Alfred Hitchcock Hour", "The F.B.I." as Barbara Erskine, the daughter of Efrem Zimbalist, Jr.'s Inspector Lewis Erskine during the first season in 1965, "The Big Valley", "Burke's Law", "The Wild Wild West", "A Man Called Shenandoah", "Bonanza", "Bob Hope Presents the Chrysler Theatre", "The Invaders", "The Man from U.N.C.L.E.", "My Three Sons", "Lancer", "The Immortal", "The Young Lawyers", "The Mod Squad", "Circle of Fear", "Return to Peyton Place", and "Police Woman". She was also seen in the tele-films "And Baby Makes Three" (1966), the horror western

"Black Noon" (1971), "The Horror at 37,000 Feet" (1973), "The Desperate Miles" (1975), and "The Kansas City Massacre" (1975). Loring quit acting in the mid-1970s to raise a family. She began working in film and television production later in the decade. She served as casting director for the 1979 tele-film "Raid on Coffeyville" (aka "The Last Ride of the Dalton Gang"). She was a production executive for the tele-films "Scared Silly" (1982), "Don't Go to Sleep" (1982), and "Making of a Male Model" (1983), and episodes of "Matt Houston", "Hotel", and "Finders of Lost Loves". Loring was a producer of the tele-films "The Return of Mod Squad" (1979), "The Best Little Girl in the World" (1981), "Sizzle" (1981), and "Making of a Male Model" (1983), and the series "Glitter" from 1984 to 1985. She produced the films "Mr. Mom" (1983) and "Me and the Kid" (1993). She worked frequently with Aaron Spelling and became president of MGM/UA Television Productions in the late 1980s. She left MGM/UA in the mid-1990s to become an independent producer. Loring was married to actor Roy Thinnes from 1967 until their divorce in 1984 and is survived by their son, Christopher Thinnes, and daughter, Casey-Leigh Thinnes. She married attorney Michael Bergman in 1988 and he predeceased her.

Lotis, Dennis

British singer and actor Dennis Lotis, who starred in the 1960 horror film "Horror Hotel", died in Norfolk, England, on February 8, 2023. He was 97. Lotis was born in Johannesburg, South Africa, on March 8, 1925. He began

performing as a singer on stage and radio as a child. He left school in his teens and worked at various jobs while singing at clubs around Johannesburg. He moved to England in the early 1950s where he joined the Ted Heath Orchestra. His first recording, a cover of Al Martino's "Here in My Heart", was released in 1952 and was followed by "Such a Night" in 1954. Lotis left Heath to perform as a solo in the mid-1950s, performing on BBC Radio and the variety circuit. His other recordings include "Cuddle Me", "Honey Love", "Tammy", and "The Only Man on the Island". He was seen on the television series "Hit Parade", "The Tin Pan Alley Show", "Festival of British Popular Songs", "Hits and Misses", "Off the Record", "Show Band Parade", "The Black and White Minstrel Show", "The Jack Johnson Show, "Crackerjack!", "Six-Five Special", "Drumbeat", "Trinder Box", "Music Shop", "Russ Conway", "Tempo 60", "Dial for Music", "The Friday Show", "Be My Guest", "The Singing Years", "Twist!", "Singalong Saturday" "Vic Parnell's Saturday Night at the London Palladium", "Thank Your Lucky Stars", "Glamour...", "The Dickie Valentine Show", and "Set 'em Up, Joe". Lotis was featured in several films including "The Extra Day" (1956), "It's a Wonderful World" (1956), "The Inbetween Age" (1958),

"Make Mine a Million" (1959), the horror film "Horror Hotel" (aka "The City of the Dead") (1960) as Richard Barlow, "Sword of Sherwood Forest" (1960) as Alan A'Dale, "Maid for Murder" (1962), and "What Every Woman Wants" (1962). He performed in the West End stage production of John Osborne's "The World of Paul Slickey" in 1959 and was seen in the 1964 "ITV Play of the Week" production of "Deep and Crisp and Stolen". He largely retired from show business by the late 1960s and worked as a restaurateur and antique store owner in Tring, Hertfordshire. He returned to the stage in the 1980s singing at nostalgia shows. Lotis married Alexandrena Maie Mackie in 1949 and they had three sons before her death in 1997. One of his sons died in 2009. He married Bronwen Z. Odell in 2000 and she also survives him.

Love, Patti

British actress Patti Love died of complications from dementia at Denville Hall, the actor's retirement home, in Northwood, London, England, on February 17, 2023. She was

75. Love was born in Glasgow, Scotland, on August 18, 1947. She studied acting at the Drama Centre in north London in the late 1960s. She began her career on stage with the Glasgow Citizens, appearing in productions of "Twelfth Night", "Saint Joan", and "Mother Courage". She also performed with the Royal Shakespeare Company and the National Theatre. She was noted for her role as psychiatrist R.D. Laing's schizophrenic patient Mary Barnes in David Edgar's 1978 play of the same name. She also appeared in such plays as Arnold Wesker's "Caritas" (1981), "Serious Money" (1987), "Three Birds Alighting on a Field" (1991), and Peter Hall's production of "Lysistrata" (1993). Love appeared in such films as "That'll Be the Day" (1973), "Butley" (1974), "The Life Story of Baal" (1978), Norman J. Warren's supernatural slasher film "Terror" (1978) as the ghostly killer Mad Dolly, the crime drama "The Long Good Friday (1980) with Bob Hoskins and Helen Miren, "Steaming" (1985), "The Krays" (1990), "A Business Affair" (1994), "An Awfully Big Adventure" (1995), "Agent Cody Banks 2: Destination London" (2004), "Mrs. Henderson Presents" (2005), and "Woman in Gold" (2015). Love was seen on television in episodes of "Trial", "Arthur of the Britons", Play for Today", "Omnibus", "Second Verdict", "Within These Walls", "Warrior Queen" as Tasca in 1978, "Shoestring", "Round and Round", "Travelling Man", "This Is David Lander", "Boon", "Casualty", "Moon and Son", "Cracker", "Middlemarch" as Mrs. Plymdale in 1994, "Grange Hill" as Mrs. Day in 1998, "The Boss", "The Bill", "Doctors", and "Galavant". Her other television credits include productions of "Escape from Sobibor" (1987), "Uncle Silas" (1989), "The Fortunes and Misfortunes of Moll Flanders" (1996), and "The Commander: Virus" (2005).

Lualdi, Antonella

Italian actress Antonella Lualdi died in Rome, Italy, on August 10, 2023. She was 92. She was born Antonietta de Pascale in Beirut, Lebanon, in July 6, 1931. She moved with  her family to Milan, Italy, at the age of ten. She studied in Florence where she began working as a model. She won a contest conducted by the film magazine "Hollywood" in 1949. She was introduced as Signorina X and readers were invited to pick her stage name. She soon began a long career in films and television. Her film credits include "Prince of Foxes" (1949), "Signorinella" (1949), "Twelve Hours to Live" (1950), "Canzoni per le Strade" (1950), "Abbiamo Vinto!" (1951), "Miracolo a Viggitiu" (1951), "L'Ultima Sentenza" (1951), "Ha Fatto 13" (1951), "Pentimento" (1952), "The Overcoat" (1952), "Three Forbidden Stories" (1952), "Adorable Creatures" (1952), "I Figli Non Si Vendono" (1952), "Il Romanzo della Mia Via" (1952), "Cani e Gati" (1952), "E Arrivato l'Accordatore" (1952), "Perdonami!" (1953), "La Cieca di Sorrento" (1953), "Die Tochter der Kompagnie" (1953), "Cavalcade of Song" (1953), "Il Piu Comico Spettacolo del Mondo" (1953), "What Scoundrels Men Are!" (1953), the short "The Story of William Tell" (1953) starring Errol Flynn, "Amori di Mezzo Secolo" (1954), "Chronicles of Poor Lovers" (1954), "Pieta per Chi Cade" (1954), "Papa Pacifico" (1954), "Avanzi di Galera" (1954), Claude Autant-Lara's historical drama "The Red and the Black" (1954), "Casta Diva" (1954), "Le Signorine Della 04" (1955), "Non c'e Amore Piu Grande" (1955), "Andrea Chenier" (1955), "Wild Love" (1956), "Altair" (1956), "I Giorni Piu Belli" (1956), "A Tailor's Maid" (1957), "Young Girls Beware" (1957), "La Cenicienta y Ernesto" (1957), "Young Husbands" (1958), "Il Cielo Brucia" (1958), "Mon Coquin de Pere" (1958), "One Life" (1958), "Polikuschka" (1958), "Delit de Fuite" (1959), "I Spit on Your Grave" (1959), "Web of Passion" (1959), "The Big Night" (1959), "Match Contre la Mort"(1959), "Silver Spoon Set" (1960), "Via Margutta" (1960), "Appuntamento a Ischia" (1960), "The Mongols" (1961) starring Jack Palance, "Disorder" (1962), "My Son, the Hero" (1962), "The Shortest Day" (1963), "Gli Imbroglioni" (1963), "Il Figlio del Circo" (1963), "Hong Kong un Addio" (1963), the horror film "Death on the Four Poster" (1964) with John Drew Barrymore, "I Maniaci" (1964), "Let's Talk About Women" (1964), "Le Repas des Fauves" (1964), "I Cento Cavalieri" (1964), "Amore Mio" (1964), "La Coda del Diavolo" (1964), "Su e Giu" (1965), "The Sea Pirate" (aka "Il Grande Colpo di Surcouf") (1966), "How to Seduce a Playboy" (1966), "Massacre in the Black Forest" (1967), "Ragan" (1968), "Columna" (1968), "Un Caso di Coscienza" (1970), "Vincent, Francois, Paul and the Others" (1974), "I Giorni della Chimera" (1975), "La Legge Violenta della Squadra Anticrimine" (1976), "Non Sparate Sui Bambini" (1978), "The Garden of Eden" (1980), "The Iron Hand of the Mafia" (1980), "Pajaros de Ciudad" (1981), "Carlotta: Amor es... Veneno" (1981), "Pe Sempe" (1982), "Zero in Condotta" (1983), "Una Spina Nel Cuore" (1986), "Diritto di Vivere" (1989), "Tutti Gli Uomini di Sara" (1992), "L'Urlo della Verita" (1992), "Nefertiti, Figlia del Sole" (1994), and "La Bella Societa" (2010). Lualdi appeared on television in productions of "Biblioteca di Studio Uno" (1964), "Don Giovannino" (1967), "D'Artagnan" (1969), "Lucien Leuwen" (1973), "E Stato Cosi" (1977), "Les Eygletiere" (1978), "Settimo Anno" (1978), "La Corde au Cou" (1978), "Goya" (1985), "Vida Privada" (1987), "Guerra di Spie" (1989), "Tango Bar" (1991), "Per Amore o per Amicizia" (1993), "Cheques en Boite" (1994), "The Sands of Time" (2000), and "On n'a Qu'une Vie" (2000). She was featured as Lucia Cordier in the series "Cordier and Son: Judge and Cop" from 1992 to 2005 and "Commissaire Cordier" from 2005 to 2008. Lualdi was married to actor Franco Interlenghi from 1955 until his death in 2015 and is survived by their two daughters, actresses Stella Interlenghi and Antonella Interlenghi.

Lucas, Pete

British singer and musician Pete Lucas, who performed with the bands Dave Dee, Dozy, Beaky, Mick & Tich and the Troggs, died of cancer at his home in Salisbury, England, on December 16, 2023. He was 73. Lucas was born  on December 16, 1950. The off-beat rock band Dave Dee, Dozy, Beaky, Mick & Tich was formed in Salisbury in 1964. The original lineup included David John Harman (Dave Dee), Charles Clark (Dozy), John Dymond (Beaky), Michael Wilson (Mick), and Ian Amey (Tich). They had several hits over the decade before breaking up in 1973. Amey and Dymond soon joined Lucas and Trevor Ward-Davies in the rock band Tracker. When the original group reunited without Wilson and Clark, Lucas and Ward-Davies became the second Mick and Dozy. Lucas played rhythm guitar and provided vocals for the group with Harman soon departing as Dave Dee. The group became known as Dozy, Beaky, Mick & Tich before Lucas left the band in 1982. He joined the rock band the Trogs in the mid-1980s, long after their popularity in the 1960s had dissipated. Lucas continued to provide bass guitar and backup vocals for the group until his retirement during the COVID-19 pandemic in the early 2020s.

Luddy, Tom

Film producer Tom Luddy, who was co-founder of the Telluride Film Festival, died of complications from Parkinson's disease at his home in Berkeley, California, on February 13, 2023. He was 79. Luddy was born in New York City on June 4, 1943. He attended college at the University of California at Berkeley. He became involved in the film community and ran the R.W. Murnau Film Society in the early 1960s. He became active with the Pacific Film Archive at Berkeley later in the decade and served as program director from 1972 to 1980. He appeared onscreen as pod person Ted Hendley in Philip Kaufman's 1978 remake of the science fiction classic "Invasion of the Body Snatchers". He became head of special projects at Francis Ford Coppola's American Zoetrope in 1980, where he supervised the restoration of Abel Gance's 1927 silent film "Napoleon". He also organized the U.S. release of Hans-Jurgen Syberberg's documentary "Our Hitler: A Film from Germany"

(1977). Luddy produced several films at Zoetrope including Paul Schrader's "Mishima: A Life in Four Chapters", Norman Mailer's "Tough Guys Don't Dance" (1987), Paul Schroeder's "Barfly" (1987), Jean-Luc Godard's "King Lear" (1987), Carroll Ballard's "Wind" (1992), Agnieszka Holland's "The Secret Garden" (1993), and Gregory Nava's "My Family" (1995). He produced several films for the Cannon Group including "Manifesto" (1988) and "Powaqqatsi" (1988). He joined film preservationist James Card and theater owners Bill and Stella Pence to launch the Telluride Festival in 1974. He served as artistic director and, with Telluride executive director Julie Huntsinger, developed the festival's program. He remained involved with Telluride festival until his death. Luddy is survived by his wife, Monique Montgomery.

Luna, Silvina

Argentine actress and model Silvina Luna died of kidney failure in Buenos Aires, Argentina, on August 31, 2023. She was 43. Luna was born in Rosario, Argentina, on June 21,

1980. She moved to Buenos Aires after high school and began working as a secretary and model. She was a finalist in the second season of "Gran Hermano", the Argentine version of the reality series "Big Brother", in 2001. She was seen frequently on television in such series as "Pone a Francella", "Maru a la Tarde", "Noche de Juegos", "La Peluqueria de los Mateos", "No Hay 2 Sin 3", "Amor en Custodia", "Los Roldan", "Casados Con Hijos", "El Patron de la Vereda" as Lucy Ferita in 2005, "Caiga Quien Caiga - CQC", "Gladiadores de Pompeya", "Son de Fierro", "El Capo", "Ciega a Citas" as Gisella from 2009 to 2010, "Todos Contra Juan", "Mistreated", "La Pelu" as Silvina Moon from 2012 to 2013, "Celebrity Splash! Argentina" as a contestant in 2013, "Futbol Para Todos" as a frequent panelist from 2013 to 2014, "La Mesa Esta Lista", "Mejor de Noche", "Sres. Papis", "Ultimatum", "Bailando Por un Sueno", "La Noche de Mirtha", "Incorrectas", "Divina Comida", "PH: Podemos Hablar", "Pasapalabra", "El Hotel de los Famosos", "Socios del Espectaculo", and "LAM". Luna was also a cabaret

artist in stage productions in the early 2000s. She reportedly had suffered from kidney stones following a problem with cometic surgery in 2014.

Lunoe, Lars

Danish actor Lars Lunoe died in Copenhagen, Denmark, on October 9, 2023. He was 87. Lunoe was born in Copenhagen on April 19, 1936. He studied acting at the Aarhus

Theater's school and performed on stage with the theater in the early 1960s. He soon made his film debut and was seen in such featurs as "Maske i Morgen" (1964), "Old Maids" (1966), "The Reluctant Sadist" (1967), "Historien om Barbara" (1967), "2 - I, a Woman, Part II" (1968), "Doctor Glas" (1968), "De Rode Heste" (1968), "Mej Och Dej" (1969), "The Man

Who Thought Life"(1969), "Praeriens Skrappe Drenge" (1970), "Nana" (1970), "Guld Til Praeriens Skrappe Drenge" (1971), "Pigen og Drommeslottet" (1974), "Ghost Train" (1976), "Stromer" (1976), "Haervaerk" (1977), "Early Spring" (1986), "Peter von Scholten" (1987), "Love on the Rails" (1989), "The Touch" (1992), "Stolen Spring" (1993), "To Mand i en Sofa" (1994), "Ondt Blod" (1996), "Klinkevals" (1999), "Facing the Truth" (2002), "Aftermath" (2004), "Springet" (2005), "Sommeren" (2005), "Morke" (2005), "Krumerne - Sa er det Jul Igen" (2006), "Terribly Happy" (2008), and "Men & Chicken" (2015). Lunoe was seen on television in productions of "Wie ein Hirschberger Danisch Lernte" (1968), "Forarsaften Med Faust" (1968), "Det er Maske Det, der Har Gjort Os Sa Smukke" (1969), "De Unge Pa 80" (1970), "Fire Portraetter" (1972), "En Aegtemand" (1976), "Ministeren Og Doden" (1976), "Ministerens Mord" (1977), "Sommeren 1807" (1970), "Uden Stotte Fra Befolkningen Kunne Vi Ingenting Udrette" (1980), "Strejferne" (1980), "Stiftelsen" (1983), "O i Reno" (1983), "For Menneskelivets Skyld" (1983), "Niels Klims Underjordiske Rejse" (1984), "August Strindberg: Ett Liv" (1985), "En Lykkelig Tragedie" (1987), "Sorgagre" (1987), "Min Vilje Ske" (1888), "Cecilia" (1991), "Kald Mig Liva" (1992), "En Fri Mand" (1996), "Bryggeren" (1997), and "Edderkoppen" (2000). His other television credits include episodes of "Ka' De Li' Osters", "Huset Pa Christianshavn", "Vores Ar", "En by I Provinsen" as Detective Hansen from 1977 to 1980, "Krigsdotre", "Froken Jensens Pensionat", "Grundtvigs Drom", "Station 13", "Gongehovdingen", "The Kingdom" as Sundhedsminster in 1994, "Hjerteflimmer", "Strisser Pa Samso" as Henrik Wessel in 1998, "Unit One", "Jul i Hjemmevaernet", "Nikolaj og Julie", "Forsvar", and "Limbo". Lunoe married Annette Hogsbro in 1989 and she survives him.

Lutvak, Steven

Composer Steven Lutvak, who was noted for his work in musical theater, died of a pulmonary embolism at his studio in Manhattan, New York, on October 9, 2023. He was 64. Lutvak was born in the Bronx, New York, on July 18, 1959. He

graduated from the State University of New York at Binghampton with a degree in music in 1980. He received a graduate degree in musical theatre writing from the Tisch School of the Arts in 1983. He frequently collaborated with Robert L. Freedman writing musicals for regional theatre and off-off Broadway including "Campaign of the Century", "The Wayside Inn", "Esmeralda", and "Almost September". Lutvak composed the score for the 2002 film and the 2005 documentary "Mad Hot Ballroom". He and Freedman were best known for the 2012 Broadway musical comedy "A Gentleman's Guide to Love and Murder" which won the Tony Award for Best Musical. He was nominated for the Tony for Best Original Score. Lutvak was a professor with the New York University Graduate Musical Theater Writing Program. He is survived by his husband, choreographer Michael McGowan and daughter, Eliot Rose Lutvak-McGowan.

Lutz, Regine

Swiss actress Regine Lutz died in Neuss, Germany, on December 17, 2023. She was 94. Lutz was born in Basel, Switzerland, on December 22, 1928. She was a student at the

Basel Conservatory and began her career on stage at Theatre Zurich in 1947. She performed with Bertolt Brecht's Berlin ensemble from 1949 until 1960. She appeared in productions of "Mother Courage and Her Children" (1952), "Life of Galileo" (1956), "The Resistible Rise of Arturo Ui" (1959), and "The Threepenny Opera" (1960). She appeared frequently on the West German stage from the 1960s at venues in Munich, Hamburg, and West Berlin. Lutz was seen in such films as "Jacke Wie Hose" (1953), "Katzgraben" (1957), "Mother Courage and Her Children" (1961), "The Lost Honor of Katharina Blum" (1975), "Die Plotzliche Einsamkeit des Konrad Steiner" (1976), "You Love Me Too" (1986), "Die Richterin" (1990), and "Es War Doch Liebe?" (1997). She appeared on television in productions of "Senora Carrar's Rifles" (1953), "Pauken und Trompeten" (1955), "Herr Puntila und Sein Knecht Matti" (1957), "Die Kassette" (1961), "Zwischen den Zugen" (1961), "Schau Heimwarts, Engel" (1961), "Golden Boy" (1962), "Affare Blum" (1962), "Dann Geh Zu Thorp" (1964), "Der Fluggast" (1964), "Der Arzt Wider Willen" (1964), "Nebeneinander" (1964), "Der Gelbe Pullover" (1964), "Das Grosse Ohr" (1965), "Adlig Sein Dagegen Sehr!" (1965), "An Einem Ganz Gewohnlichen Tag" (1966), "Palme im Rosengarten" (1967), "Die Wupper" (1967), "Vier Stunden von Elbe 1" (1968), "Die Schlacht Bei Lobositz" (1968), "Anna

Bockler" (1968), "Chopin-Express" (1971), "Play Strindberg"(1971), "Eiger" (1974), "Sechs Wochen im Leben der Bruder G." (1974), "Der Widerspenstige Heilige" (1974), "Candida" (1976), "Krock & Co." (1976), "Indiskret" (1977), "Travesties" (1978), "Diener und Andere Herren" (1978), "Wisnie" (1979), "Der Handkuss - Ein Marchen aus der Schweiz" (1980), "Faulheit Oder Der Hinkende Alois" (1980), "Francois Villon" (1981), "Mascha" (1984), "Blaubart" (1984), "Munchhausens Letzte Liebe" (1988), "Zwei an der Strippe" (1994), "Bei Hubschen Frauen Sind Alle Tricks Erlaubt" (2004), "Der Mann von Nebenan Lebt!" (2005), "Und Ich Lieb Dich Doch!" (2006), "Das Geheimnis der Wolfsklamm" (2008), and "Jeder Mensch Braucht ein Geheimnis" (2010). Her other television credits include episodes of "Der Fall Jakubowski - Rekonstruktion Eines Justizirrtums", "Kinderheim Sasener Chaussee" as Susanne Kohler in 1973, "Unter Ausschluss der Ofentlichkeit", "Gesucht Wird...", "Inspektion Lauenstadt", "Buddenbrooks" as Sesemi Weichbrodt in 1979, "Die Wilsheimer" as Luise Ziegler in 1987, "Ein Stuck aus Ihrem Leben", "The Black Forest Hospital", "Hotel Paradies", "Mrs. Harris", "Siebenbirken", "A Case for Two", "Stadtklinik", "Marienhof", "Balko", "Das Herz des Priesters", "Streit um Drei", "The Old Fox", "Sinan Toprak Ist der Unbestechliche", "Rosamunde Pilcher", "In der Mitte Eines Lebens", "Ritas Welt", "Alarm fur Cobra 11 - Die Autobahnpolizei", "Unsolved", "In Aller Freundschaft", "Leipzig Homicide", "A House of Animals", "SOKO Stuttgart", "For Heaven's Sake", and "Tatort". Her textbook for actors, "Actor, the Most Beautiful Profession", was published in 1994. She was a lecturer at the Bavarian Theater Academy in Munich and was a guest lecturer throughout Germany.

Lynch, Kathy Mills

Hairstylist and makeup artist Kathy Mills Lynch died of cancer in Lindon, Utah, on May 19, 2023. She was 54. She was born Kathy Mills in Concord, California, on June 27, 1968.

She trained at the Institute of Cosmetology after graduating high school in 1986. She began working as a hair stylist and opened her own salon. She was involved with film and television from 2013. She was makeup artist and hair stylist for the family-oriented sketch comedy series "Studio C" from 2014 to 2018. Lynch worked on such films as "Doggie B" (2013), "Just Let Go" (2015), "Great Salt Lake: Utah's Sanctuary" (2015), "6 Below: Miracle on the Mountain" (2017), "Utah's Famous Firsts" (2018), "The Night Clerk" (2020), "Joe Bell" (2020), "American Underdog" (2021), "Once I Was Engaged" (2021), "The Card Counter" (2021), "Christmas with the Chosen: The Messengers" (2021), "The Out-Laws" (2023), and "Christmas with the Chosen: Holy Night" (2023). She worked on television productions of "A Wonderama Christmas" (2016), "Snatchers" (2017), "Mosaic" (2018), "Music and the Spoken Word"

(2018), "Diesel Brothers" (2019), "Yellowstone" (2018-2020), "Show Offs" (2019-2020), "The Christmas Bow" (2020), "Dashing in December" (2020), "The Chosen" (2021), "Grey's Anatomy" (2022), "America's Got Talent" (2022), "For All Mankind" (2022), and "Jonathan & Jesus" (2024). She married Wayne Allen Lynch in 1987 and his survived by him and their four sons.

Lynch, Laura

Singer and musician Laura Lynch, who was a founding member of the country music group the Dixie Chicks, was killed in a head-on automobile collision when a car traveling in the opposite direction on an El Paso, Texas, highway attempted to pass and collided with her car on December 22, 2023. She was 65. Lynch was born in Dell City, Texas, on November 18, 1959. She teamed with Robin Lynn Macy, Martie Erwin, and Emily Erwin to form the Dixie Chicks in Dallas in 1989. She played upright bass with the group and was also a singer. Lynch and the Dixie Chicks made their debut with the Grand Ole Opry in 1991. She recorded the albums "Thank Heaven for Dale Evans" (1990), "Little Ol' Cowgirl" (1992), and "Shouldn't a Told You That" (1993) before leaving the group in 1994. She was eventually replaced by Natalie Maines, who led the Dixie Chicks to greater success. They removed the Dixie from the name and became known as the Chicks in 2020.

Lyon, Lisa

Female bodybuilding pioneer and model Lisa Lyon died of stomach cancer in Westlake Village, California, on September 8, 2023. She was 70. Lyon was born in Los Angeles, California, on May 13, 1953. She attended the University of California at Los Angeles where she majored in anthropology. She also studied dancing and began practicing kendo, a Japanese martial art using bamboo swords. She soon began weight training and bodybuilding, becoming one of the first well-known females in the sport. She won the first International Federation of Bodybuilding and Fitness Women's World Pro Bodybuilding Championship in Los Angeles in 1979. She appeared in the pages of numerous fitness magazines and was the subject of a pictorial in "Playboy" in October of 1980. Her book, "Lisa Lyon's Body Magic", was published in 1981. She met photographer Robert Mapplethorpe and began to model for him. He took numerous photographs of Lyons in various poses which resulted in a gallery show and the 1983 book "Lady: Lisa Lyon". She appeared in several films

including "Three Crowns of the Sailor" (1983) and the horror comedy "Vamp" (1986) starring Grace Jones. She also appeared in the tele-films "The Hustler of Muscle Beach" (1980) and "Getting Physical" (1984). She was the subject of the 1987 documentary short film "Lisa Lyon: A Portrait of Power". Lyons was inducted into the International Fitness and Bodybuilding Federation Hall of Fame in 2000. She had a brief marriage to ethnomusicologist and bodybuilder Robert Keeling. She subsequently married French singer and songwriter Bernard Lavilliers and they divorced in 1986. She met Dr. John C. Lilly, a neuroscientist who was involved in research with isolation tanks and communications with dolphins, in 1986. They became close and he legally adopted her as a daughter the following year. Lyon was married to actor Alan Deglin from 2009 until his death in 2020.

Lyons, Dylan

Television news reporter Dylan Lyons was shot to death while reporting from the scene of a homicide in Pine Hills, Florida, on February 22, 2023. He was 24. Lyons was born in Meadowbrook, Pennsylvania, on March 11, 1998. He graduated from the University of Central Florida where he earned degrees in journalism and political science. He worked as a reporter and anchor for WCJB-TV, and ABC affiliate in Gainesville. He later joined Spectrum News 13 in Orlando as a reporter. Lyons was covering the murder of a 9-year-old-child in the local area when the killer returned to the scene and shot him while he was reporting. His photographer, Jesse Walden, was also wounded in the shooting. The shooter then went to a nearby home and shot and killed another girl and critically wounded her mother. The shooter, 19-year-old Keith Melvin Moses, was arrested and was believed responsible for all of the shootings.

MacDonald, Dan

Canadian actor Dan MacDonald died at a hospital in Halifax, Nova Scotia, Canada, on November 23, 2023. He was 89. MacDonald was born in Pictou, Nova Scotia, on August 28, 1934. He graduated from Pictou Academy in 1953 and attended the Vancouver Theatre School and Saint Mary's University in Halifax. He began his career on stage and performed with the Old Vic Company in London, England, in the 1950s. He continued his career on stage after returning to Canada, performing with the Stratford Festival. He was also frequently heard on CBC Radio. He formed his own theatrical company, Tiroam Arts, where he produced, directed, and appeared in productions. He served as the first president of the Canadian Actors' Equity Association and was active in securing benefits for the performing arts community. MacDonald was seen in such films as "Change of Mind" (1969), "The Rowdyman" (1972), "The Neptune Factor" (1973), "Hyper Sapien: People from Another Star" (1986), "My Pet Monster" (1986), "Mr. Nice Guy" (1987), "Ordinary Magic" (1993), "Butterbox Babies" (1995), "Something More" (1999), "Now & Forever" (2002), and "Trailer Park Boys: Don't Legalize It" (2014). He appeared frequently on television with roles in episodes of "Perspective", "The Wednesday Play", the supernatural soap opera "Strange Paradise" as the Reverend Matthew Dawson from 1969 to 1970, "Police Surgeon", "Performance", "The Great Detective", "For the Record", "The Edison Twins", "Knightwatch", "The Campbells", "Friday the 13th: The Series", "Avonlea", "My Secret Identity", "Top Cops", "E.N.G.", "Street Legal", "RoboCop", "Side Effects", "Wind at My Back" as Alden Cramp from 1996 to 2001, the children's series "Incredible Story Studio" as Jacobs from 1997 to 2002, "Traders", "Due South", "Relic Hunter", "Blue Murder", "Doc" in the recurring role of General Doss from 2002 to 2004, "Puppets Who Kill", "Renegadepress.com" as Principal Taylor from 2004 to 2007, "Seed", "The Lizzie Borden Chronicles", and "Haven". His other television credits include productions of "The Discoverers" (1972), "Dracula" as Jonathan Harker on "Purple Playhouse" in 1973, "Chasing Rainbows" (1988), "Lantern Hill" (1989), "The Little Kidnappers" (1990), "Alexander Graham Bell: The Sound and the Silence" (1991), "When Innocence Is Lost" (1997), "Nothing Too Good for a Cowboy" (1998), "Gift of Love: The Daniel Huffman Story" (1999), "Seasons of Love" (1999), "The Dinosaur Hunter" (2000), "Possessed" (2000), "Without Malice" (2003), and "The Book of Negroes" (2015). MacDonald was married to Nancy Fry from 1965 until her death in 2020.

MacGowan, Shane

Irish singer Shane MacGowan, who was lead singer for the band the Pogues, died of pneumonia at his home in Dublin, Ireland, on November 30, 2023. He was 65.

MacGowan was born in Pembury, Kent, England, to Irish parents on December 25, 1957. He was expelled from Westminster School for drug use and spent time under psychiatric care in London for drugs and alcohol. He became active in the punk music scene in London under the name Shane O'Hooligan and began a punk fanzine. He and his girlfriend, Shanne Bradley, formed the punk band the Nipple Erectors, which later became the Nips, in 1977. MacGowan began playing with Peter 'Spider' Stacy' and Jem Finer in the Millwall Chainsaws, which became known as the New Republicans, in the early 1980s. They were joined by James Fearnley, who had worked with MacGowan in the Nips, to create the band known as Pogue Mahone in 1982. They were joined by Cait O'Riordan and Andrew Ranken soon after and released the 1984 single "Dark Streets of London". They shortened their name to the Pogues, partially due to some complaints to the BBC that Pogue Mahone was a version of the Gaelic phrase "kiss my arse". They recorded the albums "Red Roses for Me" (1984), "Rum Sodomy & the Lash" (1985), "If I Should Fall from Grace with God" (1988), "Peace and Love" (1989), and "Hell's Ditch" (1990). Theye had hits with their renditions of Ewan MacColl's "Dirty Old Town" and Eric Bogle's "And the Band Played Waltzing Matilda". MacGowan was often lead singer and lyricist for the group for such songs as "The Sick Bed of Cuchulainn", "Fairytale of New York", "A Pair of Brown Eyes", "Sally MacLennane", "A Rainy Night in Soho", and "Dark Streets of London". They starred in the 1988 television special "The Pogues: Live at the Town and Country". MacGowan's drug and alcohol abuse led to his being fired from the Pogues during a tour of Japan in 1991. He formed the band Shane MacGowan and the Popes, which released the albums "The Snake" (1994) and "The Crock of Gold" (1997). He rejoined the Pogues to tour and perform in 2001 and remained with them until they disbanded in 2014. MacGowan also produced solo material during his career and collaborated with such other artists as Joe Strummer, Nick Cave, and Sinead O'Connor. He was featured in several films including "Straight to Hell" (1987), "Eat the Rich" (1987), and "The Libertine" (2004). He was also seen in the 1991 tele-film "The Ghosts of Oxford Street" and an episode of "Rab C. Nesbitt" in 2011. He was featured in the television specials and documentaries "The Great Hunger: The Life and Songs of Shane MacGowan" (1997), "If I Should Fall from Grace: the Shane MacGowan Story" (2001), "The Story of Fairytale of New York" (2005), "Victoria and Shane Grow Their Own" (2009), and "Crock of Gold: A Few Rounds with Shane MacGowan" (2020). He was also a guest on the series "Top of the Pops", "The White Room", and "Late Night with Conan O'Brien". He had a lengthy relationship with Irish journalist Victoria Mary Clarke prior to their marriage in November of 2018 and she survives him.

Magoo

Rapper Melvin Barcliff, who was half of the duo Timbaland and Magoo, died in Williamsburg, Virginia, on August 13, 2023. He was 50. Barcliff was born in Norfolk, Virginia, on July 12, 1972. He became interested in rap music

while in high school and became friends with fellow enthusiast, Timothy Mosley, who became known as the rap artist and producer Timbaland. Magoo and Timbaland teamed with their friend, Larry Live, to form the group Surrounded by Idiots in 1990. They were soon joined by Pharrell Williams, who left the group after three years to pursue a solo career. Larry Live also left the group in 1993. Magoo and Timbaland continued to perform together and became part of

Da Bassment Crew collective. They signed with Blackground Records as a duo and released their debut album, "Welcome to Our World", in 1997. It contained the hit single "Up Jumps da Boogie" which also featured singers Missy Elliott and Aaliyah. They also released the albums "Indecent Proposal" (2001) and "Under Construction, Part II" (2003). Magoo largely retired from the music scene in the early 2000s. He was married to Meco Barcliff from the mid-1990s until their divorce in 2015.

Maguire, Bob

Australian Roman Catholic priest and television personality Bob Maguire died at a hospital in Malvern, Victoria, Australia, on April 19, 2023. He was 88. Maguire was born in Thronbury, Victoria, on September 14, 1934. He was an altar

boy as a child and attended Christian Brothers College, St. Kilda, from 1948 to 1953. He began studying theology at Corpus Christi College, Melbourne, in 1953. He received training for the priesthood and was ordained in 1960. He served in the Australian Army Reserve in the mid-1960 where he headed the Character Training Unit for young officers during the Vietnam War. He became priest at Sts. Peter and Paul's Church in South Melbourne in 1973. He was the founder of the Father Bob Maguire Foundation to raise funds for welfare and social justice in 2003. He was host of a ratio program in Melbourne and became co-host of "Speaking in Tongues" with John Safran on SBS television from 2005 to 2006. He was a judge on the "Strictly Speaking" competition show in 2009. He was forced to retire as parish priest in 2012. Maguire was the subject of the 2013 documentary film "In Bob We Trust".

Maguire, Hugh

Actor Hugh Maguire died in Los Angeles, California, on May 18, 2023. Maguire was born in Los Angeles on April 22, 1933. He was 80. He began his career as a child actor in the 1940s appearing in small roles in the films "Hitler's Madman" (1943), "Going My Way" (1944), "Once Upon a Time" (1944), "Meet the People" (1944), "The Seventh Cross" (1944), "Circumstantial Evidence" (1945), "Thrill of a

Romance" (1945), "Nob Hill" (1945), "This Love of Ours" (1945), "Leave Her to Heaven" (1945), and "Three Little Girls in Blue" (1946). He graduated from Loyola High School and the University of California at Berkeley where he was quarterback on the football team. He served in the United States Air Forced as a jet flight instructor. He worked as an investment banker after his discharge.

Maguire returned to acting in the late 1980s, appearing on television in episodes of "CBS Summer Playhouse", "The Slap Maxwell Story", "Knots Landing", "227", "Cheers" in the recurring role of Hugh from 1987 to 1988, "Live-In" as Ed Mathews in 1989, "Growing Pains", "Alien Nation", "Dallas", "Wings", "L.A. Law", "Martin", and "The '70s". He was also seen in the 1992 tele-film "Breaking the Silence". He was seen in the films "Deuce Coupe" (1992), "Conviction" (2010), "Vanishing on 7th Street" (2010), "All Things Fall Apart" (2011), "The Double" (2011), "Batman v Superman: Dawn of Justice" (2016) as Jack O'Dwyer, "Doctor Sleep" (2019), and "No Sudden Move" (2021). Maguire is survived by his wife, Maryly Roney, and their four children.

Maguire, Les

British musician Les Maguire, who played piano for the band Gerry and the Pacemakers, died in England on November 25, 2023. He was 81. Macguire was born in Wallasey, Merseyside, England, on December 27, 1941. He

began his career in 1959 playing tenor saxophone with the rock group Vegas Five, who later became the Undertakers. He joined Gerry and the Pacemakers in 1961, replacing Arthur 'Mack' MacMahon on piano. They signed with EMI Records in 1963 and scored a hit with "How Do You Do It?". The group had several more hits over the next few years including "I Like It", "Don't Let the Sun Catch You Crying". "Ferry Cross the Mersey", "I'm the One", and "You'll Never Walk Alone". He performed with Gerry and the Pacemakers in the concert film "The T.A.M.I. Show" and television episodes of "Beat City", "Ready, Steady, Go!", "The Ed Sullivan Show", "Top of the Pops", and "Beat Club". He also starred with the band in their 1964 film "Ferry Cross the Mersey". They disbanded later in the decade and he and bandmate opened a garage. He briefly fronted the Mississippi blues band Hog Owl in 1970. Maguire subsequently joined the Royal Navy and served during the 1982 Falkland War before his retirement. He later performed in reunion shows with the Pacemakers and played with the band Ian and the Zodiacs in the late 1990s. Marsden was predeceased by his wife, Brigitte, in 2012, and by daughter Karin in 1990. He is survived by another daughter, Stephanie.

Mahan, Larry

Rodeo cowboy and actor Larry Mahan died of bone cancer in Valley View, Texas, on May 7, 2023. He was 79. Mahan was born in Salem, Oregon, on November 21, 1943. He began competing professionally in rodeo in his early teens. He competed with the Rodeo Cowboys Association from 1963. He was a frequent winner in such events as saddle bronc riding, bareback riding, and bull Riding. He was crowned World All-Around Champion consecutively from 1966 to 1970 and again in 1973. He released an album of country music, "Larry Mahan,

King of the Rodeo", with little success in 1976. He retired from rodeo in 1977 and purchased a ranch near Phoenix, Arizona. He established a clothing line in the 1980s with his name  attached to boots, hats, and other apparel. Mahan appeared in several films including "J.W. Coop" (1971), "The Honkers" (1972), "Mackintosh and T.J." (1975), "Sixpack Annie" (1975), "Moon of the Desperados" (1990), "A Time to Revenge" (1997), "Grand Champion" (2002), and "Blood Trail" (2005). He was seen on television in the tele-films "Murder at the World Series" (1977) and "The Good Old Boys" (1995), and the mini-series "Streets of Laredo" (1995). He also appeared in episodes of "The Quest", "Tales of the Unexpected", "The Mike Douglas Show", "Hee Haw", "The Jim Nabors Show", "The Osmond Family Show", "The Streets of San Francisco", "Horse World" which he hosted in 1988. Mahan was the subject of the documentary "The Great American Cowboy", which received the Academy Award for Best Documentary Feature Film. He was inducted into the ProRodeo Hall of Fam in 1979 and was named a Legend of ProRodeo in 2010. He was married and divorced from Darlene Mahan, Robin Holtze, and Diana McNab. He was married to Julanne Read Mahan until her death in 2022. His son, Tyrone, predeceased him in 2020. His survivors include daughters Lisa and Alli.

Maharis, George

Actor George Maharis, who starred as Buz Murdock in the television series "Route 66" in the early 1960s, died of complications from hepatitis at his home in Beverley, Hills, California, on May 24, 2023. He was 94. Marharis was born  in Astoria, New York, on September 1, 1928. He left high school two serve in the U.S. Marine Corps and earned a high school diploma after his discharge. He pursued a career as a singer, performing on stage in musicals. He appeared on television in episodes of "The Philco Television Playhouse" and "Mister Peepers" in the early 1950s and studied with Sanford Meisner and Lee Strasberg at the Actors Studio. He performed on the Off-Broadway stage in productions of Jean Genet's "Deathwatch" and Edward Albee's "The Zoo Story" later in the decade. Maharis appeared frequently on television with roles in episodes of "Playwrights '56", "Lamp Unto My Feet", "Goodyear Playhouse", "The Investigator", "The Phil Silvers Show", "Brenner", "Deadline", "Alcoa Theatre", "Naked City", and the soap opera "Search for Tomorrow" as Bud Gardner in 1960. He was best known for his role as Buz Murdock opposite Martin Milner as Tod Stiles

on the CBS drama series "Route 66" from 1960 to 1963. The duo traveled around the country in a Corvette, and he earned an Emmy Award nomination in 1962. He left the series during its third series after being hospitalized for hepatitis and was replaced by Glenn Corbett before the series was canceled in 1964. Maharis recorded a handful of albums from Epic records in the early 1960s and released such singles as "Teach Me Tonight", "(Get Your Kicks On) Route 66", and "It's a Sin to Tell a Lie". He appeared in numerous variety, game, and talk shows during his career including episodes of "The New Truth or Consequences", "The Dinah Shore Chevy Show", "The Tonight Show Starring Jack Paar", "Here's Hollywood", "Password", "The Judy Garland Show", "The New Steve Allen Show", "The Les Crane Show", "Missing Links", "To Tell the Truth", "Hullabaloo", "Shindig!", "I've Got a Secret", "The Sammy Davis, Jr. Show", "Dateline: Hollywood", "Piccadilly Palace", "Everybody's Talking", "Two of a Kind", "Pat Boone in Hollywood", "The Ed Nelson Show", "Allen Ludden's Gallery", "You're Putting Me On", "The Rosey Grier Show", "The Dick Cavett Show", "Celebrity Bowling", "Chevrolet Presents the Golddiggers", "The Virginia Graham Show", "It's Your Bet", "The David Frost Show", "The Hollywood Squares", "The Merv Griffin Show", "The Bob Braun Show", "The Mike Douglas Show", "The Tonight Show Starring Johnny Carson", "Showoffs", "Shoot for the Stars", "The $10,000 Pyramid", "The Joe Franklin Show", and "Vicki!". His other television credits include episodes of "Bob Hope Presents the Chrysler Theatre", "The Danny Thomas Hour", "Journey to the Unknown", "Love Story", "The Most Deadly Game" as Jonathan Croft from 1970 to 1971, "Night Gallery", "Cade's County", "Medical Center", "Cannon", "Mission: Impossible", "Barnaby Jones", "Shaft", "Marcus Welby, M.D.", "The Snoop Sisters", "McMillan & Wife", "Movin' On", "Nakia", "Ellery Queen", "Good Heavens", "Jigsaw John", "Bert D'Angelo/Superstar", "The Bionic Woman", "Kojak", "Police Story", "The Feather and Father Gang", "Switch", "Gibbsville", "Logan's Run", "Fantasy Island", "Matt Houston", "The Master", "Superboy", and "Murder, She Wrote". Maharis was also seen in the tele-films "Escape to Mindanao" (1968), "The Monk" (1969), "The Victim" (1972), "Of Men and Women" (1973), "Murder Is a One-Act Play" (1974), "Come Die with Me" (1974), "Death in Space" (1974), "Murder on Flight 502" (1975), "Rich Man, Poor Man" (1976), "Look What's Happened to Rosemary's Baby" (1976) as Guy Woodhouse, "SST: Death Flight" (1977), and "Crash" (1978). He was featured in a handful of films during his career including "The Mugger" (1958), "Exodus" (1960), "Quick, Before It Melts" (1964), "Sylvia" (1965), "The Satan Bug" (1965), "A Covenant with Death" (1967), "The Happening" (1967), "The Desperados" (1969), "Land Raiders" (1969), "The Last Day of the War" (1970), the fantasy "The Sword and the Sorcerer" (1982) as Count Machelli, and "Doppelganger" (1993) with Drew Barrymore. Maharis also performed in Las Vegas nightclubs and posed as a nude centerfold in "Playgirl" in July of 1973. He largely retired from the screen in the early 1990s and concentrated on impressionist painting. His career was damaged during the 1960s when tabloids reported that he was involved in gay liaisons, including arrests on vice charges in 1967 and 1974.

Majors, Austin

Child actor Austin Majors died of an accidental fentanyl poisoning at a homeless shelter in Los Angeles, California, on February 11, 2023. He was 27. He was born

Austin Setmajer-Raglin in Kern County, California, on November 23, 1995. He began his career as a child in the role of Theo Sipowicz, the son of Dennis Franz's Detective Andy Sipowicz on the television police series "NYPD Blue" from 1999 to 2004. He also appeared in episodes of "Providence", "ER", the animated "Hercules" as the voice of Hyllus, "Threshold", "According to Jim", "NCIS", "American Dad!", "Desperate Housewives", and "How I Met Your Mother". He was featured in the tele-films "An Accidental Christmas" (2007) and "Night Writer" (2008). Majors appeared in the films "Nevada" (1997), "The Price of Air" (2000), and "Little Manhattan" (2005), and the shorts "Bananas" (2004), "Volare" (2004), and "Bye Bye Benjamin" (2006). He was also a voice actor in the films "Treasure Planet" (2002), "The Ant Bully" (2006), "Dead Silence" (2007), and "The Gray Man" (2007). He was a graduate of the University of Southern California's School of Cinematic Arts. He was cinematographer and editor of the 2015 short film "Hero".

Mak, Peter

Hong Kong film director Peter Mak died in Taipei, Taiwan, on March 26, 2023. He was born Tai-Kit Mak in

Saigon, South Vietnam, in 1957. He was 66. He moved to Hong Kong with his family in the 1960s during the Vietnam War. He attended college in Taiwan in 1979. He began working in films as an actor in 1982's "Lonely Fifteen". He was also seen in the films "China Scandal: Exotic Dane" (1983) and "Shu Zhi Suo Zhi" (1983). He soon began directing such films as "The Gift of A-Fu" (1984), "The Loser, the Hero" (1985), the horror comedy "Abracadabra" (aka "Loves of the Living Dead") (1986), "Lao Shi You Wen Ti" (1987), "Sir, Tell Me Why" (1987), "Ye Feng Kuang" (1989), "To Spy with Love!!" (1990), the horror fantasy "Wicked City" (1992), and "Enemy Shadow" (1995). Mak continued to appear in occasional films including "Last Eunuch in China" (1987), "Tiger Cage" (1988), "Pretty Ghost (1991), and "Twin Dragons" (1992). He later settled in Taiwan where he worked in television on the series "Meteor Garden II" (2002), "Dreams Link" (2007), "Love Catcher"

(2008), and "Fall in Love" (2010). Mak is survived by his wife and two children.

Malaret, Marisol

Puerto Rican television personality Marisol Malaret, who was crowned Miss Universe in 1970, died of a heart condition in San Juan, Puerto Rico, on March 19, 2023. She

was 73. Malaret was born in Utuado, Puerto Rico, on October 13, 1949. She worked as a secretary for the Puerto Rico Telephone Company before winning the Miss Puerto Rico pageant in 1970. She became the first Puerto Rican to be crown Miss Universe in July of 1970. Her newly found fame led to commercial endorsements and television appearances, including "The Merv Griffin Show" and co-hosting the variety series "Noche de Gala" ("Gala Night"). She also appeared in the 1971 film "Mami". Malaret opened a fashion boutique, La Femme, in San Juan in 1973 and was a co-founder and editor of the fashion magazines "Imagen" and "Caras de Puerto Rico" in the mid-1980s. She was married and divorced from Corky Stroman and Butch James. She is survived by her daughter, Sasha Stroman, and her third husband, Frank Cue.

Malcolm, Graeme

Scottish actor Graeme Malcolm died in New York City on January 10, 2023. He was 71. Malcolm was born in Dunfermline, Scotland, on July 31, 1951. He moved to New York City in the early 1980s where he performed frequently on

stage. He appeared in such Broadway productions as "Death and the King's Horseman" (1987), "Sherlock's Last Case" (1987), "The King and I" (1996), "Aida" (2000), "The Real Thing" (2000), "Translations" (2007), and "Equus" (2008). He was featured in the national tour of "M. Butterfly". He was seen on television in episodes of "As the World Turns", "Crossbow", "Law & Order: Criminal Intent", "Whoopi", "Law & Order", "Gray Matters", "Boardwalk Empire", "The Blacklist", and "The Good Wife". He also appeared in the 1995 tele-film "Follow the River". Malcolm was featured in the films "The Break" (1997), "The Adventures of Sebastian Cole" (1998), "The Eden Myth" (1999), "Everything's Jake" (2000), "Endsville" (2000), "Si' Laraby" (2003), "The Reality Trap" (2005), "In the Blood" (2006), "Rosencrantz and Guildenstern Are Undead" (2009), "The Extra Man" (2010), and "Girl Most Likely" (2012). Malcolm was noted for his work in audiobooks, narrating over 160 titles. He is survived by his two daughters.

Mang Hoi

Hong Kong actor Mang Hoi died of esophageal cancer in Hong Kong on October 9, 2023. He was 65. Mang was born in Hong Kong on May 1, 1958. He began his career in films as a juvenile in the early 1970s. He was seen in the films "Lin Chong Ye Ben" (1972), "Xiao du Long" (1972), "The Human Goddess" (1972), "Enter the Dragon" (1973), "Brue Lee and I" (1973), "Thunderfist" (1973), "Fighting Dragon vs. the Deadly Tiger"(1974), "Little Superman" (1974), "Xiangang Xiao Jiao Fu"(1974), "The Silent Guest from Peking" (1975),"Hot Potato" (1976), "Challenge of the Masters"(1976), and "Kung-Fu Sting" (1976). He continued to work as an actor and sometime stunt coordinator in action films from the mid-1970s. His credits include "Kidnap in Rome" (1976), "Executioners from Shaolin" (1977), "The Shaolin Plot" (1977), "The Fatal Flying Guillotines" (1977), "He Has Nothing But Kung Fu" (1977), "Zhui Long" (1977), "Enter the Fat Dragon" (1978), "Dirty Tiger, Crazy Frog" (1978), "Za Ma" (1978), "Warriors Two" (1978), "Way of the Black Dragon" (1978), "The Dragon and the Tiger Kids" (aka "Hell's Windstaff") (1979), "He Xing Dao Shou Tang Lang Tui" (1979), "The Buddha Assassinator" (1980), "The Ring of Death" (1980), "Hitman in the Hand of Buddha" (1981), "Dragon Lord" (1982), "Ninja in the Dragon's Den" (1982), "Esprit D'amur" (1983), "Zu: Warriors from the Magic Mountain" (1983), "Double Trouble" (1984), "Twinkle Twinkle Lucky Stars" (1985), "For Your Heart Only" (1985), "No Retreat, No Surrender" (1985), "Heart of the Dragon" (1985), "Yes, Madam!" (1985), "Millionaires' Express" (1986), "Royal Warriors" (1986), "Righting Wrongs" (1986), "Legacy of Rage" (1986), "No Retreat, No Surrender 2" (1987), "My Cousin, the Ghost" (1987), "Dragons Forever" (1988), "Profiles of Pleasure" (1988), "Mr. Vampire Saga IV" (1988), "Keep on Dancing" (1988), "Pedicab Driver" (1989), "Lady Reporter" (1989) which he also directed, "Encounter of the Spooky Kind II" (1989), "Framed" (1989), "She Shoots Straight" (1990), "Shanghai Shanghai" (1990), "The Nocturnal Demon" (1990), "The Gambling Ghost" (1991), "Mi Zong Wei Long" (1991) which he also directed, "Spiritually a Cop" (1991), "Au Revoir Mon Amour" (1991), "City Hunter" (1993), "Fight Back to School III" (1993), "Deadly Melody" (1994), "The Blade" (1995), "The Stunt Woman" (1996), "Moumantai" (1999), "Perfect Education 3" (2002), "Osaka Wrestling Restaurant" (2004), "Ip Man: The Final Fight" (2013), and "Kung Fu Jungle" (2014). Mang also appeared on television in the series "Vampire Expert" in 1995. He is survived by his wife and daughter.

Manny the Frenchie

French bulldog and internet celebrity Manny the Frenchie died in Chicago, Illinois, on June 21, 2023. He was 12. Manny was born in Chicago on February 7, 2011. He was

owned by Amber Chavez and Jon Huang and was named after Filipino boxer Manny Pacquiao. He began appearing on social media in December of 2014 with accounts on Facebook, Twitter, and Instagram. He became one of the internet's most beloved bulldogs, with his likeness on calendars, tote bags, and pillows. He made numerous personal appearances in support of charities. Manny was a model for Martha Stewart's line of Petsmart products and appeared on "The Steve Harvey Show" on television. He was credited for writing his own book, "Manny the Frenchie's Art of Happiness", in 2017.

Mantaur

Professional wrestler Mike Halac, who competed in the WWE under the name Mantaur, died at his home in Cape Coral, Florida, on July 11, 2023. He was 55. Halac was born

in Omaha, Nebraska, on May 14, 1968. He began wrestling under the name Bruiser Mastino in the early 1990s. He competed with the Catch Wrestling Association (CWA) in Germany from 1991 to 1994. He returned to the United States and joined the World Wrestling Federation (now WWE). He initially wrestled under the Bruiser Masino name before being introduced as Mantaur in early 1995. His minotaur-like character charged and trampled his opponents while mooing at them in the ring. He was managed by Jim Cornette and lost an Intercontinental Championship match against Razor Ramon. He left the WWE later in the year and resumed the Mastino name in Extreme Championship Wrestling (ECW). He briefly returned to the WWE in April of 1996 and an unnamed bodyguard for Goldust in his feud with the Ultimate Warrior. He was known as the masked Tank when he entered the United States Wrestling Association in 1997 as a member of the Truth Commission. He defeated Jerry Lawler for the USWA Unified World Heavyweight Championship in March of 1997 but lost the title back in a return match the following week. He and the Truth Commission briefly competed in the WWE in June of 1997. He was again Bruiser Mastino when he returned to Germany and the CWA. He also wrestled for NWA Germany and the European Wrestling Promotion (EWP). He continued to wrestle in the United States on the independent circuit from 2006 to 2019 under the names Mastino, the Turkish Terror Madd Mustafa, and Mantaur. Halac was part of a 2016 class action lawsuit against the WWE concerning wrestler with traumatic brain injuries during their time with the company, but the case was dismissed in September of 2018.

Mantle, Doreen

South African-British actress Doreen Mantle died in England on August 9, 2023. She was 97. Mantle was born in Johannesburg, South Africa, on June 22, 1926. She attended the University of the Witwatersrand and performed on the amateur stage and radio in South Africa. She moved the London in the late 1940s where she continued her career on stage with a repertory company in Colchester. She worked frequently on stage throughout her career, appearing in productions of "My Fair Lady", "The Seagull", "Billy Liar", and "Death of a Salesman". Mantle was seen frequently on television from the 1960s with roles in episodes of "Emergency-Ward II", "Uncle Charles", "W. Somerset Maugham", "Strange Report", "Six Days of Justice", "Kate", "Love Story", "Public Eye", "Armchair 30", "Special Branch", "The Song of Songs", "Marked Personal", "Intimate Strangers", "The Duchess of Duke Street", "All Creatures Great and Small", "Eleanor Marx", "Headmaster", "Esther Waters", "Crown Court", "Secret Army", "Thomas and Sarah", "Mystery!: Malice Aforethought", "Play for Today", "Secret Orchards", "Lady Killers", "The Gentle Touch", "BBC2 Playhouse", "The Home Front", "Connie", "Summer Season", "Screenplay", "Sunday Premiere", "Screen Two", "Lovejoy", "Mr. Wakefield's Crusade", "Sam Saturday" as Rita Sterne in 1992, "Peak Practice", "Class Act", "The Vet", "Chalk", "The Wild House", "Where the Heart Is", "One Foot in the Grave" as Mrs. Warboys from 1999 to 2000, "Casualty", "The Bill", "Shadow Play" as Queen Victoria in 2004, "Doc Martin", "Hustle", "Love Soup", "The Sarah Jane Adventures", "Clatterford" as Queenie from 2006 to 2008, "Holby City", "The Queen", "Jonathan Creek", "Dirk Gently", "Coronation Street" as Joy Fishwick from 2010 to 2011, "My Family", "The Mimic", "Inspector Lewis", "Father Brown", and "Doctors". Her other television credits include productions of "Passage to India" (1965), "Vienna 1900" (1973), "Bill Brand" (1976), "Secret Orchards" (1979), "Pride and Prejudice" (1980), "St Ursula's in Danger" (1983), "Charlie" (1984), "Home Video" (1984), "Bon Voyage" (1985), "Stanley and the Women" (1991), "The Secret Agent" (1992), "Nice Town" (1992), "Our Friends in the North" (1996), "Twenty Thousand Streets Under the Sky" (2005), "Brief Encounters" (2006), and "Bonekickers" (2008). She was heard in the BBC Radio 4 comedy series "The Attractive Young Rabbi" from 1999 to 2002. Mantle was featured in such films as "Privilege" (1967), "Frenzy" (1972), "Black Jack" (1979), "The French Lieutenant's Woman" (1981), "Yentl" (1983) as Mrs. Shaemen opposite Barbra Streisand, "Mountains of the Moon" (1990), "The Turn of the Screw" (1992), "A Man You Don't Meet Every Day" (1994), "In Love and War" (1996), "So This Is Romance?" (1997), "Suzie Gold" (2004), "Scoop" (2006), "Two Ladies and a Hill" (2010), "Late Bloomers" (2011), "The Owner" (2012), and "55

Steps" (2017). Mantle married Joshua Graham Smith in 1954 and they had two children before their divorce.

Maraden, Marti

American-Canadian actress Marti Maraden died while visiting family in Sweden on August 31, 2023. She was 78. She was born in El Centro, California, on June 22, 1945, and was raised in Minneapolis, Minnesota. She moved to Canada in 1968 with her then husband, Frank Maraden, who was seeking to avoid the draft. She performed frequently with the Stratford Festival in the 1970s, starring in productions of "Love's Labour's Lost", "The Tempest", "Hamlet", "Three Sisters", and "King Lear". She moved to New York in 1979, where she taught and directed before returning to Canada. She was featured in the 1983 film "The Wars". Maraden was seen on television in episodes of "The Beachcombers", "The Campbells", and "Street Legal", and the tele-films "A Child's Christmas in Wales" (1987) and "Mask of the Bear" (1988). She served as artistic director of the National Arts Centre English Theatre in Ottawa from 1997 to 2006. She briefly was co-artistic director of the Stratford Shakespeare Theatre in 2006. She continued to direct and perform in theaters throughout Canada during her career.

Marchand, Guy

French actor Guy Marchand, who starred in the "Nestor Burma" detective television series in the 1990s, died in Cavaillon, France, on December 15, 2023. He was 86. Marchand was born in Paris, France, on May 22, 1937. He studied at the Lycee Voltaire and played the clarinet at jazz clubs. He served as a liaison officer with the French army during the Algerian war. He was a parachute officer and was an advisor for the 1962 film "The Longest Day". He soon embarked on a career in entertainment and was a popular singer in the early 1960s. He recorded the hit song "La Passionata" in 1965. He became a popular supporting actor with role in such films as "Rum Runners" (1971), "A Gorgeous Girl Like Me" (1972), the romantic comedy "Cousin Cousine" (1975), "Let's Make a Dirty Movie" (1976), "L'Acrobate" (1976), "Le Grand Escogriffe" (1976), "Dear Inspector" (1977), "L'Hotel de la Plage" (1978), "Take It from the Top" (1978), "Le Maitre Nageur" (1979), "The Big Red One" (1980), "Loulou" (1980), "Rends-Moi la cle!" (1981), "Heat of Desire" (1981), Claude Miller's "The Grilling" (1981) earning a Cesar Award for his role as a police inspector, Bertrand Tavernier's "Coup de Torchon" (1981), "Les Sous-Doues en Vacances" (1982), "Nestor Burma, Detective de Choc" (1982), "T'es Heureuse? Moi, Toujours..." (1983), the thriller "Deadly

Circuit" (1983), "Entre Nous" (1983), "Petit Con" (1984), "Stress" (1984), "La Tete dans le Sac" (1984), "Hold-Up" (1985), "Vaudeville" (1986), "Family Council" (1986), "I Hate Actors" (1986), "La Rumba" (1987), "Grand Guignol" (1987), "L'ete en Pente Douce" (1987), "Chateauroux District" (1987), "Charlie Dingo" (1987), "Noyade Interdite" (1987), "L'ile Aux Oiseaux" (1988), "Bonjour l'Angoisse" (1988), "Les Maris, les Femmes, les Amants" (1989), "Coupe-Franche" (1989), "Un Pere et Passe" (1989), "Try This One for Size" (1989), "My New Partner at the Races" (1990), "New World" (1995), "Beaumarchais the Scoundrel" (1996), "Le Plus Beau Metier du Monde" (1996), "La Boite" (2001), "Stolen Tangos" (2001), "My Wife Maurice" (2002), "Dans Paris" (2006), "Paid" (2006), "Apres Lui" (2007), "Passe-Passe" (2008), "L'Arbre et la Foret" (2010), "The Dune" (2013), "Calomnies" (2014), "The Easy Way Out" (2014), "Paris-Willouby" (2015), "Hibue" (2016), "Just to Be Sure" (2017), "Looking for Teddy" (2018), "Heavy Duty" (2019), "Tout Nous Sourit" (2020), "Country Cabaret" (2022), and "La Plus Belle Pour Aller Danser" (2023). Marchand appeared on television in productions of "Saint-Tropez Priez Pour Eux" (1968), "Fragson, un Roi du Caf'conc'" (1969) , "Fin de Saison" (1973), "Musidora" (1973), "Le Pain Noir" (1975), "Le coeur au Ventre" (1976), "Marions les Vivantes!..." (1976), "La Mort Amoureuse" (1977), "La Voie Jackson" (1981), "Les Heroiques" (1981), "Le Petit Mitchell Illustre" (1981), "Trois Morts a Zero" (1983), "L'Homme de la Nuit" (1983), "L'Homme de Suez" (1983) as Ferdinand de Lesseps, "Le Tueur Triste" (1984), "Cinema" (1988), "Have a Nice Night" (1990), "Le Denier du Colt" (1990), "May Wine" (1990), "Bonjour la Galere" (1991), "La Memoire" (1992), "Runaway to Re" (1999), "Toute la Ville en Parle" (2000), "Suite en Re" (2000), "L'Ete Rouge" (2002), "Les Passeurs" (2004), "Pardon" (2004), "3 Jours en Juin" (2005), "The Condor Mystery" (2005), "La Fille du Chef" (2007), "Un Crime Tres Populaire" (2008), "Mother at 40" (2010), "La Residence" (2011), "Torn" (2018), and "La Derniere Partie" (2021). His other television credits include episodes of "Les Cinq Dernieres Minutes", "Actung Zoll!" as L'Inspecteur Mathieu in 1981, "L'Oeil de la Nuit", "L'Homme de la Nuit", "Sueurs Froides", "L'Histoire du Samedi", "Le Crocodile", "All Saints", "Nestor Burma" as private detective Nestor Burma from 1991 to 2003, "Fargas", "Le Grand Restaurant", "Doc Martin", "Scenes de Menages", "Nos Chers Voisins", "Call My Agent!" as Guy Marchand from 2017 to 2018, and "Priere d'Enqueter". Marchand's autobopgraphy, "Le Guignol des Buttes-Chaumont", was published in 2007. He also wrote the novels "A Razor in the Hands of a Monkey" (2008) and "The Sun of Lost Children" (2011).

Marescotti, Ivano

Italian actor Ivano Marescotti died of prostate cancer in Ravenna, Italy, on March 26, 2023. He was 77. Marescotti was orn in Villanova di Bagnacavallo, Italy, on February 4, 1946. He worked as a clerk in Ravenna before pursuing an acting career in the 1980s. He began performing on the amateur stage and was soon appearing at leading theatrical venues. He was featured in numerous films during his career including

"Ginger & Fred" (1986), "The Belt" (1989), "Tre Colonne in Cronaca" (1990), "L'Aria Serena dell'Ovest" (1990), "The Yes Man" (1991), "Il Caso Martello" (1990), "The Invisible Wall" (1991), "Especially on Sunday" (1991), "Notte di Stelle"

(1991), "Corsica" (1991), "Johnny Stecchino" (1991), "Prova di Memoria" (1992), "Quatro Figli Unici" (1992), "Gangsters" (1992), "Il Richiamo" (1992), "Il Lungo Silenzio" (1993), "Tra Due Risvegli" (1993), "Un'anima Divisa in Due" (1993), "Da Qualche Parte in Citta" (1994), "Dichiarazioni d'Amore" (1994), "I Pavoni" (1994), "Weird Tales" (1994), "The Monster" (1994), "Mario and the Magician" (!994), "Italian Village" (1994), "Terra Bruciata" (1995), "Who Killed Pasolini?" (1995), "God Willing" (1995), "Il Cielo e Sempre Piu Blu" (1996), "Italiani" (1996), "Jack Frusciante Has Left the Band" (1996), "Vesna Goes Fast" (1996), "Luna e l'Altra" (1996), "Acquario" (1996), "Messaggi Quasi Segreti" (1996), "Corti Stellari" (1997), "Consigli per Gli Acquisti" (1997), "Sorrisi Asmatici - Fiori del Destino" (1997), "Corti Stellari 2" (1998), "Asini" (1999), "The Talented Mr. Ripley" (1999) starring Matt Damon, "Twenty" (2000), "La Lingua del Santo" (2000), "Hannibal" (2001) starring Anthony Hopkins, "Come Si Fa un Martini" (2001), "Brazilero" (2001), "Un Delitto Impossibile" (2001), "Sei Come Sei" (2002), "The Legend of All, John and Jack" (2002), "The Wind in the Evening" (2004), "King Arthur" (2004) starring Clive Owen, "Berbablu" (2004), "The Moon and the Stars" (2007), "Italian Dream" (2007), "The Right Distance" (2007), "Oliviero Rising" (2007), "Lezioni di Cioccolato" (2007), "Albakiara" (2008), "Questo Piccolo Grande Amore" (2009), "Fort Apache Napoli" (2009), "Cado Dalle Nubi" (2009), "M.A.R.C.O." (2010), "What a Beautiful Day" (2011), "La Vita Facile" (2011), "Vacanze di Natale a Cortina" (2011), "All'ultima Spiaggia" (2012), "La Linea Gialla: Bologna, 2 Agosto" (2015), "Them Who?" (2015), "Nobili Bugie" (2017), "Il Crimine Non Va in Pensione" (2017), "There's No Place Like Home" (2018), "Un Figlio a Tutti i Costi" (2018), "Lovers" (2018), "Restiamo Amici" (2018), "Bentornato Presidente" (2019), "Tutto Liscio" (2019), "Il Conte Magico" (2018), "Bra Joseph" (2019), "Free - Liberi" (2020), and "Criminali Si Diventa" (2021). Marescotti appeared on television in productions of "Una Prova d'Innocenza" (1991), "Una Vita in Gioco 2" (1992), "Il Giovane Mussolini" (1993), "Ci Sara un Giorno (Il Giovane Pertini)" (1993), "Le Chateau des Oliviers" (1993), "Cuore di Ghiaccio" (2006), "E Pol c'e Filippo" (2006), "Il Pirata: Marco Pantani" (2007), "Chiara e Francesco" (2007), "Codice Aurora" (2008), "Una Buona Stagione" (2014), "Il Bosco" (2015), "Meraviglie: La Penisola dei Tesori" (2018), "Stanotte a Pompei" (2018), and "Din Don - Il Ritorno" (2019). His other television credits include episodes of "La Neve nel Bicchiere", "Verkaufte Heimat", "La Piovra" as Bellini the photographer in 1992, "Un Copmmissario a Roma", "I Ragazzi del Muretto", "Il Mastino", "Nebbie e Delitti", "Raccontami" as

Livio Sartori from 2006 to 2008, "I Liceali" as Prof. Gualtiero Cavicchioli from 2008 to 2011, "Che Cio Ci Aiuti" as Achille Gentileschi in 2014, "Don Matteo", and "Makari".

Mariuzzo, Giorgio

Italian screenwriter Giorgio Mariuzzo, who worked with director Lucio Fulci on the horror films "The Beyond" and "The House by the Cemetery", died in San Colombano al Lambro, Italy, on January 16, 2023. He was 83. Mariuzzo was  born in Venice, Italy, on July 7, 1939. He began working in films in the late 1960s as an assistant director and screenwriter for "Interrabang" (1969), "Dario di un Ialiano" (1972), "Ancora Una Volta Prima di Lasciarci" (1973), "Il Sergente Rompiglioni" (1973), "The Shameless" (1974), "Five Women for the Killer" (1974), "The Hallucinating Trip" (1975), and "Under the Sheets" (1976). Mariuzzo directed and wrote several films, some under the name George McRoots, including "Quelli Belli... Siamo Noi" (1971), "Mondo Porno Oggi" (1976), "Apache Woman" (1976), and Orazi e Curiazi 3-2" (1977). He also scripted the films "Decemeroticus" (1972), "The Novice" (1975), "Under the Sheets" (1976), 'The Novice" (1975), "Tre Sotto il Lenzuolo" (1979), "L'Insegnante al Mare Con Tutta la Classe" (1980), "Contraband" (1980), "La Moglie in Vacanza... l'Amante in Citta" (1980), and "La Moglie in Bianco... l'Amante al Pepe" (1981). Mariuzzo was best known for scripting Lucio Fulci's horror films "The Beyond" (aka "E Tu Vivrai Nel Terrore! L'Aldila") (1981), "The House by the Cemetery" (aka "Quella Villa Accanto al Cimitero") (1981), and "Aenigma" (1987). He also wrote numerous comedies and other films including "My Wife Goes Back to School" (1981), "Crema, Cioccolataa e Pa... Prika" (1981), "Pierino Medico Della SAUB" (1981), "I Carabbimatti" (1981), "Pierino la Peste alla Riscossa" (1982), "Cicciabomba" (1982), "Zero in Condotta" (1983), and "Festa di Capocanno" (1992). Mariuzzo worked frequently in television writing such productions of "Un Uomo da Ridere" (1980), "Alla Conquista di Roma" (1985), "Andi Si Nasce" (1985) which he also directed, "Doppio Misto" (1985), "Cena per Lui" (1986) which he also directed, "Ferragosto O.K." (1986), "La Famaglia Brandacci" (1987), "Diciottani - Versilia 1966" (1988), "E Non Se Ne Vogliono Andare!" (1988), "Una Casa a Roma" (1989), "E Se Poi Se Ne Vanno?" (1989), "Doris Una Diva del Regime" (1991), "Un Cane Sciolto 3" (1992), "Un Figlio a Meta" (1992), "Un Figlio a Meta un Anno Dopo" (1994), "Italian Restaurant" (1994), "Natale con Papa" (1995), "Linda e il Brigadiere" (1997), "Un Prete Tra Noi" (1997), "Il Mastino" (1998), "Il Fondo al Cuore" (1998), "Trenta Righe Per un Delitto" (1998), "Cronaca Nera" (1998), "Commesse" (1999), "Mio Figlio Ha 70 Anni" (1999), "Qualcuno da Amare" (2000), "La Memoria e il Perdono" (2001), "Mai Storie d'Amore in Cucina" (2004), "Enrico Mattei: The Man Who Looked to the Future" (2009), and "Il Restauratore" (2012). He is survived by his wife, screenwriter Paola Pascolini.

Marks, Eddie

Film costumer Eddie Marks, who was president of Western Costume Company, died while visiting Prague, Czechoslovakia, on September 11, 2023. He was 76. Marks  was born in Bayonne, New Jersey, on July 1, 1947. He moved to Los Angeles with his family in 1952. He began working in the mailroom at MGM Studios in 1965 and was soon working in the costume department for such Elvis Presley films as "Girl Happy" (1965), "Spinout" (1966), and "Stay Away, Joe" (1968). Mark worked freelance as a costumer from the early 1970s on such films as "A Man Called Horse" (1970), "Zig Zag" (1970), "Top of the Heap" (1972), "Bonnie's Kids" (1972), "Girls on the Road" (1972), "Detroit 9000" (1973), "Coma" (1978), "The China Syndrome" (1979), "Melvin and Howard" (1980), "Where the Buffalo Roam" (1980), "It's My Turn" (1980), "Taps" (1981), "Eddie Macon's Run" (1983), "Doctor Detroit" (1983), "All the Right Moves" (1983), "Revenge of the Nerds" (1984), "The Adventures of Buckaroo Banzai Across the 8th Dimension" (1984), "Windy City" (1984), "The Breakfast Club" (1985), "Cocoon" (1985), "Wildcats" (1986), "The Karate Kid Part II" (1986), "The Golden Child" (1986), "The Witches of Eastwick" (1987), "The Couch Trip" (1988), "Funny Farm" (1988), "Arthur 2: On the Rocks" (1988), "Troop Beverly Hills" (1989), "Indiana Jones and the Last Crusade" (1989), "Dead Poets Society" (1989), "National Lampoon's Christmas Vacation" (1989), and "Postcards from the Edge" (1990). He was costume supervisor for the television series "The Streets of San Francisco", "The MacKenzies of Paradise Cove", "The White Shadow", and "The Devlin Connection". He also worked on the tele-films and mini-series "Samurai" (1979), "Masada" (1981), and "Shakedown on the Sunset Strip" (1988) earning an Emmy Award. Marx headed Western Costume Company from 1989 and helped it become the world's largest costume company. He is survived by his wife, Debby, and two sons.

Marsden, Bernie

British guitarist Bernie Marsden, who was noted for his work with the band Whitesnake, died of bacterial meningitis in England on August 24, 2023. He was 72. Marsden was born in Buckingham, England, on May 7, 1951. He began playing with local bands while in his teens including Clockwork Mousetrap and Skinny Cat. He played with the bands UFO, Glenn Cornick's Wild Turkey, and Cozy Powell's Hammer in the early 1970s. He joined Babe Ruth in 1975 and played on their albums "Stealin' Home" (1975) and "Kid's Stuff" (1976). Marsden joined the group Paice Ashton Lord in 1976 and performed on their album "Malice in Wonderland" before the band folded. He joined with singer David Coverdale and guitarist Micky Moody to form the band Whitesnake in 1978. He was writer or co-writer, with Coverdale, of many of the band's hit songs including "Fool for Your Loving", "Walking in the Shadow of the Blues", "Ready

an' Willing", "Lovehunter", "Trouble", and "Here I Go Again". He was heard on Whitesnake's albums "Snakebite" (1978), "Trouble" (1978), "Lovehunter" (1979), "Ready an' Willing" (1980), "Live... in the Heart of the City" (1980), "Come an' Get It" (1981), and "Saints & Sinners" (1982) before departing the group. He also recorded the solo albums "And About Time Too" (1979) and "Look at Me Now" (1981). He subsequently formed the short-lived band Bernie Marsden's SOS. He joined singer Robert Hawthorne and keyboardist Richard Bailey in the band Alaska. They had two albums, "Heart of the Storm" (1984) and "The Pack" (1985), before disbanding. He reunited with Whitesnake bandmate Neil Murray and guitarist Mel Galley for the short-lived band MGM in 1986. He and Moody formed the Moody Marsden band in 1989 and toured Europe. They released the studio album "Real Faith" in 1994. They were joined by Norwegian singer Jorn Lande for the band the Snakes and released the 1998 album "Once Bitten". A lineup change resulted in the group's renaming as the Company of Snakes, and they released the albums "Here They Go Again (2001) and "Burst the Bubble" (2002). They became known as M3 for the album "Rough an' Ready" in 2005. Marsden produced a series of blues albums in the 2000s including "Big Boy Blue" (2003) and "Stacks" (2005). He also recorded with the artists Gary Fletcher, Jimmy Copley Tony Ashton, Don Alrey, and Jack Bruce. His later solo albums from Conquest Music include "Kings" (2021), "Chess" (2021), and "Trios" (2022). Marsden married Fran Plummer in 1980 and is survived by her and their two daughters.

Martin, Eugenio

Spanish film director Eugenio Martin Marquez, who was noted for the 1972 horror film "Horror Express", died in

Madrid, Spain, on January 23, 2023. He was 97. Martin was born in Ceuta, Spain, on May 15, 1925. He moved to Granada with his family during the Spanish Civil War. He attended the Universidad de Granada where he formed a film society. He trained at the Institute of Cinematic Investigation and Experiences in Madrid. He directed and wrote the short films "Viaje Romantico a Granada" (1955), "Adios, Rosita (Vieja Farsa Andaluza)" (1956), and "Romance de Una Batalla" (1956). Martin served as an assistant director for the fantasy

films "The 7th Voyage of Sinbad" (1958) and "The 3 Worlds of Gulliver" (1960). He made his feature debut as director with 1961's "Despedida de Soltero". He continued to direct, and frequently write, such films as "Conqueror or Maracaibo" (1961), "Hypnosis" (1962), "Golden Goddess of Rio Beni" (1964), "Captain from Toledo" (1965), "The Ugly Ones" (aka "The Bounty Killers") (1966) the first of several spaghetti westerns, "Requiem for a Gringo" (1968), "Las Leandras" (1969), "La Vida Sigue Igual" (1969), Una Senora Estupenda" (1970), "The Fourth Victimm" (1971), "Bad Man's River" (1971) starring Lee Van Cleef and Gina Lollobrigida, the horror film "Horror Express" (1972) starring Christopher Lee and Peter Cushing, "Pancho Villa" (1972) starring Tella Savalas in the title role, the horror film "A Candle for the Devil" (aka "It Happened at Nightmare Inn") (1973), "The Girl from the Red Cabaret" (1973) starring Mel Ferrer, "No Quiero Perder la Honra" (1975), "Esclava te Doy" (1976), "Call Girl (Laa Vida Privada de Una Senoirta Bien)" (1976), "Tengamos la Guerra en Paz" (1977), "Aquella Casa en las Fueras" (1980), "Sobrenatural" (1981), and "La Sal de la Vida" (1996). He directed the television mini-series "Juanita la Larga" (1982) and "Visperas" (1987). Martin married actress Lone Fleming in 1970 and she survives him.

Martin, Peter

British actor Peter Martin, who starred as Len Reynolds on the soap opera "Emmerdale" from 2001 to 2007, died in England on April 19, 2023. He was 81. Martin was born in Gainsborough, Lincolnshire, England, in December of 1941. He began his acting career in the 1960s and appeared

frequently on television. He was seen in episodes of "The Persuaders!", "The Wild West Show", "Rosie", "The Liver Birds", "BBC2 Playhouse", "Play for Today", "All for Love", "Strangers", "Juliet Bravo", "Studio", "The Gaffer", "The Outsider", "The Gathering Seed", "One by One", "Hallelujah!", "The Man from Moscow", "In Loving Memory", "Langley Bottom", "The Return of the Antelope", "Victoria Wood: As Seen on TV", "Screen Two", "Truckers", "The New Statesman", "First of the Summer Wine", "How to Be Cool", "A Bit of a Do", "Snakes and Ladders", "Victoria Wood", "Coronation Street", "Bergerac", "All Creatures Great and Small" in the recurring role of Mr. Hartley from 1988 to 1990, "Stay Lucky", "ChuckleVision", "2point4 Children", "Heartbeat", "Mother's Ruin", "Cardiac Arrest", "Last of the Summer Wine", "Dalziel and Pascoe", "Where the Heart Is", "Playing the Field" as Harry Laycock from 1998 to 1999, "dinnerladies", "City Central", "Peak Practice", "Casualty", "Water Rats", "Skins", "Walk Like a Panther", and "Doctors". He was featured as Joe Carroll, the Royle's neighbor, on the comedy series "The Royle Family" from 1998 to 2012 and was Len Reynolds in the soap opera "Emmerdale" from 2001 to 2007. Martin's other television credits include productions of "Bill Brand" (1976), "Hard Times" (1977), "The Hills of Heaven" (1978), "Nearly a Happy Ending" (1980), "Benefit of a Doubt" (1984), "Fell Tiger" (1985), "Hideaway" (1986), "First Among Equals" (1986), "The Day After the Fair" (1986), "The Beiderbecke Tapes" (1987), "The Beiderbecke Connection" (1988), "Shadow of the Noose" (1989), "Dancing Queen" (1993), and "Reckless" (1997). He was featured in a handful of films during his career including "A Matter of Innocence" (1967), "The Bronte Sisters" (1979), "Wetherby" (1985), "Ladder of Swords" (1989), "Funny Bones" (1995), "Brassed Off" (1996), "The Parole Officer" (2010), the short "Trailing Dirt" (2010), and "Walk Like a Panther" (2018). Martin was noted for his role as a confused customer in a series to television commercials for Jewsons Hardware in the 1980s.

Marx, Sue

Documentary filmmaker Sue Marx died in Birmingham, Michigan, on July 17, 2023. She was 92. She was born Suzanne Gothelf in Yonkers, New York, on November 17, 1930. She was raised in Wisconsin and Indiana

and graduated from the University of Indiana in 1952. She worked for an advertising agency in Chicago after college before settling in Detroit. She taught English in the Royal Oak suburb school district and continued her education at Wayne State University, earning a master's degree in sociology. She became interested in photography while working as a model and

became a leading freelance photographer. She became a news producer at WDIV-TV where she produced the series "Profiles in Black". She founded Sue Marx Films, Inc., in 1980, which produced numerous award-winning films and videos. She received the Academy Award for Best Documentary Short for her 1988 film "Young at Heart", which featured a romance between two octogenarians, her widowed father Lou Gothelf, and artist Reva Shwayder. Marx also produced a series of educational films for the Detroit Zoo and the tourism video "It's a Great Time in Detroit" for the Detroit Convention Bureau in 1998. She was married to Stanley 'Hank' Marx from 1953 until his death in 2007 and is survived by their three daughters.

Marziali, Marcello

Italian actor Marcello Marziali died in Livorno, Italy,

on December 1, 2023. He was 84. Marziali was born in Italy in 1939. He began acting later in life in the 1980s and performed on stage in Livorno. He appeared in several films including "Jesus" (1999), "Under the Tuscan Sun" (2003), and "Pinocchio" (2019) starring Roberto Benigni as Geppetto. He was also seen on television in an

episode of "Il Commissario Manara" and the 2019 mini-series "The New Pope". Marziali was best known for his role as Gino Rimediotti in the television series "I Delitti del BarLume" from 2013 to 2023.

Maselli, Francesco

Italian film director Francesco Maselli died in Rome, Italy, on March 21, 2023. He was 92. Maselli was born in Rome on December 9, 1930. He graduated from the Italian National Film School in 1949 and began his career as an assistant director for Michelangelo Antonioni on the short film

"Lies of Love" (1949) and the features "Story of a Love Affair" (1950) and "The Lady Without Camelias" (1953). He was also assistant director for the films "Patto Col Diavolo" (1949), "Three Girls from Rome" (1952), and "We, the Women" (1953). Maselli directed short films and documentaries from the late 1940s including "Tibet Proibito" (1949), "Finestre" (1950), "Bagnaia, Villagia Italiano" (1951), "Bambini" (1952), "Sport Minore" (1952), "Niente Va Perduto" (1952), "Ombreilai" (1952), "Zona Periscolosa" (1952), "Fioraie" (1953), "Love in the City (1953), "Citta Che Dorme" (1953), "Cantamaggio a Cervarezza" (1954), "Festa dei Morti in Siciia" (1955), "Uno Spettacolo di Pupi" (1955), "Campioni per Due Ore" (1957), "I Bambini al Cinema" (1958), "I Bambini e Gli Animali" (1958), "Un Fatto di Cronaca" (1958), "Adolescenza" (1959), and "La Scuola Romana" (1959). He made his feature debut with the 1955 World War II drama "Gli Sbandati" (aka "Abandoned"). He directed the dramas "The Doll That Took the Town" (1957) starring Virna Lisi and "Silver Spoon Set" (aka "The Dolphins") (1960) starring Claudia Cardinale. He helmed the 1964 film adaptation of Alberto Moravia's novel "Gli Indifferenti" (aka "Time of Indifference") starring Cardinale, Rod Steiger, Shelley Winters, and Paulette Goddard. Maselli was a member of the Communist Party from his youth and his films became increasingly political by the 1970s. He continued to direct "Fai in Fretta ad Uccidermi... Ho Freddo!" (1967), "A Fine Pair" (1968), the semi-autobiographical "Lettera Aperta a un Giornale Della Sera" (1970), "The Suspect" (1975), "Farewell to Enrico Berlinguer" (1984), "Sabatoventiquattromarzo" (1984), "Storia d'Amore" (1986), "Codice Privato" (1988), "Il Segreto" (1990), "L'Alba" (1991), "Roma Dodici Novembre 1994" (1995), "Cronache del Terzo Millennio" (1996), "Intolerance" (1997), "Another World Is Possible" (2001), "Firenze, il Nostro Domani" (2003), "Lettere Dalla Palestina" (2003), "Frammenti di Novecento" (2005), "Civico Zero" (2007), "All Human Rights for All" (2008), and "The Red Shadows" (2009). He appeared as an actor in small roles in several films including "Lettera Aperta a un Giornale Della Sera" (1970), Federico Fellini's "Amarcord" (1973), "La Terrazza" (1980), "And the Ship Sails On" (1983), and "The

Name of the Rose" (1986). Maselli married journalist Stefania Brai in 1986 and she survives him.

Massof, Bill

Actor Bill Massof died of complications from Alzheimer's disease in Manhattan, New York, on December 16,  2023. He was 73. Massof was born in Minneapolis, Minnesota, on January 11, 1950. He graduated from the University of Minnesota, where he earned a master's degree in philosophy. He settled in New York City where he was an actor and model. Massof was seen in the films "Bad Company" (2002), "The Guru" (2002), "The Bourne Ultimatum" (2007), "Burn After Reading" (2008), and "The Beaver" (2011). He appeared on television in episodes of "Law & Order: Special Victims Unit", "Law & Order: Criminal Intent", and "The Marvelous Mrs. Maisel". Massof is survived by his wife, painter Lisa Breslow, and daughter Shawna Lee.

Masters, Ben

Actor Ben Masters, who starred as wealthy womanizer Julian Crane on the soap opera "Passions", died of complications from COVID-19 and dementia in Palm Springs, California, on January 11, 2023. He was 75. Masters was born in Corvallis, Oregon, on May 6, 1947. He graduated from the University of Oregon in 1969 with a degree in theater. He  moved to New York City in 1972 where he appeared on Broadway in productions of "Captain Brassbound's Conversion" (1972), "The Waltz of the Toreadors" (1973), "The Cherry Orchard" (1977), and "Plenty" (1983). Masters appeared in several films during his career including "Mandingo" (1975), "All That Jazz" (1979), "Key Exchange" (1985), "Dream Lover" (1985), and "Making Mr. Right" (1987). He appeared on television in episodes "Kojak" "Petrocelli", "Kolchak: The Night Stalker", "Muggsy" as Nick Malloy from 1976 to 1977, "Barnaby Jones", "Another World" as Vic Strange in 1982, "Heartbeat" as Dr. Leo Rosetti from 1988 to 1989, "Civil Wars", "Crime & Punishment", "Murder, She Wrote", "Walker, Texas Ranger", "Diagnosis Murder", "Sweet Justice", "Kung Fu: The Legend Continues", "Sisters", "Touched by an Angel", "Spy Game", "Profit", and "Pensacola: Wings of Gold". His other television credits include productions of "Duty Bound" (1973), "One of Our Own" (1975), "Mobile Medics" (1976), "Loose Change" (1978), "The Shadow Box" (1980), "Until She Talks" (1981), "The Neighborhood" (1982), "Illusions" (1983), "Celebrity" (1984), "The Deliberate Stranger" (1986), "Kate's Secret" (1986),

"Riviera" (1987), "Noble House" (1988) as corporate raider Linc Bartlett, "Street of Dreams" (1988), "The Keys" (1992), "Cruel Doubt" (1992), "Running Mates" (1992), "A Twist of the Knife" (1993), "A Time to Heal" (1994), "Lady Killer" (1995), and "The Second Civil War" (1997). Masters was best known for his role as billionaire Julian Crane in the daytime soap opera "Passions" from 1999 through 2008.

Mastrogeorge, Harry

Television director and acting teacher Harry Mastrogeorge died in Los Angeles, California, on April 26, 2023. He was 92. Mastrogeorge was born in Pittsburgh,  Pennsylvania, on May 13, 1930. He graduated from the American Academy of Dramatic Arts in New York City in 1950. He began working in films as an extra and performed on stage in regional theater and summer stock in the 1950s. He became an acting teacher in 1956, serving for two years at Brandeis University. He subsequently taught at the American Academy of Dramatic Arts through 1974. He moved to Los Angeles where he continued to teach and direct at the Chamber Theater. Mastrogeorge began directing for television, helming episodes of "The Mary Tyler Moore Show", "Phyllis", "From Here to Eternity", "The Love Boat", "Hart to Hart", "Miami Vice", "Shell Game", and "Scarecrow and Mrs. King". He wrote and directed the 1978 documentary film "Mystery of the Sacred Shroud" and directed the 2001 film "Venus and Mars". He was married to Barbara Mastrogeorge and is survived by their three children.

Matsumoto, Leiji

Japanese manga artist Leiji Matsumoto, who created the science fiction mangas "Space Pirate Captain Harlock" and "Galaxy Express 999", died of heart failure at a hospital in Tokyo, Japan, on February 13, 2023. He was 85. He was born  Akira Matsumoto in Kurume, Japan, on January 25, 1938. He began drawing at an early age and moved to Tokyo to work as a manga artist in the mid-1950s. His first manga, "Mitsubachi No Boken", was published in "Manga Shonen" magazine in 1954. He created the manga "Otoko Oidon" in 1971 and the western comedy "Gun Frontier" for "Play Comic" magazine in 1972. He wrote and illustrated numerous short stories set during World War II from 1972 to 1975 that were collected as "The Cockpit". Matsumoto directed the science fiction anime series "Space Battleship Yamato" (aka "Star Blazers") in 1974. He also created the science fiction mangas "Space Pirate Captain Harlock" and "Galaxy Express 999" in

1977, both of which were adapted for animes. He was involved in the spin-off series "Queen Emeraldas" and "Queen Millennia". Matsumoto created the manga "Space Battleship Great Yamato" from 2000 to 2002 when the courts blocked his copyright to the Yamato franchise. He teamed with artist Koichi Shimahoshi for the manga "Captain Harlock: Dimensional Voyage", a retelling of the original manga, in 2014. He created animated music videos for the French duo Daft Punk including their song "One More Time". They worked together for on the animated DVD "Interstella 5555: The 5tory of the 5ecret 5tar 5ystem". He married fellow manga artist and frequent collaborator Miyako Maki in 1961 and she survives him.

Matt, Joe

Cartoonist Joe Matt, who was noted for the autobiographical comic "Peepshow", died of a heart attack in Los Angeles, California, on September 18, 2023. He was 60. Matt was born in Lansdale, Pennsylvania, on September 3,

1963. He began drawing as a child and graduated from the Philadelphia College of Art. He moved to New York but was unsuccessful at getting a job in magazine illustration. He began working in comics at the Philadelphia comic book store Fat Jack's Comicrypt. He also became as assistant for artist Matt Wagner, a friend from college. He was colorist for Wagner's "Grendel" comic from Comics and the DC crossovers "Batman/Grendel: Devil's Masque" and "Batman/Grendel: Devil's Riddle" in 1993. He also worked on the 1993 comic "Batman: Featuring Two-Face and the Riddler". He continued to work at Comico, coloring Steve Moncuse's "Fish Police", "Jonny Quest", and "Robotech: The Macross Saga". He began work on his autobiographical comic series "Peepshow" in 1987. It was published by Kitchen Sink Press and Drawn & Quarterly. His original series was collected for the 1992 book "Peepshow: The Cartoon Diary of Joe Matt". He continued with the comic and later collections include "The Poor Bastard" (1996), "Fair Weather" (2002), and "Spent" (2007). He became involved with Trish Schutz in 1987 and stayed with her in Toronto, Canada, for over a decade. He returned to the United States in 2002 and settled in Los Angeles. He largely quit producing comics after 2007. Matt died of a heart attack at his drawing table and a posthumous "Peepshow" comic book was scheduled for later publication by Fantagraphics.

Matthews, William F.

Production designer William F. Matthews died in Tulsa, Oklahoma, on December 30, 2023. He was 81. Matthews was born in Marietta, Ohio, on May 7, 1942. He earned a master's degree in theatre design from Carnegie-Mellon University in Pittsburgh. He began his career designing

educational films at PBS and working in stage design for live theater. He moved to Los Angeles in 1979 and worked on numerous film and television productions. He was a set designer for numerous films including "Stripes" (1981),

"Poltergeist" (1982), "Gremlins" (1984), "The Karate Kid" (1984), "In Quiet Night" (1998), "Hollywood Homicide" (2003), "Cheaper by the Dozen" (2003), "Fat Albert" (2004), "King of California" (2007), and "Larry Crowne" (2011). He was a set designer for the television series "Amazing Stories", "The Brotherhood of Poland, New Hampshire", "Boston Legal", "Carnivale", and "Monk", and the mini-series "Godless" (2017) and "The Underground Railroad" (2021). Matthews served as art director or production designer for the films "The Karate Kid Part II" (1986), "Innerspace" (1987), "Happy New Year" (1987), "Three O'Clock High" (1987), "Caddyshack II" (1988), "Hot to Trot" (1988), "The Karate Kid Part III" (1989), "Cranium Command" (1989), "Gross Anatomy" (1989), "The Marrying Man" (1991), "Shout" (1991), "Captain Ron" (1992), "Lookin' Italian" (1994), "Richie Rich" (1994), "Fair Game" (1995), "Bulletproof" (1996), "Out to Sea" (1997), and "Forgetting Sarah Marshall" (2008). He served as production designer for the television series "Beverly Hills, 90210" from 1997 to 2000 and was part of the production staff for "Lost". He was art director for the tele-films "The Flamingo Rising" (2001) and "Astronauts" (2002), and the series "The Book of Daniel" and "Life". He also began painting and assembling works of art in the 1990s and his work was frequently exhibited throughout California. Matthews received the Lifetime Achievement Award in Set Design from the Art Directors Guild in 2019. He married artist Diana Folsom in 2005 and is survived by her and two children.

Mattingly, Ken

Astronaut Ken Mattingly, who was Command Module Pilot for the Apollo 16 lunar mission in 1972, died in Arlington,

Virginia, on October 31, 2023. He was 87. He was born Thomas Kenneth Mattingly II in Chicago, Illinois, on March 17, 1936, and was raised in Hialeah, Florida, where his father worked for Eastern Airlines. He graduated from Auburn University in 1958 with a degree in aeronautical engineering. He joined the U.S. Navy in 1958 and became an aviator in 1960. He flew aircraft aboard the USS Saratoga and the USS Franklin D. Roosevelt in the early 1960s. Mattingly attended the U.S. Air Force Aerospace Research Pilot School at Edwards Air Force Base in California and was selected by NASA as an astronaut in April

1966. He served as part of the support crew for the Apollo 8 mission in 1968. He was chosen to be the Command Module Pilot for the Apollo 13 mission with James Lovell and Fred Haise in 1970. He was exposed to German measles shortly before launch and was replaced by Jack Swigert. Apollo 13 had an explosion while in flight that severely damaged the spacecraft and Mattingly, while assisting in mission control, was instrumental in helping the crew conserve power during re-entry. He accompanied John Young and Charlie Duke on the Apollo 16 lunar mission in 1982. He served as Command Module Pilot while his two crewmates walked on the moon. He subsequently worked in management for the Space Shuttle development program. Mattingly was commander of the STS-4, an orbital test flight of the Space Shuttle Columbia, in June of 1982. He was also spacecraft commander for STS-51-C, a Department of Defense mission aboard Space Shuttle Discovery in January of 1985. He subsequently retired from NASA and retired from the U.S. Navy the following year. He remained involved in aerospace with Grumman, General Dynamics, and Lockheed Martin. His many honors include induction into the International Space Hall of Fame in 1983 and the U.S. Astronaut Hall of Fame in 1997. He was a narrator for the 1989 documentary film "For All Mankind". Mattingly was portrayed by Gary Sinise in Ron Howard's 1995 film "Apollo 13" and by Zeljko Ivanek for the HBO mini-series "From the Earth to the Moon" in 1998. He also appeared in the 2009 video documentary "The Apollo Years". Mattingly married Elizabeth Dailey in 1970 and is survived by her and their son, Thomas III.

Mattinson, Burny

Animator Burny Mattinson, who worked at Walt Disney Studios for seven decades, died in Canoga Park, California, on February 27, 2023. He was 87. Mattinson was

born in San Francisco, California, on May 13, 1935. He moved to Los Angeles with his family in 1945. He was interested in animation from his youth and applied for a job at Walt Disney Studios after completing high school. He took a job with the traffic department as there were no available openings in animation. He began working as an in-betweener on the animated film "Lady and the Tramp" (1955). He became an assistant animator for Marc Davis on 1959's "Sleeping Beauty". He was an in-betweener for "One Hundred and One Dalmatians" in 1961 and provided illustrations for the film's adaptation by Little Golden Books. He began working as an assistant to Eric Larson and helped animated Ludwig von Drake for Disney's "The Wonderful World of Color" television series. He continued to work on such Disney films as "The Sword and the Stone" (1963), "Mary Poppins" (1964), "The Jungle Book" (1967), and "The Aristocrats" (1970). Mattinson became a character animator

under Ollie Johnston with "Robin Hood" in 1973. He served as animator for Tigger, Kanga, Roo, and Rabbit for "Winnie the Pooh and Tigger Too" in 1974. He was storyboard artist and title designer for "The Rescuers" (1977), "The Fox and the Hound" (1981), and "The Black Cauldron" (1985). He was producer and director of the animated short "Mickey's Christmas Carol" in 1983 which was nominated for an Academy Award for Best Animated Short Film. He directed the 1986 animated feature "The Great Mouse Detective". Mattinson was a storyboard artist or writer for the Disney films "All Dogs Go to Heaven" (1989), "Beauty and the Beast" (1991), "Aladdin" (1992), "The Lion King" (1994), "Pocahontas" (1995), "The Hunchback of Notre Dame" (1996), "Mulan" (1998), "Tarzan" (1999), "Lilo & Stitch" (2002), "Winnie the Pooh" (2011), "Big Hero 6" (2014), "Ralph Breaks the Internet" (2018), "Strange World" (2022), and "Wish" (2023) which was released posthumously and dedicated to his memory. He received the Disney Legend Award in 2008 and was featured in the short film "Once Upon a Studio" to commemorate Disney's 100th anniversary. He was Disney's longest serving employee at the time of his death. Mattinson was married to Sylvia Fry from 1962 until her death in 1986. He is survived by his second wife, Ellen Siirola, son Brett, and daughter Genny.

Maynard, Ted

British actor Ted Maynard died in Australia on December 18, 2023. He was 79. Maynard was born in England in 1944. He appeared frequently in films and television from

the mid-1980s. His film credits include "Highlander" (1986), "The American Way" (1986), "Sky Bandits" (1986), "Superman IV: The Quest for Peace" (1987), "Nightbreed" (1990), "Living Doll" (1990), "Spy Game" (2001), "xXx" (2002), "Superman Returns" (2006), "Knowing" (2009), "Mao's Last Dancer" (2009), and "Women He's Undressed" (2015). Maynard appeared on television in productions of "Ellis Island" (1984), "What Mad Pursuit?" (1985), "Murrow" (1986), "Breakthrough at Reykjavik" (1987), "The Bourne Identity" (1988), "The Care of Time" (1990), "Martin Chuzzlewit" (1994), "The Apocalypse Watch" (1997), and "Happy Birthday Shakespeare" (2000). His other television credits include episodes of "One by One", "Screen Two", "The Chef's Apprentice", "Unnatural Pursuits", "Paul Merton: The Series", "American Playhouse", "Bugs", "Strange But True?", "ChuckleVision", "Red Dwarf", Micawber", "Oscar Charlie", and "Serangoon Road" as Wild Bill in 2013. Maynard was also noted as a voice actor on commercials and narrating documentaries. He voiced roles in such video games as "Urban Chaos", "Colony Wars: Red Sun", "Gothic", "ArmA: Cold War Assault", and "Stuntman".

Mayniel, Juliette

French actress Juliette Mayniel died in San Miguel de Allende, Mexico, on July 21, 2023. She was 87. Mayniel was born in Saint Hippolyte, France, on January 22, 1936. She settled with her parents in Bordeaux after World War II. She appeared in amateur theater while in high school and later performed in repertory. She moved to Paris in 1956 to pursue an acting career. She was discovered by director Claude Chabrol in the late 1950s while appearing in a soap commercial. He cast her as Florence in his 1959 drama "Les Cousins". She was featured as Edna Gruber, the ill-fated donor of a face transplant in Georges Franju's horror classic "Eyes Without a Face" (aka "The Horror Chamber of Dr. Faustus"). Her other films include "Pecheur d'Islande" (1959), "La Nuit des Traques" (1959), "Un Couple" (1960), "Marche ou Creve" (1960), the German drama "Kirmes" (1960), "Wise Guys" (1961), "La Peau et les Os" (1961), "The Trojan Horse" (1961) opposite Steve Reeves, "Jusqu'a Plus Soif" (1962), Chabrol's "Bluebeard" (aka "Landru") (1963), "Ophelia" (1963), "Because, Because of a Woman" (1963), "Amori Pericolosi" (1964), "Assassination in Rome" (1965), "Listen, Let's Make Love" (1968), "Il Gatto Selvaggio" (1968), "L'Alibi" (1969), "That Little Differance" (1970), "Un Amore Oggi" (1970), "The Knock Out Cop" (1973), "Femmes au Soleil" (1974), "Scandal in the Family" (1975), "The Family Vice" (1975), "I Prosseneti" (1976), "Il Maetro di Violino" (1976), the bizarre psychological thriller "Dog Lay Afternoon" (aka "Bestialita") (1976), the Italian giallo "The Bloodstained Shadow" (1978), and "Molly O" (1986). Mayniel appeared on television in productions of "Les Tentations de La Fontaine" (1958), "On Roule a Deux" (1960), "Odissea" (1968), "Droga w Swietle Ksiezyca" (1973), "Un Anno di Scuola" (1977), "Madame Bovary" (1978), and "Settimo Anno" (1978). She was married to actor Robert Auboyneau until their divorce in 1964. She was the partner of Italian actor Vittorio Gassman from 1964 to 1968 and is survived by their son, actor Alessandro Gassman. Mayniel largely retired from acting in the 1980s and settled in Mexico.

McCaffrey, James

Actor James McCaffrey, who was featured as deceased firefighter Jimmy Keefe on the television series "Rescue Me" from 2004 to 2011, died of multiple myeloma at his home in Larchmont, New York, on December 17, 2023. He was 65. McCaffrey was born in Albany, New York, on March 27, 1958. He attended college at the University of New Haven in Connecticut. He subsequently moved to Boston, Massachusetts, where he worked as an artist and graphic designer. He settled in New York in the mid-1980s where he trained to become an actor. He studied at the Actors Studio and was co-owner of the Workhouse Theatre in Tribeca, New York, from 1992 to 1999. McCaffrey appeared frequently in films from the early 1990s with roles in "Bail Jumper" (1990), "Burnzy's Last Call" (1995), "The Truth About Cats & Dogs" (1996), "Nick and Jane" (1997), "The Tic Code" (1998), "Coming Soon" (1999), "The Florentine" (1999), "Fresh Cut Grass" (2002), "American Splendor" (2003), "Distress" (2003),

"She Hate Me" (2004), "Hide and Seek" (2005), "Broken English" (2007), "Feel the Noise" (2007), "Last Call" (2008), "Max Payne" (2008); "Sordid Things" (2009), "Nonames" (2010), "Meskada" (2010), "Camp Hell" (2010), "The Orphan Killer" (2011), "Montauk" (2011), "Compliance" (2012), "To Redemption" (2012), "Excuse Me for Living" (2012), "The Suspect" (2013), "A Cry from Within" (2014), "Like Sunday, Like Rain" (2014), "I Dream Too Much" (2015), "Coach of the Year" (2015), "Confidence Game" (2016), "One Fall" (2016), "Blind" (2016), "Destined" (2016), "Larchmont" (2016), "Sam" (2017), "The Big Take" (2018), "A Good Woman Is Hard to Find" (2019), and "Mob Town" (2019). McCaffrey starred in the television action series "Viper" as Michael Payton, a top driver for a crime syndicate, who is injured and has his memory wiped to become police officer Joe Astor. He becomes the driver of a heavily modified and armored vehicle known as Defender to fight crime. He played the roles during the first season of "Viper" in 1994 until his character was sent away. McCaffrey returned to the series as lead actor during its final season from 1998 to 1999. He was also seen in episodes of "Civil Wars" as Terrence Flanagan in 1992, "Swift Justice" as Mac Swift in 1996, "New York Undercover" as Captain Arthur O'Byrne in 1996, "The Big Easy", "The Job", "Sex and the City", "Queens Supreme", "Law & Order: Criminal Intent", the soap opera "As the World Turns" as Charley Spangler in 2003, "Hack", "Law & Order: Special Victims Unit", "Beautiful People" as Julian Fiske from 2005 to 2006, "3 lbs", "Canterbury's Law" as Frank Angstrom in 2008, "The Glades", "Rescue Me" as Jimmy Keefe, a deceased firefighter who frequently visits Denis Leary's Tommy Gavin in his dreams, from 2004 to 2011, "A Gifted Man", "Revenge" in the recurring role of Ryan Huntley from 2011 to 2012, "White Collar", "The Following", "Forever", "Madam Secretary", "Bull", "Jessica Jones", "Suits", "She's Gotta Have It" in the recurring role of Danton Phillips from 2017 to 2019, "Bluff City Law", and "Blue Bloods". His other television credits include the tele-films "Telling Secrets" (1993), "Schemes" (1994), "Hotel Shanghai" (1997), "Switched at Birth" (1999), "Pregnancy Pact" (2010), "Betrayed" (2014), "Gun Hill" (2014), "Romance at Reindeer Lodge" (2017), and "Engaged to a Psycho" (aka "Murder at the Mansion") (2018). McCaffrey provided the voice of Max Payne for the 2001 video game of the same name and the sequels "Max Payne 2: The Fall of Max Payne" (2003) and "Max Payne 3". He was also a voice performer for the games "Area 51" (2005), "Alone in the Dark" (2008), "Alan Wake" (2010), "Control" (2019), and "Alan

Wake II" (2023). He married actress Rochelle Bostrom in 2000 and is survived by her and their daughter, Tiarnan.

McCall, Joan

Actress and screenwriter Joan McCall died on April 14, 2023. She was 83. She was born Joan Carole Blevins in Grahn, Kentucky, on January 31, 1940. She was educated at Berea College in Kentucky. She went to New York City where she trained as an actress. She began her career on stage and performed in summer stock at the Gateway Playhouse in Bellport, Long Island. She appeared on Broadway in productions of "A Race of Hairy Men!" (1965), "The Star-Spangled Girl" (1966), and "Barefoot in the Park" (1967). She starred in the national tours of the two later productions and Woody Allen's "Don't Drink the Water". She moved to Hollywood with her husband, producer David Sheldon, later in the decade. She made her film debut in the 1974 horror film "Devil Times Five" (aka "Peopletoys") as the ill-fated Julie. She was also seen in the films "Act of Vengeance" (1974), "Grizzly" (1976), and "Project: Kill" (1976), the latter two which were produced and written by her husband. McCall began writing for television in the 1980s. She scripted such soap operas as "Days of Our Lives", "Another World", "Search for Tomorrow", "Capitol", "Divorce Court", and "Santa Barbara", sometimes using the pseudonym Joan Pommer. She scripted the 1983 film "Heart Like a Wheel" and co-wrote the sequel "Grizzly II: Revenge" (1983) with her husband. She and Sheldon co-wrote the 2005 book "When I Knew Al: The Untold Story of Al Pacino and Ed DeLeo". McCall married producer David Sheldon in 1964 and he survives her.

McCallum, David

Scottish actor David McCallum, who was noted for his roles as secret agent Illya Kuryakin in the 1960s television series "The Man from U.N.C.L.E." and as medical examiner Dr.

Donald 'Ducky' Mallard in the "NCIS" series since 2003, died at a hospital in New York City on September 25, 2023. He was 90. McCallum was born in Glasgow, Scotland, on September 19, 1933. He moved to London as a child where his father, David McCallum, Sr., led the London Philharmonic Orchestra. He attended the University College School in Hampstead, London, and played the oboe. He performed with the BBC radio repertory company from his early teens and was soon appearing in amateur theater. He served in the British Army for National Service after leaving school in the early 1950s. McCallum attended the Royal Academy of Dramatic Art after his discharge. He began his

film career later in the decade with roles in episodes of "Night Ambush" (1957), "The Secret Place" (1957), "Dangerous Youth" (1957), "Hell Drivers" (1957), "Robbery Under Arms" (1957), "Violent Playground" (1958), "A Night to Remember" (1958) as the Titanic's assistant wireless operator Harold Bride, "Jungle Street Girls" (1960), "Jungle Fighters" (1961), "Karolina Rijecka" (1961), Peter Ustinov's "Billy Budd" (1962), John Huston's "Freud" (1962) as Carl von Schlosser, the war drama "The Great Escape" (1963) as Lt. Cmdr. Eric 'Dispersal' Ashley Pitt, and the biblical drama "The Greatest Story Ever Told" (1964) as Judas Iscariot. McCallum was seen on television in productions of "The Blood Is Strong" (1956), "Amphitryon 38" (1958), "Ladies in Retirement" (1958), "Our Mutual Friend" (1958) as Eugene Wrayburn, "Cry Silence" (1958), "The Eustace Diamonds" (1959), "The Skin of Our Teeth" (1959), "Crime Passionnel" (1959), "Anouilh's Antigone" (1959), "Emma" (1969), "The Vortex" (1960), "The Unquiet Spirit" (1960), "On the Spot" (1960), "The Pot Carrier" (1960), "Midnight Sun" (1960), and "Wuthering Heights" (1962). His other television credits include episodes of "Knight Errant Limited", "Sir Francis Drake", "The Travels of Jamie McPheeters", "The Great Adventure", and "Profiles in Courage" as John Adams. He starred as Welsh miner Gwylim Griffiths, who is transformed into an evolutionary advanced human in the 1963 "The Sixth Finger" episode of the science fiction anthology series "The Outer Limits". McCallum was Tone Hobart in the 1964 "The Outer Limits" episode "The Forms of Things Unknown", which also served as the pilot for the unsold series "The Unknown" and included a different ending. McCallum was best known for his role as Russian secret agent Illya Kuryakin who starred with Robert Vaughn's Napoleon Solo in the hit series "The Man from U.N.C.L.E." from 1964 to 1968. He earned two Emmy Award nominations for his performance in 1965 and 1966. Some of the episodes of "The Man from U.N.C.L.E." were reedited as films for theatrical release including "To Trap a Spy" (1964), "The Spy with My Face" (1965), "One Spy Too Many" (1966), "One of Our Spies Is Missing" (1966), "The Spy in the Green Hat" (1966), "The Karate Killers" (1967), "The Helicopter Spies" (1968), and "How to Steal the World" (1968). He was seen in Kuryakin in a cameo in a 1966 episode of the comedy series "Please Don't Eat the Daisies" and reprised the role in the 1983 tele-film "The Return of the Man from U.N.C.L.E.: The Fifteen Years Later Affair" in 1983. He and Robert Vaughn reunited in the 1986 episode of "The A-Team", "The Say U.N.C.L.E. Affair". McCallum was also seen in episodes of "The Tonight Show with Johnny Carson", "The Andy Williams Show", "Hullabaloo", "The David Frost Show", "The Merv Griffin Show", "The Mike Douglas Show", "Night Gallery", "The Man and the City", "Marcus Welby, M.D.", "Norman Corwin Presents", "Bert D'Angelo/Superstar", "Strike Force", "Hart to Hart", "As the World Turns", and "The Master". He was featured as Flight Lt. Simon Carter in the BBC World War II prisoner-of-war drama "Colditz" from 1972 to 1974 and was Dr. Daniel Weston in the short-lived NBC science fiction series "The Invisible Man" from 1975 to 1976. He starred as Steel in the ITV science fiction series "Sapphire & Steel" opposite

Joanna Lumley from 1979 to 1982. McCallum guest-starred in episodes of "Matlock", "Alfred Hitchcock Presents", "Monsters", "Father Dowling Mysteries", "Murder, She Wrote", "Boon", "Cluedo" as Professor Plum in 1991, the short-lived British series "Trainer" as John Grey from 1991 to 1992, "SeaQuest DSV", "Babylon 5" as Dr. Vance Hendricks in the 1994 episode "Infections", "Heartbeat", "Mr. & Mrs. Smith", "VR.5" as Dr. Joseph Bloom from 1995 to 1996, the 1997 revival of "The Outer Limits", "Three", "Team Knight Rider", "Sex and the City", "Deadline", "The Education of Max Bickford" as Walter Thornhill from 2001 to 2002, and "Jeremiah". His other television credits include the tele-films and mini-series "Teacher, Teacher" (1969) earning another Emmy nomination for his role as Hamilton Cade, "The File on Devlin" (1969), the 1970 science fiction "Hauser's Memory" as Hillel Mondoro, "She Waits" (1972), "Screaming Skull" (1973), "The Six Million Dollar Man: Wine, Women and War" (1973), "Frankenstein: The True Story" (1973) as Dr. Henri Clerval, "Kidnapped" (1978), "The Corvini Inheritance" (1986) on "Hammer House of Mystery of Suspense", "Behind Enemy Lines" (1985), "Those Golden Years" (1985), Hungary's "Az Aranyifyu" (1987), "Freedom Fighters" (1988), "The Man Who Lived at the Ritz" (1989), "The Return of Sam McCloud" (1989), "Mother Love" (1989) with Diana Rigg, "Lucky Chances" (1989), "Mother Love" (1990), "Death Game" (1996), "March in Windy City" (1998), and "Coming Home" (1998). He narrated the 1994 A&E documentary "Titanic: The

Complete Story" and four NBC specials on "Ancient Prophecies" from 1994 to 1997. He was featured as chief medical examiner Dr. Donald 'Ducky' Mallard on "NCIS" from 2003 until his death. He also appeared in the role in several episodes of "JAG" and "NCIS: New Orleans". McCallun provided the voice of C.A.R. on the animated television series "The Replacements" from 2006 to 2009 and was the voice of Professor Paradox on the series "Ben 10: Alien Force" (2008-2010), "Ben 10: Ultimate Alien" (2010-2011), and "Ben 10: Omniverse" (2013-2014). He was the voice of Bruce Wayne's butler, Alfred Pennyworth, in the animated videos "Batman: Gotham Knight" (2008), "Son of Batman" (2014), and "Batman vs. Robin" (2015), and was the voice of Zeus in 2009's "Wonder Woman". His film credits also include the underwater science fiction film "Around the World Under the Sea" (1966), the concert film "The Big T.N.T. Show" (1966) as master of ceremonies and performing an instrumental version of "(I Can't Get No) Satisfaction", "Three Bites of the Apple" (1967), the thriller "Sol Madrid" (1968) in the title role, "Mosquito Squadron" (1969), "The Ravine" (1969), "The Kingfish Caper" (1975), "Dogs" (1977), "King Solomon's Treasure" (1979), the Disney horror film "The Watcher in the Woods" (1980), "Terminal Choice" (1985), "The Wind" (1986), "The Haunting of Morella" (1990), "Hear My Song" (1991), "Dirty Weekend" (1993), "Fatal Inheritance" (1993),

"Healer" (1994), and "Cherry" (1999). McCallum was a talented musician and recorded four instrumental albums from Capitol Records including "Music...A Part of Me" (1966), "Music...A Bit More of Me" (1966), "Music...It's Happening Now!" (1967), and "McCallum" (1968). He recorded three H.P. Lovecraft stories for Caedmon Records in the 1970s including "The Rats in the Walls", "The Dunwich Horror", and "The Haunter of the Dark". He performed frequently on stage and appeared on Broadway in productions of "The Flip Side" (1968), "California Suite" (186), and "Amadeus" (1999). McCallum became a naturalized United States citizen in 1999. He was author of the 2016 crime novel "Once a Crooked Man". McCallum was married to actress Jill Ireland from 1957 until their divorce in 1967. He is survived by sons Paul McCallum and guitarist Val McCallum. Their adopted son, Jason McCallum, died of an accidental drug overdose in 1989. He married fashion model and interior designer Katherine Carpenter in 1967, and is survived by her, their son Peter, and their daughter Sophie.

McCann, Peter

Songwriter and musician Peter McCann died at his home in Nashville, Tennessee, on January 26, 2023. He was 74. McCann was born in Bridgeport, Connecticut, on March 6,

1948. He graduated from Fairfield University in 1970, where he was a member of the Glee Club. He and several fellow students formed the folk-rock band the Repairs with McCann as singer, songwriter, keyboardist, and electric guitarist. They moved to Los Angeles in 1971 where they recorded the albums "Already a Household Word" (1971) and "Repairs" (1972). The band

released "Repairs Live" in 1974 and McCann was hired by ABC Records as a songwriter. He wrote the 1977 hit song "Right Time of the Night", which was Jennifer Warnes' debut single. He moved to 20th Century Fox Records where he wrote and recorded the hit "Do You Wanna Make Love" in 1977. He released his self-named debut album, "Peter McCann", later in the year. He moved to Nashville in 1978 to write for CBS and had hits with Earl Thomas Conley's Nobody Falls Like a Fool" (1985), Janie Fricke's She's Single Again" (1985), Whitney Houston's "Take Good Care of My Heart" (1985), K.T. Oslin's "Wall of Tears" (1987), Mickey Gilley's "She Reminded Me of You" (1988), Baillie & The Boys "Treat Me Like a Stranger" (1991), and Kathy Mattea's "Good News" (1993). His songs were also recorded by such artists as Karen Carpenter, Isaac Hayes, John Travolta, Ricky Nelson, Reba McEntire, Anne Murray, Kenny Rogers, Eddie Rabbitt, and Lee Greenwood. He was active with the Nashville Songwriters Association International (NSAI) and lobbied for songwriters' rights and the strengthening of copyright laws. McCann is survived by his wife of 41 years, Jacalyn Sheridan, and their son, Colin McCann.

McCarthy, Annette

Actress Annette McCarthy, who starred as Evelyn Marsh in the second season of television's "Twin Peaks" in 1990, died on January 6, 2023. She was 64. She was born on April 12, 1958, and trained as an actress in New York and Los Angeles. She appeared on stage and was featured in several television commercials. McCarthy was seen on television in the tele-films "A Cry for Love" (1980), "Crazy Times" (1981), Disney's "The Absent-Minded Professor" (1988), and "Fugitive Among Us" (1992). Her other television credits include episodes of "Happy Days", "Magnum, P.I.", "The Fall Guy", "St. Elsewhere", "The Twilight Zone", "Riptide", "Ohara", "Beauty and the Beast", "Night Court", "Twin Peaks" as Evelyn Marsh from 1990 to 1991, and "Baywatch" in the recurring role of Kathleen Huntington from 1994 to 1995. McCarthy appeared in the films "Second Thoughts" (1983) and the science fiction horror film "Creature" (1985) as Dr. Wendy Oliver. She largely retired from acting in the mid-1990s though she continued to appear on the local stage and in commercials. She was later an executive chef and director of client services at Mercury Sound Studios. McCarthy was married to sound editor Mark Mangini from 1984 and they had two sons before their subsequent divorce.

McCarthy, Cormac

Author Cormac McCarthy, who wrote the novel "No Country for Old Men" and received a Pulitzer Prize in 2007 for "The Road", died at his home in Santa Fe, New Mexico, on June 13, 2023. He was 89. He was born Charles Joseph McCarthy, Jr., in Providence Rhode Island, on July 20, 1933, and was raised in Knoxville, Tennessee. He attended the University of Tennessee in 1951 but left college after two years to join the U.S. Air Force. He returned to the University of Tennessee in 1957. He published the stories "Wake for Susan" and "A Drowning Incident" in the student literary magazine, "The Phoenix". He left college in 1959 and moved to Chicago. He changed his first name to Cormac for literary purposes. McCarthy's first novel, "The Orchard Keeper", was published in 1965. He traveled to Europe on a Rockefeller Foundation grant over the next year and settled at Spain's island of Ibiza. He wrote the novel "Outer Dark" there and returned to the United States for its publication in 1968. "Outer Dark" was adapted for a short film in 2009. His 1973 novel, "Child of God", was set in southern Appalachia and was about a cave dwelling murderer and necrophiliac. It was adapted for a film by James Franco in 2013. He moved to El Paso, Texas, in 1976. He scripted "The Gardener's Son", an episode of the PBS series "Visions", in 1977, which was nominated for two Emmy Awards. His semi-autobiographical novel, "Suttree", which he had written years before, was published in 1979. He received a MacArthur Fellowship in 1981 which provided him with funds to research his next novel, "Blood Meridian, or the Evening Redness in the West" (1985). His 1992 novel, "All the Pretty Horses", won the National Book Award and became his first bestseller. It was adapted for a film directed by Billy Bob Thornton and starring Matt Damon and Penelope Cruz in 2000. He also wrote novels "The Crossing" (1994) and "Cities of the Plain" (1998), and the play "The Stonemason" (1992). His 2005 novel "No Country for Old Men" was adapted for film by the Coen Brothers. The film starred Tommy Lee Jones, Javier Bardem, and Josh Brolin. It received four Academy Awards including Best Picture, Best Supporting Actor for Bardem, and Best Director and Best Adapted Screenplay for the Coen Brothers. McCarthy wrote the post-apocalyptic novel "The Road" in 2006 which earned him the Pulitzer Prize for Fiction. He agreed to a rare interview on "The Oprah Winfrey Show" in 2007 when "The Road" was selected for Oprah's Book Club. A film adaptation directed by John Hillcoat and scripted by Joe Penhall was released in 2009 and starred Viggo Mortensen and Kodi Smit-McPhee as a father and son traveling in the post-apocalyptic wasteland. His 2006 play "The Sunset Limited" was produced as a tele-film in 2011. He wrote the script for the 2013 crime thriller film "The Counselor" which was directed by Ridley Scott. He served as a trustee for the Santa Fe Institute, a scientific research center, despite his lack of a science background, from 2014 until his death. He wrote the non-fiction essay "The Kekule Problem" in 2017. He published two connected novels in 2022, "The Passenger" about a race car driver turned salvage diver, and "Stella Maris", about a mathematician suffering from hallucinations. He was reportedly working on a film adaptation of his novel "Blood Meridian" at the time of his death. McCarthy was married to Lee Holleman from 1961 until their divorce in 1962 and is survived by their son Chase. He was married to Anne DeLisle from 1966 until their divorce in 1981. He was married to Jennifer Claire Winkley from 1998 until their divorce in 2006 and is survived by their son John.

McCarver, Tim

Baseball player and sports commentator Tim McCarver died in Memphis, Tennessee, on February 16, 2023.

He was 81. McCarver was born in Memphis on October 16, 1941. He was signed by the St. Louis Cardinals after graduating Christopher Brothers High School in 1959. He played in the minor league teams the Keokuk Indians and the Rochester Red Wings before playing with the Cardinals. He returned to the minors in 1960, playing with the Memphis Chicks, the Charleston Charlies, and the

Atlanta Crackers. He returned to the Major Leagues with the Cardinals in 1963. He was a member of two World Series champion teams and was named to the All-Star Team in 1966 and 1967. He was traded to the Philadelphia Phillies in 1970 and they traded him to the Montreal Expos in 1972. He returned to the St. Louis Cardinals from 1973 to 1974 and played with the Boston Red Sox from 1974 to 1975. He rejoined the Phillies in 1975 where he remained until his retirement in 1979. McCarver subsequently became a sportscaster with WPHL-TV in Philadelphia. He was a backup commentator for the Game of the Week at NBC from 1980 until joining ABC in 1984. He teamed with Don Drysdale on backup "Monday Night Baseball" games and worked with Al Michaels and Jim Palmer from 1985 to 1989. He worked at CBS, teaming with Jack Buck from 1990 to 1991 and Sean McDonough from 1992 to 1993. He was co-anchor, with Paula Zahn, of the Winter Olympics in 1992 for CBS. He resumed working with Michael and Palmer at ABC from 1994 to 1995. He was partnered with Joe Buck on Fox's baseball telecasts from 1996 to 2013. He called St. Louis Cardinals games for Fox Sports Midwest from 2013 until his retirement in 2022. He was also host of the syndicated sports interview show "The Tim McCarver Show" from 2000 to 2017. He was winner of the Emmy Award for Outstanding Sports Personality - Sports Event Analyst in 2001, 2002, and 2003. He received an additional thirteen Emmy nominations. McCarver appeared in cameo roles in a handful of films including "The Naked Gun: From the Files of the Police Squad!" (1988), "Love Hurts" (1990), "Mr. Baseball" (1992), "The Scout" (1994), "BASEketball" (1998), "Fever Pitch" (2005), and "Moneyball" (2011). He also appeared in a 1997 episode of the television series "Arli$$". He was a guest on such television series as "The Ed Sullivan Show", "Late Night with David Letterman", "The Pat Sajak Show", "Sesame Street" hosting an episode in 1993, "Late Show with David Letterman", and "Charlie Rose". He was author or co-author of several books including "Oh Baby, I Love It!" (1987), "Baseball for Brain Surgeons and Other Fans" (1998), "The Perfect Season: Why 1998 Was Baseball's Greatest Year" (1999), "Few and Chosen Cardinals: Defining Cardinal Greatness Across the Eras" (2003), and "Tim McCarver's Diamond Gems" (2008). McCarver married Kathryn Anne McDaniel in 1964 and is survived by her and their two daughters, Kathy and Kelly.

McCracken, Bob

Actor Bob McCracken died of complications from gallbladder surgery at a hospital in Pasadena, California, on January 30, 2023. He was 72. McCracken was born in Philadelphia, Pennsylvania, on September 11, 1950. His father served in the military and Bob was raised around the country. He completed high school in San Juan, Puerto Rico, and studied theater at West Chester University in Pennsylvania. He began his career on the

local stage with Hedgerow Theatre Company, Pocket Playhouse, the People's Light, and others. He was also a founder of the South Street Theatre Company. He moved to Los Angeles in the early 1980s and continued his acting career in film and television. McCracken was seen on television in episodes of "Heart of the City", "What's Happening Now!", "American Playhouse", "Jake and the Fatman", "Lois & Clark: The New Adventures of Superman", "ER", "Diagnosis Murder", "Dr. Quinn, Medicine Woman", "Days of Our Lives", "Boston Common", "Dangerous Minds", "Players" in the recurring role of Malcolm O'Conner from 1997 to 1998, "C-16: FBI", "The Practice", "Nothing Sacred", "Any Day Now" also directing several episodes, "JAG", "Firefly", "Commander in Chief", "Nip/Tuck", "CSI: Crime Scene Investigation", "Sleeper Cell", "Hustle", "Journeyman", "House", "Trauma", "Chuck", "NSIC", "Law & Order: LA", "Prime Suspect",. "Shameless", "The Mentalist", "Criminal Minds", "Brooklyn Nine-Nine", "Sons of Anarchy" as Brendan Roarke from 2010 to 2014, "Hard of God" in the recurring role of Dr. Williams from 2014 to 2017, "Bosch", "Hawaii Five-O", "The Exorcist", "NCIS: New Orleans", and "Here and Now". He also directed episodes of the "Judging Amy" series. McCracken's other television credits include the tele-films "Baby Brokers" (1994), "The Innocent" (1994), and "Fast Company" (1995). He was featured in the films "Nightforce" (1987), "Spellbinder" (1988), "Mother, Mother" (1989), "Delusion" (1991), "Skyscraper" (1996), "Pay It Forward" (2000), "Rutland, USA" (2002), "Freedom Park" (2004), "Simple & Safe" (2004), "Dear Lemon Lima" (2009), "Wrong Cops" (2013), "Oscar" (2017), and "The Last Champion" (2020). McCracken married producer Kay Liberman in 2015 and is survived by her and two stepchildren.

McCutcheon, Roz

Irish actress Roz McCutcheon died in Hither Green, London, England, on March 21, 2023. She was 75. McCutcheon was born in Bandon, Ireland, on March 22, 1947. She graduated from Trinity College Dublin and moved to England to pursue a career in show business. She appeared frequently on stage and appeared in the films "The Penalty King" (2006), "Cold Earth" (2008), "Mirrors" (2008), and "Grabbers" (2012). McCutcheon was seen in television productions of "Jam" (2000), "The Lost Prince" (2003), and episodes of "The League of Gentlemen", "20 Things to Do Before You're 30", "Doctors", and "The Revolting world of Stanley Brown". She was active with the Irish Genealogical Research Society, serving on its council and producing the society's newsletter since 1991.

McDaniel, George

Actor George McDaniel died in Ventura, California, on March 24, 2023. He was 80. McDaniel was born in St. Louis, Missouri, on June 30, 1942. He attended the University of Missouri where he studied drama and was seen in numerous school productions. McDaniel performed frequently in regional theater throughout his career. He appeared often on

television from the early 1970s with roles in episodes of "Love, American Style", "Barnaby Jones", "McCloud", "Fernwood Tonight", "Days of Our Lives" as Dr. Jordan Barr from 1979 to 1980, "The Misadventures of Sheriff Lobo", "Hill Street Blues", "Little House on the Prairie", "Three's Company", "Dallas", "General Hospital", "Bring 'Em Back Alive", "Madame's Place", "The Greatest American Hero", "Knight Rider", "Wizards and Warriors", "Hardcastle and McCormick", "Remington Steele", "Emerald Point N.A.S.", "The Dukes of Hazzard", "Blue Thunder", "Cagney & Lacey", "The Rousters", "E/R", "Falcon Crest" as Alan Caldwell in 1984, "Street Hawk", "T.J. Hooker", "Scarecrow and Mrs. King", "Crazy Like a Fox", "The A-Team", "Hunter", "Magnum, P.I.", "Mama's Family", "Stingray", "Beverly Hills Buntz", "Werewolf", "Paradise", "The New Adam-12", "L.A. Law", "Saved by the Bell", "Beverly Hills, 90210", "Sliders", "ER", "The West Wing", "State of Grace", "Law & Order: Special Victims Unit", "Law & Order", "Law & Order: Criminal Intent", "All My Children" as James Beardsley from 2009 to 2010, "The Good Wife", and "All American". His other television credits include productions of "Fools, Females and Fun" (1974), "Rich Man, Boo Man - Book II" (1977), "Nichols & Dymes" (1981), "Dream West" (1986), "Nutcracker: Money, Madness & Murder" (1987), "Murder Ordained" (1987), and "Cast the First Stone" (1989). McDaniel was also seen in the films "Legacy" (1975), "This Is Spinal Tap" (1984), "The Last Starfighter" (1984), "Lionheart" (1990), "Ole" (2006), "Rickover: The Birth of Nuclear Power" (2014), and "Raunch and Roll" (2021).

McDonnell, Ross

Irish film director Ross McDonnell was reported missing in New York City on November 4, 2023. A headless and armless body was found on a beach in Breezy Point, Queens, on November 17, which was identified as McDonnell five days later. He was believed to have drowned while swimming in the ocean and foul play was not suspected. He

was 44. McDonnell was born in Dublin, Ireland, on October 29, 1979. He began working in documentary films in the early 2000s. He was cinematographer and co-director for the 2009 documentary about beekeepers, "Colony". He also directed and photographed the short films "Remember Me, My Ghost" (2011), "AKA Lonely" (2015), and "Swift Justice" (2023). He

earned an Emmy Award nomination for Outstanding Investigative Documentary for 2017's "Elian". McDonnell's credits for cinematographer also include "Dollhouse" (2012), "Snake Dance" (2012), "Life Is Sacred" (2014), "Forever Pure" (2016), "No Stone Unturned" (2017), "A Mother Brings Her Son to Be Shot" (2017), "One Million American Dreams" (2018), and "Jihad Jane" (2019). McDonnell earned Emmy Awards for Outstanding Cinematography: Documentary for "The Trade" (2021) and "The First Wave" (2022). He was cinematographer for the television series "Edge of the Unknown with Jimmy Chin" (2022) and "Photographer" (2024).

McGinty, Ian

Comic book writer and artist Ian McGinty died in Los Angeles, California, on June 8, 2023. He was 38. McGinty was born in Annapolis, Maryland, on May 6, 1985. He was

educated at St. Mary's College of Southern Maryland and the Savannah College of Art and Design in Atlanta. He began working comics in 2013 with "Adventure Time: Candy Capers" and "Suckers" from Zoetrope. He was an artist for the BOOM! Studios titles "Bee and Puppycat", "Adventure Time", and "Bravest Warrior" from 2015. He was a storyboard artist for the 2016 video game "Plants vs. Zombies Heroes" and worked on the 2019 animated television production "Invader ZIM: Enter the Florpus". He illustrated BOOM!'s "Rocko's Modern Life" series in 2018. McGinty started his on comic, "Welcome to Showside", from Z2 Comics in 2015 and was a voice performer in the subsequent animated short film. He and Sam Sattin released the graphic novel "Glint" from Lion Forge's Caracal imprint in 2019. He also drew several issues of Oni Press' "Rick and Morty" comic. He and writer Ben Katzner created the 2021 graphic novel "Hello, My Name Is Poop", from Wonderbound.

McGrath, Michael

Actor Michael McGrath, who earned a Tony Award

for his performance in the Broadway musical "Nice Work If You Can Get It" in 2012, died at his home in Bloomfield, New Jersey, on September 14, 2023. He was 65. McGrath was born in Worcester, Massachusetts, on September 25, 1957. He began his career on stage and appeared frequently on Broadway from the early 1990s. He performed in such musical productions as "My Favorite Year" (1992), "The Goodbye Girl" (1993), "Swinging on a Star" (1995), "Little

Me" (1998), "Wonderful Town" (2003), "Spamalot" (2005) earning a Tony Award nomination for his role as Patsy, "Is He Dead?" (2007), "Memphis" (2009), "Born Yesterday" (2011), "Nice Work If You Can Get It" (2012) winning a Tony and Drama Desk Award for his role as Cookie McGee, "On the Twentieth Century" (2015), "She Loves Me" (2016), "The Front Page" (2016), "Tootsie" (2019), and "Plaza Suite" (2022). McGrath appeared in a handful of films including "Boyfriends" (1996), "Changing Lanes" (2002), "Cowboys & Angels" (2003), "The Interpreter" (2005), and "Ira & Abby" (2006). He was a voice performer in the animated shorts "Escape of the Gingerbread Man!!!" (2011), "Somewhere Down the Line" (2014), and "Wolfwalkers" (2020). He appeared on television in episodes of "Mathnet", "Remember WENN", "Between the Lions", and "Madam Secretary", and the 2002 tele-film "Monday Night Mayhem". McGrath married actress Toni DiBuono in 1993 and is survived by her and their daughter, actress Katie Claire McGrath.

McGuire, Barry

Actor Barry McGuire died in Winfield, Kansas, on March 7, 2023. He was 93. McGuire was born in Caldwell, Kansas, on March 7, 1930. He graduated from the University of Denver and began his career on stage. He was seen on Broadway in a 1953 production of "Bernadine". He appeared

frequently on television from the early 1950s with roles in episodes of "The Big Story", "Kraft Theatre", "Studio One", "Robert Montgomery Presents", "Schlitz Playhouse", "The Silent Service", "Steve Canyon", "Target", "Gunsmoke", "Perry Mason", "Captain David Grief", "Father Knows Best", "Hotel de Paree", "Death Valley Days", "The Real McCoys", "Hennesey", "Two Faces West", "Bachelor Father", and "General Electric Theater". He was also featured in the 1957 film "Street of Sinners". McGuire performed puppet shows and magic acts and appeared in numerous regional productions throughout his career.

McHale, Christopher

Actor Christopher McHale died of heart disease in

Manhattan, New York, on September 12, 2023. He was 69. McHale was born in Pittsburgh, Pennsylvania, on March 30, 1954. He began performing on stage in high school and studied acting at Carnegie-Mellon University. He appeared with the Arena Stage in Washington, D.C., after graduation before moving to New York City. He appeared frequently on the Broadway stage from the early

1980s with roles in productions of "Piaf" (1981), "The Iceman Cometh" (1985), "Execution of Justice" (1986), "King Lear" (2004), "Julius Caesar" (2005), "Joe Turner's Come and Gone" (2009), "Golden Boy" (2012), "Macbeth" (2013), "Oslo" (2017), "Ink" (2019), and "The Great Society" (2019). McHale was featured in several films including "The Seduction of Joe Tynan" (1979), "F/X" (1986), and "Sunset Park" (1996). He was also seen on television in episodes of "The Equalizer", "New York News", "Law & Order", "Rescue Me", "Law & Order: Criminal Intent", "Six Degrees", "Law & Order: Special Victims Unit", and "The Deuce".

McHugh, Bill

Actor Bill McHugh died in Aurora, Illinois, on April 13, 2023. He was 88. McHugh was born in Aurora on June 14,

1934. He graduated from Notre Dame University and was a teacher at St. Edward's High School in Aurora for two decades. He moved to New York City to work as a model and actor in the 1970s. McHugh appeared in the films "Cafe Society" (1995), "You've Got Mail" (1998), "The Good Shepherd" (2006), "Pride and glory" (2008), "Listen to Your Heart" (2010), and "The Irishman" (2019). He was also seen in the short films "Plea" (2008), "New Medea" (2010), "The Man at the Counter" (2011), and "The F Bomb" (2011). He appeared on television in an episode of "Sex and the City" in 1999 and was Congressman McCulough in several episodes of "The Onion News Network" in 2011.

McKenna, Brian

Canadian documentary filmmaker Brian McKenna died in Montreal, Quebec, Canada, on May 5, 2023. He was

77. McKenna was born in Montreal on August 8, 1945. He attended Loyola College where he became editor of the student newspaper. He graduated in 1967 and became a reporter at the "Montreal Star" covering the Expo 67 World's Fair. He left the paper to join the CBS local Montreal current affairs program "The City at 6" in 1973. He was a correspondent for the "As It Happens" radio current affairs program and was founding producer of the investigative news magazine "The Fifth Estate" in 1975. He remained with the series for over a decade but also directed television productions of "The Killing Ground" (1988), "The Valour and the Horror" (1992), a documentary trilogy about Canadian leader Pierre Trudeau consisting of "The Making of a Leader (1919-1968)" (1994), "The Art of Governing (1968-1972)" (1994),

"Establishing a Just Society (1972-1984)" (1994), and "The Bribe or the Bullet" (1996), "War of 1812" (1999), "Chiefs" (2002), "Korea: The Unfinished War" (2003), "Big Sugar" (2005), "The Great War" (2007), "La Fin de la Nouvelle-France" (2009), "Famine and Shipwreck, an Irish Odyssey" (2011), and "Newfoundland at Armageddon" (2016). McKenna also directed the documentaries "War at Sea: The Black Pit" (1995), "War at Sea: U-Boats in the St. Lawrence" (1995), "A Web of War" (1996), and "Fire and Ice: The Rocket Richard Riot" (2000). He is survived by three children from Susan Purcell and two with Anne Lagace Dowson. He is also survived by his life partner, Renee Baert.

McKenzie, Richard

Actor Richard McKenzie died in Los Angeles, California, on December 1, 2023. He was 93. McKenzie was born in Chattanooga, Tennessee, on June 2, 1930. He began his career on stage and was seen in Broadway productions of "Indians" (1969), "That Championship Season" (1972), "Uncle Vanya" (1973), and "The National Health" (1974). He appeared frequently on television with roles in episodes of "My Three Sons", "Doctors' Hospital", "The Waltons", "Hawaii Five-O", "The Jeffersons",  "Rich Man, Poor Man - Book II", "Kingston: Confidential", "Quincy", "Three's Company", "Sword of Justice", "All in the Family" as Archie Bunker's younger brother Fred in a pair of episodes in 1978 and 1979, "One Day at a Time", "Carter Country", "Stone", "Family", "The Yeagers", "One in a Million", "Soap", "CBS Afternoon Playhouse", "Bring 'Em Back Alive", "Archie Bunker's Place" reprising his role as Fred Bunker in 1982, the comedy series "It Takes Two" as Walker Chaiken from 1982 to 1983, "Condo", "The Mississippi", "Oh Madeline", "You Are the Jury", "Knots Landing", "Off the Rack", "Benson", "Hail to the Chief", "Stir Crazy", "Growing Pains", "The Facts of Life", "The Colbys", "MacGyver", "Too Close for Comfort", "Comedy Factory", "Highway to Heaven", "The Wizard", "Matlock" in the recurring role of Lt. Rupert Davis from 1986 to 1987, "21 Jump Street", "Valerie", "Ohara", "Throb", "It's a Living", "ALF", "My Sister Sam", "Quantum Leap", "The Golden Girls", "The Fresh Prince of Bel-Air", "Herman's Head", "Pros and Cons", "Civil Wars", "NYPD Blue", "Empty Nest", "Picket Fences", "Grace Under Fire", "In the Heat of the Night", and "Judging Amy". He was also seen in numerous tele-films and mini-series including "Nicky's World" (1974), "McNaughton's Daughter" (1976), "The Tenth Level" (1976), "Roots" (1977), "Danger in Paradise" (1977), "Nowhere to Run" (1978), "True Grit: A Further Adventure" (1978), "Ike: The War Years" (1979), "California Fever" (1979), "Gideon's Trumpet", "Callie & Son" (1981), "Dark Night of the Scarecrow" (1981), "Splendor in the Grass" (1981), "Eleanor,

First Lady of the World" (1982) as Harry S Truman, "Life of the Party: The Story of Beatrice" (1982), "Memories Never Die" (1982), "Malibu" (1983), "Playing with Fire" (1985), "Acceptable Risk" (1986), "In Love and War" (1987), "Roses Are for the Rich" (1987), "Billionaire Boys Club" (1987), "Shootdown" (1988), "Child of Darkness, Child of Light" (1991), "Daddy" (1991), and "Deadly Medicine" (1991). McKenzie was featured in the films "Doc" (1971), "A.W.O.L." (1972), "The Stoolie" (1972), "Man on a Swing" (1974), "Corvette Summer" (1978), "Being There" (1979), "First Monday in October" (1981), "Some Kind of Hero" (1982), "Bird" (1988), "The Doctor" (1991), and "Ghost in the Machine" (1993). He largely retired from acting in the early 2000s.

McKnight, David

Actor David McKnight, who was featured as resurrected gangster J.D. Walker in the 1976 blaxploitation  horror film "J.D.'s Revenge", died of cancer in Las Vegas, Nevada, on December 3, 2023. He was 87. McKnight was born in Mound Bayou, Mississippi, on July 2, 1936, and moved to Chicago, Illinois, with his family as a child. He began acting while in high school and attended Wilson Junior College before serving in the U.S. Army. He worked as a police officer after his discharge. He was featured as David Bracy in the first all-Black television soap opera "Bird of the Iron Feather", which aired on the National Educational Television station WTTW-TV in Chicago in 1970. He was seen in such films as "The Candidate" (1972), "Lifeguard" (1976), "J.D.'s Revenge" (1976) as the vengeful murdered hustler J.D. Walker, "Coma" (1978), "The Astral Factor" (1978), Robert Townsend's "Hollywood Shuffle" (1987) as Uncle Ray, "A Taste of Hemlock" (1989), "Terror in Paradise" (1990), "Pump Up the Volume" (1990), "The Five Heartbeats" (1991) as Pastor Stone, "Pizza Man" (1991), "Under Siege" (1992), "The Glass Shield" (1994), "Sprung" (1997), and "Superhero Movie" (2008). McKnight was seen on television in episodes of "The Incredible Hulk", "Dynasty", "Cutter to Houston", "Benson", "Moonlighting", "Hill Street Blues", "CBS Summer Playhouse", "Rin Tin Tin: K-9 Cop", "Webster", "CBS Schoolbreak Special", "Friday the 13th: The Series", "War of the Worlds", "Hardball", "227", "L.A. Law", "Roc", "The Commish", "The Client", "The Parent 'Hood", "The Wayan Bros.", "ER", "Mister Sterling", "The District", "Boston Legal", and the Urban Movie Channel web series "A House Divided" as Benjamin Sanders" from 2019 to 2023. His other television credits include the tele-films "Dangerous Company" (1982), "Stop at Nothing" (1991), "Divas" (1995), "(On the Line" (1997), "A Husband for Christmas" (2016), "Sharing Christmas" (2017), and "A Christmas for Mary" (2020).

McManus, Jim

British actor Jim McManus died in England on April 11, 2023. He was 82. McManus was born in Bristol, England, on May 19, 1940. He began his acting career in films and television in the late 1950s. He was featured in the films "The Square Peg" (1958), "Breakout" (1959), "The Day the Earth Caught Fire" (1961), "Legend of the Werewolf" (1975), "Sweeney 2" (1978), "Murder by Decree" (1979), "Silver Dream Racer" (1980), "Diamond's Edge" (1988), "Buddy's Song" (1991), "Lawless Heart" (2001), "Machine" (2003), "Nella Notte" (2004), "Harry Potter and the Order of the Phoenix" (2007), "Easy Virtue" (2008), "Pride" (2014). He was seen on television in episodes of "Comedy Playhouse", "Sykes and A...", "Detective", "The Graham Stark Show", "Crossroads", "Hugh and I", "Frankie Howerd", "Softly Softly", "The Wednesday Play", "The Spanish Farm", "The Expert", "Z Cars", "Harry Worth", "The Gnomes of Dulwich", "Steptoe and Son", "Dear Mother... ...Love Albert", "The Mind of Mr. J.G. Reeder", "Armchair Theatre", "Softly Softly: Task Force", "Clochemerle", "Bless This House", "Father, Dear Father", "Doctor in Charge", "Scoop", "The Upper Crusts", "Barlow at Large", "Ooh La La!", "The Fenn Street Gang", "New Scotland Yard", "Bowler", "Dixon of Dock Green", "The Sweeney", "Rough Justice", "Doctor Who" as the Ophthalmologist in the 1977 serial "The Invisible Enemy", "The Professionals", "Juliet Bravo", "The Other 'Arf", "The Chinese Detective", "Rosie", "Roger Doesn't Live Here Anymore", "Only Fools and Horses", "Bergerac", "Screenplay", "Casting Off", "Bad Boyes", "Young Charlie Chaplin", "T.Bag and the Pearls of Wisdom", "Press Gang", "The Diamond Brothers", "Trouble in Mind", "The House of Eliott", "Screen One", "Minder", "Chef!", "Sharpe", "Jack and Jeremy's Real Lives", "Casualty", the animated children's series "The Treacle People" as the voice of Bill Wizzle and Nicko Pendle from 1996 to 1997, "Goodnight Sweetheart", "The Bill", "EastEnders', "Doctors", "Serious and Organised", and "Heartbeat". His other television credits include productions of "Harry Carpenter Never Sait It Was Like This" (1982), "Dangerous Lady" (1995), "Underworld" (1997), "Tipping the Velvet" (2002), and "Hornblower: Loyalty" (2003).

McNamara, J. Patrick

Actor J. Patrick McNamara, who was featured as Mr. Preston in the film "Bill & Ted's Excellent Adventure", died at a hospital in Jefferson, Louisiana, on January 2, 2023. He was 80. McNamara was born in New Orleans, Louisiana, on October 30, 1942. He attended De La Salle University and the University of New Orleans and graduated from the State University of New York. He earned a master's degree from the American Film Institute in Los Angeles. He pursued an acting career on stage and performed with the La MaMa Experiment

Theatre Club in New York. He taught voice at the National Academy of Drama in Carnegie Hall. He subsequently returned to New Orleans where he founded the Energy Theater. He

made his film debut in a small role in Brian DePalma's "Obsession" (1976) and appeared as the Project Leader in Steven Spielberg's science fiction classic "Close Encounters of the Third Kind" in 1977. He continued to appear in such films as DePalma's "The Fury" (1978), "Good Luck, Miss Wyckoff" (1979), Spielberg's "1941", "Blow Out" (1981), "Warning Sign" (1985), "Some Kind of Wonderful" (1987), "Phantasm II" (1988), "Bill & Ted's Excellent Adventure" (1989) as Mr. Preston, "Gross Anatomy" (1989), "The First Power" (1990), "Mom" (1990), "Flight of the Intruder" (1991), "Bill & Ted's Bogus Journey" (1991) reprising his role as Bill's father, "Dead Women in Lingerie" (1991), "Mardi Gras: Spring Break" (2011), "Never Back Down: The Beatdown" (2011), "The Hot Flashes" (2013), and "From the Rough" (2013). McNamara appeared on television in productions of "Killer on Board" (1977), "Roots: The Next Generation" (1979), "Gideon's Trumpet" (1980), "Living Proof" (2008), "Arceneaux: Melpomene's Song" (2016). His other television credits include episodes of "Barnaby Jones", "Hart to Hart", "Simon & Simon", "Dallas" in the recurring role of Jarrett McLeish in 1982, "The A-Team", "Hill Street Blues", "Stingray", "Knots Landing", "J.J. Starbuck", "Werewolf", "Head of the Class", "Star Trek: The Next Generation" as Captain Taggart in the 1989 episode "Unnatural Selection", "Freddy's Nightmares", "Roseanne", "Falcon Crest", "Tales from the Crypt", "It's Garry Shandling's Show.", "Veronica Clare", "The Big Easy", and "Orleans". He continued to perform on the local stage in New Orleans and taught acting at Tulane and Loyola. He became a tournament poker player after retiring from acting and competed at the World Series of Poker in Las Vegas. McNamara is survived by his wife, Carol Stone, and two sons.

McNulty, Patricia

Actress Patricia McNulty died on September 4, 2023. She was 80. McNulty was born in Los Angeles, California, on October 16, 1942. She left high school to pursue an acting career in the late 1950s. She was featured in the 1961 film "Tammy Tell Me True" starring Sandra Dee. McNulty appeared on television in episodes of "The Detectives", "The Many Loves of Dobie Gillis", "Hazel", "Mr. Novak", "The Tycoon", "Please Don't Eat the Daisies", and "My Three Sons". She was Yeoman Tina Lawton in the 1966 "Star Trek" episode "Charlie X". She largely retired from acting in the mid-1960s. Peterson was married to the late actor Don Dorrell.

McPhee, Tony

British guitarist and singer Tony McPhee, who was founder of the band the Groundhogs, died of complications from a fall in England on June 6, 2023. He was 79. McPhee was born in Humberston, Lincolnshire, England, on March 23, 1944. He was a founder of the Groundhogs in 1963, serving as singer, songwriter, and guitarist, with Peter Cruickshank on bass and Ken Pustelnik on drums. The Groundhogs backed Champion Jack Dupree and John Lee Hooker on their tours of England in the mid-1960s. McPhee recorded the duet single "Get Your Head Happy!" with Dupree in 1966. The Groundhogs had numerous lineup changes over the next thirty years and released such albums as "Scratching the Surface" (1968), "Thank Christ for the Bomb" (1970), "Split" (1971), "Who Will Save the World? The Mighty Groundhogs" (1972), "Hogwash" (1972), "Solid" (1974), "Black Diamond" (1976), "Razor's Edge" (1985), "Back Against the Wall" (1987), and "Hogs in Wolf's Clothing" (1998). He released his solo debut album, "The Two Sides of Tony (T.S.) McPhee" in 1973. He recorded other solo acoustic blues records and duets with Jo Ann Kelly. He also played with the groups Tony McPhee's Terraplane, Tony McPhee's Turbo, the John Drummer Band, Herbal Mixture, and Hapshash and the Coloured Coat. McPhee suffered a stroke in 2009 which affected his ability to speak and sing and officially left the Groundhogs in 2014. He was injured in a fall in 2022 and never fully recovered.

McReynolds, Jesse

Bluegrass musician Jesse McReynolds died in Gallatin, Tennessee, on June 23, 2023. He was 93. McReynolds was born in Coeburn, Virginia, on July 9, 1929. He became an accomplished mandolin player by his early teens. He began performing with his brother, Jim, as the McReynolds Brothers in the late 1940s. They were joined by guitarist Larry Roll in the early 1950s and became known as the Virginian Trio. Jim and Jesse signed with Capitol Records, where they recorded under the name Jim and Jesse and the Virginia Boys. Jesse served in the U.S. Army in Korea where he teamed with Charlie Louvin in the band the Dusty Roads Boys to entertain the troops. He reunited with his brother after his discharge. They recorded such songs as "The Flame of Love", "Gosh I Miss You All the Time", "Cotton Mill Man", "Diesel on My Tail", "Are You Missing Me", and "Paradise". They starred in the radio program "Suwannee River Jamboree" on WNER radio in Live Oak, Florida, in the late 1950s and early 1960s. Jim and Jesse were invited to join the Grand Ole Opry in 1964. They were seen on television in episodes of "The Porter Wagoner Show" and "Sing Country" and performed together until Jim's death from cancer in 2002. Jesse continued as a solo act, appearing at the Grand Ole Opry and other venues. He was featured in a pair of episodes of the television series "Nashville" as a blind musician in 2016 and 2017. McReynolds was married to Darlene McCoy from 1953 until her death in 1994. He married Joy Tipton in 1996 and she survives him. He is also survived by his daughter Gwen, and sons Michael and Randy.

Meeks, Dale

British actor Dale Meeks, who starred as Simon Meredith in the soap opera "Emmerdale" from 2003 to 2006, died of heart failure at a hospital in South Shields, Tyne and Wear, England, on April 22, 2023. He was 48. Meeks was born in South Shields on May 6, 1974. He performed frequently on stage and toured Great Britain with the musical "Chicago". He appeared frequently on television with roles in episodes of "Byker Grove" as Greg from 1990 to 1992, "Spender", "Badger", "The Bill", "The South Bank Show", "Always and Everyone", "Breeze Block" as Hips in 2002, "Swiss Toni", "Grease Monkeys", "Emmerdale" as Simon Meredith from 2003 to 2006, "Heartbeat", "Being Human", "Comedy Lab", "Hebburn", "The Dumping Ground", "Inspector George Gently", and "Casualty". His other television credits include productions of "The Wingless Bird" (1997), "Catherine Cookson's Tilly Trotter" (1999), "Close & True" (2000), "The Innocent" (2001), "Reg" (2016), and "The Hunt for Raoul Moat" (2023). Meeks was also seen in the 1997 film "Downtime" and the 2015 short "Just Life".

Mehrjui, Dariush

Iranian film director Darius Mehrjui and his wife, writer Vahidea Mohammadi, were found stabbed to death in their home in Karaj, Iran, on October 14, 2023. He was 83. Mehrjui was born in Tehran, Iran, on December 8, 1939. He became interested in films in his youth and later attended the Department of Cinema at the University of California in Los Angeles in 1959. He became dissatisfied with the film program and changed his major to philosophy before graduating in 1964. He returned to Tehran the following year and worked as a journalist and screenwriter. Mehrjui made his film debut directing and writing the 1966 James Bond parody "Diamond 33". His second film, "Gaav" ("The Cow"), proved successful internationally despite being banned by the Iranian authorities

for over a year. He continued to direct such films as "Mr. Gullible" (1970), "The Postman" (1972), and "The Cycle" (1977), and the shorts and documentaries "Isar" (1976), "Enfagh" (1977), "Kidney Transplant" (1978), and "Tehran Emergency Center" (1978). He supported the Iranian revolution that resulted in the ouster of the Shah's monarchy in February of 1979. He helmed the 1980 film "The School We Went To" before moving with his family to Paris the following year. He directed the 1983 film "Journey to the Land of Rimbaud" for French television. He returned to Iran in 1985 and continued his film career under the rule of the Ayatollah Ruhollah Kohmeini. Mehrjui was considered a leading figure in the Iranian New Wave for filmmaking. he continued to direct and frequently write such films as "The Tenants" (1987), "Shirak" (1988), "Hamoun" (1990), "The Lady" (1992), "Sara" (1993), "Pari" (1995), "Leila" (1997), "The Pear Tree" (1998), "Tales of an Island" (2000), "The Mix" (2000), "To Stay Alive" (2002), "Mom's Guest" (2004), "The Music Man" (2007), "The Carpet and the Angel" segment of "Persian Carpet" (2007), "Tehran, Tehran" (2010), "Beloved Sky" (2011), "Hame-dana" (2010), "Orange Suit" (2012), "Good to Be Back" (2013), "Ghosts" (2014), and "A Minor" (2022). He co-wrote many of his later films with his second wife, Vahidea Mohammadi. The two were murdered together at their villa in Meshkin Dahsht, Karaj. They had reportedly been victims of personal threats prior to their death, but no suspect was immediately charged.

Meisle, William

Actor William Meisle died in Doylestown, Pennsylvania, on January 26, 2023. He was 85. Meisle was born in Philadelphia, Pennsylvania, on July 23, 1937. He was

educated at Beloit College and Lawrence College. He began his acting career on stage and performed with the Attic Theater. He joined the drama department at Viterbo University in La Crosse, Wisconsin, where he worked on costume design and construction. He joined the Theater at Monmouth in Maine in 1970 during its inaugural season and remained with the company for five years. He also taught at High Mowing School in Wilton, New Hampshire. He continued to perform in regional theater throughout his career. Meisle also appeared in radio and television commercials and recorded numerous audio books. He was featured in a handful of films including "The End of August" (1981), "School Ties" (1992), "The Man Without a Face" (1993), "The Substance of Fire" (1996), "Man of the

Century" (1999), and "The Manchurian Candidate" (2004). He appeared on television in episodes of "Law & Order" and "As the World Turns". Meisle was married to Nanci Miller from 1959 until her death in 2015 and is survived by their four children.

Meisner, Randy

Musician and singer Randy Meisner, who was a founding member of the Eagles, died of complications from chronic obstructive pulmonary disease (COPD) in Los Angeles, California, on July 25, 2023. He was 77. Meisner was born in Scottsbluff, Nebraska, on March 8, 1946. He began taking

guitar lessons and playing with local bands in his youth. He took up the bass while in high school. He sang and performed with the local band Drivin' Dynamics from 1961 to 1965. They recorded several songs including the regional hit "So Fine". Meisner moved to California in 1966 to play with the band the Soul Survivors, which was renamed the Poor. They recorded several singles with little success including "She's Got the Time, She's Got the Changes" and "Come Back Baby" written by Meisner. He joined the band Poco in 1968 and was featured on the group's debut album, "Pickin' Up the Pieces" in 1969. He quit the band before the album was released. He joined Rick Nelson's Stone Canyon Band in 1969 and performed on the albums "In Concert with the Troubadour, 1969" and "Rudy the Fifth". He was featured in the music documentary "Easy to Be Free" about the band's 1969 concert tour. Meissner was a session musician for James Taylor's songs "Country Road" and "Blossom" and played on Waylon Jenning's album "Singer of Sad Songs" in 1970. He returned to Nebraska after touring Europe with the Stone Canyon Band where he played with the local band Goldrush. He resumed his career in California and joined Don Henley, Glenn Frey, and Bernie Leadon as singer Linda Ronstadt's backing musicians. The four formed the Eagles in September of 1971. He usually played bass and provided backing vocals but also wrote and performed lead on some of the band's songs including "One of These Nights", "Try and Love Again", "Is it True?", "Take the Devil", "Tryin'", and "Certain Kind of Fool". He played with the Eagles on the albums "Eagles" (1972), "Desperado" (1973), "On the Border" (1974), "One of These Nights" (1975), and Hotel California" (1976). He suffered from poor health during their final tour and quit the band after a dispute with Frey in September of 1977. He subsequently released the solo albums "Randy Meisner" (1978) and "One More Song" (1980). He formed the band Randy Meisner & the Silverados in the early 1980s. He recorded a new self-named solo album in 1982. He joined Jimmy Griffin and Billy Swan in the band Black Tie in 1985 and they recorded the 1990 album "When the Night Falls". He and Swan subsequently joined with Charlie Rich Jr. as the Meisner, Swan & Rich trio. He reunited with Poco for the 1989 "Legacy" album. He was inducted into the Rock and Roll Hall of Fame as a member of the Eagles in 1998. He toured with the group the World Classic Rockers in the early 2000s but quit performing due to health issues in 2004. Meisner was married to Jennifer Lee Barton from 1963 until their divorce in 1981 and is survived by their three children. He married long-time girlfriend Lana Rae Graham in 1996 and they remained together until her death from an accidental gunshot wound in 2016.

Melvin, Murray

British actor Murray Melvin, who was featured in Ken Russell's "The Devils" and Stanley Kubrick's "Barry Lyndon", died of complications from injuries suffered in a fall at a hospital in London, England, on April 14, 2023. He was 90.

Melvin was born in London on August 10, 1932. He began working as an office boy at a travel agency after leaving school in his teens. He spent two years with the Royal Air Force during National Service. He later studied drama at the City Literary Institute and joined Joan Littlewood's Theatre Workshop company at the Theatre Royal Stratford East as a assistant stage manager in 1957. Melvin made his acting debut on stage in a small role in a 1957 production of Shakespeare's "Macbeth". He remained a prolific stage actor throughout his career. He appeared frequently in films with roles in "The Concrete Jungle" (1960), "The Risk" (1960), "A Taste of Honey" (1961) as Geoffrey Ingham, "Petticoat Pirates" (1961), "Damn the Defiant!" (1962), "Solo for Sparrow" (1962), "Sparrows Can't Sing" (1963), "The Ceremony" (1963), "Alfie" (1966), "Kaleidoscope" (1966), "Smashing Time" (1967), "The Fixer" (1968), "Start the Revolution Without Me" (1970), Ken Russell's "The Devils" (1971) as Mignon, "The Boy Friend" (1971), "A Day in the Death of Joe Egg" (1972), "Gawain and the Green Knight" (1973), "Ghost Story" (1974), "Ghost in the Noonday Sun" (1974), Russell's "Lisztomania" (1975) as Hector Berlioz, Stanley Kubrick's "Barry Lyndon" (1975) as Rev. Samuel Runt, "Shout at the Devil" (1976), "The Bawdy Adventures of Tom Jones" (1976), "Joseph Andrews" (1977), the animated "Gulliver's Travels" (1977), "Crossed Swords" (1977), "Tales from a Flying Trunk" (1979) as Hans Christian Andersen "Nutracker" (1982), "Sacred Hearts" (1984), "Comrades" (1986), "Funny Boy" (1987), "Testimony" (1987), "Little Dorrit" (1987), "Slipstream" (1989), "The Krays" (1990), "The Fool" (1990), "Let Him Have It" (1991), "As You Like It" (1992), "Princess Caraboo" (1994), "England, My England" (1995), "The Emperor's New Clothes" (2001), "The Phantom of the Opera" (2004) based on Andrew Lloyd Webber's musical, "The Lost City of Z" (2016), and "Juqu'a la Lie" (2019). Melvin was seen on television in episodes of "Armchair Theatre", "Probation Officer", "The Avengers", "The Edgar Wallace Mystery Theatre", "The Indian Tales of Rudyard Kipling", "Six", "The Wednesday Thriller", "Knock on Any Door", "The

Informer", "Emergency-Ward 10", "Vacant Lot", "Angel Pavement" as Turgis in 1967, "Theatre 625", "Half Hour Story", "Softly Softly", "Ooh La La!", "The Tyrant King", Out of the Unknown", "Thirty-Minute Theatre", "The Flaxton Boys", "The Onedin Line", "The Little World of Don Camilo", "Take the Stage", "Bulman", "Super Gran", "Crossbow", "Chillers", "T. Bag and the Sunstones of Montezuma", "Take Off with T. Bag", the animated "Oscar's Orchestra" as the voice of Lucius in 1995, "Bugs", "Jonathan Creek", "Starhunter" as Caravaggio from 2000 to 2003, "Torchwood" in the recurring role of the villainous Bilis Manger in 2007, "Midsomer Murders", "The Spa", and "Starhunter Redux" reprising his role as Caravaggio in 2017. His other television credits include productions of "Paradise Walk" (1961), "The Jokers" (1962), "Parkin's Primitives" (1962), "Isadora" (1966), "St. Joan" (1968), "The Adventures of Don Quixote" (1973), "Harlequinade" (1973), "The Ballad of Solomon Pavey" (1977), "Clouds of Glory" (1978), "This Office Life" (1984), "Christopher Columbus" (1985), "Sunday Pursuit" (1990), "Prisoner of Honor" (1991), "Doomsday Gun" (1994), "Alice in Wonderland" (1999), "David Copperfield" (2000), "The Genius of Mozart" (2004), "Tom's Christmas Tree" (2006), and "Hepzibah - Sie Holt Dich im Schlaf" (2010).

Memisevic, Zinaid

Bosnian-Canadian actor Zinaid Memisevic died in Vancouver, British Columbia, Canada, on January 7, 2023. He was 72. Memisevic was born in Sarajevo, Bosnia (then party of Yugoslavia), on Aprikl 26, 1950. He began appearing on

stage and screen in his youth and appeared in the films "Konjuh Planinom" (1966) and "Quo Vadis Zivorade?!" (1968). He graduated from the Academy of Dramatic Arts of the University of Belgrade in 1973 and joined the National Theatre in Belgrade. He appeared in numerous theatrical productions over the next two decades. Memisevic appeared in the films "Hajka" (1977), "Bosko Buha" (1978), "Gazija" (1981), "Zadah Tela" (1983), "Braca Po Materi" (1988), and "Svedski Aranzman" (1989). He was seen on television in productions of "Vesela Kuca" (1973), "Zasto Je Pucao Alija Alijagic" (1974), "Kraj Nedelje" (1975), "Kucna Terapilja" (1977), "Bosko Buha" (1980), "Pastrovski Vitez" (1982), "Lovac Protiv Topa" (1986), and "Razgovori Stari" (1986). His other television credits include episodes of "Povoriste u Kuci", "Pricanka", "Pesma", "Dva Drugara", "Mali Program", "Svetozar Markovic", "Sedam Sekretara SKOJ-a", "Brisani Prostor", "Odlazak Ratnika, Povratak Marsala", "Smesne i Druge Price", "Bolji Zivot", "Vuk Karadzic", "Cetrdeset Osma - Zavera i Izdaja", and "TV Teatar". Memisevic moved to Canada with his family after the breakup Yugoslavia in 1994. He continued his acting career with roles in the films "Turbulence 2: Fear of Flying" (1999), "Dark Water" (2001), "I Spy" (2002), "Miracle" (2004), the short "Pappy and Speedster"

(2009), "2012" (2009) as President Sergey Makarenko, and "Countdown" (2016). He was seen on television in the tele-films "Breaking the Surface: The Greg Louganis Story" (1997), "Ronnie & Julie" (1997), "Runaway Virus" (2000), and "The Building" (2009), and episodes of "The X-Files", "The Outer Limits", "The Net", "The Adventures of Shirley Holmes", "Secret Agent Man", "Dark Angel", "Da Vinci's Inquest", "Just Cause", "Jake 2.0", and "Arrow". His survivors include his wife, Zanka, and daughter, actress Una Memisevic.

Mendoza, Rossy

Mexican actress and cabaret performer Maria del Rosario Mendoza, who performed under the name Rossy Mendoza, died of a heart attack in Nayarit, Mexico, on December 29, 2023. She was 80. Mendoza was born in Vicam, Mexico, on June 6, 1943. She began performing in burlesque

shows in cabarets in Sonora while in her teens in the 1960s. She was soon appearing in the pages of such Mexican magazines as "Cinelandia" and "Siempre" and became noted for her voluptuous and athletic appearance. She was headlining cabaret shows by the 1970s and toured with La Caravan Corona with other leading stars during the decade. Mendoza made her film debut in 1970's "Capulina Contra los Vampiros".
She was seen in numerous films including popular sexploitation features. Her films include "El Sinverguenza" (1971), "El Festin de la Loba" (1972), "Tu Camino y el Mio" (1973), "Il Imponente" (1973), "Santo vs. the Kidnappers" (1973), "El Hijo del Pueblo" (1974), "Los Perros de Dios" (1974), "Santo en Oro Negro" (1975), "El Mar" (1977(), "La Llamada del Sexo" (1977), "Sweetly You'll Die Through Love" (1977), "El Sexo Sentido" (1980), "California Dancing Club" (1981), "El Vecindario" (1981), "Pistoleros Famosos" (1982), "El Ratero de la Vecindad" (1983), "El Dia del Compadre" (1983), "Esos Viejos Rabo Verdes" (1983), "El Sexo de los Pobres" (1983), "El Dia de los Albaniles" (1984), "Juana la Cantinera" (1984), "Los Verduleros" (1984), "Los Gatos de las Azoteas" (1985), "El Ratero de la Vecindad 2" (1985), "Tres Mexicanos Ardientes" (1986), "Duro y Parejo en la Casita del Pecado" (1987), "Que Buena Esta Mi Ahijada!" (1987), "Todos Abordo" (2010), and the documentary film "Beauties of the Night" (2016). She was featured regularly on the television series "Variedades de Media Noche" in 1977 and appeared in the 1979 tele-novela "Yara".

Mengatti, John

Actor John Mengatti, who was featured as Nick Vitaglia on the television series "The White Shadow" from 1979 to 1981, died Los Angeles, California, on March 26, 2023. He was 68. Mengatti was born in New York City on September 21, 1954. He was best known for his role as a member of the Carver High School basketball team in the urban drama "The

White Shadow" from 1979 to 1981. He was also seen in episodes of "Taxi", "The Facts of Life", "CHiPs", "For Love and Honor" as Pvt. Dominick Petrizzo from 1983 to 1984, "E/R", "Stir Crazy", "Cagney & Lacey", and "Days of Our Lives". Mengatti appeared in a handful of films including "Tag: The Assassination Game" (1982), "Hadley's Rebellion" (1983), "Meatballs Part II" (1984), "Knights of the City" (1986), and "Dead Men Don't Die" (1990). He largely retired from acting in the 1990s but returned to television in the recurring role of Officer Howard in "NYPD Blue" from 2001 to 2002. He was also seen in the 2004 film "Land of the Free?". Mengatti married Lisa Nash-Jones in 2006 and she survives him.

Merlin, Joanna

Actress and casting director Joanna Merlin died complications of myelodysplastic syndrome, a bone marrow disease, in Los Angeles, California, on October 15, 2023. She was 92. She was born JoAnn Delores Ratner in Chicago, Illinois, on July 15, 1931. She began performing on stage in

community theater at the age of 11. She moved to Los Angeles with her family four years later. She attended the University of California at Los Angeles for a year in the early 1950s. She studied acting under Michael Chekhov and performed on stage in the Los Angeles area. Merlin made her film debut in a small role as Jethro's daughter in Cecil B. DeMille's "The Ten Commandments" in 1956. She was also seen in the 1958 film "Weddings and Babies" (1958). She moved to New York City where she continued to perform on stage. She made her debut on Broadway in the play "Becket" in 1961. Merlin was also seen in Broadway productions of "A Far Country" (1961), "Fiddler on the Roof" (1964) originating the role of Tzeitel, Tevye's oldest daughter, "Shelter" (1973), "Uncle Vanya" (1973), "The Survivor" (1981), and "Solomon's Child" (1982). Merlin became involved in casting while performing in "Fiddler on the Roof" and was a casting director for productions of "Company" (1970), "Follies" (1971), "A Little Night Music" (1973), "Pacific Overtures" (1976), "Side by Side by Sondheim" (1977), "On the Twentieth Century" (1979), "Sweeney Todd" (1979), "Evita" (1979), "Merrily We Roll Along" (1981), "A Doll's Life", "Play Memory" (1984), "End of the World" (1984), and "Into the Woods" (1987). She was featured in a television production of "The Power and the Glory" in 1961. She also appeared on television in episodes of "CBS Repertoire Workshop", "Naked City", "The Defenders", "East Side/West Side", "ABC Afterschool Specials", "Amazing

Stories", "Another World", "CBS Schoolbreak Special", "L.A. Law", "Baby Talk", "Northern Exposure", "New York Undercover" in the recurring role of Carmella McNamara from 1996 to 1997, "Law & Order", "Another World", "The Jury", "Law & Order: Special Victims Unit" as Judge Lena Petrovsky from 2000 to 2011, "The Good Wife", "Homeland", and "Smartphone Theatre". Her other television credits include the tele-films "The Winter's Tale" (1967), "The Last Tenant" (1978), "Nurse" (1980), "Jacobo Timerman: Prisoner Without a Name, Cell Without a Number" (1983), "Murder in Black and White" (1990), "A Marriage: Georgia O'Keeffe and Alfred Stieglitz" (1991), "In a Child's Name" (1991), "Love, Honor & Obey: The Last Mafia Marriage" (1993), "The Prosecutors" (1996), "Black and Blue" (1999), and "Witness Protection" (1999). Merlin also continued to appear in such films as "Hester Street" (1975), "All That Jazz" (1979), "Fame" (1980), "Soup for One" (1982), "Love Child" (1982), "Baby It's You" (1983), "The Killing Fields" (1984), "Prince of Darkness" (1987), "Mystic Pizza" (1988), "Class Action" (1991), "Mr. Wonderful" (1993), "Two Bits" (1995), "MURDER and murder" (1996), "City of Angels" (1998), "The Jimmy Show" (2001), "Just Another Story" (2003), "The Invasion" (2007), "The Wackness" (2008), the short "Beautiful Hills of Brooklyn" (2008) which she also produced and wrote, "Sarah's Key" (2010), and "Active Adults" (2017). She was a casting director for the films "Year of the Dragon" (1985), "Big Trouble in Little China" (1986), "The Last Emperor" (1987), "Mr. & Mrs. Bridge" (1990), "The Lover" (1992), "M. Butterfly" (1993), "Little Buddha" (1993), and "Jefferson in Paris" (1995). She taught acting at New York University's Tisch School of the Arts from 1998. She founded the Michael Chekhov Association in 1999 where she held acting workshops. She was author of the 2001 book "Auditioning: An Actor-Friendly Guide". Merlin was married to Martin Paul Lubner from 1950 until their divorce in 1957. She was married to David Dretzin from 1964 until his death in an automobile accident in 2006, and is survived by their two children, documentary filmmaker Rachel Dretzin and actress Julie Dretzin.

Meyers, Lawrence Steven

Actor and producer Lawrence Steven Meyers died in London, England, on December 5, 2023. He was 67. Meyers was born in Mount Vernon, New York, on April 7, 1956. He

attended the University of Florida in the early 1970s where he majored in communications. He subsequently worked for his uncle, Bobby Meyers, for the international sales company JAD Films. He joined New World Pictures after several years where he headed up the international sales division. He was also an executive at the companies Trilogy, Morgan Creek Entertainment, Media 8, and a decade stint with Lorimar Motion Pictures. He founded Meyers Media Group in 2011 and moved to London in 2021. Meyers was co-producer for the

1991 film "Leather Jackets" and was an executive producer for "Return of the Living Dead III" (1993), "Hugo Pool" (1997), "Unfaithful" (2002), "An American Haunting" (2005), "4 Minute Mile" (2014), and "Sacrifice" (2016). He served as consulting producer for the 2004 tele-film "The Librarian: Quest for the Spear". Meyers appeared in several films including the science fiction classic "Battle Beyond the Stars" (1980) as one of the alien Kelvin, "Dick Tracy" (1990) as Little Face, "Guncrazy" (1992), and "Chicken Park" (1994). He was also seen in a 1992 episode of "The Amazing Live Sea-Monkeys".

Migliacci, Franco

Italian lyricist and actor Franco Migliacci died in Rome, Italy, on September 15, 2023. He was 92. Migliacci was born in Mantua, Italy, on October 28, 1930. He settled in

Florence with his family where he studied acting. He moved to Rome in the early 1950s where he appeared in such films as "Carica Eroica" (1952), "Il Viale della Speranza" (1953), "Ci Troviamo in Galleria" (1953), "It Happened in the Park" (1953), "Amori di Mezzo Secolo" (1954), "The Art of Getting Along" (1954), "Di Qua di la Piave" (1954), "Una Voce, Una Chitarra, un Po' di Luna" (1956), "Noi Siamo le Colonne" (1956), "Serenata al Vento" (1956), "Ho Amato Una Diva" (1957), "He Thief, She Thief" (1958), "Giovane Canaglia" (1958), and "Nel Blu Dipinto di Blu" (1961). He was seen on television in productions of "L'Alfiere" (1956), "Il Marziano Filippo" (1956), and "Cavaliere Senza Armatura" (1957). He and Domenico Modugno wrote the song "Nel Blu Dipinto di Blu" in 1958, which became known internationally as "Volare". Migliacci was a writer on the films "Tutto e Musica" (1963) and "Per Amore... per Magia..." (1967). He also wrote several radio plays and was an illustrator for the children's magazine "The Pioneer". Migliacci is survived by his wife, Gloria Wall, and their three children.

Miles, Christopher

British film director Christopher Miles died of cancer in Devizes, England, on September 15, 2023. He was 84. Miles

was born in London, England, on April 19, 1939. He studied at Winchester College from 1953 to 1957. He was invited to show his 8mm film on the BBC children's program "All Your Own" in 1957. He also helped write and produced the variety program "The Begmillian Show", which featured his younger sister, actress Sarah Miles. He studied film director at the Institut des Hautes

Etudes Cinematographiques in the early 1960s and directed and wrote the 1962 short film "A Vol d'Oiseau". Miles' 1963 short film, "The Six-Sided Triangle", was nominated for an Academy Award. He wrote and directed the 1964 short "Rhythm 'n Greens" featuring the pop group the Shadows and helmed his first feature, the musical comedy "Up Jumped a Swagman", in 1965. His other films include "The Virgin and the Gypsy" (1970) based on D.H. Lawrence's story, Jean Anouilh's "A Time for Loving" (1972), Jean Genet's "The Maids" (1975), "That Lucky Touch" (1975), "Priest of Love" (1981), and "The Clandestine Marriage" (1998). He directed the 1972 short "Zinotchka" for television and an episode of "Full House". He also directed the controversial television production "Alternative 3" in 1977 and an adaptation of Roald Dahl's tale "Neck" for "Tales of the Unexpected" in 1979. His other television credits include productions of "Daley's Decathlon" (1982), "Marathon" (1984), "Aphrodisias - City of Aphrodite" (1984), "Lord Elgin and Some Stones of No Value" (1986), and "Love in the Ancient World" (1997). He served as professor of film and television at the Royal College of Art from 1989 to 1993. Miles married painter Suzy Armstrong in 1967 and is survived by her and their daughter, Sophie.

Millard, Irmgard

German-American actress Irmgard Millard, who worked frequently in films for her husband, director Nick Millard, died in Ave Maria, Florida, on August 31, 2023. She  was 86. She was born Irmgard Grabinger in Munich, Germany, in 1937. She moved to England and worked as a tourist guide in the mid-1950s. She settled in San Francisco in 1962, where she met filmmaker Nick Millard. They married in 1966 and she began appearing in his films in the 1970s. Irmgard was seen in such horror and exploitation films as "Alcatraz Breakout" (1975), "Satan's Black Wedding" (1976), "Death Nurse" (1987), "Cemetery Sisters" (1987), "Doctor Bloodbath" (1987), "Death Nurse 2" (1988), "The Terrorists" (1988), "A Divorce in Venice" (1989), "Dracula in Vegas" (1999), "The Blue Angel" (1999), "Bullet Ballet" (2012), "Death Sisters" (2013), and "Don't Touch That Dial" (2015). Nick Millard named his film company after his wife, IRMI Films, and she served as producer for "Gunblast" (1986), "Death Nurse" (1987), "Death Nurse 2" (1988), "The Terrorists" (1988), "The Blue Angel" (1999), "The Turn of the Screw" (2003), and "A Tribute to Priscilla Alden" (2012). She was married to Nick Millard until his death in 2022 and is survived by their two daughters, Valerie and Alexandra.

Miller, Billy

Actor Billy Miller, who was noted for his role as Billy Abbott on the television soap opera "The Young and the Restless", died of a self-inflicted gunshot wound to the head in Austin, Texas, on September 15, 2023. He was 43. Miller was born in Tulsa, Oklahoma, on September 17, 1979, and was raised in Grand Praine, Texas. He graduated from the University of Texas in Austin and moved to Los Angeles to pursue an acting career. He signed with the Wilhelmina  modeling agency and was cast in several national commercials. He was best known for his roles in soap operas, starring as the villainous Richie Novak in "All My Children" from 2006 to 2007. He played Billy Abbott on "The Young and the Restless" from 2008 to 2014, earning three Daytime Emmy Awards and two additional nominations. He played Jason Morgan and his twin, Drew Cain, on "General Hospital" from 2014 to 2019, receiving another Daytime Emmy nomination. Miller appeared as Charlie Young (aka John Delario) in the short-lived CW crime drama "Ringer" from 2011 to 2012. He was also seen in episodes of "CSI: NY", "Justified", "Castle", "Enormous", "CSI: Crime Scene Investigation", "Major Crimes", "Ray Donovan", "Suits", "Truth Be Told" as Alex Dunn from 2019 to 2021, "The Rookie", and "NCIS". His other television credits include the tele-films "Fatal Honeymoon" (2012) and "Urban Cowboy" (2016). Miller appeared in several films including "Remembering Nigel" (2009), "American Sniper" (2014), and "Bad Blood" (2015).

Miller, George T.

Scottish-Australian film director George T. Miller, who helmed the 1982 film "The Man from Snowy River", died of a heart attack in Melbourne, Australia, on February 17, 2023. He was 79. Miller was born in Edinburgh, Scotland, on November 28, 1943. He settled in Wonthaggi, Victoria, Australian with his family in 1947. He began working in the mail room at Crawford Television after completing high school.  He began working as a cameraman in the mid-1960s. He was soon directing episodes of such television series as "Homicide", "Matlock Police", "Division Four", "Ryan", "cash and Company", "The Box", "The Sullivans", "Bluey", "Against the Wind", "Young Ramsey", and "Five Mile Creek". He was best known for his 1982 feature film debut, the Australian Western "The Man from Snowy River" starring Kirk Douglas. Miller went on to direct such films as "The Aviator" (1985) starring Christopher Reeve, "Cool Change" (1986), "Les Patterson Saves the World" (1987) starring Barry Humphries, "Miracle Down Under" (1987), the fantasy classic "The NeverEnding Story II: The Next Chapter" (1990), "Over the Hill" (1992), "Frozen Assets" (1992), "Gross Misconduct" (1993), "Andre"

(1994), "Zeus and Roxanne" (1997), and "Robinson Crusoe" (1997). Miller continued to work in television, helming the mini-series and tele-films "The Last Outlaw" (1980), "Bellamy" (1981), "Der Schwarze Bumerang" (1982), "All the Rivers Run" (1983), "The Last Bastion" (1984), "Anzacs" (1985), "The Far Country" (1987), "Badlands 2005" (1988), "Goodbye, Miss 4th of July" (1988), "Spooner" (1989), "A Mom for Christmas" (1990), "In the Nick of Time" (1991), "The Great Elephant Escape" (1995), "Silver Strand" (1995), "Tidal Wave: No Escape" (1997), "In the Doghouse" (1998), "Journey to the Center of the Earth" (1999), "Tribe" (1999), and "Attack of the Sabertooth" (2005). He had a dispute with the producers of his final film, the 2009 supernatural thriller "Prey", and demanded that his name be removed from the credits. He was sometimes confused with fellow Australia director George Miller, who was noted for helming the "Mad Max" films. His survivors include sons Harvey and Geordie Miller.

Miller, Judith

Scottish antiques expert Judith Miller, who was featured frequently on the BBC's "Antiques Roadshow", died at a hospital in North London, England, on April 8, 2023. She was

71. She was born Judith Henderson Cairns in Galashiels, Scotland, on September 16, 1951. She studied history at the University of Edinburgh and began collecting antiques. She and her first husband, Martin Miller, co-wrote "Miller's Antiques Price Guide" in 1979. She wrote articles on antiques for various newspapers and magazines including "The Scotsman", "Financial Times", "The Daily Telegraph", "Antiques and Collectables", and "BBC Homes & Antiques". Miller began working in television as a consultant and co-host of "The Antiques Trail" and appeared on "The House Detectives" from 1997 to 2000. She was author or contributor to over 100 books about antiques and house interiors. Miller was frequently featured as an antiques expert on BBC's "Antiques Roadshow" from 2015. to 2021. She was married to Martin Miller from 1978 until their divorce in 1992 and they had two children together. She married John Wainwright after a lengthy relationship in 2015 and is also survived by him and their son.

Milo, Jean-Roger

French actor Jean-Roger Milo died in France on October 15, 2023. He was 66. Milo was born in Paris, France, on June 5, 1957. He trained as an actor with Sacha Pitoeff and began his career on stage. He made his film debut in the late 1970s and appeared in "The Key Is in the Door" (1978), "Le Divorcement" (1979), "Temporale Rosy" (1980), "La Femme Flic" (1980), "La Bande du Rex" (1980), "Le Jardinier" (1981), "Instinct de Femme" (1981), "Boulevard des Assassins" (1982), "Tir Groupe" (1982), "Ace of Aces" (1982) starring Jean-Paul Belmondo, "Un Dimanche de Flic" (1983), "The Moon in the Gutter" (1983), "Le Marginal" (1983), "Dog Day" (1984),

Bernard Tavernier's "A Sunday in the Country" (1984), "Les Enrages" (1985), "Les Loups Entre Eux" (1985), "Les Clowns de Dieu" (1986), "Sarraounia" (1986), "Cayenne Palace" (1987), "Radio Raven" (1989), "Life and Nothing But" (1989), "Terre Rouge" (1991), "L. 627" (1992), Claude Berri's "Germinal" (1993), "Lucie Aubrac" (1997), "Le Pari" (1997), "Asterix and Obelix vs. Caesar" (1999), "House Arrest" (1999) "Mamirolle" (2000), "Sauve-Moi" (2000), "Daughter of Keltoum" (2001), and "San Antonio" (2004). Milo appeared on television in producitons of 'Histoire Contemporaine' (1981), "Toutes Griffes Dehors" (1982), "Pablo Est Mort" (1983), "Manon Roland" (1989), "Femme de Voyou" (1991), and "Les Sagards" (2000).

Minow, Newton N.

Attorney Newton N. Minow, who declared that television was a "vast wasteland" in a speech while chairman of the Federal Communications Commission in the early 1960s,

died of a heart attack at his home in Chicago, Illinois, on May 6, 2023. He was 97. Minow was born in Milwaukee, Wisconsin, on January 17, 1926. He served in the U.S. Army during World War II and was stationed in India from 1944 to 1946. He attended Northwestern University after his discharge and earned a law degree from Northwestern University School of Law in 1950. He served as a law clerk to Chief Justice Fred Vinson of the U.S. Supreme Court from 1951 to 1952. He was an assistant counsel to Adlai Stevenson, the Governor of Illinois, from 1952 to 1953 and worked in his presidential campaigns in 1952 and 1956. He was part of his law firm, Stevenson, Rifkind & Wirtz, from 1955 to 1961. Minow worked for John F. Kennedy's presidential campaign in 1960 and was appointed by him as chairman of the Federal Communications Commission in 1961. He became noted as a critic of commercial television and described it as a "vast wasteland" at a speech before the National Association of Broadcasters in May of 1961. He also commented that "when television is good, nothing - not the theater, not the magazines or newspapers - nothing is better. But when television is bad, nothing is worse." He was instrumental in persuading the U.S. Congress to establish communications satellites and mandated UHF reception for television receivers, increasing the number of television stations around the country. He left the FCC in June of 1963 and joined the international law firm Sidley Austin LLP in Chicago as a managing partner in 1965. He became a senior counsel in 1991. He was instrumental in recruiting Barack Obama to work for the firm in 1988 and later became a leading supporter of Obama's presidential candidacy. Minow served on numerous corporate and philanthropic boards and served as co-chairman of the presidential debates in 1976 and 1980. Minow served on the Board of Governors for the Public Broadcasting Service (PBS) from 1973 and was chairman from 1978 to 1980. He was co-author of several books including "Equal Time: The Private Broadcaster and the Public Interest" (1964), "Abandoned in the Wasteland: Children, Television, and the First Amendment" (1995), and "Inside the Presidential Debates: Their Improbably Past and Promising Future" (2008). He was awarded the Presidential Medal of Freedom from President Obama in 2016. Minow was married to Josephine Baskin from 1949 until her death in 2022. He is survived by their son and two daughters.

Minutoli, Domenico

Italian actor Domenico Minutoli died in Italy on May 23, 2023. He was 76. Minutoli was born in Messina, Sicily,

Italy, on January 11, 1947. He began performing on stage from an early age. He was seen on television in productions of "La Mano Sugli Occhi" (1979), "L'Uomo Che Sognava Con le Aquile" (2006), and "The Murder of a General" (2007). His other television credits include episodes of "I Racconti del Maresciallo", "Il Maresciallo Rocca", "Un Prete Tra Noi" as Quinto in 1997, "Detective Montalbano", "Don Matteo", and "1992". Minutoli appeared in the films "Volevo i Pantaloni" (1990), Roberto Benigi's "Johnny Stecchino" (1991) as the Chief of Police, "S.P.Q.R. 2000 e 1/2 Anni Fa" (1994), "Dio C'e" (1998), "Fantozzi 2000 - La Clonazione" (1999), and "Barney's Version" (2010).

Mirisch, Walter

Film producer Walter Mirisch, who won the Academy Award for the 1967 film "In the Heat of the Night", died in Los Angeles, California, on February 24, 2023. He was 101.

Mirisch was born in New York City on November 8, 1921. He worked as a movie theater usher in his teens and later moved into management positions. He graduated from the University of Wisconsin at Madison in 1942 and earned a graduate degree from Harvard's School of Business Administration the following year. He moved to Burbank, California, to write technical articles at a bomber plant during World War II after a heart murmur kept him from serving in the U.S. Navy. He made his debut as a producer at Monogram for 1947's "Fall Guy". Mirisch continued to produce such films as "I Wouldn't Be in

Your Shoes" (1948), "Bomba, the Jungle Boy" (1949) the first in a series of jungle thrillers, "The Lost Volcano" (1950), "County Fair" (1950), "The Hidden City" (1950), "The Lion Hunters" (1951), "Cavalry Scout" (1951), "Elephant Stampede" (1951), the science fiction film "Flight to Mars" (1951), "Fort Osage" (1952), "Rodeo" (1952), "Wild Stallion" (1952), "African Treasure" (1952), "The Rose Bowl Story" (1952), "Bomba and the Jungle Girl" (1952), and "Hiawatha" (1952). Mirisch became head of production at Allied Artists Studios, then a division of Monogram, in the early 1950s. He was a producer or executive producer for the films "Flat Top" (1952), "Safari Drums" (1953), "Fighter Attack" (1953), the horror film "The Maze" (1953), "The Golden Idol" (1954), "Riot in Cell Block 11" (1954), "Killer Leopard" (1954), "The Human Jungle" (1954), "The Big Combo" (1955), "Seven Angry Men" (1955), "An Annapolis Story" (1955), "The Warriors" (1955), "Lord of the Jungle" (1955) the final Bomba film, "Wichita" (1955), "The Phenix City Story" (1955), the science fiction classic "Invasion of the Body Snatchers" (1956), "World Without End" (1956), "Crime in the Streets" (1956), "The First Texan" (1956), "Hold Back the Night" (1956), "Friendly Persuasion" (1956), Roger Corman's "The Undead" (1957), "The Oklahoman" (1957), and "The Tall Stranger" (1957). He and his brothers, Marvin and Harold Mirisch formed a production company, The Mirisch Company, and signed a distribution deal with United Artists. Walter produced the first film from the new company, "Man of the West", starring Gary Cooper, in 1958. He also produced the films "Fort Massacre" (1958), "The Man in the Net" (1959), "The Gunfight at Dodge City" (1959), "The Horse Soldiers" (1959), "Cast a Long Shadow" (1959), the western classic "The Magnificent Seven" (1960), "By Love Possessed" (1961), the musical "West Side Story" (1961), "The Children's Hour" (1961), the Elvis Presley films "Follow That Dream" (1962) and "Kid Galahad" (1962), "Two for the Seesaw" (1962), the World War II drama "The Great Escape" (1963), "Toys in the Attic" (1963), "The Pink Panther" (1963), "633 Squadron" (1964), "A Shot in the Dark" (1964), "The Russians Are Coming the Russians Are Coming" (1966) "Hawaii" (1966), "How to Succeed in Business Without Really Trying" (1967), "In the Heat of the Night" (1967) earning an Academy Award for Best Picture, "Fitzwilly" (1967), "The Party" (1968), "The Thomas Crown Affair" (1968), "Sinful Davey" (1969), "Some Kind of Nut" (1969), "Halls of Anger" (1970), "The Landlord" (1970), "The Hawaiians" (1970), "They Call Me Mister Tibbs!" (1970), "The Organization" (1971), "Fiddler on the Roof" (1971), "Scorpio" (1973), "The Spikes Gang" (1974), "Mr. Majestyk" (1974), "Midway" (1976), "Gray Lady Down" (1978), "Same Time, Next Year" (1978), "The Prisoner of Zenda" (1979), "Dracula" (1979) starring Frank Langella, and "Romantic Comedy" (1983). He was a producer for the "Pink Panther" animated shorts in the 1960s under the company name Mirisch-Geoffrey-DePatie-Freleng. Mirisch also moved into television in the late 1950s, co-producing such series as "Wichita Town", "Peter Loves Mary", "The Rat Patrol", "Hey Landlord", and "The Magnificent Seven". He was a producer of the tele-films "High Midnight" (1979), "Desperado" (1987), "Trouble Shooters:

Trapped Beneath the Earth" (1993), "A Case for Life" (1996), and "Bridal Wave". He was executive producer of the animated series "The Pink Panther" and "Pink Panther & Pals". He served as president of the Academy of Motion Picture Arts and Sciences from 1973 to 1977. Mirisch received the Irving G. Thalberg Memorial Award from the Academy in 1978 and the Jean Hersholt Humanitarian Award in 1983. He was author of the 2008 memoir "I Thought We Were Making Movies, Not History". Mirisch was married to Patricia Kahan from 1947 until her death in 2004. He is survived by his sons Andrew and Lawrence and daughter Anne.

Miroshnichenko, Irina

Russian actress Irina Miroshnichenko died in Moscow, Russia, on August 3, 2023. She was 81. Miroshnichenko was born in Barnaul, Russia, on July 24, 1942. She trained as an actress at the Moscow Art Theater School

from 1961. She made her film debut in "Walking the Streets of Moscow" in 1964. She continued to appear in such films as "Avariya" (1965), "Korolevskaya Regata" (1966), "Andrei Rublev" (1966) as Mary Magadalene, "Ikh Znali Tolko v Litso" (1967), "Shtrikhi k Portretu V.I. Lenina" (1967), "The Secret Agent's Blunder" (1968), "Nikolay Bauman" (1968), "Kremlyovskie Kuranty" (1970), "Uncle Vanya" (1970), "Mission in Kabul" (1971), "A Soldier Came Back from the Front" (1972), "That Sweet Word: Liberty!" (1972), "Zdes Nash Dom" (1974), "Avariya" (1974), "Okovani Soferi" (1975), "Doverie" (1976), "Strakh Vysoty" (1976), "...And Other Officials" (1976), "Ferhat ile Sirin" (1978), "Komissiya Po Rassledovaniyu" (1979), "Agent Sekrotnoy Sluzhby" (1979), "Chudak" (1979), "Vernemsya Osenyu" (1979), "Staryy Novyy God" (1981), "Love and Lies" (1981), "Shlyapa" (1982), "Mera Presecheniya" (1983), "Priznat Vinovnym" (1984), "Nasledstvo" (1985), "Neudobnyy Chelovek" (1985), "Tayny Madam Vong" (1986), "Zhaloba" (1986), "Nayezdniki" (1987), "Repetitor" (1987), "Winter Cherry 2" (1990), "The World in Another Dimension" (1990), and "Klyukva v Sakhare" (1995). She appeared on television in productions of "Zagovor" (1971), "Yedinstvennyy Svidetel" (1973), "Solo Dlya Chasov s Boyem" (1974), "Chayka" (1974), "V Odnom Mikrorayone" (1976), "Chekhovskiye Stranitsy" (1977), "Odnokashniki" (1978), "Babushki Nadvoe Skazali..." (1979), "Kristalybirodalom" (1982), "Professiya - Sledovatel" (1984), "Tri Sestry" (1984), "Ryzhiy Chestnyy Vlyublyonnyy" (1984), "Ne Soshlis Kharakterami" (1989), "Zimnyaya Vishnya 3" (1995), "Proshchalnoe Ekho" (2004), and "Sesta Po Nasledstvu" (2018). Miroshnichenko was married to playwright Mikhail Shatrov from 1960 until their divorce in 1972. She was briefly married to film director Vytautas Zalakevicius in 1972 and was married to actor Igor Vasilev from 1975 until their divorce in 1980.

Mistretta, Sal

Actor Sal Mistretta died in Palm Springs, California, on January 26, 2023. He was 78. Mistretta was born in Brooklyn, New York, on January 9, 1945. He studied drama at

Ithica College in New York. He performed frequently on stage in plays, musicals, and revues. He was seen on Broadway in productions of "Something's Afoot" (1976), "On the Twentieth Century" (1978), "Evita" (1978), "Welcome to the Club" (1989), "Sunset Boulevard" (1994) as Police Chief Sheldrake, and "Cabaret" (1998). Mistretta was featured in several films including "Stepmom" (1998), "Building Girl" (2005), "The Immaculate Misconception" (2006), "The Narrows" (2008), and "Step Up 3D" (2010). He appeared on television in productions of "Sweeney Tood: The Demon Barber of Fleet Street" (1982) and "Having It All" (1982), and episodes of "Simon & Simon", "Third Watch", "Law & Order", "Law & Order: Criminal Intent", and "Rescue Me". Mistretta is survived by his husband of 46 years, Jeff Jelineo.

Mitani, Noboru

Japanese actor Noboru Mitani died of chronic heart failure in Tokyo, Japan, on January 15, 2023. He was 90. Mitani was born in Fukuyama, Hiroshima, Japan, on April 9, 1932. He appeared in numerous films from the late 1960s

including Akira Kurosawa's "Dodes'ka-den" (1970), "Kigeki: Onna Ikitemasu" (1971), "Watch Your Heart, Tamegoro" (1971), "Under the Flag of the Rising Sun" (1972), "Flowers at the Crossing" (1972), "Gendai Yakuza: Hito-kiri Yota" (1972), "Outlaw Killers: Three Mad Dog Brothers" (1972), "Tabi No Omosa" (1972), "The Music" (1972), "The Black Battlefront Kidnappers" (1973), "Graveyard of Honor" (1975), "Challenge Me Dragon" (1975), "Violent Panic: The Big Crash" (1976), "The Sun Never Cries" (1976), Kon Ichikawa's horror thriller "The Inugami Family" (1976), "Japanese Belly Button" (1977), "Dannoura Pillow War" (1977), "Inugami No Tatari" (1977), "Yumeno Kyusaku's Girl Hell" (1977), "The Devil's Island" (1977), "Teacher Deer" (1978), the science fiction film "Message from Space" (1978) with Vic Morrow and Sonny Chiba, "Young Beast: Secret Pleasures" (1978), "The Demon" (1978), "Devil's Flute" (1979), "The Woman with Red Hair" (1979), "Oretachi Ni Haka Wa Nai" (1979), "Marital War in Kibogaoka" (1979), "Dog of Fortune" (1979), "Beautiful Girl Hunter" (1979), "Path of the Beast" (1980), "Koichiro Uno's Shell Competition" (1980),

"Nippon Keishicho Na Haji to Iwareta Futari: Keiji Chindochu" (1980), "Female Teacher: Dirty Afternoon" (1981), "Samurai Reincarnation" (1981), "Lonely Heart" (1981), "Angel Guts: Red Porno" (1981), "Tantei Monogatari" (1983), "Sex Crime" (1983), "Nozoki" (1983), "Izakaya Choji" (1983), "Yudono-Sanroku Noroi Mura" (1984), "Shanhai Bansukingu" (1984), "Big Magnum Kuroiwa Sensei" (1985), "The Legend of the Stardust Brothers" (1985), "The Second Is a Christian" (1985), "Love Letter" (1985), "Congratulatory Speech" (1985), "Ora Tokyo Sa Iguda" (1985), "Atami Satsujin Jiken" (1986), "Shinshi Domei" (1986), "Too Much" (1987), "A Taxing Woman's Return" (1988), the gruesome horror film "Evil Dead Trap" (1988), "Bee Bop Highschool: Koko Yotaro Ondo" (1988), "Sweet Home" (1989), "Black Rain" (1989), "Buddies" (1989), "Hagure Keiji: Junjoha" (1989), "Youkai Tengoku: Ghost Hero" (1990), "Minbo" (1992), "Kantsubaki" (1992), "O-Roshiya-Koku Suimu-Tan" (1992), "Hold Me and Kiss Me" (1992), "The Last Dance" (1993), "Kowagaru Hitobito" (1994), "Elephant Song" (1994), "A Quiet Life" (1995), "Parasite Eve" (1997), "Marutai No Onna" (1997), "Kagi" (1997), "Glassy Ocean: Kujira No Choyaku" (1998), "The Geisha House" (1998), "Atsumono" (1999), "I Went To" (2000), "Iki-Jigoku" (2000), "Deracine" (2003), "In Za Puru" (2005), "Ubume No Natsu" (2005), "Semishigure" (2005), "The Insects Unlisted in the Encyclopedia" (2007), "Kissho Tennyo" (2007), "Sakura No Hito Tachi" (2009), "Play Cards When You Die" (2009), "The Storyteller's Apprentice" (2013), "The Ark in the Mirage" (2015), and "Reason of Life" (2015). Mitani also appeared in television productions of "Jikan Desuyo" (1965), "Matsumoto Seicho No Uma Wo Uru Onna" (1982), "Rirakkusu: Matsubara Katsumi No Nichijo Seikatsu" (1982), "Kyotaro Nishimura's Travel Mystery 4" (1983), "Dansen" (1983), "Kage No Kokuhatsu-Sha" (1983), "The Kosuke Kindaichi Series 4: The Foggy Mountain Lodge" (1985), "The Asami Mitsuhiko Mystery 4" (1988), "Kikyo" (1988), "Izakaya Choji" (1992), "Hiroshima" (1995), "Kyoto Sekushi Yokai Satsujin Annai" (1997), , "Kaseifu Wa Mita! 16" (1997), "Kagemusha Tokugawa Leyasu" (1998), "Ninjo Kyoju Natsume Ryunosuke 2: Izu No Odoriko Satsujin Jiken" (1998), "Kyotaro Nishimura's Travel Mystery 36" (2001), and "The Vulture" (2007). His other television credits include episodes of "The Guard Man", "Return of Ultraman", "Horror Theater Unbalance", "Ultraman Taro" as Kazumi Futani in 1974, "Fight! Dragon", "The Gorilla Seven", "G-Men '75", "Daitokai - Tatakai No Hibi", "Yokomizo Seishi Shirizu", "The Detective Story", "Tennou No Ryouriban", "Shin Jikin: Waga Uta Wa Hana Ichimonme", "Space Sheriff Gavan" as Witch Kiba in 1983, "Space Sheriff Shaider", "Magical Girl Chukana Ipanema", "Aishiatterukai!", the anime "Princess Tutu" as the voice of Drosselmeyer in 2003, and "Sengoku Jietai Sekigahara No Tatakai".

Moder, Lee

Comic book artist Lee Moder, who was co-creator of the DC superhero Courtney 'Stargirl' Whitmore, died on January 15, 2023. He was 53. Moder was born in Pittsburgh, Pennsylvania, in 1970. He graduated from La Roche University with a degree in graphic design in 1992. He began working on comics in the early 1990s at Malibu Comics. He joined DC in 1993 where he served as artist for the series "Wonder Woman"

and "Legion of Super-Heroes". He was best known for collaborating with writer Geoff Johns for the "Stars & S.T.R.I.P.E." comic in 1999 which introduced the character of Courtney Whitmore. The series also re-imagined the Golden Age character of Pat Dugan's Stripesy, former sidekick of the Star-Spangled Kid, as Courtney's stepfather who commands a giant robot as S.T.R.I.P.E. Courtney, wielding the cosmic staff of Starman as Star. She later joined the Justice Society of America as Stargirl. The characters were stars of the CW's "Stargirl" television series for three seasons from 2020 to 2022 starring Brec Bassinger as Courtney and Luke Wilson as Pat. Stargirl was also featured in several DC animated series including "Justice League Action" and "Young Justice". Moder also provided art for such titles as Marvel's "X-Factor" and "Captain American Annual" in 2001, Dynamite's "Highlander", "Red Sonja", and "Painkiller Jane", Top Cow's "Dragon Prince", CrossGen's "Scion", Boom! Studios' "Zombie Tales", and the digital comic strip "The Mucker: The Adventures of Billy Byrne".

Mohawk, Essra

Singer and songwriter Essra Mohawk, who wrote several tunes for "Schoolhouse Rock" television series, died of cancer at her home in Nashville, Tennessee, on December 11, 2023. She was 85. She was born Sandra Elayne Hurvitz in

Philadelphia, Pennsylvania, on April 23, 1948. She recorded her first single, "The Boy with the Way" with Liberty Records in 1964 under the name Jamie Carter. She used her own name when writing the songs "I'll Never Learn" for the Shangri-Las and "The Spell Comes After" for the Vanilla Fudge. She briefly performed with Frank Zappa and the Mothers of Invention in 1967 and released her first album, "Sandy's Album Is Here At Last!", from Bizarre in 1968. She signed with Reprise Records for the 1969 album "Primordial Lovers". She soon married producer Frazier Mohawk and became known as Essra Mohawk. She planned to perform at the Woodstock Festival in 1969 but her driver got lost and she arrived too late. She was noted for singing several songs for the television series "Schoolhouse Rock!" in the mid-1970s including "Interjections!", "Mother Necessity", and "Sufferin' Till Suffrage". She also sang the theme for the "Sesame Street" segment "Teeny Little Super Guy" in the 1980s. Mohawk was well received when she performed the song "Appointment with a Dream" on "The Gong

Show" in 1977. She had success with several of the songs she had written including "Change of Heart" by Cyndi Lauper in 1987 and "Stronger Than the Wind" by Tina Turner in 1989. She continued to release such albums as "Essra Mohawk" (1974), "Burnin' Shinin'" (1982), "E-Turn" (1985), "Essie Mae Hawk Meets the Killer Grove Band" (1999), "Essra Live at Genghis Cohen" (2001), "You're Not Alone" (2003), "Love Is Still the Answer" (2006), "Revelations of the Secret Diva" (2007), and "The One and Only" (2019). Mohawk was lead vocalist for the animated short film "Sufferin' Till You're Straight" in 2011. She and Frazier Mohawk were married until his death in 2012.

Mohyeddin, Zia

British-Pakistani actor Zia Mohyeddin died in Karachi, Pakistan, on February 13, 2023. He was 91. Mohyeddin was born in Lyallpur, Punjab, British India (now Faisalabad, Pakistan), on June 20, 1931. He was raised in Lahore, Pakistan, and traveled to London to attend the Royal Academy of Dramatic Art from 1953 to 1955. He began his career on stage and was featured in theatrical productions of "Long Day's Journey into Night" and "Julius Caesar". He made his West End debut in 1960 with the play "A Passage to India" as Dr. Aziz. He reprised the role on Broadway in 1962 and in a television adaptation on "BBC Play of the Month" in 1965. He returned to the Broadway stage in 1968 in the play "The Guide". He was also seen on television in productions of "Let Me Ever Escape Them" (1954), "The Three Princes" (1954), and "The Alien Sky" (1956), and in episodes of "Lilli Palmer Theatre", "Danger Man", "Drama '61", "Sir Francis Drake", "The Doctors and the Nurses", and "Armstrong Circle Theatre". Mohyeddin made his film as Tafas, the Arab guide of Peter O'Toole's T.E. Lawrence, who is shot to death by Omar Sharif's Sherif Ali ibn el Kharish for drinking water from the wrong well, in David Lean's 1963 Oscar-winning epic "Lawrence of Arabia". He was also featured in the films "A Boy Ten Feet Tall" (1963), "Behold a Pale Horse" (1964), "Khartoum" (1966) with Charlton Heston and Alec Guinness, "Deadlier Than the Male" (1967), "The Sailor from Gibraltar" (1967), the science fiction film "They Came from Beyond Space" (1967), and the off-beat comedy "Work Is a Four-Letter Word" (1968). He appeared on television in productions of "She's a Free Country" (1963), "Vicky and the Sultan" (1963), "The Joel Brand Story" (1965), and "After Many a Summer" (1967). His other television credits include episodes of "The Hidden Truth" as Dr. Hamavid de Silva in 1964, "The Indian Tales of Rudyard Kipling", "Secret Agent", "The Avengers", "Thirteen Against Fate", "Armchair Theatre", "Orlando" as Abdul in 1966, "Jackanory", "Trapped", "Public Eye", "Man in a Suitcase", "Champion House", "City '69", "The Expert", "The Champions", "Hadleigh", and "Detective". He returned to Pakistan in the late

1960s where he hosted the television talk show "The Zia Mohyeddin Show" from 1969 to 1973. He also helped fund the PIA Arts and Dance Academy and appeared in the films "Bombay Talkie" (1970) and "Mujram Kaun" (1971). He again left Pakistan to return to England in the late 1970s because of political problems with General Zia-ul-Haq's military regime. Mohyeddin resumed his acting career in the films "Ashanti" (1979), "The Assam Garden" (1985), "Partition" (1987), and "Immaculate Conception" (1992). He was also seen in television productions of "Death of a Princess" (1980), "Staying On" (1980), "Salt on a Snake's Tail" (1983), "The Jewel in the Crown" (1984), "Lord Mountbatten - The Last Viceroy" (1986) as V.P. Menon, "We Are the Children" (1987), "Shalom Salaam" (1989), "Gummed Labels" (1992), "Doomsday Gun" (1994), and "L'Enfant des Rues" (1995). He appeared in episodes of such series as "Gangsters" as Iqbal Khan in 1978, "Z Cars", "Turtle's Progress", "Minder", "Live from Pebble Mill", "Bergerac", "King of the Ghetto" as Timur Hussein in 1986, "Arena", "Tickle on the Tum" as Mayor Choudhury in 1988, "Saracen", "Chancer", "Family Pride", and "Casualty". He later returned to Pakistan where he was founder and president of the National Academy of Performing Arts in Karachi from 2005. He was author of several books including "A Carrot Is a Carrot: Memoires and Reflections" (2008) and "The God of My Idolatry: Memories and Reflections" (2016). He was the subject of the 2018 documentary "Some Lover To Some Beloved". Mohyeddin was married and divorced from Sawar Zamani with whom he had two children. He married Pakistani Kathak dancer Nahid Siddiqui in the early 1970 and in survived by their son, percussionist Hassan 'Moyo' Mohyeddin. He married actress Azra Bano Zaidi in 1994 and is also survived by her and their daughter, Aaliya.

Moissi, Bettina

German actress Bettina Moissi died in Zurich, Switzerland, on November 21, 2023. She was 100. Moissi was

born in Berlin, Germany, on October 15, 1923. She was the daughter of acclaimed stage actor Alexander Moissi. She was raised in Switzerland when her family moved there in the early 1930s. She trained as an actress under Otto Falckenberg in Munich and appeared frequently on stage. She appeared in a handful of films in the 1940s including "The Comedians" (1941), "Jakko" (1941), "Seven Journeys" (1947), "Lang Ist der Weg" (1948), "The Original Sin" (1948), and "Epilog - Das Geheimnis der Orplid" (1950). Moissi was married to art collector Heinz Berggruen from 1960 until his death in 2007 and is survived by their two sons.

Moll, Richard

Actor Richard Moll, who was featured as Bailiff Bull Shannon on the television comedy series "Night Court" from 1984 to 1992, died at his home in Big Bear Lake, California, on

October 26, 2023. He was 80. He was born Charles Richard Moll in Pasadena, California, on January 13, 1943. He was very tall from his youth, reaching a height of 6'8". He attended the University of California at Berkeley and graduated in 1964. He worked as a deputy probation officer in Alameda County and was a clerk in a San Francisco ladies' hosiery story. Moll moved to Los Angeles in 1968 to pursue an acting career. He  initially had little success but was featured in a commercial for Hertz. He made his film debut as Mormon leader Joseph Smith in the 1977 feature "Brigham". He was featured in the 1980 horror film "Cataclysm", which was reedited to become "The Case of Claire Hansen" segment of the anthology film "Night Train to Terror" in 1985. Moll's imposing size led to numerous roles in films and television, often portraying thugs. He was seen in episodes of "Welcome Back, Kotter", "The Rockford Files", "How the West Was Won", "Happy Days", "Bigfoot and Wildboy", "B.J. and the Bear", "The Misadventures of Sheriff Lobo", "Buck Rogers in the 25th Century", "The Bad News Bears", "Nobody's Perfect", "Best of the West", "Here's Boomer", "Laverne & Shirley", "Code Red", "Bret Maverick", "Mork & Mindy", "The Fall Guy", "T.J. Hooker", "Remington Steele", "The Hollywood Squares", "The $10,000 Pyramid", "Fantasy Island", "Alice", "Just Our Luck", "The Dukes of Hazzard", "The A-Team", "Santa Barbara", "The Facts of Life", "Sledge Hammer!", "Super Password", "Wordplay", "My Two Dads", "Monsters", "227", "Out of This World", "The Munsters Today", "Highlander", "Martin", "The Wil Shriner Show", "The Pat Sajak Show", "The Arsenio Hall Show", "The Marsha Warfield Show", "To Tell the Truth", and "CBS Schoolbreak Special". Moll was best known for his role as the hulking but lovable bailiff, Nostradamus 'Bull' Shannon, on the NBC comedy series "Night Court" from 1984 to 1992. He continued to appear in such series as "Getting By" in the recurring role of Boo from 1993 to 1994, "Due South", "Hercules: The Legendary Journeys", "Babylon 5", "Dr. Quinn, Medicine Woman", "Baywatch", "Weird Science", "Married... with Children", "7th Heaven", "Sabrina the Teenage Witch", "The Parent 'Hood", "100 Deeds for Eddie McDowd" as the Drifter from 1999 to 2002, "Smallville", "Cold Case", "Anger Management", and "Kirby Buckets". He was the voice of Harvey 'Two-Face' Dent in "Batman: The Animated Series" from 1992 to 1994 and was Norman in the animated series "Mighty Max" from 1993 to 1994. He also voiced roles in such animated productions as "The Twisted Tales of Felix the Cat" (1996), "Superman: The Animated Series" (1996), "Freakazoid!" (1996), "Aaahh!!! Real Monsters" (1996), "The Legend of Calamity Jane" (1997), "Happily Ever After: Fairy Tales for Every Child", "The Incredible Hulk" (1996-1997) voicing the Abomination, "Spider-Man: The Animated Series" (1997) as the voice of Mac 'Scorpion' Gargan, "Cow and Chicken" (1998), "Oh Yeah! Cartoons" (1998), "The New

Batman Adventures" (1997-1998) again voicing Two-Face, "The Zeta Project" (2002), "Justice League" (2002), "Batman: The Brave and the Bold" (2001), and "Scooby-Doo! Curse of the Lake Monster" (2010). He also voiced characters in the video games "The Adventures of Batman & Robin Activity Center" (1996), "Fallout: A Post-Nuclear Role-Playing Game" (1997), "Outlaws" (1997), "The Incredible Hulk: Ultimate Destruction" (2005), and "Dante's Inferno" (2010). His other television credits include the tele-films "The Jericho Mile" (1979), "Mark Twain: Beneath the Laughter" (1979), "The Archer: Fugitive from the Empire" (1981), "Though the Magic Pyramid" (aka "The Time Crystal") (1981), "Savage Journey" (1983) a reedited version of his earlier film "Brigham", "Combat High" (1986), "If It's Tuesday, It Still Must Be Belgium" (1987), "Dream Date" (1989), "Class Cruise" (1989), "The Last Halloween" (1991), "Summertime Switch" (1994), "The Ransom of Red Chief" (1998), "Call Me Claus" (2001), "The Defectors" (2001), "The Fantastic Two" (2007), "Lake Effects" (2012), "Ghost Shark" (2013), and "Pub Quiz" (2016). He continued to appear frequently in films throughout his career with such credits as "Hard Country" (1981), "Liar's Moon" (1981), the horror film "Evilspeak" (1981) as Father Esteban, the prehistoric comedy "Caveman" (1981) as the Abominable Snowman, the animated "American Pop" (1981) as the voice of the beat poet, the adventure fantasy "The Sword and the Sorcerer" (1982) as Xusia of Delos, the science fiction "Metalstorm: The Destruction of Jared-Syn" (1983) as the villain Hurok, "Under Arrest" (1983), "The Dungeonmaster" (1984), the horror comedy "House" (1985) as Big Ben, "Survivor" (1987), the horror anthology "Pulse Pounders" (1988) in the "Dungeonmaster 2" segment, "Wicked Stepmother" (1989), "Think Big" (1989), "Driving Me Crazy" (1991), "Let's Kill All the Lawyers" (1992), "Sidekicks" (1992), "Marilyn Alive and Behind Bars" (1992), "Loaded Weapon 1" (1993), "Storybook" (1994), "The Flintstones" (1994), "No Dessert, Dad, Till You Mow the Lawn" (1994), "Beanstalk" (1994), "Galaxis" (1995), "The Secret Agent Club" (1996), "The Glass Cage" (1996), "Jingle All the Way" (1996), "The Elevator" (1996), "Little Cobras: Operation Dalmatian" (1997), "Living in Peril" (1997), "Snide and Prejudice" (1997), "Farticus" (1997), "Casper: A Spirited Beginning" (1997), "Casper Meets Wendy" (1998), "The Survivor" (1998), "Monkey Business" (1998), "Route 66" (1998), "Foreign Correspondents" (1999), "But I'm a Cheerleader" (1999), "Dish Dogs" (2000), "Shadow Hours" (2000), "Boltneck" (2000), "Flamingo Dreams" (2000), "The Summer in LA" (2000), "Dumb Luck" (2001), "Spiders II: Breeding Ground" (2001), "Evolution" (2001), "Scary Movie 2" (2001), "Angel Blade" (2002), "No Place Like Home" (2002), "The Work and the Story" (2003), "Cats and Mice" (2003), "Boy-Next-Door" (2004), "Uh Oh!" (2004), "The Biggest Fan" (2005), "Diamond Zero" (2005), "Angels with Angles" (2005), "Nightmare Man" (2006), "Headless Horseman" (2007), the short "A Four Cent Carol" (2008), "Thomas Kinkade's Christmas Cottage" (2008), "Love at First Hiccup" (2009), "DaZe: Vol. Too (sic) - NonSeNse" (2016), "Assassins' Code" (2011), "DisOrientation" (2012), the short "The End, My F.R.E.N.D."

(2012), "Sorority Party Massacre" (2012), "Hemingway" (2012), "Jurassic: Stoned Age" (2013), "BFFs" (2014), "Kids vs. Monsters" (2015), "Razor" (2016), "Circus Kane" (2017), and "Slay Belles" (2018). Moll was married to Laura Class from 1988 until their divorce in 1992. He was married to Susan Brown from 1993 until their divorce in 2005 and is survived by their children, Chloe and Mason.

MoneySign Suede

Rapper Jaime Brugada Valdez, who performed under the name MoneySign Suede, was stabbed to death at The

Correctional Training Facility in Soledad, California, on April 25, 2023. He was 22. Valdez was born in Los Angeles, California, on August 7, 2000. He began recording and uploading rap songs in his teens and soon signed with Atlantis Records. He scored a hit with his track "Back to the Bag" in 2020. He released a self-titled EP and his debut album, "Parkside Baby", in 2022. He served nearly a year in prison in 2020. He was charged with two counts of firearm possession and parole violations and was sentenced to a 32-month prison sentence in Soledad in January of 2023.

Montaldo, Giuliano

Italian film director Giuliano Montaldo died in Rome, Italy, on September 6, 2023. He was 93. Montaldo was born in Genoa, Italy, on February 22, 1930. He began working in

films as an actor in Carlo Lizzani's 1951 World War II drama "Attention! Bandits!". He continued to appear in such films as "La Cieca di Sorrento" (1953), "Ai Margini Della Metropoli" (1953), "Chronicle of Poor Lovers" (1954), "High School" (1954), "Gli Sbandati" (1955), "The Doll That Took the Town" (1957), "Kean: Genius or Scoundrel" (1957), "Il Momento Piu Bello" (1957), "Il Marito Bello: Il Nemico di Mia Moglie" (1959), "The Assassin" (1961), "Extraconiugale" (1964), "Una Bella Grinta" (1965), and "Il Morbidine" (1965). Montaldo began working behind the cameras as an assistant director on "La Grande Strada Azzurra" (1957), "Eserina" (1959), "Kapo" (1960), and "The Assasin" (1961). He was second unit director for such films as Gillo Pontecorvo's "The Battle of Algiers" (1966) and "A Genius, Two Partners and a Dupe" (1975). He directed, and frequently wrote, numerous films from the early 1960s including "Tiro al Piccione" (aka "Pigeon Shoot") (1961), "Nudi per Vivere" (1963), "Extraconiugale" (1964), "Una Bella Grinta" (1965), "Grand Slam" (1967) starring Edward G. Robinson and Janet Leigh, the crime drama

"Machine Gun McCain" (1969) starring John Cassavetes and Peter Falk, "The Fifth Day of Peace" (1970), "Sacco & Vanzetti" (1971), "Giordano Bruno" (1973), "L'Agnese Va a Morire" (aka "And Agnes Chose to Die") (1976), "Il Giocattolo" (1979), "Farewell to Enrico Berlinquer" (1984), "Sabatoventiquanttromarzo" (1984), "Control" (1987), "The Gold Rimmed Glases" (1987), "Time to Kill" (1989) starring Nicolas Cage, "Ci Sara Una Volta" (1992), "La Stagioni dell'Aquila" (1997), "The Demons of St. Petersburg" (2008), "L'Oro di Cuba" (2009), and "The Entrepreneur" (2011). Montaldo helmed the television productions "Closed Circuit" (1978) and "Marco Polo" (1982). He returned to acting in the 1990s, appearing in the films "Il Lungo Silenzio" (1993), "Un Eroe Borghese" (1995), "The Caiman" (2006), "The Haunting of Helena" (2012), "The Big Score" (2016), and "Tutto Quello Che Vuoi" (2017). Montaldo is survived by his wife, Vera Pesarolo, who often worked as his assistant director, and his daughter, costume designer Elisabetta Montalo.

Montanari, Giuseppe

Italian comic book artist Giuseppe Montanari, who was noted for his work on the "Dylan Dog" comic series, died in Italy on August 5, 2023. He was 86. Montanari was born in

San Giovanni in Persiceto, Italy, on November 26, 1936. He trained as an artist and began his career at Roy d'Ami's studios in 1954. He worked on the comic series "I Tre Bill" with d'Ami for Bonelli. He also worked on western stories for the comic magazines "Cucciolo" and "Tiramolla". He began working at La Corno in 1962 where he illustrated "Atomik" and provided covers for "Maschera Nera" and "Gordon". He worked with the RG publishing house in the 1970s on such comic series as "Goldrake il Playboy", "Alamo Kid", "Le Streghe", and "Sharon Shade", often with Ernest Grassini. He and writer Giuseppe Pederiali created the 1979 comic "La Discussione" about the history of the Christian Democratic Party. He began working with Sergio Bonelli Editore in the late 1970s illustrating "Il Piccolo Ranger" and the "Dylan Dog" series. Montanari illustrated stories featuring Warner Bros. characters and "James Bond Junior" written by his daughter, Federica, for Corrierino dei Piccoli. He illustrated "Teenage Mutant Ninja Turtles", "Il Piccolo Zorro", and "Zia Aghata" for "Il Giornalino". Montanari was cover artist for "Dylan Dog Oldboy" from 2021.

Monteith, Kelly

Comedian Kelly Monteith, who was star of several British comedy series in the 1980s, died of complications from a stroke at his home in Los Angeles, California, on January 1, 2023. He was 80. Monteith was born in St. Louis, Missouri, on October 17, 1942. He began performing comedy from an early age. He later moved to California and trained at the Pasadena Playhouse's College of Theatre Arts. He was soon appearing at nightclubs and casinos across the country. He was seen on television in episodes of "Jack Paar Tonite", "The Dean Martin Comedy World", "Dean's Place", "Sammy and Company", "The Peter Marshall  Variety Show", "The Alan Thicke Show", "The Comedy Shop", "The Hollywood Squares", "The Mike Douglas Show", "The Toni Tennille Show", "The Merv Griffin Show", "The Jim Nabors Show", "The Tonight Show Starring Johnny Carson", "Family Feud", "The Arsenio Hall Show", and "Late Show with David Letterman". He was host of his own short-lived series "The Kelly Monteith Show" in 1976. He worked frequently in England from the late 1970s and starred in the comedy series, "Kelly Monteith", from 1979 to 1984. The two-part one-man show "Kelly Monteith in One" followed in 1985. He was also a guest in episodes of "The Alan Hamel Show", "The Val Doonican Music Show", "Des O'Connor Tonight", "Blankety Blank", "The Bob Monkhouse Show", "A Royal Night of One Hundred Stars", "Wogan", "The Bruce Gold Show", "The John Longthorne Show", and "Kelly Monteith's BBC Memories" from 2019 to 2020. He was featured in several films including "Screwball Hotel" (1988), "Hollywood Boulevard II" (1990), "A Lousy 10 Grand" (2004), "Fuel" (2009), and "Too Hip for the Room" (2015). Monteith was also seen in episodes of "The Love Boat", "New Love, American Style", "Isabel's Honeymoon Hotel", "Out of This World", and "The Real Geezers of Beverly Hills-Adjacent" which he also wrote in 2019. He recorded the comedy album, "Lettuce Be Cool", in 1984. He married his second wife, Caroline Alexander, in 1985. They later divorced and he is survived by their two children, daughter Tierney and son Kyle.

Montell, Lisa

Actress Lisa Montell, who starred in the science fiction film "World Without End", died of complications from heart failure and sepsis in Van Nuys, California, on March 7, 2023. She was 89. She was born  Irena Ludmilla Vladimirovna Augustinovich in Warsaw, Poland, on July 5, 1933. She fled Poland with her family before World War II. They settled in New York City where they changed their family name to Montwill. She attended the high School of Performing Arts in the late 1940s. She completed her high school education in Fort Pierce, Florida, after her family moved there in her senior year. She attended the University of Miami before accompanying her family to Peru where her father worked for an iron mining company. She became involved with the local English-language theater. She made her film debut in "Daughter of the Sun God" which was filmed in 1953 but remained unreleased until 1962. She subsequently moved to Hollywood to pursue an acting career after the death of her father. She appeared frequently on television with roles in episodes of "Public Defender", "The Gene Autry Show", "Lux Video Theatre", "Jane Wyman Presents the Fireside Theatre", "The Millionaire", "Broken Arrow", "The O. Henry Playhouse", "Cavalcade of America", "Wire Service", "Tales of Wells Fargo", "Matinee Theatre", "Colt .45", "The Adventure of Jim Bowie", "Mike Hammer", "The Ann Southern Show", Disney's "The Nine Lives of Elfego Baca" as Anita Chavez in 1958, "Northwest Passage", "Frontier Doctor", "Have Gun - Will Travel", "Sugarfoot", "Westinghouse Desilu Playhouse", "The Dennis O'Keefe Show", "Bat Masterson", "Cheyenne", "One Step Beyond", "Johnny Midnight", "Maverick", "The Deputy", "Surfside 6", "77 Sunset Strip", and "Combat!". Montell was seen in the films "Escape to Burma" (1955) with Barbara Stanwyck and Robert Ryan, "Jump Into Hell" (1955), "Daddy Long Legs" (1955), "Finger Man" (1955), "Pearl of the South Pacific" (1955), "The Wild Dakotas" (1956), the science fiction film "World Without End" (1956) with Rod Taylor, "Gaby" (1956), "Naked Paradise" (1957), "Tomahawk Trail" (1957), "Ten Thousand Bedrooms" (1957) with Dean Martin, "The Lone Ranger and the Lost City of Gold" (1958), Roger Corman's "She Gods of Shark Reef" (1958), and "The Firebrand" (1962). Montell joined the Baha'i Faith in the mid-1950s and largely abandoned her acting career by the early 1960s. She became an active spokesperson for the religion and was involved in social activism for racial unity. She served as a delegate to the national Baha'i convention frequently. She worked with Los Angeles Mayor Tom Bradley and served as a liaison with various committees dealing with poverty, youth programs, the elderly, and the arts. She left Bradley's staff in the early 1980s to attend graduate courses. She taught holistic education at the School of Education at National University near San Diego. She remained active in religious and social affairs for the remainder of her life and authored the 2005 book "Baha'i: The New Vision". Montell married David Janti in 1957. They later divorced and she is survived by their daughter Shireen Janti.

Moonbin

South Korean singer and actor Moonbin died of a reported suicide at his home in Seoul, South Korea, on April 19,  2023. He was 25. He was born Moon Bin in Cheongju, South Korea, on January 26, 1998. He began working as a child model in 2004 and appeared in the music video for TVXQ's "Balloons" in 2006. He was featured in the television drama "Boys Over Flowers" in 2009. He began working with Fantagio entertainment company while in elementary school. He graduated from the Hanlim Multi Art School where he studied music. Moonbin became part of the boy group Astro in 2016, and they

314

released the EP "Spring Up". He was a regular on the television series "The Ultimate Watchlist of Latest Trends" for two seasons from 2018 to 2019. He appeared as Jung Oh-je in the series "Moments of Eighteen" in 2019. He returned to perform with Astro after an absence due to health reasons in 2020. He became a host of the music series "Show Champion" from 2020 to 2022 and starred in the series "The Mermaid Prince" in 2020. He and Astro bandmate Sanha (Yoon San-ha) teamed for the EP "In-Out" featuring the lead single "Bad Idea". He joined the second season of "Saturday Night Live Korea" in 2021. His survivors include his younger sister, Moon Sua, who performs with the girl group Billie.

Morath, Max

Ragtime pianist and composer Max Morath died in Duluth, Minnesota, on June 19, 2023. He was 96. Morath was born in Colorado Springs, Colorado, on October 1, 1926. He learned the piano from his mother as a child. He graduated from

Colorado College in 1948. He worked at a radio station as an announcer and pianist while in college. He continued to work in radio, television, and theater. He developed an interest in ragtime music and created the PBS series "The Ragtime Era" for the Denver affiliate KRMA from 1959 to 1961. His performances on the show in syndication gave him national recognition and was followed by the series "Turn of the Century". Morath began touring with a one-man ragtime show, "Max Morath at the Turn of the Century". He appeared on television in episodes of "The Merv Griffin Show", "The Mike Douglas Show", "The Bell Telephone Hour", "The Kraft Music Hall", "The Tonight Show Starring Johnny Carson", "The David Frost Show", and "Dinah!". He was a regular guest on Arthur Godfrey's CBS radio show from 1965 to 1972. Morath continued to perform and tour in one-man shows including "The Ragtime Years", "Living the Ragtime Life", "The Ragtime Man", "Ragtime Revisited", and "Ragtime and Again". He retired from touring in 2007. He returned to school to earn a master's degree from Columbia University in 1996. His thesis about songwriter Carrie Jacobs-Bond led to his 2008 biographical novel about her, "I Love You Truly: A Biographical Novel Based on the Life of Carrie Jacobs-Bond". Morath was married to Norma Loy Tackitt from 1953 until their divorce in 1992 and is survived by their son and two daughters. He married Diane Fay Skomars in 1993 and she also survives him.

Morgan, Cindy

Actress Cindy Morgan, who starred in such films as "Tron" and "Caddyshack" in the early 1980s, was found dead at her home in Lake Worth Beach, Florida, on December 30, 2023. She was 69. She had last been seen alive on December 19. She was born Cynthia Ann Cichorski in Chicago, Illinois, on September 29, 1954. She attended Northern Illinois

University in DeKalb, where she studied communications. She also served as a disc jockey on the campus radio station. She was a weather forecaster at a television station in Rockford,

Illinois, after graduation and worked at a local rock radio station. She returned to Chicago to work at radio station WSDM and as a model for Fiat Automobiles before moving to Los Angeles in 1978. She appeared in advertisements for Irish Spring while training as an actress. Morgan made her film debut as the sexy blonde Lacey Underall in the 1980 comedy classic "Caddyshack" starring Chevy Chase, Rodney Dangerfield, and Bill Murray. She starred as computer programmer Lora and her video game doppelganger Yori in the computer-generated film "Tron" in 1982. Her other films include "Up Yours" (1979), "American Gigolo" (1980), "Silent Fury" (1994), "Galaxis" (1995), and "Open Mic'rs" (2006). Morgan appeared frequently on television with roles in episodes of "The Love Boat", "Vega$", "CHiPs", the short-lived adventure series "Bring 'Em Back Alive" as Gloria Marlowe from 1982 to 1983, "The Tonight Show Starring Johnny Carson", "Hawaiian Heat", "Masquerade", "The Fall Guy", "Tough Cookies", "Crazy Like a Fox", "Amazing Stories", "Beverly Hills Buntz", the prime-time soap opera "Falcon Crest" as Gabrielle Short from 1987 to 1988, "The Highwayman", "She's the Sheriff", "Matlock", "Mancuso, FBI", "Hunter", "Harry and the Hendersons", "The Larry Sanders Show", and "Under Suspicion". Her other television credits include the tele-films "The Midnight Hour" (1985), "Solomon's Universe" (1985), and "The Return of the Shaggy Dog" (1987). Morgan was associate producer and appeared in small roles in a trio of science fiction tele-films in 1995, "Dead Weekend", "Amanda & the Alien", and "Out There". She was featured in several short films later in her career including "Summer Waters" (2009), "Empty Sky" (2011), "Face of the Father" (2016), and "Face of the Trinity" (2022).

Morghen, John

see Lombardo Radice, Giovanni

Morowitz, Arthur

Adult film producer and home video pioneer Arthur Morowitz died in New Jersey on September 11, 2023. He was 89. Morowitz was born on August 24, 1943. He teamed with Howard Farber in 1965 to form Distribpix, a low-budget production and distribution company. He produced, and occasionally appeared in, such sexploitation films as "The Bed and How to Make It!" (1966), "Skin Deep in Love" (1966), "Anything for Money" (1967), "Pamela, Pamela, You Are..." (1968), "All the Sins of Sodom" (1968), and "Vibrations" (1968). He created the Video Shack rental chain in 1979 and was a founding member of the Video Software Dealers Association (VSDA). Morowitz served as executive producer

of the adult films "Inside Jennifer Welles" (1977), "All About Gloria Leonard" (1978), "Tigresses and Other Man-Eaters" (1979), "Inside Seka" (1980), "Deep Inside Annie Sprinkle" (1981), "The Erotic World of Angel Cash" (1982), and "...in the Pink" (1983). He formed the WWF Coliseum Video label in the 1980s and was executive producer of the wrestling videos "Andre the Giant" (1985), "Wrestling's Country Boys" (1985), "The British Bulldogs" (1986), and "Jake the Snake Roberts" (1987). Morowitz later bought and sold collectible stamps and currency through his Champion Stamp Company.

Morris, Olin

Television personality Olin Morris, who was host of the local series "Good Morning from Memphis", died in Memphis, Tennessee, on February 15, 2023. He was 87. Morris was born in Inman, South Carolina, on November 25, 1935. He attended high school in Oak Ridge, Tennessee, and joined the U.S. Army in 1956. He served as a communications

and personnel specialist and was known as the Voice of the U.S. Army Band. He began working in television after his discharge as a station manager at WATE-TV in Knoxville, Tennessee, in 1958. He continued his career in television in Fort Wayne and Evansville, Indiana, before joining WREG-TV in Memphis, Tennessee. He rose to become president and general manager of the station. Morris was co-host with Frances Kelly of the "Good Morning from Memphis" program during the 1970s. He was also announcer for the AutoZone Liberty Bowl Football Classic Halftime, St. Jude Telethons with Danny Thomas, and local telecasts for the Muscular Dystrophy Telethon with Jerry Lewis. He was involved in civic and community affairs serving as president of the Memphis Area Chamber of Commerce. He is survived by his wife, Sandi Morris, and predeceased by their son, Lindle Morris.

Morrisett, Lloyd

Experimental psychologist Lloyd Morrisett, who helped create the children's television show "Sesame Street", died at his home in San Diego, California, on January 15, 2023. He was 93. Morrisett was born in Oklahoma City, Oklahoma, on November 2, 1929. He moved to Yonkers, New York, with his family as an infant. He graduated from Oberlin College in Ohio in 1951. He attended the University of California at Los Angeles for graduate work in psychology for two years. He subsequently attended Yale, where he earned a doctorate in experimental psychology in 1956. He began teaching at the

University of California at Berkeley. He joined the Social

Science Research Council in New York in 1958. He began working for the Carnegie Corporation in 1959 and later became vice president. He spent a decade at Carnegie where he was instrumental in the creation of the National Assessment of Educational Programs (NAEP). His interest in early education and psychology inspired him to utilize television in teaching young children. He joined with Joan Ganz Cooney to create and obtain funding for the Children's Television Workshop in 1968. The following year the landmark children's series "Sesame Street", starring Jim Henson's Muppets, debuted on television. He and Cooney also helped create the children's program "The Electric Company". Morrisett became president of the John and Mary Markle Foundation in 1969 and guided it towards work in communications and information technology through the late 1990s. He served as chairman of the Children's Television Workshop (later known as Sesame Workshop) from 1970 to 2000. He and Cooney shared Kennedy Center Honors for their creation of "Sesame Street" in 2019. He is survived by his wife, Mary Pierre, and their two daughters, Julie and Sarah.

Mortensen, Lia

Actress Lia Mortensen died of lung cancer in Chicago, Illinois, on June 7, 2023. She was 57. Mortensen was born in Illinois on June 15, 1965. She was the daughter of Dale

Mortenson, who later won the Nobel Prize for Economics. She graduated from Indiana University and returned to Chicago in 1987. She became a leading performer on the Chicago stage with roles in productions of "The Voice of the Turtle", "Night and Day", "Faith Healer", "Rabbit Hole", "Company", and "Four Places" which she directed in 2019. Mortensen appeared in the films "Blink" (1993), "Sex, Love & Intimacy" (1996), "A Nightmare on Elm Street" (2010) as Nora Fowles, "Consumed" (2015), "The View from Tall" (2016), "Resurrecting McGinn(s)" (2016), "Marked Value" (2017), "Soul Sessions" (2018), and "Deep Woods" (2022). She was seen on television in episodes of "The Chicago Code", "Chicago Fire", "Dr. Good" as Dr. Lisa in 2013, "Crisis", "Empire", "Shameless", "Chicago Med", "Electric Dreams", "Easy Abby", and "Soundtrack". She was married and divorced from fellow Chicago actor Si Osborne and is survived by their two daughters.

Moss, Jerry

Recording executive Jerry Moss, who was co-founder of A&M Records, died at his home in Bel Air, California, on

August 16, 2023. He was 88. Moss was born in New York City on May 8, 1935. He graduated from Brooklyn College and served in the U.S. Army. He began working in music by

promoting the Crests' 1958 hit recording "16 Candles". He moved to California in 1962 where he founded a record company with trumpeter Herb Alpert. The company became known as A&M Records and initially released recordings by Herb Alpert and the Tijuana Brass. They recorded hits by such top artists as Burt Bacharach, Sergio Mendes & Brasil '66, the Sandpipers, Quincy Jones, the Carpenters, Peter Frampton, Joan Baez, Billy Preston, Cat Stevens, Janet Jackson, Joe Cocker, Carole King, Sting, and the comedy Cheech & Chong. A&M became the largest independent record company in the world until Moss and Alpert sold to PolyGram in 1989 for $500. They continued to manage the label until 1993. They received an additional $200 after suing PolyGram in 1998. They managed the Almo Sounds record label in the 1990s, recording Alpert, Gillian Welch, and others. He and Alpert were inducted into the Rock and Roll Hall of Fame in the non-performer category in 2006. Moss was also a noted horse breeder and art collector. He was married to Helen Sandra Wingert from 1965 until their divorce in 1983. She was subsequently married and divorced from Ann Holbrook. He was married and divorced from Helen Sandra Rusetos and Ann Holbrook. He married Tina Littlewood Morse in 2019 and she survives him. He is also survived by two sons and two daughters.

Mowbray, Malcolm

British director and screenwriter Malcolm Mowbray died of complications from dementia in England on June 23, 2023. He was 74. Mowbray was born in Knebworth,

Hertfordshire, England, on June 24, 1949. He was educated at Ravensbourne College of Art and Design and the National Film and Television School. He began working in television in the late 1970s, directing episodes of "Premiere", "BBC2 Playhouse", and "Objects of Affection". He was best known for directing and writing the 1984 comedy film "A Private Function" starring Michael Palin and Maggie Smith. He helmed the television mini-series "Crocodile Shoes" (1994) and "Monsignor Renard" (2000), and episodes of "Once Upon a Time in the North", "Cadfael", and "Pie in the Sky". Mowbray also directed the films "Out Cold" (1989), "The Boyfriend School" (1990), "The Revengers' Comedies" (1998) which he also wrote, and "Meeting Spencer" (2011). He taught at the Northern Film School in Leeds and was named head of

the directing department in 2016. Mowbray was married to Valerie Hill from 1977 until her death in 2006 and is survived by their two sons.

Mowry, Pat

Actress Pat Mowry, who also performed under the name Patricia Winters, died in Escondido, California, on March 14, 2023. She was 90. Mowry was born in Manchester, New Hampshire, on February 4, 1933. She was crowned Miss New Hampshire U.S.A. in 1955 and competed in the subsequent Miss Universe pageant. She subsequently moved to the San

Fernando Valley and embarked on an acting career. She was seen in such films as "Slander" (1957), "Jeanne Eagels" (1957), "Until They Sail" (1957), "Marjorie Morningstar" (1958), the science fiction film "Missile to the Moon" (1958) as a Moon Girl, "A Very Special Favor" (1965), "Valley of the Dolls" (1967), and "This Is a Hijack" (1973). Mowry appeared on television in episodes of "General Electric Theater", "Maverick", "Perry Mason", "Dragnet", "The Joey Bishop Show", "Run for Your Life", "The Beverly Hillbillies", "Adam-12", "Mannix", and "Longstreet". She also was seen in the 1971 tele-film "The Feminist and the Fuzz". Mowry largely retired from the screen in the early 1970s and spent the next two decades working in real estate. She was founder of the Purrfect Solutions Feline Rescue company, a sanctuary for cats, in 2000. She was married and divorced from William Donnelly and they had two daughters together. She was married to actor Chuck Wassil from 1959 until their divorce in 1980.

Murguia, Ana Ofelia

Mexican actress Ana Ofelia Murguia, who was the voice of Mama Coco in the 2017 animated film "Coco", died in Mexico on December 31, 2023. She was 90. Murguia was born

in Mexico City on December 8, 1933. She began appearing in films from the late 1960s with roles in "Pax?" (1968), "El Juego de Zuzanka" (1970), "Para Servir a Usted" (1971), "El Aguila Descalza" (1971), "El Profeta Mimi" (1973), "Mexico, Mexico, Ra Ra Ra" (1976), and "El Apando" (1976). She was recipient of the Ariel Award for Best Supporting Actress for her roles in "Life Sentence" (1979), "Los Motivos de Luz" (1985), and "The Queen of the Night" (1994). She was nominated for Ariels for her supporting and minor roles in "Las Poquianchis (De los Pormenores y Otros Sucedidos del Dominio Publico que Acontecieron a las Hermanas de Triste Memoria a Quienes la Maledicencia asi las Bautizo)" (1976), "Ora Si Tenemos Que

317

Ganar" (1981), "Chido Guan, el Tacos de Oro" (1986), "Los Confines" (1987), "El Jardin del Eden" (1994), "Morena" (1995), "Esmeralda Comes by Night" (1997), "Ave Maria" (1999), and "Su Alteva Serenisima" (2001). Murguia shared the record for most nominations for Best Actress Ariels without a win for her work in "Naufragio (1978)", "Mi Querido Tom Mix" (1992), "El Anzuelo" (1996), "De Muerte Natural" (1996), and "Escrito en el Cuerpo de la Noche" (2001). Her other films include "Maten al Leon" (1977), "Pedro Paramo" (1977), "The Black Widow" (1977), "Amor Libre" (1979), "Constelaciones" (1980), "Mary My Dearest" (1981), "El Corazon de la Noche" (1984), David Lynch's "Dune" (1984) in a small role as a palace maid, "Mexicano Tu Puedes!" (1985), "Como Ves?" (1986), "Las Inocentes" (1986), "Gaby: A True Story" (1987), "El Jinete de la Divina Providencia" (1989), "Goitia, un Dios Para Si Mismo" (1989), "Intimidad" (1989), "Las Asesinas del Panadero" (1989), "Morir en el Golfo" (1990), "Diplomatic Immunity" (1992), "Ambar" (1994), "Nobody Will Speak of Us When We're Dead" (1995), "Luces de la Noche" (1998), "Sexo por Compasion" (2000), "Pachito Rex: I'm Leaving But Not for Good" (2001), "Su Alteza Serenisima" (2001), "Otilia Rauda" (2001), "El Eden" (2004), "A Good Death Beats a Dull Life" (2005), "Bandidas" (2006), "Senas Particulares" (2007), "Parpados Azules" (2007), "El Viaje de la Nonna" (2007), "Tear This Heart Out" (2008), "Walking Vengeance" (2008), "I Miss You" (2010", "Las Buenas Hierbas" (2010), "El Mar Muerto" (2010), "The Compass Is Carried by the Dead Man" (2011), "Fecha de Caducidad" (2012), and "The Last Call" (2013). She was awarded a Special Golden Ariel in 2011. Murguia provided the voice of Mama Coco in the Disney-Pixar animated musical "Coco" in 2017. She was seen on television in episodes of "La Tormenta", "El Padre Guernica", "Las Fieras", "La Pasion de Isabela", "Hora Marcada", "El Abuelo y Yo" as Senorita Estrada in 1992, "Entre Vivos y Muertos", "Tric Trac", "te Dejare de Amar" as Alicia Larios in 1996, "El Amor di Mi Vida" as Mama Lupe in 1998, "Cuentos Para Solitarios", "Lo Que Callamos la Mujeres", "Uroboros" as Portera in 2001, "La Hija del Jardinero" as Dona Rigoberta 'Rigo' Rondon in 2003, "Mientras Haya Vida", "Gregoria la Cucaracha", "Quererte Asi", "Mozart in the Jungle", and "Jose Jose: El Principe de la Cancion".

Myers, Addison

Actor Addison Myers died at his home in Columbia, Missouri, on December 23, 2023. He was 92. He was born in Philadelphia, Pennsylvania, on November 5, 1931. He graduated from Bluffton College in 1952 and earned a master's degree from Ohio State University two years later. He served in the U.S. Army in Korea for two years. He taught and directed the theater program at Hollywood High School in Los Angeles from 1964 to 1968. He taught acting and theater history at Stephens College in Columbia from 1968 to 1974 and from 1976 until his retirement in 1998. He began performing on stage in the late 1950s. He was active in summer stock and appeared frequently on the local stage. He was an actor and stage manager at the Macklanburg Playhouse in Columbia from

its opening in 1984. He was seen occasionally on television from the early 1960s with roles in episodes of "Shannon", "The Twilight Zone", "Adventures in Paradise", "Hazel", and

"Combat!". Myers also appeared in the tele-films "Back to Hannibal: The Return of Tom Sawyer and Huckleberry Finn" (1990), "They've Taken Our Children: The Chowchilla Kidnapping" (1993), and "Truman" (1995). He was also seen in several films including "The Horizontal Lieutenant" (1962), "Mr. & Mrs. Bridge" (1990), and "Ride with the Devil" (1999). Myers is survived by his wife of 42 years, Darcy Wells, and his daughter, Alison.

Myers, Larry, Jr.

Larry Myers, Jr., who was featured on the television series "My 600-lb. Life", died of a heart attack at his home in

Houston, Texas, on June 13, 2023. He was 49. Myers was born on June 10, 1974. He was an aspiring gospel singer who was featured on the 10th season of TLC's television reality series "My 600-lb. Life" in January of 2022. He weighed 950 lbs. before having gastric-bypass surgery. He became known as Mr. Buttermilk Biscuits due to him singing about his favorite meal during the show. He launched "The Buttermilk Biscuit Show" on YouTube after his appearance on the series that featured motivational speeches and updates on his condition.

Myles, Lynda

Television writer Lynda Myles died in New York City on April 15, 2023. She was 83. Myles was born in New York City on July 22, 1939. She was educated at Michigan State

University. She began her career as an actress and appeared on the Broadway stage in productions of "Plaza Suite" (1968) and "6 Rms Riv Vu" (1972). She and her husband, Jan Leighton, starred as George Washington and Sally Fairfax in the 1973 television documentary "The World Turned Upside Down". She began writing plays and "Wives" was performed in 1979. Myles also wrote the play "Thirteen" and the short story "A Lucky Man". She was noted for her work with television soap operas, earning a Daytime Emmy Award for writing "Santa Barbara" in 1989 and 1991 and an addition nomination in 1990. She was also nominated for Daytime

Emmys for "General Hospital" in 1998, "As the World Turns" in 2000, and "One Life to Live" in 2002. Her other soap opera credits include "Loving" and "Guiding Light". Myles was married and divorced from actor Jan Leighton, who died in 2009. Their daughter, Hallie Leighton, died in 2013.

Myrberg, Per

Swedish actor Per Myrberg died in Sweden on December 28, 2023. He was 90. Myrberg was born in Stockholm, Sweden, on July 11, 1933. He was a prolific actor in films and television from the late 1950s. His film credits include "Varmlanningarna" (1957), "Domaren" (1960), "The  Pleasure Garden" (1961), "The Swedish Mistress" (1962), "Adam och Eva" (1963), "The Cats" (1965), "On" (1966), "Myten" (1966), "Made in Sweden" (1969), "A Handful of Love" (1974), "The Garage" (1975), "Hallo Baby" (1976), "Paradistorg" (1977), "The Simple-Minded Murderer" (1982), "Malacca" (1987), "Los Duenos del Silencio" (1987), "Hamkligheten" (1990), "Honungsvargar" (1990), "Sunday's Children" (1992), "Alfred" (1995), "Blind Light" (1998), "Elias og Kopngeskipet" 1999), the thriller "The Girl with the Dragon Tattoo" (2011) as Harald, "The Hidden Child" (2013), and "For Better and Worse" (2015). Myrberg was seen in television productions of "Aventyr Med Gammal Bil" (1958), "Vald" (1960), "Eurydike" (1961), "Dacke" (1961), "Ett Resande Teatersallskap" (1961), "Taggen" (1961), "Pa Jakt Efter Lyckan" (1962), "Varmalanningarna" (1962), "M. Ljung, Valhallavagen 117, 2 tr. o.g." (1964), "Tigerlek", "En Lille Dosis Strindberg - Eller Selvforsvarets Brutale Kunst" (1970), "Reservatet" (1970), "Alberte" (1972), "Spoksonaten" (1972), "Revisorn" (1973), "Kontrollanten" (1973), "Embargo" (1976), "Kalkonen" (1977), "Isgraven" (1977), "Jarnspisrum" (1978), "Strandvaskeren" (1978), "Hyenan Ler Faktiskt Inte..." (1980), "Babels Hus" (1981), "Fanrik Stals Sagner" (1981), "Mannen Utan Sjal" (1983), "Rosmersholm" (1984), "Kontoret" (1985), Ingmar Bergman's "The Blessed Ones" (1986), "Paganini Fran Saltangen" (19877), "Manguden" (1988), "Kopplingen" (1991), "Fallet Paragon" (1994), "Staden" (1998), "Spoksonaten" (2007), and "Gentlemen & Gangsters" (2016). He also appeared in episodes of "Hedebyborna" as Carl-Gustaf Urse in 1978, "Spanarna", "Nya Dagbladet", "Det Var Da...", "Din Vredes Dag" as Overste Lagercrantz in 1991, "Rosenbaum", "Rederlet" as Robert Boisse de Blaque from 1999 to 2000, "S.P.U.N.G.", "Svensson Svensson", "Livet i Fagervik", "Salton" as William McFie from 2005 to 2010, and "Gynekologen i Askim" as Sten from 2007 to 2011. He is survived by his wife, Sara Myrberg, and six children.

Mystic Meg

British astrologer Margaret Anne Lake, who was known by the name Mystic Meg, died of influenza at a hospital in Paddington, London, England, on March 9, 2023. She was 80. Lake was born in Accrington, Lancashire, England, on July 27, 1942. She attended the University of Leeds and later  worked at the "News of the World". She became the paper's regular astrologer in the 1980s. She had a short weekly segment with "The National Lottery Live" from 1994 to 2000, attempting to predict things about the future winner. She was spokesperson for bookmaker Gala Coral Group's Grand National marketing campaign in 2015. She ran a website featuring horoscopes and astrological readings and operated a psychic telephone hotline. Meg appeared on television in episodes of "Jools's Hootenanny", "Noel's House Party", "The Lily Savage Show", "Des O'Connor Tonight", "Comic Relief", "McCoist and MacAulay", and "Harry Hill".

Nair, Aparna P.

Indian actress Aparna P. Nair died of a suicide by hanging at her home in Karamana, Thiruvananthapuram, India, on August 31, 2023. She was 33. Nair was born in Kerala, India, on November 30, 1989. She made her film debut in the  2009 Malayalam-language feature "Meghatheertham". Her other films include "Mudhugauv" (2016), "Mythily Veendum Varunnu" (2017), "Achayans" (2017), "Neeranjana Pookkal" (2017), "Devasparsham" (2018), "Pen Masala" (2018), "Kodatha Samaksham Balan Vakeel" (2019), "British Bungalow" (2019), "Nalla Vishesham" (2019), "Kalki" (2019), and "Kadalu Paranja Kadha" (2022). She was noted for her work in television serials, starring as Asianet in "Chandanamazha" from 2014 to 2018 and as Mazhavil Manorama in "Athmasakhi" from 2016 to 2018. She is survived by two children.

Naka, Yosuke

Japanese voice actor Yosuke Naka, who was noted for his role as Nobita's Dad in the "Doraemon" anime series, died in Tokyo, Japan, on October 20, 2023. He was 93. He was born  Kazuo Nakajima in Chiba Prefecture, Japan, on March 30, 1930. He voiced numerous roles in animes and cartoons from the 1960s. His credits include "Daraku Suru Onna", "Kawado's Sanpei Youkai Daisakusen", "Talyo Ne Hoero!", "Lupin the Third: The Strange Psychokinetic Strategy", "Battle Hawk", "Special Investigation Unit", "Daitokai - Tatakai No Hibi",

"Kamin Rider" as Admiral Majin in 1980, "Dai Sentai Google-V", "Future Police Urashiman", "Space Cobra", "Lupin III: Part III", "Yawara!", "Yajikita Gakuen Dochuki", "Konchu Monogatari Miinashigo Hatchi", "Kentouchi", "Mad Bull 34", "21 Emon: Sora Ike! Haradhi No Purinsesu", "Berserk", "Panzer Dragoon Saga", "Master Keaton", "Ghost in the Shell: Stand Alone Complex", and "Nitaboh".

Nakajima, Sadao

Japanese film director Sadao Nakajima, who was noted for his numerous yakuza crime films, died of pneumonia in Kyoto City, Japan, on June 11, 2023. He was 88. Nakajima was born in Togane, Japan, on August 8, 1934. He attended the University of Tokyo before going to work for Toei studio in 1959. He served as an assistant to such directors as Tadashi Imai, Masahiro Makino, and Tomotaka Tasaka. Nakajima made his directorial debut with 1964's "Female Ninja Magic". He directed and often scripted numerous films, many of which accentuated the violence in the yakuza genre, over the next five decades. His film include "The Spying Sorceress" (1964), "Hatamoto Yakuza" (1966), "Yakuza Gurentai" (1966), "Otoko No Shobu" (1966), "Ninkyo Yawara Ichidai" (1966), "Aa Doki No Sakura" (1967), "Zoku o-Oku Maruhi Monogatari" (1967), "O-Oku Maruhi Monogatari" (1967), "Kyodai Jingi: Kanto Aniki-Bun" (1967), "Amadera Maruhi Monogatari" (1968), "Nippon '69 Sekkusu Ryoki Chitai" (1969), "Nihon Ansatsu Hiroku" (1969), "Postwar Secrets" (1970), "Hot Springs Konjac Geisha" (1970), "Nippon Yokujo Monogatari" (1971), "Twisted Sex" (1971), "Gendai Yakuza: Chizakura San Kyodai" (1971), "Choeki Taro: Mamushi No Kyodai" (1971), "Mamushi No Kyodai: Choeki Jusankai" (1972), "Mamushi No Kyodai: Shogai Kyokatsu Juhappan" (1972), "Kogarashi Monjiro" (1972), "Kogarashi Monjiro: Kakawari Gozansen" (1972), "Sekkusu Dokyumento: Poruno No Shojo" (1973), "Teppodama No Bigaku" (1973), "The Kyoto Connection" (1973), "Girl Boss: Escape from Reform School" (1973), "Tokyo-Seoul-Bangkok" (1973), "Karajishi Keisatsu" (1974), "Gokudu Tai Mamusi" (1974), "Violent Fraternity" (1974), "The Rapacious Jailbreaker" (1974), "Jinzu Burusu: Asu Naki Buraiha" (1974), "Mamushi to Aodaisho" (1975), "Company Buggers" (1975), "Riot at Shimane Prison" (1975), "Gokudo Shacho" (1975), "Authentic True Account: Osaka Shock Tactics" (1976), "A Savage Beast Goes Mad" (1976), "Bakamasa Horamasa Toppamasa" (1976), "The Great Okinawa Yakuza War" (1976), "Piraniya-Gundan" (1976), "Yakuza Senso: Nihon No Don" (1977), "Nihon No Jingi" (1977), "Nippon No Don: Yabohen" (1977), "Shag" (1978), "Nihon No Don: Kanketsuhen" (1978), "Socho No Kubi" (1979), "The Shogun Assassins" (1979), "Renegade Ninjas" (1979), "Saraba, Wagatomo: Jitsuroku o-Mono Shikeishutachi" (1980), "Ageinsuto" (1981), "Conquest" (1982), "Theater of Life" (1983), "Appassionata" (1984), "The Seburi Story" (1985), "1750 Days of Turbulence" (1990), "Lady Kasuga" (1990), "Yakuza Ladies Revisited" (1991), "Gokudo Senso: Butoha" (1991), "The Man Who Shot the Don" (1994), "Yakuza Ladies 6" (1996), "Yakuza Ladies: decision" (1998), "Chambara: The Art of Japanese Swordplay" (2015), and "Tajuro Jun'ai-ki" (2018). Nakajima also worked in television, directing productions of "Takeda Shingen" (1990) and "Oda Nobunaga" (1992). He was a professor at the Osaka University of Arts from 1987 to 2008.

Napoleon XIV

Singer Jerrold Samuels, who performed the hit novelty song "They're Coming to Take me Away, Ha-Haaa!" under the name Napoleon XIV, died of complications from dementia at a hospital in Phoenixville, Pennsylvania, on March 10, 2023. He was 84. Samuels was born in New York City on May 3, 1938. He began playing the piano at an early age. He wrote songs from his teens and Johnnie Ray recorded a rendition of his "To Ev'ry Girl — To Ev'ry Boy" in 1954. He co-wrote "As If I Didn't Know", which was recorded by Adam Wade in 1961. His song, "The Shelter of Your Arms", was later recorded by Sammy Davis, Jr. He recorded the novelty song "They're Coming to Take Me Away, Ha-Haaa!" under the pseudonym Napoleon XIV, which became a hit in 1966. An album of the same name was released by Warner Bros. later in the year and included other songs adhering to the mental illness theme including "Bats in My Belfry" and "I Live in a Split Level Head". A second album, "For God's Sake, Stop the Feces!", was recorded in 1968 but was not released due to the controversial nature of some of the songs. Needlejuice Records released it a month after Samuels' death. He was a singer and pianist at bars and other local venues for many years. He also performed frequently at retirement communities. He formed the Jerry Samuels Agency in 1984 to book musical acts for seniors until his retirement in 2021. Samuels was married to Rosemary Djivre until their divorce in 1968. He is survived by their son, Scott. He was involved with Petra Vesters from 1973 until 1987 and is survived by their son, Jason. He married Bobbie Simon in 1996 and she also survives him. Another son, Eric, died in 1991.

Naraoka, Tomoko

Japanese actress Tomoko Naraoka died of pneumonia in Tokyo, Japan, on March 23, 2023. She was 93. Naraoka was born in Tokyo on December 1, 1929. She was a graduate of the Joshibi University of Art and Design. She began working in films in the late 1940s as an actress. Her numerous film credits include "Chijin no Ai" (1949), "Hito Kui Kuma" (1950), "Children of Hiroshima" (1952), "Epitome" (1953), "Konketsuji" (1953), "Utsukushii" (1954), "The Heart" (1955), "Wolf" (1955), "Aya Ni Itoshiki" (1956), "Night Drum" (1958), "Ballad of the Cart" (1959), "Sekai o Kakeru Koi" (1959),

"Season of Affairs" (1959), "Everything Goes Wrong" (1960), "Pigs and Battleships" (1961), "Asu No Hanayome" (1962), "Kaze No Shisen" (1963), "Futari Dake No Toride" (1963), "Utsukushii Koyomi" (1963), "Hikaru Umi" (1963), "The Scent of Incense" (1964), "Shonin No Isu" (1965), "The Song of  Love" (1965), "Eddy Currents of Life" (1966), "Your Life" (1966), "Zessho" (1966), "Oyuki San" (1966), "Koi No Highway" (1967), "Hymn to a Tired Man" (1968), "Retsuden Shumei Tobaku" (1969), "Apart from Life" (1970), "Dodes'ka-den" (1970), "Tekkaba Boo" (1970), "Asagiri" (1971), "Kaigun Tokubetsu Nensho-hei" (1972), "Ballad of Orin" (1977), "Take Me Away!" (1978), "Tobe Ikarosu No Tsubasa" (1980), "May Love Be Restored" (1980), "The Young Rebels" (1980), "The Imperial Navy" (1981), "Yasha" (1985), "Haru No Kane" (1985), "River of Fireflies" (1987), "Tora-san's Salad-Day Memorial" (1988), "Ruten no Umi" (1990), "Noh Mask Murders" (1991), "Sensou to Seishun" (1991), "My Sons" (1991), "Railroad Man" (1999), "Poppoya" (1999), "The Firefly" (2001), "Han-Ochi" (2004), the animated "Ponyo" (2008) as the voice of Yoshie, "Railways" (2010), "Tatara Samurai" (2016), "Takatsu-gawa" (2022), and "The Zen Diary" (2022). Naraoka was featured as Hisae Suzuki in eight films in the "Tsuribaka Nisshi" series in the late 1990s and early 2000s. She appeared on television in such productions as "Ten To Chi To" (1969), "Haru No Sakamichi" (1971), "Kaze To Kumo To Niji" (1976), "Taiyo Ni Hoero! Part 2" (1986), "Princess Go" (2011), and "55 Sai Kara No Hello Life" (2014). Naraota was narrator for "Oshin" from 1983 to 1984, "Inochi" (1986), "Kasuga No Tsubone" (1989), "Onna Wa Dokyo" (1992), "Haru Yo, Koi" from 1994 to 1995, and "Nankyoku Tairiku" (2011).

Nash, Noreen

Actress Noreen Nash, who starred in the 1953 science fiction film "Phantom from Space", died at her home in Beverly Hills, California, on June 6, 2023. She was 99. She was born Norabelle Jean Roth in Wenatchee, Washington, on April 4,  1924. She was crowned Apple Blossom Queen in her hometown in 1942. She subsequently began her career in films as a showgirl with MGM. She appeared in largely decorative roles over the next several years in such films as "Girl Crazy" (1943), "Meet the People" (1944), "Bathing Beauty" (1944), "Maisie Goes to Reno" (1944), "An American Romance" (1944), "Mrs. Parkington" (1944), "Thirty Seconds Over Tokyo" (1944), and "Ziegfeld Follies" (1945). She starred as Becky in Jean Renoir's 1945 film "The Southerner". Nash continued her career in films with such credits as "Monsieur

Beaucaire" (1946), "The Devil on Wheels" (1947), "The Big Fix" (1947), "The Perils of Pauline" (1947), "The Red Stallion" (1947), "The Tender Years" (1948), "Adventures of Casanova" (1948), "Assigned to Danger" (1948), "The Checkered Coat" (1948), the western "Storm Over Wyoming" (1950) starring Tim Hold, "Charlie's Haunt" (1950), "Aladdin and His Lamp" (1952), "Road Agent" (1952), "We're Not Married!" (1952), the science fiction film "Phantom from Space" (1953) as Barbara Randall, "The Body Beautiful" (1953), "Giant" (1956) in the small role of actress Lona Lane, "The Lone Ranger and the Lost City of Gold" (1958) as Frances Henderson opposite Clayton Moore, and "Wake Me When It's Over" (1960). She was seen on television in episodes of "Fireside Theatre", "Hopalong Cassidy", "Your Favorite Story", "The Lone Ranger", "My Hero", "Big Town", "Ramar of the Jungle", "City Detective", "The Abbott and Costello Show", "Four Star Playhouse", "My Little Margie", "Dragnet", "It's a Great Live", "The Charles Farrell Show" as Doris Mayfield in 1956, "Schlitz Playhouse", "State Trooper", "The Lineup", "77 Sunset Strip", "Yancy Derringer", "General Electric Theater", and "The Dick Powell Theatre". Nash retired from acting in the early 1960s. She later attended the University of California at Los Angeles, graduating in 1971. She published the historical drama "Love Fulfilled" in 1980. She also wrote the 2013 book "Agnes Sorel, Mistress of Beauty" and 2015's "Titans of the Muses: When Henry Miller Met Jean Renoir" with Jeanne Rejaunier. Nash was married to Dr. Lee Siegel from 1942 until his death in 1990 and is survived by their sons, novelist Lee Siegel, Jr., and cardiologist Robert James Siegel. She was married to actor James Whitmore from 2001 until his death in 2009.

Nastase, Silvia

Romanian actress Silvia Nastase, who was featured in a trio of science fiction films from Full Moon Entertainment in the late 1990s, died in Bucharest, Romania, on June 11, 2023. She was 80. Nastase was born in Bucharest on February 4,  1943. She trained as an actress with the Institute of Theatrical Arts and Cinematography, graduating in 1965. She performed frequently on stage throughout her career with roles in the National Ion Luca Caragiale theater in Bucharest. She appeared in films from the 1960s with roles in "Sah la Rege" (1966), "The Green Grass of Home" (1977), "Cine Iubesta si Lasa" (1982), "Al Patrulea Gard, Langa Debarcader" (1986), "Morometii" (1987), "Train of Life" (1998), "Cindres et Sang" (2009), "Tuesday, After Christmas" (2010), "Aurora" (2010), "Sieranevada" (2016), and "Zavera" (2019). Nastase was featured in a trio of juvenile science fiction films from Full Moon Entertainment that were filmed in Romania including "Phantom Town" (1999), "Teenage Space Vampires" (1999), and "Aliens in the Wild, Wild West" (1999).

Ndlovu, Patrick

South African actor Patrick Ndlovu died in South Africa on May 30, 2023. He was 84. Ndlovu was born in Mohlakeng, South Africa, on November 15, 1938. He was a popular performer in films and television from the 1980s. He was featured in such films as "Bullet on the Run" (1982), "The Devil & the Song" (1989), "Oddball Hall" (1999), "Serafina!" (1992), "Kalahari Harry" (1994), "Cry, the Beloved Country" (1995), "Danger Zone" (1996), "Jump the Gun" (1997), "Lettre d'Amour Zoulou" (2004), "Running Riot" (2006), "Everyman's Taxi" (2012), "The Killing Floor" (2017), "Knuckle City" (2019), and "The Queenstown Kings" (2023). Ndlovu appeared on television in productions of "Shaka Zulu" (1986), "Le Crime de Monsieur Stil" (1995), "Manshowe" (1996), "Rhodes" (1996), and "Dr. Lucille: The Lucille Teasdale Story" (2001). His other television credits include episodes of "Rosie", "Honeytown", "Missionnaire", "Tarzan: The Epic Adventures", "Yizo Yizo" as Principal Thembu in 1999, and "Zone 14" as Sizwe Moloi from 2005 to 2008.

Negreba, Aleksandr

Russian actor Aleksandr Negreba died of lung cancer in Russia on April 7, 2023. He was 61. Negreba was born in Kharkiv, Ukraine (then part of the Soviet Union), on April 28, 1968. He trained at the Russian Institute of Theatre Arts and began his career on stage with the Riga Youth Theater. He moved to Moscow in the 1980s and was a performer and director with the Small Drama Troupe. He was seen in such films as "Aborigen" (1987), Vasily Pichul's "Little Vera" (1988) as the title character's older brother, "V Gorode Sochi Tyomnye Nochi" (1989), "Neustanovlennoe Litso" (1990), "Za Den Do" (1991) which he also directed, "Dyuba-Dyuba" (1992), "Vremya Sobirat Kamni" (1992), "Mechty Idiota" (1993), and "Ligne de Vie" (1996). Negreba continued to work on stage as a producer, director, and writer. He was married to Yelena Koptseva-Negreba until her death on March 24, 2023.

Nehr, Jean

French actor Jean Nehr died at a retirement home in Aix-en-Provence, France, on January 2, 2023. She was 93. Nehr was born in Douai, France, on June 12, 1929. He was director of the Maison des Jeunes et de la Culture Jacques Prevert in Aix-en-Provence from 1962 to 1970. He then served as director of the Regional Federation of MJC Mediterranee4 youth center. Nehr made his television debut in the 1969 production of "The Aeronauts". He was also seen in television productions of "L'Affaire Bougrat" (1973), "L'Etrange Histoire d'Une Aboyeuse" (1973), "L'Affaire Bernardi de Sigoyer" (1974), "Le Fol Amour de Monsieur de Mirabeau" (1974), "La Ville, la Nuit" (1979), "So Long, Reveuse" (1980), "Fair Stood the Wind for France" (1980), "Le Devine-Vent" (1980), "Changements de Decors" (1980), "Le Vie Fantastique des Figures Peintes" (1981), "La Steppe" (1982), "Liebe Lafft alle Blumen Bluhen" (1987), "The Free Frenchman" (1989),

"Alcyon" (1990), "Strangers Dans la Nuit" (1991), "Pour Une Fille en Rouge" (1992), "La Controverse de Valladolid" (1992), "La Voyageuse du Soir" (1993), "Association de Bienfaiteurs" (1994), "Coup de Chien" (1994), "La Bastide Blanche" (1997), "Marseille" (1998), "Le Blanc et le Rouge" (2000), "Le Vol de la Colombe" (2001), "Le Chatiment du Makhila" (2001), "Les Filles du Calendrier" (2002), "Le Don Fait a Catchaires" (2003), "Entrusted" (2003), "Troubled Waters" (2004), "Le Miroir de l'Eau" (2004), "93, Rue Lauriston" (2004), "L'Affaire Christian Ranucci: Le Combat d'Une Mere" (2007), "La Victoire au Bout du Baton" (2012), and "Imposture" (2017). His other television credits include episodes of "L'Hiver d'Un Gentilhomme", "Les Enquetes du Commissaire Maigret", "Cinema 16", "Les Cinq Dernieres Minutes", "Les Coeurs Brules", "Puissance 4", "Docteur Sylvestre", "L'Avocate", "L'Histoire du Samedi", "Le Tuteur", "Vive les Vacances!", "Enquetes Reservees" as Ange Albertini in 2010, "Cain", "Meurtres a...", "Marjorie", and "Plus Belle la Vie". Nehr was also seen in several films including "Doux Amer" (1989), "Hercule & Sherlock" (1996), "Cartouches Gauloises" (2007), and "Marseille" (2016). He was the father of five children.

Neigher, Geoffrey

Television writer and producer Geoffrey Neigher died of complications from cancer at his home in Los Angeles, California, on August 10, 2023. He was 78. Neigher was born in Springfield, Massachusetts, in 1945. He graduated from

Yale University and Yale Law School. He moved to Los Angeles in 1973 where he began writing for television with Coleman 'Chick' Mitchell. They worked at MTM Enterprises on the series "The Bob Newhart Show", "Rhoda", and "Paul Sand in Friends and Lovers". The duo wrote and produced the 1978 unsold pilot "Annie Flynn" and the comedy series "Gimme a Break!" from 1981 to 1983. Neigher scripted episodes of "We Got It Made" and wrote and produced for the 1987 series "Roomies". He was also a producer for the series "Who's on Call?", "The New Odd Couple", "Spencer", and "I Married

Dora". He shared an Emmy Award nomination for writing an episode of "Northern Exposure" in 1993 and shared an Emmy as producer for "Picket Fences" in 1994. He was also a writer and producer for the series "Murder One", "Total Security", "Murder One: Diary of a Serial Killer", "Law & Order: Criminal Intent", and "John Doe". He wrote episodes of "Law & Order: Criminal Mind" and "Paris Criminal Investigations". Neigher's survivors include his wife Karen, and children, Julie and Eric.

Neil, Hildegarde

British actress Hildegarde Neil, who was Cleopatra to Charlton Heston's Mark Antony in 1972's "Antony and Cleopatra", died in England on September 19, 2023. She was 84. She was born Hildegard Zimmermann in Cape Town,  South Africa, on May 20, 1939. She moved to England in 1961 and studied at the Royal Academy of Dramatic Art for two years. She made her television debut as Calpurnia in a BBC production of "Julius Caesar" in 1963. She was soon performing in repertory at theaters in Ipswich, Leatherhead, and Worthing. She was a member of the Royal Shakespeare Company during the 1969 season. She was also seen on television in episodes of "No Hiding Place", "Dixon of Dock Green", "The Mind of Mr. J.G. Reeder", "The Expert", "W. Somerset Maugham", "Mystery and Imagination", "Doomwatch", "Codename", "Ace of Wands", "The Adventures of Don Quick", "The Main Chance", "Happy Ever After", "Man at the Top", "Jason King", "Six Faces", "Play for Today", "The Protectors", "Orson Welles' Great Mysteries", "Boy Dominic" as Emma Bulman in 1974, "The Early Life of Stephen Hind", "Whodunnit?", "Couples", "Crown Court" as Virginia Matheson in 1977, "Space: 1999", "Van der Valk", "The Professionals", "ITV Playhouse", "Diamonds" as Margaret Coleman in 1981, "Kelly Monteith", "Hotel Babylon", "Above Suspicion", and "Doctors". Neil's other television credits include productions of "Resurrection" (1968), "Imperial Palace" (1969), "Put Out More Flags" (1970), "A Spy at Evening" (1981), and "A Talent for Murder" (1984). She starred with Roger Moore in the psychological thriller "The Man Who Haunted Himself" in 1970 and was Cleopatra to Charlton Heston's Mark Antony in 1972's "Antony and Cleopatra". Her other films include "A Touch of Class" (1973) with George Segal and Glenda Jackson, "England Made Me" (1973), the horror film "The Legacy" (1978), the Agatha Christie adaptation "The Mirror Crack'd" (1980) starring Angela Lansbury as Miss Marple, "Seaview Knights" (1994), "The Bruce" (1996), "Macbeth" (1997), "King Lear" (1999), and "Upstaged" (2005). Neil was featured in the short films "Mr. Bojagi" (2009) and "Leni. Leni" (2016) as Leni Riefenstahl. She appeared with her daughter, Rosalind Blessed, in the 2020 film "Lullabies for the Lost". Neil also performed frequently on stage throughout her career, with roles in productions of "Macbeth" (1971) as Lady Macbeth, "The Doctor's Dilemma" (1981), and "The Lion in Winter" (1994) as Eleanor of Aquitaine opposite Brian Blessed's Henry II. She married Barry Wenn in 1961 and they later divorced. She married John Cartmel-Crossley in 1971 and they also divorced. Neill married actor Brian Blessed in 1978 and is survived by her and their daughter, Rosalind.

Nero, Peter

Concert pianist and conductor Peter Nero died at an assisted living facility in Eustis, Florida, on July 6, 2023. He was 89. He was born Bernard Nierow in Brooklyn, New York, on May 22, 1934. He began studying piano as child and attended New York City's High School of Music & Art in his early teens. He continued his studies at the Juilliard School of Music and graduated from Brooklyn College in 1956. He performed on television with a rendition of "Rhapsody in Blue"  for a Paul Whiteman special in 1952. He recorded an album under the name Bernie Nerow in 1957 and performed in Las Vegas with a jazz trio. He signed a contract with RCA in 1960 under the name Peter Nero and showed great range in his artistry with the 1961 album "Piano Forte". He received a Grammy Award for best new artist in 1961 and earned another for best performance with an orchestra for 1962's "The Colorful Peter Nero". He received an additional eight Grammy nominations during his career. Nero performed on television in the variety and talk shows "The George Gobel Show", "The Bob Newhart Show", "The Tonight Show Starring Jack Paar", "The Tonight Show", "The Lively Ones", "The Dinah Shore Chevy Show", "Alcoa Premiere", "The Jonathan Winters Specials", "Perry Como's Kraft Music Hall", "The Kathy Kirby Show", "The Bell Telephone Hour", "Hullabaloo", "The Hollywood Palace", "The Jackie Gleason Show", "Two of a Kind", "Lulu's Back in Town", "The London Palladium Show", "The Merv Griffin Show", "Life with Linkletter", "The Ed Sullivan Show", "The Barbara McNair Show", "The Ice Palace", "The Lee Phillip Show", "The David Frost Show", "The Tonight Show Starring Johnny Carson", "The Bob Braun Show", "The Mike Douglas Show", and "Dinah!". He scored the 1963 film "Sunday in New York" and appeared on screen performing "Thou Swell". He moved to Columbia Records later in the decade. He had a hit single and album featuring an instrumental version of the theme from the 1971 film "Summer of '42" and received another Grammy award. Nero starred in the 1972 television special "S'Wonderful, S'Marvelous, S'Gershwin" honoring George Gershwin. He recorded numerous hit albums with RCA during the 1960s. He also toured with the Peter Nero Trio in Las Vegas and Atlantic City, and composed a cantata based on the writing of Anne Frank, "The Diary", in the early 1970s. Nero served as conductor and music director for the Philly Pops from the late 1970s. He marked national holidays with patriotic musicales with the Pops through 2013.He was also a conductor and director with the Tulsa Philharmonic and the Florida Philharmonic. Nero married Marcia Dunner in 1956. They later divorced and he is survived by their two children, Jedd and Beverly. He married Peggy Altman in 1977 and they also divorced. He was also married and divorced from Rebecca Edie, a pianist with the Philly Pops.

Nettleton, John

British actor John Nettleton, who was noted for his role as Sir Arnold Robinson in the British television comedy series "Yes Minister" and "Yes, Prime Minister" in the 1980s, died in England on July 12, 2023. He was 94. Nettleton was born in Sydenham, London, England, on February 5, 1929. He trained at the Royal Academy of Dramatic Art, graduating in 1951. He began his career on stage and appeared in numerous productions with the Royal Shakespeare Company and the Old Vic. He accompanied a production of "As You Like It" to Broadway in 1974. Nettleton was seen frequently on television from the mid-1950s with roles in episodes of "Nom-de-Plume", "The Black Tulip", "Escape", "Mister Charlesworth", "ITV Television Playhouse", "Charlesworth at Large", "Starr and Company", "Maigret", "The Marriage Lines", "Softly Softly", "Seven Deadly Virtues", "The Fellows", "Comedy Playhouse", "Armchair Theatre", "Haunted" as Professor Alec Ritchie in 1967, "Theatre 625", "Oh La La"!", "The Champions", "Gazette", "The Expert", "ITV Playhouse", "The Avengers", "Charge!", "Her Majesty's Pleasure" as Pongo Little from 1968 to 1969, "Fraud Squad", "Detective", "Not in Front of the Children", "Department SS", "Please Sir!", "Smith", "The Wednesday Play", "The Culture Vultures", "Bachelor Father", "If It Moves, File It" as Froggett in 1970, "Conceptions of Murder", "Doctor at Large", "Out of the Unknown", "Birds on the Wing", "Thirty-Minute Theatre", "The Organization", "Six Days Justice", "Upstairs, Downstairs", "Dead of Night", "The Adventures of Black Beauty", "The Protectors", "The Rivals of Sherlock Holmes", "Justice", "A Pin to See the Peepshow" as George Beale in 1973, "How's Your Father?, "All Creatures Great and Small", "Churchill's People", "Village Hall", "The Main Chance", "Shadows", "My Brother's Keeper", "Z Cars", "The Professionals", "Feet First", "Spy!", "Play for Today", "Tales of the Unexpected", "Only When I Laugh", "The Happy Apple" as Arthur Spender in 1983, "Crown Court in the recurring role of Mr. Justice Sylvester from 1981 to 1984, "Blue Peter", "Brass", "Victoria Wood: As Seen on TV", "Fairly Secret Army" as Smith in 1986, "Worlds Beyond", "Rude Health", "Theatre Night", "The Russ Abbot Show" "Minder", "The New Statesman" as Sir Stephen Baxter from 1987 to 1989, "Gentlemen and Players", "Doctor Who" as Reverend Ernest Matthews in the 1989 two-part episode "Ghost Light", "Victoria Wood", "Haggard", "Screen Two", "Rumpole of the Bailey",

"Degrees of Error", "Douglas (Pilot)", "Wing and a Prayer", "Midsomer Murders", "The Bill", "Casualty", "Foyle's War", and "Kingdom". Nettleton starred as Cabinet Secretary Sir Arnold Robinson in the series "Yes Minister" from 1980 to 1985, and Robinson was the president of the Campaign for Freedom of Information in the sequel series "Yes, Prime Minister" from 1985 to 1988. His other television credits include productions of "Macbeth" (1958), "Yvette" (1958), "The Little Key" (1961), "Walk a Crooked Mile" (1961), the science fiction mini-series "A for Andromeda" (1961) as Harries, "Gina" (1964), "One Fat Englishman" (1967), "The Undoing" (1969), "The Girl Upstairs" (1971), "Elizabeth R" (1971) as Sir Francis Bacon, "Alice Dancing" (1971), "Fly on the Wall: The General" (1971), "The Edwardians" (1972), "The Staff Room" (1973), "The Pallisers" (1974), "The Fortune Hunters" (1976), "Abide with Me" (1976), "The Country Wife" (1977), "Henry VIII" (1979), "The Tempest" (1980), "Sheppey" (1980), "The Flame Trees of Thika" (1981), "Brideshead Revisited" (1981), "Anyone for Denis?" (1982), "The Plot to Murder Lloyd George" (1983), "The Citadel" (1983), "Martin Luther, Heretic" (1983), "Newstime" (1985), "A Perfect Spy" (1987), "Bomber Harris" (1989), "Longitude" (2000), and "Dad" (2005). Nettleton was seen in occasional films during his career including "A Man for All Seasons" (1966), "The Last Show You Hear" (1969), "Some Will, Some Won't" (1970), "And Soon the Darkness" (1970), "Black Beauty" (1971), "Burning Secret"(1988), "American Friends" (1991), "Jinnah" (1998), "Oliver Twist" (2005), and "Fishtales" (2007). He married actress Deirdre Doone in 1954 and is survived by her and their three children.

Newby, Chas

British musician Charles Newby, who briefly played the bass for the Beatles in December of 1960, died in England on May 22, 2023. He was 81. Newby was born in Liverpool, England, on June 18, 1941. He performed with Pete Best's group, the Black Jacks, as a bass guitarist in the late 1950s. He briefly joined the Beatles in the late 1960s, filling in for Stuart Sutcliffe on bass for a handful of engagements in December. He was invited to go to West Germany with the group but declined to return to school. He was later a mathematics teacher in Droitwich Spa in Wyachovan, England. He began playing with the Quarrymen, the reincarnation of an early version of the Beatles, in 2016

Newman, Barry

Actor Barry Newman, who starred in the 1971 cult film "Vanishing Point" and the television legal drama "Petrocelli", died at a hospital in New York City on May 11, 2023. He was 84. Newman was born in Boston, Massachusetts, on November 7, 1938. He played the saxophone and clarinet while attending high school and studied anthropology at

Brandeis University. He graduated in 1952 and served in the U.S. Army as part of the 3rd Army Band in Atlanta. He returned to New York after his discharge to pursue a master's degree in anthropology at Columbia University. He left  Columbia soon after to study acting with Lee Strasberg. He began his career on stage and appeared on Broadway in productions of "Nature's Way" (1957), "Maybe Tuesday" (1958), "Night Life" (1962), and "What Makes Sammy Run?" (1964). Newman made his film debut as Al Riccardo in the 1960 crime drama "Pretty Boy Floyd". He appeared on television in episodes of "Way Out", "The Defenders", "The United States Steel Hour", "Naked City", "Armstrong Circle Theatre", and "Get Smart", and was attorney John Barnes in the daytime soap opera "The Edge of Night" from 1964 to 1965. Nelson starred as attorney Anthony J. Petrocelli in the 1970 film "The Lawyer" and the 1974 tele-film "Night Games" and reprised the role in the "Petrocelli" series on NBC from 1974 to 1976. He earned an Emmy Award for his work in "Petrocelli" in 1975. He was also seen in the tele-films "Sex and the Married Woman" (1977), "King Crab" (1980), "Fantasies" (1982), "...Deadline..." (1982), "Having It All" (1982), "Second Sight: A Love Story" (1984), "Fatal Vision" (1984), "My Two Loves" (1986), "Miss Marple: The Mirror Crack'd from side to Side" (1992), "Der Blaue Diamant" (1993), and "MacShayne: Winner Takes All" (1994). His other television credits include episodes of "Quincy", "The Fall Guy", the short-lived medical drama "Nightingales" as Dr. Garrett Braden in 1989, "L.A. Law", "Murder, She Wrote", "JAG", "NYPD Blue", "Cupid", "The O.C." in the recurring role of Professor Max Bloom in 2005, "The Cleaner", and "Ghost Whisperer". He also appeared in the talk and variety shows "The Irv Kupcinet Show", "The Tonight Show Starring Johnny Carson", "The Peter Marshall Variety Show", "The Mike Douglas Show", "Celebrity Sweepstakes", "The Merv Griffin Show", "Dinah!", "The Alan Thicke Show", "The New Hollywood Squares", and "Night of 100 Stars". Newman starred as Kowalski in the 1971 action film "Vanishing Point" by Richard C. Sarafian about a race driver transporting a 1970 Dodge Challenger from Colorado to California while being pursued by the police. It was initially unsuccessful at the box office but soon developed a cult following. His other films include "The Salzburg Connection" (1972), "Far Is the Key" (1972), "City on Fire" (1979), "Amy" (1981), "Daylight" (1996), "Next Year in Jerusalem" (1997), "Goodbye Lover" (1998), "Brown's Requiem" (1998), "Fugitive Mind" (1999), "The Limey" (1999), "Bowfinger" (1999), "G-Men from Hell" (2000), "Jack the Dog" (2001), "Good Advice" (2001), "True Blue" (2001), "40 Days and 40 Nights" (2002), "Manhood" (2003), "What the #$! Do We (K)now!?" (2004), "What the Bleep!?" Down the Rabbit Hole" (2006), "Grilled" (2006), and "Raise Your Kids on Seltzer" (2015). Newman is survived by his wife, Angela.

Newstone, Pauline

Canadian actress Pauline Newstone, who voiced characters in such animated series as "Beast Wars: Transformers" and "Dragon Ball Z", died in Los Angeles, California, on May 5, 2023. She was 79. Newstone was born  in Sainte-Therese, Quebec, Canada, on August 13, 1943. She provided the English dubbing voice for numerous animes and cartoons from the late 1980s. She was the voice of Airazor in "Beast Wars: Transformers" from 1996 to 1998, Heka in "Mummies Alive!" in 1997, and Frieza in "Dragon Ball Z" from 1997 to 2003. Newstone was also heard on such series as "Captain N: The Game Master", "G.I. Joe", "Bucky O'Hare and the Toad Wars!", "Captain Zed and the Zee Zone", "Bitsy Bears", "Adventures of Sonic the Hedgehog", "Littlest Pet Shop",, "Vortech: Undercover Conversion Squad", "Mister Keaton", "Fat Dog Mendoza", "Z-Mind", "Hamtaro", "Yvon of the Yukon", "Infinite Ryvius", "Monster Rancher", "Aaagh! It's the Mr. Hell Show", "Project ARMS", "Ulltimate Book of Spells", "Sitting Ducks", "X-Men: Evolution" as the voice of Agatha Harkness from 2002 to 2003, "Inuyasha", "Being Ian", "The Cramp Twins" as Lily Parsons from 2001 to 2005, "Kong: The Animated Series" as Harpy from 2005 to 2006, "A Kind of Magic", "Bratz", "Cosmic Quantum Ray" as Olga and Contessa De Worm in 2009, "Gingama", and "Ninjago" as Aspheera in 2019. Newstone was also a voice actress in the animated films "Snow White" (1991), "Mummies Alive! The Legend Begins" (1998), "Grandma Got Run Over by a Reindeer" (2000), "Robin and the Dreamweavers" (2000), "A Fish Tale" (2000), "Bratz: Desert Jewelz" (2012), and "Cats & Dogs 3: Paws Unite" (2020).

Ng, Richard

Hong Kong actor Richard Ng died at a hospital in Hong Kong on April 9, 2023. He was 83. He was born Richard  Ng Yiu-hon in Guangzhou, China, on December 17, 1939. He was a popular comic performer in Hong Kong films from the mid-1970s. His films include "Golden Needles" (1974), "The Good, the Bad and the Loser" (1976), "The Private Eyes" (1976) his first of many films starring Sammo Hung, "Money Crazy" (1977), "Winner Takes All" (1977), "Murder Most Foul" (1979) which he also wrote and directed, "Itchy Fingers" (1979), "Carry on Pickpocket" (1982), "It Takes Two" (1982), "Winners & Sinners" (1983), "Pom Pom" (1984) as Chau in the first of a comedy series,

"Heaven Can Help" (1984), "The Return of Pom Pom" (1984), "Wheels on Meals" (1984), "My Lucky Stars" (1985) as Sandy in this comedy series, "Mr. Boo Meets Pom Pom" (1985), "These Merry Souls" (1985), "Twinkle Twinkle Lucky Stars" (1985), "Yes, Madam!" (1985), "From Here to Prosperity" (1986), "My Family" (1986), "Millionaires' Express" (1986), "Lucky stars Go Places" (1986), "Shuang Long Tu Zhu" (1986), "My Cousin, the Ghost" (1987), "Dynamite Fighters" (1987), "Bat Si Yuen Ga Bat Jui Tau" (1987), "Mr Handsome" (1987), "Golden Swallow" (1987), "Mr. Vampire Part 3" (1987), "Carry on Hotel" (1988), "In the Line of Duty III" (1988), "Wu Long Zei Ti Shen" (1988), "Gui Meng Jiao" (1988), "Faithfully Yours" (1988), "Gaston en Leo in Hong Kong" (1988), "Unfaithfully Yours" (1989), "Little Cop" (1989), "Return of the Lucky Stars" (1989), "Miracles: The Canton Godfather" (1989), "Beyond the Sunset" (1989), "Run, Don't Walk" (1989), "Mr. Sunshine" (1989), "Meng Gui Shan Fen" (1989), "Wu Ming Jia Zu" (1990), "Shuai Gui Qiao Qiang Jiao" (1990), "Licence to Steal" (1990), "Red Dust" (1990), "The Nocturnal Demon" (1990), "The Gambling Ghost" (1991), "Slickers vs. Killers" (1991), "The Banquet" (1991), "Ghost Punting" (1992), "Now You Seet It, Now You Don't" (1992), "Saviour of the Soul II" (1992) as the Devil King, "Handsome Siblings" (1992), "Banana Spirit" (1992), "Future Cops" (1993), "Jie da Huan Xi" (1993), "Boys Are Easy" (1993), "Kung Fu Cult Master" (1993), "Doctor Mack" (1995), "Don't Give a Damn" (1995), "Once in a Lifetime" (1995), "Heaven Can't Wait" (1995), "Whatever Will Be, Will Be" (1995), "How to Meet the Lucky Stars" (1996), "The Stunt Woman" (1996), "Once Upon a Time in China and America" (1997), "Hong Kong Night Club" (1997), "The Pale Sky" (1998), "King of Stanley Market" (1998), "Sausalito" (2000), "Jiang Hu: The Triad Zone" (2000), "Beijing Rocks" (2001), "My Wife Is 18" (2002), and "My Dream Girl" (2003). Ng moved to London, England, in the late 1990s, though he continued to appear on films in Hong Kong and England. He appeared under the pseudonym Richard Woo in a small role in the 2003 film "Lara Croft: Tomb Raider - The Cradle of Life" starring Angelina Jolie. His other films include "Legend of the Dragon" (2005), "Saam Fun Chung Sin Saan" (2008), "Bodyguard: A New Beginning" (2008), "Echelon Conspiracy" (2009), "Here Comes Fortune" (2010), "Flirting Scholar 2" (2010), "Detective Dee: The Mystery of the Phantom Flame" (2010), "Perfect Wedding" (2010), "Men Suddenly in Love" (2011), "Jin Chou Fu Lu Shou" (2011), "Repeat I Love You" (2012), "Supercapitalist" (2012), "Rigor Mortis" (2013), "Little Big Master" (2015), "Already Tomorrow in Hong Kong" (2015), "Skiptrace" (2016), "The Moment" (2016), "Vampire Cleanup Department" (2017), "Bio Raiders" (2017), "Mr. Zombie" (2918), "A House of Happiness" (2018), "Chinatown: The Three Soldiers" (2018), "Hotel Soul Good" (2018), "Dearest Anita" (2019), "A Lifetime Treasure" (2019), "Go Back to China" (2019), "The Invincible Dragon" (2019), the horror film "Walk with Me" (2019), "Dead Packet" (2019), "Ga Yau Hei See" (2020), "A Moment of Happiness" (2020), and "Theory of Ambitions" (2022). Ng was seen on television in productions of "Under One Roof" (1999), "The Monkey King" (2001), "Life Beyond the Box: Norman Stanley Fletcher"

(2003), "The First Emperor" (2006), "The Great Wall of China" (2007), "Phoo Action" (2008), "Pulau Hantu (2008), and "Fragments of Summer" (2019). He also appeared in episodes of "River City", "The Bill", "Genie in the House", "Red Dwarf", "Sayang Sayang", "Love Thy Family", and "Silver Lining". He is survived by his wife, English hair stylist Susan Ng, who he married in 1965, and four children.

Ngema, Mbongeni

South African playwright Mbongeni Ngema, who was noted for the musical "Sarafina!", was killed in an automobile accident while returning from Lusikisiki, South Africa, on December 27, 2023. He was 68. Ngema, an ethnic Zulu, was  born in Verulam, South Africa, on May 10, 1955. He was raised in a rural area in kwaHlabisa and returned to Verulam and Durban to attend high school. He left to perform in local bands. He moved to Johannesburg in the late 1970s where he began performing in local theater. He co-wrote the play "Woza Albert!" with Percy Mtwa in 1981. He formed his own theatrical company, Committed Artists in the early 1980s. He and wrote the musical "Asinamali!", which deals with racist laws and police violence, in 1983. The first performance was raided by South African police and the actors were arrested. "Asinmali!" was performed on Broadway and earned Ngema a Tony Award nomination for his direction. He directed and starred as Comrade Washington in a film version in 2017. His 1988 play "Serafina!", based on the Soweto uprising of 1976, earned five Tony Award nominations when it was performed on Broadway. "Serafina!" was adapted for a film in 1992 starring Whoopi Goldberg and Miriam Makeba, which featured Ngema, who was also librettist for the soundtrack, in the role of Sabela. He also wrote the plays "Township Fever" and "Sheila's Day" in 1990. He was a vocal arranger for the Disney animated film "The Lion King" in 1994. He wrote the 1995 musical "Mama!: The Musical of Freedom" after Nelson Mandela became president of South Africa. His sequel, "Serafina II", dealing with South Africa's AIDS epidemic, premiered in 1996. He was composer and producer for his 1997 solo album "Woza My Fohloza". He wrote the 2005 play "The House of Shaka"in 2005. His later works include "Lion of the East" (2009) and "The Zulu" (2013). Ngema was married to Xoliswa Nduneni-Ngema from 1982 until their divorce in 1992. She later published a memoir which accused him of abuse during their marriage. He had affair with actress Leleti Khumalo during his first marriage and their married in 1992. He and Khumalo divorced in 2005.

Niane, Adama

French actor Adama Niane died in Paris, France, on January 28, 2023. He was 56. Niane was born in Paris on August 23, 1966. He trained as an actor at the Sorbonne

Nouvelle University in Paris and began his career on stage with Philippe Duclos' theatrical troupe. He appeared in films and

television from the early 1990s with roles in production of "Commissaire Moulin", "No Hiding Place", "Gabriel", "Le JAP, Juge d'Application des Peines", "Suite en Re", "Julie Lescaut", "Frank Riva", "Ambre a Disparu", "Lost Signs" as Paolo Bruni in 2007, "P.J." as Lorenzo Dantzer in 2009, "Plus Belle la Vie" as Sebstien Sanga in 2009, "Flics", "Boulevard du Palais", "The Last Panthers" as Nadim in 2015, "Nicolas Le Floch", "Chefs", "Imposture", "La Mante" as Stern in 2007, "Troubled Waters", "Prise au Piege", "Maroni" in the recurring role of Dialo from 2018 tom 2021, "Sam" as Issa from 2019 to 2021, "Inhuman Resources" as David Fontana in 2020, "Lupin" as Leonard Kone in 2021, "Alex Hugo", and "L'ile Aux 30 Cercueils" as Yannick Lantry in 2022. Niane appeared in the films "Mo'" (1996), "Baise-moi" (2000), "35 Shots of Rum" (2008), "SK1" (2014), "Gang of the Caribbean" (2016), "Get In" (2019), "The Bare Necessity" (2019), and "Felicita" (2020).

Nichols, John

Novelist John Nichols, who was best known for his books "The Milagro Beanfield War" and "The Sterile Cuckoo", died after a long illness in Taos, New Mexico, on November 28, 2023. He was 83. Nichols was born in Berkeley, California, on July 23, 1940. His mother died at an early age and he

relocated frequently in his youth. He graduated from Hamilton College in Clinton, New York, in 1962. His first novel, "The Sterile Cuckoo", was published in 1965. A film version, directed by Alan J. Pakula, was released in 1969 and earned Liza Minnelli an Academy Award nomination for her starring role. Nichols' novel, "The Wizard of Loneliness", followed in 1966 and it was adapted for film in 1988.

He settled in Taos, New Mexico, in the late 1960s where he wrote the historical fiction "The Milagro Beanfield War" (1974). A film version, directed by Robert Redford and starring Ruben Blades, was released in 1988. "The Milagro Beanfield War" was the first part of a trilogy that included "The Magic Journey" (1978) and "The Nirvana Blues" (1981). Nichols also penned the novels "A Ghost in the Blood" (1979), "American Blood" (1987), "An Elegy for September" (1992), "Conjugal Bliss: A Comedy of Martial Arts" (1994), "The Voice of the Butterfly" (2001), "The Empanada Brotherhood" (2007), "On Top of Spoon Mountain" (2012), "The Annual Big Arsenic Fishing Contest!" (2016), and "Goodbye, Monique" (2019). He also wrote the non-fiction trilogy "If Mountains Die: A New

Mexico Memoir" (1979), "The Last Days of Autumn" (1982), and "On the Mesa" (1986). His other non-fiction includes "A Fragile Beauty: John Nichols' Milagro Country" (1987), "Keep It Simple: A Defense of the Earth" (1992), "Dancing on the Stones: Selected Essays" (2000), "An American Child Supreme: The Education of a Liberation Ecologist" (2001), and "I Got Mine: Confessions of a Midlist Writer" (2022). Nicholas was the subject of director Kurt Jacobsen's documentary feature" The Milagro Man: The Irrepressible Multicultural Life and Literary Times of John Nichols" in 2012. He is survived by a son and daughter from his first marriage to Ruth Wetherell Harding.

Niekerk, Louis van

South African actor Louis van Niekerk died in South Africa on February 7, 2023. He was 87. Niekerk was born in South Africa on June 27, 1935. He had a long career on stage, screen, and television from the 1960s. he was featured in the

films "Die Voortreflike Familie Smit" (1965), "Danie Bosman: Die Verhaal van die Grootste S.A. Komponis" (1969), "Stop Exchange" (1970), "Pressure Burst" (1971), "Die Sersant en die Tiger Moth" (1973), "Siener in die Suburbs" (1974), "Die Saboteurs" (1974), "Skadu's van Gister" (1974), "Vrou Uit die Nag" (1974), "Elsa se Geheim" (1979), "40 Days" (1979), "Tawwe

Tienies" (1984), "Jobman" (1989), "Damned River" (1989), "The Fourth Reich" (1990), "The Road to Mecca" (1991), "Taxi to Soweto" (1991), "Orkney Snork Nie! 2 (Nog 'n Movie)" (1993), "Promised Land" (2002), "In My Country" (2004), "Goo0dbyen Bafana" (2007), "Susanna von Biljon" (2010), "Mandela: Long Walk to Freedom" (2013), "Ladygrey" (2015), and the short "Bittersoet" (2022). Niekerk appeared on television in productions of "Die Heks" (1976), "Die Vlakte Duskant Hebron" (1982), "Mauwie" (1985), "Heroes" (1986), "Inside" (1996), "Die Staat se Bul" (2014), and "Bus 7070" (2021). His other television credits include episodes of "Diamantendetektiv Dick Donald", "Mattewis en Meraai", "Kooperasiestories", "Kampus", "Agter Elke Man", "Die Hoffman", "Moordspeletjies", "Die Binnekring", "Die Sonkring", "Konings", "MMG Engineers", "Torings", "Grondbaronne", "Cycle Simenon", "Die Laksman", "Jackpot", "Hagenheim: Streng Privaat", "Die Vierde Kabinet", "Amalia", "Amalia 2", "Feast of the Uninvited", "Wild at Heart", "Geraamtes in die Kas", "Swartwater", "Vlug na Egipte", and "Gertroud Met Rugby" as Festus from 2009 to 2022.

Nienhuis, Terry

Actor Terry Nienhuis died in Williamsburg, Virginia, on November 30, 2023. He was 78. He was born in Grand Rapids, Michigan. He graduated from Western Michigan University and earned a PhD from the University of Michigan at Ann Arbor. He moved to Cullowhee, North Carolina in 1972 and taught English at Western Carolina University. He returned from Western Carolina University in 2008. He was active with  the school theater, appearing in numerous productions. He also appeared on stage with the Southern Appalachian Repertory Theatre and the Hayward Arts Regional Theatre. He continued to perform on the local stage through the early 2000s. Nienhuis was featured in the films "The Journey of August King" (1995), "This World, Then the Fireworks" (1997), "Carolina Low" (1997), "October Sky" (1999), "Angel with a Kick" (2005), "Wesley" (2009), and "Moon Europa" (2009). He appeared in television productions of "What the Deaf Man Heard" (1997), "Having Our Say: The Delany Sisters' First 1000 Years" (1999), and "The Water Is Wide" (2006). He began involved with helping Chinese speakers improve their English language skills in Nanjing. He began working with Bei Zhang, owner of an English language institute, and she became his third wife in 2015. He is survived by her and their son, Nick.

Niesp, Sharon

Actress Sharon Niesp died of complications of pulmonary fibrosis in Provincetown, Massachusetts, on  September 20, 2023. She was 80. Niesp was born in Buffalo, New York, on August 8, 1943. She moved to Provincetown in the early 1970s and soon became involved with actress Cookie Mueller. Niesp joined Mueller in John Waters' cult trash classic "Desperate Living" (1977) in the role of Shotsie. She also appeared in Waters' films "Polyester" (1981) and "Pecker" (1998). She and Mueller also performed in the off-beat musical group B.B. Steele Revue with Ben Syfu, Susan Lowe, and Edith Massey. Niesp and Mueller broke up in 1981 and she moved to New Orleans several years later. She returned to Provincetown to work as a cook at Spiritus Pizza and appeared on the local stage in Gary, Indiana. She would remain close to Mueller until her death by AIDS-related pneumonia in 1989. Niesp was a contributor to Chloe Griffin's 2014 book "Edgewise: A Picture of Cookie Mueller".

Nilsson, Stefan

Swedish pianist and film composer Stefan Nilsson died of complications from ALS in Saltsjobaden, Sweden, on May 25, 2023. He was 67. Nilsson was born in Kukasjarvi, Sweden, on July 27, 1955. He began playing piano in his youth and continued his studies in college under Gunner Karl Hagen. He began a jazz rock band, Kornet, in the 1970s, and they released three albums. He performed and recorded frequently with Tommy Korberg. He scored numerous films and television productions from the early 1980s including "Sally and Freedomm" (1983), "Kalabaliken i Bender" (1983), "Lyckans Ost" (1983), "Slagskampen" (1984), "Smugglarkungen" (1985), "False as Water" (1985), "Morrhar & Artor" (1986), "The Serpent's Way" (1986), "Jim & Piraterna Blom" (1987), the Oscar-winning foreign language film "Pelle the Conqueror" (1987), "The Time of the Wolf" (1988), "Sweetwater" (1988), "Den Ofrivillige Golfaren" (1991), "My Best Intentions" (1992), "Lotta pa Brakmakargatan" (1992),  "Brandbilen Som Forsvann" (1993), "Lotta 2 - Lotta Flyttar Hemifran" (1993), "Murder at the Savoy" (1993), "Roseanna" (1993), "Mannen Pa Balkongen" (1993), "The Police Murderer" (1994), "Stockholm Marathon" (1994), "Yrrol - En Kolossalt Genomtankt Film" (1994), "Stora Och Sma Man" (1995), "Body Switch" (1995), "Alskar Alskar Inte" (1995), "Jerusalem" (1996), "Juloratoriet" (1996), "Ogifta Par... en Film Som Silkjer Sig" (1997), "En Sang for Martin" (2001), "Wolf Summer" (2003), "As It Is In Heaven" (2004), which included the hit song "Gabriella's Song", "Carambole" (2005), "Kim Novak Never Swam in Genesaret's Lake" (2005), "Munsters Fall" (2005), "Borkmann's Point" (2005), "Svalan, Katten Rosen, Doden" (2006), "Fallet G" (2006), "Moreno and the Silence" (2006), "Himlens Hjarta" (2008), "Fri Os Fra Det Onde" (2009), "Gornedel Og Det Onde - Bag Kameraet" (2009), "Kvinden der Dromte om en Mand" (2010), "Liv & Ingmar" (2012), "Marie Kroyer" (2012), "The Optimists" (2013), "Let the Scream Be Heard" (2013), and "Wars Don't End" (2018). Nilsson composed for such television productions as "Voyeur - For the Millions" (1980), "Tamara - La Donna d'Oro" (1981), "Ett Hjarta Av Guld" (1982), "Cirkus Skrot" (1983), "Kara Faror" (1990), "The Best Intentions" (1991), "Kvallspressen" (1992), "Min Van Percys Magiska Gymnastikskor" (1994), "Lotta Pa Brakmakargatan" (1995), "Persons Parfymeri" (1997), "Skargardsdoktorn" (1997), "Det Grovmaskiga Natet" (2000), "Aterkomsten" (2001), "Kvinna Med Fodelsemarke" (2001), and "Detaljer" (2003).

Nolen, Timothy

Actor and singer Timothy Nolen died on August 31, 2023. He was 82. Nolen was born in Rotan, Texas, on July 9, 1941. He began his career performing small roles in operas in the 1960s. He performed with the San Francisco Opera in Darius Milhaud's "Christophe Colomb" in 1968. He appeared in supporting roles in productions of "Romeo et Juliette", "Rigoletto', "Otello", "La Boheme", and "Carmen". He starred with the San Francisco Opera in "The Babara of Seville" (1976) as Figaro, "Don Pasquale" (1980) as Dr. Malatesta, and "Die Fledermaus" (1990) as Dr. Falke. Nolen starred in the title role of the first operatic version of Stephen Sondheim's "Sweeney

Todd: The Demon Barber of Fleet Street" in 1984. He made his debut in Broadway as Doyle in Larry Grossman's "Grind"

in 1985. Nolen replaced Michael Crawford in the title role of Andrew Lloyd Webber's "The Phantom of the Opera" on Broadway in October of 1988 and remained with the production through March of 1989. He also starred as Comte de Guiche in Broadway's "Cyrano: The Musical" in 1994. He continued to star in the title role in productions of "Sweeney Todd". He took the role of Judge Turpin in a 2001 New York Philharmonic concert version of "Sweeney Todd" which was broadcast on PBS's "Great Performances". He debuted at the Metropolitan Opera as Krusina in a production of Bedrich Smetana's "The Bartered Bride" in 1996. His other performances at the Met including "The Merry Widow" (2000) as Baron Zeta and "Die Frau Ohne Schatten" (2001) as the One-Eyed Man. Norman was seen on television in episodes of "The Guiding Light", "The Sopranos", and "Wildfire".

Norell, Michael

Actor and screenwriter Michael Norell, who starred as Captain Hank Stanley on the television series "Emergency!", died in Huntingdon, Pennsylvania, on May 12, 2023. He was 85. Norell was born in Wallace, Idaho, on October 4, 1937. He

and his family lived in Tokyo, Japan, while his father served in the U.S. Army during the Korean War. He later attended high school in Virginia and majored in journalism at Washington and Lee University in Lexington, Virginia. He served in the U.S. Army for five years after graduating achieving the rank of captain. He worked for the "Richmond Times-Dispatch" newspaper before moving to New York City to pursue an acting career. He soon moved to Hollywood where he was cast as Captain Hank Stanley in the medical drama series "Emergency!" from 1972 to 1978. Norell also wrote several episodes of the series and largely worked as a screenwriter after the series ended. He scripted the tele-films "Sex and the Married Woman" (1977), "Three on a Date" (1978), "What's Up Doc" (1978), "Featherstone's Nest" (1979) which he also produced, "Revenge of the Gray Gang" (1981), "In Love with an Older Woman" (1982), "Dead Man's Folly" (1986), "Barnum" (1986), "Pals" (1987), "Murder by the Book" (1987), "Long Gone" (1987), "Christmas Comes to Willow Creek" (1987), "The Cover Girl and the Cop" (1989), "She Knows Too Much" (1989), "The Incident" (1990) earning an Emmy Award nomination, "Against Her Will: An Incident in Baltimore" (1992), "The Diamond Fleece" (1992), "The Streets of Beverly Hills" (1992), "River of Rage: The Taking of Maggie Keene"

(1993), "I Spy Returns" (1994), "Remember Me" (1995), and "Doomsday Rock" (1997). He also wrote episodes of "The Love Boat", "Aloha Paradise", "Love Boat: The Next Wave", "Tales of the South Seas", "The Magnificent Seven", and "Nash Bridges". He produced episodes of the short-lived "Aloha Paradise" which he also co-created and "Nash Bridges". Norell was script coordinator for the series "Murder One", "Brooklyn South", and "NYPD Blue", and assistant to the producer for "Flying Blind". He was married to Elizabeth Ingleson from 1965 until her death in 1983. He married television producer Cynthia A. Cherback in 1991 and is survived by her and their two children.

Norman, Vera

French actress Vera Norman died in Saint-Arnoult, France, on May 19, 2023. She was 98. She was born Marguerite Trediakowski in Paris, France, on December 28, 1924. She began her career in films in the mid-1940s and was

seen in "Echec au Roy" (1945), "La Rose de la Mer" (1946), "Rouletabille Joue et Gagne" (1947), Maurice Cloche's "Monsieur Vincent" (1947) as Mademoiselle de Chatillon, "La Renegate" (1948), "Mission a Tanger" (1949), "Retour a la Vie" (1949), "Le Grand Rendez-vous" (1950), "Lady Paname" (1950), "Le Tampon du Capiston" (1950), "Just Me" (1950), "L'Homme de la Jamaique" (1950), "Serenade au Bourreau" (1951), "Les Petites Cardinal" (1951), "Au Pays du Soleil" (1951), "Un Jour Avec Vous" (1951), the short "Torticola Contre Frankensberg" (1952), "Violetas Imperiales" (1952), "Caroline Cherie" (1963), "Cet Homme est Dangereux" (19530, "The Snow Was Black" (1954), "Les Corsaires du Bois de Boulogne" (1954), and "La Cancion del Penal" (1954). She ended her acting career in the mid-1950s and married radio and television game designer Pierre Henry. She retired to Deauville with her family to become an antique dealer and an artist in the mid-1980s.

Norris, Charlie

Professional wrestler Charlie Norris died in Red Lake, Minnesota, on February 6, 2023. He was 59. Norris, a Chippewa Indian, was born in the Red Lake Indian Reservation in Minnesota on October 21, 1963. He trained as a wrestler with Eddie Sharkey in 1988 and began his career with his promotion, Pro Wrestling America (PWA). He defeated Ricky Rice for the PWA's Heavyweight Championship in October of 1989. He lost the title in a rematch in May of 1990. He briefly held the title in February of 1991 after defeating Terminator Riggs and then losing a rematch four days later. He held the championship three more times against competitors the Golden Idol, Teijo Khan, and Punisher Sledge before leaving the promotion in early 1993. Norris soon joined World Championship Wrestling (WCW) where he feuded with Maxx

Payne, Steve Austin, Vader, and Lord Steven Regal. He returned to the PWA in 1994 and teamed with Sam Houston as the Renegades to defeat the Storm Troopers for the tag team championship. He and Derrick Dukes formed the Thunderblood tag team in 1996 and again captured the tag titles from the Storm Troopers. They held the belts until the promotion folded later in 1996. He briefly competed in the American Wrestling Federation (AWF) in 1996 and wrestled on the independent circuit over the next decade. Norris retired from the ring in 2006 and worked as a personal trainer at a Red Lake gym.

Norris, Terry

Australian actor Terry Norris died in Australia on March 20, 2023. He was 92. Norris was born in Richmond, Victoria, Australia, on June 9, 1930. He trained as an actor at the Melbourne Tivoli Theatre in the late 1950s. He performed on stage in repertory in England before returning to Australia in 1963. Norris appeared on television in productions of "A Man

for All Seasons" (1963) as King Henry VIII, "Nude with Violin" (1964), "The Sponge Room" (1964), "Corruption in the Palace of Justice" (1964), "Othello" (1964), "Luther" (1964), "The Physicists" (1964), "Six Characters in Search of an Author" (1964), "Romanoff and Juliet" (1965), "The Winds of Green Monday" (1965), "Topaze" (1966), "The Proposal and the Bear" (1968), "The Shifting Heart" (1968), "I'm Damned If I Know" (1972), "Power Without Glory" (1976), "The Damnation of Havey McHugh" (1994), "Noah's Ark" (1999), "Waiting at the Royal" (2000), "Changi" (2001), "Marshall Law" (2002), "The Society Murders" (2006), "Valentine's Day" (2008), "Hawke" (2010), "Killing Time" (2010), and "Romper Stomper" (2018). He starred as Eric Tanner in the tele-films "Jack Irish: Bad Debts" (2012), "Jack Irish: Black Tide" (2012), and "Jack Irish: Dead Point" (2014), and the series "Jack Irish" from 2016 to 2021. His other television credits include episodes of "The Eggheads", "Barley Charlie", "Consider Your Verdict", "Australian Playhouse", "Hunter", "Dynasty", "Homicide", "Ryan", "Matlock Police", "Division 4", "The Last of the Australians" as Blue Dawson from 1975 to 1976, "Solo One", "Bellbird" as Joe Turner from 1969 to 1977, "Young Ramsay", "Bobby Dazzler" as Uncle Oz from 1977 to 1978, "Cop Shop" as Senior Sgt. Eric O'Reilly from 1977 to 1984, "Driven Crazy", "Pig's Breakfast", "Blue Heelers" as Max Arnold from 1996 to 1999, "Something in the Air", "Horace & Tina", "Stingers", "CrashBurn", "City Homicide", "Miss Fisher's Murder Mysteries", and "Bloom" as Herb Webb from 2019 to 2020.

Norris was seen in the films "Stork" (1971), "The Great Macarthy" (1975), "High Rolling in a Hot Corvette" (1977), "Paperback Romance" (1994), "Road to Nhill" (1997), the short "Mr., Craddock's Complaint" (1998), "Innocence" (2000), "Hostage to Fate" (2001), the short "Bowl Me Over" (2001), "Human Touch" (2004), "Three Dollars" (2005), "Irresistible" (2006), "Romulus, My Father" (2007), "Salvation" (2007), "Zyco Rock" (2008), "The Chronicles of Narnia: The Voyage of the Dawn Treader" (2010) as Lord Bern, "Paper Planes" (2014), "Force of Destiny" (2015), "Looking for Grace" (2015), "The Dressmaker" (2015) starring Kate Winslet, "Mortal Engines" (2018) as Professor Arkengarth, "Judy & Punch" (2019), and "The King's Daughter" (2022). Norris' acting career went on hiatus in 1982 when he entered politics. He was a member of the Australian Labor Party and was elected to the Victorian Legislative Assembly. He rose to become deputy speaker of the assembly before retiring from politics and returning to acting in 1992. Norris married actress Julia Lake in 1962 and is survived by her and three children.

Nugent, Judy

Actress Judy Nugent, who began her career as a child in the late 1940s, died of cancer at her ranch in Montana on October 26, 2023. She was 83. Nugent was born in Los Angeles, California, on August 22, 1940. She made her film debut at the age of six in 1947's "It Had to Be You", which also

featured her older sister, Carol Nugent, in the same role at different ages. She was also seen in juvenile roles in such films as "The Big Clock" (1948), "City Across the River" (1949), "Angels in the Outfield" (1951), "Here Comes the Groom" (1951), "The Greatest Show on Earth" (1952), "Night Stage to Galveston" (1952), "Down Laredo Way" (1953), "Ma and Pa Kettle at Home" (1954) as Judy Kettle, "Magnificent Obsession" (1954), "There's Always Tomorrow" (1956), "Navy Wife" (1956), "The Girl Most Likely" (1957), "Go, Johnny, Go!" (1959), and "High School Caesar" (1960). She starred as young Donna Ruggles in the early television comedy series "The Ruggles" from 1949 to 1952 and was Ann Carson, the little blind girl who flies around the world with Superman, in a 1954 episode of "Adventures of Superman". Nugent's other television credits include episodes of "The Lone Ranger", "Annie Oakley", "The Life of Riley", "The Ford Television Theatre", "The Man Behind the Badge", "Lassie", "Celebrity Playhouse", "Matinee Theatre", "Playhouse 90", "The Mickey Mouse Club" as Jet Maypen in the 1958 serial "Annette", "The Thin Man", "The Danny Thomas Show", "The Ann Sothern Show", "Sugarfoot", "The Millionaire", "The Dennis O'Keefe Show", "77 Sunset Strip", "Rawhide", "The Brothers Brannagan", "The Many Loves of Dobie Gillis", "The Gertrude Berg Show", "The Tall Man" in the recurring role of June McBean from 1960 to 1962, and "Saints and Sinners". She largely retired from acting in the early 1960s. She briefly returned to the screen in the 1970s with roles in "Summer Run" (1974) and "Beartooth" (1978) opposite her husband, Buck Taylor. Nugent married Taylor in 1961 but their marriage was soon annulled. She and Taylor remarried in 1963 and remained together until their divorce in 1983. She is survived by their daughter and three sons.

Nussbaum, Mike

Actor Mike Nussbaum died in Chicago, Illinois, on December 23, 2023. He was 99. Nussbaum was born in Chicago on December 29, 1923. He served in the U.S. Army during World War II. He worked with his brother as a pest exterminator for two decades after his discharge. He began performing on stage in community theater in the 1950s. He

became a popular performer on the Chicago stage over the next decade. He became friends with a young David Mamet, and the playwright cast him as Teach in his production of "American Buffalo". Nussbaum appeared on Broadway as George Aaronow in Mamet's play "Glengarry Glen Ross" in 1984. He also appeared in the Broadway comedy "The House of Blue Leaves" (1986). He appeared frequently in films with roles in the science fiction satire "The Monitors" (1969), "T.R. Baskin" (1971), "Harry and Tonto" (1974), "Towing" (1978), "House of Games" (1987), "Fatal Attraction" (1987), "Things Change" (1988), "Field of Dreams" (1989), "Desperate Hours" (1990), "Gladiator" (1992), "Losing Isaiah" (1995), "Steal Big Steal Little" (1995), "Men in Black" (1997) as Gentle Rosenburg, "The Game of Their Lives" (2005), "Dirty Work" (2006), "Osso Bucco" (2008), "Tom of Your Life" (2020), and "The Old Country" (2021). Nussbaum was seen on television in the tele-films and mini-series "Vital Signs" (1986), "Fatal Confession: A Father Dowling Mystery" (1987), "Archie: To Riverdale and Back Again" (1990) as Pop Tate, "Separate But Equal" (1991) as Justice Felix Frankfurter, "The Water Engine" (1992), "Overexposed" (1992), "Condition: Critical" (1992), "Love, Honor & Obey: The Last Mafia Marriage" (1993), "Gypsy" (1993), "Shadow of a Doubt" (1995), and "The Con" (1998). His other television credits include episodes of "Spencer: For Hire", "The Equalizer", "227", "L.A. Law", "Brooklyn Bridge", "Class of '96", "Frasier", "The Commish" in the recurring role of Ben Metzger from 1992 to 1996, "The X-Files", "Early Edition", "Cupid", and "The Chicago Code". Nussbaum was married to Annette Brenner from 1949 until her death in 2003 and is survived by a son and daughter. Another daughter, actress and disability activist Susan Nussbaum, died in 2022. He married Julie Brudios in 2004 and she also survives him.

Nuti, Francesco

Italian actor and director Francesco Nuti of complications from a injuries he had received in a fall years

earlier in Rome, Italy, on June 12, 2023. He was 68. Nuti was born in Prato, Italy, on May 17, 1955. He began performing in the cabaret group Giancativi with Alessandro Benvenuti and Athina Cenci in the late 1970s. The trio appeared in the 1981

film "Ad Ovest di Paperino". Nuti soon embarked on a solo appeared in appeared in several films by director Maurizio Ponzi, "What a Ghostly Silence There Is Tonight" (1982), "The Pool Hustlers" (1982), and "Son Contento" (1983). He directed, wrote, and starred in many of his subsequent films including "Casablanca, Casablanca" (1985), "Tutta Colpa del Paradiso" (1985), "Stregati" (1986), "Caruso Paskoski, Son of a Pole" (1988), "Willy Signori e Vengo da Lontano" (1989), "Donne Con le Gonne" (1991), "OcchioPinocchio" (1994) appearing as Pinocchio, "Il Signor Quindicipalle" (1998), "Io Amo Andrea" (2000), "Caruso, Zero in Condotta" (2001), and "Concorso di Colpa" (2004). Nuti was planning to shoot a new film when he suffered a severe fall from the stairs at his home in September of 2006. He suffered serious brain damage which was aggravated when he suffered another fall in September of 2016. He had a daughter, Ginevra Nuti, with actress Anna Maria Malipiero, in 1999 and she became his legal guardian the following year in 2017.

O'Brien, Brendan

Actor Brendan O'Brien, who was noted as the original voice of Crash Bandicoot in video games, died at his home in California on March 23, 2023. He was 60. O'Brien was born in Hollywood, California, on May 9, 1962. He was the son of

Actors Edmond O'Brien and Olga San Juan. He made his film debut as a child in the 1973 tele-film "Honor Thy Father". He played guitar and performed in bands while in high school. He later graduated from Loyola Marymount University. He was best known for voicing Crash Bandicoot in various video games from 1996 through the early 2000s. O'Brien voiced other roles for the video game series including Dr. Neo Cortez, Dr. Nitrus Brio, Dr. N. Gin, Tiny Tiger, and Pinstripe Potoroo. He was also a voice actor for the animated television series "Spawn" and Ralph Bakshi's "Spicy City". He appeared on television in episodes of "Candid Camera", "The Amazing Live Sea-Monkeys" and "Riverdale", and productions of "Busker's Odyssey" (1994), "Wild Grizzly" (1999), "The Trial of Old Drum" (2000), and "The Slowest Show" (2021). O'Brien appeared in a handful of films including "Hollywood Chaos" (1989), "The Legend of Galgameth" (1996), "Casper: A Spirited Beginning" (1997), "3 Ninjas: High Noon at Mega Mountain" (1998), "P.U.N.K.S." (1999), "Race to Space" (2001), "Grindhouse" (2003), and "Totally Killer" (2023). O'Brien married Ingrid K. Behrens in 2000 and she survives him.

O'Connor, Raymond

Actor Raymond O'Connor died on October 9, 2023. He was 71. O'Connor was born in the Bronx, New York, on September 13, 1952. He was a prolific actor on television from

the mid-1980s with roles in episodes of "Hill Street Blues", "Hunter", "The Wizard", "Ohara", "L.A. Law", "The Law and Harry McGraw", "J.J. Starbuck", "Hard Time on Planet Earth", "Tales from the Crypt", "Hooperman", "Growing Pains", "Northern Exposure", "Who's the Boss?", "Sisters", "Baby Talk", "Down the Shore", "Roc", "Beverly Hills, 90210", "Sirens", "Dark Justice", "Phenom", "Rebel Highway", "Diagnosis Murder", "Seinfeld", "Vanishing Son", "Minor Adjustments", "Fudge", "Sister, Sister", "Wings", "Land's End", "Hudson Street", "Boy Meets World", "The Steve Harvey Show", "The Sentinel", "Silk Stalkings", "The Wayan Bros.", "Babylon 5", "Damon", "Two of a Kind", "Brutally Normal", "Becker" (2000), "V.I.P.", "City of Angels", "The Michael Richards Show", "That's Life", "Days of Our Lives", "Dead Last", "Buffy the Vampire Slayer", "Six Feet Under", "Providence", "Boomtown", "NYPD Blue", "The Handler", "Monk", "CSI: Crime Scene Investigation", "Malcolm in the Middle", and "Saving Grace". He was also seen in the 1985 mini-series "Kane & Abel", and the tele-films "Hollywood Dog" (1990), "Tagteam" (1991), "Cast a Deadly Spell" (1991), "Girls in Prison" (1994), "Skeletons" (1997), "Audrey's Rain" (2003), "Sands of Oblivion" (2007), and "Shark Swarm" (2008). O'Connor appeared frequently in films with minor roles in "Off Limits" (1988), "Arthur 2: On the Rocks" (1988), "Traxx" (1988), "Halloween 4: The Return of Michael Myers" (1988), "Dr. Alien" (1989), "My Blue Heaven" (1990), "Megaville" (1990), "Life Stinks" (1991), "Pyrates" (1991), "Mr. Nanny" (1993), "Prehysteria! 3" (1995), "The Rock" (1996), "Opposite Corners" (1997), "My Giant" (1998), "Breakfast of Champions" (1999), "Inspector Gadget" (1999), "Drowning Mona" (2000), "April's Shower" (2003), "The Bug in My Ear" (2003), "See This Movie" (2004), "Serial Killing 4 Dummys" (2004), "Bananas" (2004), "Careful What You Wish For" (2004), "Don't Come Knocking" (2005), "Just Like Heaven" (2005), "Bottoms Up" (2006), "Love Made Easy" (2006), "Crazy" (2008), "Diamonds and Guns" (2008), "The Intervention" (2009), "Off the Ledge" (2009), and "Balls to the Walls" (2011).

O'Connor, Sinead

Irish singer and political activist Sinead O'Connor, who had a hit song with "Nothing Compares to You", was found at her flat in Herne Hill, South London, England, on July

26, 2023. She was 56. O'Connor was born in Dublin, Ireland, on December 8, 1966. She attended Dominican College Sion Hill school in Blackrock, County Dublin. She was Roman Catholic Magdalene reform school due to her propensity for

shoplifting and truancy at age 15. She later attended Maryfield College in Drumcondra, and Newtown School in Waterford. She became involved in music, singing and writing songs. She recorded a song, "Take My Hand", with the band Tua Nua and formed her own band, Ton Ton Macoute, with Col Farrelly in 1984. She left school to travel with the band to Dublin. She signed with Ensign Records and co-wrote the song "Heroine" with U2 guitarist the Edge for the film "Captive" soundtrack. Her first album, "The Lion and the Cobra", was released by Chrysalis Records in 1987. The album contained the singles "Mandinka", "I Want Your (Hands on Me)", and Troy". She appeared on an episode of "Late Night with David Letterman" the following year and received a Grammy Award nomination for Best Female Rock Vocal Performance. O'Connor wrote music and starred in the 1989 Northern Irish film "Hush-a-Bye-Baby". She released the album "I Do Not Want What I Haven't Got" in 1990, and she gained attention for her now shaved head. The album contained her rendition of Prince's song "Nothing Compares 2 U", "The Emperor's New Clothes", and "I Am Stretched on Your Grave". Her controversial stands, including allegations that the American music industry was racist, caused an outcry. She received a Grammy for Best Alternative Music Performance in 1991 and three additional nominations. She covered jazz standard and torch songs for her 1992 album "Am I Not Your Girl?". She toured and recorded with Peter Gabriel on the album "Us" and appeared in the 1991 tele-film "The Ghosts of Oxford Street". O'Connor appeared on "Saturday Night Live" in October of 1992. After performing an updated rendition of Bob Marley's "War" she tore up a photograph of Pope John Paul II on camera in protest of the Catholic Church's abuse of children. Her rendition of "You Made Me the Thief of Your Heart" was featured on the soundtrack for the 1993 film "In the Name of the Father". Her 1994 album "Universal Mother" featured the songs "Fire on Babylon" and "Famine", which both became hit music videos. O'Connor was seen in the uncredited role of Emily Bronte in the film "Wuthering Heights" in 1992 and was featured as the Virgin Mother in Neil Jordan's 1997 film "The Butcher Boy". Her later albums include "Faith and Courage" (2000), "Sean-Nos Nua" (2002), the reggae-themed "Throw Down Your Arms" (2005), "Theology" (2007), "How About I Be Me (and You Be You)?" (2012), and "I'm Not Bossy, I'm the Boss" (2014). She covered Dolly Parton's song "Dagger Through the Heart" for Parton's 2003 album "Just Because I'm a Woman". She performed the song "Lay Your Head Down" for the soundtrack of the 2011 film "Albert Nobbs". O'Connor announced that she had converted to Islam in 2018 and changed her name to Shuhada Sadaqat. She released her memoirs, "Rememberings", in 2021 and she was the subject of the 2022 documentary "Nothing Compares". O'Connor was married to music producer John Reynolds from 1989 until their divorce in 1991 and is survived by their son Jake. She had a daughter, Brigidine Roisin Waters, with Irish columnist John Waters in 1995, which resulted in a lengthy custody battle. She was married to British journalist Nick Sommerlad for less than a year between 2001 to 2002. She and Irish musician Donal Lunny had a son, Shane, in 2004. Shane died by suicide in January of 2022. She had another son, Yeshua, with Frank Bonadio in 2006. She was married to musician and frequent collaborator Steve Cooney from 2010 until their divorce in 2011. She married Irish therapist Barry Herridge in 2011 but they later separated.

Oe, Kenzaburo

Japanese writer Kenzaburo Oe, who received the Nobel Prize in Literature in 1994, died in Tokyo, Japan, on March 3, 2023. He was 88. Oe was born in Ose, Japan, on

January 31, 1935. He attended high school in Matsuyama in the early 1950s and began studying French Literature at the University of Tokyo in 1954. His first published work was the short-story "Lavish Are the Dead" in 1957 and he earned acclaim for his short-story "Shiiku" the following year. It was adapted by director Nagisa Oshima for the film "The Catch"

in 1961. He produced a series of works in the late 1950s and early 1960s that utilized sexual metaphors to examine the Japanese during and after the country's occupation. His first novel, "Nip the Buds, Shoot the Kids", was published in 1958. His 1961 novella, "The Death of a Political Youth", about a young right-wing radical who had assassinated the leader of the Socialist Party and later committed suicide in prison, resulted in him receiving numerous death threats and a physical assault by militants on the far right. The birth of his son, Hikari, in 1963 with a brain hernia that resulted in a learning disability influenced his 1964 novel "A Personal Matter". Oe's other works include "Hiroshima Notes" (1965), "The Silent Cry" (1967), the short-story collection "Teach Us to Outgrow Our Madness" (1969), "The Pinch Runner Memorandum" (1976), "Coeval Games" (1979), "Rise Up O Young Men of the New Age!" (1983), "An Echo of Heaven" (1989), the memoir "A Healing Family" (1996), "The Changeling" (2000), "Death by Water" (2009), and "In Late Style" (2013). He was recipient of the Nobel Prize for Literature in 1994 and was cited "who with poetic force creates an imagined world, where life and myth condense to form a disconcerting picture of the human predicament today." He was active in pacifist and anti-nuclear campaigns throughout his life. Oe married Yukari Itami in 1960 and is survived by her and their three children.

O'Grady, Paul

British comedian and television personality Paul O'Grady, who was noted for his drag persona Lily Savage, died from sudden cardiac arrhythmia in Aldington, Kent, England, on March 28, 2023. He was 67.

O'Grady was born in Tranmere, Cheshire, England, on June 14, 1955. He left school in his early teens and worked at various jobs in Liverpool. He became active in the local gay scene and worked as a bartender and a clerk. He was a social worker for disabled children in the mid-1970s. He moved to London later in the decade and worked with Camden Social Services. He became involved with drag in 1978, creating the character of Lily Savage. He began performing with the Glamazons and teamed with Hush for the drag mime act, the Playgirls. O'Grady continued to perform sporadically and resurrected the Playgirls in the early 1980s. They soon became a popular act in London and Northern Europe. He worked at a gay pub in Vauxhall in 1984 where he perfected his routine as Lily and was soon appearing on television. O'Grady was a guest, usually in his Lily Savage persona, on such series as "The Last Resort with Jonathan Ross", "Ring My Bell", "Top of the Pops", "The South Bank Show", "Eurotrash", "The Big Breakfast", "That's Showbusiness", "Des O'Connor Tonight", "Celebrity Ready, Steady, Cook", "Steve Wright's People Show" "Harry Enfield and Chums", "Richard & Judy", the game show "Blankety Blank" hosting from 1997 to 2002, "V Graham Norton", "Patrick Kielty... Almost Live", "Who Wants to Be a Millionaire", "Today with Des and Mel", "The Late Late Show", "Call My Bluff", "Parkinson", "Comic Aid", "The Catherine Tate Show", "The Charlotte Church Show", "Dawn French's Boys Who Do Comedy", "Celebrity Ding Dong", "Friday Night with Jonathan Ross", "Ant & Dec's Saturday Night Takeaway", "Celebrity Mastermind", "The Graham Norton Show", "Piers Morgan's Life Stories", "Good Morning Britain", "Gogglebox", "Most Haunted", "Loose Women", and "Lorraine". He starred in the television specials and series "Lily Savage Live from the Hackney Empire" (1991), "Viva Cabaret" as host in 1994, "Live from Lilydrome" in 1995, "Glam O Rama" (1995), "An Evening with Lily Savage" (1996), "The Lily Savage Show" in 1997, "Paul O'Grady's America" (2001), "Lily Live!" (2001), "The Paul O'Grady Show" from 2004 to 2015, "Paul O'Grady Live" from 2010 to 2011, "Paul O'Grady: For the Love of Dogs" from to 2012 to 2023, "Paul O'Grady's Working Britain" in 2013, "Paul O'Grady's Hollywood" in 2017, "Blind Date" as host from 2017 to 2019, "The One Show", "This Morning", and "Paul O'Grady's Saturday Night Line-Up" in 2021. He was billed as Paul Savage in the 1991 television mini-series "Chimera", the 1993 film "In the Name of the Father", and episodes of "The Bill" and "The New Statesman" as Marlene Dietrich. He also appeared in episodes of "The Inspector Lynley Mysteries", "Eyes Down" as Ray Temple from 2003 to 2004, "The Life and Times of Vivienne

Vyle", "Doctor Who" in a cameo role as himself in the 2008 episode "The Stolen Earth", "Playhouse Presents", "Little Crackers", "Holby City" as Tim Connor in 2013, and "The Madame Blanc Mysteries". He was featured as Miss Hannigan in a production of "Annie" at the Edinburgh Playhouse several days before his death. He had suffered several heart attacks from the early 2000s. O'Grady had a daughter, Sharon Lee Jansen, with a female friend in 1974, and she survives him. He married a Portuguese lesbian friend, Teresa Fernandes, in 1977 to prevent her deportation. They lost contact and were not legally divorced until 2005. He was involved with Brendan Murphy, who also served as his manager, from the mid-1980s until his death from brain cancer in 2005. He married Andre Portasio in 2017 and is survived by him and his daughter.

Oh, Jacky

Actress Jacky O died of complications from cosmetic surgery in Miami, Florida, on May 31, 2023. She was 32. She was born Jacklyn Smith in Oakland, California, on November  3, 1990. She was a regular performer on Nick Cannon's improvisational comedy series "Wild 'n Out" on MTV for five seasons between 2014 and 2018. She was also seen on television in episodes of "Shift Drinks", "Marc + Jenni", and "The World Couple". She appeared in the films "Del Playa" (2017), "Switched at Love" (2021), "Scheme Queens" (2022), "Clout" (2022), and "The 4th Quarter: Legacy" (2023). Jacky Oh also sold real estate and began her own lip gloss line. Her survivors include her longtime partner, DC Young Fly, and their three children.

O'Hara, Gerry

British film and television director Gerry O'Hara died in England on January 9, 2023. He was 98. O'Hara was born in Boston, Lincolnshire, England, on October 1, 1924. He left school in his early teens and began working as a junior reporter  for the "Boston Guardian" and the "Lincolnshire Standard". He began working in films as a trainee in the script department of the documentary company Verity Films in 1941. He was a production assistant for the short "Song of the People" and second assistant director for "Old Mother Riley at Home" in 1945. He soon rose to assistant director and worked on such films as "Loyal Heart" (1946), "Meet the Navy" (1946), "The Three Weird Sisters" (1948), "Miranda" (1948), "Quartet" (1948), "Here Come the Huggetts" (1948), "Vote for Huggett" (1949), "The Huggetts Abroad" (1949), "Boys in Brown" (1949), "So Long at the Fair" (1950), "Trio" (1950), "The Clouded Yellow" (1950), "Both Sides of the Law" (1953),

"Meet Mr. Callaghan" (1954), "The Divided Heart" (1954), "Companions in Crime" (1954), "Quentin Durward" (1955), "Richard III" (1955), "The Man Who Never Was" (1956), "Bhowani Junction" (1956), "Pacific Destiny" (1956), "It's a Wonderful World" (1956), "Anastasia" (1956), "Island in the Sun" (1957), "The Truth About Women" (1957), "The Key" (1958), "The Journey" (1959), "Third Man on the Mountain" (1959), "Our Man in Havana" (1959), "Exodus" (1960), "The Four Horsemen of the Apocalypse" (1962), "The Playboy of the Western World (162), "Maid for Murder" (1962), "Term of Trial" (1962), "The L-Shaped Room" (1962), "Cleopatra" (1963), "Tom Jones" (1963), "The Cardinal" (1963), "Rattle of a Simple Man" (1964), and "Judith" (1966). O'Hara was also directing and frequently scripting films by the early 1960s including "That Kind of Girl" (1963), "The Pleasure Girls" (1965), "Game for Three Losers" (1965), "Maroc 7" (1967), "Amsterdam Affair" (1968), "All the Right Noises" (1970), "Professor Popper's Problem" (1974), "Whose Child Am I?" (1976), "Paganini Strikes Again" (1977), "The Brute" (1977), "Blind Man's Bluff" (1977), "Leopard in the Snow" (1978), "The Bitch" (1979), "Fanny Hill" (1983), and "The Mummy Lives" (1993). He also wrote the films "Hot Target" (1985), "Ten Little Indians" (1989), "The Phantom of the Opera" (1989), and "The Sandgrass People" (1990). O'Hara directed television episodes of "The Edgar Wallace Mystery Theatre", "The Avengers", "Man in a Suitcase", "Journey to the Unknown", "The Professionals", and "Press Gang". He scripted episodes of "Bergerac", "The Professionals", "Special Squad", and "C.A.T.S. Eyes", and the tele-films "Operation Julie" (1985) and "Sherlock Holmes: Incident at Victoria Falls" (1992). He married his third wife, Penny Chalmers, in 1997 and she survives him.

Ohlsson, Fredrik

Swedish actor Fredrik Ohlsson died in Sweden on November 18, 2023. He was 92. Ohlsson was born in Ulricehamn, Sweden, on June 12, 1931. He studied at the Royal Academy of Dramatic Art in London in 1956 and made his  stage debut in a 195 production of "Hedda Gabler" in London. He continued his career on stage in Sweden and was a long-time member of the Royal Dramatic Theatre in Stockholm. He appeared frequently in films and television from the late 1950s. His film credits include "48 Hours to Live" (1959), "Himmel Och Pannkaka" (1959), "Siska" (1962), "Het Sno" (1968), "Pippi Longstocking" (1969), "Pippi Goes on Board" (1969), "Pippi in the South Seas" (1970), "Pippi on the Run" (1970), Jerry Lewis' unreleased 1972 film "The Day the Clown Cried", "Haervaerk" (1977), 'You're Out of Your Mind Maggie" (1979), "En Flicka Pa Halsen" (1982), "Jonssonligan Far Guldfeber" (1984), "PS Sista Sommaren" (1988), "Rattornas Vinter" (1988), "The Searchers" (1993), "Jerusalem" (1996), "Selma & Johanna - En

Roadmovie" (1997), "Aphelium" (2005), "Den Enskilde Medborgaren" (2006), "The Girl with the Dragon Tattoo" (2009) as Gunnar Brannlund, "So Different" (2009), "Oskar, Oskar" (2009), and "Between Two Fires" (2010). Ohlsson was seen on television in productions of "I Sista Minuten" (1961), "Henrik IV" (1964), "Herr Dardanell Och Hans Upptag Pa Landet" (1965), "Roda Rummel" (1970), "Korsbarstadgarden" (1970), "Soderkakar" (1970), "Hon Kallade Mej Javla Mordare" (1971), "Har Ligger en Hund Begraven" (1971), "Flagga for Trygghet" (1971), "Larare" (1973), "Nagonstans i Sverige" (1974), "Jorden Runt Pa 80 Dagar" (1975), "Engeln II" (1976), "Predikare-Lena" (1976), "Arliga Bla Ogon" (1977), "Semlons Grona Dalar" (1977), "Pa Banken" (1980), "Lita Pa Mig!" (1981), "Skulden" (1982), "Amedee" (1982), "Distrikt 5" (1983), "Colombe" (1983), "Hemma Hoz" (1985), "Glasmastarna" (1986), "Beskyddarna" (1986), "Utmaningen" (1994), "Saltkrakan" (1995), "Millennium" (2010), and "Arne Dahl: Europa Blues" (2012). His other television credits include episodes of "Nikalsons" as Harry Njutgarde in 1965, "Pippi Longstocking" as Herry Settergren in 1969, "Pappas Pojkar", "Broderna Malm", "Spanarna", "Obergs Pa Lilloga", "Madicken", "Nya Dagbladet", "Varuhuset" as Jens Josefsson in 1988, "Det Var Da...", "Rosenbaddarna", "Uppfinnaren", "Rederiet", "Du Bestammer", "Anna Holt - Polis", "Sjukan", "Snoken", "Beck", and "Tjuvarnas Jul". He was married to Anita Ohlsson from 1964 to 1972 and is survived by three children.

Oko, Iyabo

Nigerian actress Iyabo Oko died in Nigeria on June 28, 2023. She was 62. She was born Sidikat Odunkanwi in Iwo,

Osun, Nigeria, on November 15,1960. She began performing on stage in her teens in 1973 with the Eda Onileola Theatre Troupe. She went on to be a popular film and television performer. She was featured in the films "Mayowa" (1999), "Idunno Okan" (2006), "Okobo Dimeji" (2008), "Atitale" (2013), and "Aromimawe" (2016). Oko was seriously ill in early 2022 and was pronounced dead, but the reports proved premature.

Oldoini, Enrico

Italian film director and writer Enrico Oldoini died of complications from amyotrophic lateral sclerosis (ALS) and leukemia in Rome, Italy, on May 10, 2023. He was 77. Oldoini was born in La Spezia, Italy, on May 4, 1946. He attended the Silvio D'Amico National Academy of Dramatic Art in Rome, though did not graduate. He began working in films in the early 1970s as an assistant director for "Metti lo Diavolo Tuo ne lo Mio Inferno" (1972) and "Il Lumascone" (1974). He appeared on screen in small roles in the films "Plot of Fear" (1976) and "Il Giacattolo" (1979). Oldoini soon began writing films including "Plot of Fear" (1976), "Questo Si Che e Amore"

(1978), "Stay As You Are" (1978), "Ciao, les Mecs" (1979), "Il Corpo della Ragassa" (1979), "Qua la Mano" (1980), "Manolesta" (1981), "Tais-Toi Quand Tu Parles!" (1981), "Talcum Powder" (1982), "La Casa Stregata" (1982), "Bingo

Bongo" (1982), "Heads I Win, Tails You Lose" (1982), "The Pool Hustlers" (1983), "Al Bar dello Sport" (1983), "Sing Sing" (1983), "Acqua e Sapone" (1983), "Son Contento" (1983), "Softly, Softly" (1984), "I Love You" (1986), and "Una Spina nel Cuore" (1986). He was director and writer of the films "Cuori Nella Tormenta" (1984), "He's Worse Than Me" (1985), "Yuppies 2" (1986), "Bellifreschi" (1987), "Bye Bye Baby" (1988), "Una Botta di Vita" (1988), "Vacanze di Natale '90" (1990), "Vacanze di Natale '91" (1991), "Anni 90" (1992), "Anna 90 - Parte II" (1993), "Miracolo Italiano" (1994), "Un Bugiardo in Paradiso" (1998), "13dici a Tavola" (2004), "La Fidenzata di Papa" (2008), and "I Mostri Oggi" (2009). Oldoini director and often wrote such television productions of "Dio Vede e Provvede" (1995), "Nuda Proprieta Vendesi" (1997), "Incompreso" (1998), "I Diavolo e l'Acqua Santa" (1999), "La Crociera" (2001), and "Anna's World" (2004). He also directed episodes of "Don Matteo", "Il Giudice Mastrangelo", "Capri", "Un Passo dal Cielo", "Il Restauratore", and "The Teacher".

Oliphant, Peter

Video game designer Peter Oliphant, who was a child actor on television in the early-1960s, died on May 24, 2023.

He was 72. Oliphant was born on September 1, 1950. He was a child actor in the early 1960s with roles in episodes of "Playhouse 90", "Hong Kong", "The Donna Reed Show", and "Daniel Boone". He was featured as Freddie Helper in several episodes of "The Dick Van Dyke Show" from 1962 to 1965. Oliphant was also seen in the films "Deadly Duo" (1962), "Mr. Hobbs Takes a Vacation" (1962), "Take Her, She's Mine" (1963), "Hot Rods to Hell" (1966), and "The Roommates" (1973). He worked as a computer game programmer and designer in the 1980s for such games as "Dragon's Keep", "WallWar", "Troll's Tale", and "Mr. Cool". He created handheld electronic games for Mattel Electronics. He worked for Interplay Productions in the 1990s, designing the games "Lexi-Cross" (1991) and "Stonekeep" (1995).

Oliver, Clifton

Actor Clifton Oliver, who played Simba in the Broadway production of "The Lion King" in 2011, died after a long illness in New York on August 2, 2023. He was 47. Oliver was born in Jacksonville, Florida, on December 3, 1975. He attended the Douglas Anderson School of the Arts. He moved to New York City in 2010 to pursue an acting career. He took

over the role of Simba in "The Lion King" for several months in 2011 and appeared in the national tour. He also appeared on Broadway in the musicals "Wicked" and "In the Heights". He toured in productions of "Dreamgirls" and "Motown the Musical" and was featured in off-Broadway's "Miracle Brothers" and "Bella: An American Tall Tale". Oliver appeared on television in an episode of "Law & Order: Criminal Intent" and was featured in the 2007 film "Whirlwind".

Oliveros, Ramiro

Spanish actor Ramiro Oliveros died in Madrid, Spain, on April 27, 2023. He was 82. Oliveros was born in Madrid on March 13, 1941. He appeared in numerous films from the early 1970s including "La Leyenda del Alcalde de Zalamea" (1973),

"The Killer Is One of 13" (1973), "Al Otro Lado del Espejo" (1973), "Vida Conyugal Sana" (1974), "The Student Connection" (1974), "The Swamp of the Ravens" (1974), "Una Mujer Prohibida" (1974), "Novios de la Muerte" (1975), "Cross of the Devil" (1975), "Ya Soy Mujer!" (1975), "Sensualidad" (1975), "Terapia al Desnudo" (1975), "Imposible Para una Solterona" (1976), "Spanish Fly" (1976), "Tu Dios y Mi Infierno" (1976), "Los Viajes Escolares" (1976), "Rape" (1976), "Mas Alla del Deseo" (1976), "Volvoreta" (1976), "Wifemistress" (1977), "The Pyjama Girl Case" (1977), "Las Locuras de Jane" (1978), "Let's Go, Barbara" (1978), "Cabo de Vara" (1978), "Memorias de Leticia Valle" (1979), "Viaje al Mas Alla" (1980), "El Oreja Rajada" (1980), Antonio Margheriti's horror film "Cannibal Apocalypse" (aka "Cannibals in the Streets") (1980) as Dr. Phil Mendez, "El Poderoso Influjo de la Luna" (1981), "El Ser" (1982), "Black Commando" (1982), "Power Game" (1983), the action fantasies "Hundra" (1983) and "Yellow Hair and the Fortress of Gold" (1984), "El Cafre" (1986), "Dark Tower" (1987), and "Cancion Triste de..." (1989). Oliveros was seen on television in episodes of "Hora Once", "Teatro de Siempre", "Ficciones", "El Teatro", "Original", "La Saga delos Rius" as Ernesto in 1976, "Teatro Estudio", "Novela", "Los Mitos", "Estudio 1", "La Mascara negra", "Manana es Primavera", "Regimen Abierto", "Brigada Central", "No Se Bailar", "Todos los Hombres Sois Iguales" as Inaki from 1996 to 1998, "Que Grande es el Teatro!", and "Se Puede?". He also appeared in the 1986 tele-film "El Rey y la Reina" and the 1992 mini-series "Piazza di Spagna". He retired in the early 2000s. Oliveros was married to singer Concha Marquez Piquer from 1982 until her death in 2021.

O'Malley, William

Actor and priest William O'Malley, who was a technical advisor for the 1973 film "The Exorcist", died in Newton, Massachusetts, on July 15, 2023. He was 91. O'Malley was born in Buffalo, New York, on August 18, 1931.

He was ordained a Jesuit priest in 1951 and graduated from the College of the Holy Cross in 1953. He taught English and theology at McQuaid Jesuit High School in Rochester, New York, from 1966 to 1986, and at Fordham Prep in the Bronx from 1986 to 2012. He performed on stage while in Rochester in productions of "The Power and the Glory" and "The Glass Menagerie". O'Malley was technical advisor for the 1973 horror film "The Exorcist" and appeared onscreen as Father Dyer. He was a guest on television's "The Mike Douglas Show". He was author of numerous books on religion including "Building Your Own Conscience (Batteries Not Included)" (1992), "Why Be Catholic?" (1993), "Redemptive Suffering: Understanding Suffering, Living With It, Growing Through It" (1997), "Meeting the Living God" (1998), "The Fifth Week" (1998), God: The Oldest Question: A Fresh Look at Belief and Unbelief - And Why the Choice Matters" (2000), "Choosing to Be Catholic" (2001), "Daily Prayers for Busy People" (2002), "Help My Unbelief" (2008), "The Wow Factor: Bringing the Catholic Faith to Life" (2011), "You'll Never Be Younger: A Good News Spirituality for Those Over 60" (2015), "God Questions: Meeting the Living God" (2015), and "Being There: The Parables of Jesus in a Different Voice" (2016).

O'Neal, Kevin

Actor Kevin O'Neal, who starred as Private Ben Whitledge in the 1964 comedy series "No Time for Sergeants", died in Thousand Oaks, California, on January 28, 2023. He

was 77. He was born Geoffrey Garrett O'Neal in Los Angeles, California, on March 26, 1945. He was the son of screenwriter Charles 'Blackie' O'Neal and actress Patricia Callaghan and younger brother of actor Ryan O'Neal. He began his acting career on the early 1960s and appeared in episodes of "The Deputy", "The Danny Thomas Show", "The Donna Reed Show", "The Twilight Zone" as Butler in the 1962 episode "The Changing of the Guard", "My Three Sons", "The Jimmy Durante Show", "Wagon Train", the military comedy "No Time for Sergeant" as Private Ben Whitledge from 1964 to 1965, "Gidget", "Perry Mason", "The Fugitive", "Gunsmoke", "Please Don't Eat the Daisies", "The Time Tunnel", "Bonanza", "Mod Squad", "The New People", "Daniel Boone", "Lancer", and "Room 222". O'Neal was also

seen in the films "Kisses for My President" (1964), "Young Fury" (1964), "Village of the Giants" (1965), "The Big Bounce" (1969), "The Trouble with Girls" (1969), "Love Story" (1970), "What's Up, Doc?" (1972), "The Mechanic" (1972), "The Thief Who Came to Dinner" (1973), and "At Long Last Love" (1975). He retired from acting by the late 1970s. O'Neal was married to Sheila Stubbs from 1965 until their divorce in 1967. His survivors include his brother, Ryan, and son Garrett.

O'Neal, Ryan

Actor Ryan O'Neal, who was a leading star in the 1970s with such films as "Love Story", "Paper Moon", and "Barry Lyndon", died after a long illness on December 8, 2023. He was 82. O'Neal was born in Los Angeles, California, on April 20, 1941, the son of novelist and screenwriter Charles O'Neal and actress Patricia Callaghan. He trained as a Golden Gloves boxer while a student at University High School in Los Angeles. He compiled an amateur boxing record of 18 wins and four losses. He accompanied his family to Munich, Germany, in the late 1950s, where his father was writing for a television series. He continued high school there and made his acting debut as an extra and stuntman on the series "Tales of the Vikings". He continued to pursue an acting career after returning to the United States in the early 1960s. O'Neal appeared in episodes of "The Many Loves of Dobie Gillis", "The Untouchables", "General Electric Theater", "The DuPont Show with June Allyson", "Bachelor Father", "Laramie", "Two Faces West", "Westinghouse Playhouse", "Leave It to Beaver", "My Three Sons", "The Virginian", "Perry Mason", "The Merv Griffin Show", "The Joey Bishop Show", "Wagon Train", "The Mike Douglas Show", "The Dick Cavett Show", "The David Frost Show", and "The Tonight Show Starring Johnny Carson". He starred as Tal Garrett in the western series "Empire" from 1962 to 1963 and was Rodney Harrington in the prime-time soap opera "Peyton Place" from 1964 to 1969. He was a judge in the series "Dream Girl of '67". He appeared in the unsold television pilot "European Eye" in 1968 and the tele-films "Under the Yum Yum Tree" (1969) and "Love Hate Love" (1971). He made his film debut in the 1969 feature "The Big Bounce" with his then-wife, Leigh Taylor-Young. He starred as Olympic athlete Scott Reynolds in the 1970 film "The Games". O'Neal received an Academy Award nomination for his role as Oliver Barrett in the 1970 romantic drama "Love Story" opposite Ali MacGraw. He also appeared in the films "Wild Rovers" (1971) with William Holden, Peter Bogdanovich's comedy farce "What's Up, Doc?" (1972) opposite Barbra Streisand, and "The Thief Who Came to Dinner" (1973) with Jacqueline Bisset. He reunited with director Bogdanovich for the 1973 film "Paper Moon", as con artist Moses Pray, co-starring with his young daughter, Tatum O'Neal, who received an Academy Award for Best Supporting Actress for the film at the age of ten. O'Neal starred in the title

role in Stanley Kubrick's historical drama "Barry Lyndon" in 1975. The film was a commercial and critical disappointment and O'Neal's career suffered as a result. His next film, Bogdanovich's "Nickelodeon", co-starred Burt Reynolds and daughter Tatum, and also proved unsuccessful. He had a small role as General James Gavin in the all-star war epic "A Bridge Too Far" in 1977. He starred in the 1978 action film "The Driver" directed by Walter Hill. He reprised his role from "Love Story" in the 1978 sequel "Oliver's Story" opposite Candice Bergen. He reunited with Barbra Streisand in the 1979 film "The Main Event" as boxer Eddie 'Kid Natural' Scanlon. O'Neal continued his career in largely forgettable films including "Green Ice" (1971), "So Fine" (1981), "Partners" (1982), "Irreconcilable Differences" (1984), "Fever Pitch" (1985), Norman Mailer's off-beat crime drama "Tough Guys Don't Dance" (1987), "Chances Are" (1989), "Man of the House" (1995), "Faithful" (1996), "Hacks" (1997), the mockumentary "An Alan Smithee Film: Burn Hollywood Burn" (1997), "Zero Effect" (1998), "Coming Soon" (1999), "Gentleman B." (2000), "The List" (2000), "People I Know" (2002), "Malibu's Most Wanted" (2003), the horror thriller "Slumber Party Slaughter" (2012), and "Knight of Cups" (2015). He returned to television in the late 1980s with roles in productions of "Sam Found Out: A Triple Play" (1988), "Small Sacrifices" (1989) opposite partner Farrah Fawcett, "1775" (1992), "The Man Upstairs" (1992), the documentary "Farrah's Story" (2009) recounting the Farrah Fawcett's final battle with cancer, and the science fiction "Epoch" (2001). He starred as Bobby Tannen in the short-lived CBS series "Good Sports" with Fawcett in 1991. His other television credits include episodes of "The Larry Sanders Show", "The Arsenio Hall Show", "The Tonight Show with Jay Leno", "The Jamie Kennedy Experiment", "Bull" as Robert Roberts Jr. from 2000 to 2001, "Miss Match" as Jerry Fox in 2003, "Desperate Housewives", "90210", "The Oprah Winfrey Show", and "Bones" in the recurring role of Max Keenan, the father of Emily Deschanel's title character, Temperance 'Bones' Brennan, from 2006 to 2017. O'Neal's estranged relationship with daughter Tatum and their reconciliation was the subject of the 2011 reality series "Ryan and Tatum: The O'Neals" on the Oprah Winfrey Network. He continued to appear in such talk shows as "Live with Kelly and Mark", "The Talk", "Piers Morgan Live", "Rachael Ray", and "Tavis Smiley". O'Neal's memoir, "Both of Us: My Life with Farrah", was published in 2012. He reunited with Ali MacGraw for a national tour of the stage production "Love Letters". O'Neal was diagnosed with leukemia in 2001 and prostate cancer in 2012. O'Neal was married to actress Joanna Moore from 1963 until their divorce in 1967. He is survived by their daughter, actress Tatum O'Neal, and son, actor Griffin O'Neal. He was married to actress Leigh Taylor-Young, his "Peyton Place" co-star, from 1967 to 1974 and is survived by their son, sportscaster Patrick O'Neal. He was in a relationship to actress Farrah Fawcett from 1979 until they separated in 1997. They reunited in 2001 and remained together until Fawcett's death in 2009. He is also survived by their son, Redmond James Fawcett O'Neal. His brother, actor Kevin O'Neal, died in January of 2023.

Onetto, Maria

Argentine actress Maria Onetto was found dead of a suicide at her apartment in Buenos Aires, Argentina, on March 2, 2023. She was 56. Onetto was born in Buenos Aires on August 18, 1966. She studied psychology at the University of Buenos Aires, graduating in 1987. She began studying acting at Ricardo Bartis' theatrical workshop, Sportivo Teatral, in 1991. She was soon working as an acting teacher and coach. She made her debut on stage in Rafael Spregelburd's 1997 production of "Dragging the Cross". She continued to perform on stage in such productions as "La Escala Humana" (2002) and "Nunca Estuviste Tan Adorable" (2008). She reprised her role as Blanca in the film version the following year. Her films also include "Cuatro Mujeres Descalzas" (2005), "Arizona Sur" (2006), "The Other" (2007), "The Headless Woman" (2008), "Horizontal/Vertical" (2009), "Puzzle" (2010), "Lock Charmer" (2014), "Wild Tales" (2014), "La Vida Despues" (2015), "2001: Mientras Kubrick Estaba en el Espacio" (2016), "El Peso de la Ley" (2017), "Perdida" (2018), "Aire" (2018), and "Yo Nena, Yo Princesa" (2021). Onetto appeared on television in productions of "El Disfraz" (2014), "Montecristo" (2006) as Leticia Monserrat, "Tratame Bien" (2009) as Elsa Lipis, "Lo Que el Tiempo Nos Dejo" (2010), "Television Por la Inclusion" (2011), "23 Pares" (2012), "Santos y Pecadores" (2013), "La Celebracion" (2014), "Doce Casas" (2014), "Vestir a la Nacion" (2014), "En Terapia" (2014), "La Casa" (2015), "Estocolmo" (2016), "Mis Noches Sin Ti" (2017), "La Pulera" (2017), "Mi Hermano es un Clon" (2018), "Mardona: Blessed Dream" (2021), and "Ringo: Glory and Death" (2023).

Origa, Graziano

Italian artist and cartoonist Graziano Origa died in Quartu Sant'Elena, Italy, on June 18, 2023. He was 70. Origa was born in Dolianova, Italy, on November 22, 1952. He began working in comics for his own StudioOriga in 1972. The studio produced various illustrated pocket series including "Lady Lust', "Zordon", "Bonnie', "Bian-caneev", "Karzan", "Misterlady", and "Lucifera". He also oversaw the monthly underground music magazine "Gong" from 1977 to 1979 and fashion magazine "Punk Artist Magazine". He closed StudioOriga in 1982 and spent the next five years in New York City. He was an illustrator for the Italian newspaper "Progresso Italoamericano" and the gay magazines "The Advocate", "Torso", and "Blueboy". He continued his career after returning to Italy in 1987 and was editor and art director for the comics news magazine "Fumetti d'Italia" from 1992 to 2002. He was editor of the "Grande Blek" and "Capitan Miki" reprints in the early 2000s and was art consultant at the Museo del Fumetto di Lucca. Origa was author of numerous books about comics including "Enciclopedia del Fumetto" (1977), "Diary of a Punk Artist" (1980), "I Mondi di Dylan Dog" (1992), "Videomax" (1994), "Monografia Corrado roi" (1994), "L'Isola dei Fumetti" (1994), "Magnus: Lo Sconosciuto" (1999), "Edifumetto Index" (2002), "Incredibili Comics!" (2003), and "Vietato ai Minori (2007).

Ormeny, Tom

Actor Tom Ormeny died of a cancerous brain tumor in California on July 16, 2023. He was 77. Ormeny was born in Budapest, Hungary, on April 17, 1946. He mother was leading actress Eva Szorenyi. He fled Hungary with his family in 1956 when the Soviet army entered the country to put down an anti-Communist uprising. The went to Austria before settling in the United States. He attended high school in Sherman Oaks, California, and earned a master's degree at the University of California at Los Angeles. He appeared on stage and screen from the 1970s. He was featured in episodes of such series as "Medical Centeer", "Cannon", "Police Story", "General Hospital", "The Streets of San Francisco", "Wonder Woman", "MacGyver", "Newhart", the soap opera "Days of Our Lives" as Lloyd Garrison in 1990, "Star Trek: The Next Generation", "L.A. Heat", "Nothing Sacred", "7th Heaven", "Profiler", "The District", "Providence", "The Guardian", "JAG", "Boston Public", "Boston Legal", "Grey's Anatomy", "Heartland", "Mad Men", and "Scrubs". His other television credits include the tele-films 'Sergeant Matlovich vs. the U.S. Air Force" (1978), "Ernie Kovacs: Between the Laughter" (1984), "Wallenberg: A Hero's Story" (1985), "Roseanne & Tom: Behind the Scenes" (1994), and "When Billie Beat Bobby" (2001). Ormeny was featured in several films including "Only When I Laugh" (1981), "Agent on Ice" (1985), and "Gang Related" (1997). He and his wife, Maria Gobetti, founded the Victory Theatre Centre in Burbank, California, in 1980. He directed and acted in numerous plays with the company. He also taught acting in Orange County, California, at Cypress College. Ormeny and Maria Gobetti married in 1980 and she survives him.

Orwin, Anne

British actress Anne Orwin died in England on October 8, 2023. She was 68. Orwin performed frequently on stage and screen from the 1970s. She appeared on television in episodes of "Full House", "Play for Today", "Barriers", "Super Gran", "Young, Gifted and Broke", "Coronation Street" as Nurse Lucy Clark in 1992, "The Return of the Psammead", "Crimewatch Files", "Knight School", "Emmerdale" as Gwen Dingle in 1999, "Dalziel and Pascoe", "Barbara", "The League

of Gentlemen", "Holby City", "55 Degrees North", and "Byker Grove" as Lou Gallagher from 1990 to 2006. Orwin also appeared in television productions of "Lost Yer Tongue?" (1975), "Crime and Punishment" (1979), "White Peak Farm" (1988), "The Tide of Life" (1996), "Our Friends in the North" (1996), "The Wingless Bird" (1997), and "Catherine Cookson's Tilly Trotter" (1999). She was featured in several films including "Ladder of Swords" (1989), "Purely Belter" (2000), and "Public Sex" (2009).

Osborne, Bobby

Bluegrass musician Bobby Osborne, who was half of the duo the Osborne Brothers who were noted for their recording of the hit song "Rocky Top", died at a hospital in Gallatin, Tennessee, on June 27, 2023. He was 91. Osborne

was born in Thousandsticks, Kentucky, on December 7, 1931. He and his brother, Sonny Osborne, began performing with the Lonesome Pine Fiddlers. He served in the U.S. Marine Corps during the Korean War. He was wounded in action and received a purple heart before his discharge in 1953. He reunited with his brother as the Osborne Brothers, with Bobby on mandolin and Sonny on banjo, and they became noted for their bluegrass recordings. They joined with guitarist Red Allen (aka Stanley Alpine) and recorded with Gateway Records in 1956. They soon signed a contract with MGM Records and scored a hit with 1958's "Once More". They continued to record such songs as "Blame Me", "Sweethearts Again", and "Fair and Tender Ladies". They signed with Decca Records in 1963 and the brothers became members of the Grand Ole Opry the following year. They had a major hit with their 1967 recording of "Rocky Top", which became an official state song for Tennessee. Their other hits include "Up This Hill & Down", "Making Plans", "Kentucky", "Tennessee Hound Dog", and "Midnight Flyer". They were inducted into the International Bluegrass Music Association's Hall of Fame in 1994. They continued to tour and perform until Sonny retired from the group in 2005. He died in 2021. Bobby continued to play with the band Rock Top X-press, which included his sons, Bobby, Jr. He is survived by his wife, Karen Osborne, and three sons.

Ostrosky, David

Mexican actor David Ostrosky Vinograd died in Mexico City, Mexico, on August 17, 2023. He was 66. Ostrosky was born in Mexico City on December 1, 1956. He began his career on television in the early 1980s and was seen

in such series and tele-novelas as "Principesa" (1984), "Marionetas" (1986), "Dos Vidas" (1988), "Rosa Salvaje" as Carlos Manrique from 1987 to 1988, "Teresa" as Willy from

1989 to 1990, "Simplemente Maria" as Rodrigo de Penalvert from 1989 to 1990, "Alcanzar Una Estrella", "Carrusel" as Isaac Ravinovich from 1989 to 1990, "Alcanzar Una Estrella II" (1991), "The Mischievous Dreamer" (1991), "Los Secretas Intenciones" (1992), "Maria Mercedes" (1992), "Valentina" (1993), "Aguejetas de Color de Rosa" (1994), "Bajo un Mismo Rostro" as Ruben in 1995, "Humble Maria" (1995), "Marisol" as Mariano Ruiz in 1996, "La Antorcha Encendida" as Mariano Abasolo in 1996, "Alguna Vez Tendremos Alas" (1997), "El Secreto de Alejandra" as Ruben in 1997, "El Diario de Daniela" as Gustavo Corona from 1998 to 1999, "El Nino Que Vino del Mar" (1999), "The Beach House" as Cesar Villarreal in 2000, "Carita de Angel" (2000), "The Right to Be Born" as Jose Rivera in 2001, "Blameless Love" (2001), "El Juego de la Vida" (2001), "Vivan los Ninos!" (2002), "Bajo la Misma Piel" as Jaime Sandoval from 2003 to 2004, "Amy, la Nina de la Mochila Azul" (2004), "Barrera de Amor" (2005), "Alborada" (2005), "La Parodia" (2005), "Duel of Passions" (2006), "Vecinos" (2007), "Objetos Perdidos" (2007), "Destilando Amor" as Eduardo Saldivar in 2007, "Mujer, Casos de la Vida Real" (2007), "Incognito" (2008), "La Rosa de Guadalupe" (2008), "In the Name of Love" as Dr. Rodolfo Bermudez from 2008 to 2009, "Central de Abasto" (2009), "Ugly Betty" (2009), "Adictos" (2009), "Mujeres Asesinas" (2009), "Hermanos y Detectives" (2009), "Los Simuladores" (2009), "Alma de Hirro" (2009), "Soy Tu Duena" as Moises Macotela" in 2010, "Timeless Love" as Benjamin Casillas in 2011, "El Encanto del Agila" (2011), "A Shelter for Love" as Claudio Linares in 2012, "Porque el Amor Manda" as Astudillo from 2012 to 2013, "Por Siempre Mi Amor" as Gilberto from 2013 to 2014, "Until the End of Time" as Martin Coria in 2014, "A Que No Me Dejas" as Clemente from 2015 to 2016, "Nosostros los Guapos" (2017), "Papis Muy Padres" (2017), "Por Amar Sin Ley" (2018), "Como Dice el Dicho" (2018), "Sin Miedo a a Verdad" as Dr. Jaramillo from 2018 to 2019, "Preso No. 1" (2019), "The House of Flowers" as Dr. Salomon Cohen from 2018 to 2020, "Vis a Vis: El Oasis" as Victor Ramala in 2020, "The Search" (2020), "Vencer la Ausencia" as Hoero Runes in 2022, "La Mujer de Mi Vida" (2023), and "C.H.U.E.C.O." as Roberto in 2023. Ostrosky was also seen in the films "Triste Recuerdo" (1991), "Amor y Venganza" (1991), "Like Water for Chocolate" (1992), "La Segunda Noche" (2001), "La Ultima Noche" (2005), "My Mexican Shivah" (2007), "Spam" (2008), "Secretos de Familia" (2009), "Morgana" (2012), "Como Filmar Una XXX" (2017), "Souvenir" (2019), and "The House of Flowers: The Movie" (2021) reprising his role as Dr. Salomon Cohen.

Ottoni, Filippo

Italian film director and screenwriter Filippo Ottoni died in Rome, Italy, on May 7, 2023. He was 84. Ottoni was born in Cellere, Italy, on May 17, 1938. He graduated from the London Film School and began his career working on documentaries for the BBC. He returned to Italy to work as an assistant for directors Romolo Guerrieri and Mario Bava in the 1960s. He directed and wrote the 1971 film "The Big Black Sow". He scripted Bava's early slasher film "Bay of Blood" (aka "Twitch of the Death Nerve") in 1971. Ottoni was also director and writer of the films "Questo Si Che e Amore" (1978), "Detective School Dropouts" (1986), "I Giorni Randagi" (1988), and "L'Assassino e Quello Con le Scarpe Gialle" (1995). He scripted the 1993 film "Jonah Who Lived i the Whale". Ottoni worked as dubbing director for the Italian language version of numerous films. He is survived by is wife, actress Elettra Bisetti.

Pacho el Antifeka

Puerto Rican rapper Neftali Alvarez Nunez, who performed under the name Pacho El Antifeka, was shot to death at a shopping center in Bayamon, Puerto Rico, on June 1, 2023. He was 42. Alvarez was born in Puerto Rico on March 24, 1981. He was performing from the early 2000s and was half of the rap duo Pacho & Cirilo. He recorded "Como Soy" under the name Pacho Al-Queda with Bad Bunny and Daddy Yankee in 2018. He later collaborated with such artists as Nio Garcia, Alex Rose, Nicky Jam, and Casper Magico. He released his first single, "All Star Game", with Lunay in 2021.

Palter, Lew

Actor Lew Palter, who was featured as Isidor Straus in the 1997 film "Titanic", died of lung cancer at his home in Los Angeles, California, on May 21, 2023. He was 94. Palter was born in New York City on November 3, 1928. He graduated from Tufts University in Boston and received a master's degree from Alfred University in New York. He earned a Ph.D. in theater from Northwestern University in Evanston, Illinois. Palter also served a stint in the U.S. Army. He began his acting career on stage and performed in productions of "The Madwoman of Chaillot" and "An Enemy of the People" in New York. He also directed Off-Broadway plays as "Let Man Live", "Overruled", and "The Trial of Lucullus". He acted and directed in summer stock and joined the Millbrook Playhouse in Mill Hall, Pennsylvania, in the mid-1960s. Palter was seen frequently on television with roles in episodes of "Run for Your Life", "It Takes a Thief", "The Virginian", "Days of Our Lives" as Mr. Mackowitz in 1968, "Gunsmoke", "Mission: Impossible", "The High Chaparral", "The Flying Nun", "Nanny and the Professor", "The Doris Day Show", "The F.B.I.", "Here's Lucy", "Ironside", "Griff", "Columbo", "The Brady Bunch", "Kojak", "The Six Million Dollar Man", "The Invisible Man", "McMillan & Wife", "Doctors' Hospital", "Three for the Road", "Baretta", "The Bionic Woman", "McCloud", "Delvecchio", "Charlie's Angels", "Soap", "The Incredible Hulk", "The Waltons", "Bosom Buddies", "Too Close for Comfort", "Cagney & Lacey", "The A-Team", "Hill Street Blues", "L.A. Law" in the recurring role of Judge Leon Ruben from 1986 to 1987, "Day by Day", and "Madman of the People". His other television credits include the tele-films and mini-series "Lieutenant Schuster's Wife" (1972), "The Law" (1975), "Richie Brockelman: The Missing 24 Hours" (1976), "Stonestreet: Who Killed the Centerfold Model?" (1977), "Police Story: Confessions of a Lady Cop", "The Rules of Marriage" (1982), "Badge of the Assassin" (1985), "Glory Years", "Alien Nation: Dark Horizon" (1994), and "Alien Nation: The Udara Legacy" (1997). Palter appeared in a handful of films during his career including "The Steagle" (1971), "First Monday in October" (1981) as Justice Benjamin Halperin, and James Cameron's "Titanic" (1997) as ill-fated passenger Isidor Straus. He joined the faculty of the CalArts School of Theater in Santa Clarita, California in 1971, where he taught until his retirement in 2013. Palter was married to actress Nancy Vawter from 1956 until her death in 2020 and is survived by their daughter, Catherine Palter.

Panettiere, Jason

Actor Jason Panettiere, the younger brother of actress Hayden Panettiere, died of aortic valve complications caused by an enlarged heart in New York City on February 19, 2023. He was 28. Panettiere was born in Palisades, New York, on September 25, 1994. He began his career in the early 2000s with voices roles in the animated series "Midori's Nintendoland Bakery", "Brand Central Bennetts", "Blue's Clues", "Evelyn: The Rocketeer", "100 Things to Do Before Middle School", "The Male Contestant's New School", "The X's" as the voice of Truman X from 2005 to 2006, and "Holly Hobbie & Friends". He also voiced roles in the animated films "Racing Stripes" (2005), "Robots" (2005), and "Ice Age: The Meltdown" (2006). Panettiere appeared in the films "The Babysitters" (2007), "The Secrets of Jonathan Sperry" (2008), "The Perfect Game" (2008), "The Forger"

(2012), "The Lost Medallion: The Adventures of Billy Stone" (2013), "The Martial Arts Kids" (2015), "Summer Forever" (2015), "Del Playa" (2017), "Bart Bagalzby and the Garbage Genie" (2021), and "Love and Love Not" (2022). He appeared on television in episodes of "Even Stevens", "Hope & Faith", "Third Watch", "Everybody Hates Chris", "Major Crimes", and "The Walking Dead". His other television credits include the tele-films "Tiger Cruise" (2004) with sister Hayden, "The Last Day of Summer" (2007), "8" (2012), and "How High 2" (2019).

Panfilov, Gleb

Russian film director Gleb Panfilov died in Moscow, Russia, on August 26, 2023. He was 89. Panfilov was born in Magnitogorsk, Russia, on May 21, 1934. He graduated from

the Ural Polytechnic University with a degree in chemistry in 1957. He worked at a medical equipment factory and started an amateur film studio later in the decade. He produced the short films "Little Nylon Jacket" and "National Militia" in 1958. He soon began working for a local television station where he made the documentary short "Regain Our Ranks" (1959), the short films "Killed at War" (1962) and "Nina Melovisinova" (1962), and the feature tele-film "The Case of Kurt Clausewitz" (1963). He studied cinematography at the Gerasimov Institute of Cinematography (VGIK) in the early 1960s, graduating in 1963. He earned a degree in directing in 1966. Panfilov was hired by Lenfilm and made his first feature, "No Path Through Fire", in 1967. The historical drama starred his wife, actress Inna Churikova. He continued to direct such films as "The Beginning" (1970) and "I Wish to Speak" (1975). He began working for Mosfilm in Moscow and taught courses in film directing. He helmed the 1979 film "The Theme" which was banned by officials for nearly a decade. He filmed "Valentina", an adaptation of the play "Last Summer in Chullmsk", in 1981. He also began directing theatrical productions in the 1980s. His other films include "Vassa" (1983), "Gamlet" (1989), "Mat" (1990), "Romanovs: The Imperial Family" (2000), "Bez Vini Vinovatiye" (2009), "Khranit Vechno" (2008), and "100 Minutes" (2021). Panfilov was married to his frequent leading lady, Inna Churikova, from the 1960s until her death in January of 2023.

Panich, Yulian

Russian actor Yulian Panich died in Rambouillet, France, on October 9, 2023. He was 92. Panich was born in Kirovohrad, Ukraine (then Zinovievsk, part of the Soviet Union), on May 23, 1931. He graduated from Moscow's Shchukin Acting School in 1954. He appeared in such films as "Road to Life" (1955), "Za Vlast Sovetov" (1956), "Raznye Sudby" (1956), "Trista Let Tomu..." (1956), "Krovavyy Rassvet" (1957), "Vsego Dorozhe" (1957), "Leningrad Symphony" (1957), "Kochubey" (1958), "O Moyom Druge" (1959), "Be Careful, Grandma!" (1961), "Zelyonaya Kareta"

(1967), and "Pervorossiyanye" (1967). He appeared on

television in the 1967 production of "Mashina Kilimandzharo" and directed the tele-films "Doroga Domoy" (1968) and "Provody Belykh Nochey" (1969). Panich left the Soviet Union for Israel in 1972. He settled in Munich, Germany, the following year where he worked with Radio Liberty/Free Europe radio. He became a symbol of anti-Soviet resistance. He was featured in the 1978 film "Brass Target" starring Sophia Loren and George Kennedy and the 1979 German television mini-series "Ein Kapitel fur Sich". Panich married Ludmila Zweig in 1956 and is survived by her and their son, Igor.

Parady, Hersha

Actress Hersha Parady, who was featured as Alice Garvey in the television series "Little House on the Prairie" in the late 1970s, died of a brain tumor in Norfolk, Virginia, on

August 23, 2023. She was 78. She was born Betty Sandhoff in Berea, Ohio, on May 25, 1945. She began performing on stage in the Cleveland area during her early teens. She moved to California in the early 1970s and was soon appearing on television. She was seen in episodes of "Bearcats!", "Mannix", "The Waltons", "The Quest", the "CBS Afternoon Playhouse" serial "Joey and Redhawk" as Laura Harker in 1978, "NBC Special Treat", "ABC Weekend Specials", "The Phoenix", "Unsolved Mysteries", "Second Noah", and "Kenan & Kel". Parady was featured as Alice Garvey on "Little House on the Prairie" from 1977 to 1980 when her character perished in a fire. Her other television credits include the tele-films "The $5.20 an Hour Dream" (1980), "The Babysitter's Seduction" (1996), and "Our Son, the Matchmaker" (1996). She was featured in several films including "Courage" (1984), "Hyper Sapien: People from Another Star" (1986), and "The Break" (1995). She largely retired from the screen after her marriage to Oscar-winning producer John Peverall in 1994. They later divorced and she is survived by their son, Jonathan.

Paramor, John

Australian actor John Paramor died in Sydney, Australia, on September 22, 2023. He was 80. Paramor was born in Sydney on April 29, 1943. He studied acting at the National Institute of Dramatic Art in the late 1960s. He appeared frequently on stage, starring as Brad in the original Australian production of "The Rocky Horror Show" and starring as the title character in the premiere of "The Legend of King O'Malley" in 1970. He was featured as Eustace in the television series "The Unisexers" in 1975. He was Matt Barrington in the series "Number 96" in 1974 and returned as

Peter Raikes in 1976. He also was seen in episodes of "Homicide", "Cop Shop", "Sons and Daughters", "Rafferty's Rules", "A Country Practice", "The Flying Doctors", and "Heartbreak High" as Geoff Miller from 1994 to 1995. His other television credits include productions of "Shout! - The Story of Johnny O'Keefe" (1985), "Shark's Paradise" (1986), and "Fields of Fire II" (1988). Paramor appeared in several films including "Private Collection" (1972), "The Night, the Prowler" (1978), "The Everlasting Secret Family" (1988), "Stones of Death" (1988), and "Children of the Revolution" (1996). He produced and starred in the 2008 short film "A Chair with a View".

Parker, Jim

British film composer Jim Parker died on July 28, 2023. He was 88. Parker was born in Hartlepool, Durham, England, on December 18, 1934. He graduated from the

Guildhall School of Music in London. He played with orchestras and became a member of the Barrow Poets. He provided incidental music and frequently accompanied them on a variety of folk instruments. He was a conductor and composer from the 1970s, putting the poetry of Sir John Betjeman to music in such recordings as "Banana Blush" (1974), "Late Flowering Love" (1974), "Sir John Betjeman's Britain" (1977), and "Varsity Rag" (1981). He set the poetry of Jeremy Lloyd to music for the hit recording "Captain Bleaky and His Band" in 1977 and a 1980 sequel. The albums inspired BBC television shows, a pantomime, and a West End musical. Parker composed frequently for television, receiving a BAFTA Award nomination in 1991 for his work on "House of Cards". He received four BAFTA Awards for Best Original Television Music for "To Play the King" (1994), "The Fortunes and Misfortunes of Moll Flanders" (1997), "The History of Tom Jones, a Foundling" (1998), and "A Rather English Marriage" (1999). He was also composer for television productions and series including "Red Letter Day" (1976), "Tales of the Unexpected" (1982), "Pictures" (1983), "Good Behaviour" (1983), "Man of Letters" (1984), "Six English Towns" (1984), "Hay Fever" (1984), "The Man from Moscow" (1985), "Remember the Lambeth Walk" (1985), "Absurd Person Singular" (1985), "Mapp & Lucia" (1985-1986), "Watching" (1986), "Season's Greetings" (1986), "Our Geoff" (1987), "The Finding" (1987), "The Moneymen" (1987), "The Giftie" (1988), "Every Breath You Take" (1988), "Dreams, Secrets,

Beautiful Lies" (1988), "Watch with Mother" (1988), "Deadline" (1988), "Mike & Angelo" (1989), "Snakes and Ladders" (1989), "Relatively Spaking" (1989), "Wish Me Luck" (1989-1990), "Pirate Prince" (1991), "The House of Eliott" (1991-1994), "Body & Soul" (1993), "Soldier Soldier" (1994), "Treasures in Trust" (1995), "An Independent Man" (1995), "The Final Cut" (1995), "The Happy Prince" (1996), "Change That" (1997), "Deadly Summer" (1997), "Midsommer Murders" (1997-2021), "Storm Over 4" (1998), "My Summer with Des" (1988), "Lost for Words" (1999), "Murder Rooms: Mysteries of the Real Sherlock Holmes" (2000), "The Law" (2000), "Dirty Tricks" (2000), "Born and Bred" (2002-2005), "Foyle's War" (2002-2008), "The Booze Cruise" (2003), "The Booze Cruise II: The Treasure Hunt" (2005), and "Betjeman's West Country" (2006). He was also composer for numerous concert works. Parker married Sonia Levy in 1961 and they later divorced. He is survived by their daughter. He married Pauline George in 1969 and is also survived by her and their two daughters.

Parker, Lara

Actress Lara Parker, who starred as Angelique in the gothic soap opera "Dark Shadows", died of cancer in Los Angeles, California, on October 12, 2023. She was 84. She

was born Mary Lamar Rickey in Knoxville, Tennessee, on October 27, 1938. She was raised in Memphis, Tennessee, where her parents, Albert and Ann Rickey, were prominent political and civic figures. She attended Vassar College before graduating from Rhodes College (formerly Southwestern) in Memphis. She earned a master's degree in speech and drama from the University of Iowa. She began her career on stage and performed with the Millbrook Playhouse in Pennsylvania. Parker moved to New York City in the late 1960s and appeared in the 1968 Broadway production of "Woman Is My Idea". She was seen in the Off-Broadway plays "Lulu" (1970) and "A Gun Play" (1971). Parker was best known for her role as Angelique Bouchard, the 17th century witch who cursed Jonathan Frid's Barnabas Collins to become a vampire. She portrayed Angelique from 1967 until the character's supposed death in 1968 but soon returned to "Dark Shadows" as modern-day counterpart Cassandra Blair Collins. Parker remained with "Dark Shadows" as Angelique and various other roles including Alexis Stokes and Catherine Collins until it finished airing in April of 1971. She reprised the role in the 1971 film version "Night of Dark Shadows" and was featured in a cameo role in Tim Burton's 2012 "Dark Shadows" starring Johnny Depp. She was also seen on television in episodes of "N.Y.P.D.", "Kung Fu", "The F.B.I.", "Insight", "Medical Center", "Owen Marshall, Counselor of Law", "Lucas Tanner", "Police Woman", "The Rockford Files", "Kolchak: The Night Stalker", "S.W.A.T.", "Mobile One",

"Emergency!", "Doctors' Hospital", "The Six Million Dollar Man", "Jigsaw John", "City of Angels", "Kojak", "Alice", "The Incredible Hulk", "Switch", "Baretta", "Quincy", "The Lazarus Syndrome", "Sword of Justice", "The Misadventures of Sheriff Lobo", "Barnaby Jones", "Hawaii Five-O", "Mrs. Columbo", "Hagen", "Galactica 1980", "This Is the Life", "The Fall Guy", "Jessica Novak" as Katie Robbins in 1981, "A New Day in Eden", "Manimal", "Remington Steele", "One Life to Live", the soap opera "Capitol" as Linda Vandenburg from 1985 to 1986, "Highway to Heaven", "The Highwayman", "P.S.I. Luv U", and the web anthology series "Theatre Fantastique". Her other television credits include the tele-films and mini-series "My Darling Daughters' Anniversary" (1973), "The Chadwick Family" (1974), "Adventures of the Queen" (1975), "Stranded" (1976), "Washington: Behind Closed Doors" (1977), "The Solitary Man" (1979), "Once Upon a Family" (1980), "Desperate Voyage" (1980), "Rooster" (1982), "The China Lake Murders" (1990), and "People Like Us" (1990). Parker made her film debut in Brian De Palma's 1970 feature "Hi, Mom!" with Robert De Niro. Her other films include "Save the Tiger" (1973) starring Jack Lemmon, "Airport 1975" (1974), the horror film "Race with the Devil" (1975) opposite Peter Fonda, "Foxfire Light" (1983). Parker worked as a high school English teacher after retiring from acting in the late 1980s. She later wrote several books based on "Dark Shadows" including "Angelique's Descent" (1998), "The Salem Branch" (2006), "Wolf Moon Rising" (2013), and "Heiress of Collinwood" (2016). She was also active in the Big Finish Productions audio franchise of the series. She was married to artist Tom Parker from 1959 until their divorce in 1974 and is survived by two sons. She married Jim Hawkins in 1985 and is also survived by him and their daughter.

Parkinson, Michael

British television host and journalist Michael Parkinson died at his home in Bray, Berkshire, England, on August 16, 2023. He was 88.

Parkinson was born in Cudworth, West Riding of Yorkshire, England, on March 28, 1935. He began his career as a journalist for local newspapers. He was later a feature writer for the "Manchester Guardian" and the "Daily Express" in London. He served in the British Army during National Service from 1955 to 1957 and was a press liaison officer in Egypt during the Suez Canal Crisis. He began working in television in the 1960s and was a host of the BBC1 daily news show "Twenty-Four Hours" from 1966 to 1968. He hosted Granada Television's late-night film review show "Cinema" from 1969 to 1971. He returned to the BBC to host his own program, "Parkinson" from 1971 to 1982 and again from 1998 to 2007. He was a host of "Good Morning, Britain" from 1983 to 1984 and hosted Thames Television's game show "Give Us a Clue" from 1984 to 1985. He was host of the Yorkshire Television interview show "Parkinson One to One" from 1987 to 1988. Parkinson was featured as himself in the paranormal drama "Ghostwatch" in 1992 and had a cameo role in the 2003 romantic comedy film "Love Actually". He was host of the BBC One daytime game show "Going for a Song" from 1995 to 1999. He appeared as himself in the Australian soap opera "Neighbours" in 2007 and retired from "Parkinson" later in the year. He returned to television as host of "Parkinson: Masterclass" on Sky Arts in 2012. He also worked in radio, hosting the series "Desert Island Discs" from 1986 to 1988, "Parkinson on Sport" from 1994 to 1996, and "Parkinson's Sunday Supplement" from 1997 to 2007. He penned a series of children's books, "The Woolfits", during the early 1980s and was narrator of the Yorkshire Television animated series from 1981 to 1982. His autobiography, "Parky", was published in 2008. Parkinson married journalist Mary Heneghan in 1959 and is survived by her and their three children.

Parr, Chris

British theatrical and television producer and director Chris Parr died of pneumonia and complications from Parkinson's disease in England on November 24, 2023. He was 80. Parr was born in Littlehampton, Sussex, England, on

September 25, 1943. He attended Queen's College, Oxford, but left without earning a degree. He pursued a career in theater and was a director at the Nottingham Playhouse from 1965 to 1966. He attended the University of Bradford from 1969 to 1972. He served as artistic director of the Traverse Theatre in Edinburgh, Scotland, from 1975 to 1981. He oversaw the production of numerous plays by emerging Scottish playwrights including Howard Brenton and David Edgar. He began working for the BBC and was script editor for the science fiction anthology series "Play for Tomorrow" in 1982. Parr was a producer for many television productions including "Phonefun Limited" (1982), "Aunt Suzanne" (1984), "After You've Gone" (1984), "Fire at Magilligan" (1984), "A Woman Calling" (1984), "This Is History, Gran" (1986), "The Daily Woman" (1986), "Fighting Back" (1986), "The Continental" (1987), "The Rainbow" (1988), "Shalom Salaam" (1989), "Nice Work" (1989), "My Kingdom for a Horse" (1991), "Bad Company" (1993), "Takin' Over the Asylum" (1994), "Martin Chuzzlewit" (1994), "Cruel Train" (1995), "Neverwhere" (1996), "The Moonstone" (1996), "Ivanhoe" (1997), "The Ice House" (1997), "The Scold's Bridle" (1998), "The Law" (2000), "Beech Is Back" (2001), "Promoted to Glory" (2003), and "Falling" (2005). He was also producer for such series as "Play for Today", "Summer Season", "The Ritz", "Screen Two", "Chalkface", "Children of the North", "Screenplay", "All Quiet on the Preston Front", "Blood & Peaches", "Backup", "Dangerfield", "Dalziel and Pascoe", "Madson", "Wing and a Prayer", and "The Bill". Parr married actress Tamara Ustinov in 1973 and they later divorced. His marriage to Theresa Crichton in 1980 also ended in divorce. Parr married television writer Anne Devlin in 1985 and is survived by her and their son, Connal.

Patitz, Tatjana

German model Tatjana Patitz died of breast cancer in Santa Barbara, California, on January 11, 2023. She was 56. Patitz was born in Hamburg, West Germany, on May 25, 1966,

and was raised in Skanor, Sweden. She began modeling after becoming a finalist in the Elite Model Look competition in 1983. She was soon being photographed for such magazines as "Vogue", "Elle", "Cosmopolitan", and "Harper's Bazarre". She modeled for numerous designers on the catwalk and worked with such photographers as Peter Lindbergh, Irving Penn, Herb Ritts, and Helmut Newton. She was credited as one of the original supermodels of the late 1980s and was subject of the 1988 "Vogue" article "Tatjana: Million Dollar Beauty". She appeared with several other leading models in the music video for George Michael's song "Freedom! '90" in 1990. She settled in Los Angeles where she worked in advertising campaigns for such fashion houses as Chanel, Valentino, Karl Lagerfeld, Versace, Donna Karan, and Vivienne Westwood. She was a cover model for over 200 magazines by the late 1990s. Her final appearance on the catwalk was during Milan Fashion Weeks in 2019. Patitz was also seen in music videos for Duran Duran's "Skin Trade" and "Burning the Ground" and Korn's "Make Me Bad" and "Deuce". She was featured in the films "Rising Sun" (1993) as murder victim Cheryl Lynn Austin, "Ready to Wear" (1994), and "Restraining Order" (1999), and episodes of "The Larry Sanders Show" and "The Single Guy". Patitz was married to businessman Jason Johnson from 2003 until their divorce in 2009 and is survived by their son.

Patrick, Robert

Playwright Robert Patrick died at his home in Los Angeles, California, on April 23, 2023. He was 85. Patrick was

born in Kilgore, Texas, on September 27, 1937. He traveled around with his family in his youth and graduated high school in Roswell, New Mexico. He went to New York in 1961 where he began working in off-off Broadway theaters including Caffe Cino and La Mama. He appeared in numerous productions and began writing poetry and plays. His first play, "The Haunted Host", was produced at Caffe Cino in 1964, and he starred in the central role. He was a pioneer in gay theater and penned over 60 plays. His works include "Joyce Dynel" (1969), "Salvation Army" (1969),

"Camera Obscura" (1969), "Kennedy's Children" (1974) which was performed on Broadway the following year, "My Cup Runneth Over" (1976), "T-Shirts" (1979), "Blue Is for Boys" (1983), and "Untold Decades" (1988). He moved to California in the early 1990s. He appeared in several documentaries about gay theater and published his memoirs, "Film Moi or Narcissus in the Dark", in 2004. He produced a DVD of his lecture, "Caffe Cino: Birthplace of Gay Theatre", in 2010, and several collections of poems. He gave a solo performance about his career, "What Doesn't Kill Me... Makes a Great Story Later", in 2014. A short film of him reciting his poetry, "Robert Patrick's The Theory of Romance", was produced by L.A. Art Documents in 2020.

Patrick, Vincent

Author and screenwriter Vincent Patrick, who was noted for the crime novel "The Pope of Greenwich Village",

died of complications from Lewy body dementia at his home in Manhattan, New York, on October 6, 2023. He was 88. Patrick was born in the Bronx, New York, on January 19, 1935. He dropped out of his school and took jobs in a bowling alley and as a door-to-door Bible salesman. He returned to school in the 1950s and earned a degree in mechanical engineering at New York University. He left a successful career in engineering to write the 1979 crime novel "The Pope of Greenwich Village". He scripted the 1984 film version starring Eric Roberts, Mickey Rourke, and Daryl Hannah. His 1985 book, "Family Business", became a 1989 film starring Sean Connery, Matthew Broderick, and Dustin Hoffman as three generations of the McMullen family, who concoct a criminal scheme. Patrick also wrote the 1999 novel "Smoke Screen". He wrote for the short-lived comedy series "Tough Cookies" in 1986. He was also involved with writing early treatments of the films "Beverly Hills Cop" (1984), "The Godfather Part III" (1990), "At Play in the Fields of the Lord" (1991), and "Money Train" (1995). He co-scripted the 1997 film "The Devil's Own" and the 1999 television mini-series "To Serve and Protect". Patrick married Carole Unger in 1954 and is survived by her and their two sons, Richard and Glen.

Patridge, Joe

Actor Joe Patridge, who starred as Detective Sgt. Dave Kennedy in 1960 horror film "The Hypnotic Eye", died at a hospital in Panorama City, California, on June 3, 2023. He was 92. Patridge was born in Arcola, Illinois, on July 21, 1930. He graduated from Eastern Illinois University in 1952 where he was a football and track star. He served in the U.S. Army from 1953 to 1955 and studied acting at the Pasadena Playhouse after his discharge. He appeared on television in episodes of "West Point", "The Adventures of Jim Bowie", "Highway Patrol" as an officer in a handful of episodes from 1957 to 1958, "77 Sunset Strip", "Sky King", "State Trooper", "Maverick",

"Wanted: Dead or Alive", "Colt. 45", "Bronco", "Wichita Town", "Rawhide", "Bonanza", "Michael Shayne", and "The New Phil Silvers Show". Patridge also appeared in the films "Cast a Long Shadow" (1959), the horror film "The Hypnotic Eye" (1960), "The Wizard of Baghdad" (1960), "Sanctuary" (1961), "Fate Is the Hunter" (1964), "Fort Coura-geous" (1965), and "Convict Stage" (1965). He largely retired from the screen in the mid-1960s. He remained active on stage and later was an actor and director at Theater East in Studio City, California. Patridge is survived by his wife, Barbara, and was predeceased by his daughter, Debbie Dunagan.

Pavan, Marisa

Italian actress Marisa Pavan, who received an Academy Award nomination for her role in the 1955 film "The

Rose Tattoo", died at her home in Saint-Tropez, France, on December 6, 2023. She was 91. She was born Maria Luisa Pierangeli in Cagliari, Sardinia, Italy, on June 19, 1932. Her twin sister, Anna Maria Pierangeli, became the noted actress, Pier Angeli. Maria Louisa moved to Rome with her family in the late 1940s. Her sister was cast in Vittorio De

Sica's 1950 film "Tomorrow Is Too Late". The family subsequently moved to Hollywood where Anna Maria became known as Pier Angeli. Maria Luisa was initially uninterested in a film career but reconsidered when she was cast as Nicole Bouchard in John Ford's 1952 feature "What Price Glory" under the name Marisa Pavan. She continued to appear in films in the United States and Europe over the next decade including "I Choose Love" (1953), "Down Three Dark Streets" (1954), the western "Drum Beat" (1954) with Alan Ladd, "The Rose Tattoo" earning an Oscar nomination for Best Supporting Actress for her role as Rosa Delle Rose, "Diane" (1956) as Catherine de Medici, "The Man in the Gray Flannel Suit" (1956) with Gregory Peck, "The Midnight Story" (1957) opposite Tony Curtis, "John Paul Jones" (1959) opposite Robert Stack, "Solomon and Sheba" (1959) as Abishag, and "Three Faces of Sin" (1961). She later appeared in the French films "A Slightly Pregnant Man" (1973) and "Antoine and Sebastian" (1974). Pavan was seen frequently on television from the early 1950s with roles in episodes of "Fireside Theatre", "Studio One", "Front Row Center", "Alfred Hitchcock Presents", "The Kaiser Aluminum Hour", "ITV Television Playhouse", "Climax!", "The Frank Sinatra Show", "Playhouse 90", "Westinghouse Desilu Playhouse", "The Arthur Murray Party", "The United States Steel Hour", "Hallmark Hall of Fame" in the

musical fantasy "Shangri-La" in 1960, "Naked City", "Breaking Point", "77 Sunset Strip", "Combat!", "Bob Hope Presents the Chrysler Theatre", "The F.B.I.", "Court Martial", "Seaway", "The Merv Griffin Show", "What's My Line?", "The Hollywood Palace", "Wonder Woman", "McMillan & Wife", "Switch", "Hawaii Five-O", "The Rockford Files", "La Vie des Autres", the soap opera "Ryan's Hope" as Chantal Dubujak in 1985, "Cinema 16", "Renseignements Generaux", and "Haute Tension". Her other television credits include productions of "The Diary of Anne Frank" (1967) as Margot Frank, "Cutter's Trail" (1970), "Arthur Hailey's the Moneychangers" (1976), and "The Trial of Lee Harvey Oswald" (1977). She was the subject of Margaux Soumoy's 2021 biograph "Drop the Baby; Put a Veil on the Broad!". Her sister, Pier Angeli, died of a drug overdose in 1971. Pavan was married to French actor Jean-Pierre Aumont from 1956 until his death in 2001. She is survived by their two sons, Jean-Claude and Patrick Aumont.

Peacock, Justin

Television writer and producer Justin Peacock died of heart disease at his home in Los Angeles, California, on July

13, 2023. He was 52. Peacock was born in Detroit, Michigan, in October of 1970. He graduated from the University of Michigan and earned a master's degree from Columbia University. He graduated from Yale Law School and worked as an intellectual property and First Amendment attorney in New York City. His first novel, "A Cure for the Night", was published in 2008. He moved

to Los Angeles in 2011 and was a writer and story editor for the USA series "Suits" from 2012 to 2015. He also wrote and produced the series "The Lincoln Lawyer" in 2022 and "Alert: Missing Persons Unit" in 2023.

Pearce, Eve

Scottish actress Eve Pearce died in Denville Hall, London, England, on January 13, 2023. She was 93. Pearce was born in Aberdeen, Scotland, on April 17, 1929. Her mother

died when she was a child and she moved to London with her father after he remarried. She entered the Royal Academy of Dramatic Art in 1948 and began her career on stage in repertory in the early 1950s. She later performed in many productions with the Royal Shakespeare Company. Pearce appeared on television in episodes of "Family Solicitor", "Drama '63", "Love Story", "Theatre 625", "This Man Craig", "King of the River", "Coronation Street", "City '68", "The First Lady", "Plays of Today", "Wicked Women", "Z Cars", "Dr. Finlay's Casebook", "Tales of

Unease", "Menace", "The Expert", "The Rivals of Sherlock Holmes", "Softly Softly: Task Force", "The Befrienders", "The Brothers", "Six Faces" as Miss Haverford in 1972, "Crown Court" as Helen Musgrove in 1972, "The Fenn Street Gang", "Adam Smith", "The Frighteners", "Between the Wars", "Spy Trap", "Bedtime Stories", "Whatever Happened to the Likely Lads?", "Late Night Drama", "Dixon of Dock Green", "The Main Chance", "Play for Today", "Yes, Honestly" as Lily's Mother in 1976, "Beryl's Lot", "ITV Playhouse", "Thomas and Sarah", "A Fine Romance", "Just Good Friends", "Brookside", "Lytton's Diary" as Beryl in 1985, "Blood Red Roses", "Bulman", "The Campbells", "The Two of Us", "Close to Home", "Taggart", "Take the High Road", "Poirot", "The 10%ers", "Bramwell", "Midsomer Murders", "The Cazalets", "Born and Bred", "Torchwood", "The Bill", "Him & Her", "Holby City", "Getting On", "Doctors", "WPC 56", and "The Durrells". Her other television credits include productions of "Love and Miss Figgis" (1954), "Kipps" (1960), "Four Triumphant: St. Patrick" (1966), "Love on the Dole" (1967), "The Investigation" (1967), "The Gold Robbers" (1969), "The Crib" (1971), "Man of Straw" (1972), "The Edwardians" (1972), "Total Eclipse" (1973), "Fall of Eagles" (1974) as Empress Dona, "No Hard Feelings" (1976), "Grey Granite" (1983), "Sorrell and Son" (1984), "Reunion at Fairborough" (1985), "Great Expectations" (1989), "Milner" (1994), "Into the Blue" (1997), "The 10th Kingdom" (2000) as the Gypsy Queen, and "Funland" (2005). Pearce appeared in occasional films throughout her career including "Can Heironymus Merkin Ever Forget Mercy Humppe and Find True Happiness?" (1969), "Please Sir!" (1971), "Beg!" (1994), "Topsy-Turvy" (1999), "The Lake" (2002), "Wimbledon" (2004), "Mirrormask" (2005), "Penelope" (2006), "Sezon Tumanov" (2009), "The Wee Man" (2013), "The Woman in Black 2: Angel of Death" (2014), and "London Unplugged" (2018). She was featured in the short films "A Loving Act" (2001), "Plenty of Spoons" (2005), "Quietus" (2009), "Cherry Cake" (2015), "Hands" (2015), and "The Elder" (2016). She was also a poet with her first collection, "Capturing Snowflakes", which was published in 2012.

Peluso, Chris

Broadway actor and singer Chris Peluso died in London, England, on August 15, 2023. He was 40. Peluso was born in Hoboken, New Jersey, on July 1, 1983. He was a graduate of the University of Michigan, where he performed frequently on stage. He appeared on Broadway from the early 2000s with roles in productions of "Mamma Mia!" (2001) as Sky, "Assassins" (2004), Elton John's "Lestat" (2006), and "Beautiful: The Carol King Musical" (2014). He starred as Fiyero in the touring company productions of "Wicked" and appeared Off-Broadway in "The Glorious Ones". He moved to London where he appeared in West End productions of "Funny Girl", "Show Boat", "Death Takes a Holiday", "Miss Saigon", and "The Woman in White". Peluso had been diagnosed with schizoaffective disorder in the year before his death. Peluso is survived by his wife, Jessica Gomes, and their son and daughter.

Pepperell, Ian

British actor Ian Pepperell, who starred as Roy Tucker in the radio soap opera "The Archers", died after a long illness on December 22, 2023. He was 53. Pepperell was born in Oxford, England, in 1970. He was featured as Russell in the television soap opera "East-Enders" in 1993. He was also seen in episodes of "The Bill", "Pie in the Sky", "Beck", and "Get Real". He starred as hotel operator Roy Tucker in the BBC rural radio drama "The Archers" from 2006 to 2023. Pepperell also performed frequently on stage.

Perak, John

Actor John Perak died in Laguna Woods, California, on November 2, 2023. He was 83. Perak was born in Chicago,

Illinois, on October 10, 1940. He began performing on the Chicago stage while in high school. He enlisted in the U.S. Army and earned a Purple Heart after losing his left eye due to a hand grenade while serving in Vietnam. Perak moved to Hollywood after leaving the military to pursue an acting career. He appeared frequently on television from the late 1960s through the early 1980s. He was seen in episodes of "The Virginian", "Adam-12", "Ironside", "The F.B.I.", "Bonanza", "Cannon", "Police Story", "Barnaby Jones", "Most Wanted", "The Rockford Files", "Charlie's Angels", "Bret Maverick", and "The A-Team". His other television credits include the tele-films "Brinks: The Great Robbery" (1976), "Deadly Game" (1977), "True Grit: A Further Adventure" (1978), "A Woman Called Moses" (1978), and "Love's Savage Fury" (1979). Perak was featured in several films during his career including "Living Venus" (1961), "Coffy" (1973), and "Beyond Reason" (1985). He worked behind the scenes at CBS Studios after ending his acting career. He worked on such series as "Seinfeld", "Will & Grace", and "Evening Shade" before his retirement in 2003. He continued to perform and direct for the local stage after settling in Laguna Woods in 2007. He was married to Darlene Ann Hazlett from 1966 until her death in 2006 and is survived by their son and daughter. He married Elizabeth Perak in 2007 and she also survives him.

Perfort, Holger

Danish actor Hoger Perfort died in Denmark on April 29, 2023. He was 97. Perfort was born in Aarhus, Denmark, on June 9, 1925. He trained as an actor and performed with the Aarhus Teater from 1948. He moved to Copenhagen in 1954 where he performed frequently on stage and screen. He was chairman of the Danish Actors' Association from 1969 to 1976. He was a noted character actor in such films as "Min Datter Nelly" (1955), "Once Upon a War" (1966), "Det Var en Lordag Aften" (1968), "De Rode Heste" (1968), "Og Sar er der Bal Bagefter" (1970), "The Missing Clerk" (1971), "Olsen-Banden Gar Amok" (1973), "Olsen-Bandens Sidste Bedrifter" (1974), "Olsen-Banden Deruda'" (1977), "Haervaerk" (1977), "Skytten" (1977), "Mirror, Mirror" (1978), "The Olsen Gang Goes to War" (1978), "Rend Mig i Traditionerne" (1979), "Olsen-Banden Over Alle Bjerge!" (1981), Gabriel Axel's Oscar-winning foreign film "Babette's Feast" (1987) as Karlsen, "Europa" (1991), "Crumb at a Gallop" (1992), "Black Harvest" (1993), "White Lies" (1995), "The Olsen Gang - Final Mission" (1998), "Fruen pa Hamre" (2000), "Baenken" (2000), "Kat" (2001), and "Jolly Roger" (2001). Perfort was seen on television in productions of "Sparekassen" (1957), "Hexerie Eller Blind Alarm" (1959), "En Lordag Pa Ama'r" (1959), "Naevningen" (1960), "Orfeus i Underverdenen" (1960), "En Tur i Byen" (1961), "Helligtrekongersaften" (1961), "Jeppe Pa bjerget" (1963), "Salad Days" (1963), "Regnvejr Og Ingen Penge" (1965), "I Braendingen" (1965), "I Sandhed en Helt" (1967), "Billet til Manen" (1967), "En Mand fra La Mancha" (1967), "Skaert Kod Til Frk. Afsenius" (1967), "Farvel Thomas" (1968), "Henrik IV" (1968), "Huset Pa Graensen" (1969), "Tango Jalousi" (1970), "Til Lykke Hansen" (1971), "De Fremmede" (1975), "Ministeren Og Doden" (1976), "Ministerens Mord" (1977), "Matine Pa Rode Molle" (1978), "Sanct Hansaften-Spil" (1979), "Dette er et TV-Apparat" (1980), "Uden Stotte Fra Befolkningen Kunne Vi Ingenting Udrette" (1980), "En Folkefjende" (1983), "Hver Dag Forsvinder" (1984), "Anthonsen" (1984), "Renters Rente" (1996), "Bryggeren" (1997), and "1864" (2014). His other television credits include episodes of "Cabaret la Blonde", "Smuglerne", "Huset Pa Christianshavn", "Ret Beset", "En By i Provinsen", "Strandvaskeren", "Vores Ar", "Krigsdotre", "Matador" as Tjener Olsen from 1978 to 1982, "Nissebanden", "Eldorado for Dyr", "Station 13", "Ugeavisen", "Tre Karlekar", "Landsbyen", "Gongehovdingen" as Tambouren in 1992, "The Kingdom" as Professor Ulrich from 1994 to 1997, "Taxa", "Pas Pa Mor", "Pyrus i Alletiders Eventyr", "Hotellet", "Jesus & Josefine", "Kroniken", and "Osman Og Jeppe". Perfort was married to actress Lillian Tillegreen from 1952 until her death in 2002 and is survived by their son.

Perry, Anne

British writer Anne Perry, who helped murder her best friend's mother as a teenager in a crime that was depicted in the 1994 film "Heavenly Creatures", died of a heart attack at a hospital in Los Angeles, California, on April 10, 2023. She was 84. She was born Juliet Hulme in London, England, on October 28, 1938.

She moved to New Zealand in her early teens where she became best friends with Pauline Yvonne Parker. Juliet and Pauline invented a fantasy world, writing stories and plays about their experiences there. They envisioned a parallel dimension they called the Fourth World and created a hierarchy of saints based on celebrities. The two were going to be separated after Hulme's parents planned to send her to South African for her health while they returned to England. The girls hoped that they could persuade their parents to allow them to go there together, but Parker felt that her mother would not allow it. Hulme and Parker had afternoon tea with Parker's mother, Honorah Rieper, on June 22, 1954. They then went for a walk in a wooded area where they bashed her head repeatedly with a brick in a sock. They were both convicted of the murder and sentenced to five years in prison. Juliet served her sentence in Auckland's Mount Eden prison. She left the country after her release in 1959 and joined her father in Italy. She subsequently spent time in England and the United States, where she joined the Mormon Church, before settling in Scotland. She began writing historical detective novels under the name Anne Perry in the 1970s. Her first work, "The Cater Street Hangman", set in the 1880s and featuring her recurring characters, Thomas and Charlotte Pitt, was published in 1979. It was adapted for a tele-film in 1998 starring Eoin McCarthy and Keeley Hawes. The Pitts were the protagonists of over thirty subsequent novels including "Callander Square" (1980), "Paragon Walk" (1981), "Resurrection Row" (1981), "Rutland Place" (1983), "Bluegate Fields" (1984), "Death in the Devil's Acre" (1985), "Cardington Crescent" (1987), "Silence in Hanover Close" (1988), "Bethlehem Road" (1990), "Highgate Rise" (1991), "Belgrave Square" (1992), "Farrier's Lane" (1993), "The Hyde Park Headsman" (1994), "Traitors Gate" (1995), "Pentecost Alley" (1996), "Ashworth Hall" (1997), "Brunswick Gardens" (1998), "Bedford Square" (1999), "Half Moon Street" (2000), "The Whitechapel Conspiracy" (2001), "Southampton Row" (2002), "Seven Dials" (2003), "Long Spoon Lane" (2005), "Buckingham Palace Gardens" (2008), "Betrayal at Lisson Grove" (2011), "Dorchester Terrace" (2012), "Midnight at Marble Arch" (2013), "Death on Blackheath" (2014), "The Angel Court Affair" (2015), "Treachery at Lancaster Gate" (2016), and "Murder on the Serpentine" (2016). The couple's son, Daniel Pitt, later had his own series of mysteries that included "Twenty-One Days" (2018), "Triple Jeopardy" (2019), "One Fatal Flaw" (2020), "Death with a Double Edge" (2021), "Three Debts Paid" (2022), and "The Fourth Enemy" (2023). Perry created the fictional detective Inspector William Monk, an amnesiac who is assisted by Crimean War nurse Hester Latterly, in the 1990 novel "The Face of a Stranger". Their investigations take place in the mid-1800s and include the novels "A Dangerous Mourning" (1991), "Defend and Betray" (1992), "A Sudden, Fearful Death" (1993), "The Sins of the Wolf" (1994), "Cain His Brother" (1995), "Weighed in the Balance" (1996), "The Silent City" (1997), "A Preach of Promise" (aka "Whited Sepulchres") (1997), "The Twisted Root" (1999), "Slaves of Obsession" (2000), "A Funeral in Blue" (2001), "Death of a Stranger" (2002), "The Shifting Tide" (2004), "Dark Assassin" (2006), "Execution Dock" (2009), "Acceptable Loss" (2011), "A Sunless Sea" (2012), "Blind Justice" (2013), "Blood on the Water" (2014), "Corridors of the Night" (2015), "Revenge in a Cold River" (2016), "An Echo of Murder" (2017), and "Dark Tide Rising" (2018). The adventures of photographer Elena Standish were set in pre-World War I England and included "Death in Focus" (2019), "A Question of Betrayal" (2020), "A Darker Reality" (2021), "A Truth to Lie For" (2022), and "The Traitor Among Us" (2023). Perry set another series during World War I that was composed of "No Graves as Yet" (2003), "Shoulder in the Sky" (2004), "Angels in the Gloom" (2005), "At Some Disputed Barricade" (2006), and "We Shall Not Sleep" (2007). She began a series of Christmas stories with 2003's "A Christmas Journey" which continued through 2023's "A Christmas Vanishing". Perry was also the author of the fantasy novels "Talthea" (2000) and "Come Armageddon" (2002), and the "Timepiece" series of young adult novels including "Tudor Rose" (2011), "Rose of No Man's Land" (2011), "Blood Red Rose" (2012), and "Rose Between Two Thorns" (2012). Her short story, "Heroes", earned her an Edgar Award in 2000. Her earlier identity remained largely unknown until Peter Jackson began filming an account of the murder, 1994's "Heavenly Creatures", which starred Kate Winslet as Hulme and Melanie Lynskey as Parker. She was subject of the 2009 documentary film "Anne Perry Interiors" and also received an Agatha Award for lifetime achievement in 2009. Perry moved to Los Angeles in 2017 to try and promote film adaptations of her novels. She suffered a heart attack in December of 2022 and died the following April.

Perry, Ernest, Jr.

Actor Ernest Perry, Jr., died in Schiller Park, Illinois, on November 23, 2023. He was 76. He was born in Chicago, Illinois, on May 30, 1947. He began his career on the Chicago stage in the 1970s and was a founder of the black theatrical company, Amistad, later in the decade. He appeared in numerous productions with Chicago's Goodman Theatre including "Two Trains Running", "Puddin 'n' Pete", "Ma Rainey's Black Bottom", and "Cry, the Beloved Country". He also appeared with the Chicago Shakespeare Theatre, Court Theatre, Victory Gardens Theater, Northlight Theatre, the Royal Shakespeare Company in London, the Abbey Theatre in Dublin, and Thalia Theatre in Germany. He was featured on Broadway in the 1987 production of "Death and the King's Horseman". Perry also appeared in such films as "The Big Score" (1983), "Running Scared" (1986), "The Color of

Money" (1986), "A Rage in Harlem" (1991), "Cold Justice" (1991), "Dunston Checks In" (1996), "Liar Liar" (1997), "Live

Liza" (2002), "Roll Bounce" (2005), "The Trouble with Dee Dee" (2005), "The Promotion" (2008), "The Express" (2008), "The Last Rites of Joe May" (2011), and "Animator" (2018). He was seen on television in episodes of "T.J. Hooker", "Lady Blue", "Courthouse", "ER", "Star Trek: Deep Space Nine" as Admiral Charles Whatley in the 1996 episode "Rapture", "Turks", "The Chi", "Chicago P.D.", and "Proven Innocent". His other television credits include the tele-films "Unnatural Causes" (1986), "Howard Beach: Making the Case for Murder" (1989), "Memphis" (1992), and "In the Shadow of a Killer" (1992). Perry was predeceased by his wife, Alice Carol, in 2017 and daughter, Alison, in 2018. He is survived by daughters Mary and Jaisy.

Perry, Matthew

Actor Matthew Perry, who starred as Chandler Bing in the hit comedy series "Friends" from 1994 to 2004, was found dead in the hot tub at his home in Pacific Palisades, California, on October 28, 2023. An autopsy revealed he died from the

acute effects of the anesthetic ketamine, with coronary artery disease and buprenorphine as contributing factors. He was 54. Perry was born in Williamstown, Massachusetts, on August 19, 1969. He was the son of actor John Bennett Perry and Canadian journalist Suzanne Marie Morrison, who served as press secretary to Prime Minister Pierre Trudeau. His parents divorced when he was a child, and he was largely raised with his mother in Canada. He became a leading junior tennis player in his teens. He moved to Los Angeles to live with his father in 1983 where he studied acting at the Buckley School during high school. He also trained in improv and comedy at the L.A. Connection. He appeared in episodes of "240-Robert" in a bit role with his father, "Charles in Charge", "Silver Spoons", "The Tracey Ullman Show", "Just the Ten of Us", "Highway to Heaven", and "Empty Nest". He starred as Chazz Russell in the Fox sitcom "Second Chance" (aka "Boys Will Be Boys") from 1987 to 1988. He was featured as Sandy, Carol Seaver's boyfriend who dies from injuries received in a drunk driving accident, in three episodes of "Growing Pains" in 1989. Perry was featured as Billy Kells, the younger brother of Valerie Bertinelli's character, on the short-lived CBS comedy series "Sydney" in 1990. He was also featured in episodes of "Who's the Boss?", "Beverly Hills, 90210", "Dream On", and "The John Larroquette Show", and the tele-films "Morning Maggie"

(1987), "Dance 'Til Dawn" (1988), "Call Me Anna" (1990) as Desi Arnaz, Jr., "Deadly Relations" (1993), "Parallel Lives" (1994), and the unsold science fiction comedy pilot "L.A.X. 2194" (1994). He starred as Matt Bailey in the short-lived ABC comedy series "Home Free" in 1993. Perry had much greater success with his subsequent series, starring as Chandler Bing in the ensemble comedy series "Friends" from 1994 until 2004. He and his co-stars, Jennifer Aniston, Courteney Cox, Lisa Kudrow, Matt LeBlanc, and David Schwimmer, initially received $22,500 per episode when the series began and were earning $1 million per episode by the time the series ended. Perry received an Emmy Award nomination for his performance in 2002. He had a cameo role as Chandler in an episode of "Caroline in the City" and provided a cameo voice role in the animated series "The Simpsons" in 2001. He was featured as Joe Quincy on several episodes of "The West Wing" and earned Emmy nominations for his guest role in 2003 and 2004. He appeared in episodes of such series as "Ally McBeal", "Scrubs" also directing an episode, "Childrens Hospital", Cougar Town", and "Playhouse Presents". He received another Emmy nomination for starring in the title role of the 2006 tele-film "The Ron Clark Story". He starred as Matt Albie in Aaron Sorkin's "Studio 60 on the Sunset Strip" from 2006 to 2007 and was also seen in the 2008 tele-film "The End of Steve", also serving as co-creator and executive producer. He was creator and executive producer for the short-lived series "Mr. Sunshine" in 2011 and starred in the role of Ben Donovan. He appeared in the recurring role of smarmy politician Mike Kresteva on the drama series "The Good Wife" from 2012 to 2013 and the sequel series "The Good Fight" in 2017. He starred as sportscaster Ryan King in the series "Go On" from 2012 to 2013. He was Tyler Bishop in a pair of episodes of "Web Therapy" starring Lisa Kudrow in 2015. He was executive producer and writer of the remake of "The Odd Couple" series from 2015 to 2017 and co-starred in the role of Oscar Madison. He was featured as Ted Kennedy in the 2017 mini-series "The Kennedys After Camelot". Perry was also seen on the talk and variety shows "Comic Relief", "Saturday Night Live" hosting in 1997, "Jerry Lewis MDA Labor Day Telethon", "The Rosie O'Donnell Show", "Last Call with Carson Daly", "Punk'd", "The Oprah Winfrey Show", "Celebrity Poker Showdown", "The Reichen Show", "Late Night with Conan O'Brien", "Up Close with Carrie Keagan", "Late Night with Jimmy Fallon", "Celebrity Liar", "The Daily Show", "The Tonight Show with Jay Leno", "Hollywood Game Night", "Piers Morgan Live", "Late Night with David Letterman", "Kevin Pollak's Chat Show", "The Late Late Show with Craig Ferguson", "The Late Late Show with James Corden", "Conan", "The Graham Norton Show", "Late Night with Seth Meyers", "The Ellen DeGeneres Show", "Jimmy Kimmel Live!", "Ca$h Cab", "The Talk", "Live with Kelly and Mark", "The Tonight Show Starring Jimmy Fallon", and "Watch What Happens Live with Andy Cohen". He was a voice performer as Benny in the 2010 video game "Fallout: New Vegas". He was an executive producer for the 2021 special "Friends: The Reunion", sharing an Emmy nomination for Outstanding Variety Special. Perry was also seen in the films

"A Night in the Life of Jimmy Reardon" (1988), "She's Out of Control" (1989), "Getting In" (1994), "Fools Rush In" (1997), the western comedy "Almost Heroes" (1998) with Chris Farley in his final role, "Three to Tango" (1999), "The Whole Nine Yards" (2000) as Oz Oseransky opposite Bruce Willis as an ex-con in witness protection, "The Kid" (2000), "Serving Sara" (2002) opposite Elizabeth Hurley, "The Whole Ten Yards" (2004) reprising his role as Oz, "Numb" (2007) also serving as executive producer, "Birds of America" (2008), and "17 Again" (2009). He starred on stage in a production of David Mamet's "Sexual Perversity in Chicago" in 2003. He wrote and starred in the play "The End of Longing" in 2016 and reprised the role in an Off-Broadway production in 2017. His autobiography, "Friends, Lovers, and the Big Terrible Thing", was published in 2022. He revealed that he became an alcoholic in his early teens. He became addicted to pain medication following a jet-ski accident in 1997 and attended rehab on several occasions. He suffered from numerous health issues caused by his addictions including alcohol-induced pancreatitis and gastrointestinal perforation. Perry never married but had relationships with such stars as Yasmine Bleeth, Julia Roberts, Lizzy Caplan, and literary manager Molly Hurwitz, who was his fiancee from 2020 to 2021.

Pesch, Jean-Louis

French cartoonist Jean-Louis Pesch died in Chateauneuf-sur-Sarthe, France on May 17, 2023. He was 94. He was born Jean-Louis Poisson in Paris, France, on June 29,  1928. His parents were both arts and he began drawing from an early age. He studied at L'Ecole des Arts Appliques in Paris. He served in the French Navy for several years after World War II. He began working in animation after his discharge and began an advertising studio in 1950. He worked on various children's magazines from the mid-1950s including "Capucine", "Mireille", "Bernadette", "Ames Vaillantes", "Le Pelerin", and "Tintin". He created the "Pinpinville" series and took over "Sylvain et Sylvette" after the death o Maurice Cuvillier in 1956. He continued to work on the fairy tale series through the early 2000s. He and Henriette Robitaillie created the "Bec-en-Fer" series for "Le Pelerin" in 1964 and resumed working on the comic in the 1980s. Pesch also worked on the "Les Pieds Nickeles" series and "Les Primeurs" in the 1980s. He continued to work on comics and advertising projects until his death.

Peterson, Melinda

Actress Melinda Peterson died of cardiac arrest in Benedict Canyon, California, on July 31, 2023. She was 73. Peterson was born in Hartford, Connecticut, on August 20, 1949. She graduated from Hofstra University where she studied drama. She appeared on television in the role of nurse Pat Holland Dixon on the soap opera "As the World Turns"

from 1975 to 1977. She was also seen in episodes of "The Young and the Restless", "MacGyver", "The Twilight Zone", "Cagney & Lacey", "The Bronx Zoo", "Santa Barbara", and "JAG". Her other television credits include the tele-films "Terror Out of the Sky" (1978), "A Last Cry for Help" (1979), "Police Story: Confessions of a Lady Cop" (1980), "All God's Children" (1980), "Emergency Room" (1983), "Voices Within: The Lives of Truddi Chase" (1990), and the animated "The Town Santa Forgot" (1993). She was also a voice actress for various radio plays. Peterson was featured in the films "The Independent" (2000), "Alex in Wonder" (2001), the short "Barrier Device" (2002), "The Selling" (2011), "I'm Harry Clark" (2013), "Window of Opportunity" (2015), and "Love Addict" (2016). She was a founding member of the Antaeus Theater Company in Glendale, California, from 1991. Peterson married comedian Phil Proctor of the comedy troupe Firesign Theatre in 1992 and he survives her. She is also survived by their daughter, Kristin.

Peterson, Nan

Actress Nan Peterson, who was featured in Robert Clarke's 1958 science fiction film "The Hideous Sun Demon",

died in Corona del Mar, California, on August 15, 2023. She was 92. Peterson was born in Minneapolis, Minnesota, on July 7, 1931. She made her film debut as Trudy Osborne in the 1958 cult science fiction film "The Hideous Sun Demon", which was produced, directed, written, and starred Robert Clarke. She starred in the 1959 crime drama "The Louisiana Hussy" and appeared in the films "Girls Town" (1959) and "Shotgun Wedding" (1963). Peterson was seen frequently on television from the late 1950s through the early 1960s. She appeared in episodes of "Zane Grey Theatre", "The Texan", "Rawhide", "Lawman", "Men into Space", "Black Saddle', "Gunsmoke", "Perry Mason", "Dante", "Lock Up", "Sea Hunt", "The Dick Powell Theatre", "Frontier Circus", "Don't Call Me Charlie", "The Untouchables", and "The Twilight Zone" in small roles in four episodes. She largely retired from the screen in the early 1960s. She was interviewed by Tom Weaver in his 2010 book "A Sci-Fi Swarm and Horror Horde" and wrote the afterword for Weaver's "Scripts from the Crypt: The Hideous Sun Demon" (2011). Peterson was married to James Edwin Moore from 1955 until their divorce 1958. She was married to Dr. James Clifford Doyle from 1963 until his death in 2008 and is survived by their son.

Piaz, Gianna

Italian actress Gianna Piaz died in Rome, Italy, on January 27, 2023. She was 99. Piaz was born in Bologna, Italy,

on December 9, 1923. She began her career on stage in the 1940s and worked with Vittorio Gassman. She acted in radio dramas from the early 1950s. She was seen in several films including "Solo per te Lucia" (1952), "Il Seduttore" (1954), the horror film "Atom Age Vampire" (1960) as a nurse, "Regalo di Natale" (1986), and "500!" (2001). Piaz appeared on television in productions of "La Cittadella" (1964), "Quinta Colonna" (1966), "La Felicita Domestica" (1966), "L'Affare Kubinsky" (1967), "Brodo di Pollo con l'Orzo" (1969), "Il Mulino del Po" (1971), "Il Crogiuolo" (1971), "Marty" (1971), "Un Affare Privato" (1972), "Qui Squadra Mobile" (1978), "E.S.P." (1973), "Dov'e Anna?" (1976), "La Paga del Sabato" (1977), "L'Esercito di Scipione" (1977), "Zio Vanja" (1979), "Quattro Grandi Giornalisti" (1980), "La Vigna di Uve Nere" (1984), "Affari di Famiglia" (1986), and "Lapin Lapin" (1997). Her other television credits include episodes of "Nero Wolfe", "Aeroporto Internazionale", and "Detective Montalbano". Piaz worked frequently as a voice dubber for films. She made her final stage appearance in a production of "La Nemica" in 2003.

Pignatelli, Micaela

Italian actress Micaela Pignatelli Cendali died in Rome, Italy, on October 30, 2023. She was 78. Pignatelli was born in Naples, Italy, on March 11, 1945. She was the daughter

of General Guido Cendali and Princess Andreina Pignatelli. She appeared frequently in films from the mid-1960s with such credits as "Our Agent Tiger" (1965), "Dio, Come ti Amo!" (1966), "Lo Scandalo" (1966), the superhero action films "Flashman" (1967) and "Goldface, the Fantastic Superman" (1967), the spaghetti western "Piluk, the Timid One" (1968), Ruggero Deodato's jungle action film "Gungala, the Black Panther Girl" (1968), "Candy" (1968), "Gangsters' Law" (1969), "Amarsi Male" (1969), "May Morning" (1970), "The Last Day of the War" (1970), "Spacco Alla Mafia" (1970), "La Ragazza Dalle Mani di Corallo" (1971), "Night of the Flowers" (1972), "What Have They Done to Your Daughters?" (1974), "Farfallon" (1974), "La Vita Nova" (1974), "I Giorni Della Chimera" (1975), "Perche Si Uccidono (La Merde)" (1976), "Um Uomo da Nulla" (1977), "Maledetti vi Amero" (1980), "Great White" (aka "The Last Shark") (1981) opposite James Franciscus and Vic Morrow in a film that was pulled from U.S. release after Universal Pictures won an injunction due to its similarities to "Jaws", "Io So Che Tu Sai Che Io So" (1982), "Private Affairs" (1988), Michael Soavi's horror film "The Church" (1989), "C'era un Castello Con 40 Cani" (1900),

"Gangsters" (1992), and Dario Argento's thriller "The Card Player" (2003) as Professor Terzi. She was seen on television in productions of "Sotto il Placido Don" (1974), "Circuito Chiuso" (1978), "Colpo di Grazia alla Sezione III" (1981), "Storia di Anna" (1981), "Delitto di Stato" (1982), "La Sconosciuta" (1982), "Il Diavolo al Pontelungo" (1982), "Quer Pasticciaccio Brutto de Via Merulana" (1983), "Festa di Capodanno" (1988), and "Rita da Cascia" (2004). She also appeared in episodes of "Luigi Ganna Detective", "Turno di Notte", "The Teacher", and "Verdetto Finale". Pignatelli also provided the Italian dubbing voice for Jamie Lee Curtis in "Halloween", Catherine Bach in "The Dukes of Hazzard", and Daryl Hannah in "Wall Street". She was married and divorced from actor Flavio Bucci and is survived by their two sons.

Pilgrim, Mark

South African television host Mark Pilgrim died of cancer in Johannesburg, South Africa, on March 5, 2023. He

was 53. Pilgrim was born in Kent, England, on September 20, 1969. He came to South Africa at an early age and graduated high school in 1986. He studied industrial psychology and business economics at Wits University and worked as a consumer researcher for nearly a decade. He aspired for a career in radio and began hosting a weekend late-night program in 1995. He became a popular radio personality and disc jockey. He was also working in television by the end of the decade. He was host of the first two seasons of "Big Brother South Africa" from 2001 to 2002 and "Big Brother Africa" in 2003. His other television credits include "Retail Therapy" (2002-2005), "Face 2 Face" (2004), "Sex Etc." (2005), and "Power of 10" (2008). Pilgrim was originally diagnosed with testicular cancer in 1988 which went into remission following chemotherapy. He suffered a major heart attack in 2008 and was diagnosed with stage 4 lung cancer in 2022. Pilgrim was married to Nicole Torres from 2007 until their divorce in 2020 and is survived by their two daughters. He married Adrienne Watkins in 2022 and she also survives him.

Pinner, Laura

Actress and model Laura Pinner died of complications

from amyotrophic lateral sclerosis (ALS) at her home in Lakeland, Florida, on July 7, 2023. She was 53. Pinner was born in Lakeland on November 30, 1969. She learned to dance at an early age and was a cheerleader in high school. She competed in two Miss Florida pageants. She graduated from the University of Florida in 1992 and moves to Los Angeles to pursue an acting career. She worked as a

model and was a product spokesperson for Subaru at auto shows. She was also a model with Home Shopping Network. She was featured in the 2004 film "Dog Gone Love". She also appeared on television in a 2003 episode of "Still Standing" and the 2017 tele-film "A Woman Deceived".

Pinsent, Gordon

Canadian actor Gordon Pinsent, who was featured in the films "Colossus: The Forbin Project" and "Blacula", died of complications from a cerebral hemorrhage at a hospital in Toronto, Ontario, Canada, on February 25, 2023. He was 92.

Pinsent was born in Grand Falls, Newfoundland, Canada, on July 12, 1930. He began performing on stage in his teens in the late 1940s. He served in the Royal Canadian Army for four years in the early 1950s. He appeared frequently on stage after his discharge from the Royal Manitoba Theatre Centre and at the Stratford Festival. He also performed in radio dramas and in television productions of "The Man at the Window" (1957), "The Bird in a Gilded Cage" (1958), "The Man Born to Be King" (1961), "The Long Knight" (1961), "Cyrano De Bergerac" (1962), "A Very Close Family" (1964), "Twelfth Night" (1964), "Quarantined" (1970), "Invitation to a March" (1972), "Incident on a Dark Street" (1973), "Horse Latitudes" (1975), "A Gift to Last" (1976), "The Suicide's Wife" (1979), "Escape from Iran: The Canadian Caper" (1981) as Ambassador Ken Taylor, "The Life and Times of Edwin Alonzo Boyd" (1982) in the title role, "A Case of Libel" (1983), "Sam Hughes' War" (1984), "And Miles to Go" (1985), "In the Eyes of a Stranger" (1992),. "Bonds of Love" (1993), "A Vow to Kill" (1995), "Les Amants de Riviere Rouge" (1996), "A Holiday for Love" (1996), "Win, Again!" (1999), "Blind Terror" (2001), "Hemingway vs. Callaghan" (2003) as Morley Callaghan, "Fallen Angel" (2003), "Ambulance Girl" (2005), "Heyday!" (2006), "Yours, Al" (2006), "The Pillars of the Earth" (2010), "Sunshine Sketches of a Little Town" (2012), and the animated "Pirate's Passage" (2015) as the voice of Harry Freelove. His television credits also include episodes of "The Unforeseen", "Startime", "First Person", "Encounter", "Summer Circuit", "Playdate", "Scarlett Hill", "Quest", "The Forest Rangers" as Sergeant Scott from 1963 to 1965, "The Serial" as Quentin Durgens in 1965, "Seaway", "Festival", "Quentin Durgens, M.P." reprising his role as Durgens in 1968, "It Takes a Thief", "Adventures in Rainbow Country", "The Young Lawyers", "Dan August", "Corwin", "Hogan's Heroes", "Stone", "Banacek", "Cannon", "Marcus Welby, M.D.", "The Play's the Thing", "The Collaborators", "The Beachcombers", "A Gift to Last", "People Talking Back", "For the Record", "Seeing Things", "American Playhouse", "Danger Bay", "Friday the 13th: The Series", the animated "Babar" as the voice of King Babar from 1989 to 1991, "The Hidden Room", "The Ray Bradbury Theater", "Beyond Reality", "Counterstrike",

"E.N.G.", "Street Legal" in the recurring role of Harold Vickers from 1989 to 1993, "Secret Service", "The Red Green Show" as Hap Shaughnessy from 1991 to 2004, "Avonlea", "Kung Fu: The Legend Continues", "Lonesome Dove: The Series", "The Outer Limits", "Due South" as Robert Fraser, Sr. from 1994 to 1999, "Relic Hunter", "Power Play" as Duff McArdle from 1998 to 2000, "Wind at My Back" in the recurring role of Leo McGinty from 1997 to 2000, "Mentors", "Blue Murder", "Just Cause", "The Industry", "Bury the Lead", "H2O", "Puppets Who Kill", "Angela's Eyes", "Corner Gas", "The Listener", "The Ron James Show", "Republic of Doyle" in the recurring role of Maurice Becker from 2010 to 2013, "Satisfaction", the animated "Babar and the Adventures of Badou" reprising his role as King Babar from 2010 to 2013, "Reel East Coast", "The Detour", and "Private Eyes". Pinsent appeared frequently in films with roles in "Lydia" (1964), "Affair with a Killer" (1966), "The Thomas Crown Affair" (1968), "Colossus: The Forbin Project" (1970) as the President, "Chandler" (1971), "The Rowydman" (1972), the horror film "Blacula" (1972) as Lt. Jack Peters, "Newman's Law" (1974), "Only God Knows" (1974), "The Heatwave Lasted Four Days" (1975), "Who Has Seen the Wind" (1977), "Draga Kisfiam!" (1978), "Klondike Fever" (1979), "Silence of the North" (1981), "John and the Missus" (1987), "Blood Clan" (1990), "Pale Saints" (1997), "The Shipping News" (2001), "Nothing" (2003), "The Confessor" (2004), "Saint Ralph" (2004), "Away from Her" (2006), "Eating Buccaneers" (2008), "Sex After Kids" (2013), "The Grand Seduction" (2013), "Big News from Grand Rock" (2014), and "Two Lovers and a Bear" (2016). He was a voice performer in the animated films "Babar: The Movie" (1989) as the voice of King Babar, "Pippi Longstocking" (1997), "The Old Man and the Sea" (1999), and "The Spine" (2009). Pinsent directed the films "Once" (1981) and "John and the Missus" (1987), and the tele-films "A Far Cry from Home" (1981), "Two Men" (1988), and "Heyday!" (2006). He also scripted television productions of "A Gift to Last" (1976), "Up at Ours" (1979), "A Gift to Last" (1978), "And Miles to Go" (1985), "Win, Again!" (1999), and "Heyday!" (2006). Pinsent hosted the CBC Radio One documentary series "The Late Show" from 2008 to 2011. His memoir, "By the Way", was published in 1992 and the sequel, "Next", was released in 2012. He was the subject of the 2016 documentary "The River of My Dreams". Pinsent was married to actress Charmion King from 1962 until her death in 2007. He is survived by their daughter, actress Leah Pinsent. He is also survived by two children, actor Barry Kennedy and Beverly Kennedy, from a previous marriage to Irene Reid.

Piro, Sal

Sal Piro, the founder and president of "The Rocky Horror Picture Show" Fan Club who helped turn the film into an interactive cult phenomenon, died of an esophageal aneurysm at his home in Manhattan, New York, on January 22, 2023. He was 71. Piro was born in Jersey City, New Jersey, on June 29, 1950. He attended Seton Hall University in South Orange, New Jersey, but left without receiving a degree. He later taught theology and was a theater director in New Jersey.

"The Rocky Horror Picture Show" opened in 1975 with poor reviews. It soon became a popular midnight movie at the Waverly Theater in Greenwich Village. Piro was a regular member of the audience that frequently shouted responses to much of the film's dialogue. He soon helped create a floor show among the audience members that became an elaborate ritual during the showings. He was founder and president of The Rocky Horror Picture Show Fan Club from 1977 until his death. Piro appeared as a Rocky Horror M.C. in the 1980 film "Fame" and was seen in a cameo role as a guy on a payphone in the "Rocky Horror" semi-sequel "Shock Treatment" in 1981. He had small roles in the films "My X-Girlfriend's Wedding Reception" (1999) and "Four Deadly Reasons" (2002). He was also seen in the tele-film "Hey Paisan!" (2001) and an episode of "Third Watch". He was featured as a photographer in the 2016 tele-film "The Rocky Horror Picture Show: Let's Do the Time Warp Again". Piro wrote a memoir about his experience with fandom, "Creatures of the Night", in 1990.

Plank, Leo

German stuntman Leo Plank died of injuries from an accident in Berlin, Germany, on May 18, 2023. He was 57. Plank was born in Germany in 1966. He began working in films

in the early 1990s as a stunt man and driver. He was involved with such films as "Attention, Papa Arrives!" (1991), "No More Mr. Nice Guy" (1993), "Deadly Maria" (1993), "The Passion of Darkly Noon" (1994), "Jailbirds" (1996), "Obsession" (1997), "Winter Sleepers" (1997), "Cascadeur" (1998), "Run Lola Run" (1998), "Love Scenes from Planet Earth" (1998), "Anatomy 2" (2003), "Autobahnraser" (2004), "V for Vendetta" (2005), "Treasure Island" (2007), "Auf dem Vulkan" (2007), "Der Seewolf" (2008), "Speed Racer" (2008), "Inglorious Basterds" (2009), "Ninja Assassin" (2009), "Cloud Atlas" (2012), "Hansel & Gretel: Witch Hunters" (2013), "Alien Rising" (2013), "The Book Thief" (2013), "The Innocents" (2013), "The Voices" (2014), "The Monuments Men" (2014), "Dracula Untold" (2014), "Head Full of Honey" (2014), "The Hunger Games: Mockingjay - Part 1" (2014), "Jupiter Ascending" (2015), "Hitman: Agent 47" (2015), "Bridge of Spies" (2015), "The Hunger Games: Mockingjay - Part 2" (2015), "Point Break" (2015), "Captain America: Civil War" (2016), "A Cure for Wellness" (2016), "Jason Bourne" (2016), "Berlin Syndrome" (2017), "War Machine" (2017), "Atomic Blonde" (2017), "Spider-Man: Homecoming" (2017), "Out of Control" (2017), "Don't. Get.

Out!" (2018), "Never Look Away" (2018), "The Girl in the Spider's Web" (2018), "Charlie's Angels" (2019), "Extraction" (2020), "Cherry" (2021), "Without Remorse" (2021), "The Matrix Resurrections" (2021), "Tar" (2022), "All Quiet on the Western Front" (2022), "John Wick: Chapter 4" (2023), "Blood & Gold" (2023), "Retribution" (2023), and "The Expendables 4" (2023). Plank worked on such television series as "Doppelter Einsatz", "Homeland", "Berlin Station", "Dark", and "Counterpart".

Poffo, Lanny

Professional wrestler Lanny Poffo, who was known in the ring as Leaping Lanny and the Genius, died of heart failure in New York City on February 2, 2023. He was 68. Poffo was born in Calgary, Alberta, Canada, on December 28, 1954. He was the son of professional wrestler Angelo Poffo and younger brother of Randy Poffo, who achieved fame in the wrestling ring as the Macho Man Randy Savage. Lanny began his career with the All-South Wrestling Alliance in Atlanta, Georgia, in April of 1974. He remained with the promotion for several months and teamed with his father. They began working at Big Time Wrestling, a National Wrestling Alliance (NWA) promotion out of Detroit. They feuded with the team of Bobo Brazil and Fred Curry and captured the NWA World Tag Team Championship in 1974. They lost the belts the following year. Lanny began competing in singles matches and lost to NWA World Heavyweight Champion Terry Funk in May of 1976. He soon joined Jim Crockett's Mid Atlantic Championship Wrestling where he began teaming with his brother Randy as the Poffo Brothers. He resumed singles competition after Randy left the promotion in early 1977. He challenged Harley Race for the NWA championship in February of 1978 in a bout that ended in a draw. Lanny moved to Atlantic Grand Prix Wrestling two months later where he became the promotion's first International Heavyweight Champion. He began feuding with his brother, now billed as Randy Savage, and exchanged the championship several times. He competed with Pacific Northwest Wrestling for several months. He joined his father's new independent promotion International Championship Wrestling (ICW) in the summer of 1979 where he was frequently billed as Leaping Lanny. He and brother Randy frequently battled each other for the ICW championship until the promotion folded in 1984. He also held the ICW U.S. Tag Team Championship several times with partner George Weingeroff. Lanny competed with Bill Watt's Mid South Wrestling, where he teamed with Rick Rude in a feud against the Midnight Express. He also battled Buddy Landell in singles competition. He joined the Continental Wrestling Association (CWA) in Memphis in June of 1984 where he teamed with brother Randy against the Rock 'n' Roll Express. They also feuded with Eddie Gilbert and Tommy Rich and the Fabulous

Ones. Randy signed with the World Wrestling Federation (WWF/now WWE) in June of 1985 and Lanny soon followed him. The relationship between the brothers was never acknowledged by the WWF. Lanny would read a poem before his matches and throw frisbees into the crowd of spectators. He displayed high-flying athleticism with such moves as the "leaping backflip" though usually wrestled on the undercard. He turned heel in the promotion in March of 1989, insulting the crowds and dubbing himself the Genius while wearing a collegiate cap and gown. He feuded with Koko B. Ware and was consultant and occasional partner for Curt 'Mr. Perfect' Hennig. He and Hennig challenged Hulk Hogan in tag matches with various partners and he feuded with Brutus 'the Barber' Beefcake, losing much of his hair in a match. He continued to compete against such stars as Greg Valentine, Jim Duggan, and Bret Hart. He began managing Mike Enos and Wayne Bloom, who wrestled in the WWF as the Beverly Brothers, in September of 1991. He appeared with them in six-man matches and remained their manager until leaving the WWF in December of 1992. He wrestled for various independent promotions before signing with World Championship Wrestling (WCW) in 1995, though he was seldom used during his five years under contract. He made occasional returns to the ring over the next decade. His brother died in 2011 and Lanny represented him when he was inducted into the WWE Hall of Fame in 2015. He was author of poetry book "Leaping Lanny: Wrestling with Rhyme" in 1988 and the 2004 anti-smoking children's book "Limericks from the Heart (and Lungs!)". Poffo appeared in various wrestling documentaries and was featured in the low-budget horror films "Curse of the Wolf" (2006) and "Ninja: Prophecy of Death" (2011). He was featured in an episode of the Investigation Discovery network's "I (Almost) Got Away with It" in 2013. His biographical comic book, "The Genius Lanny Poffo", was released by Squared Circle Comics in 2018. He was host of the weekly podcast "The Genius Cast with Lanny Poffo" from 2018 to 2019. He subsequently moved to Ecuador but continued to return to the United States to attended wrestling conventions.

Pollack, Rachel

Science fiction and comic book writer Rachel Pollack died of non-Hodgkin lymphoma in Rhinebeck, New York, on April 7, 2023. She was 77. She was born Richard A. Pollack in New York City on August 17, 1945. She graduated from New York University and received a master's degree in English from Claremont Graduate University. Her first short story, "Pandora's Bust", was published in the "New Worlds" anthology in 1971. She came out as a transgender and lesbian in 1971 and underwent transition surgery in the Netherlands five years later. She continued writing fiction and became a leading authority on tarot cards. Her guide to the history and interpretation of tarot, "Seventy-Eight Degrees of Wisdom", was published in two parts in the early 1980s. She wrote 1985's "Salvador Dali's Tarot", a guidebook to the artist's paintings. She met author Neil Gaiman in 1990 when he sought her guidance about tarot reading for a comic book he was writing. She wrote the comic book series "Doom Patrol" from 1993 to 1995, taking over from Grant Morrison. She created DC's first transgender superhero, Kate 'Coagula' Godwin, who had the power to dissolve things with one hand and coagulate them with the other, during her run on the series. She joined with Gaiman and artist Dave McKean to create the "Vertigo Tarot", a guidebook and card set featuring mystical characters from DC Comics, in 1995. Pollack's other work in comics include the 1995 mini-series "Time Breakers" from DC's Helix imprint in 1995, "New Gods" from 1995 to 1996, and "Vertigo Visions: Tomahawk" in 1998. She continued to write numerous science fiction and fantasy short fiction. She also wrote the novels "Golden Vanity" (1980), "Alqua Dreams" (1987), "Unquentionable Fire" (198), "Temporary Agency" (1994), "Godmother Night" (1996) which earned her the World Fantasy Award for Best Novel, "A Secret Woman" (2002), "The Child Eater" (2015), and "The Fissure King: A Novel in Five Stories" (2017). Pollack is survived by her wife, Zoe Matoff.

Porter, Beth

American-British actress Beth Porter died in England on August 1, 2023. She was 81. Porter was born in New York City on May 23, 1942. She began performing on stage with a

touring company before her teens and studied at the Stratford Connecticut Shakespeare Festival and the American Theatre Wing. She continued her studies as Bard College, New York University, and Hunter College at the City University of New York. She performed on stage in the 1961 production of Jules Romains' "Donogoo" at the Greenwich Mews Theatre. She joined the original New York LaMaMa Troupe in 1966 and was featured in Tom O'Horgan's experimental satire "Futz!". She reprised the role of Marjorie Satz in the 1969 film version. Porter was also seen in such films as Andy Milligan's "The Naked Witch" (1967), "Me and My Brother" (1968), "The Great Gatsby" (1974), and Woody Allen's "Love and Death" (1975). She was also featured on television in episodes of "Baretta" and "Kojak". Porter largely settled in England in the mid-1970s and became a citizen in 2014. Her other film credits include "Dick Deadeye, or Duty Done" (1975), "Whose Child Am I?" (1976), the animated "Lucky Luke: Ballad of the Daltons" (1978) as the English language voice of Miss Worthlesspenny, "What's Up Superdoc!" (1978), "On a Paving Stone Mounted" (1978), "Superman II" (1980), "Reds" (1981), and "Yentl" (1983). Porter was also seen on television in episodes of "Full House", "Thirty-Minutes Theatre", "Armchair Theatre", "Mousey", "Seven Faces of Woman", "Rock Follies of '77" as Kitty

Schreiber in 1977, "Crown Court", "The Deep Concern" and Carrie Stone in 1979, "Tales of the Unexpected" (1980), "ITV Playhouse", "The Hitchhiker's Guide to the Galaxy", "Floodtide", "Square Deal" as Hannah in 1988, and "Ruth Rendell Mysteries". She was the voice of Jadis, the White Witch, in the animated television production of "The Lion, the Witch & the Wardrobe" (1979) and appeared in productions of "Blue Money" (1985), "Queen of Hearts" (1985), "The Men's Room" (1991), and "Pleasure" (1994). She was featured as the voice of the wife on Roger Waters' 1984 album "The Pros and Cons of Hitch Hiking". She worked as a script editor on the 1986 mini-series "Fighting Back", and was producer of BBC Television's "The Husband, the Wife and the Stranger" (1986) and Channel 4's "Unusual Ground Floor Conversion" (1989). Porter also worked as a film critic for "Film Journal International" from 1988 to 1998. She subsequently served as senior web producer for Online Magic, contributing to various web-related magazines. Her book, "The Net Effect", was published in 2002. She published a collection of short fiction, "Resident Aliens", in 2013, and a collection of her scripts, "Drama Queen", in 2014. Her autobiography, "Walking on my Hands: How I Learned to Take Responsibility for My Life with the Help of Woody Allen, Barbra Streisand, Greta Garbo, Harvey Milk, Idi Amin, Guy The Gorilla, and Frank Sinatra, Among Others", was published in 2014. She also wrote the collection "Settling Beyond the Pale" (2016), the fantasy/horror novella "Feeding the Twins" (2018), the novels "ScreenSaver!" (2018) and "Becca's Providing" (2019), and the short story collections "Painted Ladies" (2019) and "Locks: A Quartet of Short Fiction" (2021). Porter was married to Peter Reid from 1969 until the separation in 1974. She was romantically involved with director Jack Clayton from 1974 to 1979 and with Kerry Lee Crabbe from 1979 to 1985.

Povey, Jon

British drummer and keyboardist Jon Povey, who played with the rock band Pretty Things, died of leukemia in

Spain on May 9, 2023. He was 80. Povey was born in London, England, on August 20, 1942. He was raised in Dartford, Kent, and began playing drums in the rhythm and blues band Bern Elliott and the Bluecaps in the early 1960s. They became known as Bern Elliott and the Fenmen in 1961 and signed with Decca Records. They recorded a hit cover of "Money (That's What I Want)" in 1963. Povey and his three remaining bandmates became the Fenmen when Elliott left the band in early 1964. He and Wally Waller left the Fenmen to join the band Pretty Things in 1967. He switched to keyboard with the group and was heard on their third album "Emotions" in 1967. He appeared with them in the 1969 film "What's Good for the Goose". He briefly left Pretty Things in 1971 but soon returned until 1976. He was with the band from 1978 to 1981, when they disbanded after appearing in the horror anthology film "The Monster Club". He again reunited with Pretty Things from 1994 to 2007. He was featured on the albums "S.F. Sorrow" (1968), "Parachute" (1970), "Freeway Madness" (1972), "Silk Torpedo" (1974), "Savage Eye" (1976), "Cross Talk" (1980), and "Balboa Island" (2007). He also recorded several solo albums. Povey moved to Spain later in life and was working on an autobiography, "Dartford Boys", at the time of his death.

Powell, Dinny

British stuntman and actor Dinny Powell, who worked on numerous films for the James Bond franchise, died in England on June 6, 2023. He was 90. He was born in London, England, on July 27, 1932. His older brother, Nosher Powell,

also worked as a stuntman and the brothers were both professional boxers. Dinny followed him into the film business in the late 1950s. He performed stunts and appeared in small roles in numerous films including "Dunkirk" (1958), "Dr. No" (1962), "From Russia with Love" (1963), "The Fall of the Roman Empire" (1965), "Those Magnificent Men in Their Flying Machines" (1965), "Town Tamer" (1965), "Clarence, the Cross-Eyed Lion" (1965), "The Sons of Katie Elder" (1965), "The Singing Nun" (1966), "Casino Royale" (1967), "You Only Live Twice" (1967), "Carry on Up the Khyber" (1968), "Great Catherine" (1968), "The Magic Christian" (1969), "Those Daring Young Men in Their Jaunty Jalopies" (1969), "On Her Majesty's Secret Service" (1969), "You Can't Win 'Em All" (1970), "The Blood on Satan's Claw" (1971), "1,000 Convicts and a Woman" (1971), "Steptoe & Son" (1972), "Innocent Bystanders" (1972), "Get Charlie Tully" (1972), "The MacKintosh Man" (1973), "Brannigan" (1975), "Side by Side" (1975), "Never Too Young to Rock" (1976), "The Spy Who Loved Me" (1976), "The Pink Panther Strikes Again" (1976), "Revenge of the Pink Panther" (1978), "the Boys from Brazil" (1978), "The Golden Lady" (1979), "Moonraker" (1979), "North Sea Hijack" (aka "ffolkes") (1980), "Superman II" (1980), "Victor/Victoria" (1982), "Krull" (1983), "Curse of the Pink Panther" (1983), "Never Say Never Again" (1983), "Space Riders" (1984), "Sword of the Valiant" (1984), "Lassiter" (1984), "The Company of Wolves" (1984), "Brazil" (1985), "A View to a Kill" (1985), "Lifeforce" (1985), "The Bride" (1985), "Revolution" (1985), "Biggles: Adventures in Time" (1986), "Sky Bandits" (1986), "Willow" (1988), "The Adventures of Baron Munchausen" (1988), "Bullseye!" (1990), "Robin Hood: Prince of Thieves" (1991), "The Three Musketeers" (1993), "First Knight" (1995), "GoldenEye" (1995), "Mission: Impossible" (1996), "Tomorrow Never Dies" (1997), "Legionnaire" (1998), "The Mummy" (1999), "Shiner" (2000), "The Mummy Returns" (2001), "Buffalo Soldiers" (2001), "Gosford Park" (2001), "Finding Neverland" (2004), and "The Phantom of the Opera" (2004). Powell worked in television on

episodes of "Captain Moonlight: Man of Mystery", "The Avengers", "Garry Halliday", "Moonstrike", "Detective", "The Midnight Men", "The Man from U.N.C.L.E.", "The Time Tunnel", "Adam Adamant Lives!", "The Saint", "the Prisoner", "Man in a Suitcase", "The Champions", "The Wednesday Play", "Z Cars", "Manhunt", "Doctor Who", "Softly Softly: Task Force", "The Adventurer", "Special Branch", "Armchair Cinema", "The Sweeney", "The New Avengers", "Space: 1999", "The New Avengers", "The Losers", "Blake's 7", "Minder", "The Professionals", "The Jim Davidson Show", "The Gathering Seed", "Big Deal", "Cannon and Ball", "EastEnders", "Dempsey and Makepeace", "Robin Hood", "Bergerac", "Campion", "Wish Me Luck", "Spender", "Comedy Playhouse", "Red Dwarf", "Between the Lines", "Sharpe", and "Raging Planet". His other television credits include productions of "Under Western Eyes" (1975), "Wolcott" (1981), "Brideshead Revisited" (1981), "The Zany Adventures of Robin Hood" (1984), "Family Ties Vacation" (1985), "The Lady and the Highwayman" (1988), "Winners and Losers" (1989), "A Ghost in Monte Carlo" (1990), "The Blackheath Poisonings" (1992), "Jane Eyre" (1997), "The Magical Legend of the Leprechauns" (1999), and "The Last King" (2003).

Pradhan, Shahnawaz

Indian actor Shahnawaz Pradhan died of cardiac arrest in Mumbai, India, on February 17, 2023. He was 56. Pradhan

was born in Raj Khariar, India, on December 6, 1963. He was best known for his role as Sindbad the Sailor in the Arabian Nights television series "Alif Laila" from 1993 to 1995. He starred as Nanda Baba in the series "Shri Krishna" from 1993 to 1997 and was Mataprasad Shukla in "Kahe Diya Pardes" in 2006. His other television credits include episodes of "Hari Mirchi Lal Mirchi", "Savdhaan India: Crime Alert", "The Suite Life of Karan & Kabir", "Crime Patrol", "24: India", "Better Life Foundation", "Bisht, Please!", "Hankaar", "Hostages", "The Family Man", "Mirzapur", and "Staff Room - Teacheron Ka Adda". Pradhan appeared in the films "Chal Pichchur Banate Hain" (2012), "Ekk Albela" (2016), "M.S. Dhoni: The Untold Story" (2016), "Raees" (2017), "Manto" (2018), "Hum Chaar" (2019), "Dolly Kitty and Those Twinkling Stars" (2019), "Khuda Haafiz" (2020), "Khuda Haafiz: Chapter 2 - Agni Pariksha" (2022), "Chakki" (2022), "Mid Day Meeal" (2022), and "IB 71" (2023). He was also the Hindi dubbing actor for such South Indian performers as Kota Srinivasa, Cochi Hanifa, and Nedumudi Venu, and for British actors Michael Gough, Michael Caine, and Jonathan Pryce.

Precht, Robert

Television producer Robert Precht, who produced the popular variety series "The Ed Sullivan Show" for over twenty years, died at his home in Missoula, Montana, on November 26, 2023. He was 93. Precht was born in Douglas, Oklahoma, on May 12, 1930. He moved to San Diego, California, with his

family in the early 1940s. He attended the University of California at Los Angeles. He was selected by his fellow students as a "great lover" in 1949, earning the opportunity to escort actress Elizabeth Taylor to the school's junior prom during a promotion for the Bob Hope film "The Great Lover". He transferred to the University of California at Berkeley where he graduated in 1952. He also married Betty Sullivan, the daughter of band leader and impresario Ed Sullivan, in 1952. He spent four years in the U.S. Navy and began working in television after his discharge. He served as an assistant producer for the children's show "Winky Dink and You" and was associate producer for "The Verdict Is Yours". He became associate producer of his father-in-law's popular television program "The Ed Sullivan Show" in 1958 and produced the television special "Ed Sullivan's Invitation to Moscow" in 1959. Precht replaced Marlo Lewis as the show's producer in 1960 and later served as executive producer. He oversaw the series when the Beatles performed on the show in 1964 and oversaw the documentary of the band's concert at Shea Stadium in Queens, New York, the following year. Precht remained producer and occasional director for "The Ed Sullivan Show" until it was cancelled in 1971. He was producer for the 1973 television series "Calucci's Department" and the tele-films "Change at 125th Street" (1974) and "Sonny Boy" (1974). He produced and directed the tele-films "The Norming of Jack 243" and "Too Easy to Kill" in 1975. He produced numerous television specials including "The Lily Tomlin Show" (1973), "Carroll O'Connor Special" (1973), "Andy Williams Presents" (1974), "Grand Ole Opry 50th Anniversary" (1975), "The Sullivan Years: A Tribute to Ed Sullivan" (1975), "The Soupy Sales Show" (1976), "TV Guide: The First 25 Years" (1979), "The Crystal Gayle Special" (1979), "NBC Family Christmas" (1981), "Screen Actors Guild 50th Anniversary Celebration" (1984), "Grand Ole Opry 60th Anniversary" (1986), and "Grand Ole Opry 65th Anniversary" (1991). He also produced televised presentations of the Entertainer of the Year Awards, the Country Music Association Awards, the Daytime Emmy Awards, and the People's Choice Awards. Precht was married to Betty Sullivan from 1952 until her death in 2014. He is survived by two sons and two daughters. Another son, Andrew, died in 1995.

Presley, Lisa Marie

Singer Lisa Marie Presley, who was the daughter of Elvis and Priscilla Presley, died from cardiac arrest at a hospital in Los Angeles, California, on January 12, 2023. She was 54. Presley was born in Memphis, Tennessee, on February 1, 1968. Her parents separated in the early 1970s and she frequently stayed with her father at Graceland in Memphis. She became joint heir to Elvis' estate after his death in August of 1977 with her grandfather, Vernon Presley, and Vernon's mother, Minnie

Mae Presley. She became sole heir after Vernon's death in 1979 and Minnie Mae's in 1980 and inherited the estate on her 25th birthday in 1993. Lisa Marie made a posthumous duet with her father in the 1997 music video "Don't Cry Daddy". She released her debut album, "To Whom It May Concern", in 2003 and co-wrote most of the songs. She frequently performed in concerts and released the album "Now What" in 2005. She performed another posthumous duet with her father with the single "In the Ghetto" in 2007. Her third album, "Storm & Grace", was released in 2012. Presley was active in numerous philanthropic endeavors. Presley was a member of the Church of Scientology from the 1990s until leaving the religion in 2014. She sold 85 percent of her father's estate in 2004. Lisa Marie was a guest on such television shows as "Friday Night with Jonathan Ross", "This Morning", "Late Night with Conan O'Brien", "Late Show with David Letterman", "Biography", "The View", "Howard Stern", "The Ellen DeGeneres Show", "The Oprah Winfrey Show", "American Idol", "The Tonight Show with Jay Leno", "Jimmy Kimmel Live!", "Today", "The Talk", and "Entertainment Tonight". She was also seen in various documentaries about her father including "Elvis by the Presleys" (2005), "Elvis Lives: The 25th Anniversary Concert, 'Live' from Memphis" (2007), and "Elvis: Viva Las Vegas" (2008). Lisa Marie was married to musician Danny Keough from 1988 until their divorce in 1994. They had two children, actress Riley Keough, and son Benjamin Keough, who died of a suicide in 2020. She was briefly married to singer Michael Jackson from 1994 until their divorce in 1996 and to actor Nicholas Cage from 2002 until their divorce in 2004. She married Michael Lockwood, her guitarist and music producer, in 2006. They had twin girls before their divorce in 2021. Presley suffered from cardiac arrest at her home in Calabasas, California, on January 12, 2023. She was revived after receiving CPR on route to a Los Angeles hospital but died later in the day.

Pressman, Edward R.

Film producer Edward R. Pressman, who produced such films as "The Crow" and "American Psycho", died in Los Angeles, California, on January 17, 2023. He was 79. Pressman was born in New York City on April 11, 1943. His father was Jack Pressman, founder of the Pressman Toy Corporation. His mother, Lynn Rambach Pressman, helped to toy business grow and later was an actress in producer for her son's films. Edward began his career producing three of director Paul Williams' films, the short "Girl" (1966), "Out of It" (1969), and "The Revolutionary" (1970). He formed his own film production company in 1969 and served as producer or executive producer for numerous films including "Dealing: Or the Berkeley-to-Boston Forty-Brick Lost-Bag Blues" (1972), Brian De Palma's horror film "Sisters" (1972), Terrence Malick's crime drama "Badlands", DePalma's rock musical horror "Phantom of the Paradise" (1974), Sylvester Stallone's "Paradise Alley", "Victoria" (1979), "Heart Beat" (1980), Oliver Stone's horror film "The Hand" (1981), the director's cut of "Das Boot" (1981), "Conan the Barbarian" (1982) starring Arnold Schwarzenegger, "The Pirates of Penzance" (1983), "Flicks" (1983), "Conan the Destroyer" (1984), Sam Raimi's "Crimewave" (1985) also appearing on screen as Ernest Trent,

"Plenty" (1985), "Half Moon Street" (1986), "True Stories" (1986), "Good Morning Babylon" (1987), "Masters of the Universe" (1987), the science fiction film "Cherry 2000" (1987), "Walker" (1987), "Wall Street" (1987), "Paris by Night" (1988), "Talk Radio" (1988), "Martians Go Home" (1989), "To Sleep with Anger" (1990), "Blue Steel" (1990), "Waiting for the Light" (1990), "Reversal of Fortune" (1990), "Stranger in the House" (1990), "Iron Maze" (1991), "Homicide" (1991), "Year of the Gun" (1991), "Bad Lieutenant" (1992), "Storyville" (1992), "Hoffa" (1992), "Dream Lover" (1993), "The Crow" (1994), "Street Fighter" (1994) also appearing in a small role, "Judge Dredd" (1995), "City Hall" (1996), "The Island of Dr. Moreau" (1996), "The Crow: City of Angels" (1996), "The Blackout" (1997), "The Winter Guest" (1997), "Two Girls and a Guy" (1997), "Endurance" (1998), "New Rose Hotel" (1998), "Legionnaire" (1998), "Black & White" (1999), "Nichts als die Wahrheit" (1999), "American Psycho" (2000), "The Crow: Salvation" (2000), "The Endurance" (2000), "Happy Times" (2000), "Wendigo" (2001), "Harvard Man" (2001), "The Guys" (2002), "The Cooler" (2003), "Party Monster" (2003), "Owning Mahowny" (2003), "The Hebrew Hammer" (2003), "Love Object" (2003), "Rick" (2003), "Never Die Alone" (2004), "The Beautiful Country" (2004), "Undertow" (2004), "The King" (2005), "The Crow: Wicked Prayer" (2005), "Thank You for Smoking" (2005), "Driving Lessons" (2006), "Fur: An Imaginary Portrait of Diane Arbus" (2006), "Amazing Grace" (2006), the 2006 remake of "Sisters", "Mutant Chronicles" (2008), "Bad Lieutenant: Port of Call New Orleans" (2009), "Wall Street: Money Never Sleeps" (2010), "The Moth Diaries" (2011), "Red Wing" (2013), "The Man Who Knew Infinity" (2015), "Reconquest of the Useless" (2015), "Phantom of Winnipeg" (2019), "Dear Mr. Brody" (2021), "She Will" (2021), "Evolver" (2022), "Daliland" (2022), and "Catching Dust" (2023). He was also executive producer of the television series "The Crow: Stairway to Heaven" from 1998 to 1999 and the 2018 tele-film "Paterno". Pressman married actress Annie McEnroe in 1983 and is survived by her and their son, Sam Pressman.

Priestley, Tom

British film editor Tom Priestley died in England on December 25, 2023. He was 91. Priestley was born in London, England, on April 22, 1932. He was the son of playwright J.B. Priestely. He graduated from King's College, Cambridge,

before going to work at Shepperton Studios. He did various jobs, becoming assistant sound editor by the end of the decade. He was an assistant sound editor on the films "Dunkirk" (1958), "Nowhere to Go" (1958), "Left Right and Centre" (1959), "The Scapegoat" (1959), "This Other Eden" (1959), and "The Angry Silence" (1960). He was assistant film editor for "Tommy the Toreador" (1959), "The Boy Who Stole a Million" (1960), "Whistle Down the Wind" (1961), "Waltz of the Toreadors" (1962), and "This Sporting Life" (1963). He served as editor for the 1963 science fiction film "Unearthly Stranger". Priestley was sound editor of the films "Repulsion" (1965), "Dr. Who and the Daleks" (1965), and "The Skull" (1965). He continued to edit such films as "Father Came Too!" (1964), "Morgan – A Suitable Case for Treatment" (1966) earning a BAFTA Award, "Marat/Sade" (1967), "Our Mother's House" (1967), "Isadora" (1968), "Leo the Last" (1970), "Deliverance" (1972) receiving and Academy Award nomination, Lindsay Anderson's "O Lucky Man!" (1973), "The Great Gatsby" (1974), "The Return of the Pink Panther" (1975), "That Lucky Touch" (1975), "Voyage of the Damned" (1976), "Exorcist II: The Heretic" (1977), "Jubilee" (1978), "Son of Hitler" (1979), "Tess" (1979), "Times Square" (1980), the short "A Shock Accident" (1982), "Another Time, Another Place" (1983), "1984" (1984), "Dream One" (1984), "Nanou" (1986), the short "Dreamless Sleep" (1986), "White Mischief" (1987), "The Kitchen Toto" (1987), and "Lord of the Flies" (1990). His father died in 1984 and Priestley left films later in the decade to care of his father's estate. He also toured and lectured about film editing.

Pritchard, Christine

Welsh actress Christine Pritchard died in Bangor, Wales, on February 14, 2023. She was 79. Pritchard was born

in Caernafon, Wales, on August 6, 1943. She graduated from Bristol University where she studied language and drama. She later taught English French on Saint Kitts in the Caribbean. She taught drama in Putney, London, after returning after returning to Great Britain. She joined the Cwmni Theatr Cymru in Bangor in 1970 and performed frequently on stage with Theatr Genedlaethol Cymru, the Welsh national theatre founded in 2003. She starred as Dilys Mainwaring in the television series "Taff Acre" in 1981.

She was also seen in episodes of "The District Nurse", "Night Beat News", "The Magnificent Evans", "Screen One", "Stella", "The Indian Doctor" as Mrs. Daniels in 2013, "Love Me" as Nancy Hopkins in 2014, "Doctors", "Deian a Loli", "Tourist Trap", 35 Awr" as Moira in 2019, "Right Non", "Cyswillt (Lifelines)", "Keeping Faith", and "Casualty". She also appeared in the tele-films "The Extremist" (1984), "A Relative Stranger" (1996), "Plainissimo" (2012), and "Down the Caravan" (2018). She was a voice performer in television productions of "A Winter Story" (1986), "The Easter Egg" (1987), "Turkey Love" (1988), and "Testament: The Bible in Animation" (1996). Pritchard was featured in several films including "Wild Justice" (1996), "Buffalo Heart" (1996), and "A Way of Life" (2004). She wrote and was a voice performer in the animated shorts "Ben and the Hot Cross Bunny" (2011) and "Ben and the Box of Surprises" (2012). She was heard on the BBC Radio Cymru soap opera "Eileen/Rhydeglwys".

Pupella, Mario

Italian actor Mario Pupella died in Palermo, Italy, on January 22, 2023. He was 77. Pupella was born in Castelvetrano, Italy, on April 10, 1945. He began his acting

career on stage. He was an actor and director for productions at the Teatro Europa, Teatro Crystal, and Teatro Sant'Eugenio in Sicily. Pupella appeared in occasional films during his career including "Servo Suo" (1973), "I Grimaldi" (1997), "Angela" (2002), "La Passione di Giosue l'Ebreo" (2005), "La Mafia dei Nuovi Padrini" (2005), "Me, the Other" (2006), "I Vicere" (2007), "La Siciliana Ribelle" (2008), "La Matassa" (2009), "Sins" (2012), "Salvo" (2013), "At War with Love" (2016), "Quel Bravo Ragazzo" (2016), "Titanium White" (2016), "Scappo a Casa" (2019), "Padrenostro" (2020), and "School of Mafia" (2021). He appeared on television in productions of "Il Cortile Degli Aragonesi" (1973), "Callas e Onassis" (2005), and "Giovanni Falcone, l'Uomo Che Sfido Cosa Nostra" (2006), and episodes of "Quadra Antimafia - Palermo Oggi", "Detective Montalbano", and "The Bad Guy".

Quadflieg, Christian

German actor Christian Quadflieg died in Hamburg, Germany, on July 16, 2023. He was 78. Quadflieg was born in Vaxjo, Sweden, on April 11, 1945. He was the son of German actor Will Quadflieg and Swedish countess Benita von Vegesack. He was raised in Hamburg and trained as an actor at the Westfalische Schauspielschule Bochum. He performed on stage in Oberhausen (under the name Christian Urs), Wuppertal, and Basel in the late 1960s and early 1970s. He continued to perform on stage with the Thalia Theatre in Hamburg and theaters in Munich, Vienna, and Zurich. Quadflieg appeared frequently on television from the early 1970s with roles in productions of "Das Wunder" (1971), "Sie Hatten im Sommer Kommen Sollen" (1972), "Die

Unfreiwilligen Reisen des Moritz August Benjowski" (1975), "Das Anhangsel" (1975), "Des Christoffel von Grimmelshausen Abenteuerlicher Simplicissimus" (1975), "Ein Badeunfall" (1976), "Der Winder, der ein Sommer War" (1976), "Das Rentenspiel" (1977), "Ein Frieden fur die Armen Seelen" (1980), "Kummert Euch Nicht um Sokrates" (1979), "Dantos Tod" (1981), "Urlaub am Meer" (1982), "Flohe Hutten ist Leichter" (1982), "Elisabeth von England" (1983), "Feuerwanzen Kuss ich Nicht" (1985), "Die Frau Mit den Karfunkelsteinen" (1985), "Das Andere Leben" (1987), "Auch Handwerker Sind Menschen" (1991), "Das Grosste Fest des Jahres - Weihnachten bei Unseren Fernsehfamilien" (1991), "W.P.Anders - Jugendgerischtshelfer" (1993), "Im Zweifel Fur..." (1995), "Der Preis der Schonheit" (2000), and "Eine Offentliche Affare" (2001). His other television credits include episodes of "Unter Ausschluss der Offentlichkeit", "Wie Wurden Sie Entscheiden?", "Star Maidens" as Rudi in 1976, "Polizeiinspektion 1", "Tatort", "Derrick", "Das Traumschiff", "Steckbriefe", "Urlaub am Meer", "Die Krimistunde", "Alles was Recht Ist", "A Case for Two", "Die Manner vom K3", "The Country Doctor" (aka "Der Landarzt") as Dr. Karsten Mattiesen from 1987 to 1992, "Ein Unvergessliches Wochenende", "Mit Leib und Seele" as Manfred Stehlin from 1992 to 1993, "Sonntag & Partner" as Michael Sonntag from 1994 to 1995, "Anwalt Martin Berg - Im Auftrag der Gerechtigkeit", "Vater Wider Willen", "Siska", and "The Old Fox". Quadflieg also directed television productions of "Ewald - Rund um die Uhr" (1990), "Urlaub Mal Ganz Anders" (1990), "Liebes Leben" (1990), "Sonne, Meer und 1000 Palmen" (1991), "Kleinstadtgeschichten" (1991), and "W.P.Anders - Jugendgerishtshelfer" (1993), and episodes of "The Country Doctor" and "Ein Unvergessliches Wochenende". He toured Germany frequently giving poetry recitals and recorded numerous audio books. Quadflieg married actress Renate Reger in 1974 and she survives him.

Quant, Mary

British fashion designer Mary Quant, who was credited with designing the miniskirt, died at her home in Surrey, England, on April 13, 2023. She was 93. Quant was born in Woolwich, London, England, on February 11, 1930. She studied illustration and art at Goldsmiths College, graduating in 1953. She aspired to a career in fashion and worked as an apprentice for a Mayfair milliner. She opened a fashion boutique, initially selling clothing from wholesalers. She began creating her own dress designs and the bolder styles became a huge success in the 1960s. Her boutique, Bazaar, was noted for its hip elegance and including music and drinks with the shopping experience. Quant was among the designers credited with popularizing the miniskirt and played a prominent role in London's Swinging Sixties. She also accompanied the miniskirt with brightly colored and patterned tights. She was noted for her beret designs produced by Kangol later in the 1960s. Quant's designs extended to household goods including  the duvet in the 1970s and 1980s. She also headed the cosmetics company, Mary Quant Ltd., until 2000. She was involved in films, designing clothes for Clair Bloom in "The Haunting" (1963), Cilla Black and Julie Samuels in "Ferry Cross the Mersey" (1964), Nancy Kwan in "The Wild Affair" (1965), Charlotte Rampling in "Georgy Girl" (1966), and Audrey Hepburn in "Two for the Road" (1967). She was seen on television in episodes of "What's My Line?", "The David Frost Show", and "The Eamonn Andrews Show". Quant was appointed Dame Commander of the Order of the British Empire (DBE) in 2015 for services to British fashion. She was author of the books "Quant by Quant: The Autobiography of Mary Quant" (1996) and "Mary Quant Autobiography" (2011). Quant was married to Alexander Plunket Greene from 1957 until his death in 1990, and is survived by their son, Orlando.

Quinton, Everett

Actor Everett Quinton died of glioblastoma in Brooklyn, New York, on January 23, 2023. He was 71. Quinton was born in Brooklyn on December 18, 1951. He served in the U.S. Air Force and was stationed in Thailand. He subsequently attended Hunter College for two years. He met actor and playwright Charles Ludlam in 1975 and became his professional and personal partner. Ludlam was the founder  of Greenwich Village's Ridiculous Theatrical Company in 1967. The two appeared together in numerous productions written by Ludlam, with Quinton often portraying female roles. His plays include "The Enchanted Pig" (1979) and "The Mystery of Irma Vep" (1984). Quinton headed the RTC after Ludlam's death from complications from AIDS in 1987 through its closing in 1997. He continued to direct and perform on the New York stage. Quinton appeared in the films "Legal Eagles" (1986), "Forever, Lulu" (1986), "The Sorrows of Dolores" (1986), "From the Hip" (1987), "Deadly Illusion" (1987), "Hello Again" (1987), "Big Business" (1988), "Natural Born Killers" (1994) as Deputy Warden Wurlitzer, "Pollock" (2000), "After Louie" (2017), and "Bros" (2022). He was seen on television in episodes of "Miami Vice", "Law & Order", "Guiding Light", "Nurse Jackie", and "The Louise Log" as Ethelred in 2014.

Quitak, Oscar

British actor Oscar Quitak, who starred as the crippled hunchback Karl in the Hammer horror film "The Revenge of Frankenstein", died in Ibiza, Spain, on December 31, 2023. He was 97. Quitak was born in Kensington, London, England, on  March 10, 1926. He performed frequently on stage throughout his career with roles at the Old Vic and the National Theatre. He starred as Nathaniel Winkle in the musical "Pickwick" in the original West End production in 1963 and accompanied the musical to Broadway in 1965. Quitak was seen frequently on television with roles in productions of "As You Like It" (1946), "Richard of Bordeaux" (1947), "London Wall" (1948), "Heaven and Charing Cross" (1950), "Shadow Scene" (1951), "The Bespoke Overcoat" (1954), "Barbara's Wedding" (1954), "The Power and the Glory" (1957), "Tomorrow Mr. Tompion! And About Time Too!" (1958), "Who Killed Menna Lorraine?" (1960), "The Nightwalkers" (1960), "Cousin Bette" (1971), "The Death of Adolf Hitler" (1973) as Joseph Goebbels, "David Copperfield" (1974), "A Suitable Case for Killing?" (1975), "The Changes" (1975), "Holocaust" (1978), "The Clifton House Mystery" (1978), "Suez 1956" (1979) as Hugh Gaitskell, "The Ghost Sonata" (1980), "Kessler" (1981) as Joseph Mengele, "Nye" (1982), "Red Monarch" (1983), "The Fasting Girl" (1984), "Black Carrion" (1984), "Anna Karenina" (1985), "Jenny's War" (1985), "Christmas Hamper" (1985), "Silas Marner" (1985), "The Last Days of Patton" (1986), "The Alamut Ambush" (1986), "Cold War Killers" (1986), "A Very British Coup" (1988), and "Murderers Among Us: The Simon Wiesenthal Story" (1989). His other television credits include episodes of "The Man in Armour", "Rheingold Theatre", "The Grove Family" as Charlie Mead in 1954, "Lilli Palmer Theatre", "Assignment Foreign Legion", "O.S.S.", "The New Adventures of Charlie Chan", "Armchair Theatre", "Sailor of Fortune", "The Adventures of Brigadier Wellington-Bull", "The Four Just Men", "Interpol Calling", "Somerset Maugham Hour", "About Religion", "Saturday Playhouse", "ITV Television Playhouse", "Top Secret", "Man of the World", "Zero One", "The Wednesday Play", "Man in a Suitcase", "Virgin of the Secret Service", "Thirty-Minute Theatre", "Canterbury Tales", "Doomwatch", "ITV Playhouse", "Paul Temple", "Rules, Rules, Rules", "Ace of Wands", "The Rivals of Sherlock Holmes", "Z Cars", "Colditz", "Dial M for Murder", "Ski-Boy", "The New Avengers", "Crown Court", "The Famous Five", "Play for Today", "Open All Hours", "The Nation's Health", "Chessgame", "The Kenny Everett Television Show", "Yes, Prime Minister", "Lovejoy", "Howards' Way" as Richard Shellet from 1985 to 1986, "French and Saunders", "Ten Great Writers of the Modern World", "Theatre Night", "Screenplay", "Screen One", "Saracen", "10x10", "Outside Time", "Telltale", and "Every Silver Lining" as Willie in 1993. Quitak appeared in such films as "The Outsider" (1948), "It's Hard to Be Good"

(1948), "Cairo Road" (1950), the short "Four Men in Prison" (1950), "The Dark Man" (1951), "Hell Is Sold Out" (1951), "So Little Time" (1952), "Something Money Can't Buy" (1952), "Top of the Form" (1953), "Shop Spoiled" (1954), "The Colditz Story" (1955), "The Prisoner" (1955), "Zarak" (1956), "Town on Trial" (1957), "The Accursed" (1957), the Hammer horror film "The Revenge of Frankenstein" as the crippled hunchback Karl, "Operation Amsterdam" (1959), "Tangiers" (1982), "Bloodbath at the House of Death" (1984), "Brazil" (1985), and "Code Name: Emerald" (1985). He largely retired from acting in the late 1980s and settled with his family in Ibiza, Spain. He was married to actress Andree Melly from 1964 until her death in 2020 and is survived by their two children, Natasha and Mark.

Rabanne, Paco

Spanish fashion designer Francisco Rabaneda y Cuervo, who was better known under the name Paco Rabanne, died at his home in Portsall, Ploudalmezeau, France, on February 3, 2023. He was 88. Rabaneda was born in Pasaia,

Spain, on February 18, 1934. His mother was chief seamstress for fashion designer Cristobal Balenciaga, and she moved the family to Paris after Balenciaga opened a fashion house there. Rabanne studied architecture at l'Ecole Nationale des Beaux-Arts. He worked with Auguste Perret's architectural firm for over a decade. He began making fashion sketches for Dior and Givenchy and also created jewelry for them. He opened his own fashion house in 1966 and created flamboyant designs using metal, plastic, and paper. He became noted for his futuristic space age designs and provided many of the costumes worn by Jane Fonda in the 1968 science fiction film "Barbarella". He also served as designer for the films "The Last Adventure" (1967) and "Les Poneyttes" (1968) and appeared in small roles in "Money-Money" (1969) and "Cameroon Connection" (1985). Rabanne began marketing perfumes in 1969 with the scent called Calandre. He was author of the 1994 book "Has the Countdown Begun? Through Darkness to Enlightenment". Rabanne was also known for his sometimes-bizarre public statements. He claimed to have been visited by extraterrestrials, visited with God, and murdered the pharaoh Tutankhamun during his 75,000 years of life.

Ragalyi, Elemer

Hungarian cinematographer Elemer Ragalyi died in Hungary on March 30, 2023. He was 83. Ragalyi was born in Budapest, Hungary, on April 18, 1939. He began his career working at Mafilm in 1957 where he was a laboratory technician, lighting engineer, and recording manager. He earned a degree in cinematography from the Academy of Theater and Film Arts in 1968. He became a prolific cinematographer in Hungarian cinema and television. He also

worked on productions throughout Europe and the United States. His film credits include "Meddig el Az Ember? I-II" (1968), "Sziget a Szarazfoldon" (1969), "Arc" (1970), "The Falcons" (1970), "A Nagy Kek Jelzes" (1970), "Befejezetlenul" (1970), "Stafeta" (1971), "Sarika, Dragam" (1971), "Madarkak" (1971), "Fotografia" (1973), "Kakuk Marci" (1973), "Football of the Good Old Days" (1973), "Egy Kis Kely a Nap Alatt"

(1973), "Istenmezejen 1972-73-ban" (1974), "Dreaming Youth" (1974), "Bastyasetany Hetvennegy" (1974), "Strange Masquerade" (1976), "Egyszeru Tortenet" (1976), "Voros Rekviem" (1976), "Talpuk Alatt Futyul a Szel" (1976), "Pokfoci" (1977), "Saman" (1977), "A Ketfeneku Dob" (1978), "Csatater" (1978), "Kihojolni Veszelyes" (1978), "Deliver Us from Evil" (1979), "The Trumpeter" (1979), "Vasarnapi Szulok" (1980), "Utolso Elotti Itelet" (1980), "Majd Holnap" (1980), "The Heiresses" (1980), "Vammentes Hazassag" (1980), "Ripacsok" (1981), "Mascot" (1982), "Dogkeselyu" (1982), "A Koncert" (1983), "Szerencses Daniel" (1983), "The Long Ride" (1983), "Flowers of Reverie" (1985), "Tarasutazas" (1985), "Csak Egy Mozi" (1985), "Der Schwarze Tanner" (1986), "Embriok" (1986), "A Nagy Generacio" (1986), "Queen Live in Budapest" (1986), "Csok, Anyu!" (1987), "A Hungarian Fairy Tale" (1987), "Miss Arizona" (1988), "Hanna's War" (1988), "Tusztortenet" (1989), "Mack the Knife" (1989), "The Phantom of the Opera" (1989), Xavier Koller's Oscar-winning foreign language film "Journey to Hope" (1990), "Mesmer" (1994), "A Kid in King Arthur's Court" (1995), "Never Talk to Strangers" (1995), "Sztracsatella" (1996), "A Miniszter Felrelep" (1997), "Jakob the Liar" (1999), "An American Rhapsody" (2001), "Down by Love" (2003), "A Rozsa Enekei" (2003), "A Long Weekend in Pest and Buda" (2003), "Apam Beajulna" (2003), "Nincs Kegyelem" (2006), "The Moon and the Stars" (2007), "The Door" (2012), "Corn Island" (2014), "Think of Me" (2016), "1945" (2017), and "Budapest Noir" (2017). Ragalyi worked in television as cinematographer for such productions as "Murderers Among Us: The Simon Wiesenthal Story" (1989), "Red King, White Knight" (1989), "Max and Helen" (1990), "Judgment" (1990), "The Josephine Baker Story" (1991), "The Gravy Train Goes East" (1991), "Teamster Boss: The Jackie Presser Story" (1992), "Maigret" (1992-1993), "Charlemagne" (1993), "Passport to Murder" (1993), "Family Pictures" (1993), "Catherine the Great" (1995), "Rasputin" (1996) earning an Emmy Award, "Trilogy of Terror II" (1996), "The Hunchback of Notre Dame" (1997), "Ms. Scrooge" (1997), "Crime and Punishment" (1998), "A Knight in Camelot" (1998), "Mary, Mother of Jesus" (1999), "In the Beginning" (2000), "David Copperfield" (2000), "Anne Frank: The Whole Story" (2001) receiving another Emmy nomination, "Dracula" (2002), "Ring of the Nibelungs" (2004), and "Republica" (2010).

Ramakers, Ben

Dutch actor Ben Ramakers died on the set of the television mini-series "Elixir" in the Netherlands on November 2, 2023. He was 69. Ramakers was born in Hoensbroek, Netherlands, on November 25, 1953. He began his career on stage and studied at the Theater Academy in Maastricht. He was seen frequently on television with roles in episodes of "De Weg Naarr School", "Een Galerij", "Coverstory", "Achter Het Scherm", "Toen Was Geluk Heel Gewoon", "In Voor- en Tegenspoed", "12 Steden, 13 Ongelukken", "Flodder", "Unit 13" as Commissionar Mooldijk from 1996 to 1998, "Onderweg Naar Morgen" as Miguel Zwart from 1999 to 2000, "Westenwind", "Dok 12", "Spangen", "Baantjer", "Meiden van De Wit", "Rozengeur & Wodka Lime", "Grijpstra & De Gier", "Van Speijk", "St. Nick & Friends", "A'dam 0 E.V.A.", "Moordvrouw", and "I.M" as Vader Palmen in 2020. Ramakers also appeared in such films as "The Northerners" (1992), "The Flying Liftboy" (1998), "Leak" (2000), "Het Zwijgen" (2006), "Winter in Wartime" (2008), "Saint" (2010), and "Wonderbroeders" (2014).

Ramsess, Taraja

Stuntman Taraja Ramsess was killed in an automobile accident on a highway in Atlanta, Georgia, on October 31, 2023. He was 41. His vehicle crashed into a tractor trailer broken down on the left lane of the expressway, killing him two daughters, and a son. A third daughter survived the crash. Ramsess was born in Atlanta on March 9, 1982. He began working in films in the 2000s and served as a set dresser for "8Dazeaweakend" (2009), "Halloween II" (2009), "Preacher's

Kid" (2010), "Why Did I Get Married Too?" (2010), "Due Date" (2010), "Fast Five" (2011), "Contagion" (2011), "Footloose" (2011), "Wanderlust" (2012), "Lawless" (2012), "Madea's Witness Protection" (2012), "Flight" (2012), "Identity Thief" (2013), "The Hunger Games: Catching Fire" (2013), "Project Almanac" (2015), "The DUFF" (2015), "Furious 7" (2015), "90 Minutes in Heaven" (2015), "Barbershop: The Next Cut" (2016), "Taple 19" (2017), "All Eyez on Me" (2017), "Escape Plan 2: Hades" (2018), and "What Men Want" (2019). He also worked as a set dresser for such television series as "The Glades", "Detroit 1-8-7", "The Vampire Diaries", "Single Ladies", "Teen Wolf", "The Walking Dead", "Revolution", "Halt and Catch Fire", "Resurrection", "Devious Maids", "Constantine", "Game of Silence", "MacGyver", "24: Legacy", and "When the Streetlights Go On". His other television credits include productions of "Marry Me" (2010), "Coma" (2012), and "CrazySexyCool: The TLC Story" (2013). Ramsess was a stunt performer for the 2018 Marvel film "Black Panther". He also performed stunts in such films as "Avengers: Infinity War" (2018), "What Men Want" (2019), "Avengers: Endgame" (2019), "Shaft" (2019), "Bad Boys for Life" (2020), "The 24th" (2020), "Chaos Walking" (2021), "The Suicide Squad" (2021), "The Harder They Fall" (2021), "A Jazzman's Blues" (2022), "Black Adam" (2022), "Black Panther: Wakanda Forever" (2022), "Emancipation" (2022), "Creed III" (2023), and "They Cloned Tyrone" (2023). He was a stuntman in episodes of the television series "Constantine", "Containment", "Game of Silence", "MacGyver", "24: Legacy", "The Gifted", "Valor", "Star", "Black Lightning", "American Soul", "Boomerang", "Step Up: High Water", "Dynasty", "All the Queen's Men", "She-Hulk: Attorney at Law", "Atlanta", and "BMF", and the 2023 tele-film "Cruel Encounters".

Rankine, Alan

Scottish musician Alan Rankine, who was keyboardist for the rock band the Associates, died of heart disease on January 2, 2023. He was 64. Rankine was born in Bridge of Allan, Scotland, on May 17, 1958. He learned to play the guitar

in his teens and began performing with vocalist Billy Mackenzie as the Associates in 1979. They recorded a cover version of David Bowie's "Boys Keep Swinging" and received a contract with Fiction Records. They were joined by bassist Michael Dempsey and drummer John Murphy and recorded their debut album "The Affectionate Punch" in 1980. The Associates released the 1981 singles compilation "Fourth Drawer Down" and the album "Sulk" in 1982. Rankine subsequently left the band to work as a producer. He was associated with such artists as Anna Domino, the Cocteau Twins, Paul Haig, and the Pale Fountains. He recorded the solo albums "The World Beings to Look Her Age" (1986), "She Loves Me Not" (1987), and the instrumental "The Big Picture Sucks" (1989). He became a teacher at Stow College in Glasgow where he assisted students in creating the in-house record label Electric Honey. He discussed a reunion album with Mackenzie in the 1990s and wrote several songs together. Mackenzie committed suicide in 1997 ending any reunion hopes. Rankine married Belinda Pearse Henderson in the 1980s. They later divorced and he is survived by his sons, Callum and Hamish.

Rapp, Carol

Canadian singer and actress Carol Rapp died in Toronto, Canada, on July 7, 2023. She was 88. She was born Carol Starkman in Toronto on December 18, 1934. She began modeling as a child and later became an actress and singer. She performed on stage and appeared on Canadian television from the early 1950s. She was seen on television in episodes of

"Encounter", "Folio", "The Adventures of Tugboat Annie", "On Camera", "Hudson's Bay", "Playdate", "Scarlett Hill", "The Wayne and Shuster Hour", and "Festival". Her only film credit was a small role in the off-beat crime drama "The Bloody Brood" starring Peter Falk in 1959. Rapp was active in women's rights issues and promoting the arts. She and her husband established the Carol & Morton Rapp Gallery at the Art Gallery of Ontario. She married Mortimer Harvey Rapp in 1952 and is survived by him and their daughters, Lee and Laura.

Rauch, Lee

Drummer Lee Rauch, who performed with the thrash metal band Megadeath, died in Lakeview, Ohio, on June 23,

2023. He was 58. Rauch was born in Toledo, Ohio, on September 10, 1964. He graduated from high school in 1982. He joined guitarist Dave Mustaine's band Megadeth in the fall of 1983, replacing Dijon Carruthers on drums. He performed with Mustaine, guitarist Kerry King, and bassist David Ellefson in several live performances in 1984. He was also heard on the recording demo "Last Rites" before leaving the band later in the year. He was replaced by drummer Gar Samuelson, who performed on the band's first two studio albums. Rauch subsequently played drums from live shows with Dark Angel. He joined Michelle Meldrum's band Wargod in 1986 and recorded two demo tracks before they broke up in 1987. He also played with the short-lived thrash band Grimace later in the decade. He largely retired from his music career but would continue to perform locally on occasion.

Raucher, Herman

Author Herman Raucher, who was noted for the novel and screenplay for the 1971 film "Summer of '42", died in a

hospital in Stamford, New York, on December 28, 2023. He was 95. Raucher was born in New York City on April 13, 1928. He studied advertising at New York University and became a successful advertising agent after graduation. He was part of the advertising team that promoted the opening of Disneyland in 1955. He also began writing plays, several of which were adapted for television anthology shows in the 1950s. He wrote "Finkle's Comet" (1956) and

"The Magic Horn" (1956) for "The Alcoa Hour" and "Stardust II" (1956) for "Goodyear Playhouse". His "The Lonely Look" aired on "Matinee Theatre" in 1957 and "The Fair-Haired Boy" on "Studio One" in 1958. Raucher's play "Pioneer, Go Home" was adapted for the 1962 Elvis Presley film "Follow That Dream", and "Harold" was staged on Broadway in 1962. He also wrote the films "Sweet November" (1968) which was remade in 2001, "Can Heironymus Merkin Ever Forget Mercy Humppe and Find True Happiness?" (1969) with Anthony Newley, and "Watermelon Man" (1970) directed by Melvin Van Peebles. His coming-of-age experiences with an older war widow when he was in his teens served as the basis for his script for the 1971 film "Summer of '42" and earned him an Academy Award nomination. He also wrote the best-selling novelization of the film and the 1973 sequel "Class of '44". Raucher also wrote the films "Ode to Billy Joe" (1976) and "The Other Side of Midnight" (1977). He was author of the novels "A Glimpse of Tiger" (1971) and "There Should Have Been Castles" (1978). He was married to dancer Mary Kathryn Martinet from 1960 until her death in 2002 and is survived by their two daughters.

Rauh, Dick

Special effects designer Dick Rauh died at his home in Westport, Connecticut, on October 9, 2023. He was 98. Rauh was born in Brooklyn, New York, on January 31, 1925. He

served as a communications officer in the U.S. Navy in the 1940s. He later graduated from Hobart College and studied at the Art Students League. He worked in films as an artist and animator and was part-owner of the special effects business Optical House. He worked in graphics and special effects for the films "Little Shop of Horrors" (1986), "Working Girl" (1988), "Star Trek V: The Final Frontier" (1989), and "Second Sight" (1989). He became interested in botany and flower drawing after retiring in the 1990s. He earned a doctorate in botany from Lehman College. He served as president of the Guild of Natural Science Illustrators and the American Society of Botanical Artists. Rauh was married to Harriette Lyford from 1951 until her death in 2018. He is survived by his daughter Helen and two sons, Daniel and David.

Reaves, Michael

Television writer Michael Reaves, who was noted for his work on animated series, died of complications from Parkinson's disease in Los Angeles, California, on March 20, 2023. He was 72. Reaves was born in San Bernardino, California, on September 14, 1950. He studied at the Clarion Science Fiction Writers' Workshop in East Lansing, Michigan, in the early 1970s. He moved to Los Angeles in 1974 where he worked at various jobs while trying to become a writer. He scripted an episode of "The Secrets of Isis" in 1975 and continued to write episodes of such animated and live-action

series as "Shazam!", "The New Archie/Sabrina Hour", "Space Sentinels", "Tarzan, Lord of the Jungle", "The New Shmoo", "Space Stars", "Blackstar", "Flash Gordon", "He-Man and the Masters of the Universe", "The Incredible Hulk", "Spider-Man and His Amazing Friends", "The Smurfs", "The Biskitts", "Benji, Zax & the Alien Prince", "Pole Position", "The Mighty Orbots", "CBS Storybreak", "Dungeons & Dragons", "The Littles", "Challenge of the GoBots", "Star Wars: Droids", "Star Wars: Ewoks", "Teen Wolf", "The Transformers", "Centurions", "Potato Head Kids", "Bionic Six", "My Little Pony", "Jem", "Starcom: The U.S. Space Force", the 1987 "Star Trek: The Next Generation" episode "Where No One Has Gone Before", "Captain Power and the Soldiers of the Future", "Spiral Zone", "Superman", "The Twilight Zone", "Dink, the Little Dinosaur", "Swamp Thing", "Tiny Toon Adventures", "Monsters", "The Real Ghostbusters", "The Flash", "Teenage Mutant Ninja Turtles", "Father Dowling Mysteries", "Peter Pan and the Pirates", "The New Adventures of He-Man", "Full Eclipse", "Cadillacs and Dinosaurs", "Conan and the Young Warriors", "Batman: The Animated Series" receiving a Daytime Emmy Award in 1993 and another nomination in 1994, "Phantom 2040", "Gargoyles", "Invasion America" which he also produced in 1998, "Young Hercules", "Sliders", "Roughnecks: The Starship Troopers Chronicles", "Spider-Man Unlimited", "Beast Machines: Transformers", "He-Man and the Masters of the Universe", "Godzilla: The Series", "Max Steel", and "Star Trek Phase II" also serving as executive producer in 2007. He also scripted the 1993 animated film "Batman: Mask of the Phantasm". Reaves with also writer of the science fiction and fantasy novels "I - Alien" (1978), "Dragonworld" (1979) with Byron Preiss, "Hellstar" (1984) with Steve Perry, "Dome" (1987), "Street Magic" (1991), "Night Hunter" (1995), "Thong the Barbarian Meets the Cycle Sluts of Saturn" (1998) with Perry, and "Voodoo Child" (1998). His "Kamus of Kadizhar" series included "The Big Spell" (1977), "The Maltese Vulcan" (1977), "Murder on the Galactic Express" (1982), and "The Man with the Golden Raygun" (1982). He co-wrote the 2007 Batman novel "Fear Itself" with Steven-Elliot Altman. He co-wrote the 2007 young adult novel "InterWorld" with Neil Gaiman and co-wrote the sequels, "The Silver Dream" (2013) and "Eternity's Wheel" (2015), with his daughter, Mallory Reaves. He wrote several novels in the Star Wars Universe including "Darth Maul: Shadow Hunter" (2001), "Star Wars: Clone Wars: Medstar" (2004), "Star Wars: Death Star" (2007), and "Coruscant Nights: Jedi Twilight" (2008). Reaves was married and divorced from Brynne Chandler and is survived by their three children.

Reaves-Phillips, Sandra

Actress and singer Sandra Reaves-Phillips died in Queens, New York, on December 29, 2023. She was 79.

Reaves-Phillips was born in Mullins, South Carolina, on December 23, 1944. She was raised by her grandmother until the age of 15 when she moved to New York City to live with her mother. She began performing at local clubs and joined the Al Fann Theatrical Ensemble in Harlem. She starred in the national tours of the Broadway musicals "Raisin" (1975) and "One Mo' Time" (1980). She appeared in the 1990 off-Broadway sequel "And Further Mo'" and on Broadway in "Hot Feet" in 2006. She toured in several one-woman shows including "The Late, Great Ladies of Blues & Jazz", "Bold and Brassy Blues", and "Heart to Heart". Reaves-Phillips was seen in the films "The Happy Hooker" (1975), "'Round Midnight" (1986) as Buttercup, "Lean on Me" (1989) as music teacher Mrs. Powers, "For Love or Money" (1993), "Don't Explain" (2002), and "Good Funk" (2016). She appeared on television in the 1994 tele-film "Following Her Heart" and episodes of "ABC Weekend Specials", "Homicide: Life on the Street", "A Prairie Home Companion with Garrison Keillor", "Strangers with Candy", and "Law & Order". Reaves-Phillips had suffered from poor health since falling off a stage during a production in St. Louis in 2004 and having serious automobile accidents in New York in 2014 and 2015. She is survived by her son, singer and director Lacy Darryl Phillips, and daughter, actress and singer Marishka Shanice Phillips.

Rebney, Jack

Advertising agent Jack Rebney, who was star of the 2009 documentary "Winnebago Man" and one of the internet's

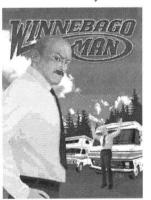

first viral personalities, died in Oregon on May 10, 2023. He was 93. Rebney was born in Minnesota on December 17, 1929. He was a former journalist who became spokesman for a Winnebago recreation vehicle commercial in 1988. He continually interrupted filming with angry and profanity-laced outbursts. The production crew later compiled a VHS of his more bombastic outtakes and shared them with friends. Joe Pickett and Nick Prueher, who ran the Found Footage Festival, were given access to the commercial shoot's raw footage in the early 2000s. They put together their own edit which was featured at their festival and had millions of views on YouTube and other streaming sites. Ben Steinbauer found Rebney, who was unaware of his internet fame, at his home in a remote area of California. He began interviewing the still irascible Rebney for what became the 2009 documentary "Winnebago Man". He later moved to Southern Oregon.

Reddick, Lance

Actor Lance Reddick who starred as Cedric Daniels in "The Wire" television series and was Charon, concierge at the Continental hotel, in the "John Wick" film franchise, died at his home in Los Angeles, California, on March 17, 2023. He was 60. Reddick was born in Baltimore, Maryland, on June 7, 1962.

He studied classical music composition at the University of Rochester's Eastman School of Music. He graduated from the Yale School of Drama with a Master of Fine Arts degree in 1994. He was soon appearing on television in episodes of "New York Undercover", "Swift Justice", "The Nanny", "The West Wing", "Falcone" in the recurring role of Detective Willis Simms in 2000, "Oz" as undercover cop Detective Johnny Basil (aka Desmond Mobay) from 2000 to 2001, "100 Centre Street", "Law & Order: Criminal Intent", "Law & Order", "CSI: Miami" in the recurring role of FBI Agent David Park from 2005 to 2006, "Numb3rs", "The Wire" as Cedric Daniels from 2002 to 2008, "Lost" in the recurring role of Matthew Abaddon from 2008 to 2009, "Svetlana", "It's Always Sunny in Philadelphia", "Drone", "Fringe" as Homeland Security Special Agent Phillip Broyles from 2008 to 2013, "Comedy Bang! Bang!", "American Horror Story" as Papa Legba in the 2014 serial "The Coven", "Wanda Sykes Presents Herlarious", "Wilfred", "NTSF:SD:SUV", "The Blacklist", "Intelligence" as DCI Jeffrey Tetazoo in 2014, "Key and Peele", "Bosch" as Police Chief Irvin Irving, "Castle", "Tim and Eric's Bedtime Stories", "Quantum Break", "Mary + Jane", "Corporate" as Christian DeVille" from 2018 to 2020, "Young Sheldon", and "Resident Evil" as Albert Wesker in 2022. He appeared posthumously as Zeus in the 2023 series "Percy Jackson and the Olympians". His other television credits include productions of "What the Deaf Man Heart" (1997), "The Fixer" (1998), "Witness to the Mob" (1998), "The Corner" (2000), and "Keep the Faith, Baby" (2002). Reddick appeared frequently in films from the late 1990s and was noted for his authoritative voice, shaved head, and tall statute. He was seen in the films "Great Expectations" (1998), "The Siege" (1998), "I Dreamed of Africa" (2000), "Don't Say a Word" (2001), "Bridget" (2002), "Brother to Brother" (2004), "Dirty Work" (2006), "Tennessee" (2009), "The Way of War" (2009), "Jonah Hex" (2010), "Remains" (2011), "Won't Back Down" (2012), "White House Down" (2012) as General Caulfield, "Oldboy" (2013), "The Guest" (2014), "Faults" (2014), "Search Party" (2014), "Fun Size Horror: Volume One" (2015) in "The Collection" segment, the short film "Spoken Word" (2016) which he also produced, "Lawman" (2017), "Little Woods" (2018), "Canal Street" (2018), "The Domestics" (2018), the serial killer thriller "Monster Party" (2018), "Angel Has Fallen" (2019), "Business Ethics" (2019), "Faith Based" (2020) also serving as executive producer, "Sylvie's Love" (2020), "One

Night in Miami..." (2020), "Godzilla vs. Kong" (2021) as Guillermin, and the short "Man of Fire" (2021). He was Charon, the Continental hotel manager, in the films "John Wick" (2014), "John Wick: Chapter 2" (2017), "John Wick: Chapter 3 - Parabellum" (2019), and "John Wick: Chapter 4" (2023) starring Keanu Reeve in the title role. Reddick was a voice actor in animated television series "The Avengers: Earth's Mightiest Heroes" as Sam 'Falcon' Wilson, "Tron: Uprising", "Beware the Batman" as Ra's Al Ghul, "Rick & Morty", "DuckTales", "Castlevania" as the Captain in 2020, "Farzar", "Paradise PD" from 2020 to 2022, "The Vindicators" as Alan Rails in 2022, and "The Legend of Vox Machina" as Thordak in 2023. He also provided voiced roles for such video games as "50 Cent: Blood on the Sand" (2009), "Payday 2" (2013), "Destiny" (2014) and its sequels as Commander Zavala, "Quantum Break" (2016), "Horizon Zero Dawn" (2017) as Sylens, "John Wick Hex" (2019), and "Horizon Forbidden West" (2022). Reddick was married to Suzanne Yvonne Louis from 1986 until their subsequent divorce and is survived by their two children, Yvonne and Christopher. He married Stephanie Diane Day in 2011 and she also survives him.

Redding, Otis, III

Singer Otis Redding III died of cancer in Macon, Georgia, on April 14, 2023. He was 59. Redding was born in

Macon on December 17, 1963. He was the son of soul singer Otis Redding, who was killed in an airplane crash in December of 1967. Otis III later joined with his brother, Dexter, and cousin, Mark Lockett, to form the funk band the Reddings. He was the group's guitarist and they recorded six albums in the 1980s. They had minor hits with their recordings of "Remote Control" and "Call the Law". He later toured with singer Eddie Floyd and was called upon to sing some of his father's songs including "(Sittin' on) the Dock of the Bay". Redding later worked with his family's foundation to teach children to play music during summer camps.

Reed, Deborah

Actress Deborah Reed, who starred as the Goblin

Queen in the 1990 cult classic "Troll 2", died of complications from cancer in Bountiful, Utah, on November 18, 2023. She was 73. She was born Deborah Hansen in Salt Lake City, Utah, on October 29, 1950. She lived in Lafayette, California, from the age of five to fifteen. She returned to Utah and performed in drama while in high school. She moved to Spokane, Washington, with her family in 1970 where she began performing in musical theater. She worked as a model and actress from the 1980s, appearing in numerous print ads and commercials. She was featured as the villainous Creedence Leonore Gielgud, the Queen of the Goblins, in Claudio Fragasso's 1990 horror film "Troll 2". The movie has gained a reputation of being one of the worst of all time with Reed's over-the-top performance being a highlight. Michael Stephenson, a child star of the film, directed the 2009 documentary "Best Worst Movie" about "Troll 2". Reed was seen in a small role in the 1994 television mini-series "The Stand" and was a makeup artist on the Jim Carrey comedy film "Dumb and Dumber" (1994). She worked as an executive assistant to U.S. Congressman Merrill Cook in the late 1990s. She was also producer and co-host of his Radio program, "The Merrill Cook Show". She and her third husband, Randy Holman, produced and starred in the television series "It's All About Homes" in 2007. They also operated a production company that made documentaries and commercials. Reed was the author of the children's books "When Bugs Are Bugging You" and "Flump - Book One: The Gaseous Ghost". She was married and divorced from Peter Anderegg and Philip Reed, and is survived by her sons, Gavin and Remington Reed. She was married to Randy Holman until his death in 2012.

Reenberg, Jorgen

Danish actor Jorgen Reenberg died in Denmark on November 9, 2023. He was 96. Reenberg was born in Frederiksberg, Denmark, on November 8, 1927. He performed frequently on stage with numerous roles at the Royal Theatre. He made his film debut in the late 1940s and was seen in the features "Tre ar Efter" (1948), "We Want a Child!" (1949), "I Gabestokken" (1950), "Fodboldpraesten" (1951), "Father of

Four" (1953), "Ild og Jord" (1955), "Ingen Tid Til Kaertegn" (1957), "Krudt og Klunker" (1958), "Seksdageslobet" (1958), "Skibet er Ladet Med" (1960), "Flemming og Kvik" (1960), "Logn og Lovebrol" (1961), "Tine" (1964), "I, a Woman" (1965), "Pas pa Ryggen, Professor!" (1977), "Haervaerk" (1977), "Oviri" (1986), "Europa" (1991), and "I Am Dina" (2002). Reenberg appeared on television in productions of "Scapins Gavtyvestreger" (1955), "Virilius" (1956), "Var Det en Drom?" (1957), "Livsflammen" (1957), "Manden i Manen" (1957), "Paske" (1960), "Den Gode Fregat »Pinafore«" (1960), "Man Kan Aldrig Vide" (1960), "En Dor Skal Vaere Aben Eller Lukket" (1961), "For Cannae" (1962), "Midsommerdrom i Fattighuset" (1962), "Indenfur Murene" (1963), "Eurydike" (1964), "Vildanden" (1966), "Fjernsynets Onskeprogram - Giro 413" (1966), "Kongelig Underholdning Med Danske Digtere" (1968), "Troubadouren" (1968), "Natlig Samtale Med et Foragtet Menneske" (1968), "Ardele" (1968), "Flagermusen" (1968), "Kirsebaerhaven" (1969), "Solens Born" (1972), "Den Levende Vare" (1972), "Den Stundeslose" (1973), "Det Lykkelige Skibbrud" (1974), "Flagermusen" (1975), "Figaros

Bryllup", "Helligtrekongersaften" (1981), "Braendende Talmodighed" (1984), "Fra Regnormenes Liv" (1985), "Kong Lear" (1987), "Blodsband" (1998), "Don Ranudo" (1998), "Sandhedens Haevn" (1999), "Gengangere" (2000), and "Vores Sensommer" (2006). His other television credits include episodes of "To Generationer Pa Scenen", "Ret Beset", and "Mor er Major" as Oberst Love in 1985. He was the brother of film director Annelise Reenberg, who died in 1994.

Rees, Lanny

Juvenile actor Lanny Rees, who starred as Junior Riley in the "Life of Riley" film and television series, died of cancer in Tacoma, Washington, on February 7, 2023. He was 89. Rees was born in Veradale, Washington, on December 14, 1933. He

trained as a dancer from an early age and entertained troops in the Spokane area during World War II. He moved to Los Angeles soon after to pursue a career in films. He attended Maurie Reubens' talent school and was signed by RKO. He made his film debut as Barbara Hale's younger brother in 1947's "A Likely Story". He was also seen in the Republic Pictures western "Home in Oklahoma" (1946) with Roy Rogers and Dale Evans. His other films include "Little Iodine" (1946), "My Dog Shep" (1946), "Banjo" (1947), "The Law Comes to Gunsight" (1947), "Overland Trails" (1948), "Reaching from Heaven" (1948), "California Firebrand" (1948), "Fighting Father Dunne" (1948), "The Time of Your Life" (1948), "Kim" (1950), "Count the Hours!" (1953), and "Dragonfly Squadron" (1954). Rees was featured as Junior Riley in the 1948 film "Life of Riley" starring William Bendix. He reprised the role on television for a season with Jackie Gleason taking on the role of Riley from 1949 to 1950. He was also seen in episodes of "The Lone Ranger", "Schlitz Playhouse", and "Your Favorite Story". He served in the U.S. Army in the 1950s and later worked at Rocketdyne testing component parts. He moved back to Washington State in the 1960s to work as a truck mechanic in the Spokane area. He became active in the local theater before moving to the Seattle area in 1986. He briefly returned to the screen in the 1990 horror film "Class of 1999". He retired in 2003. Rees was married and divorced from Myrna Jackson and is survived by their three sons, and a daughter. His oldest son, Mark, predeceased him. He married actress and singer Natalie Monte in 1972 and is also survived by her and his two stepsons.

Refoua, John

Film editor John Refoua, who received an Oscar nomination for his work on the 2009 film "Avatar", died of complications from bile duct cancer in Santa Monica, California, on May 14, 2023. He was 62. Refoua was born in Tehran, Iran, on August 20, 1960. He came to the United States in 1976 and graduated from Oberlin College with a degree in economics in 1980. He moved to Los Angeles in 1983 where he worked at various jobs. He took a course in film editing at the University of California at Los Angeles and began work as an editor on television. He was an assistant editor for David Lynch's "Twin Peaks" series in 1990 and for the 1991 tele-film "Nightmare in Columbia County". Refoua edited episodes of

such series as "Raven", "The Adventures of Brisco County, Jr.", "Touched by an Angel", "Extreme", "Legend", "Players", "Roar", "New York Undercover", "L.A. Doctors", "To Have & to Hold", "Law & Order", "Soul Food", "Ally McBeal", "Dark Angel", "CSI: Miami", "Reno 911!", "Sleepy Hollow", and "The Whispers". He also worked frequently in films, editing for such directors as James Cameron, Antoine Fuqua, and Michael Bay. Refoua edited the films "Soft Toilet Seats" (1999), James Cameron's documentary "Ghosts of the Abyss" (2003), "L.A. Twister" (2004), "Reno 911!: Miami" (2007), "Balls of Fury" (2007), "Avatar" (2009) sharing an Oscar and BAFTA nomination with Cameron and Stephen E. Rivkin, "21 & Over" (2013), "Olympus Has Fallen" (2013), "The Equalizer" (2014), "Southpaw" (2015), "The Magnificent Seven" (2016), "Transformers: The Last Knight" (2017), "Geostorm" (2017), and "Avatar: The Way of Water" (2022). He was working of Cameron's forthcoming film "Avatar 3" at the time of his death. He married Serena Bell Refoua in 1990 and is survived by her and their son.

Regala, John

Filipino actor John Regala, who was noted for his roles as villains in action and crime films, died of complications from

liver and kidney disease in Queson City, Philippines, on June 3, 2023. He was 55. He was born John Paul Guido Boucher Scherrer in Manilla, Philippines, on September 12, 1967. His parents were actors Mel Francisco and Ruby Regala. he was featured on the Filipino television variety series "That's Entertainment" in the mid-1980s. He soon embarked on a career in films appearing in "Anak ng Tondo" (1985), "The Life Story of Julie Vega" (1986), "Bagets Gang" (1986), "Kamandag ng Kris" (1987), "Balandra Crossing" (1987), "Bloody Mary, the Movie" (1987), "Arturo Lualhati" (1988), "Langit at Lupa" (1988), "Aguilar, May Oras Ka Rin" (1988), "Ang Lihim ng Golden Buddha" (1989), "Pamilya Banal" (1989), "Boy Kristiano" (1999), "Target: Central Luzon Bank Robbery" (1989), "Kunin Mo Ang Ulo Ni Ismael" (1990), "Ako Ang Batas: General Karingal" (1990), "Kristobal: Tinik sa Korona" (1990), "Huling Lalaki sa Bityan" (1990), "Alyas Baby Face" (1990), "Iputok Mo... Dadapa Ako! (Hard to Die)" (1990), "Don Pepe" (1991), "Boyong Manalac: Hoodlum Terminator" (1991), "Amok: Patrolman 2" (1991),

"Bukas... Tatakpan Ka Ng Dyaryo" (1991), "Lintik Lang Ang Walang Ganti!" (1991), "Kalabang Mortal Ni Baby Ama" (1992), "Totoy Buang: Mad Killer ng Maynila" (1992), "Tondo: Libingan Ng Mga Siga" (1992), "Ano Ba Iyan?" (1992), "Fatal Chase" (1992), "Jerry Marasigan WPD" (1992), "Kapatid ni Hudas" (1993), "Sgt. Lando Liwanag, Vengador: Batas Ng Api" (1993), "The Vizconde Massacre: God, Help Us!" (1993), "Angel Cremenal" (1993), "Tony Bagyo: Daig Pa Ang Asong Ulol" (1993), "Nandito Ako" (1994), "The Maggie dela Riva Story (God... Why Me?)" (1994), "The Fatima Buen Story" (1994), "Silya Elektrika" (1994), "Lipa 'Arandia' Massacre: Lord Deliver Us from Evil" (1994), "Pards" (1994), "Deadly Brothers" (1994), "Bukas Bibitayin Si Itay" (1995), "Kana" (1995), "Pamilya Valderama" (1995), "Tomboy: The Movie" (1995), "Hindi Lahag Ng Ahas Ay Nasa Gubat" (1996), "Batas Ko Ay Bala" (1996), "Batang Estero" (1996), "Labanang Lalake" (1997), "Cesar Hudas" (1996), "Moises Archanghel: Sa Guhit Ng Bala" (1996), "Si Mokong, Si Astig, At Si Gamol" (1997), "Saturnino Anghel, Asal Demonyo" (1997), "Bobby Barbers: Parak" (1997), "Pards 2" (1997), "Askal" (1997), "Lucio San Miguel: Walang Kaluluwa" (1999), "Squala" (1998), "Notoryus" (1998), "Type Kita... Walang Kokontra" (1999), "Anino" (1999), "Gatilyo" (1999), "Col. Elmer jamias: Barako Ng Maynila" (2000), "Eskort" (2000), "Total Aikido" (2001), "Pilak" (2001), "Parehas Ang Laban" (2001), "Amasona... Kumakasa, Pumuputok" (2001), "Tomagan" (2003), "Animal" (2004), "Paraiso" (2005), "Ligalig" (2006), "Butchered" (2009), the horror comedy "Zombadings 1: Patayin Sa Shokot Si Remington" (2011), "The Road" (2011), "Manila Kingpin: The Asiong Salonga Story" (2011), "El Presidente" (2012), "Magnum Muslim .357" (2014), "Chain Mail" (2015), "Lumayo Ka Nga Sa Akin" (2016), "Teniente Gimo" (2016), "Ang Panday" (2017), and "OFW: The Movie" (2019). Ragala was seen on television in productions of "Akin Ang Paghihiganti" (1995), "Encantadia" as Apitong in 2005, "Impostora" (2007), "Joaquin Bordado" (2008), "Pieta" as Miguel from 2008 to 2009, "Star Confessions" (2011), "Juan Dela Cruz" (2013) asw Coco Martin, "Little Champ" (2013), "Dyesebel" (2014), "Beki Boxer" (2014), "#ParangNormal Activity" (2015), "Ang Probinsyano" as Congressman Randolf Subito in 2016, and "Ipaglaban Mo" (2017). Regala's acting career was damaged in the early 2000s due to alcohol and drug abuse. He became a born-again Christian after going to a drug rehabilitation center. He was also active in the environmental movement. Ragala was married to Aurina Manansala from 1996 until the marriage was annulled in 2004. he was married to Victoria Alonzo from 2005 until her death in 2020.

Reid, Keith

British songwriter Keith Reid, who co-wrote the lyrics for most of Procol Harum's albums, died of colon cancer in London, England, on March 23, 2023. He was 76. Reid was born in Welwyn Garden City, Hertfordshire, England, on October 19, 1946. He left school at an early age to pursue a career in songwriting. He met Gary Brooker, the lead singer for the Paramounts, who would soon become Procol Harum, in

1966. They soon began collaborating on songs. They wrote the 1967 hit song "A Whiter Shade of Pale", which was the band's first single. The band also recorded the hit song "Conquistador". Reid was considered an official member of

Procol Harum and attended their recording sessions and live performances, though he did not perform with the group. He continued to write lyrics for Procol Harum until they disbanded in 1977. Reid was also lyricist for the songs "You'll Be on My Mind" and "Time Will Tell" for French singer Michel Polnareff in 1966 and was co-writer of John Farnham's "You're the Voice" in 1986. He also wrote songs for Annie Lennox, Willie Nelson, and Heart. He moved to New York City to start a management company in 1986. He was lyricist and producer for the 2008 album "The Common Thread", featuring various musicians under the name the Keith Reid Project. Another album from the Keith Reid Project, "In My Head", was released in 2018. Reid is survived by his wife, Pinkey, who he married in 2004.

Reston, James, Jr.

Author and journalist James Reston, Jr., died of pancreatic cancer in Chevy Chase, Maryland, on July 19, 2023. He was 82. Reston was born in Manhattan, New York, on March 8, 1941. His father, James 'Scotty' Reston, was an editor

off the "New York Times" and his mother, Sally Fulton, was a journalist and photographer. Reston moved to Washington, D.C., with his family at the age of two. He graduated from the University of North Carolina at Chapel Hill with a degree in philosophy in 1963. Reston worked for U.S. Secretary of the Interior Stewart Udall as an assistant and speechwriter from 1964 to 1965. He served in the U.S. Army as an intelligence officer from 1965 to 1968. He began writing about people had left the United States to avoid the Vietnam War in the late 1960s. Two collections of his essays on this subject were published, "When can I Come Home" (1972) and "The Amnesty of John David Herndon" (1973). He was an adviser to David Frost for his interviews with former President Richard M. Nixon from 1976 to 1977. His book about the interviews, "The Conviction of Richard Nixon: The Untold Story of the Frost/Nixon Interviews" was the subject of the 2008 film "Frost/Nixon". Reston is portrayed by Sam Rockwell in the film. He wrote articles for numerous publications including "Saturday Review", "National Geographic", "Esquire", "Playboy", "George", "American Heritage", "Omni", "The New Yorker", and "The New York

Times Magazine". He was author of numerous books of non-fiction including "Perfectly Clear: Nixon from Whittier to Watergate" (1973), "The Innocence of Joan Little: A Southern Mystery" (1977), "Our Father Who Are in Hell: The Life and Death of Jim Jones" (1981) which was the basis of his 1982 play "Jonestown Express", "Sherman's March and Vietnam" (1985), "The Lone Star: The Life of John Connally" (1989), "Collision at home Plate: The Lives of Pete Rose and Bart Giamatti" (1991), "Galileo: A Life" (1994) which he adapted for the play "Galileo's Torch" in 2014, "The Last Apocalypse: Europe in the Year 1000 A.D." (1998), "Warriors of God: Richard the Lionheart and Saladin in the Third Crusade" (2001), "Dogs of God: Columbus, the Inquisition, and the Defeat of the Moors" (2005), "Fragile Innocence: A Father's Memoir of His Daughter's Courageous Journey" (2006), "Defenders of the Faith: Charles V, Suleyman the Magnificent, and the Battle for Europe, 1520-1536" (2009), "The Accidental Victim: JFK, Lee Harvey Oswald, and the Real Target in Dallas" (2013), "Luther's Fortress: Martin Luther and His Reformation Under Siege" (2015) which he adapted for the play "Luther's Trumpet" in 2018, "A Rift in the Earth: Art, Memory, and the Fight for a Vietnam War Memorial" (2017), and "The Impeachment Diary: Eyewitness to the Removal of a President" (2019). He wrote several novels including "To Defend, to Destroy" (1971), "The Knock at Midnight" (1975), and "The 19th Hijacker: A Novel of 9/11" (2021). Reston married Denise Leary in 1971 and is survived by her and their three children.

Reubens, Paul

Comedian and actor Paul Reubens, who portrayed Pee-wee Herman, the child-like host of the children's television series "Pee-wee's Playhouse", died of cancer in Los Angeles, California, on July 30, 2023. He was 70. He was born Paul

Rubenfeld in Peekskill, New York, on August 27, 1952, and was raised in Sarasota, Florida. He began performing for family and friends in his youth. He later appeared in high school productions and plays with local theatrical groups. He attended Plymouth State University and Boston University and studied acting at the California Institute of the Arts. He performed at local comedy clubs from the mid-1970s and teamed with Charlotte McGinnis for the comedy act the Hilarious Betty and Eddie. He was featured in over a dozen episodes of "The Gong Show" from 1977. He became part of the improvisational comedy team the Groundlings, writing and performing with fellow troupe members Phil Hartman, John Paragon, and Bob McClurg. He created the character of Pee-wee Herman while with the Groundlings. He appeared on television in episodes of "Working Stiffs" and "Mork & Mindy", and the tele-film "Things We Did Last Summer" (1978). He provided the voice of Freaky Frankenstone on the animated "The Flintstone Comedy Show" in 1980. He was also seen in several comedy specials starring Steve Martin. He was featured in several films including "Midnight Madness" (1980), "Pray TV" (1980), and "The Blues Brothers" (1980). He usually wore a too-small plaid gray suit and a bright red bow tie while performing as child-like Pee-wee. Reuben failed to win a spot on "Saturday Night Live" after an audition in 1980. He and his friends subsequently created "The Pee-wee Herman Show" which was performed live for five months at the Roxy Theatre in West Hollywood. He gained a national audience after HBO aired "The Pee-wee Herman Show" in 1981 and he gained a cult following. He appeared in the film "Cheech and Chong's Next Movie" (1980) and the comedy duo's subsequent film "Nice Dreams" (1981). He was a guest on such television series as "Late Night with David Letterman" "The Tonight Show Starring Johnny Carson", "Dolly", "The Late Show", and "The Arsenio Hall Show", often in character as Pee-wee. He starred in the title role in a 1984 production of "Pinocchio" on "Faerie Tale Theatre". Reubens was featured in the films "Dream On!" (1981), "Pandemonium" (1982), "Meatballs Part II" (1984), and "Flight of the Navigator" (1986) as the voice of Max. He starred in the hit films "Pee-wee's Big Adventure" (1985) directed by Tim Burton and "Big Top Pee-wee" (1988). He was host of a 1985 episode of "Saturday Night Live" and appeared in a cameo as Pee-wee in the 1987 film "Back to the Beach". He was Pee-wee in episodes of "227" and "Sesame Street",. and voiced the character in the cartoon series "All Star Rock 'n' Wrestling Saturday Spectacular". Reuben became star of the CBS Saturday morning children's series "Pee-wee's Playhouse" from 1986 to 1990. His Playhouse in Puppetland included talking furniture and appliances including Chairry and Magic Screen, and the puppets Conky the Robot and Pterri the baby Pteranodon. Other frequent denizens of the Playhouse included John Paragon as Jambi the Genie, Phil Hartman as Captain Carl, Lynne Marie Stewart's Miss Yvonne, Laurence Fishburne's Cowboy Curtis, S. Epatha Merkerson's Reba the Mail Lady, and William Marshall's King of Cartoons. "Pee-wee's Playhouse" received 15 Daytime Emmy Awards and 44 addition nominations during its five seasons, including four for Reuben as Outstanding Performer in Children's Programming. He and the network had mutually agreed to end the series in 1990 but reruns were pulled off the air after Reuben's arrest for indecent exposure at an adult theater in Sarasota, Florida in 1991. He subsequently pleaded no contest to the charges and the resulting publicity damaged his career, despite the support of many of his friends in Hollywood. He resumed acting in the early 1990s appearing as the Penguin's Father in "Batman Returns" (1992) and as Amilyn, a vampire henchman with an uncomfortably long death scene, in the 1992 film version of "Buffy the Vampire Slayer". His other films include "The Nightmare Before Christmas" (1993) as the voice of Lock, "Dunston Checks In" (1996), "Matilda" (1996), "Buddy" (1997), "Doctor Dolittle" (1998) as the voice of the Raccoon, "Mystery Men" (1999) as the flatulence powered superhero Spleen, "South of Heaven, West of Hell" (2000), and "Blow" (2001) as a drug dealer. He was featured in the recurring role of Andrew J. Lansing III, the off-beat nephew of network president Stan Lansing on Candice Bergen's television series

"Murphy Brown" from 1995 to 1997 and earned an Emmy Award nomination. His other television credits include episodes of "Everybody Loves Raymond", "Ally McBeal", "Campus Ladies", "Reno 911!", "Late Show with David Letterman", "Late Night with Conan O'Brien", "The Jay Leno Show", "The Bonnie Hunt Show", "30 Rock", "Dirt" in the recurring role of Chuck Lafoon in 2007, "Tim and Eric Awesome Show, Great Job!", "Pushing Daisies", the 2007 unsold pilot "Area 57" as the Alien, "WWE Raw", "The Tonight Show with Conan O'Brien", "Comedy Bang! Bang!", "The Wendy Williams Show", "Late Night with Jimmy Fallon", "Rachael Ray", "Top Chef", "Face Off", "The Tonight Show Starring Jimmy Fallon", "Late Night with Seth Meyers", "Live with Kelly and Mark", "Today", "Jimmy Kimmel Live!", "Conan", "Portlandia", "The Blacklist" in the recurring role of Mr. Vargas, an ill-fated associate of James Spader's Red

Reddington, from 2014 to 2015, "Gotham" in the recurring role of Elijah Van Dahl, the wealthy father of Robin Lord Taylor's Oswald 'The Penguin' Cobblepot, from 2016 to 2017, "Mosaic" as JC Schiffer in 2018, "Celebrity Family Feud", "Celebrity Wheel of Fortune", "To Tell the Truth", "What We Do in the Shadows", "Legends of Tomorrow" in the recurring role of the voice of the Dybbuk from 2018 to 2019, and "The Conners". He provided voice roles in such animated productions of "Beauty and the Beast: The Enchanted Christmas" (1997), "Hercules" (1998-1999) as Mr. Herodotus, "The Groovenians" (2002), "Rugrats" (2002) as Hermie the Elf, "Teacher's Pet" (2004), "Hopeless Pictures" (2005), "Tripping the Rift" (2005), "Dirt Squirrel" (2005), "Tom Goes to the Mayor" (2006), "Re-Animated" (2006), "Chowder" (2007-2009), "Adventure Time" (2010), "Batman: The Brave and the Bold" as the voice of Bat-Mite from 2009 to 2011, "The Smurfs" (2011) as the voice of Jokey Smurf, "Robot Chicken" (2012), "Tron: Uprising" as the voice of Pavel from 2012 to 2013, "Tom and Jerry's Giant Adventure" (2013), "Scooby-Doo! Mecha Mutt Menace" (2013), "The Smurfs 2" (2013), "Kung Fu Panda: Legends of Awesomeness" (2014), "Teenage Mutant Ninja Turtles" (2014), "Snajay and Craig" (2014), "Lego DC Comics: Batman Be-Leaguered" (2014), "Star Wars: Rebels" (2014), "Phineas and Ferb" (2014), "Randy Cunningham: 9th Grade Ninja" (2015), "Turbo FAST" (2015), "American Dad!" (2014-2016), "Pickle and Peanut" (2015-2016), "Penn Zero: Part Time Hero" (2015-2017), "Minecraft: Story Mode" (2018) as the voice of Ivor, "Voltron: Legendary Defender" (2017-2018), "Tigtone" (2019), "The Crown with a Shadow" (2021), "The Tom and Jerry Show" (2021), and "Bob's Burgers" (2023). He also provided voice roles for various video games including "The Nightmare Before Christmas: Oogie's Revenge" (2004), "The Smurfs 2" (2013), "Call of Duty: Infinite Warfare" (2016), "Wilson's Heart" (2017), and "Minecraft: Story Mode- Season 2" (2017).

Reuben again became the subject of a legal proceeding when his home was searched for child pornography in 2002. The city attorney claimed to have found dozens of photos of child pornography in his collection of kitsch memorabilia that included 70,000. Reuben and his lawyer denied the charges and said whatever items he possessed were vintage erotica that they considered innocent art. The child pornography charges were dropped in 2004 after Reuben's plead guilty to a lesser misdemeanor obscenity charge. His later films include "The Tripper" (2006), "Reno 911!: Miami" (2007), "Life During Wartime" (2009), the short "The Final Moments of Karl Brant" (2013), the documentary "Above and Beyond" (2014), and "Accidental Love" (2015). Reuben revived the character of Pee-wee in the 2009 stage production "The Pee-wee Herman Show on Broadway" which was televised on HBO in 2011, and the 2016 film "Pee-wee's Big Holiday". He had been diagnosed with cancer six years earlier but declined to reveal his condition to the public.

Reynolds, Norman

British production designer Norman Reynolds, who shared Academy Award for his work on "Star Wars" and "Raiders of the Lost Ark", died in England on April 6, 2023. He was 89. Reynolds was born in Willesden, London, England,

on March 26, 1934. He was working for an illuminated sign company when he was hired to create signs for the film "The Road to Hong Kong" in 1962. He soon began a career in films at Elstree Studios as a designer for "Come Fly with Me" (1963) and "Thunderball" (1965), and the television series "The Saint". He was an assistant art director by the late 1960s for such films as "Battle of Britain" (1969), "Zeppelin" (1971), "A Warm December" (1973), "Phase IV" (1974), and "The Fifth Musketeer" (1979). He soon graduated to art director for "The Little Prince" (1974), "Mr. Quilp" (1975), "Lucky Lady" (1975), "The Incredible Sarah" (1976) sharing an Academy Award nomination, "Star Wars" (1977) sharing an Oscar, "Superman" (1978), and "Superman II" (1980). Reynolds was productions designer for the films "The Empire Strikes Back" (1980) receiving another Oscar nomination, "Raiders of the Lost Ark" (1981) sharing his second Oscar, "Return of the Jedi" (1983) earning another Academy Award nomination, "Return to Oz" (1985), "Young Sherlock Holmes" (1985), "Empire of the Sun" (1987) receiving his final Oscar nomination, "Mountains of the Moon" (1990), "The Exorcist III" (1990) serving as special effects unit director, "Avalon" (1990), "Alien 3" (1992), "Alive" (1993) also serving as second unit director, "Clean Slate" (1994), "Mission: Impossible" (1996), "Sphere" (1998), and "Bicentennial Man" (1999). He directed two episodes of Steven Spielberg's anthology series "Amazing Stories" in 1986. Reynolds is survived by his wife, Ann, and their three daughters.

Reynolds, Sheldon

Guitarist and singer Sheldon Reynolds, who performed with the band Earth, Wind & Fire, died in Los

Angeles, California, on May 23, 2023. He was 63. Reynolds was born in Cincinnati, Ohio, on September 13, 1959. He began playing the guitar at an early age. He graduated from the University of Cincinnati and began touring with singer Millie Jackson. He joined the Commodores in 1983 and played on the albums "Nightshift" (1985) and "United" (1986). He recorded several albums with the R&B band Sun. Reynolds played guitar for Maurice White's 1985 self-titled album and Philip Bailey's "Family Affair" in 1989. He joined Earth, Wind & Fire, as their lead guitarist and co-vocalist in 1986. He was heard on their albums "Touch the World" (1987), "The Best of Earth, Wind & Fire, Vol. 2" (1988), "Heritage" (1990), "Millennium" (1993), and "In the Name of Love" (1997). Je was received a Grammy nomination with the band for the song "Sunday Morning" in 1994. He later recorded and performed with Urban Knights, Alfonzo Blackwell, Chicago, and Brian Culbertson. Reynolds was formerly married to Janie Hendrix, the adopted sister of Jimi Hendrix. His survivors include a son and a daughter.

Rhodes, Michael

Television director Michael Rhodes died in California on December 29, 2023. He was 78. Rhodes was born in Estherville, Iowa, on July 11, 1945. He graduated from Yale University and earned master's degrees from Pacific School of Religion and the University of Southern California Film

School. He produced and directed the 1979 short film "Blessed Be...". He continued to direct, and sometimes produce, the tele-films "Girl on the Edge of Town" (1981), "To Climb a Mountain" (1982), "High Powder" (1982), "The Juggler of Notre Dame" (1982), "Leadfoot" (1982), "Josie" (1983), "The Bet" (1984), "The Pilot" (1985), "The Fourth Wise Man" (1985), "Safe Harbor" (1985), "Babies" (1990), "Matters of the Heart" (1990), "The Killing Mind" (1991), "Reason for Living: The Jill Ireland Story" (1991), "In the Best Interest of the Children" (1992), "Seduction: Three Tales from the Inner Sanctum" (1992), "Visions of Murder" (1993), "Heidi" (1993), "Not Our Son" (1995), "Co-ed Call Girl" (1996), and "Shaughnessy" (1996). Rhodes also directed episodes of "CBS Afternoon Playhouse", "Little House on the Prairie", "Bay City Blues", "Insight", "Buchanan High", "Fame", "Star Trek: The Next Generation", "A Year in the Life", "The Bronx Zoo", "Paradise", "In the Heat of the Night", "Island Son", "China Beach", "Baywatch", "H.E.L.P.", "Wolf", "Equal Justice", "Ned Blessing: The Story of My Life and Times", "Christy", "Promised Land", "Hyperion Bay", "Beverly Hills, 90210", "Dark Angel", "So Weird", "The Jersey", and "Miracles". He was supervising producer for the 1989 film "Romero" and directed the 1996 film "Entertaining Angels: The Dorothy Day Story". Rhodes married Diane Krafft in 1967 and is survived by her and their two daughters.

Rich, Adam

Child actor Adam Rich, who starred as Nicholas Bradford on the television series "Eight Is Enough", died at his home in Los Angeles, California, on January 7, 2023. He was 54. Rich was born in New York City on October 12, 1968. He

made his acting debut in an episode of "The Six Million Dollar Man" in 1976. He appeared in television commercials for Betty Crocker Snackin' Cakes. He was best known for his role as Nicholas Bradford, the youngest of child of Dick Van Patten's brood in the comedy-drama "Eight Is Enough from 1977 until 1981. With his pageboy haircut and crooked smile, he became the quintessential little brother. Rich was a winner of the Young Artist Award for Best Young Actor in 1980 and 1981. He reprised his role as Nicholas Bradford in the reunion tele-films "Eight Is Enough: A Family Reunion" (1987) and "An Eight Is Enough Wedding" (1989). He received another Young Artist Award for "CBS Children's Mystery Theatre" production of "The Zertigo Diamond Caper" in 1983 and was nominated for his role as Danny Blake which he played in the series "Code Red" from 1981 to 1982. Rich was also seen on television in episodes of "The Love Boat", "3-2-1 Contact", "Fantasy Island", "CHiPs", "Gun Shy" as Clovis in 1983, the animated "Dungeons & Dragons" as the voice of Presto the Magician from 1983 to 1985, "St. Elsewhere", "Silver Spoons", "Small Wonder", "Baywatch", and "Reel Comedy". His other television credits include the tele-films "The City" (1977) and the animated "Tukiki and His Search for a Merry Christmas" (1979) as the voice of Tukikli. Rich was featured in the 1981 film "The Devil and Max Devlin" starring Bill Cosby and had a cameo role in 2003's "Dickie Roberts: Former Child Star". Rich dropped out of high school in his teens and experiment with drugs in the 1980s. He had several incidents with the law including and attempted burglary of a pharmacy in 1991 and a driving under the influence charge in 2002. He went through rehab on several occasions.

Richards, Ted

Underground cartoonist Ted Richards died of lung cancer in California on April 21, 2023. He was 76. Richards was born in Fort Bragg, North Carolina, on October 20, 1946. His father served in the Green Berets, and he traveled with his family to various locations in his youth. Richards moved to San

Francisco in 1969 after serving in the U.S. Air Force. He began working as a cartoonist, contributing to Gilbert Shelton's "The Fabulous Furry Freak Brothers". He also worked on the comic titles "Dopin' Dan", "E.Z. Wolf", and "Mellow Cat". He was part of the underground comix collective Air Pirates from the early 1970s. He worked on Rip Off Press' "Give Me Liberty" comic in 1975 and illustrated the comic strip "The Forty Year Old Hippie". Richards graduated from San Francisco State University in 1977. He left comics in 1981 to work in the computer division of Atari. He founded AdWare, to provide software products and design services for computer users in the late 1980s. He was a web site developer in the 1990s.

Ricochet

Ricochet, a Golden Retriever dog who was a pioneer in the dog surfing cicuit, died of liver cancer in Escondido, California, on March 31, 2023. She was 15. Ricochet was born in San Diego, California, on January 25, 2008. She was raised

by Judy Fridno as part of the Puppy Prodigies Neo-Natal & Early Learning Program. She climbed on a boogie board in a kiddie pool when she was eight weeks old and was able to balance herself. Ricochet became noted on social media when a video of her surfing with a quadriplegic boy was posted on YouTube in 2009. She began entering dog surfing contests in 2010, placing third in the Purina Incredible Dog Challenge Surf Dog competition. She was a contestant in many other surf dog competitions, usually placing in the top three. She was a therapy dog who worked with surfers with disabilities, particularly children with special needs. She also worked with active duty military service members suffering from PTSD, brain injuries, or other combat related disabilities. Fridno wrote the 2014 book "Ricochet: Riding a Wave of Hope with the Dog Who Inspires Millions". She was featured on calendars, t-shirts, stuffed animals, trading cards, and other merchandise. Ricochet appeared in the pages of such magazines as "People", "Guideposts", "Modern Dog", "Cesar's Way", "Women's World", and "Woof". She appeared on television in episodes of "Good Morning America" and "ABC Evening News with Diane Sawyer" and was a dog extra in the 2010 film "Marmaduke". Ricochet was diagnosed with liver cancer in August of 2022.

Riddle, George

Actor George Riddle died of cancer in North Plainfield, New Jersey, on June 2, 2023. He was 86. Riddle was born in Auburn, Indiana, on May 21, 1937. He began his career working as a high wire performer in the circus before turning to acting. He performed on stage at the Fred Miller

Theatre in Milwaukee from the mid-1950s. He was a member of the original cast of the off-Broadway play "The Fantasticks", appearing as Hucklebee in over 5,000 performances from 1963. He was featured as the Major General in the Broadway revival of Gilbert & Sullivan's "The Pirates of Penzance" in 1981. He was seen in stage productions of "The Glorious Age" (1975), "Tarantara! Tarantara!" (1980), and "Anything Goes" (1988), and was Clem Rogers in the touring production of "The Will Rogers Follies" from 1992 to 1995. Riddle was featured in the films "Simon" (1980), "Arthur" (1981), "True Blood" (1989), "The Pompatus of Love" (1995), "BlackMale" (2000), "Little Manhattan" (2005), "The Legacy of Walter Frumm" (2005), "Flannel Pajamas" (2006), "Eavesdrop" (2008), "The Blind" (2009), "Every Day" (2010), "The Innkeepers" (2011), "The Automatic Hate" (2015), "Most Likely to Murder" (2018), "Diane" (2018), and "The Kitchen" (2019). He was also seen in the short films "Sometimes the Neighbor" (2003), "Numskull" (2009), "Blood Country" (2012), "A Time to Speak" (2012), "Whiskey 'n Ditch" (2012), "La Boite Noir", "Snapper Magee's", and "Mildred & The Dying Parlor" (2016). Riddle appeared in the tele-films "The Trial of Standing Bear" (1988) as Civil War General George Crook and "The Superagent" (2009), and episodes of "The Baby-Sitters Club", "The Sopranos", "The Onion News Network" as Joad Cressbeckler in 2011, "Inside Amy Schumer", "Dave & Ethan: Lovemakers", "Betty", and "Little Voice". Riddle is survived by a son, Rene.

Rimmer, David

Canadian experimental filmmaker David Rimmer died in Vancouver, British Columbia, Canada, on January 26, 2023. He was 81. Rimmer was born in Vancouver on January 20, 1942. He graduated from the University of British Columbia in

1963. He traveled the world before returning to Canada in 1965. He took a filmmaking course from producer Stan Fox and left graduate school at Simon Fraser University in 1968 to become an artist. He was soon making such experimental films as "Square Inch Field" (1968) and "Migration" (1969). Rimmer moved to New York City from 1971 to 1974. He worked mainly on documentaries from the late 1970s. His numerous films include "Landscape" (1969), "Surfacing on the Thames" (1970), "Variations on a Cellophane Wrapper" (1970), "Blue Movie" (1970), "The Dance" (1970), "Forest Industry" (1970),

"Treefall" (1970), "Seashore" (1971), "Real Italian Pizza" (1971), "Watching for the Queen" (1973), "Fracture" (1973), "Canadian Pacific" (1974), "Canadian Pacific II" (1975), "Al Neil / A Portrait" (1979), "Narrows Inlet" (1980), "Shades of Red" (1982) co-directed with Paula Ross, "Bricolage" (1984), "Sisyphus" (1984), "Along the Road to Altamira" (1986), "As Seen on TV" (1986), "Roadshow" (1988), "Divine Mannequin" (1989), "Black Cat, White Cat It's a Good Cat if it Catches the Mouse" (1989), "Beaubourg Boogie-Woogie" (1992), "Local Knowledge" (1992), "Perestroyka" (1992), "Tiger" (1994), "Under the Lizards" (1994), "Codes of Conduct" (1997), "Jack Wise – Language of the Brush" (1998), "Traces of Emily Carr" (1999), "Early Hand-Painted" (2002) a series of ten shorts, "An Eye for an Eye" (2003), "Gathering Storm" (2003), "On the Road to Kandahar" (2003), "Padayatra: Walking Meditation" (2005), "Digital Psyche" (2007), and "Collective" (2008).

Rissien, Edward L.

Film producer Edward L. Rissien died in Los Angeles, California, on April 8, 2023. He was 98. Rissien was born in Des Moines, Iowa, on October 20, 1924. He attended Grinnell College before serving in the U.S. Army Air Force during

World War II. He resumed his education at Stanford where he graduated in 1949. He decided on a career in show business and moved to New York City. He began working in summer stock and regional theater. He was an assistant stage manager on Broadway for "South Pacific" in 1952 and was stage manager for "Mid-Summer" in 1953. Rissien moved to Hollywood the following year and worked as an assistant to the producer for the series "Big Town". He was an associate producer for the films "Time Table" (1956) and "Gun Fever" (1958). He worked in production at Screen Gems at Columbia and helped form Harry Belafonte's production company, HarBel Productions, in 1959. He became a program supervisor at ABC and a producer at NBC, working on such series as "Combat, "The Donna Reed Show", "Decision", "The Man from Blackhawk", "Peter Loves Mary", and "The Jane Powell Show". He became vice president of production for Bing Crosby Productions in the early 1960s where he works on the series "Hogan's Heroes", "Ben Casey", and "The Bing Crosby Show". He subsequently held the same position at Filmways where he produced the series "The Beverly Hillbillies" and "Green Acres" and the 1969 film "Castle Keep". Rissien produced the 1972 film "Snow Job" and was a production executive for the tele-films "The Third Girl from the Left" (1973), "A Summer Without Boys" (1973), "The Great Niagara" (1974), "Beyond the Bermuda Triangle" (1975), and "The Death of Ocean View Park" (1979). He joined Playboy as executive vice president of production in 1972 and rose to become president overseeing television movies and specials before leaving in the late 1980s. He produced the films "The Crazy World of Julius Vrooder" (1974) and "Saint Jack"

(1979). He was also a producer for the tele-films "The Family Kovack" (1974), "Minstrel Man" (1977), "Big Bob Johnson and His Fantastic Speed Circus" (1978), "Detour to Terror" (1980), and "A Whale for the Killing" (1981). Rissien was married to actress Joanne Gilbert from 1958 until their divorce in 1964. He married Laurie Rissien in 1978 and is survived by her and their daughter, Jenna.

Rivers, Bobby

Television personality Bobby Rivers died of cancer at a hospital in Minneapolis, Minnesota, on December 26, 2023. He was 70. Rivers was born in Los Angeles, California, on September 20, 1953. He graduated from Marquette University in Wisconsin and began his career on radio in Milwaukee. He moved to television in 1979 becoming the first African-American film critic on television at the ABC affiliate WISN-TV's "PM Magazine". He served as co-host of a live daily show of WISN from 1985 to 1985. He subsequently was an entertainment reporter for WPIX-TV in New York City. He became a VJ for the VH1 cable channel in 1987 and was soon hosting the show "Watch Bobby Rivers". He hosted the short-lived syndicated game show "Bedroom Buddies" in the early 19990s. He became lifestyles and entertainment reporter for WNYW-TV's "Good Day New York" in 1992. He joined ABC News/Lifetime as entertainment editor of the weekday magazine series "Lifetime Live" in 2000. He subsequently moved to the Food Network where he hosted "Top 5" from 2002 to 2004. Rivers was the weekly film critic and entertainment reporter for Whoopi Goldberg's "Wake Up with Whoopi" show on Premiere Radio from 2006 to 2008. He was seen on television in episodes of "The Equalizer", "Identity Crisis", "The Pat Sajak Show", "The Joan Rivers Show", and "The Sopranos". He appeared on The Onion news network podcast as Professor Robert Haige in the satirical segment "In the Know" from 2008 to 2009. He also began writing a blog, "Bobby Rivers TV", in 2011. He was featured in the 2020 documentary "The Sit-In: Harry Belafonte Hosts the Tonight Show".

Rivers, Larry 'Gator'

Basketball player Larry 'Gator' Rivers, who performed with the Harlem Globetrotters, died of cancer in Savannah, Georgia, on April 29, 2023. He was 73. Rivers was born in Savannah on May 6, 1949. He played basketball at Alfred E. Beach High School in his teens and led the team to three state titles before graduating in 1969. He continued to play basketball in college at Moberly Junior College and Missouri Western State College. He tried out for the Harlem Globetrotters in 1973 and they were impressed by his dribbling skills. He played with the teams through 1977. Reynolds returned to Missouri Western to assist with coaching and recruiting for two years before rejoining the Globetrotters in

1979. He took over as the team's main dribbler from Curly Neal in 1982. He and four other teammates were featured on an episode of "The Love Boat" on television in 1984. He became a player-coach in 1985 before leaving the Globetrotters over a disagreement with new management in 1986. He subsequently joined Meadowlark Lemon's exhibition basketball team Shooting Stars. He joined other former Globetrotters with the Basketball Magic team in January of 1987. He retired from touring later in the decade and founded Gatorball Academy to train children in basketball in 1990. He also coached high school basketball in Missouri and Kansas in the 1990s. Rivers returned to Savannah in 2008 where he continued to operate Gatorball Academy. He was elected to the Chatham County Commission in 2020. His survivors include his wife, Jean Brown Rivers.

Rivet, Gilberte

French actress Gilberte Rivet died in Bagnois-sur-Ceze, France, on March 4, 2023. He was 96. Rivet was born in Pont-Saint-Esprit, France, on September 15, 1926. She was a piano prodigy from an early age and performed concerts from the age of seven. She later studied acting from Henri Rollan at the Conservatory. She performed frequently on stage throughout her career and was part of the Sacha Pitoeff Company. Rivet was seen in the films "Heureaux Qui Comme Ulysse..." (1970), "Lacombe, Lucien" (1974) as Lucien's Mother, "Aloise" (1975), "Le Pays Bleu" (1977), "Retour a Marseille" (19890), "At the Top of the Stairs" (1983), the short "La Lettre a Dede" (1985), and "Les Enfants du Diable" (1992). She appeared on television in productions of "Nemo" (1970), "Les Cousins de la Constance" (1970), "Pourquoi Tuer le Pepe" (1978), "Le Facteur de Fontcabrette" (1979), "Le Jeune Homme Vert" (1979), "Ciboulette" (1980), "Fini de Rire, Fillette" (1981), "Le Sage de Sauvenat" (1982), "La Terre et le Moulin" (1984), "L'Ami Giono" (1990), "Les Mouettes" (1991), "Liebesreise" (1992), and "Dans un Grand Vent de Fleurs" (1996). Her other television credits include episodes of "En Votre Ame et Conscience", "Aubrac City" as Leonide from 1971 to 1982, "Les Gens de Mogador" as Philomene in 1972, "Nans le Berger", "Bergeval et Fils", "Bonsoir Chef" as Louise in 1977, "Medecins de Nuit", "Heidi", and "Cinema 16".

Robertson, George R.

Canadian actor George R. Robertson, who starred as Commissioner Henry Hurst in the "Police Academy" film series, died at a health center in Toronto, Ontario, Canada, on January 29, 2023. He was 89. Robertson was born in Brampton, Ontario, on April 20, 1933. He excelled as an athlete in high school and attended Columbia University in New York, where he earned a master's degree in business in 1959. He made his film debut in a small role in the 1968 supernatural film "Rosemary's Baby". He was also seen in the films "Marooned" (1969), "Airport" (1970), "The Girl in Blue" (1973), "Paperback Hero" (1973), "Power Play" (1978), "Norma Rae" (1979), "The Amateur" (1981), and "Murder by Phone" (1982). Robertson appeared a Commissioner Henry Hurst in the films

"Police Academy" (1984), "Police Academy 2: Their First Assignment" (1985), "Police Academy 3: Back in Training" (1986), "Police Academy 4: Citizens on Patrol" (1987), "Police Academy 5: Assignment: Miami Beach" (1988), and "Police Academy 6: City Under Siege" (1989). His other film credits include "Deceived" (1991), "JFK" (1991), "National Lampoon's Senior Trip" (1995), "Murder at 1600" (1997), and "Still Mine" (2012). Robertson appeared frequently on television with roles in episodes of "The F.B.I.", "The Most Deadly Game", "Cool Million", "House of Pride", "Police Surgeon", "The Littlest Hobo", "The Great Detective", "ABC Weekend Specials", "CBS Summer Playhouse", "The Twilight Zone", "Street Legal", "War of the Worlds", "Top Cops", "E.N.G." as Kyle Copeland from 1989 to 1994, "Side Effects", "The Great Defender", "The Adventures of Shirley Holmes",. "Police Academy: The Series" reprising his role as Commissioner Hurst in 1998, "PSI Factor: Chronicles of the Paranormal", "Leap Years", "Doc", and "Haven". His other television credits include productions of "The Mad Trapper" (1972), "Deedee" (1974), "The Canary" (1975), "The Dawson Patrol" (1978), "F.D.R.: The Last Year" (1980) as Gen. Leslie Groves, "Escape from Iran: The Canadian Caper" (1981), "Evergreen" (1985), "The High Price of Passion" (1986), "Shades of Love: Sunset Court" (1988), "Day One" (1989) as Edward Condon, "Small Sacrifices" (1989), "Hitler's Daughter" (1990), "Iran: Days of Crisis" (1991) as Secretary of State Cyrus Vance, "Devlin" (1992), "Teamster Boss: The Jackie Presser Story" (1992) as Senator Howard Cannon, "The Good Fight" (1992), "Shattered Trust: The Shari Karney Story" (1993), "A Perfect Stranger" (1994), "Dancing in the Dark" (1995), "Hiroshima" (1995) as Admiral William D. Leahy, "The Silence of Adultery" (1995), "Double Jeopardy" (1996), "The Boys Next Door" (1996), "Devil's Food" (1996), "Holiday Affair" (1996), "Lies He Told" (1997), "The Familiar Stranger" (2001), "We Were the Mulvaneys" (2002), "America's Prince: The John F. Kennedy Jr. Story" (2003) as Maurice Templesman, "The Pentagon Papers" (2003) as Senator J.W. Fulbright, "The Reagans" (2003) as Barry Goldwater, "The Path to 9/11" (2006) as Vice President Dick Cheney, "Sundays at Tiffany's" (2010), "Crossfire" (2016), and "Cradle to Grave" (2017). Robertson

married Adele Marie Probst in 1961 and is survived by her and their two daughters.

Robertson, Pat

Religious broadcaster and political commentator Marion Gordon 'Pat' Robertson, who was a candidate for the Republican presidential nomination in 1988, died at his home in Virginia Beach, Virginia, on June 8, 2023. He was 93. Robertson was born in Lexington, Virginia, on March 22, 1930. He was the son of A. Willis Robertson, who served in the U.S. Senate representing Virginia from 1946 to 1966. He graduated magna cum laude from Washington and Lee University with a

degree in history. He served in combat with the U.S. Marine Corps in Korea in the late 1940s and early 1950s. He was discharged as a First Lieutenant in 1952 and graduated from Yale Law School in 1955. He decided to pursue a religious career after becoming a born again Christian and attended the Biblical Seminary of New York. He received a Master of Divinity degree in 1959. He was ordained a Southern Baptist minister in 1961. Robertson began the Christian Broadcasting Network in Virginia Beach, Virginia, in 1960. He purchased WYAH-TV which began broadcasting the following year. The network was best known as the home of the Christian variety and talk show "The 700 Club". Robertson served as co-host of the show from its inception through 2021. He was founder of CBN University in 1977 in Virginia Beach. It became known as Regent University in 1990 with Robertson serving as chancellor and CEO. He was also founder of the American Center for Law and Justice, International Family Entertainment Inc., Operation Blessing International Relief and Development Corporation, and The Flying Hospital, Inc. Robertson's conservative political activities led him to seek the Republican nomination for President of the United States. He announced his intention to challenge Vice President George H.W. Bush for the nomination in September of 1986. He performed poorly in many of the early primaries and withdrew from the campaign before the primary season ended in spring of 1988. He had taken a break from "The 700 Club" during his campaign and resumed his role as co-host. He also became a founder of the Christian Coalition, a right-wing organization that supported conservative candidates. Robertson's political and religious viewpoint often brought controversy. He was an outspoken critic of abortion, homosexuality, feminism, and liberalism in general. He stated that Hinduism was demonic, Islam was Satanic, and compared Buddhism to a disease. He seemed to blame the terrorist attack on September 11, 2001, and Hurricane Katrina, which devastated New Orleans and other areas in 2005 were punishments from God for America's abortion policy and other issues. Robertson co-wrote his autobiography, "Shout It from the Housetops", in 1972. He wrote numerous books including "My Prayer for You" (1977), "The Secret Kingdom" (1982), "Beyond Reason: How Miracles

Can Change Your Life" (1985), "America's Dates with Destiny" (1986), "The New World Order" (1991), "Turning Tide: The Fall of Liberalism and the Rise of Common Sense" (1993), the novel "The End of the Age" (1995), "The Ten Offenses" (2004), "Courting Disaster" (2004), "On Humility" (2009), "Right on the Money: Financial Advice for Tough Times" (2009), "I Have Walked with the Living God" (2020), "The Power of the Holy Spirit in You: Understanding the Miraculous Power of God" (2022), and "The Shepherd King: The Life of David" (2023). Robertson was married to model and beauty queen Adelia 'Dede' Elmer from 1954 until her death in 2022. He is survived by their four children, including Gordon P. Robertson, who succeeded his father as president of the Christian Broadcasting Network and host of "The 700 Show".

Robertson, Robbie

Canadian musician Robbie Robertson, who was lead guitarist and songwriter with the rock group the Band, died of prostate cancer in Los Angeles, California, on August 9, 2023. He was 80. Robertson was born in Toronto, Ontario, Canada, on July 5, 1943. His mother was a Mohawk who often took him to the Six Nations Reserve when he was a child. He learned to play the guitar at an early age. He began playing with the band Little Caesar and the Colonels in his early teens. He joined the Suedes in 1959 and soon wrote a pair of songs with rockabilly singer Ronnie Hawkins. He soon joined Hawkins' band, the Hawks. He performed and recorded with the backing band, which included Levon Helm and other future members of the Band, for several years. The Hawks broke with Hawkins in 1964 and began performing as Levon and the Hawks, with Robertson writing most of their songs. Bob Dylan recruited him to be part of his backing band, which soon included most of his Hawks bandmates, in 1965. He was heard on Dylan's 1966 album "Blonde on Blonde". Robertson and his fellow band members rented a place that became known as Big Pink and was near Dylan's Woodstock, New York, headquarters. The musicians wrote and recorded music, some of which was later released as "The Basement Tapes" in 1975. They changed the name of their group to the Band, which included Robertson, Levon Helms on drums, Richard Manuel on piano, Rick Danko on bass, and Garth Hudson on keyboards. The Band released their debut album, "Music from Big Pink", in 1968 which was followed by a self-named album in 1969. Robertson wrote or co-wrote all the songs that included the hits "Up on Cripple Creek" and "The Night They Drove Old Dixie Down". More successful albums followed including "Stage Fright" (1970), "Cahoots" (1971), the live album "Rock of Ages" (1972), "Moondog Matinee" (1973) featuring blues and R&B covers, "Northern Lights - Southern Cross" (1975) featuring the single "Acadian Driftwood", and "Islands" (1977). The Band briefly rejoined Dylan, backing him on the 1974 album "Planet Waves". They were musical guests on an episode of "Saturday Night Life" in 1976. They scheduled what was billed as their final concert, "The Last Waltz", in San Francisco in 1976. They were joined on stage by numerous guest artists and the event was filmed by Martin Scorsese for the 1978 concert film "The Last Waltz". Robertson went on to produce Neil Diamond's albums "Beautiful Noise" and "Love at the Greek". The remaining members of the band recorded several albums without Robertson in the 1990s. He recorded his first self-named solo album in 1987 which was nominated for a Grammy Award. It was followed by "Storyville" in 1991, which also received a Grammy nomination. Robertson returned as musical guest on "Saturday Night Live" in 1988 and 1992 and starred in the 1995 television special "Robbie Robertson: Going Home". He was a guest on such series as "Late Night with David Letterman", "The Whoopi Goldberg Show" also composing the opening theme, "Late Night with Conan O'Brien", "The Tonight Show with Jay Leno", "Later... With Jools Holland", "Jimmy Kimmel Live!", "Late Night with Jimmy Fallon", "Tavis Smiley", "The Tonight Show Starring Jimmy Fallon", and "The Big Interview with Dan Rather". His later solo albums include "Music for the Native Americans" (1994), "Contact from the Underworld of Redboy" (1998), "How to Become Clairvoyant" (2011), and "Sinematic" (2019). Robertson starred as Patch in the 1980 film "Carny" opposite Jodie Foster and Gary Busey. He also co-produced the soundtrack album for the film. He was featured as Roger in Sean Penn's 1995 film "The Crossing Guard". He continued to work with Martin Scorsese, supplying music to underscore his 1980 film "Raging Bull". He scored the films "The King of Comedy" (1983), "The Color of Money" (1986), "Jimmy Hollywood" (1994), and "The Irishman" (2019). He also worked with Scorsese on the films "Casino" (1995), "Gangs of New York" (2002), "Shutter Island" (2010), "The Wolf of Wall Street" (2013), and "Silence" (2016). Robertson scored the 2023 film "Killers of the Flower Moon" shortly before his death and received a posthumous Academy Award nomination for his work. He and the Band were inducted into the Rock and Roll Hall of Fame in 1994 and he received a Lifetime Achievement Award from the National Academy of Songwriters in 1997. His memoirs, "Testimony", were published in 2016 and he was featured in the 2019 documentary film "Once Were Brothers: Robbie Robertson and the Band". Robertson was married to journalist Dominique Bourgeois from 1968 until their divorce in 2000 and is survived by their three children. He married his girlfriend, restaurateur Janet Zuccarini, in March of 2023 and she also survives him.

Robison, Charlie

Country music singer and songwriter Charlie Robison died of cardiac arrest at a hospital in San Antonio, Texas, on September 10, 2023. He was 59. Robison was born in Houston, Texas, on September 1, 1964. He played football with Southwest Texas State University until he was sidelined with a knee injury. He moved to Austin, Texas, in the late 1980s where he performed with the bands Chaparral, Millionaire Playboys, and Two Hoots. He released the solo album

"Bandera" in 1996. His second album, "Life of the Party", was released through Sony's Lucky Dog Records subsidiary in 1998 and included his hit single "My Hometown". Robison released the live albums "Unleashed Live" and "Step Right Up" and 2001 which contained the hit "I Want You So Bad". He was a judge on the first season of the television singing competition "Nashville Star" in 2003. He released the album "Good Times" through the independent label Dualtone in 2004 and self-produced the 2009 follow-up "Beautiful Day". He continued to tour and perform until 2018 when he announced his retirement due to complications from throat surgery. He resumed his career on stage in 2022. He appeared in several films including "The Big Day" (1999), "Grand Champion" (2002), "Blood Trail" (2005), "ExTerminators" (2009), and "Javelina" (2011). Robison was married to Emily Erwin of the Dixie Chicks (now Chicks) from 1999 until their divorce in 2008 and is survived by their three children. He married Kristen Robison in 2015 and is also survived by her and their son.

Rodriguez, Sixto

Musician Sixto Rodriguez, who was the subject of the 2012 Oscar-winning documentary "Searching for Sugar Man", died of complications from a stroke in Detroit, Michigan, on August 8, 2023. He was 81. Rodriguez was born in Detroit on July 10, 1942. He released his first single, "I'll Slip Away",

under the name Rod Riguez in 1967. He signed with Sussex Records in 1970 and recorded the albums "Cold Fact" (1970) and "Coming from Reality" (1971) under the name Rodriguez. He had a minor hit with his signature song "Sugar Man" in 1972. He abandoned his music career in 1976 to work at low-income jobs in demolition and production lines. He was active in politics and civic affairs and ran unsuccessfully for several public offices, including races for Mayor of Detroit in 1981 and 1993. Despite the lack of public attention his recording received in the United States they became popular in Australia, New Zealand, and southern Africa. Concert promoters in Australia tracked him down to Detroit and he had two concert tours in 1979 and 1981. He was unaware of the huge popularity he had gained in South Africa until 1997 when his daughter found a website dedicated to him. He soon went on the first of several South African tours and was subject of the 2001 documentary "Dead Men Don't Tour: Rodriguez in South Africa 1998". There had previously been rumors the Rodriguez had died in the 1960s and 1970s. Director Malik Bendjelloul made a documentary film about the efforts of two South African fans to find him in the late 1990s. The film, "Search for Sugar Man", was released

in 2012 and won the Academy Award and BAFTA Award for Best Documentary Feature. Rodriguez received a resurgence of publicity in the United States and was a guest on "Late Show with David Letterman", "The Tonight Show with Jay Leno", "The Jeff Probst Show", and "Later... with Jools Holland". He is survived by his second wife, Konny Koskos, and three daughters.

Roe, Bart

Film and television assistant director Bart Roe died in Hollywood, California, on January 14, 2023. He was 90. Roe was born in New York City on April 2, 1932. He began his

career as a child actor on radio and appeared on the Broadway stage in the 1947 revival of "A Young Man's Fancy". He served in the U.S. Army during the Korean War. He worked in television from the 1950s serving as an assistant director for episodes of "The Ernie Kovaks Show", "The Hollywood Palace", "Young Dr. Kildare", "General Hospital", "Lucan", and "V". He also served as a second assistant director for the tele-films "The Secret Life of John Chapman" (1976), "Having Babies II" (1977), "Ants!" (1977), "Dark Night of the Scarecrow" (1981), "Love Leads the Way: A True Story" (1984), and "Everybody's Baby: The Rescue of Jessica McClure" (1989). Roe was second assistant director for the films "The Master Gunfighter" (1975), "Sweet Revenge" (1976), "Final Chapter: Walking Tall" (1977), "Damnation Alley" (1977), and "The Electric Horseman" (1979). He left the film industry in the 1980s to work in real estate.

Rogow, Stan

Television producer Stan Rogow, who was noted for the Disney series "Lizzie McGuire", died at a hospital in Los Angeles, California, on December 7, 2023. He was 75. Rogow

was born in Brooklyn, New York, on November 30, 1948. He graduated from Boston University and earned a law degree from the Boston University School of Law. He worked as a lawyer in Boston before becoming involved with films. He served as a production executive for the CBS tele-film "Playing for Time" in 1980. Rogow moved to Los Angeles where he was a producer for the television series "Fame". He shared an Emmy nomination in 1982. He was a producer for the tele-films and mini-series "Help Wanted: Kids" (1986), "Rock 'n' Roll Mom" (1988), "Murder in High Places" (1991), "Nowhere to Hide" (1994), "Desert Breeze" (1996), "The Defenders: Payback" (1997), "The Defenders: Choice of Evils" (1998), "The Defenders: Taking the First" (1998), "Man Made"

(1998), "Bad Cop, Bad Cop" (1998), "What's Stevie Thinking?" (2005), "Flight 29 Down: The Hotel Tango" (2007), "Valemont" (2009), and "Gulliver Quinn" (2012). Rogow was executive producer for the series "Shannon's Deal", "Middle Ages" which he co-created, "South of Sunset" which he co-created in 1993, "Nowhere Man", "State of Grace", "Darcy's Wild Life", and "Flight 29 Down" which he created in 2005. He was executive producer for the "Lizzie McGuire" series and shared Emmy nominations in 2003 and 2004. He also produced the 2004 film "The Lizzie McGuire Movie". He began the Electric Farm Entertainment production company in 2007 and produced and directed the internet series "Afterworld", "Gemini Division", and "Woke Up Dad". Rogow was co-producer for the 1986 prehistoric film "The Clan of the Cave Bear". He was executive producer for the films "All I Want for Christmas" (1991) and "Men of War" (1994). His survivors include his son, actor Jackson Rogow.

Rohr, Tony

Irish actor Tony Rohr died of prostate cancer on October 29, 2023. He was 84. Rohr was born in Carrick-on-Suir, County Tipperary, Ireland, on May 21, 1939. He served in the Irish army before pursuing an acting career. He  performed with the New Irish Players in Killarney in the early 1960s. He worked with the Traverse Theatre Workshop company in the early 1970s. Rohr performed frequently on stage and was a founding member of the Joint Stock Theatre Group in 1974. He often performed in the works by playwright Samuel Beckett and was a founder of the theatre cooperative the Godot Company in 2004. He was seen frequently on television with roles in episodes of "Adam Adamant Lives!", "Doctor Who", "Softly Softly", "Sherlock Holmes", "Special Branch", "Orson Welles' Great Mysteries", "The Ventures", "Second City Firsts", "Life at Stake", "The Sweeney", "The Other Side", "Spearhead", "BBC2 Playhouse", "Crown Court", "Screen Two", "Hard Cases", "Taggart", "The Paradise Club", "Screenplay", "Van der Valk", "Maigret", "Lovejoy", "The Bill", "The Chief", "Cracker", "The Vet", "Father Ted", "Chef!", "The Lakes" as Grandad Anthony from 1997 to 1999, "On Home Ground" as Brian Horan in 2001, "Waking the Dead", "Hustle", "Horne & Corden", "Casualty", "The Street", "New Tricks", "Inspector George Gently", and "Derek". His other television credits include productions of "The School for Scandal" (1975), "Three Men in a Boat" (1975), "Sheppey" (1980), "The Patricia Neal Story" (1981), "Harry's Game" (1982), "Grace Kelly" (1983), "Enemies of the State" (1983), "Jamaica Inn" (1983), "The Old Men at the Zoo" (1983), "Johnny Jarvis" (1983), "Much Ado About Nothing" (1984), "The Rockingham Shoot" (1987), "A Perfect Spy" (1987), "Small World" (1988), "Coppers" (1988), "Not Mozart: Letters, Riddles and Writs" (1991) as Ludwig van Beethoven,

"Middlemarch" (1994), "Prime Suspect: The Lost Child" (1995), "Painted Lady" (1997), "Colour Blind" (1998), "Perfect Day: The Funeral" (2006), and "The Time of Your Life" (2007). He was also seen in numerous films including "Terror" (1978), "The Long Good Friday" (1980), "McVicar" (1980), "Angel" (1982), "Ascendancy" (1983), "No Surrender" (1985), "Code Name: Emerald" (1985), "Rocinante" (1986), "High Spirits" (1988), "I Hired a Contract Killer" (1990), "The Playboys" (1992), "Into the West" (1992), "The Butcher Boy" (1997), "The Nephew" (1998), "Titanic Town" (1998), "Sweety Barrett" (1998), "Most Important" (1999), "Dead Man Running" (2009), "Leap Year" (2010), "Mr. Nice" (2010), "Round Ireland with a Fridge" (2010), "Les Miserables" (2012), and "The Double" (2013). Rohr and actress Pauline Collins had a daughter, Louise, which they gave up for adoption in 1964. He and Collins were reunited with her child over twenty years later. He was married to Janet Revell from 1981 until her death in 2003 and is also survived by their three daughters.

Roizman, Owen

Cinematographer Owen Roizman, who received Oscar nominations for the films "The French Connection" and "The Exorcist", died at his home in Encino, California, on January 6, 2023. He was 86. Roizman was born in New York City on September 22, 1936. His father, Sol Roizman, was a newsreel  photographer for Fox Movietone News. Owen attended Gettysburg College in Pennsylvania and worked in New York for a camera rental company. He began working in film after graduation, serving as an assistant to cinematographer Akos Farkas for commercials. Roizman made his film debut with the low-budget 1970 film "Stop!", filmed in Puerto Rico. He earned an Academy Award nomination for his work on his next film, William Friedkin's "The French Connection" (1971). He was cinematographer for the 1972 television special "Liza with a Z". He was also director of cinematography for the films "The Gang That Couldn't Shoot Straight" (1971), Woody Allen's "Play It Again, Sam" (1972), "The Heartbreak Kid" (1972), William Friedkin's horror classic "The Exorcist" (1973) receiving another Oscar nomination, "The Taking of Pelham One Two Three" (1974), "The Stepford Wives" (1975), "Three Days of the Condor" (1975), "The Return of a Man Called Horse" (1976), Sidney Lumet's "Network" (1976) earning his third Academy Award nomination, "Straight Time" (1976), "Sgt. Pepper's Lonely Hearts Club Band" (1978), "The Electric Horseman" (1979), "The Rose" (1979) photographing concert scenes, "The Black Marble" (1980), "True Confessions" (1981), "Absence of Malice" (1981), "Taps" (1981), Sydney Pollack's "Tootsie" (1982) receiving another Oscar nomination, "Vision Quest" (1985), "I Love You to Death" (1990), "Havana" (1990) also appearing onscreen in the small role of Santos, "The Addams Family" (1991), and "Grand Canyon" (1991).

Roizman received a fifth Academy Award nomination for cinematography for Lawrence Kasdan's "Wyatt Earp" (1994) also appearing in the small role of Danny. His final film as director of photography was Kasdan's "French Kiss" in 1995. He was cinematographer for several Madonna music videos in the mid-1980s. He was president of the American Society of Cinematographers (ASC) from 1997 to 1998 and received their Lifetime Achievement Award in 1997. He was a recipient of an honorary Academy Award in 2017. Roizman married Mona Lindholm in 1964 and is survived by her and their son, camera operator Eric.

Roland, John

Television newscaster John Roland died of complications from a stroke in North Miami Beach, Florida, on May 7, 2023. He was 81. He was born John Roland Gingher, Jr., in Pittsburgh, Pennsylvania, on November 25, 1941. He

graduated from California State University at Long Beach in 1964. He began working in television as a researcher for NBC News in Los Angeles in 1966. He soon became a reporter at KTTV in Los Angeles where he covered the assassination of Robert F. Kennedy in 1968 and the murder of actress Sharon Tate in 1969. He moved to WNEW-TV in New York where he became a weekend anchor and produced a cooking show. He took over as weeknight anchor in 1979. He remained with WNEW, which later became Fox's WNYW, until his retirement in 2004. Roland appeared in cameo roles in several films including "Hero at Large" (1980), "Eyewitness" (1981), "The Scout" (1994), and "The Object of My Affection" (1998). Roland is survived by his fourth wife, Zayda Galasso.

Romaguera, Joaquin

Operatic tenor and actor Joaquin Romaguera died in Mount Dora, Florida, on May 9, 2023. He was 90. Romaguera was born in Key West, Florida, on September 5, 1932. He

began his career as a tenor with the Miami Opera Company in 1950. He performed frequently with the New York City Opera from the late 1960s, with roles in Hugo Weisgall's "Nine Rivers from Jordan" (1968) as the Dead Man, and Gian Carlo Menotti's "The Most Important Man" (1971) as Professor Risselberg. He was noted for his portrayal of Adolfo Pirelli in the original Broadway production of "Sweeney Todd: The Demon Barber of Fleet Street" in 1979. He was featured as Teddy in an off-Broadway revival of Cole Porter's "Gay Divorce" in 1987. Romaguera performed at venues around the country including the Opera Company of Boston, the Opera Society of Washington, and Broadway Sacramento, where he gave his final performance in a production of Andrew Lloyd Webber's "Evita". He was predeceased by his life partner, Broadway hair designer Robert Cybula, in 2000.

Romanus, Richard

Actor Richard Romanus, who was the voice of Weehawk in Ralph Bakshi's 1977 animated fantasy classis "Wizards", died at a hospital in Volos, Greece, on December 23, 2023. He was 80. Romanus was born in Barre, Vermont, on February 8, 1943. He graduated from Xavier University in

Cincinnati, Ohio, in 1964. He briefly studied law at the University of Connecticut Law School. He moved to New York City where he trained as an actor with Lee Strasberg at the Actors Studio. He made his film debut in Andy Milligan's 1968 horror film "The Ghastly Ones" and was seen in a small role in 1970's "Walk the Walk". Romanus was featured in Martin Scorsese's 1973 crime drama "Mean Streets". His other films include "The Gravy Train" (aka "The Dion Brothers") (1974), "Russian Roulette" (1975), Ralph Bakshi's animated fantasy "Wizards" (1977) as the voice of Weehawk, "Sitting Ducks" (1980), the animated "Heavy Metal" (1981) starring in the "Harry Canyon" segment, the comedy slasher film "Pandemonium" (1982), the animated "Hey Good Lookin'" (1982), "Strangers Kiss" (1983), "Protocol" (1984), "Murphy's Law" (1986), "The Couch Trip" (1988), "Hollywood Heartbreak" (1990), "Final Stage" (1990), "Oscar" (1991), "To Protect and Serve" (1992), the action thriller "Point of No Return" (1993), "Cops and Robbersons" (1994), "Urban Relics" (1998), "Carlo's Wake" (1999), "Nailed" (2001), and "The Young Black Stallion" (2003). Romanus was seen frequently on television with roles in episodes of "Mission: Impossible", "Mod Squad", "Rhoda", "Kojak", "Charlie's Angels", "Starsky and Hutch", "Hawaii Five-O", "The Rockford Files", "Tenspeed and Brown Shoe" as Crazy Tommy Tedesco in 1980, "Hart to Hart", "Fantasy Island", "Foul Play" as Captain Vito Lombardi in 1981, the crime series "Strike Force" as Lieutenant Charlie Gunzer from 1981 to 1982, "Matt Houston", "Hardcastle and McCormick", "Hunter", "Fame", "Tales from the Darkside", "Stir Crazy", "Shadow Chasers", "Hill Street Blues", "MacGyver", "The A-Team", "Cagney & Lacey", "Midnight Caller", "Mission: Impossible", "Jake and the Fatman", "Reasonable Doubts", "Johnny Bago" as Vinnie in 1993, "Chicago Hope", "Northern Exposure", "Charlie Grace", "Diagnosis Murder", "NYPD Blue", "Providence", and "The Sopranos" in the recurring role of Richard La Penna from 1999 to 2002. His other television credits include the tele-films "Night Chase" (1970), "Night Drive" (1977), "Gold of the Amazon Women" (1979), "More Than Murder" (1984), "Second Sight: A Love Story" (1984), "Crackups" (1984), "Ghost of a Chance" (1987), "Married to the Mob" (1989), "The Entertainers" (1991), and "The Rockford Files: A Blessing in Disguise" (1995). He and his wife, Anthea Sylbert, wrote and produced the Lifetime tele-films "Giving Up the Ghost" (1998) and "If You Believe" (1999), and Romanus also appeared in them. The couple moved to the Greek island of Skiathos in 2004 where he began writing. His memoirs, "Act III: A Small Island in the Aegean", were published in 2011. He also wrote the novels "Chrysalis" (2011) and "Matoula's Echo" (2014). Romanus was married to actress and singer Tina Bohlmann from 1967 until their divorce in 1980 and is survived by their son. He married costume designer Anthea Sylbert in 1985 and she also survives him.

Romita, John, Sr.

Comic book artist John Romita, Sr., who co-created such Marvel Comic characters as Wolverine, the Punisher, and Luke Cage, died at his home in Floral Park, Florida, on June 12, 2023. He was 93. Romita was born in Brooklyn, New York,  on January 24, 1930. He began drawing at an early age and graduated from Manhattan's School of Industrial Art in 1947. He was working at Forbes Lithograph in 1949 when he began working as a ghost artist for Lester Zakarin at Timely Comics, the predecessor of Marvel. He continued to collaborate with Zakarin at Timely and Trojan Comics until being drafted into the U.S. Army in 1951. He was stationed in New York where he did layouts for recruitment posters. He was still in the army when he approached Stan Lee at Atlas Comics (the former Timely and future Marvel) about working on comics. He was given a science fiction tale to illustrate that appeared in the pages of "Strange Tales" #4 in December of 1951. He continued to provide art of tales of horror, war, and romance at Atlas. He had a brief run as artist for the reboot of the "Captain America" comic in 1954. He was creator for the character M-11 the Human Robot for "Menace" #11 in May of 1954, who was resurrected many years later for the "Agents of Atlas" team. Romita also illustrated the "Waku, Prince of the Bantu" series for "Jungle Tales" in 1954. He began working at DC Comics in the late 1950s on such romance titles as "Heart Throbs", "Falling in Love", and "Young Love". He was soon the primary artist for the romance covers and began inking his own pencils by the early 1960s. He returned to Marvel Comics in 1965 as an inker for "The Avengers" #23 and was soon working on the "Daredevil" title. Stan Lee selected him to replace Steve Ditko on "The Amazing Spider-Man" in 1966. He was co-creator of Spider-Man's girlfriend, Mary Jane Watson, and villains the Kingpin, the Shocker, and Rhino. Romita began cutting back on his work on Spider-Man later in the decade, doing layouts or covers. He relinquished the title to Gil Kane in 1971 but returned as penciller from 1972 to 1974. He was artist and editor for the "Spider Super Stories" comic book series in the 1970s in coordination with the Children's Television Workshop's series "The Electric

Company". He illustrated the "Spider-Man" newspaper comic strip from 1977 to 1980. Romita served as Marvel's art director from 1973 through the 1980s. He was instrumental in the creation and design of such characters as the Punisher, Wolverine, Luke Cage, Tigra, Brother Voodoo, a restyled Black Widow, and Bullseye. He inked Jack Kirby's oversized comic "Captain America's Bicentennial Battles" in 1976. He was inker for the first appearance of Monica Rambeau's Captain Marvel in 1982 and the Hobgoblin in 1983. He worked with Marvel's special projects department before announcing his semi-retirement in 1996. He continued to do occasional cover art and illustrated one of the "TV Guide" covers promoting the new "Spider-Man" film in 2002. His Spider-Man illustration and a Rick Buckler Hulk image Romita had inked were among the Marvel Super Heroes postage stamps released in 2007. He was inducted into the Will Eisner Award Hall of Fame in 2002, and the Inkwell Awards Joe Sinnott Hall of Fame in 2020. Romita married Virginia Bruno in 1952 and she survives him. They had two sons, Victor and John Jr., who also became a leading comic book artist.

Roos, Casper

Actor Casper Roos died in Newport, Rhode Island, on August 18, 2023. He was 98. Roos was born in the Bronx, New York, on March 21, 1925. He served in the Merchant Marine after graduating high school in 1943. He pursued a career on  stage after World War II ended. He was seen in numerous Broadway productions including "First Impressions" (1959), "Once Upon a Mattress" (1959), "How to Succeed in Business Without Really Trying" (1961), "Do I Hear a Waltz?" (1965), "Skyskraper" (1965), "Mame" (1966), "Walking Happy" (1966), "Here's Where I belong" (1968), "Minnie's Boys" (1970), "Ari" (1971), "The Merchant of Venice" (1973), "Shenandoah" (1975), "Kings" (1976), "Brigadoon" (1980), "My One and Only" (1983), "Into the Light" (1986), and the 1989 revival of "Shenandoah". He was seen in small roles as a minister or undertaker in various television soap operas. He was also featured in a 1974 television production of "Enemies" and an episode of "Finders of Lost Loves" in 1984. Roos appeared in the films "Deadtime Stories" (1986) and "The Heat" (2013). He was married to Shirley Anne Richolson from 1961 until her death in 2017 and is survived by their son Pieter.

Rose, Patrick

Canadian actor Patrick Rose died of cancer at a hospital in Toronto, Canada, on July 1, 2023. He was 79. Rose was born in Dauphin, Manitoba, Canada, on February 1, 1944. He attended the University of British Columbia where he began performing on stage. He went to London, England, in 1968 where he was featured in a production of George Gershwin's "Lady, Be Good!". He returned to Canada in the early 1970s and performed frequently at the Arts Club Theatre in Vancouver. He moved to Toronto with his family later in the decade.

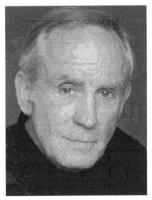

Rose was a recurring performer on the "Inside Canada" television comedy series from 1973 to 1974. He was also seen in episodes of "King of Kensington", "The Littlest Hobo", "Seeing Things", "Today's Special", "Night Heat", "Air Waves", "Alfred Hitchcock Presents", and "Street Legal". He was featured in several films including "Improper Channels" (1981), the tele-film "A Far Cry from Home" (1981), "Mr. Nice Guy" (1987), and "This Is My Life" (1992). Rose married Susan Rose in 1969 and is survived by her and their two children.

Ross, Elizabeth

British actress Elizabeth Ross died in England on

January 10, 2023. She was 98. Ross weas born in Kenya on January 24, 1924. She performed on stage after World War II and was part of the Donald Wolfit Acting Company. She appeared on television in her later years with roles in episodes of "Doctors", "EastEnders", "Casualty", and "Psychoville". Ross also appeared in the shorts "And the Red Man Went Green" (2003), "Patience", "Out of Sight" (2014), and "At Dawn" (2015), and the 2016 film "Criminal".

Rossington, Gary

Guitarist Gary Rossington, who was co-founder of the southern rock band Lynyrd Skynyrd, died at his home in Milton, Georgia, on March 5, 2023. He was 71. Rossington

was born in Jacksonville, Florida, on December 4, 1951. He was in his early teens when he joined with Ronnie Van Zandt, Bob Burns, Allen Collins, and Larry Junstrom to form the band the Noble Five in 1964. The later became the One Percent before changing their name to Lynyrd Skynyrd, after gym teacher Leonard Skinner who frequently hassled them about their long hair, in 1969. They band played at bars around Florida and evolved into a seven-piece unit, with Rossington, Collins, and Ed King on guitars backing Van Zant's vocals. The group recorded their first album, "Lynyrd Skynyrd (pronounced 'lĕh-'nérd 'skin-'nérd)", in 1973. The album contained such iconic hit songs as "Free Bird", "Gimme Three Steps", and "Simple Man". They recorded four more albums over the next

several years including "Second Helping" (1974) featuring the hit single "Sweet Home Alabama", "Nuthin' Fancy" (1975), "Gimme Back My Bullets" (1976), and "Street Survivors" (1977). He was involved in an automobile accident in 1976 while under the influence of drugs and alcohol, forcing the band to postpone a tour schedule. He was a passenger on the chartered plane crash in Mississippi on October 20, 1977, that killed bandmates Ronnie Van Zant, Steve Gaines, and Cassie Gaines, and three others. He was badly injured in the crash with steel rods in his right arm and right leg. He became addicted to pain medication during his recovery. He and Allen Collins played in the Rossington Collins Band from 1980 until 1982. He and his wife, Dale Krantz-Rossington, formed the Rossington Band and released albums in 1986 and 1988. He was instrumental in reuniting the surviving members of Lynyrd Skynyrd with Van Zant's younger brother, Johnny, as vocalist for a tour commemorating the tenth anniversary of the plane crash. The new group, with an ever changing lineup, continued to tour and perform through 2023, though Rossingon's participation became limited due to health issues. He suffered a heart attack in 2014 and underwent emergency heart surgery in 2021. He was the last surviving member of the band's original lineup at the time of his death. Rossington married Dale Krantz in 1982 and is survived by her and their two daughters.

Roundtree, Richard

Actor Richard Roundtree, who starred as detective John Shaft in the 1971 action film "Shaft", died of pancreatic cancer at his home in Los Angeles, California, on October 24,

2023. He was 81. Roundtree was born in New Rochelle, New York, on July 9, 1942. He attended Southern Illinois University in Carbondale, Illinois, after graduating high school in 1961. He left college in 1963 to pursue an acting career. He worked as a model for the Ebony Fashion Fair and joined the Negro Ensemble Company in 1967. He appeared on stage with the company's production of "The Great White Hope". He was best known for his role as John Shaft in the pioneer blaxploitation classic "Shaft" in 1971. It became a hit film and Isaac Hayes earned an Academy Award for his original song "Theme from Shaft". Roundtree reprised the role in the less successful sequels "Shaft's Big Score" (1972) and "Shaft in Africa" (1973), and the short-lived "Shaft" television on CBS from 1973 to 1974. He was featured as Uncle John Shaft in the 2000 "Shaft" film starring Samuel L. Jackson in the title role. He was seen in numerous other films including "Embassy" (1972), "Charley-One-Eye" (1973), the all-star disaster epic "Earthquake" (1974) as motorcycle daredevil Miles Quade, "Man Friday" (1975) in the title role opposite Peter O'Toole's Robinson Crusoe, "Diamonds" (1975), "Escape to Athena" (1979), "Portrait of a Hitman" (1979), "Game for Vultures" (1979), "Days of the

Assassin" (1979), "Gypsy Angels" (1980), the Korean War epic "Inchon" (1981), "An Eye for an Eye" (1981) with Chuck Norris and Christopher Lee, Larry Cohen's cult horror film "Q: The Winged Serpent" (1982), the blaxploitation action film "One Down, Two to Go" (1982) with Fred Williamson, Jim Brown, and Jim Kelly, "Young Warriors" (1983), "The Big Score" (1983), "Killpoint" (1984), "City Heat" (1984) with Clint Eastwood and Burt Reynolds, "Opposing Force" (1986), "Jocks" (1986), the horror film "Maniac Cop" (1988) as Commissioner Pike, "Party Line" (1988), "Angel III: The Final Chapter" (1988), "Miami Cops" (1989), "Night Visitor" (1989), "Crack House" (1989), "The Banker" (1989), "Bad Jim" (1990), "Gypsy Angels" (1990), "A Time to Die" (1991), "Bloodfist III: Force to Fight" (1991), "Sins of the Night" (1993), "Deadly Rivals" (1993), "Mind Twister" (1993), "Body of Influence" (1993), "Amityville: A New Generation" (1993), "Ballistic" (1995), "Se7en" (1995) starring Brad Pitt and Morgan Freeman, "Once Upon a Time... When We Were Colored" (1995), "Theodore Rex" (1995), "Original Gangstas" (1996), "George of the Jungle" (1997), the super hero film "Steel" starring Shaquille O'Neal in the title role, "Antitrust" (2001), "Hawaiian Gardens" (2001), "Corky Romano" (2001), "Capone's Boys" (2002), "Boat Trip" (2002), "Men Cry in the Dark" (2003), "Max Havoc: Curse of the Dragon" (2004), "Brick" (2005), "Wild Seven" (2006), "All the Days Before Tomorrow" (2007), "Vegas Vampires" (2007), "Speed Racer" (2008) as Ben Burns, "Set Apart" (2009), "The Confidant" (2010), "This Bitter Earth" (2012), "Whatever She Wants" (2014), "Collar" (2015),

"Retreat!" (2016), "What Men Want" (2019), "The Sin Choice" (2020), "Haunting of the Mary Celeste" (2020), and "Moving On" (2022). Roundtree returned to the role of John Shaft in one of his final films, starring Samuel L. Jackson as his son and Jessie T. Usher and grandson J.J. Shaft. He appeared frequently on television with roles in productions of "Parachute to Paradise" (1972), "Firehouse" (1973), the mini-series "Roots" (1977) as Sam Bennett, "The Baron and the Kid" (1984), "A.D." (1985), "The Fifth Missile" (1986), "Cadets" (1988), "Christmas in Connecticut" (1992), "Bonanza: The Return" (1993), "Moscacieca" (1993), "Nero Come il Cuore" (1994), "Shadows of Desire", "Bonanza: Under Attack" (1995), "Any Place But Home" (1997), "Having Our Say: The Delany Sisters' First 100 Years" (1999) as Booker T. Washington, the 2002 PBS documentary mini-series "The Rise and Fall of Jim Crow" as the narrator, "Joe and Max" (2002), "Painkiller Jane" (2005) as Colonel Watts, "Final Approach" (2007), "Point of Entry" (2007), "Ladies of the House" (2008), and "A Family Reunion Christmas" (2019). His many television credits also include episodes of "The Love Boat", "CHiPs", "Magnum, P.I.", "Masquerade", "Hollywood Beat", the short-lived western science fiction "Outlaws" as Isaiah 'Ice' McAdams from 1986 to 1987, "ABC Afterschool Specials", "Murder, She Wrote", "A

Different World", "Amen", "Beauty and the Beast", "21 Jump Street", "MacGyver", the soap opera "Generations" as Dr. Daniel Reubens in 1990, "The Young Riders", "Beverly Hills, 90210", "Hearts Are Wild", "L.A. Law", "Roc" in the recurring role of Russell Emerson from 1991 to 1994, "Hangin' with Mr. Cooper", "Renegade", "The Wayans Bros.", "Dream On", "Touched by an Angel", "Buddies" as Henry Carlisle in 1996, "The Fresh Prince of Bel-Air", "Profiler", the short-lived Fox drama "413 Hope St." as Phil Thomas from 1997 to 1998, "Dr. Quinn, Medicine Woman", "Rescue 77" as Captain Durfee in 1999, "Linc's", "Soul Food" as Hardy Lester from 2000 to 2001, "Resurrection Blvd.", "As the World Turns" as Oliver Travers from 2002 to 2003, "1-800-Missing", "Alias", "Desperate Housewives" in the recurring role of Mr. Shaw from 2004 to 2005, "The Closer", "Blade: The Series" (2006), "Grey's Anatomy" (2006), "Close to Home" (2006), "Heroes" as Charles Deveaux from 2006 to 2007, "Knight Rider", "Lincoln Heights" in the recurring role of Coleman Bradshaw from 2007 to 2009, "Meet the Browns", "The Mentalist", "Diary of a Single Mom" as Lou Bailey from 2009 to 2011, "Private Practice", "Being Mary Jane" as Paul Patterson, Sr. from 2013 to 2019, "Chicago Fire" as Wallace Boden, Sr. in 2015, "The Player", "Star" as Charles Floyd from 2017 to 2018, "Lethal Weapon, "Game On! A Comedy Crossover Event", "Sacrifice", "Family Reunion" as Grandpa from 2019 to 2022, and "Cherish the Day" as Mandeville 'MV' St. James from 2021 to 2022. He appeared on the talk and game shows "The Tonight Show Starring Johnny Carson", "The David Frost Show", "Donahue", "The Dean Martin Show", "The Merv Griffin Show", "Jerry Lewis MDA Labor Day Telethon", "The Hollywood Squares", "Dinah!", "Celebrity Bowling", "The Mike Douglas Show", "Circus of the Stars", "The Marsha Warfield Show", "Maury", "Vicki!", "The Tonight Show with Jay Leno", "The Arsenio Hall Show", "Today", and "Tavis Smiley". Roundtree voiced the title character in the 1998 video game "Akuji the Heartless" and provided the voice of Burt Campana in 2006's "Scarface: The World Is Yours". He was diagnosed with breast cancer in 1993 and underwent a radical double mastectomy and chemotherapy. Roundtree was married to Mary Jane Grant from 1963 until their divorce in 1973 and is survived by their two children. He was married to Karen M. Ciernia from 1980 until their divorce in 1998 and they had three children.

Rourke, Andy

British musician Andy Rourke, who was bassist for the indie rock band the Smiths, died of pancreatic cancer in a hospital in New York City on May 19, 2023. He was 59. Rourke was born in Manchester, England, on January 17, 1964. He was given his first guitar as a child and soon began playing music with school friend Johnny Marr. The two formed a band and Rourke switched to bass. He left school in 1979 and worked at various jobs while playing in rock bands. He performed with the short-lived funk band Freak Party with Marr. He was invited by Marr and Morrissey to join the Smiths in 1982 after their first performance. The group released their first self-named debut album in 1984. Rourke was noted for his performance on the song "Barbarism Begins at Home" for the

"Meat Is Murder" album. He was also heard on such songs as "Rusholme Ruffians", "Nowhere Fast", "This Charming Man", and "How Soon Is Now?". Rourke's ongoing heroin addiction led to his arrest for drug possession in early 1986. He was

briefly fired from the band but was reinstated for a tour of the United States two weeks later. Their album, "The Queen Is Dead", was released later in the year. The Smiths released their final album, "Here We Come", in 1987 and disbanded soon after. Rourke and drummer Mike Joyce began playing with Sinead O'Connor and were featured on her 1990 album "I Do Not Want What I Haven't Got". He also played bass on several songs by former bandmate Morrissey including "November Spawned a Monster" and "Piccadilly Palare". He was a session bassist for the Pretenders in 1994. He also played with Killing Joke, Badly Drawn Boy, Aziz Ibrahim, Ian Brown, and Paul 'Bonehead' Arthurs. Rouke joined with fellow bassists Mani and Peter Hook in the band Freebass from 2007 to 2010. He moved to New York City in 2009 where he teamed with Ole Korretsky and singer Dolores O'Riordan to form the alternative rock band D.A.R.K. They released the album "Science Agrees" in 2016. He formed Blitz Vega with singer and guitarist Kev Sandhu after the death of O'Riordan and their first single, "Hey Christo", was released in 2019. They continued to perform and record together with their most recent single, "Strong Vampire", released in 2022. Rourke married Francesca Mor in 2012 and she survives him.

Rowe, Douglas

Actor Douglas Rowe died at a hospital in Medford, Oregon, on May 13, 2023. He was 85. Rowe was born in Patterson, New Jersey, on February 28, 1938, and was raised in

Newburyport, Massachusetts. He attended Bates College in Maine where he began performing on stage. He spent some time in New York City before moving to Los Angeles. He was active on stage, serving as managing director of the Laguna Playhouse from 1964 to 1996 and was artistic director from 1976 to 1991. Rowe was seen often on television with roles in episodes of "The Lieutenant", "Get Smart", "The Wild Wild West", "Room 222", "Nanny and the Professor", "Emergency!", "Spencer's Pilot", "M*A*S*H", "Billy", "Hart to Hart", "St. Elsewhere", "Hill Street Blues", "The Mississippi", "Newhart", "Knots Landing", "Star Trek: The Next Generation" as Debin in the 1988 episode "The Outrageous Okona", "Murder, She Wrote", "Silk Stalkings", "Northern Exposure", "Viper", "Wings", "ER", "Melrose Place", "Legend" in the recurring role of Sheriff Sam Motes in 1995, "Fired Up", "Pensacola: Wings

of Gold", "Providence" in the recurring role of Dr. Kendrick from 2000 to 2001, "Gilmore Girls", and "The OA". His other television credits include the tele-films "Frankie & Annette: The Second Time Around" (1978), "Scandal Sheet" (1985), "Run Till You Fall" (1988), "Incident at Dark River" (1989), "The Incident" (1990), "To My Daughter" (1990), "Deadly Desire" (1991), "Cry in the Wild: The Taking of Peggy Ann" (1991), "Writer's Block" (1991), "Precious Victims" (1993), "The Colony" (1995), and "Sins of the Mind" (1997). Rowe appeared in numerous films including "Flareup" (1969), "The Legend of Nigger Charley" (1972), "Appointment with Fear" (1985), "In the Mood" (1987), "Critters 2: The Main Course" (1988), "Impulse" (1990), "No More Dirty Deals" (1993), "The Hard Truth" (1994), "Raspberry Heaven" (2004), "Conversations with God" (2006), "Babysitter Wanted" (2008), "Stephanie's Image" (2009), "Calvin Marshall" (2009), "Redwood Highway" (2013), "Black Road" (2016), "Besetment" (2017), and the short "The Bullet of Time" (2018). He and his family moved to Oregon in the mid-1990s where he was active in local theater, serving as director of the Ashland New Plays Festival. Rowe married Catherine Rowe in 1980 and is survived by her and their two sons, Bill and Jackson.

Roy, Mandeep

Indian actor Mandeep Roy, who was noted for his appearances in Kannada language films, died of a heart attack in Bengaluru, India, on January 29, 2023. He was 73. Roy was born in Karnataka, India, on April 4, 1949. He began his film

career in the early 1980s, often appearing in comic roles. He was featured in over 500 Kannada films during his career. His numerous film credits include "Minchina Ota" (1980), "Devara Aata" (1981), "Baadada Hoo" (1982), "Benkiya Bale" (1983), "Hosa Theerpu" (1983), "Makkaliralavva Mane Thumba" (1984), "Bidugadeya Bedi" (1985), "Nannavaru" (1986), "Digvijaya" (1987), "Anthima Ghatta" (1987), "Elu Suttina Kote" (1988), "Gajapathi Garvabhanga" (1989), "Manmatha Raja" (1989), "Aasegobba Meesegobba" (1990), "Ashwamedha" (1990), "Bhairavi" (1991), "Golmaal Part 2" (1991), "Agni Panjara" (1992), "Aathanka" (1993), "Aakasmika" (1993), "Kumkuma Bhagya" (1993), "Apoorva Samsara" (1994), "Bal Nan Maga" (1995), "Aayudha" (1996), "Agni IPS" (1997), "Arjun Abhimanyu" (1998), "King" (1998), "Chandramukhi Pranasakhi" (1999), "Deepavali" (2000), "Aunty Preethse" (2001), "Nagarahavu" (2002), "Aathma" (2002), "Preethsod Thappa" (2003), "Kushee" (2003), "Avale Nanna Gelathi" (2004), "Ayya" (2005), "Hatavadi" (2006), "Sixer" (2007), "VIP 5" (2007), "Beladingalagi Baa" (2008), "Taxi No-1" (2009), "Aptharakshaka" (2010), "Rangappa Hogbitna" (2011), "Alemari" (2012), "Victory" (2013), "Amanusha" (2014), "Ond Chance Kodi" (2015), "Maduveya Mamatheya Kareyole" (2016), "...Re" (2016), "Pushpaka

Vimana" (2017), "Raajakumara" (2017), "#0 Premave" (2018), "Sankashta Kara Ganapathi" (2018), "Mane Maratakkide" (2019), "Auto Ramanna" (2021), "Trikona" (2022), "Bettada Dari" (2022), and "Mandala: The UFO Incident" (2023).

Royale, Betty Jane

Actress Betty Jane Royale died in Bakersfield, California, on September 29, 2023. She was 76. She was born Betty Jane Hermann in Los Angele, California, on October 12, 1946. She was the daughter of businessman J. Carter Hermann and actress Polly Ann Young. Her aunts were actresses Loretta Young, Sally Blane, and Georgiana Montalban. She had a brief career as an actress in the mid-1960s appearing in the comedy "The Trouble with Angels" (1966) and the science fiction film "Cyborg 2087" (1966). She also appeared on the television series "The Dating Game" and worked as a model. She was married to Robert Tornstrom and they had two sons and a daughter before their divorce.

Rozier, Jacques

French film director Jacques Rozier, who was considered the last of the French New Wave directors, died in Theoule-sur-Mer, France, on May 31, 2023. He was 96. Rozier was born in Paris, France, on November 10, 1926. He attended the Institute for Advanced Film Studies and began his career in television as an assistant. He aided Jean Renoir with his production of the 1955 musical "French Cancan" and was assistant director for the 1956 tele-film "Eugenie Grandet". Rozier wrote and directed the short films "Rentree des Classes" (1955) and "Blue Jeans" (1958). He helmed his first feature, "Adieu Philippine", in 1962. He continued to direct such shorts as "Dans le-Vent" (1963), "Paparazzi" (1964), "Le Parti des Choses: Bardot et Godard" (1964), "Romeos et Jupettes" (1966), "Nono Nenesse" (1976), and "Comment Devenir Cineaste Sans se Prendre la Tete" (1995). He also directed and wrote the features "Near Orouet" (1971), "Les Naufrages de l'ile de la Tortue" (1976), "Maine Ocean" (1986), "Fifi Martingale" (2001), and "Oh, Oh, Oh, Jolie Tournee!" (2001). Rozier was married and divorced from Michele O'Glor who died in 2022. Their only son, Jean Jacques Rozier, died in 2021.

Rubin, Arthur

Singer and actor Arthur Rubin died in New York City on July 22, 2023. He was 97. Rubin was born on June 16, 1926. He began his career on Broadway in the 1951 musical revue

"Two on the Aisle" where he provided off-stage vocals for Bert Lahr. He appeared in Broadway productions of "Can-Can" (1953), "Silk Stockings" (1955), "The Most Happy Fella" (1956), "Juno" (1959), "Kean" (1961), and "Here's Love" (1963). He also served as an assistant stage manager for such Broadway shows as "The Music Man" (1957) and "West Side Story" (1960). Rubin appeared on television in episodes of "Car 54, Where Are You?" and "The Patty Duke Show". He was a performer auditioning the role of Hitler for the 1967 film "The Producers" and had a small singing role in "Crossing Delancey" in 1988. Rubin provided the singing voice of Robin Hood in the 1993 film "Robin Hood: Men in Tights". His survivors include his children, Ronnie, Anne, Alan, and Jane.

Ruffo, Johnny

Australian singer and actor Johnny Ruffo died of brain cancer in Sydney, Australia, on November 10, 2023. He was

35. Ruffo was born in Perth, Western Australia, on March 8, 1988. He learned to play the guitar and piano in his youth and aspired to a career in music. He began working as a concreter after attending high school. He also performed with the electropop band Supanova around Perth. Ruffo auditioned for the third season of "The X Factor Australia" in 2011. He was selected for live shows and was mentored by singer Guy Sebastian. He placed third in the finals. He was a celebrity contestant on "Dancing with the Stars" in 2012 and won the competition. He signed with Sony Music Australia and his first single, "On Top", was released later in 2012. He served as host of the digital live stream show, "The X Stream", for the fourth Season of "The X Factor". He starred as Chris Harrington on the television series "Home and Away" from 2013 to 2016. He also appeared in the 2017 mini-series "House of Bond" and was Owen Campbell in "Neighbours" in 2020. He continued to record such singles as "Take It Home", "Untouchable", "She Got That O", "White Christmas", "Broken Glass", and 2021's "Let's Get Lost". Ruffo was diagnosed with brain cancer in 2017 and had surgery to remove a brain tumour. He went into remission after two years of treatment but returned in 2020.

Rundell, Matthew

Film and television editor Matthew Rundell died in an automobile accident in Los Angeles, California, on May 1, 2023. He was 55. Rundell was born in Dallas, Texas, on November 12, 1967. He attended Menlo College and Chapman College and graduated from the University of Southern

California. He directed the short films "The Line" (1996) and "Allegedly So" (2004). Rundell served as editor of the films "Hellraiser: Revelations" (2011), "The Wayshower" (2011), "Cheesecake Casserole" (2012), "Mystical Traveler" (2014),

"The Benefactor" (2015), "Approaching the Unknown" (2015), "Bent" (2018), "Wilding" (2018), "The New Mutants" (2020), "The Believer" (2021), and "Beautiful Disaster" (2023). He was assistant editor for the films "Stuck in Love" (2012), "The Fault in Our Stars" (2014), "Dying of the Light" (2014), and "Last Seen Alive" (2022). Rundell was an editor for such television productions as "LA LA Land" (2008), "Hit Factor" (2008), and "Murder in Manhattan" (2013). He was also an editor on the series "Knockout Sportsworld", "Dating After Divorce", "American Odyssey", "T@gged", "Blood Drive", "New Amsterdam", "Midnight, Texas", "The Stand", "Nova Vita", and "Yellowstone". He was married and divorced from Courtney Rundell and is survived by his son, Morgan.

Russell, Mark

Political satirist and comedian Mark Russell died of complications from prostate cancer in Washington, D.C., on March 30, 2023. He was 90. He was born Marcus Ruslander in Buffalo, New York, on August 23, 1932. He graduated from

high school in Buffalo and briefly attended the University of Miami and George Washington University before joining the U.S. Marine Corps. He began playing piano at local bars in the Washington, D.C., area after his discharge in 1956. He changed his name to Mark Russell and soon began adding political humor to his routines at the Carroll Arms cocktail lounge. He began incorporating song parodies relating to political figures and events into his act in 1959 which became a must see show in the capital. Democrats and Republicans alike were skewered by Russell's biting musical satires. His audience included such major political figures as Richard Nixon, Hubert Humphrey, and Robert F. Kennedy. He moved his act to the Shoreham Hotel in 1961, where remained for twenty years. He performed in act in a deadpan manner sporting a bow tie on a patriotic set. He jabbed presidents from Eisenhower to Trump and brought musical humor to events including Watergate and Bill Clinton's sexual antics. He scoured the newspapers and the Congressional Record for fodder for his parodies. When he was asked if he had any writers Russell replied, "Oh, yes - 100 in the Senate and 435 in the House of Representatives". He had a series of comedy specials on PBS that ran from 1975 to 2004. He was a guest on such television series as "The Merv Griffin

Show", "The Steve Allen Show", "Della", "The David Frost Show", "Life with Linkletter", "The Dean Martin Comedy World", "The Starland Vocal Band Show", "The Mike Douglas Show", "Real People", "Match Game/Hollywood Squares Hour", and the Pat Sajak Show". He was host of "Mark Russell's 25th Anniversary Special" in 2007. He announced his retirement from public performances in 2010. He resumed touring in 2013 before again retiring three years later. His autobiography, "Presenting Mark Russell", was published in 1980. Russell was married to Rebekah Ward from 1955 until their divorce in 1975 and is survived by their three children. He married Alison Kaplan in 1978 and she also survives him.

Ruzicka, William

Animator William Ruzicka died after experiencing cold and flu symptoms for a week on February 1, 2023. He was

45. Ruzicka was born on October 14, 1977. He began his career in 2012 working as a storyboard revisionist for the Hasbro Studios cartoons "Transformers Prime", "G.I. Joe Renegades", and "Transformers Rescuebots". He was a storyboard artist for the series "Ultimate Spider-Man", "The Legend of Korra", "Ben 10: Omniverse", "Justice League Action", "DuckTales", "Rise of

the Teenage Ninja Turtles", "Blood of Zeus", "Snap Ships: Dawn of Battle", "Onyx Equinox", "Star Trek: Lower Decks", "Batman Unlimited", "High Guardian Spice", "Kung Fu Panda: The Dragon Knight", and "Invincible". Ruzicka was also storyboard artist for the animated videos "Batman: Bad Blood" (2016), "Justice League vs. Teen Titans" (2016), "Lego Scooby-Doo!: Haunted Hollywood" (2016), "Wonder Woman: Bloodlines" (2019), and "Scooby-Doo! The Sword and the Scoob" (2021). He directed episodes of "Bunnicula", "Invincible", "High Guardian Spice", and "Kung Fu Panda: The Dragon Knight".

ryuchell

Japanese social medial personality, singer, and LGBTQ advocate Ryuji Higa, who was known as ryuchell, was found dead of a suicide by their manager at a talent agency

office in Shibuya, Tokyo, Japan, on July 12, 2023. They were 27. Higa was born in Ginowan, Japan, on September 29, 1995. They moved to Tokyo after graduating high school and began working as a model and clothing store clerk. Ryuchell debuted as a singer with the song "Hands Up!! If You're Awesome" in 2018. A second song, "Link", in honor of their son, was released later in the year. They became a leading figure in the genderless fashion subculture in Japan and appeared frequently on television variety shows and at LGBTQ events. Their album, "Super Candy Boy", was released in 2019. Another album, "Time Machine", was released in early 2023. They were a voice performer in the 2019 animated film "Crayon Sin-chan: Honeymoon Hurricane - The lost Hiroshi" and appeared in the 2022 feature "Aishiteru!". Ryuchell married model and social media personality Tetsuko Okuhira, better known as Peco, in 2016 while still identifying as a male. They had a son, Link, two years later. They divorced in 2022 after ryuchell announced his gender nonconformity. Ryuchell is survived by their son.

Saad, Margit

German actress Margit Saad died in Munich, Germany, on August 7, 2023. She was 94. Saad was born in

Munich on May 30, 1929. She took acting classes at the Otto Falckenberg Academy and worked as a model. She made her film debut in 1951's "Eva Erbt das Paradies... Ein Abenteuer im Salzkammergut". She appeared in numerous films over the next two decades including "Heidelberger Romanze" (1951), "The Unholy Intruders" (1952), "Sudliche Nachte" (1953), "Hab' Ich Nur Deine Liebe" (1953), "The Gypsy Baron" (1954), "Baron Tzigane" (1954), "Ehesanatorium" (1955), "Sommarflickan" (1955), "Drei Madels vom Rhein" (1955), "If All the Guys in the World..." (1956), "Beichtgeheimnis" (1956), "Was die Schwalbe Sang" (1956), "Drei Birken auf der Heide" (1956), "Made in Germany - Die Dramatische Geschichte des Hauses Zeiss" (1957), "Ein Stuck vom Himmel" (1957), "Ein Amerikaner in Salzburg" (1958), "Man ist Nur Zweimal Jung" (1958), "Hoppla, Jetzt Kommt Eddie" (1958), "Peter Voss, der Millionendieb" (1958), "Rendezvous in Wien" (1958), "The Chasers" (1959), "Heisse Ware" (1959), "Wenn das Mein Grosser Bruder Wusste" (1959), "Melodie und Rhythmus" (1959), "Paradies der Matrosen" (1959), Joseph Losey's British crime drama "The Concrete Jungle" (1960) with Stanley Baker, "Call Me Genius" (1961), "Playback" (1962), "Das Geheimnis der Drei Dschunken" (1965), "I Deal in Danger" (1966), the British comedy "The Magnificent Two" (1967) with Morecambe & Wise, and "The Last Escape" (1970). Saad was seen on television in such productions as "Der Trojanische Krieg Findet Nicht Statt" (1957), "Es Bleibt in der Familie" (1958), "Lauter Lugen" (1961), "Becket Oder Die Ehre Gottes" (1962), "Das Verflixte Erste Mal - Ein Feuilleton Mit Musik" (1962), "Die Launen der Marianne" (1963), "Gehen Sie zu Paul Potter; Ein Detektiv in Tausend Noten" (1964), "Robin Hood, the Noble Robber" (1966), and "Jahreszeiten der Liebe" (1979). Her other television credits include episodes of "The Edgar Wallace Mystery Theatre", "Curd Jurgens Erzahlt...", "The Saint", "Die Funfte Kolonne", "The Third Man", "Bob Morane", "Jorg Prea Berichtet", "Blue Light", "Der Kriminalmuseum", "Graf Yoster Gibt Sich die Ehre",

"Engadiner Bilderbogen", "Die Falle des Herrn Konstantin", "Eine Schone Wirtschaft", and "Tatort". She appeared frequently on stage in Germany and Austria throughout her career. She largely retired from acting by the early 1980s and began directing for television. She directed and often wrote productions of "Abenteuer Aus dem Englischen Garten" (1984), "Die Geschichte Vom Guten Alten Herrn und Dem Schonen Madchen" (1985), "Das Lied der Taube" (1989), and "Die Erzahlung der Magd Zerline" (1990). Saad was married to French opera director Jean-Pierre Ponnelle from 1957 until his death in 1988 and is survived by their son, conductor Pierre-Dominique Ponnelle.

Sabatelli, Luca

Italian costume designer Luca Sabatelli died in Milan, Italy, on November 24, 2023. He was 87. Sabatelli was born in Florence, Italy, on June 3, 1936. He graduated from the

Academy of Fine Arts in Florence. He began his career as a set and costume designer on stage in Milan in 1959. He was costumer designer for numerous films from the mid-1960s including "Come Imparai ad Amare le Donne" (1966), "Avenger X" (1967), "Ti Ho Sposato per Allegria" (1967), "La Pecora Nera" (1968), "Colpo de Stato" (1969), "Detective Belli" (1969), "Dove Vai Tutta Nuda?" (1969), "Viva Cangaceiro" (1969), "Basta Guardarla" (1970), "The Pacifist" (1970), Dario Argento's horror thriller "The Cat o'Nine Tails" (1971), "The Dead Are Alive!" (1972), "Indian Summer" (1972), "Even Angels Eat Beans" (1973), "Watch Out, We're Mad" (1974), "Anche Gli Angeli Tirano di Destro" (1974), "Erotomania" (1974), "The Immortal Bachelor" (1975), "Africa Express" (1975), "Amoe Vuol dir Gelosia" (1975), "Vai Gorilla" (1975), "Duck in Orange Sauce" (1975), "Sex with a Smile" (1976), "Safari Express" (1976), "Cattivi Pensieri" (1976), "Spogliamoci Cosi, Senza Pudor..." (1976), "L'Altra Meta del Cielo" (1977), "Wifemistress" (1977), "Slave of the Cannibal God" (1978), "Per Vivere Meglio, Divertitevi Con Noi" (1978), "Tigers in Lipstick" (1979), Aldo Lado's science fiction film "The Humanoid" (1979), "To Forget Venice" (1979), "Mani di Velluto" (1979), "Barbara" (1980), "Mia Moglie e Una Strega" (1980), "Asso" (1981), "Nudo di Donna" (1981), "La Poliziotta a New York" (1981), "Talcum Powder" (1982), "Il Buon Soldato" (1982), "Porca Vacca" (1982), "Grand Hotel Excelsior" (1982), "Sesso e Volentieri" (1982), "Attila Flagello di Dio" (1982), "Il Ras del Quartiere" (1983), "Acqua e Sapone" (1983), "I due Carabinieri" (1984), "Grandi Mgazzini" (1986), "Io e Mia Sorella" (1987), "Racconti di Donne" (1988), "Compagni di Scuola" (1988), "Pigmalione 88" (1988), and "Il Bambino e il Poliziotto" (1989). Sabatelli designed costumes for television productions of "Dal Primo Momento Che Ti Ho Visto" (1976), "Il Barone e il Servitore" (1978), "Progetti di Allegria" (1982), and "Un Posto Freddo in Fondo al Cuore"

(1992). His other television credits include episodes of "Ma Che Sera", "Profumo di Classe", Heather Parisi's variety show "Fantastico 6" from 1983 to 1993, "La Corrida", "Immagina", and "Odiens".

Sabato, Mario

Argentine film director Mario Sabato died in Buenos Aires, Argentina, on June 3, 2023. He was 78. Sabato was born in La Plata, Argentina, on February 15, 1945. He was the son

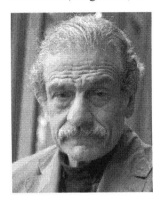

of novelist Ernest Sabato. He began working in films in the early 1960s as an assistant to director Ricardo Alventosa. He wrote and directed the 1963 short film "El Nacimiento de un Libro". He continued to direct such films as "El Homenaje a Don Segundo Sombra" (1969), "Juego Solitario" (1970), "Y Que Patatin, Y Que Patatan" (1971), "Juegos" (1971), "Hola, Senor Leon" (1973), "Los Golpes Bajos" (1974), "Un Mundo de Amor" (1975), "The Power of Darkness" (1979), "Tiro al Aire" (1980), "To the Heart" (1996), "Porque te Quiero" (2001), and "India Pravile" (2003). Sabato helmed several children's films and comedies under the alias Adrian Quiroga including "Los Superagentes y el Tesoro Maldito" (1978), "Los Parchis Contra el Inventor Invisible" (1981), "Los Magia de Los Parchis" (1982), "La Gran Aventura de los Parchis" (1982), and "Superagentes y Titanes" (1983). He directed the 2009 documentary film about his father, "Ernesto Sabato, Mi Padre". Sabato directed episodes of the television series "Libre-Mente" in 1999 and the 2001 tele-film "Visita".

Sakamoto, Ryuichi

Japanese composer and pianist Ryuichi Sakamoto, who earned an Academy Award for his score to the 1987 film

"The Last Emperor", died of cancer in Tokyo, Japan, on March 28, 2023. He was 71. Sakamoto was born in Nakano, Japan, on January 17, 1952. He studied piano from an early age and began composing at the age of ten. He attended the Tokyo National University of Fine Arts and Music in 1970 and earned a master's degree in music composition. He continued to study ethnomusicology and experiment with electronic music. He formed the early electronic music band Yellow Magic Orchestra with Haruomi Hosono and Yukihiro Takashi in 1977. Sakamoto wrote, composed, and played keyboard on many of the band's hits including "Yellow Magic (Tong Poo)" (1978), "Technopolis" (1979), "Nice Age" (1980), "Ongaku" (1983), and "You've Got to Help Yourself" (1983). He released the solo albums "Thousand Knives of Ryuichi Sakamoto" in 1978 ad "B-2 Unit" in 1980. The latter included the electro-music hit "Riot in Lagos". He began a long association with British musician and singer David Sylvian in 1980 and collaborated with him on the 1982 single "Bamboo Houses/Bamboo Music". He continued to make a long series of solo albums including "Left-Handed Dream" (1981), "Ongaku Zukan" (1984), "Esperanto" (1984), "Futurista" (1986), "Neo Geo" (1987), "Beauty" (1989), "Heartbeat" (1991), "Sweet Revenge" (1994), "Smoochy" (1995), "1996" (1996), "Discord" (1997), "BTTB" (1999), "Comica" (2002), "Elephantism" (2002), "Chasm" (2004), "Out of Noise" (2009), "Playing the Piano" (2009), "Async" (2017), and "12" (2023). Sakamoto was featured as Captain Yonoi in Nagisa Oshima's 1983 film "Merry Christmas Mr. Lawrence" starring David Bowie. He received a BAFTA Award for composing the film's score. He worked on numerous films as a composer including "It's All Right, My Friend" (1983), "The Adventures of Milo and Otis" (1986), "Wings of Honneamise" (1987), "The Last Emperor" (1987) sharing an Academy Award and a Grammy and appearing onscreen in the role of Masahiko Amakasu, "The Handmaid's Tale" (1990), "Butoh: Body on the Edge of Crisis" (1990), "High Heels" (1991), "Tokyo Decadence" (1992), "Wuthering Heights" (1992), "Little Buddha" (1993) earning a Grammy nomination, "Wild Side" (1995), "Love Is the Devil: Study for a Portrait of Francis Bacon" (1998), "Snake Eyes" (1998), "Taboo" (1999), "Alexei to Izumi" (2002), "Derrida" (2002), "Femme Fatale" (2002), "The Blonds" (2003), "Life Is Journey" (2003), "Appleseed" (2004), "Original Child Bomb" (2004), "Toy Takitani" (2004), "Hoshi Ni Natta Shonen" (2005), "Silk" (2007), "The Moment After" (2009), "Women Without Men" (2009), "Hara-Kiri: Death of a Samurai" (2011), "Futaba Kara Tooku Hanarete" (2012), "Light Up Nippon" (2012), "I Have to Buy New Shoes" (2012), "Ana Ana" (2013), "Metamorphosis" (2013), "Haga to Kuraseba" (2015), "The Revenant" (2015) receiving a BAFTA and Grammy nomination, "Any Other Normal" (2016), "Rage" (2016), "Star Sand" (2017), "Haiku on a Plum Tree" (2017), "Baigun Ga Mottomo Osoreta Otoko, Sono Na Wa Kamejiro" (2017), "The Fortress" (2017), "Your Face" (2018), "My Tyrano: Together, Forever" (2018), "Draw a Line" (2019), "Paradise Next" (2019), "Agniyogana" (2019), "Proxima" (2019), "Minamata" (2020), "Love After Love" (2020), "Beckett" (2021), "L'ile Invisible - Fukushima, a la Recherche de l'Esprit de la Zone" (2021), "Monster" (2023), and "Ryuichi Sakamoto: Opus" (2023). He also composed music for television productions of "Wild Palms" (1993) and the "Black Mirror" episode "Smithereens" (2019). He composed music for the opening ceremony for the Olympics in Barcelona, Spain, in 1992. He was married to Natsuko Sakamoto from 1972 until their divorce in 1982 and is survived by their daughter. He married pianist and singer Akiko Yao in 1982. They separated in the early 1990s and divorced in 2006. He is survived by their daughter, singer Miu Sakamoto. He subsequently married his manager, Norika Sara, and is also survived by her and their two children.

Saki, Eileen

Japanese-American actress Eileen Saki, who portrayed the proprietor of Rosie's Bar in the television series

"M*A*S*H", died of pancreatic cancer in Los Angeles, California, on May 1, 2023. She was 79. She was born Minako Saki in Japan on November 18, 1943. She had a small role in an episode of the Korean War comedy series "M*A*S*H" in 1976. She returned to "M*A*S*H" as Rosie, the proprietor of Rosie's Bar, becoming the third and final actress in the recurring role from 1979 to 1981. Saki was also seen in episodes of

"Good Times", "CHiPs", "The Greatest American Hero", "Gimme a Break!", "Sidekicks", and "Without a Trace". She appeared in several tele-films including "Enola Gay: The Men, the Mission, the Atomic Bomb" (1980), "Victims for Victims: The Theresa Saldana Story" (1984), and "Boys Will Be Boys" (1999). Saki was featured in the films "Black Gunn" (1972), "Policewoman" (1974), "Meteor" (1979), "History of the World: Part I" (1981), and "Splash" (1984). She is survived by her husband, producer Bob Borgen.

Saluga, Bill

Comedian Bill Saluga, who was noted for his comic persona Raymond J. Johnson, Jr., known for the catchphrase "You Can Call Me Ray, or You Can Call Me Jay, or You Can Call Me...:, died of cardiopulmonary arrest in Los Angeles, California, on March 28, 2023. He was 85. Saluga was born in Youngstown, Ohio, on September 16, 1937. He served in the

U.S. Navy for two years before he began performing as a comedian at local clubs. He performed on stage frequently during the 1960s and worked for Steve Allen as talent coordinator for his television show. He became a member of the Ace Trucking Company comedy troupe later in the decade where he created the character of cigar-smoking Raymond J. Johnson, Jr. His shtick would entail him reciting a lengthy litany of alternate names someone could use when they addressed him as Mr. Johnson. Saluga was featured in television commercials for Miller Lite beer in the 1970s and for Anheuser-Busch Natural Light in the early 1980s. He was featured in several films including "Dynamite Chicken" (1971), "The Harrad Experiment" (1973), "Harrad Summer" (1974), "Tunnel Vision" (1976), and "Going Berserk" (1983). He was a regular performer on the "Redd Foxx" variety television series in 1977. He also appeared in episodes of "The Tonight Show Starring Johnny Carson", "This Is Tom Jones", "The Midnight Special", "The David Steinberg Show", "The Mike Douglas Show", "The Gong Show", "Hollywood Squares", "Teachers Only", "Going Bananas", "Charlie & Co." (1985), "Tall Tales & Legends", "Murphy Brown", "Seinfeld", "Designing Women", "Home Improvement", the animated "Garfield and Friends", "Blossom", "The Parent 'Hood", "Sisters", "The Steve

Allen Comedy Hour", "Vicki!", "Mad About You", "Playboy's Really Naked Truth" as a regular performer from 1995 to 1996, "The Simpsons" and "King of the Hill" voicing his Johnson character, "Curb Your Enthusiasm", and "Sons & Daughters". His other television credits include productions of "Cher... and Other Fantasies" (1979), "The Jerk, Too" (1984), "Coconut Downs" (1991), and "The American Clock" (1993). He made his final film appearance in 2008's "The Great Buck Howard" starring John Malkovich.

Sanderford, John

Actor John Sanderford died in Burbank, California, on September 22, 2023. He was 71. Sanderford was born in

Orlando, Florida, on February 6, 1952. He attended high school in Greensboro, North Carolina, where he performed in school plays. He studied drama at the North Carolina School of the Arts. He appeared frequently on television from the early 1980s with roles in episodes of "Bosom Buddies", "Madame's Place", "T.J. Hooker", "Airwolf", "General Hospital" as Ian Shelton from 1983 to 1984, "Partners in Crime", "Riptide", "St. Elsewhere", "Hunter", "Hardcastle4 and McCormick", "Ryan's Hope" as Frank Ryan from 1985 to 1989, "Murphy Brown", "Santa Barbara" as Jerry Calhoun in 1989, "The Munsters Today", "Who's the Boss?", "McGee and Me!", "Saved by the Bell", "Models Inc.", "Baywatch", "Melrose Place", "Matlock", "Live Shot", "Baywatch Nights", "Mike Hammer, Private Eye", "Crusade", "Titans", "Monk", "CSI: Miami", "Judging Amy", "Eyes", "Close to Home", "Justice", "What About Brian", "The Riches", "Cold Case", "Women's Murder Club", "Days of Our Lives" as Crawford Decker from 2007 to 2008, "Mind of Mencia", "Prison Break", "Desperate Housewives", "The Finder", "Enlightened", "The Bridge", and "Yellowstone". Sanderford was also seen in the tele-films and mini-series "Fantasies" (1982), "The Winds of War" (1983), "Kids Don't Tell" (1985), "Hostage Flight" (1985), "Triplecross" (1986), "A Father's Homecoming" (1988), "War and Remembrance" (1988), "My Boyfriend's Back" (1989), "Coins in the Fountain" (1990), "The Woman Who Sinned" (1991), "Lady Boss" (1992), "Saved by the Bell: Wedding in Las Vegas" (1994), "Black Scorpion" (1995), "Bound by a Secret" (2009), "Undercover Bridesmaid" (2012), "Law & Order True Crime" (2017) as Dominick Dunne, "Sharing Christmas" (2017), and "Murder In-Law" (2019). He appeared in a handful of films including "Looker" (1981), "The Alchemist" (1983), "Firestarter" (1984), "Leprechaun" (1992), "Excessive Force II: Force on Force" (1995), "Born Bad" (1997), "Recoil" (1998), "Live!" (2007), "Transformers: Revenge of the Fallen" (2009), "Hollywoo" (2011), and "All About the Money" (2017). Sanderford is survived by is wife of 42 years, Judi, and their two children.

Sanders, Anita

Swedish actress and model Anita Sanders died in Italy on April 18, 2023. She was 81. She was born Anita Johannesson in Sweden on April 8, 1942. She made her film debut in the 1965 drama "La Fuga". She was featured as a topless party guest in Federico Fellini's fantasy "Juliet of the Spirits" (1965) and appeared in Elio Petri's science fiction "The 10th Victim" (1965). Her other films include "Ridera! (Cuore Matto)" (1967), "Assalto al Tesoro di Stato" (1967), "Bandits in Rome" (1968), Tinto Brass' "Nerosubianco" (aka "Attraction") (1969) in the lead role of Barbara, "La Donna Invisible" (1969), "Ostia" (1970), Torgny Wickman's Swedish horror film "Sensuous Sorceress" (aka "Fear Has a 1000 Eyes") (1970), "Thomas... ...Gli Indemoniati" (1970), Pier Paolo Pasolini's "The Canterbury Tales" (1972), "La Coppia" (1973), and "That Malicious Age" (1975). She subsequently worked at the Italian film studio Cinecitta as an assistant director.

Sandon, Henry

British antiques expert Henry Sandon, who appeared frequently on the BBC One series "Antiques Roadshow" for over four decades, died at a care facility in Malvern, Worcestershire, England, on

December 25, 2023. He was 95. Sandon was born in the East End of London, England, on August 10, 1928. He studied at the Guildhall School of Music and was a singer and music teacher. He also became an archaeologist and developed an interest in ceramics. He collected ceramic art from buildings in Worcester that were being torn down in the 1950s. He was named curator of the Dyson Perrins Museum at the Royal Worcester factory in 1966. He began making appearances on "Antiques Roadshow" during its second season in 1979. He became the series' resident expert on porcelain and pottery. Sandon also appeared on television in episodes of "Going for a Song", "It's Patently Obvious", "Noel's House Party", "This Is Your Life", "The Weakest Link", and "The Green Green Grass". He made his final appearance on "Antiques Roadshow" in September of 2018. he was married to Barbara Sandon for 56 years prior to her death in 2013. He is survived by their three sons, including fellow antiques expert John Sandon.

Sands, Julian

British actor Julian Sands, who starred in such horror films as "Warlock", "Arachnophobia", and 1998's "The Phantom of the Opera" in the title role, went missing while

hiking in Mount Baldy, California, in the San Gabriel Mountains northeast of Los Angeles on January 13, 2023. He was 65. A series of severe storms hindered the initial search and his car was located several days later. There had been eight official search missions before human remains were found by hikers near the area where Sands had disappeared on June 24, 2023. They were positively identified as the actor several days later. Sands was born in Otley, West Riding of Yorkshire, on January 4, 1958. The tall and thin actor began his career in the

early 1980s and was seen in the films "Privates on Parade" (1983), "Oxford Blues" (1984), "The Killing Fields" (1984), and "After Darkness" (1985). He was featured as Dr. Murray in the body snatching horror film "The Doctor and the Devils" (1985) and was George Emerson in the Merchant Ivory romance film "A Room with a View" (1985). He continued to appear in such films as Ken Russell's "Gothic" (1986) as Percy Bysshe Shelley, "Siesta" (1987), "Vibes" (1988), "Wherever You Are..." (1988), the horror film "Warlock" (1989) in the title role, "Manika, the Girl Who Lived Twice" (1989), "Tennessee Waltz" (1989), "Night Sun" (1990), the horror film "Arachnophobia" (1990) as spider expert Dr. James Atherton, "Impromptu" (1991) as Franz Liszt, "The Wicked" (1991), "Grand Isle" (1991), "Husbands and Lovers" (1991), David Cronenberg's adaptation of William S. Burroughs' "Naked Lunch" (1991) as Yves Cloquet, "The Turn of the Screw" (1992), "Tale of the Vampire" (1992), "America" (1992), the off-beat "Boxing Helena" (1993) as Dr. Nick Cavanaugh, who amputates the arms and legs of Sherlyn Fenn's lovely title character to prevent her from leaving him, "Warlock: The Armageddon" (1993) reprising his role as the Warlock, "The Browning Version" (1994), "Lamerica" (1994), "Mario und der Zauberer" (1994), "Leaving Las Vegas" (1995) starring Nicholas Cage, "Never Ever" (1996), "One Night Stand" (1997), "Long Time Since" (1998), "The Loss of Sexual Innocence" (1998), Dario Argento's "The Phantom of the Opera" (1998) in the title role of Erik, "Mercy" (2000), "The Million Dollar Hotel" (2000), "Love Me" (2000), Mike Figgis' experimental film "Timecode" (2000), "Vatel" (2000) as King Louis XIV, "Hotel" (2001), "The Scoundrel's Wife" (2002), "The Medallion" (2003), "Easy Six" (2003), "Romasanta" (2004), "Her Name Is Carla" (2005), "The Trail" (2006), "Ocean's Thirteen" (2007), "Cat City" (2008), "Blood and Bone" (2009), "Heidi 4 Paws" (2009), "Golf in the Kingdom" (2010), "Assisting Venus" (2010), "The Girl with the Dragon Tattoo" (2011) as young Henrik Vanger, "Hirokin: The Last Samurai" (2012), "Suspension of Disbelief" (2012), the short "The Facts in the Case of M. Valdemar" (2013) as the Narrator, "All Things to All Men" (2013), "Cesar Chavez" (2014), "GHB: To Be or Not to Be" (2014), "Me" (2014), "Six Dance Lessons in Six Weeks" (2014), the fantasy "Sariel" (2015) as God, "The Persian Connection" (2016), "The Chosen" (2016), "Crooked

House" (2017), "Toy Gun" (2018), "Walk Like a Panther" (2018), "The Keeper" (2018), the animated "Bongee Bear and the Kingdom of Rhythm" (2019) as the voice of King Jason, "The Painted Bird" (2019), "The Garden of Evening Mists" (2019), "Yeh Ballet" (2020), the animated "Bobbleheads: The Movie" (2020) as the voice of Purrbles, "Death Rider in the House of Vampires" (2021) as Count Holiday, "Benediction" (2021), "The Survivalist" (2021), "The Ghosts of Borley Rectory" (2021), "The Ghosts of Monday" (2022), "Seneca: On the Creation of Earthquakes" (2023), and "The Piper" (2023). Sands appeared on television in productions of "A Married Man" (1983), "The Sun Also Rises" (1984), "Romance on the Orient Express" (1985), "The Holy Experiment" (1985), "Harem" (1986), "Basements" (1987), "Murder by Moonlight" (1989), "Blood Royal: William the Conqueror" (1990), "Crazy in Love" (1992), "Witch Hunt" (1994), "The Great Elephant Race" (1995), "The Tomorrow Man" (1996), "End of Summer" (1997), Stephen King's "rose Red" (2002), "Napoleon" (2002), "Ring of the Nibelungs" (2004), "Kenneth Tynan: In Praise of Hardcore" (2005) as Sir Laurence Olivier, "The Haunted Airman" (2006), "Beyond Sherwood Forest" (2009), "We're Doomed! The Dad's Army Story" (2015) as John Le Mesurier, "Man in an Orange Shirt" (2017), and "What/If" (2019). His other television credits include episodes of "Play for Today", "The Box of Delights", "Chicago Hope", "Strangers", "The L Word", "Stargate SG-1", "Law & Order: Special Victims Unit", "Law & Order: Criminal Intent", "24" as Russian terrorist mastermind Vladimir Bierko in 2006, "Marple", "Blood Ties", "Ghost Whisperer", "Lipstick Jungle" as Hector Matrick in 2009, "Bollywood Hero" as Reg Hunt in 2009, "Castle", "Smallville" in the recurring role of Clark Kent's Kryptonian father Jor-El from 2009 to 2010, "Above Suspicion", "NTSF:SD:SUF", "Person of Interest", "Dexter" as Miles Castner, the wealthy husband on Dexter Morgan's former lover, Hannah McKay, in a 2013 episode, who is dispatched by his wife and Dexter assists her in disposing of the body at sea, "Banshee" as the Priest in 2014, "Rosamunde Pilcher", "Chronica de Castas", "Crossbones" as William Jagger in 2014, "The Village", "Banshee Origins", "Gotham" in the recurring role of Gerald Crane, the Scarecrow's father, in 2015, "Will" as Barrett Emerson in 2017, "The Blacklist", "Elementary", "Medici", and "Into the Dark". He was a voice actor in the animated series "Biker Mice from Mars", "Adventures from the Book of Virtues", "The Real Adventures of Jonny Quest", "Jackie Chan Adventures", and "Ozzy & Drix". Sands starred on stage in "A Celebration of Harold Pinter" at the Edinburgh Fringe Festival in 2011. He remained in the role when it was transferred to the Irish Repertory Theatre in New York City and was nominated for a Drama Desk Award for his performance in 2013. He was a voice actor in the video games "Star Wars: The Old Republic" (2011) and "Call of Duty: Black Ops II" (2012) and was the voice of Q in several James Bond radio plays from 2012 to 2018. Sands was married to journalist and author Sarah Harvey from 1984 until their divorce in 1987 and is survived by their son. He married playwright Evgenia Citkowitz in 1990 and is also survived by her and their two daughters.

Sano, Nami

Japanese manga artist Nami Sano died of ovarian cancer in Japan on August 5, 2023. She was 36. Sano was born in Nishinomiya, Japan, on April 17, 1987. She began drawing manga while in high school and continued to study manga art at Kyoto Seika University. She made her debut as a manga artist with the one-shot "Non-Sugar Coffee" in 2010. She was best known for her series "Haven't You Heard? I'm Sakamoto" from 2012 to 2015 and "Mag & Dali" from 2017 to 2021. Both were adapted into anime series.

Sarno, Janet

Actress Janet Sarno died of cancer in New York City on March 15, 2023. She was 89. Sarno was born in Bridge Port, Connecticut, on November 18, 1933. She earned a master's degree from the Yale School of Drama. She began her career on stage and performed with the Williamstown Summer Theatre for fourteen years. She was seen frequently in Off-Broadway plays and appeared on Broadway in productions of "Dylan" (1964), "Equus" (1974), "Knockout" (1979), "The Apple Doesn't Fall" (1996), and "Fish in the Dark" (2015). Sarno appeared in the films "The People Next Door" (1970), "The Hospital" (1971), "Across 100th Street" (1972), "Family Honor" (1973), "Gorp" (1980), "Power" (1986), "The Hard Way" (1991), "Italian Movie" (1995), "Requiem for a Dream" (2000), "Passing Stones" (2001), "Rock the Paint" (2005), "Carlito's Way: Rise to Power" (2005), "Split Ends" (2009), the short "The Couch" (2009), "All Is Bright" (2013), "The Savage Beast" (2013), the short "The Sweet Sublime" (2016), and "To Dust" (2018). She was seen on television in the 1980 tele-film "Hardhat and Legs" and episodes of "All My Children", "The Edge of Night" as Mrs. Arnold in 1981, "The Baby-Sitters Club", "The Wright Verdicts", "100 Centre Street", "Law & Order", "Conviction", and "New Amsterdam". Sarno was married to Michael Joseph Dontzin from 1977 until his death in 2012 and is survived by their son and daughter.

Sarnoff, Robert W.

Television executive Thomas W. Sarnoff died in Woodland Hills, California, on June 4, 2023. He was 96. Sarnoff was born in New York City on February 23, 1927. His father was David Sarnoff, who was a radio and television pioneer who headed the media conglomerate that included RCA and NBC. Thomas was said to be the first live television subject as a child when he appeared in a demonstration of the medium for the RCA/NBC World's Fair in the 1930s. He attended Princeton University before serving in World War II as a combat engineer. He was also a signal corps instructor at the

U.S. Military Academy at West Point. He continued his education at Stanford University after the war and graduated with a degree in electrical engineering in 1948. He became a floor manager at ABC in Los Angeles in 1949. Sarnoff was hired at NBC as an assistant to the finance director in 1952 and became vice president of production and business affairs in 1957. He served as president of NBC Entertainment Corp. from 1965 to 1977. He was instrumental in negotiating deals for television specials starring Bob Hope and Elvis Presley. He was also chairman of the National Academy of Television Arts & Sciences from 1973 to 1974. He continued to serve on the academy's executive committee and became chairman of the Television Academy Foundation in the 1990s. He was recipient of the Syd Cassyd Founder's Award from the Television Academy in 1997. He founded Sarnoff International Enterprises Inc. after leaving NBC and produced the live-arena show "Yabba Dabba Doo" with Hanna-Barbera and "Peter Pan" and "Disney on Parade" with Walt Disney Productions. Sarnoff was executive producer of the 1981 television special "The Funtastic World of Hanna-Barbera Arena Show" and helped revive "Gumpy" for a television series in 1987. He was also executive producer of the tele-films "Bonanza: The Next Generation" (1988), "Bonanza: The Return" (1993), and "Bonanza: Under Attack" (1995). Thomas' father, David Sarnoff, died in 1971. His eldest brother, Robert W. Sarnoff, succeeded his father as chairman of RCA and died in 1997. Janyce Lundon Sarnoff, his wife of 67 years, died in 2021. He is survived by sons Daniel and Timothy and daughter Cynthia.

Satsuma, Kenpachrio

Japanese actor and stuntman Kenpachiro Satsuma, who portrayed Godzilla in films from 1984 to 1995, died of complications from pneumonia in Japan on December 16, 2023.

He was 78. He was born Yasuaki Maeda in Kagoshima, Japan, on May 27, 1947. He began his career in films in the late 1960s and appeared in small roles in samurai films and other dramas. He was seen in "Aa Himeyuri No To" (1968), "Incident at Blood Pass" (1970), "The Militarists" (1970), and "Kaigun Tokubetsu Nensho-Hei" (1972). Satsuma began working in the Godzilla franchise under the stage name Kengo Nakayama, appearing as the monster Hedorah in 1971's "Godzilla vs. Hedorah" (aka "Godzilla vs.

the Smog Monster") opposite Haruo Nakajima in the Godzilla suit. He again fought Nakajima's Godzilla as the space monster cyborg Gigan in "Godzilla vs. Gigan" (1972) and "Godzilla vs. Megalon" (1973). Satsuma took over as Godzilla for the 1984 film "The Return of Godzilla" (aka "Godzilla 1985") and remained the kaiju antagonist for the remainder of the series Heisei era. He continued to don the suit for "Godzilla vs. Biollante" (1989), "Godzilla vs. King Ghidorah" (1991), "Godzilla and Mothra: The Battle for Earth" (1992), "Godzilla vs. Mechagodzilla II" (1993), "Godzilla vs. SpaceGodzilla" (1994), and "Godzilla vs. Destoroyah" (1995). His other films include "Prophecies of Nostradamus" (1974), "I Want To" (1979), "The Imperial Navy" (1981), "Station" (1981), the North Korean kaiju film "Pulgasari" (1985) as the title creature, "Hong Kil-dong" (1986), "Yamato Takeru" (1994), Teruo Ishii's horror films "Japanese Hell" (1999) as the Blue Ogre and "Blind Beast vs. Dwarf" (2001) as Yasukawa the doll-maker, and "Kawana Mariko: Sakuragai No Amai Mizu" (2002). The character of Godzilla was resurrected several years after Satsuma's last interpretation of the character for the Millennium era. Tsutomu Kitagawa took over as the man beneath the suit for 1999's "Godzilla 2000" and films in the series.

Saunders, Kate

British author and actress Kate Saunders died of complications from cancer and multiple sclerosis at her home in London, England, on April 21, 2023. She was 62. Saunders

was born in London on May 5, 1960. She attended the Camden School for Girls and studied with the Anna Scher theatre group. She began her career as an actress on television in the 1970s with roles in episodes of "You Must Be Joking!", "A Place to Hide", "Angels" as Brenda Cotteral in 1978, "ITV Playhouse", "A Family Affair", "Only Fools and Horses", "Just Good Friends", and the "American Playhouse" production of "Displaced Person" in 1985. She was featured in a small role in the 1979 film "Birth of the Beatles" and appeared on stage with the National Theatre. Saunders wrote for newspapers and magazines including "The Sunday Time", "Daily Telegraph", and "Cosmopolitan". She appeared on such Radio 4 programs as "Woman's Hour", "Start the Week", and "Kaleidoscope", and was a guest on the first episode of the television news quiz show "Have I Got News for You" in 1990. Her debut novel, "The Prodigal Father", was published in 1986. She also wrote the novels "Storm in the Citadel" (1989), "Night Shall Overtake Us" (1993), "Wild Young Bohemians" (1995), "Lily-Josephine" (1998), "The Marrying Game" (2002), "Bachelor Boys" (2004), "Crooked Castle" (2013), and "Mariana". Saunders co-wrote the 1992 non-fiction "Catholics and Sex" with Peter Stanford and the co-hosted the subsequent television mini-series. Her series of Laetitia Rodd Mysteries include "The Secrets of Wishtide" (2016), "The Case of the

Wander Scholar" (2019), and "The Mystery of the Sorrowful Maiden" (2021). The children's television series "Belfry Witches", which aired on BBC One from 1999 to 2000, was based on her series of children's stories. Saunders's children stories include "A Spell of Witches" (1999), "Cat and the Stinkwater War" (2003), "The Little Secret" (2006), "Beswitched" (2010), "Magicalamity" (2011), "The Whizz Pop Chocolate Shop" (2012), "The Curse of The Chocolate Phoenix" (2013), "Five Children on the Western Front" (2014), "The Land of Neverendings" (2017), and the posthumously published "A Drop of Golden Sun" (2024). She contributed to the 2016 authorized Winne-the-Pooh sequel, "The Best Bear in All the World". Saunders married Philip Wells in 1985 and they divorced in the early 2000s. Their son, Felix, died of a suicide in 2012.

Saura, Carlos

Spanish film director Carlos Saura Atares, who was considered one of Spain's leading filmmakers in the latter half of the 20th Century and was nominated for three Academy

Awards for Best Foreign Language Film, died of respiratory failure at his home in Collado Mediano, Spain, on February 10, 2023. He was 91. Saura was born in Huesca, Spain, on January 4, 1932. He attended the University of Madrid where he studied engineering. He also began working as a photographer and transferred to the National Film School in 1952. He began directing in the mid-1950s with the short films "El Pequeno Rio Manzanares" (1956), "La Tarde del Domingo" (1957), and "Cuenca" (1958). He made his featured debut with the 1960 film set in the Madrid slums, "The Delinquents". Saura did his best to avoid the Spanish censors during the regime of Generalissimo Francisco Franco while still alluding to the country's troubled history. He continued to direct such films as "Llanto Por un Bandido" (1964), "The Hunt" (1966), "Peppermint Frappe" (1967), "Stress Is There" (1968), "Honeycomb" (1969), and "The Garden of Delights" (1970). He ran afoul of the censors with the script for the film "Anna and the Wolves", which was eventually made starring his companion, Geraldine Chaplin, in 1973. He helmed the 1973 film "Cousin Angelica" and the allegorical "Cria Cuervos" in 1975 which received a special jury prize from the Cannes Film Festival. He was able to express his visions on film with less restrictions after Franco's death in 1975. His other films include "Elisa, My Life" (1977), "Los Ojos Vendados" (1978), "Mama Turns 100" (1979) which received an Oscar nomination for best foreign language film, "Deprisa, Deprisa" (1981), "Sweet Hours" (1982), "Antonieta" (1982), and "Los Zancos" (1984). He directed a trilogy of films featuring flamenco dancer Antonio Gades, "Blood Wedding" (1981), "Carmen" (1983) earning another Oscar nomination, and "El Amor Brujo" (1986). He continued to direct and write such films as "El

Dorado" (1988), "The Dark Night of the Soul" (1989), "Oh, Carmela!" (1990), "Sevillanas" (1992), "Outrage" (1993), "Marathon" (1993) the official film of the 1992 Olympics in Barcelona, the dance documentary "Flamenco" (1995), "Taxi" (1995), "Little Bird" (1997), "Tango" (1998) earning another Oscar nomination, "Goya in Bordeaux" (1999), "Bunuel y la Mesa del Rey Salomon" (2001), "Salome" (2002), "El 7o Dia" (2004), "Ieria" (2005), "Fados" (2007), "Sinfonia de Aragon" (2008), "Io Don Giovanni" (2009), the dance documentary "Flamenco Flamenco" (2010), "Argentina" (2015), "Jota de Saura" (2016), the shorts "Rosa Rosae: A Spanish Civil War Elegy" (2021) and "Goya 3 de Mayo" (2021), "The King of All the World" (2021), and "Las Paredes Hablan" (2022). He was due to receive a Goya lifetime achievement the day after his death. Saura married Adela Medrano in 1957 and they had two sons, Carlos and Antonio, before their divorce. He had a relationship with actress Geraldine Chaplin, and they had a son, Shane Saura Chaplin, in 1974. He was married to Mercedes Perez from 1982 until their divorce in 1993 and they had three sons, Manuel, Adrian, and Diego. He was involved with actress Eulalia Ramon from the early 1990s and they had a daughter, Anna Saura, who later worked as his producer. He and Ramon married in 2006 and she also survives him.

Savage, Herschel

Adult actor Herschel Savage, who starred in the 1978 porn classic "Debbie Does Dallas", died in California on October 8, 2023. He was 70. He was born Harvey Cohen in

New York City on November 25, 1952. He studied acting with Uta Hagen and Stella Adler and aspired for a career on stage and screen. He was encouraged to enter the adult film industry in the mid-1970s. He usually appeared under the stage name Herschel Savage and was seen in over 1000 films and videos during his fifty-year career. He was also billed by a host of other pseudonyms including Bill Berry, Billy Bell, Cornell Hayes, Dan Hues, Gerald Graystone, Greg Falcon, Harvey Cowan, Harvey Crain, Harvey Savage, Herschel Steed, Howard Gibs, Jack Blake, Jack Sin, Jack Soft, Joel Kane, Martin Quincy, Norman Vain, Paul Hues, Skip Brooks, Van Ayasit, and Vic Falcon. His numerous films include "Teenage Housewife" (1976), "The Awakening of Emily" (1976), "Odyssey: The Ultimate Trip" (1977), "Captain Lust" (1977), "Sharon" (1977), "Jail Bait" (1977), "Breaker Beauties" (1977), "Honeymoon Haven" (1977), "The Night Bird" (1977), "Her Total Response" (1977), "Prey of the Call Girl" (1977), "Hollywood Goes Hard" (1978), "Sweet Temptations" (1978), the blockbuster adult film "Debbie Does Dallas" (1978), "Hot Honey" (1978), "The Fur Trap" (1978), "Safari Club" (1978), "Candi Girl" (1979), "Hot Child in the City" (1979), Roberta Findlay's "Honeysuckle Rose" (1979), "For Richard for Poorer" (1979), "Satin Suite" (1979), "Tigresses and Other Man-Eaters"

(1979), "Blonde in Black Silk" (1979), "Playthings" (1979), "The Sexpert" (1979), "The Girls of Godiva High" (1980), "Dracula Exotica" (1980) with Jamie Gillis as Count Dracula, "The Filthy Rich: A 24 K-Dirty Movie" (1980), "Ladies Night" (1980), "On White Satin" (1980), "The Blonde" (1980), "11" (1980), "Hotline" (1980), "A Woman's Dream" (1980), "Inside Hollywood: The John Barfield Story" (1980), "Blonde Ambition" (1981), Gerard Damiano's science fiction porn "The Satisfiers of Alpha Blue" (1981), "Aunt Peg's Fulfillment" (1981), "Oriental Madam" (1981), "8 to 4" (1981), "Cheryl Hansson: Cover Girl" (1981), "Amanda by Night" (1981), "Cells of Passion" (1981), "Seka's Fantasies" (1981), "Same Time Every Year" (1981), "Lips" (1981), "Every Which Way She Can" (1981), "A Thousand and One Erotic Nights" (1982), "Fox Holes" (1982), "N*u*r*s*e*s of the 407th" (1982), "Inspirations" (1982), "Expose Me Now" (1982), "Campus Capers" (1982), "Nightlife" (1982), "That's My Daughter" (1982), "Nasty Nurses" (1982), "I Like to Watch" (1982), "Memphis Cathouse Blues" (1982), "Body Magic" (1982), "Little Orphan Dusty Part II" (1982), "Mai Lin vs. Serena" (1982), "The Challenge of Desire" (1982), "Summer Camp Girls" (1983), "San Fernando Valley Girls" (1983), "Up 'n' Coming" (1983), "Moments of Love" (1983), "Private Moments" (1983), "Bold Obsession" (1983), "The Young Like It Hot" (1983), "Sorority Sweethearts" (1983), "Bad Girls II" (1983), "Bodies in Heat" (1983), "Erotic Radio WSEX" (1983), "A Taste of Money" (1983), "A Bit Too Much Too Soon" (1983), "Tuesday's Lover" (1983), "Pleasure Zone" (1983), "Working It Out" (1983), "Let's Talk Sex" (1983), "Eat at the Blue Fox" (1983), "Carnal Olympics" (1983), "Coffee, Tea or Me" (1983), "Sex Star" (1983), "Sulka's Daughter" (1984), "China and Silk" (1984), "What Gets Me Hot!" (1984), "Making It Big" (1984), "Sister Dearest" (1984), "Erotic Aerobics" (1984), "Matinee Idol" (1984), "Stiff Competition" (1984), "Young Girls Do" (1984), "Bachelorette Party" (1983), "Kissin' Cousins" (1984), "The Pleasure Hunt" (1984), "Sexdance Fever" (1984), "Scared Stiff" (1984), "Sexsations" (1984), "The X-Team" (1984), "Brooke Does College" (1984), "Nasty Lady" (1984), "Space Virgins" (1984), "Cathouse Fever" (1984), "Intimate Couples" (1984), "Temptation: The Story of a Lustful Bride" (1984), "Trashy Lady" (1985), "Fleshdance" (1985), "Wild Things" (1985), "Tower of Power" (1985), "Corporate Assets" (1985), "Some Kind of Woman" (1985), "Yank My Doodle, It's a Dandy!" (1985), "Sex-a-Vision" (1985), "California Valley Girls" (1985), "Country Girl" (1985), "It's My Body" (1985), "Poonies" (1985), "Blue Ice" (1985), "Squalor Motel" (1985), "Erotic Zone" (1985), "Beverly Hills Wives" (1985), "Blue Dream Lover" (1985), "Futuresex" (1985), "Ginger on the Rocks" (1985), "Naked Eyes" (1985), "Family Heat" (1985), "The Heartbreak Girl" (1985), "Losing Control" (1985), "Marina Heat" (1985), "Nice n' Tight" (1985), "Orifice Party" (1985), "The Pornbirds" (1985), "One Night in Bangkok" (1985), "The Backdoor Club" (1985), "Bootsie" (1985), "A Coming of Angels: The Sequel" (1984), "Sex Toys" (1985), "2002: A Sex Odyssey" (1985), "Hot Blooded" (1985), "Inspector Cliteau in... The Pink Panties" (1985), "The Pleasure Seekers" (1985), "Letters of

Love" (1985), "The Best Little Whorehouse in San Francisco" (1985), "Inside Candy Samples" (1985), "Lust in Space" (1985), "Passage to Ecstasy" (1985), "A Taste of Candy" (1985), "If My Mother... Only Knew" (1985), "Getting Personal" (1985), "Erotic Zone" (1985), "Angel's Revenge" (1986), "I've Never Done This Before!" (1986), "Chocolate Kisses" (1986), "Night Prowlers" (1986), "Hypersexuals" (1986), "Flesh for Fantasies" (1986), "Winner Takes All" (1986), "Lucy Has a Ball" (1986), John Frankenheimer's mainstream film "52 Pick-Up" (1986) in a small role, "Merry X Miss" (1986), "Debbie Duz Dishes" (1986), "Hotel California" (1986), "Sweethearts" (1986), "Porn in the U.S.A." (1986), "The Black Chill" (1986), "Club Exotica" (1986), "Club Exotica II: Part Two - The Next Day..." (1986), "Down & Dirty in Beverly Hills" (1986), "Ex-Connection" (1986), "Innocent Taboo" (1986), "Mouth Watering" (1986), "Science Friction" (1986), "Stripteaser" (1985), "This Butt's for You" (1986), "The Ultimate Lover" (1986), "Winner Take All" (1986), "Doctor Penetration" (1986), "Black to the Future" (1986), "Breakin In" (1986), "Busty Wrestling Babes" (1986), "Dangerous Curves" (1986), "Debbie Goes to College" (1986), "Funky Brewster" (1986), "Harem Girls" (1986), "Hot Gun" (1986), "I Am Curious Black" (1986), "In All the Right Places" (1986), "In and Out in Beverly Hills" (1986), "Jewel of the Nite" (1986), "Kiss of the Married Woman" (1986), "The Red Garter" (1986), "Pink and Pretty" (1986), "Luscious Lucy in Love" (1986), "Pleasure Spot" (1986), "The Postman Always Comes Twice" (1986), "Rambone Does Hollywood" (1986), "Sailing into

Ecstasy" (1986), "Shades of Passion" (1986), "Twins" (1986), "White Trash" (1986), "Wild Nurses in Lust" (1986), "Double Standards" (1986), "Ginger & Spice" (1987), "In Search of the Golden Bone" (1987), "Ginger Snaps" (1987), "She's a Boy Toy" (1987), "The Adventures of Dick Black, the Black Dick" (1987), "The Bride" (1987), "Pretty Peaches 2" (1987), "The Adulteress" (1987), "Blow-Off!" (1987), "The Boss" (1987), "The Cat Club" (1987), "Charmed & Dangerous" (1987), "Phone Sex Girls" (1987), "The Sex Detective" (1987), "Barbara the Barbarian" (1987), "The Brazilian Connection" (1987), "Cabaret Sin" (1987), "Furburgers (Home of the Box Lunch)" (1987), "Jane Bond Meets Golden Rod" (1987), "Nymphette Does Hollywood" (1987), "Ladies Room" (1987), "Living Doll" (1987), "The Long Ranger" (1987), "Sexy Delights II" (1987), "WPINK-TV 3" (1987), the crime thriller "Fatal Pulse" (1988), "Empire of the Sins" (1988), "Honeybuns 2: Grecian Formula" (1988), "The Screwdriver Saloon" (1988), "This Is Your Sx Life" (1988), "Amanda by Night 2" (1988), "La Boomba" (1988), "Mammary Lane" (1988), "Sins of Angel Kelly" (1988), the science fiction film "Droid" (1988), "Soul Games" (1988), "Tawnee Be Good" (1988), "Air Erotica" (1988), "Have Body Will Travel" (1989), "Bodies in Heat... the Sequel" (1989), and "Sheer Haven" (1989). He left acting in adult films in the late

1980s. Savage directed and frequently produced the videos "The Maddams Family" (1991), "Dances with Foxes" (1991), "The Naked Bun 8 1/2" (1992), "Jugsy" (1992), "Cape Lere" (1992), "The Last Girl Scout" (1992), "The Sexual Limits" (1992), "Bazooka County 5: The Jugs" (1993), "Ass Ventura: Crack Detective" (1995), "The Malibu Madam" (1995), and "Joannie Pneumatic" (1997). He resumed acting in porn in the late 1990s with roles in "Persona" (1997), "Sins of the Flesh" (1997), "Blown Out" (1997), "Deep Throat the Quest" (1997), "Boobsville Cabaret" (1998), "The Brad Pack" (1998), "Country Comfort" (1998), "Nude World Order" (1998), "Heartache" (1998), "The Other Side of Serenity" (1998), "White Angel" (1998), "Confessions of Hollywood Housewives" (1998), "Love's Passion" (1998), "Cravings" (1998), "This Little Piggy Went to Porno" (1998), "Married, Yes... Dead, No!" (1998), "Eyes of Desire" (1998), "Thunder Pussy" (1998), "Masseuse 3" (1998), "She's Got Milk" (1998), "Rage" (1998), "Always Lily White" (1998), "Boomerang" (1998), "Possession" (1998), "Trial by Copulation" (1999), "Ladies Night" (1999), "Double Feature" (1999), "Sports Spectacular" (1999), "Phoenix Rising" (1999), "Scenes from the Oral Office!!" (1999), "The Kissing Game" (1999), "Eternal Excesses" (1999), "The Trophy" (1999), "Amnesiac" (1999), "Barely Legal" (1999), "Knockout" (1999), "Millennium" (1999), "Midas Touch" (1999), "Ka$h" (1999), "The Boxer and the Stripper" (1999), "Intimate Memories" (1999), "Little White Lies" (1999), "Buried Alive Bukkake" (1999), "Knocking at Heaven's Backdoor" (1999), "Sexed to Death" (1999), ""Stray Cat" (1999), "Taxi Dancer' (1999), "The Sopornos" (1999), "Extreme Teen" (1999), "Suitcase Pimps" (1999), "High Heels 'N' Hot Wheels" (1999), "Trigger" (1999), "Brown Eyes Blondes" (1999), "Intrigue" (1999), "For His Eyes Only" (1999), "Naughty Little Nymphos" (1999), "Plaid" (1999), "Very Naughty Angels" (1999), "Wang Dang That Sweet Poon Tang" (1999), "Kickin' It with Anna Malle" (1999), "Seymore Butt's Tushy Anyone?" (1999), "No Regrets' (1999), "Last Breath" (2000), "Shrink Wrapped" (2000), "Trick Baby" (2000), "Blue Matrix" (2000), "Dark Chambers" (2000), "Spellbound" (2000), "Emmanuelle 2000" (2000), "Dreamquest" (2000), "Dirty Deeds Done Dirt Cheap" (2000), "Ally McFeal" (2000), "True Blue" (2000), "Torrid Tramps" (2000), "Gapes of Wrath" (2000), "Asia Is in Too Deep" (2000), "The Bride of Double Feature" (2000), "L.A. Unforgiven" (2000), "Lust in Paradise" (2000), "Freak Show" (2000), "Sodomy on the Menu" (2000), "Foreign Bodies" (2000), "Indigo Nights" (2000), "Screamers" (2000), "Idiots Guide to Making Porno Movies" (2000), "Underworld" (2001), "A Wolf's Tail" (2001), "Reflections of Lust" (2001), "Taken" (2001), "Infidelity" (2001), "Cracked" (2001), "Sex Merchants" (2001), "Delinquent Teens" (2001), "Disturbed" (2001), "Mafioso" (2001), "Succubus" (2001), "Caveman Humping" (2001), "A Passion" (2001), "Lady Be Good" (2001), "The Gate" (2001), "After Midnight" (2001), "Fast Cars and Tiki Bars" (2001), "Teacher's Pet" (2001), "Dark Hart" (2002), "Madame Hollywood" (2002), "Big Bottom Sadie" (2002), "Crime & Passion" (2002), "Blue Angel" (2002), "Play with Fire" (2002), "The Fear of Speed" (2002), "La Femme Nikita

Denise" (2002), "Roadblock" (2002), "Naked Movie" (2002), "Easy Cheeks" (2002), "Red Hot Redheads" (2002), "Makin' It" (2002), "Love @ First Byte" (2002), "Strip Bowling" (2002), "Sindee the Campus Slut" (2002), "Body Illusion" (2003), "No Limits" (2003), "Photo Club" (2003), "Czechmate" (2003), "Third Date" (2003), "Cargo" (2003), "Retro Lust" (2003), "Something Wicked" (2003), "The Contortionist" (2003), "Dark Dimension" (2003), "The Hitman" (2003), "The Legends of Sex" (2003), "Lust Will and Testament" (2003), "The Scandal of Nicky Eros" (2003), "Servicing Sara" (2003), "Video Dames" (2003), "Roommate from Hell" (2003), "Apocalypse Babylon" (2003), "Love and Bullets" (2004), "Impact" (2004), "Sex Crazed College Coeds" (2004), "Blue Angels: The Second Coming" (2004), "Love on the Run" (2004), "Chasing Destiny" (2004), "Get Lucky" (2004), "Desperate Desires" (2004), "Slave to Love" (2004), "Uranus or Bust" (2004), "To Protect and Service" (2004), "Wonderland" (2005), "The Animal" (2005), "DarkSide" (2005), "Butt Pirates of the Caribbean" (2005), "American Sex Idol" (2006), "Federal Breast Inspectors" (2006), "The Sphincter Chronicles" (2006), "Manhunters" (2006), "Corruption" (2006), "The Reincarnation of Betty Page 2" (2006), "Hannah Goes to Hell" (2006), "Extreme Idols" (2006), "Ass Good Ass It Gets" (2006), "Guide to Porn Stars Sex Secrets" (2006), "Farmer's Daughters Make You Go Yee-Haw!" (2006), "Stiffer Competition" (2006), "Lady Scarface" (2007), "Mobster's Ball" (2007), "Delilah" (2007), "Strippers Need Love Too" (2007), "Sentenced" (2007), "Reform School Girls" (2007), "A Slice of Pie" (2007), "Spunk'd: The Movie" (2007), "Minutes to Midnight" (2007), "The Doll Underground" (2007), "Dawg the Booty Hunter" (2007), "Bad Girls" (2008), the horror porn "Texas Vibrator Massacre" (2008), "The Erotic Ghost Whisperer" (2008), "Fallen" (2008), "One Wild & Crazy Night" (2008), "Carpool" (2008), "MILFwood USA" (2008), "The Chauffeur's Daughter" (2008), "Swingtown" (2009), "Faithless" (2009), "Throat: A Cautionary Tale" (2009), "Heaven" (2009), "30 Rock: A XXX Parody" (2009), "Cougar 101" (2009), "My Wife's a Tramp" (2009), "Everybody Needs MILF" (2009), "Celebrity Apprentass" (2009), "18 and Dangerous" (2009), "3 Days in June" (2010), "Gia: Portrait of a Porn Star" (2010), "Not M*A*S*H XXX" (2010), "This Ain't Fox News XXX" (2011), "A Pornstar Is Born" (2011), "The Graduate XXX" (2011), "Mary Pops in the Magical Nanny" (2011), "Dallas XXX: A Parody" (2012), "The New Behind the Green Door" (2013), "Fallen II: Angels & Demons" (2018), and "Machine Gunner" (2023). He appeared on television in an episode of the comedy series "Just Shoot Me!" in 2001. Savage performed frequently on stage from the early 2000s with roles in productions of "The Prisoner of Second Avenue", "The Deep Throat Sex Scandal" as director Gerard Damiano, and "Pretty Filthy" as himself in a musical about the adult film business. His autobiographical one-man show, "Porn Star: My Life in the Sex Industry", premiered in 2016. Savage was inducted into the AVN and XRCO Halls of Fame celebrating the adult film industry. Savage was married to production manager Inez Ochoa from

1983 until their divorce in 1995. He was briefly married to fellow adult performer Wanda Curtis in 2001.

Savage, Joan

British singer and actress Joan Savage died at the Brinsworth House retirement home in Twickenham, London, England, on November 1, 2023. She was 89. Savage was born in Blackpool, England, on January 2, 1934. She was the daughter of comedian Norman Savage. She began performing on stage at the age of 12 with the Children's Tower Ballet and the Blackpool Tower Circus. She met fellow performer Ken Morris while touring with George and Alfred Black's revue "Music and Madness". They married in 1955 and they formed a double act. They were frequent performers on television's "The Arthur Haynes Show" from 1956 to 1962. They were also seen in various television advertisements and episodes of "The Jack Jackson Show", "Dancing with the Stars", "The Saturday Show", "This Is the Henry Hall Show", "Variety Parade", "The Music Goes Round", "Hi, Summer!", "Blackpool Show Parade", "The Dick Emery Show", and "The Black and White Minstrel Show". She was later seen on television in episodes of "Sex Les", "Dad's Army", and "Come Back Lucy". Savage was featured as dancer Celeste Pickersgill in five episodes of the television soap opera "Coronation Street" in 2000. She and Ken Morris were married until his death in 1969 and she is survived by their daughter, Kelly. She is also survived by her second husband, Bryan, who she married in 1972.

Sawyer, Brett

Professional wrestler Brett Woyan, who was known in the ring under the name Brett Sawyer, died on September 8, 2023. He was 63. Woyan was born in Orlando, Florida, on August 10, 1960. He began wrestling in his teens in the late 1970s under the name Brett Wayne. He took the name Hacksaw Brett Sawyer in the early 1980s and teamed with his older brother, Buzz Sawyer, in a tag team with Pacific Northwest Wrestling. The brothers held the National Wrestling Association (NWA) Pacific Northwest Tag Team Championship several times. He was also tag team champion teaming with Rocky Johnson, Steve Pardee, and Tom Prichard in the early 1980s. Sawyer was the NWA Pacific Northwest Heavyweight Champion four times in 1982. He and his brother competed for Georgia Championship Wrestling where the defeated the Road Warriors for the NWA National Tag Team Championship in 1983. He also captured the NWA National Heavyweight Championship in Atlanta in 1983. Sawyer joined Southwest Championship Wrestling in San Antonio, Texas, in 1984, and teamed with Chicky Starr to hold that promotion's tag team titles. He and Buzz joined Jim Crockett Promotions in North Carolina in early 1985 and lost a loser leaves town match to the Midnight Express later in the year. He captured the NWA Central States Heavyweight Championship in Kansas City, Missouri, in late 1985. He toured with his brother in Japan with New Japan Pro-Wrestling in 1987. He teamed with Jim Backlund as the Playboys in Championship Wrestling Florida, and they held the tag belts there in 1989. He wrestled briefly in World Championship Wrestling (WCW) as Brett Wayne in 1991. His brother died of a drug overdose in 1992 and Brett retired from the ring in 1998. He later opened a wrestling school in St. Petersburg, Florida. His survivors include two children.

Sawyer, Toni

Actress Toni Sawyer died on May 11, 2023. She was 83. Sawyer was born in Westfield, Massachusetts, on October 15, 1939. She began her acting career on stage and played Becky Thatcher in a touring production of "The Adventures of Tom Sawyer" in her early teens. She appeared frequently on television from the early 1980s with roles in episodes of "Secrets of Midland Heights", "Lou Grant", "Flamingo Road", "Crisis Counselor", "Days of Our Lives", "Family Ties", "ABC Afterschool Specials", "Bare Essence", "Tucker's Witch", "The Dukes of Hazzard", 'Three's Company", "Finders of Lost Loves", "Call to Glory", "The A-Team", "Hardcastle & McCormick", "The Twilight Zone", "Not Necessarily the News", "Santa Barbara" as Nurse Hodgers in 1986, "Matlock", "Webster", "Moonlighting", "The Oldest Rookie", "Mathnet", "Baby Boom", "The Golden Girls", "Nurses", "Evening Shade", "Civil Wars", "Knots Landing", "Love & War", "Seinfeld", "Land's End", "Providence", "The Jamie Foxx Show", "The Bold and the Beautiful", "ER", "Rodney", "Close to Home", "Kitchen Confidential", "Cold Case", "General Hospital: Night Shift", "NCIS", "All My Children", "Criminal Minds", "The Young and the Restless", and "Decker". Sawyer also appeared in the tele-films and mini-series "Please Don't Hit Me, Mom" (1981), "Drop-Out Father" (1982), "North & South: Book 2, Love & War" (1986), "Blue de Ville" (1986), "The Betty Ford Story" (1987), "The Stepford Children" (1987), "Cracked Up" (1987), "The Nerd" (1989), "Jury Duty: The Comedy" (1990), "Doing Time on Maple Drive" (1992), "A Time to Heal" (1994), "The O.J. Simpson Story" (1995) as Nicole's Mother, and "A Face to Die For" (1996). Sawyer was seen in such films as "Hughes and Harlow: Angels in Hell" (1977), "Wacko" (1982), "Down on Us" (1984), "Mask" (1985), "Sweet Dreams" (1985), "Stewardess School" (1986), "18 Again!" (1988), "High Strung" (1992), "My Life" (1993), "Wildly Available" (1996), "The Thirteenth Floor" (1999), and "The Sky Is Falling" (1999).

Schacht, Sam

Actor Sam Schacht died in New York City on January 5, 2023. He was 86. Schacht was born in New York City on April 19, 1936. He graduated from the City College of New York and studied at the Actor's Studio under Lee Strasberg. He performed frequently on stage and appeared in Broadway productions of "The Magic Show" (1974) and "Golda" (1977). Schacht was featured in the films "Puzzle of a Downfall Child" (1970), "Badge 373" (1973), "A Secret Space" (1977), "Tattoo" (1981), "Heart of Midnight" (1988), and "A Shock to the System" (1990). He appeared on television in episodes of "N.Y.P.D.", "Kojak", "The Doctors", "The Edge of Night", "Guiding Light", "The Equalizer", "As the World Turns", and "Law & Order". His other television credits include productions of "Paradise Lost" on "Great Performances" in 1971, "First Ladies Diaries: Rachel Jackson" (1975), "Woman of Valor" (1977), "The Four of Us" (1977), "The Last Tenant" (1978), "Doctor Franken" (1980), "True West" on "American Playhouse" in 1984, and "Sentimental Journey" (1984). He was also a teacher at the Actors Studio Drama School and the Stella Adler Studio of Acting. He was co-founder of the New York theatrical companies the New Group and the Workshop. Schacht later earned a master's degree in psychoanalytic studies through the Center for Modern Psychoanalytic Studies. He married Sybil Blaufeld in 1962 and is survived by her and their two sons.

Scheckman, Richard

Television archivist Richard Scheckman, who worked with David Letterman's television shows for over three decades, died at a hospital in Manhattan, New York, on March 10, 2023. He was 67. Scheckman was born in Queens, New York, on December 1, 1955. He attended New York University and earned a master's degree from Baruch College. He collected decades of film footage that could be used for commercials or television shows. He began working with "Late Night with David Letterman" in March of 1982, shortly after the show debuted on NBC. He was called upon to supply so much obscure footage that he was hired full-time as the show's film coordinator. Scheckman came to CBS with Letterman in 1994 and remained with "Late Show with David Letterman" until it went off the air in 2015. He also became a performer in front of the camera in various comedy skits including playing Elvis Presley. Scheckman was a director of film programming for the classic film festival, Cinefest, from 1980 and was chairman of F.I.L.M. Arhices since 1986.

Schmidt, Arthur

Film editor Arthur Schmidt, who received Academy Awards for his work on the films "Who Framed Roger Rabbit" and "Forrest Gump", died at his home in Santa Barbara, California, on August 5, 2023. He was 86. Schmidt was born in Los Angeles, California, on June 17, 1937. His father was film editor Arthur P. Schmidt. He graduated from Santa Clara University. He began his career in films assisting Dede Allen as a standby editor for the 1970 film "Little Big Man". He was an assistant editor for "Macho Callahan" (1970), "Scream Blacula Scream" (1973), "The Fortune" (1975), and "Maathon Man" (1976). He was assistant editor for the tele-films "Second Chance" (1972), "Guess Who's Been Sleeping in My Bed?" (1973), and "I Heard the Owl Call My Name" (1973). He worked as editor for the films "The Last Remake of Beau Geste" (1977), "Jaws 2" (1978), "Coal Miner's Daughter" (1980) receiving an Academy Award nomination, "The Idolmaker" (1980), "The Escape Artist" (1982), "The Buddy System" (1984), "Firstborn" (1984), "Fandango" (1985), "Back to the Future" (1985), "Ruthless People" (1986), "Beaches" (1988), "Who Framed Roger Rabbit" (1988) earning an Academy Award, "Back to the Future II" (1989), "Back to the Future III" (1990), "The Rocketeer" (1991), "Deth Becomes Her" (1992), "The Last of the Mohicans" (1992), "Addams Family Values" (1993), "Forrest Gump" (1994) receiving a second Oscar, "Congo" (1995), "The Birdcage" (1996), "Chain Reaction" (1996), "Contact" (1997), "Primary Colors" (1998), "What Lies Beneath" (2000), "Cast Away" (2000), "Pirates of the Caribbean: The Curse of the Black Pearl" (2003), "The Chumscrubber" (2005), and "Flight" (2012). Schmidt also edited the tele-films "The Jericho Mile" (1979) and "You Ruined My Life" (1987), and an episode of "Tales from the Crypt". He was executive producer of the 2010 documentary short "The Labyrinth". His book, "We Don't Need Roads", was published in 2015. He was recipient of the American Cinema Editors Career Achievement Award in 2009. Schmidt is survived by his wife, Susan Craig.

Schmidt-Reitwein, Jorg

German cinematographer Jorg Schmidt-Reitwein, who worked frequently with director Werner Herzog, died in Germany on August 21, 2023. He was 84. Schmidt-Reitwein was born in Konigs Wusterhausen, Germany, on February 21, 1939. He moved to Berlin in 1959 to pursue a career in film. He spent three years in prison in East Germany on charges he attempted to smuggle his girlfriend to West Berlin. He became an assistant cameraman in Munich on television productions of "Der Zirkus Stirbt - Es Lebe der Zirkus" (1965), "Reichtum

Verpflichtet. Mazene Einst und Heute" (1966), and "Die Chassidim" (1966), and the film "Even Dwarfs Started Small" (1970). He was cinematographer for the shorts "Heimatmuseum" (1968) and "Precautions Against Fanatics" (1969), and the films "Cardillac" (1969) and "Anglia" (1970). Schmidt-Reitwein worked as cinematographer with Werner Herzog on the feature documentary "Fata Morgana" (1971). He and Herzog worked together on 17 subsequent films and documentaries. He continued to serve as cinematographer on such films as "Land of Silence and Darkness" (1971), "The Enigma of Kaspar Hauser" (1974), "The Great Ecstasy of Woodcarver Steiner" (1974), "Das Andechser Gefuhl" (1975), "Die Atlantikschwimmer" (1976), "Heart of Glass" (1976), "There Is a Criminal Touch to Art" (1976), "Mit Mir Will Niemand Spielen" (1976), "Ob's Sturmt Oder Schneit" (1976), "Bierkampf" (1977), "Bye-bye Bavaria!" (1978), "Germany in Autumn" (1978), Herzog's "Nosferatu the Vampyre" (1979), "Woyzeck" (1979), "Der Komantsche" (1979), "Die Patriotin" (1979), "Der Kandidat" (1980), "Der Neger Erwin" (1981) also appearing on screen in a small role, "Das Letzte Loch" (1981), "Liebeskonzil" (1982), "Der Depp" (1982), "Das Gespenst" (1982), "Land of Look Behind" (1982), "Die Olympiasiegerin" (1983), "Rita Ritter" (1984), "Wanderkrebs" (1984), "Where the Green Ants Dream" (1984), "The Practice of Love" (1985), "Kaiser und Eine Nacht" (1985), "Der Nachbar" (1986), the short "Portrait Werner Herzog" (1986), "Triumph der Gerechten" (1987), "Zimmer 36" (1988), "Gesucht: Monika Ertl" (1989), "In Meinem Herzen, Schatz..." (1989), "Bavaria Blue" (1990), "Echoes from a Somber Empire" (1990), "Brandnacht" (1992), "Probefahrt ins Paradies" (1993), "Bells from the Deep: Faith and Superstition in Russia" (1993), "Erotic Tales III" (1999), "Der Onkel vom Meer" (2000), "Fisimatenten" (2000), "Poem: I Set My Foot Upon the Air and It Carried Me" (2003), "Marmorera" (2007), "Der Ruf der Geckos" (2007), "Problema" (2010), and "Escape from Tibet" (2012). He was cinematographer for television productions of "Behinderte Zukunft" (1971), "Indien Zwischen Gestern und Morgen" (1972), "Der Damm" (1972), "Drachensteigen" (1972), "Seniorenschweiz" (1976), "Zeit der Empfindsamkeit" (1977), "Die Menschen, die das Staufer-Jahr Vorbereiten" (1977), "Baldauf" (1979), "Max und Traudl" (1979), "Deutschland Kann Manchmal Sehr Schon Sein" (1982), "The French As Seen By..." (1988), "Seefahrer" (1988), "Herdsmen of the Sun" (1989), "Wilma Wohnt Weit Weg" (1991), "Heiss - Kalt" (1993), "Verbotene Zone" (1995), "The Transformation of the World Into Music" (1996), "Im Rausch der Liebe" (1996), "Rot Wie das Blut" (1998), and "Jessye Norman - Ich Leb Allein in Meinem Himmel, meinem Lieben, Meinem Lied" (2005). He also worked on episodes of the series "Eurocops" and "Tatort". He was subject of the 2017 documentary "Jorg Schmidt-Reitwein: Ways of Seeing". Schmidt-Reitwein is survived by a daughter from his first wife, Erika Kaul, and a son and two daughters from his second wife, Susanne Rupprecht. He is also survived by his third wife and their daughter.

Schroeder, Bernd

German screenwriter and author Bernd Schroeder died in Mecklenburg-Vorpommern, Germany, on June 18, 2023. He was 79. Schroeder was born in Aussig an der Elbe, Germany, on June 6, 1944. He attended the University of Munich in the mid-1960s. He began working as an assistant director for the television network Bayerischer Rundfunk while attending college. He wrote numerous television productions from the early 1970s including "8051 Grinning" (1972), "Sitten-gemalde" (1973), "Nestwarme" (1973), "Hahnenkampf" (1975), "Die Herausforderung" (1975), "Die Stadt im Tal" (1975), "Munchnerinnen" (1976), "Menschenfresser" (1976), "Notwehr" (1977), "Qualverwandtschaften" (1982), "Kein Schoner Land" (1985), "Fraulein - Ein Deutsches Melodram" (1986), and "Der Einbruch" (1991). Schroeder scripted episodes of such television series as "Munchner Geschichten", "Wie Wurden Sie Entscheiden?", "Bier und Spiele", and "Der Eiserne Weg". He wrote the films "Gefundenes Fressen" (1977) and "Pizza Colonia" (1991). He scripted numerous audio plays for radio, frequently working with his wife Elke Heidenreich. They continued to work together after their separation, penning the films "Rudernde Hunde" (2002) and "Elke Heidenreich" (2009). His other books include "Versunkenes Land" (1993), "Die Madonnina" (2001), "Mutter & Sohn" (2004), "Auf Amerika" (2012), "Wir Sind Doch Alle Da" (2013), and "Warten Auf Goebbels" (2017). Schroeder was married to Elke Heidenreich from 1972 until their divorce in 1995.

Schulman, Arnold

Screenwriter Arnold Schulman, who earned Oscar nominations for his scripts for "Love with a Proper Stranger" and "Goodbye, Columbus", died at his home in Santa Monica, California, on February 4, 2023. He was 97. Schulman was born in Philadelphia, Pennsylvania, on August 11, 1925. He attended the University of North Carolina before serving in the U.S. Navy during World War II. He moved to New York City after his discharge in 1946 where he studied writing with Robert Anderson at the American Theatre Wing. He appeared in a small role in the Broadway plays "Come Back, Little Sheeba" (1950) and "An Enemy of the People" (1950). He was writing for television by the early 1950s, scripting episodes of "Cosmopolitan Theatre", "Danger", "Schlitz Playhouse", "You Are There", "Suspense", "Studio One", "Omnibus", "Kraft Theatre", "Windows", "Matinee Theatre", "Playwrights '56", "The United States Steel Hour" adaptation of "Bang the Drum Slowly" in 1956, "General Electric Theater", "First Person", and "The Danny Thomas Hour". Schulman penned the hit Broadway comedy "A Hole in the Head" (1957) and scripted the 1959 film adaptation, directed by Frank Capra and starring Frank Sinatra. Schulman wrote the 1957 film "Wild Is the Wind" and scripted the film adaptation of Edna Ferber's "Cimarron" in 1960. He received Academy Award nominations for writing the 1963 film "Love with the Proper Stranger" and adapting Philip Roth's "Goodbye, Columbus" to film in 1969. He also scripted "The Night They Raided Minsky's" (1968) and wrote Francis Ford Coppola's "Tucker: The Man and His Dream" (1988). He was credited as a writer for the films "To Find a Man" (1972), "Funny Lady" (1975), "Won Ton Ton: The Dog Who Saved Hollywood" (1976), "Players" (1979), and "A Chorus Line" (1985) but claimed that little of his work appeared in the finished products. He was scripter and co-producer for the 1993 tele-film "And the Band Played On".

Scotto, Renata

Italian operatic soprano Renata Scotto died in Savona, Italy, on August 16, 2023. She was 89. Scotto was born in  Savona on February 24, 1934. She studied music at the Milan Conservatory. She sang the title role of Verdi's "La Traviata" at the Teatro Nuovo in Milan in 1952. She was featured in the role of Walter in Alfredo Catalani's "La Wally" at La Scala the following year. She was Sophie in Massenet's "Werther" at the Rome Opera in 1955 and starred in a production of "La Traviata" at La Fenice in Venice in 1956. She became a member of the ensemble at La Scala in 1957. She earned international acclaim for her performance as Amina in Bellini's "La Sonnambula" at the Edinburgh Festival in 1957. She starred in such operas as "Zair", "La Straniera", "Maria di Rohan", and "Robert le Diable" over the next several years. She made her U.S. debut as Mimi in Puccini's "La Boheme" in 1960 at the Lyric Opera of Chicago. She starred in "Madama Butterfly" at the Metropolitan Opera in 1965. She starred in over 300 performances at the Met including Mozart's "La Clemenza di Tito", in Meyerbeer's "Le Prophete", and Ponchielli's "La Gioconda". Scotto starred in television productions of "La Boheme" (1977) as Mimi, "Otello" (1978), "Luisa Miller" (1979), "Don Carlo" (1980), "Manon Lescaut" (1980), "Il Trittico" (1981), "La Boheme" (1982) as Musetta, and "Francesca da Rimini" (1984) on "The Metropolitan Opera Presents". She was a guest on several episodes of "The Mike Douglas Show" and "The Merv Griffin Show". She began

directing operas in the late 1980s including her final appearance with the Met in "Madama Butterfly" in 1987, and a televised production of "La Traviata" in 1995. Her memoir, "Scotto: More Than a Diva", was published in 1984. She was married Lorenzo Anselmi, a violinist in the La Scala orchestra who became his wife's business manager, from 1960 until his death in 2021. She is survived by their two children. Laura and Filippo.

Seacat, Sandra

Acting teacher and actress Sandra Seacat died of primary biliary cholangitis in Santa Monica, California, on January 17, 2023. He was 86. Seacat was born in Greensburg, Kansas, on October 2, 1936. She studied method acting at  Northwestern University and moved to New York City after graduation. She trained under Michael Howard and at the Actors Studio with Lee Strasberg. She performed on stage from the early 1960s appearing in productions of "The Noble Spaniard" and "The Waltz of the Dog" under her married name Sandra Kaufman. She appeared on Broadway in productions of "The Three Sisters" (1964), "A Streetcar Named Desire" (1973), and "Sly Fox" (1976). She was an original member of the improvisation troupe Second City Revue in the mid-1960s and performed frequently on stage in Toronto, Atlanta, and New Orleans later in the decade. She taught acting at the Lee Strasberg Theatre Institute, City College of New York's Leonard Davis Center for the Performing Arts, and the Actors Studio in the 1970s and had such students as Christopher Reeve, Meg Ryan, Laura Dern, Lance Henricksen, Mickey Rourke, Marlo Thomas, Jessica Lange, and Steve Railsback. She utilized dream work to help actors play characters with Melanie Griffith and Gina Gershon crediting the technique with improving their performances. Seacat appeared in such films as "The Rose" (1979), "Jane Austen in Manhattan" (1980), "The Kidnapping of the President" (1980), "Frances" (1982), "The Golden Seal" (1983), "Country" (1984), "Promised Land" (1987), "Wildfire" (1988), "The New Age" (1994), "The Destiny of Marty Fine" (1996), "Crazy in Alabama" (1999), "Nailed" (2001), "Daddy and Them" (2001), "The Want" (2001), "Prey for Rock & Roll" (2003), "A Little Crazy" (2003), "In the Land of Milk and Money" (2004), "Illusion" (2004), "Fade" (2007), "Tattered Angel" (2008), "Sympathy for Delicious" (2010), "The Time Being" (2012), "Palo Alto" (2013), "Alex of Venice" (2014), and "Buster's Mal Heart" (2016). She was also seen in the short films "Liv" (1998), "Shale" (2012), "The Scarecrow" (2015), "The Strangeness You Feel" (2017), and "Lina" (2022). Seacat directed the 1990 film "In the Spirit" starring Marlo Thomas and Elaine May. She appeared on television in productions of "First Ladies Diaries: Edith Wilson" (1976), "Fame" (1978), "Nobody's Child" (1986), "Held Hostage: The Sis and Jerry Levin Story" (1991), "The Baby Dance" (1998), "You Don't

Know Jack" (2010), "Enlightened" (2011), "Guest Appearances" (2020), and "Under the Banner of Heaven" (2022). Seacat was married to Arthur Kaufman from 1959 until their divorce in 1970 and is survived by their daughter, acting coach Greta Seacat. She was married to actor Michael Ebert from 1972 until their divorce in 1978. She married actor Thurn Hoffman in 1982 and he also survives her.

Sebaldt, Maria

German actress Maria Sebaldt died in Munich, Germany, on April 4, 2023. She was 92. Sebaldt was born in Steglitz, Berlin, Germany, on April 26, 1930. She began

training as an actress in 1946 and made her stage debut in a production of "Krach im Hinterhaus" in Sondershausen in 1947. She continued to appear frequently on stage throughout her career. She made her film debut in 1953's "When the Village Music Plays on Sunday Nights". Sebaldt was also seen in such films as "So Ein Affentheater" (1953), "Die Starkere" (1953), "Geliebtes Leben" (1953), "Strassenserenade" (1953), "Das Ideale Brautpaar" (1954), "The Gupsy Baron" (1954), "Der Zarewitsch" (1954), "Ihre Grosse Prufung" (1954), "Sacred Lie" (1955), "Liebe Ohne Illusion" (1955), "Vatertag" (1955), "Madchen Ohne Grenzen" (1955), "Alibi" (1955), "Urlaub auf Ehrenwort" (1955), "Nacht der Entscheidung" (1956), "Dany, Bitte Schreiben Sie" (1956), "The Captain from Kopenick" (1956), "Die Rosel vom Schwarzwald" (1956), "Anastasia: The Csar's Last Daughter" (1956), "Heisse Ernte" (1956), "Frauen Sind fur die Liebe Da" (1957), "The Zurich Engagement" (1957), "Tolle Nacht" (1957), "Lemkes Sel. Witwe" (1957), "Eine Frau, die Weiss, Was Sie Will" (1958), "Der Greifer" (1958), "Hoppla, Jetzt Kommt Eddie" (1958), "Grabenplatz 17" (1958), "Zauber der Montur" (1958), "Vater, Mutter and Neun Kinder" (1958), "The Kidnapping of Miss Nylon" (1959), "Mein Ganzes Herz Ist Voll Musik" (1959), "Peter Schiesst den Vogel Ab" (1959), "Tausend Sterne Leuchten" (1959), "Ich Bin Kein Casanova" (1959), "The Buddenbrooks" (1959), "Das Hab Ich in Paris Gelernt" (1960), "Frauen in Teufels Hand" (1960), "Eine Frau Furs Ganze Leben" (1960), "Hauptmann - Deine Sterne" (1960), "Das Schwarze Schaf" (1960), "The Last of Mrs. Cheyney" (1961), "Barbara - Wild Wie ds Meer" (1961), "Im Sechsten Stock" (1961), "Der Vogelhandler" (1962), "Bekenntnisse Eines Moblierten Herrn" (1963), "Charley's Tante" (1963), "Vorsicht Mister Dodd" (1964), "Five Thousand Dollars on One Ace" (1965), "Peter und Sabine" (1968), and ...Aber Jonny!" (1973). She appeared frequently on television with roles in productions of "Drei Mann auf Einem Pferd" (1957), "Blatter im Einde" (1958), "Drei Kleine Helle" (1959), "Menschen, Lire, Vollpensionen - Ein Urlaubskabarett Ohne Pass und..." (1959), "Das Grosse Messer" (1959), "Das Nasse Leben: Erinnerungen Einer Brutschwimmerim" (1961), "Der Marquis von Keith" (1962), "Schones Wochenende" (1962),

"Has der Schonheit" (1963), "Die Zwiebel" (1964), "Kein Ersatz fur Perlen" (1964), "Oh, Diese Geister" (1966), "Das Abgrundige in Herrn Gerstenberg" (1966), "Die Schwarze Sonne" (1968), "Das Hohere Leben" (1968), "Christoph Kolumbus Oder Die Entdeckung Amerikas" (1969), "Auf und Davon" (1970), "Mancher Lernt's Nie" (1972), "Scheidung Auf Musikalisch" (1972), "Manolescu - Die Fast Wahre Biographie Eines Gauners" (1972), "Zu Einem Mord Gehoren Zwei" (1973), "Diamantenparty" (1973), "Gruss Nach Vorn" (1975), "Heitere Episoden Mit Hans Joachim Kulenkampff" (1975), "Erben Ist Menschlich" (1977), "Endstation Paradies" (1977), "Der Grosse Karpfen Ferdinand und Andere Weihnachtsgeschichten" (1978), "Ein Mann fur alle Falle" (1979), "Die Grossen Sebastians" (1979), "Pension Scholler" (1980), "Keine Angst vor Verwandten!" (1981), "Zuruck an den Absender" (1981), "Streichquartett" (1981), "Schuld Sind Nur die Frauen" (1982), "Urlaub am Meer" (1982), "Toutes Griffes Dehors" (1982), "Rendezvous der Damen" (1983), "Frau Juliane Winkler" (1983), "Herbert Ist Hermann" (1985), "Zerbrochene Brucken" (1986), "So Ein Schlawiner" (1990), "Mit Herz und Schnauze" (1992), "Dreamboy Macht Frauen Glucklich" (1999), "Eine Liebe auf Mallorca 2" (2000), "Eine Liebe auf Mallorca 3" (2001), "Mein Taum von Venedig" (2008), "1:0 Fur das Gluck" (2008), and "Plotzlich Onkel" (2009). Her other television credits include episodes of "Adieu, Prinzessin", "Das Kriminalmuseum", "Gewagtes Spiel" as Babette Bollmann from 1964 to 1966, "Lerchenpark - Moderne Geschichten aus Einer Satellitenstadt", "Der Kommissar", "Unter Einem Dach", "Wir Warten Auf's Christkind", "Lemmi und die Schmoker", "Karl, der Gerechte" as Else in 1976, "Tatort", "Frau Uber Vierzig", "Derrick", "Die Unsterblichen Methoden des Franz Josef Wanninger", "The Old Fox", "Tegtmeier Klart Auf", "Lach Mal Wieder", "Schone Ferien", "Ich Heirate Eine Familie..." as Sybille 'Bille' Vonhoff from 1983 to 1986, "Berliner Weisse Mit Schuss", "Edgar, Huter der Moral", "Die Wicherts von Nebenan" as Hannelore Wichert from 1986 to 1991, "Gluckliche Reise", "Liebe ist Privatsache", "Wolffs Revier", "Evelyn Hamann's Geschichten aus dem Leben", "Park Hotel Stern", "Fast Ein Gentleman", "Grosstadtrevier", "Der Bulle von Tolz", "Heimatgeschichten", "Rosamunde Pilcher", "Hallo Robbie!", "Siska", "SOKO Munchen", "Coast Guard", "Meine Wunderbare Familie", and "Das Traumschiff". Sebaldt worked frequently in radio and was the German dubbing voice for such actresses as Joanne Woodward, Eva Marie Saint, and Antonella Lualdi. She and her husband's first wife, actress Maria Becker, wrote the cookbook "Eat and Drink and Be Happy in 1997, Favorite Dishes from Maria Becker & Maria Sebaldt". Sebaldt was married to actor and director Robert Freitag from 1965 until his death in 2010. She is survived by their daughter, Katharina Freitag.

Sebesky, Don

Musician and arranger Don Sebesky died of complications from dementia in Maplewood, New Jersey, on April 29, 2023. He was 85. Sebesky was born in Perth Amboy, New Jersey, on December 10, 1937. He studied the trombone

at the Manhattan School of Music, graduating in the late 1950s. He was a multi-instrumentalist, also playing electric piano, organ, and accordion. He performed with such artists as Stan Kenton, Kai Winding, Tommy Dorsey, Maynard Ferguson, and Warren Covington. He concentrated on arranging and conducting from the early 1960s. His debut album, "The Distant Galaxy", was released in 1968 and "Don Sebesky and the Jazz-Rock Syndrome" came out later in the year. He became house arranger for the jazz label Creed Taylor Inc. (CTI) in the 1970s, working with Paul Desmond, George Benson, Chet Baker, Astrud Gilberto, and Wes Montgomery. Sebesky was orchestrator for numerous Broadway productions including "Peg" (1983), "Prince of Central Park" (1989) which he scored, "Tommy Tune Tonite" (1992), "The Boys Choir of Harlem and Friends" (1993), "Cyrano - The Musical" (1993), "The Life" (1997) receiving a Tony nomination, "Parade" (1998) earning another Tony nomination, "Kiss Me, Kate" (1999) receiving a Tony Award, "Minnelli on Minnelli" (1999), "Bells Are Ringing" (2001), "The Boys from Syracuse" (2002), "Flower Drum Song" (2002), "The Look of Love" (2003), "Sweet Charity" (2005), "Liza's at the Place..." (2008), "Pal Joey" (2008), "Come Fly Away" (2010), "Baby It's You!" (2011), "Honeymoon in Vegas" (2015), "An American in Paris" (2015) receiving a second Tony Award, and "Parade" (2023). He was composer or orchestrator for the films "The People Next Door" (1970), "Some of My Best Friends Are..." (1971), "The Rosary Murders" (1987), and "Julie & Julia" (2009). Sebesky composed for the tele-films "F. Scott Fitzgerald and 'the Last of the Belles'" (1974), "How to Pick Up Girls!" (1978), "Hollow Image" (1979), and "Smoke Alarm: The Unfiltered Truth About Cigarettes" (1997). He also composed for the 1994 television series "Allegra's Window". He was a band leader at the Fat Tuesday's nightclub in Manhattan in 1984. Sebesky was nominated for 31 Grammy Awards during his career and won three in the late 1990s. His marriage to Janet Sebesky ended in divorce and he is survived by their son sons, Ken and Kevin. He was predeceased by their two daughters, Cymbaline and Alison. He married Janina Serden in 1986 and is also survived by her and their two daughters, Olivia and Elizabeth.

Seigler, Tommy

Professional wrestler Tommy Seigler died in South Carolina on July 25, 2023. He was 85. Seigler was born in Fieldale, Virginia, on September 24, 1938, and was raised in Anderson, South Carolina. He graduated high school in 1956 and moved to Flint, Michigan, to work in a car factory. He returned to South Carolina the following year to work in construction. He was on a construction job in Pensacola, Florida, in 1963 when he was approached by some local wrestlers while working out at a gym. He began wrestling part-time while maintaining his construction job. He began

wrestling full time by the end of the decade. He captured the NWA Macon Tag Team Championship with Argentina Apollo in 1972. He defeated Ox Baker for the All-South Wrestling Georgia Television Championship in July of 1973 and won the

promotion's tag team belts with Super Gladiator later in the year. He teamed with Charlie Cook to beat the Interns for the NWA Southern Tag Team Championship in Nashville in October of 1975. He was a two-time NWA Southeastern Television Champion and the NWA Florida Television Champion in 1976. Seigler defeated the Iron Sheik for the NWA British Commonwealth Heavyweight Championship in 1977 and retained the belt until his retirement the following year due to several ruptured disks in his lower back. He returned to Anderson, South Carolina, where he worked in local law enforcement for two decades. Seigler is survived by four children.

Seiler, Sonny

Attorney Frank W. 'Sonny' Seiler, who was the owner of the University of Georgia Bulldog's Uga bulldog mascots,

died of cancer in Savannah, Georgia, on August 28, 2023. He was 90. Seiler was born in Savannah on February 20, 1933. He graduated from the University of Georgia in 1956 and earned a law degree there in 1958. He practiced law in Savannah where he was a senior partner at Bouhan Falligant LLP. He became best known as defense attorney in the murder trial of antiques dealer Jim Williams who was accused of the shooting death of his employee, Danny Hansford, in 1981. Seiler took over the defense after the Georgia Supreme Court overturned a guilty verdict in 1983. A second trial also resulted in a guilty verdict that was overturned in 1985 and a third trial in 1987 ended with a hung jury. Williams was acquitted in a fourth trial in May of 1989 but collapsed and died at his home the following January. The murder and trial were featured in John Berendt's true crime novel "Midnight in the Garden of Good and Evil" in 1994. Clint Eastwood directed a film version in 1997 starring John Cusack and Kevin Spacey as Williams. Seiler was portrayed by Jack Thompson and Seiler played Judge Samuel L. White, who presided over the trial. He was also seen in the films "The Gingerbread Man" (1998) and "The Legend of Bagger Vance" (2000). Seiler's family were owners of a line of English bulldogs who became mascots for the University of Georgia Bulldogs' football team. The first dog, Hood's Ole Dan, accompanied Seiler to a football game in 1956 and coach Wally Butts suggested that he become the team's official mascot. He took the name Uga for the University of Georgia and attended all home games and most away games from 1956 until his death in 1966. He was succeeded by his son, Uga II, from 1966 to 1972, and the line continued through Uga XI who took over the role of mascot in 2023. He was married to Cecelia Gunn Seiler for 59 years before her death in 2014. He is survived by three daughters and a son.

Selwyn, Charlotte

British actress Charlotte Selwyn died in England on July 12, 2023. She was 87. She was born Charlotte Anne  Pudney in Paddington, London, England, on March 15, 1936. She performed on stage in musicals and on television in the 1960s. She was seen in episodes of "Probation Officer", "Drama '62'", "The Avengers", "Suspense", "Love Story", "Taxi!", "Festival", "First Night", "Silas Marner", "Undermind", "The Wednesday Play", "Knock on Any Door", "Mrs. Thursday", "Emergency-Ward 10", "Armchair Theatre", "The Saint", and "Thirty-Minute Theatre". She also appeared in the television mini-series "Martin Chuzzlewit" (1964) and "The Possessed" (1969). Selwyn was seen in small roles in several films including "The Private Right" (1966), "Cop-Out" (1967), and "Anne of the Thousand Days" (1969).

Sereys, Jacques

French actor Jacques Sereys died in Paris, France, on January 1, 2023. He was 94. Sereys was born in Saint-Maurice, France, on June 2, 1928, and was raised in Marseilles. He  trained as an actor at the Conservatoire National Superieur d'Art Dramatique, where he studied under Henri Rollan. He began his career on stage with the Comedie-Francaise in 1955. He left the Comedie-Francaise in 1964 but returned in 1977. He remained a member until his retirement in 1997 and made occasional appearances on stage until 2014. Sereys was seen in the films "Les Demons de Minuit" (1961), "The Fire Within" (1963), "Heartbeat" (1968), "Murmur of the Heart" (1971), "A Season in Hell" (1971), "Le Gang" (1977), "L'Etat Sauvage" (1978), "A Simple Story" (1978), "Le Mors Aux Dents" (1979), "I... For Icarus" (1979), "T'inquiete Pas, Ca Se Soigne" (1980), "Le Bon Plaisir" (1984), "L'Addition" (1984), "La Galette du Roi" (1986), "La Petite Amie" (1988), "Le Bal du Gouverneur" (1990), "L'Elegant Criminel" (1990), "Operation Corned Beef" (1991), "The Horseman on the Roof" (1995), "La Serva Amorosa" (1996), "Kings for a Day" (1997), "On Guard" (1997), "Chouchou" (2003), "Towards Zero" (2007), "Disco" (2008), and "Du Cote

de Chez Proust" (2010). He was seen on television in productions of "La Bonne Mere" (1957), "La Meprise" (1960), "Adieux de Tabarin" (1996), "Un Crime de Bon Ton" (1970), "Les Thibault" (1972), "La Conciliation ou Anatomie d'un Otage" (1974), "Meurtre a Credit" (1974), "Sara" (1975), "Desire" (1976), "Adios" (1976), "La Folle de Chaillot" (1980), "Les Plaisirs de l'Ile Enchantee" (1981), "Le Bourgeois Gentilhomme" (1981), "La Locandiera" (1982), "Toutes Griffes Dehors" (1982), "Le Tartuffe" (1983), "La Derapade" (1985), "Le Paria" (1985), "The Gravy Train" (1990), "The Gravy Train Goes East" (1991), "C'Est Quoi Ce Petit Boulot?" (1991), "L'Elixir d'Amour" (1992), "La Vie de Galilee" (1992), "Notre Homme" (1996), "La Chanson du Macon" (2002), and "Ruy Blas" (2002). His other television credits include episodes of "Comment Ne Pas Espouser un Milliardaire" as Archibald Canfield in 1966, "Presence du Passe", ""Au Theatre Ce Soir", "Les Dossiers de l'Ecran", "Emmenez-Moi au Theatre", "Les Amours des Annees 50", "Les Passions de Celine", "Palace", "Le Mari de l'Ambassadeur", "The Young Indiana Jones Chronicles", "Les Mercredis de la Vie", "Nestor Burma", and "Maigret". He was married to actress Philippine Pascal, the stage name of Philippine de Rothschild, from the early 1960s until their divorce in 1999. He is survived by their two children, Camille and Philippe.

Serrano, Irma

Mexican actress and singer Irma Serrano died of a heart attack in Mexico on March 1, 2023. She was 89. Serrano was born in Comitan, Mexico, on December 9, 1933. She began her career as a dancer in the 1950s. She also began  singing and signed with Columbia Records in 1962. She became a popular Mexican folk music singer and was noted for the song "La Martina". She became known as La Tigresa. She made her film debut in the wrestling horror film "Santo vs. the Zombies" in 1962. Her other films include "El Extra" (1962), "Tiburoneros" (1963), "El Corrido de Maria Pistolas" (1964), "Gabino Barrera" (1965), "El Zurdo" (1965), "La Conquista de El Dorado" (1965), "Los Sheriffs de la Frontera" (1965), "El Higo de Gabino Barrera" (1965), "Los Gavilanes Negros" (1966), "El Higo del Diablo" (1966), "Los Malvados" (1966), "El Caudillo" (1966), "Los Amores de Juan Charrasqueado" (1968), "La Chamuscada (Tierra y Libertad)" (1971), "La Venganza de Gabino Barrera" (1971), "La Martina" (1972), "The Royal Eagle" (1973), "La Tigresa" (1973), "El Monasterio de los Buitres" (1973), "Carnival Nights" (1978), "Nana" (1979) which she also directed and wrote, "Adriana del Rio, Actriz" (1979), "Lola the Truck Driving Woman" (1985), the horror film "Lovers of the Lord of the Night" (1986), and "Juana la Cubana" (1994). Serrano appeared on television in productions of "La Tierra" (1974), "Yara" (1979), "Que Nos Pasa?", "Hospital el Paisa" (2004), "Stepmother" as La Duquesa de Walterrama y San Calixto in 2005, and "La Hora

Pico" (2005). She opened Teatro Fru Fru in Mexico City in 1972 where she staged a controversial production of "Nana" in 1973. Her other plays at the venue include "A Lady Without Camelias"(1977), "Oh... Calcutta" (1977), "Yocasta Reina" (1978), "The Cross-Legged War" (1979), and "A Catzon Amarrado" (1980) based on her autobiography, "The Two Emanuele" (1984), and "The Well of Solitude" (1985). Serrano was elected a senator from her home state of Chiapas, serving from 1994 to 2000. Serrano was the subject of various scandals and controversies including an affair Mexico's president, Gustavo Diaz Ordaz, during his time in office in the late 1960s.

Serrano, Lupe

Chilean-American ballet dancer Guadalupe Martínez Desfassiaux 'Lupe' Serrano died of complications from Alzheimer's disease in Syosset, New York, on January 16, 2023. She was 92. Serrano was born in Santiago, Chile, on

December 7, 1930. She began studying dance from an early age. She moved to Mexico City with her family in 1943 where she began training with Nelsy Dambre. She made her professional debut with the Mexico City Ballet the following year. She toured with the Cuban company Ballet Alicia Alonso in Central America in 1948. She joined her former teacher's new

company Ballet Nelsy Dambre after returning to Mexico City. She moved to New York to perform with the Ballet Russe de Monte-Carlo in 1951 and toured throughout the Americas. She toured South America with Ballet Concerts in 1952. She returned to New York the following year to join the American Ballet Theatre (ABT). She starred in such leading ballets as "Swan Lake", "Giselle", and "Aurora's Wedding". She created roles in Eugene Loring's "Capital of the World", Herbert Ross' "Paean", Agnes de Mille's "Sebastian", and Birgit Cullberg's "Lady from the Sea". She performed in the operas "La Gioconda" and "Die Fledermaus" with the Metropolitan Opera Ballet in the late 1950s. Serrano toured the Soviet Union with the ABT in 1960. She began a brief dance partnership with Rudolf Nureyev after he defected in 1961. They performed a piece from "Le Corsaire" on television's "The Bell Telephone Hour" in 1962. She also performed on episodes of "Camera Three" and "The Merv Griffin Show". She danced for the ABT as a guest performer in the late 1960s and began teaching. Serrano retired from the stage in 1971. She was assistant director at the National Academy of Arts in Champaign, Illinois, in 1971 and was a teacher at the Pennsylvania Ballet in 1974. She became head of the Pennsylvania Ballet School in 1977. She moved to Washington, D.C., in 1988 and was artistic director of the Washington Ballet for a decade. She also taught classes at Juilliard School, the ABT, and the Jacqueline Kennedy Onassis School. Serrano married composer Kenneth Schermerhorn in 1957 and they had two daughters, Erica and Veronica, before their divorce in 1973.

Serre, Henri

French actor Henri Serre, who starred as Jim in Francois Truffaut's classic film "Jules and Jim", died in Saint-

Jean-du-Bruel, France, on October 9, 2023. He was 92. Serre was born in Sete, France, on February 6, 1931. He studied at the Paris Conservatory of Dramatic Art. He began his career in films in the 1950s with roles in "Women of Paris" (1953), Louis Malle's "Les Amant" (1957), "The Army Game" (1960), and "Le Combat dans l'Ile" (1962). He received international recognition for his starring role in Francois

Truffaut's "Jules and Jim" in 1962. He continued to appear in such films as "The Verona Trial" (1963), "The Fire Within" (1963), "Hong Kong un Addio" (1963), "Atout Coeur a Tokyo Pour OSS 117" (1966), "Fantomas vs. Scotland Yard" (1967), "The Hand" (1969), "Winter in Mallorca" (1970), "Romance of a Horsethief" (1971), "La Vie Facile" (1971), "Galaxie" (1972), "Le Sourire Vertical" (1973), "House of 1000 Pleasures" (1974), "Special Section" (1975), "Last In, First Out" (1978), "Street of the Crane's Foot" (1979), "L'Oeil du Maitre" (1980), "Une Nuit Revee Pour un Poisson Banal" (1980), "Svarta Faglar" (1983), "Vertiges" (1985), "The Satin Slipper" (1985), "Mon Cas" (1986) in a voice role, "Engagements of the Heart" (1987), "The French Revolution" (1989), "Je t'ai Dans la Peau" (1990), and the horror thriller "Mister Frost" (1990) starring Jeff Goldblum. Serre was seen on television in productions of "La Dame d'Outre-Nulle Part" (1965), "Mon Fils" (1971), "Yvette" (1971), "Die Eltern" (1974), "Entre Toutes les Femmes" (1974), "Les Amants d'Avignon" (1975), "Le Devoir de Francais" (1978), "Le Mandarin" (1980), "Un Jour Sombre Dans la Vie de Marine" (1981), "Le Sud" (1982), "L'Epingle Noire" (1982), "Lundi Noir" (1989), "Des Voix Dans la Nuit - Le Mains d'Orlac" (1990), "Moi, General de Gaulle" (1990), "Alcyon" (1990), and "Belle Epoque" (1995). He also appeared in episodes of "Une Chambre a Louer" as Sylvain Lambert in 1965, "En Votre Ame et Conscience", "Le Service des Affaires Classees", "Les Cinq Dernieres Minutes", "Les Borgia ou le Sang Dore", "Les Heritiers", "L'Inspecteur Mene l'Enquete", "Les Amours de la Belle Epoque", "Les Dossiers de l'Ecran", "Cinema 16", "La Vie des Autres", "Messieurs les Jures", "La Sonate Pathetique", "La Belle Anglaise", "Sixieme Gauche", "Riviera", and "Beaumanoir". Serre was married to actress Francois Brion from 1958 until their divorce in 1975 and is survived by their two children.

Setterfield, Valda

British-American dancer and actress Valda Setterfield died in Manhattan, New York, on April 9, 2023. She was 88. Setterfield was born in Margate, Kent, England, on September 17, 1934. She studied ballet under Dame Marie Rampert and trained in mime with Tamara Karsavina. She performed on stage in pantomime productions. She moved to New York City in 1958 where she continued her studies. She married dancer and choreographer David Gordon in 1961. She was featured in the WNET documentary about dance "America's Beyond the Mainstream" in 1987 and appeared with Mikhail Baryshnikov

in "David Gordon's Made in USA" for "Great Performances" in 1988. Setterfield performed in such venues as Pantages Theater in Minneapolis, the ODC Theater in San Francisco, Barbican Theater in London, New York City's Danspace, and the Brooklyn Academy of Music's Next Wave Festival. She was featured in the films "The Wedding Party" (1969), "Film About a Woman Who..." (1974), "The Cold Eye (My Darling, Be Careful)" (1980), Woody Allen's "Mighty Aphrodite" (1995), "Everyone Says I Love You" (1996), "The Guru" (2002), and "Doubt" (2008). Setterfield was married to David Gordon from 1961 until his death in 2022. She is survived by their son, actor and playwright Ain Gordon. The three received an Obie Award for their performances in "The Family Business" in 1995.

Sevilla, Carmen

Spanish actress and singer Carmen Sevilla, who was featured as Mary Magdalene in the 1961 film "King of Kings", died of complications from Alzheimer's disease at a hospital in

Madrid, Spain, on June 27, 2023. She was 92. She was born Maria del Carmen Garcia Galisteo in Seville, Spain, on October 16, 1930. She moved to Madrid with her family later in the decade and began performing on stage at an early age. She was soon training in dance and studying at the Conservatory of Music. She made her film debut in the 1946 documentary "Hombres Ibericos". She was a contestant in the Miss Spain contest the following year and was featured in the 1947 film "Serenata Espanola". Sevilla starred in the film "Jalisco Sings in Seville" (1948) and continued to appear in such features as "Filigrana" (1949), "La Guitarra de Gardel" (1949), "La Revoltosa" (1950), "Cuentos de la Alhambra"(1950), "Andalousie" (1951), "El sueno de Andalucia" (1951), "Le Desir et l'Amour" (1952), "La Hermana San Sulpicio" (1952), "Plume au Vent" (1952), "Babes in Bagdad" (1952), "Violetas Imperiales" (1952), "Reportaje" (1953), "La Belle de Cadix" (1953), "Gitana Tenias Que Ser" (1953), "Amor Sobre Ruedas" (1954), "Un Caallero Andaluz" (1954), "La Picara Molinera" (1955), "Requiebro" (1955), "Congreso en Sevilla" (1955), "La Fierecilla Domada" (1956), "Don Juian" (1956), "Spanish Affair" (1957), "Desert Warrior" (1957), Juan Antonio Bardem's Oscar nominated foreign film "La Venganza" (1958),

"Pan, Amor y Andalucia" (1958), "Secretaria Para Todo" (1958), and "European NIghts" (1959). Sevilla starred as Mary Magdalene in Nicholas Ray's religious epic "King of Kings" (1961) with Jeffrey Hunter as Jesus. Her other films include "Buscando a Monica" (1962), "El Balcon de la Luna" (1962), "Crucero de Verano" (1964), "Operacion Plus Ultra" (1966), "Camino del Rocio" (1966), "La Guerrillera de Villa" (1967), "El Taxi de los Conflictos" (1969), "Un Adulterio Decente" (1969), "El Relicario" (1970), "Ensenar a un Sinverguenza" (1970), "Una Senora Llamada Andres" (1970), "Glass Ceiling" (1971), "El Apartamento de la Tentacion" (1971), "Embrujo de Amor" (1971), "La Cera Virgen" (1972), "Antony and Cleopatra" (1972) as Octavia with Charlton Heston as Mark Antony, "The Boldest Job in the West" (1972), "No One Heart the Scream" (1973), "No es Bueno Que el Hombre Este Solo" (1973), "Dormir y Ligar: Todo es Empezar" (1974), "Sex o No Sex" (1974), "La Loba y la Paloma" (1974), "Una Mujer de Cabaret" (1974), "Cross of the Devil" (1975), "Terapia al Desnudo" (1975), "Nosotros, los Decentes" (1976), "Beatriz" (1976), "La Noche de los Cien Pajaros" (1976), "Guerreras Verdes" (1976), "La Promesa" (1976), "El Apolitico" (1977), "Mueerte de un Quinqui" (1977), and "Rostros" (1978). She performed on television in such series as "The Ed Sullivan Show", "Noche de Estrellas", "Noche del Sabado", "Einer Wird Gewinnen", and "Night-Club". She retired from the screen in the late 1970s but continued to perform on television. She appeared in the series "La Viuda Blance" as Alejandra in 1986 and in "Ada Madrina" as Ada from 1999 to 2000. She served as host for numerous shows and specials including "Telecupon" from 1991 to 1997, "La Noche de Carmen" from 1997 to 1998, and "Cine de Barrio" from 2004 to 2010. Sevilla was married to composer and conductor August Alguero from 1961 until their divorce in 1974 and is survived by their son, Augusto Jr. She was married to Vicente Patuel from 1985 until his death in 2000.

Seymour, Lynn

Canadian ballet dancer Lynn Seymour died in London, England, on March 7, 2023. She was 83. She was born Berta Lynn Springbett in Wainwright, Alberta, Canada, on March 8,

1939. She studied ballet in Vancouver, British Columbia, and earned a scholarship to London's Sadler's Wells Ballet School in 1953. She joined the Covent Garden Opera Ballet in 1956 and danced with the Touring Roya Ballet from 1957. She became a principal dancer with the Royal Ballet in 1959. She created roles for several of Kenneth MacMillan's ballets including "The Burrow" (1958), "The Invitation" (1960), and "Le Baiser de la Fee" (1960). She starred in MacMillan's staging of "Romeo and Juliet" in 1965. Seymour worked with MacMillan at the Berlin Opera Ballet, serving as prima ballerina from 1966 to 1969. She created the lead role in a 1967 version of "Anastasia". She performed at the London Festival Ballet, National Ballet of Canada, Alvin Ailey American Dance Theater, and American Ballet Theatre. She was a guest artist with the Royal Ballet from 1971 to 1978, dancing in MacMillan's "Anastasia" (1971) and "Mayerling" (1978) in the role of Mary Vetsera, and Frederick Ashton's "Five Brahms Waltzes in the Manner of Isadora Duncan" (1976) and "A Month in the Country" (1976). She also became a choreographer in the early 1970s and her first ballet, "Night Ride", was staged in 1973. Her other works include "Gladly, Sadly, Badly, Madly" (1975), "The Court of Love" (1977), "Intimate Letters" (1978), and "Bastet" (1988). She served as artistic director at the Bavarian State Ballet in Munich from 1978 to 1980 and returned to the Royal Ballet in 1981. She subsequently retired from performing on stage. She was the subject of Karin Altman's 1979 documentary film "Lynn Seymour: In a Class of Her Own", and her autobiography, "Lynn", was published in 1980. Seymour was featured as Aunt Hildegard in the television series "The Little Vampire" from 1986 to 1987 and appeared in the films "Dancers" (1987) and "Wittgenstein" (1993). She married Colin Jones in 1963 and they later divorced. She had twin sons, Adrian and Jerszy, with Polish dancer Eike Walcz in 1968. She married photographer Philip Pace in 1974 and they had a son, Demian, before their subsequent divorce. She was married to Vanya Hackel from 1983 until their divorce in 1988.

Shade, Beverly

Professional wrestler Beverly Wenhold, who competed in the ring under the name Beverly Shade, died of lung cancer in Southaven, Mississippi, on June 2, 2023. She

was 87. Wenhold was born in Nashville, Tennessee, on March 21, 1936. She was trained as a wrestler by Ella Waldek in the late 1950s and earned the nickname the Hammer. She competed as a wrestler for about three years. She returned to the ring in 1968 and occasionally wrestled under the names Beverly Bates and Beverly Blue River. She competed in the ring with such opponents as the Fabulous Moolah, Cora Combs, Mae Weston, and Judy Martin. She was the All-Wrestling Champion in Florida on two occasions. She teamed with Natasha the Hatchet Lady, and they captured the NWA Women's Tag Team Championship in 1978. She retired from the ring in 1989 but continued to appear at wrestling conventions and reunions. Wenhold married wrestler Bill Wenhold, who competed under the name Billy Blue River, in 1969. She is survived by him and their two sons.

Shakeel

Pakistani actor Yousuf Kamal, who was known as Shakeel, died in Karachi, Pakistan, on June 29, 2023. He was 85. Kamal was born in Bhopal, British India, on May 29, 1938. he moved to Karachi, Pakistan, with his family in 1952. He

made his film debut in the mid-1960s with "Honehar" in 1966. He was also seen in the films "Josh-e-Intiqaam" (1968), "Nakhuda" (1968), "Dastaan" (1969), "Badal Aur Bijli" (1973), and "Jeedar" (1981). He starred as Uncle Urfi in the 1972 television series of the same name. he also appeared on television in the series "Aangan Terha" (1984) as Mehboob Ahmed and "Ankahi" (1982) as Taimoor Ahmad. He was featured as Pakistan's first Prime Minister, Liaquat Ali Khan, in the 1998 film "Jinnah", starring Christopher Lee in the title role.

Shamray, Gerry

Comic book artist Gerry Shamray, who worked with Harvey Pekar on the series "American Splendor", died

suddenly in Cleveland, Ohio, on September 25, 2023. He was 66. Shamray was born in Cleveland on February 19, 1957. He was educated at Cayahoga Community College from 1975 to 1977 and the Cooper School of Art from 1977 until graduating in 1980. He began working with Harvey Pekar in 1979 and illustrated his autobiographical comic book series "American Splendor" from 1979 to 1983. He also drew the "Cleveland" comic strip featuring caricatures of notable citizens, in the "Cleveland Pess". He was artist for Tom Batiuk's comic strip "John Darling" from 1985 to 1990. He joined the staff of the Sun Newspapers in Cleveland in 1988, serving as graphics editor for over twenty years. He later taught at the Cleveland Institute of Art.

Shay, Anna

Socialite and television personality Anna Shay, who starred on the television reality series "Bling Empire", died of

complications from a stroke in Los Angeles, California, on June 1, 2023. She was 62. Shay was born to a wealthy family in Tokyo, Japan, on January 30, 1961. She moved to Los Angeles with her family in 1968. She was a graduate of the Buckley School and attended the University of Southern California and other colleges. She worked with the Edward A and Ai O Shay Family Foundation after it was formed by her mother in 2010. Her philanthropic works focused on education, performing arts, and music. She was an heiress to Pacific Architects and Engineers,

which had been founded by her father in the 1950s. The company was sold to Lockheed Martin after her father's death for $1.2 billion. Shay joined the cast of the Netflix reality television series "Bling Empire" in 2021. She remained with the series for three seasons until it was cancelled earlier in 2023. She also appeared in an episode of "Celebrity Family Feud". Shay was married and divorced four times. Her three-year marriage to firefighter Kenneth John Kemp resulted in the birth of a son, Kenny Shay-Kemp, who survives her.

Shebib, Donald

Canadian film director Donal Shebib died in Toronto, Ontario, Canada, on November 5, 2023. He was 85. Shebib was born in Toronto on January 27, 1938. He attended the University of Toronto and entered the University of California at Los Angeles School of Theater, Film and Television in 1961. He worked on several Roger Corman productions, serving as

cinematographer and assistant editor for "Dementia 13" (1962), the first film of his classmate Francis Ford Coppola. He was also assistant editor for the films "The Terror" (1963) and "Summer Children" (1965) and was cinematographer for "Surfin'" (1964). He graduated from UCLA with a master's degree in 1965 before returning to Canada. Shebib directed the short films "Satan's Choice" (1965), "Revival" (1965), and "A Search for Learning" (1967) before making his feature debut with "Goin' Down the Road" in 1970. He continued to direct such films as "Rip-OFf" (1971), "Between Friends" (1972), "Second Wind" (1976), "Fish Hawk" (1979), "Heartaches" (1981), "Running Brave" (1983), "The Climb" (1986), "Change of Heart" (1993), "The Ascent" (1994), and "Down the Road Again" (2011). Shebib worked frequently in television, directing productions of "Deedee" (1974), "The Canary" (1975), "Good Times Bad Times" (1977), "The Fighting Men" (1977), "The Little Kidnappers" (1990), and "The Pathfinder" (1996). His other television credits include episodes of "The Collaborators", "For the Record", "The Edison Twins", "T and T", "My Secret identity", "Night Heat", "Diamonds", "Rin Tin Tin: K-9 Cop", "The Campbells", "Top Cops", "Street Justice", "E.N.G.", "Counterstrike", "Lonesome Dove: The Series", "Dead Man's Gun", "Police Academy: The Series", "The New Addams Family", "Wind at My Back", "Code Name: Eternity", "The Zack Files", and "Radio Free Roscoe". His son, Noah '40' Shebib was executive producer of his final film, 2022's "Nightalk". Shebib was married to actress Tedde Moore and is survived by their two children, actress Suzanna Shebib and music executive Noah '40' Shebib.

Shepherd, Suzanne

Actress Suzanne Shepherd died at her home in New York City on November 17, 2023. She was 89. She was born Suzanne Stern on October 31, 1934. She attended Bennington College and studied acting with Stanford Meisner. She was an early member of the Compass Players in the late 1950s. She later became a teacher of Meisner's acting program. She served on the faculty of Trinity Square Conservatory, Hartman Conservatory, the Berghof Studio, and her own studio in New York City. She performed frequently on stage in regional

theater productions with The Roundabout, Yale Repertory, Long Wharf, Berkeley Repertory, Vineyard Theatre, and Ensemble Studio Theatre. She also directed production at the Nederlander Theatre, Dallas Theatre Center, Trinity Square Repertory Theatre, Steppenwolf, Ensemble Studio Theatre, and the Whole Theatre. Shepherd made her film debut as Aunt Tweedy in the 1988 film "Mystic Pizza". Her other films include "Working Girl" (1988), "Uncle Buck" (1989), "Second Sight" (1989), "Goodfellas" (1990) as the mother of Lorraine Bracco's Karen Hill, "Jacob's Ladder" (1990), "The Jerky Boys" (1995), "Palookaville" (1995), "Bullet" (1996), "Trees Lounge" (1996), "Lolita" (1997), "Illuminata" (1998), "Living Out Loud" (1998), "American Cuisine" (1998), "On the Run" (1999), "Requiem for a Dream" (2000), "Never Again" (2001), the short "The Wormhole" (2002), "A Dirty Shame" (2004), "Choke" (2008), "Harold" (2008), "I Hate Valentine's Day" (2009), "Delivering the Goods" (2012), "Where Is Kyra?" (2017), "Furlough" (2018), "The Week Of" (2018), and "The Performance" (2023). She was seen on television in the 1998 tele-film "Vig" and episodes of "Law & Order", "Third Watch", "Deadline", "Law & Order: Criminal Intent", "Law & Order: Special Victims Unit", "Ed", "The Sopranos" as Mary DeAngelis, the mother of Edie Falco's Carmela Soprano, on the HBO series "The Sopranos" from 2000 to 2007, "Gravity", and "Blue Bloods". Her survivors include her daughter, actress Kate Shepherd.

Sherbanee, Maurice

Iraqi-American actor Maurice Sherbanee died after a

long illness inn Sherman Oaks, California, on December 13, 2023. He was 93. Sherbanee was born in Baghdad, Iraq, on October 23, 1930. He was a Mizrahi Jew with an Iraqi father and a mother from Singapore. He fled Baghdad with his family during World War II to live in India. The family was again uprooted during the civil war and partition in India in the late 1940s. They spent nearly two decades in Japan before Sherbanee and his surviving family settle in Los Angeles. He had begun performing in nightclubs while in Japan and continued to pursue a career after coming to the United States. He performed on stage and in musical theater. Sherbanee appeared in ethnic roles in such films as

"Jud" (1971), "The Don Is Dead" (1973), "Sons of Sassoun" (1975), "Promise of Love" (1978), "First Family" (1980), "Forty Days of Musa Dagh" (1982), "Mausoleum" (1983), "W.B., Blue and the Bean" (1989), "Indecent Proposal" (1993), "In the Army Now" (1994), "Eye for an Eye" (1996), "The Pursuit of Happyness" (2006), and "Charlie Wilson's War" (2007). He was seen frequently on television with roles in episodes of "The Six Million Dollar Man", "Cannon", "The F.B.I.", "The Rookies", "Get Christie Love!", "Barnaby Jones", "Wonder Woman", "The Rockford Files", "Small & Frye", "Super Bloopers and Practical Jokes", "The A-Team", "MacGyver", "The New Adam-12", "NYPD Blue", "ER", "Party Girl", "Tracey Takes On...", "Arli$$", "USA High", "The District", "Joan of Arcadia", "The Shield", and "Rules of Engagement". His other television credits include the tele-films and mini-series "The Girl Who Came Gift-Wrapped" (1974), "Death Cruise" (1974), "Jacqueline Susann's Valley of the Dolls" (1981), "Desperate Rescue: The Cathy Mahone Story" (1993), "Don't Look Back" (1996), and "Journey of the Heart" (1997).

Sherman, Philip

Orthodox Jewish cantor and actor Philip Sherman died of pancreatic cancer at his home in Englewood, New Jersey, on August 9, 2023. He was 67. Sherman was born in Syracuse, New York, on April 26, 1956. He

graduated from a joint program with Columbia University and the Jewish Theological Seminary of America with a degree in music and Jewish studies in 1979. He was certified as a mohel and performed his first ritual circumcision while in college. He became known as "the busiest mohel in New York" during his 45-year career and circumcised thousands of babies. Sherman was also a cantor in Jewish synagogues in Manhattan for over thirty years. He began acting in the late 1990s and appeared in a commercial for the digital currency Flooz.com. He was also seen on "Storage Wars" as an expert appraiser. Sherman was featured in the 2011 film "Our Idiot Brother" and appeared in episodes of "Z Rock", "Orange is the New Black", and "The Marvelous Mrs. Maisel". He was married to Dr. Naomi Freistat from 1980 until their divorce in 1993 and is survived by their daughter and two sons. He was married to author Andrea Raab from 1994 until their divorce in 2022.

Shima, Yvonne

Japanese-Canadian actress Yvonne Shima died of cancer in British Columbia, Canada, on September 1, 2023. She was 88. Shima was born in British Columbia in 1935. She moved to England in 1958 where she appeared on stage as Lotus Blossom in a production of "The Teahouse of the August Moon". She was soon appearing in such films as "The Savage Innocents" (1960), "The World of Suzie Wong" (1960),

"Passport to China" (1960), "The Sinister Man" (1961), and the Bob Hope and Bing Crosby comedy "The Road to Hong Kong" as Poon Soon. Shima was featured as receptionist Sister Lily in the first James Bond film "Dr. No" in 1962. Shima was also seen in the films "The Cool Mikado" (1963) and "Genghis Khan" (1963), and television episodes of "Armchair Theatre" and "The Avengers". She retired from film and television in the mid-1960s after an automobile accident.

Shorter, Wayne

Jazz saxophonist and composer Wayne Shorter died in Los Angeles, California, on March 2, 2023. He was 89. Shorter was born in Newark, New Jersey, on August 25, 1933. He played the saxophone while in high school and graduated in

1952. He performed in Newark with the Nat Phipps Band. He graduated from New York University in 1956 before serving in the U.S. Army from two years at Fort Dix in New Jersey. He played tenor saxophone and was a composer for Art Blakey's Jazz Messengers and the Miles Davis Quintet in the 1960s. He was noted for his compositions for Davis including "E.S.P." in 1965 and "Nefertiti" in 1968. He recorded 11 solo albums with Blue Note in the 1960s including "Night Dreamer" (1964), "JuJu" (1964), "The All Seeing Eye" (1966), "Adam's Apple" (1967), "Super Nova" (1969), and "Schizophrenia" (1969). Shorter formed the fusion group Weather Report in 1971. The group included a variety of musicians with Shorter and bassist Miroslav Vitous the only constants until breaking up in 1985. He wrote numerous songs for the band including "Tears", "Palladium", and "Mysterious Traveler". He teamed with singer and guitarist Milton Nascimento for the album "Native Dancer" in 1974. He continued to record and lead groups. He toured with guitarist Carlos Santana in 1988. He released the solo album "High Life" in 1995 which received the Grammy Award for Best Contemporary Jazz Album. He worked with Herbie Hancock on the 1997 album "1+1" which earned Grammies for both artists. He formed an acoustic quartet with pianist Danilo Perez, bassist John Patitucci, and drummer Brina Blade in 2000. He was the subject of the 2015 documentary film "Wayne Shorter: Zero Gravity". He toured with the supergroup Mega Nova with Herbie Hancock, Carlos Santana, and others in 2016. His 2018 album "Emanon" was accompanied by a science fiction comic book he co-wrote with Monica Sly and artist Randy DuBurke. He retired from performing on 2018 but continued to compose. He created the operatic work "Iphigenia", which was staged in 2021. Shorter was the recipient of twelve Grammy Awards and received the Grammy Lifetime Achievement Award in 2014. He received the Kennedy Center Honors Award in 2018. Shorter was married to Teruko 'Irene' Nakagami from 1961 until separating in 1964 and is survived by their daughter Miyako. He married Ana Maria Patrico in 1966 and she perished in an airplane crash in 1996. Their daughter Iska died of a grand mal seizure in 1985. He married Brazilian dancer Carolina Dos Santos in 1999 and she survives him.

Shulman, Ray

British musician and songwriter Ray Shulman, who was co-founder of the band Gentle Giant, died in London, England, on March 30, 2023. He was 73. Shulman was born in Portsmouth, Hampshire, England, on December 8, 1949. He  learned to play the guitar and violin in his youth. He joined the band Simon Dupree and the Big Sound with his brothers, Derek and Phil, in 1966. They had a hit record with the son "Kites" the following year and released the album "Without Reservation' in 1967. They released the single "We Are the Moles" under the pseudonym the Moles the following year. The brothers had grown frustrated by the pop style direction their music was going in and disbanded Simon Dupree and the Big Sound in 1969. They joined with multi-instrumentalists Gary Green and Kerry Minnear and drummer Martin Smith to form Gentle Giant in 1970. They soon released their self-named debut album followed by "Acquiring the Taste" the following year. Smith left the band in 1971 and was replaced by Malcolm Mortimore as drummer. He was replaced by John 'Pugwash' Weathers in 1973 after a motorcycle accident. Ray Shulman and Minnear continued to write most of the band's songs. They released the album "Octopus" in 1972 and Phil Shulman departed the band after the subsequent tour. Gentle Giant also recorded the albums "In a Glass House" (1973), "The Power and the Glory" (1973), "Free Hand" (1975), "Interview" (1976), "Playing the Fool - The Official Live" (1977), "The Missing Piece" (1977), "Giant for a Day" (1978), and "Civilian" (1980). The band broke up after playing a final concert in California in June of 1980. Ray began working with television soundtracks and advertising before becoming a record producer in the late 1980s. He worked with such artists as the Sugarcubes, Echo and the Bunnymen, the Sundays, the Trash Can Sinatras, and Ian McCulloch. He also composed music for such video games as "Privateer 2: The Darkening" (1996) "Silver" (1999), and "Attack of the Saucerman" (1999). Shulman is survived by his wife, Barbara Tanner, and his two brothers.

Silver, Stu

Screenwriter Stu Silver, who was noted for the 1987 film "Throw Momma from the Train", died of complications from prostate cancer in Rochester, New York, on July 18, 2023.

He was 76. Silver was born in Los Angeles, California, on June 29, 1947, and was raised in Rochester. He moved to New York City after graduating high school. He began working as an actor  and appeared in the 1970 film "The Cross and the Switchblade". He performed on Broadway in a 1975 production of "Dance with Me". He wrote and frequently produced such television series "Soap" sharing an Emmy Award nomination in 1981, "Benson", "Bosom Buddies", "The New Odd Couple", and "Brothers", and the 1985 tele-film "Joanna". Silver created and wrote for the comedy series "Star of the Family" (1982), "It's a Living" (1980-1989), "Webster" (1983-1989), and "Good Grief" (1990-1991). He also appeared in small roles in episodes of "Mork & Mindy" and "Good Grief". He scripted the 1987 comedy film "Throw Momma from the Train" and appeared onscreen in the role of Ramon. He later retired to Rochester where he was active in local theater.

Silverstein, Elliot

Film and television director Elliot Silverstein, who was noted for the films "Cat Ballou" and "A Man Called Horse", died in Los Angeles, California, on November 24, 2023. He was 96. Silverstein was born in Boston,  Massachusetts, on August 2, 1927. He attended Boston College and Yale University, where he studied directing. He began producing and directing plays at Brandeis University and staged productions for the television series "Omnibus" in the mid-1950s. He directed the Broadway play "Maybe Tuesday" in 1958. Silverstein continued to work frequently in television, directing episodes of "The United States Steel Hour", "Suspicion", "Goodyear Theatre", "The Furth Adventures of Ellery Queen", "Alcoa Theatre", "Black Saddle", "Assignment: Underwater", "The Westerner", "Checkmate", "Route 66:, "Have Gun - Will Travel", "Naked City", "Cain's Hundred", "The Dick Powell Theatre", "The Eleventh Hour", "Dr. Kildare", "Channing", "Breaking Point", "The Twilight Zone" helming the episodes "The Obsolete Man", "The Passerby", "The Trade-Ins", and "Spur of the Moment", "The Doctors and the Nurses", "Arrest and Trial", "The Defenders", "Kraft Suspense Theatre", "The Firm", "Picket Fences", and "Tales from the Crypt". His other television credits include the tele-films "Betrayed by Innocence" (1986), "Night of Courage" (1987), "Fight for Life" (1987), and "Rich Men, Single Women" (1990). He made his film debut directing the comedy western "Cat Ballou" in 1965. His other films include "The Happening" (1967), "A Man Called Horse" (1970), "Nightmare Honeymoon" (1974), the horror film "The Car" (1977) which he also produced, and "Flashfire" (1994). Silverstein was instrumental in formulating the Bill of Creative Rights in 1964 that gave directors more control over their work. The Director's Guild of America was able to include it in a new contract with producers later in the year. He continued to campaign for director's rights and was founder of the Artists Rights Foundation in the 1990s. Silverstein was married to actress Evelyn Ward from 1960 until their divorce in 1968. He married Alana King in 1982 and they later separated.

Simic, Charles

Serbian-American poet Charles Simic, who received the Pulitzer Prize for Poetry in 1990, died of complications from dementia in Dover, New Hampshire, on January 9, 2023. He

was 84. Simic was born in Belgrade, Yugoslavia, on May 9, 1938. He was raised during and after World War II in a devastated Europe. He came to the United States with his family in 1954, settling in Oak Park, Illinois. He was drafted in the U.S. Army in 1961. He attended New York University after his discharge and graduated in 1966. He began writing and publishing poems in the late 1960s. His first book, "What the Grass Says", was published in 1967. He taught American literature and creative writing at the University of New Hampshire from 1973. He published numerous collections of poems, translations, and essays. He was a Pulitzer Prize finalist for the poetry collections "Selected Poems, 1963-1983) in 1986 and "Unending Blues" in 1987. He received the Pulitzer Prize for Poetry in 1990 for the prose poem "The World Doesn't End". His later collections include "The Lunatic" (2015), "Scribbled in the Dark" (2017), "Come Closer and Listen: New Poems" (2019), and "No Land in Sight: Poems" (2022). Simic was elected to the American Academy of Arts and Letters in 1995 and became chancellor of the Academy of American Poets in 2000. He became United States Poet Laureate in 2007. Simic married Helen Dubin in 1964 and she survives him. He is also survived by their daughter, Anna, and son, Philip.

Simonischek, Peter

Austrian actor Peter Simonischek, who starred in the Oscar nominated film "Toni Erdmann" in 2016, died in Vienna, Austria, on May 29, 2023. He was 76. Simonischek was born in Graz, Austria, on August 6, 1946. He began his acting career on stage and screen in the 1970s. He appeared in such films as "Die Auslieferung" (1974), "Three Sisters" (1988), "Sukkubus" (1989), "Der Achte Tag" (1990), "Der Berg" (1990), "Erfolg" (1991), "Krucke" (1993), "Tief Oben" (1995), the thriller "Assignment Berlin" (1998) with Cliff Robertson, "Love Your Neighbour!" (1998), "Beresina or The Last Days of Switzerland" (1999), "Geburtig" (2002), "Hierankl" (2003), "Mozart in China" (2008), "Ludwig II" (2012), the fantasy film

"Ruby Red" (2013), "Oktober November" (2013), "Biest" (2014), "Sapphire Blue" (2014), the Academy Award for Best Foreign Film nominee "Toni Erdmann" (2015) as Winfried Conradi, "Emerald Green" (2016), "Wunderlich's World" (2016), "Lou Andreas-Salome, The Audacity to be Free" (2016), "Only God Can Judge Me" (2017), "The Interpreter" (2018), "The Command" (2018), "Crescendo" (2019), "Army of Thieves" (2021), "Fantastic Beasts: The Secrets of Dumbledore" (2022), "Lieber Kurt" (2022), "Measures of Men" (2023), and "Das Beste Kommt Noch!" (2023). Simonischek was seen on television in productions of "Das Eine Gluck und das Andere" (1980), "Harrenjahre" (1983), "Das Dorf an der Grenze" (1983), "Der Park" (1985), "Drei Schwestern" (1986), "Lenz Oder die Freiheit" (1986), "Geblendeter Augenblick - Anton Weberns Tod" (1986), "Die Affare Rue de Lourcine" (1989), "Der Veruntreute Himmel" (1990), "Der Einsame Weg" (1991), "Kein Platz fur Idioten" (1995), "Family of Lies" (1995), "Die Grube" (1995), "Der Blinde" (1996), "Agentenfieber" (1997), "Portrat Eines Richters" (1997), "Reise in die Dunkelheit" (1997), "Kunst" (1997), "Speer" (1998), "Vertrauen Ist Alles" (2000), "Liebst du Mich" (2000), "Blumen fur Polt" (2001), "Alles Gluck Dieser Erde" (2003), "Jedermann" (2004), "Daniel Kafer - Die Villen der Frau Hursch" (2005), "Einmal So Wie Ich Will" (2005), "Eine Folgenschwere Affare" (2007), "Daniel Kafer - Die Schattenuhr" (2008), "Mit Einem Schlag" (2008), "Gott Schutzt die Liebenden" (2008), "Anna and the Prince" (2009), "Oh Shit!" (2010), "Tod in Istanbul" (2010), "Der Briefwechsel" (2010), "Years of Love" (2011), "Der Kaktus" (2013), "Clara Immerwahr" (2014), "Verhangnisvolle Nahe" (2014), "Das Konzert" (2015), "Bergfried" (2016), "Das Sacher. In Bester Gesellschaft" (2016), "Die Fledermaus" (2020), and "At His Side" (2021). His other television credits include episodes of "Derrick", "Ein Starkes Team", "Stockinjger", "HeliCops - Einsatz Uber Berlin" as Hagen Dahlberg from 1998 to 2001, "Tatort", "Einsatz in Hamburg", "The Old Fox", "Bella Block", and "Kranitz - Bei Trennung Geld Zuruck". Simonischek was a leading stage performer and a regular member of the Burgtheater in Vienna from 1999. He also performed frequently at the Salzburg Festival. He was married and divorced from actress Charlotte Schwab and is survived by their son, actor Maximilian Simonischek. He married actress Brigitte Karner in 1989 and is also survived by her and their two children, director Benediikt Simonischek and actor Kaspar Simonischek.

Sizemore, Tom

Actor Tom Sizemore, who starred in such films as "Saving Private Ryan" and "Black Hawk Down", died at a hospital in Burbank, California, on March 3, 2023. He had suffered a brain aneurysm on February 18, 2023, and had remained in a coma until he was taken off life support two weeks later. He was 61. Sizemore was born in Detroit, Michigan, on November 29, 1961. He graduated from Wayne State University in 1983 and earned a master's degree in theater from Temple University in

Philadelphia in 1986. He subsequently moved to New York City where he waited tables while appearing in plays. He was featured in a small role in Oliver Stone's 1989 film "Born on the Fourth of July". He continued to appear in such films as "Lock Up" (1989), "Rude Awakening" (1989), "Penn & Teller Get Killed" (1989),"A Matter of Degrees" (1990), "Blue Steel" (1990), "Flight of the Intruder" (1991), "Guilty by Suspicion" (1991), "Point Break" (1991), "Harley Davidson and the Marlboro Man" (1991), "Where Sleeping Dogs Lie" (1991), "Bad Love" (1992), "Passenger 57" (1992), "Watch It" (1993), and "Striking Distance" (1993). He had prominent supporting roles as Milo Peck in the 1993 fantasy "Heart and Souls", Cody Nicholson in the 1993 crime film "True Romance", and Bat Masterson in 1994's "Wyatt Earp" starring Kevin Costner. He was Detective Jack Sagnetti in Oliver Stone's "Natural Born Killers" (1994) and Michael Cheritto in Michael Mann's "Heat" (1995). Sizemore was also seen in the films "Strange Days" (1995), "Devil in a Blue Dress" (1995), the horror film "The Relic" (1997) as Lt. Vincent D'Agosta, Steven Spielberg's World War II classic "Saving Private Ryan" (1998) as Sergeant Mike Horvath, "Enemy of the State" (1998), "The Florentine" (1999), "The Match" (1999), Martin Scorsese's "Bringing Out the Dead" (1999), "Play It to the Bone" (1999), "Get Carter" (2000), "Red Planet" (2000), "Pearl Harbor" (2001), "Ticker" (2001), Ridley Scott's "Black Hawk Down" (2001), "Big Trouble" (2002), "Swindle" (2002), and "Welcome to America". Sizemore's drug addiction and legal difficulties damaged his career and he primarily appeared in increasingly lower budget films in the 2000s. His later films include "Pauly Shore Is Dead" (2003), "Dreamcatcher" (2003), "Paparazzi" (2004), "The Nickel Children" (2005), "Born Killers" (2005), "No Rules" (2005), "Zyzzyx Rd" (2006), "Ring Around the Rosie" (2006), "Shut Up and Shoot!" (2006), "Splinter" (2006), "The Genius Club" (2006), "White Air" (2007), "Bottom Feeder" (2007), "Game of Life" (2007), "Protecting the King" (2007), "Furnace" (2007), "A Broken Life" (2007), "American Son" (2008), "Sky Kids" (2008), "Red" (2008), "The Acquirer" (2008), "The Last Lullaby" (2008), "Super Capers: The Origins of Ed and the Mission Bullion" (2008), "Stiletto" (2008), "Toxic" (2008), "Commute" (2009), "The Grind" (2009), "21 and a Wake-Up" (2009), "Double Duty" (2009), "Big Money Rustlas" (2010), "Shadows in Paradise" (2010), "The Auctioneers" (2010), "Bad Ass" (2010), "Black Gold" (2011), "Cross" (2011), "Cellmates" (2011), "The Saints of Mt. Christopher" (2011), "Contractor's Routine" (2011), "Suing the Devil" (2011), "The Speak" (2011), "The Snitch Cartel" (2011),

"Slumber Party Slaughter" (2012), "El Bosc" (2012), "Visible Scars" (2012), "The Banksters, Madoff with America" (2013), "5 Hour Friends" (2013), "Meth Head" (2013), "Chlorine" (2013), "Company of Heroes" (2013), "Paranormal Movie" (2013), "Crosshairs" (2013), "Remnants" (2013), "Five Thirteen" (2013), "Before I Sleep" (2013), "Seal Team Eight: Behind Enemy Lines" (2014), "The Drunk" (2014), "Flashes - The Director's Cut" (2014), "The Colombian Connection" (2014), "Murder 101" (2014), "Private Number" (2014), "Bordering on Bad Behavior" (2014), "Reach Me" (2014), "The Age of Reason" (2014), "SWAT: Unit 887" (2015), "The Intruders" (2015), "Laugh Killer Laugh" (2015), "Assassin's Game" (2015), "6 Ways to Die" (2015), "Night of the Living Dead: Darkest Dawn" (2015), "If I Tell You I Have to Kill You" (2015), "Collar" (2015), "Clandestine" (2016), "Durant's Never Closes" (2016), "WEAPONiZED" (2016), "Halloweed" (2016), "Devil's Doors" (2016), "Crossing Point" (2016), "Wolf Mother" (2016), "Hunting Season" (2016), "Traded" (2016), "The Bronx Bull" (2016), "Beyond Valkyrie: Dawn of the 4th Reich" (2016), "USS Indianapolis: Men of Courage" (2016), "Better Criminal" (2016), "Calico Skies" (2016), "Cross Wars" (2017), "Secrets of Deception" (2017), "Atomica" (2017), "Joe's War" (2017), "Adrenochrome" (2017), "The Immortal Wars" (2017), "Bad Frank" (2017), "The Assault" (2017), "College Ball" (2017), "Mark Felt: The Man Who Brought Down the White House" (2017), "The Slider" (2017), "A Chance in the World" (2017), "I Believe" (2017), "Blood Circus" (2017), "Radical" (2017), "The Second Coming of Christ" (2018), "The Litch" (2018), "Unkillable" (2018), "The Martyr Maker" (2018), "Black Wake" (2018), "Dead Ringer" (2018), "Nazi Overlord" (2018), "Speed Kills" (2018), "Wish Man" (2019), "Myra" (2019), "Hell Girl" (2019), "The Pining" (2019), "Killing Me" (2019), "7 Deadly Sins" (2019), "I Am Not for Sale: The Fight to End Human Trafficking" (2019), "John Wynn's Mirror Mirror" (2019), "Abstruse" (2019), "Cross: Rise of the Villains" (2019), "Adam" (2020), "The Runners" (2020), "Monster Hunters" (2020), "Ole Bryce" (2020), "Nowheresville" (2020), "Apocalypse of Ice" (2020), "C.L.E.A.N." (2020), "Central Park Dark" (2021), "Alien Conquest" (2021), "Whack the Don" (2021), "Megalodon Rising" (2021), "The Shipment" (2021), "#Unknown" (2021), "Hustle Down" (2021), "Blood Runs Thick" (2021), "Vampfather" (2022), "Damon's Revenge" (2022), "The Electric Man" (2022), "Project Skyquake" (2022), "Bullet Train Down" (2022), "Night of the Tommyknockers" (2022), "Battle for Pandora" (2022), "Amber Road" (2022), "Impuratus" (2022), "Bermuda Island" (2023), "The Legend of Jack and Diane" (2023), and "Breakout" (2023). He also appeared frequently in short films and had numerous features in various stages of production at the time of his death. Sizemore appeared on television in productions off "An American Story" (1992), "Witness to the Mob" (1998) as John Gotti, "Witness Protection" (1999), "Sins of the Father" (2002), "Hustle" (2004), "Superstorm" (2007), "Dark Haul" (2014), and "Exit Strategy" (2015). He was also seen on television in episodes of "Gideon Oliver", "China Beach" as Sgt. Vinnie 'the Dog Man' Ventresca from 1989 to 1990, "Against the Law", "The Rosie

O'Donnell Show", "The Tonight Show with Jay Leno", "Late Night with Conan O'Brien", "Howard Stern", the animated "Justice League" as the voice of Rex 'Metamorpho' Mason in 2002, "Robbery Homicide Division" as Lt. Sam Cole from 2002 to 2003, "Dr. Vegas" in the recurring role of Vic Moore from 2004 to 2006, "Head Case", "CSI: Miami", "Crash" as Adrian Cooper from 2008 to 2009, "Larry King Live", "Southland", "Entourage", "It's Always Sunny in Philadelphia", "Hawaii Five-O" in the recurring role of Captain Vincent Fryer from 2011 to 2012, "Perception", "The Red Road" as Jack Kropus from 2014 to 2015, "Law & Order: Special Victims Unit", "Lucifer", "Undercover", "Shooter" as Hugh Meachum from 2016 to 2017, "Twin Peaks" as Anthony Sinclair in 2017, "Cobra Kai", and Dine n' Dashians". Sizemore struggled with addition to methamphetamine and heroin for many years. He had various legal problems resulting in charges of drug abuse and domestic violence. He was sentenced to seven months in jail following a conviction of domestic violence against his girlfriend, the former Hollywood Madam Heidi Fleiss in 2003. He had several more charges of drug possession and attempts to fake a urine test while on probation. His battles with drug addiction were depicted in the 2007 VH1 reality series "Shooting Sizemore" and in such series as "Celebrity Rehab with Dr. Drew", "Celebrity Rehab Presents Sober House", and "Dr. Phil". He pleaded no contest to charges of domestic abuse against his girlfriend in 2017 and was sentenced to three years of probation. His memoirs, "By Some Miracle I Made It Out of There: A Memoir", was published in 2013. Sizemore was married to actress Maeve Quinlan from 1996 until their divorce in 1999. He had twin sons with girlfriend Janelle McIntire in 2005 and they survive him.

Skeates, Steve

Comic book writer Steve Skeate, who co-created the DC characters Hawk and Dove, died in Rochester, New York, on March 30, 2023. He was 80. Skeates was born in Rochester on January 29, 1943. He graduated from Alfred University in New York in 1965. He moved to New York City to work as an assistant to Stan Lee at Marvel Comics. His job with Lee was short-lived and he was soon writing western comics for Marvel. He wrote for Tower Comics in the mid-1960s, penning such titles as "T.H.U.N.D.E.R. Agents", "Noman", and "Undersea Agents". Skeates wrote "The Many Ghosts of Doctor Graves" for Charlton Comics from 1967 to 1969. His other work at Charlton included such titles as "Abbott & Costello", "Outlaws of the West", the "Thane of Bagarth" backup stories in "Hercules", "Sarge Steel" in "Judomaster", and "Fightin' 5" in "Peacemaker". He worked frequently at DC where he co-created "Hawk and Dove" with Steve Ditko in "Showcase" #75 in 1968. He also wrote the first four issues of their own title. His other work at DC included the comics "Aquaman", "House

of Secrets", "House of Mystery", "Date with Debi", "The Flash", "Adventure Comics", "The Witching Hour", "Teen Titans", "Plop!", "Phantom Stranger", "Plastic Man", "Star Spangled War Stories", "The Mighty Isis", "Blackhawk", and "Superman's Pal, Jimmy Olsen". He penned numerous stories for the Warren Publishing comic magazines "Creepy", "Eerie", and "Vampirella" in the early 1970s. He wrote several Gold Key titles in the late 1970s including "Underdog", "The Twilight Zone", and "Yosemite Sam and Bugs Bunny". Skeates returned to Marvel in the 1980s to write for the titles "Peter Porker, the Spectacular Spider-Ham", "Howard the Duck", "Bizarre Adventures", and "Savage Tales". He left comics by the end of the decade and soon moved back to Rochester. He served as editor of the Peoples' Comic Book Newsletter" fanzine from 1996 to 2012. He began writing articles about comics for "Charlton Spotlight" in 2000 and created the self-published comic "Could I Have My Reality Check Please?". He wrote for "The Charlton Arrow" anthology series in 2014.

Smart, Andy

British comedian Andy Smart died in England on May 16, 2023. He was 63. Smart was born in Southsea, Hampshire, England, on June 16, 1959. He became a comedian in the early 1980s and teamed with Angelo Abela as the Vicious Boys. They won the Time Out Street Entertainer Award in 1984. The Vicious Boys were seen on television in episodes of "Saturday Night Out", "Lift Off!", the children's series "Get Fresh" in 1986, "Open Space", "Craig Goes Mad in Melbourne", "Jools Holland's Happening", and "Ghost Train". Smart began performing with the Comedy Store Players in 1994 and soon became a full member. He remained with them through 2008. He appeared in the tele-films "The Preventers" (1996), "Bostock's Cup" (1999), and "Sex 'n' Death" (1999), and an episode of "Murder City". He was seen in the 2001 film "Endgame" and the shorts "The Suicidal Dog" (2000) and "The Goodbye Girls" (2006). Smart's memoirs, "A Hitch in Time: From Liverpool to Pamplona on a 72,000-Mile Road Trip", in 2019. He is survived by a daughter, Grace, with actress Victoria Willing, and a son, Joe.

Smith, Brandon

Actor Brandon Smith, who was featured as police officer Davis Tubbs in the 2001 horror film "Jeepers Creepers", died in Houston, Texas, on October 27, 2023. He was 71. Smith was born in Harris County, Texas, on August 13, 1952. He made his acting debut in a small role in the 1970 tele-film "My Sweet Charlie". He appeared frequently on television over the next fifty years with roles in episodes of "Number 96", "Magnum, P.I.", "The Young Riders", "Dangerous Curves", "Pointman", "Walker, Texas Ranger", "The F.B.I. Files", "Prison Break" in the recurring role of Warden Ed Pavelka in 2006, "Laws of Chance", "The Deep End", "Friday Night

Lights" in the recurring role of Vice Principal Trucks from 2008 to 2010, "Lone Star", "The Good Guys", "Hysteria", "From  Dusk Till Dawn: The Series" as Captain Chance Holbrook from 2014 to 2015, "Hawaii Five-O", and "5th Ward". His other television credits include the tele-films and mini-series "License to Kill" (1984), "Lonesome Dove" (1989), "The Fulfillment of Mary Gray" (1989), "Margaret Bourke-White" (1989), "Challenger" (1990), "In Broad Daylight" (1991), "A Seduction in Travis County" (1991), "Trial: The Price of Passion" (1992), "A Taste for Killing" (1992), "The Habitation of Dragons" (1992), "Fatal Deception: Mrs. Lee Harvey Oswald" (1993), "Witness to the Execution" (1994), "North & South: Book 3, Heaven & Hell" (1994), "Shadows of Desire" (1994), "Texas Justice" (1995), "Forgotten Sins" (1996), "From the Earth to the Moon" (1998), "Still Holding On: The Legend of Cadillac Jack" (1998), "Mr. Murder" (1998), "ATF" (1999), "King of the World" (2000), "Heartless" (2005), "Into the West" (2005), "Living Proof" (2008), and "Sex and Lies in Sin City" (2008). Smith was featured in such films as "Full Moon in Blue Water" (1988), "Night Game" (1989), "Blaze" (1989), "Dark Angel" (1990), "Dan Turner, Hollywood Detective" (1990), "RoboCop 2" (1990), "Hard Promises" (1991), "Rush" (1991), "A Perfect World" (1993), "Powder" (1996), "The Only Thrill" (1997), "The Rage" (1997), "Jeepers Creepers" (2001) as Sergeant Davis Tubbs, "She Gets What She Wants" (2002), "The Rookie" (2002), "The Face of the Serpent" (2003), "The Alamo" (2004), "Paradise, Texas" (2006), "Bordertown" (2007), "No Country for Old Men" (2007), "Cook County" (2008), "Maidenhead" (2008), "Spirit Camp" (2009), "A Gangland Love Story" (2010), "Bernie" (2011), "The Last Mark" (2012), "Dawn of the Crescent Moon" (2014), and "Jeepers Creepers III" (2017) reprising his role as Sergeant Tubbs. Smith is survived by his wife, Margaret.

Smith, Broderick

British-Australian singer and songwriter Broderick Smith died in Australia on April 30, 2023. He was 75. Smith  was born in Hertfordshire, England, on February 17, 1948. He moved to Australia with his family in 1959, settling in St. Albans. He left school in 1963 and worked as a messenger and store clerk for several years. He began playing and singing with various blues bands in the 1960s including the Smokey Hollows and the Adderley Smith Blues Band. He participated in National Service for two years at the end of the decade. He briefly played with Kerryn Tolhurst in the country music group Sundown after his discharge. He

joined the blues-boogie band Carson in 1971. They recorded such songs as "Travelling South" and "Moonshine" and released the albums "Blown" and "On the Air". Smith recorded the solo singles "Goin' on Down to the End of the World" and "Yesterday It Rained" in 1972. He starred as he Father in an orchestral version of the Who's rock opera "Tommy" in Australia in 1973. He joined Tolhurst and other musicians for the band the Dingoes in April of 1973. They released their self-named debut album the following year. The Dingoes relocated to the United States in 1976 where they released the albums "Five Times the Sun" (1977) and "Orphans of the Storm" (1979). Smith returned to Australia where he performed with various bands including Broderick Smith's Hired Hands, Broderick Smith's Big Combo releasing the single "Faded Roses" and "My Father's Hands", Broderick Smith Band, and Broderick Smith and the Noveltones. He appeared on television in the 1985 mini-series "Anzacs" and in episodes of "Janus", "Blue Heelers", "Snowy River: The McGregor Saga", and "State Coroner". He continued to write songs and perform in the 2000s. He teamed with Mick O'Connor on piano, Pip Avent on tuba, and Tim O'Connor on drums for the 2002 recording "Too Easy". He performed with the groups the Backsliders, the Woodpickers, and Tabasco Tom and Doc White, touring throughout Australia and New Zealand. His son, Ambrose Kenny-Smith, was part of the group King Gizzard & the Lizard Wizard, and Brandon wrote the lyrics and narrated their second album, "Eyes Like the Sky", in 2013. His autobiography, "Man Out of Time", was published in 2018. He is survived by his son.

Smith, Dean

Olympic athlete and stuntman Dean Smith died on June 24, 2023. He was 91. Smith was born in Breckenridge, Texas, on January 15, 1932. He was a track and field athlete  and competed at the 1952 Olympics in Helsinki. He placed fourth in the 100-meter dash and earned a gold medal as part of the relay team. He graduated from the University of Texas at Austin and briefly played football for the Los Angeles Rams and the Pittsburgh Steelers. Smith also competed in rodeo events including bareback bronc riding and calf roping. Smith began working in films and television as a stuntman and occasional actor in the late 1950s. He served as a stunt double for such actors as Strother Martin, Alex Cord, Claude Akins, Dale Robertson, Ben Johnson, Robert Forster, Robert Duvall, Bruce Dern, and James Garner. His film credits include "Quantrill's Raiders" (1958), "The Law and Jake Wade" (1958), "Cat on a Hot Tin Roof" (1958), "Born Reckless" (1958), "Auntie Mame" (1958), "Rio Bravo" (1959), "Pork Chop Hill" (1959), "Darby O'Gill and the Little People" (1959), "They Came to Cordura" (1959), "Seven Ways from Sundown" (1960), "The Alamo" (1960), "Two Rode Together" (1961), "The Comancheros" (1961), "How the West Was Won"

(1962), "The Birds" (1963), "PT 109" (1963), "McLintock!" (1963), "Kings of the Sun" (1963), "A Distant Trumpet" (1964), "Cheyenne Autumn" (1964), "Blood on the Arrow" (1964), "Rio Conchos" (1964), "In Harm's Way" (1965), "The Great Race" (1965), "Stagecoach" (1966), "What Did You Do in the War Daddy?" (1966), "El Dorado" (1966), "The War Wagon" (1967), "Hurry Sundown" (1967), "The Scalphunters" (1968), "The Stalking Moon" (1969), "Sweet Charity" (1969), "True Grit" (1969), "Stiletto" (1969), "Butch Cassidy and the Sundance Kid" (1969), "Airport" (1970), "The Cheyenne Social Club" (1970), "Little Big Man" (1970), "Rio Lobo" (1970), "Big Jake" (1971), "Evel Knievel" (1971), "Sometimes a Great Notion" (1971), "Squares" (1972), "The Legend of Nigger Charley" (1972), "Jeremiah Johnson" (1972), "Hickey & Boggs" (1972), "Ulzana's Raid" (1972), "The Life and Times of Judge Roy Bean" (1972), "The Train Robbers" (1973), "Westworld" (1973), "The Sting" (1973), "The Sugarland Express" (1974), "Airport 1975" (1974), "Earthquake" (1974), "The Towering Inferno" (1974), "Seven Alone" (1974), "The Great Waldo Pepper" (1975), "The Drowning Pool" (1975), "Three Days of the Condor" (1975), "Hearts of the West" (1975), "Mackintosh and T.J." (1975), "The Captive: The Longest Drive 2" (1976), "Fraternity Row" (1977), "Black Sunday" (1977), "FM" (1978), "The Astral Factor" (1978), "Hardcore" (1979), "The Concorde... Airport '79" (1979), "Christine" (1983), "The Lonely Guy" (1984), "Cloak & Dagger" (1984), "Rhinestone" (1984), "Raw Deal" (1986), "Creepshow 2" (1987), "Hot to Trot" (1988), "Three Fugitives" (1989), "Maverick" (1994), "The Quick and the Dead" (1995), "Michael" (1996), and "Keys to Tulsa" (1997). Smith worked on the television series "Cheyenne", "Cimarron City", "Laramie", "The Nine Lives of Elfego Baca", "Texas John Slaughter", "The Swamp Fox", "Bat Masterson", "Overland Trail", "Have Gun - Will Travel", "Target: The Corruptors!", "The Tall Man", "Wagon Train", "Tales of Wells Fargo", "The Virginian", "The Legend of Jesse James", "The Loner", "The F.B.I.", "Ironside", "Iron Horse", "Cimarron Strip", "The Name of the Game", "The Outcasts", "Search", "The Bold Ones: The New Doctors", "Search", "How the West Was Won", "The Six Million Dollar Man", "Police Story", "Three for the Road", "The Quest", "Bret Maverick", "Simon & Simon", "The Fall Guy", "Paradise", and "Silk Stalkings". He also worked in the tele-films and mini-series "Mrs. Sundance" (1974), "Scream of the Wolf" (1974), "The Legend of the Golden Gun" (1979), "The Last Rider of the Dalton Gang" (1979), "Timestalkers" (1987), and "Rough Riders" (1997). Smith received the Golden Boot Award for his contributions to Western films and television and was inducted into the Texas Rodeo Cowboy Hall of Fame in 2006. His autobiography, "Cowboy Stuntman from Olympic Gold to the Silver Screen", was published in 2013. Smith was married and divorced from Abigail Gowan, and they had a child together. He married Debra Stoker in 1996 and is also survived by their son.

Smith, Huey 'Piano'

Pianist Huey 'Piano' Smith, who was noted for the classic song "Rockin' Pneumonia and the Boogie Woogie Flu",

died at his home in Baton Rouge, Louisiana, on February 13, 2023. He was 89. Smith was born in New Orleans, Louisiana, on January 26, 1934. He began writing songs as a child and was playing local clubs in his teens. He signed with Savoy Records in 1952 and released the single "You Made Me Cry" the following year. He was a session musician for Specialty

Records in the mid-1950s and performed with Little Richard's first band. He led the Rhythm Aces in 1956 and recorded a version of "Little Liza Jane". He formed the band Huey 'Piano' Smith and His Clowns the following year and signed by Ace Records. They scored a major hit with their recording of "Rockin' Pneumonia and the Boogie Woogie Flu". Scarface John Williams usually sang lead with the band on such songs as "Genevieve", "Tu-Ber-Cu-Lucas and the Sinus Blues", "Beatnik Blues", and "Quit My Job". The Clowns had another major hit with "Don't You Just Know It" in 1958. Smith's song "Sea Cruise" was overdubbed by singer Frankie Ford before it was released by Ace. He left Ace for Imperial Records by the end of the decade but had little success with future releases. He recorded with smaller labels from the 1960s. He continued to perform in the New Orleans area until moving to Baton Rouge in 1980. Smith filed numerous lawsuits in attempts to get royalty payments without much success and filed bankruptcy in 1997. Smith married Doretha Ford in 1957 and they had five children before divorcing in the mid-1960s. He married Margrette Riley in 1971 and is survived by her and eight children.

Smith, Sheila

Actress Sheila Smith, who was noted for her roles in such Broadway productions as "Mame" and "Follies", died on

November 30, 2023. She was 90. Smith was born in Conneaut, Ohio, on April 3, 1933. She began her career on stage, performing in Chicago and in Off-Broadway productions of "Taking My Turn", "Fiorello!", and "Anything Goes". She made her Broadway debut in the 1963 musical "Hot Spot". Smith was understudy for both Angela Lansbury's Mame and Bea Arthur's Vera in the original Broadway production of "Mame" in 1966. Her other Broadway credits include the musicals "Company" (1970), "Follies" (1971), "Sugar" (1972), "42nd Street" (1980), "The Five O'Clock Girl" (1981), and "Show Boat" (1994). Smith appeared on television in an episode of "Charlie's Angels" in 1978 and in the 1984 tele-film "Taking My Turn".

Smith, Shelley

Actress and fashion model Shelley Smith, who starred as Sara James in the short-lived television comedy series "The Associates" in 1979, died of cardiac arrest in Los Angeles, California, on August 8, 2023. She was 70. Smith was born in Princeton, New Jersey, on October 25, 1952. She graduated from Connecticut College in the early 1970s and began her career as a model. She was a cover model for numerous magazines including "Vogue", "Glamour", "Harper's Bazaar", and "Mademoiselle". Smith made her acting debut later in the decade in the 1979 tele-film "Mirror, Mirror". She was also seen in the tele-films "Swan Song" (1980), "The Night the City Screamed" (1980), "This House Possessed" (1981), "Scruples" (1981), and "The Fantastic World of D.C. Collins" (1984). She starred as Bostonian lawyer Sara James in the short-lived legal comedy "The Associates" with Martin Short from 1979 to 1980. She appeared in episodes of "Tenspeed and Brown Shoe", "Ryan's Hope", "The Stockard Channing Show", "Angie", "The Phoenix", "Hart to Hart", the military drama "For Love and Honor" as Captain Carolyn Engel from 1983 to 1984, "Fantasy Island", "Cover Up", "Hotel", "Lady Blue", "The Love Boat", "Diff'rent Strokes", "The New Mike Hammer", "Hunter", "Magnum, P.I.", "Webster", "Simon & Simon", "Dragnet", and "Murder, She Wrote". She was a guest on such television game shows as "Battle of the Network Stars", "The Hollywood Squares", "Chain Reaction", "All-Star Family Feud", "Body Language", "Celebrity Double Talk", "Super Password", "The $10,000 Pyramid", and "Blackout". Smith was featured in the films "Class Reunion" (1982) and "Fatal Charm" (1990). She earned a master's degree in psychology from Antioch University and was licensed as a marriage family therapist from 1993. She was also founder of the Egg Donor Program, later known as Hatch Fertility, to assist infertile couples in having children. Smith was married to producer Jonathan Axelrod from 1978 until their divorce in 1978. She was married to producer Reid Nathan from 1987 until their divorce in 2001 and is survived by their twin children, Nicholas and Miranda. She married actor Michael Maguire in 2004 and he also survives her.

Smothers, Tom

Comedian and musician Tom Smothers, who formed the popular musical comedy duo The Smothers Brothers with his brother, Dick, died of lung cancer at his home in Santa Rosa, California, on December 26, 2023. He was 86. Smothers was born in New York City on February 2, 1937. His father was a U.S. Army major who died as a prisoner of war of the Japanese in April of 1945. He moved to California with his family where he attended high school. He competed in gymnastics and pole vaulting at San Jose State College. Tom and his younger brother, Dick, began performing folk music with the Casual

Quartet. They soon became a duo with appearances at the Purple Onion in San Francisco in 1959. The brothers were guests on such television shows as "The Tonight Show Starring Jack Paar", "The New Steve Allen Show", "The Steve Allen Playhouse", "Hootenanny", "The Judy Garland Show", "The Garry Moore Show", "I've Got a Secret", "The Tennessee Ernie Ford Show", "The Hollywood Palace", "The Jack Paar Program", "The Jack Benny Program", "Password", "Gypsy", "The Dean Martin Summer Show", "The Danny Thomas Show", "The Andy Williams Show", "The Val Doonican Show", "The Eamonn Andrews Show", "The Jack Benny Hour", "What's My Line?", "Pat Boone in Hollywood", and "Dee Time". They were popular nightclub performers and recorded several albums including "The Two Sides of the Smothers Brothers" (1962) and "Curb Your Tongue, Knave!" (1964). Tom and Dick guest-starred in an episode of the crime series "Burke's Law" in 1964. They were stars of the short-lived CBS fantasy sit-com "The Smothers Brothers Show" (aka "My Brother the Angel") with Tom as an apprentice angel trying to earn his wings by helping out his brother. They were Tweedledee and Tweedledum in a 1966 television production of "Alice Through the Looking Glass". Their ground-breaking variety series "The Smothers Brothers Comedy Hour" aired from 1967 to 1969. The popular and controversial gave a new generation of comics a showcase including Steve Martin, Don Novello, Rob Reiner, Bob Einstein, Albert Brooks, and Pat Paulsen. Music acts were geared to younger audiences and featured artists not normally found on variety shows of the day including Joan Baez, The Doors, Janis Ian, Jefferson Airplane, The Who, Simon and Garfunkel, and Pete Seeger. They were guests on the 1968 television special "Pat Paulsen for President", which featured their deadpan resident comedian as a real candidate for president. The shows outspoken opposition to the Vietnam War and President Lyndon B. Johnson frequently brought the brothers into conflict with CBS censors. Continued problems with the network led to the abrupt cancellation of "The Smothers Brothers Comedy Hour" in April of 1969. The series won an Emmy Award for best writing that year and the brothers successfully sued CBS for breach of contract. The show's cancellation was later the subject of the 2002 documentary "Smothered". Tom and Dick were stars of the ABC summer series "The Return of the Smothers Brothers" in 1970 and "The Smothers Brothers Show" form NBC in 1975. They were hosts of "The Tom and Dick Smothers Brothers Special I" and "The Tom and Dick Smothers Brothers Special II" in 1980. They were also seen in such series as "The Tonight Show Starring Johnny Carson", "The Rosey Grier Show", "The Jonathan Winters Show", "What's It All About, World?", "Della", "The Joey Bishop Show", "The Bob Hope Show", "The Andy Williams Show", "Pat Paulsen's Half a Comedy Hour", "The David Frost Show", "The Irv Kupcinet Show", "Playboy After

Dark", "The Ray Stevens Show", "The Dean Martin Show", "The Ed Sullivan Show", "Rollin' on the River", "The Glen Campbell Goodtime Hour", "Flip", "The Dick Cavett Show", "Dean Martin Presents: The Bobby Darin Amusement Co.", "The New Bill Cosby Show", "NBC Follies", "The Julie Andrews Hour", "The Hollywood Palladium", "The Mike

Douglas Show", "The Carol Burnett Show", "Ben Vereen... Comin' at Ya", "Cher", "Dinah!", "The Sonny and Cher Show", "The David Steinberg Show", "Van Dyke and Company", "The Merv Griffin Show", "The Bob Braun Show", "Barbara Mandrell and the Mandrell Sisters", "The Glen Campbell Music Show", "Saturday Night Live" as co-hosts in 1982 and 1983, "The New Hollywood Squares", "Dolly", "Super Dave", "The Pat Sajak Show", "Late Night with Conan O'Brien", "The Martin Short Show", "Life with Bonnie", "Hollywood Squares", "Last Call with Carson Daly", "The Late Late Show with Craig Ferguson", "Tavis Smiley", "The Green Room with Paul Provenza", and "CBS News Sunday Morning with Jane Pauley". They starred as cameraman Bones Howard and reporter Ryan Fitzpatrick in tele-film "Terror at Alcatraz" and the subsequent short-lived series "Fitz and Bones" in 1982. They also appeared in various comedy specials. They returned to CBS for a 20th anniversary special in 1988 and a short-lived return of "The Smothers Brothers Comedy Hour" from 1988 to 1989. Tom appeared in a handful of films including Brian De Palma's 1972 comedy "Get to Known Your Rabbit" as tap-dancing magician Donald Beeman, "Silver Bears" (1977), "A Pleasure Doing Business" (1979), "Serial" (1980), "There Goes the Bride" (1980), the comedy horror "Pandemonium" (1982), "Speed Zone" (1989), and "The Informant!" (2009). He was the voice of Ted E. Bear in the animated television specials "The Bear Who Slept Through Christmas" (1973) and "The Great Bear Scare" (1983). His other television credits include episodes of "Love, American Style", "Fantasy Island", "The Love Boat", "Hotel", "Tales of the Unexpected", "Benson", "Dream On", "Suddenly Susan", "Maggie", and "Norm". Tom was King Sextimus in the Disney tele-film "Once Upon a Mattress" in 2005 and provided voices for episodes of the animated series "Dr. Katz, Professional Therapist" and "The Simpsons". The brothers starred in the 1978 Broadway musical satire "I Love My Wife" and the tele-film "Cinemax Comedy Experiment Rap Master Ronnie" in 1989. Tom starred in the VHS release "The Yo Yo Man Instructional Video" in 1988. The Smothers Brothers announced their retirement after a performance at the Orleans Hotel and Casino in Las Vegas in 2010. The reunited at a charity event in Sarasota, Florida, in 2019. They announced in 2022 that they would resume touring the following year, but Tom was diagnosed with lung cancer in July of 2023. They were given a star on the Hollywood Walk of Fame in 1989 and were inducted into the Television Academy Hall of Fame in 2010. Tom Smothers was the owner of the Remick Ridge Vineyards in Sonoma County, California,

from 1977 until 2023. He was married to Stephanie Shorr from 1963 until their divorce in 1967 and to Rochelle Robley from 1974 until their divorce in 1976. He married Marcy Carriker in 1990 and is survived by her and their two children. A son from his first marriage died in April of 2023.

Sneed, Floyd

Canadian drummer Floyd Sneed, who was a member of the band Three Dog Night, died in Canada on January 27, 2023. He was 80. Sneed was born in Calgary, Alberta, Canada,

on November 22, 1942. He began playing drums in his youth and received his first drum kit from his older sister who was married to actor Tommy Chong a the time. Sneed and his older brother, pianist Bernie Sneed, played in the band called the Calgary Shades. He soon began playing in Chong's band, Little Daddy and the Bachelors, in the Vancouver area in the early 1960s. He moved to Los Angeles in 1966 to form his own band. Sneed joined the band Three Dog Night in 1968. They released their self-named first album later in the year and had hits with the songs "Try a Little Tenderness" and "One". A string of hits followed over the next several years including "Eli's Coming", "Celebrate", "Mama Told Me (Not to Come)", "Out in the Country", "One Man Band", "Joy to the World" with Sneed singing backup, "An Old Fashioned Love Song", "Never Been to Spain", "The Family of Man", and "Shambala". He left Three Dog Night in 1974 and the band broke up soon after. He continued to play drums with other groups including the Ohio Players and the SS Fools, working with other backing musicians from Three Dog Night. He briefly rejoined a newer version of Three Dog Night in the mid-1980s. Sneed was featured in a small role as a drummer in Tommy Chong's 1990 film "Far Out Man". He later worked with the band K.A.T.T. and formed his own band, Same Dog New Tricks. He worked with former Three Dog Night lead singer Chuck Negron on various projects in the 1990s and 2000s.

Snow, Michael

Canadian artist and experimental filmmaker Michael

Snow died of pneumonia in Toronto, Ontario, Canada, on January 5, 2023. He was 94. Snow was born in Toronto on December 10, 1928. He attended Upper Canada College and the Ontario College of Art, where he graduated in 1952. He made his first film, an animated short entitled "A to Z", in 1956. He had his first art exhibition the following year. He created a stylized female silhouette he called the Walking Woman in 1961. The piece was featured in his painting, sculptures, photographs and films. He moved to New York City in 1963 where he continued to incorporate the Walking Woman symbol in his art. He became part of the avant garde set and created numerous experimental films including "New York Eye and Ear Control" (1964), "Short Shave" (1965), "Wavelength" (1967) considered an underground masterpiece, "Standard Time" (1978), "Dripping Water" (1969) with his then wife Joyce Wieland, "<----> or Back and Forth" (1969), and "Side Seat Paintings Slides Sound Film" (1970). Snow subsequently returned to Canada where made the three-hour landscape study film "La Region Centrale" in 1971. He continued to produce such shorts and films as "Two Sides to Every Story" (1974), "Rameau's Nephew by Diderot (Thanx to Dennis Young) by Wilma Schoen" (1974), "Breakfast (Table Top Dolly)" (1976), "Presents" (1981), "So Is This" (1982), "Seated Figures" (1988), "See You Later" (1990), "To Lavoisier, Who Died in the Reign of Terror" (1991), "Prelude" (2000), "The Living Room" (2000), "Solar Breath" (2002), the digitally produced "*Corpus Callosum" (2002), "WVLNT ("Wavelength For Those Who Don't Have the Time")" (2003), "Triage" (2004) with Carl Brown, "SSHTOORRTY" (2005), "Reverberlin" (2006), "Puccini Conservato" (2008), and "Cityscape" (2019). His other works include a 1979 installation piece for the Toronto mall the Eaton Center in 1979. It included 60 fiberglass Canadian geese suspended from the ceiling and was called "Flight Stop". The mall decorated the geese with red ribbons for Christmas and Snow sued to have the decorations removed. He won the case which affirmed an artist's rights to protect the integrity of his work. Snow was married to Joyce Wieland from 1956 until their divorce in 1976. He married curator and writer Peggy Gale in 1990 and is survived by her and their son.

Soderblom, Irene

Swedish actress Irene Soderblom died in Lidingo, Sweden, on July 27, 2023. She was 101. Soderblom was born

in Gothenburg, Sweden, on November 19, 1921. She learned to play the accordion in her teens and was soon touring with other musicians. She became an accordion soloist at Chinavarieten in 1944. She trained in acting at the Terserus Theater School and appeared on stage with the Casino Theater. She was also a founder of the Sallskapet Stallfaglarnas in 1947. Soderblom appeared frequently in films in the 1940s and 1950s with roles in "Tre Soner Gick Till Flyget" (1945), "Hotell Kakbrinken" (1946), "91: an Karlssons Permis" (1947) as Elvira Jansson, "Loffe Som Miljonar" (1948), "Lattjo Med Boccaccio" (1949), "Stjarnsmall i Frukostklubben" (1950), "Pahittiga Johansson" (1950), "Spoke Pa Semester" (1951), "91: an Karlssons Bravader" (1951), "Kungen av Dalarna" (1953), "Alla Tiders 91: an Karlsson" (1953), "Sju Svarta Be-ha" (1954), "Far Och Flyg" (1955), "91: an Karlsson Rycker in" (1955), "91: an

Karlsson Slar Knockout" (1957), "Enslingen Johannes" (1957), and "Enslingen i Blasadar" (1959). She continued to perform on stage through the early 1960s. Soderblom was married to actor and director Gosta Bernhard from 1947 until their divorce in 1970 and is survived by their daughter, Lillemor. She was married to journalist Torsten Adenby from 1971 until their divorce in 1980.

Solli, Sergio

Italian actor Sergio Solli died in Naples, Italy, on February 3, 2023. He was 78. Solli was born in Naples on

November 19, 1944. He worked as a hairdresser in the 1960s and appeared on the amateur stage. He joined Eduardo De Filippo's theatrical troupe in the early 1970s where he performed and directed for many years. Solli was seen on television in productions of "The Age of the Medici" (1972), "Il Marsigliese" (1975), "Uomo e Galantuomo" (1975), "De Pretore Vincenzo" (1976), "Gli Esami Non Finiscono Mai" (1976), "Natale in Casa Cupiello" (1977), "Il Cilindro" (1978), "Gennareniello" (1978), "Quei Figuri di Tanti Anni Fa" (1978), "Le Voci di Dentro" (1978), "Un Paio di Scarpe per Tanti Chilometri" (1981), "Il Berretto a Sonagli" (1981), "Padre Part-Time" (1984), "Les Heritiers" (1997), "Anni '50" (1998), "Anni '60" (1999), "La Omicidi" (2004), "Matilde" (2005), "Scusate il Disturbo" (2009), "Il Bosco" (2015), and "Romanzo Siciliano" (2016). His other television credits include episodes of "Investigatori d'Italia", "Il Giudice Istruttore", "Un Commissario a Roma", "Nonno Felice", "Un Prete Tra Noi", "Elisa di Rivombrosa", "Un Posto al Sole d'Estate", "Recipe for Crime", "Il Clan dei Camorristi", and "Le Mani Dentro la Citta". Solli appeared in numerous films including "No Grazie, il Caffe Mi Rende Nervoso" (1982), "A Joke of Destiny, Lying in Wait Around the Corner Like a Bandit" (1983), "Il Petomane" (1983), "Softly, Softly" (1984), "Uno Scandalo Perbene" (1984), "Cosi Parlo Bellavista" (1984), "Il Mistero di Bellavista" (1985), "Stregati" (aka "Bewitched") (1986), "32 Dicembre" (1988), "L'Ultima Scena" (1988), "'O Re" (1989), "Basta! Adesso Tocca a Noi" (1990), "C'e Posto per Tutti" (1990), "Nessuno Mi Crede" (1992), "Deat of a Neapolitan Mathematician" (1992), "Ciao, Professore!" (1992), Massimo Troisi's Oscar nominated feature "Il Postino" (aka "The Postman") (1994), "Croce e Delizia" (1995), "A Spasso Nel Tempo - L'Avventura Continua" (1997), "E Adesso Sesso" (2001), "Stregati Dalla Luna" (2001), "Pater Familias" (2003), "A Children's Story" (2004), "L'Aria Salata" (2006), "La Seconda Volta Non Si Scorda Mai" (2008), "Come Undone" (2010), "The Wholly Family" (2011), "Box Office 3D: The Filmest of Films" (2011), "Kryptonite!" (2011), "Piazza Fontana: The Italian Conspiracy" (2012), Woody Allen's "To Rome with Love" (2012), "Dimmelo Con il Cuore" (2014), "I Can Quit Whenever I Want" (2014), "A Napoli Non Piove Mai"

(2015), "Effetti Indesiderati" (2015), "Le Verita" (2017), "E Se Mi Comprassi Una Sedia?" (2017), and "I Can Quit Whenever I Want: Ad Honorem" (2017).

Somers, Suzanne

Actress Suzanne Somers, who starred as Chrissy Snow on the popular television comedy series "Three's Company", died of breast cancer at her home in Palm Springs, California, on October 15, 2023. She was 76. She was born Suzanne

Mahone in San Bruno, California, on October 16, 1946. She had a troubled childhood, suffering from dyslexia and an abusive father. She began performing in plays while in high school and briefly attended Lone Mountain College in San Francisco after her graduation in 1964. She left college after becoming pregnant and marriedd the following year. She soon embarked on an acting career and was seen in small roles in the films "Bullitt" (1968), "Daddy's Gone A-Hunting" (1969), "Fools" (1970), and "Magnum Force" (1973). Somers made an impact in a bit role in George Lucas' 1973's "American Graffiti" as the blonde in the white Thunderbird. She made her television debut in the comedy series "Lotsa Luck!" in 1974 and was seen in episodes of "The Rockford Files", "One Day at a Time", "The Love Boat", "Starsky and Hutch", and "The Six Million Dollar Man". She was also seen in the tele-films "Sky Heist" (1975), "It Happened at Lakewood Manor" (aka "Ants!") (1977), "Happily Ever After" (1978), and "Zuma Beach" (1978). Somers seen in the films "Billy Jack Goes to Washington" (1977), "Yesterday's Hero" (1979), and "Nothing Personal" (1980). She was best known for her role as Chrissy Snow, roommate with John Ritter's Jack Tripper and Joyce DeWitt's Janet Wood, on the comedy series "Three's Company" from 1977 to 1981. Somers was featured as Chrissy in a small role in the spin-off series "The Ropers" in 1979. She left "Three's Company" in 1981 at the start of the fifth season in a financial dispute with the network, requesting parity with her male co-star, Ritter, who was earning five times her salary. She had little success with subsequent court cases and was replaced on the series by Jenilee Harrison and Priscilla Barnes over the final three seasons. Somers was the subject of a nude pictorial in "Playboy" magazine without her permission in 1980 from a photo session a decade earlier. She sued "Playboy" and received a settlement that was donated to charity. She accepted an offer by "Playboy" for another pictorial in 1984, feeling she would have more control of the quality of the photographs published. She continued her career on television with roles in episodes of "Billy", "Sisters", "The Larry Sanders Show", "Full House", "The Naked Truth", and "The Simpsons" in a voice role. Somers was featured as Gina Germaine in the 1985 mini-series "Hollywood Wives", and starred in the tele-films "Goodbye Charlie" (1985), "Totally Minnie" (1988), "Rich Men, Single Women" (1990), "Keeping Secrets" (1991),

"Exclusive" (1992), "Seduced by Evil" (1994), "Devil's Food" (1996), "Love-Struck" (1997), "No Laughing Matter" (1998), and "The Darklings" (1999). She starred as Sheriff Hildy Granger in the comedy series "She's the Sheriff" from 1997 to 1989 and was Carol Foster Lambert in the sit-com "Step by Step" opposite Patrick Duffy from 1991 to 1998. Her later film credits include small roles in "Serial Mom" (1994), "Rusty: A Dog's Tale" (1998) as the voice of Malley, and "Say It Isn't So" (2001). Somers was featured in numerous talk, variety, and game shows during her career including "Match Game", "Celebrity Challenge of the Sexes", "The Hollywood Squares", "Celebrity Challenge of the Stars", "Dinah", "Dean Martin Celebrity Roast" as celebrant in 1978, "Donny and Marie", "The Tim Conway Show", "The Mike Douglas Show", "Donahue", "The Regis Philbin show", "The Tonight Show Starring Johnny Carson", "Jerry Lewis MDA Labor Day Telethon", "The Late Show", "The Wil Shriner Show", "Hour Magazine", "The Home Show", "Intimate Portrait", "One on One with John Tesh", "Sally Jesse Raphael", "The Tonight Show with Jay Leno", "Maury", "The Daily Show", "The Howard Stern Show", "The Martin Short Show", "Late Night with Conan O'Brien", "The Rosie O'Donnell Show", "Jimmy Kimmel Life", "The Wayne Brady Show", "The Sharon Osbourne Show", "The Factor", "Good Day Live", "The Tony Danza Show", "The Late Late Show with Craig Ferguson", "Scarborough Country", "The View", "The Ellen DeGeneres Show", "Kathy Griffin: My Life on the D-List", "The Fran Drescher Show", "Larry King Live", "The Hour", "Piers Morgan Live", "Rachael Ray", "Anderson Live", "Larry King Now", "Marie", "Katie", "Hannity", "Fox and Friends", "The Meredith Vieira Show", "Dancing with the Stars" as a contestant in 2015, "Live with Kelly and Mark", "Watch What Happens Live with Andy Cohen", "The Talk", "Good Morning America", "Today", "The Wendy Williams Show", "Home & Family", "The Dr. Oz Show", and "The Drew Barrymore Show". She hosted the specials "The Suzanne Somers Special" (1982) and "Suzanne Somers... And 10,000 G.I.'s" (1983), and "The Suzanne Somers Show" in 1994. Sommers was also noted for her role as the spokesperson for the ThighMaster exercise equipment in the 1990s. She was co-host of the revised television series "Candid Camera" from 1997 to 1999. She was also seen frequently on the Home Shopping Network in the early 2000s selling her designs for clothing, jewelry, and household items. She starred in the short-lived one-woman show "The Blonde in the Thunderbird" on Broadway in 2005. She hosted the online talk show "Suzanne Somers Breaking Through" from 2012, where she reunited and reconciled with her "Three's Company" co-star Joyce DeWitt. She was host of the short-lived "The Suzanne Show" in 2012, earning an Emmy nomination while dealing with health and fitness topics, on Lifetime. She was a contestant on "Dancing with the Stars" in 2015, finishing in 9th place. She also starred in a Las Vegas revue, "Suzanne Sizzles", in 2015. Somers suffered from health issues from her 20s and was diagnosed with skin cancer in her 30s. She underwent a lumpectomy and received radiation treatment for stage II breast cancer in 2001. She wrote the 1979 autobiography "Keeping Secrets" and the 1980 collection

"Touch Me: The Poems of Suzanne Somers". She was a sometimes controversial proponent of alternate medical responses to cancer and other health issues, penning such books as "After the Fall: How I Picked Myself Up, Dusted Myself Off, and Started All Over Again" (1998), "Suzanne Somers' Get Skinny on Fabulous Food" (1999), "Suzanne Somers' Get Skinny on Fabulous Food" (1999), "Suzanne Somers' 365 Ways to Change Your Life" (1999), "Suzanne Somers' Eat, Cheat, and Melt the Fat Away" (2001), "Somersize Desserts" (2001), "Suzanne Somers' Fast and Easy: Lose Weight the Somersize Way with Quick, Delicious Meals for the Entire Family!" (2004), "The Sexy Years: Discover the Hormone Connection – The Secret to Fabulous Sex, Great Health, and Vitality, for Women and Men" (2004), "Somersize Chocolate" (2004), "Suzanne Somers' Slim and Sexy Forever: The Hormone Solution for Permanent Weight Loss and Optimal Living" (2005), "Somersize Cocktails: 30 Sexy Libations from Cool Classics to Unique Concoctions to Stir Up Any Occasion" (2005), "Somersize Appetizers: 30 Scintillating Starters to Tantalize Your Tastebuds at Every Occasion" (2005), "Ageless: The Naked Truth About Bioidentical Hormones" (2008), "Breakthrough: Eight Steps to Wellness" (2008), "Knockout: Interviews with Doctors Who Are Curing Cancer – And How to Prevent Getting It in the First Place " (2009), "Stay Young & Sexy with Bio-Identical Hormone Replacement: The Science Explained. Smart Publications" (2009), "Sexy Forever: How to Fight Fat after Forty" (2010), "The Sexy Forever Recipe Bible" (2011), "Bombshell: Explosive Medical Secrets That Will Redefine Aging" (2012), "I'm Too Young for This!: The Natural Hormone Solution to Enjoy Perimenopause" (2013), and "TOX-SICK: From Toxic to Not Sick" (2015). Her inspirational memoir "Two's Company: A Fifty-Year Romance with Lessons Learned in Love, Life & Business" was published in 2017. She married Bruce Somers in 1965 and they had a son, Bruce Jr., later in the year. They divorced in 1968 and she became involved with television producer and host Alan Hamel. They married in 1977 and he also survives her.

Sonni, Jack

Musician Jack Sonni, who played the guitar with the band Dire Straits, died on August 30, 2023. He was 68. Sonni was born in Indiana, Pennsylvania, on December 9, 1954. He learned to play the piano and trumpet as a child before taking up the guitar in his early teens. He attended the University of Connecticut before leaving to study at the Hartford

Conservatory of Music. He was mentored by guitarist Elliott Randall and moved to New York City in 1976. He did session work and formed his own band, the Leisure Class. He met members of the Dire Straits while working at Rudy's Music Shop in New York. He was invited to join the band for a recording session of the "Brothers in Arms" album in 1984 and subsequently performed with them on their world tour. He replaced Hal Lindes on rhythm guitar and became noted as the band's "other guitarist". He played with Dire Straits at the Live Aid concert in 1985 and was featured in several videos. He left music after the birth of twin daughters in 1988 and began working as a marketing executive. Sonni was employed by Rivera Guitar Amplifiers and became director of marketing communications for the musical equipment manufacturer Line 6. He served as vice president of marketing communications for Guitar Center from 2001 to 2006. He began writing in the 2000s and continued to participate in the music scene. He returned to his band the Leisure Class in 2017 and frequently joined with other former Dire Straits members in the Dire Straits Legacy project. Sonni's daughter, Nadine, was killed in an automobile accident in 2018. He is survived by her sister, Caitlin.

Soriano, Pepe

Argentine actor Jose Carlo 'Pepe' Soriano died in Buenos Aires, Argentina, on September 13, 2023. He was 93. Soriano was born in Buenos Aires on September 25, 1929. He attended the University of Buenos Aires Law School before

abandoning law to pursue a career in theater. He staged several plays while in school in the early 1950s and made his professional debut with a production of "A Midsummer Night's Dream" in 1953. He appeared frequently in films from the mid-1950s with roles in "Adios Muchachos" (1955), "El Protegido" (1956), "Hotel Alojamiento" (1966), "Cuando los Hombres Hablan de Mujeres" (1967), "Tute Cabrero" (1968), "Psexoanalisis" (1968), "Juan Lamaglia y Senora" (1970), "El Ayudante" (1971), "Heroina" (1962), "Las Venganzas de Beto Sanchez" (1973), "Rebellion in Patagonia" (1974), "The Jewish Gauchos" (1975), "No Toquen a la Nena" (1976), "Netri el Martir de Alcorta" (1977), "Grandma" (1979), "Sentimental" (1981), "Pubis Angelical" (1982), "La Invitacion" (1982), "Asesinato en el Senado de la Nacion" (1984), "Escapada Final (Scapegoat)" (1985), "Te Amo" (1986), "Poor Butterfly" (1986), "Esperame en el Cielo" (1988), "Matar al Nani" (1988), "El Tesoro" (1988), "El Mary y el Tiempo" (1989), "La Taberna Fantastica" (1991), "El Rey Pasmado" (1991), "Funes, un Gran Amor" (1993), "A Shadow Yu Soon Will Be" (1994), "New Hope" (1996), "A School Teacher" (1996), "Tangos Are for Two" (1997), "Momentos Robados" (1997), "Cohen vs. Rosi" (1998), "Angel, the Diva and I" (1999), "Porque te Quiero" (2001), "El Ultimo Tren" (2002), "Common Ground" (2002), "La Suerte Dormida" (2003), "Cargo de Conciencia" (2005), "A Traves de Tus Ojos" (2006), "El Brindis" (2007), "Babilonia, la Noticia Secreta" (2010), "Pecados" (2011), "My First Wedding" (2011), "Nocturna: Side A - The Great Old Man's Night" (2021), and "Nocturna: Side B - Where the Elephants Go to Die" (2021). Soriano was seen on television in productions of "Hamlet" (1964), "Romeo y Julieta" (1966),

"Los Vecinos" (1966), "Los Dias de Julian Bisbal" (1966), "El Monstruo No Ha Muerto" (1970), "El Abuelo" (1971), "El Angel de la Muerte" (1971), "El Tobogan" (1971), and "La Huella del Crimen" (1991). He was a regular performer in the series "Yo Soy Porteno" n 1963 and appeared in episodes of "La Familia Falcon", "Senoritas Alumnas", "El Departamento", "Teatro Trece", "Carola y Carolina", "Operacion Ja-Ja" from 1963 to 1967, "Domingos de Mi Ciudad" from 1966 to 1970, "Domingos de Teatro Comico", "El Boton" in 1969, "El Chaleco" in 1970, "Uno Entre Nosotros", "Narciso Ibanez Menta Presenta", "La Comedia del Domingo", "Juguemos al Amor", "Persona", "Alta Comedia", "Historias de Medio Pelo", "La Batalla de los Angeles", "Los Especiales de ATC", "Los Reporteros", "Miguel Servet (La Sangrey y la Ceniza)", "Historias del Otro Lado", "Alta Comedia", "Farmacia de Guardia" as Don Rnrique Cano from 1991 to 1992, "Una Gloria Nacional", "Cha Cha Cha", "La Casa de la Esquina", "R.R.D.T." as Isidro from 1997 to 1998, and "Trillizos, Diljo la Partera!" as Domenico Gargiulo in 1999.

Sorkin, Arleen

Actress Arleen Sorkin, who provided the inspiration and the voice for the Batman comic book character Harley Quinn, died of complications from pneumonia and multiple sclerosis on August 24, 2023. She was 67. Sorkin was born in Washington, D.C., on October 14, 1957. She began her career

in the 1970s performing in cabarets and with a comedy troupe. She was featured as Calliope Jones on the daytime television soap opera "Days of Our Lives" from 1984 to 1990. She made return visits to the show in 1992, 2001, 2006, and 2010. She was also seen on television from the early 1980s with roles in episodes of "Saturday Night Live", "The New Mike Hammer", "The Wil Shriner Show", "Win, Lose or Draw", the comedy series "Duet" as Geneva from 1987 to 1989, "Family Feud", "The New Hollywood Squares", "The Marsha Warfield Show", "Open House", "Dream On", "Room for Romance", "Ameria's Funniest People" as co-host with Dave Coulier from 1990 to 1992, and "Frasier". She also appeared in the tele-films "From Here to Maternity" (1986) and "Perry Mason: The Case of the Killer Kiss" (1993). Sorkin was noted for her voice role as Harley Quinn (aka Dr. Harleen Quinzel) on various animated series. She had inspired Batman writer Paul Dini to create the character after he saw her playing a harlequin in a dream sequence of "Days of Our Lives". She made her debut in "Joker's Favor", a 1992 episode of "Batman: The Animated Series". Harley was originally designed to only make one appearance, but her popularity led to her recurring often as the Joker's sidekick. Sorkin voiced the role in episodes of "Batman: The Animated Series", "Superman: The Animated Series",

"The New Batman Adventures", "Gotham Girls", "Static Shock", and "Justice League". She was also Harley Quinn in the animated features "The Batman Superman Movie: World's Finest" (1997) and "Batman Beyond: Return of the Joker" (2000), and various video games. The character of Harley Quinn became highly popular in the DC Universe, appearing in numerous comic books and films. She was played by Margot Robbie in the films "Suicide Squad" (2016), "Birds of Prey (and the Fantabulous Emancipation of One Harley Quinn)" (2020), and "The Suicide Squad" (2021). She was later voiced in animated productions by Tara Strong, Melissa Rauch, Laura Post, Kaley Cuoco, and others. Sorkin was also a voice actress for episodes of "Taz-Mania" and the 1993 animated film "Batman: Mask of the Phantasm". She appeared in a handful of films during her career including "Trading Places" (1983), "Odd Jobs" (1986), "Oscar" (1991), "Ted & Venus" (1991), "I Don't Buy Kisses Anymore" (1992), and "Comic Book: The Movie" (2004). She wrote the 1997 film "Picture Perfect" and episodes of "Down Home" and "Tiny Toon Adventures". She was a writer and executive producer for episodes of the series "Fired Up" and "How to Marry a Billionaire". Sorkin married television producer Christopher Lloyd in 1995 and is survived by him and their two sons, Eli and Owen.

Spellos, Peter

Actor Peter Spellos, who starred in the slasher film "Slumber Party Massacre II" and provided voice dubbing for numerous animes, died of pancreatic cancer at a hospital in Indianapolis, Indiana, on November 19, 2023. He was 69. Spellos was born in New York City on March 1, 1954. He

appeared in such films as "Opportunity Knocks" (1990), "Sorority House Massacre II" (1990) as the unkillable Orville Ketchum, "Smoothtalker" (1990), "The Guyver" (1991), "Freddy's Dead: The Final Nightmare" (1991), "Munchie" (1992), "Bad Love" (1992), "Hoffa" (1992), "Joshua Tree" (1993), "Little Miss Millions" (1993), "Body Shot" (1994), "Dinosaur Island" (1994), "Munchie Strikes Back" (1994), "In the Army Now" (1994), "Inner Sanctum II" (1994), "Possessed by the Night" (1994), "Victim of Desire" (1995), "Bikini Drive-In" (1995), "Attack of the 60 Foot Centerfolds" (1995), "Droid Gunner" (1995), "Masseuse" (1996), "Night Shade" (1996), "Demolition High" (1996), "Vampirella" (1996) as the Robot voice, "Fugitive Rage" (1996), "Bound" (1996), "Living in Peril" (1997), "Sexual Roulette" (1997), "Mystery on Makeout Mountain" (1997), "Hybrid" (1997), "Vice Girls" (1997), "City of Angels" (1998), "Little Miss Magic" (1998), "Invisible Dad" (1998), "Maximum Security" (1998), "Phoenix" (1998), "The Assault" (1998), "One Hell of a Guy" (1998), "Billy Frankenstein" (1998), "Stealth Fighter" (1999), "Sideshow" (2000), "Brother" (2000), "Agent Red" (2000), "Heartbreakers" (2001), "Love & Support" (2001), "Men in Black II" (2002), "Thirteen Erotic

Ghosts" (2002), "Glass Trap" (2005), "Bikini Chain Gang" (2005), and "Bikini Escort Company" (2006), and "Yes Man" (2008). Spellos was sometimes billed under the name G. Gordon Baer. He was seen on television in episodes of "Growing Pains", "Get a Live", "FBI: The Untold Stories", "Red Shoes Diaries, "The Wonder Years", "Sisters", "Dream On", "VR.5", "Married... with Children", "Sliders", "Weird Science", "Step by Step", "Lois & Clark: The New Adventures of Superman", "Caroline in the City", "Life's Work", "NewsRadio", "Two Guys, a Girl and a Pizza Place", "Rude Awakening", "The Voyeur", "NYPD Blue", "ER", "American Dreams" as Gus from 2002 to 2005, and "Without a Trace". He also appeared in the tele-films "A Child Lost Forever: The Jerry Sherwood Story" (1992), "Perry Mason: The Case of the Telltale Talk Show Host" (1993), "Tyson" (1995), "A Wing and a Prayer" (1998), and "Radio Needles" (2009). Spellos was noted for his numerous voice roles in anime films and television. He was heard in the animes "Lupin the 3rd Part 2", "Eagle Riders", "Mobile Suit Gundam", "Akira", "Fist of the North Star", "El-Hazard: The Wanderers", "Street Fighter II V", "Rurouni Kenshin", "Cowboy Bebop", "Flint the Time Detective", "Outlaw Star", "Trigun", "The Big O", "Digimon: Digital Monsters", "Android Kikaider: The Animation", "Carried by the Wind: Tsukikage Ran", "Transformers: Robots in Disguise" as Sky-Byte, "Cosmo Warrior Zero", "Cyborg 009", "Digimon Tamers" as Meramon, "Rave Master", "s-CRY-ed", "Digimon Frontier", "Ghost in the Shell", "Narut", "The Twelve Kingdoms", "Saiyuki Reload", "Wolf's Rain", "Zatch Bell!", "Bleach", "Samurai Champloo", "Code Geass: Lelouch of the Rebellion", "Ghost Slayers Ayashi", "Kekkaishi", "Blue Dragon", "Gurren Lagann", "Moribito: Guardian of the Spirit".

Spicer, Jerry

Actor and stuntman Jerry Spicer died in Johnson City, Tennessee, on June 6, 2023. He was 64. Spicer was born in Hamilton, Ohio, on September 27, 1958. He served in the U.S.

Army after graduating high school. He made training films for the military during his service. Spicer worked in films and television after his discharge, performing stunts and appearing in small roles. His film credits include "Kiss My Grits" (1982), "No Man's Land" (1987), "Under the Gun" (1987), "Less Than Zero" (1987), "Jack's Back" (1988), "The Wizard of Speed and Time" (1988), "License to Drive" (1988), "Earth Girls Are Easy" (1988), "Dangerous Love" (1988), "Skin Deep" (1989), "Twister" (1989), "Cold Feet" (1989), "Caddie Woodlawn" (1989), "Bad Influence" (1990), "Pump Up the Volume" (1990), "White Palace" (1990), "Peacemaker" (1990), "Highlander II: The Quickening" (1991), "True Colors" (1991), "Rich Girl" (1991), "Alligator II: The Mutation" (1991),

"Liquid Dreams" (1991), "Mobsters" (1991), "Live Wire" (1992), "Miracle Beach" (1992), "The Vagrant" (1992), "Seedpeople" (1992), "Storyville" (1992), "Mom and Dad Save the World" (1992), "The Double O Kid" (1992), "Guncrazy" (1992), "To Protect and Serve" (1992), "Out for Blood" (1992), "Sunset Grill" (1993), "Ring of Fire II: Blood and Steel" (1993), "Relentless 3" (1993), "Betrayal of the Dove" (1993), "Night Eyes Three" (1993), "Firepower" (1993), "Dream Lover" (1993), "No Escape No Return" (1993), "L.A. Wars" (1994), "Save Me" (1994), "Witchcraft VI" (1994), "Naked Gun 33 1/3: The Final Insult" (1994), "Bad Blood" (1994), "The Fantastic Four" (1994), "Prehysteria! 3" (1995), "Serial Killer" (1995), "Cyber-Tracker 2" (1995), "Live Nude Girls" (1995), "Guns & Lipstick" (1995), "One Man's Justice" (1996), "Baby Face Nelson" (1996), "Squanderers" (1995), "Bigfoot: The Unforgettable Encounter" (1995), "Mars" (1997), "The Gravedancers" (2006), and "The Sorcerer's Apprentice" (2010). He worked in television on the tele-films "Stark: Mirror Image" (1986), "Desperate for Love" (1989), "Children of the Bride" (1990), "Stepfather 3" (1992), "The Heart of Justice" (1992), "Sexual Response" (1992), "Based on an Untrue Story" (1993), "Sketch Artist II: Hands That See" (1995), "Suspect Device" (1995), "Piranha" (1995), "Midnight Heat" (1996), "The Outsider" (1997), "The Lost" (2009), and "Battledogs" (2013). Spicer was also a stuntman and actor for such television series as "ABC Afterschool Specials", "Star Trek: The Next Generation", "Star Trek: Voyager", "The Client", "Signs and Wonders", and "L.A. Heat".

Springer, Jerry

Television host Jerry Springer, who oversaw a controversial tabloid talk show for three decades, died of pancreatic cancer in Evanston, Illinois, on April 27, 2023. He was 79. Springer was born in London, England, on February 13, 1944. He immigrated to the United States with his family in

1949 and was raised in New York City. He graduated from Tulane University in 1965 and earned a law degree from Northwestern University in Evanston, Illinois, in 1968. Springer became an adviser to Senator Robert F. Kennedy during his campaign to become the Democratic presidential nominee in 1968. He joined a law firm in Cincinnati after Kennedy's assassination later in the year. He was partner in the law firm Grinker, Sudman & Springer from 1973 to 1985. Springer was the Democratic nominee for the U.S. House of Representatives in 1970 but failed to unseat the Republican incumbent. He was elected to the Cincinnati City Council in 1971. He resigned from the council in April of 1974 after it became public that he had solicited a prostitute and paid for her services by check. He easily returned to the council in the 1975 election and was selected to serve as mayor in 1977.

He left the council in 1981 to make an unsuccessful attempt at attaining the Democratic nomination for Ohio governor in 1982. Springer subsequently joined the local NBC affiliate, WLWT, and political reporter. He rose to become the station's lead news anchor and received ten local Emmy Awards. He began a political talk show, "Jerry Springer", in 1991. He also remained a commentator with WLWT until 1993. He changed the format of "The Jerry Springer Show" in early 1994 and achieved a large audience with his new tabloid-style sensationalism. He was producer and host of the ever-controversial series that was targeted by such groups as the Parents Television Council and American Family Association. It remained popular with the audience and became the inspiration for 2003's "Jerry Springer: The Opera", in England. He also hosted several short-lived series for the British market, "Jerry Springer UK" in 1999 and "The Springer Show" in 2005. "The Jerry Springer Show" eventually ended first-run syndicated episodes in July of 2018. He served as star of the courtroom series "Judge Jerry" from 2019 to 2022. Springer starred as Jerry Farrelly, a talk show host based on himself, in the 1998 film "Ringmaster", which he also produced. His autobiography of the same name was also published in 1998. He appeared in various other films, frequently in cameo roles, including "Meet Wally Sparks" (1997), "Killer Sex Queens from Cyberspace" (1998), "Kissing a Fool" (1998), "The 24 Hour Woman", "A Fare to Remember" (1999), "Austin Powers: The Spy Who Shagged Me" (1999), "Sugar & Spice" (2001), "Undertaking Betty" (2002), "Citizen Verdict" (2003), "Pauly Shore Is Dead" (2003), "The Defender" (2004) as the President of the United States, "Domino" (2005), "And the Winner Is..." (2009), and "Indie Guys" (2016). He was seen on television in episodes of "Married... with Children", "Roseanne", "The X-Files", "NightMan", "The Wayans Bros.", "The Simpsons" voicing himself, "Love Boat: The Next Wave", "Early Edition", "V.I.P.", "Sabrina the Teenage Witch", "Malcolm & Eddie", "Sunset Beach", "Suddenly Susan", "Son of the Beach", "George Lopez", "Days of Our Lives", "Cubed", "Are We There Yet?", "Happy!", "Random Acts of Flyness", "Circus of Chaos", and "The House Arrest Rooneys". He also appeared in the tele-films "Since You've Been Gone" (1998) and "Sharnado 3: Oh Hell No!" (2015). He was host of "America's Got Talent" for the series second and third seasons from 2007 to 2008. Springer was a contestant on the third season of "Dancing with the Stars" in 2006 and performed as the Beetle on "The Masked Singer" in 2022. He hosted the Miss World competition in 2000 and 2001 and Miss Universe in 2008. He was host of episodes of "WWE Raw" in 2010 and 2014 and hosted "Jerry Springer Presents "WWE: Too Hot for TV" for the WWE Network in 2014. He was host of the dating game show "Baggage" on GSN from 2010 to 2015 and the Investigation Discovery series "Tabloid" from 2014 to 2015. Springer was also a guest on numerous other series including "The Bob Braun Show", "An Evening at the Improv", "Crook & Chase", "The Rosie O'Donnell Show", "Night Stand", "Maury", "Talk Soup", "Ruby Wax Meets...", "America's Most Wanted", "Jerry Lewis MDA Labor Day Telethon", "The Chris Rock Show", "The Roseanne Show", "The Basement", "TFI Friday", "This Morning", "Des O'Connor Tonight", "Space Ghost Coast to Coast", "MTV Spring Break", "The Brian Conley Show", "Now or Never, Face Your Fears", "The Cindy Margolis Show", "Celebrity Deathmatch", "Politically Incorrect", "Say What? Karaoke", "The Test", "The Daily Show", "Greed", "Jenny Jones", "Weakest Link", "Rendez-View", "Beat the Geeks", "Revealed with Jules Asner", "Hollywood Squares", "The Late Show with Craig Kilborn", "Whose Line Is It Anyway?", "The Tonight Show with Jay Leno", "V Graham Norton", "On-Air with Ryan Seacrest", "Hell's Kitchen", "Hannity & Colmes", "Crossfire", "Cheap Sets: Without Ron Parker", "Strictly Come Dancing", "The Tony Danza Show", "I've Got a Secret", "The Friday Night Project", "The Megan Mullally Show", "Late Show with David Letterman", "Happy Hour", "Thank God You're Here", "Larry King Live", "American Idol", "Live with Kelly and Mark", "Close-Up", "Last Comic Standing", "Svengoolie", "Nothing But the Truth", "Ant & Dec's Saturday Night Takeaway", "Late Night with Conan O'Brien", "Saturday Kitchen", "Who Do You Think You Are?", "Have I Got News for You", "The Xtra Factor", "Anytime with Bob Kushell", "Planet Soap", "The Late Late Show", "Md TV", "Chris Moyles Quiz Night", "Countdown", "Richard & Judy's New Position", "Britain's Got More Talent", "The Wright Stuff", "Alan Carr: Chatty Man", "Meet the Hasselhoffs", "Holly's World", "Shatner's Raw Nerve", "The Late Late Show with Craig Ferguson", "Sharon Osbourne: A Comedy Roast", "The Soup", "Chelsea Lately", "Piers Morgan's Life Stories", "Conan", "Lopez Tonight", "Jimmy Kimmel Live!", "Joy Behar: Say Anything!", "The Talk", "I Get That a Lot", "Hannity", "Trust Us with Your Life", "Piers Morgan Live", "Hollywood Uncensored with Sam Rubin", "Question Time", "Full Throttle Saloon", "Rachael Ray", "The Neighbors", "The Arsenio Hall Show", "The Steve Wilkos Show", "Big Morning Buzz Live", "PoliticKING with Larry King", "Sidewalks Entertainment", "Hello Ross!", "Loose Women", "8 Out of 10 Cats", "Bethenny", "The Mommy Show", "Who Wants to Be a Millionaire", "The View", "Huffpost Live", "Celebrity Name Game", "Ice & Coco", "Through the Keyhole", "At Home with Steph & Dom", "Celebrity Juice", "The Meredith Vieira Show", "The Edge and Christian Show Totally Reeks of Awesomeness", "Steve Harvey", "The Saturday Show", "Original Sin: Sex", "Ridiculousness", "The Domenick Nati Show", "The Raw World", "Drop the Mic", "The One Show", "Steve", "All Round to Mrs. Brown's", "The Sit Down with Patrick Bet-David", "Good Morning Britain", "Celebrity Family Feud", "Today", "GMA3: Strahan, Sara & Keke", "Larry King Now", "The Kelly Clarkson Show", "Access Hollywood", "First Look", "A Little Late with Lilly Singh", "Nick Cannon", "The Simonetta Lein Show", "The Wendy Williams Show", "The Good Dish", and "Daily Blast Live". He briefly appeared on Broadway as the Narrator in "The Rocky Horror Show" in late 2001 and was Billy Flynn in the musical revival of "Chicago" in 2009. He considered a return to politics in the early 2000s but decided against runs for the U.S. Senate in 2000 and 2004. Springer married Micki Velton in 1973 and is survived by her and their daughter, Katie.

Squires, Dougie

British choreographer Dougie Squires died in England on May 21, 2023. He was 91. Squires was born in Long Eaton, Derbyshire, England, on February 16, 1932. He was active in local amateur drama groups and worked as an accountant. He moved to London in the early 1950s where he studied dance with Audrey de Vos while working as a waiter. He began touring the country in revues and pantomimes in 1954 and staged variety programs in Glasgow. He made his television debut in the groundbreaking pop music series "Cool for Cats" on ITV in 1956. He soon became choreographer of the show's dancers, who became known as the Dougie Squires Dancers, during its five-year run. He continued to choreograph for such television series as "The Alma Cogan Show", "On the Bright Side", "Russ Conway", "The Jimmy Logan Show", "Showtime", "Ask Anne", "The Singing Years", "The Country and Western Show", "The Dick Emery Show", "Singalong Saturday", "Song Boat", "Zodiac", "The George Mitchell Choir: Around the World in Song", "Something Special", "Glamor...", "International Cabaret", and "Man in a Suitcase". Squires formed and trained the Young Generation dancing troupe, which consisted of 15 male and 15 female dancers. They became regular performers on "The Rolf Harris Show" in 1967. They starred in their own "The Young Generation" show in 1970. They performed regularly on the "It's Lulu" series from 1970 to 1970 and appeared in specials with Shirley Bassey, Rod McKuen, Vera Lynn, and Engelbert Humperdinck. He also developed a similar group, the Second Generation, in the early 1970s. They had a short-lived series, "2Gs and the Pop People", on ITV in 1972. Squires also directed various stage productions. He continued to work in television on such series as "Max Bygraves Says 'I Wanna Tell You a Story'", "Hi! Summer", "The Les Dawson Show", "Lena Zavaroni and Music", "Mike Yarwood in Persons", "Show-Express", and "Grace Kennedy". He was choreographer and stage director for numerous royal pageants. Squires is survived by his life-partner of 45 years, Antony Jones, who he married in 2015.

Squires, Rosemary

British singer Rosemary Squires died in England on August 8, 2023. She was 94. She was born Joan Rosemary Yarrow in Bristol, England, on December 7, 1928. She began singing and playing piano while in secondary school in Salisbury. She performed at army bases and became a singer with big bands led by Ted Heath, Geraldo, and Cyril Stapleton. Squires moved to London in 1948 where she was featured on BBC radio programs "Melody Time" and "Workers' Playtime". She also made numerous recordings in the 1950s and 1960s. She starred as the Wife in the television comedy series "Let's Stay Home" in 1956. Squires performed frequently on television in such series as "Off the Record", "Six-Five Special", "The Lenny the Lion Show", "After Hours", "The

Melody Dances", "Musical Playhouse", "The Black and White Minstrel Show", "Music Shop", "Saturday Spectacular", "Words and Music", "Home in Time", "The Arthur Haynes Show", "Young at Heart", "The Ken Dodd Show", "The Charlie Chester Music Hall", "A Swingin' Time", "Two of a Kind", "Thank Your Lucky Stars", "Open House", "Five O'Clock Club", "The Mike Douglas Show", "The Tonight Show Starring Johnny Carson", "Juke Box Jury", "The Dickie Valentine Show", "The Norman Vaughan Show", "Doddy's Music Box", "Dee Time", "Zingalong", "Glamour...", "The Good Old Days", "Looks Familiar", and The Sooty Show". Squires was married to Frank Lockyer from 1991 until his death in 2020.

St. John, Betta

American-British actress Betta St. John, who was featured in the horror films "Corridors of Blood" and "Horror Hotel", died at an assisted living facility in Brighton, England, on June 23, 2023. She was 93. She was born Betty Jean Striegler in Hawthorne, California, on November 26, 1929. She began her career as a child actress and was part of the Meglin Kiddies troupe of young performers. She made her film debut as an uncredited child singer in the 1939 western "Destry". She was a tap dancer in the 1940 "Our Gang" short "Waldo's Last Stand" and played orphans in "Lydia" (1941) and "Jane Eyre" (1943). St. John was featured in the Broadway musical "Carousel" from 1945 to 1947 and was part of the touring company through 1949. She starred as Liat in the Rodgers and Hammerstein musical "South Pacific" in 1949 and accompanied the production to London. She met British actor and singer Peter Grant while performing in London and they married in 1952. She returned to the screen as the exotic Princess Tarji in the 1953 romantic comedy "Dream Wife" with Cary Grant and Deborah Kerr. St. John was featured as Miriam in the Biblical epic "The Robe" (1953) starring Richard Burton. Her other films include "All the Brothers Were Valiant" (1953), "Dangerous Mission" (1954), "The Saracen Blade" (1954), "The Student Prince" (1954), the William Castle western "The Law vs. Billy the Kid" (1954), "The Naked Dawn" (1955), the psychological mystery "Alias John Preston" (1955) opposite Christopher Lee, "High Tide at Noon" (1957), and the Hammer thriller "The Snorkel" (1958). She was leading lady in two films starring Gordon Scott as Tarzan, 1957's "Tarzan and the Lost Safari" as Diana Penrod and 1960's "Tarzan the Magnificent" as Fay Ames. St. John was featured as Susan in body snatching period thriller "Corridors of Blood" (1958) with

Boris Karloff and Christopher Lee and was Patricia Russell in the 1960 supernatural horror film "Horror Hotel" (aka "The City of the Dead") with Christopher Lee and Dennis Lotis. She appeared on television in productions of "All My Sons" (1958), "Johnny Belinda" (1958), and "Proud Passage" (1959), and episodes of "The Vise", "The Count of Monte Cristo", "Rheingold Theatre", "the Errol Flynn Theatre", "The Invisible Man", "Armchair Theatre", "The Four Just Men", "International Detective", "Rendezvous", and "The Third Man". She retired from the screen in the early 1960s to raise a family. St. John was married to actor Peter Grant from 1952 until his death in 1992. She is survived by their son, television producer Roger Grant, and daughters Karen and Deanna.

Stafford, Baird

Actor Philip 'Baird' Stafford, who starred in the extreme 1981 slasher film "Nightmare", died of respiratory

failure at a hospital in West Melbourne, Florida, on February 4, 2023. He was 75. Stafford was born in Boulder, Colorado, on April 23, 1947. he attended the University of Colorado at Boulder from 1965 to 1968, studying English and literature. He became active on stage, appearing in productions of numerous plays in the Florida area. He was an actor, director and teacher at the Surfside Playhouse, Playwrights Workshop of Brevard, and the Brevard Community College Experimental Theatre. Stafford starred as George Tatum in Romano Scavolini's graphic horror film "Nightmare" in 1981. The extreme violence in the film resulted in it receiving a X rating in the United States and was banned for obscenity as a "video nasty" in the United Kingdom. Clips from the film were featured in several documentaries including "Fear, Panic & Censorship" (2000), "Ban the Sadist Videos!" (2005), and "Video Nasties: Moral Panic, Censorship & Videotape" (2010), and the 2021 psychological horror film "Censor". Stafford reunited with director Scavolini for the violent Vietnam War film "Dog Tags" in 1987. He later worked as a photographer, writer, and editor for various small publishers. He an early contributor to the internet, working with several Pagan and Wiccan groups. He was co-founder of the Information Systems Security Association, serving as president for nearly three decades. Stafford is survived by his husband of 33 years, Harvey Newstrom.

Stafford, Maeliosa

Irish-Australian actor Maeliosa Stafford died in Sydney, Australia, on April 11, 2023. He was 66. Stafford was born in Galway, Ireland, on December 15, 1956. He made his debut on the local stage at the age of five. He joined the student drama society while attending University College, Galway, and joined the newly formed Druid Theatre Company in 1978. He performed with the group over the next decade. He settled in

Australia in 1989 and was a co-founder of the O'Punksky's Theatre Company in Sydney in 1990 with John O'Hare. He

returned to Ireland for three years to serve as artistic director of Druid in the early 1990s. He rejoined O'Punsky's in Australia in 1994. Stafford appeared on television in productions of "Cuirt an Mhean Oiche" (1985) and "The Playboy of the Western World" (1986). He was also seen in episodes of "Acropolis Now", "Stingers", "White Collar Blue", and "Rake". He was featured as Grandad in the series "Drop Dead Weird" from 2017 to 2019. Stafford also appeared in the films "Eat the Peach" (1986), "The Fantasist" (1986), "Quigley Down Under" (1990), "Me Myself I" (1999), "Burke & Wills" (2006), "Ride Like a Girl" (2019), and "Evicted! A Modern Romance" (2022). He was married and divorced from Joyce McGreevy, and is survived by their son, Eoghan. He met Carolyn Forde in 1988 and they soon married. He is also survived by her and their three children.

Stanley, Ginger

Actress and model Ginger Stanley, who was the underwater stunt double for Julie Adams in the 1954 Universal horror classic "Creature from the Black Lagoon", died in Orlando, Florida, on January 19, 2023. She was 91. Stanley was born in Sandersville, Georgia, on December 19, 1931. She

moved to Sebring, Florida, in her early teens to live with an older sister. She met swimming promoter Newt Perry in the early 1950s and he hired her as a professional mermaid at the Weeki Wachee Springs tourist attraction. She appeared in a small role in the 1951 film "Distant Drums". She was a swimmer and underwater model for photographer Bruce Mozert at Silver Springs from 1953 to 1956. Stanley served as the swimming double for actress Julie Adams in the 1954 horror classic "Creature from the Black Lagoon", working with Ricou Browning, who portrayed the Creature in underwater sequences. She was swimming double for Lori Nelson in the 1955 sequel "Revenge of the Creature". She did underwater stunts for the films "Jupiter's Darling" (1955) and "Don't Give Up the Ship" (1959), and later appeared in small roles in the films "The Meal" (1975), "Splash, Too" (1988), and "Passenger 57" (1992). She worked as a fashion model for many years and taught at the Lisa Maile Image Modeling and Acting School. Stanley was married to Albert V. Hallowell, Jr., from 1956 until his death in 1987 and they had three daughters, Dawn, Heather, and Shannon.

Steeger, Ingrid

German actress Ingrid Steeger died of an intestinal obstruction in Bad Hersfeld, Germany, on December 22, 2023. She was 76. She was born Ingrid Stengert in Berlin, Germany, on April 1, 1947. She worked as a secretary while attending school and was discovered by a photographer for men's magazines. She was soon appearing on covers and pinups. The attractive blonde was soon appearing in films, frequently in decorative roles in adult comedies. She was featured in such films as "A Belles Dents" (1966), "Gorilla Gang" (1968), "Der Partyphotograph" (1968), "The

Swingin' Pussycats" (1969), the adult short "Die Perverse Herrin und ihre Opfer" (1969), "Die Liebestollen Baronessen" (1970), "Higher and Higher" (1970), "The Sex Adventures of the Three Musketeers" (1971), "Der Lusterne Turke" (1971), "Angels of Terror" (1971), "The Young Seducers" (1971), "Husbands-Report" (1971), "Die Goldene Banane von Bad Porno" (1971), "Die Stewardessen" (1971), "Ready, Willing and Able" (1971), "Ein Langer Ritt Nach Eden" (1971), "Lonely Wives" (1972), "Swingin' Models" (1972), "Young Seducers 2" (1971), "Wedding Night Report" (1972), "The Swinging Co-eds" (1972), "Massagesalon der Jungen Madchen" (1972), "Schoolgirl Report Part 4: What Drives Parents to Despair" (1972), "Nurses Report" (1972), "Blutjenge Verfuhrerinnen 3. Teil" (1972), "Hausfrauen Report International" (1973), "Liebe in Drei Dimensionen" (1973), "Hostess in Heat" (1973), "Schoolgirl Report Part 5: What All Parents Should Know" (1973), "Junge Madchen Mogen's Heiss, Hausfrauen Noch Heisser" (1973), "Swap Meet at the Love Shack" (1973), "Drei Manner im Schnee" (1974), "Andre Schafft Sie Alle" (1985), "Paul Is Dead" (2000), and "Goldene Zeiten" (2006). Steeger was seen frequently on television with roles in episodes of "Die Theaterwerkstatt", "Der Kommissar", "Munchner Geschichten", "Lokalseite Unten Links", "Beschlossen und Verkundet", "Die Gimmicks", "Blauer Dunst", the comedy series "Klimbim" as the host, Gabi Klimbim, from 1973 to 1979, "Susi" as Susi Paschke from 1980 to 1981, "Lach Mal Wieder", "Zwei Schwarze Schafe (Geschichten aus Kalmusel)", "Glucklich Geschieden...", "Die Krimistunde", "Unternehmen Kopenick", "Urlaub auf Italienisch", "Loberg", "Kontakt Bitte...", "Derrick", "Justitias Kleine Fische", "Pension corona", "Edgar, Huter del Moral", "Gluckliche Reise", "Der Millionar", "Familie Heinz Becker", "Geschichten aus der Heimat", "Zwei Schlitzohren in Antalya", "Zwei alte Hasen", "Corinna", "Grosstadtrevier", "Rosamunde Pilcher", "Heimatgeschichten", "Manner Sind was Wunderbares", "A Case for Two", "CityExpress", "SOKO Munchen", "Freunde furs Leben" as Loni from 1999 to 2001, "Klinikum Berlin Mitte - Leben in Bereitschaft", "Gute Zeiten, Schlechte Zeiten" as Karin Blum in 2002, "Bewegte Manner", "Edel & Starck", "Our Charly", and "Der Pfundskerl". Her television credits also include productions of "Auf Befehl

Erschossen - Die Bruder Sass, Einst Berlins Grosse Ganoven" (1972), "Die Autozentauren" (1972), "Ein Haus Voll Zeit" (1973), "Strychnin und Saure Drops" (1974), "Berlin Grusst Bern" (1975), "Manchmal Marchen" (1976), "Die Klempner Kommen" (1976), "Zwei Himmlische Tochter" (1978), "Warten auf Hugo" (1986), "Wilder Western Inclusive" (1988), "Von Mord Wird Abgeraten" (1989), "Der Neue Mann" (1990), "Sonne, Meer und 1000 Palmen" (1991), "Der Grosse Bellheim" (1993), "Ein Bock Zuviel" (1993), "Die Blaue Kanone" (1999), and "Crazy Race 2 - Warum die Mauer Wirklich Fiel" (2004). Steeger was married to cameraman Lothar E. Stickelbrucks from 1973 until their divorce in 1975. She was married to Tom LaBlanc from 1992 until their divorce in 1995. She had numerous romantic partners including Peter Koenecke, French actor Jean-Paul Zehnacker, director Dieter Wedel, and Swiss actor Bernd Seebacher.

Steelman, Ron

Actor Ron Steelman died in Holmdel, New Jersey, on July 31, 2023. He was 77. Steelman was born in Columbus, Ohio, on May 20, 1946. He

graduated from Ohio State University. He performed as an actor on stage with numerous regional theatrical companies in the 1970s and 1980s. He appeared on local television station WBNS as Ron the Mailman on the children's television program "Friendly Junction" from 1972 to 1975. He also appeared in episodes of the children's series "Luci's Toyshop". Steelman was seen on television in episodes of "ALF", "Murder, She Wrote", and Seinfeld". He also appeared in the 1992 film "Out for Blood". He worked in advertising with Steelman Media, producing local television and radio commercials. He is survived by his wife of 34 years, Elaine Rowe Smith, a son, and a daughter.

Stein, Seymour

Music executive Seymour Stein, who was co-founder of Sire Records, died of cancer in

Los Angeles, California, on April 2, 2023. He was 80. He was born Seymour Steinbigle in New York City on April 18, 1942. He began working as a clerk at the music industry magazine "Billboard" in his early teens. He assisted Tommy Noonan in developing the Billboard Hot 100 charts in 1958. He began working for Syd Nathan at King Records in Cincinnati, Ohio, in the late 1950s. He returned to New York City in 1963 and briefly worked for Herb Abramson. He soon became an assistant to George Goldner at Red Bird Records. Stein and record producer Richard Gottehrer founded Sire Productions in 1966. Gottehrer left Sire in 1974 and Stein signed the Ramones to the label the following year. He soon had such artists as Talking Heads, Richard Hell & the Voidoids, the Pretenders, and the Rezillos at Sire. He was instrumental in promoting new wave genre music, a term he preferred to punk. He signed Madonna to the label in 1982 and other artists who recorded at Sire include Depeche Mode, the Smiths, the Replacements, the Cure, Ice-T, the Undertones, Ministry, and Echo & the Bunnymen. He remained as president of Sire Records and vice president of Warner Bros. Records until his retirement in 2018. Stein was inducted into the Rock and Roll Hall of Fame in 2005. His autobiography, "Siren Song: My Life in Music", was published in 2018. He was married to music promoter Linda Stein from 1970 until their divorce in 1979. He is survived by their daughter, filmmaker Mandy Stein, who directed the 2009 film "Burning Down the House: The Rise and Fall of CBGB". Another daughter, Samantha, died of brain cancer in 2013.

Steinberg, Norman

Screenwriter and producer Norman Steinberg, who co-wrote Mel Brooks' 1974 comedy classic "Blazing Saddles",  died in Hudson Valley, New York, on March 15, 2023. He was 83. Steinberg was born in Brooklyn, New York, on June 6, 1939. He graduated from the University of Maryland in 1961 and earned a law degree from the University of Pittsburgh School of Law in 1964. He worked in copyright law in Manhattan before he began writing comedy for television. He wrote for David Frye's comedy album "I Am the President" in 1969 which earned a Grammy Award. He wrote for the CBS summer replacement series "Comedy Tonight" in 1970 and shared an Emmy Award for writing the NBC comedy series "Flip" in 1971. Steinberg wrote for the series "The Corner Bar" in 1972 and for television productions of "Aquacade in Acapulco" (1972), "The Wonderful World of Aggravation" (1972), "Season's Greetings from Mike Douglas" (1972), "Alan King Looks Back in Anger: A Review of 1972" (1973), "The Many Faces of Comedy" (1973), "Free to Be... You and Me" (1974), "Energy Crisis" (1974), and "Ann in Blue" (1974). He and writing partner, Alan Uger, a former dentist, co-wrote Mel Brooks' 1974 comedy classic "Blazing Saddles". He was a producer and script consultant for Brooks' 1975 television series "When Things Were Rotten". Steinberg also co-wrote the films "Yes, Giorgio" (1982), "My Favorite Year" (1982), "Mr. Mom" (1983) providing uncredited revisions, "Out of Order" (1984), "Johnny Dangerously" (1984), "Wise Guys" (1986), "Funny About Love" (1990), and "Paws of Fury: The Legend of Hank" (2022). He appeared in small roles in several films including "Yes, Giorgio" (1982), "My Favorite Year" (1982), "Johnny Dangerously" (1984), and "Miami Rhapsody" (1995). He wrote and frequently produced such television productions as "Roosevelt and Truman" (1977),

"The Bay City Amusement Company" (1977) which he also directed, "In the Beginning" (1978), "The Six O'Clock Follies" (1980), "The Ellen Burstyn Show" (1986), "Doctor Doctor" (1989-1991), "Teech" (1991), "Cosby" (1998), "Raising Dad" (2002), "Touch 'Em All McCall" (2003), "The 76th Annual Academy Awards" (2004), "Paradise" (2004), and "Chemistry" (2011). He was executive producer of the tele-films "Paradise" (2004), "Then Comes Marriage" (2004), "Red Hook (2012), and "Fireside" (2018). He also directed episodes of "The Ellen Burstyn Show", "Doctor Doctor", and "Raising Dad". He was married and divorced from Bonnie Steinberg and is survived by their son and daughter. He is also survived by his wife, Serine.

Stephens, Garn

Actress Garn Stephens died on April 14, 2023. She was 87. Stephens was born in Tulsa, Oklahoma, on November 7, 1944. She began her career on stage and appeared on  Broadway in productions of "Father's Day" (1971) and "Grease" (1972). She was seen on television in episodes of "All in the Family", "Phyllis" as Harriet Hastings from 1976 to 1977, "Charlie's Angels", "Barney Miller", "Family Ties", "Foley Square", "Buck James", "Have Faith", "Falcon Crest", and "Quantum Leap" as Gladys Presley. Her other television credits include productions of "Please Call It Murder" (1975), "Blind Ambition" (1979), "Portrait of a Rebel: The Remarkable Mrs. Sanger" (1980), "The Seduction of Miss Leona" (1980), "Princess Daisy" (1983) as Candice Bloom, "Children in the Crossfire" (1985), "Killer Instinct" (1988), "Family of Spies" (1990), and "Something to Live For: The Alison Gertz Story" (1992). Stephens was featured in several films including "The Sunshine Boys" (1975), the horror film "Halloween III: Season of the Witch" (1982) as the ill-fated Marge Guttman, and "Jake's M.O." (1987). She also worked as a screenwriter, scripting episodes of "St. Elsewhere" earning an Emmy Award nomination in 1984, "Trapper John, M.D.", "Hotel", and "Trial by Jury". Stephens was married to her "Halloween III" co-star Tom Atkins from 1976 until their divorce in 1985. She was later involved with guitarist Stuart Niemi and is survived by their son, Spencer Baird Niemi.

Sterlin, Jenny

Actress Jenny Sterlin died on December 23, 2023. She was born in England and trained as an actress at Birmingham Theatre School. She began her career on stage in England with a repertory company. She was a founder of the experimental Living Theater. She later moved to the United States where she earned a degree in psychology and English literature. Sterlin appeared frequently on stage and was seen in Broadway productions of "Design for Living" (2001), "Major Barbara" (2001), "Heartbreak House" (2006), and "Macbeth" (2013). Sterlin was seen on television in episodes of "Hope & Faith",

"Law & Order", "Gossip Girl", "White Collar", "Divorce", "The Marvelous Mrs. Maisel", "New Amsterdam", and "Evil". She was featured in several films including "Happy End" (2003), "Blood, Sand and Gold" (2018), and "Tower of Silence" (2019). Sterlin was noted as an audiobook narrator for numerous works including Laurie King's mysteries "Pirate King" and "The Language of Bees" and Deborah Crombie's Duncan Kincaid/Gemma James series. She narrated children's books including Eva Ibbotson's "The Beasts of Clawstone Castle".

Sterling, Lester

Jamaican musician Lester 'Ska' Sterling, who was a founding member of the band the Skatalites, died in Jamaica on May 16, 2023. He was 87. Sterling was born in Kingston, Jamaica, on January 31, 1936. He performed alto saxophone with the Jamaica Military Band in the 1950s. He joined Val Bennett's band in 1957 and was a session musician at Kingston studios in the late 1950s and early 1960s. He was a founding member of the ska band the Skatalites in 1964. They recorded the 1964 album "Ska Authentic" in 1964 and broke up the following year. Sterling subsequently joined Byron Lee & the Dragonaires. He had a solo debut album, "Bangarang", from Pama Records in 1969. He reunited with the Skatalites in 1975 and remained a constant presence in their often-changing lineup through 2014. He released a second solo album, "Sterling Silver", in 2002.

Sternhagen, Frances

Actress Frances Sternhagen, who received two Tony Awards for her work on Broadway and was featured in the recurring role of Cliff Claven's mother, Esther, on the television comedy series "Cheers", died at her home in New Rochelle, New York, on November 27, 2023. She was 93. Sternhagen was born in Washington, D.C., on January 13, 1930. She graduated from Vasser College in 1951 and did graduate work at the Catholic University of America. She trained as an actress at the Perry Mansfield School of the Theatre and the Neighborhood Playhouse in New York City. She taught song and dance to children at the Milton Academy in Massachusetts. She made her stage debut at the summer theater at Bryn Mawr in 1948. She performed at the Arena Stage in Washington, D.C., from 1953 to 1954. Sternhagen made her Broadway debut as Miss T. Muse in a 1955 production of "The Skin of Our Teeth". She appeared frequently on Broadway during the next fifty years appearing in productions of "The Carefree Tree" (1955), "Viva Madison Avenue!" (1960), "Great Day in the

Morning" (1962), "The Right Honourable Gentleman" (1965), "You Know I Can't Hear You When the Water's Running" (1967), "The Cocktail Party" (1968), "Cock-A-Doodle Dandy" (1969), "Blood Red Roses" (1970), "The Playboy of the Western World" (1971), "All Over" (1971), and "Mary Stuart" (1971). She received a Tony Award nomination for her

featured role as Mavis Parodus Bryson in the 1972 play "The Sign in Sidney Brustein's Window". Sternhagen received a Tony for Best Featured Actress for 1973's "The Good Doctor" and 1995's "The Heiress" as Lavinia Penniman. She earned additional Tony nominations for the plays" Equus" (1975) as Dora Strang, "Angel" (1978), "On Golden Pond" (1979) originating the role of Ethel Thayer, and "Morning's at Seven" (2002). Her other Broadway credits include "Enemies" (1972), "The Father" (1981), "Grown Ups" (1981), "You Can't Take It with You" (1983), "Home Front" (1985), "The Heiress" (1995), "Steel Magnolias" (2005), and "Seascape" (2005). Sternhagen appeared in numerous off-Broadway plays and received an Obie Award for life-time achievement in 2013. She was also seen on television from the mid-1950s with roles in episodes of "Producers' Showcase", "Omnibus", "Studio One", "Goodyear Playhouse", "Play of the Week", "The Doctors and the Nurses", "The Defenders", "Profiles in Courage", "For the People", "NET Playhouse, "Great Performances", "The American Parade", and "The Andros Targets". She was featured in the soap operas "Love of Life" as Toni Prentiss Davis from 1967 to 1968, "The Doctors" as Phyllis Corrigan" in 1970, "Another World" as Jane Overstreet in 1971, and "The Secret Storm" as Jessie Reddin from 1973 to 1974. She was Millie Sprague in the comedy series "Spencer" in 1985 and was Gina Williams in Stephen King's "Golden Years" in 1991. She appeared in the recurring role of Esther Clavin in the hit sit-com "Cheers" from 1986 to 1993, earning two Emmy Award nominations, and was Charlotte Babineaux in the short-lived drama series "The Road Home" in 1994. She also had recurring roles as Millicent 'Gamma' Carter in "ER" from 1997 to 2003, as Bunny MacDougal in "Sex and the City" from 2000 to 2002, earning another Emmy nomination, and as Willie Ray Johnson in "The Closer" from 2006 to 2012. Her other television credits include episodes of "The Days and Nights of Molly Dodd", "Tales from the Crypt", "The Outer Limits", "Law & Order", the animated "The Simpsons" in a voice role, "Becker", and "Parenthood". Sternhagen appeared in such tele-films and mini-series as "Who'll Save Our Children?" (1978), "Mother and Daughter: The Loving War" (1980), "The Man That Corrupted Hadleyburg" (1980), "Prototype" (1983), "The Dining Rome" (1984), "Resting Place" (1986), "At Mother's Request" (1987), "Once Again" (1987), "Follow Your Heart" (1990), "She Woke Up" (1992), "Labor of Love: The Arlette Schweitzer Story" (1993), "Reunion" (1994), "The Con" (1998), "To Live Again"

(1998), and "The Laramie Project" (2002). She made her film debut as librarian Charlotte Wolf in the 1967 schoolhouse drama "Up the Down Staircase". She was also seen in the films "The Tiger Makes Out" (1967), the black comedy "The Hospital" (1971) as Mrs. Cushing, "Two People" (1973), "Fedora" (1978), "Starting Over" (1979), the science fiction "Outland" (1981) as Doc Marian Lazarus opposite Sean Connery's Marshal William T. O'Niel, "Independence Day" (1983), "Romantic Comedy" (1983), "Bright Lights, Big City" (1988), "See You in the Morning" (1989), The science fiction "Communion" (1989), "Sibling Rivalry" (1990), the Stephen King thriller "Misery" (1990) as Deputy Virginia, "Doc Hollywood" (1991) starring Michael J. Fox, King's Brian DePalma's psychological horror "Raising Cain" (1992) as Dr. Waldheim, "It All Came True" (1998), "The Rising Place" (2001), "Landfall" (2001), "Highway" (2002), the 2007 adaptation of King's horror novella "The Mist" as Irene Reppler, "Julie & Julia" (2009), "Dolphin Tale" (2011), and "And So It Goes" (2014). Sternhagen was married to actor Thomas A. Carlin from 1956 until his death in 1991. She is survived by their four sons and two daughters.

Stevens, April

Singer April Stevens died in Scottsdale, Arizona, on April 17, 2023. She was 93. She was born Caroline Vincinette LoTempio in Niagara Falls, New York, on April 29, 1929. Her younger brother, Anthony LoTempio, began singing as a child.

The family moved to Los Angeles where April attended high school. She began her career as a recording artist at RCA Victor in 1951. She had hits with the singles "I'm in Love Again", "Gimme a Little Kiss, Will Ya, Huh?", and "And So to Sleep Again". Stevens was featured in a cameo role in the 1955 film "The Big Tip Off". She returned to the charts later in the decade with the 1959 hit "Teach Me Tiger". An album of the same name was released the following year. Stevens was best known for her 1963 recording of "Deep Purple" with her young brother, now known as Nino Tempo. The duo performed on "American Bandstand" and the song earned a Grammy Award for Best Rock and Roll Recording. They continued to sing together over the next decade on such records as "Whispering", "All Strung Out", and "The Coldest Night of the Year". She retired from singing by the early 1980s. Her autobiography, "Teach Me Tiger", was released in 2013. Stevens married William Perman in 1985 and he survives her.

Stevens, Rory

Child actor Rory Stevens died in Calabasas, California, on November 30, 2023. He was 69. He was born Rory Shevin in Los Angeles, California, on April 9, 1954. He began acting at the age of five under the name Rory Stevens. He appeared frequently on television from the early 1960s with roles in episodes of "Wagon Train", "The Andy Griffith Show",

"General Electric Theater", "Dr. Kildare", "Leave It to Beaver", "McKeever and the Colonel", "Going My Way", "Sam Benedict", "Alcoa Premiere", "The Lloyd Bridges Show", "Bonanza", "My Favorite Martian", "Slattery's People", "Kraft Suspense Theatre", "Gomer Pyle, USMC", "The Legend of Jesse James", "Bewitched", "The Virginian", "The Long, Hot Summer", "Please Don't Eat the Daisies", "The Munsters", "Laredo", "The Fugitive", "My Three Sons", "Pistols 'n' Petticoats", "The Felony Squad", "This Is the Life", "Adam-12", "Daniel Boone", "The Brady Bunch", "Room 222", "One Day at a Time", and "Lou Grant". Stevens was seen in several films including "The Birds" (1963), "Carrie" (1976), "Ruby" (1977), and "Malibu Beach" (1978). He retired from the screen by the late 1970s. His autobiography, "My Life as a Child Actor: Chaos, Cruelty, & Laughter", was published in 2022.

Stevens, Stella

Actress Stella Stevens, who starred with Jerry Lewis in "The Nutty Professor" and Elvis Presley in "Girls! Girls! Girls!", died from complications from Alzheimer's disease in

Los Angeles, California, on February 18, 2023. She was 84. She was born Estelle Eggleston in Yazoo City, Mississippi, on October 1, 1938, and moved to Memphis, Tennessee, with her parents at the age of four. She attended Memphis State University where she appeared in a stage production of "Bus Stop". She moved to Los Angeles in 1959 where she signed with 20th Century Fox. She made her film debut in a small role in 1959's "Say One for Me". She was also seen in "The Blue Angel" (1959). She was soon signed by Paramount and starred as sultry Appassionata Von Climax in the 1959 film version of the Broadway musical "Li'l Abner". Stevens was featured as Playboy's Playmate of the Month in January of 1960. The pictorial gave a boost to her film career, and she became a celluloid sex symbol. She appeared in the films "Man-Trap" (1961) and "Too Late Blues" (1961) opposite Bobby Darin. She starred as Robin Gantner in Elvis Presley's 1962 film "Girls! Girls! Girls!" and was Stella Purdy, the sexy student and love interest of Jerry Lewis' "The Nutty Professor" in 1963. Her other films include "The Courtship of Eddie's Father" (1963) as Dollye Daly, the comedy western "Advance to the Rear" (1964), the drama "Synanon" (1965), "The Secret of My Success" (1965), the spy spoof "The Silencers" (1966) starring Dean Martin as Matt Helm, "Rage" (1966), "How to Save a Marriage and Ruin Your Life" (1968), "Sol Madrid"

(1968), "Where Angels Go Trouble Follows!" (1968) as Sister George, and the horror film "The Mad Room" (1969) with Shelley Winters. Stevens appeared frequently on television in the early 1960s with roles in episodes of "Alfred Hitchcock Presents", "Johnny Ringo", "Hawaiian Eye", "Bonanza" as a deaf mute in the 1960 episode "Silent Thunder", "Riverboat", "General Electric Theater", "Follow the Sun", "Frontier Circus", "Vacation Playhouse", "Ben Casey" in the recurring role of Jane Hancock in 1964, "The Bob Hope Show", "The Bing Crosby Show", "The Joey Bishop Show, "The Irv Kupcinet Show", "The David Frost Show", and "The Tonight Show Starring Johnny Carson". She continued her film career in the 1970s, starring as Hildy opposite Jason Robards, Jr., in the Sam Peckinpah comedy western "The Ballad of Cable Hogue". Her other films include the spaghetti western "A Town Called Hell" (1971), "Stand Up and Be Counted" (1972), and the blaxploitation film "Slaughter" (1972) with Jim Brown. Stevens starred as Linda Rogo, the ex-prostitute wife of Ernest

Borgnine's retired policeman, in Irwin Allen's all-star disaster epic "The Poseidon Adventure" (1972) with Gene Hackman, Shelley Winters, Jack Albertson, and Roddy McDowall. She also appeared in the horror comedy "Arnold" (1973), "Cleopatra Jones and the Casino of Gold" (1975) as Bianca Javin, the Dragon Lady, foe of Tamara Dobson's Cleopatra Jones, "Las Vegas Lady" (1975), Peter Bogdanovich's "Nickelodeon" (1976), the horror film "The Manitou" (1978) starring Tony Curtis, "Wacko" (1982), "Ladies Night" (1983), the women-in-prison exploitation film "Chained Heat" (1983), "Mister Deathman" (1983), "The Longshot" (1986), "Monster in the Closet" (1987), "Down the Drain" (1990), "Mom" (1990), the horror film "The Terror Within II" (1991) directed by her son Andrew Stevens, "Last Call" (1991), "The Nutt House" (1992), "Exiled in America" (1992), "Eye of the Stranger" (1993), "South Beach" (1993), "Little Devils: The Birth" (1993), "Hard Drive" (1994), Point of Seduction: Body Chemistry III" (1994), "Molly & Gina" (1994), "Illicit Dreams" (1994), the horror comedy "The Granny" (1995) in the title role, "Virtual Combat" (1995), "Body Chemistry 4: Full Exposure" (1995), Fred Olen Ray's science fiction film "Star Hunter" (1996), "Invisible Mom" (1996), "Bikini Hotel" (1997), "The Long Ride Home" (2003), "Blessed" (2004), "Glass Trap" (2005), "Hell to Pay" (2005), "Popstar" (2005), the short "Dante's Inferno: Abandon All Hope" (2010), and the monster movie "Megaconda" (2010). She concentrated more on television from the 1970s with roles in the tele-films and mini-series "In Broad Daylight" (1971), "Climb an Angry Mountain" (1972), "Linda" (1973), "Honky Tonk" (1974), "The Day the Earth Moved" (1974), "Kiss Me, Kill Me" (1976), "Wanted: The Sundance Woman" (1976), "Charlie Cobb: Nice Night for a Hanging" (1977), "Murder in Peyton Place" (1977), "The Night They Took Miss Beautiful"

(1977), "Cruise Into Terror" (1978), "The Jordan Chance" (1978), "The French Atlantic Affair" (1979), "Friendships, Secrets and Lies" (1979), "Make Me an Offer" (1980), "Children of Divorce" (1980), "Twirl" (1981), "Women of San Quentin" (1983), "Amazons" (1984), "No Man's Land" (1984), "A Masterpiece of Murder" (1986), "The History of White People in America: Volume II" (1986), "Fatal Confession: A Father Dowling Mystery" (1987), "Tales from the Hollywood Hills: A Table at Ciro's" (1987), "Man Against the Mob" (1988), "Jake Spanner, Private Eye" (1989), "Attack of the 5 Ft. 2 Women" (1994), "Subliminal Seduction" (1996), "In Cold Blood" (1996), "The Dukes of Hazzard: Reunion!" (1997) as Mama Jo Max, "The Christmas List" (1997), and "By Dawn's Early Light" (2001). Her other television credits include episodes of "Circle of Fear", "Hec Ramsey", "The Hollywood Squares", "The Mike Douglas Show", "The Merv Griffin Show", "Banacek", "Police Story", "Wonder Woman" as Marcia in the 1975 pilot, "The Oregon Trail", "The Eddie Capra Mysteries", "Supertrain", "Hart to Hart", the prime-time soap opera "Flamingo Road" as Lute-Mae Sanders from 1980 to 1982, "The Alan Thicke Show", "Matt Houston", "The Love Boat", "Newhart", "Fantasy Island", "Hotel", "Highway to Heaven", "Night Court", "Murder, She Wrote", "Magnum, P.I.", "The New Hollywood Squares", "Vicki!", "Adventures Beyond Belief" as Mrs. Loretta Kemble in 1988, "Alfred Hitchcock Presents", "Dream On", the soap opera "Santa Barbara" as Phyllis Blake from 1989 to 1990, "In the Heat of the Night", "Dangerous Curves", "The Commish", "Burke's Law", "Highlander", "Marker", "Dave's World", "Up All Night", "Renegade", "Arli$$", "Silk Stalkings", "Nash Bridges", "Viper", "General Hospital" in the recurring role of Jake from 1996 to 1999, "Strip Mall" as Doreen Krudup in 2001, and "Twenty Good Years". Stella was married to Noble Herman Stephens from 1954 until their divorce in 1957. She later had a bitter custody battle with her husband over their son after her acting career took off. She eventually won full custody. She is survived by their son, actor and producer Andrew Stevens. Her partner of nearly forty years, rock guitarist Bob Kulick, died in 2020. Stevens spent her finals years in a long-term Alzheimer's care facility in Los Angeles.

Stevenson, John

British television writer John Stevenson, who was

noted for his work on the soap opera "Coronation Street", died of complications from Alzheimer's disease in England on September 5, 2023. He was 86. Stevenson was born in Manchester, England, on May 10, 1937. He attended the London School of Economics and began working as a journalist for the "Oldham Evening Chronicle" from 1958 to 1964. He then moved to the "Daily Mail" in Manchester as an entertainment writer and theater critic. He began writing for television in the late 1960s with the comedy series "Her Majesty's Pleasure". Stevenson continued to write for such series as "A Family at War", "The Last of the Baskets", "Nearest and Dearest", "Shabby Tiger", "Once Upon a Time", "How's Your Father", "Crown Court", "Yanks Go Home", "Dead Ernest", "Brass", "The Brothers McGregor", "Capstick's Law", "All Change", "It's a Girl", "Mother's Ruin", "Heartbeat", "Oh Doctor Beeching!", and "The Grimleys". He began writing for the ITV soap opera "Coronation Street" in 1976 and scripted over 400 episodes through 2006. Stevenson married Barbara Sutcliffe in 1957 and they later divorced. He is survived by their daughter and son. He married Sheila McGregor in 1977 and they also divorced. He married Myra Davies in 1985 and he is also survived by her and their three daughters.

Stevenson, Ray

Northern Irish actor Ray Stevenson, who starred as Titus Pullo in the television series "Rome" and was Volstagg in Marvel's "Thor" films, died at a hospital on the island of Ischia, Italy, on May 21, 2023. He was

58. Stevenson was born in Lisburn, Northern Ireland, on May 25, 1964. He moved to Newcastle upon Tyne, England, with his family as a child. He later attended Bath Lane College where he studied interior design. He worked in London at an architectural film before pursuing an acting career. He graduated from the Bristol Old Vic Theatre School in 1993. He appeared frequently on television with roles in productions of "The Dwelling Place" (1994), "The Return of the Native" (1994), "The Tide of Life" (1996), "Some Kind of Life" (1996), "Drovers' Gold" (1997), "Real Women II" (1999), "Green-Eyed Monster" (2001), "Life Line" (2007), "Babylon Fields" (2007), and "Saints & Strangers" (2015). He was also seen in such series as "A Woman's Guide to Adultery", "Brand of Gold" as Steve Dickson from 1995 to 1996, "Peak Practice", "City Central" as DI Tony Baynham from 1998 to 1999, "Love in the 21st Century", "Holby City", "The Bill", "Dalziel and Pascoe", "At Home with the Braithwaites" as Graham Braithwaite from 2001 to 2002, "Red Cap", "Murphy's Law", "Waking the Dead", the BBC/HBO historical drama "Rome" as Titus Pullo from 2005 to 2007, "Dexter" as Russian gangster Isaak Sirko in 2012, "Crossing Lines", "Black Sails" as Blackbeard the Pirate from 2016 to 2017, "Rellik" as Detective Superintendent Edward Benton in 2017, "Reef Break" as Jake Elliot in 2018, "Medici", "The Spanish Princess" as King James in 2020, "Vikings" as Othere in 2020, and "Das Boot" as Jack Swinburne in 2022. Stevenson was featured as the voice of Gar Saxon in the animated television series "Star Wars: Rebels" from 2016 to 2017 and "Star Wars: The Clone Wars" in 2020. He appeared as Dark Jedi Baylan Skoll in the "Star Wars" television series "Ahsoka" later in 2023. Stevenson appeared in the films "The Theory of Flight" (1998), "G: MT Greenwich Mean Time"

(1999), "King Arthur" (2004) as the ill-fated knight Sir Dagonet, "Outpost" (2008) battling Nazi zombies, "Punisher: War Zone" (2008) as the title character Frank Castle, "Cirque du Freak: The Vampire's Assistant" (2009) as Murlaugh, "The Book of Eli" (2010), "The Other Guys" (2010), the crime drama "Kill the Irishman" (2011), "The Three Musketeers" (2011) as Porthos, "Jayne Mansfield's Car" (2012), "G.I. Joe: Retaliation" (2013) as Firefly, "Big Game" (2014), "The Transporter Refueled" (2015), "Cold Skin" (2017), "Accident Man" (2018) as Big Ray, "Final Score" (2018), the Indian Teluga-language epic "RRR" (2022) as Scott Buxton, "Memory" (2022), and "Accident Man: Hitman's Holiday" (2022). He was Marcus in the trilogy "Divergent" (2014), "Insurgent" (2015), and

"Allegiant" (2016). Stevenson was featured as Volstagg, Thor's Asgardian comrade, in the Marvel Cinematic Universe productions of "Thor" (2011), "Thor: The Dark World" (2013) and "Thor: The Dark World" (2013). He appeared frequently on stage during his career with roles in London stage productions of "Mouth to Mouth" and "The Duchess of Malfi" in the early 2000s. He was filming "Cassino in Ischia" in Italy at the time of his death. He was married to actress Ruth Gemmell from 1997 until their divorce in 2005. He was involved with Italian anthropologist Elisabetta Caraccia, with whom he had three children.

Stewart, Mark

British singer Mark Stewart, who was a founding member of the band the Pop Group, died in England on April 21, 2023. He was 62. Stewart was born in Bristol, England, on August 10, 1960. He began his career in music founding the

pioneering post-punk band the Pop Group in 1977 with John Waddington, Simon Underwood, Gareth Sager, and Bruce Smith. They recorded the albums "Y" (1979) and "For How Much Longer Do We Tolerate Mass Murder?" (1980) and released such singles as "She Is Beyond Good and Evil" and "We Are All Prostitutes". The Pop Group disbanded in 1981 and Stewart moved to London. He joined Adrian Sherwood's dub music collective New Age Steppers and their recordings were released by On-U Sound. Stewart released the 1982 single "Who's Hot". His EP "Jerusalem" (1983) and album "Learning to Cope with Cowardice" (1983) were released under the name Mark Stewart & the Mafia. He released the album "As the Veneer of Democracy Starts to Fade" in 1985 and had a self-titles solo album in 1987. His other albums include "Metatron" (1990), "Control Data" (1996), "Kiss the Future" (2005), and "Edit" (2008). He was featured in the 2009 documentary film "On/Off - Mark Stewart

- from The Pop Group to the Mafia". The Pop Group reunited in 2010 for a live show. They released the compilation album "We Are Time" in 2014. Two more albums followed, "Citizen Zombie" (2015) and "Honeymoon on Mars" (2016). Stewart was also involved in conceptual art and collaborated with Rupert Goldsworthy on the 2012 show "I AM THE LAW". He collaborated with Bobby Gillespie of Primal Scream and experimental filmmaker Kenneth Anger on his final solo album "The Politics of Envy" in 2012.

Sticky Vicky

Spanish dancer and vaginal magician Victoria Maria Aragues Gadea, who performed under the names Vicky Leyton and Sticky Vicky, died of uterine cancer in La Nucia, Alicante, Spain, on November 29, 2023. She was 80. She was born in

Santa Cruz de Tenerife, Spain, on April 15, 1943. She soon moved to Barcelona with her mother and studied ballet from an early age. She performed as a dancer and had a musical act with her sister, a contortionist. She took the stage name Vicky Leyton and managed a theater in Barcelona. She began performing in more sexually explicit shows after censorship restrictions were lifted following the death of Spanish dictator Francisco Franco in 1975. A magician suggested an act that entailed Vicky removing various objects from her vagina. The act proved a success in Spain, and she was a featured attraction in shows in Benidorm on the Mediterranean coast in the mid-1980s. Taking the name Sticky Vicky, she would slowly undress on stage before removing such objects as ping pong balls, eggs, sausages, handkerchiefs, razor blades, machetes, and a lit lightbulb from her vagina. She had cameo appearances in several episodes of the British television comedy series "Benidorm" in 2009. Vicky maintained a busy schedule on stage until retiring following hip surgery and a diagnosis of uterine cancer in 2016. She is survived by a son, Eduardo Romero Aragues, and a daughter, Maria Gadea Aragues, who developed her own exotic dance routine using her mother's pseudonym Sticky Vicky.

Stinnette, Dorothy

Actress Dorothy Stinnette died in Manhattan, New

York, on October 23, 2023. She was 95. Stinnette was born in Wichita, Kansas, on May 22, 1928. She began performing on stage during high school and graduated from Northwestern University. She moved to New York City in the early 1950s to pursue an acting career. She performed frequently on stage throughout the country and was seen on Broadway in productions of "New Girl in Town" (1957) and "The Man Who Came to Dinner" (1980). She appeared on television in the late 1950s in episodes of "The Phil Silvers Show", "Highway Patrol", and "The Big Story". Stinnette appeared frequently in television soap operas including "Somerset" as Laura Delaney Cooper from 1970 to 1973, "The Edge of Night" as Nadine Scott from 1980 to 1981, "Another Life" as Kate Phillips Carothers from 1982 to 1984, "Loving" as Rose Donovan from 1984 to 1986, and "One Life to Live" as Luann Cummings in 1989. She was seen in the films "Murder, Inc." (1960) and "An Empty Bed" (1989).

Stockwell, Alec

Canadian actor Alec Stockwell died at his home in Thornhill, Ontario, Canada, on April 14, 2023. He was 78. He was born Alexander McKee Stephenson in Canada on December 29, 1944. He graduated from the University of

Windsor and later pursued post graduate work and taught at York University in Toronto. He pursued an acting career and performed and directed in theaters across Canada. Stockwell was also seen in the films "April One" (1994), "True Blue" (2001), "Spider" (2002), "Cypher" (2002), "The Republic of Love" (2003), "Cinderella Man" (2005), "You Are Here" (2010), Guillermo del Toro's horror film "Crimson Peak" (2015), "My Big Fat Greek Wedding 2" (2016), "The Second Time Around" (2016), and "The Silencing" (2020). He appeared on television in episodes of "Street Legal", "The Campbells", "Rin Tin Tin: K-9 Cops", "Queer as Folk", "1-800-Missing", "Slings and Arrows", "Puppets Who Kill", "The Murdoch Mysteries", "This Is Wonderland" in the recurring role of Mr. Kaslowski from 2004 to 2006, "Saving Hope", "Killjoys", "People of Earth", "Shadowhunters", "In the Dark", and "Mary Kills People" in the recurring role of William in 2019. His other television credits include the tele-films "Our Fathers" (2005) and "Anne of Green Gables: A New Beginning" (2008).

Street, Adrian

Welsh professional wrestler Exotic Adrian Street died of sepsis at a hospital in Cwmbran, Wales, on July 24, 2023. He was 82. Street was born in Brynmawr, Wales, on December 5, 1940. He began bodybuilding in his teens and began his professional wrestling career in 1957. He originally wrestled under the name Kid Tarzan Jonathan. He soon bleached his hair blonde and wrestled as the Nature Boy Adrian Street. He teamed with Tony Charles as the Welsh Wizards and Bad Boy Bobby Barnes as the Hell's Angeles. He began using the maneuver of kissing an opponent to escape a hold and covering him in makeup after he was tagged. His attire and personality became increasingly flamboyant by the time he joined All-Star Wrestling in 1970. He became known as Exotic Adrian Street and was a multiple winner of the middleweight championship. Miss Linda became Street's valet, originally being billed as Blackfoot Sue, and would frequently interfere in matches in his

behalf. He left Great Britain in 1981 and briefly competed with Stampede Wrestling in Calgary, Canada. Street was soon a memorable bad guy with wrestling promotions in the United States. His effeminate ring persona and attire belied a ruthless tough as nails competitor. He feuded with Superstar Bill Dundee in Mid-South Wrestling in Memphis and battled Dusty Rhodes in Florida and the Mid-Atlantic. He appeared frequently with Ron Fuller's Continental Championship Wrestling, feuding with Austin Idol, Wendall Cooley, and Norvell Austin. He competed with the promotion until it closed in 1989, with feuds against Hustler Rip Rogers and the team of Terry Garvin and Marc Gulleen, known as Beauty and the Beast. He retired from wrestling full-time in the 1990s and ran the Skull Krushers Wrestling School in Gulf Breeze, Florida. He made occasional returns to the ring, capturing the NWA Alabama title in 2010. He wrestled his final match in Birmingham in 2015. The school was badly damaged by Hurricane Ivan in 2004, and he returned to Wales in 2018. Street was featured in several films including "The Canterbury Tales" (1972), "Quest for Fire" (1981), and "Grunt! The Wrestling Movie" (1985). He and his band, the Pile Drivers, released the 1986 album "Shake, Wrestle, and Role". He was the subject of the 2019 documentary "You May Be Pretty, But I Am Beautiful: The Adrian Street Story". He was author of a series of memoirs including "I Only Laugh When It Hurts" (2012), "Sadist in Sequins" (2012), "My Pink Gas Mask" (2012), "Imagine What I Could Do to You" (2013), and "Violence Is Golden" (2015). Street married Jean Dawe in 1962 and they later divorced. He is survived by their three children, Adrian, Vince, and Amanda. He married his long-time manager Miss Linda (Linda Gunthorpe Hawker) in 2005 and she survives him.

Strong, Barrett

Singer and songwriter Barrett Strong died at his home

in San Diego, California, on January 28, 2023. He was 81. Strong was born in West Point, Mississippi, on February 4, 1941. He moved to Detroit, Michigan, with his family as a child and soon began playing the piano. He began singing while attending middle school. He signed with Berry Gordy's new label, Tamla Records, and had a hit with the single "Money (That's What I Want)". Strong was credited as co-writer of the song. He

became a lyricist at Motown in the mid-1960s, working with producer Norman Whitfield. They penned such hit songs as Marvin Gaye's "I Heard It Through the Grapevine" and "Wherever I Lay My Hat (That's My Home)", Edwin Starr's "War", the Undisputed Truth's "Smiling Faces Sometimes", and the Temptations "Cloud Nine", "Psychedelic Shack", "Ball of Confusion (That's What the World Is Today)", "I Can't Get Next to You", "Just My Imagination (Running Away with Me)", and "Papa Was a Rolling Stone", which earned him a Grammy Award in 1973. He left Motown to resume his singing career and signed with Epic in 1972. He soon moved to Capitol Records where he recorded the albums "Stronghold" (1975) and "Live & Love" (1976). He continued to write and record in the 1980s and founded the Detroit record label Blarritt Records in 1995. He released the 2001 album "Stronghold II" through Blarritt. He and Whitfield were inducted into the Songwriters Hall of Fame in 2004. Strong was married to Sandy White from 1967 until her death in in 2002 and is survived by seven children.

Sturm, Betty

Actress Betty Sturm, who was featured in Timothy Carey's off-beat 1962 film "The World's Greatest Sinner", died of complications from Alzheimer's disease at her home in

Clinton, New Jersey, on January 22, 2023. She was 89. Sturm was born in Spain in 1933 and was raised in Germany. She came to Los Angeles in the late 1950s. She was cast as a follower of Timothy Carey's cult leader in the film "The World's Greatest Sinner" (1962). Carey produced, directed, wrote, and starred in the film. Sturm originally had a larger role but she decided not to complete work on the film due to financial disputes with the producer and a year-long shooting schedule. She sold custom hairpieces of characters at Disneyland park and for Disney films in the early 1970s. She operated the Elizabeth Sturm Talent Agency in the 1990s. Sturm recounted her experiences making "The World's Greatest Sinner" in the 2012 documentary "Making Sinner", where she was interviewed by Timothy Carey's son, Romeo. She was married to former child actor Robert Winckler from 1962 until his death in 1982. She is survived by her son, director and writer William Winckler, and daughter, Patricia.

Sulcova, Jana

Czech actress Jana Sulcova died of heart failure in Prague, Czech Republic, on July 28, 2023. She was 76. Sulcova was born in Prague on February 12, 1947. She trained as an actor at Prague's Academy of Performing Arts, graduating in 1969. She performed frequently on stage with the Municipal Theaters of Prague through 1992. She made her film debut in a small role in the 1968 horror film "The Cremator". Sulcova was also seen in the films "Kulhavy Dabel" (1968), "A

Quelques Jours Pres" (1969), "Velka Neznama" (1970), "Game of a Handsome Dragoon" (1971), "Pet Muzu a Jedno Srdce" (1971), "Smrt Si Vybira" (1973), "Pulnocni Kolona" (1973), "Hvezda Pada Vzhuru" (1975), "Hrozba" (1978), "Postaveni

Mimo Hru" (1979), "Romaneto" (1981), "I Enjoy the World with You" (1983), "Horky Podzim s Vuni Manga" (1984), "Hubert the Smart Boy" (1985), "Oldrich a Bozena" (1985), "Dobre Svetlo" (1986), "Operace Me Dcery" (1986), "Muka Obraznosti" (1990), "Sukromne Zivoty" (1991), "Duse Jako Kaviar" (2004), "Doktor Od Jezera Hrochu" (2010), "Identity Card" (2010), "Bastardi" (2010), "The Snake Brothers" (2015), "The Price of Happiness" (2019), and "Daria" (2020). She was seen on television in productions of "Kresadlo" (1968), "Sest Uprchliku" (1970), "Mata Hari" (1970), "Manon Lescaut" (1970), "Dlouha Bila Nit" (1971), "Konfrontace" (1971), "Kraska a Zvire" (1971), "Nemaluj Si Certa Na Zed" (1971), "Opory Spolecnosti" (1972), "Ohnivy Maj" (1974), "Princ Chocholous" (1974), "Akce Byci Oko" (1976), "Ja Zustanu Verny" (1977), "Theodore Chindler - Die Geschichte Einer Deutschen Familie" (1979), "Zlate Rybicky" (1979), "Kotva u Privozu" (1980), "Panenka" (1980), "Vzorna Tchyne" (1980), "Death on the Hour" (1981), "Ubohy Pan Kufalt" (1981), "Prichazeji Bosi: Nezralost" (1982), "Diplomat" (1982), "Horka Vune Leta" (1982), "Ples v Opere" (1983), "Pratele" (1986), "Penize a Krev" (1986), "XYZ" (1987), "Jsem Vrah?" (1988), "Detinske Hry Dospelych" (1990), "Pres Padaci Mosty" (1991), "Milostive Leto" (1991), "Spolecenska Hra" (1991), "Dno" (1991), "Ariadnina Nit" (1992), "Pomale Sipy" (1993), "Spolecnice" (2000), "Miluj Blizniho Sveho" (2005), "Opravdova Laska" (2008), "Svedomi Denisy Klanove" (2009), and "Vzteklina" (2018). Her other television credits include episodes of "Hrisni Lide Mesta Prazskeho", "Alexander Dumas Starsi", "Byl Jednou Jeden Dum" as Jarmila Klabikova in 1974, "Nejmladsi z Rodu Hamru" as Marie Zajickova in 1975, "Tajemstvi Prouteneho Kosiku" as Hana Karasova in 1978, "Zakony Pohybu" as Milada Serakova in 1978, "Bakalari", "Dnes v Jednom Dome" as Jitka Strachotova in 1980, ""My Vsichni Skolou Povinni" as Helena Olivova in 1984, "Circus Humberto", "Dobrodruzstvi Kriminalistiky", "Nahrdelnik" as Luisa von Bruckner in 1992, "Hrichy Pro Patera Knoxe", "Co Ted a Co Potom?" as Nora from 1991 to 1992, "Horakovi" as Zdena Kadlecova from 2006 to 2007, "Ordinace v Ruzove Zahrade", "Cukrarna" as Miluse Mila from 2010 to 2011, "Wonderful Times" as Pani Pastorova from 2010 to 2013, "Kouzelna Skolka" as Babicka Jana from 2011 to 2012, "Helena", "Major Case Squad", "Doctor Martin", "Trpaslik" as Bozena Janackova in 2017, and "Vesnican". She was married to actor Oldrich Vizner until their divorce in 1988 and is survived by their two daughters.

Sullivan, Dean

British actor Dean Sullivan, who starred as Jimmy Corkhill on the soap opera "Brookside" from 1986 to 2003, died of complications from prostate cancer in Birkenhead,

Merseyside, England, on November 29, 2023. He was 68. Sullivan was born in Liverpool, England, on June 7, 1955. He graduated from Lancaster University and worked as a primary school teacher for six years from the late 1970s. He was cast as Jimmy Corkhill on the Channel 4 soap opera "Brookside" in 1986. He continued to work as a substitute teacher for several years before becoming a regular on the series. He remained with "Brookside" until its cancellation in 2003. He performed on stage with Liverpool's Epstein Theatre and the Liverpool Playhouse. Sullivan also appeared on television in episodes of "The Word", "Blankety Blank, "The John Daly Show", "Doctors", "My North West", "Pointless Celebrities", "Crime Stories", and "Forward Slash/Jobs". He was seen in the films "Forgotten Word" (2022) and "Wings" (2023).

Sullivan, Leo D.

Animator Leo D. Sullivan died of heart failure in Los Angeles, California, on March 25, 2023. He was 82. Sullivan was born in Lockhart, Texas, on September 10, 1940. He moved to Los Angeles in 1952 and began working in animation

in his teens. He worked at Bob Clampett Productions as a cel polisher before becoming an artist and animator. He served as an assistant animator on the "Beany and Cecil" cartoon in 1960. Sullivan teamed with fellow Black animation pioneer Floyd Norman to form Vignette Films in 1960. They worked on producing short films for high school students in the Black community. Vignette also created the original animated logo for television's "Soul Train" in 1971. He was an animator, storyboard artist, or timing director for numerous cartoon series over the next thirty years including "Fat Albert and the Cosby Kids", "Jabberjaw", "Scooby's Laff-A-Lympics", "I Am the Greatest! The Adventures of Muhammad Ali", "Posse Impossible", "Undercover Elephant", "C.B. Bears", "Blast-Off Buzzard", "Shake, Rattle and Roll", "The New Adventures of Mighty Mouse and Heckle and Jeckle", "Caspar and the Angels", "The New Schmoo", "Super Friends", "Richie Rich", "The Flintstone Comedy Show", "The Richie Rich/Scooby-Doo Show", "The Little Rascals", "Flash Gordon", "Pac-Man", "BraveStarr", "Tiny Toon Adventures", "Animaniacs", "Taz-Mania", "Fantastic Four: The Animated Series", "Dumb and Dumber", "Iron Man", "The Incredible Hulk", "Extreme

Dinosaurs", "Moon Dreamers", "The Transformers", "My Little Pony", "Bill & Ted's Excellent Adventures", and "Make Way for Noddy". He also worked on the animated features "Mighty Mouse in the Great Space Chase" (1982) and "Pinocchio and the Emperor of the Night" (1987). Sullivan is survived by his wife, Ethelyn Stewart, a son, and a daughter.

Sutherland, David

Scottish comic artist David Sutherland died in Scotland on January 19, 2023. He was 89. Sutherland was born in Invergordon, Scotland, on March 4, 1933. He left school at age fifteen to work as an assistant at an advertising agency. He was soon illustrating promotion material about upcoming films for cinemas. He trained at the Glasgow School of Art before serving in Egypt during National Service. He was hired by the Scottish publishing company DC Thomson in 1959 as a ghost artist for David Law and Dudley D. Watkins for "The Beano" comic magazine. Sutherland illustrated the adventure strips "Danny on a Dolphin", "The Great Flood of London", "The Cannonball Crackshots", "Lester's Little Circus", and "General Jumbo" in the 1960s. He worked on the gag series "The Bash Street Kids" for "The Beano" from 1962 until he became seriously ill early in 2023. His other cartoon work includes the series "Billy the Cat and Katie" from 1967 to 1974, "Biffo the Bear" from 1969 to 1971, "Dennis the Menace" from 1970 to 1998, "Rasher" from 1984 to 1995, "The Germs" from 1988 to 1992, "Oscar Knight - Child Actor" from 1992 to 1993, "Korky the Cat" from 1999 to 2000, and "Fred's Bed" from 2008 to 2012. Sutherland married Margaret Robertson in 1958 and is survived by her and their two daughters.

Suzuki, Mizuho

Japanese actor and voice dubber Mizuho Suzuki died in Tokyo, Japan, on November 19, 2023. He was 96. Suzuku was born in Manchuria, China, on October 23, 1927. He dropped out of Kyoto University to pursue a career in films. He was featured in numerous movies from the early 1950s including "Before Dawn" (1953), "Utsukushii Hito" (1954), "Kikenna Onna" (1959), "Otona To Kodomo No Ainoko Dai" (1961), "Dorodarake No Junjo" (1963), "Youth of the Beast" (1963), "Alibi" (1963), "Okami No Oji" (1963), "Hanayome Wa Jugo Sai" (1964), "Teigin Jiken: Shikeishu" (1964), "A Man's Crest: Fight Challenge" (1964), "Gun Demon Without Form" (1964), "Nippon Dorobo Monogatari" (1`965), "A Chain of Islands" (1965), "Shinobi No Mono: Iga-Yashiki" (1965), "Aoi Kuchizuke" (1965), "Ashita Wa Sako Hana Sako" (1965), "Akai Glass" (1966), "Fusha No Aru Machi" (1966),

"Watashi, Chigatteiru Kashira" (1966), "Shoiroi Kyoto" (1966), "Yogiri Yo Kon'ya Mo Arigato" (1967), "Zatoichi the Outlaw" (1967), "Yubue" (1967), "The Sands of Kurobe" (1968), "The Snow Woman" (1968), "Dorei Kojo" (1968), "Sworn Brothers" (1969), "Tengu-to" (1969), "Apart from Life" (1970), "The Battle of Manchuria" (1970), "Konketsuji Rika: Hitoriyuku Sasuraitabi" (1973), "Hatachi No Genten" (1973), "Submersion of Japan" (1973), "Police Tactics" (1974), "The Family" (1974), "Lady Snowblood 2: Love Song of Vengeance" (1974), "The Legend of Love & Sincerity" (1974), "Prophecies of Nostradamus" (1974), "The Legend of Love & Sincerity: Continuation" (1975), "Cops vs. Thugs" (1975), "The Perennial Weed" (1975), "Bullet Train" (1975), "Tenpo Suiko-den: Ohara Yugaku" (1976), "Inugami No Tatari" (1977), "High Seas Hijack" (1977), "Proof of the Man" (1977), "Shag" (1978), "The Demon" (1978), "Yasei No Shomei" (1978), "Nihon No Don: Kanketsuhen" (1978), "Juhassai, Umi E" (1979), "I Want To" (1979), "A Distant Cry from Spring" (1980), "Hadashi No Gen Part 3: Hiroshima No Tatakai" (1980), "Jishin Retto" (1980), "Summer of Evil" (1981), "Samurai Reincarnation" (1981), "Shosetsu Yoshida Gakko" (1983), "Legend of the Eight Samurai" (1983), "The Miracle of Umitsubame Joe" (1984), "Make-up" (1984), "The Return of Godzilla" (aka "Godzilla 1985") (1984) as the Foreign Minister, "Kizudarake No Kunsho" (1986), "The Shogunate's Harem" (1986), "Rock Requiem" (1988), "Tonko" (1988), "Four Days of Snow and Blood" (1989), "Fukuzawa Yukichi" (1991), "Kacho Shima Kosaku" (1992), "Kabei: Our Mother" (2008), "Battle Under Orion" (2009), "Patisserie Coin De Rue" (2011), "Until the Break of Dawn" (2012), and "Don't Lose Heart" (2013). Suzuki provided the dubbing voice of Darth Vader in a Japanese release of the original "Star Wars" trilogy. He also provided the Japanese voice for Curt Jurgens in the Bond film "The Spy Who Loved Me", Richard Harris' Marcus Aurelius in "Gladiator, Marlon Brando's Carmine Sabatin in "The Freshman", and George C. Scott's William F. Kinderman in "The Exorcist III".

Swan, Robert

Actor Robert Swan died of liver cancer in Rolling Prairie, Indiana, on August 9, 2023. He was 78. Swan was born in Chicago, Illinois, on October 20, 1944. He sang in the chorus at the Lyric Opera and the Chicago Symphony in his youth. He performed on the Chicago stage and appeared on Broadway in the 1974 play "The Freedom of the City". He made his film debut in 1980's "Somewhere in Time" as a stagehand who fights with Christopher Reeve in 1912. Swan was also seen in the films "Take This Job and Shove It" (1981), "Doctor Detroit" (1983), "Grandview, U.S.A." (1984), "That Was Then... This Is Now" (1985), "Hosiers" (1986) as Rollin Butcher, "The Untouchables" (1987), "Who's That Girl" (1987), "Betrayed"

(1988), "Backdraft" (1991), "The Babe" (1993) as Babe Ruth's father, "Mo' Money" (1992), "Rudy" (1993), "The Childhood Friend" (1994), Oliver Stone's "Natural Born Killers" (1994) as Deputy Napalatoni, "Going All the Way" (1997), "Cold Night Into Dawn" (1997), "C.S.A.: The Confederate States of America" (2004), and "The Owner" (2012). He appeared on television in episodes of "The Duke", "Walking Tall", "The Misadventures of Sheriff Lobo", "Wildside", "The Twilight Zone", "Stingray", "Spencer: For Hire", "All My Children" as Jeb Tidwell in 1988, "The Equalizer", and "Missing Persons" as Dan Manaher from 1993 to 1994. His other television credits include the tele-films "Heart of Steel" (1983), "The Dollmaker" (1984), and "The Trial of Standing Bear" (1988). He was a voiceover actor for numerous commercials for such products as United Airlines, Busch, Schlitz, and Nine Lives cat food. His survivors include his wife, Barbara.

Swenson, Inga

Actress Inga Swenson, who was featured as Gretchen Kraus in the television comedy series "Benson", died in Los Angeles, California, on July 23, 2023. She was 90. Swenson  was born in Omaha, Nebraska, on December 29, 1932. She was active in speech and drama while in high school and was winner of the National Forensic League's state and national speech contests. She attended Northwestern University in Evanston, Illinois, where she continued to study drama in the early 1950s. She also trained as a lyric soprano and began her career on stage. She made her Broadway debut in the musical revue "New Faces of 1956". She was also seen in Broadway productions of "The First Gentleman" (1957), "Peer Gynt" (1960), "Camelot" (1960) as a standby for Julie Andrews' Guinevere, "110 in the Shade" (1963) earning a Tony Award nomination for her role as Lizzie Curry, and "Baker Street" (1965) receiving another Tony nomination for her role as Irene Adler opposite Fritz Weaver's Sherlock Holmes. She appeared frequently on stage around the country throughout her career. She was seen often on television from the late 1950s with roles in episodes of "Goodyear Playhouse", "The Seven Lively Arts", "Folio", "The United States Steel Hour", "Playhouse 90", "Play of the Week", "The Defenders", "Dr. Kildare", "The Doctors and the Nurses", "Bonanza" as Inger Borgstrom Cartwright, mother of Hoss Cartwright, in the 1962 episode "Inger, My Love", "CBS Playhouse", "The Tonight Show Starring Johnny Carson", "The Jack Paar Program", "Password", "Medical Center", "The Merv Griffin Show", "Owen Marshall, Counselor at Law", "Griff", "The Rookies", "Sara", "ABC Weekend Specials", "Barnaby Jones", "Vega$", "Soap" as Ingrid Swenson from 1978 to 1979, "All-Star Family Feud", "ABC Afterschool Specials", "Highcliffe Manor", "Hotel", "Newhart", "The Golden Girls" as the younger sister of Betty White's Rose, "Doctor Doctor" in the recurring role of Connie Stratford from 1989 to 1990, and

the animated "Life with Louie" as the voice of Grandma Helga from 1997 to 1998. Swenson was best known for her role as Gretchen Wilomena Kraus, the governor's Germanic chef, in the comedy series "Benson" from 1979 to 1986. She was the frequent foil for Robert Guillaume's Benson and earned three Emmy Award nominations. Her other television credits include productions of "Heart of Darkness" (1958), "The Wings of the Dove" (1959), "Oliver Twist" (1959), "Victoria Regina" (1961), "Androcles and the Lion" (1967), "My Father and My Mother" (1967), "The Tape Recorder" (1970), the science fiction tele-film "Earth II" (1971) as Ilyana Kovalefskii, "Testimony of Two Men" (1977), "Ziegfeld: The Man and His Women" (1978), "North & South: Book 1, North & South" (1985) and "North & South: Book 2, Love & War" (1986) as Maude Hazard, "Nutcracker: Money, Madness & Murder" (1987), and "Bay Cove" (1987). Swenson was featured in several films including the political drama "Advise & Consent" (1962) as Ellen Anderson, "The Miracle Worker" (1962) as Helen Keller's mother Kate, "Lipstick" (1976), "The Betsy" (1978), and "The Mountain Men" (1980). Swenson married sound engineer Lowell Harris in 1953 and he survives her. They had two sons, James, who died in a motorcycle accident in 1987, and Mark, who works as a film editor.

Swinny, Wayne

Guitarist Wayne Swinny, who was co-founder of the band Saliva, died of a brain hemorrhage at a hospital in  Nashville, Tennessee, on March 22, 2023. He was 59. Swinny was born in Memphis, Tennessee, on October 31, 1963. He played guitar in local bands including Roxy Blue. He was a founding member of the hard rock band Saliva in Bartlett, Tennessee, in 1996. The original line-up included Swinny and Chris D'Abaldo on guitar, Dave Novotny on bass, Todd Poole on drums, and Josey Scott Sappington as lead singer. They performed at local venues and band competitions in the Memphis area. They released eleven albums and had popular singles with "Always", "Rest in Pieces", "Click Click Boom", "Ladies in Gentlemen", and "Survival of the Sickest". Saliva's song "I Walk Alone" was used as the entrance theme for Dave Batista's wrestling matches in World Wrestling Entertainment in the early 2000s. Swinney suffered a brain hemorrhage while on tour with the band in Nashville. He was the last remaining founding member of Saliva still performing with the group.

Syms, Sylvia

British actress Sylvia Syms , who appeared in the films "Expresso Bongo" and the Amicus horror anthology "Asylum", died in Northwood, London, England, on January 27, 2023. She was 89. Syms was born in Woolwich, London, on January 6, 1934. She decided to become an actress in her teens and graduated from the Royal Academy of Dramatic Art in 1954.

She began her career in repertory in Eastbourne and Bath and appeared in a production of "The Apple Cart" in the West End. Syms was soon appearing in films and television. Her film  credits include "Teenage Bad Girl" (1956), "Woman in a Dressing Gown" (1957) earning a BAFTA Award nomination for her role as Georgie, "No Time for Tears" (1957), "The Birthday Present" (1957), "The Moonraker" (1958), "Ice Cold in Alex" (1958), "Bachelor of Hearts" (1958), "No Trees in the Street" (1959) receiving another BAFTA nomination for her role as Hetty, "Ferry to Hong Kong" (1959), "Expresso Bongo" (1959) as Masie King opposite Cliff Richard and Laurence Harvey, "Conspiracy of Hearts" (1960), "The World of Suzie Wong" (1960), "Amazons of Rome" (1961), "Flame in the Streets" (1961), "Victim" (1961) opposite Dirk Bogarde, "The Quare Fellow" (1962) with Patrick McGoohan, "The Punch and Judy Man" (1963) as Tony Hancock's wife, "The World Ten Times Over" (1963), "East of Sudan" (1964), "Operation Crossbow" (1965), "The Big Job" (1965), "Danger Route" (1967), "The Fiction-Makers" (1968), "The Desperados" (1969), "Run Wild, Run Free" (1969), "Hostile Witness" (1969), the Amicus horror anthology "Asylum" (1972) as Ruth in the "Frozen Fear" segment, "The Tamarind Seed" (1974) earning a BAFTA nomination for her supporting role as Margaret Stephenson, "Give Us Tomorrow" (1978), "There Goes the Bride" (1980), "Absolute Beginners" (1986), "A Chorus of Disapproval" (1989), "Shirley Valentine" (1989), "Shining Through" (1992), "Dirty Weekend" (1993), "Staggered" (1994), "Food of Love" (1997), "The House of Angelo" (1997), the short "Mavis and the Mermaid" (2000), "What a Girl Wants" (2003), "I'll Sleep When I'm Dead" (2003), "The Queen" (2006) as the Queen Mother opposite Helen Mirren's Queen Elizabeth II, "Is Anybody There?" (2008), "Bunny and the Bull" (2009), the short "The Long Lonely Walk" (2010), "Booked Out" (2012), "Run for Your Wife" (2012), the short "A Cake for Mabel" (2013), "The Hatching" (2014), and "Together" (2018). She appeared frequently on television throughout her career with roles in such productions as "The Romantic Young Lady" (1955), "The Powder Magazine" (1955), "The Devil's Disciple" (1956), "The House in Athens" (1956), "The Valley and the Peak" (1956), "Broken Journey" (1959), "Bat Out of Hell" (1966), "Boswell's Life of Johnson" (1971), "Nancy Astor" (1982), "It's Your Move" (1982), "Miss Marple: A Murder Is Announced" (1985), "Intimate Contact" (1987), "Mr. H Is Late" (1988), "Thatcher: The Final Days" (1991) as Margaret Thatcher, "The Glass Virgin" (1995), "Original Sin" (1997), "Neville's Island" (1998), "Doctor Zhivago" (2002) as Madame Fleury, "The Poseidon Adventure" (2005) as Belle Rosen, "Child of Mine" (2005), "Collision" (2009), and "Bouquet of Barbed Wire" (2010). Syms other television credits include episodes of "Terminus", "Life with the Lyons", "After Hours", "Suspense", "The Human Jungle", "Love Story", "Secret Agent", "The

Baron", "Armchair Theatre", "Half Hour Story", "The Root of All Evil?", "The Saint", "Strange Report", "Thirty-Minute Theatre", "ITV Playhouse", "Brian Rix Presents...", "Paul Temple", "The Adventurer", "My Good Woman" in the recurring role of Sylvia Gibbons from 1972 to 1974, "Comedy Premiere", "Jackanory Playhouse", "I'm Bob, He's Dickie", "Time for Murder", "Rockliffe's Folly", "Doctor Who" as Mrs. Pritchard in the 1989 serial "Ghost Light" starring Sylvester McCoy as the Doctor, "May to December", "Natural Lies", "Mulberry", "Ghosts", "Peak Practice" as Isabel de Gines from 1993 to 1995, "Screen Two", "Kavanagh QC", "Heartbeat", "Ruth Rendell Mysteries", "The Jury" as Elsie Beamish in 2002, "Holby City", "A Home with the Braithwaites" as Marion Riley from 2000 to 2003, "Where the Heart Is", "Born and Bred", "Family Affair", "Judge John Deed", "Dalziel and Pascoe", "New Tricks", "Marple", "Blue Murder", "Above Suspicion", "Casualty", "Missing", "Doctors", "EastEnders", "Case Histories", "Rev.", "Playhouse Presents", and "Gentleman Jack". She was married to Alan Edney from 1956 until their divorce in 1989 and is survived by their two children, actors Benjamin and Beatie Edney.

Taka, Miiko

Actress Miiko Taka, who was noted for her role opposite Marlon Brando in the 1957 Korean war drama "Sayonara", died in Las Vegas, Nevada, on January 4, 2023.  She was 97. She was born Miiko Shikata in Seattle, Washington, on July 24, 1925, and was raised in Los Angeles, California. She and her family, who had immigrated from Japan, were interned at the Gila River War Relocation Center in Arizona during World War II. She later returned to Los Angeles where she worked as a travel agency clerk. Taka was cast by director Joshua Logan to star as dancer Hana-Ogi in the 1957 film adaptation of James Michener's novel "Sayonara" opposite Marlon Brando. She continued to appear in such films as "Hell to Eternity" (1960), "Cry for Happy" (1961) opposite Glenn Ford, "Operation Bottleneck" (1961), "A Global Affair" (1964) with Bob Hope, "The Art of Love" (1965), "Walk Don't Run" (1966) starring Cary Grant, George Pal's "The Power" (1968), "Lost Horizon" (1973), "Paper Tiger" (1975), "Mister Yoso" (1976), "Midway" (1976), "The Big Fix" (1978), and "The Challenge" (1982). Taka was seen on television in episodes of "Hawaiian Eye", "Alcoa Theatre", "The Arlene Francis Show", "Peter Como's Kraft Music Hall", "The Howard Miller Show", "I've Got a Secret", "The Les Crane Show", "Adventures in Paradise", "The Man from U.N.C.L.E.", "The F.B.I.", "I Spy", "The Girl from U.N.C.L.E.", "The Wild Wild West", "Anna and the King", and "The Little People". Her other television credits include productions of "Judge Dee and the Monastery Murders" (1974), "The Lives of Jenny Dolan" (1975), "Arthur Hailey's The Moneychangers" (1976), "Billy: Portrait of a Street Kid"

(1977), "A Family Upside Down" (1978), and "Shogun" (1980) as Kiri. Taka was married to actor Dale Ishimoto from 1944 until their divorce in 1958 and is survived by their son and daughter. She was married to Los Angeles news director Lennie Blondheim from 1963 until his death in 2002. She married Reginald Hsu in 2003.

Takahashi, Yukihiro

Japanese drummer and singer Yukihiro Takahshi, who was a pioneer of electronic pop music, died of complications

from a brain tumor and pneumonia in Karuizawa, Japan, on January 11, 2023. He was 70. Takahashi was born in Tokyo, Japan, on June 6, 1952. He was the drummer for Kazuhiko Kato's rock group the Sadistic Mika Band in the early 1970s. Takahashi and several bandmates formed the the Sadistics when the earlier band broke up in 1975. He recorded the solo album, "Saravah", in 1977. He teamed with Ryuichi Sakamoto and Haruomi Hosono in the Yellow Magic Orchestra in 1978, serving as drummer and lead singer. He released numerous solo albums in the 1980s and 1990s and collaborated with such musicians as Bill Nelson, Iva Davies, Keitchi Suzuki, and Steve Jansen. Takahashi reunited with the Sadistic Mika Band for reunions in 1985, 1989, and from 2006 to 2007. He helped compose the soundtrack for the 1989 anime series "Nadia: Secret of the Blue Water". He and Haruomi Hosono formed the Sketch Show duo in the early 2000s and released two albums. He is survived by his wife, Kiyomi Takahashi.

Takeyema, Yo

Japanese screenwriter Hiroshi 'Yo' Takeyama died of septic shock in Tokyo, Japan, on April 12, 2023. He was 76. Takeyema was born in Tokorozawa City, Japan, on July 28, 1946. He graduated from Waseda University and became a

writer for television. He moved to films in the late 1970s, working for Nikkatsu studios. He scripted Kichitaro Negishi's "Never in the Morning" (1980). Takeyama worked on several softcore films for director Shogoro Nishimura including "Nurses' Journal: Nasty File" (1980), "Koichiro Uno's Girl Dormitory" (1980), and My Girlfriend Wears a Uniform" (1981). He also wrote the films "Gynecology Ward: Caress Me Tenderly" (1981) and "The Pursuit of Happiness" (1988). He co-wrote the 1994 film "47 Ronin" with director Kon Ichikawa. His other films include "Gimu to Engi" (1997), "The Firefly" (2001), and "Futo Fukutsu" (2007). Takeyama wrote several tele-films in the "Inspector Totsugawa" series in the early 1990s. He also

scripted six tele-films in the "Taxi Driver no Suiri Nisshi" series. His other television credits include productions of "Toki Yo Tomare" (1995), "Moike Mariko No 'Kagi Rojin'" (2001), "Sabu" (2002), "Tenka" (2004), "Towering Waves" (2006), "Ri Koran" (2007), "Ten to Sen" (2007), "Giwaku" (2009), "Ijiwaru Baasan" (2010), "Suna No Utsuwa" (2011), "Ai Inochi - Shinjuku KabukichoKakekomi Dera -" (2011), "Matsumoto Seicho No Atsui Kuki" (2012), "3 Oku Yen Jiken" (2014), "Kaseifu Wa Mita!" (2014), "Silver Jack" (2014), "Revenge Court" (2015), Kaseifu Wa Mita!" (2015), "The Woman Who Buys the Local Newspaper" (2016), "Kichiku" (2017), "Paddington Hatsu 4ji 50pun: Shindai Tokkyuu Satsuhin Jiken" (2018), and "Giwaku" (2019).

Tarantino, Tony

Actor Tony Tarantino, the father of film director Quentin Tarantino, died in Los Angeles, California, on December 8, 2023. He was 83. Tarantino was born in Queens,

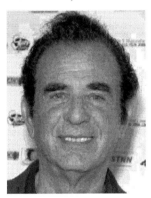

New York, on July 4, 1940. He graduated from high school in 1958 and studied acting at the Pasadena Playhouse. He appeared in a small role in the 1960 film "Where the Boys Are". Tarantino claimed that an altercation with a Hollywood talent agent ended his acting career. He and Connie McHugh were parents of Quentin Tarantino in 1963, though Tony left the family before his son was

born. Quentin became a leading film director and writer in the 1990s. He later stated in an interview that he had never met his father. Tony joined with other celebrity parents as the Silver Foxes and was featured in the 2000 exercise video "Silver Foxes: Power Pilates". He also appeared in a handful of films including "All the Rage" (1999), "Family Tree" (1999), "Blood Money" (2003) which he also co-directed, the short "Saved" (2009), "Underbelly Blues" (2011) also serving as an executive producer, "Mediterranean Blue" (2012), and "Holy Hollywood" (2021).

Tardioli, Sergio

Italian actor Sergio Tardioli died in Civitavecchia, Italy, on October 4, 2023. He was 85. Tardioli was born in Spello, Italy, on July 14, 1938. He began his career on stage and appeared frequently with theater groups throughout Italy. He was seen in supporting roles in numerous films including "La Polizia Ha le Mani Legate" (1975), "The Boss and the Worker" (1975), "San Babili: 8 P.M." (1976), "L'Italia in Pigiama" (1977), "A Man Called Magnum" (1977), "A Man Called Blade" (1977), "A Policewoman on the Porno Squad" (1979), "Supersexymarket" (1979), "Sabato, Domenica a Venerdi" (1979), "Mani di Velluto" (1979), "Il Ficcanaso" (1980), "Crime at the Chinese Restaurant" (1981), "Pierino Colpisce Ancora" (1982), "Identification of a Woman" (1982), "Giovani, Belle... Probabilmente Ricche" (1982), "Vai Avanti Tu Che Me Vien da Ridere" (1982), "Sbirulino" (1982),

"Apocalisse di un Terremoto" (1982), "Pin il Monello" (1982), "Mystere" (1983), "Uno Scandalo Perbene" (1984), "Una Spina Nel Cuore" (1986), "Voyage a Rome" (1992), "Senza Pelle" (1994), "Celluloide" (1996), "Banzai" (1997), "La Via Degli Angeli" (1999), "Amici Ahrarara" (2001), and "Il Signor Diavolo" (2019). Tardioli appeared on television in productions of "Paganii" (1976), "Il Passatore" (1977), "Diario di un Giudice" (1978), "La Vedova e il Piedipiatti" (1979), "L'Affare Stavisky" (1979), "Un Uomo da Ridere" (1980), "Arabella" (1980), "L'Assedio" (1980), "Un Paio di Scarpe per Tanti Chilometri" (1981), "Turno di Notte" (1981), "George Sand" (1981), "Don Luigi Sturzo" (1981), "L'Elemento D" (1981), "Il Caso Murri" (1982), "L'Amante dell'Orsa Maggiore" (1983), "Un'isola" (1986), "La Scalata" (1993), "Il Grande Fuoco" (1995), and "The Murder of a General" (2007). His other television credits include episodes of "Quadi Davvero", "Un Commissario a Roma", "Casa Vianello", "Detective De Luca", "Don Matteo", "Rocco Schiavone", "Blanca", "Che Dio Ci Aiuti", and "DOC - Nelle Tue Mani".

Tater Tot

Tater Tot, an orange tabby kitten whose physical deformities made him an internet sensation, died suddenly of suspected pneumonia at his foster home in Utah on August 2, 2023. She was 6 weeks old. Tater Tot was born in Utah on June 16, 2023. The tiny kitten was found with four legs that were malformed and a cleft palate and was later handed over to Kitty CrusAIDe, a Salt Lake City animal rescue, where he was fostered out. His foster parents splinted his legs in hopes that he'd learn to walk, which he did shortly before his death. His life was documented on Facebook and TikTok and videos of Tater Tot had millions of viewers.

Taylor, Gilbert W.

Canadian film director and writer Gilbert W. Taylor died in Toronto, Ontario, Canada, on May 27, 2023. He was 86. Taylor was born in Oshawa, Ontario, on September 5, 1936. He graduated from Ryerson University in Toronto and worked at Procter and Gamble. He teamed with Bill Marshall to create Marshall Taylor Productions, a public relations and film production company, in the 1960s. Taylor produced, directed, and wrote the 1969 short film "The Mississauga Movie" and directed and scripted the 1970 horror film "Dr. Frankenstein on Campus". He served as producer of the films "Pinocchio's Birthday Party" (1973) and "Klondike Fever" and various stage shows. He later served as president of the Royal Canadian Military Institute for five years. Taylor is survived by his wife of sixty years, Anne.

Taylor, Teresa

Rock drummer and actress Teresa Taylor, who performed with the experimental band Butthole Surfers, died of lung disease in Austin, Texas, on June 18, 2023. She was 60.

Taylor was born in Arlington, Texas, on November 10, 1962. She was the drummer for several high school marching bands in the Fort Worth and Austin area. She joined singer Gibby Haynes, guitarist Paul Leary, and fellow drummer King Coffey in the Butthole Surfers in 1983. She was billed as Teresa Nervosa and performed on the albums "Live PCPPEP" (1984), "Psychic... Powerless... Another Man's Sac" (1984), "Cream corn from the Socket of Davis" (1985), "Rembrandt Pussyhorsse" (1986), "Locust Abortion Technician" (1987), and "Hairway to Steven" (1988). She left the band in 1989 after undergoing brain surgery for an aneurysm. Taylor was featured in Richard Linklater's 1990 film "Slacker". She returned to the Butthole Surfers to tour with the band in 2008 and 2009.

Teo, Pearry Reginald

Singapore film director Pearry Reginald Teo died of an accidental drug overdose at his home in North Hollywood, California, on March 9, 2023. He was 44. He born Pearry Reginald Teo Zhang Pingli in Singapore on July 23, 1978. He moved to the United States in 2001 to pursue a career in films.

He produced, directed, and wrote several short horror films including "Liberata Me" (2002), "Children of the Arcana" (2003), and "Take Me Somewhere Nice" (2004). He helmed his first feature, "The Gene Generation", starring Bai Ling and Faye Dunaway, in 2007. Teo continued to work primarily in the horror genre, directing and frequently writing such films as "Necromentia" (2009), the tele-film "Witchville" (2010), "The Evil Inside" (2011), the short "Tekken: Reload" (2012), "Dracula: The Dark Prince" (2013), "The Curse of Sleeping Beauty" (2016) also appearing onscreen as the Shadow Djinn, "Ghosthunters" (2016), "The Assent" (2019) featuring Tatum O'Neal, "Methuselah" (2021), "Fast Vengeance" (2021) starring DMX, and "Shadow Master" (2022) also appearing as

Hanuman. He was an executive producer of the Wachowskis' "Cloud Atlas" (2012) and co-producer of "Day of the Dead: Bloodline" (2017). Teo reportedly had several films in post-production including "Nikola Tesla 19hz", "How to Make a Deal with the Devil", and "Pale Horse". Teo and author Christine Converse wrote the 2013 horror novel "Bedlam Stories" together. His survivors include his son, Teo.

Terasawa, Buichi

Japanese manga artist Buichi Terasawa died of a heart attack in Japan on September 8, 2023. He was 68. Terasawa was born in Asahikawa, Japan, on March 30, 1955. He became interested in comics from an early age. He moved to Tokyo in 1976 and studied under artist Osamu Tezuka. He worked in the

manga department of Tezuka Productions. He was a pioneer in the use of personal computers in creating comic book art. He was best known for creating the series "Cobra" (1978), "Karasu Tengu Kabuto" (1987), and "Midnight Eye Goku" (1987), all of which were adapted for anime series. He created the early digital manga series "Takeru" in 1992. He was diagnosed with a malignant brain tumor in 1998 and was paralyzed on the left side of his body. He continued to work as a manga artist despite his disabilities.

Thallaug, Anita

Norwegian singer and actress Anita Thallaug died in Norway on March 30, 2022. She was 85. Thallaug was born in Baerum, Norway, on February 14, 1938. She began performing at the Spider Theater in Oslo under the name Vesla Rolfsen at the age of seven. She also appeared in children's

programs from the Norwegian Broadcasting Corporation in the 1950s. Thallaug sang "Solhverv" in the Eurovision Song Contest in 1963 and placed last among the 13 competitors. She was featured in several films including "I Moralens Navn" (1954), "Blonde in Bondage" (1957), "Operasjon Lovsprett" (1962), and "Bells in the Moonlight (1964). She appeared on television in productions of "Fru Luna" (1962) and "Anything Goes" (1962). She largely retired in the mid-1960s and wrote her autobiography, "Veien Mot Nord", in 1978. She resumed performing in the late 1980s, appearing in musicals and the 1990 television production "The Spanish Fly". She recorded the album "Me, and My Friends" in 1998. Her older sister, opera singer Edith Thallaug, died in 2020.

Thomas, Charlie

Singer Charlie Thomas, who performed with the vocal group the Drifters from the late-1950s, died of liver cancer in

Bowie, Maryland, on January 31, 2023. He was 85. Thomas was born in Lynchburg, Virginia, on April 7, 1937. He was

performing with the vocal group the Five Crowns in the late 1950s. They were appearing at the Apollo Theater in 1958 when George Treadwell, the manager of the Drifters, fired the group's members and replaced them with Thomas and three other of the Five Crowns. He sang tenor with the new lineup which included lead singer Ben E. King, baritone, Dock Green, and bass Elsbeary Hobbs. They recorded their first hit song, "There Goes My Baby", in 1959. Thomas sang lead vocals on the songs "Sweets for My Sweet" and "When My Little Girl Is Smiling". Thomas left the Drifters in 1967. He began a splinter group known as Charlie Thomas' Drifters in 1971 and continued to perform with them until his death. Thomas was inducted into the Rock and Roll Hall of Fame in 1988 as a member of the Drifters.

Thomas, Mark

British film composer Mark Thomas died at his home in Wales after a long illness on July 19, 2023. He was 67. Thomas was born in Penclawde, Wales, on April 9, 1956. He studied music composition and orchestration and began his

professional career as a session violinist in London. He played violin on numerous film soundtracks including "Supergirl" (1984), "A View to a Kill" (1985), "Death Wish 3" (1985), "Eleni" (1985), "Revolution" (1985), "Highlander" (1986), "Link" (1986), "Clockwise" (1986), "Mona Lisa" (1986), "Haunted Honeymoon" (1986), "Shanghai Surprise" (1986), "Duet for One" (1986), "The Living Daylights" (1987), "Superman IV: The Quest for Peace" (1987), "Someone to Watch Over Me" (1987), "Willow" (1988), "Rambo III" (1988), "Licence to Kill" (1989), and "Batman" (1989). He worked as a composer on numerous films including ""Moonchild" (1989), "Avalon" (1989), "Torment" (1990), "Atlantis" (1991), "Un Nos Ola' Leuad" (1991), "Wild Justice" (1994), "Y Mapiwr" (1995), "Twin Town" (1997) earning a BAFTA Cymru Award, "Chameleon" (1997), "Up 'n' Under" (1998), "The Sea Change" (1998), "Mad Cows" (1999), "The Big Tease" (1999), "House!" (2000), "Taliesin Jones" (2000), "Merlin: The Return" (2000), "The Little Unicorn" (2001), "The Sorcerer's Apprentice" (2001), "The Meeksville Ghost" (2001), "Askari" (2001), "Dog Soldiers" (2002), "The Great Dome Robbery" (2002), "Re-Inventing Eddie" (2002), "Hooded Angels" (2002), "The Final Curtain" (2002), "Pets to the Rescue" (2002), "Hoodlum & Son" (2003), "Agent Cody Banks 2: Destination London" (2004), "Berserker" (2004),

"School for Seduction" (2004), "The Magic Roundabout" (2005), "Rottweiler" (2004), "Shadows in the Sun" (2005), "Blood of Beasts" (2005), "Last Best Chance" (2005), "The Adventures of Greyfriars Bobby" (2005), "Doogal" (2006), "Wilderness" (2006), "Hot Tamale" (2006), "Calon Gaeth" (2006), "Back in Business" (2007), "Moondance Alexander" (2007), "The Magic Door" (2007), "Tales of the Riverbank" (2008), "Goal! III" (2009), "Flicka 2" (2010), "Marley & Me: The Puppy Years" (2011), "Swinging with the Finkels" (2011), "Foster" (2011), "Flicka: Country Pride" (2012), "So You Want to Be a Pirate!" (2012), "Y Syrcas" (2013), "Under Milk Wood" (2015), "Zoo" (2017), "Last Summer" (2018), the short "Death Meets Lisolette" (2020), "La Cha Cha" (2021), and "The Lady from the Sea" (2023). Thomas worked frequently on television, composing for productions of "Richard Burton's Christmas Story" (1991), "Trauma" (1991), "The Jazz Detective" (1992), "The Marshal" (1993), "Wycliffe and the Cycle of Death" (1993), "Daisies in December" (1995), "The Final Passage" (1996), "Aristocrats" (1999), "The Real Eve" (2002), "Out of Eden" (2002), "Doc Martin and the Legend of the Cloutie" (2003), "The Deputy" (2004), "Big Dippers" (2005), "The Booze Cruise III: The Scattering" (2006), "May Contain Nuts" (2009), "Most Shocking Celebrity Moments 2010" (2010), "A Princess for Christmas" (2011), "The Sweeter Side of Life" (2013), "Love by Design" (2014), and "Brief Encounters" (2016). His other television credits include the series "Merched Lasarus", "Testament: The Bible in Animation", "Raging Planet", "Mysteries of Magic", "Jack of Hearts", "Equinox", "Doc Martin", "Any Time Now", "A Mind to Kill", "Treflan", "Seriously Weird", "Home Farm Twins", "Ace Lightning", "Dalziel and Pascoe", "Purple and Brown", "Cowbois Ac Injans", "Hyperdrive", "Star Stories", "Plus One", "Krod Mandoon and the Flaming Sword of Fire", "The Kevin Bishop Show", "The Great Outdoors", "Ladies of Letters", "Reggie Perrin", "Frankie Boyle's Tramadol Nights", "Comedy Showcase", "Mossy Bottom Shorts", "Being Eileen", "DC's World's Funnest", "Shaun the Sheep", "Harry & Bip", "Episodes" earning an Emmy Award nomination for composing the theme, "Stella", and "Benidorm". Thomas is survived by his wife, Luz Marie, and three children.

Thorne, Angela

British actress Angela Thorne died at her home in Battersea, London, England, on June 16, 2023. She was 84.

Thorne was born in Karachi, British India (now Pakistan), on January 25, 1939. Her father served in the army there as a doctor and she settled in England with her family at the age of five. She studied at the Guildhall School of Music and Drama. She began her career with the Caryl Jenner Children's Theatre and performed in repertory in York and Sheffield. She appeared in stage productions throughout her career. Thorne was seen on television in episodes of "The Avengers", "The Liars", "Mystery and Imagination", "Knock on Any Door", "Sergeant Cork", "Conflict", "Blandings Castle", "World in Ferment" as Nancy Chuff in 1969, "The Woodlanders" as Felice Charmond in 1970, "The Culture Vultures", "Seasons of the Year", "Love Story", Kate", "Justice", "Then and Now", "Heil Caesar!", "Ten from the Twenties", "Within These Walls", "Get Some In!", "Aquarius", "Well Anyway", "The Good Life", "Mr. Big", "Horizon", "Crown Court", "Emmerdale" as Charlotte Verney in 1978, "House of Caradus", "After Julius", "Cowboys", "The Bagthorpe Saga" as Laura Bagthorpe in 1981, "Drummonds", "Shades of Darkness", "Screenplay", "Farrington of the F.O." as Harriet Harrington from 1986 to 1987, "Three Up Two Down" as Daphne Trenchard from 1985 to 1989, "The Good Guys", "Noah's Ark" as Valerie Kirby from 1997 to 1998, "Heartbeat", "Midsomer Murders", "Foyle's War", "The Royal", "To the Manor Born" as Marjory Frobisher from 1979 to 1981, "Call My Bluff", "Wallander", "Wogan", "The Life of Rock with Brian Pern", and "Talking Comedy". Her other television credits include productions of "Take a Sapphire" (1968), "Elizabeth R" (1971), "Haunted: Poor Girl" (1974), "Ballet Shoes" (1975), "The Rocking Horse Winner" (1977), "Anyone for Denis?" (1982) as Margaret Thatcher, "Mistral's Daughter" (1984), "The Lady's Not for Burning" (1987), "Dunrulin" (1990) again as Thatcher, "Cold Comfort Farm" (1995), and "Silent Hours" (2015). Thorne was featured in several films including "Oh! What a Lovely War" (1969), "Yellow Dog" (1973), "Lady Oscar" (1979), "The Human Factor" (1979), "ffolkes" (aka "North Sea Hijack") (1980), "Bullshot" (1983), the animated "The BFG" (1989) as the voice of the Queen of England, "Bright Young Things" (2003), and "Lassie" (2005). Thorne was married to actor Peter Penry-Jones from 1967 until his death in 2009. She is survived by their two sons, actors Laurence and Rupert Penry-Jones.

Thorpe, Marc

Special effects artist Marc Thorpe, who worked in the

"Star Wars" and "Indiana Jones" franchises, died of complications from Parkinson's disease at a hospice facility in Alamo, California, on November 24, 2023. He was 77. Thorpe was born in San Francisco, California, on November 9, 1946. He attended Cal State University and earned a master's degree from the University of California at Davis in 1971. He worked on a behavioral sculpture at Marineland in Florida in 1974, training two female dolphins to perform synchronized swimming routines. He joined Industrial Light and Magic at Lucasfilm in 1979 as a model maker and animatronic designer. He was involved with the optical effects of the second "Star Wars" film, "The Empire Strikes Back", in 1980. He was a model maker and visual effects artist on the films "Raiders of the Lost Ark" (1981), "Dragonslayer" (1981), "Poltergeist" (1982), "Return of the Jedi" (1983), "Indiana

Jones and the Temple of Doom" (1984), "Explorers" (1985), "Howard the Duck" (1986), "*batteries not included" (1987), "Indiana Jones and the Last Crusade" (1989), and "The Hunt for Red October" (1990). He was a senior designer at LucasToys and came up with the idea for Robot Wars. They were basically death matches for mechanical devices that would battle in an arena. The championships were televised in the early years. He continued to produce Robot Wars Events until losing creative control of the business in lengthy legal proceedings to Profile Records in 1997. He founded the independent design consultancy service, Marc Thorpe Designs in 2011. It lasted until 2003 and again from 2007 to 2013. Thorpe was diagnosed with Parkinson's disease in 1993. His survivors include his daughter, Megan.

Tibbles, Doug

Television writer Doug Tibbles died in Massachusetts on April 12, 2023. He was 83. Tibbles was born in California on January 19, 1940. He attended the University of California at Los Angeles after graduating high school. He began writing for television comedy series in the mid-1960s. He penned episodes of "The Munsters", "Family Affair", "The Andy Griffith Show", "Bewitched", "Room 222", "The Doris Day Show", "My Three Sons", "Love, American Style", "Chico and the Man", "The Krofft Supershow", "Magic Mongo", "Hello, Larry", and "The New Gidget". Tibbles also wrote for the television specials "Raquel" (1970) and "Robert Young with the Young" (1973). He soon married singer Barbara Keith and they left Hollywood for Massachusetts. Doug and Helen formed the band the Stone Coyotes, with Doug on drums. The band was later joined by sons John and Doug, Jr. The Stone Coyotes recorded their first album, "Church of the Falling Rain", in 1998. They recorded 15 albums from Red Cat Records over the next three decades. Tibbles is survived by his wife and three children from a previous marriage.

Tickner, George

Guitarist George Tickner, who was a founding member of the band Journey in 1973, died on July 5, 2023. He was 76. Tickner was born in Syracuse, New York, on September 8, 1946. He performed with the San Francisco band Frumious Bandersnatch in the early 1970s. He and bassist Ross Valory were founding members of Journey in 1973, joining with lead guitarist Neal Schon and drummer Prairie Prince. Journey's self-titled debut album was released in

April of 1975. Tickner soon left the band to attend Stanford Medical School. He received a medical degree and practiced as a doctor. He continued to be involved in music and formed the Hive recording studio with Valory. They were joined by Stevie 'Keys' Rosenman in the band VTS and released the 2005 album "Cinema". Tickner reunited with his former bandmates when Journey received a star on the Hollywood Walk of Fame in 2005.

Tidelius, Kerstin

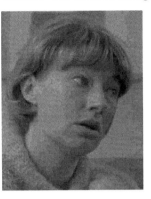

Swedish actress Kerstin Tidelius died in Naca, Stockholm, Sweden, on February 15, 2023. She was 88. Tidelius was born in Kungsholm, Stokholm, on October 14, 1934. She trained as an actress at the Gothenburg City Theatre from 1954. She began her career on stage in 1957 and performed frequently with Gothenburg's Stadsteater until her retirement in 1995. Tidelius was seen in the films "Marianne" (1953), "Karlek Pa Turne" (1955), "Adamsson i Sverige" (1966), "Roseanna" (1967), "Who Saw Him Die?" (1968), "Adalen 31" (1969), "Snacka Gar Ju..." (1981), "Avskedet" (1982), Ingmar Bergman's "Fanny and Alexander" (1982) as Henrietta Vergerus, and "Juloratoriet" (1996). She appeared on television in productions of "En Fortrollad Natt" (1966), "Mannen Som Blev Bjuden Pa Somnmedel" (1967), "Huset Vid Gransen" (1968), "Froken Julie" (1969), "Vad Sager Du, Tomas?" (1971), "Sandladan" (1972), "Fiskelaget" (1974), "Galenpannan" (1974), "Gyllene Ar" (1975), "Polisen Som Vagrade Ge Upp" (1984), "Sparvoga" (1989), and "Glenn & Gloria Eller Nar Vinder Vander" (1989). Her other television credits include episodes of "Magnus", "Jourhavande" as Gudrun from 1974 to 1975, "Stjarnhuset", "Hall Huvet Kallt" (1994), and "Alskade Lotten". She was featured in the recurring role of Ingrid Lofgren in the long-running television series "Hem Till Byn" (aka "Home to the Village") from 1971 to 2006.

Tidy, Bill

British cartoonist Bill Tidy died in England on March 11, 2023. He was 89. Tidy was born in Tranmere, Cheshire, England, on October 9, 1933. He began creating cartoons for the school magazine while attending St. Margaret's Church of England Academy in his early teens. He served in the military with the Royal Engineers from 1952 to 1955. He worked in advertising after his discharge and began freelancing as a cartoonist. His work began appearing in the pages of "The Daily Sketch" and "Daily Mirror". He soon moved to London where he was co-founder of the British Cartoonists'

Association. He was noted for the cartoon strip "The Cloggies" that ran in the satirical magazine "Private Eye" from 1967 to 1981, and "The Fosdyke Saga", a parody of "The Forsyte Saga", which appeared in the "Daily Mirror" from 1971 to 1984. "The Fosdyke Saga" was adapted for a television series in 19778 and a radio series on the BBC in 1983. Tidy's works were also seen in the pages of "New Scientist", "What's Brewing", and "Punch". He was a guest on such television series as "2nd House", "World of Laughter", "Celebrity Squares", "Quick on the Draw", "3-2-1", "It's a Knockout", "Tell the Truth", "Babble", "You Bet!", "Countdown", "The Stuart Hall Show", "This Is Your Life", and "A Word in Your Ear". His autobiography, "Is There Any News of the Iceberg?" was published in 1995. Tidy was married to Rosa Colotti from 1960 until her death in 2019 and they had three children together.

Tiller, Nadja

Austrian actress Nadja Tiller died at a retirement home in Hamburg, Germany, on February 21, 2023. She was 93.

Tiller was born in Vienna, Austria, on March 16, 1929. She was the daughter of stage actor and director Anton Tiller and opera singer Erika Korner. She began training at the Max Reinhardt Seminar in 1945 and continued to study dance and acting at the University of Music and Performing Arts until 1949. She began her career on stage with the Theatre in der Josefstadt. She also won the Miss Austria beauty competition in 1949 and again in 1951. Tiller made her film debut in 1949's "Marcheen vom Gluck" and continued to appear in such films as "Kleiner Schwinel am Wolfgangsee" (1949), "Marika" (1950), "Scham' Dich, Brigitte!" (1952), "Ich Hab' Mich So an Dich Gewohnt" (1952), "Illusion in Moll" (1952), "Einmal Keine Sorgen Haben" (1953), "Die Kaiserin von China" (1953), "Ein Tolles Fruchtchen" (1953), "Schlagerparade" (1953), "Liebe und Trompetenblasen" (1954), "Madchen Mit Zukunft" (1954), "Sie" (1954), "The Last Summer" (1954), "Gestatten, Mein Name Ist Cox" (1955), "Ball im Savoy" (1955), "Reaching for the Stars" (1955), "Wie Werde Ich Filmstar?" (1955), "Hotel Adlon" (1955), Rolf Thiele's historical drama "Die Barrings" (1955), "The Life and Loves of Mozart" (1955), "Das Bad auf der Tenne" (1956), "Ich Suche Dich" (1956), "Friedericke von Barring" (1956), "Fuhrmann Henschel" (1956), "Spy for Germany" (1956), "Banktresor 713" (1957), "Die Grosse Chance" (1957), "Drei Mann Auf Einem Pferd" (1957), "El Hakim" (1957), "King on Horseback" (1958), "The Night Affair" (1958), "Rosemary" (1958), "Riff Raff Girls" (1959), "Labyrinth" (1959), "Portrait of a Sinner" (1959), "The Buddenbrooks" (1959), "Meet Peter Voss" (1959), "Die Botschafterin" (1960), "The World in My Pocket" (1961), "The Nina B. Affair" (1961), "Geliebte Hochstaplerin" (1961), Julien Duvivier's supernatural thriller "The Burning Court" (1962), "Lulu" (1962) in the title role, "Anima Nera" (1962), "L'Amore

Diffiile" (1962), "Moral 63" (1963), "Schloss Gripsholm" (1963), "Das Grosse Liebesspiel" (1963), "Tonio Kroger" (1964), "Killer Spy" (1965), "Das Liebeskarussell" (1965), "The Upper Hand" (1966), "Dymky" (1966), "Tender Scoundrel" (1966) with Jean-Paul Belmondo, "Come Imparai ad Amare le Donne" (1966), "L'Estate" (1966), "Emma Hamilton" (1968), "Death Knocks Twice" (1969), "Slap in the Face" (1970), "O Happy Day" (1970), "Engel, die Ihre Flugel Verbrenne" (1970), "Die Feuerzangenbowle" (1970), "Le Leonesse" (1971), "The Dead Are Alive!" (1972), "Le Moine" (1972), "Il Baco da Seta" (1974), "Wanted: Babysitter" (1975), "Der Sommer des Samurai" (1986), "The Sunset Boys" (1995), "Barefoot" (2005), and "Dinosaurier" (2009) joined by her husband, Walter Giller, as a senior citizen couple. Tiller appeared on television in productions of "The Poppy Is Also a Flower" (1966), "Waterloo" (1969), "Hotel Royal" (1969), "11 Uhr 20" (1970), "Das Sexte Programm" (1971), "Hallo, Wer Dort?" (1971), "Geschichten Zu Zweit" (1973), "Ein Mann fur Alle Falle" (1979), "Liebling, Ich Lass' Mich Scheiden!" (1981), "Er-Goetz-Liches" (1984), "Die Ziepflanze" (1985), "Mutter und Tochter" (1985), "Boses Blut" (1993), "Liane" (1996), "Champagner und Kamillentee" (1997), "Spending Nights with Joan" (1998) as Joan Crawford, "Holstein Lovers" (1999), "Zwischen Liebe und Leidenschaft" (2000), "Das Weibernest" (2001), "Ein Albtraum von 3 1/2 Kilo" (2002), "Der Zweite Fruhling" (2003), "Das Bernstein-Amulett" (2004), "Laura's Wish List" (2005), "Ich Heirate Meine Frau" (2007), "Liebling, Wir Haben Geerbt!" (2007), "Und Ewig Schweigen die Manner" (2008), "Liebe Ist Verhandlungssache" (2009), and "Es Liegt Mir Auf der Zunge" (2009). Her other television credits include episodes of "Der Rasende Lokalreporter", "Der Kommissar", "Hallo - Hotel Sacher... Portier!", "Es Muss Nicht Immer Kaviar Sein", "Die Schone Marianne" as Marianne in 1978, "Sternensommer" as Gena Marquardt in 1981, "Die Laurents", "Die Krimistunde", "Tatort", "Locker vom Hocker", "The Black Forest Hospital", "Il Ricatto", "Geschichten Aus der Heimat", "Alles Gluck Dieser Erde", "Ein Unvergessliches Wochenende", "Mordslust", "Guten Morgen Mallorca", "Freunde Furs Leben", "Das Traumschig", "Sylter Geschicthen", "Die Drei", "Sturmzeit", "Rosamunde Pilcher", "Fur Alle Falle Stefanie", and "Der Ferienarzt". She continued to perform frequently on stage throughout her career appearing at the Salzburg Festival, Theater Lubeck, and the Hamburger Kammerspiele. Tiller was married to actor Walter Giller from 1956 until his death in 2011. She is survived by their son and daughter.

Tindall, Blair

Oboist and author Blair Tindall, who wrote the 2005 memoir "Mozart in the Jungle", died of heart disease in Los Angeles, California, on April 12, 2023. She was 63. Tindall was born in Chapel Hill, North Carolina, on February 2, 1960. She learned to play the piano as a child and switched to the oboe to join her junior high school band. She subsequently graduated from the North Carolina School of the Arts in 1978 and earned a master's degree with the Manhattan School of Music. She performed with such groups as the New York Philharmonic,

Orpheus chamber Orchestra, and the Orchestra of St. Luke's. Tindall played in the pit orchestras for Broadway productions of "Miss Saigon" and "Les Miserables". She was heard on the soundtracks of such films as "Mr. & Mrs.

Bridge" (1990), "Malcolm X" (1992), "Mad Dog and Glory" (1993), "The Inkwell" (1994), "Crooklyn" (1994), "4 Little Girls", "Twilight" (1998), and "Snake Eyes" (1998). She moved to California in 1999 to study journalism at Stanford, where she earned a master's degree. She worked for several newspapers including "The Contra Costa Times" and "The San Francisco Examiner". She penned her memoir, 2005's "Mozart in the Jungle: Sex, Drugs, and Classical Music", which was showed the seamy underside of classical music. The controversial "Mozart in the Jungle" was adapted for a television series by Amazon in 2014. Lola Kirke starred as a young oboist and Gael Garcia Bernal was conductor of a New York orchestra. The series lasted four seasons before ending in 2018 and Tindall appeared in a cameo role as an usher. She married science educator Bill Nye ("the science guy") in February of 2006. The relationship was brief and tumultuous as the marriage was declared invalid by the State of California. Nye later accused her of breaking into his house and killing his plants with herbicides and she received a restraining order. Tindall is survived by her fiance, photographer Chris Sattlberger.

Ting Chiang

Taiwanese actor Ting Chiang died of complications from a fall at a hospital in Taoyuan, Taiwan, on January 27, 2023. He was 86. Ting was born

in Zhejiang, China, on April 26, 1936. He was seen in numerous films from the early 1960s including "Ke Nu" (1963), "Wan Jun Biao Mei" (1965), "Zhen Jia Qing Fu" (1965), "Ying Xiong Lie Nu" (1966), "Yan Nu" (1968), "Xia Zhong Xia" (1968), "In the Flat Field" (1969), "A Battle of Magog" (1969), "Storm Over the Yangtse River" (1969), "Dao Wang Jian Wang" (1970), "Ge Wang Ge Hou" (1970), "Tai Tai Hui Niang Jia" (1970), "Yin Juan Nu Xia" (1970), "Yi Dai Ge Wang" (1970), "Ti Ying" (1971), "Zhu Hong Wu" (1971), "Al Qing Yi Er San" (1971), "Tie Quan Zheng Ba" (1972), "Jing Tian Dong Di" (1972), "Wu Jia Zhi Bao" (1972), "Two Ugly Men" (1973), "Da San Yuan" (1974), "Shang Xing Lie Che" (1981), "Exit No. 6" (2006), "War Game 229" (2011), "Love" (2012), "Bear It" (2012), "Joyful Reunion" (2012), "A Moment of Love" (2012), "Love Transplantation" (2013), "Black Sheep" (2016), "The Mad King of Taipei" (2017), "Manhattan Cop" (2017), and "The

Bold, the Corrupt and the Beautiful" (2017). Ting was seen on television in productions of "Ji Zhu, Wang Le" (2001), "Nie Zi" (2003), "Fu Qi You An Kang" (2009), "Police Et Vous" (2009), "Xing Fu Xiao Gong Yuan" (2010), "Year of the Rain" (2010), "Ranger" (2011), "I Love You So Much" (2012), "Happy 300 Days" (2013), "Zhuan. Da Ren" (2014), "Shi Shang Zui Qiang Fang Shou Dui, Ho Tann Mai Tsau!" (2014), "Ai Qing Duo Yi Kou" (2015), "Ba Ji Teenagers"(2015), "Moon River" (2015), "A Touch of Green" (2016), "Refresh Man" (2016), "700 Sui Lu Cheng"(2016-2017), "Suan Tian Zhi Wei" (2017), "The Eternal Flower Yong Sheng Hua" (2018), "Hun Qiu Xi Men" (2019), "CSIC: I Hero" (2019), "Zui Jia Li Yi" (2019), "The North-Ming Fish" (2020), "The Haunted Heart" (2020), "Tears of Fire" (2021), "Ni Hau, Wo Shi Shei?" (2022), and "Mom, Don't Do That!" (2022). Ting married actress Hsuan Li in 1971 and is survived by her and their three children.

Topham, Top

British musician Anthony 'Top' Topham, who was lead guitarist for the Yardbirds, died of complications from dementia in England on January 23, 2023. He was 75. Topham was born in Southall, England, on July 3, 1947. He and his secondary school friend, rhythm guitarist Chris Dreja met fellow several fellow musicians, vocalist/harmonica player Keith Relf, drummer Jim McCarty, and bassist Paul Samwell-

Smith, at a jazz music venue in Norbiton, England, in May of 1963. They decided to form a band, the Blue-Sounds, which soon became the Yardbirds. Topham was lead guitarist though tenure with the band was short-lived as he left the band the following October. He was fifteen at the time and faced parental disapproval and feared a full-time band schedule would disrupt his education. Topham was replaced by Eric Clapton, with Jeff Beck and Jimmy Page later taking on the role of lead guitarist. The Yardbirds became one of the leading rock bands of the 1960s. Topham attended Epsom Art School where he studied fine art. He continued to play guitar, working with Duster Bennett and Marc Bolan in the band Winston G and the Wicked. He became a session musician at the Blue Horizon record label and recorded a solo album, "Ascension Heights" in 1968. His music career was again interrupted when he became seriously ill in 1970. He joined the Subud spiritual movement and began working in fine arts and interior decorating. He again returned to music in 1988 when he reunited with former Yardbird Jim McCarty. They formed the Topham-McCarty Band and performed together for two years. Topham began playing country blues and returned to work as a session musician. He rejoined McCarty and Dreja in a new version of the Yardbirds in the 2000s and was a member of the band from 2013 until 2015. Topham changed his name to Sanderson Rasjid after joining the Subud movement. He is survived by three daughters, including musician Leanie Kaleido, and seven sons.

Topol, Chaim

Israeli actor Chaim Topol, who starred as Tevye in the stage and screen productions of the musical "Fiddler on the Roof", died of complications from Alzheimer's disease in Tel Aviv, Israel, on March 8, 2023. He was 87. Topol was born in Tel Aviv, in what was then part of the Palestine Mandate, on September 9, 1935. He graduated from high school in 1952 and

moved to the Kibbutz Geva. He enlisted in the Israeli army the following year and served with the entertainment troupe. He settled at the Kibbutz Mishmar David after the Sinai War in 1956 where he formed a theatrical company. He sang and acted with the group through the early 1960s. He joined the satirical theatre company Batzal Yarok (Green Onion) in 1960 and toured the country. He was also co-founder of the Haifa Municipal Theatre. Topol made his film debut in "I Like Mike" in 1961 and was also seen in the films "El Dorado" (1963), "Sallah" (1964), "Cast a Giant Shadow" (1966) with Kirk Douglas, "Ervinka" (1967), "Before Winter Comes" (1968), and "The Rooster" (1971). He starred in the role of Tevye the Dairyman in an Israel production of the musical "Fiddler on the Roof" in 1966. He joined the London production the following year, where he learned to speak English phonetically for the part. He also began being billed only under the name Topol. He was cast as Tevye in the 1971 film version of "Fiddler", earning an Academy Award nomination for his performance. He returned to the role in a revival in London's West End in 1983 and starred in a Broadway revival from 1990 to 1991, where he was nominated for a Tony Award. He toured England with "Fiddler" in 1994 and Israel from 1997 to 1998. He also performed the role in several productions of the musical in Australia in the 2000s. He made his farewell tour with "Fiddler in the United States in 2009 but was forced to withdraw due to a shoulder injury. He played the part on stage over 3,500 times during his career. Topol co-starred with Mia Farrow in the 1972 film "The Public Eye" (aka "Follow Me"). His other films include "A Talent for Loving" (1973), "Galileo" (1975) in the title role of astronomer Galileo Galilei, the science fiction cult classic "Flash Gordon" (1980) as Dr. Hans Zarkov, "For Your Eyes Only" (1981) as Milos Columbo with Roger Moore's James Bond, "Again, Forever" (1985), "Left Luggage" (1998), and the short "Time Elevator" (1998). He appeared on television in such series as "The Danny Kaye Show", "The Eamonn Andrews Show", the short-lived BBC variety series "It's Topol" in 1968, "Frost on Sunday", "The Lee Philip Show", "The Merv Griffin Show", "The David Frost Show", "The Don Lane Show", "This Is Your Life", and "Wogan". Topol starred in television productions of "The Going Up of David Lev" (1973), "The Best of Times" (1974), "The House on Garibaldi Street" (1979), "The Winds of

War" (1983) as Berel Jastrow, "Queenie" (1987), and "War and Remembrance" (1988) reprising his role as Berel Jastrow. He was also seen in episodes of "Tales of the Unexpected" and "SeaQuest DSV". He was active in philanthropic endeavors, founding Variety Israel to help children with special needs in 1967. He was also co-founder of Jordan River Village in 2012, a vacation camp for Jewish and Arab children with serious illnesses. His autobiography, "Topol by Topol", was published in 1981. He was also author of the books "To Life!" (1994) and "Topol's Treasury of Jewish Humor, Wit and Wisdom" (1995). He was also a talented artist who illustrated numerous books in Hebrew and English. He was recipient of the Israel Prize for lifetime achievement in 2015. He married Galia Topol in 1956 and is survived by her and three children, Anat, Omer and Adi Topol. His family revealed after his death that Topol of a secret operative with the Mosad, Israel's espionage agency. His star status allowed him to visit country's where Israel had no official presence.

Toy, Camden

Actor Camden Toy, who was noted for horror roles under special effects makeup in such series as "Buffy the Vampire Killer" and "Angel", died of pancreatic cancer in Los Osos, California, on December 11, 2023. He was 68. Toy was

born in Pittsburgh, Pennsylvania, on May 31, 1955. He moved to New York City to pursue an acting career, where he was a founding member of the off-off-Broadway Nada Theatre in the late

1980s. He studied martial arts, clowning, and mime. Toy subsequently moved to Los Angeles and appeared in numerous films including "The Genius" (1993), "Faith" (1997), "My Chorus" (2000), "Backgammon" (2001), "Irascible" (2004), "All Souls Day: Dia de los Muertos" (2005), "The Works" (2005), "The Black Door" (2006), "Outta Sync" (2006), "Morning Glory" (2007), "The Recruited" (2007), "Naya Din" (2007), "Trickery Mimicry" (2008), "The League" (2008) as Lenin, "Immortally Yours" (2009), "Running Away with Blackie" (2009), "Mansfield Path" (2009), "Klikt" (2009), "Privateer" (2009), "The Godmother" (2010), "The Next Word" (2010), "The Morning Routine" (2010), "Overlords, Incorporated" (2010), "The Damage Done" (2010), "Bare Knuckles" (2010), "Carnies" (2010), "Vidor" (2010), "Runt" (2011), "Chromeskull: Laid to Rest 2" (2011), "Hard Love" (2011), "The Way I Saw You" (2011), "Sebastian" (2011), "Big Bad Bugs" (2012), "Dark Splinter" (2013), "Feed Me" (2013), "Now Hiring" (2014), "Valiant" (2014), "Disciples" (2014), "A Blood Story" (2015), "Bedeviled" (2016), "Boogey-Man" (2021), and "Average Joe" (2021). He served as an editor on the films and shorts "Betaville" (2001), "Deeper Mark" (2002), "Zen Noir" (2004), "Irascible" (2004), "Lightning Bug" (2004), and "Over Breakfast" (2005). Toy was noted for his work on

"Buffy the Vampire Slayer", portraying one of the ghoulish Gentlemen in the 1999 episode "Hush", the skin-eating Gnarl in 2002's "Sam Time, Same Place", and the Ubervamp in four episodes in 2002 and 2003. He was also seen in episodes of "Angel" as the Prince of Lies in the 2004 episode "Why We Fight", "The Mentalist", "The Insider's Guide to Film School" as Professor Strauss from 2008 to 2009, "Goodnight Burbank" as Yan Bobek in 2011, "The Bay" as Igor Chambers from 2010 to 2014, "Shameless", "Into the Dark", "Geeking Out with Al and Candace", and "The Indie Escape Network". His survivors include his partner, Bethany Henderson.

Trent, Buck

Country musician Buck Trent, who appeared regularly on the "Hee Haw" television series, died in Branson, Missouri, on October 9, 2023. He was 85. Trent was born in Spartanburg,  South Carolina, on February 17, 1938. He began performing on local radio stations by the age of eleven. He played with Cousin Wilbur and Blondie Brooks in Asheville, North Carolina, in 1955. He settled in Nashville in 1959 and joined the Bill Carlisle Show. He appeared on the Grand Ole Opry stage and was a member of Bill Monroe's Bluegrass Boys from 1960 to 1961. He was skilled with various instruments including the five-string banjo, dobro, steel guitar, mandolin, and electric bass and guitar. He played with Porter Wagoner's Wagon Masters from 1962 to 1973 and appeared regularly on television's "The Porter Wagoner Show". He played banjo on Dolly Parton's hit recordings "I Will Always Love You" and "Jolene" in 1973. Trent was a regular performer with Roy Clark's band on the country music variety series "Hee Haw" from 1974 to 1983. He was also seen in episodes of "The Jimmy Dean Show", "The Midnight Special", "The Tonight Show Starring Johnny Carson", "The Mike Douglas Show", "Nashville on the Road", "The Bob Braun Show", "Dolly", "Nashville Now", "Gilley's Place", and "The Marty Stuart Show". He performed frequently at theaters in Branson, Missouri, from the 1990s. He appeared with Clark and other musicians as a performer in Branson in the 1994 comedy film "Gordy". He is survived by his wife of 27 years, Jean Marie Trent, son Charles, and daughter Melissa.

Trilling, Zoe

Actress Zoe Trilling, who starred as Shirley Finnerty in the 1994 horror film "Night of the Demons 2", died in El Cajon, California, on September 8, 2023. She was 57. She was born Geralyn Marie Betzler in Wausau, Wisconsin, on May 27, 1966. She moved to Los Angeles in the mid-1980s to pursue an acting career. She worked at various jobs including teaching aerobics while studying acting and dance. She made her film debut under her real name in 1985's Girls Just Want to Have Fun". She was noted for her roles in horror and exploitation films over the next decade including "Fear" (1988), "The Borrower" (1991), "Nervous Ticks" (1992), "Dr. Giggles"

(1992) as Normi, "To Protect and Serve" (1992), "Night Terrors" (1993), "Hellbound" (1994), "Night of the Demons 2" (1994), "Leprechaun 3" (1994), and "The Sunchaser" (1996).  Trilling was seen on television in episodes of "Hunter", "Guiding Light" as Lacey Bauer in 1987, "21 Jump Street", "CBS Summer Playhouse", "Married... with Children", "They Came from Outer Space", "MacGyver", and "Jake and the Fatman". Her other television credits include the tele-films "Children of the Night" (1985), "Amityville Horror: The Evil Escapes" (1989), "Thanksgiving Day" (1990), "Reason for Living: The Jill Ireland Story" (1991), and "Last Exit to Earth" (1996). She abandoned her acting career in the mid-1990s to move to New York City, where she worked as a choreographer and yoga instructor.

Tristan, Dorothy

Actress Dorothy Tristan, who was featured as prostitute Arlyn Page in the 1971 film "Klute", died of complications from Alzheimer's disease in La Porte, Indiana,  on January 7, 2023. She was 88. She was born Dorothy Behrndt in Yorkville Heights, New York City, on May 9, 1934. She began her career as a model and appeared on the covers of such magazines as "Vogue" and "Life". She began performing on stage in the early 1960s, starring as Charlotte Corday in a touring production of "Marat/Sade". She made her film debut in the 1970 film "End of the Road" directed by her then-husband Aram Avakian. She continued to appear in such films as "Klute" (1971) with Jane Fonda, "Man on a Swing" (1974), "Pigeon" (1974), "Swashbuckler" (1986), "Rollercoaster" (1977), "California Dreaming" (1979), and "Down and Out in Beverly Hills" (1986). Tristan appeared on television in the tele-films "Isn't It Shocking?" (1973), "The Trial of Chaplain Jensen" (1975), "Journey from Darkness" (1975), "Fear on Trial" (1975) as Laura Faulk, "Griffin and Phoenix" (1976), and "The Sad and Lonely Sundays" (1976). Her other television credits include episodes of "Gunsmoke", "Kojak", "The Rookies", "The Incredible Hulk", and "The Waltons". She scripted the tele-film "Steal the Sky" (1988) and the films "Weeds" (1987), "A Piece of Eden" (2000), and "Suspended Animation" (2001) based on her novel. She co-wrote and starred in her final film, 2015's "The Looking Glass", which was directed by her husband, John D. Hancock, and set in the couple's home in La Porte County, Indiana. Tristan was married to director Aram Avakian from 1957 until their divorce in 1972 and is survived by their two children, photojournalist Alexandra Avakian and musician Tristan Avakian. She married John D. Hancock in 1975 and he also survives her.

Trpcic, Shawna

Costume designer Shawna Trpcic, who was noted for her work on the television series "Firefly" and "The Mandalorian", died suddenly in Palm Desert, California, on October 4, 2023. She was 56. She was born Shawna Leavell in Artesia, California, on October 18, 1966. She began working in films with the 1990 films "Megaville" and "Mom". She served as a wardrobe assistant or assistant costume designer for the films "Stone Cold" (1991), "Toys" (1992), "Payback" (1995), "The First $20 Million Is Always the Hardest" (2002), "The Core" (2003), and "This Is the End" (2013). She was a costume illustrator for "What Lies Beneath" (2000) and "Hidalgo" (2004). She served as a wardrobe supervisor for the television series "Red Shoe Diaries" in 1992. She was costume designer for the 1993 juvenile series "Mighty Morphin Power Rangers". Trpcic designed costumes for numerous science fiction and action series from the early 2000s including "Firefly", "Angel", "Point Pleasant", "K-Ville", "Dr. Horrible's Sing-Along Blog", "Dollhouse", "Torchwood: Miracle Day", "Dragon Age: Redemption", "Husbands", "Witches of East End", "Second Chance", "Powers", "Swedish Dicks", and "Another Period". She was involved with the "Star Wars" television franchise, sharing Emmy Award nominations for her costumes for "The Mandalorian" in 2021 and 2023 and "The Book of Boby Fett" in 2022. She also designed for the 2023 series "Ahsoka". She was also costume designer for the tele-films "The Madness of Jane" (2008), "Pleading Guilty" (2010), and "Frankenstein's Monster's Monster, Frankenstein" (2019). She designed costumes for such films as "Leather Jackets" (1991), "Star Time" (1992), "Mikey" (1992) also appearing onscreen as a stewardess, "Slaughter of the Innocents" (1993), "The Cabin in the Woods" (2011), "Much Ado About Nothing" (2012), "Lust for Love" (2014), "The SpongeBob Movie: Spong on the Run" (2020), "The Never List" (2020), and numerous shorts. Trpcic usually attempted to include a pink flamingo design on her costumes as her signature mark. She was married to musician Joseph Trpcic until their divorce in 2018 and is survived by her son Joseph Jr. and daughter Sarah.

Tsuchida, Yoshiko

Japanese manga artist Yoshiko Tsuchida died in Tokyo, Japan, on September 15, 2023. He was 75. Tsuchida was born in Musashino, Japan, on February 26, 1948. She began her career after graduating high school as an assistant to manga artist Fujio Akatsuka at Fujio Pro. She created the manga series "Harenchi-kun" for "Shosetsu June" magazine in 1968. She was best known for her "It's Princess Tsuru!" manga that appeared in the magazines "Margaret" from 1973 to 1979. It was adapted for an anime television series in 1990. Her other manga's include "I am Yoshko" for "Margaret" and "Kimidori", "Midoru" and "Aomidori" for "Ribbon". She largely retired from manga in the 1990s.

Tuber, Rick

Emmy Award-winning television editor Rick Tuber died of a heart attack in Los Angeles, California, on January 7, 2023. He was 69. Tuber was born on May 10, 1953. He graduated from California State University at Northridge. He

began working as an assistant editor in television for the series "Cagney & Lacey" in 1985. He was also assistant editor for the tele-films "Reed Down Under" (1988), "The Fatal Image" (1990), "Seduction: Three Tales from the 'Inner Sanctum'" (1992), "Cagney & Lacey: Together Again" (1995) and "Cagney & Lacey: True Convictions" (1996), and episodes of "Baywatch Nights" and "Nash Bridges". He served as an assistant editor for the films "Arthur 2: On the Rocks" (1988), "The Karate Kid Part III" (1989), and "Sister Act 2: Back in the Habit" (1993). He was editor for the 1992 horror film "Maniac Cop 3: Badge of Silence". Tuber continued to work in television, editing episodes of "Downtown", "Crime Story", "Wiseguy", "ER" receiving an Emmy Award in 1995, "Flipper", "Fame L.A.", "Martial Law", "The Strip", "Nash Bridges", "Flatland", "Black Lash", "Trace Evidence: The Case Files of Dr. Henry Lee", "Vanished", "Women's Murder Club", "The Unit", "Raising the Bar", "Lie to Me", "The Chicago Code", "Breakout Kings", "The Protector", "Awake", "Chicago Fire", "The Haves and the Have Nots", "Ravenswood", "If Love You Is Wrong", "The Bastard Executioner", "Salem", and "Bones". He also edited the tele-films "Living a Lie" (1991) and "Exit Strategy" (2015). Tuber was the author of three novels featuring film editor Rick Potter as the protagonist, "Should Have Seen It Coming" (2017), "Just My F***ing Luck" (2018), and "Well, I'll Be Damned" (2020). He also wrote the book "Shanghai Cuts: A Hollywood Film Editor's Misadventures in China" (2014), a memoir about working with Dennis Hopper in the television series "Flatland". He is survived by his wife, Shirley Reiser, and four sons.

Tufano, Brian

British cinematographer Brian Tufano, who was noted for his work with director Danny Boyle, died in England on January 12, 2023. He was 83. Tufano was born in Shepherd's Bush, London, England, on December 1, 1939. He began working at the BBC as a projectionist and became a cameraman in 1973. He worked on such television series as "Cluff", "Man Alive", "The Wednesday Play", "Villette", "Sense and Sensibility", "The Brothers", "Scene", "All in a Day", "Blue Peter Special Assignment", "Inside Story", and "The Lively

Arts". He was also a camera operator for television productions of "The Long Journey" (1964), "The Violent Universe" (1969), "Vile Bodies" (1970), "The Resistible Rise of Arturo Ui" (1972), "The Edwardians" (1972), and "Rogue Male" (1976).

He served as a cinematographer or director of photography for numerous films from the late 1960s including "The Big Switch" (1968), "The Sailor's Return" (1978), "Quadrophenia" (1979), "Riding High" (1981), Ridley Scott's "Blade Runner" (1982) providing addition photography, "The Lords of Discipline" (1983), "Dreamscape" (1984), "War Party" (1988), "Windprints" (1989), "Ruby" (1992), Danny Boyle's debut film "Shallow Grave" (1994), "Trainspotting" (1996), "True Blue" (1996), "The Life of Stuff" (1997), "A Life Less Ordinary" (1997), "The MatchMaker" (1997), "What Rats Won't Do" (1998), "East Is East" (1999), "Virtual Sexuality" (1999), "Women Talking Dirty" (1999), "Tube Tales" (1999), "Billy Elliot" (2000) earning a BAFTA Award nomination, "Late Night Shopping" (2001), "Last Orders" (2001), "Once Upon a Time in the Midlands" (2002), "Millions" (2004), "Kidulthood" (2006), "I Could Never Be Your Woman" (2007), "Adulthood" (2008), Boyle's short film "Alien Love Triangle" (2008), "Sex & Drugs & Rock & Roll" (2010), "Everywhere and Nowhere" (2011), and "Gymnast" (2011). Tufano was cinematographer for television productions of "A Few Castles in Spain" (1966), "Isadora" (1966), "Papillons" (1970), "The Search for the Nile" (1971), "Steven" (1974), "The Enemy Within" (1974), "Robinson Crusoe" (1974), "The Evacuees" (1975), "Daft As a Brush" (1975), "Moll Flanders" (1975), "Three Men in a Boat" (1975), "The Glittering Prizes" (1976), "Arnhem: The Story of an Escape" (1976), "She Fell Among Thieves" (1978), "Murder Is Easy" (1982), "The Wall" (1982), "Trapped in Silence" (1986), "The Endless Game" (1989), "Mr. Wroe's Virgins" (1993), "Middlemarch" (1994) receiving another BAFTA nomination, "The Choir" (1995), "Silent Witness" (1996), "Element of Doubt" (1996), and "My Zinc Bed" (2008). He also served as cinematographer for episodes of "Out of the Unknown", "Take Three Girls", "Thirty-Minute Theatre", "Music on 2", "Omnibus", "The Sextet", "Full House", "Wessex tales", "Dial M for Murder", "BBC2 Playhouse", "Play for Today", "Supernatural", "Centre Play" directing an episode in 1977, "Five-Minute Films", "Common As Muck", and "Silent Witness". He received a special BAFTA Award for Outstanding Contribution to Film and Television in 2001. Tufano served as head of cinematography at the National Film and Television School in Beaconsfield from 2003 to 2016. Tufano was married to Pamela J. Copeland from 1964 until their divorce in 1990 and they had a child together. He married Sarah Pykett in 2005 and she survives him.

Turen, Kevin

Film and television producer Kevin Turen who produced the "Euphoria" television series and Ti West's "X"

horror film trilogy, died at a hospital in Los Angeles, California, on November 12, 2023. Turen was driving his Tesla vehicle on autopilot mode on a California freeway when he suffered from congestive heart failure and was taken to a nearby hospital. He was 44. Turen was born in New York City on August 16, 1979. He graduated from Columbia University where he studied film.

He worked at First Look Pictures and later became its president. He also worked at infinity Media and Treehouse Films and became head of the production company Phantom Four in 2014. He subsequently joined with Sam and Ashley Levinson to found Little Lamb Productions om 2-18. He worked in films from the early 2000s and served as a producer for "Wassup Rockers" (2005), "The Dead Girl" (2006), "An American Crime" (2007), "Smiley Face" (2007), "Operation Endgame" (2010), "Arbitrage" (2012), "At Any Price" (2012), "All Is Lost" (2013), "The Awkward Moment" (2014), "99 Homes" (2014), "The Benefactor" (2015), "Mediterranea" (2015), "The Birth of a Nation" (2016), "Assassination Nation" (2018), "Tau" (2018), "A-X-L" (2018), "Villains" (2019), "Waves" (2019), "The Last Days of American Crime" (2020), "Pieces of a Woman" (2020), "Malcolm & Marie" (2021), "North Hollywood" (2021), "Those Who Wish Me Dead" (2021), "Antlers" (2021), "Breaking" (2022), "Sharp Stick" (2022), and "The Unbearable Weight of Massive Talent" (2022) starring Nicholas Cage. Turen produced Ty West's 2022 horror film "X" starring Mia Goth, the 2022 prequel "Pearl", and the forthcoming sequel "MaXXXine". He served as executive producer of the television series "Irma Vep", "Fables", "Euphoria" earning an Emmy Award nomination in 2022, and "The Idol". He married Evelina Turen in 2012 and is survived by her and their two sons.

Turman, Lawrence

Film producer Lawrence Turman, who received an Academy Award nomination for the 1967 film "The Graduate", died at the Motion Picture & Television Country House and Hospital in Los Angeles, California, on June 1, 2023. He was

96. Turman was born in Los Angeles on November 28, 1936. He attended the University of California at Los Angeles and served in the U.S. Navy for two years. He worked for his father's textile business for several years before becoming a talent agent at Kurt Frings Agency in the late 1950s. He served as agent for actress Joan Fontaine and director Alan J. Pakula. He joined with Stuart Millar to produce the 1961 film "The Young Doctors". They also produced Judy Garland's final film, "I Could Go on Singing". He teamed with David Foster to head the Turman

Foster production company from 1974 until 1991. He formed the Turman-Morrissey Co. with John Morrissey in 1996. Turman produced such films as "Stolen Hours" (1963), "The Best Man" (1964), "The Flim-Flam Man" (1967), "The Graduate" (1967) earning an Oscar nomination, "Pretty Poison" (1968), "The Great White Hope" (1970), "The Marriage of a Young Stockbroker" (1971) which he also directed, "The Nickel Ride" (1974), "The Drowning Pool" (1975), "First Love" (1977), "Heroes" (1977), "Walk Proud" (1979), "Tribute" (1980), the prehistoric comedy "Caveman" (1981) starring Ringo Starr, John Carpenter's "The Thing" (1982), "Second Thoughts" (1983) which he also directed, "Mass Appeal" (1984), "The Mean Season" (1984), "Short Circuit" (1986), "Running Scared" (1986), "Short Circuit 2" (1988), "Full Moon in Blue Water" (1988), "Gleaming the Cube" (1989), "The Getaway" (1994), "The River Wild" (1994), "Booty Call" (1997), "American History X" (1998), "Kingdom Come" (2001), "What's the Worst That Could Happen?" (2001), and the prequel "The Thing" (2011). Turman was executive producer for the tele-films "The Flim-Flam Man" (1969), "She Lives!" (1973), "Get Christie Love!" (1974), "The Morning After" (1974), "Unwed Father" (1974), "Between Two Brothers" (1982), "The Gift of Life" (1982), "News at Eleven" (1986), "Pretty Poison" (1996), "The Long Way Home" (1998), and "Miracle on the Mountain: The Kincaid Family Story" (2000). He was director of the Peter Stark Producing Program at the University of Southern California from 1991 until his retirement in 2021. He was author of the 2005 book "So You Want to Be a Producer" and was guest critic on the web series "On Cinema" in 2014. His survivors include three sons, screenwriter John Turman, cinematographer Andrew Turman, and Peter Turman.

Turner, Tina

Legendary singer and actress Tina Turner, who was noted for such hits as "Proud Mary" and "What's Love Got to Do with It", died after a long illness at her home in Kusnacht, Switzerland, on May 24, 2023. She was 83. She was born Anna Mae Bullock in Brownsville, Tennessee, on November  26, 1939, and was raised in Nutbush, Tennessee. Her mother left her and her two older sisters when Tina was in her early teens. She spent several years with her maternal grandmother before her death. She then joined her mother in St. Louis where she completed high school. She worked at a hospital as a nurses' aide. She began attending local night clubs and was soon performing with Ike Turner and his band, the Kings of Rhythm, in 1957. She made her first recording, the single "Box Top", the following year under the name Little Ann. She recorded Ike's song, "A Fool for Love", in 1960. The record was a hit, and she was renamed Tina Turner to headline the band, now named the Ike and Tina Turner Revue. She and Ike married in 1962 and they continued to record such hits as "It's Gonna Work Out Fine", earning them a Grammy nomination, "I Idolize You", "Poor Fool", and "Tra La La La La". She and the band toured the country over the next two years. They recorded with various labels throughout the decade and released the hit album "Live! The Ike & Tine Show" in 1965. They also had success with the singles "Tell Her I'm Not Home" and "Good Bye, So Long". They were featured in the 1966 music documentary film "The Big T.N.T. Show". They were also seen in the films "It's Your Thing" (1970), "Gimme Shelter" (1970), "Taking Off" (1971), and "Soul to Soul" (1971). Turner performed on television in episodes of "Hollywood Discotheque", "Shindig!", "Hollywood a Go Go", "Where the Action Is", "The Lloyd Thaxton Show", "Ready, Steady, Go!", "The Joey Bishop Show", "The Hollywood Palace", "The Donald O'Connor Show", "The Smothers Brothers Comedy hour", "Della", "The Ed Sullivan Show", "Playboy After Dark", "The Everly Brothers Show", "The Andy Williams Show", "The Name of the Game", "American Bandstand", "Starparade", "The Pearl Bailey Show", "Soul Train", "Beat-Club", "The Dick Cavett Show", "The New Bill Cosby Show", "The Burns and Schreiber Comedy Hour", "Dinah!", "Cher", "The Mac Davis Show", "The Tonight Show Starring Johnny Carson", "The Alan Hamel Show", "The Merv Griffin Show", and "The Mike Douglas Show". Ike and Tina Turner signed with Phil Spector's Philles label in 1966 and recorded the hit "River Deep - Mountain High". Their 1969 album "Outta Season" contained a hit cover of Otis Redding's "I've Been Loving You Too Long". Tina earned a Grammy nomination for her recording of the title track for the 1969 album "The Hunter". They were soon performing at music festivals and headlining Las Vegas shows. They recorded the albums "Come Together" and "Workin' Together" in 1970 and had a major hit with their 1971 cover of Creedence Clearwater Revival's "Proud Mary", when received a Grammy Award. They recorded the hit live album "What You Hear Is What You Get" at Carnegie Hall in 1971. The Turners opened their own recording studio, Bolic Sound, in 1972. Tina wrote most of her own songs for the 1972 album "Feel Good" and they had a hit single with "Nutbush City Limits" in 1973. They recorded the hits "Sweet Rhode Island Red" and "Sexy Ida" in 1974 and received a Grammy nomination for the 1974 album "The Gospel According to Ike & Tina". She also had her first solo album, "Tina Turns the Country On!", in 1974. Tina was featured as the Acid Queen in the film version of the Who's rock opera "Tommy" in 1975. Her next album took its title from her character role, "Acid Queen", and contained the hits "Baby, Get It On" and "Whole Lotta Love". Ike's addiction to cocaine and a long history of domestic violence against Tina resulted in their separation in July of 1976. Two more albums were credited to the duo, "Delilah's Power" (1977) and "Airwaves", before the divorce was final in March of 1978. Tina continued to appear on television in such variety series as "The Hollywood Squares", "Rock Concert", "Donny and Marie", "The Brady Bunch Variety Hour", "The Sonny and Cher Show", "Laugh-In", "Luna Park", "The Kenny Everett Video Show", "The Midnight Special", "Tom Jones Now!", and "Solid Gold". She appeared in a small role in the 1978 musical film "Sgt. Pepper's Lonely Hearts Club Band". Tina reinvented her concert performances in 1977, headlining cabaret shows in Las Vegas with new costumes created by Bob Mackie. Her albums "Rough" (1978) and "Love Explosion" (1979) met with little success. Tina was featured in the television special "Olivia Newton-John: Hollywood Nights" in 1980. She performed  "Hot Legs" with Rod Stewart on an episode of "Saturday Night Live" in 1981 and opened for the Rolling Stones during their U.S. tour in 1981. Her music video for "Ball of Confusion" was seen frequently during the early days of MTV in 1982. Her career received a resurgence with her 1983 cover of Al Green's "Let's Stay Together" and the 1984 album "Private Dancer". They scored major hits with the title track and the singles "What's Love Got to Do with It" and "Better Be Good to Me". She received three Grammy Awards in 1985 including record of the year for "What's Love Got to Do with It". Turner co-starred with Mel Gibson in the 1985 post-apocalyptical film "Mad Max Beyond Thunderdome" as Bartertown ruler Aunty Entity. She recorded the songs "We Don't Need Another Hero" and "One for the Living" for the film and earned a Grammy Award for the latter. She performed with Mick Jagger at Live Aid in 1985 and her duet with Bryan Adams, "It's Only Love", scored a Grammy nomination. Her 1986 album "Break Every Rule" contained the singles "Typical Male", "Two People", "What You Seen Is What You Get", and "Back Where You Started", which earned her another Grammy. Turner's autobiography, "I Tina", was published in 1986. Another Grammy followed with the 1988 album "Tina Life in Europe". She recorded the 1989 album "Foreign Affair" and had a major hit with the single "The Best". Her European tour in support of the album was a major success as was the greatest hits recording "Simply the Best" (1991). Ike & Tina Turner were inducted into the Rock and Roll Hall of Fame in 1991, but neither attended the ceremony. A semi-autobiographical film, "What's Love Got to Do with It", was released in 1993. Angela Bassett and Laurence Fishburne received Academy Award nominations for their roles as Tina and Ike Turner. Turner was featured as the Mayor in Arnold Schwarzenegger's action-comedy film "Last Action Hero" in 1993. She recorded the title song for the 1995 James Bond film "GoldenEye" and released the album "Wildest Dreams" in 1996. Her solo album, "Twenty Four Seven" was released in 1999 and she was seen in a cameo role in an episode of the television series "Ally McBeal" in 2000. A DVD of her concerts at Wembley Stadium, "One Last Time Live in Concert", was released in 2001 after she announced her retirement from touring. She recorded the 2004 album "All the Best" and received the Kennedy Center Honors at the John F. Kennedy Center for the Performing Arts in Washington, DC, in 2005. She recorded the 2006 duet "Teach Me Again" with the singer Elisa for the anthology film "All the Invisible Children"

in support of the World Food Programme and UNICEF. Tina performed with Beyonce at the Grammy Awards in 2008 and earned a Grammy Award as a featured artist on the album "River: The Joni Letters". She made a return to touring with 2008's "Tina! 50th Anniversary Tour" before again retiring. Turner resided primarily in Switzerland in recent years where she was co-founder of Beyond Foundation, a global music group. She co-released several spiritual albums including "Beyond: Buddhist and Christian Prayers" (2009), "Children - With Children United in Prayer" (2011), "Love Within" (2014), and "Awakening" (2017). She worked on the musical play "Tina", based on her life story, which opened in London in 2018 with Adrienne Warren starring as Turner. Warren reprised the role on Broadway in 2019. She received the Grammy Lifetime Achievement Award in 2018 and another memoir, "My Love Story", was published later in the year. She co-wrote the 2020 book "Happiness Becomes You: A Guide to Changing Your Life for Good". She was featured in the 2021 documentary film "Tina". She was inducted into the Rock and Roll Hall of Fame as a solo artist in 2021. A Barbie doll in her image was released in 2022. She had suffered from multiple illnesses over her last decade including a stroke in 2013 and intestinal cancer in 2016. She received a kidney transplant from her husband in 2017. Turner was involved with saxophonist Raymond Hill while performing with the Ike's Kings of Rhythm in the late 1950s and they had a son, Craig, who committed suicide in 2018. She had a son, Ronnie, in 1960 with Ike Turner. He died of colon cancer in December of 2022. She also adopted Ike's two sons after their marriage. Tina became involved with German music executive Erwin Bach in 1986 and they married in 2013. He survives her.

Tweto, Jim

Alaska bush pilot Jim Tweto, who starred in the Discovery Channel television reality series "Flying Wild Alaska", was killed when his aircraft crashed while taking off  near Shaktoolik, Nome, Alaska, on June 16, 2023. He was 68. He was piloting a Cessna 180H from a remote mountain ridgeline airstrip when he struck a tree. His passenger, outdoor guide Shane Reynolds, was also killed in the crash. Tweto was born in Wichita, Kansas, on November 26, 1954, and was raised in Silver Bay, Minnesota. He moved to Anchorage, Alaska, in the early 1970s to play hockey at the University of Alaska at Anchorage. He became a pilot and moved to Unalakleet, Alaska, in 1980. He began his own airline and became chief operating officer with Era Alaska in 2009. He was the star of the reality television series "Flying Wild Alaska" on the Discovery Channel from 2011 to 2012. His wife, Ferno Tweto, who he married in 1988, and their two daughters, Ariel and Ayla Tweto, were frequently seen on the series. His wife and daughters survive him.

Twilley, Dwight

Singer and songwriter Dwight Twilley died after suffering a stroke while driving and crashing into a tree in Tulsa, Oklahoma, on October 18, 2023. He was 72. Twilley  was born in Tulsa on June 6, 1951. He met fellow musician and songwriter Phil Seymour while in their teens in 1967. They soon formed the band Oister with Twilley writing songs and playing guitar and piano, and Seymour on drums and bass. They both sang lead and were later joined by Bill Pitcock IV on guitar. Twilley and Seymour went to Los Angeles in 1974 and signed with Leon Russell's Shelter Records. They were renamed the Dwight Twilley Band and had a hit with their debut single "I'm on Fire" in 1975. They performed on television's "American Bandstand" and released the albums "Sincerely" (1976) and "Twilley Don't Mind" (1977) with Tom Petty contributing vocals to the song "Looking for the Magic". The band performed on the short-lived children's television series "Wacko!" in 1977. Their albums had little success and Seymour left the band to pursue a solo career in 1977. Twilley continued to perform and record with Pitcock and Susan Cowsill as the Dwight Twilley Band. His 1979 album "Twilley" and the singles "Somebody to Love" and "You're Gonna Get It" also proved unsuccessful. The band moved to EMI American for the 1982 album "Scuba Divers". The 1984 album "Jungle" featured the hit singles "Girls" and "Little Bit of Love". He recorded the album "Wild Dogs" with Private I Records in 1986 shortly before the label collapsed. Pitcock left the band and Twilley had difficulty finding a new label. Many of the band's unreleased early songs were compiled for the recording "The Great Lost Twilley Album" shortly before Seymour's death in 1993. The Dwight Twilley Band albums were rereleased by EMI in 1996. His later albums include "The Luck" (2001), "47 Moons" (2005), "Live: All Access" (2006), "Green Blimp" (2010), and "Always" (2014). Twilley is survived by his wife, Jan and daughter Dionne.

Two Rivers, Billy

Canadian Mohawk professional wrestler and actor Billy Two Rivers died in Kahnawake, Quebec, Canada, on February 12, 2023. He was 87. Two Rivers was born in Kahnawake on May 5, 1935. He met leading wrestler Don Eagle in the early 1950s who took him to Columbus, Ohio, to train to be a wrestler. Two Rivers made his professional ring debut in Detroit, Michigan, in 1953. He battled such wrestlers as Wild Bull Curry and Larry Hamilton and formed a tag team with Don Eagle from 1956 to 1959. He also teamed with Antonino Rocca and Red Bastien in the North Carolina territory. He and George Becker captured the NWA Southern Tag Team Championship in April of 1959. They lost the belts three months later and Two Rivers traveled overseas to wrestle

in England and Scotland. He was a popular attraction in England, with a feathered headdress, Mohawk haircut, and frequent war dance performances during his matches. He returned to the United States and resumed wrestling in North  Carolina in 1965. He went to Japan to wrestle the following year. Two Rivers began wrestling in Canada in the early 1970s where he frequently teamed with Johnny War Eagle. He wrestled in England from 1973 to 1974 before again returning to Canada. He competed with Grand Prix Wrestling (GPW) in Montreal and captured the promotion's tag titles with Jean War Eagle in 1974. He battled such wrestlers as Sailor White, the Sheik, and Kurt Von Hess, and captured the Canadian International Heavyweight Championship from Serge Dumon in August of 1976. Two Rivers retired from the ring in 1977. He became active with the Mohawk nation on the Kahnawake reservation, serving as an elder and chief. Two Rivers appeared in several films including "Black Robe" (1991), "Bolt" (1995), "Pocahontas: The Legend" (1995), "Musketeers Forever" (1998), and "Taking Lives" (2004). He appeared on television in the 1989 tele-film "Red Earth, White Earth" and episodes of "Heritage Minutes", "Tales of the Wild", and "Mohawk Girls". He is survived by his wife, Pauline Lahache Two Rivers, and children Kasennie, Dawn, and Karen. He is also survived by a son, British fashion designer Wayne Hemingway, from a relationship with Maureen Hemingway during his time in England in the early 1960s.

Ubaldi, Marzia

Italian actress Marzia Ubaldi died in Narni, Italy, on October 21, 2023. She was 85. Ubaldi was born in Milan, Italy, on June 2, 1938. She was featured in the films "Il Medico Delle  Donne" (1962), "Countersex" (1964), "La Moglie Giapponese" (1968), "L'Assassino Speranza Delle Donne" (1972), "E Comincio il Viaggio Nella Vertigine" (1974), Mario Caiano's exploitation film "Nazi Love Camp 27" (1977) as Frau Gruber, "Farfalle" (1997), "The House of Chicken" (2001), "Non c'e Campo" (2017), "Euphoria" (2018), and "The Predators" (2020). Ubaldi was also a dubbing voice for such actresses as Rosalba Neri, Teresa Gimpera, Martine Beswick, Virna Lisi, Sylva Koscina, Anna Massey, and Lucia Bose. Her numerous television credits include productions of "La Coscienza di Zeno" (1966), "Una Coccarda per il Re" (1970), "Un Certo Harry Brent" (1970), "E.S.P." (1973), "Diagnosi" (1975), "L'Armadietto Cinese"

(1975), "Nella Tua Vita" (1976), "L'Uomo Difficile" (1978), "Ricatto Internazionale" (1980), "Arabella" (1980), "La Pulce Nell'Orecchio" (1980), "Indiscretion of an American Wife" (1998), "Casa e Bottega" (2013), and "I Nostri Figli" (2018). Ubaldi was also seen in episodes of "Nero Wolfe", "Aeroporto Internazionale", "Investigatori d'Italia", "Frederick Forsyth Presents", "Professione Fantasma" as Serena Baldini in 1998, "Valeria Medico Legale", "Incantesimo" as Amalia Forti in 2003, "Elisa di Rivombrosa", "7 Vite" as Sole Vardelli from 2007 to 2009, "Questo Nostro Amore" as Alberta Ferraris from 2012 to 2014, "L'Allieva" as Nonna Amalia from 2016 to 2020, "Suburra: Blood on Rome" as Sibilla Mancini in 2020, "I Hate Christmas" as Matilde in 2022, and "Call My Agent - Italia" as Elvira Bo in 2023. She was married to actor Gastone Moschin from 1970 until his death in 2017. Her survivors include their daughter, actress Emanuela Moschin.

Urbankova, Nada

Czech singer and actress Nada Urbankova died of complications from cancer and COVID-19 in Prague, Czech Republic, on February 3, 2023. She was 83. She was born Nadezda Balazbanova in Nova Paka, Czech Republic (then part of the Protectorate of Bohemia and Moravia), on June 30, 1939.

She studied nursing in Trutnov and began performing on stage in productions with the Pardubice Theatre in the late 1950s. She moved to Prague after her marriage to actor Karel Urbanek and performed with the Magician's Lantern theater. She had a ten-year association with the Semafor theater from the mid-1960s. Urbankova was seen in such films as "If a Thousand Clarinets" (1965), "Zlocin v Divci Skole" (1966), "Closely Watched Trains" (1966), "Pension Pro Svobodne Pany" (1968), "Larks on a String" (1969), "Lucie a Zazraky" (1970), "Raduz a Mahulena" (1970), "My, Ztraceny Holky" (1972), "Na Samote u Lesa" (1976), "Hodinarova Svatebni Cesta Koralovym Morem" (1979), "Frando, o Fandy" (1983), and "Nenozna" (1988). She appeared on television in productions of "Sest Zen" (1963), "Benefice S + S" (1965), "Lysistrata" (1965), "Wandersanger - Chansons aus Prag" (1967), "Sedm Zen Alfonse Karaska" (1967), "Bahno" (1969), "Lasky Emanuela Pribyla" (1971), "Milacek" (1972), "Pristi Leto v Locarnu" (1973), "Slecna Ze Sporitelny" (1973), "To Byla Svatba, Strycku" (1976), "Romanek Za Tri Krejcary" (1982), "Zluty Kvitek" (1982), "Pet Prani" (1987), "Dvojcata" (1988), and "Herbert v Ringu" (2009). Her other television credits include episodes of "Bejvavalo", "Navstevni Den", "Bakalari", "Galasupersou", "Vesele Prihody z Nataceni", "Stopy Zivota", "Head Over Heels", "Doktori z Pocatku" as Jasna from 2014 to 2015, and "The Fury" as Matka Machy" in 2019. Urbankova was married and divorced from Karel Urbanek and Jan Nemejovka and is survived by a daughter, singer Yanna Fabian. She married Josef Havlik in 1990 and he also survives her.

Urbano, Jun

Filipino actor and comedian Manuel 'Jun' Urbano, Jr. died from a ruptured abdominal aortic aneurysm in the Philippines on December 2, 2023. He was 84. Urbano was

born in the Philippines on June 8, 1939. His father was actor and director Manuel Urbano, Sr., who was better known was Manuel Conde. Jun graduated from the Ateneo de Manila University with a degree in journalism. He briefly worked as a reporter for "The Manila Times" before embarking on a career in advertising. He created thousands of television commercials for such products as San Miguel Beer, Coca-Cola, Pepsi, and Tide. Urbano created the Mongol-styled character, Mr. Shooli, in the 1980s, who would give satirical takes on Philippine politics and pop culture. The character, complete with bright red robes and a Fu Manchu mustache, became the star of the weekly television show "Mongolian Barbecue". He starred as the character in several films including "Juan Tamad at Mister Shooli: Mongolian Barbecue" (1991) and "M.O.N.A.Y. (Misteys Obda Neyson Andres Yata) Ni Mr. Shooli" (2007), both of which he directed and wrote. Urbano was also seen in the films "Boy Anghel: Utak Pulburon" (1992), "Magic Temple" (1996), "Magic Kingdom: Ang Alamat Ng Damortis" (1997), "Litsonero" (2009), "Miss You Like Crazy" (2010), "I Do" (2010), "Hostage Ko... Multo!" (2011), "Law Law Gang" (2011), "Huling Biyahe" (2012), "Otso" (2013), "ABCs of Death 2" (2014), "Kid Julafu" (2015), "Everyday I Love You" (2015), "Hiblang Abo" (2016), "Unli Life" (2018), "Magikland" (2020), and "Sugapa" (2023). He starred as Steven Go in the television series "Be Careful with My Heart" in 2013 and was Mang Damian in "Ang Probinsyano" in 2016. He also appeared in episodes of "Midnight DJ", "Ang Probinsyano", "Maalaala Mo Kayaa", and "Windflower". Urbano is survived by his wife, VIctoria, and four sons.

Valdemarin, Mario

Italian actor Mario Valdemarin died of complications

from COVID-19 in Rome, Italy, on December 12, 2023. He was 97. Valdemarin was born in Gorizia, Italy, on December 31, 1931. He was a contestant on Mike Bongiorno's television game show "Lascia o Raddoppia" (aka "Fold or Double?"), the Italian version of "The $64,000 Question", in the mid-1950s before embarking on an acting career. Valdemarin was featured in such films as "March's Child" (1958), "Vacanze d'Inverno" (1959), "The Great War" (1959), "Arrangiatevi" (1959), "Il

Carro Armato dell'8 Settembre" (1960), "Le Ambriziose" (1961), "Una Spada Nell'Ombra" (1961), "Hercules and the Captive Women" (aka "Hercules Conquers Atlantis") (1961) starring Reg Park as Hercules, "Rocco e le Sorelle" (1961), "The Last Charge" (1962), Umberto Lenzi's "Sandokan the Great" (1963) starring Steve Reeves in the title role, "Death on the Fourposter" (1964), "Le Consequenze" (1964), the espionage drama "Spy in Your Eye" (1965), "Mutiny at Fort Sharpe" (1966), "Me, Me, Me... and the Others" (1966), "Stress" (1971), "A.A.A. Massaggiatrice Bella Presenza Offresi..." (1972), "24 Ore... Non un Minuto di Piu" (1972), "Non Ho Tempo" (1973), "Commissariato di Notturna" (1974), "La Citta dell'Ultima Paura" (1975), "Tre Sotto il Lenzuolo" (1979), "The Fascist Jew" (1980), and "La Fine della Notte" (1989). Valdemarin appeared on television in productions of "Formiche - Ferragosto in Citta" (1958), "Peg del Mio Cuore" (1958), "Il Vicario di Wakefield" (1959), "Donne Brutte" (1961), "Un Caso di Coscienza" (1964), "La Baruffe Chiozzotte" (1966), "Holiday (Incantesimo)" (1967), "Il Leone di San Marco" (1969), "L'Amica delle Mogli" (1970), "...e le Stelle Stanno a Guardare" (1971), "Qui Squadra Mobile" (1973), "Il Galatuomo per Transazione" (1973), "Roma" (1974), "Sotto il Placido Don" (1974), "Anna Karenina" (1974), "Una Pistola nel Cassetto" (1974), "La Contessa Lara" (1975), "Extra" (1976), "La Gatta" (1978), "Accadde a Zurigo" (1981), "Il Processo di Stabio" (1991), "Chiara D'Assasi - Storia di Una Cristiana" (1992), and "L'Illazione" (2011). He also performed on stage in productions at the Piccolo Teatro of Milan.

Valdez, Ronaldo

Filipino actor Ronaldo Valdez, who was featured in the 1969 horror film "The Mad Doctor of Blood Island", died  of a self-inflicted gunshot wound in the head in Manila, Philippines, on December 17, 2023. He was 76. He was born Ronald James Dulaca Gibbs in Manila on November 27, 1943. He made his film debut opposite Susan Roces in 1966's "Pepe En Pilar". He was featured as Carlos Lopez in the 1968 horror cult classic "Mad Doctor of Blood Island" with John Ashley. Valdez appeared in hundreds of films during his career including "The Jukebox Queen" (1966), "Chinatown" (1966), "Buhay Artista" (1967), "Anna Lizza" (1967), "Close to You" (1967), "Hey Boy! Hey Girl" (1967), "Brainwash" (1968), "Eskinita 29" (1968), "Lady Untouchable" (1968), "Brownout" (1969), "At the Top" (1971), "Lumuha Pati Mga Anghel" (1971), "Daluyong!" (1971), "Lilet" (1971), "Kung Bakit Dugo Ang Kulay Ng Gabi" (1973), "Fe, Esperanza, Caridad" (1974), "Daigdig Ng Sindak at Lagim" (1974), "Banaue: stairway to the Sky" (1975), "Nino Valiente" (1975), "Ang Pag-ibig Ko'y Huwag Mong Sukatin" (1975), "Pandemonium" (1976), "Electrika Kasi, Eh!" (1977), "Hagkan Mo Ang Dugo Sa Kamay Ni Venus" (1977), "Tatlong Bulaklak" (1979), "Candy" (1980), "Kanto Boy" (1980),

"Lumakad Kang Hubad... Sa Mundong Ibabaw" (1980), "Langis at Tubig" (1980), "Mahinhin vs. Mahinhin" (1981), "Dear Heart" (1981), "Mr. One-Two-Three Part 2" (1981), "The Betamax Story" (1981), "Karma" (1981), "Gaano Kadalas Ang Minsan?" (1982), "Palabra de Honor" (1983), "Apoy Sa Iyong Kandungan" (1984), "Kaya Kong Abutin Ang Langit" (1984), "May Daga Sa Labas Ng Lungga" (1984), "Lalakwe" (1985), "Bomba Queen" (1985), "Heartache City" (1985), "Miguelito" (1985), "Paano Ang Aking Gabi?" (1985), "Yvonne" (1985), "Napakasakit, Kuyu Eddie" (1986), "Laban Kung Laban" (1986), "Huwag Mo Kaming Isumpa" (1986), "Ang Daigdig Ay Isang Butil Na Luha" (1986), "Bunsong Kerubin" (1987), "Gatas" (1988), "Lady L" (1989), "Huwag Kang Hahalik Sa Diablo" (1989), "Kolehiyala" (1990), "I Want to Live" (1990), "Hot Summer" (1990), "Bad Boy" (1990), "Above Everything Else" (1991), "Joey Boy Munti: 15 Anyos Ka Sa Muntinglupa" (1991), "Padre Amante Guerrero" (1992), "Estribo Gang: The Jinggoy Sese Story" (1992), "Rosang Tatoo" (1992), "Adan Ronquillo: Tubong Cavite... Laking Tondo" (1993), "Abel Morado: Ikaw Ang May Sala" (1993), "Tumbasan Mo Ng Buhay" (1993), "Loving Someone" (1993), "Isa Lang Ang Buhay Mo! Sgt. Bobby Aguilar" (1993), "Biboy Banal: Pagganti Ko Tapos Kayo" (1994), "Muntik Na Kitang Minahal" (1994), "Campus Girls" (1995), "Redeem Her Honor" (1995), "Kapitan Tumba: The Capt. Jose Huevos Story" (1995), "I Love You Sabado!!!" (1995), "The Flor Contemplacion Story" (1995), "Grepor Butch Belgica Story" (1995), "Karanasan: The Claudia Zobel Story" (1995), "Tubusin Mo Ng Bala Ang Puso Ko" (1996), "Cedie" (1996), "Virgin People 2" (1996), "Iskalawag: Ang Batas Ay Batas" (1997), "Dahil Tanging Ikaw" (1997), "Ambisyosa" (1997), "Puerto Princesa" (1997), "Hanggang Kailan Kita Mamahalin?" (1997), "Nasaan Ang Puso" (1997), "Roberta"(1997), "Isinakdal Ko Ang Aking Ina" (1997), "Ikaw Pala Ang Mahal Ko" (1997), "Silaw" (1998), "Ben Delubyo" (1998), "Nagbibinata" (1998), "I Love You, If That's Okay" (1998), "Armadong Hudas" (1998), "Tik Tak Toys: My Kolokotoys" (1999), "Yes, It's Loved If Loved" (1999), "Pedro Penduko, Episode II: The Return of the Comeback" (2000), "Trip" (2001), "Till There Was You" (2003), "Annie B." (2004), "Sukob" (2006), "When Loves Begins..." (2008), "Rosario" (2010), "yesterday Today Tomorrow" (2011), "The Mistress" (2012), "My Lady Boss" (2013), "All You Need Is Pag-ibig" (2015), "Girlfriend for Hire" (2016), "Seven Sundays" (2017), "I Love You, Hater" (2018), "Jack Em Popoy: The Puliscredibles" (2018), "Mang Jose" (2021), and "Ikaw at Ako" (2012). He was seen on television in productions of "Iduyan Mo Ang Duyan Ko" (1995), "Mula Sa Puso" (1997), "Ang Munting Paraiso" (1999), "Sa Dulo Ng Walang Hanggan" (2001), "Bituin" (2002), "Marinara" (2004), "Sugo" (2005), "Bahay Mo Ba'To" (2005), "Asian Treasures" (2007), "Kamandag" as Lolo Pepe in 2007, "My Girl" (2008), "I Heart Betty La Fea" (2008), "Full House" as Lorenzo in 2009, "Kung Tayo'y Magkakalayo" as Supremo in 2010, "Minsan Lang Kita Iibigin" as Jaime Sebastiano in 2011, "100 Days to Heaven" as Attorney Galileo Fonacier in 2011, "Glamorosa" (2011), "Dahil Sa Pag-ibig" as Don Ramon Belasco in 2012, "Ina, Kapatid, Anak" (2012),

"Wansapanataym" (2013), "Seasons of Love" (2014), "Pasion de Amor" (2015), "Meant to Be" (2017), "Dear Uge" (2017), "Pamilya" (2018), "Los Bastardos" as Don Roman Cardinal, Sr. in 2018, and "2 Good 2 Be True" as Hugo Agcaoili in 2022. Valdez was selected as the first Filipino Colonel for KFC commercials in 2017. He was married to Maria Fe Ilagan and they had two children, Janno and Melissa, before their separation.

Valenzuela, Laura

Spanish actress and television host Laura Valenzuela died of complications from Alzheimer's disease at a hospital in Madrid, Spain, on March 17, 2023. She was 92. She was born Rocia Espinosa Lopez-Cepero in Seville, Spain, on February 18, 1931. Her father was a pilot and she frequently moved around Spain in her youth. She spent time in France before turning to Spain. She began working as a model in Madrid in the early 1950s. She appeared frequently in films including "El Pescador de Coplas" (1954), "Alta Costura" (1954), "La Ciudad de los Suenos" (1954), "Sucedio en Sevilla" (1955), "Day of Fear" (1957), "La Guerra Empieza en Cuba" (1957), "El Inquilino" (1958), "Aquellos Tiempos del Cuple" (1958), "La Violetera" (1958), "Muchachas en Vacaciones" (1958), "Viva lo Imposible!" (1958), "Ana Dice Si" (1958), "Patio Andaluz" (1958), "Luna de Verano" (1959), "Los Tramposos" (1959), "La Fiel Infanteria" (1960), "Trio de Demas" (1960), "Los Economicamente Debiles" (1960), "Madame" (1961), "Los Que No Fuimos la Guerra" (1962), "Eva 63" (1963), "Las Hijas de Helena" (1963), "The Black Tulip" (1964), "Cyrano et d'Artagnan" (1964), "Faites vos Jeux, Mesdames" (1965), "La Tete du Client" (1965), "La Visita Que No Toco el Timbre" (1965), "Z7 Operation Rembrandt" (1966), "An Ace for Four Queens" (1966), "Amor a la Espanola" (1967), "Las Que Tienen Que Servir" (1967), "Los Subdesarrollados" (1968), "La Dinamita Esta Servida" (1968), "Do Profesion, Sus Labores" (1970), "Pierna Creciente, Falda Menguante" (1970), and "Espanolas en Paris" (1971). She was a host of early television programs from Spain's Television Espanola (TVE) from its inception in 1956. She co-hosted the musical series "Galas del Sabado" with Joaquin Prat from 1968 to 1970. Valenzuela was noted as the host of the 1969 Eurovision Song Contest in 1969. She retired from acting after her marriage to producer Jose Luis Dibildos in 1971. She resumed working in television in the 1980s on such productions as "25 Primeros Anos Television Espanol" (1981), "Bla, Bla, Bla" (1981), "Plato Vacio" (1986), "Tel 5 Digame? (1990), "VIP Noche" (1991), "Date un Respiro" (1993), "Querida Concha" (1993), "Las Mananas de Tele 5" (1993), "Las Mananas de Tele 5" (1993), "Mi Querida Espana" (1994), "Con Luz Propia" (1995), "Grand Prix" (1995), "What's the Bet?" (1995), "Entre Tu y Yo" (1997), "Mananas de Primera" (1996), "Dia a Dia" (1998), "Espejo Secreto" (1998), "Todo en Familia" (1999), "Donde Estas, Corazon?" (2003), "Querida Lola" (2005), "Salsa Rosa" (2005), "Corazon de..." (2005), "El Club" (2007), "La Noria" (2011), "Cine de Barrio" (2012), and "Tenemos Que Hablar" (2013). Valenzuela retired from show business in 2013. She and Jose Luis Dibildos remained married until his death in 2002 and she is survived by their daughter, actress Lara Dibildos.

van Dijk, Cilia

Dutch animator and film producer Cilia van Dijk died in the Netherlands on April 26, 2023. She was 81. She was born Cilia van Lieshout in Uden, the Netherlands, on November 22, 1941. She began working as a teacher in the 1960s and operated a modeling agency and a nursery school. She married filmmaker Gerrit van Dijk in 1963 and became involved with making animated films with him. She was founder of the distribution company Animated People in 1978. Van Dijk served as producer for the animated shorts "A Good Turn Daily" (1983), "Haast Een Hand" (1983), "Anna & Bella" (1984) earning an Academy Award for Best Animated Short, "Pas a Deux" (1988), "Frieze Frame" (1991), "De Houten Haarlemmers" (1995), "Dada" (1997), "Ik Beweeg, Dus Ik Besta" (1998), "Radio Umanak" (2000), "The Last Words of Dutch Schultz" (2001), "Stiltwalker" (20023), and "Animation Has No Borders" (2015). She and her husband were involved in the Haarlem theatrical community, and she handled business affairs for Het Volk, a local theater company. She and Gerrit van Dijk were married from 1963 until his death in 2012 and is survived by their two children.

Van Dyke, Conny

Actress and singer Conny Van Dyke died of complications from vascular dementia at her home in Los Angeles, California, on November 11, 2023. She was 78. Van Dyke was born in Cape Charles, Virginia, on September 28, 1945. She worked as a model in her teens was crowned "Teen" magazine's Miss Teen of the United States in 1960. She signed with Motown Records the following year and recorded the songs "Oh Freddy" by Smokey Robinson and "It Hurt Me Too" by Marvin Gaye. in 1963. She made her film debut in a small role in Tom Laughlin's 1961 film "The Young Sinner" (aka "Like Father, Like Son", "Among the Thorns"). She was featured in the 1969 biker film "Hell's Angels '69" and was seen on television in episodes of "Ironside", "Adam-12", "Hee Haw", "Pop! Goes the Country", "Nakia", "Sunshine", "Barbary Coast", "The Merv Griffin Show", "Dinah!", "Tattletales", "You Don't Say", "Showoffs",

"Rhyme and Reason", "The Cross-Wits", "Match Game", and "Police Woman". She also released a pair of albums, "Conny Van Dyke" and "Conny Van Dyke Sings for You". Van Dyke appeared with Burt Reynolds in 1975's "W.W. and the Dixie Dancekings" and with Joe Don Baker in "Framed", also in 1975. She retired from acting in the mid-1970s to raise her son. She returned to the screen after thirty years to appear in 2004's "Shiner". She was also seen on television in episodes of "Cold Case" and "CSI: Crime Scene Investigations". She subsequently suffered a stroke which again ended her career. Van Dyke was married and divorced multiple times including to George Fisher from 1963 to 1966, Robert Runyon Page from 1968 to 1970, "Larry Coates from 1971 to 1976, Douglas Dunham from 1978 to 1985, Emilio Acevedo from 1988 to 1990, and Ernest Guerra from 1997 to 2003. She is survived by her son from her second marriage, Bronson Page.

Varga, Veronika

Hungarian-French actress Veronika Varga died in Paris, France, on September 30, 2023. She was 54. Varga was born in Budapest, Hungary, on June 10, 1969. She studied at a

music school in Budapest and began performing with the alternative rock group A Ceg. She began training as an actress and attended the Royal Conservatory of Brussels, Belgium, and the National Conservatory of Dramatic Art in Paris. She began her career on stage and film in the late 1980s. She starred in the title role in the 1994 French short film "Emilie Muller". Varga was also seen in the films "The King of Paris" (1995), "Nina's House" (2005), "The Snake" (2006), "Long Live Freedom" (2013), "Nice and Easy" (2014), "Those Who Remained" (2019), "A Call to Spy" (2019), "Small Country: An African Childhood" (2020), "Garbage Theory" (2021), "Simone: Woman of the Century" (2022), and "Halfway Home" (2022). She appeared on television in productions of "Des Mots Qui Dechirent" (1995), "Egy No Igaz Tortenete" (2007), "A Bad Encounter" (2011), and "The Jewish Cardinal" (2013). Her other television credits include episodes of "Les Anees Lycee", "L'Histoire du Samedi", "Maigret", "Konyveskep", "The Witcher", and "FBI: International".

Vasilyeva, Vera

Russian actress Vera Vasilyeva died in Moscow, Russia, on August 8, 2023. She was 97. Vasilyeva was born in Moscow on September 30, 1925. She studied at the Moscow City Drama School in 1943. She made her debut in films in 1945's "The Call of Love". She starred as Nastenka Petrovna Gusenkova in 1948's "Symphony of Life" (aka "Ballad of Siberia"). Vasilyeva was seen in numerous films over the next sixty years including "V Mirnye Dni" (1951), "Chuk and Gek" (1953), "Bride with a Dowry" (1953), "They Met on the Road" (1957), "Lyudi Moey Doliny" (1961), "Na Zavtrashney Ulitse" (1965), "Pogonya" (1965), "Pokhozhdeniya Zubnogo Vracha"

(1965), "Priezzhayte Na Baykal" (1966), "Za Vsyio v Otvete" (1973), "Zhrebiy" (1974), "Zvezda Ekrana" (1974), "Eto My Ne Prokhodili" (1976), "Razvlechenie Dlyaa Starichkov" (1977), "Legenda o Tile" (1977), "Nesovershennoletnie" (1977), "Podarok Sudby" (1977), "Karnaval" (1982), "My Zhili Po Sosedstvu" (1982), "Zhenatyy Kholostyak" (1982), "Kak Ya Byl Vunderkindom" (1983), "Prikazano Vzyat Zhivym"

(1984), "Vyyti Zamuzh Za Kapitana" (1986), "Zlovrednoye Voskresenye" (1986), "Window to Paris" (1993), "Liza i Eliza" (1995), and the animated "Serafima's Extraordinary Travel" (2015) as the voice of Aunt Lisa. Vasileva was seen on television in productions of "Togda v Yanvare..." (1967), "Zhenskiy Monastyr" (1971), "Ofitser Flota" (1971), "Neschastnyy Sluchay" (1972), "Megre i Chelovek Na Skameyke" (1973), "Bezumnyy Den ili Zhenitba Figaro" (1974), "Vot Takiye Istorii" (1974), "Benefis. Vera Vasileva" (1974), "Vesna Dvadtsat Devyatogo" (1975), "Poshchyochina" (1976), "Kaz Vazhno Byt Seryoznym" (1976), "Mesyats Dlinnykh Dney" (1978), "Tabletku Pod Yazyk" (1978), "U Vremeni v Plenu" (1980), "Revizor" (1983), "Vino iz Oduvanchikov" (1997), "Sledstvie Vedut Znatoki" (2002), "Vremena Ne Vybirayut" as Olga Kiknadze in 2002, "Maska i Dusha" (2002), "Poka Tsvetet Paporotnik" (2012), and "Derevenshchina" (2014). Vasilyeva was married to actor Vladimir Ushakov from 1956 until his death in 2011.

Vassilikos, Vassilis

Greek author Vassilis Vassilikos, who was best known for writing the 1967 political novel "Z", died in Athens, Greece, on November 30, 2023. He was 90. Vassilikos was born in Kavala, Greece, on November 18, 1933. He was raised in

Thessaloniki, where he graduated from law school. He then attended Yale University's Drama School to study television directing. He returned to Greece to work as a journalist in Athens. He went into exile after the military coup in 1967. His novel about events leading up to the coup, "Z", was published in 1967 and was adapted for film by Costa-Gavras in 1969. Many of his works were adapted for film including "Young Aphrodites" (1963), "Epitafios Gia Ehthrous Kai Filous" (1966), "The Steps" (1966), "I Nyhta Me Ti Silena" (1986), "Broken April" (1987), "Monaxia Mou, Ola..." (1998), "The Jews of Salonka" (1999), "Leilatontas Mia Matomeni Hora" (2010), and "Shanghai" (2012) an Indian adaptation of "Z". Television adaptations of his works include "Kaeneio Emigrec" (1986) "Mia Syzitisi Me Ton Zografo Gianni Kounelli" (1988), "Des Annees Dechirees" (1993), "Les Yeus de Cecile" (1993), "To Teleftaio Antio" (1994), "Thymata

Eirinis" (1999-2000), and "Erotomenos Angelos" (2000). Vassilikos appeared in a handful of films including "The Steps" (1966), "The Strangler" (1970), "Sto Dromo Tou Lamore" (1979), "Variete" (1985), "Pater Familias" (1997), "I Limouzina: Komodia Paraxigiseon" (2013), and "Adults in the Room" (2019). He returned to Greece after the collapse of the military dictatorship and served as deputy director of the Greek state television station (ET1) from 1981 to 1984. He was Greece's ambassador to UNESCO from 1996 to 2004. He was elected to the Greek Parliament in 2019, serving until April of 2023. He was divorced from his first wife, Dimitra 'Mimi' Vassilikos, who became a nun before her death. He married soprano Vaso Papantroniou in 1983 and is survived by her and their daughter, Euridice.

Vaughan-Clarke, Peter

British actor Peter Vaughan-Clarke, who starred as Stephen Jameson in the juvenile science fiction series "The Tomorrow People" in the 1970s, died in England in August of 2023. He was 66. Vaughan-Clarke was born in Wandsworth, London, England, on June 16, 1957. He began his acting career in the early 1970s. He was featured as Ronnie Page in the series "Both Ends Meet" in 1972. Vaughan-Clarke was best known for his role as Stephen Jameson, whose budding psychic powers brought him to "The Tomorrow People" ITV television series from 1973 to 1976. He was also seen in episodes of "New Scotland Yard", "The Pallisers", "Late Call", "The Duchess of Duke Street", and "Shoestring". He retired from acting by the early 1980s and later worked as a lighting technician and key grip.

Velasco, Concha

Spanish actress and entertainer Concha Velsasco died of complications of lymphatic cancer at a hospital in Majadahonda, Spain, on December 2, 2023. She was 84. She was born Concepcion Velasco Varona in Valladolid, Spain, on November 29, 1939. She moved to Madrid in the late 1940s where she studied dance at the National Conservatory. She began performing as a dancer with the La Coruna opera. She was also a flamenco dancer and performed in revues. She made her film debut while in her teens in 1955's "La Reina Mora". Velasco was featured in numerous films including "La Fierecilla Domada" (aka "The Moorish Queen") (1956), "Dos Novias Para un Torero" (1956), "Los Maridos No Cenan en Casa" (1957), "El Bandido Generoso" (1957), "Mensajeros de Paz" (1957), "Muchachas en Vacaciones" (1958), the comedy "Red Cross Girls" (1958), "El Dia de los Enamorados" (1959), "Los Tramposos" (1959), "Crimen Para Recien Casados" (1960), "Amor Bajo Cero" (1960), "Vida Sin Risas" (1960), "The Reprieve" (1960), "La Paz Empieza Nunca" (aka "Peace Never Comes") (1960), "Festival en Benidorm" (1961), "My

Wedding Night" (1961), "Julia y el Celacanto" (1961), "Martes y Trece" (1962), "Sabian Demasiado" (1962), "Trampa Para Catalina" (1963), "La Verbenaz de la Paloma" (aka "The Fair of the Dove") (1963), "La Boda Era a las Doce" (1964), "Casi un Caballero" (1964), "La Frontera de Dios" (1965), "Historias de la Television" (1965), "El Arte de no Casarse" (1966), "Las Locas del Conventillo" (1966), "Hoy Como Ayer" (1966), "El Arte de Casarse" (1966), "Honeymoon, Italian Style" (1966), "Las Que Tienen Que Servir" (1967), "Pero... en Que Pais Vivimos?" (1967), "Los Que Tocan el Piano" (1968), "Una Vez al Ano Ser Hippy No Hace Dano" (1969), "El Taxi de los Conflictos" (1969), "Relaciones Casi Publicas" (1969), "Cuatro Noches de Boda" (1969), "Juicio de Faldas"(1969), "Matrimonios Separados" (1969), "Susana" (1969), "El Alma Se Serena" (1970), "Despues de los Nueve Meses" (1970), "En un Lugar de La Manga" (1970), "La Decente" (1971), "La Casa de los Martinez" (1971), "Prestame Quince Dias" (1971), "Los Gallos de la Madrugada" (1971), "La Red de Mi Cancion" (1971), "Me Debes un Muerto" (1972), "Venta Por Pisos" (1972), "El Vikingo" (1972), "The Lonely Woman" (1973), "Las Senoritas de Mala Compania" (1973), "El Amor Empieza a Medianoche" (1974), "Tormento" (1974), "Mi Mujer es Muy Decente, Dentro de lo Que Cabe" (1975), "Un Lujo a Su Alcance" (1975), "El Love Feroz o Cuando los Hijos Juegan al Amor" (1975), "Pim, Pam, Pum... Fuego!" (1975), "Pais S.A." (1975), "Yo Soy Fulana de Tal" (1975), "Las Bodas de Blanca" (1975), "Yo Creo Que..." (1975), "Las Largas Vacaciones del 36" (1976), "Libertad Provisional" (1976), "Wifemistress" (1977), "Jaque a la Dama" (1978), "Ernesto" (1979), "Cinco Tenedores" (1980), "La Colmena" (aka "The Beehive") (1982), "The Witching Hour" (1985), "Esquilache" (1989), "Yo Me Bajo en la Proxima, y Usted?" (1992), "Mas Alla del Jardin" (aka "Beyond the Garden") (1996), "Paris Tombuctu" (1999), "Km. 0" (2000), "The Lost Steps" (2001), "El Oro de Morscu" (aka "Moscow Gold") (2003), "Los Ninos del Jardin" (2003), "Bienvenido a Casa" (2006), "Chuecatown" (2007), "Enloquecidas" (2008), "Rage" (2009), "Flow" (2014), and "Malasana 32" (2020). Velasco appeared on television in episodes of "Sabado 64", "Gran Teatro", "Confidencias", "Primera Filaz", "Tiempo y Hora", "Las Doce Caras de Eva", "Estudio 1", "Este Senor de Negro", "Teresa de Jesus" as Teresa de Avila in 1984, "La Comedia Musical Espanola", "Yo, Una Mujer" as Elena Andrade in 1996, "Mama Quiere ser Artista" as Leonor in 1997, "Companeros" as Charo from 1998 to 1999, "Se Puede?", "Motivos Personales" as Aurora Acosta in 2005, "Heirs" as Carmen Orozco Argenta from 2007 to 2009, "Las Chicas de Oro" as Doroti in 2010, "Hospital Center", "Gran Hotel" as Angela Salinas from 2011 to 2013, "Bajo Sospecha" as Adela Valcarcel in 2016, "Velvet" as Petra in 2016, and "Cable Girls" as Dona Carmen from 2017 to 2020. She was also seen in television productions of "Cinco Minutos Nada Menos" (1984), "Mama, Quiero ser Artista!" (1989), La

Cerezas del Cementerio" (2005), and "Parte de Tu Vida" (2014). She performed frequently on stage throughout her career. Velasco was married to actor Francisco Marso from 1977 until their divorce in 2005 and they had two children.

Velez, Karen

Model Karen Velez, who was Playboy's Playmate of the Year in 1985, died in Downey, California, on July 2, 2023.

She was 62. Velez was born in Rockville Centre, Long Island, New York, on January 27, 1961. The buxom brunette was chosen as Playmate of the Month for the December of 1984 edition of "Playboy". She was selected as Playmate of the Year in 1985. Velez was also featured in several Playboy videos and was the cover model for the first issue of "Playboy's Playmate Review". She later worked as a hypnotist and certified hypnotherapist. Velez was married to actor Lee Majors from 1988 until their divorce in 1994 and is survived by their three children, daughter Nikki, who also posed for a "Playboy" pictorial, and twin sons Dane and Trey. She was married to Vic Ventimiglia, Jr., from 1999 until their divorce in 2004.

Velle, Louis

French actor Louis Velle died in Morainvilliers, France, on February 3, 2023. He was 96. Velle was born in Paris, France, on May 29, 1926. He began his career on stage in the 1940s and performed in numerous productions through the early 2000s. He appeared in numerous films from the early 1950s including "Agence Matrimoniale" (1952), "L'Oeil en Coulisses" (1953), "Une Vie de Garcon" (1953), "The Three

Musketeers" (1953), "My Seven Little Sins" (1954), "Danger Flight 931" (1955), "The Impossible Mr. Pipelet" (1955), "La Meilleure Part" (1955), "Le Coin Tranquille" (1957), "L'Inspecteur Aime la Bagarre" (1957), "Par-dessus le Mur" (1961), "Because, Because of a Woman" (1963), "Amongst Vultures" (1964), "Martin Soldat" (1966), "La Nuit Infidele" (1968), "Docteur Caraibes" (1970), "Touch and Go" (1971), "Les Anges" (1973), "La Ligne de Sceaux" (1973), "Le Permis de Condire" (1974), "Les Murs Ont des Oreilles" (1974), "L'Intrepide" (1975), "Quand la Ville s'Eveille" (1977), "Un Marui, c'est un Mari" (1976) which he also wrote, "Private Passions" (1984), "Duo Solo" (1987), and "Kings for a Day" (1997). Ville was seen on television in productions of "Hotel des Neiges" (1958), "Vient de Paraitre" (1962), "Les Choses Voient" (1963), "Le Misere et la Gloire" (1965), "Le Miroir a Trois Faces: Louise" (1967), "Adeline

Venecian" (1967), "Le Regret de Pierre Guilhem" (1968), "I Giovedi della Signora Giulia" (1970), "L'Homme Qui Revient de Loin" (1972), "Les Temoins" (1972), "Petite Flamme dans la Tourmente" (1973), "L'Arc de Triomphe" (1975), "Paris-Porto-Vecchio" (1981), "Adieu Ma Cherie" (1981), "La Nuit de Matignon" (1982), "Le Lys" (1982), "Ultimatum" (1982), "Pazuvre Eros" (1983), "Taxi Girl" (1992), "Tout ou Presque" (1992), "Le Chateau des Oliviers" (1993), "Il Padre di Mia Figlia" (1997), "Le Grant Batre" (1997), "Tous les Chagrins se Ressemblent" (2002), "Mon Fils Cet Inconnu" (2004), "On Ne Prete Qu'aux Riches" (2005), "Les Secrets du Volcan" (2006), and "Les Chetaigniers du Desert" (2010). His other television credits include episodes of "Plasir du Theatre", "L'abonne de la Ligne U" as Roux in 1964, "L'Age Heureux", "Le Train Bleu s'Arrete 13 Fois", "Comment ne Pas Epouser eun Milliardaire" as Robert de Gissac in 1966, "Allo Police", "Le Monde Parallele", "La Demoiselle d'Avignon" as Francois Fonsalette in 1972, "Le Seize a Kerbriant", "Les Evasions Celebres", "Temoignages", "Docteur Caraibes" in the title role in 1973, "L'Etrange Monsieur Duvallier" as Duvalier/Raner in 1979, "Au Theatre ce Soir", "Julien Fontanes, Magistrat", "Le Bonheur d'en Face", "Le Marie de l'Ambassadeur", "L'Histoire du Samedi", "Louis Page", and "L'Agence Coup de Coeur". Ville was married to actress and writer Frederique Hebrard from 1949 until his death and is also survived by their three children, Catherine, Nicholas, and director Francois.

Veloz, Jean

Dancer and actress Jean Veloz died at her home in Los Angeles, California, on January 15, 2023. She was 99. She was born Jean Phelps in Los Angeles on March 1, 1924. She began dancing from an early age and competed in jitterbug dance contests in her teens. She was featured as a dancer in several films including "Swing Fever" (1943), "Where Are Your Children?" (1943), "Jive Junction" (1943), the shorts "The

Joint's Jumping at Juke Box Joe's" (1944) and "Groovie Movie" (1944), and "The Horn Blows at Midnight" (1945). She danced in the chorus line for Nick Castle's productions in Las Vegas in 1946 and began training with dancer Frank Veloz. She soon became his dance partner, and they were involved with the choreography for the films "Valentino" (1951) and "Latin Lovers" (1953). They also worked together on a Los Angeles television show "Fare for Ladies" from 1956 to 1957. She retired after her husband's death in 1981 but resumed dancing in the early 1990s. She was inducted into the California Swing Dance Hall of Fame in 1996. Veloz was also a dance instructor for the television reality series "The Bachelorette" in 2016 and performed on the Steve Harvey series "Little Big Shorts: Forever Young" in 2017. She continued to attend dance festivals well into her 90s, with her most recent in 2020. She married Harold 'Babe' Davi" in 1947

452

but they later divorced. She was married to her dance partner, Frank Veloz, from 1963 until his death in 1981.

Ventura, Anna

Adult film actress Anna Ventura died of upper gastrointestinal bleed and peptic ulcers in Mayodan, North Carolina, on August 4, 2023. She was 63. She was born Patricia Susanne Roesch in Los Angeles, California, on June 9, 1960. She was a

model for men's magazines in the late 1970s and early 1980s including "Oui", "Expose!", "Penthouse", "Playboy", and "Companion". She made her adult film debut with Michelle Bauer in 1981's "Bad Girls" under the name Jasmine du Bai. She was also seen in the films "Class Reunion" (1980), "Society Affairs" (1982) under the name Carla Russel, "The Devil in Miss Jones Part II" (1982), "Tight Assets" (1982), "Wild Dallas Honey" (1982), "Oui, Girls" (1982), "Girlfriends" (1983), "Hot Dreams" (1983), "That's Outrageous" (1983), "Daddy's Little Girls" (1983), "When She Was Bad" (1983), and "Never Sleep Alone" (1984). She left the film industry after several years and went to Japan where she continued modeling. Her drug and alcohol abuse led to her returning to the United States where she checked into rehab. She left modeling and married someone she met in rehab. She had three girls and a boy, and the family moved around the country. They divorced after a decade and another brief and turbulent marriage followed. Another more successful marriage followed but drug and alcohol, combined with failing health, eventually ended it as well. She is survived by her four children.

Verlaine, Tom

Guitarist and singer Tom Verlaine, who led the rock band Television in the 1970s, died of prostate cancer in New York City on January 28, 2023. He was 73. He was born Thomas Miller in Denville, New Jersey, on December 13, 1949.

He was raised in Wilmington, Delaware, and played the piano and saxophone. He attended Sanford Preparatory School but moved to New York City without graduating, changing his name to Tom Verlaine. He and classmate Richard Meyers, who became known as Richard Hell, teamed with drummer Billy Ficca to form the early punk band the Neon Boys in 1972. The band reformed as Television the following year. They added guitarist Richard Lloyd to their lineup and performed at punk clubs around New York. Fred Smith replaced Hell as Television's bassist for the albums "Marquee Moon" (1977) and "Adventure" (1978). The band subsequently broke up and Verlaine embarked on a successful solo career. He composed the score for the 1994

indie film "Love and a .45". Television reformed for a self-titled third album in 1992 and continued to tour and perform together irregularly. Lloyd left the group for reasons of health in 2007 and Johnny Rip joined the band on guitar. He was part of a super-group along with fellow guitarists Nels Cline and Lee Ranaldo in the Million Dollar Bashers. They recorded songs for the soundtrack of the 2007 film "I'm Not There". Verlaine's later solo albums include "The Wonder" (1990), "Warm and Cool" (1992), "The Miller's Tale: A To Verlaine Anthology" (1996), "Songs and Other Things" (2006), and "Around" (2006).

Vidal, Francisco

Spanish actor Jose Francisco Vidal Bornay died in Spain on October 6, 2023. He was 82. Vidal was born in Ibi, Spain, in 1941. He attended the University of Madrid and

studied acting under Miguel Narros at the Circulo Medina. He began performing with the Teatro Estudio in Madrid in the 1960s and worked with the Independent Experimental Theater from 1968 to 1978. Vidal taught acting at the Institute of Community Education from 1998. He appeared in such films as "Oscuros Seunos de Agosto" (1968), "El Desastre de Annual" (1970), "La Gioconda esta Triste" (1977), "Pasion" (1977), "Caperucita y Roja" (1977), "Tengamos la Guerra en Paz" (1977), "Cabo de Vara" (1978), "Pero No Vas a Cambiar Nunca, Margarita?" (1978), "Tobi" (1978), "Madrid al Desnudo" (1979), "7 Dias de Enero" (1979), "Con Unas y Dientes" (1979), "Gary Cooper, Que Estas en los Cielos" (1980), "El Crack" (1981), "La Segunda Guerra de los Ninos" (1981), "Asesinato en el Comite Central" (1982), "En Busca del Huevo Perdido" (1982), "Corazon de Papel" (1982), "Fermenino Singular" (1982), "El Gran Mogollon" (1982), "Los Pajaritos" (1983), "Mar Brava" (1983), "Parchis Entra en Accion" (1983), "Padre Nuestro" (1985), "De Hombre a Hombre" (1985), "Caso Cerrado" (1985), "Marbella, un Golpe de Cinco Estrellas" (1985), "Mabru Se Fue a la Guerra" (1986), "El Lute: Run for Your Life" (1987), "The Enchanted Forest" (1987), "Amanece Como Puedas" (1988), "El Tesoro" (1988), "Ella el y Benjamin" (1990), "Ovejas Negras" (1990), "Don Juan, Mi Querido Fantasma" (1990), "The Fencing Master" (1992), "Eso" (1996), "Burn with Me" (2002), "Pan's Labyrinth" (2006), "GAL" (2006), "Cowards" (2008), "Antes de Morir Plensa en Mi." (2008), "Instrucciones Para Una Nueva Vida" (2008), "La Luz Con el Tiempo Dentro" (2015), and "Ana by Day" (2018). Vidal appeared on television in productions of "El Si de las Ninas" (1970), "Las Picaras" (1983), "Nunca es Tarde" (1984), "Pedro I el Cruel" (1989), "El Obispo Leproso" (1990), "La Regena" (1994), "Viento del Pueblo (Miguel Hernandez)" (2002), "Cartas de Sorolla" (2006), "Alfonso, el Principe Maldito" (2010), and "Rescatando a Sara" (2012). He was also seen in episodes of "Plinio", "Hora Once", "Cronicas de un Pueblo" as D. Marcelino from 1971 to

1974, "Los Pintores del Prado", "El Teatro", "Manuel de Falla. 7 Cantos de Espana" as Manuel de Falla in 1977, "Los Libros", "Estudio 1", "Teatro Breve", "Cervantes" as Torralba in 1981, "Verano Azul", "La Mascara Negra", "Don Baldomero y Su Gente" as Luis in 1982, "La Comedia", "Gatos en el Tejado", "Amores Dificiles", "Miguel Servet (La Sangre y le Ceniza)", "Brigada Central", "Supercan y Su Banda", "La Huella del Crimen", "Farmacia de Guardia", "Tango", "Cronicas del Mal", "Habitacion 503", "Villarriba y Villabajo", "El Sexologo", "Compuesta y Sin Novio", "Canguros", "Los Ladrones Van a la Oficina", "Ay, Senor, Senor!", "Hermanos de Leche", "Vidas Cruzadas", "Todos los Hombres Sois Iguales", "La Banda de Perez", "Pasen y Vean", "Este es Mi Barrio" as Angel from 1996 to 1997, "Hermanas", "Manos a la Obra", "Antivicio", "Un Hombre Solo", "Robles, Investigador", "Cuentame Como Paso", "La Verad de Laura", "El Comisario", "Al Filo de la Ley", "7 Vidas", "Amar en Tiempos Revueltos", "Hermanos & Detectives", "Countdown", "La Senora" as Doctor Freire from 2008 to 2009, "Hospital Central", "El Secreto de Puenta Vieja" as Don Julian in 2011, "Aida", "Victor Ros", and "La Sonata del Silencio".

Vieau, Michael

Actor Michael Vieau died in Chicago, Illinois, on June 29, 2023. He was 52. Vieau was born in Roselle, Illinois, on

June 9, 1971. He appeared frequently on television from the late 1990s with roles in episodes of "Cupid", "Prison Break" in the recurring role of Christopher Trokey in 2005, "The Beast", "The Playboy Club", "Chicago Fire", "The Mob Doctor" in the recurring role of Benny in 2012, "Shameless", and "Chicago P.D.". He was featured as Rossi in Christopher Nolan's 2008 film
"The Dark Knight" starring Christian Bale as Batman, and was Ed Shouse in 2009's "Public Enemies". Vieau performed frequently on the Chicago stage throughout his career.

Vienhage, Rocco

Actor Rocco Vienhage died in Los Angeles, California, after a long illness on June 28, 2023. He was 60.

He was born in Springfield, Missouri, on October 7, 1962. He performed on the local stage with the Springfield Little Theater. He moved to California in the 1980s and appeared with the West Coast Ensemble in Los Angeles. Vienhage was featured in the films "What I Did for Love" (1998) and "The Wedding Planner" (2001). He was seen frequently on television with roles in episodes of "Murphy Brown", "Sliders", "The Burning

Zone", "Nick Fresno: Licensed Teacher", "Nothing Sacred", "USA High", "Sabrina the Teenage Witch", "Clueless", "Sister, Sister", "Nash Bridges", "The Parkers", "Girlfriends", "Malibu County", and "Extant". He was seen in the tele-films "Blood Money" (2000) and "Super Sweet 16: The Movie" (2007). Vienhage also worked in finance.

Villaronga, Agusti

Spanish film director Agusti Villaronga, who was noted for the 1989 fantasy film "Moon Child", died in

Barcelona, Spain, on January 22, 2023. He was 69. Villaronga was born in Palma de Mallorca, Spain, on March 4, 1953. He worked in films as an actor from the 1970s, appearing in "Robin Hood Nunca Muere" (1975), "El Fin de la Inocencia" (1977), "El Ultimo Guateque" (1978), "Perros Callejeros II" (1979), "Souvenir" (1994), "Presence of Mind"
(1999), "The Uninvited Guest" (2004), "Atlas of Human Geography" (2007), "Little Indi" (2009), "Difuminado" (2014), and "The Whistlers" (2019). He wrote and directed the short films "Anta Mujer" (1976), "Al Mayurka" (1980), and "Laberint" (1980). He made his feature debut as director and writer for the 1986 horror film "In a Glass Cage". He also directed and wrote the films "Moon Child" (1989), "Al-Andalus: The Art of Islamic Spain" (1992), "99.9" (1997), "The Sea" (2000), "Aro Tolbukhin: In the Mind of a Killer" (2002), "Black Bread" (2010), "The King of Havana" (2015), "Uncertain Glory" (2017), "Born a King" (2019), "The Belly of the Sea" (2021), and the comedy "Stormy Lola" (2023). He directed television productions of "Miquel Bauca, Poeta Invisible" (2007), "After the Rain" (2007), and "Letter to Eva" (2012), and episodes of "Cycle Simenon", "Croniques de la Veritat Oculta", and "50 Anos De".

Vlaming, Jeff

Television writer and producer Jeff Vlaming, who was noted for his work on the series "The X-Files" and "Hannibal", died of cancer at a hospital in Pasadena, California, on January 30, 2023. He was 63. Vlaming was born in Edina, Minnesota,

on September 23, 1959. He graduated with a degree in television productions from the University of Minnesota. He worked as an advertising art director in Minneapolis before moving to Los Angeles in the early 1990s. He was soon writing scripts for the series "Northern Exposure". Vlaming was writer for numerous series including "Lucky Luke",
"The Adventures of Brisco County, Jr.", "Catwalk", "The X-Files" serving as story editor from 1995 to 1996, "Weird Science", "Lois & Clark: The New Adventures of Superman"

serving as executive story editor from 1996 to 1997, "Honey, I Shrunk the Kids: The TV Show", "Animorphs", "Xena: Warrior Princess", "The Magnificent Seven", "Cleopatra 2525", "So Weird", "Murder in Small Town X", "Numb3rs", "Battlestar Galactica", and "Stargate Universe". Vlaming was a producer and writer for the series "Rescue 77", "NCIS", "Keen Eddie", "Touching Evil", "Reaper", "Fringe", "Teen Wolf", "Hannibal", "Outcast", "The 100", and "Debris". He was author of the 2023 graphic novel "Twelve O'Clock Somewhere". Vlaming is survived by his wife, Kathy, and their two sons.

Wagner, Robin

Scenic designer Robin Wagner, who was recipient of three Tony Award for his works on Broadway, died at his home in New York City on May 29, 2023. He was 89. Wagner was

born in San Francisco, California, on August 31, 1933. He attended the California School of Fine Arts and began his career working on the local stage on such productions as "Amahl and the Night Visitors" and "Waiting for Godot". He moved to New York City in 1958 where he continued to design sets for off-Broadway plays. He made his Broadway debut as an assistant designer to Ben Edwards for the 1961 play "Big Fish, Little Fish". Wagner served as an assistant to designers Edwards and Oliver Smith on subsequent productions of "The Aspern Papers" (1962), "Harold" (1962), "110 in the Shade" (1963), "Hello, Dolly!" (1964), "Luv" (1964), "Baker Street" (1965), and "Baker Street" (1965). He was scenic designer for Jean-Paul Sartre's "The Condemned of Altona" in 1966. He continued to work on such Broadway productions as "Galileo" (1967), "The Trial of Lee Harvey Oswald" (1967), "Hair" (1968), "Lovers and Other Strangers" (1968), "The Cuban Thing" (1968), "The Great White Hope" (1968), "Promises, Promises" (1968), "The Watering Place" (1969), "My Daughter, You Son" (1969), "Gantry" (1970), "The Engagement Baby" (1970), and "Lenny" (1971). Wagner was nominated for Tony Awards for his scenic design for "Jesus Christ Superstar" (1971) and "Mack & Mabel" (1974) and earned the Tony for 1978's "On the Twentieth Century". He also won the Tony for "City of Angels" (1989) and "The Producers" (2001) and received additional nominations for "Dreamgirls" (1981), "Jelly's Last Jam" (1992), "Angels in America: Millennium Approaches" (1993), "Kiss Me, Kate" (1999), and "Young Frankenstein" (2007). His numerous Broadway credits also include "Inner City" (1971), "Sugar" (1972), "Lysistrata" (1972), "Seesaw" (1973), "Full Circle" (1973), "Rachael Lily Rosenbloom and Don't You Ever Forget It" (1973), "The Fifth Dimension with Jo Jo's Dance Factory" (1974), "A Chorus Line" (1975), the American Ballet Theatre's production of "Hamlet Connotations" (1975), "Hair" (1977), "Ballroom" (1978), "Comin' Uptown" (1979), "42nd Street" (1980), "One Night Stand" (1980), "Merlin" (1983),

"Song and Dance" (1985), the 1987 revival of "Dreamgirls", "Teddy & Alice" (1987), "Chess" (1988), "Jerome Robbins' Broadway" (1989), "Crazy for You" (1992), "Angels in America: Perestroika" (1993), "Victor/Victoria" (1995), "Big" (1996), "The Life" (1997), "Side Show" (1997), "Saturday Night Fever" (1999), "The Wild Party" (2000), "Flower Drum Song" (2002), "The Boy from Oz" (2003), "Never Gonna Dance" (2003), "A Chorus Line" (2006), and "Leap of Faith" (2012). His sets were used for several films including "Sgt. Pepper's Lonely Hearts Club Band" (1978), "42nd Street" (1986), "Victor/Victoria" (1995), and "The Producers" (2005). He also designed sets for the Metropolitan Opera, the Vienna State Opera, the New York City Ballet, the Royal Opera House at Covent Garden, and regional productions around the country. He was inducted into the Theater Hall of Fame in 2001. Wagner was married and divorced from Joyce Workman and is survived by their three children. He was also married and divorced for film executive Paula Kauffman.

Walker, Geordie

British rock musician Geordie Walker, who was the guitarist for the post-punk group Killing Joke, died of complications from a stroke in Prague, Czech Republic, on November 26, 2023. He was 64. He was born Kevin Walker in Chester-le-Street, County Durham, England, on December

18, 1958. He learned to play the guitar in his teens. He moved to London to study architecture in 1979. He answered an ad by singer Jaz Coleman to form a band and joined with Paul Ferguson on drums and Martin 'Youth' Glover on bass to form Killing Joke. The band released the LP "Turn to Red" later in the year and their self-titled debut album came out in 1980. Killing Joke had frequent line-up changes though Walker played guitar on all of their subsequent albums including "What's THIS For...!" (1981), "Revelations" (1982), "Fire Dances" (1983), "Night Time "(1985), "Brighter Than a Thousand Suns" (1986), "Outside the Gate" (1988), "Extremities, Dirt and Various Repressed Emotions" (1990), "Pandemonium" (1994), and "Democracy" (1996). Killing Joke went on hiatus in 1996. Walker also performed with the supergroups Murder, Inc. and the Damage Machine. Killing Joke began recording again in 2002 and another self-named album was released the following year. The album "Hosannas from the Basements of Hell" followed in 2006. Bassist Paul Raven, who had played with the band from the early 1980s, died in 2007. The original Killing Joke line-up reunited in 2008 and embarked on a world concert tour. They released the albums "Absolute Dissent" (2010), "MMXII" (2012), and "Pylon" (2015). Walker moved to Prague in 2006 where he worked with Studio Faust Records. He was married to Ginny Kiraly from 1989 until their divorce in 2012 and is survived by their son, Atticus. He became involved with

Alexander Kocourkova and is survived by her and their daughter, Isabella.

Walker, Lillias

Scottish actress Lillias Walker died of complications from vascular disease in Great Britain on August 10, 2023. She was 93. Walker was born in Longforgan, Scotland, on December 31, 1929. She appeared frequently on stage and television from the 1960s. She was seen in episodes of "This Man Craig", "Sir Arthur Conan Doyle", "Vendetta", "Armchair Theatre", "The Newcomers", "Out of the Unknown", "The Wednesday Play", "The First Churchills", "Paul Temple", "The Borderers", "Manhunt", "Dr. Finlay's Casebook", "Public Eye", "New Scotland Yard", "Van der Valk", "Crime of Passion", "Sporting Scenes", "Softly Softly: Task Force", "You're on Your Own", "Doctor Who" as Sister Lamont in the 1975 serial "Terror of the Zygons", "Within These Walls", and "The Cedar Tree" as Rosemary Cartland from 1976 to 1978. Walker was featured in television productions of "The Nicest Man in the World" (1976), "Beasts" (1976), "The Walls of Jericho" (1981), and "Charlie" (1984). She was seen in several films including "Mr. Brown Comes Down the Hill" (1965), "What Became of Jack and Jill?" (1972), "Malachi's Cove" (1973), "The Romantic Englishwoman" (1975), "The Hiding Place" (1975), and "Intimate Reflections" (1975). Walker was married to actor Peter Vaughan from 1966 until his death in 2016 and is survived by their son.

Walser, Martin

German author Martin Walser died in Nussdorf, Germany, on July 26, 2023. He was 96. Walser was born in Wasserburg am Vodensee, Germany, on March 24, 1927. He served in the German Wehrmacht during World War II. He resumed his education after the war and studied at the Uniersity of Regensburg and the University of Tubingen. He earned a

doctorate in literature with a thesis on Franz Kakfa in 1951. He also worked as a reporter for a Munich broadcasting company and began writing audio plays. He became an active member of the writer conference Gruppe 47. His first novel, the satirical "Marriage in Philippsburg", was published in 1957. Walser penned the trilogy that included "Halbzeit" (1960), "Das Einhorn" ("The Unicorn") (1966) which was adapted for a 1978 film, and "Der Sturz" ("The Fall") (1973) which became a film in 1975. He was noted for his 1978 novella "Ein Fliehendes Pferd" ("Runaway Horse"), which was adapted for television in 1986 and for a film in 2007. He also wrote the films "Havoc" (1972) and "La Faille" (1975) and episodes of the television series "Tatort" and "Tassilo - Ein Full fur Sich". Several of his other novels and plays were adapted for film and television including "Der Abstecher" (1962), "Eiche und Angora" (1964), "Die Zimmerschlacht" (1969), "Uberlebensgross Herr Krott" (1971), "Alles aus Liebe" (1986), and "Ohne Einander" (2007). He married Kathe Neuner-Jehle in 1950 and is survived by her and their four children, actress Franziskaa Walser, writer and painter Alissa Walser, and writers Johanna and Theresa Walser.

Warda, Arnold

Actor Arnold 'Arne' Warda died while in hospice care in Elmhurst, Illinois, on January 25, 2023. He was 88. Warda was born in Chicago, Illinois, on January 18, 1935. He served

in the U.S. Army after graduating high school in 1952. He returned to Chicago after his discharge where he pursued an acting career on stage. He moved to Los Angeles in the early 1960s where he worked as a male model and appeared frequently in television commercials. Warda made his film debut as Sgt. Grimaldi in Al Adamson's horror film "Blood of Ghastly Horror" (aka "Psycho a Go-Go!" and "Fiend with the Electronic Brain") (1967). His other films include "Angels' Wild Women" (1971), "Love, Swedish Style" (1972), and "Pushing Up Daisies" (1973). He was seen on television in episodes of "Police Story", "Police Woman", "CHiPs", "Quincy", and "Whiz Kids". He also served as host of Hugh Hefner's television variety series "Playboy After Dark" and ran the Playboy Club in Century City, California, in the early 1970s. He left acting in the late 1980s and settled in Naperville, Illinois, where he designed and built homes. Warna married Barbara Anderson in 1986 and is survived by their daughter, Marne.

Wardlow, John

Canadian stuntman John Wardlow died in Surrey, British Columbia, Canada, on January 15, 2023. He was 77. Wardlow was born in Driffield, East Yorkshire, England, on

August 15, 1945. He emigrated to Canada when he was a child. He began working in the film industry in the late 1960s and served as a location manager and assistant director for commercials and films. He became one of Canada's first stuntmen and was co-founder of Stunts Canada. Wardlow performed and coordinated stunts and occasionally appeared in small roles in such films as "One Minute Before Death" (1972), "The Oval Portrait" (1973), "Shadow of the Hawk" (1976), "The Keeper" (1976), "Bear Island" (1979), "Harry Tracy: The Last of the Wild Bunch" (1982), "Spacehunter: Adventures in the Forbidden Zone" (1983), "Never Cry Wolf" (1983), "Iceman" (1984), "The Journey of Natty Gann" (1985), "The Clan of the Cave Bear" (1986), "April Fool's Day" (1986), "The Stepfather" (1987), "American Gothic" (1987), "Roxanne" (1987), "Stakeout" (1987), "Shoot to Kill" (1988), "The Experts" (1989), "The Fly II" (1989), "Friday the 13th Part VIII: Jason Takes Manhattan" (1989), "Ax 'Em" (1992), "Another Stakeout" (1993), "The Hunteds" (1995), "Suspicious Agenda" (1995), "Mind Ripper" (1995), "Crying Freeman" (1995), "Man with a Gun" (1995), "Car Pool" (1996), "Air Bud" (1997), "Free Willy 3: The Rescue" (1997), "Deep Rising" (1998), "Wrongfully Accused" (1998), "A Twist of Faith" (1999), "Epicenter" (2000), "My 5 Wives" (2000), "Bear with Me" (2000), "Chain of Fools" (2000), "Cats & Dogs" (2000), "Ballistic: Ecks vs. Sever" (2002), "The Core" (2003), "Paycheck" (2003), "Air Bud: Spikes Back" (2003), "Walking Tall" (2004), "The Wild Guys" (2004), "I, Robot" (2004), "Fascination" (2004), "Alone in the Dark" (2005), "Edison" (2005), "Fantastic Four" (2005), "X-Men: The Last Stand" (2006), "Fantastic Four: Rise of the Silver Surfer" (2007), "Postal" (2007), "Aliens vs. Predator: Requiem" (2007), "Afghan Knights" (2007), "Beneath" (2007), "Wrong Turn 2: Dead End" (2007), "Vice" (2008), "12 Rounds 2: Reloaded" (2013), and "A Dog's Way Home" (2019). He was unit production manager for the tele-films "Who'll Save Our Children?" (1978), "The Plutonium Incident" (1980), and "A Piano for Mrs. Cimino" (1982) and assistant director for the television series "Huckleberry Finn and His Friends" (1980) and "The Minikins" (1982). Wardlow worked in stunts for such tele-films and mini-series as "The Glitter Dome" (1984), "Spot Marks the X" (1986), "A Stranger Waits" (1987), "Deep Dark Secrets" (1987), "Tracks of Glory" (1992), "Relentless: Mind of a Killer" (1993), "Sherlock Holmes Returns" (1993), "Futuresport" (1998), "Poison" (2000), "Snow Queen" (2002), "Jinnah: On Crime - White Knight, Black Widow" (2003), "The Love Crimes of Gillian Guess" (2004), "Human Cargo" (2004), "Behind the Camera: The Unauthorized Story of Mork & Mindy" (2005), "Murder at the Presidio" (2005), "Eight Days to Live" (2006), "The Mermaid Chair" (2006), "Ogre" (2008), "The Most Wonderful Time of the Year" (2008), and "A Firehouse Christmas" (2016). He also worked on the series "Danger Bay", "Airwolf", "Palace Guard", "The Commish", "Madison", "Highlander" serving as stunt coordinator from 1992 to 1995, "The Lone Gunmen", "The Outer Limits" serving as stunt coordinator from 1995 to 2001, "Dead Like Me", "The 4400", "Cold Squad", "Psych", "Motive", "Arrow", "Shut Eye", and "Rogue". Wardlow is survived by his wife, Margaret Long.

Waterman, Stan

Cinematographer and underwater film producer Stan Waterman died on August 10, 2023. He was 100. Waterman was born in Maine on April 5, 1923. He served in the U.S. Navy during World War II. He subsequently graduated from Dartmouth College in 1946. He purchased an early version of the aqualung and operated a diving charter business in the Bahamas from 1954 to 1958. He filmed a family trip to Tahiti in 1965 which was purchased and aired on television by

"National Geographic" as "The Call of the Running Tide". Waterman was producer and underwater photographer for the 1971 shark film "Blue Water, White Death". He was also an underwater cinematographer for the films and television productions "The Deep" (1977), "Jaws of Death", "The Bermuda Depths" (1978), "The Lost Treasure of the Concepcion" (1979), "A Whale for the Killing" (1981), and "Tails of the South Pacific" (2000). He shared an Emmy Award with his son, George Waterman, for the "National Geographic Explorer" production of "Dancing with Stingrays" in 1987. He was the subject of the Discovery Channel documentary "The Man Who Loves Sharks" in 1992. Waterman's book, "Sea Salt: Memories and Essays", was published in 2005. He made his final dive in the Cayman Islands in 2013 at the age of 90. He is survived by his wife, Susanna, and three children.

Watts, Andre

Classical pianist Andre Watts died of prostate cancer in Bloomington, Indiana, on July 12, 2023. He was 77. Watts

was born in Nuremberg, Germany, on June 20, 1946, where his father was stationed with the U.S. Army. He spent his childhood in Europe living near Army posts where his father was stationed. He began studying violin at an early age but switched to piano at the age of six. He settled in Philadelphia, Pennsylvania, with his family in 1954. He continued studying the piano and made a public performance in 1956. He graduated from the Philadelphia Musical Academy in 1963 and performed with the Philadelphia Orchestra Children's Concerts. He appeared on television in Leonard Bernstein's "Young People's Concert" series in 1963, performing Liszt's "Piano Concert No. 1 in E-Flat". He was asked by Bernstein to join the New York Philharmonic and soon released the album "The Exciting Debut of Andre Watts". He continued his studies at the Peabody Institute in Baltimore, graduating in 1972. He performed in numerous concerts around the United States and Europe and signed a recording contract with Columbia Masterworks Records. He later signed with EMI from 1985 through the early 1990s. Watts served on the faculty at Indiana University from 2004. He appeared on television in such series as "Camera Three", "Andre Previn's Music Night", "Mister Rogers' Neighborhood", and "Tavis Smiley". He was nominated for five Grammy Awards and won Most Promising New Classical Recording Artist in 1964. He was nominated for a 1995 Emmy Award for Outstanding

Cultural Program. He was recipient of the National Medal of Arts in 2011 and was inducted into the American Classical Music Hall of Fame in 2013. His survivors include his wife, Joan Brand, and two stepchildren.

Weaver, Cheryl

Actress Cheryl Weaver died in her home in Lawrence, Kansas, on June 4, 2023. She was 65. She was born Cheryl Virginia Rawlings in Wichita, Kansas, on January 28, 1958. She briefly attended the University of Missouri after graduating

high school. She subsequently transferred to the University of Kansas where she began performing on stage. She moved to Dallas with her husband after graduation where she worked at various jobs and appeared frequently on the local stage. She continued to pursue an acting career after moving to East Lansing, Michigan. She and her family resettled in Lawrence, Kansas, in the 1990s where she was a leading performer on the Kansas City stage. Weaver was featured in the tele-films "Truman" (1995) and "Gone in the Night" (1996) and the films "Ride with the Devil" (1999) and "Raising Jeffrey Dahmer" (2006). She is survived by her husband, Doug, and son, Ian.

Webb, Chris

British stuntman and actor Chris Webb, who worked on over a dozen James Bond films from the 1970s through the

1990s, died in Littlehampton, West Sussex, England, on November 27, 2023. He was 86. Webb was born in Lambeth, London, England, on March 16, 1937. He began working in films and television in the mid-1960s. He performed stunts and appeared in small roles in numerous films including "Carry on Cowboy" (1965), "The Brides of Fu Manchu" (1966), "You Only Live Twice" (1967), "The Assassination Bureau" (1969), "On Her Majesty's Secret Service" (1969) as George Lazenby's stunt double, "Diamonds Are Forever" (1971), "Family Life" (1971), "All Coppers Are..." (1972), "Rentadick" (1972), "Live and Let Die" (1973), "Brannigan" (1975), "The Squeeze" (1977), "Star Wars" (1977), "A Bridge Too Far" (1977), "The Spy Who Loved Me" (1977), "Valentino" (1977), "The Wild Geese" (1978), "Superman" (1978), "The London Connection" (1979), "Hanover Street" (1979), "Superman II" (1980), "Flash Gordon" (1980), "For Your Eyes Only" (1981), "Victor/Victoria" (1982), "Britannia Hospital" (1982), "Tangiers" (1982), "Octopussy" (1983), "Krull" (1983), "Curse of the Pink Panther" (1983), "Space Riders" (1984), "Banana Cop" (1984), "Indiana Jones and the Temple of Doom" (1984), "Brazil" (1985), "Morons from Outer Space" (1985), "A View

to a Kill" (1985), "Lifeforce" (1985), "The Holcroft Covenant" (1985), "Eleni" (1985), "Revolution" (1985), "Biggles: Adventures in Time" (1986), "Aliens" (1986), "The Living Daylights" (1987), "A Time of Destiny" (1988), "Buster" (1988), "Without a Clue" (1988), "Indiana Jones and the Last Crusade" (1989), "Slipstream" (1989), "Batman" (1989), "Nightbreed" (1990), "Midnight Breaks" (1990), "Company Business" (1991), "Different for Girls" (1996), "Macbeth" (1997), "FairyTale: A True Story" (1997), "Photographing Fairies" (1997), "The Borrowers" (1997), "Tomorrow Never Dies" (1997), "Sexy Beast" (2000), "Formula 51" (2001), "The Gathering" (2002), "The Heart of Me" (2002), "The Da Vinci Code" (2006), "Stormbreaker" (2006), "National Treasure: Book of Secrets" (2007), "Harry Brown" (2009), "Harry Potter and the Deathly Hallows: Part 1" (2010), "One Day" (2011), "Hugo" (2011), "The Anomaly" (2014), and "Playing with Fire" (2019). Webb worked on such television series and productions as "The Scales of Justice", "Softly Softly", "The First Lady", "The Wednesday Play", "Journey to the Unknown", "Ace of Wands", "Special Branch", "Catweazle", "Doctor Who", "The Brothers", "Z Cars", "Shades of Greene", "Arthur of the Britons", "Star Maidens", the 1977 tele-film "The Man in the Iron Mask", "Raffles", "Target", "Holding On", "Blake's 7", "People Like Us", "The Sweeney", "The Last of the Summer Wine", "Wolcott", "The Treachery Game", "Going Out", "The Chinese Detective", "Reilly: Ace of Spies", "Brideshead Revisited", "The Professionals", "Minder", "Widows", "Driving Ambition", 1984's "The Zany Adventures of Robin Hood", "Travelling Man", "Juliet Bravo", "The Practice", "Dempsey and Makepeace", "Now, Something Else", "Bowen A'i Bartner", "Blott on the Landscape", "Super Gran", "The Tripods", "First Among Equals", "The Return of Sherlock Holmes", "Floodtide", "The Comic Strip Presents", 1988's "The Face of Trespass", "Coronation Street", "Blind Justice", "Confessional", 1989's "The Return of Sam McCloud", 1990's "Spymaker: The Secret Life of Ian Fleming", "Cracker", "Between the Lines", 1997's "Our Boy", "Taggart", "Messiah", "Band of Brothers", "William and Mary", "Mike Bassett: Manager", "1000 Ways to Die", and "Debris". Webb was given a lifetime achievement award from the British Stunt Register in 2018.

Wei Wei

Chinese actress Wei Wei died in Hong Kong on November 2, 2023. She was 101. She was born Miao

Mengying in Zhenjiang, China, on May 17, 1922. She began her acting career in the late 1940s, appearing in "Night Inn" (1947). She was noted for her role as Zhou Yuwen in the classic film "Spring in a Small Town" in 1948. She continued to appear in such films as "The Great Reunion" (1948), "Jiang Hu Er Nu" (1952), "Zi Mei Qu" (1954), "Shan Dian Lian Ai" (1955), "Yi Nian Zhi Ji" (1955),

"Shui Huo Zhi Jian" (1955), "Ji Mo De Xin" (1956), "Tai Tai Quan Qi" (1957), "Feng Chun You Wu" (1957), "Chun Man Ren Jian" (1959), "Cao Mu Jie Bing" (1960), "Kinmonto Ni Kakeru Hashi" (1962), and "Nan Nan Nu Nu" (1964). Wei's career in films ended in the mid-1960s for over three decades. She resumed acting in the 1990s with such credits as "I Want to Go on Living" (1995), "The Age of Miracles" (1996), "Anna Magdalena" (1998), "The Truth About Jane and Sam" (1999), "And I Hate You So" (2000), "Sang Yat Fai Lok" (2007), "Fire of Conscience" (2010), "The Drunkard" (2010), and "The Assassins" (2012).

Weinstein, Samantha

Canadian actress Samantha Weinstein died of ovarian cancer at a hospital in Toronto, Ontario, Canada, on May 14, 2023. She was 28. Weinstein was born in Toronto on March  20, 1995. She began her career as a child actress in the early 2000s and appeared in such films as "Siblings" (2004), the award-winning short film "Big Girl" (2005) as Josephine, "Ninth Street Chronicles" (2006), "The Stone Angel" (2007), "The Rocker" (2008) "Toronto Stories" (2008), "Jesus Henry Christ" (2011), "Haunter" (2013), the 2013 remake of the horror film "Carrie" as Heather Mason, and "Reign" (2015). Weinstein was seen on television in episodes of "The Red Green Show", "XPM", "72 Hours: True Crime", "Wild Card", "At the Hotel" as Piper in 2006, "The Border", "Being Erica", "Less Than Kind", "Copper", "Darknet", "Burden of Truth", and "Riley Rocket". Her other television credits include productions of "The Seeking Reveals" (2004), "Swarmed" (2005), "Celine" (2009), "Maggie Hill" (2009), "Alias Grace" (2017), and "Angry Angel" (2017). She was also a voice actress in such animated series as "Gerald McBoing Boing", "Super Why!", "Barbar and the Adventures of Badou", "The ZhuZhus", "Wishfart", "D.N. Ace" as the voice of Sloane Plunderman from 2019 to 2020, "Kingdom Force", "Let's Go Luna!", "Mittens & Pants" as the voice of Ms. McRooster in 2023, "Dino Ranch", and "FLCL: Grunge". She was also singer, songwriter, and lead guitarist with the Toronto garage rock band Killer Virgins. Weinstein married Michael Knutson in October of 2022 and he survives her.

Weis, Heidelind

Austrian actress Heidelind Weis died of heart failure at a hospital in Villach, Austria, on November 24, 2023. She was 83. Weis was born in Villach on September 17, 1940. She began performing in plays while in school and completed her training at the Max Reinhardt Seminar in Vienna in 1958. She married theatrical producer Hellmuth Duna in 1960 and performed frequently with his theatrical troupe. She was also featured in such films as "Ich Heirate Herrn Direktor" (1960), "Dead Woman from Beverly Hills" (1964), "Verdammt Zut

Sunde" (1964), "Lausbubeneschichten" (1964) as Cousin Cora Thomas, "Erzahl Mir Nichts" (1964), "Serenade fur Zwei Spione" (1965), "Madchen Hinter Gittern" (1965), "Tante Frieda - Neue Lausbubengeschichten" (1965), "Liselotte von der Pfalz" (1966), "Onkel Filser - Allerneueste Lausbubengeschichten" (1966), "The Man Outside" (1967), "Der Lugner und die Nonne" (1967), "Wenn Ludwig ins Manover Zieht" (1967), "Something for Everyone" (1970),  "Der Paukenspieler" (1971), "The Woman from Sarajevo" (1980), "Umwege Nach Venedig" (1989), and "Die Grunen Hugel von Wales" (2010). Weis was seen on television in productions of "Mary Rose" (1961), "Die Probe Oder Die Bestrafte Liebe" (1963), "Wasw Ihr Wollt" (1963), "Detective Story" (1963), "Der Geisterzug" (1963), "Die Kleinste Schau der Welt" (1963), "Two Gentlemen of Verona" (1964), "Eurydike" (1964), "Zweierlei Mass" (1964), "Colombe" (1965), "Der Seidene Schuh" (1965), "Antigone" (1965), "Die Geschichte von Vasco" (1968), "Othello" (1968) as Desdemona, "Jean der Traumer" (1969), "Liebe Gegen Paragraphen" (1969), "Ein Dorf Ohne Manner" (1969), "Die Marquise von B." (1970), "Die Frau in Weiss" (1971), "Hallo, Wer Dort?" (1971), "Diamantenparty" (1973), "Ein Abend Mit O.E. Hasse" (1973), "Vabanque" (1973), "Nie Wieder Mary" (1974), "Eine Frau Zieht Ein" (1975), "Eifersucht" (1978), "Ein Sommertagstraum" (1978), "Wo die Liebe Hinfallt" (1979), "...es Ist die Liebe" (1979), "Colombe" (1981), "Manche Mogen's Leis'" (1981), "Die Gerechten" (1981), "Die Erbin" (1982), "Der Heuler" (1982), "Funkeln im Auge" (1984), "Abgehort" (1984), "Gold Oder Leben - Vier Heitere Geschichten" (1984), "Im Amt und Wurden" (1985), "Spates Erroten" (1986), "Quadrille" (1986), "Acht Stunden Zeit" (1986), "Die Selige Edwina Black" (1987), "Flohr und die Traumfrau" (1987), "Alte Zeiten" (1988), "Falsche Spuren" (1990), "Kann Ich Noch Ein Bisschen Bleiben?" (1990), "Ausgetrickst" (1991), "Eine Phantastische Nacht" (1992), "Nervenkrieg" (1993), "Gabriellas Rache" (1994), "Ein Richter Zum Kussen" (1995), "Drei im Fremden Kissen" (1995), "Drei in Fremden Betten" (1996), "Haus der Vergeltung" (1997), "Am Anfang War der Seitensprung" (1999), "Nicht Mit Uns" (2000), "Am Anfang War der Eifersucht" (2001), "Sommerwind" (2001), "Fliege Kehrt Zuruck" (2003), "Drei Unter Einer Decke" (2003), "Lotti auf der Flucht" (2003), "Fliege Hat Angst" (2004), "Neue Freunde, Neues Gluck" (2005), "Heirate Meine Frau" (2005), "Cluck Auf Vier Radern" (2006), "Ein Ferienhaus auf Ibiza" (2008), "Liebe fur Fortgeschrittene" (2008), "Nichts als Arger Mit den Mannern" (2009), "Vorzimmer Zur Holle" (2009), "Das Gluck Ist ein Kaktus" (2011), "Vorzimmer Zur Holle - Streng Geheim!" (2011), and "Lebe Dein Leben" (2012). Her other television credits include episodes of "Familie Leitner", "Meine Frau Susanne" as Susanne Koldewey from 1963 to 1964, "Dem Tater auf der Spur", "Der Kommissar", "Die Krimistunde", "The

Black Forest Hospital" as Dr. Elena Bach in 1985, "Der Elegante Hund", "Das Erbe der Guldenburgs", "Auf der Suche Nach Salome", "A Case for Two", "Eurocops", "Faust", "Wir Konigskinder", "Ein Mord for Quandt", "Derrick", "The Old Fox", "In der Mitte Eines Lebens", "Rosamunde Pilcher", "Typisch Sophie", "Lilly Schonauer", "SOKO Munchen", "Das Traumschiff", "Pfarrer Braun", "Utta Danella", "Das Traumhotel", and "Weissblaue Geschichten". Her autobiography, "The Best Is Yet to Come", was published in 2022. Weis was married to Hellmuth Duna from 1960 until his death in 1998.

Weisbecker, Allan

Surfer and writer Allan Weisbecker died on October 9, 2023. Weisbecker was born in Montauk, New York, in 1948. He was 75. He learned to surf at Ditch Plains Beach in Montauk, New York, in 1965. He continued to surf around the world from Hawaii to Costa Rica. He also wrote for various surfing magazines and was a photojournalist for such publications as "Smithsonian", "Popular Photography",

"American Photo", "Surfing", and "The Surfer's Journal". He wrote the 1985 film "Beer" and scripted episodes of "Crime Story" and "Miami Vice". He was noted for his gonzo memoirs "In Search of Captain Zero: A Surfer's Road Trip Beyond the End of the Road" (2001), "Can't You Get Along With Anyone?: A Writer's Memoir and a Tale of a Lost Surfer's Paradise" (2007), and "Cosmic Banditos: A Contrabandista's Quest for the Meaning of Life" (2009). Weisbecker produced, directed, wrote, and appeared in the 2014 film "Water Time: Surf Travel Diary of a MadMan" and the short "Fundy; A Study of Time and Tide" (2014).

Weisberg, Steven

Film editor Steven Weisberg died of complications from Alzheimer's disease at the Motion Picture Hospital in Los

Angeles, California, on October 16, 2023. He was 68. Weisberg was born in New York City on January 16, 1956. He graduated from Syracuse University and Binghamton University. He began working in films as an associate editor for 1987's "Gaby: A True Story". He also served as associate editor of the tele-film "Third Degree Burn" (1989). He was editor for numerous films including "Vietnam War Story: The Last Days" (1989), "The Color of Evening" (1990), "Mistress" (1992), "Miami Rhapsody" (1995), "A Little Princess" (1995), "The Cable Guy" (1996), Alfonso Cuaron's "Great Expectations" (1998), "Permanent Midnight" (1998),

"Message in a Bottle" (1999), "Nurse Betty" (2000), "Big Trouble" (2002), "Men in Black II" (2002), "I Am David" (2003), "Harry Potter and the Prisoner of Azkaban" (2004), "Asylum" (2005), "The Producers" (2005), "Man of the Year" (2006), "Mr. Magorium's Wonder Emporium" (2007), "Mother and Child" (2009), The Chronicles of Narnia: The Voyage of the Dawn Treader" (2010), "Morning Glory" (2010), "Albert Nobbs" (2011), "Sir Billi" (2012), and "Hope Springs" (2012). Weisberg was also editor of the television productions "The Wickedest Witch" (1989), "Mrs. Cage" (1992), and "Last Light" (1993), and episodes of "Bakersfield P.D." and "The Tick". He was diagnosed with early onset Alzheimer's in 2010 and retired from editing soon after. He was married and divorced from Susan Ellicott and is survived by two sons.

Welch, Raquel

Actress and sex symbol Raquel Welch, who starred in such films as "Fantastic Voyage" and "One Million Years B.C.", died in Los Angeles, California, on February 15, 2023. She was 82. She was born Jo Raquel Tejeda in Chicago, Illinois, on September 5, 1940. She moved with her family to

San Diego, California, at the age of two. She aspired for a career as a performer from an early age and studied ballet for a decade. She entered various beauty contests winning the titles Miss La Jolla, Miss San Diego, and Maid of California. She graduated high school in 1958 and attended San Diego State College. She married James Welch in 1959 and kept his name throughout her career. She starred in the outdoor play "The Ramona Pageant" in Hemet, California, in 1959. She began working as a weather girl at San Diego television station KFMB in 1960. She soon separated from her husband and moved to Dallas, Texas, with her two children. She worked as a cocktail waitress and as a model for Neiman Marcus. She relocated to Los Angeles in 1973 where she pursued a film career. Agent Patrick Curtis became her personal and business manager, and she appeared in small roles in the films "A House Is Not a Home" (1964), "Roustabout" (1964) starring Elvis Presley, and "Do Not Disturb" (1965). Welch was featured in the beach film "A Swingin' Summer" and was a miniaturized doctor in the 1966 science fiction classic "Fantastic Voyage". The buxom and exotic brunette secured her role as a sex symbol starring as Loana, the prehistoric maiden in a fur bikini, in the Hammer prehistoric film "One Million Years B.C." in 1966. She continued to appear in the films "Shoot Loud, Louder... I Don't Understand" (1966), "The Queens" (aka "Sex Quartet") (1966), the anthology film "The Oldest Profession" (1967) in "The Gay Nineties" segment, the spy comedy "Fathom" (1967), "Bedazzled" (1967) as Lillian Lust opposite the comic team of Peter Cook and Dudley Moore, the caper thriller "The Biggest Bundle of Them All" (1968), the western "Bandolero!" (1968) opposite Dean Martin and James Stewart, the mystery thriller

"Lady in Cement" (1968) starring Frank Sinatra, the western "100 Rifles" (1969) with Jim Brown and Burt Reynolds, "Flareup" (1969), "The Magic Christian" (1969) in a cameo role as the Priestess of the Whip, "The Boodle" (1969), the sex comedy "Myra Breckinridge" (1970) in the title role, "The Beloved" (1971), "Hannie Caulder" (1971) also serving as executive producer, "Fuzz" (1972), "Kansas City Bomber" (1972) as roller derby star K.C. Carr, "Bluebeard" (1972) opposite Richard Burton, "The Last of Sheila" (1973), "The Three Musketeers" (1973) and "The Four Musketeers: Milady's Revenge" (1974) as the ill-fated Constance de Bonacieux, "The Wild Party" (1975), "Mother, Jugs & Speed" (1976) as Jugs opposite Bill Cosby's Mother and Harvey Keitel's Speed, "Crossed Swords" (aka "The Prince and the Pauper") (1977), the French action comedy "Animal" (aka "Stuntwoman") (1977), "Naked Gun 33 1/3: The Final Insult" (1994) in a cameo role as herself, "Chairman of the Board" (1997), "What I Did for Love" (1998), "Tortilla Soup" (2001), the comedy "Legally Blonde" (2001) as Mrs. Windham Vandermark, "Forget About It" (2006), and "How to Be a Latin Lover" (2017). Welch appeared on television from the early 1960s with roles in episodes of "The Virginian", "McHale's Navy", "Bewitched", "Shindig!", "What's My Line?", "The Eamonn Andrews Show", "The Rogues", "Wendy and Me", "The Hollywood Palace", "The Baileys of Balboa", "The Merv Griffin Show", "The Dean Martin Show", "The Joey Bishop Show", "This is Tom Jones", "The David Frost Show", "The Dick Cavett Show", "Bracken's World", "Rowan & Martin's Laugh-In", "The Mike Douglas Show", "Cher", "Saturday Night Live" as guest host in 1976, "The Muppet Show", "Dinah!", "Donny and Marie", "Mork & Mindy" as the alien Captain Nirvana in 1979, "The Toni Tennille Show", "Evening Shade", "Wogan", "Night of 100 Stars", "The Tonight Show Starring Johnny Carson", "Lois & Clark: The New Adventures of Superman", the animated "Happily Ever After: Fairy Tales for Every Child" in a voice role, "Live with Kelly and Ryan", "Late Night with David Letterman", "Late Show with David Letterman", "Biography", "Late Night with Conan O'Brien", "Maury", "C.P.W." as Dianna Brock in 1996, "Sabrina the Teenage Witch", "Seinfeld", "Spin City" in the recurring role of Abby Lassiter from 1997 to 2000, "Holly Squares", "Larry King Live", "American Family" as Aunt Dora in 2002, "8 Simple Rules", "Welcome to the Captain" as Charlene Van Ark in 2008, "The View", "Martha", "Rachael Ray", "The Oprah Winfrey Show", "Good Morning America", "The Bonnie Hunt Show", "The Late Late Show with Craig Ferguson", "Piers Morgan's Life Stories", "CSI: Miami", and "The Talk", "Date My Dad" as Rosa in 2017. Welch starred in the specials "Raquel" (1970), "Really, Raquel" (1974), and "From Raquel with Love" (1980).

Her other television credits include productions of "The Legend of Walks Far Woman" (1980), "This Girl's Back in Town" (1987), "Right to Die" (1987), "Right to Die" (1987), "Scandal in a Small Town" (1988), "Trouble in Paradise" (1989), "Tainted Blood" (1993), "Torch Song" (1993), "Hollywood-a-Bye Baby" (1993), "House of Versace" (2013), and "The Ultimate Legacy" (2016). She performed in nightclubs from the early 1970s and was an opening act for Elvis Presley at the Las Vegas Hilton in 1972. She starred on Broadway in a production of "Woman of the Year", filling in for Lauren Bacall for two weeks in 1981. Welch released the dance single and video "This Girl's Back in Town" in 1988. She also starred in Broadway in the musical "Victor/Victoria" in 1997. Welch received a star on the Hollywood Walk of Fame in 1996. She also became a spokesman for health and beauty routines. Her book and videos "The Raquel Welch Total Beauty and Fitness Program", which included her hatha yoga fitness program, were released in 1984. She also had a jewelry and skincare line and a successful wig collection, HAIRuWEAR. Welch was married to James Welch from 1959 until their divorce in 1964 and is survived by their two children, Damon Welch and actress Tahnee Welch. She was married to her publicist Patrick Curtis from 1967 until their divorce in 1972. She was married to producer Andre Weinfeld from 1980 until their divorce in 1990. Welch was married to pizzeria owner Richie Palmer from 1999 until their divorce in 2003.

Weldon, Fay

British author Fay Weldon, who was noted for her 1983 novel "The Life and Loves of a She-Devil", died at a nursing facility in Northampton, England, on January 4, 2023.

She was 91. She was born Franklin Birkinshaw in Birmingham, England, on September 22, 1931. She was raised in Christchurch, New Zealand, where her father was a doctor. Her parents divorced in 1940 and she returned to England in 1946. She was overweight as a child and her later novels were populated with women in a similar condition. She studied psychology and economics at the University of St. Andrews in Scotland and moved to London after earning her master's degree in 1952. She worked at various jobs before becoming a clerk for the Foreign Office. She later worked at Crawford's Advertising Agency and became head of copywriting at Ogilvy, Benson & Mather. Weldon began writing for radio and television in the early 1960s. Her tele-plays "A Catching Complaint" (1966), "The Fat Woman's Tale" (1966), and "Dr. De Waldo's Therapy" (1967) were produced for "ITV Play of the Week". She also wrote episodes of "Trapped", "Love Story", "Half Hour Story", "For Amusement Only", "The Sex Game", "The Wednesday Play", "Scene", "Happy Ever After", "The Doctors", "Armchair Theatre", "Trial", "Suspicion", "Thirty-Minute Theatre", "ITV

Playhouse", "Kate", "Menace", "Owen, M.D.", "Then and Now", "Upstairs, Downstairs", "Marked Personal", "Against the Crowd", "Ten from the Twenties", "Rooms", "The Velvet Glove", "Jubilee", "Send in the Girls", "Shadows", "Leap in the Dark", "Time for Murder", "Mountain Men", "Growing Rich", and "Good Ideas of the 20th Century". Weldon wrote the tele-films "The Tale of Timothy Bagshott" (1975), "Act of Rape" (1977), "Life for Christine" (1980), BBC television mini-series adaptation of Jane Austen's "Pride and Prejudice" (1980), "Little Miss Perkins" (1982), "A Dangerous Kind of Love" (1986), and "Action Replay" (1989). Her first novel, "The Fat Woman's Joke", was published in 1967. She wrote numerous novels, usually with a feminist outlook, including "Down Among the Women" (1971), "Words of Advice" (1974), "Little Sisters" (1975), "Female Friends" (1975), "Remember Me" (1976), "Praxis" (1978), the supernatural drama "Puffball" (1980) which was made into a film by Nicolas Roeg in 2007, and "The President's Child" (1982) which was adapted for a tele-film in 1992. Her best-known novel, "The Life and Loves of a She-Devil", was published in 1983. It was adapted for a television mini-series in 1986 starring Julie T. Wallace and Patricia Hodge. A film version by Susan Seidelman, "She-Devil", starring Roseanne Barr and Meryl Streep, was released in 1989. A radio adaptation aired in 2016 and she penned a sequel, "Death of a She Devil", in 2017. Her other novels include "The Shrapnel Academy" (1986), "The Heart of the Country" (1987) which was adapted for a television mini-series the same year, "The Hearts and Lives of Men" (1987), "Leader of the Band" (1988), the science fiction "The Cloning of Joanna May" (1989) which was adapted for television in 1992, "Darcy's Utopia" (1990), "Growing Rich" (1992), "Life Force" (1992), "Question of Timing" (1992), "Trouble" (1993), "Affliction" (1994), "Splitting (1995), "Worst Fears" (1996), "Big Women" (1997) which was adapted for a television mini-series in 1998, "Rhode Island Blues" (2000), "The Bulgari Connection" (2000), "Mantrapped" (2004), "She May Not Leave" (2006), "The Spa Decameron" (2007), "The Stepmother's Diary" (2008), "Chalcot Crescent" (2009), and "Kehua!" (2010). She also wrote the "Love and Inheritance" trilogy including "Habits of the House" (2012), "Long Live the King" (2013), and "The Newcountess" (2013), and the "Spoils of War" series, "Before the War" (2017) and "After the Peace" (2018). Weldon wrote several works of non-fiction including "Letters to Alice: On First Reading Jane Austen" (1984), "Rebecca West" (1985), "Sacred Cows: A Portrait of Britain, Post-Rushdie, Pre-Utopia" (1989), "Godless in Eden" (1999), the autobiography of her early years "Auto da Fay" (2002), "What Makes Women Happy" (2006), and "Why Will No-One Publish My Novel?" (2018). She is survived by a son, Nicolas, from a relationship with musician Colyn Davies in the early 1950s. Weldon was married to Ronald G. Bateman from 1956 until their divorce in 1959. She was married to Ron Weldon from 1963 until his death in 1994, hours before their divorce could be finalized. She is survived by their three sons, Dan, Tom, and Sam. She married her manager, poet Nick Fox, in 1994 but they filed for divorce in 2020.

Weldon, Jimmy

Ventriloquist and voice actor Jimmy Weldon, who created the character of Webster Webfoot the duck, died in Paso Robles, California, on July 6, 2023. He was 99. He was born  Ivy Laverne Shinn in Dale, Texas, on September 23, 1923. He joined the U.S. Army in 1943 and was deployed to Europe during World War II. He was part of the squad that liberated the Buchenwald Death Camp near the end of the war. He began his career in radio as a disc jockey and announcer at KWCA after his discharge. He created and voiced the character of Webster Webfoot, a little duck who visited him while he was playing record requests. The imaginary duck became an important part of Weldon's show. He moved to Duncan, Oklahoma, to work at KRHD-AM in 1948. Webster became a puppet character when he and Weldon moved to television for "The Webster Webfoot Show" in 1950. They joined KCOP-TV in Hollywood in 1952 where they continued their children's show and also served as hosts for the new game show "Funny Boners". They briefly moved to Fresno in 1956 until being called upon to replace Shari Lewis on the NBC "Hi, Mom" series in New York. They returned to Hollywood in 1959 and he was Uncle Jimmy as co-host with Webster for the "Cartoonery" series from 1959 to 1961. He continued to work throughout California during the 1960s. Weldon appeared as Lt. Webb in the science fiction film "The Phantom Planet" in 1961. He later appeared in several films including "Americathon" (1979), "Chattanooga Choo Choo" (1984), and "The Wrong Guys" (1988). He was a guest on such television series as "The Halls of Ivy", "Alfred Hitchcock Presents", "Dragnet", "The Waltons", "S.W.A.T.", "The Family Holvak", "The Oregon Trail", "B.J. and the Bear", "Dallas", "The Rockford Files", "Diff'rent Strokes", "Father Murphy", "Knight Rider", and "It's a Living". His other television credits include the tele-films "The New Daughters of Joshua Cabe" (1976), "The Best Place to Be" (1979), and "Portrait of a Rebel: The Remarkable Mrs. Sanger" (1980). Weldon was a voice actor for numerous cartoons, notably channeling Webster Webfoot for the voice of cartoon duck Yakky Doodle on "The Yogi Bear Show" in 1961. He was heard on other animated series including "Fred Flintstone and Friends", "Scooby-Doo and Scrappy-Doo", "The Little Rascals", "Richie Rich", "The New Scooby and Scrappy-Doo Show", "Super Friends" as the voice of Solomon Grundy, "Shirt Tales", "Challenge of the GoBots", "CBS Storybreak", "Yogi's Treasure Hunt", "Popeye and Son", "Fantastic Max", "Tom & Jerry Kids Show", "Adventures in Odyssey", and "The 7D". Weldon was married to Muriel Jones from 1947 until her death in 1988.

Wellander, Lasse

Swedish guitarist Lars-Ove 'Lasse' Wellander, who performed with the band ABBA, died of cancer in Overgran, Sweden, on April 7, 2023. He was 70. Wellander was born in

Viker, Sweden, on June 18, 1952, and was raised in the small village of Skrekarhyttan. He began performing with bands in Sweden in the late 1960s including Peps & Blues Quality and

Nature. He was touring with Ted Gardestad when he began working with ABBA, consisting of Bjorn Ulvaeus, Benny Andersson, Agnetha Faltskog, and Anni-Frid Lyngstad, in 1974. He recorded and toured frequently with the band throughout the decade. He was heard on the albums "ABBA" (1975), "Arrival" (1976), "The Album" (1977), "Voulez-Vous" (1979), "Super Trouper" (1980), and "The Visitor" (1981). Wellander worked on various solo albums for the members of ABBA after the group disbanded in 1982. He recorded a handful of albums and singles with his most recent recording, "Oh Come, All Ye Faithful", released in 2022. He was heard on the soundtracks for the films "Mamma Mia!" (2007) and "Mamma Mia! Here We Go Again" (2018). Wellander reunited with ABBA for the hit comeback album, "Voyage", in 2021.

Wendel, David

Actor David Wendel died in Escondido, California, on April 20, 2023. He was 85. Wendel was born in Cresco, Iowa, on July 20, 1937, and was raised in Eugene, Oregon. He briefly

attended the University of Oregon and worked odd jobs before joining the U.S. Army in 1960. He moved to San Francisco after his discharge in 1962 and played tenor sax and several jazz clubs. He went to New York City in 1964 where he studied acting under Uta Hagen. Wendel settled in Santa Monica, California, the following year to pursue an acting career. He was seen in the films "Ice Station Zebra" (1968), "Changes" (1969), "Suppose They Gave a War and Nobody Came" (1970), and "R.P.M." (1970). He also appeared in an episode of "Daniel Boone". He and his family moved to British Columbia, Canada, in 1970, where he worked as a third-grade teacher for over a decade. He briefly returned to acting in the 1980s with a role in an episode of "Charlie's Angels" and appeared as an Army general in the 1987 horror comedy "The Monster Squad". Wendel eventually settled back in Oregon where he worked as a medical transcriber. He was divorced from his wife Donna and is survived by their two daughters.

Wepper, Elmar

German actor Elmar Wepper died in Planegg, Bavaria, Germany, on October 31, 2023. He was 79. Wepper was born in Augsburg, Germany, on April 16, 1944, and was raised in Munich. His older brother was Fritz Wepper and they appeared together in the 1957 film "Heute Blau und Morgen Blau". His other films include "Schmetterlinge Weinen Nicht" (1970),

"Beinah Trinidad" (1985), "Cafe Europa" (1990), "Lammbock" (2001), "Der Fischer und Seine Frau" (2005), "Kirschbluten - Hanami" (2008), "Three Quarter Moon" (2011), "Alles ist Liebe" (2014), "Lommbock" (2017), "As Green as It Gets" (2018), and "Cherry Blossoms and Demons" (2019). Wepper appeared frequently on television with roles in productions of "Ein Weihnachtslied in Prosa Oder Eine Geistergeschichte Zum Christfest" (1960), "General Quixotte" (1961), "Die Feuertreppe" (1962), "Der Strohhalm" (1964), "Ein Unheimlich Starker Abgang" (1973), "Die Leute von Feichtenreut" (1976), "Der Grosse Karpfen Ferdinand und Andere Weihnachtsgeschichten" (1978), "Tipfehler" (1981), "Die Tochter des Bombardon" (1982), "Flohe Huten ist Leichter" (1982), "Das Hinterturl zum Paradies" (1987), "Das Grosste Fest des Jahres - Weihnachten bei Unseren Fernsehfamilien" (1991), "Geschichten aus der Heimat - Battschuss" (1993), "Dier Heiratsvermittler" (1994), "Knallhart Daneban" (1995), "Bitter Unschuld" (1999), "Einmal Leben" (2000), "Hochzeit Zu Viert" (2001), "Ein Dorf Sucht Seinen Morder" (2002), "Auch Erben Will Gelernt Sein" (2003), "Mutter Kommt in Fahrt" (2003), "Drei Unter Einer Decke" (2003), "Der Traum vom Suden" (2004), "Im Zweifel fur die Liebe" (2004), "Mathilde Liebt" (2005), "Die Sturmflut" (2006), "Leo" (2006), "Fight for Justice" (2007), "Ich Heirate Meine Frau" (2007), "Ich Trag Dich Bis ans Ende der Welt" (2010), "Adel Dich" (2011), "Hopfensommer" (2011), "Das Unsichtbare Madchen" (2011), and "Zwei Allein" (2014). His other television credits include episodes of "Unternehmen Kummerkasten" as Bert Bohm from 1961 to 1962, "Isar 12", "Der Kommissar" as Erwin Klein from 1974 to 1976, "Derrick", "Zeit Genug", "Die Wiesingers", "Der Millionenbauer" as Andreas Hartinger from 1979 to 1980 and again in 1988, "Schone Ferien", "Unsere Schonsten Jahre" as Raimund Sommer from 1983 to 1985, "Irgendwie und Soweiso" (1986) as Josef 'Sepp' Gruber in 1986, "Weissblaue Geschichten", "Polizeiinspektion 1" as Helmut Heinl from 1977 to 1988, "Zwei Munchner in Hamburg" as Dr. Ralf Maria Sagerer from 1989 to 1993, "Geschichten aus der Heimat", "Florian III", "Unsere Schule ist die Beste" as Harald Schonauer from 1994 to 1995, "Cafe Meineid", "Rosamunde Pilcher", the detective series "Zwei Bruder" with his brother Fritz starring as brothers Peter and Christoph Thaler from 1994 to 2001, "Schuhbecks", "Evelyn Hamann's Geschichten aus dem Leben", "Utta Danella", "Tatort", "Das Traumschiff", "Zwei Arzte Sind Einer Zu Viel" as Dr. Stefan Wolf from 2006 to 2009, "Kanal Fatal", "Schuhbecks Meine Kuchengeheimnisse", and "Kommissarin Lucas". Wepper was also a prolific dubbing actor for numerous films and television productions, providing the German voiceover for Mel Gibson and other stars. He married Anita Schlierf in 2004 and she survives him.

Werner, Peter

Film and television director Peter Werner died of complications from a torn aorta in Wilmington, North Carolina, on March 21, 2023. He was 76. Werner was born in New York City on January 17, 1947. He graduated from Dartmouth College and earned a master's degree from Antioch University. He continued his studied at the American Film Institute where he directed the 1976 short film "In the Region of Ice" which won the Academy Award for Best Live-Action Short". He worked primarily in television from the late 1970s, helming episodes of "Family", "Call to Glory", "Hometown", "Moonlighting" receiving an Emmy Award nomination in 1986, "Outlaws", "Hooperman", "Men", "DEA", "The Wonder Years", "A Different World", "Middle Ages", "Winnetka Road", "Nash Bridges", "Ghost Cop", "The Expert", "The '70s", "Maybe It's Me", "Philly", "Grounded for Life", "For the People", "Boomtown", "Raines", "Kidnapped", "Law & Order: Criminal Intent", "Army Wives", "Ghost Whisperer", "Medium", "No Ordinary Family", "Hawthorne", "A Gifted Man", "Elementary", "The Blacklist", "Unforgettable", "The Lottery", "Justified", "UnREAL", "Proof", "The Mysteries of Laura", "Limitless", "Outsiders", "Blue Blood", "Ice", "Grimm", "Bull", "Instinct", "Six", and "Law & Order: Special Victims Unit". He also directed the tele-films and mini-series "Battered" (1978), "Aunt Mary" (1979), "Barn Burning" (1980), "Hard Knox" (1984), "I Married a Centerfold" (1984), "Sins of the Father" (1985), "LBJ: The Early Years" (1987) receiving another Emmy nomination, "The Image" (1990), "Hiroshima: Out of the Ashes" (1990), "Ned Blessing: The True Story of My Life" (1992), "Doorways" (1993), "The Good Policeman" (1993), "The Substitute Wife" (1994), "The Four Diamonds" (1995), "Almost Golden: The Jessica Savitch Story" (1995) earning another Emmy nomination, "The Unspoken Truth" (1995), "Inflammable" (1995), "Two Mothers for Zachary", "Blue Rodeo" (1996), "On the Edge of Innocence" (1997), "House of Frankenstein" (1997), "Soul Mates" (1997), "Tempting Fate" (1998), "Mama Flora's Family" (1998), "Hefner: Unauthorized" (1999), "After Amy" (2001), "Ruby's Bucket of Blood" (2001), "Call Me Claus" (2001), "We Were the Mulvaneys" (2002), "The Pact" (2002), "Killer Instinct: From the Files of Agent Candice DeLong" (2003), "Gracie's Choice" (2004), "Vinegar Hill" (2005), "Mom at Sixteen" (2005), "Amber Frey: Witness for the Prosecution" (2005), "Snow Wonder" (2005), "Why I Wore Lipstick to My Mastectomy" (2006) sharing an Emmy nomination, "Girl, Positive" (2007), "The Circuit" (2008), "Front of the Class" (2008), "A Dog Named Christmas" (2009), "Bond of Silence" (2010), and "Prosecuting Casey Anthony" (2013). Werner directed several films including "Don't Cry, It's Only Thunder" (1982) also appearing onscreen in a small role, "Prisoners" (1983), "No Man's Land" (1987), and "Death Merchants" (1991). He was married and divorced from Marie Ashton. Werner is survived by his second wife, Kendren Jones, and three children, Lillie, Katharine, and James.

Wersching, Annie

Actress Annie Wersching, who starred as Leslie Dean in the series "Runaways" and was the Borg Queen in "Star Trek: Picard", died of cancer in Los Angeles, California, on January 29, 2023. She was 45. Wersching was born in St. Louis, Missouri, on March 28, 1977. She graduated from Millikin University School of Theater and Dance in Decatur, Illinois in 1999. She performed on the local stage and performed with the St. Louis Celtic Stepdancers. Wersching moved to Los Angeles in 2001 and performed in a production of "Do I Hear a Waltz?" with the Pasadena Playhouse. She made her television debut as Liana the "Oasis" episode of "Star Trek: Enterprise" in 2002. She went on to appear in episodes of "Birds of Prey", "Frazier", "Angel", "Charmed", "Out of Practice", "Killer Instinct", "E-Ring", "Cold Case", "Boston Legal", "Supernatural", "General Hospital" as Amelia Joffe in 2007, "Journeyman", "24" as ill-fated FBI Special Agent Renee Walker from 2009 to 2010, "CSI: Crime Scene Investigation", "NCIS", "Nor Ordinary Family", "Rizzoli & Isles", "Hawaii Five-0", "Harry's Law", "Body of Proof", "Dallas" in the recurring role of Alison Jones in 2013, "Touch", "Revolution", "Intelligence", "Blue Bloods", "Extant" as Femi Dodd in 2014, "Castle" in the recurring role of Dr. Kelly Nieman from 2013 to 2015, "Bosch" in the recurring role of rookie police officer Julia Brasher from 2014 to 2021, "Code Black", "The Vampire Diaries" as Lily Salvatore from 2015 to 2016, "The Catch", "Major Crimes", "Doubt", "Timeless" as Emma Whitmore from 2017 to 2017, "Runaways" as cult leader Leslie Dean from 2017 to 2019, "The Rookie" in the recurring role of Rosalind Dyer" from 2019 to 2023, and "Star Trek: Picard" as the Borg Queen in 2022. She also appeared in the tele-films "Company Man" (2007), "Partners" (2011), "Blue-Eyed Butcher" (2012), "The Surrogate" (2013), and "The Other Mother" (2017). She appeared in a handful of films including "Bruce Almighty" (2003), the short "The Showdown" (2006), and "Below the Beltway" (2010). Wersching was the voice of Tess in the video game "The Last of Us" in 2013 and was Tassyn in "Anthem" in 2019. She was diagnosed with cancer in 2020 but kept the illness private and continued to act. She married comedian Stephen Full in 2009 and is survived by him and their three sons, Freddie, Ozzie, and Archic.

West, James Douglass

Television writer James Douglass West, who worked on the "Lassie" series in the 1960s, died in Studio City, California, on March 5, 2023. He was 93. West was born in

Redwood City, California, on July 17, 1929. He began his career as a child actor on stage in a production of "On Borrowed Time" in the mid-1930s. He soon signed with MGM and appeared in several films including "The Way of All Flesh"  (1940), "On the Sunny Side" (1942), and "Happy Land" (1943). He attended Los Angeles City College in his early teens. He served in the U.S. Army in the late 1940s and returned to acting in the film "Our Very Own" (1950) after his discharge. He began writing for films and television in the 1950s, working with Jack DeWitt on the western film "Battles of Chief Pontiac" (1952). West also wrote the films "Hey Boy! Hey Girl!" and "California" (1963). He scripted an episode of the television series "The Gray Ghost" and was story editor for "The Virginian". He served on the writing staff for CBS's "Lassie" series from 1963 through 1973. He also penned the Disney tele-films "Two Against the Arctic" for "The Wonderful World of Disney" in 1974. He left television in 1980 to open a medical transmission business. His wife of 47 years, Geri, died in 2007.

Westbury, Ken

British cinematographer Ken Westbury died of complications of skin cancer in England on April 28, 2023. He  was 96. Westbury was born in Shepherd's Bush, London, England, on January 5, 1927. He began working in films at Ealing Studios in 1942. He initially ran errands before advancing to clapper loader and focus puller. He worked on numerous films including "Far into the Night" (1943), "For Those in Peril" (1944), "The Halfway House" (1944), "Champagne Charlie" (1944), "Dreaming" (1944), "Whisky Galore!" (1949), "Kind Hearts and Coronets" (1949), "The Blue Lamp" (1950), "The Magnet" (1950), "The Man in the White Suit" (1951), "Secret People" (1952), "Crash of Silence" (1952), "Meet Mr. Lucifer" (1953),"West of Zanzibar" (1954), and "The Third Key" (1956). Westbury moved to the BBC in 1956 where he served as a camera operator and director of photography. He worked on television productions of "The Frog" (1959), "The Spur of the Moment" (1959), "Medico" (1959), "The Adventures of Alice" (1960), "Persuasion" (1960), "The Wind and the Sun" (1960), "Old Mick Mack" (1961), "Town Vet" (1961), "Television and the World" (1961), "The Andromeda Breakthrough" (1962), "The Man Who Opted Out" (1962), "The Wall" (1962), "I'm Not Stopping" (1963), "The Full Chatter" (1963), "Don't I Look Like a Lord's Son?" (1964), "The Man Shakespeare" (1964), "Ninety Years On" (1964), "The Burning Fiery Furnace" (1967), "Benjamin Britten and His Festival" (1967), "The Callas Conversations" (1968), "The

Siegfried Idyll" (1969), "The Last of the Mohicans" (1971), "Casanova" (1971), "Shelley" (1972), "The Mad Trapper" (1972), "The British Empire: Echoes of Britannia's Rule" (1972), "Emma" (1972), "Wessex Tales" (1973), "Shoulder to Shoulder" (1974), "Anna Karenina" (1977), "Nicholas Nickleby" (1977), "Pennies from Heaven" (1978), "The Vanishing Army" (1978), "The Rainhill Story: Stephenson's Rocket" (1979), "We, the Accused" (1980), "To the Lighthouse" (1983), "St. Ursula's in Danger" (1983), "Dr. Fischer of Geneva" (1984), "Tender Is the Night" (1985), "The Singing Detective" (1986), "Tears in the Rain" (1988), "The Man in the Brown Suit" (1989), "Magic Moments" (1989), "Hands of a Murderer" (1990), "The Gravy Train" (1990), "The Tragedy of Flight 103: The Inside Story" (1990), "The Black Velvet Gown" (1991), "Chimera" (1991), "On Dangerous Ground" (1996), "Silent Witness" (1997), "Midnight Man" (1997), and "Far from the Madding Crowd" (1998). His other television credits include episodes of "The Sky Larks", "Solo for Canary", "Spy-Catcher", "The Days of Vengeance", "The Charlie Drake Show", "Detective", "Maigret", "Compact", "Viewpoint", "Dial RIX", "Moonstrike", "Gala Performance", "First Night", "Festival", "Dixon of Dock Green", "Six", "Sherlock Holmes", "Monitor", "R3", "Dr. Finlay's Casebook", "Cluff", "The Troubleshooters", "Sunday Night", "Five More", "Adam Adamant Lives!", "The Forsyte Saga", "The Wednesday Play", "Omnibus", "Doomwatch", "Paul Temple", "The Onedin Line", "The Brothers", "Z Cars", "Bedtime Stories", "Steptoe and Son", "The Wednesday Play", "Music on 2", "2nd House", "Supernatural", "Open Door", "Blue Peter", "The Duchess of Duke Street", "When the Boat Comes In", "Inside Story", "Warship", "1990", "Doctor Who", "Six English Towns", "Target", "The Magic of Dance", "Secret Army", "Everyman", "Penmarric", "Escape", "BBC2 Playhouse", "Shoestring", "Break in the Sun", "Play for Today", "Bergerac", "One Pair of Eyes", "Q.E.D.", "Tenko", "Headhunters", "Pie in the Sky", "An Independent Man", "Silent Witness", "Bugs", and "Ruth Rendell Mysteries". He left the BBC in 1987 and continued to work in television and films until his retirement in 2003. Westbury was married to Doreen White from 1949 until her death in 2013 and is survived by their four children.

Weston, Jay

Film producer Jay Weston died at the Motion Picture & Television Country House and Hospital in Woodland Hills,  California, on February 28, 2023. He was 93. He was born John Weinstein in New York City on March 9, 1929. he graduated from New York University in 1949 and served in the U.S. Army during the Korean War. He worked for the military newspaper during his service and continued to work in journalism after his discharge. He moved into public relations in 1953 and was involved with promoting Cinerama Inc. He became head of ABC's feature film division at Palomar Pictures in 1967. Weston served as producer of the films "For Love of Ivy" (1968), "They Shoot Horses, Don't They?" (1969), "Lady Sings the Blues" (1972), "W.C. Fields and Me" (1976). "Night of the Juggler" (1980), "Underground Aces" (1981), "Chu Chu and the Philly Flash" (1981), and "Buddy Buddy" (1981). He also produced the 1968 Broadway play "Does a Tiger Wear a Necktie?" which earned actor Al Pacino a Tony Award. He became noted as a restaurant critic and began "Jay Weston's Restaurant Newsletter" in the early 1980s. He later produced the 1990 film "Side Out" and the tele-films "Laguna Heat" (1987) and "Invisible Child" (1999). He was married and divorced from Annabelle Weston and is survived by their daughter, Teresa.

White, Fred

Drummer Fred White, who was a member of the band Earth, Wind, & Fire, died in Los Angeles, California, on January 1, 2023. He was 67. He was born Frederick Adams in  Chicago, Illinois, on January 13, 1955. He began playing drums as a child and was playing in nightclubs by his early teens. He accompanied soul singer Donny Hathaway while performing in the Chicago area. He also toured with the rock band Little Feat and performed on their album "Feats Don't Fail Me Now" (1974). His brother, Verdine, and half-brother, Marcus, led the popular band Earth, Wind & Fire and invited Fred to join them in 1974. He was initially a dual drummer with Ralph Johnson. He made his album debut with the band's "That's the Way of the World" in 1975. White played drums on some of the band's leading hits including "Let's Grove", "September", "Boogie Wonderland", and "Shining Star". He played with Earth, Wind & Fire until the band went on hiatus in 1984 and was not invited to rejoin when they regrouped several years later. He and his brothers, along with six other bandmates, were inducted into the Rock & Roll Hall of Fame as part of Earth, Wind & Fire in 2000. Maurice White died in 2016 and he is survived by brother Verdine and a sister, Geri.

White, Jennifer

British actress Jennifer White died in Wiltshire, England, on August 20, 2023. She was 80. White was born in  Cardiff, Wales, on February 16, 1943. She performed in films from the late 1950s with roles in "Jack the Ripper" (1959), "Only Two Can Play" (1962), "All Night Long" (1962), "The L-Shaped Room" (1962), "A Stitch in Time" (19763), "They All Died Laughing" (1964), "Night Train to Paris" (1964), "The Murder Game" (1965), "Press for Time"

(1966), the James Bond spoof "Casino Royale" (1967), "Carry on Doctor" (1967), "Assignment K" (1968), and "If It's Tuesday, This Must Be Belgium" (1969). White was seen on television in episodes of "Yorky", "ITV Television Playhouse", "Harpers West One", "The Marriage Lines", "Crane", "The Human Jungle", "The Dick Emery Show", "Armchair Theatre", "Mr. Rose", "The Caesars" as Julia Livilla in 1968, "The Avengers", and "Juliet Bravo". White largely retired from the screen following her marriage to businessman Eddie Shah, with who she had three children.

White, Peter

Actor Peter White, who starred as Linc Tyler on the soap opera "All My Children" for nearly thirty years, died of cancer in Los Angeles, California, on November 1, 2023. He was 86. White was born in New York City on October 10, 1937. He graduated from Northwestern University in  Evanston, Illinois, and attended the Yale School of Drama where he studied acting. He began his career on stage in the 1960s and was understudy for Robert Redford in the Broadway comedy "Barefoot in the Park" in 1963. He starred as Alan McCarthy in the 1968 off-Broadway play "The Boys in the Band" and reprised the role in the subsequent film version in 1970. White was also featured in the films "The Pursuit of Happiness" (1971), "Blade" (1973), "Diary of a Hitman" (1991), "Dave" (1993), "Mr. Wrong" (1996), "Mother" (1996), "Flubber" (1997), "Armageddon" (1998) as the Secretary of Defense, "Passport to Paris" (1999), "Thirteen Days" (2000) as CIA Director John McCone, "First Daughter" (2004), "South of Pico" (2007), and "Punching Henry" (2016). He appeared frequently on television with roles in episodes of "The Secret Storm" as Jerry Ames from 1965 to 1966, "N.Y.P.D.", "The Bold Ones: The Senator", "Dan August", the soap opera "Love Is a Many Splendored Thing" as Dr. Sanford Hiller in 1971, "Banyon", "Cannon", "The Feather and Father Gang", "Hill Street Blues", "The Greatest American Hero", "Falcon Crest", "The Jeffersons", "Gavilan", "Insight", "Hart to Hart", "Boone", "Dynasty", "Legmen", "Knots Landing", "Simon & Simon", "Hardcastle and McCormick", "Cover Up", "The Paper Chase", "Crazy Like a Fox", "Scarecrow and Mrs. King", "Matlock", "The Colbys" as Arthur Cates from 1985 to 1986, "The Law and Harry McGraw", "L.A. Law", "Superboy", "Amen", "Designing Women", "Hooperman", "Who's the Boss?", "Monsters", "Hunter", "Dallas", "The New Lassie", "Pros and Cons", "Life Goes On", "Star Trek: Deep Space Nine" as Ambassador Sharat in the 1994 episode "Armageddon Game", "The Naked Truth", "Murder, She Wrote", "Sisters" in the recurring role of Dr. Thomas Reed from 1991 to 1996, "Mad About You", "Profiler", "Ally McBeal", "The X-Files", "The West Wing", "JAG", "NYPD Blue", "Miracles", "Mister Sterling", "Strong Medicine", "The D.A.", "Cold Case", and "Saving Grace". White starred as Linc Tyler of the daytime soap opera "All My Children" from 1976 to 2005. His other television credits include the tele-films "Between Two Brothers" (1982), "Eleanor, First Lady of the World" (1982) as James Roosevelt, "I Want to Live" (1983), "Sins of the Past" (1984), "The Execution" (1985), "Daughter of the Streets" (1990), "Voices from Within" (1994), "Weapons of Mass Distraction" (1997), "See Arnold Run" (2005), and "Though None Go with Me" (2006).

Whitehead, Paxton

British actor Paxton Whitehead, who received a Tony Award nomination for his role as King Pelinore in the Broadway play "Camelot" in 1980, died of complications from a fall at a hospital in Arlington, Virginia, on June 16, 2023. He  was 85. Whitehead was born in East Malling and Larkfield, Kent, England, on October 17, 1937. He trained at the Webber Douglas Academy of Dramatic Art in London in the mid-1950s. He began his career performing in repertory and joined the Royal Shakespeare Company in 1958. He made his Broadway debut in 1962's "The Affair". He served as artistic director of the Shaw Festival at Niagara-on-the-Lake, Canada, from 1966 to 1977. He performed frequently on stage in the United States and England throughout his career. Whitehead was seen on Broadway in productions of "Beyond the Fringe" (1962), "Candida" (1970), "Habeas Corpus" (1975), "The Crucifer of Blood" (1978) as Sherlock Holmes, "Camelot" (1980) earning a Tony Award nomination for his role as King Pelinore, "Noises Off" (1983), "Run for Your Wife" (1989), "Artist Descending a Staircase" (1989), "Lettice and Lovage" (1990), "A Little Hotel on the Side" (1992), "My Fair Lady" (1993), "Absurd Person Singular (2005), "The Importance of Being Earnest" (2011), and "Bernhardt/Hamlet" (2018). He appeared on television in episodes of "Knight Errant Limited", the "Golden Showcase" production of "The Picture of Dorian Gray" in 1961, "Performance", "The Naked Mind", "The National Dream: Building the Impossible Railway", "Magnum, P.I.", "Hart to Hart", "Brothers", "The A-Team", "Silver Spoons", "Down and Out in Beverly Hills", "Marblehead Manor", "Great Performances", "Baby Boom", "Murder, She Wrote", "The Nutt House", "Law & Order", "The General Motors Playwrights Theater", "Almost Home", "Dinosaurs", "Simon" as Duke Stone from 1995 to 1996, "Caroline in the City", "Ellen" in the recurring role of Dr. Whitcomb from 1995 to 1996, "3rd Rock from the Sun", "Frasier", "Early Edition", "Friends", "Mad About You" in the recurring role of Hal Conway from 1997 to 1999, "Dead Last", "The Drew Carey Show", "The West Wing", and "Desperate Housewives". He also provided voices for the animated series "Garfield and Friends" and "The Real Adventures of Jonny Quest". His other television credits include productions of "The First Night of 'Pygmalion'" (1975), "Riel" (1979), "The Alan King Show" (1986), "Chips, the War

Dog" (1990), "Child of Darkness, Child of Light" (1991), "An Inconvenient Woman" (1991), "Boris and Natasha" (1992), "Monster in My Pocket: The Big Scream" (1992) as the voice of the Invisible Man, "12:01" (1993), "Where Are My Children?" (1994), "Trick of the Eye" (1994), "London Suite" (1996), "Liberty! The American Revolution (1997) as Horace Walpole, and "The Importance of Being Earnest" (2011). Whitehead was featured in several films including "Back to School" (1986), "Jumpin' Jack Flash" (1986), "Baby Boom" (1987), the animated "Rover Dangerfield (1991) as the voice of the Count, "Nervous Ticks" (1992), "The Adventures of Huck Finn" (1993), "My Boyfriend's Back" (1993), "Goldilocks and the Three Bears" (1995), "RocketMan" (1997), "The Duke" (1999), "Kate & Leopold" (2001), and "The Aristocrat" (2009). Whitehead was married to actress Patricia Gage from 1971 until their divorce in 1986. He was married to Katherine Robinson from 1987 until her death in 2009 and is survived by two children.

Whiting, Margaret

British actress Margaret Whiting, who was the evil Zenobia in 1977's "Sinbad and the Eye of the Tiger", died in Wimbledon, London, England, on December 13, 2023. She was 90. Whiting was born in Bristol, England, on February 8,  1933. She trained as an actress with the Royal Academy of Dramatic Art and began her career on stage in the 1950s. She performed frequently at the Old Vic Theatre in such productions as "Timon of Athens", "Titus Andronicus", "Equus", "Hamlet", and "The Misanthrope". Whiting was featured in several films during her career including "The Password Is Courage" (1962), "Underworld Informers" (1963), "The Counterfeit Constable" (1964), "Mr. Quilp" (1975), and "Sinbad and the Eye of the Tiger" (1977) as the witch Zenobia. She was seen on television in productions of "A Midsummer Night's Dream" (1958), "Till Murder Do Us Part" (1960), "The Old Road" (1961), "Somewhere for the Night" (1961), "The Plough and the Stars" (1961), "A Letter from the General" (1962), "The Wife of Knightsbridge" (1964), "Before Paris" (1972), "The Strauss Family" (1972), "Disraeli: Portrait of a Romantic" (1978), "Langrishe Go Down" (1978), "The Trespasser" (1981), "Artemis 81" (1981), "Shroud for a Nightingale" (1984), and "The Secret Garden" (1987). Her other television credits include episodes of "The Count of Monte Cristo", "ITV Television Playhouse", "The Cheaters", "The Avengers", "Studio 4", "Festival", "The Human Jungle", "Crane", "Thursday Theatre", "No Hiding Place", "Undermind", "Armchair Mystery Theatre", "The Wednesday Thriller", "Knock on Any Door", "Love Story", "Suspicion", "Two Women", "Play for Today", "Public Eye", "The Sweeney", "BBC2 Playhouse", "Jury" as Ann Coombs in 1983, "C.A.T.S. Eyes", "Rumpole of the Bailey", "McCallum", and "Let Them Eat Cake". Whiting was married to actor Colin

Blakely from 1961 until his death in 1987 and they had three children together.

Whitlock, Lee

British actor Lee Whitlock died after a long illness in England on February 17, 2023. He was 54. Whitlock was born in Hammersmith, London, England, on April 17, 1968. He began his acting career as a juvenile, appearing in episodes of "The Gentle Touch" and "Sherlock Holmes and Doctor

Watson" in 1980. He was also seen in such series as "Cribb", "Legacy of Murder", "Spooner's Patch", "Tears Before Bedtime", "Dramarama", "Behind the Bike Sheds", "Comrade Dad", "C.A.T.S. Eyes", "Me and My Girl", "Starting Out", "Young Charlie Chaplin" as Sydney Chaplin in 1989, "Split Ends" as Lee in 1989, "The Two of Us", "Harry Enfield's Television Programme", "Lovejoy", "Soldier Soldier", "Boon", "A Touch of Frost", "The Detectives", "Grange Hill" as Bevis Loveday in 1993, "Get Back", "99-1", "Scene", "Silent Witness", "McCallum", "Maisie Raine", "London's Burning", "Holby City, "The Bill", "EastEnders" as Rob Hedges from 1997 to 1998, "Casualty", "Law & Order: UK", and "Lucky Man". Whitlock starred as Stanley Moon, the son of the title character, in the ITV series "Shine on Harvey Moon" from 1982 to 1985 and reprised the role when the series returned a decade later in 1995. His other television credits include productions of "The Merry Wives of Windsor" (1982), "Hold the Back Page" (1985), "The Best Years of Your Life" (1986), "Two of Us" (1987), "Bloodlines", "Ghostboat", "That Summer Day", "Prime Suspect 7: The Final Act", "He Kills Coppers", "Parade's End" (2012), and "Complicit" (2013). Whitlock also appeared in such films as "Wish You Were Here" (1987), "Under Suspicion" (1991), "Shopping" (1994), "Command Approved" (2000), "Cassandra's Dream" (2007), "Love Me Still" (2007), "Sweeney Todd: The Demon Barber of Fleet Street" (2007), "Beyond the Rave" (2008) "Wild Bill" (2011), "Comes a Bright Day" (2012), "Ill Manors" (2012), "The Sweeney" (2012), "Rock and Roll Fuck'n'Lovely" (2013), "Jack the Giant Killer" (2013), "Their Finest" (2016), "Rise of the Footsoldiers 3" (2017), and "D Is for Detroit" (2022).

Whitlock, Tom

Songwriter Tom Whitlock, who received an Academy Award for the song "Take My Breath Away" from the film "Top Gun", died of complications from Alzheimer's disease in Nashville, Tennessee, on February 18, 2023. He was 68. Whitlock was born in Springfield, Missouri, on February 20, 1954. He learned to play the drums in his youth and worked as a session musician. He performed with local bands and wrote songs while attending high school. He attended Drury University in the early 1970s. Whitlock went to Los Angeles in 1983 and began working at Giorgio Moroder's studio. He

and Moroder co-wrote five songs for the 1986 film "Top Gun", including "Take My Breath Away", Kenny Loggins' hit "Danger Zone", "Radar Radio", "Lead Me On", and "Through the Fire". They shared an Oscar for Best Original Song for "Take My Breath Away". He and Moroder also wrote songs for the films "American Anthem" (1986) "Over the Top" (1987) including Sammy Hagar's hit "Winner Takes It All". Whitlock co-wrote songs for numerous other films including "Revenge of the Nerds II: Nerds in Paradise" (1987), "Fatal Be3auty" (1987), "Dream a Little Dream" (1989), "Let It Ride" (1989), "Navy SEALs" (1990), "Fire, Ice and Dynamite" (1990), "Out for Justice" (1991), "Boris and Natasha" (1992), and "10 Things I Hate About You" (1999). He co-wrote the song "Hand in Hand", that was the theme for the 1988 Summer Olympics.

Whitney, John

British television writer and producer John Whitney died in England on November 4, 2023. He was 92. Whitney

was born in Gerrards Cross, Buckinghamshire, England, on December 20, 1930. He left school in the late 1940s and began working for Ross Radio Productions Ltd. He produced radio programs for Radio Luxembourg and founded the Local Radio Association to promote commercial radio in England. He wrote for such television series as "Shadow Squad", "Crime Sheet", "The Case Before You", "The Verdict Is Yours", "Knight Errant Limited", "Suspense", "Deadline Midnight", "ITV Television Playhouse", "Theatre 70", "The Avengers", "Our Mister Ambler", "Ghost Squad", "Harper's West One", "Drama '63", "The Plane Makers" which he also produced, "About Religion", "The Villains", "Blackmail", "The Informer", and "In for a Penny". He became managing director of London's Capital Radio in the early 1970s. He also teamed with John Hawkesworth to form Sagitta Productions and created the television productions "Upstairs, Downstairs" and "Danger UXB". Whitney was director general of the Independent Broadcasting Authority from 1982 to 1989. He subsequently became managing director of the Really Useful Group Ltd. He was chairman of the Royal Academy of Dramatic Art from 2003 until his retirement in 2007. Whitney married ballet dancer Roma Duncan in 1956 and is survived by her, daughter Fiona, and son Alexander.

Whittaker, Roger

British singer and musician Roger Whittaker died at a hospital near Toulouse, France, on September 13, 2023. He was 87. Whittaker was born to English parents in Nairobi,

Kenya, on March 22, 1936. He learned to play the guitar and sang while in high school in Kenya. He spent two years with the Kenya Regiment fighting the Mau Mau rebellion during National Service. He attended the University of Cape Town in South Africa after his discharge in 1956. He left without graduating and worked as a teacher with the civil service education department. Whitaker moved to England in 1959 where he continued teaching. He also attended University College of North Wales where he earned a degree in science.

He began singing at local clubs and was signed by Fontana Records for his first official single, 1962's "The Charge of the Light Brigade". He moved to EMI's Columbia label in 1966. He had a minor hit with his own composition, "Durham Town (The Leavin')" in 1969. He also had success with the 1970 song "New World in the Morning" and wrote and recorded "No Blade of Grass", the title theme for 1970 science fiction film of the same name. His whistling came to the forefront with his 1974 song "The Finnish Whistler", which became the theme for the Finnish television cooking series "Patakakkonen". He had his biggest hit with "The Last Farewell" in 1975. He was also a popular recording artist in Germany during the 1970s and 1980s and had several successful concert tours. He also toured extensively in the United States, where his low-key style, whistling, and yodeling made him a popular performer for his audiences. He performed frequently on television throughout his career, appearing in episodes of "All That Jazz", "The Saturday Show", "Discs a Go-Go", "Thank Your Lucky Stars", "Open House", "Godzooks! It's All Happening", "Now for Nixon", "Dee Time", "Whistle Stop" as host from 1967 to 1968, "Bandstand", "Discorama", "Zingalong", "The Engelbert Humperdinck Show", "The Kenneth Williams Show", "It's Lulu", "The Val Doonigan Show", "4-3-2-1 Hot and Sweet", "The Sound of...", "David Nixon's Magic Box", "It's Cliff Richard", "Whittaker's World of Music", "Mary's Music", "The Golden Shot", "The Rolf Harris Show", "Presenting Lena Martell", "The Young Generation", "Pebble Mill at One", "The Animal Game", "Lift Off", "George Hamilton IV and Other Folk", "Dinah!", "The Vera Lynn Show", "Nana Mouskouri", "Going for a Song", "Musik aus Studio B", "Die Montagsmaler", "The Wheeltappers and Shunters Social Show", "Die Drehscheibe", "Starparade", "It's a Knockout", "The Roger Whittaker Show" which he hosted in 1977, "Session", "Crackerjack!", "Muaik Ist Trumpf", "The Mike Douglas Show", "Look Who's Talking", "The Alan Thicke Show", "Muiskladen", "The Bob Braun Show", "Nashville on the Road", "This Is Your Life", "Show-Express", "The Main Attraction", "The Merv Griffin Show", "Cannon and Ball", "Des O'Connor Now", "The Val Doonican Music Show", "Live from Her Majesty's", "Top of the Pops", "Hudson and Halls", "Jerry Lewis MDA Labor Day Telethon", "Flitterabend", "Wetten, Dass..?", "Today with Des and Mel", "Kelly", "Die Goldene Stimmgabedl", "Musikantenstadl",

"Willkommen Bei Carmen Nebel", "Feste der Volksmusik", "Die Feste Mit Floria Silbereisen", and "Die Helene Fischer Show". Whittaker was dropped by his record label, RCA, in the mid-1970s. He marketed his 1977 album "All My Best" on television himself and sold nearly a million copies. He was subject of the 1982 documentary film, "Roger Whittaker in Kenya: A Musical Safari". His autobiography, "So Far, So Good", was co-written with his wife in 1986. He lived in Ireland before moving to the south of France in 2012. He retired from performing the following year. Whittaker married Natalie O'Brien in 1964 and is survived by her, their two sons, and their three daughters.

Whittenshaw, Jane

British actress Jane Whittenshaw died in England on August 12, 2023. She was 53. Whittenshaw was born in London, England, on August 27, 1969.

She performed on stage and appeared in productions with the Royal Shakespeare Company. She appeared frequently on television with roles in episodes of "Screen Two", "Tears Before Bedtime", "Peak Practice", "Silent Witness", "EastEnders" as Anita Banks in 1997, "Wing and a Prayer", "Grange Hill", "Kiss Me Kate", "Doctors", "Murder City", "The Bill", "Green Wing", "Twenty Twelve", "Casualty", "Endeavour", and "Call the Witness". He was seen in the tele-films "What a Way to Run a Revolution" (1986) and "Pollyanna" (2003) and was a voice performer in the animated series "Eddy and the Bear", "Pigeon Boy", "Olivia", "Henry Hugglemonster", and "Ninja Express". She performed with the BBC Radio Drama Company and was featured in over 500 radio plays. She was featured in several films including "Mrs. Dalloway" (1997), "Golden Years" (2016), and "Above the Clouds" (2018). Whittenshaw married actor Hugh Kermode in 2004 and he survives her.

Wiggins, Spencer

Soul singer Spencer Wiggins died in Memphis, Tennessee, on February 13, 2023. He was 81. Wiggins was born in Memphis on January 8, 1942.

He began performing with gospel groups in his youth including the New Rival Gospel Singers. He teamed with his brother Percy and David Porter in the R&B group the Four Stars after leaving school. He performed in local clubs in Memphis in the early 1960s and was signed by Goldwax Records. He released his first recording, "Lover's Crime", in 1964. Wiggins continued to record the singles "Uptight Good Woman" and "I Never Loved a Woman (The Way I Love

You)". He moved to Fame Records in Muscle Shoals in 1969 and charted with "Double Lovin'". He settled in Miami, Florida, in 1973 where he returned to his gospel roots. He served as choir director at the New Birth Baptist Church in Miami and released the gospel recording "Keys to the Kingdom" in 2004. His work as a soul singer received a rebirth in the late 1980s when much of his work was reissued in Europe and Japan.

Wilbur, George P.

Actor and stuntman George P. Wilbur, who was featured as masked killer Michael Myers in "Halloween 4: The Return of Michael Myers", died on February 1, 2023. He was 81. Wilbur was born in Kent, Connecticut, on March 6, 1941. He served in the U.S. Navy and worked as a ranch wrangler in Tucson Arizona, in the early 1960s. He began his film career as an extra and stunt double for the 1966 John Wayne film "El Dorado". He subsequently moved to California to pursue a

career in films and television. He worked on numerous films as a stuntman and bit actor including "Hombre" (1967), "Planet of the Apes" (1968), "Escape from the Planet of the Apes" (1971), "Hammer" (1972), "Conquest of the Planet of the Apes" (1972), "Blacula" (1972), "The Poseidon Adventure" (1972), "High Plains Drifter" (1973), "Cleopatra Jones" (1973), "Blazing Saddles" (1974), "99 & 44/100% Dead" (1974), "The Towering Inferno" (1974), "Lepke" (1975), "Framed" (1975), "Johnny Firecloud" (1975), "The Hindenburg" (1975), "Grizzly" (1976), "Death Journey" (1976), "Drum" (1976), "The White Buffalo" (1977), "Black Oak Conspiracy" (1977), "Hanging on a Star" (1978), "Movie Movie" (1978), "Beyond the Poseidon Adventure" (1979), "Every Which Way But Loose" (1979), "Parts: The Clonus Horror" (1979), "Virus" (1980), "The Mountain Men" (1980), "Coast to Coast" (1980), "Delusions" (1981), "Escape from New York" (1981), "Cannonball Run" (1981), "Under the Rainbow" (1981), "Pennies from Heaven" (1981), "The Sword and the Sorcerer" (1982), "Poltergeist" (1982), "Star Trek II: The Wrath of Khan" (1982), "White Dog" (1982), "The Beastmaster" (1982), "They Call Me Bruce" (1982), "Hysterical" (1982), "Max Dugan Returns" (1983), "The Sting II" (1983), "Blue Thunder" (1983), "Yellowbeard" (1983), "The Osterman Weekend" (1983), "Firestarter" (1984), "Ghostbusters" (1984), "City Limits" (1984), "City Heat" (1984), "The Mean Season" (1985), "Re-Animator" (1985), "Fletch" (1985), "Murphy's Romance"

(1985), "The Check Is in the Mail..." (1985), "Poltergeist II: The Other Side" (1986), "Raw Deal" (1986), "A Fine Mess" (1986), "Extreme Prejudice" (1987), "Slam Dance" (1987), "The Monster Squad" (1987), "The Running Man" (1987), "The Couch Trip" (1988), "Split Decision" (1988), "Remote Control" (1988), "Colors" (1988), "Two Moon Junction" (1988), "Dead Heat" (1988), "Die Hard" (1988), "Halloween 4: The Return of Michael Myers" (1988), "Moonwalker" (1988), "Winter People" (1989), "The 'Burbs" (1989), "Ghostbusters II" (1989), "Lock Up" (1989), "A Nightmare on Elm Street: The Dream Child" (1989), "An Innocent Man" (1989), "Halloween 5: The Return of Michael Myers" (1989), "Loose Cannons" (1990), "Secret Agent OO Soul" (1990), "Come See the Paradise" (1990), "Total Recall" (1990), "The Exorcist III" (1990), "Pump Up the Volume" (1990), "Repossessed" (1990), "Eve of Destruction" (1991), "The Silence of the Lambs" (1991), "The Marrying Man" (1991), "Suburban Commando" (1991), "Defenseless" (1991), "Leatherjackets" (1991), "The Last Boy Scout" (1991), "The Vagrant" (1992), "Unlawful Entry" (1992), "Dr. Giggles" (1992), "Boiling Point" (1993), "Excessive Fore" (1993), "Hot Shots! Part Deux" (1993), "Undercover Blues" (1993), "Me and the Kid" (1993), "Monkey Trouble" (1994), "Holy Matrimony" (1994), "Cobb" (1994), "Cops and Robbersons" (1994), "Bad Blood" (1994), "There Goes My Baby" (1994), "Outbreak" (1995), "Halloween: The Curse of Michael Myers" (1995), "Casino" (1995), "Spider the Dead: The First Chapter" (1995), "Broken Arrrow" (1996), "Set It Off" (1996), "Mars Attacks!" (1996), "Vegas Vacation" (1997), "The Corporate Ladder" (1997), "Homegrown" (1998), "Rush Hour" (1998), "P.U.N.K.S." (1999), "What Planet Are You From?" (2000), "The Perfect Storm" (2000), "Bedazzled" (2000), "Spider-Man" (2002), "The First $20 Million Is Always the Hardest" (2002), "The Notebook" (2004), "The Aggression Scale" (2012), "The Thompsons" (2012), "Cheap Thrills" (2013), and "American Muscle" (2014). Wilbur worked frequently in television, performing stunts and appearing in small roles in episodes of "Gunsmoke", "Mission: Impossible", "Search", "Switch", "The Six Million Dollar Man", "Masquerade", "The Master", "The New Mike Hammer", "Simon & Simon", "Hardcastle and McCormick", "Magnum, P.I", "Dynasty", "Tales from the Crypt", "Days of Our Lives", "Renegade", "The Practice", "The District", and "Deadwood". His other television credits include the tele-films and mini-series "Dead Man on the Run" (1975), "Sky Heist" (1975), "Pearl" (1978), "Silent Victory: The Kitty O'Neil Story" (1979), "Stunt Seven" (aka "The Fantastic Seven") (1979), "Goldie and the Boxer" (1979), "Goldie and the Boxer Go to Hollywood" (1981), "Hardcase" (1981), "Best of Friends" (1981), "The Fighter" (1983), "Ewoks: The Battle of Endor" (1985), "Fatal Exposure" (1991), "Not of This World" (1991), and "Cast a Deadly Spell" (1991), "Behind the Action: Stuntmen in the Movie" (2002), and "Wedding Daze" (2004).

Wilcox, Shannon

Actress Shannon Wilcox died in Los Angeles, California, on September 2, 2023. She was 80. She was born Mary Wilcox in Ohio on May 21, 1943, and raised on a farm in

Indiana. She moved to Boulder, Colorado, to attend high school and college. Wilcox worked in Paris, France, as a dancer before settling in Los Angeles to be an actress in the late 1970s. She

was seen frequently on television with roles in episodes of "Sirota's Court", "Starsky and Hutch", "Dog and Cat", "Hawaii Five-O", "Kaz", "Family", "Hart to Hart", "Mrs. Columbo", "Cagney & Lacey", "Crazy Like a Fox", "Magnum, P.I.", "Remington Steele", "Tales from the Darkside", "Buck James" as Jenny James, the ex-wife of Dennis Weaver's title character, from 1987 to 1988, "Alien Nation", "1st & Ten", "Jake and the Fatman", "Over My Dead Body", "Dallas" in the recurring role of Anita in 1990, "The Fanelli Boys", "Civil Wars", "In the Heat of the Night", "Angel Falls", "Matlock", "L.A. Law", "Beyond Belief: Fact or Fiction", "Rescue 77", "Boston Public", "ER", "NCIS", "NCIS: Los Angeles", "The Romanoffs", "The Resident", "Truth Be Told", "Grey's Anatomy", "Trailerville USA", and "Smartphone Theatre". She was also seen in the tele-films "Thou Shalt Not Commit Adultery" (1978), "Mysterious Two" (1982), "When Your Lover Leaves" (1983), "Triplecross" (1986), "Dangerous Passion" (1990), "83 Hours 'Til Dawn" (1990), "The Set Up" (1995), and Hallmark's "A Boyfriend for Christmas" (2004) with her daughter Kelli Williams. Wilcox made her film debut in the 1980 comedy "Cheaper to Keep Her". Her other films include "The Border" (1982), "Six Weeks" (1982), "The Karate Kid" (1984), "Songwriter" (1984) as Anita, the ex-wife of Willie Nelson's Doc Jenkins, "Hollywood Harry" (1985), "Legal Eagles" (1986), "Zapped Again!" (1990), "For the Boys" (1991), "There Goes My Baby" (1994), "Criminal Passion" (1994), "Se7en" (1995), "The Annihilation of Fish" (1999), "Restive Planet" (2004), "Crazylove" (2005), "A Year and a Day" (2005), "Ready or Not" (2009) also serving as executive producer, "Scammerhead" (2014), and "The Atticus Institute" (2015). She frequently worked with director Gerry Marshall, with roles in such films as "Frankie and Johnny" (1991), "Exit to Eden" (1994), "Dear God" (1996), "The Other Sister" (1999), "Runaway Bride" (1999), "The Princess Diaries" (2001), "The Princess Diaries 2: Royal Engagement" (2004), and "Raising Helen" (2004). Wilcox was married to plastic surgeon John Williams from 1965 until their divorce in 1984. She is survived by their children, actress Kelli Williams and director Sean Doyle. She was married to actor Alex Rocco from 2005 until his death in 2015.

Wilde, Larry

Comedian and actor Larry Wilde died on September 3, 2023. He was 95. He was born Herman Wildman in Jersey City, New Jersey, on February 6, 1928. He served in the U.S. Marines from 1946 to 1948 and staged and performed in shows at Camp Lejeune, North Carolina. He graduated from the University of Miami after his discharge. He began working as

a stand-up comedian at Florida nightclubs in the early 1950s while attending college. He became a popular performer at

clubs around the country. He made his television debut in an episode of "The United States Steel Hour" in 1958. Wilde was also seen in episodes of "The Woody Woodbury Show", "The Peter Martin Show", "The Mike Douglas Show", "The Irv Kupcinet Show", "Allen Ludden's Gallery", "Della", "The Barbara McNair Show", "The Real Tom Kennedy Show", "The Virginia Graham Show", "Dan August", "The Partners", "Adam-12", "Barnaby Jones", "Sanford and Son", "The Mary Tyler Moore Show", "The Paul Ryan Show", and "Rhoda". He was noted for his books "The Great Comedians Talk About Comedy" (1968) and "How the Great Comedy Writers Create Laughter" (1976). He also wrote numerous joke books in the 1970s and 1980s. He continued to perform at conventions, concerts, cruise ships, and nightclubs throughout his career. Wilde was married to Dana Slawson from 1955 until their divorce in 1957, and to Julie Heater from 1968 until their divorce in 1971. He married Maryruth Poulos in 1974 and she survives him.

Wildmon, Donald

Methodist clergyman Donald Wildmon, who was an outspoken critic of immorality in media and the founder of the American Family Association, died of Lewy body dementia in

Tupelo, Mississippi, on December 28, 2023. He was 94. Wildmon was born in Dumas, Mississippi, on January 18, 1938. He graduated from Millsaps College in 1960. He served in the U.S. Army Special Services from 1961 to 1963 and was ordained a minister of the United Methodist Church in 1964. He earned a Master of Divinity from Emory University's Candler School of Theology the following year. Wildmon served was a United Methodist Church pastor in several Mississippi towns until 1977 when he founded the National Federation of Decency in Tupelo. He felt most primetime television programs were unfit for a family with young children. His group described itself as "a Christian organization promoting the biblical ethic of decency in American society with primary emphasis on television and other media," and added emphasis to "moral issues that impact the family." He organized an advertiser boycott against such programs as "Charlie's Angels", "All in the Family", and "Three's Company". He was interviewed on such television shows as "The Phil Donohue Show" and "Meet the Press" and was featured in the pages of "Time", "Newsweek", "People", "TV Guide", and the "New York Times". The National Federation of Decency evolved into the American

Family Association (AFA). Wildmon founded the American Family Radio network in 1991 to promote conservative Christian-oriented programming on nearly 200 stations. He was heard on the radio programs "AFA Report" and "My Turn with Don Wildmon". Wildmon and the AFA organized boycotts against 7-Eleven, WaldenBooks, and other stores seeking to eliminate the sale of "Playboy", "Penthouse", and other adult magazines. He helped instigate a boycott against the Walt Disney Company for promoting a "gay agenda" by offering employees benefits for domestic partnerships. Other campaigns included protests of the film "The Last Temptation of Christ", Madonna's song "Like a Prayer", and Blockbuster Video for carrying NC-17 rated films. Wildmon's battle with artists Andres Serrano and Robert Mapplethorpe was the subject of the 1991 British documentary film "Damned in the U.S.A.". He was author of several books including "Stand Up to Live" (1975), "Home Invaders" (1985), "The Case Against Pornography" (1986), "Don Wildmon: The Man the Networks Love to Hate" (1989) with Randall Nolton, and "Speechless: Silencing the Christians: How Secular Liberals and Homosexual Activists are Outlawing Christianity (and Judaism) to Force Their Sexual Agenda on America". Wildmon stepped down as chairman of the American Family Association due to poor health in 2010 and was succeeded by his son, Tim Wildmon. He married Lynda Lou Bennett in 1961 and is survived by her and their four children.

Wilhelm, Wimie

Dutch actress Wilhelmina 'Wimie' Wilhelm died of cancer in Amsterdam, Netherlands, on September 16, 2023. She was 62. Wilhelm was born in Amsterdam on August 21, 1961. She performed as a cabaret artist and appeared frequently in films and television from the early 1990s. She was seen in the films "Antonia's Line" (1995), "Missing Link" (1999), "Little Crumb" (1999), "Pietje Bell" (2002), "Deuce Bigalow: European Gigolo" (2005), "Black Book" (2006), "Dennis P." (2007), "Frogs and Toads" (2009), "Nothing Personal" (2009), "IJspaard" (2014), "Familieweekend" (2016), "Herrie in Huize Gerri" (2021), and "Melk" (2023). Wilhelm was seen on television in productions of "Bruin Goud" (1994), "Maten" (1999), "Dichter op de Zeedijk" (2000), "De Middeleeuwen" (2001), "Groen Is Toch de Mooiste Kleur Voor Gras" (2007), "Hitte/Harara" (2008), "Godenzoon" (2008), "Ghost Corp" (2017), and "Get Lost!" (2018). Her other television credits include episodes of "Niemand e Deur Uit!", "Bureau Kruislaan", "De Victorie", "Madelief: Met de Poppen Gooien", "Oppassen!!!", "Unit 13", "Sterker dan Drank", "Zebra", "Oud Geld", "Flodder", "Blauw Blauw", "Wildschut & De Vries", "De Vloer Op", "Najib en Julia", "Gooische Vrouwen", "Baantjer" as Els Peeters from 2000 to 2006, "S1ingle", "Dol", "Sorry Minister", "De Co-Assistent", "Koen Kampioen", "Dokter Tinus", "Doris", "Danni

Lowinski", "Smeris", "The Neighbors" as Psychologist Hetty in 2014, "Bakker", "Toren C", "Alleen Op de Wereld", "Vechtershart", "Connie & Clyde 2", "Opslaan als de Serie", "De Regels van Floor", "Undercover", "Bestseller Boy", "Sinterklaasjournaal", "Panduloria", "Flikken Maastricht", and "Ferry: The Series".

Wilkinson, Tom

British actor Tom Wilkinson, who was noted for his roles in the films "The Full Monty" and "In the Bedroom", died at his home in London, England, on December 30, 2023. He was 75. Wilkinson was born in Leeds, Yorkshire, England, on February 5, 1948. He moved to Canada with his family in 1959 where they remained for five years before returning to England. Wilkinson studied literature at the University of Kent at Canterbury. He began acting and directing with the university's drama society. He attended the Royal Academy of Dramatic Art, graduating in 1973 and performed with the Nottingham Playhouse. He appeared in the West End as Horatio in a 1981 production of "Hamlet" by the Royal Shakespeare Company, earning a Laurence Olivier Award nomination for his supporting role. He earned the Laurence Olivier Award for best actor for his role as Dr. Stockmann in Henrik Ibsen's "An Enemy of the People" (1988). Wilkinson made his film debut in a small role in 1976's "The Shadow Line". He appeared in numerous films including "Bones" (1984), "Wetherby" (1985), "Sylvia" (1985), "The Lost Secret" (1986), "Paper Mask" (1990), "In the Name of the Father" (1993), "A Business Affair" (1994), "Royal Deceit" (1994), "Priest" (1994), Ang Lee's "Sense and Sensibility" (1995) as Mr. Dashwood, "The Ghost and the Darkness" (1996) starring Michael Douglas and Val Kilmer, the Nordic mystery "Smilla's Sense of Snow" (1997), the comedy "The Full Monty" (1997) earning a BAFTA Award for Best Actor for his role as Gerald Cooper, "Wilde" (1997) as the Marquess of Queensberry, "Oscar and Lucinda" (1997), "The Governess" (1998), "Rush Hour" (1998) with Jackie Chan and Chris Tucker, "Jilting Joe" (1998), "Shakespeare in Love" (1998) receiving a BAFTA Award nomination for his role as Hugh Fennyman, "Molokai" (1999), "Ride with the Devil" (1999), "The Patriot" (2000) as General Lord Cornwallis, "Essex Boys" (2000), "Chain of Fools" (2000), "In the Bedroom" (2001) earning an Academy Award and BAFTA Award nomination for his leading role as Matt Fowler, "Another Life" (2001), "Black Knight" (2001), "The Importance of Being Earnest" (2002), "Before You Go" (2002), "Girl with a Pearl Earring" (2003), "If Only" (2004), Jim Carrey's "Eternal Sunshine of the Spotless Mind" (2004) as Dr. Howard Mierzwiak, "Stage Beauty" (2004), "A Good Woman" (2004), "Piccadilly Jim" (2004), "Batman Begins" (2005) as mob boss Carmine Falcone, the horror film "The Exorcism of Emily Rose" (2005) as Father

Moore, "Separate Lies" (2005), "Ripley Under Ground" (2005), "The Night of the White Pants" (2006), "The Last Kiss" (2006), "Dedication" (2007), Woody Allen's "Cassandra's Dream" (2007), "Michael Clayton" (2007) receiving an Oscar nomination and a BAFTA Award for his supporting role as attorney Arthur Edens, Guy Ritchie's "RocknRolla" (2008), "Valkyrie" (2008) as General Friedrich Fromm, "Duplicity" (2009), "44 Inch Chest" (2009), Roman Polanski's "The Ghost Writer" (2010), "Jackboots on Whitehall" (2010), "The Debt" (2010), "The Conspirator" (2010), "Burke and Hare" (010) as Dr. Robert Knox, "The Green Hornet" (2011) as James Reid, "The Best Exotic Marigold Hotel" (2011) as Graham Dashwood, "Mission: Impossible - Ghost Protocol" (2011), "The Samaritan" (2012), "The Lone Ranger" (2013), "Belle" (2013), "Felony" (2013), Wes Anderson's "The Grand Budapest Hotel" (2014), "Good People" (2014), "Selma" (2014) as President Lyndon B. Johnson, "Unfinished Business" (2015), "Bone in the Throat" (2015), "Little Boy" (2015), "Jenny's Wedding" (2015), "The Choice" (2016), "Snowden" (2016), "Denial" (2016), "This Beautiful Fantastic" (2016), "The Catcher Was a Spy" (2018), "The Happy Prince" (2018), "Burden" (2018), "The Titan" (2018), "Dead in a Week or Your Money Back" (2018), "Dr. Bird's Advice for Sad Poets" (2021) as the voice of Dr. Bird, and the action thriller "SAS: Red Notice" (2021). Wilkinson appeared in such television productions as "Crime and Punishment" (1979), "Spyship" (1983), "Sharma and Beyond" (1984), "Squaring the Circle" (1984), "Sakharov" (1984), "Miss Marple: A Pocketful of Rye" (1985), "First Among Equals" (1986), "The Woman He Loved" (1988), "The Attic: The Hiding Place of Anne Frank" (1988), "First and Last" (1989), "Parnell and the Englishwoman" (1991), "Prime Suspect" (1991) as Peter Rawlins, "Resnick: Lonely Hearts" (1992) as Detective Inspector Charlie Resnick, "Resnick: Rough Treatment" (1993) reprising his role as Resnick, "Martin Chuzzlewit" (1994) receiving a BAFTA Award nomination for portraying Seth Pecksniff, "A Very Open Prison" (1995), "Interview Day" (1996), "Cold Enough for Snow" (1997) earning another BAFTA Award nomination for his role as Hugh Lloyd, "David Copperfield" (1999) as the Narrator, "The Gathering Storm" (2002), "An Angel for May" (2002), "Normal" (2003) receiving an Emmy Award nomination for his role as Roy Applewood, "John Adams" (2008) winning an Emmy Award for his role as Benjamin Franklin, "Recount" (2008) receiving another Emmy nomination for portraying James A. Baker, "A Number" (2008), the animated "The Gruffalo" (2009) as the voice of the Fox, "The Kennedys" (2011) earning an Emmy Award for his role as Joe Kennedy Sr., "The Gruffalo's Child" (2011) reprising the voice of the Fox, "Watership Down" (2018) as the voice of Threarah, "Belgravia" (2020) as Earl of Brockenhurst, and the Disney+ sequel "The Full Monty" (2023) reprising his role as Gerald. His other television credits include episodes of "2nd House", "Panorama", "All for Love", "Strangers and Brothers", "Travelling Man", "Happy Families", "Ruth Rendell Mysteries", "Inspector Morse", "TECX", "Counterstrike", "Lovejoy", "Underbelly", "An Exchange of Fire", "Stay Lucky", "Alleyn Mysteries", "Shakespeare: The Animated Tales" as the voice of Buckingham in "King Richard III" in 1994, "Performance", and "Screen Two". Wilkinson married actress Diana Hardcastle in 1988 and is survived by her and their two daughters, Alice and Molly.

Williams, Cindy

Actress Cindy Williams, who starred as Shirley Feeney on the television comedy series "Laverne & Shirley", died in Los Angeles, California, on January 25, 2023. She was 75. Williams was born in Van Nuys, California, on August 22, 1947. She spent her childhood with her parents in Dallas and returned to Los Angeles at age ten. She performed on stage  during high school and majored in theater at Los Angeles City College. She began her acting career in the late 1960s and appeared in commercials for TWA and Foster Grant sunglasses. She was seen on television from the early 1970s with roles in episodes of "My World and Welcome to It", "Barefoot in the Park", "Nanny and the Professor", "Room 222", "Getting Together", "The Funny Side", "Hawaii Five-O", "Cannon", "Insight", "Police Story", and "Petrocelli". Williams made her film debut in Roger Corman's off-beat black comedy "Gas! -Or- It Became Necessary to Destroy the World in Order to Save It". She also appeared in the films "Drive, He Said" (1971) directed by Jack Nicholson, "Beware! The Blob" (aka "Son of the Blob") (1972) directed by Larry Hagman, "Travels with My Aunt" (1973), and the psychological horror film "The Killing Kind" (1973). She was noted for her performance as Laurie Henderson, girlfriend of Ron Howard's Steve Bolander, in George Lucas' hit coming-of-age film "American Graffiti" (1973). She reprised the role in, now as wife Laurie Henderson Bolander, in the 1979 sequel "More American Graffiti". She also appeared in such films as Francis Ford Coppola's acclaimed thriller "The Conversation" (1974) whose conversation with Frederic Forrest served as the backdrop of the film, the tele-film "The Migrants" (1974), "Mr. Ricco" (1975), and the musical comedy "The First Nudie Musical". She worked with Penny Marshall at Francis Ford Coppola's Zoetrope as comedy writers when Marshall's brother, Garry, asked if they would appear on an episode of his hit comedy series "Happy Days". She and Marshall starred as fun-loving roommates Shirley Feeney and Laverne De Fazio, who go on a date with Ron Howard's Richie Cunningham and Henry Winkler's Fonzie. Their characters proved popular enough that they became stars of a spin-off series, "Laverne & Shirley". The two made occasional guest appearances in subsequent "Happy Days" episodes. "Laverne & Shirley" was a hit comedy series and Williams remained in the role until the start of the eighth, and last, season in 1982. She left the series due to a pregnancy in real life and ongoing conflicts with Penny Marshall. She also voiced the role of Shirley in the cartoon series "Laverne & Shirley in the Army" from 1981 to 1982 and

"Mork & Mindy/Laverne & Shirley/Fonz Hour" in 1982. Williams continued to appear on television with roles in the tele-films "Suddenly, Love" (1978), "Joanna" (1985), "When Dreams Come True" (1985), "Help Wanted: Kids" (1986), "The Leftovers" (1986), "Save the Dog!" (1988), "Tricks of the Trade" (1988), "Perry Mason: The Case of the Poisoned Pen" (1990), "Menu for Murder" (1990), "Earth Angel" (1991), "Crimes of Passion: Escape from Terror - The Teresa Stamper Story" (1995), "The Stepford Husbands" (1996), "The Patty Duke Show: Still Rockin' in Brooklyn Heights" (1999), "Strawberry Summer" (2012), and "A Dream of Christmas" (2016). Her other television credits include episodes of "Saturday Night Live", "Laugh-In", "CHiPs", "The Billy Crystal Comedy Hour", "Just Like Family" as Lisa Burke in 1989, the short-lived comedy "Normal Life" as Anne Harlow in 1990, the unsold pilot "Steel Magnolias" as M'Lynn Eatenton in 1990, the comedy series "Getting By" as Cathy Hale from 1993 to 1994, "Lois & Clark: The New Adventures of Superman", "The Magic School Bus" in a voice role, "Night Stand", "Touched by an Angel", "Hope & Gloria", the Comedy Central series "Strip Mall" in the recurring role of herself from 2000 to 2001, "Son of a Beach", "The Brothers Garcia", "For Your Love" in the recurring role of Ronnie from 2000 to 2002, "7th Heaven", "Less Than Perfect", "8 Simple Rules", "Law & Order: Special Victims Unit", "Girlfriends", "Drive" as the House Mother in 2007, "Are We There Yet?", "Sam & Cat", and "The Odd Couple". Williams appeared in occasional films from the 1980s including "The Creature Wasn't Nice" (1981), the science fiction comedy "UFOria" (1984), "Big Man on Campus" (1989), "Rude Awakening" (1989), "Bingo" (1991), "Meet Wally Sparks" (1997), "The Biggest Fan" (2005), "The Legend of William Tell" (2006), "Stealing Roses" (2012) also serving as associate producer, "Still Waiting in the Wings" (2018), and "Canaan Land" (2020), and the shorts "For Goodness Sake" (1993), "The Happiest Man Alive" (2012), and "Peter at the End" (2012). She served as a co-producer for the comedy films "Father of the Bride" (1991) and "Father of the Bride Part II" (1995) starring Steve Martin. She starred in the television specials "The Cindy Williams Comedy Special" (1994) and "The Laverne & Shirley Reunion" (1995). She appeared in episodes of such talk and games shows as "The Merv Griffin Show", "Dinah!", "Cos", "Dean Martin Celebrity Roast", "Celebrity Challenge of the Sexes", "Circus of the Stars", "America 2-Night", "Donny and Marie", "The Tonight Show Starring Johnny Carson", "The Mike Douglas Show", "The Andy Kaufman Show", "An Evening at the Improv", "Richard Rossi Live", "One on One with John Tesh", "The Rosie O'Donnell Show", "Hollywood Squares", "Who Wants to Be a Millionaire", "The Test", "Weakest Link", "Intimate Portrait", "Pet Star", "Biography", "The Rosie Show", "Celebrity Ghost Stories", "Today", and "The Talk". Williams performed on stage in national tour productions of "Grease", "Deathtrap", and "Moon Over Buffalo". She was featured as Mrs. Tottendale in the Broadway comedy "The Drowsy Chaperone" in 2007. Her memoir, "Shirley, I Jest!", was published in 2015. Williams was married to musician Bill Hudson of the Hudson Brothers from 1982 until their divorce

in 2000. She is survived by their son, William Hudson, and daughter, Emily Hudson.

Williams, Treat

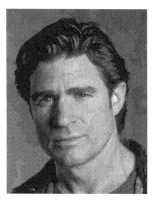

Actor Treat Williams who starred in such films as "Hair", "Dead Heat", and "The Phantom", died of injuries received when his motorcycle crashed into a vehicle in Dorset, Vermont, on June 12, 2023. He was airlifted to a hospital in Albany, New York, where he was pronounced dead. He was 71. Williams was born in Stamford, Connecticut, on December 1, 1951. He played football while in high school and college and became performing on stage in theatrical productions. He abandoned football to concentrate on acting while attending Franklin & Marshall College in Lancaster, Pennsylvania. He began performing in musical theater and was an understudy for several male leads in the Broadway production of "Grease" in the 1970s. He took over the lead role of Danny Zuko in 1978. Williams was also featured in other Broadway musicals and plays including "Over Here!" (1974), "Once in a Lifetime" (1978), "The Pirates of Penzance" (1981), "Love Letters" (1989), and "Follies" (2001). He made his film debut in 1975's "Deadly Hero". He was seen in numerous films throughout his career including "The Ritz" (1976), "Marathon Man" (1976), "The Eagle Has Landed" (1976), the counterculture musical "Hair" (1979) as Berger, Steven Spielberg's comedy "1941" (1979), the "Star Wars" sequel "The Empire Strikes Back" (1980) as an uncredited rebel soldier extra, "Why Would I Lie?" (1980), the crime drama "Prince of the City" (1981) as Detective Daniel Ciello, "Neapolitan Sting" (1983), Sergio Leone's crime epic "Once Upon a Time in America" (1984) as Jimmy O'Donnell, "Flashpoint" (1984), "Smooth Talk (1985), "The Men's Club" (1986), "Sweet Lies" (1987), "Night of the Sharks" (1988), "The Third Solution" (1988), "Dead Heat" (1988) as zombie cop Roger Mortis, "Heart of Dixie" (1989), "Where the Rivers Flow North" (1993), "Hand Gun" (1994), "Things to Do in Denver When You're Dead" (1995), "Mulholland Falls" (1996), "The Phantom" (1996) as the villainous Xander Drax, "The Devil's Own" (1997), "Cannes Man" (1997), the underwater horror film "Deep Rising" (1998), "The Deep End of the Ocean" (1999), "Crash Point Zero" (2001), "Critical Mass" (2001), "Skeletons in the Closet" (2001), "The Substitute: Failure Is Not an Option" (2001), "Venomous" (2001), "Gale Force" (2002), "Hollywood Ending" (2002), "The Circle" (2002), "Miss Congeniality 2: Armed & Fabulous" (2005), "Moola" (2007), "Il Nascondiglio" (2007), "What Happens in Vegas" (2008), "Howl" (2010), "127 Hours" (2010) as the father of James Franco's Aron Ralston, "Martino's Summer" (2010), "A Little Bit of Heaven" (2011), "Oba: The Last Samurai" (2011), "Mask Maker" (2011), "Deadfall" (2012), "Attack of the 50 Foot Cheerleader" (aka "Blue Residents") (2012), "Reaching for the Moon" (2013),

"Age of Dinosaurs" (2013), "Barefoot" (2014), "In the Blood" (2014), "Operation Rogue" (2014), "The Congressman" (2016), "The Etruscan Smile" (2018), "Second Act" (2018), "Drunk Parents" (2019), "The Great Alaskan Race" (2019), "Run Hide Fight" (2020), "Dolly Parton's Christmas on the Square" (2020), "12 Mighty Orphans" (2021), and "American Outlaws" (2023). Williams starred as boxer Jack Dempsey in the 1983 tele-film "Dempsey" and was Stanley Kowalski in a 1984 television adaptation of "A Streetcar Named Desire". He was also seen in television productions of "Some Men Need Help" (1985) for "American Playhouse", "J. Edgar Hoover" (1987) in the title role, "Echoes in the Darkness" (1987), "Third Degree Burns" (1989), "Max and Helen" (1990), "Drug Wars: The Camarena Story" (1990), "Final Verdict" (1991), "Till Death Us Do Part" (1992), "The Water Engine" (1992), "Deadly Matrimony" (1992), "Bonds of Love" (1993), "Parallel Lives" (1994), "Texan" (1994) which he also directed, "Ho un Segreto Con Papa" (1994), "In the Shadow of Evil" (1995), "Johnny's Girl" (1995), "The Late Shift" (1996) earning an Emmy Award nomination for his role as network executive Michael Ovitz, "Escape: Human Cargo" (1998), "The Substitute 2: School's Out" (1998) as Karl Thomasson, "Every Mother's Worst Fear" (1998), "36 Hours to Die" (1999), "The Substitute 3: Winner Takes All" (1999), "Journey to the Center of the Earth" (1999), "Hopewell" 2000", "Guilty Hearts" (2002), "The Staircase Murders" (2008), "Front of the Class" (2008), "Good Behavior" (2008), "Chasing a Dream" (2009), "Safe Harbor" (2009), "The Story" (2009), "Boston's Finest" (2010), "Beyond the Blackboard" (2011), "Eve of Destruction" (2013), "Confirmation" (2016) as U.S. Senator Ted Kennedy, "Rocky Mountain Christmas" (2017), "The Christmas House" (2020), "The Christmas House 2: Deck Those Halls" (2021), and "We Own This City" (2022). His other television credits include episodes of "Faerie Tale Theatre" in a 1987 production of "The Little Mermaid", the short-lived drama series "Eddie Dodd" in the title role in 1991, "Tales from the Crypt", the animated "Batman: The Animated Series" as the voice of Dr. Achiles Milo, "Avonlea", the comedy series "Good Advice" as Jack Harold from 1993 to 1994, "UC: Undercover", "Maury", "The Rosie O'Donnell Show", "Late Night with Conan O'Brien", "Late Show with David Letterman", "Going to California", the WB drama series "Everwood" as Dr. Andy Brown from 2002 to 2006, "Brothers & Sisters" as David Morton in 2006, "The Ellen DeGeneres Show", "Heartland" as Dr. Nathaniel Grant in 2007, "Against the Wall" as Don Kowalski in 2011, "Law & Order: Special Victims Unit", "The Simpsons" in a cameo voice role, "Leverage", "White Collar" in the recurring role of Sam Phelps/James Bennett from 2012 to 2013, "Hawaii Five-O", "CSI: Crime Scene Investigation", "American Odyssey" as Colonel Stephen Glen in 2015, "All Downhill from Here", "Chicago Fire" in the recurring role of Benny Severide from 2013 to 2018, "Nightbirds", "Chesapeake Shores" as Mick O'Brien from 2016 to 2022, "Blue Bloods" in the recurring role of Lenny Ross from 2016 to 2023, and "Feud: Capote's Women". Williams was a certified pilot and scuba diver and was author of the 2010 children's book "Air Show!". He

married Pam Van Sant in 1988 and is survived by her and two children, Gill and Elinor.

Wilson, Cal

New Zealand comedian and television host Cal Wilson died of cancer at a hospital in Sydney, Australia, on October 11, 2023. He was 53. Wilson was born in Christchurch, New Zealand, on October 5, 1970. She earned a degree from the

University of Canterbury in the early 1990s. She was co-founder of the Court Jesters comedy improv group in 1990. She became a full-time stand-up comic later in the decade. She was a regular performer on the "Pulp Comedy" series from 1997 to 1998. She wrote for the comedy series "Willy Nilly" from 2001 to 2003. Wilson also wrote and appeared in the series "Skitz", "Telly Laughs", "Flatmates", "Skithouse", "The Wedge", "The Weekly with Charlie Pickering", and "Rosehaven". She was seen in the television series "The Panel", "Rove Live", "Stand Up!", "The Glass House", "Aussie Gold", "Dancing with the Stars" as a contestant in 2008, "Thank God You're Here", "The Project", "Hey Hey It's Saturday", "Home Cooked! With Julie Goodwin", the comedy improv game show "Sleuth 101" as the host in 2010, "Statesmen of Comedy", "You Have Been Watching", "Good News Week", "Pictures of You", "Can of Worms", "QI", "The Unbelievable Truth", "Comedy Up Late", "Tractor Monkeys", "SlideShow", "Back Seat Drivers", "Fishcam", "The Chaser's Media Circus", "The Weekly with Charlie Pickering", "The Big Music Quiz", "Whose Line Is It Anyway? Australia", "Show Me the Movie!", "7 Days", "Behave Yourself!", "Whovians", "Hughesy, We Have a Problem", "Have You Been Paying Attention", "I'm a Celebrity, Get Me Out of Here!" as a contestant in 2022, "Spicks and Specks", "Celebrity Letters and Numbers", "Would I Lie to You?", "Who the Bloody Hell Are We?", and "The Great Australian Bake Off" as host in 2023. She was featured as Yelena in the television series "Street Legal" in 2000. She was also seen in episodes of "Duggan", "Flatmates", "Last Man Standing" as Nurse Vanderwert in 2005, "It's a Date", and "Kitty Is Not a Cat" as the voice of petal and Thorn from 2018 to 2019. She had a cameo role in the 2001 tele-film "Zenon: The Zequel" and appeared in the films "Orphans and Angles" (2003) and "Locks of Love" (2014). Wilson married Chris Woods in 2008 and is survived by him and their son.

Winding, Romain

French cinematographer Romain Winding died at his home in Ardeche, France, on July 20, 2023. He was 71. Winding was born in Boulogne-Billancourt, France, on December 25, 1951. His father was cinematograph Andreas Winding, and his mother was film editor Genevieve Winding. He began working in films in the early 1970s as an intern to his father for "A Time for Loving" (1972) and "Paulina 1980"

(1972). He was a second assistant cameraman for the films "The Infernal Trio" (1974), "Seven Deaths by Prescription" (1975), and "The Accuser" (1977). He was soon working as an assistant cameraman or camera operator for the films "A Young Emmanuelle" (1976), "L'Imprecateur" (1977), "The Bronte Sisters" (1979), "Laisse- Moi Rever" (1979), "French Postcards" (1979), "The Aviator's Wife" (1981), "A Good Marriage" (1982), "Entre Nois" (1983), "Liberty Belle" (1983), "Les Malheurs d'Octavie" (1983), and "Dandin" (1988). He served as cinematographer for the short films "Ne Me Parlez Plus Jamais d'Amour" (1981), "Les Atours de l'Oeil Foudre" (1982), "Ballades" (1983), and "Incognito" (1985), and a segment of "Paris Seen By... 20 Years After" (1984). His feature debut was 1987's "Yagmur Kacaklari". He was cinematographer for numerous films over the next thirty years including "Sound and Fury" (1988), "White Wedding" (1989), "Un Jeu d'Enfant" (1990), "La Discrete" (1990), "Celine" (1992), "The Stolen Diary" (1992), "Lettre Pour L..." (1993), "L'Ange Noir" (1994), "Consentement Mutuel" (1994), "Le Geographe Manuel" (1996), "Tire a Part" (1996), "Seventh Heaven" (1997) the first of seven films with director Benoit Jacquot, "Vicious Circles" (1997), "The Revengers' Comedies" (1998), "The Misadventures of Margaret" (1998), "Beautiful Mother" (1999), "Keep It Quiet" (1999), "La Fausse Suivante" (2000), "Workers for the Good Lord" (2000), "Room to Rent" (2000), "Tosca" (2001), "A Moment of Happiness" (2001), "Bienvenue Chez les Rozes" (2003), "Le Cou de la Girafe" (2004), "Tideline" (2004), "La Cloche a Sonne" (2005), "La Fille du Juge" (2006), "Le Candidat" (2007), "Je Vous Aime Tres Beaucoup" (2010), "When Pigs Have Wings" (2011), "Farewell, My Queen" (2012) winning a Cesar Award, "Looking for Hortense" (2012), "Being President" (2013), "Josephine" (2013), "Supercondriaque" (2014), "The Belier Family" (2014), and "Journal d'Une Femme de Chambre" (2015). Winding worked in television as a cinematographer for productions of "Bonjour la Galere" (1991), "Le Chasseur de la Nuit" (1993), "Devil's Game" (1994), "La Reve d'Esther" (1996), "Pigeon Vole" (1996), "Les Liens du Coeur" (1996), "On N'a Qu'une Vie" (2000), "L'Abaye du Revoir" (2004), "Eliane" (2005), "Gaspard le Bandit" (2006), "Pas Tout de Suite..." (2007), "Le Choix de Myriam" (2009), "Revivre" (2009), "The Counterfeiters" (2010), "La Maison des Rocheville" (2010), and "A l'Elysee" (2013). His other television credits include episodes of "Monologues", "Cuentos de Borges", "Master of the Spirits", "Sartre, Years of Passion", and "Clara Sheller". He is survived by his wife, Josiane, and two children.

Wingrove, Ian

British special effects artist Ian Wingrove, who received an Academy Award nomination for his work on the film "Return to Oz", died in England on December 30, 2023.

He was 79. Wingrove was born in Windsor, England, on March 15, 1944. He began working as a special effects technician in television in the mid-1960s for Gerry Anderson's series "Stingray", "Thunderbirds", and "UFO". He was an effects assistant on the 1971 film "The Last Valley" (1971) and the James Bond films "Live and Let Die" (1973) and "The Man with the Golden Gun" (1974). Wingrove continued to work on special effects for such films as "The Land That Time Forgot" (1974), "Shout at the Devil" (1976), "A Dirty Knight's Work" (1976), "At the Earth's Core" (1976), "A Bridge Too Far" (1977), "The People That Time Forgot" (1977), "Golden Rendezvous" (1977), "The Hound of the Baskervilles" (1978), "The Legacy" (1978), "The Deer Hunter" (1978), "The Great Train Robbery" (1978), "Game for Vultures" (1979), "The Long Good Friday" (1980), "Loophole" (1981), "The Final Conflict" (1981), "Reds" (1981), "Treasure of the Yankee Zephyr" (1981), "The Dark Crystal" (1982), "Return of the Jedi" (1983), "Never Say Never Again" (1983), "White Nights" (1985), "Return to Oz" (1985) sharing an Oscar nomination, "Sky Bandits" (1986), "Devil's Paradise" (1987), "Consuming Passions" (1988), "Without a Clue" (1988), "Henry V" (1989), "Diamond Skulls" (1989), "Edge of Sanity" (1989), "Chicago Joe and the Showgirl" (1990), "Hamlet" (1990), "Kafka" (1991), "Blame It on the Bellboy" (1992), "Four Weddings and a Funeral" (1994), "Princess Caraboo" (1994), "The Run of the Country" (1995), "Mission: Impossible" (1996), "Prince Valiant" (1997), "Mortal Kombat: Annihilation" (1997), "The Land Girls" (1998), "The Avengers" (1998), "Sleepy Hollow" (1999), "Black Hawk Down" (2001), "The Sleeping Dictionary" (2003), "The League of Extraordinary Gentlemen" (2003), "Troy" (2004), "Alien vs. Predator" (2004), "The Omen" (2006), "Flyboys" (2006), "Mirrors" (2008), "Blood Creek" (2009), "The Wolfman" (2010), and "Captain America: The First Avenger" (2011). Wingrove also designed special effects for the television series "The Protectors", "The Storyteller: Greek Myths", and "Monsignor Renard, and the tele-films "Lace II" (1985), "Doomsday Gun" (1994), and "A Christmas Reunion" (1994). He married Kathleen Dickens in 1968. They later divorced and he is survived by the son. He married Maggie Wingrove in 1974 and is also survived by her and their son, Gareth, who also worked in special effects.

Winsted, Keith

Actor and director Keith Winsted died of leukemia in Brooklyn, New York, on January 18, 2023. He was 57. Winsted was born in Russellville, Alabama, on August 9, 1965. He graduated from the University of Montevallo in Alabama. He moved to New York where he earned a master's degree in playwright from the Actors Studio Drama Program at the New School. He wrote such plays as "Cockfight", "The Perils of

Nadine", "Reel to Real", and "Not About Nathan". He was creator and director of the "Mister New York" (MRNY) short documentary interview series. He performed frequently on stage and was featured as Preacher John in the 2003 comedy horror film "Gory Gory Hallelujah". He also appeared in the film "Chicken" (2013) and the shorts "Fire Pit" (2011) and "The Red Marsh". Winsted produced, directed, and wrote the 2009 short "The Heartbreak of Acting". He became a professor of playwriting and acting at the Borough of Manhattan Community College in 2007. He was co-creator of the City University of New York (CUNY) Theatre Festival in 2015. Winsted is survived by his partner, Jeremy Pagirsky.

Winston, George

Pianist George Winston, who was noted for his instrumental piano solos, died of cancer in Williamsport, Pennsylvania, on June 4, 2023. He was 74. Winston was born in Hart, Michigan, on February 11, 1949. He was raised in

Montana, Mississippi, and Florida. He graduated from high school in Coral Gables, Florida, in 1967. He attended Stetson University in DeLand, Florida, but left before completing his studies. He began playing the piano in the early 1970s and made his debut album, "Piano Solos", with John Fahey's Takoma Records. He had success with his subsequent albums "Autumn" (1980), "Winter into Spring" (1982), and "December" (1982). He composed the score to the 1985 television production "Little Ears: The Velveteen Rabbit", narrated by Meryl Streep, which earned a Grammy nomination for Best Children's Music Album. He composed the music for the 1988 television mini-series "This Is America Charlie Brown". Winston's album "Forest" received a Grammy Award for Best New Age Album in 1996. His later albums "Plains" (1999) and "Montana: A Love Story" (2004) were also nominated in the new age category. He was a long-time fan of the work of Vince Guaraldi and released two albums in his honor, "Linus and Lucy: The Music of Vince Guaraldi" (1996) and "Love Will Come: The Music of Vince Guaraldi, Volume 2" (2020). He played the solo guitar soundtrack for the 1995 short film "Sadako and the Thousand Paper Cranes". He provided solo piano renditions for the 2002 album "Night Divides the Day - The Music of the Doors". Winston suffered from increasingly poor health due to various forms of cancer during the 2010s. He released the 2019 solo piano album "Restless Wind", and his final album, "Night", was released in 2022.

Woloshyn, Illya

Canadian actor Illya Woloshyn died suddenly at his home in Barrie, Ontario, Canada, on January 19, 2023. He was 43. Woloshyn was born in Toronto, Canada, in 1979. He began

his career on stage as a child, starring as Jacob in the 1986 production of "Jacob Two-Two Meets the Hooded Fang" at the Young People's Theatre in Toronto. He was featured as Gavroche in a production of "Les Miserables" at Toronto's Royal Alexandra Theatre in 1988. Woloshyn was featured in the films "The Last Season" (1989) and "I'll Never Get to Heaven" (1992), and the shorts "Exposed" (1989) and "Letters to a Street Child" (1999). He appeared on television in episodes of "Night Heat", "The Twilight Zone", "Friday the 13th: The Series", "War of the Worlds", "Forever Knight", "Are You Afraid of the Dark?", "The Kids in the Hall", and "Mythic Warriors: Guardians of the Legend". He was also seen in the tele-films "A Nest of Singing Birds" (1987), the animated "Johann's Gift to Christmas" (1991) as the voice of Johann, "Beethoven Lives Upstairs" (1992), "Hush Little Baby" (1994), and "Vanished Without a Trace" (1999). Woloshyn was best known for his role as Jay Ziegler in the children's fantasy series "The Odyssey" from 1992 to 1994. He retired from acting in the late 1990s.

Wood, Anita

Singer Anita Wood, who was Elvis Presley's girlfriend in the late 1950s, died of pneumonia at a hospital in Jackson,

Mississippi, on June 29, 2023. She was 85. Wood was born on May 27, 1938. She met Elvis Presley in 1957 and the two soon began dating. Elvis referred to her as his No. 1 Girl and they remained together until he went into the Army the following year. She recorded with ABC-Paramount in 1958 and performed on several episodes of the television series "The Chevy Showroom Starring Andy Williams". She also appeared on an episode of "The Tonight Show Starring Jack Paar". She later appeared in several documentaries about Presley including "Elvis: His Life and Times" (1993), "Presley" (1987), "The Definitive Elvis" (2002), and "There's Only One Elvis" (2002). Wood was married to football player Johnny Brewer from 1965 until his death in 2011 and they had three children together.

Wood, Bennett

Actor Bennett Wood, who was a leading figure in the Memphis, Tennessee, theatre community, died in League City, Texas, on September 3, 2023. He was 91. Wood was born in Mooreville, Mississippi, on July 12, 1932. He moved to

Memphis with his family as a child. He attended Yale University and returned to Memphis after his graduation. He began performing on the local stage in the 1950s and was a volunteer at Memphis Little Theatre, now Theatre Memphis, from 1952. He was an actor, director, stage manager, and held various other roles for nearly 70 years. He served on the theatre's board for over 30 years and was an editor of a book celebrating Theatre Memphis' 75th anniversary. He also acted and directed at Rhodes College's McCoy Theatre, the Memphis Shakespeare Festival, Front Street Theater, and Ballet Memphis. Wood was narrator for numerous documentaries by local filmmaker Willy Bearden and was heard in regional museums including the Cotton Museum, the Elvis Presley Birthplace Museum, and the Tunica River Museum. Wood was featured in several films including "The Old Forest" (1985) and "The People vs. Larry Flynt" (1996). Wood also worked as a copywriter and advertising executive for nearly forty years. He remained in Memphis until December of 2022 when he moved to League City, Texas, to be closer to his sister.

Wood, Dee Dee

Choreographer Dee Dee Wood died in Cave Creek, Arizona, on April 26, 2023. She was 95. She was born Audrey Wood Donella in Boston, Massachusetts, on June 7, 1927. She took ballet while in high school studied at the School of American Ballet. She joined Katherine Dunham's

Experimental Dance Group and began her career as a dancer in New York City. She performed in such Broadway plays as "Can-Can" (1953) and "Li'l Abner" (1953). She married fellow dancer Marc Breaux in 1955 and they served as assistants to choreographer Michael Kidd on the 1959 musical "Destry Rides Again" (1959). She and Breaux choreographed the musical comedy "Do Re Mi" in 1960. The couple choreographed for numerous television variety series and specials in the 1960s and early 1970s including "Coke Time", "The United States Steel Hour", "The Bell Telephone Hour", "The Andy Williams Show", "The Judy Garland Show", "The Bing Crosby Show", "The Danny Thomas Special", "The Hollywood Palace", "ABC Stage '67", "The King Family Show", "Debbie Reynolds and the Sound of Children", "Burlesque Is Alive and Living in Beautiful Downtown Burbank", and 1972's "If Thee I Sing". She and Breaux were choreographers for the films "Li'l Abner" (1959), "Mary Poppins (1964), "The Sound of Music" (1965), "The Happiest Millionaire" (1967), and "Chitty Chitty Bang Bang" (1968). The couple divorced in the early 1970s and both

continued to choreograph separately. Wood worked on such television productions as "The Shape of Things", "Cher", "John Denver and Friend", 1978's "Benji's Very Own Christmas Story", "Pat Boone and Family Easter Special", "The Billy Crystal Comedy Hour", "The Love Boat", "Los Angeles 1984: Games of the XXIII Olympiad", "Grand Ole Opry 60th Anniversary" in 1986, "Las Vegas: An All-Star 75th Anniversary", "Disneyland's All-Star Comedy Circus" in 1988, and "Dream On". She also choreographed three Super Bowl halftime shows and the films "In God We Trust" (1980) and "Beaches" (1988). She shared an Emmy Award for Outstanding Achievement in Choreography for her work on the closing ceremonies for the televised 100th Anniversary of the Statue of Liberty in 1986. Wood's survivors include her son, Michael Breaux.

Wood, Oliver

British cinematographer Oliver Wood died of cancer at his home in Los Angeles, California, on February 13, 2023.

He was 80. Wood was born in London, England, on February 21, 1942. He moved to New York City in the early 1960s to pursue a career in films. He served as an assistant cameraman on the 1968 film "A Little of What You Fancy". He was cinematographer for the science fiction musical "Popdown" in 1969. Wood was cinematographer or director of photography for numerous films including "The Honeymoon Killer" (1970), "Danny" (1979), "Don't Go in the House" (1979), "Feedback" (1979), "Maya" (1981), "The Returning" (1983), "Alphabet City" (1984), "The Sex O'Clock News" (1985), "Joey" (1986), "Neon Maniacs" (1986), "Die Hard 2" (1990), "The Adventures of Ford Fairlane" (1990), "Bill & Ted's Bogus Journey" (1991), "Hammerin' Home" (1992), "Mystery Date" (1991), "Rudy" (1993), "For Love or Money" (1993), "Sister Act 2: Back in the Habit" (1993), "Terminal Velocity" (1994), "Mr. Holland's Opus" (1995), "Celtic Pride" (1996), "2 Days in the Valley" (1996), "Face/Off" (1997), "Switchback" (1997), "Mighty Joe Young" (1998), "U-571" (2000), "The Bourne Identity" (2002), "The Adventures of Pluto Nash" (2002), "I Spy" (2002), "National Security" (2003), "Freaky Friday" (2003), "Scooby-Doo 2: Monsters Unleashed" (2004), "The Bourne Supremacy" (2004), "Fantastic Four" (2005), "Talladega Nights: The Ballad of Ricky Bobby" (2006), "The Bourne Ultimatum" (2007) earning a BAFTA Award nomination, "Step Brothers" (2008), "Surrogates" (2009), "The Other Guys" (2010) also appearing onscreen in the role of Captain Salty, "Safe House" (2012), "2 Guns" (2013), "Anchorman 2: The Legend Continues" (2013), "Two Plans, Two Sisters & a Parade" (2014), "Child 44" (2015), "The Brothers Grimsby" (2016), "Ben-Hur" (2016), "Jack Reacher: Never Go Back" (2016), "The Equalizer 2" (2018), "Holmes & Watson" (2018), and "Morbius" (2022). He was also a camera operator for the films "Fat Chance" (1981), "In Our Hands"

(1983), "Body Rock" (1984), "Death of an Angel" (1985), and "Seven Minutes in Heaven" (1986). Wood provided additional or second unit photography for "Q: The Winged Serpent" (1982), "Rappin'" (1985), "Quiet Cool" (1986), "Hoosiers" (1986), "Cutthroat Island" (1995), "Breach" (2007), "The Town" (2010), "Little Fockers" (2010), "Battle Los Angeles" (2011), "Wrath of the Titans" (2012), and "Bird Box" (2018). He was cinematographer for numerous episodes of the television series "Miami Vice" from 1986 to 1989. He also worked on the tele-films "City Boy" (1985), "Nasty Hero" (1987), and "Angel City" (1991). Wood was married to Andy Warhol superstar Jane Forth for 22 years before their divorce and is survived by their two daughters, Katharine and Fiona. He later married costumer Sabine Groth and she also survives him.

Woodruff, Teeuwynn

Role-playing game designer Teeuwynn Woodruff died of cardiac arrest in Bellevue, Washington, on August 28, 2023. She was 56. Woodruff was born in Philadelphia, Pennsylvania, on October 25, 1966. She graduated from Widener University with a double major in psychology and sociology. She began

working in role-playing games in the early 1990s after sending some material to TSR for their "Advanced Dungeons & Dragons" game. She also wrote for West End Games' "Galitia Citybook" for "Bloodshadows" and "Indiana Jones and the Tomb of the Templars". Woodruff was hired by White Wolf in 1993 as their first female game designer.

She wrote "World of Darkness: Gypsies" and contributed to their games "Vampire: The Masquerade", "Werewolf: The Apocalypse", "Mage: The Ascension", and "Wrath: The Oblivion". She moved to Seattle in 1995 to work for Wizards of the Coast. She worked on numerous projects including "Battle Tech", "Magic: The Gathering", "Netrunner", "Duel Masters", "Dreamblade", and the "Pokemon Trading Card Game". She worked on Avalon Hill's "Betrayal at the House on the Hill" in 2004. Woodruff formed Lone Shark Games in 2005 and specialized in creating large puzzles for corporate events. She also interviewed participants for the television reality shows "The Amazing Race" and "Survivor" for the RealityNewsOnline website. Woodruff is survived by her husband, Mike Cooper, and sons Griffin, Frost, and Ember.

Woodward, Tim

British actor Tim Woodward died of cancer in England on November 9, 2023. He was 70. Woodward was born in Kensington, London, England, on April 24, 1953. He was the son of actors Edward Woodward and Venetia Barrett. His siblings, Peter Woodward and Sarah Woodward, also became actors. Tim attended the Haileybury and Imperial Service College and trained as an actor at the Royal Academy of Dramatic Art in London. Woodward appeared frequently on

television from the mid-1970s with roles in episodes of "Play for Today", "Within These Walls", "The Expert", "The Cost of Loving", "Wings" as Alan Farmer from 1976 to 1978, "BBC2

Playhouse", "Q.E.D.", "Tales of the Unexpected", "Cousin Phillis" as Edward Holdsworth in 1982, "The Irish R.M.", "Spooky", "Crown Court", "Father's Day", "The Equalizer", "Families" as John Thompson from 1990 to 1991, "Absolutely Fabulous", "The Good Guys", "Pie in the Sky", "The Governor" as Mr. Turnbull in 1996, "Ruth Rendell Mysteries", "Bramwell", "Space Island One", "The Vice", "In Defence", "Silent Witness", "Outside the Rules", "New Tricks", "Crossroads" as Bishop Black in 2003, "Midsomer Murders", "William and Mary", "Murphy's Law", "Space Race", "Rosemary & Thyme", "Poirot", "Murder City" as DCI Turner from 2004 to 2006, "Vital Signs", "The Bill", "Heartbeat", "Casualty 1909", "Doctors", "MI-5", "Mr. Selfridge" as Musker in 2013, "Mad Dogs" in the recurring role of Dominic from 2011 to 2013, "Genius", "Vera", "Peaky Blinders", "Casualty", and "Agatha Raisin". His other television credits include productions of "Prometheus: The Life of Balzac" (1975), "Chips with Everything" (1975), "French Without Tears" (1976), "Frost in May" (1982), "East Lynne" (1982), "Partners in Crime" (1983), "The Files of Jill Hatch" (1983), "The Case of the Frightened Lady" (1983), "All the World's a Stage" (1984), "Pope John Paul II" (1984), "Lady Windermere's Fan" (1985), "A Killing on the Exchange" (1987), "Piece of Cake" (1988), "Uncle Silas" (1989), "Iphigenia at Aulis" (1990), "Traitors" (1990), "MacGyver: Lost Treasure of Atlantis" (1994), "Go Back Out" (1995), "Prime Suspect: The Scent of Darkness" (1995), "David" (1997), "Holding On" (1997), "Heat of the Sun" (1998), "Vanity Fair" (1998), "The Colour of Justice" (1999), "RKO 281" (1999), "Blue Murder" (2000), "Murder Rooms: Mysteries of the Real Sherlock Holmes" (2001), ""The Second Coming" (2003), "Danielle Cable: Eyewitness" (2003), "Nuremberg: Nazis on Trial" (2006), "Clapham Junction" (2007), "He Kills Coppers" (2008), "Hunter" (2009), "The Fattest Man in Britain" (2009), "Any Human Heart" (2010), "Without You" (2011), "Fleming" (2014) as Air Chief Marshall 'Bomber' Harris, "Houdini" (2014), "Jekyll and Hyde" (2015) as Sir Marion Carew, and "Decline and Fall" (2017). Woodward was also seen in numerous films including "Galileo" (1975), "The Europeans" (1979), "King David" (1985), "Salome" (1986), "Personal Services" (1987), "Passion & Paradise: Part 2" (1989), "Closing Numbers" (1993), "The Scarlet Letter" (1995), "Some Mother's Son" (1996), "The House of Angelo" (1997), "B. Monkey" (1998), "K-19: The Widowmaker" (2002), "Pierrepoint: The Last Hangman" (2005), "Flight of Fury" (2007), "Legend" (2015), "London Has Fallen" (2016), "Criminal" (2016), "Beast" (2017), "The Marine 6: Close Quarters" (2018), "Radioactive" (2019), and "Denmark" (2019). Woodward married Amanda Smith in 1997 and is survived by her and their three children. He is also survived by a son with actress Jan Campbell and a daughter with Kate Barnwell.

Woudenberg, Helmert

Dutch actor Helmert Woudenberg died of a heart attack in Amsterdam, the Netherlands, on November 23, 2023. He was 78. Woudenberg was born in Elspe, Germany, on February 15, 1945, and was raised by a foster family in  Hilversum, the Netherlands, after his father was killed during World War II. He trained as an actor at the Amsterdam Theater School, graduating in 1968. He was a founder of the theater collective Het Werkteater the following year. He performed on stage throughout his career and taught his improvisational acting style in the training course Studio5. Woudenberg appeared frequently in films from the early 1970s with roles in "Blue Movie" (1971), "Wat Zien Ik" (1971), "Daniel" (1971), "VD" (1972), "Frank & Eva" (1973), "Because of the Cats" (1973), "Dakota" (1974), "Alicia" (1974), "Mens Erge Je Niet" (1975), "De Laatste Trein" (1975), "Alle Dagen Feest" (1976), "Max Havelaar" (1976), "Barocco" (1976), "Toestanden" (1976), "Eeen Radiodroom" (1976), "Doctor Vlimmen" (1977), "Camping" (1978), "Opname" (1979), "Rigor Mortis" (1981), "Two Queens and One Consort" (1981), "Een Zwoele Zomeravond" (1982), "Parfait Amour" (1985), the horror film "Amsterdamned" (1988) as the Chief Commissioner, "Zwerfsters" (1989), "Godforsaken" (2003), "Polleke" (2003), "Ellis in Glamourland" (2004), "Paid" (2006), "'n Beetje Verliefd" (2006), "Kicks" (2007), "Matterhorn" (2013), and "Secrets of War" (2014). He was seen on television in productions of "Woyzeck" (1972), "Diagnose - Wat is er Aan de Hand Met Misdaad?" (1974), "De Wilde Eend" (1981), "Avandrood" (1981), "Ons Soort Mensen" (1988), "De Laatste Held" (1993), "Maten" (1999), "Bij Ons in de Jordaan" (2000), and "Fred" (2000). His other television credits include episodes of "We Zijn Weer Thuis" as Dr. Paalhof in 1990, "Niemand de Deur Uit!", "Het Labyrint", "Loenatik", "De Keerzijde", "Otje", "Wilhelmina", "De Vloer Op", "Russen", "Hartslag", "Baantjer", "Spoorloos Verdwenen", "Keyzer & De Boer Advocaten", "Flikken Maastricht" as Eugene Hoeben from 2008 to 2010, "Feuten", and "Dokter Tinus". Woudenberg had two sons with actress Marja Kok.

Wright, Gary

Musician and songwriter Gary Wright, who was the keyboardist and singer for the band Spooky Tooth and wrote the hit song "Dream Weaver", died of complications from Lewy Body dementia and Parkinson's disease at his home in Palos Verde, Estates, California, on September 4, 2023. He was 80. Wright was born in Cresskill, New Jersey, on April 26, 1943. He began his career as a child actor, appearing the the juvenile science fiction series "Captain Video and His Video Rangers" in 1950. He also appeared in the Broadway play  "Fanny" in 1954. He soon abandoned acting but became involved with music while attending high school. He and his friend, Bill Markle, formed the duo Gary and Billy and released the single "Working After School". He attended college at William & Mary in Virginia before transferring to New York University to study medicine. He graduated in 1965 and moved to West Germany to attend the Free University of Berlin. He abandoned his medical ambitions to return to music and formed the band the New York Times. They toured Europe supporting the band Traffic. Wright was invited to London where he joined pianist Mike Harrison and drummer Mike Kellie in the band Art. They soon changed their name to Spooky Tooth and Wright served as joined lead vocalist and keyboard player. Their first album, "It's All About", was released in 1968, and was followed by "Spooky Two" in 1969. Wright composed most of the band's songs including "Sunshine Help Me", "That Was Only Yesterday", and "Better by You, Better Than Me". He left Spooky Tooth in early 1970 after the release of their third album "Ceremony". He recorded the 1970 album "Extraction" that included the songs "Get on the Right Road" and "The Wrong Time". He was invited to play on George Harrison's 1970 triple album "All Things Must Pass". He and Harrison became close friends and he played on most of his subsequent albums. He played keyboard on Ringo Starr's hits "It Don't Come Easy" and "Back Off Boogaloo" in the early 1970s. Wright formed the band Wonderwheel in 1971 and recorded the album "Footprint". The band appeared on "The Dick Cavett Show" and performed the song "Two Faced Man" with George Harrison on slide guitar. He wrote the soundtrack for the 1972 film "Benjamin". He soon disbanded Wonderwheel and reformed Spooky Tooth with Mike Harrison, Wonderwheel members Mick Jones on guitar and Bryson Graham on drums, and bassist Chris Stewart. The new version of Spooky Tooth released with 1973 album "You Broke My Heart So I Busted Your Jaw", which included Wright's songs "Cotton Growing Man", "Wildfire", and "Self Seeking Man". Graham left the group later in the year and original drummer Mike Kellie returned for the 1973 album "Witness". His association with George Harrison led to his adopting Eastern mysticism after the two went to India in 1974. The experience became an important part of his life and music. He recorded a final album with Spooky Tooth, "The Mirror", before again disbanding in 1974. Wright signed with Warner Bros. for his 1975 solo album "The Dream Weaver". The album primarily used keyboard instruments including synthesizers instead of guitars. Wright became one of the first musicians to perform with a portable keyboard for the subsequent tour. The album's single, "Dream Weaver", became a major hit. His association with Eastern mysticism deeply influenced his next album,

1977's "The Light of Smiles". He was featured in a cameo role in the 1978 film "Sgt. Pepper's Lonely Hearts Club Band". He had limited success with his subsequent albums from Warner including "Touch and Gone" (1977), "Headin' Home" (1979), and "The Right Place" (1981) which had the popular single "Really Wanna Know You". He worked frequently in films from the 1980s, scoring the 1982 thriller "Endangered Species" and the skiing film "Fire and Ice" in 1986. He wrote the song "Hold on to Your Vision" for the 1986 Sylvester Stallone film "Cobra" and "Am I the One" for the surf movie "North Shore" in 1987. Wright re-recorded his hit song "Dream Weaver" for the comedy film "Wayne's World" in 1992. He released albums including "Who I Am" (1988), "First Signs of Life" (1995), and "Human Love" (1999). He reunited with Harrison and Kellie for the 2004 Spooky Tooth reunion tour and the album "Nomad Poets Live in Germany" (2007). He toured with Ringo Starr & His All-Star Band in 2008 and 2010. His later albums include "Waiting to Catch the Light" (2008) and "Connected" (2010). His autobiography, "Dream Weaver: Music, Meditation, and My Friendship with George Harrison", was released in 2014. Wright was divorced from Dori Accordino and Christina Uppstrom, who was also known as Tina Wright, and is survived by their sons, Dorian and Justin. He married Rose Anthony in 1985 and she also survives him.

Wright, John

Film editor John Wright died of cancer in Calabasas, California, on April 20, 2023. He was 79. Wright was born in Glendale, California, in 1943. He began working in films in the

1970s and served as an assistant film editor for "The Bad News Bears" in 1976. He also served as editor of the spaceship sequences for 1985's "Explorers" and was additional editor for the films "Sea of Love" (1989) and "Freejack" (1992). Wright was editor for the films "Acapulco Gold" (1976), "Dogs" (1977), "Life Goes to War: Hollywood and the Home Front" (1977), "Convoy" (1978), "Separate Ways" (1981), "Only When I Laugh" (1981), "Frances" (1982), "Mass Appeal" (1984), "The Running Man" (1987), "Gleaming the Cube" (1989), "The Hunt for Red October" (1990) sharing an Academy Award nomination, "Teenage Mutant Ninja Turtles II: The Secret of the Ooze" (1991), "Necessary Roughness" (1991), "Last Action Hero" (1993), "Speed" (1994) receiving another Oscar nomination, "Die Hard with a Vengeance" (1995), "Broken Arrow" (1996), "Deep Rising" (1998), "The Thomas Crown Affair" (1999), "The 13th Warrior" (1999), "X-Men" (2000), "Rollerball" (2002), Mel Gibson's "The Passion of the Christ" (2004), "Glory Road" (2006), Gibson's "Apocalypto" (2006), "The Incredible Hulk" (2008), "Secretariat" (2010), "A Belfast Story" (2013), and "Heaven Is Real" (2014). Wright was editor for the television productions of "Cruise Into Terror" (1978), "The Corn Is Green" (1979), "Sanctuary of Fear" (1979), "Blind

Ambition" (1979), "The Family Man" (1979), "The Women's Room" (1980), "Crisis at Central High" (1981), "Heartsounds"(1984), "Double Switch" (1987), "My Name Is Bill W." (1989) sharing an Emmy Award nomination, and "Sarah, Plain and Tall" (1991) receiving the Emmy Award. His other television credits include episodes of "The Paper Chase", and "Amazing Stories". Wright is survived by his wife of 57 years, Jane, and a son and daughter.

Wyatt, Bray

Professional wrestler Windham Rotunda, who was best known for his work with World Wrestling Entertainment (WWE) under the name Bray Wyatt, died of a heart attack in Clearmont, Florida, on August 24, 2023. He was 36. Rotunda was born in Brooksville, Florida, on May 23, 1987. He was the son of wrestler Mike Rotunda (aka Irwin R. Schyster (IRS) & V.K. Wallstreet) and Stephanie Windham. His grandfather was

leading wrestler Blackjack Mulligan and his uncles were Barry and Kendall Windham. His younger brother, Taylor Rotunda, wrestled in the WWE under the name Bo Dallas. He began competing with Florida Championship Wrestling (FCW) in 2009 under the names Alex Rotundo and Duke Rotundo.

He brother joined the promotion several years later as Bo Rotundo and they captures the FCW Florida Tay Team Championship. He joined the WWE developmental television competition show NXT under the name Husky Harris in 2010. He continued to wrestle at FCW under the Husky Harris name and feuded with Percy Watson. He made his debut in WWE at the Hell in a Cell pay-per-view in October of 2010 and soon joined Wade Barrett's faction the Nexus. He remained in the WWE until January of 2011 when he was written off television after being badly beaten by Randy Orton. He returned to FCW and reteamed with his brother to feud with Lucky Cannon and Damien Sandow. He lost several matches for the FCW championship and feuded with Richie Steamboat. He and his brother recaptured the FCW tag titles in February of 2012 but lost the belts the following month. Rotunda became known as Bray Wyatt in April of 2012 and competed with the WWE's repackaging of FCW as NXT. He teamed with Luke Harper and Erick Rowan as the cultish Wyatt Family and began appearing in a series of bizarre vignettes on WWE Raw. They began making attacks on Kane and other WWE wrestlers. They feuded with Daniel Bryan, John Cena, and Chris Jericho. Wyatt began a feud with Dean Ambrose in late 2014 without the rest of the Wyatt Family. He also unsuccessfully challenged the Undertaker. He reunited with Luke Harper in 2015, battling Roman Reigns and Dean Ambrose and the team of the New Day. They were soon joined by Braun Strowman as part of the family. He parted with Harper and Strowman and began teaming with Randy Orton in 2016. The duo defeated Heath Slater and Rhyno for the SmackDown Tag Team Championship in December of 2016 for a brief reign. Wyatt won the WWE Championship in an Elimination Chamber match in February of 2017. He was defeated for the title for Orton at WrestleMania 33 in April of 2017. He continued to feud with such wrestlers as Seth Rollins, Finn Balor, and Matt Hardy. He soon began to team with Hardy and they won the vacant Raw Tag Team Championship in April of 2018. They lost the belts

three months later to Bo Dallas and Curtis Axel. Wyatt began dropping another series of bizarre vignettes in April of 2019 and presented himself as the host of the children's program "Firefly Fun House". He was soon wearing a demonic mask and became known as the Fiend. He defeated Set Rollins for the Universal Championship in October of 2019. He feuded with the Miz and Daniel Bryan before losing the title to Goldberg in February of 2020. He won the belt from former partner Brawn Strowman the following August but relinquished the belt to Roman Reigns in a triple threat match later in the month. He began working with female wrestler Alexa Bliss and renewed his feud with Randy Orton. Wyatt was released from the WWE in July of 2021. Another series of vignettes ushered in the return of Wyatt in October of 2022 along with various Firefly Fun House characters including the masked Uncle Howdy. He feuded with LA Knight and began a feud with Bobby Lashley before failing health ended his wrestling run. He was the subject of the 2024 biofilm "Bray Wyatt: Becoming Immortal". He was married to Samantha Krieger from 2012 until their divorce in 2017 and is survived by their two daughters, Kendyl and Cadyn. He was subsequently involved with WWE announcer JoJo Offerman and is survived by her, their son Knash Sixx, and their daughter Hyrie Von.

Yale, Stan

Actor Stan Yale died on July 3, 2023. He was 86. Yale was born in Queens, New York, on January 26, 1937. He

was a character actor in films and television from the late 1970s, often playing bums and street people. His film credits include "Gas City" (1978), "Rhinestone" (1984), "The Terminator" (1984), "A Minor Miracle" (1985), "House" (1985), "Terminal Exposure" (1987), "P.I. Private Investigations" (1987), "Two Idiots in Hollywood" (1988), "Watchers II" (1990), "Party Plane" (1991), F.A.R.T.: The movie" (1991), "Dead On: Relentless II" (1992), "Trancers III" (1992), "Monolith" (1993), "The Force" (1994), "Save Me" (1994), "Bad Blood" (1994), "Persons Unknown" (1996), and "Living in Peril" (1997). Yale appeared on television in episodes of "Hill Street Blues", "Hot

Pursuit", "It's Your Move", "General Hospital", "Moonlighting", "Matlock", "L.A. Law", "Dragnet", "The Bold and the Beautiful", "In Living Color", "Madman of the People", "Guideposts Junction", "Sabrina the Teenage Witch", "The Pretender", "Black Scorpion", "Nikki", "Judging Amy", and "My Name Is Earl". His other television credits include the tele-films "The Other Side of Hell" (1978), "Hell Town" (1985), and "The Children of Times Square" (1986).

Yamamoto, Nizo

Japanese art director Nizo Yamamoto, who worked on numerous animated films with Hayao Miyazaki, died of stomach cancer in Hanno City, Japan, on August 19, 2023. He

was 70. Yamamoto was born in Goto City, Japan, on June 27, 1953. He began working in anime in the 1970s at Ad Cosmo and joined Nippon Animation by 1978. He was involved with such animated productions as "Conan: The Boy in the Future" (1978), "Anne of Green Gables" (1979), "The Castle of Cagliostro" (1979), "Chie the Brat" (1981), "Sherlock Hound" (1984), and "Little Nomo - Adventures in Slumberland" (1989). Yamamoto joined Studio Ghibli in 1985 and is noted for his work for films from directors Hayao Miyazaki and Isao Takahata including "Castle in the Sky" (1986), "Grave of the Fireflies" (1988), "Only Yesterday" (1991), "Whisper of the Heart" (1995), "Princess Mononoke" (1997), and "Spirited Away" (2001). He left Studio Ghibli in the early 2000s and was founder of the animation company Kaieisha. His later work as a background artist includes "Fullmetal Alchemist the Movie: Conqueror of Shamballa" (2005), "Highlander: The Search for Vengeance" (2007), "Mai Mai Miracle" (2009), "Welcome to the Space Show" (2010), and "Rainbow Fireflies" (2012). He directed the 2007 animated tele-film "Miyori's Forest".

Yarwood, Mike

British comedian and impressionist Mike Yarwood died at Brinsworth House, the actor's retirement home in Tuickenham, London, England, on September 8, 2023. He was

82. Yarwood was born in Bredbury, Cheshire, England, on June 14, 1941. He left secondary school in his teens and worked at odd jobs including a messenger and garment salesman. He tried his hand at comedy and was a runner-up at a talent show at a pub in Dunkinfield. He was noted for his impressions and began touring clubs in Northern England. He began working in television in 1963 with the comedy revue series "Comedy Bandbox". He impersonated such stars as Frankie Howerd, Max Bygrave,

Michael Crawford, and Ken Dodd, as well as political figures including Prince Charles, Harold Wilson, James Callaghan, Denis Healey, and Edward Heath. He continued to appear in such series as "Club Night", "Let's Laugh", "Tom Jones!", "The London Palladium Show", "Cilla", "Billy Cotton Band Show", "Three of a Kind", "A Spoonful of Sugar", the comedy series "Will the Real Mike Yarwood Stand Up?" which he hosted from 1968 to 1969, "Anything You Can Do", "It's Lulu", "The Golden Shot", "Crowther's Back in Town", "A Question of Sport", "An Hour With...", "The Royal Variety Performance", "We Want to Sing", "What's My Line?", the series "Look, Mike Yarwood!" which he starred in from 1971 to 1976, "Saturday Night at the Mill", "The Jack Jones Show", "Multi-Coloured Swap Shop", "Parkinson", "Mike Yarwood in Persons" from 1976 to 1978, the 1977 special "The Mile Yarwood Christmas Show", "Friday Night, Saturday Morning", "The Generation Game", "Sunday, Sunday", "Aspel & Company", "Mike Yarwood in Persons" from 1982 to 1987, "Wogan", "Des O'Connor Tonight", "Comic Relief", "Bruce Forsyth's Generation Game", "This Is Your Life", "Esther", "Have I Got News for You", and "Heroes of Comedy". Yarwood's career largely ended by the early 2000s due to problems with anxiety and depression. His autobiography, "And This Is Me!", was released in 1975. Yarwood was married to actress Sandra Burville from 1969 until their divorce in 1985 and is survived by their daughters, Charlotte and Clare.

Yasulovich, Igor

Russian actor Igor Yasulovich died in Russia on August 19, 2023. He was 81. Yasulovich was born in Reinsfeld (now Zalesye), Koshkinsky District, Russia, on September 24, 1941. He studied as an actor with the Gerasimov Institute of Cinematography, graduating in 1962. He soon began performing in experimental theater. He was seen frequently in films from the early 1960s with roles in "Nine Days of One Year" (1962), "Posledniy Khleb" (1963), "Cherez Kladbishche" (1965), "Pomni, Kaspar!" (1965), "Vremya, Vperyod!" (1965), "Gorod Masterov" (1966), "Pervyy Posetitel" (1966), "Pedejais Bledis" (1966), "Aybolit-66" (1967), "Ne Samyy Udachnyy Den" (1967), "Net i Da" (1967), "Arena" (1967), "The Golden Calf" (1968), "The Diamont Arm" (1969), "Semeynoe Schaste" (1970), "Waterloo" (1970), "Twelve Chairs" (1971), "Chelovek s Drugoy Storony" (1972), "Ekhali v Tramvaye Lif i Petrov" (1972), "Boy Posle Pobedy" (1972), "Mogila Iva" (1972), "Fuslan i Lyudmila" (1972), "Bez Trokh Minut Rovno" (1972), "Privalovskiye Miliony" (19763), "Za Oblakami - Nebo" (1973), "Parashuty Na Derevyakh" (1973), "Kazhdyy Den Doktora Kelinnikovoy" (1974), "It Can't Be!" (1975), "Chudo s Kosichkami" (1976), "Tam, Za Gorizontom" (1976), "Legenda o Tile" (1977), "100 Gramm Dlya Khrabrosti" (1977), "Front Za Liniey Fronta" (1978), "Pol Ulitsam Komod Vodili..."

(1978), "Life Is Beautiful" (1979), "V Odno Prekrasnoye Detstvo" (1980), "Odnazhdy Dvadtsat Let Spustya" (1981), the science fiction film "To the Stars by Hard Ways" (1981), "Kto Zaplatit Ze Udachu?" (1981), "Tovarishch Innokentiy" (1981), "Predchuvstviye Lyubvi" (1982), "Ostavit Sled" (1983), "Po Zakonam Voennogo Vremeni" (1983), "I Don't Want to Be a Grown-Up" (1983), "Pokhozhdeniya Grafa Nevsorova" (1983), "K Svoim!" (1983), "Nezhdanno-Negadann" (1983), "Vitya Glushakov, Drug Apachey" (1983), "Polosa Vezeniya" (1983), "Molodye Lyudi" (1983), "Shans" (1984), "Zudov, vy Uvoleny" (1984), "Vosem Dney Nadezhdy" (1984), "No More Jokes!" (1985), "Gorod Nevest" (1985), "Zhil Otvazhnyy Kapitan" (1985), "Tantsy Na Kryshe" (1985), "Kak Stat Scfhastlivym" (1986), the fantasy film "Mio in the Land of Faraway" (1987), "Silnee Vsekh Inykh Veleniy" (1987), "Lilac Ball" (1988), "Lovkachi" (1988), "Drug" (1988), "Rokovaya Oshibka" (1989), "Kriminalnyy Kvartet" (1989), "His Nickname Is Beast" (1990), the science fiction film "The Witches Cave" (aka "Podzemelye Vedm") (1990), "Ay Lav Yu, Petrovich" (1990), "Scarlet Flower" (1991), "Sestrichki Liberti" (1991), "Chyornyy Kvadrat" (1992), "Byron: Ballad for a Daemon" (1992), "Den Russiske Sangerinde" (1993), "Osennie Soblazny" (1993), "Marquis de Sade" (1996), "Melankaya Printsessa" (1997), "Ne Poslat li Nam... Gontsa?" (1998), "Dazhe Ne Dumay!" (2003), "White Gold" (2004), "4 Taxidrivers and a Dog" (2004), "Barabashka" (2004), "Statskiy Sovetnik" (2005), "Treasure Raiders" (2007), "Wind Man" (2007), "Sad" (2008), "Chetyre Vozrasta Lyubvi" (2008), "Probka" (2009), "Spasti Pushkina" (2017), "Korotkie Volny" (2017), "Tri Sestry" (2017), "Convoy 48" (2019), "Dorogoy Papa" (2019), "Kniga Zhizni" (2021), and "Dobro Ooizhalovat v Semyu" (2022). He directed several films including "Everyone Dreams About a Dog" (1975), "He Is Missing and Found" (1976), and "Hello, River!" (1978). Yasulovich also appeared on television in productions of "Teper Pust Ukhodit" (1963), "Schit i Mech" (1968), "...I Snova May!" (1968), "O Druzyakh-Tovarishchakh" (1970), "Peterburg" (1971), "Obratnoy Dorogi net" (1971), "31 Iyunya" (1978), "The Very Same Munchausen" (1980), "Sem Schastlivkykh Not" (1981), "Otpusk Za Svoy Schyot" (1982), "Kafedra" (1982), "Assol" (1982), "Chelovek Iz Strany Grin" (1983), "Meri Poppins, do Svidaniya" (1984), "Guest from the Future" (1984), "Dom Na Dyunakh" (1987), "Midshipmen, Onwards!" (1988), "Artistka Iz Gribova" (1988), "Prestuplenie Lorda Artura" (1993), "Grafinya Sheremeteva" (1994), "Koroli Rossiykogo Syska" (1994), "Tribunal" (1995), "Volshebnoe Kreslo" (1996), "Chasy Bez Strelok" (2001), "Kamenskaya: Ya Umer Vchera" (2002), "The State Counsellor" (2005), "Brezhnev" (2005) as Mikhail Suslov, "Devyat Neizvestnykh" (2006), "Poroki i Ikh Poklonniki" (2006), "Vyiti Zamuzh Za Generala" (2008), "When We Were Happy" (2009), "Okhotniki Za Brilliantami" (2011), "Krasotka" (2013), "I'll Overcome Everything I'll Overcome Everything" (2014), "Mosgaz: Formula Mesti" (2019), and "Sedmaya Simfoniya" (2021). His other television credits include episodes of "Fuse", "Mayor 'Vikhr'", "Peterburgskie Tayny" as Yuzica from 1994 to 1996, "Koroleva Margo", "Volshebnoe Kreslo", "Razvyazka Peterburgskikh

Tayn" reprising his role as Yuzicz in 1998, "Kamenskaya - 1", "Dose Detektiva Dubrovskogo", "Rostov-papa", "Kamenskaya - 2", "Moskva, Tsentralnyy Okrug", "Sibirochka", "Adyutanty Lyubvi" as Graf von der Pahlen in 2005, "Schastye Ty Moyo", "Geroy Nashego Vremeni", "Fotograf", "Vsegda Govori Vsegda" (2009), "Poor Relatives" as Ustin Demidko in 2012, "Tvoy Mir", "Pandora", "The Blood Lady" as Ts Itsianov" in 2018, "The Diplomat" as Luchnikov Sr. in 2019, "Two Sisters", and "Dokumentalist. Okhotnik za Prizrakami". Yasulovich married Natazlia Egorova in 1963 and is survived by her and their son, Alexey Yasulovich.

Yoda, Yoshio

Japanese-American actor Yoshio Yoda, who was featured as Fuji in the television series "McHale's Navy", died in Fullerton, California, on January 13, 2023. He was 88. Yoda was born in Tokyo, Japan, on March 31, 1934. He studied law at Keio University before deciding to come to the United States and pursue an acting career. He enrolled at the University of Southern California in 1958 with the intention of becoming a film producer. His acting career began when MGM approached the faculty about a young man fluent in Japanese and English. Yoda was subsequently cast as Sgt. Roy Tada in the 1962 film "The Horizontal Lieutenant". He soon joined the cast of the military comedy series "McHale's Navy" as Imperial Japanese Navy Seaman 3rd Class Fujiwara 'Fuji' Takeo Kobiashi. He played Fuji in the series that also starred Ernest Borgnine and Tim Conway from 1962 to 1966. He also reprised the roles in the spin-off films "McHale's Navy" (1984) and "McHale's Navy Joins the Air Force" (1965). Yoda appeared in an episode of "Love, American Style" in 1969. He later left acting to work as an executive for Toyota in Honolulu, Hawaii. He retired to Fullerton, California, in 2012.

Yoon Jeong-hee

South Korean actress Yoon Jeong-hee died of complications from Alzheimer's disease in Paris, France, on January 19, 2023. She was 78. She was born Son Mi-ja in Busan, Korean, on July 30, 1944. She made her film debut in 1967 with Hapdong Films and appeared in over 200 features during the next decade. Her numerous film credits include "A Swordsman in the Twilight" (1967), "Sound of Magpies" (1967), "Sorrowful Youth" (1967), "I Am Not Lonely" (1967), "Mist" (1967), "Is Wild Apricot an Apricot?" (1967), "I Live as I Please" (1967), "Dolmuji" (1967), "A Miracle of Gratitude" (1967), "Legend of Ssarigol" (1967), "The First Night" (1967), "Gang Myeong-hwa" (1967), "A Secret Royal Inspector" (1967), "Longing in Every Heart" (1967), "The Third Class Inn" (1967), "A Man of Great Strength: Im Ggyeok-jeong" (1968), "The Sorrow of Separation" (1968), "Snowstorm" (1968), "Lonely Marriage Night" (1968), "Great Swordsman"

(1968), "Secret of Motherly Love" (1968), "Kisaeng" (1968), "Bell Daegam" (1968), "Students of Karl Marx" (1968), "Shining Sadness" (1968), "A Cliff" (1968), "Pure Love" (1968), "Glory of Barefoot" (1968), "A Devoted Love" (1968), "Yeong" (1968), "Jade Binyeo" (1968), "A Japanese" (1968),

"Hard to Forget" (1968), "Three-Thousand Miles of Legend" (1968), "A Man of Windstorm" (1968), "Grudge" (1968), "A Young Gisaeng" (1968), "Warm Wind" (1968), "Eunuch" (1968), "Scared of Night" (1968), "Snow Lady" (1968), "Enraged Land" (1968), "Dreams of Sora" (1968), "Sorrow Over the Waves" (1968), "Good Bye Dad" (1968), "A Journey" (1968), "Potato" (1968), "Correspondent in Tokyo" (1968), "Nightmare" (1968), "Chorus of Trees" (1968), "Mother Is Strong" (1968), "Crossed Love" (1968), "the General's Mustache" (1968), "Sobbing Swan" (1968), "The Crossroads of Hell" (1968), "Winds and Clouds" (1968), "Women's Quarter" (1968), "Sunset" (1968), "Blue Writings of Farewell" (1968), "Beautiful Land" (1968), "Dangerous Blues" (1968), "Trumpet in Night Sky" (1968), "Hard to Forget" (1968), "The Geisha of Korea" (1968), "In Your Arms" (1969), "Temptation" (1969), "A Native of Myeong-dong" (1969), "Devoting the Youth" (1969), "Love Is the Seed of Tears" (1969), "A Nicknamed Woman" (1969), "Immortal Rivers and Mountains" (1969), "Condemned Criminals" (1969), "Jin and Min" (1969), "An Old Potter" (1969), "The Three Female Swordsmen" (1969), "The Past" (1969), "Foggy Shanghai" (1969), "Woman Captain" (1969), "Castle of Rose" (1969), "Deer in the Snow Field" (1969), "Destiny of My Lord" (1969), "The 4th Man" (1969), "Window" (1969), "First Night" (1969), "Youth" (1969), "Reminiscence" (1969), "Gallant Man" (1969), "Embrace" (1969), "Girl of Heuksan Island" (1969), "Until That Day" (1969), "Day Dream" (1969), "Yoejin Tribe" (1969), "Calm Life" (1969), "Forget-Me-Not" (1969), "The Magical Ship" (1969), "Women of Yi-Dynasty" (1969), "Housekeeper's Legacy" (1969), "Friend's Husband" (1969), "Parking Lot" (1969), "One Step in the Hell" (1969), "Love and Hate" (1969), "Seven People in the Cellar" (1969), "I Love You" (1969), "A Left-Hander in Tokyo" (1969), "Under the Roof" (1969), "Blues at Midnight" (1969), "A Wonderer in Myeong-dong" (1969), "I Like it hot" (1969), "If We Didn't Meet" (1969), "Darling" (1969), "Six Shadows" (1969), "Regret" (1969), "First Experience" (1970), "Cutest of Them All" (1970), "Lonely Father" (1970), "Why She Doesn't Marry" (1970), "Two Women in the Rain" (1970), "Oh! My Love" (1970), "Because You Are a Woman" (1970), "Rain Outside the Porthole" (1970), "Thy Name Is Woman" (1970), "Answer My Question" (1970), "Chastity" (1970), "Turtle" (1970), "The Javelin Killer in the Wild" (1970), "Yearning for a Lover" (1970), "A Wild Girl" (1970), "Sunday Night and Monday Morning" (1970), "The Woman Who Wanted an Apartment" (1970), "An Abandoned Woman" (1970), "Between My Father's Arms" (1970), "If He Were the Father" (1970), "Angel,

Put Your Clothes On" (1970), "Chase That Woman" (1970), "The Woman Who Grabbed the Tiger's Tail" (1970), "Old Gentleman in Myeongdong" (19790), "A Woman's Battleground" (1970), "Man of Desires" (1970), "Golden Operation 70 in Hong Kong" (1970), "Affair on the Beach" (1970), "Marriage Classroom" (1970), "Escape" (1970), "Twisted Fate of Man" (1970), "Escape in the Mist" (1970), "An Idiot Judge" (1970), "My Life in Your Heart" (1970), "Separation at the Station" (1970), "A Woman Who Came a Long Away" (1970), "A Queen of Misfortune" (1970), "We Wish You a Long Life, Mom and Dad!" (1970), "Tears of an Angel" (1970), "Big Brother's Marriage" (1970), "Today's Men" (1971), "The Women of Kyeongbokgung" (1971), "The Last Flight to Pyongyang" (1971), "Saturday Afternoon" (1971), "Mother of Two Daughters" (1971), "Leaving in the Rain" (1971), "Not a Good Wife" (1971), "A Guilty Woman" (1971), "Madame Mist" (1971), "A Woman Who Came in Straw Sandals" (1971), "Two Daughters" (1971), "My Wife" (1971), "Two Sons" (1971), "Why Do You Abandon Me" (1971), "Woman in a Red Mask" (1971), "Gapsun-i" (1971), "Best of Them All" (1971), "Between You and Me" (1971), "Impetuous Mother-in-Law" (1971), "A Family of Brother and Sister" (1971), "Two Guys" (1971), "What Happened That Night" (1971), "Light in the Field" (1971), "My Father" (1971), "Two Weeping Women" (1971), "A Hotel Room" (1971), "Bun-Rye's Story" (1971), "Sergeant Kin's Return from Vietnam" (1971), "The Golden Harbor in Horror" (1971), "East and West" (1971), "His Double Life" (1971), "A Sworn Brother" (1971), "Happy Farewell" (1971), "Tomorrow's Scenery of Korea" (1971), "My Love, My Foe" (1971), "New Year's Soup" (1971), "Two Women Ridden with Han" (1971), "A Woman Gambler" (1971), "Time on Myungdong" (1971), "The Last Marine in Vietnam" (1971), "Tragic Death of Ambition" (1971), "Seven Jolly Sisters" (1971), "I Can't Forget You" (1971), "Brother and Sister in the Rain" (1971), "Twelve Women" (1971), "Sorrow in Tears" (1971), "Bye, Mom" (1971), "To Love and to Die" (1971), "A Family Tree" (1971), "Courtesan" (1972), "30 Years of Love" (1972), "Where Should I Go?" (1972), "On a Star Shining Night" (1972), "Cruel History of Myeong Dong" (1972), "Kneel Down and Pray" (1972), "The Fugitive in the Storm" (1972), "Drum Sound of Sae Nam Teo" (1972), "Don't Go" (1972), "The Partner" (1972), "A Ghost Affair" (1972), "Oh, Frailty" (1972), "A Crossroad" (1972), "Daughter-in-Law" (1972), "Voices" (1972), "A Shaman's Story" (1972), "Hatred Becomes..." (1972), "Our Land Korea" (1972), "Sim Cheong" (1972), "Oyster Village" (1972), "Ever Smiling Mr. Park" (1972), "Mother, Why Did You Give Birth to Me?" (1972), "One Who Comes Back and the Other Who Has to Leave" (1972), "Gab Sun Yi the Best Driver" (1972), "Looking for Sons and Daughters" (1972), "When a Little Dream Blooms..." (1972), "Don't Forget Love, Though We Say Good Bye" (1972), "Sister" (1973), "A Cafe of September" (1973), "20 Years After the Independent and Baek Beom Kim Ku" (1973), "A Field Full of Happiness" (1973), "Tto Sun Yi, a College Girl" (1973), "During Mother's Lifetime" (1973), "The Three-Day Reign" (1973), "The Military Academy" (1973), "A Wrecked Fishing Boat" (1973), "Special Investigation Bureau: Kim So-San, the Kisaeng" (1973), "Love Class" (1973), "Azaleas in my Home" (1973), "A Flowery Bier" (1974), "Ecstasy" (1974), "Woman Like a Crane" (1975), "Bird of Paradise" (1975), "Truth of Tomorrow" (1975), "The Tae-Baeks" (1975), "Night Journey" (1977), "A Splendid Outing" (1977), "Flowers and Birds" (1978), "the Loneliness of the journey" (1978), and "The Terms of Love" (1979). Yoon continued to appear in occasional films in the 1980s and 1990s including "Liberal Wife '81" (1981), "Bird that Cries at Night" (1982), "The Chrysanthemum and the Clown" (1982), "A Woman on the Verge" (1987), "The Isle of Shiro" (1988), "Flower in the Snow" (1992), and "Manmubang" (1994). She retired from films in the mid-1990s and settled in France. She made a brief return to the screen in Lee Chang-dong's 2010 feature "Poetry". Yoon married pianist Kun-Woo Paik in 1974 and is survived by him and their daughter, a violinist.

Young, Barbara

British actress Barbara Young, who was noted for her role as Agrippina, the mother of Nero, in the 1976 "I, Claudius" television mini-series, died at a hospital in Cambridge, Cambridgeshire, England, on April 27, 2023. She was 82.

Young was born in Brighouse, West Riding of Yorkshire, England, on February 9, 1931. She appeared frequently on television from the late 1950s with roles in productions of "Fred Emney Picks a Pop" (1960), "The Chopping Block" (1960), "Poor Sidney" (1960), "The Primitive" (1961), "Jane Eyre" (1970), "I, Claudius" (1976), "On Giant's Shoulders" (1979), "Crime and Punishment" (1979), "The Good Companions" (1980), "Praying Mantis" (1982), "A Perfect Spy" (1987), "Sleepers" (1991), and "The Vacillations of Poppy Carew" (1995). Her other television credits include episodes of "On Stage - London", "Probation Officer", "Bootsie and Snudge", "Knight Errant Limited", "Emergency-Ward 10", "Armchair Theatre", "No Hiding Place", "Bulldog Breed", "Crying Down the Lane", "Moonstrike", "Pardon the Expression", "Dr. Kildare", "Homicide", "The Root of All Evil?", "Nearest and Dearest", "The Main Chance", "War & Peace", "Public Eye", "ITV Playhouse", "Crown Court", "Love Story", "How's Your Father?" as Doreen Cropper in 1974, "2nd House", "Looking for Clancy", "Angels", "Hazell", "Play for today", "Bless Me, Father", "The Gentle Touch", "Dempsey and Makepeace", "A Dorothy L. Sayers Mystery", "Witness", "Split Ends", "All Good Things", "Virtual Murder", "Lovejoy", "The Memoirs of Sherlock Holmes", "Casualty", "Cracker", "The Bill", "The Broker's Man", "Four Fathers", "Midsomer Murders", "Holby City", "Hollyoaks", and "Doctors". Young was featured on "Coronation Street" in several roles including Betty Ridgeway in 1961, Mrs. Stockwell in 1982, Barbara Platt in 1991, and Doreen Fenwick in 2007. She was Sadie Hargreaves in "Family

Affair" from 1999 to 2005, and Stella on "Last of the Summer Wine" from 2008 to 2010. Young appeared in several films during her career including "White City" (1985), "Hidden City" (1987), and "The Keeper" (2018). She was married to screenwriter Jack Pulman, who scripted the "I, Claudius" series, until his death in 1979. She is survived by their daughters, singer Liza Pulman and actress Cory Pulman.

Young, Burt

Actor Burt Young, who was featured as Paulie, the brother-in-law of Sylvester Stallone's Rocky Balboa, in the "Rocky" film franchise, died in Los Angeles, California, on October 8, 2023. He was 83. He was born Gerald DeLouise in New York City on April 30, 1940. He left high school to join the U.S. Marines, serving from 1957 to 1959. He was also a successful boxer while serving in the marines. Young later decided on a career in acting and studied at the Actors Studio under Lee Strasberg. He made his film debut under the name John Harris as Gimpy, the hunchbacked red herring, in the 1970 horror film "Carnival of Blood". He had a successful career portraying a variety of hoods and low-life characters over the next fifty years. He took the name Burt Young for such subsequent films as "Born to Win" (1971), "The Gang That Couldn't Shoot Straight" (1971), "Across 100th Street" (1972), "Cinderella Liberty" (1973), Roman Polanski's "Chinatown" (1974) starring Jack Nicholson, "The Gambler" (1974), "Murph the Surf" (1975), "The Killer Elite" (1975), and "Harry and Walter Go to New York". He was best known for his role as Paulie Pennino, the brother of Talia Shire's Adrian and best friend and eventual corner man of Sylvester Stallone's boxing icon Rocky Balboa in the first "Rocky" film in 1976. He earned an Academy Award nomination for Best Supporting Actor for his role. He reprised the role of Paulie in the five sequels, "Rocky II" (1979), "Rocky III" (1982), "Rocky IV" (1985), "Rocky V" (1990), and "Rocky Balboa" (2006). He remained a popular character actor in such films as "The Choirboys" (1977), the nuclear thriller "Twilight's Last Gleaming" (1977), Sam Peckinpah's "Convoy" (1978) as renegade trucker Pigpen, "Uncle Joe Shannon" (1978) which he scripted and starred in the title role, the horror film "Blood Beach" (1980), "...All the Marbles" (1981) as sleazy wrestling manager Eddie Cisco, the horror film "Amityville II: The Possession" (1982) as ill-fated patriarch Anthony Montelli, "Lookin' to Get Out" (1982), "Over the Brooklyn Bridge" (1984), Sergio Leone's crime epic "Once Upon a Time in America" (1984), "The Pope of Greenwich Village" (1984), the comedy "Back to School" (1986) starring Rodney Dangerfield, "Medium Rare" (1987), "Last Exit to Brooklyn" (1989), the western "Blood Red" (1989), "Beverly Hills Brats" (1989), "Going Overboard" (1989), "Wait Until Spring, Bandini" (1989), "Betsy's Wedding" (1990), "Club Fed" (1990), "Backstreet Dreams" (1990), "Driving In" (1990),

"Bright Angel" (1990), the Italian comedy "Americano Rosso" (1991), "Alibi Perfecto" (1992), "Bad Girls" (1992), "Excessive Force" (1993), "Berlin '39" (1993), "North Star" (1996), "Hit & Run" (1997), "Kicked in the Head" (1997), "She's So Lovely" (1997), "The Undertaker's Wedding" (1997), "The Deli" (1997), "The Good Life" (1997), "Heaven Before I Die" (1997), "Red-Blooded American Girl II" (1997), "Stone Cutter" (1998), "One Deadly Road" (1998), "The Florentine" (1999), "Loser Love" (1999), the Hugh Grant comedy "Mickey Blue Eyes" (1999) as mob boss Vito Graziosi, "The Wasteland" (1999), "Blue Moon" (2000), "L'Uomo della Fortuna" (2000), "Table One" (2000), "Very Mean Men" (2000), "The Day the Ponies Come Back" (2000), "The Boys Behind the Desk" (2000), "Never Look Back" (2000), "The Boys from Sunset Ridge" (2001), "Plan B" (2001), "Cugini" (2001), "Checkout" (2002), the science fiction comedy "The Adventures of Pluto Nash" (2002) starring Eddie Murphy, "Kiss the Bride" (2002), "And She Was" (2002), "Crooked Lines" (2003), "Shut Up and Kiss Me!" (2004), "The Wager" (2004), "Land of Plenty" (2004), "Downtown: A Street Tale" (2004), "Transamerica" (2005), "Carlito's Way: Rise to Power" (2005), "Nicky's Game" (2005), ."Revolution" (2006), "Blue Lake Butcher" (2007), "Go Go Tales" (2007), "Hack!" (2007), "Il Nascondiglio" (2007), "Oliviero Rising" (2007), "Camera: The Walking Mountain" (2008), "New York, I Love You" (2008), "Kingshighway" (2010), "Win Win" (2011), "The Shoemaker" (2012), "Abigail Harm" (2012), "Ci Vediamo Domani" (2013), "Rob the Mob" (2014), "Zarra's Law" (2014), "Tom in America" (2014), "The Elevator" (2015), "Lostland" (2015), "King Rat" (2017), "The Neighborhood" (2017), "6 Children & 1 Grandfather" (2018), "Road to the Lemon Grove" (2018), "Sarah Q" (2018), "The Amityville Murders" (2018), "Tapestry" (2019), "The Brawler" (2019), "Smothered by Mothers" (2019), "Epiphany" (2019), "Vault" (2019), "Bottom of the 9th" (2019), "Beckman" (2020), "Whack the Don" (2021), "Tomorrow's Today" (2021), and "The Final Code" (2021). Young was seen on television in episodes of "The Doctors", "M*A*S*H", "Little House on the Prairie", "Serpico", "Baretta", "The Rockford Files", "You and Me Kid", "Miami Vice", "The Equalizer", "Alfred Hitchcock Presents", the short-lived NBC comedy "Roomies" as Nick Chase in 1987, "Tales from the Crypt", "Bless This House", "The Outer Limits", "Law & Order", "Walker, Texas Ranger", "Thinking About Africa", "The Sopranos", "Alternate Realities", "The Handler", "I'm with Her", "Law & Order: Special Victims Unit", "Medium Rare", "Baciamo le Mani: Palermo-New York 1958" as Don Gillo Draghi in 2013, "Kevin Can Wait", and "Russian Doll". His other television credits include the tele-films and mini-series "The Connection" (1973), "The Great Niagara" (1974), "Hustling" (1975), "Woman of the Year" (1976), "Daddy, I Don't Like This" (1978) which he also wrote, "Murder Can Hurt You!" (1980), "A Summer to Remember" (1985), "Vendetta: Secrets of a Mafia Bride" (1990), "Due Vite, un Destino" (1993), "Double Deception" (1993), "Vendetta II: The New Mafia" (1993), "Undercover" (1994), "Crocodile Shoes" (1994), "The Maharaja's Daughter" (1994), "Firehouse" (1996), "The Last Don" (1997), "Before Women Had Wings" (1997), "Cuori in Campo" (1998), "Gioco di Specchi" (2000), and "Horace and Pete" (2016). Young was also an artist whose works appeared in galleries around the world. He was married to Gloria Young from 1961 until her death in 1974 and is survived by their daughter, Anna Morea.

Young, Gary

Musician Gary Young, who was the original drummer for the indie rock band Pavement, died at his home in Stockton, California, on August 17, 2023. He was 70. Young was born in Mamaroneck, New York, on May 3, 1953. He performed

with the punk band the Fall of Christianity in the early 1980s. Stephen Malkmus and Scott Kannberg formed the indie rock band Pavement in 1989, and their first EP, "Stay Tracks (1933-1969)", was recorded at Young's Louder Than You Think home studio. Young played drums for the recording as their two subsequent EPs. He also was drummer on Pavement's debut album "Slanted and Enchanted" in 1992. Young was noted for his eccentric activities at live shows, handing out cabbages and mashed potatoes to audience members at the door and performing handstands on stage. His battles with alcohol abuse led to problems with the band and he departed in 1993 after the release of their EP "Watery, Domestic". He released the albums "Hospital" (1994), "Things We Do for You" (1999), and "The Grey Album" (2004) under the name Gary Young's Hospital. He reunited with Pavement for a pair of shows for the reunion tour in 2010. Young recorded the 2016 solo album "Malfunction". He was the subject of Jed I. Rosenberg's documentary film "Louder Than You Think" in 2023.

Young, Rob

Canadian sound engineer Rob Young, who received

an Academy Award nomination for his work on the 1992 film "Unforgiven", died in Albi, France, on June 11, 2023, of complications from a fall while on a trip to Morocco. He was 76. Young was born in Sussex, New Brunswick, Canada, in 1947. He studied radio and television at Ryerson University in Toronto. He began working as a sound mixer at Spence-Thomas Productions. He worked on numerous films as a boom operator or sound mixer from the early 1970s including "Kemek" (1970), "Volcano: An Inquiry Into the Life and Death of Malcolm Lowry" (1976), "The Food of the Gods" (1976), "Buffalo Bill and the Indians, or Sitting Bull's History Lesson" (1976), "Shadow of the Hawk" (1976), "La Menace" (1977), "Bear Island" (1979), "Jack Hodgins' Island" (1981), "The Grey Fox" (1982), "First Blood" (1982), "Ladies and Gentlemen, the Fabulous Stains" (1982), "Running Brave"

(1983), "Runaway" (1984), "Gifted Kids" (1984), "Rambo: First Blood Part II" (1985), "Stripper" (1985), "The Boy Who Could Fly" (1986), "Roxanne" (1987), "John and the Missus" (1987), "The Accused" (1988), "Cousins" (1989), "The Fly II" (1989), "Kingsgate" (1989), "The First Season" (1989), "The NeverEnding Story II: The Next Chapter" (1990), "The Russia House" (1990), "Run" (1991), "Crooked Hearts" (1991), "Mystery Date" (1991), "Leaving Normal" (1991), Clint Eastwood's "Unforgiven" (1992) sharing an Oscar and BAFTA Award nomination, "Look Who's Talking Now" (1993), "White Fang 2: Myth of the White Wolf" (1994), "Hideaway" (1995), "Man of the House" (1995), "Crying Freeman" (1995), "Jumanji" (1995), "Homeward Bound II: Lost in San Francisco" (1996), "Romeo + Juliet" (1996) receiving another BAFTA nomination, "Mr. Magoo" (1997), "Deep Rising" (1998), "Wrongfully Accused" (1998), "Disturbing Behavior" (1998), "I'll Be Home for Christmas" (1998), "Double Jeopardy" (1999), "Reindeer Games" (2000), "Mission to Mars" (2000), "Romeo Must Die" (2000), "The Guilty" (2000), "The Pledge" (2001), "Antitrust" (2001), "Ignition" (2001), "Snow Dogs" (2002), "Life or Something Like It" (2002), "I Spy" (2002), "X2: X-Men United" (2003), "The Chronicles of Riddick" (2004), "Catwoman" (2004), "The Exorcism of Emily Rose" (2005), "The Pink Panther" (2006), "Final Destination 3" (2006), "She's the Man" (2006), "Night at the Museum" (2006), "Shooter" (2007), "Elegy" (2008), "The Uninvited" (2009), "Night at the Museum: Battle of the Smithsonian" (2002), "Jennifer's Body" (2009), and "Percy Jackson & the Olympians: The Lightning Thief" (2010). Young also worked in sound for television productions of "Hey, I'm Alive" (1975), "Revenge for a Rape" (1976), "Who'll Save Our Children?" (1978), "the Plutonium Incident" (1980), "Al Oeming: Man of the North" (1980), "A Piano for Mrs. Cimino" (1982), "The Haunting Passion" (1983), "The Best Christmas Pageant Ever" (1983), "Secrets of a Married Man" (1984), "The Glitter Dome" (1984), "Picking Up the Pieces" (1985), "Mrs. Delafield Wants to Marry" (1986), "A Stranger Waits" (1987), "The Red Spider" (1988), "Higher Ground" (1988), "The Penthouse" (1989), "Anything to Survive" (1990), "The Man Upstairs" (1982), "For the Love of My Child: The Anissa Ayala Story" (1993), "Moment of Truth: To Walk Again" (1994), "Seasons of the Heart" (1994), "A Dream Is a Wish Your Heart Makes: The Annette Funicello Story" (1995), "A Kidnapping in the Family" (1996), "Harvey" (1996), "Murder in My Mind" (1997), "Big and Hairy" (1998), "Hostage Negotiator" (2001), "No Place Like Home" (2003), and "Reefer Madness: The Movie Musical" (2005). His other television credits include episodes of such series as "Here Come the Seventies", "W5", "New Newcomers", "Huckleberry Finn and His Friends", "The Minikins", "The Hitchhiker", "Stir Crazy", "The New Adventures of Beans Baxter", "Danger Bay", "Wiseguy", "Glory Days", "Jack's Place", "Sliders", "Millennium", "John Doe", "House", and "Psych". He retired from films in 2010 and settled in France, where he was working on a novel and screenplay. He is survived by his wife, Yvonne Wetherall, and three children.

Zehetgruber, Rudolf

Austrian film director Rudolf Zehetgruber, who was noted for directing and writing the "Superbug" fantasy comedy film series, died in Vienna, Austria, on July 2, 2023. He was 96. Zehetgruber was born in Vienna on September 16, 1926. He began working in films in the 1950s as an assistant director for "Der Vogelhandler" (1953), "Cabaret" (1954), "Ein Haus Voll Liebe" (1954), "Der Kongress Tanzt" (1955), "Sissi" (1955), "Bademeister Spargel" (1956), "Opernball" (1956), "Sissi - Die Junge Kaiserin" (1956), "Sissi - Schicksalsjahre Einer Kaiserin" (1957), "Der Arzt von Stalingrad" (1958), "Der Priester und das Madchen" (1958), "Der Schatz vom Toplitzsee" (1959), and "The Bashful Elephant" (1961). He directed numerous films from the early 1960s, which he also frequently produced, scripted, and appeared in small roles. His films include "Das Dorf Ohne Moral" (1960), "The Black Cobra" (1963), the crime drama "The Nylon Noose" (1963), "Piccadilly Zero Hour 12" (1963), "Inn on Dartmoor" (1964), "The Secret of the Chinese Carnation" (1964), "Seven Vengeful Women" (1965), the spy thrillers "Kommissar X - Three Yellow Cats" (1966) and "Kommissar X - "Drei Grune Hunde" (1967). Zehetgruber was noted for his "Superbug" series of comedy films featuring a sentient Volkswagen Beetle. He usually played the driver, Jimmy Bondi, under such aliases as Richard Lynn, Robert Mark, and Rudolf Rittberg, and his wife, Kathrin Oginski, was leading lady. The films include "Superbug Goes Wild" (1971), "Superbug, Super Agent" (1972), "Superbug Rides Again" (1973), "The Maddest Car in the World" (1975), and "Return of Superbug" (1978). His final film, the fantasy adventure "Nessie, das Verruckteste Monster der Welt", was released in 1985. Zehetgruber was married to actress Kathrin Oginski until her death in 2009.

Zehme, Bill

Author Bill Zehme, who co-wrote books with such celebrities as Jay Leno and Hugh Hefner, died of colorectal cancer in Chicago, Illinois, on March 26, 2023. He was 64. Zehme was born in South Holland, Illinois, on October 28, 1958. He graduated from Loyola University in Chicago with a degree in journalism in 1980. He wrote articles for numerous magazines including "Playboy", "Rolling Stone", and "Vanity Fair". Zehme and Bonnie Schiffman wrote "The Rolling Stone Book of Comedy" in 1991. He co-wrote "I'm Only One Man" with Regis Philbin in 1995 and "Leading with My Chin" with Jay Leno in 1996. He conducted an interview with Frank Sinatra for an article in "Esquire" in 1996 and expanded it for the 1997 book "The Way You Wear Your Hat: Frank Sinatra and the Lost Art of Livin'". Zehme's other books include "Who Wants to Be Me?" (2000) with Regis Philbin, "Intimate Strangers: Comic Profiles and Indiscretions of the Very Famous" (2002), "Hef's Little Black Book" (2004) with Hugh Hefner, "Carson the Magnificent: An Intimate Portrait" which was scheduled for publication in 2007 but was never completed, and "Lost in the Funhouse: The Life and Mind of Andy Kaufman" (2009). He was featured on television in the documentaries "Playboy: Inside the Playboy Mansion" (2002), "Wait 'Til Next Year: The Saga of the Chicago Cubs" (2006), "The Battle for Late Night" (2010), and "The Story of Late Night" (2021). Zehme was married and divorced from Tina Zimmel and is survived by their daughter, Lucy Reeves. He is also survived by his partner, Jennifer Engstrom.

Zeller, Bibiana

Austrian actress Bibiana Zeller died in Vienna, Austria, on July 16, 2023. She was 95. Zeller was born in Vienna on February 25, 1928. She trained as an actress at the Franz Schubert Conservatory and began her career on stage with the Theater in der Josefstadt in 1951. She performed at theaters throughout Austria and Germany including the Theatre am Kurfurstandamm in Berlin, the Theater Bonn, and the Burgtheater in Vienna, which she joined in 1972. Zeller was a prolific television actress from the late 1950s with roles in productions of "Akt Mit Geige" (1958), "Die Conways und die Zeit" (1958), "Liselott" (1961), "Ende Schlecht - Alles Gut" (1962), "Der Fidele Bauer" (1962), "Parlez-vous Francais?" (1962), "Die Verhangnisville Faschingsnacht" (1962), "Ein Netter Kerl" (1963), "Komodie der Irrungen" (1963), "Der Fischbecker Wandteppich" (1964), "Ein Sommernachtstraum" (1965), "Minister Gesucht" (1966), "Das Marchen" (1966), "Ein Monat auf dem Lande" (1967), "Das Veilchen" (1967), "Fruhere Verhaltnisse" (1968), "Von der Schwierigkeit, Sich Zu Konzentrieren" (1969), "Kampl" (1969), "Wer War Mr. Hilary?" (1969), "Schwester Bonaventura" (1969), "Das Weite Land" (1969), "Smeraldina" (1969), "Zug Fahrt Wiental" (1970), "Pasion Eines Politikers" (1970), "Blaues Wild" (1970), "Die Prinzessin und der Schweinehirt" (1970), "Wiener Totentanz" (1971), "Der Illegale" (1972), "Elisabeth Kaiserin von Osterreich" (1972), "Ein Junger Mann aus dem Innviertel - Adolf Hitler" (1973), "Der Abituriententag" (1974), "Vor Gericht Seh'n Wir uns Wieder" (1978), "Die Enfalle der Helligen Klara" (1980), "Kurt Sowinetz - Mei Team und I" (1980), "Es Hat Sich Eroffnet..." (1981), "Es Fing Ein Knab' Ein Vogelein" (1982), "Der Vorhang Fallt" (1986), "Heldenplatz" (1989), "Duett" (1993), "Die Skandalosen Frauen" (1993), "Lamorte" (1997), "Wie Eine Schwarze Mowe" (1998), "Jetzt Bringen Wir Unsere Manner Um" (2001), "Glaube und Heimat" (2001),

"Zuckeroma" (2004), "Feine Dame" (2006), "Meine Liebe Familie" (2008), "Die Spatzunder" (2010), "Oh Shit!" (2010), "Lug Weiter, Liebling" (2010), "Adel Dich" (2011), "Der Wettbewerb" (2011), "Homecoming with Obstacles" (2012), "The Hunt for the Amber Room" (2012), "Hochzeiten" (2012), "Obendruber da Schneit Es" (2012), "Alles Schwindel" (2013), "Flaschenpost an Meinen Mann" (2013), "Die Letzte Fahrt" (2013), "Just Married - Hochzeiten Zwei" (2013), and "Live Is Life - Der Himmel Soll Warten" (2013). Her other television credits include episodes of "Les Aventures du Capitaine Luckner", "Das Jahrhundert der Chirurgen", "Hallo - Hotel Sacher.. Portier!", "Unter Ausschluss der Offentlichkeit", "Die Abenteuer des Braven Soldaten Schwejk", "Mein Lieber Mann", "Familienalbum", "Kottan Ermittelt" as Ilse Kottan from 1977 to 1983, "Waldheimat", "Der Leihopa", "Heiteres Bezirksgericht", "MA 2412" as Frau Ziegler from 1999 to 2001, "Der Bulle von Tolz", "Julie - Eine Ungewohnliche Frau" as Hertha Mahr from 1999 to 2000 and as Ann Miller from 2002 to 2003, "Tom Turbo", "Four Women and a Funeral", "Hilfe! Hochzeit! - Die Schlimmste Woche Meines Lebens" as Johanna von Schanz in 2007, "SOKO Kitzbuhel", "Polly Adler", "Lilly Schonauer", "Tatort", "Fast Forward", "Braunschlag", "Pastewka", "Oben Ohne" as Hilde Horrowitz from 2008 to 2012, "CopStories", and "For Heaven's Sake". She appeared in occasional films during her career including "Abenteuer im Schloss" (1952), "Die Hexe" (1954), "Kain" (1973), "The Uppercrust" (1981), "Ferien Mit Silvester" (1992), "The Knickerbocker Gang: The Talking Grave" (1995), "Ant Street" (1995), "Zum Gluck Gibt's Meine Frau" (1995), "The Unfish" (1997), "Qualtingers Wien" (1997), "Wanted" (1999), "Fink Fahrt Ab" (1999), "Ene Mene Muh - Und Tot Bist Du" (2001), "Taxi fur Eine Leiche" (2002), "Elisabeth II" (2003), "Kottan Ermittelt: Rien Ne Va Plus" (2010), "The Way to Live" (2011), "Das Pferd auf dem Balkon" (2012), "Ghosthunters: On Icy Trails" (2015), and "The Bloom of Yesterday" (2016). Zeller was married and divorced from director Otto Anton Eder and is survived by their two sons. She was subsequently married to actor Eugen Stark until his death in 2021.

Zeman, Jacklyn

Actress Jacklyn Zeman, who starred as nurse Bobbie Spencer on the soap opera "General Hospital" for over four

decades, died of cancer at a hospital in Thousand Oaks, California, on May 9, 2023. She was 70. Zeman was born in Englewood, New Jersey, on March 6, 1953. She studied dance at New York University and worked as a bunny at the Playboy Club in the early 1970s. She made her film debut in a small (nonsexual) role in the 1974 adult film "Deep Throat Part II". She appeared in the daytime soap opera "The Edge of Night" in 1976 and was Lana McLain in "One Life to Live" from 1976 to 1977. Zeman was best known for her role as Nurse Bobbie Spencer, the sister of Anthony Geary's Luke Spencer, on the soap opera "General Hospital" from 1977 until her death. She received Daytime Emmy Award nominations for her work in 1981, 1995, 1997, and 1998. She also appeared as Bobbie in the 1996 tele-film "General Hospital: Twist of Fate". Zeman's other television credits include episodes of "The New Mike Hammer", "Sledge Hammer!", ABC Afterschool Specials", "Chicago Hope", and "Misguided". She appeared in the tele-film "Jury Duty: The Comedy" (1990) and the mini-series "This Show Sucks Truth + Consequences" (2022). She starred as Sofia Madison in the streaming series "The Bay" from 2010 to 2022, earning another Daytime Emmy nomination. Zeman was a guest on such talk and game shows as "Dinah!", "The Mike Douglas Show", "Family Feud", "The Star Games", "The Merv Griffin Show", "Win, Lose or Draw", "The Hollywood Squares", "Donahue", "Match Game", "Maury", "The Chuck Woolery Show", "One on One with John Tesh", "The Suzanne Somers Show", "Crook & Chase", "Mad TV", "The Rosie O'Donnell Show", "Dog Whisperer with Cesar Millan", "SoapTalk", "The Florence Henderson Show", "Celebrity Ghost Stories", and "One on One with Jasper Cole". She was seen in several films including "The Day the Music Died" (1977), "Young Doctors in Love" (1982), "Class Reunion" (1982), the short "The Mission" (2005), and "Deep in the Valley" (2009). She was married to disc jockey Murray Kaufman, who was known as Murray the K, from 1978 until their divorce in 1981. She was briefly married to Steve Gribbin in 1986. Zeman was married to Glenn Gorden from 1988 until their divorce in 2007 and is survived by their two daughters.

Zephaniah, Benjamin

British poet and actor Benjamin Zephaniah, who was featured as Jeremiah Jesus in the BBC crime drama "Peaky Blinders" from 2013 to 2022, died of complications from a brain tumor in England on December 7, 2023. He was 65. Zephaniah was born in Handsworth, Birmingham, England, on

April 15, 1958. He left school in his early teens and moved to London in 1979. He became an activist with a workers' co-operative and wrote poetry. His first collection, "Pen Rhythm", was published in 1980. He released the 1982 album "Rasta" featuring the Wailers. He also wrote the books "The Dread Affair: Collected Poems" (1985), "Rasta Time in Palestine" (1990), the children's poetry collection "Talking Turkeys" (1994), "Too Black, Too Strong" (2001), and "We Are Britain!" (2002). He also wrote the novels "Face" (1999) and "Refugee Boy" (2001), which was adapted as a play in 2013. His autobiography, "The Life and Rhymes of Benjamin Zephaniah", was published in 2018. He was featured in the 1990 film "Farendj" and appeared on television in episodes of "A Beetle Called Derek", "The Comic Strip Presents", "EastEnders", "The Bill", "Life & Rhymes", "Crucial Tales", "The Jonathan Ross Show", and

"Zen Motoring". He was featured in the recurring role of Jeremiah Jesus in the crime drama "Peaky Blinders" from 2013 to 2012. He active an opposing racism in Great Britain and was an animal rights activist and vegan. His book, "The Little Book of Vegan Poems", was published in 2001. Zephaniah was married to Amina from 1990 until their divorce in 2000.

Zeus

Zeus, a Great Dane who was recognized as the tallest dog in the world by the "Guinness Book of World Records", died of complications of bone cancer and pneumonia died in Buford, Texas, on September 12, 2023. He was 3. Zeus was born in Buford in November of 2019. He was the largest of a litter and grew to the size of 3'5.18". Zeus was owned by Brittany Davis and was named the tallest living male dog in 2022 by Guinness World Records.

Zonfrillo, Jock

Scottish chef and television host Barry 'Jock' Zonfrillo was found dead at his hotel room in Melbourne, Australia, on April 30, 2023. He was 46. Zonfrillo was born in

Glasgow, Scotland, on August 4, 1976. He began working in restaurant kitchens in his teens and soon began cooking. He worked at the Turnberry Hotel and was named Young Scottish Chef of the Year in 1993. He worked at several restaurants in London before moving to Australia in 1994. He worked as a sous chef in Sydney before returning the London the following year. He held his first position as head chef at the Treseanton Hotel there in 1998. His career had been impacted by addiction to drugs when he quit before immigrating to Australia in 2000. He became head chef at Restaurant 41 but was dismissed after setting fire to an apprentice chef who he felt was working too slow. He eventually filed for bankruptcy to avoid paying damages to his victim. He continued to work in restaurants before opening his own in 2013. His restaurant Orana became a popular Adelaide establishment. He operated several bars and restaurants in the Adelaide area. Zonfrillo was host of the Discovery Channel series "Nomad Chef" in 2014 where he visited various countries to study their cooking techniques. He was host of the reality cooking series "Restaurant Revolution" in 2015 and co-hosted "Chef Exchange" the following year. Zonfrillo was programming director for Tasting Australia from 2016 to 2019. He was a host of "MasterChef Australia" in 2019 and for "Junior MasterChef Australia" in 2020. His memoir, "Last Shot", was published in 2021. He married his third wife, Lauren Fried in 2017 and is survived by her and their son and

daughter. He is also survived by two daughters from previous marriages.

●●●

Todd, Sally

Actress Sally Todd, who starred in the 1950s horror films "The Unearthly" and "Frankenstein's Daughter", died in France on November 21, 2022. She was 88. She was born

Sarah Joan Todd in Boone, Missouri, on June 7, 1934, and was raised in Arizona. She won a trip to Hollywood in 1952 after placing first in the Miss Tucson Beauty Contest. She began working as a model and made her film debut in a small role in 1953's "The French Line". She was featured as one of The Carson Cuties on "The Johnny Carson Show" in New York from 1955 to 1956. She returned to California where she was signed by 20th Century Fox. She was seen in the films "The Revolt of Mamie Stover" (1956), "The Best Things in Life Are Free" (1956), the horror film "The Unearthly" (1957) as Natalie Andries, Roger Corman's "The Saga of the Viking Women and Their Voyage to the Waters of the Great Sea Serpent" (1957), the horror cult classic "Frankenstein's Daughter" (1958) as Suzie Lawler, "Al Capone" (1959), and "G.I. Blues". Todd appeared on television in episodes of "The Bob Cummings Show", "Flight", "Dragnet", "M Squad", "Rescue 8", "The Untouchables", "Lock Up", "Johnny Ringo", "The Many Loves of Dobie Gillis", "77 Sunset Strip", "The Tab Hunter Show", and "Holiday Lodge". She appeared in "Playboy" magazine as Playmate of the Month in February of 1957. Todd retired from the screen in the early 1960s. Her autobiography, "Notorious, Sally Todd, the Life of a Hollywood Icon", was published in 2015.

Made in the USA
Columbia, SC
25 June 2024

37482238R00267